T0181101

Lecture Notes in Computer Science 4278

Commenced Publication in 1973
Founding and Former Series Editors:
Gerhard Goos, Juris Hartmanis, and Jan van Leeuwen

Editorial Board

David Hutchison
Lancaster University, UK
Takeo Kanade
Carnegie Mellon University, Pittsburgh, PA, USA
Josef Kittler
University of Surrey, Guildford, UK
Jon M. Kleinberg
Cornell University, Ithaca, NY, USA
Friedemann Mattern
ETH Zurich, Switzerland
John C. Mitchell
Stanford University, CA, USA
Moni Naor
Weizmann Institute of Science, Rehovot, Israel
Oscar Nierstrasz
University of Bern, Switzerland
C. Pandu Rangan
Indian Institute of Technology, Madras, India
Bernhard Steffen
University of Dortmund, Germany
Madhu Sudan
Massachusetts Institute of Technology, MA, USA
Demetri Terzopoulos
University of California, Los Angeles, CA, USA
Doug Tygar
University of California, Berkeley, CA, USA
Moshe Y. Vardi
Rice University, Houston, TX, USA
Gerhard Weikum
Max-Planck Institute of Computer Science, Saarbruecken, Germany

Robert Meersman Zahir Tari
Pilar Herrero et al. (Eds.)

On the Move to Meaningful Internet Systems 2006: OTM 2006 Workshops

OTM Confederated International Workshops and Posters
AWeSOMe, CAMS, COMINF, IS, KSinBIT, MIOS-CIAO, MONET,
OnToContent, ORM, PerSys, OTM Academy Doctoral Consortium,
RDDS, SWWS, and SeBGIS 2006
Montpellier, France, October 29 – November 3, 2006
Proceedings, Part II

Springer

Volume Editors

Robert Meersman
Vrije Universiteit Brussel (VUB), STARLab
Bldg G/10, Pleinlaan 2, 1050 Brussels, Belgium
E-mail: meersman@vub.ac.be

Zahir Tari
RMIT University, School of Computer Science and Information Technology
Bld 10.10, 376-392 Swanston Street, VIC 3001, Melbourne, Australia
E-mail: zahirt@cs.rmit.edu.au

Pilar Herrero
Universidad Politécnica de Madrid, Facultad de Informática
Campus de Montegancedo S/N, 28660 Boadilla del Monte, Madrid, Spain
E-mail: pherrero@fi.upm.es

Library of Congress Control Number: 2006935257

CR Subject Classification (1998): H.2, H.3, H.4, C.2, H.5, I.2, D.2, K.4

LNCS Sublibrary: SL 3 – Information Systems and Application, incl. Internet/Web
and HCI

ISSN   0302-9743
ISBN-10   3-540-48273-3 Springer Berlin Heidelberg New York
ISBN-13   978-3-540-48273-4 Springer Berlin Heidelberg New York

Springer is a part of Springer Science+Business Media

springer.com

© Springer-Verlag Berlin Heidelberg 2006
Printed in Germany

Typesetting: Camera-ready by author, data conversion by Scientific Publishing Services, Chennai, India
Printed on acid-free paper   SPIN: 11915072   06/3142   5 4 3 2 1 0

Volume Editors

Robert Meersman
Zahir Tari
Pilar Herrero

AWeSOMe
Daniel Grosu
Pilar Herrero
Gonzalo Medez
Marta Sabou

CAMS
Annika Hinze
George Buchanan

COMINF
Aldo de Moor
Michael Gurstein

IS
Mario Freire
Simao Melo de Sousa
Vitor Santos

KSinBIT
Maja Hadzic
Bart De Moor
Yves Moreau
Arek Kasprzyk

MIOS-CIAO
Antonia Albani
Jan L.G. Dietz

MONET
Fernando Ferri
Maurizio Rafanelli
Arianna D'Ulizia

OnToContent
Mustafa Jarrar
Claude Ostyn
Werner Ceusters
Andreas Persidis

ORM
Terry Halpin
Robert Meersman

PerSys
Skevos Evripidou
Roy Campbell

OTM Academy Doctoral Consortium
Antonia Albani
Gabor Nagypal
Johannes Maria Zaha

RDDS
Eiko Yoneki
Pascal Felber

SWWS
Katia Sycara
Elizabeth Chang
Ernesto Damiani
Mustafa Jarrar
Tharam Dillon

OTM 2006 General Co-chairs' Message

Dear OnTheMove Participant or Reader of these Proceedings,

The General Chairs of OnTheMove 2006, Montpellier, France, are happy to observe that the conference series that was started in Irvine, California in 2002 and subsequently held in Catania, Sicily in 2003 and in Cyprus in 2004 and 2005 clearly continues to attract a growing representative selection of today's worldwide research on the scientific concepts underlying distributed, heterogeneous and autonomous yet meaningfully collaborative computing, with the Internet and the WWW as its prime epitomes.

Indeed, as such large, complex and networked intelligent information systems become the focus and norm for computing, it is clear that there is an acute and increasing need to address and discuss in an integrated forum the implied software and system issues as well as methodological, theoretical and application issues. As we all know, e-mail, the Internet, and even video conferences are not sufficient for effective and efficient scientific exchange. This is why the OnTheMove (OTM) Federated Conferences series has been created to cover the increasingly wide yet closely connected range of fundamental technologies such as data and Web semantics, distributed objects, Web services, databases, information systems, workflow, cooperation, ubiquity, interoperability, mobility, grid and high-performance. OnTheMove aspires to be a primary scientific meeting place where all aspects of the development of Internet- and Intranet-based systems in organizations and for e-business are discussed in a scientifically motivated way. This fifth 2006 edition of the OTM Federated Conferences event therefore again provided an opportunity for researchers and practitioners to understand and publish these developments within their individual as well as within their broader contexts.

The backbone of OTM was originally formed by the co-location of three related, complementary and successful main conference series: DOA (Distributed Objects and Applications, since 1999), covering the relevant infrastructure-enabling technologies, ODBASE (Ontologies, DataBases and Applications of SEmantics, since 2002) covering Web semantics, XML databases and ontologies, CoopIS (Cooperative Information Systems, since 1993) covering the application of these technologies in an enterprise context through, for example, workflow systems and knowledge management. For the 2006 edition, these were strengthened by a fourth conference, GADA (Grid computing, high-performAnce and Distributed Applications, a successful workshop at OTM since 2004), covering the large-scale integration of heterogeneous computing systems and data resources with the aim of providing a global computing space. Each of these four conferences encourages researchers to treat their respective topics within a framework that incorporates jointly (a) theory , (b) conceptual design and development, and (c) applications, in particular case studies and industrial solutions.

Following and expanding the model created in 2003, we again solicited and selected quality workshop proposals to complement the more "archival" nature of the main conferences with research results in a number of selected and more "avant garde" areas related to the general topic of distributed computing. For instance, the so-called Semantic Web has given rise to several novel research areas combining linguistics, information systems technology, and artificial intelligence, such as the modeling of (legal) regulatory systems and the ubiquitous nature of their usage. We were glad to see that several earlier successful workshops (notably WOSE, MIOS-INTEROP, AweSOMe, CAMS, SWWS, SeBGIS, ORM) re-appeared in 2006 with a second, third or sometimes fourth edition, and that not less than seven new workshops could be hosted and successfully organized by their respective proposers: IS (International Workshop on Information Security), COMINF (International Workshop on Community Informatics), KSinBIT (International Workshop on Knowledge Systems in Bioinformatics), MONET (International Workshop on MObile and NEtworking Technologies for social applications), OnToContent (Ontology content and evaluation in Enterprise), PerSys (International Workshop on Pervasive Systems), and RDDS (International Workshop on Reliability in Decentralized Distributed Systems). We know that as before, their audiences will mutually productively mingle with those of the main conferences, as is already visible from the overlap in authors! The OTM organizers are especially grateful for the leadership and competence of Pilar Herrero in managing this complex process into a success for the second year in a row.

A special mention for 2006 is again due for the third and enlarged edition of the highly attractive OnTheMove Academy (formerly called Doctoral Consortium Workshop). Its 2006 Chairs, Antonia Albani, Gábor Nagypál and Johannes Maria Zaha, three young and active researchers, further refined the original set-up and interactive formula to bring PhD students together: they call them to submit their research proposals for selection; the resulting submissions and their approaches are presented by the students in front of a wider audience at the conference, where they are then independently and extensively analyzed and discussed in public by a panel of senior professors. This year these were Johann Eder, Maria Orlowska, and of course Jan Dietz, the Dean of the OnTheMove Academy, who provided guidance, support and help for the team. The successful students are also awarded free access to all other parts of the OTM program, and only pay a minimal fee for the Doctoral Symposium itself (in fact their attendance is largely sponsored by the other participants!). The OTM organizers expect to further expand the OnTheMove Academy in future editions of the conferences and so draw an audience of young researchers into the OTM forum.

All four main conferences and the associated workshops share the distributed aspects of modern computing systems, and the resulting application-pull created by the Internet and the so-called Semantic Web. For DOA 2006, the primary emphasis was on the distributed object infrastructure; for ODBASE 2006, it became the knowledge bases and methods required for enabling the use of formal semantics; for CoopIS 2006, the topic was the interaction of such technologies and methods with management issues, such as occur in networked organizations, and for GADA 2006, the topic was the scalable integration of heterogeneous computing systems and data resources with the aim of providing a global computing space. These subject areas naturally overlap and many submissions in fact also treat an envisaged mutual impact among them. As for the earlier editions, the organizers wanted to stimulate this cross-pollination by a shared program of famous keynote speakers: this year we were proud to announce Roberto Cencioni (European Commission), Alois Ferscha (Johannes Kepler Universität), Daniel S. Katz (Louisiana State University and Jet Propulsion Laboratory), Frank Leymann (University of Stuttgart), and Marie-Christine Rousset (University of Grenoble)! We also encouraged multiple event attendance by providing all authors, also those of workshop papers, with free access or discounts to one other conference or workshop of their choice.

We received a total of 361 submissions for the four main conferences and an impressive 493 (compared to the 268 in 2005 and 170 in 2004!) submissions for the workshops. Not only may we indeed again claim success in attracting an increasingly representative volume of scientific papers, but such a harvest of course allows the Program Committees to compose a higher quality cross-section of current research in the areas covered by OTM. In fact, in spite of the larger number of submissions, the Program Chairs of each of the three main conferences decided to accept only approximately the same number of papers for presentation and publication as in 2003, 2004 and 2005 (i.e., average one paper out of four submitted, not counting posters). For the workshops, the acceptance rate varies but was much stricter than before, about one in two to three, to less than one quarter for the IS (Information Security) international workshop. Also for this reason, we separated the proceedings into two books with their own titles, with the main proceedings in two volumes, and we are grateful to Springer for their suggestions and collaboration in producing these books and CDROMs. The reviewing process by the respective Program Committees as usual was performed very professionally and each paper in the main conferences was reviewed by at least three referees, with arbitrated e-mail discussions in the case of strongly diverging evaluations. It may be worthwhile to emphasize that it is an explicit OnTheMove policy that all conference Program Committees and Chairs make their selections completely autonomously from the OTM organization itself. Continuing a costly but nice tradition, the OnTheMove Federated Event organizers decided again to make all proceedings available to all participants of conferences and workshops, independently of one's registration to a specific conference or workshop. Each participant also received a CDROM with the full combined proceedings (conferences + workshops).

The General Chairs are once more especially grateful to all the many people directly or indirectly involved in the setup of these federated conferences who contributed to making it a success. Few people realize what a large number of people have to be involved, and what a huge amount of work, and sometimes risk, the organization of an event like OTM entails. Apart from the persons in the roles mentioned above, we therefore in particular wish to thank our 12 main conference

PC Co-chairs (GADA 2006: Pilar Herrero, María S. Pérez, Domenico Talia, Albert Zomaya; DOA 2006: Judith Bishop, Kurt Geihs; ODBASE 2006: Maurizio Lenzerini, Erich Neuhold, V.S. Subrahmanian; CoopIS 2006: Mike Papazoglou, Louiqa Raschid, Rainer Ruggaber) and our 36 workshop PC Co-chairs (Antonia Albani, George Buchanan, Roy Campbell, Werner Ceusters, Elizabeth Chang, Ernesto Damiani, Jan L.G. Dietz, Pascal Felber, Fernando Ferri, Mario Freire, Daniel Grosu, Michael Gurstein, Maja Hadzic, Pilar Herrero, Terry Halpin, Annika Hinze, Skevos Evripidou, Mustafa Jarrar, Arek Kasprzyk, Gonzalo Méndez, Aldo de Moor, Bart De Moor, Yves Moreau, Claude Ostyn, Andreas Persidis, Maurizio Rafanelli, Marta Sabou, Vitor Santos, Simao Melo de Sousa, Katia Sycara, Arianna D'Ulizia, Eiko Yoneki, Esteban Zimányi).

All, together with their many PC members, did a superb and professional job in selecting the best papers from the large harvest of submissions.

We also heartily thank Zohra Bellahsene of LIRMM in Montpellier for the considerable efforts in arranging the venue at their campus and coordinating the substantial and varied local facilities needed for a multi-conference event such as ours. And we must all also be grateful to Mohand-Said Hacid of the University of Lyon for researching and securing the sponsoring arrangements, to Gonzalo Méndez, our excellent Publicity Chair, to our extremely competent and experienced Conference Secretariat and technical support staff Daniel Meersman, Ana-Cecilia Martinez Barbosa, and Jan Demey, and last but not least to our hyperactive Publications Chair and loyal collaborator of many years, Kwong Yuen Lai, this year bravely assisted by Peter Dimopoulos.

The General Chairs gratefully acknowledge the academic freedom, logistic support and facilities they enjoy from their respective institutions, Vrije Universiteit Brussel (VUB) and RMIT University, Melbourne, without which such an enterprise would not be feasible.

We do hope that the results of this federated scientific enterprise contribute to your research and your place in the scientific network... We look forward to seeing you again at next year's edition!

August 2006   Robert Meersman, Vrije Universiteit Brussel, Belgium
                                         Zahir Tari, RMIT University, Australia
                                         (General Co-chairs, OnTheMove 2006)

Organization Committee

The OTM (On The Move) Federated Workshops aim at complementing the more "archival" nature of the OTM Federated Conferences with research results in a number of selected and more "avant garde" areas related to the general topic of distributed computing. In 2006, only 14 workshops were chosen after a rigourous selection process by Pilar Herrero. The 2006 selected international conferences were: AWeSOMe (International Workshop on Agents, Web Services and Ontologies Merging), CAMS (International Workshop on Context-Aware Mobile Systems), COMINF (International Workshop on Community Informatics), IS (International Workshop on Information Security), KSinBIT (International Workshop on Knowledge Systems in Bioinformatics), MIOS+CIAO (International Workshop on Inter-organizational Systems), MONET (International Workshop on MObile and NEtworking Technologies for social applications), OnToContent (International Workshop on Ontology content and evaluation in Enterprise), ORM (International Workshop on Object-Role Modeling), PerSys (International Workshop on Pervasive Systems), OTM Academy Doctoral Consortium, RDDS (International Workshop on Reliability in Decentralized Distributed Systems), SWWS (IFIP WG 2.12 and WG 12.4 International Workshop on Web Semantics), and SeBGIS (International Workshop on Semantic-based Geographical Information Systems).

OTM 2006 Federated Workshops are proudly supported by CNRS (Centre National de la Researche Scientifique, France), the City of Montpellier (France), Ecole Polytechnique Universitaire de Montepellier, Université de Montpellier II (UM2), Laboratoire d'Informatique de Robotique et de Microélectronique de Montpellier (LIRMM), RMIT University (School of Computer Science and Information Technology), and Vrije Universiteit Brussel (Department of Computer Science).

Executive Committee

OTM 2006 General Co-chairs: Robert Meersman (Vrije Universiteit Brussel, Belgium), Zahir Tari (RMIT University, Australia), and Pilar Herrero (Universidad Politécnica de Madrid, Spain).

AWeSOMe 2006 PC Co-chairs: Daniel Grosu (Wayne State University, USA), Pilar Herrero (Universidad Politécnica de Madrid, Spain), Gonzalo Médez (Universidad Complutense de Madrid, Spain), and Marta Sabou (The Open University, UK).

CAMS 2006 PC Co-chairs: Annika Hinze (University of Waikato, New Zealand) and George Buchanan (University of Wales Swansea, UK).

COMINF 2006 PC Co-chairs: Aldo de Moor (Vrije Universiteit Brussel, Belgium) and Michael Gurstein (Community Informatics Research Network, Canada).

IS 2006 PC Co-chairs: Mário Freire (University of Beira Interior, Portugal), Simão Melo de Sousa (University of Beira Interior, Portugal), and Vitor Santos (Microsoft Lisbon, Portugal).

KSinBIT 2006 PC Co-chairs: Maja Hadzic (Curtin University of Technology, Australia), Bart De Moor (Katholieke Universiteit Leuven, Belgium), Yves Moreau (Katholieke Universiteit Leuven, Belgium), and Arek Kasprzyk (European Bioinformatics Institute, UK).

MIOS-CIAO 2006 PC Co-chairs: Antonia Albani (University of Augsburg, Germany) and Jan L.G. Dietz (Delft University of Technology, Netherlands).

MONET 2006 PC Co-chairs: Fernando Ferri (National Research Council, Italy), Maurizio Rafanelli (National Research Council, Italy) and Arianna D'Ulizia (National Research Council, Italy).

OnToContent 2006 PC Co-chairs: Mustafa Jarrar (Vrije Universiteit Brussel, Belgium), Claude Ostyn (IEEE-LTSC, USA), Werner Ceusters (University of Buffalo, USA), and Andreas Persidis (Biovista, Greece).

ORM 2006 PC Co-chairs: Terry Halpin (Neumont University, USA) and Robert Meersman (Vrije Universiteit Brussel, Belgium).

PerSys 2006 PC Co-chairs: Skevos Evripidou (University of Cyprus, Cyprus) and Roy Campbell (University of Illinois at Urbana-Champaign, USA).

OTM 2006 Academy Doctoral Consortium PC Co-chairs: Jan Dietz, OTM Academy Dean (Tu Delft, Netherlands), Antonia Albani (University of Augsburg, Germany), Gábor Nagypál (Forschungszentrum Informatik - FZI, Germany) and Johannes Maria Zaha (Queensland University of Technology, Australia).

RDDS 2006 PC Co-chairs:	Eiko Yoneki (University of Cambridge, UK) and Pascal Felber (Université de Neuchâtel, Switzerland).
SWWS 2006 PC Co-chairs:	Katia Sycara (Carnegie Mellon University, USA), Elizabeth Chang (Curtin University of Technology, Australia), Ernesto Damiani (Milan University, Italy), Mustafa Jarrar (Vrije Universiteit Brussel, Belgium), and Tharam Dillon (University of Technology Sydney, Australia) .
SeBGIS 2006 PC Co-chair:	Esteban Zimány (Université Libre de Bruxelles, Belgium).
Publication Co-chairs:	Kwong Yuen Lai (RMIT University) and Peter Dimopoulos (RMIT University).
Local Organizing Chair:	Zohra Bellahsene (University of Montpellier II, France).
Publicity Chair:	Gonzalo Méndez (Universidad Complutense de Madrid, Spain).
Secretariat:	Ana-Cecilia Martinez Barbosa, Jan Demey, and Daniel Meersman.

AWeSOMe (Agents, Web Services and Ontologies Merging) 2006 Program Committee

José Luis Bosque
Juan A. Botía Blaya
Liliana Cabral
Isaac Chao
Adam Cheyer
Ian Dickinson
John Domingue
Antonio Garcia Dopico
Jorge Gómez
Dominic Greenwood
Jingshan Huang
Margaret Lyell
Dan Marinescu
Gregorio Martinez
Michael Maximilien
Mauricio Paletta
Juan Pavón
José Mariía Peña

Marí Pérez
Ronald Poell
Debbie Richards
Víctor Robles
Paul Roe
Manuel Salvadores
Alberto Sánchez
Weisong Shi
Marius-Calin Silaghi
Henry Tirri
Santtu Toivonen
Rainer Unland
Chris van Aart
Sander van Splunter
Julita Vassileva
Niek Wijngaards
Cheng-Zhong Xu

CAMS (Context-Aware Mobile Systems) 2006 Program Committee

Susanne Boll
Dan Chalmers
Keith Cheverst
Trevor Collins
Gill Dobbie
Tiong Goh
John Grundy
Reto Krummenacher

Diane Lingrand
Dave Nichols
Michel Scholl
Goce Trajcevski
Mark van Setten
Agnes Voisard

COMINF (Community Informatics) 2006 Program Committee

Mark Aakhus
Mark Ackerman
Anjo Anjewierden
Michael Bieber
Andy Bytheway
Stijn Christiaens
Tanguy Coenen
Fiorella De Cindio
Peter Day
Dan Dixon
Lilia Efimova
Hamid Ekbia
Marcus Foth

Mark Gaved
Tom Horan
Driss Ketani
Rolf Kleef
Ulrike Lechner
Peter Mambrey
Dave Newman
Jack Park
Larry Stillman
Beverly Trayner
Bartel Van de Walle
Brian Whitworth

IS (Information Security) 2006 Program Committee

Andre Adelsbach
Manuel Bernardo Barbosa
Carlo Blundo
Fernando Boavida
Thierry Brouard
Ilyoung Chong
Nathan Clarke
Miguel P. Correia
Gwenaël Dërr
Paul Dowland
Mahmoud T. El-Hadidi

Steven Furnell
Michael Gertz
Javier Herranz
Sushil Jajodia
Lech J. Janczewski
Hyun-KooK Kahng
Stamatios Kartalopoulos
Kwok-Yan Lam
Benoit Libert
William List
Henrique S. Mamede

Evangelos Markatos
Sjouke Mauw
Natalie Miloslavskaya
José Pina Miranda
Edmundo Monteiro
Yi Mu
Nuno Ferreira Neves
Maria Papadaki
Manuela Pereira
Hartmut Pohl
Carlos Ribeiro

Henrique Santos
Ryoichi Sasaki
Sung-Won Sohn
K.P. Subbalakshmi
Stephanie Teufel
José Esgalhado Valen
Serge Vaudenay
Jozef Vyskoc
Paulo Veríssimo
André Zúquete

IS (Information Security) 2006 Additional Referees

Anyi Liu
Chao Yao
Filipe Caldeira
João Abrunhosa
Jorge Granjal
José Carlos Bacelar Almeida
Lingyu Wang
Nuno Garcia

Pedro Inácio
Romeu Silva
Sérgio Nunes
Shiping Chen
Sotiris Ioannidis
Stéahine Cuachie

KSinBIT (Knowledge Systems in Bioinformatics) 2006 Program Committee

Robert Meersman
Werner Ceusters
Georges De Moor
Elizabeth Chang
Peter Dawyndt
Jan Van den Bussche
Antoon Goderis
Paolo Romano
Marie-Dominique Devignes
Bert Coessens
Mark Wilkinson
Katy Wolstencroft
Peter Li
Robert Stevens

Carole Goble
Phillip Lord
Chris Wroe
Michael Bada
Ilkay Altintas
Stephen Potter
Vasa Curcin
Armin Haller
Eyal Oren
M. Scott Marshall
Marco Roos
Iwei Yeh

MIOS+CIAO (Inter-organizational Systems) 2006 Program Committee

Wil van der Aalst
Paer Agerfalk
Antonia Albani
Bernhard Bauer
Emmanuel delaHostria
Jan L.G. Dietz
Johann Eder
Joaquim Filipe
Rony G. Flatscher
Kees van Hee
Jan Hoogervorst
Christian Huemer
Zahir Irani
Peter Loos
Graham McLeod
Arturo Molina

Aldo de Moor
Moira Norrie
Maria Orlowska
Erik Proper
Gil Regev
Dewald Roode
Pnina Soffer
Arne Solvberg
Jose Tribolet
Klaus Turowski
Vijay K. Vaishnavi
Rene Wagenaar
Christian Winnewisser
Robert Winter
Johannes Maria Zaha

MONET (MObile and NEtworking Technologies for social applications) 2006 Program Committee

Russell Beale
Tiziana Catarci
Richard Chbeir
Karin Coninx
Peter Dimopoulos
Juan De Lara
Anna Formica
Patrizia Grifoni
Otthein Herzog
Irina Kondratova
Steve Marsh

Rebecca Montanari
Michele Missikoff
Nuria Oliver
Marco Padula
Andrew Phippen
Tommo Reti
Tim Strayer
Henri Ter Hofte
Riccardo Torlone
Mikael Wiberg

OnToContent (Ontology content and evaluation in Enterprise) 2006 Program Committee

Adil Hameed
Alain Leger
Aldo Gangemi
Andre Valente

Andrew Stranieri
Avigdor Gal
Barry Smith
Bill Andersen

Bob Colomb
Christiane Fellbaum
Christopher Brewster
Ernesto Damiani
Fausto Giunchiglia
Francesco Danza
Francky Trichet
Giancarlo Guizzardi
Giorgos Stamou
Hans Akkermans
Jeff Pan
Jens Lemcke
John Sowa
Joost Breuker
Karl Stroetmann
Kewen Wang
Luk Vervenne

Miguel-Angel Sicilia
Mohand-Said Hacid
Nikolay Mehandjiev
Paolo Bouquet
Paul Piwek
Robert Meersman
Robert Tolksdorf
Sergio Tessaris
Silvie Spreeuwenberg
Simon White
Stephen McGibbon
Theo Mensen
Yannick Legre
Yannis Charalabidis
Yaser Bishr

ORM (Object-Role Modeling) 2006 Program Committee

Guido Bakema
Herman Balsters
Linda Bird
Anthony Bloesch
Scott Becker
Peter Bollen
Andy Carver
Dave Cuyler
Necito dela Cruz
Aldo de Moor
Olga De Troyer
Jan Dietz
David Embley
Ken Evans
Gordon Everest
Henri Habrias
Pat Hallock

Terry Halpin
Hank Hermans
Stijn Hoppenbrouwers
Mike Jackson
Mustafa Jarrar
Alberto Laender
Inge Lemmens
Robert Meersman
Tony Morgan
Maurice Nijssen
Sjir Nijssen
Erik Proper
Peter Spyns
Sten Sundblad
Theo van der Weide
Gerd Wagner

PerSys (Pervasive Systems) 2006 Program Committee

Jalal Al-Muhtadi
Jean Bacon

Christain Becker
Roy Campbell

Adrian David Cheok

Hakan Duman

Hesham El-Rewini

Skevos Evripidou

Hans Gellersen

Markus Huebscher

Yunhao Liu

Wallid Najjar

Das Sajal

George Samaras

Anja Schanzenberger

Behrooz Shirazi

Sotirios Terzis

Gregory Yovanof

Arkady Zaslavsky

OTM Academy (International Doctoral Symposium) 2006 Program Committee

Antonia Albani

Domenico Beneventano

Sonia Bergamaschi

Jaime Delgado

Jan Dietz

Johann Eder

Maria Orlowska

Gábor Nagypál

Johannes Maria Zaha

RDDS (Reliability in Decentralized Distributed Systems) 2006 Program Committee

Licia Capra

Mariano Cilia

Vittorio Cortellessa

Simon Courtenage

Patrick Eugster

Ludger Fiege

Maria Gradinariu

Eli Katsiri

Michael Kounavis

Marco Mamei

Jon Munson

Maziar Nekovee

Andrea Passarella

Peter Pietzuch

Matthieu Roy

Francois Taïani

Niki Trigoni

Einar Vollset

SWWS (Web Semantics) 2006 Program Committee

Aldo Gangemi

Amit Sheth

André Valente

Andrew Stranieri

Avigdor Gal

Carole Goble

Carole Hafner

Cecilia Magnusson Sjoberg

Chris Bussler

David Bell

Elisa Bertino

Elizabeth Chang

Enrico Franconi

Ernesto Damiani

Feng Ling
Frank van Harmelen
Giancarlo Guizzardi
Grigoris Antoniou
Guiraude Lame
Hai Zhuge
Jaime Delgado
Jaiwei Han
John Debenham
John Mylopoulos
Joost Breuker
Jos Lehmann
Katia Sycara
Kokou Yetongnon
Layman Allen
Leonardo Lesmo
Ling Liu
Lizhu Zhou
Lotfi Zadeh
Manfred Hauswirth
Mariano Lopez
Masood Nikvesh
Mihaela Ulieru
Mohand-Said Hacid

Mukesh Mohania
Mustafa Jarrar
Nicola Guarino
Peter Spyns
Pieree Yves Schobbens
Qing Li
Radboud Winkels
Ramasamy Uthurusamy
Richard Benjamins
Rita Temmerman
Robert Meersman
Robert Tolksdorf
Said Tabet
Stefan Decker
Susan Urban
Tharam Dillon
Trevor Bench-Capon
Usuama Fayed
Valentina Tamma
Wil van der Aalst
York Sure
Zahir Tari

SeBGIS (Semantic-based Geographical Information Systems) 2006 Program Committee

Gennady Adrienko
Yvan Bédard
David Bennett
Michela Bertolotto
Roland Billen
Alex Borgida
Bénédicte Buch
Christophe Claramunt
Eliseo Clementini
Nadine Cullot
Fernando Ferri
Anders Friis-Christensen
Antony Galton

Marinos Kavouras
Werner Kuhn
Robert Laurini
Sergei Levashkin
Thérèse Libourel
Peter van Oosterom
Dimitris Papadias
Maurizio Rafanelli
Simonas Saltenis
Emmanuel Stefanakis
Nectaria Tryfona
Stephan Winter

Table of Contents – Part II

Competence Ontologies

Workshop on Obect-Role Modeling(ORM)

Modeling Extensions

Data Warehousing

Language and Tool Issues

Dynamic Rules and Processes

The Modeling Process and Instructional Design

Workshop on Pervasive Systems (PerSys)

Infrastructure for Pervasive Systems

Service Discovery and Personalization

Pervasive Environments

Security and Privacy

Wireless and Sensor Networks

Doctoral Consortium

Enterprise Systems

System Development

Workshop on Reliability in Decentralized Distributed Systems (RDDS)

P2P

Distributed Algorithms

Reliability Evaluation

Networks 1540
   Joos-Hendrik Böse, Andreas Thaler

Traceability and Timeliness in Messaging Middleware 1551
   Brian Shand, Jem Rashbass

Transaction Manager Failover: A Case Study Using JBOSS Application
Server 1555
   A.I. Kistijantoro, G. Morgan, S.K. Shrivastava

Workshop on Semantic-Based Geographical Information Systems (SeBGIS)

GIS Integration and GRID

Semantic Information 1566
   Christoph Quix, Lemonia Ragia, Linlin Cai, Tian Gan

Towards a Context Ontology for Geospatial Data Integration 1576
   Damires Souza, Ana Carolina Salgado, Patricia Tedesco

Spatial Data Access Patterns in Semantic Grid Environment 1586
   Vikram Sorathia, Anutosh Maitra

Spatial Data Warehouses

   Sandro Bimonte, Pascal Wehrle, Anne Tchounikine, Maryvonne Miquel

Affordable Web-Based Spatio-temporal Applications for Ad-Hoc
Decisions 1606
   Vera Hernández Ernst

IFIP WG 2.12 and WG 12.4 International Workshop on Web Semantics (SWWS)

Security, Risk and Privacy for the Semantic Web

Semantic Web and Querying

Ontologies

Applications of Semantic Web

Concepts for the Semantic Web

Workshop on Context Aware Mobile Systems (CAMS)

Models of Context

Service Models

Data Handling

Users and Uses

Filtering and Control

Table of Contents – Part I

Posters of the 2006 CoopIS (Cooperative Information Systems) International Conference

Posters of the 2006 DOA (Distributed Objects and Applications) International Conference

Posters of the 2006 ODBASE (Ontologies, Databases, and Applications of Semantics) International Conference

Posters of the 2006 GADA (Grid Computing, High Performance and Distributed Applications International Conference

Workshop on Agents, Web Services and Ontologies Merging (AweSOMe)

Invited Talk

Combing Agent and Web Service Technology

Web Services in E-Commerce and Business

Modeling and Re-using Ontologies

Workshop on Community Informatics (COMINF)

Community Informatics Foundations

Capturing Community Meaning

Improving Community Communications

Analyzing and Designing Community IS

Community Evaluation and Assessment Methodologies

Plenary Discussion: Towards a Socio-technical Research Agenda for Community Informatics

Workshop on Information Security (IS)

Multimedia Security

RFID Security

Network Security

Cryptographic Algorithms and Protocols

Mobile and Wireless Network Security

Information Security and Service Resilience

Workshop on Knowledge Systems in Bioinformatics (KsinBIT)

Bioinformatics Ontologies, Terminologies and Knowledge Bases

Use of Ontologies in Bioinformatics

Bioinformatics Data Manipulation, Integration and Associated Tools

Workshop on Modeling Inter-Organizational Systems (MIOS-CIAO)

Architecture in Inter-organizational Cooperation

Ontology and Project Management

Inter-organizational Business Processes

Workshop on Mobile and Networking Technologies for Social Applications (MONET)

Social Networks

Studies and Methodologies for Mobile and Networking Technologies

Mobile and Networking Technologies in Different Context

Architecture and Middleware

OnToContent 2006 PC Co-chairs' Message

Welcome to the proceedings of the first international workshop on ontology content and evaluation in enterprise (OnToContent 2006). This book reflects the issues raised and presented during the workshop, which paid attention to ontology content, specially ontologies in human resources and employment, and healthcare and life sciences.

This workshop was organized and partially funded by the Ontology Outreach Advisory OOA (Knowledge Web NoE, FP6-507482). The OOA is devoted to developing strategies for ontology recommendation and standardization, thereby promoting and providing outreach for verifiable quality ontological content.

This first year, a total of 35 papers were submitted to OnToContent. Each submission was reviewed by two to four experts. The papers were judged according to their originality, validity, significance to theory and practice, readability and organization, and relevancy to the workshop topics and beyond. This resulted in the selection of 12 papers for presentation at the workshop and publication in these proceedings (34% acceptance rate). We feel that these proceedings will inspire further research and create an intense following. The Program Committee comprised: Adil Hameed, Alain Leger, Aldo Gangemi, André Valente, Andrew Stranieri, Avigdor Gal, Barry Smith, Bill Andersen, Bob Colomb, Christiane Fellbaum, Christopher Brewster, Ernesto Damiani, Fausto Giunchiglia, Francesco Danza, Francky Trichet, Giancarlo Guizzardi,Giorgos Stamou, Hans Akkermans, Harith Alani, Jeff Pan, Jens Lemcke, John Sowa, Joost Breuker, Karl Stroetmann,Kewen Wang, Luk Vervenne, Lina Al-Jadir, Miguel-Angel Sicilia, Mohand-Said Hacid, Nikolay Mehandjiev, Paolo Bouquet, Paul Piwek, Robert Meersman, Robert Tolksdorf, Sergio Tessaris, Silvie Spreeuwenberg, Simon White, Stephen McGibbon, Theo Mensen, Yannick Legré, Yannis Charalabidis, Yaser Bishr.

We would like to express our deepest appreciation to the authors of the submitted papers and thank all the workshop attendees and the Program Committee members for their dedication and assistance in creating our program and turning the workshop into a success. Producing this book would not have been possible without the much-appreciated contribution of Pilar Herrero, Peter Dimopoulos, and Kwong Lai.

Thank you and we hope you will enjoy the papers as much as we do.

August 2006   Mustafa Jarrar, Vrije Universiteit Brussel, Belgium
                                          Claude Ostyn, IEEE-LTSC, USA
                               Werner Ceusters, University of Buffalo, USA
                                      Andreas Persidis, Biovista, Greece

R. Meersman, Z. Tari, P. Herrero et al. (Eds.): OTM Workshops 2006, LNCS 4278, p. 1011, 2006.
© Springer-Verlag Berlin Heidelberg 2006

Unit Tests for Ontologies

Denny Vrandečić[1] and Aldo Gangemi[2]

[1] Institute AIFB, University of Karlsruhe, Germany
denny@aifb.uni-karlsruhe.de
[2] LOA Laboratory of Applied Ontology, Rome, Italy
aldo.gangemi@istc.cnr.it

Abstract. In software engineering, the notion of unit testing was successfully introduced and applied. Unit tests are easy manageable tests for small parts of a program – single units. They proved especially useful to capture unwanted changes and side effects during the maintenance of a program, and they grow with the evolution of the program.

Ontologies behave quite differently than program units. As there is no information hiding in ontology engineering, and thus no black box components, at first the idea of unit testing for ontologies seems not applicable. In this paper we motivate the need for unit testing, describe the adaptation to the unit testing approach, and give use cases and examples.

1 Introduction

In software engineering, the idea of unit testing [1] was introduced to counter the complexities of modern software engineering efforts. Unit tests are meant to facilitate the development of program modules or units, and to ensure the interplay of such units in the combined system. It results in more loosely coupled code, that is easier to refactor and simpler to integrate, and that has a formalized documentation (although not necessarily complete). Unit tests can be added incrementally during the maintenance of a piece of software, in order to not accidentally stumble upon and old bug and hunt it down repeatedly.

Unit tests are not complete test suites: there are several types of errors that unit tests will not catch, including errors that result from the integration of the units to the complete system, performance problems, and, naturally, errors that were not expected when writing the unit tests.

Unit tests in software engineering became popularized with the object oriented language Smalltalk, and still to this today remain focused on languages with strong possibilities to create smaller units of code. They are based on several decomposition techniques, most important of all information hiding.

Ontologies are different. As of now, no form of information hiding or interfaces are available – and it remains an open research issue in the field of ontology modularization how this will be taken care of.

In this paper we will take a look at the benefits of unit testing applied to ontologies, i.e. their possibilities to facilitate regression tests, to provide a test

R. Meersman, Z. Tari, P. Herrero et al. (Eds.): OTM Workshops 2006, LNCS 4278, pp. 1012–1020, 2006.

framework that can grow incrementally during the maintenance and evolution phase of the ontology, and that is reasonably simple to use. In order for the unit testing for ontologies to be useful, they need to be reasonably easy to use and mantain. This will depend heavily on the given implementation (which is underway). The task of this paper is to investigate different ideas that are inspired by the idea of unit testing, and to work out the intuitions of how these ideas could be used in the context of the ontology lifecycle. Especially in the enterprise application of ontologies, some easy to use form of ontology evaluation will be required in order to let ontology based technologies become more widespread. We will show a number of ideas and examples of how this goal can be achieved.

The paper will first show a typical use case, as encountered in a project setting in Section 2. We will then discuss five different approaches, that all are inspired by the unit testing frameworks in software engineering: first we look at the idea of design by contract, i.e. of stating what statements should and should not derive from an ontology being developed or maintained, either as explicit ontology statements or as competency questions using a query language (Sections 3 and 4). Then we investigate the relationship of heavy- to lightweight ontologies, and how they can interplay with regards to ontology evaluation in Section 5. Autoepistemic operators lend themselves also to be used in the testing of ontologies, especially with regards to their (relative) completeness, since they are a great way to formalize the introspection of ontologies (Section 6). We also regard a common error in ontology modelling with description logics based language, and try to turn this error into our favour in Section 7, before we discuss related work and give an outlook on possible further work and open issues.

For this work, the term ontologies refers to web ontologies as defined by the OWL DL standard [15]. This means that the ontologies are a variant based on the description logics $\mathcal{SHOIN}(\mathbf{D})$, and, especially, that ontologies mean to encompass both the so called TBox, where the vocabulary of the ontology is defined (which some call the whole ontology), and the ABox, where facts using the vocabulary defined are stated (which some call the knowledge base).

2   Motivation

In the SEKT project[1], one of the case studies aims at providing an intelligent FAQ system to help newly appointed judges in Spain [2]. The system depends on an ontology for finding the best answers and to find references to existing cases in order to provide the judge with further background information. The applied ontology is built and maintained by legal experts with almost no experience in formal knowledge representation [4].

As the ontology evolved and got refined (and thus changed), the legal experts noticed that some of their changes had undesired side effects. To give a simplified example, consider the class hierarchy depicted in Figure 1. Let's take for granted that this ontology has been used for a while already, before someone notices that not every academic needs necessarily be a member of an university. So *Academic*

---

[1] http://www.sekt-project.com

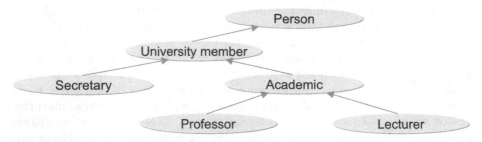

Fig. 1. Example class hierarchy

becomes a direct subclass of *Person*, instead of *University member*. But due to this change, also *Professor* is no subclass of *University member* any more (a change that maybe was hidden from the ontology engineer, as the ontology development environment may not have displayed the subclasses of *Academic*).

The resulting ontology remains perfectly satisfiable. But a tool, that, for example, creates a web page for all members of the university may now skip the professors, since they are not classified as university members any more – an error that would only become apparent in the use of the tool much later and will be potentially hard to track down to that particular ontology change operation.

Unit testing for ontologies can discover such problems, and a few other ones as well, as we will see in the following sections.

3   Affirming Derived Knowledge

We create two test ontologies T^+ (called the positive test ontology) and T^- (the negative test ontology), and define that an ontology O, in order to fulfil the constraints imposed by the test ontologies, needs to fulfil the following conditions: each axiom $A_1^+...A_n^+ \in T^+$ must be derivable from O, i.e.

$$O \models A_i^+ \forall A_i^+ \in T^+$$

and each axiom $A_1^-...A_n^- \in T^-$ must not be derivable from O, i.e.

$$O \not\models A_i^- \forall A_i^- \in T^-$$

Note that T^+ trivially fulfils the first condition if O is not satisfiable, whereas an empty ontology trivially fulfils the second condition. So it is not hard to come up with ontologies that fulfil the conditions, which shows that unit tests are not meant to be complete formalizations of the requirements of an ontology, but rather helpful indicators towards possible errors or omissions in the tested ontologies. Note also that T^- could be unsatisfiable, i.e. there are two sets of axioms (both subsets of T^- that contradict each other. This still makes sense, as it means that O must not make a decision about the truth of either of these sets (thus formalizing the requirement that O must be agnostic towards certain statements).

To come back to our previous example in Section 2 a simple test ontology T^+ that consists of the single axiom *Professor* $\sqsubseteq$ *University member* would have been sufficient to discover the problem described. So after the discovered error, this statement is added to the test ontology, and now this same error will be detected by running the unit tests.

The test ontologies are meant to be created and grown during the maintenance of the ontology. Every time an error is encountered in the usage of the ontology, the error is formalized and added to the appropriate ontology (like in the example above). Experienced ontology engineers may add appropriate axioms in order to anticipate and counter possible errors in maintenance.

In software engineering it is often the case, that the initial development of a program is done by a higher skilled, better trained, and more consistent team, whereas the maintenance is then performed by a less expensive group, with less experienced members, that change more frequently. So in software engineering, the more experienced developers often anticipate frequent errors that can happen during maintenance, and create unit tests accordingly in order to put appropriate constraints on the future evolution of the software. We expect a similar development in ontology engineering and maintenance, as soon as ontologies become more common components of information systems. The framework proposed in this paper offers the same possibilities to an ontology engineer.

Why should an ontology engineer not just add the axioms from T^+ to O, and $\neg A_i^-$ for each A_i^- in T^-? There are several reasons: 1) not every axiom A_i^- can be negated. For example, the simple statement $R(a, b)$ stating a relation R between the individuals a and b can not be negated in OWL DL. 2) adding such axioms increases redundancy in the ontology, and thus makes it harder to edit. 3) the axioms may potentially increase reasoning complexity, or else use language constructs that are not meant to be used within the ontology, for whatever reason. 4) as stated above, the axioms in T^- may be contradictory. 5) Finally, due to the open world assumption, $O \not\models A_i^- \forall A_i^- \in T^-$ is not the same as $O \models \neg A_i^- \forall A_i^- \in T^-$, so that the negative test ontology can actually not be simulated with the means of OWL DL.

4   Formalized Competency Questions

Competency questions, as defined by some methodologies for ontology engineering (like OTK [17] or Methontology [6]), describe what kind of knowledge the resulting ontology is supposed to answer. These questions can always be formalized in a query language (or else the ontology will actually not be able to answer the given competency question, and thus will not meet the given requirements). Formalizing the queries, instead of writing them down in natural language, and formalizing the expected answers as well, allows for a system that automatically checks if the ontology meets the requirements stated with the competency questions.

We consider this approach especially useful not for the maintenance of the system, but rather for its initial build, in order to define the extent of the ontology. Note that competency questions usually are just exemplary questions – answering all competency questions does not mean that the ontology is complete. Also note that sometimes, although the question is formalizable, the answer does not necessarily need to be known at the time of writing the question. This is especially true for dynamic ontologies, i.e. ontologies that reflect properties of the world that keep changing often (like the song the user of the system is listening to at query time). In that case we can define some checks if the answer is sensible or even possible (like that the answer indeed needs to be a song). Often these further checks will not go beyond the abilities defined by the other approaches to unit testing in this paper.

5   Expressive Consistency Checks

Ontologies in information systems often need to fulfil the requirement of allowing reasoners to quickly answer queries with regards to the ontology. Light weight ontologies usually fulfil this task best. Also, many of the more complex constructors of OWL DL often do not add further information, but rather are used to restrict possible models. This is useful in many applications, like ontology mapping and alignment, or information integration from different sources.

For example, a minimal cardinality constraint will, due to the open world assumption, hardly ever lead to any inferred statements in an OWL DL ontology (this can only become the case if range of the minimal cardinality restricted relation is a class consisting of nominals). Nevertheless the statement can be useful as an indicator for tools that want to offer a user interface to the ontology, or for mapping algorithms that can take this information into account.

Further expressive constraints on the ontology, like disjointness of classes, can be used to check the ontology for consistency at the beginning of the usage, but after this has been checked, a light weight version of the ontology, that potentially enables reasoners to derive answers with a better response time, could be used instead.

Also, for these pre-use consistency checks, more expressive logical formalisms could be used, like reasoning over the ontology metamodel [13,3], using SWRL [11], or using the transformation of the ontology to a logic programming language like datalog [8] and then add further integrity constraints to that resulting program (that may easily go far beyond the expressivity available in the original ontology language: with a logic programming language it would be easy to state that, by company policy, a supervisor is required to have a higher income than the persons reporting to her – which is impossible in OWL DL).

Formally, we introduce a test ontology T^C for an ontology O, that includes the high axiomatization of the terms used in O, and check for the satisfiability of the merged ontology $O \cup T^C$. In the case of using the logic programming translation, we merge (concatenate) the translation of the ontology to datalog

$(LP(O))$ with the test program T_{LP}^C, and test the resulting program for violation of the integrity constraints.

Let us consider an example ontology O_x:

$tradesStocks(Jim, MegaCorp)$
$CEO(MegaCorp, Jack)$
$bestBuddy(Jim, Jack)$
$bestBuddy \sqsubseteq hasNoSecrets$

This example ontology is equivalent to the translated logic program $LP(O_x)$:

$tradesStocks(Jim, MegaCorp)$.
$CEO(MegaCorp, Jack)$.
$bestBuddy(Jim, Jack)$.
$hasNoSecrets(X, Y) : -bestBuddy(X, Y)$.

The test program T_{LP}^C (that checks for insider trading) may consist of the following line, a single integrity constraint:

$: -hasNoSecrets(X, Y), tradesStocks(Y, C), CEO(X, C)$.

Evaluating the program should now raise a violated integrity constraint. We could also name the integrity constraints (by putting *insiderTrading* into its head and then explicitly evaluate *insiderTrading* to see if it evaluates to true or false. We also could use the head *insiderTrading*(Y) and then query for the same head, to get a list of people who actually do the insider trading (and thus uncover problems in the program much faster).

6   Use of Autoepistemic Operators

In [7] an extension of OWL DL with autoepistemic operators is described. Especially the **K**-operator can be useful to check an ontology not only with regards to its consistent usage, but also with regards to some explicitly defined understanding of completeness. In a geographic ontology, we may define that every country has a capital, $Country \sqsubseteq \exists capital.City$. But stating the existence of a country without stating its capital will not lead to an error in the ontology, because the reasoner (correctly) assumes, that the knowledge is not complete. Using the **K**- and **A**−operators instead, we would define that $\mathbf{K}Country \sqsubseteq \exists\mathbf{A}capital.\mathbf{A}City$, i.e. for every known country the capital must also be known (i.e. either stated explicitly or inferrable) in the ontology, or else the ontology will not satisfiable (the example follows ex. 3.3 in [5]). Thus we are able to state what *should* be known, and a satisfiability check will check if, indeed this knowledge is present.

On the Semantic Web, such a formalism will prove of great value, as it allows to simply discard data that does not adhere to a certain understanding of completeness. For example, a crawler may gather event data on the Semantic Web. But instead of simply collecting all instances of event, it may decide to only accept events that have a start and an end date, a location, a contact email, and a classification with regards to a certain term hierarchy. Although this will decrease the recall of the crawler, the data will be of a higher quality, i.e. of a bigger value, as it can be sorted, displayed, and actually used by calendars, map tools, and email clients in order to support the user.

The formalisation and semantics of autoepistemic operators for the usage in web ontologies is described in [7], and thus will not be repeated here.

7   Domain and Ranges as Constraints

Users often complain that their intuitive usage of relation domain and ranges contradict their actual semantics. They expect domain and ranges to be used like constraints, i.e. if they say that *brideOf* is a relation with the domain *Woman* and one applies it to *John*, who is a *Man*, instead of getting an inconsistency *John* will be classified as a *Woman* by the reasoner (for the sake of the example, we take it for granted that *Man* and *Woman* are not disjoint). In the following we will try to use this error to the benefit of the user.

As the domain and range declarations in the ontology will usually render these checks trivially true, we need to remove them first from the ontology. Therefore we take an ontology, and delete all domain and range declarations that are to be understood as constraints (in the example in the previous paragraph, we would remove the declaration of *brideOf*'s domain as *Woman*). Now we check for all instantiations of the removed domain or range declaration's relation if the subject (in case of a removed domain declaration) or the object (in case of a removed range declaration) indeed gets classified with the supposed class (in the example, we ask if *John* is indeed a *Woman*).

Note that these removals may have further implications on the ontology's inferred statements, depending on the further axioms of the ontology, and its planned usage. Experiments need to be performed to be able to judge the described approach with regards to its impact on the inferred knowledge in real world scenarios. This approach actually will not necessarily highlight errors, but only indicate possible places for errors. It will probably make more sense to introduce a new relation that let us define constraints for relations, and then to check these explicitly. We expect to learn from the planned experiments how to exactly bring this approach to use.

8   Related Work

A Protégé Plug-In implementing an OWL Unit Test framework[2] exists, that allows to perform what we have described with T^+ testing for affirming derived knowledge in Section 3.

In [16] the theory and practice of ontology evolution is discussed. Ontology change operations and ontology evolution strategies are introduced. Based on this, [9] extends this work for OWL DL ontologies, and investigates the evolution of ontologies with regards to consistency, implemented in the so called evOWLution framework. As the theoretical work allows generic and user defined consistency checks, the ideas presented here could be regarded as a number of ways to formalize further aspects of the ontology, and enable more expressive consistency checks beyond simple logical satisfiability.

---

[2] http://www.co-ode.org/downloads/owlunittest/

Some parts of the presented ideas – especially the test ontologies in Section 3 and the consistency check against heavy weight descriptions in Section 5 – may often lead to unsatisfiable ontologies when the unit testing uncover problems. In this case, research done in debugging [14] and revising [12], especially evolving ontologies [10], will provide the tools and techniques to actually resolve the problems.

9 Outlook

The approaches described in this paper address problems in ontology engineering and maintenance that have been discovered during the work with ontologies within the SEKT case studies. As they often reminded us of problems that occurred in software engineering, a solution that was successfully introduced to software engineering was examined – unit testing. Although the notion of unit testing needed to be changed, it inspired a slew of possible approaches, that have been described in this paper. Also, examples for these approaches have been given to illustrate how they can be used within the lifecycle of an ontology.

As of now, we are working on an implementation of the presented ideas in order to experimentally verify their usefulness. Although we have shown that several problems we have encountered can be solved with the presented approaches, it is unclear if the idea behind them is simple enough to be understood by non-experts in ontology engineering. Also it needs to be investigated, how often certain classes of problems appear in real world ontologies, and which of the ideas presented here are most effective to counter these problems.

Like in software engineering, we do not expect unit tests to cover the whole field of ontology evaluation. But we expect it to become (and remain) an important building block within an encompassing framework, that will cover regression tests and (relative) completeness, and help to indicate further errors in the initial development, and especially further maintenance of an ontology.

We expect modularization of ontologies and networked ontology to become more important in the next generation of web ontology based technologies. Unit testing provides a framework to formalize requirements about ontologies. We expect the approaches described in this paper, and maybe further similar approaches, to become much more investigated and discussed in the close future.

Acknowledgements

Research reported in this paper was supported by the IST Programme of the European Community under the SEKT project, Semantically Enabled Knowledge Technologies (IST-1-506826-IP, http://www.sekt-project.com). We want to thank our colleagues for fruitful discussions, especially Stephan Grimm, Boris Motik, Peter Haase, Sudhir Agarwal, Jos Lehmann, and Malvina Nissim.

This publication reflects the authors' view.

References

1. K. Beck. Simple Smalltalk testing: With patterns. http://www.xprogramming. com/testfram.htm.
2. V. Benjamins, P. Casanovas, J. Contreras, J. L. Cobo, and L. Lemus. Iuriservice: An intelligent frequently asked questions system to assist newly appointed judges. In V. Benjamins, P. Casanovas, A. Gangemi, and B. Selic, editors, *Law and the Semantic Web*, LNCS, Berlin Heidelberg, 2005. Springer.
3. S. Brockmans and P. Haase. A Metamodel and UML Profile for Rule-extended OWL DL Ontologies –A Complete Reference. Technical report, Universität Karlsruhe, March 2006. http://www.aifb.uni-karlsruhe.de/WBS/sbr/ publications/owl-metamodeling.pdf.
4. P. Casanovas, N. Casellas, M. Poblet, J. Vallbé, Y. Sure, and D. Vrandečić. Iuriservice ii ontology development. In P. Casanovas, editor, *Workshop on Artificial Intelligence and Law at the XXIII. World Conference of Philosophy of Law and Social Philosophy*, May 2005.
5. F. M. Donini, D. Nardi, and R. Rosati. Description logics of minimal knowledge and negation as failure. *ACM Transactions on Computational Logic*, 3(2):177–225, 2002.
6. M. Fernández-López, A. Gómez-Pérez, J. P. Sierra, and A. P. Sierra. Building a chemical ontology using Methontology and the Ontology Design Environment. *IEEE Intelligent Systems*, 14(1), 1999.
7. S. Grimm and B. Motik. Closed world reasoning in the semantic web through epistemic operators. In B. C. Grau, I. Horrocks, B. Parsia, and P. Patel-Schneider, editors, *OWL: Experiences and Directions*, Galway, Ireland, Nov 2005.
8. B. Grosof, I. Horrocks, R. Volz, and S. Decker. Description Logic Programs: Combining Logic Programs with Description Logic. In *Proceedings of the Twelfth International World Wide Web Conference, WWW2003, Budapest, Hungary, 20-24 May 2003*, pages 48–57. ACM, 2003.
9. P. Haase and L. Stojanovic. Consistent evolution of OWL ontologies. In A. Gómez-Pérez and J. Euzenat, editors, *Proc. of the 2nd European Semantic Web Conf. ESWC*, volume 3532, pages 182–197, Heraklion, Crete, Greece, 2005. Springer.
10. P. Haase, F. van Harmelen, Z. Huang, H. Stuckenschmidt, and Y. Sure. A framework for handling inconsistency in changing ontologies. In Y. Gil, E. Motta, V. R. Benjamins, and M. A. Musen, editors, *Proceedings of the ISWC2005*, volume 3729 of *LNCS*, pages 353–367. Springer, NOV 2005.
11. I. Horrocks, P. Patel-Schneider, H. Boley, S. Tabet, B. Grosof, and M. Dean. SWRL: a semantic web rule language combining OWL and RuleML, 2003.
12. S. J. Lam, D. Sleeman, and W. Vasconcelos. Retax++: a tool for browsing and revising ontologies. In *Proc. ISWC 2005 Demo Session*, Galway, Ireland, 2005.
13. B. Motik. On the properties of metamodeling in OWL. In *Proc. of the 4th International Semantic Web Conference, Galway, Ireland, November 2005*, NOV 2005.
14. B. Parsia, E. Sirin, and A. Kalyanpur. Debugging OWL ontologies. In *Proc. of the 14th World Wide Web Conference (WWW2005)*, Chiba, Japan, May 2005.
15. M. K. Smith, C. Welty, and D. McGuinness. OWL Web Ontology Language Guide, 2004. W3C Rec. 10 February 2004, avail. at http://www.w3.org/TR/owl-guide/.
16. L. Stojanovic. *Methods and Tools for Ontology Evolution*. PhD thesis, University of Karlsruhe, 2004.
17. Y. Sure and R. Studer. On-To-Knowledge methodology. In J. Davies, D. Fensel, and F. van Harmelen, editors, *On-To-Knowledge: Semantic Web enabled Knowledge Management*, chapter 3, pages 33–46. J. Wiley and Sons, 2002.

Issues for Robust Consensus Building in P2P Networks

A-R. Mawlood-Yunis, M. Weiss, and N. Santoro

School of Computer Science, Carleton University
Ottawa, Ontario, K1S 5B6, Canada
{armyunis, santoro, weiss}@scs.carleton.ca

Abstract. The need for semantic interoperability between ontologies in a peer-to-peer (P2P) environment is imperative. This is because, by definition participants in P2P environment are equal, autonomous and distributed. For example, the synthesis of concepts developed independently by different academic researchers, different research labs, various emergency service departments and, hospitals and pharmacies, just to mention a few, are an assertive request for cooperation and collaboration among these independent peers. In this work we are looking at issues that enable us to build a robust semantic consensus to solve the interoperability problem among heterogeneous ontologies in P2P networks. To achieve a robust semantic consensus we focus on three key issues: i. semantic mapping faults, ii. consensus construction iii. fault-tolerance. All these three issues will be further elaborated in this paper, initial steps to address theses issues will be described and fault-tolerant semantic mapping research directions will be further identified.

1 Introduction

There has been considerable work on semantic interoperability, i.e. the mapping between different concepts from different ontologies. Some of this work suggests achieving interoperability through a global ontology mediator [6], while others suggest building consensus incrementally from local mapping [1, 7, 8]. We favor the latter approach and it is the focus of our research. To build a robust semantic consensus system we focus on three key issues: i. semantic mapping faults, i.e. semantic mapping conflicts, ii. consensus construction iii. fault-tolerance. The existing works on building semantic consensus among distributed ontologies do not distinguish between permanent and temporary **semantic mapping faults**. The failure to distinguish between permanent and temporary mapping faults could result in the erroneous labeling of peers with incompatible knowledge representation. Incompatible knowledge representation could have the further consequence of preventing labeled peers from teaming up with other knowledge-comparable peers. Our hypothesis is that to be able to extract the most consensus possible among related peers we should focus not only on the cooperative peers, which most of the existing works do, but also on uncooperative peers as well. Observing the fact that **consensus building** technique used in semantic mapping

R. Meersman, Z. Tari, P. Herrero et al. (Eds.): OTM Workshops 2006, LNCS 4278, pp. 1021–1027, 2006.
© Springer-Verlag Berlin Heidelberg 2006

is similar to the *majority voting* technique used in the designing fault-tolerance hardware and software systems opens up a new avenue for consensus construction research. We believe that there are opportunities to build a more robust semantic consensus systems using other applied majority voting and fault-tolerance techniques. The need for **fault-tolerance** capability of software have been determined by the fact that the real-world applications require a highly reliable, continuously available, safe and accurate softwares. Therefore, we believe that semantic mapping systems should be constructed with the built-in capability to tolerate faults.

The rest of this paper is organized as follows: in section 2, we look at the temporary fault issue in consensus building. In section 3, we describe the similarity between majority voting and consensus building and its effect on future research. In section 4, we discuss the construction of the consensus-based systems with fault-tolerance capabilities and finally in section 5, the conclusion of the paper with some future research directions are presented.

2   Semantic Mapping Faults

Consensus formation in a P2P network is identified by the greatest(lowest) possible common knowledge (GCK) among all the peers of the network. Current consensus building procedure obeys the following steps: Every-time a peer P encounters another peer $\bar{P}$ that could handle its request (i.e. a peer with similar semantic knowledge representation), that peer $\bar{P}$ will be added to the list of related peers to peer P. This knowledge will be used for the subsequent cooperation and encounters, for example, when answering a query. However, if a peer P meets another peer $\hat{P}$ with a different semantic knowledge representation, that peer $\hat{P}$ will not be considered for subsequent tasks [1, 7, 4]. Two key elements in the described consensus formation are semantic *mapping operation* and *peers participation*. In other words, correct mapping relates peers with semantic comparable concepts. Most of the existing works on concept mapping are concern with the *precision* of mapping. It is implemented as threshold variable δ and the user of the system decides on its value at a run time. The δ and GCK are inversely related, i.e. the higher the δ the lower the result of GCK and vise-versa. The following represents this relation.

$$f(GCK) : 1/\delta \hspace{4cm} \text{Eq.1}$$

Others such as [8, 7] tried to improve the result of GCK by increasing the number of peers ρ who participate in consensus formation. This is done by accepting partial results. Hence Eq.1 could be rewritten as follows:

$${}'f(GCK) : 1/\delta, P(\rho) \hspace{4cm} \text{Eq.2}$$

where $'f(GCK)$ represents the improved $f(GCK)$ and $P(\rho)$ is the probability of extra peers participating in consensus formation because of their ability to provide partial results to the query. In the described consensus formation, peers' past collaborations used for future decisions on further collaborations. We will rewrite Eq.2 to reflect this reality where χ represents cooperative peers.

$$'f(GCK) : (1/\delta, P(\rho))[\chi]$$ Eq.3

One shortcoming with the above described method is that, once a peer is unable to fulfill a particular request, for example answering a query, it will not be considered for the subsequent tasks. In other words, the described method sees the peers' inability to answer a query as a permanent fault - permanent non-cooperation. We see this as a deficiency because peers' inability to answer a query could be a result of temporary dis-connection, noise or incompetency to answer a particular request. Therefore, writing the Eq.3 to account for temporary uncooperative peers ϵ yields the following relation.

$$''f(GCK) : (1/\delta, P(\rho))[\chi, \epsilon]$$ Eq.4

To be able to include temporary uncooperative peers for future tasks, we have to distinguish between permanent and temporary uncooperative peers. Classification of different types of faults along the temporal dimension: transient, intermittent and permanent is the enabling mechanism which facilitates the differentiation between permanent and temporary uncooperative peers. A detailed description of fault types, fault source and fault classification will be considered in future work.

3   Constructing Semantic Consensus

In this section, we highlight some similarities between concepts and techniques used in two different fields and those used in the semantic mapping process, i.e., consensus formation. These fields are: i. theory of cooperation and evolution and ii. fault-tolerant computing systems. The possibility of misunderstanding or misimplementation between players, i.e. noise, has been heavily studied in **Cooperation and Evolution** fields [2, 13, 11]. Strategies applied to bring autonomous selfish peers to a *consensus* with existing noise in the system is an attractive proposition for solving semantic mapping problem with existing faults in the process. We believe that there are similarities between handling faults in consensus building and coping with noise in autonomous agent cooperation. We see noise as fault, more specifically, as a transient fault. Therefore, strategies for coping with noise in agent cooperation could be adapted to tolerate faults in consensus formation.

Majority voting is used to design **Fault-Tolerant computing systems** and it has similarity with techniques used by [1, 7, 8, 5, 12] to perform mapping and to eliminate the disambiguation between concepts, i.e., the *consensus* formation technique. Lets consider both the majority voting, consensus and their similarities in more details.

In the **consensus based system** concepts are translated along the query translation or query propagation path. Hence, if the semantic of the concepts are preserved along the query propagation path the query yields a correct (consensus) answer. We could restate this as follow:

For every query to yield an acceptable answer, the translation of the query element semantics have to be approved by multiple peers. This could be considered as a form of a voting.

Please note that, not every consensus answer is a correct answer. There is a possibility that even when several peers reach a consensus about a particular query answer their conclusion might not to be the correct one when compared to some predefined or known facts.

Figure 1 represents the consensus based system where each node represents a peer P and each directed edge $M_{i,j}$ represents a query mapping from source peer P_i to target query P_j. Each cycle in the graph, $P_{i1}, P_{i2}.....P_j, P_{i1}$ represents the query translation path. The selection (deselection) of a query result among multiple results returned from different translation paths by *query initiator* is an approve (disapprove) to the voting decision made by different peers on the translation path. A dished circle in Fig. 1 represents one circle, i.e. translation query path, which peers on the path might reach a consensus.

There are other types of systems such as those described in [5, 12] that do not use *translation* to achieve consensus. Here, consensus is achieved through *counting* the number of times a *concept* or the *relation* between two concepts appears among different ontologies. We see that both described methods, translation and reinforcement, uses the notion of voting to reach consensus.

The **majority voting** techniques is a well-known technique used to determine a consensus result from the results delivered by multiple computation sources. We will concentrate on the TMR (Triple Modular Redundancy) majority voting technique for its simplicity. The TMR system is based on using extra hardware components. More specifically, the TMR system uses three components in place of one component. The TMR system also has an extra component called *Voter*. The Voter is the place where the voting on the different results takes place, i.e., consensus made. The main idea of this technique is that the system tries to build a consensus result from three results [10]. This technique is used to prevent the computation process from relying on a single result. Figure 2 is an illustration for this technique where three peers (components) produce data and a voter combine their output. From figure 2 we can notice that the role of the Voter component becomes an essential role and the reliability of entire system now depends upon the reliability of the Voter. We can notice that the same drawback does exist in the consensus technique as well. In Figure 1, the P8 plays this critical role.

We could replace T which stands for the Triplicate in the TMR technique by N where $N > 2$. This leads to a system with N components redundancy, the NMR system, instead of the TMR system.

Other voting methods such as plurality voting, threshold voting and weighted k-out-of-n are also used to reach consensus. There are tradeoffs involved in using each of these method. Some methods are more suitable than others for certain

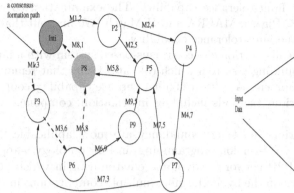

Fig. 1. Query Translation Along Query Paths, P8 plays similar role of voter in Fig. 2

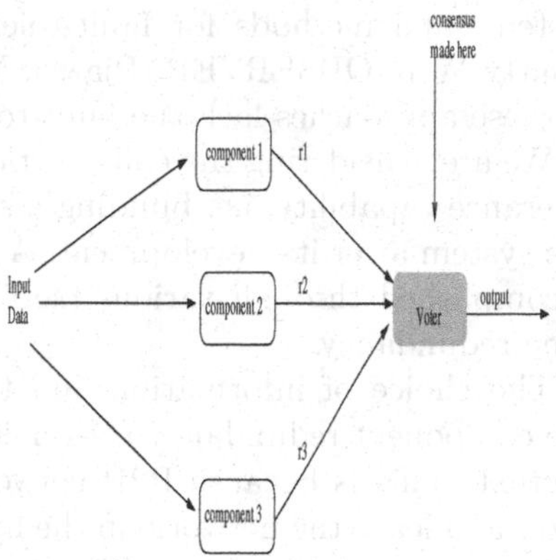

Fig. 2. Triple Modular Redundancy

applications. For example, the plurality voting method is usually used to determine a winner in a given election. In the plurality method two parameters are important: i. the number of voters that voted for the consensus, i.e. L voters agree and ii. the number of voters which vote for consensus is grater than number of voters which do not vote for consensus, i.e. $M < L$. In other words, the winner does not need to have n/2+1 votes to win, where n is the number of total participants in the voting. The winner needs only L votes where L is the number of participants who voted for the winner and it exceeds the number M were voted against the winner.

It worth to re-emphasis that what we trying to convey here is that the *voting is a form of consensus reaching*. We believe that both the *voting technique* which is used by fault-tolerance systems and a *consensus reaching* used by semantic mapping process have a lot in common. This leads us to the next issues: the feasibility of adapting other forms of voting and fault-tolerance techniques to build consensus and to measure the certainty [1] and the confidences [2] in the consensus reaching. Examples of such techniques include a weighted majority voting, plurality voting and time and information redundancy techniques. We believe that the equivalences between consensus and majority voting will open up new avenues for research. Currently we are researching this issues further.

4   Fault-Tolerance

Software components are human made products and since humans are subject to make mistakes, real-world software components cannot guaranteed to be error free. Hence, we should strive to achieve highly reliable, continuously available and safe software [3]. We scrutinized several promising ontology mapping

---

[1] Weight of peers participated in consensus formation.

[2] Number of peers participated in consensus formation [14].

systems and methods for fault-tolerance capability. The examination covered Chatty Web, OBSERVER, Piazza, MAFRA and H-Match. We find out that all of these approaches lack the fault-tolerance capability.

We are considering the construction of a consensus-based system with a fault-tolerance capability, i.e. building a system which tolerates faults that remain in the system after its development. A software fault-tolerance capability could be accomplished through various methods including information, component and time redundancy.

The choice of information and time redundancy are more applicable than the component redundancy (N-version programming) in P2P ontology mapping context. This is because P2P network is dynamic environment in which peers enter and leave the network on the fly. Performing multiple computations in such a dynamic environment is difficult and subject to termination, thus depriving peers from opportunities to produce responses. A reasonable alternative would be the duplication of critical variables and/or blocks of code and comparing the output of these code blocks and variables at different stages of the execution of the same program.

The time-redundancy technique could be used to add fault-tolerance capabilities to the consensus formation methods in at least two ways including: i. querying the peer service provider more than once at different times and comparing the obtained results, and ii. preparing a test query for which a querying peer knows the answer. In both of the above cases a querier could directly verify whether the related peers execute correctly [9]. Similarly, information redundancy technique could be used for building consensus formation with fault-tolerance abilities. This is could be done by incorporating extra information about the query and performing checking on the query response for the query added information.

We strongly believe that fault-tolerance capability should be used as a criterion to determine the quality of consensus based systems. The fault tolerant capability is particularly important in critical applications such as security and business applications. This particularity arises from the fact that excluding a useful source of information or a valuable business partner just for a transient type error will have severe consequences on the level of accuracy of the collected information and could jeopardize financial gain for the peers.

5   Conclusion and Future Work

We started by observing that there are several shortcoming of the incremental building semantic consensus among distributed ontologies. We proposed to solve the problem by focusing on three key issues: i. considering cooperative and temporary uncooperative peers in building semantic consensus, ii. adapting other applied voting techniques to semantic mapping reaching and iii. building semantic mapping systems with fault-tolerance capability. Some first steps of these key issues were described. Future works include: i. implementing a bottom-up semantic consensus system with ability to tolerate the non-permanent faults. ii. exploring and adapting some new techniques to build a robust semantic consensus.

References

1. K. Aberer and P. Cudre-Mauroux and M. Hauswirth. Start making sense: The Chatty Web approach for global semantic agreements. In *Journal of Web Semantics*, 1(1): 89-114, 2003.
2. R. Axelrod. The Complexity of Cooperation. Princeton University Press, 1997.
3. M. R. Lyu. Software Fault Tolerance. *Wiley publishing*, 1995.
4. S. Castano, A. Ferrara, S. Montanelli. H-Match: an Algorithm for Dynamically Matching Ontologies in Peer-based Systems. In *Proc. of the 1st VLDB Int. Workshop on Semantic Web and Databases (SWDB)*, P: 231-250, 2003.
5. P. Fergus, A. Mingkhwan, M. Merabti,and M. Hanneghan . Distributed emergent semantics in P2P networks. In *Proc. of the Second IASTED International Conference on Information and Knowledge Sharing*, P: 75-82, 2003.
6. A. Gomez-Perez, M. Fernandez-Lopez and and O. Corcho. Ontological Engineering. Springer publishing, 2003.
7. A. Halevy, Z. Ives, P. Mork, and I. Tatarinov. Piazza: Mediation and integration infrastructure for semantic web data. In *proceedings of the International World-Wide Web Conference WWW-03*, 2003.
8. E. Mena, A. Illarramendi, V. Kashyap and A. Sheth. OBSERVER: an approach for query processing in global information systems based on interpretation across pre-existing ontologies. In *Distributed and Parallel Databases*, 8(2):223-71, 2000.
9. E. Papalilo, T. Friese, M. Smith, B. Freisleben. Trust Shaping: Adapting Trust Establishment and Management to Application Requirements in a Service-Oriented Grid Environment In *Proceedings of the 4th International Conference on Grid and Cooperative Computing (GCC)*, pp. 47-58, LNCS 3795, 2005.
10. D. K. Paradhan. Fault-Tolerant Computing System Design. *Prentice Hall PTR* publication, 1996.
11. B. Sainty. Achieving greater cooperation in a noisy prisoner's dilemma: an experimental investigation In *Journal of Economic Behavior and Organization*, 39(4):421-435, 1999.
12. L.M. Stephens, M.N. Huhns. Consensus ontologies. Reconciling the semantics of Web pages and agents. In *IEEE Internet Computing*, 5(5): 92-95, 2001.
13. J. Wu and R. Axelrod. How to Cope with Noise in the Iterated Prisoner's Dilemma. In *Journal of Conflict Resolution*, 39(1): 183-189, 1995.
14. S. Yacoub, X. Lin, S. Simske, and J. Burns. Automating the analysis of voting systems. In *14th International Symposium on Software Reliability Engineering*, p 203-214, 2003.

Ontology and Agent Based Model for Software Development Best Practices' Integration in a Knowledge Management System

Nahla Jlaiel and Mohamed Ben Ahmed

Riadi Lab, National School of Computer Sciences
University of La Manouba, La Manouba 2010, Tunisia
{Nahla.Jlaiel, Mohamed.Benahmed}@Riadi.rnu.tn

Abstract. In this paper, we will focus on the importance of management of knowledge held by the organization's human resources and gained through experience and practice. For this issue, we propose a model for software best practices' integration in a Knowledge Management System (KMS) of a Software Development Community of Practices (SDCoP). This model aims on the one hand, to integrate human, organizational, cultural and technical dimensions of the Knowledge Management (KM) discipline and on the other hand, to cover all the KM's process. In response to these needs, the proposed model, purpose of this paper, is founded on the basis of ontologies and intelligent agents' technologies.

Keywords: Best Practices, competencies, Knowledge Management, Software Development Process, Ontology, Intelligent Agents, OWL, Jena, Nuin.

1 Introduction

In the new knowledge centred age, most organizations have recognized the importance of their immaterial assets in addition to the material ones (buildings, equipments, etc.). The first one consists in external knowledge (knowledge about customers, competitors, partners, etc.) and in internal knowledge dealing with organization's employees (know-how, competencies, skills, best practices) and processes. Thus, knowledge became a strategic asset leading to organization's growth and survival [1] requiring new methods and tools designed for its management giving hence, rise to the new discipline of KM. In the research work, purpose of this paper, we will focus on the management of the knowledge held by the organization's employees and gained through the experience. For this problem, we propose a model for software best practices' integration in a KMS of an SDCoP. This model, baptized SoBestPractIM (**So**ftware **Best Pract**ices Integration **M**odel), allows and supports not only knowledge integration in a KMS, but also knowledge creation and sharing so as to reach the new KM generation's goals.

R. Meersman, Z. Tari, P. Herrero et al. (Eds.): OTM Workshops 2006, LNCS 4278, pp. 1028–1037, 2006.

2 Knowledge Management and Best Practices

Through this section, we will try to define certain key concepts that are needed for our study and on the basis of which we have designed our proposed model.

2.1 Knowledge Management

As defined by Malhotra [2], "Knowledge Management caters to the critical issues of organisational adoption, survival and competence in face of increasingly discontinuous environmental change. Essentially, it embodies organizational processes that seek synergistic combination of data and information processing capacity of information technologies, and the creative and innovative capacity of human beings." KM is then, a multidisciplinary field of study implying other disciplines (Sociology, Psychology, Management, Artificial Intelligence, etc.) taking therefore, into account four principal aspects: Human, Organizational, Technical and Cultural (HOTC). The human ones are fundamental and critical since human beings are the unique knowledge holders (know-how, competencies, skills, experiences, best practices, etc.) as well as for their creation and innovation capacities representing the core of the new KM initiatives. The KM is a cyclical process [3] consisting of three principal activities: knowledge creating, integrating and sharing. In this process, actors are considered as active members trying to resolve problems encountered during the exercise of their work leading hence, to new knowledge creation. Once integrated in a KMS, knowledge can be shared, updated and consequently enriched.

2.2 Best Practices

As a particular kind of knowledge, Best Practices (BP) are considered as procedural knowledge having proven their value through the practice [4]. Stemming from experiences, BP are not static, they follow according to us and to Snowden's Cynefin Model [5] a cycle during which they are identified, formalized, evaluated and validated giving then, raise to new competencies. This model presents the dynamic aspect of the knowledge represented by its various domains (Chaos, Complex, Known and Knowable). This knowledge flow shows that BP are the ability to move from Knowable to Known through capturing added knowledge, more know-how, acquiring dedicated skills and identifying the context. So, BP are the consequence of a cyclic reflection process allowing according to us, BP' identification, maturity and then new knowledge creation.

3 State of the Art: Experience Management's Approaches

Our literature review has revealed a great range of approaches dealing with the experience and BP' management topic. In this section, we will present four principal and recent projects.

3.1 Case-Based Approach: BORE

Started in 1997 by an American group of researchers at the university of Nebraska-Lincoln and directed by its inventor Henninger [6], BORE (Building an Organizational Repository of Experiences) aims to provide a flexible methodological framework for project management consisting in a living experience memory for software development BP' context capture. The BORE's approach is based on a case based technique in which problem resolution activity is considered as past experiences adaptation to similar present cases. Each experience or BP is represented by a case in BORE. A case specifies the context in which a methodology, activity or a task may be adopted supporting its adaptation to projects' specificities and evolution by the use of rules. BORE adopts the Experience Factory's methodology [7] for experience and BP's management all along the software development process. This methodology supports the QIP (Quality Improvement Paradigm) so as to simplify and to make more efficient the experience management's process.

3.2 Ontology-Based Approach: LiSER

Recently developed in 2004 by a group of researchers from the University of Malaysia directed by Abdulmajid [8], the LiSER's approach proposes a specific representation model of knowledge acquired from software development's experiences and provides a Web environment for experience management and sharing. The proposed model is built on the definition of ontologies[1] of different types so as to make explicit knowledge assets acquired during software development's processes. In their proposed model, Abdulmajid *et al.* describe software development's knowledge assets through four ontologies' types. The competence ontology is designed for competencies categorization forming a taxonomy of useful skills. The type ontology classifies the different kinds of knowledge. The information ontology defines the attributes employed for knowledge assets' description depending on their types. The deliberation ontology arguments and documents decisions made about the captured knowledge assets.

3.3 Case-Based and Ontology-Based Approach: KMIR

Developed in 2004 by Hefke [10] at the German research center of the University of Karlsruhe, the KMIR's approach aims to provide a framework for KM recommendations and BP' implementation. KMIR uses the Case Based Reasoning and the Semantic Web techniques for the management of experiences and BP of KM implementation. In KMIR, BP are represented by cases and are structured through a defined ontology: the KMIR's ontology [10]. The proposed ontology considers a BP as a profile instance describing the organization's profile, problems faced during its KM project's implementation and solutions adopted to overcome these problems.

---

[1] As defined by Gruber, an ontology is a specification of a shared conceptualization: "In the context of knowledge sharing, I use the term ontology to mean a specification of a conceptualization. That is, an ontology is a description (like a formal description of a program) of the concepts and the relationships that can exist for an agent or a community of agents…" [9].

Similarity between cases in KMIR is measured with tradionnal (cases' attributes values) and ontological measures [11] (similarity of relations, similarity of taxonomies).

3.4 Storytelling-Based Approach: HSKM

In this approach, Soulier *et al.* [12] exploit the storytelling's technique, considered as a natural act of knowledge transfer, for experience's sharing within an organization. This approach aims to facilitate the interiorization and socialization's phases through a story model. The project HSKM (Hyper-Storia Knowledge Management) is an implementation of this approach consisting in the development of an assistance tool for experience capitalization which is centered on the narration technique and is intended for a KM consultants' team. In this approach, stories are indexed according to two principal dimensions: intentional and contextual dimensions setting histories with reference to a given domain. In the contextual dimension, scriplets represent actor's cognitive skills and know-how and consist in procedures or groups of actions that are frequently applied for their effectiveness.

3.5 Comparative Study of Experience Management's Approaches

Having studied four main approaches of experience and BP' management, we present a comparaison putting forward the strong and weak points of the ones compared to the others. With this intention, we fixed a set of criteria on the basis of which the comparative study will be undertaken. The choice of these criteria was based on the HOTC aspects of the new KM's generation as well as on the particularities deduced from the study of the BP' concept.

Table 1. Evaluation's Criteria

Criterion	Description	Values and notations
Integration	The integration level of the experience management process in organization's business processes.	++: very strong, +: strong, ~: average, -: weak, --: very weak.
Formalization	The formalization degree of experience and BP.	++: very strong, +: strong, ~: average, -: weak, --: very weak.
Context	The representation method of experience's context.	+: intelligent, ~: simple.
Creation	Knowledge creation level supported by the approach.	++: very strong, +: strong, ~: average, -: weak, --: very weak.
Event	Types of events taken into account by the approach.	+: positive events, -: negative events, +-: positive and negative events.
Exploitation	The Exploitation methods of experiences and BP.	+: intelligent, ~: simple.
Implication	The human implication level in the experience management process.	++: very strong, +: strong, ~: average, -: weak, --: very weak.
Automatization	The automatization degree supported by the approach.	++: very strong, +: strong, ~: average, -: weak, --: very weak.
Domain	The application domain of the approach.	++: SD^2 and T, +: SD and non T, ~: OD^3 and T, -: OD and non T.

---

[2] SD: Software Development.
[3] OD : Other Domain.

The following table clarifies the value of each criterion for the presented approaches.

Table 2. The Comparative Table of the Experience Management's Approaches

	BORE	LiSER	KMIR	HSKM
Integration	++ Experience Factory methodology	-- A process apart	+ CBR cycle	-- A process apart
Formalization	- Problem and solution's specification	~ Recommended actions' set	++ KMIR's ontology	- Implicit induction of BP through models
Context	~ Rules' engine (if-then)	+ Information ontology	+ Ontology's concepts	~ Historiet's attributes
Creation	+ Rules creation and adaptation	-- Experiences' packaging	++ New recommendations creation	-- Stories' packaging
Event	+- Positve/negative experiences	- Problems resolution's situations	+- Users' positive/negative feedbacks	- Anomaly's notion
Exploitation	~ tasks' analysis (cases' links exploitation)	+ Semantic exploitation	+ traditional/ontological similarity's measures	~ Intentional/contextual attributes of the Stories
Implication	~ Project and experience factory's activities separation	- Deliberation ontology	-- Case base alimentation	++ All levels Human intervention
Automatization	~ Human knowledge adaptation/validation	- Automatic memorization and searching	++ Automatic generation of new recommendations	~ Experience and BP' socialization and interiorization
Domain	++ Applicable in other domains	+ Non applicable	~ Applicable in other domains	~ Applicable in other domains

The comparative study of the presented approaches has revealed a set of facets affecting the experience and BP management's process. In fact, the strong and weak points identified through this study and our litterature review helped us to design a model that combines positive facets found in each approach and taking into account KM new generation's demands and BP management's specificities.

4 The Proposed Model: SoBestPractIM

In this section, we specify the best criteria for our model in order to tackle in a better way the experience and BP management. For doing so, we are presenting the theoretical fundamentals, the meta-model and the architecture of our proposed model.

4.1 Model's Theoretical Fundamentals

These are our considerations for the above mentionned criteria: concerning the integration's criterion, we suggest the entire integration of the experience and BP' management process in organization's business processes. This integration will give more meaning to BP created during the software development's process by capturing their context of creation without additional efforts of documentation, out of the context of activity, at the end of the development's process. Regarding the formalization's criterion, we vote for the most natural and structured level of formalization of experiences and BP by using the storytelling's technique since it was proven that it's an efficient means for knowledge sharing and BP's transfer within an organization. Concerning the context's criterion, we propose to put emphasis on the context in which experiences and BP are captured by means of ontologies specifically designed for software development's knowledge representation. These ontologies deal with a shared semantic giving a precise idea about context and its components without ambiguities. For the creation's criterion, we consider that the knowledge creation's need may be fulfilled by supporting the communication between software development process's actors promoting thus, experiences and BP' sharing, cooperation and adding values through annotation. Regarding the event's criterion, we propose to take into account both positive events (successful experiences) and negative ones (anomalies, problems) that are sources for new BP'capture. Concerning the exploitation's criterion, as experience and BP are integrated using ontologies, their exploitation method will be also founded on the designed ontologies. Ontologies' concepts and the corresponding relations will be then, useful for the semantic exploitation of knowledge captured during the software develompent's processes. For the implication's criterion which is a key for KM's success, we think that actors must be sensitized to the importance of an experience and BP's management approach and to its integration in the software development's process. In order to support actors in integrating experiences and in BP' management, we propose to reinforce the KMS implementing SoBestPractIM by a rewards' system (best contributor's election, most used BP' classification). Concerning the automatization's criterion, we propose the minimization of the automatization's degree by according more importance to the human intervention and interpretation, so the targeted KMS will provide an intelligent assistance to the software development process's actors supporting thus, the experiences and BP management's process that must be human centered to fulfil its goals.

4.2 The SoBestPractIM's Meta Model

On the basis of previous assumptions and specificities, we designed a Meta model representing the key concepts and relations that must be taken into consideration in the design of SoBestPractIM (cf. Fig. 1). To each key meta-concept (ontology is a concept tree, graph or lattice) we have assigned an ontology making more explicit knowledge related to the concept. Our study of the software development's process has revealed nine ontologies:

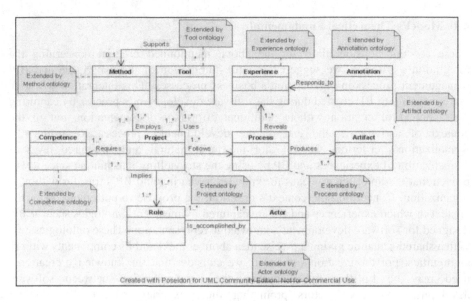

Fig. 1. The SoBestPractIM's Meta Model

The project's ontology describes project's characteristics as well as the different implied roles and corresponding actors, the required competencies, the adopted process and the various methods, tools and artefacts used during the project. The process's ontology aims to describe an adopted software development's process using the concepts of process, activity and role. A process is composed of activities of various granularities (iteration, phase, activity, and task) that can be subdivided into sub-activities. The competencies' ontology allows the description and the classification of the various types of competencies that are required during a software development's process. This classification depends on activity's nature (analysis, design, implementation, and test). The actor's ontology allows the representation of knowledge concerning software developpent process actors' profile, the acomplished roles and the acquired competencies. The experience's ontology represents knowledge describing a software development's experience, including the deduced BP, the employed or created competencies, the implied roles, the adopted methods, the used tools and the created or used artefacts during the experience. The annotation's ontology allows the representation of various forms of observations posted by a worker in response to a given experience and BP. These annotations lead to experiences and BP' enrichment and refinement. The tools' ontology is used for the characterization and the categorization of the various types of tools that can be employed during a software development's project according to the activity for which they are used. It also represents the different competencies required for tools' use. The method's ontology is designed to represent knowledge concerning methods being able to be used during a software development's process. This knowledge deals with the activity using the method, the competencies required for method's adoption, the method's language, the supporting tool(s) as well as other possible required methods.

The artefacts' ontology is used for the characterization and categorization of the different artefacts' types that are created or used during the software development's process.

4.3 Model's Architecture

Having developed the SoBestPractIM's core elements, we present the targeted architecture that we decided to reinforce it by developing a multi agents system (cf. Fig. 2):

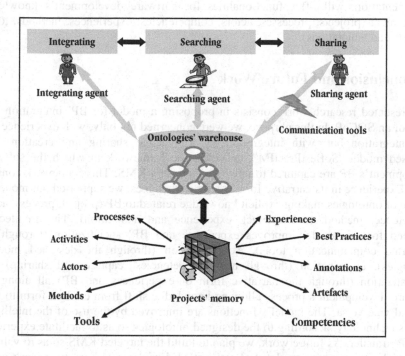

Fig. 2. The SoBestPractIM's Architecture

In this architecture, we notice three principal components: the ontologies' warehouse which is composed of the designed model's ontologies and according to which knowledge will be integrated searched and communicated. The projects' memory, which aims to memorize projects' characteristics, "activities' definition, history and results" [13] as well as "lessons and experiences from given projects" [14], will be able to conserve all the knowledge types presented in the figure 2. Concerning the model's functions, the integrating function allows users of the targeted KMS, to integrate any knowledge's type following the respective ontology. The searching function allows actors to find any useful concept needed for a specific situation (activity in progress, concerned worker's profile), either on demand (pull mode) by means of queries, or proactively (push mode) guided by the context. This function is carried out according to the ontologies of the proposed model serving as sources of knowledge and as patterns for searching queries. The sharing function permits the communication between actors and members of an SDCoP. This function is supported by communication tools (synchronous and asynchronous) and concerns any concept of the model offering thus, a private semantic Web environment (Intranet) for knowledge sharing, annotation and enrichment. These functions are interconnected and interdependent, improved by the use of the intelligent agents' technology so as to facilitate experience and BP' transfer. The model's ontologies are built with OWL [15]. The Java's toolkit component: Jena [16] is selected for ontologies' management and the Nuin's agent platform [17] is designated for the BDI agent's model creation [18]. As outcome the KMS, target of SoBestPractIM's implementation, will offer functionalities for software development's knowledge management (projects, processes, actors, competencies, experiences, methods, tools, artefacts and annotations).

5 Conclusion and Future Work

The presented research work consists in proposing a model for BP' integration in a KMS of an SDCoP. In this purpose, we were concerned not only, with experience and BP' integration but, with integration for knowledge sharing and creation. The proposed model "SoBestPractIM", considers the framework in which the software development's BP are captured to integrate them in a KMS. This framework consists in the Experience in its narrative form. As far as that goes, we supported our model by the use of ontologies making explicit knowledge related to BP (project, process, actor, competence, method, tool, artefact, experience and annotation). The architecture designed for this model improves experience and BP' socialization (through the supported communication tools), externalization (through the designed model's ontologies), combination (through new competencies' capture and sharing) and internalization (through the narrative form of experiences and BP) all along the software development's process allowing knowledge shift from explicit form to tacit one and vice versa. The model's functions are improved by the use of the intelligent agent's technology, according to the designed ontologies so as to facilitate experience and BP' transfer. As future work, we plan to build the targeted KMS so as to validate and enrich our proposed model: SoBestPractIM. For doing so, we must work on an Intranet of a great SDCoP whose members are geographically distant needing to share their experiences, competencies, skills and BP.

References

1. Ermine, J. L., « La gestion des connaissances, un levier stratégique pour les entreprises », Actes du IC'2000, journées francophones de l'ingénierie des connaissances, Toulouse, 10-11 mai 2000
2. Malhotra, Y., "Deciphering the Knowledge Management Hype", The Journal for Quality & Participation, Vol. 21 No. 4, pp. 58-60, July-August, 1998
3. Fischer, G., Ostwald, J., "Knowledge Management: Problems, Promises, Realities, and Challenges", IEEE Intelligent Systems Journal, Vol.16, No.1, pp. 60-72, January-February 2001

4. Perrin, A., "Knowledge Management and Performance", 2005, http://km.typepad.com/index/
5. Snowden, D., "Complex Acts of Knowing: Paradox and Descriptive Self-awareness", Special Edition Journal of Knowledge Management, Vol. 6, No. 2, pp. 1-14, May 2002
6. Henninger, S., Maurer, F., "Tool Support for Experience-Based Methodologies", LSO 2002, LNCS 2640, Springer-Verlag, Berlin Heidelberg, pp. 44–59, 2003
7. Basili, Victor R., Gianluigi, C., Rombach, H. D., "The Experience Factory". In Encyclopaedia of Software Engineering, Vol. 1, New York: John Wiley & Sons, pp. 470-476, 1994
8. Abdulmajid, H. M., Sai, P. L., Siti, S. S., "An Ontology-Based Knowledge Model For Software Experience Management", Journal of Knowledge Management Practice, The Knowledge Garden, Vol. 5, May 2004
9. Gruber, T., "What is an Ontology ?", 1993, http://wwwksl.stanford.edu/kst/what-is-an-ontology.html
10. Hefke, M., "A Framework for the Successful Introduction of KM using CBR and Semantic Web Technologies", Journal of Universal Computer Science, Vol. 10, No. 6, pp. 731-739, 2004
11. Maedche, A., Zacharias, V., "Clustering Ontology-based Metadata in the Semantic Web", 2002
12. Soulier, E., Caussanel, J., « Médiatiser la narration pour le transfert d'expériences : Une application au domaine du conseil en Knowledge Management », CITE'2003 (Coopération, Innovation et TEchnologie), Troyes, 3-4 novembre 2003
13. Matta, N., Ribière, M., Corby, O., « Définition d'un modèle de mémoire de projet », Rapport de Recherche n° 3720, INRIA (Institut National de Recherche en Informatique et en Automatique), juin 1999
14. Pomian, J., « Mémoire d'entreprise, techniques et outils de la gestion du savoir ». Editions Sapientia. In [MAT et al., 1999]
15. McGuinness, D.L., Van Harmelen, F.., "OWL Web Ontology Language Overview", W3C Recommendation, 10 February 2004, http://www.w3.org/TR/owl-features/
16. Dollin, C., J. Caroll, J., Dickinson, I., Reynolds, D., Seabome, A., Wilkinson, K., "Jena: Implementing the Semantic Web Recommendations", WWW 2004, pp. 74-83, New York, May 17-22, 2004
17. Dickinson, I., Wooldridge, M., "An Initial Response to the OAS'03 Challenge Problem", Workshop on Ontologies and Agent Systems (OAS-03) at the conference on Autonomous Agents and Multi-Agent Systems (AAMAS-03), Melbourne, Australia, July 2003
18. Rao, A., Georgeff, M., "BDI Agents: From Theory to Practice", Proceedings of the First International Conference on Multi-Agent Systems (ICMAS-95), San Francisco, USA, pp. 312-319, June 1995

Extracting Ontological Relations of Korean Numeral Classifiers from Semi-structured Resources Using NLP Techniques

Youngim Jung[1], Soonhee Hwang[2], Aesun Yoon[3], and Hyuk-Chul Kwon[1]

[1] Pusan National University, Department of Computer Science and Engineering,
[2] Pusan National University, Center for U-Port IT Research and Education,
[3] Pusan National University, Department of French,
Jangjeon-dong Geumjeong-gu, 609-735 Busan, S. Korea
{acorn, soonheehwang, asyoon, hckwon}@pusan.ac.kr

Abstract. Many studies have focused on the facts that numeral classifiers give decisive clues to the semantic categorizing of nouns. However, few studies have analyzed the ontological relationships of classifiers or the construction of classifier ontology. In this paper, a semi-automatic method of extracting and representing the various ontological relations of Korean numeral classifiers is proposed. Shallow parsing and word-sense disambiguation were used to extract semantic relations from natural language texts and from wordnets.

1 Introduction

Korean is a typical 'classifier language', in which most nouns are quantified by a specific numeral-classifier structure. This contrasts with English, in which numerals directly quantify nouns. As for the research on Korean classifiers, the majority of studies have focused on describing classifiers and analyzing them from a linguistic point of view [1, 9]. However, these studies lacked refined categorizations of classifiers to be applied to practical tasks. Thus, classifier ontology and its applicability are highly required as language resources for NLP and MT, but relevant research is still insufficient. This study focuses on building Korean classifier ontology.

The present paper is structured as follows. In Section 2, we examine related studies on the attempts to the construction of classifier ontology. In Section 3, we present a semi-automatic method of extracting ontological relations by exploiting NLP techniques, and then the result compared to other studies will be discussed in Section 4. Conclusions and future work follow in Section 5.

2 Related Studies

In spite of the relative paucity of studies on classifiers, an important motivation in building classifier ontology is found in a series of studies [3, 4], and recent studies [7, 8, 10] have been conducted focusing on the analysis of semantic properties of Chinese and Korean numeral classifiers, respectively for the application to NLP domain. [3, 4]

R. Meersman, Z. Tari, P. Herrero et al. (Eds.): OTM Workshops 2006, LNCS 4278, pp. 1038–1043, 2006.
© Springer-Verlag Berlin Heidelberg 2006

proposed a method for the automatic generation of Korean and Japanese numeral classifiers using semantic categories from a thesaurus and dictionaries. However, the studies dealt with only a few Japanese and Korean classifiers and they did not mentioned the syntactic or semantic ambiguities derived from processing natural language texts. One semantic category was given to a noun as to generate a default numeral classifier and thus the noun-classifier pairs were limited in their practical application. [10] built a database of Korean numeral classifiers. 942 Korean numeral classifiers were collected and subcategorized; however, more than 500 classifiers fell into dummy categories without any semantic criteria, and neither the correlation of classifiers nor the salient semantic properties of co-occurring nouns were   sufficiently described; thus, the relations between classifiers and co-occurring nouns were not constructed.

3   Extraction of Ontological Relations for Building Korean Classifier Taxonomy

In extracting ontological relationships from unstructured or semi-structured resources such as large-scale corpora, dictionaries, and ontologies, an entire processing pipeline comprising sentence splitting, tokenizing, morphological analyzing, part-of-speech tagging, chunking, and other processes, is required. In this section, we will discuss a method of extracting ontological relations from our resources. Although none of the previous studies corresponds to our aim for building ontological relations of Korean classifiers, all available knowledge resources is gathered as shown in Table 1.

Table 1. Knowledge Resources for Building Korea Numeral Classifier Ontology

Resources	Characteristics	Size
Standard Korean Dictionary	sense distinguished definitions	500,000 entries
List of high-frequency Korean classifiers	frequent Korean numeral classifiers extracted from large corpus in previous study	676 classifiers
Corpus	newspaper articles, middle school text books, scientific papers, literary texts, and law documents	7,778,848 words, (450,000 occurrences of classifiers)
WordNet Noun 2.0	general-purpose lexical database	79,689 synsets
KorLex Noun 1.5	Korean wordnet based on WordNet 2.0	58,656 synsets

3.1   Extraction of Ontological Relations with NLP

Since most available resources are not structured as natural language texts, natural language processing is the prerequisite to efficiently and accurately extracting ontological relations from semi-structured dictionaries or raw corpus [2, 6].

Collection of lexical information from structured resources: Lexical information such as the POS, origin, polysemy, and definition of Korean classifiers were collected from the *Standard Korean Dictionary*. 'Units of measure' included in KorLex and their semantic relations such as synonyms, hypernyms/hyponyms, holonyms/meronyms, and antonyms were obtained without additional processing.

Shallow parsing of semi-structured definitions: Since many Korean classifiers are dependent nouns and few of them are found among KorLex nouns, most semantic relations were extracted from the dictionary definitions by shallow parsing. For example, as '*doe*', a traditional Korean classifier, is not included among the KorLex nouns, its semantic relations are generated from the following definition.

Table 2. Definition of Classifier '*doe*' from *Standard Korean Dictionary*

Classifier	Transcribed Sentences in definition	Translated sentences in definition
Doe	*bupi-ui dan-wi*	① (It is a) unit of volume.
	gogsig, galu, aegche-ui bupileul jael	② (It is) used for measuring the volume of <u>grain, powder, or liquid</u>;
	ttae sseunda;	
	han doeneun <u>*han mal-ui* 10*bun-ui* 1*e*</u>	③ one *doe* <u>is one tenth of one *mal*</u>;
	haedanghanda; *yag* 1.8 *liteo*;	about 1.8 liter

The syntactic pattern of Sentence ①, '*bupi* (volume) *–ui* (adjectival postposition representing 'of') *dan-wi* (unit),' typically, is composed of compound words combining a modifier and a head word. In this pattern, the compound word is the hypernym of the classifier, *doe*. Further, the head word '*dan-wi*' becomes the hypernym of the compound word '*bupi-ui dan-wi*'. In Sentence ②, the objective phrases '*gogsig, galu, aegche-ui bupi+leul* (accusative case marker)' of a verb '*jae-* (measure)' are analyzed. Words representing attributes such as *bupi* (volume) and the referred nouns such as *gogsig, galu, aegche* are separated. The verb, '*jae-*', and the word attributing the referred noun, '*bupi*', are translated into English and then combined to form an ontological relation, 'MeasureVolume'. From Sentence ③, the syntactic pattern, 'A *neun* Bui 10+*bun-ui*+1' represents that 'A is one-tenth of B'. Thus, the holonym/meronym relation between A and B can be derived.

POS-tagging and parsing of unstructured texts: Classifiers can indicate what kind of noun or noun categories will appear in the text, since they select co-occurring nouns very restrictively. Many co-occurring nouns can be collected from unstructured texts in corpus. The simplest combination pattern of a numeral classifier and its context is shown in (E1):

(E1)   a. **3 *doe*** -*ui ssal*   b. *ssal* **3 *doe***
       3 '*doe*' -of rice   rice 3 '*doe*'
       "5.4 liter of rice"   "5.4 liter of rice"

However, according to [13], a classifier can be combined not only with numerals and nouns but also with pre-numerals, post-numerals, and post-classifiers, and their combined pattern varies in real texts. Through POS-tagging and parsing of sentences including the classifiers, the syntactic patterns of the combination can be recognized and be processed.

Word-Sense Disambiguation: Polysemies or homonyms are common in Korean classifiers, since many homographic classifiers have been borrowed from Chinese. For example, the homographic classifier '*gu*' has three senses:

(1) unit of a dead body;   (2) borough ;   (3) unit of counting a pitch

These ambiguities can be resolved with the context of the homographic classifier. If *sache* (dead_body) or *siche* (corpse) comes with '*gu*', the meaning of '*gu*' selects 'a unit of dead bodies'. When *haengjeong gu-yeog* (administrative district) appears as its context, then the meaning of '*gu*' is 'borough', whereas when *cheinji-eob* (change-up), *bol* (ball) appears, the meaning of '*gu*' is 'unit of counting a pitch'.

3.2 Taxonomy of Korean Classifier Based on Semantic-Feature Analysis

In order to establish a hierarchy of Korean classifiers, their taxonomy is required. Classifiers showing selectional restrictions for co-occurring nouns, a set of co-occurring nouns with classifiers is to be analyzed closely. Korean typically has four major types of classifiers: mensural-classifier (CL), measuring the amount of some entity; sortal-CL, classifying the kinds of quantified noun-referents; event-CL, quantifying abstract events; and generic-CL, restricting quantified nouns to generic kinds. Apart from the taxonomy of mensural-CL capable of being extracted easily by means of KorLex[1] or dictionary-based definitions, three types of classifier, sortal, generic and event-CL, have to be analyzed semantically either by dictionary-based definitions or by corpus-based contexts.

Sortal-CL classifies the kind of quantified noun phrase they collocate with, and can be divided into two sub-classes by [+/-living thing]. Generic-CL limits the noun phrase to be interpreted as a generic kind, which relates to only [-living thing]. Event-CL quantifies abstract events. We can classify this class into at least two kinds by its most salient features, [+/-time], for example, [+event] and [+attribute].

Table 3. Classification of Korean Classifiers by Semantic Features

Types	Sub-Category (Semantic Features)				Example
Mensural	-				*doe* (CL of measuring volume of grain, powder), *liteo* (liter)
Sortal	Entity	[+living thing]	[+animacy]	[+human being]	*myeong* (CL of counting people)
				[-human being]	*mali* (CL of counting animals)
			[-animacy]	[+plant]	*songi* (CL of counting flowers)
				[-plant]	*gu* (CL of counting dead bodies)
		[-living thing]	[+shape]*	[+round] [+long], [+thin], [+short], [+square] etc.	*hwan* (CL of counting tablets)
			[-shape]	-	*gwon* (CL of counting books)
Generic	Entity-Abstract	[-living thing]	-		*gae* (CL of counting entities), *jonglyu* (kind)
Event	Abstract events		[+time] [+event] [+action] [+repetition]		*bal* (CL of counting shots) *beon* (CL of repetitive work)
			[-time] [+attribute]		*deunggeub* (magnitude)

---

[1] The classification of mensural-CL, such as time, space, metric unit or monetary unit, follows the hierarchy of KorLex.

4 Results and Discussions

By exploiting the NLP techniques, we extracted the lexical information and semantic relations necessary for building the ontological relations of Korean classifiers efficiently. In total, 1,138 numeral classifiers were collected, and their taxonomy was constructed according to the 'Is-A' relations extracted from the dictionary, the Kor-Lex noun hierarchy and a semantic-feature analysis by linguists. The size of the ontology is applicable to NLP applications, considering the size of classifier inventories created in a previous study. According to [7], 427 Chinese classifiers were sufficient in size for studying the Mandarin classifier systems comprehensively. We found that the sense granularity of noun classes quantified by classifiers differs depending on the types of the classifiers. For instance, mensural-CL and generic-CL can quantify a wide range of noun classes. By contrast, each sortal-CL and event-CL can combine only with a few specific noun classes. Table 4 shows the size of the classifiers constructed into the ontology as well as examples of semantic classes of nouns quantified by the classifiers.

Table 4. Semantic classes of nouns quantified by Korean classifiers

Types	Size	Classifiers	Nouns quantified by the classifier	Class of Nouns
Mensural	772	*liteo* (liter)	*gogsig* (grain2), *galu* (powder1), *aegche* (liquid3)	substance1
Sortal	270	*mali* (CL of counting animals except human beings)	*nabi* (butterfly1), *beol* (bee1)	invertebrate1
			gae (dog1), *go-yang-i* (cat1)	carnivore1
			geomdung-oli (scoter1), *mae* (hawk1)	bird1
			baem (snake1), *badageobug* (turtle1)	reptile1
			ogdom (tilefish1), *chi-eo* (fingerling1)	fish1
Generic	7	*jongryue* (kind)	*seolyu* (paper5), *sinbal* (footwear2)	artifact1
			jipye (paper money1), *menyu*(menu1)	communication2
Event	89	*bal* (CL of counting shots)	*jiloe* (land mine1), *so-itan* (incendiary2)	explosive device1
			gonggichong (air gun1)	gun1
			chong-al (bullet1), *hampo* (naval gun1)	weaponry1
			lokes (rocket1), *misa-il* (missile1)	rocket1

In the present study, we tried to represent and formalize various ontological aspects of Korean numeral classifiers by constructing various relations. Table 5 presents the numbers of representative relations constructed in KCLOnto.

Table 5. Results of Korean Classifier Ontology

Relations	Size	Relations	Size
IsHypernymOf	1,350	HasDomain	696
IsHolonymOf	258	HasOrigin	657
IsSynonymOf	142	HasStdIdx	442
QuantifyOf	2,973	IsEquivalntToKL	696
QuantifyClassOf	287	IsEquivalntToWN	734

All the procedures were performed semi-automatically for the improvement of efficiency and consistency. Compared with the previous studies noted in Section 2, this result shows that the comprehensive approach for building a Korean classifier ontology includes seventeen types of relations based on refined semantic analysis. With this comprehensive and refined result, more accurate and wide application to NLP is expected. In addition, the constructed linkages to WordNet guarantee easier and prompter connections to ontologies in other languages.

5 Conclusions and Further Studies

As explained in this paper, the ontological relations of Korean numeral classifiers were semi-automatically extracted using NLP techniques, and those various relations were formalized with OWL, which supports strong expressiveness in knowledge representation and expandability and linkage to other ontologies. The results show that the constructed ontology is sufficiently large to be applied to NLP subfields. 'IsEquivalentTo' and 'HasOrigin' relations can be used to improve performance in machine translation. As future work, we will study the applicability of the suggested KCLOonto to e-Learning, especially to the domain of foreign-language education, which requires sophisticated and easy-to-use learning-support systems.

Acknowledgement

This work was supported by the National Research Program under Grant M10400000332-06J0000-33210.

References

1. Allan, K.: Classifiers. Language 53(2) (1977) 285-311
2. Alani, H., Kim, S., Millard, D.E., Weal, M.J., Hall, W., Lewis, P.H., Shadbolt, N.R.: Automatic Ontology-Based Knowledge Extraction from Web Documents, IEEE Intelligent Systems (2003) 14-21
3. Bond, F., Paik, K.: Classifying Correspondence in Japanese and Korean. In : 3rd Pacific Association for Computational Linguistics Conference: PACLING-97 (1997) 58-67
4. Bond, F., Paik, K.: Reusing an Ontology to Generate Numeral Classifiers. In : Proceedings of the 18th Conference on Computational Linguistics (2000) 90-96
5. Fellbaum, C. (ed.): WordNet - An Electronic Lexical Database. MIT Press, Cambridge (1998)
6. Garcia, R.V., Nieves, D.C., Breis, J.F., Vicente, P.V.: A Methodology for Extracting Ontological Knowledge from Spanish Documents, LNCS 3878 (2006) 71-80
7. Huang, C.R., Ahrens, K.: Individuals, Kinds and Events: Classifier Coercion of Nouns. Language Sciences 25 (2003) 353-373
8. Hwang, S.H., Jung. Y.I., Yoon, A.S., Kwon, H.C.: Building Korean Classifier Ontology Based on Korean WordNet. TSD-LANI (2006) Accepted, to be published
9. Lyons, J.: Semantics I. Cambridge University Press, Cambridge (1979)
10. Nam, J.S.: A Study of Korean Numeral Classifiers for the Automatic French-Korean Translation of the Expression with Quantifiers. Review of French Studies (54) (2006) 1-28

A Transfusion Ontology for Remote Assistance in Emergency Health Care (Position Paper)

Paolo Ceravolo, Ernesto Damiani, and Cristiano Fugazza

Università degli studi di Milano,
Dipartimento di Tecnologie dell'Informazione via Bramante, 65
26013 Crema (CR), Italy
{ceravolo, damiani, fugazza}@dti.unimi.it
http://ra.crema.unimi.it/kiwi

Abstract. Transfusion Ontology is a simple task-based ontology developed in the emergency health care domain. Taking the assumption that ontologies are instruments for supporting exchange of information among parties, the principles governing the design of this ontology was mainly based on the identification of the interactions of messages to be exchanged among parties. This paper shows how this simple design principle is able to guide a whole ontology construction.

1 Introduction

Complex organizations are defined by the scope of their internal languages more than by any physical boundary. When two or more different organizations need to cooperate and exchange information, matching their internal vocabularies is nearly always one a main concern. Strategies to bridge inter-organizational language barriers when, say, exchanging business documents have historically been based on meeting and putting common terms and concepts in a standard format. In web-based environments the more successful technologies are definitely XML vocabularies and protocols. In this case, the common vocabulary relies on a semi-structured data model, that is used for defining both the content of messages and the protocol for exchanging messages. Examples of such kind of vocabulary can be SOAP [10] or ebXML [7]. But usually XML vocabularies are used as protocols for enforcing messages according to a standard format. The vocabulary strongly bound the data format predefining a set of terms but also constraining the structural position of elements. This approach can be very effective if parties completely agree on the data format to be exchanged. But a more abstract level of agreement among parties can be achieved by means of the adoption of an ontology. An ontology is an explicit specification of a conceptualization [3]. The specification of an ontology allows parties to achieve a common conceptual ground for enabling interoperability. But this specification is not tasked to describe data itself. The goal is to describe the semantics of data without involving the data format and this can be done adopting a metadata layer. But the centrality of the notion of interaction used in web-based

R. Meersman, Z. Tari, P. Herrero et al. (Eds.): OTM Workshops 2006, LNCS 4278, pp. 1044–1049, 2006.

protocols can be preserved as a design principle able to guide a whole ontology construction. Metadata are tasked to describe the resources exchanged as well as the services provided and the actors interacting during transactions among parties. This paper describes the construction of the Transfusion Ontology according to this design principle[1]. Section 2 gives some reference marks in the field of knowledge management and ontology modeling literature. Section 3 preliminarily introduces the domain we are going to model. Section 4 underlines the interactions characterizing the domain. On the basis of these interactions we can now model all the other elements of the ontology. In section 5 we provide a list of the principal concepts of the ontology. Section 6 explains how organize this concepts according to the interaction structure. Section 7 introduces properties tasked to describe classes and distinguish instances in a class. Finally, in section 8 we show our ontology in work by means of a simple example.

2   Ontology Modeling

Knowledge management research focuses on the development of concepts, methods, and tools supporting the companys knowledge management throughout human interactions. The capability to create and utilize knowledge has been suggested as the key inimitable resource contributing to the creation of sustainable rents [9]. Other researches focus on the key notion of competence based competition [8], and dynamic capabilities [1] highlights organizational knowledge as the central factors to take in consideration in the strategic competition. The notion of process was proposed as a general dimension enabling to correlate business process, information system and user behavior [5]. Transferring these notions in the field of ontology modeling brings to the consequence to propose methodologies enabling to take into account domain modeling by the perspective of application requirements [6]. This approach allows to extend traditional methodologies for modeling domain conceptualizations, well summarized in [4] and [2], toward a process-oriented direction. Our work is inserted in this vision, but in addition we try to simplify as much as possible the design principles to be followed during the modeling work.

3   Defining the Domain

In the preliminary step, we need to decide what will be the boundaries of our domain. What is the state of affair, i.e. the portion of the world that our ontology will model? What types of questions should the ontology enable us to answer? Our example will deal with a single specialpurpose ontology, partially covering the domain of emergency health care. When performing the scope definition step, it is necessary to provide an application scenario, clarifying who will be

[1] This work was partly funded by the Italian Ministry of Research Fund for Basic Research (FIRB) under projects **RBAU01CLNB_001** "Knowledge Management for the Web Infrastructure" (KIWI).

the parties that will share the ontology, which information will be exchanged and which resources contain this information. For instance, our sample ontology could be used for ensuring intelligent communication between people working at a remote location (say, an oildrilling offshore platform) and physicians with whom the paramedics may get in touch via a teletype device connected to long-distance communication link in case of an emergency. When sending a message to the physicians providing remote support, the paramedic on the oil-drilling platform will use a vocabulary that will be used also in the responses travelling in the opposite direction. Besides ensuring that both sides of the communication line will use the same set of symbols, we need to make sure that both sides of the communication will associate those symbols with the same concepts. To achieve this we need both parties to agree on a shared ontology.

4   Defining Interactions

If our ontology is aimed at ensuring that the paramedic and the remote support will speak the same language about how a transfusion need to be administered, the ontology scope has to involve the communication that may take place while administering an emergency transfusion. A good way to identify the interactions to be supported by an ontology is listing some questions the ontology should help to understand (and, therefore, to answer correctly and unambiguously). In our case, these questions are the ones that will be asked via the Teletype by the remote physician to our paramedic (or viceversa) in the framework of the medical supervision required for a blood transfusion to take place. Here are some examples:

1. Is the transfusion kit that you are using compatible with the patient?
2. Have you checked that the transfusion kit has not expired yet?
3. Have you disposed of the empty blood pack?

Answers must be provided in accordance to the provisions adopted by the organizations. For instances in our scenario each transfusion must be provided with a transfusion report signed by a physician. Also we shall assume sets of transfusion kits to be available on the platform and that they have already been pre-selected in order to match the blood types of the people working there.

5   Defining the Classes of the Ontology

Of course, we need to include all concepts one is likely to need to answer the questions listed above. Let us start to list some of the concepts we will include in our domain analysis:

- Blood packs, i.e. the sterile containers normally used for transfusions and the blood component (plasma, whole blood or other) they contain.
- Filters, to be placed between the blood pack and the needle when administering the transfusion

- Needles to be inserted in the patients vein when administering the transfusion
- Compatibility labels, showing the ABO group and Rh factor data of a blood component, as well as the results of tests performed on it to determine the antigens it contains.
- Transfusion kits composed of a pack, plus a needle, a filter and a compatibility label.

But in order to fully describe interactions we need to define agents and roles interacting, and messages to be exchanged. In our scenario we have:

- Agents such as organizations or persons.
- Roles that can be played by organizations as well as by persons, such as suppliers or insurance providers.
- Roles that can be played by persons only, such as blood donators, patients, technician paramedic or physician.
- Messages to be exchanged are official documents such as donation reports, transfusion reports or authorizations to transfusion.

It is as important to store all the concepts of the domain as to define all the disjointness relations among classes. For instance if we define that a `Technician` is disjoint from a `Physician` we are stating that in our domain they must play different roles in transactions.

6   Defining Task-Oriented Properties

A typical interaction involve two agents playing a specific role and exchanging the suitable documents, signed by an authorized role. Documents speak about domain concepts. These concepts can be linked one to the other by means of a set of particular properties. The role of these properties is to organize concept according to the tasks and the interaction required in the system. We call these properties task-oriented properties. This terminology is related to the ontology engineering tradition that call task ontology an ontology designed in order to describe a task or an activity. For instance in our scenario a class `Agent` is linked to an instance of a class `Role` by means of the property `has_role`. Each class describing a document contains a set of properties setting the roles and the domain concepts involved in the document. For instance the class `Transfusion_Report` has a property `on_patient` linking to an instance of `Agent` linked to an instance of a class `Patient` and a property `signed_by` that must be signed by an agent playing the role of paramedic.

Organizing concepts according to the interactions to be supported by the systems provides our ontology with a satisfactory degree of modularization. If the interaction schema does not evolve agents, roles, and documents can be added and removed without damages to the ontology. Task-oriented properties can be viewed as a fixed backbone of the ontology, and all other classes of the ontology are organized around it. On the contrary, domain evolutions involving the structure of the interactions among parties require to redesign a great part of the ontology.

The definition of a ontology backbone, coupled to the definition of all disjoint classes of the domain, is an important point in order to verify the ontology validity. In fact if a task oriented property has in its domain or range two disjoint classes this means the general organization of the ontology must be reviewed (excepting if the classes are not truly disjoint in the domain).

7   Defining Descriptive Properties

Other properties describe classes features with the aim of distinguishing instances in a class. For instance a pack's properties include its capacity (usually around 300 ml.) and the material it is made of (usually, PVC plastics). The blood component's properties include its expiry date and anti-coagulant additives, while the compatibility label's properties hold the values it shows: the associated component's blood type, Rh factor and, possibly, the results of various tests performed on it. Finally, the filter and the needle included in the kit will have many properties, some of them being codes specified by their supplier (such as the supplier's code and model number), and others being numbers expressing their dimensions and physical characteristics. Note that ontology classes' properties are very versatile. They can be used to denote intrinsic properties of a class, whose values cannot be changed for a given instance (e.g., the ABO group of a blood unit or the diameter of a needle). Also, they may contain extrinsic properties that, at least in principle, could be changed at will by an external authority (e.g. a blood unit's expiry date). A class' property may also denote the smaller parts that, when put together, constitute the class' instances, such as the blood component and pack properties of a transfusion kit. Finally, the properties may model a class' relations to other classes. Class properties may be simple or complex: simple properties contain primitive values (such as strings or numbers), while complex ones contain (or point to) instances of other classes.

8   Putting Ontologies to Work

Now that we have completed the steps to create our ontology, we may briefly comment on how it relates to the application scenario we identified in the first step. Our ontology was designed as a common conceptual framework to be used when the oil-drilling platform paramedic and the remote support physician need to communicate. Basically, what the physician needs to do is to supervise the compatibility check between the transfusion kit being used on a patient and the patient herself/himself. Thanks to the blood transfusion ontology, the compatibility check can be precisely defined in terms of the properties of the involved instances of the `Transfusion_Kit` and `Patient` classes, even if the paramedic and the physician have never met before and were trained in different environments. Let us consider a pair formed by a `Patient` class' instance (patient) requiring the transfusion and a candidate `Transfusion_Kit` class' instance (kit). Checking compatibility means that the (distinct) instances of the `Compatibility_Label` class contained respectively in the label property of the patient and in the `comp_label` property of the kit must contain the same values of blood group, Rh factor and antibodies. A looser version of this constraint could also be added, requiring that the `comp_label` property of the kit to hold value 0 for the blood group and value "+' for the Rh factor, regardless of the `Patient` instance's `label` property. At this point, the first question listed in the scope definition phase of our ontology has been given a precise definition in terms of the shared ontology. The fact that the supervision procedure for the transfusion is clearly expressed in terms of the ontology ensures that the paramedic and the remote physician will actually mean the same things when performing and supervising compatibility check.

9   Conclusions

We have seen how the definition of interactions of messages exchanged in a specific domain can be adopted as a criteria for modeling a whole ontology. Identifying an interaction we can highlight roles acting in the domain, resources exchanged, and concepts described by the resources. These elements are a very important base for enumerating the classes of the ontology of the domain. But more important, analyzing domain interactions we can also deduce a set of properties, that we called task-oriented properties, relating classes of the ontology according to a structure suitable to its scopes. This way we get a modular organization of the ontology were task-oriented properties can be maintained as a fixed backbone of the ontology while other classes can be modified and evolved.

References

1. A. Sheun, J. Teece, G. Pisano. Dynamic capabilities and strategic management. *Strategic Management Journal*, 18:509–533, 1997.
2. A. Gomez-Perez, D. Manzano-Macho A survey of ontology learning methods and techniques OntoWeb Deliverable, 2003.
3. T. Gruber. A translation approach to portable ontology specifications. *Knowledge acquisitions*, 5(2):199–220, 1993.
4. N. Guarino. Formal ontology in information systems. *Proceedings of FOIS*, pages 3–15, 1998.
5. H. Takeuchi, I. Nonaka. The knowledge-creating company. *Oxford University Press*.
6. M. Jarrar. Towards methodological principles for ontology engineering. *PhD Thesis*, 2005.
7. OASIS – UN/CEFACT. *Business Process Project Team, ebXML Business Process Specification Schema (BPSS), Version 1.01, ebXML*, 2001. http://www.ebxml.org.
8. H. Thomas, R Sanchez, A. Heene. Dynamics of competence-based competition. 1998.
9. Schendel. Knowledge and the rm. *Strategic Management Journal*, 17, 1996.
10. World Wide Web Consourtium. *SOAP Version 1.2, W3C Recommendation*, June 2003. http://www.w3.org/TR/soap/.

Ontological Distance Measures for Information Visualisation on Conceptual Maps

Sylvie Ranwez[1], Vincent Ranwez[2], Jean Villerd[1], and Michel Crampes[1]

[1] LGI2P Research Centre, EMA/Site EERIE, Parc scientifique G. Besse,
F – 30 035 Nîmes cedex 1, France
Firstname.Lastname@ema.fr
[2] Laboratoire de Paléontologie, Phylogénie et Paléobiologie, Institut des Sciences de
l'Evolution (UMR 5554 CNRS), Université Montpellier II, CC 064,
F – 34 095 MONTPELLIER Cedex 05, France
ranwez@isem.univ-montp2.fr

Abstract. Finding the right semantic distance to be used for information research, classification or text clustering using Natural Language Processing is a problem studied in several domains of computer science. We focus on measurements that are real distances: i.e. that satisfy all the properties of a distance. This paper presents one *ISA*-distance measurement that may be applied to taxonomies. This distance, combined with a distance based on relations other than *ISA*, may be a step towards a real semantic distance for ontologies. After presenting the purpose of this work and the position of our approach within the literature, we formally detail our *ISA*-distance. It is extended to other relations and used to obtain a MDS projection of a musical ontology in an industrial project. The utility of such a distance in visualization, navigation, information research and ontology engineering is underlined.

Keywords: *ISA*-distance, Semantic Distance, MDS, Ontology Visualisation, Conceptual Maps, Ontology Engineering.

1 Introduction

Searching for information in a huge amount of data is a challenging task. Visual assistance, such as conceptual and knowledge maps, may help the human operator by showing him/her data that are close to each other: which papers concern a given subject, which people are interested in a given molecule, which picture may best illustrate his/her speech, etc. We underlined the interest of conceptual and knowledge maps for indexing, navigating or retrieving information through massive data sets in [7]. The objective is now to reinforce the semantic of the maps by projecting ontologies onto those maps, using a MultiDimensional Scalling (MDS) method, in such a way that concepts and other *objects* are gathered together by means of semantic distance.

In face of the growth in the amount of available information, various domains of computer science propose solutions often based on ontologies or taxonomy and use

R. Meersman, Z. Tari, P. Herrero et al. (Eds.): OTM Workshops 2006, LNCS 4278, pp. 1050–1061, 2006.

similarity or semantic distance measurements. Few of these distances respect the three properties of distance: *positiveness*, *symmetry* and *triangle inequality*. This paper presents an ISA-distance (based on the *ISA* relationship) that respects those properties. It may be a first step towards a real semantic distance and can be used to apply MDS onto the concepts of an ontology.

The remainder of the paper is organised as follows. The next section presents the state-of-the-art concerning semantic distance measurement and positions our approach within the literature. Our method is then introduced, formally described and illustrated by means of simple examples. This distance measurement was applied to an industrial project where musical landscapes are used to visually index music titles and compose playlists semi-automatically. The distance measurement is therefore extended to other semantic relations. Then it is used to obtain a knowledge map in the music domain, through the MDS projection of the concepts of the ontology. We also demonstrate how this distance may support engineers and domain specialists in assessing semantic consistency when designing an ontology for a particular domain. These results, together with their limits and perspectives are discussed before the conclusion.

2 State-of-the-Art Concerning Semantic Distance

The different strategies and methodologies used for semantic distance measurement aim at estimating a kind of similarity between concepts. Several domains of computer science have tried to find a semantic distance measurement. The state-of-the-art below presents the various approaches and their vocabulary.

The major reason for finding such a distance concerns information retrieval. Initially, information systems used exact correspondence between request and data but, to avoid silence, current methods allow approximate requests and use distance measures to find pertinent information, widening the scope of the search. One of the first methods was proposed by J. Sowa in [16]: given a lattice of concept types, the distance between concept a and concept b is given by the length of the shortest path from a to b that does not pass through the absurd concept ($\perp$).

Other distance measurements have been proposed by the *Object* community. For example Jérome Euzenat uses the unary distance proposed by [2] in order to determine the neighbourhood of an object in classification systems [9]. This distance between two concepts corresponds to the number of edges between them in the graph.

People working in the NLP (*Natural Language Processing*) community, are often interested in analysing and comparing sets of documents, and applying clustering methods to them. Several similarity measurements are therefore used [1, 12]. A document is commonly represented as a vector of terms. The basis of the vector space corresponds to distinct terms in a document collection. The components of the document vector are the weights of the corresponding terms, which represent their relative importance in the document and the whole document collection. The measurement of distances may be ensemblist, using Dice or Jaccard coefficients, or geometric, using cosines, Euclidian distance, distributional measure or Jensen-Shannon divergence. The problem with these approaches is the lack of precision due to vectorisation and the fact that some concepts may be considered as totally independent even if they are semantically close. For example, considering synonyms as independent concepts may adversely affect the distance estimation. Some solutions have been proposed using *Synonym Rings[1]*, as in the WordNet ontology [4].

However, this context is rather remote from ours. While in NLP people search for the most representative set of concepts that may characterise a document and find a similarity distance between them, we are looking for a distance between the concepts themselves. This is also the problematic of [3], in which semantic relatedness and semantic distance are distinguished. Semantic relatedness uses all the relations in the ontology (WordNet), while semantic distance only takes into consideration the hyponymy relation. In our approach, initially, we also limit the calculus to the hyponym relation and then we extend it to other semantic relations.

To determine the semantic distances between concepts, it is possible to use a vectorial representation of each concept, as proposed in [11]. Each dimension of this vector consists of a concept, as in the above mentioned approach, except that concepts are associated with other concepts and not with documents. Using these vectors, a numeric distance can be calculated between two concepts, using numeric methods (cosines, Euclidian distance, etc.). In our application, there is no correspondence between concepts using vectors and, more generally, it is always difficult to associate a numeric value to a non-numeric parameter in order to apply traditional mathematical calculus. We therefore prefer directly to use the links available in the ontology and their semantics.

Concerning the database community, one semantic distance model has been proposed in [15]. However, the formalism used is very generic and, while we try to comply with most of the recommendations given, it is difficult to satisfy all of them.

The semantic web community, in particular researchers interested in ontologies, has also proposed several algorithms to determine the distance between concepts[2] [5]. Most of them are based on edge-measurement of the shortest path between concepts, which is not satisfactory because it does not take into account the degree of detail of the ontology. Other methods are based on the lowest super-ordinate (most specific common subsumer); in ontologies, concepts often have several *parents* and only taking the closest one into account may hide other aspects of the concepts. Moreover, it compromises the respecting of triangle inequality. The probabilistic measure of similarity proposed by Resnik [14], takes multiple inheritances into account, but does not satisfy all the properties of a distance.

3   From Ontology to Semantic Distance

This section details the semantic distance that we propose. It starts with an intuitive description, followed by formalisation and examples. We follow the notation of [5], using upper case for sets of concepts and lower case for single concepts.

---

[1] http://en.wikipedia.org/wiki/Synonym_Ring
[2] See for example: Laakso, A.: Semantic similarity. Wikipedia web pages at
     http://www.laakshmi.com/aarre/wiki/index.php/Semantic_similarity

3.1 Intuitive Approach

Two concepts are close if there is a concept that subsumes both of them and if this concept is slightly *more general*; to estimate its degree of generalisation we consider the number of concepts encompassed by it. In the simple case where the ontology is a tree and concept a subsumes concept b, we want the distance from a to b to be the number of concepts encompassed by a but not b. The number of such concepts is thus used to estimate the degree of generalisation of a compared to b.

NOTE – If a subsumes b and b subsumes c, using such a distance ensures that:

$$d(a,c) = d(a,b) + d(b,c) \tag{1}$$

In a concept hierarchy supporting multiple inheritances the subsumers of a concept (for example s and s', which subsume y in Fig. 1) may be seen as several points of view regarding this concept. The intuitive approach presented above needs to be extended to the general case. Considering a concept hierarchy like the one modelled in Fig. 1, one can easily understand that concepts a and x, which are subsumed by s, are closer than a and b. More generally, all concepts subsumed by s are closer to a than b, with respect to the point of view of s. Therefore, the higher the number of concepts subsumed by s, the greater the distance between a and b.

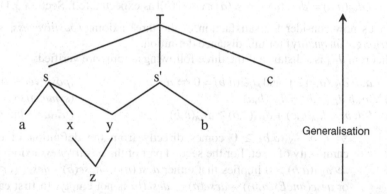

Fig. 1. Hierarchy that may represent a taxonomy of concepts. Note that the orientation of edges is top-down, i.e. "*z is an x*".

Using these two intuitive notions of distance, we set out to define a distance measurement where the distance between two concepts (for example a and b) is a function of the number of concepts closer to a than b, and to b than a, respectively. This means that the distance must take into account all points of view with regard to a concept. To be more significant, common sub-concepts must be removed from the distance.

3.2 Definition and Proof

Using an ontology, the similarity between concepts can be estimated on the basis of several indicators. The concepts can be linked by various kinds of relations, and the similarity can hardly be estimated without taking into account their semantics. Among these relations, the ISA relation defining the generalization between concepts plays a key role as the backbone of any ontology. Since one concept can be a specialization of several others, the ISA part of the ontology can be represented by a Direct Acyclic Graph (DAG) whose nodes represent the concepts of the ontology and whose oriented edges represent the specialization relation.

Given a graph (V,E) where V is the set of vertices and E the set of edges, a is a father of b if edge $(a,b) \in V$, and a is an ancestor of b iff there is a path between a and b. The set of concepts having a as ancestor is denoted by $desc(a)$, while its set of ancestors is denoted by $ansc(a)$. Given two nodes a and b, node x is one of their exclusive ancestors iff it is the ancestor of exactly one of them i.e. $x \in ansc(a) \cup ansc(b) - ansc(a) \cap ansc(b)$. The set of the exclusive ancestors of a and b is denoted by $anscEx(a,b) = anscEx(b,a)$.

We use $d_{ISA}(a,b)$ to denote the distance between two concepts a and b based on the ISA relationship, defining it as follows:

$$d_{ISA}(a,b) = |desc(ancEx(a,b)) \cup desc(a) \cup desc(b) - desc(a) \cap desc(b)| \qquad (2)$$

If the ISA-graph is a tree and $b \in desc(a)$, we can observe that the exclusive ancestors of a and b are on the path between a and b. Thus, $desc(ancEx(a,b)) \subset desc(a)$ and $desc(b) \subset desc(a)$, therefore:

$$d_{ISA}(a,b) = |desc(a) - desc(a) \cap desc(b)| \text{ as expected (c.f. Section 3.1)}$$

Let us now consider the satisfaction of the three axioms (*positiveness, symmetry and triangle inequality*) for this distance definition.

Theorem d_{ISA} is a distance if the three following axioms are verified:

i) $\forall \; a, b \; d_{ISA}(a,b) \geq 0$ and $d_{ISA}(a,b) = 0 \Leftrightarrow a = b$ (*positiveness*)
ii) $\forall \; a, b \; d_{ISA}(a,b) = d_{ISA}(b,a)$ (*symmetry*)
iii) $\forall \; a, b, c \; d_{ISA}(a,c) + d_{ISA}(c,b) \geq d_{ISA}(a,b)$ (*triangle inequality*)

i) $\forall \; a, b \; d_{ISA}(a,b) \geq 0$ comes directly from the definition of d_{ISA} as a cardinality of a set. For the second part of the *positiveness* axiom we have: $\Rightarrow d_{ISA}(a,b) > 0$ implies that either $desc(a) \cup desc(b) - desc(a) \cap desc(b)$ or $desc(ancEx(a,b)) - desc(a) \cap desc(b)$ is not empty. In first case, there is at least one x such that $(x \in desc(a)$ et $x \notin desc(b))$ or $(x \in desc(b)$ et $x \notin desc(a))$. The existence of x ensures that $a \neq b$. In second case, there is at least one ancestor that is not common to a and b (otherwise $desc(ancEx(a,b))$ will be empty). The existence of this exclusive ancestor ensures that $a \neq b$.
$\Leftarrow$ having $a = b$ trivially implies that both $desc(a) \cup desc(b) - desc(a) \cap desc(b)$ and $desc(ancEx(a,b))$ are empty sets and therefore that $d_{ISA}(a,b) = 0$

ii)   By definition of the distance, since $anscEx(a,b) = anscEx(b,a)$

iii)   It is sufficient to prove that any element of the set $S_{ab}=\{desc(ancEx(a,b)) \cup desc(a) \cup desc(b) - desc(a) \cap desc(b)\}$ is an element of at least one of the two sets $S_{ac}= \{desc(ancEx(a,c)) \cup desc(a) \cup desc(c) - desc(a) \cap desc(c)\}$ and $S_{bc}=\{desc(ancEx(c,b)) \cup desc(c) \cup desc(b) - desc(c) \cap desc(b)\}$.

If $x \in S_{ab}$, either
- $x \in \{desc(a) \cup desc(b) - desc(a) \cap desc(b)\}$
- or $x \in \{desc(ancEx(a,b)) - desc(a) \cap desc(b)\}$.

In the first case, let us assume $x \in desc(a)$ and $x \notin desc(b)$ the proof is similar for the alternative case where $x \in desc(b)$ and $x \notin desc(a)$. Therefore either $x \notin desc(c)$, and $x \in \{desc(a) \cup desc(c) - desc(a) \cap desc(c)\}$ or $x \in desc(c)$ and thus $x \in \{desc(c) \cup desc(b) - desc(c) \cap desc(b)\}$. In both cases $x \in S_{bc}$.

In the second case, $x \in \{desc(y) - desc(a) \cap desc(b)\}$ with $y \in ancEx(a,b))$, note that this implies that x is not a descendant of both a and b. Let us now assume that y is an ancestor of a and not of b (the proof is similar for the alternative case where y is an ancestor of b and not of a). Either $y \in Anc(c)$ or not. If it does, $y \in AncEx(c,b)$. In this case if $x \in desc(c)$ and since x is not a descendant of both a and b, then $x \in \{desc(a) \cup desc(c) - desc(a) \cap desc(c)\}$ or $x \in \{desc(c) \cup desc(b) - desc(c) \cap desc(b)\}$. If $x \notin desc(c)$ then $x \notin \{desc(b) \cap desc(c)\}$ and therefore $x \in \{desc(c) \cup desc(b) - desc(c) \cap desc(b)\}$.

If $y \notin Anc(c)$, $y \in AncEx(a,c)$ and the proof is the same as above, inversing a and b.

3.3 Simplified Example

To illustrate our ISA-distance calculus, let us consider some distances using a small example. Considering the hierarchy given in Fig. 1, the ISA-distance between x and y is obtained as follows:

$$
\begin{aligned}
d_{ISA}(x,y) &= | \ desc(ancEx(x,y)) \cup desc(x) \cup desc(y) - desc(x) \cap desc(y) \ | \\
&= | \ desc(s') \cup desc(x) \cup desc(y) - \{z\} \ | \\
&= | \ \{s',y,b,z\} \cup \{x, z\} \cup \{y, z\} - \{z\}| = | \ \{s',y,b,x\}| = 4.0
\end{aligned}
$$

The full distance matrix concerning the hierarchy given in Fig. 1 is presented in Table 1. One can verify the three distance properties on this matrix.

Table 1. Distance Matrix between the Nodes given in Fig. 1

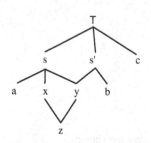

	T	b	y	a	x	s'	s	z	c
T	0.0	8.0	7.0	8.0	7.0	5.0	4.0	8.0	8.0
b	8.0	0.0	6.0	7.0	7.0	3.0	7.0	7.0	5.0
y	7.0	6.0	0.0	5.0	4.0	5.0	5.0	4.0	8.0
a	8.0	7.0	5.0	0.0	3.0	7.0	4.0	4.0	6.0
x	7.0	7.0	4.0	3.0	0.0	6.0	3.0	2.0	6.0
s'	5.0	3.0	5.0	7.0	6.0	0.0	5.0	6.0	5.0
s	4.0	7.0	5.0	4.0	3.0	5.0	0.0	4.0	6.0
z	8.0	7.0	4.0	4.0	2.0	6.0	4.0	0.0	6.0
c	8.0	5.0	8.0	6.0	6.0	5.0	6.0	6.0	0.0

Moreover, note that proposition (1) holds for concepts having tree-like relationship; for instance $dist(\top,a) = dist(\top,s) + dist(s,a) = 5 + 3 = 8$.

4 Applications, Results and Perspectives

4.1 Results in Ontology Visualisation

The following example is extracted from a current industrial project[3] which aims at modelling and representing music knowledge as an ontology which is projected onto a two dimensional map for navigation and indexing purpose [7]. In this simple extract, we only consider two types of concepts: music periods and composers (music works are not considered to keep the discussion simple). The semantics of the relations between them is *BELONGS-TO*. Periods are children of the root. This model can be represented as a Direct Acyclic Graph (DAG). The traditional approach for an aesthetic visualisation of a DAG is a hierarchical model whereby nodes are displayed in layers according to their rank in the graph hierarchy [17, 8]. We now show how our semantic distance produces an alternative representation that conserves part of semantic information which is otherwise poorly represented.

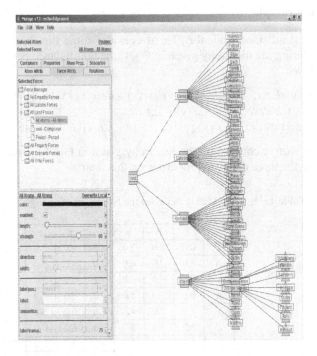

Fig. 2. Hierarchical visualisation of the ontology (works are not shown)

---

[3] This project was realised with Nétia *inc. http://www.netia.net/us/*

In the following snapshots, all the displays were performed using our knowledge mapping environment called Molage that implements different graph drawing algorithms among which MultiDimensional Scaling (MDS) and Force Directed Placement [6, 7]. Fig. 2 presents an aesthetic hierarchical display[4] of the music model performed with Molage (with a limited number of edge crossings [8]). The periods are on the second layer, most of composers are on the third layer, two sub-periods for the xx[th] century ('Le groupe des Six' and 'Ecole de Vienne') are also on this third layer, and their children on the fourth layer. In order to read the labels, another Molage force called the 'Limit force' was applied to separate the different nodes that are on the same layer along the y axis. The result is understandable, but presents several pitfalls. It looses particular semantic information since those composers that are linked to two periods like *Alberti*, *Debussy* or *Malher* are not highlighted in the mass of all composers. The different periods are not separated according to their respective influence, but merely because of the fact that we want to limit the number of edge crossings in the display. It is necessary to keep visible links to associate each composer to his (her) period(s). A display with most of the composers on the third layer is a sub-optimal usage of the plane with empty and cluttered spaces. Finally, with such a display, a concept, such as *Romantic*, is far on the Euclidian plane from its instances which are the composers that represent this period. This is a problem when we want to use the Euclidian plane for indexing as we do in our application [7].

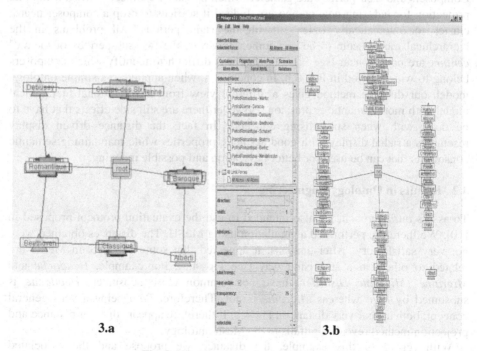

3.a   **3.b**

Fig. 3. Visualisation using our distance

---

[4] Note that labels are in French because it has been done in a French project.

Our distance measurement may now be applied to this ontology in order to maintain strong semantics. In this application we consider concepts to be defined in an extensive way. For example, each musical period is characterised by composers who composed works during a certain period. In the same way, a composer may be considered through his complete works.

Fig. 3.a shows the result of applying the distance described in Section 0 followed by an MDS projection. Music periods are identified as *pink squares*[5], and composers as *blue triangles*. One can see that all composers of a unique period are piled up under their period. However, some composers are between several musical periods. *Beethoven* is considered as a turning point between the *classical* and *romantic* periods. He is therefore positioned in a cluster between the two periods (like *Schubert*). One can also notice a kind of chronological circle around the root (square without label) from *Baroque* period to the *Classical*, then the *Romantic* ending with the XXth Century. In order to identify the composers beneath a period, in Fig. 3.b we applied the 'Limit force' as we did for the hierarchical display in Fig. 2.

The semantic distance in Fig. 3.b can now be compared to the hierarchical model in Fig. 2. The belonging of composers to a particular period is clearer and their links to their period is no longer necessary. The space is better utilized and there is less cluttering. Composers that belong to two different periods like *Alberti* or *Beethoven* are better identified since they are positioned between the corresponding periods. Composers and their periods are gathered which is what we expected when using this projection for indexing new composers. Indeed it suffices to drop a composer near a cluster to automatically index it with the right periods. All problems in the hierarchical model seem to be overcome. However, the two sub-periods of the XXth century are now so near (see Fig. 3.a) that it is difficult to identify which composers belong to which period in Fig. 3.b. In conclusion, when applied to a simple ontology model, our distance method gives a different view from the traditional hierarchical model with more semantic expression. However there are still side effects that have to be dealt with when specialising concepts. In fact, the distance driven display resembles a radial display with good aesthetic properties while maintaining semantic constraints that can be used for better navigation and possible indexing.

4.2 Results in Ontology Engineering

To assess our approach, we also intended to use the evaluation protocol proposed in [10]. We therefore performed a simulation using MeSH. The distances obtained were not very satisfactory. After analysis, it appeared that some concepts in MeSH are related to others in a surprising way (see Fig. 4.a). For example, *Headache* and *Migraine (Migraine Disorder)* have no common close subsumer. *Headache* is subsumed by *Pain* whereas *Migraine* is not. Therefore, *Pain* being a very general concept, both appear very distant on Fig. 4.b. It therefore appears that our distance and projection method reveals a pitfalls in the Mesh ontology.

With regard to this example, the distance we propose and the associated visualisation may be used by ontology modellers. During the building of an ontology

---

[5] Shapes enable readers of the black and white printed version to ignore colours.

the projection emphasises ontological inconsistencies, e.g. semantically closed concepts that appear far from one another on the projection, thus revealing bad or missing relations. It may also be used for ontology validation.

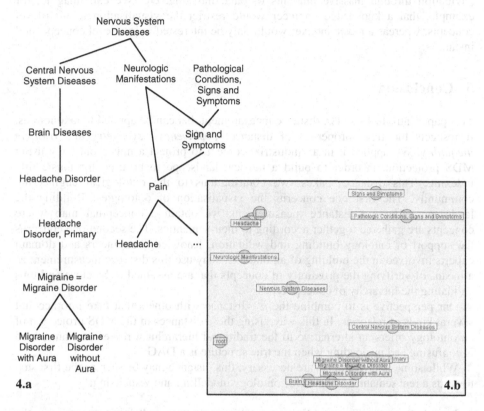

Fig. 4. A Fragment of the MeSH Taxonomy and is projection in Molage

4.3 Perspectives

For better results, our method needs to be completed. Only considering the ISA relation is not sufficient. It would be interesting to combine this distance with others that take into account the meronymy relation or some functional relations. Our future work will concern this extension to other relations.

Another perspective concerns the inclusion of a level of detail that can be associated with each concept of the ontology. Building an ontology often consists in listing the "words" that are used in a particular domain, determining which are synonyms and the concepts that are designated by those words. From the list of domain concepts, relations between them are defined, in particular the ISA-relation, which is used to structure them in a concept hierarchy. However, knowledge engineers and domain experts may describe some parts of the ontology at a high level of granularity (very deeply) whereas some other parts are described more succinctly. It is necessary to associate a value to each concept that specifies whether the concept is close to instances or a general concept and that represents the level of detail [13]. Combining this level of detail with the distance measurement presented in this paper would enable different visualisations in function of usage: ontology engineering, navigation through massive amounts of data, indexing, etc. We can imagine, for example, that a knowledge engineer would restrict the visualisation to high-level concepts, whereas a music indexer would only be interested in low-level concepts and instances.

5   Conclusion

This paper introduces an ISA-distance measurement that can be applied to taxonomies. It respects the three properties of distance: *positiveness*, *symmetry* and *triangle inequality*. We applied it in an industrial context to project a music ontology using MDS projection, in order to build a musical landscape to be used for music title indexing. This distance makes two contributions to the ontological engineering community. The first one concerns the visualisation of ontologies. Building the landscape using our distance measurement, we obtain a conceptual map where concepts are gathered together according to their semantics. The second one concerns the support of ontology building and validation. Knowledge engineers and domain experts involved in the building of an ontology may use this distance measurement as a means of verifying the proximity of concepts that are assumed to be close and thus validating the hierarchy of concept types.

Our perspective is to combine the *ISA*-distance with others that take into account several kinds of relations. In this way, using these distances in the MDS projection of an ontology offers an alternative to the traditional hierarchical representation, which is confusing and misleading when the true structure is a DAG.

While some improvements are necessary, this distance may be seen as the first step towards a real semantic distance for ontology modelling and visualising.

Acknowledgments. This publication is the result of a collaboration between the "Institut des Sciences de l'Evolution de Montpellier" (UMR 5554 - CNRS) and the "LGI2P Research Centre from Ecole des Mines d'Alès".

References

1. Besançon, R.: Intégration de connaissances syntaxiques et sémantiques dans les représentations vectorielles de textes – application au calcul de similarités sémantiques dans le cadre du modèle DSIR. Thèse de sciences EPFL, n° 2508 (2001)
2. Barthémemy, J.P., Guénoche, A.: Trees and Proximity Representation. Chichester, New-York: Wiley & sons (1991)
3. Budanitsky, A., and Hirst, G.: Semantic Distance in WordNet: An Experimental, Application-oriented Evaluation of Five Measures. Workshop on WordNet and Other Lexical Resources, in the North American Chapter of the Association for Computational Linguistics, NAACL-2000, Pittsburgh, PA, June (2001)
4. Collective of authors: WordNet. An electronic lexical database. Edited by Christiane Fellbaum, with a preface by George Miller. Cambridge, MA: MIT Press (1998) 422 p

5. Cordì, V., Lombardi, P. Martelli, M. Mascardi, V.: An Ontology-Based Similarity between Sets of Concepts. In Proceedings of WOA 2005, F. Corradini, F. De Paoli, E. Merelli and A. Omicini eds. Pitagora Editrice Bologna, ISBN 88-371-1590-3 (2005) 16-21
6. Crampes, M., Ranwez, S., Villerd, J., Velickovski, F., Mooney, C., Emery, A., Mille, N.: Concept Maps for Designing Adaptive Knowledge Maps, in Concept Maps, A Special Issue of Information Visualization, Vol. 5, Issue 3, Guest Editors: S.-O. Tergan, T. Keller and R. Burkhard, Palgrave - Macmillan, sept. 2006.
7. Crampes, M., Ranwez, S., Velickovski, F., Mooney, C., Mille, N.: An integrated visual approach for music indexing and dynamic playlist composition, in proc. 13th Annual Multimedia Computing and Networking (MMCN'06), San Jose, CA, US. Jan 18-19 (2006)
8. Di Battista, G., Eades, P., Tamassia, R., Tollis, I.: Graph drawing. Algorithms for the visualisation of graphs. Prentice Hall , Upper Saddle River (1999)
9. Euzenat, J.: Représentations de connaissance : de l'approximation à la confrontation. Habilitation à diriger des recherches, Univ Grenoble 1, 116 pages, (1999) *English title : Knowledge representations : from approximation to confrontation*
10. Hliautakis, A.: Semantic Similarity Measures in MeSH Ontology and their application to Information Retrieval on Medline. Dissertation Thesis, Technical Univ. of Crete (TUC), Dept. of Electronic and Computer Engineering, Chania, Crete, Greece, (2005)
11. Jaillet, S., Teisseire, M., Dray, G., Plantié, M.: Comparing Concept-Based and Statistical Representations for Textual Categorization. In proceedings of 10th Conference on Information Processing and Management of Uncertainty in Knowledge-Based Systems (IPMU'04), (2004) 91-98
12. Jing, L., Zhou, L., Ng, M.K., Huang, J.Z.: Ontology-based Distance Measure for Text Clustering. In proceedings of the Fourth Workshop on Text Mining, Sixth SIAM International Conference on Data Mining, Hyatt Regency Bethesda, Maryland (2006)
13. Ranwez, S.: Composition Automatique de Documents Hypermédia Adaptatifs à partir d'Ontologies et de Requêtes Intentionnelles de l'Utilisateur, PhD thesis in computer science, Montpellier II University (2000)
14. Resnik, P.: Semantic Similarity in a Taxonomy: An Information-Based Measure and its Application to Problems of Ambiguity in Natural Language. Journal of Artificial Intelligence Research, Vol. 11 (1999) 95-130
15. Roddick, J., Hornsby, K., de Vries, D.: A unifying semantic distance model for determining the similarity of attribute values. In Proceedings of the 26th Australian Computer Science Conference (ACSC2003), Adelaide, Australia (2003)
16. Sowa, J.F.: Conceptual Structures: Information Processing in Mind and Machine. Addison-Wesley (1984)
17. Sugiyama, K., Tagawa, S. and Toda, M.: Methods for visual understanding of hierarchical systems. IEEE Trans. Syst. Man Cybern., SMC Vol. 11, Issue 2 (1981) 109–125

The Management and Integration of Biomedical Knowledge: Application in the Health-e-Child Project (Position Paper)

E. Jimenez-Ruiz[1], R. Berlanga[1], I. Sanz[1], R. McClatchey[2],
R. Danger[1], D. Manset[3], J. Paraire[3], and A. Rios[3]

[1] University Jaume I, Castellon, Spain
{ejimenez, berlanga, isanz, danger}@uji.es
[2] CCS Research Centre, University of the West of England (UWE), Bristol, UK
Richard.McClatchey@uwe.ac.uk
[3] Maat Gknowledge, Valencia, Spain
{dmanset, jparaire, arios}@maat-g.com

Abstract. The Health-e-Child project aims to develop an integrated healthcare platform for European paediatrics. In order to achieve a comprehensive view of children's health, a complex integration of biomedical data, information, and knowledge is necessary. Ontologies will be used to formally define this domain knowledge and will form the basis for the medical knowledge management system. This paper introduces an innovative methodology for the vertical integration of biomedical knowledge. This approach will be largely clinician-centered and will enable the definition of *ontology fragments*, connections between them (*semantic bridges*) and enriched ontology fragments (*views*). The strategy for the specification and capture of fragments, bridges and views is outlined with preliminary examples demonstrated in the collection of biomedical information from hospital databases, biomedical ontologies, and biomedical public databases.

Keywords: Vertical Knowledge Integration, Approximate Queries, Ontology Views, Semantic Bridges.

1 Introduction

The Health-e-Child (HeC) project [1] aims for the construction of a Grid-based service-oriented environment to manipulate distributed and shared heterogeneous biomedical data and knowledge sources. This biomedical knowledge repository will allow clinicians to access, analyze, evaluate, enhance and exchange integrated biomedical information and will also enable the use of integrated decision support and knowledge discovery systems. The biomedical information sources will cover six distinct levels (also referred to as vertical levels), classified as molecular, cellular, tissue, organ, individual, population, and will focus on paediatrics, in particular, on some carefully selected representative diseases in three different categories: paediatric heart diseases, inflammatory diseases, and brain tumours.

R. Meersman, Z. Tari, P. Herrero et al. (Eds.): OTM Workshops 2006, LNCS 4278, pp. 1062–1067, 2006.

The HeC project will have several medical institutions contributing diverse biomedical data for the different vertical levels. It is likely that data sources for each level will have different schemata, using different software packages with varying types of access controls. In order to bring these disparate sources together it is necessary to identify the core entities for each level, to build an intermediary data model per level to capture the entities' structures, and to unify these level data models. A set of biomedical ontologies will be used to formally express the HeC medical domain with the mentioned *vertical abstraction levels*. This paper also introduces the concept of an Integrated Disease Knowledge Model (IDKM), which captures the core entities for each vertical level and provides the valid concepts for a particular disease.

1.1   Issues in Biomedical Data Integration

Data source integration has been a traditional research issue in the database community. The main goal of an integrated database system is to allow users to access a set of distributed and heterogeneous databases in a homogeneous manner. The key aspect of data integration is the definition of a global schema, but it is worth pointing out that we must distinguish between three kinds of global schemata: the database schemata, the conceptual schemata and domain ontologies. The first describes the data types with which information is locally stored and queried; the second generalizes these schemata by using a more expressive data model like UML (TAMBIS [2] and SEMEDA [3] follow this approach). Finally, domain ontologies describe the concepts and properties involved in a domain (such as Biomedicine) independently of any data model, facilitating the expression of the semantics of the application resources (e.g. via semantic annotation) as well as reasoning about them.

Medical research has a long tradition in unifying terminological concepts and taxonomies (e.g. through the Unified Medical Language System (UMLS) [4]), and in using ontologies to represent and query them in medical information systems. Recently, several approaches to integrating medical and bioinformatics public databases have been ontology based (e.g. ONTOFUSION [5]). However, new issues and challenges arise from the introduction of domain ontologies when integrating information sources. Firstly, many domain ontologies in Biomedicine do not cover completely the requirements of specific applications. Moreover, these concepts can involve different abstraction levels (e.g. molecular, organ, disease, etc.) that can be in the same or in different domain ontologies. Secondly, domain ontologies are normally rather large, resulting in two main effects: users find them hard to use for annotating and querying information sources and only a subset of those are used by system applications. Finally, in current integration approaches, it is necessary to manually map the existing data sources to domain concepts, which implies a bottleneck in large distributed scenarios.

This paper mainly focuses on the two first issues: managing multiple domain ontologies and presenting personalised ontology views to end-users and applications involved in an integrated biomedical information system. The proposed approach consists of a new ontology-based methodology that spans the entire integration process. This methodology relies on both the definition of ontology-based views and their construction from domain ontology fragments.

2 Methodology for the Vertical Knowledge Integration

The most important aspect of HeC, in contrast to current biomedical integration projects (e.g. INFOGENMED [7], MyGrid [6], TAMBIS, etc.), is to integrate patient information according to disease models, instead of integrating public biomedical databases. An Integrated Disease Knowledge Model (IDKM) is proposed as a solution to specify the concepts of particular diseases, taking into account all the biomedical abstraction layers. Patient-centric information collected in the hospitals will be semantically annotated in terms of a particular IDKM. Following the Description Logic terminology, the distributed repositories that store the patient semantic annotations are called ABoxes (or Assertional Boxes).

The methodology presented here provides the necessary mechanisms to build IDKMs from well-known biomedical ontologies and public databases. Most simply stated, it enables building ontology-based *views* from consistent fragments of biomedical ontologies, which are interrelated by means of so-called *semantic bridges*. Each ontology fragment is intended to capture the main concepts involved in a disease for a particular abstraction layer (e.g. genetic, organ, etc.). Bridges perform the actual vertical integration, where they relate selected elements of an abstraction layer to those of a more abstract one. In this methodology, bridges can be found explicitly in the biomedical ontologies (e.g. NCI, GO, FMA, etc.) or implicitly in text-rich public biomedical databases (e.g. UNIPROT, OMIM, EMBL, etc.).

Constructing such IDKM models requires going through the following stages (see Figure 1 for a graphical representation of methodology steps):

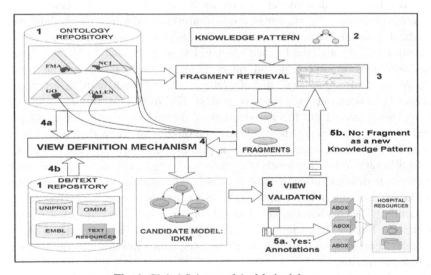

Fig. 1. Global Schema of the Methodology

1. **Creation of a Knowledge Repository.** To apply the presented methodology, a set of well-known domain ontologies and public databases have been collected.
2. **Definition of a Knowledge Pattern.** We start the construction of IDKMs from a knowledge pattern: a set of concepts, a hierarchy of concepts (tree), a graph, etc.

3. **Ontology fragments retrieval.** Candidate regions, with respect to a knowledge pattern, are identified in the ontologies through approximate tree matching.
4. **View Definition Mechanism**
   a. *Definition of complete views.* Previously introduced fragments are then enriched with other concepts and roles from the ontologies by means of a set of inference rules.
   b. *Connecting view fragments.* Views are merged using mapping techniques and inferring connections (*semantic bridges*) from the public databases.
5. **Validation of Views:** The resulting view will be an IDKM candidate model.
   a. *Annotating.* Patient information collected in hospitals has to be annotated according to validated IDKM concepts and roles. The annotation information (or semantic representation) constitutes the A-Boxes.
   b. *Feedback.* If the view is not sufficiently complete, it can be used as a new knowledge pattern and start again the methodology cycle.

3   Retrieving Ontology Fragments with ArHex

For the purposes of this study, the tool ArHex [8] has been adopted to retrieve ontology fragments in order to guide the building of the IDKMs. Thus, starting from a collection of ontologies and a knowledge pattern, users can query the knowledge and progressively construct the required IDKM. However, using multiple ontologies raises the problem of semantic heterogeneity, as different concepts can have similar lexical expressions. In the presented approach these problems have been addressed by the introduction of approximate queries [9]. Basically, an approximate query is a *tree pattern* whose nodes specify which concepts and roles have to be found, and arcs that express the different approximate relationships between them (e.g. parent/child, ancestor/descendant, etc.). The retrieval system provides a list of ontology fragments ranked with respect to a similarity measure that compares candidate regions and patterns. We are currently developing a set of base similarity measures suitable for the HeC project, as well as extending the pure tree-oriented ArHeX indexing engine to support directed acyclic graphs, which are required for more powerful ontology querying facilities.

4   Definition of Consistent View Fragments

Obtained ontology fragments cannot be directly used to build a consistent IDKM for several reasons. Firstly, some of the selected ontology fragments can conflict and secondly, ontology fragments are sometimes too small and/or incomplete for an IDKM. Therefore, it is necessary to complete these retrieved fragments and to check possible conflicts between their extensions. Fragments provide information about the context of the query concepts, and help in defining views over an ontology, since they bring more information about neighbour concepts and relations. Thus, the view mechanism can be seen as a technique to enrich, with other concepts and relations, the extracted or identified fragments.

At this point in time, the definition of such views has been achieved through the use of a traversal-based view definition language, called OntoPathView [10]. In this language, views over an ontology consist of the union of a set of traversal queries (paths) and a set of inference rules in order to get closed, consistent and complete views [10].

5 Representation of Vertical Levels: Modules and Mappings

The identification of the knowledge represented in the ontologies and the coverage over the identified vertical levels is a crucial aspect in the application of this methodology. Figure 2 illustrates the example of a possible coverage of four biomedical ontologies. In the figure ovals represent possible modules identified in the ontologies that cope, partially or totally, with the HeC levels, while arrows represent connections. The connections between modules of the same ontology are easy to establish because they are defined during the modularization; whereas the connections between modules of different ontologies involves a complex mapping process.

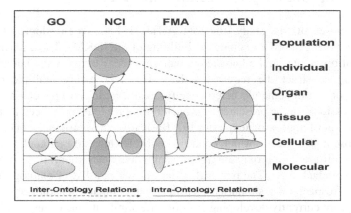

Fig. 2. Vertical levels and modules in ontology representations

Classical mapping discovery processes only try to find similarities between two ontologies, by determining which concepts and properties represent the same reality (so-called syntactic and lexical matching) [11]. However modern approaches, such as C-OWL [12] or E-Connections [13], try to find more complex relations (or bridges) between concepts (e.g.: causes-disease, located-at, encodes, involves, etc.). These works refer to these complex relations as *bridge rules* or *E-Connection*, respectively, and infer them by means of external sources (i.e. document repositories such as PubMed, Meta-thesaurus, etc.). In the approach presented in this paper the definition of bridges is mainly based on an earlier work [14] in which a technique for automatically generating ontology instances from texts was applied. The extracted instances not only populate the ontology but also should yield some additional information, potentially useful for completing and refining the ontology definition, or for adding new semantic relations between concepts (semantic bridges). To extract such bridges, for the biomedical domain, public biomedical databases like UNIPROT, OMIM, EMBL, etc. are mined.

6 Conclusions

In this paper we have presented a novel methodology for the integration of biomedical knowledge. It specifically addresses vertical integration over diverse granularity levels and describes several techniques to enforce the methodology. Text mining facilities are used to automatically populate ontology instances, providing complementary information for completing the ontology definition and discovered bridges. Semantic bridges are the key to integration and discovery of new knowledge. We believe these powerful concepts will drive us towards the construction of an integrated view of child's health in the European Health-e-Child project.

Acknowledgements

The authors wish to acknowledge the support provided by all the members of the Health-e-Child (IST 2004-027749) consortium in the preparation of this paper. This work has been also partially funded by the UJI-Bancaixa project P1B2004-30 and the Spanish Ministry of Education and Science project TIN2005-09098-C05-04.

References

1. J. Freund, et al. "Health-e-Child: An Integrated Biomedical Platform for Grid-Based Pediatrics", Studies in Health Technology & Informatics # **120,** pp 259-270 IOS Press 2006
2. C. Goble et al. "Transparent Access to Multiple Bioinformatics Information Sources (TAMBIS)". IBM System Journal, **40(2)**, pp.532-551, 2001.
3. J. Kohler, S. Phillipi & M. Lange., "SEMEDA: ontology based semantic integration of biological databases". Bioinformatics 19(18), 2003.
4. The Unified Medical Language System (UMLS) fact sheet available at the National Institutes of Health Library of Medicine: http://www.nlm.nih.gov/pubs/factsheets/ umls. html
5. D Perez-Roy et al.,"ONTOFUSION: Ontology-based integration of genomic and clinical databases". Computers in Biology & Medicine **36(7-8)**, 2006.
6. R. Stevens, A. Robinson, and C.A. Goble., "myGrid: Personalised Bioinformatics on the Information Grid" Bioinformatics Vol. **19**, Suppl. 1, i302-i304, 2003.
7. I. Oliveira et al., "On the Requirements of Biomedical Information Tools for Health Applications: The INFOGENMED Case Study". BioENG 2003. Lisbon, Portugal.
8. I. Sanz, M. Mesiti, G. Guerrini, R. Berlanga. "ArHeX: An Approximate Retrieval System for Highly Heterogeneous XML Document Collections". Demo at EDBT 2006.
9. I. Sanz, M. Mesiti, G. Guerrini, R. Berlanga. "Highly Heterogeneous XML Collections: How to retrieve precise results?" In Proc. of FQAS. 2006.
10. E. Jiménez, R. Berlanga, I. Sanz, M. J. Aramburu, R. Danger: "OntoPathView: A Simple View Definition Language for the Collaborative Development of Ontologies". Artificial Intelligence Research and Development, pp 429-436. IOS Press, 2005.
11. N. F. Noy. "Semantic Integration: A Survey of Ontology Based Approaches" ACM SIGMOD Record, Special Issue on Semantic integration, 2004.
12. Bouquet, F. Giunchiglia, F. Van Harmelen, L. Serafini, H. Stuckenschmidt. "Contextualizing ontologies", Journal of Web Semantics **1(4)**, pp. 325-343, 2004
13. Cuenca-Grau, B. Parsia, E. Sirin. "Combining OWL Ontologies using E-Connections". Journal of Web Semantics **4 (1)**, pp. 40-59, 2005.
14. R. Danger, R. Berlanga, J. Ruíz-Shulcloper "CRISOL: An approach for automatically populating a Semantic Web from Unstructured Text Collections". In Proc. of DEXA 2004.

Ontology-Based Systems Dedicated to Human Resources Management: An Application in e-Recruitment

Vladimir Radevski and Francky Trichet

SEEU - South East European University
Ilindenska p.n. - 1200 Tetovo - Republic of Macedonia
v.radevski@seeu.edu.mk
LINA - Computer Science Research Institute
University of Nantes
2 rue de la Houssinière - BP 92208
44322 Nantes Cedex 3, France
francky.trichet@univ-nantes.fr

Abstract. This paper presents the CommOn framework (Competency Management through Ontologies) which aims at developing operational Knowledge-Based Systems founded on ontologies and dedicated to the management of competencies. Based on two different models (implemented within specific tools developped with the Protégé-2000 framework), Common allows a Knowledge Engineering (i) to build competency reference systems related to particular domains such as Healthcare or Information and Telecommunication, (ii) to identify and formally represent competency profiles (related to a job seeker, a job offer or a training offer) and (iii) to automatically match competency profiles. Developed in the context of Semantic Web Technology, the CommOn framework permits the building of domain ontologies and knowledge bases represented with Semantic Web Languages and the development of Competency-Based Web Services dedicated to Human Resources Management. The use of CommOn is illustrated in the context of a project (related to e-recruitment) which aims at developing the first Macedonian web-based platform dedicated to the definition of an efficient networking of employment and training operators. However, Common is not limited to e-recruitment application and it can be used for different purposes such as staff development and deployment, job analysis or economic evaluation.

Keywords: Knowledge-Based System, Ontology, Semantic Web, Competency, Human Resources Management, e-recruitment.

1 Introduction

People-Finder Knowledge Management Systems (also known as yellow pages) are repositories that allow managing knowledge by holding pointers to experts

R. Meersman, Z. Tari, P. Herrero et al. (Eds.): OTM Workshops 2006, LNCS 4278, pp. 1068–1077, 2006.

who possess specific knowledge within an organization [1]. CommOn (*Competency Management through Ontologies*) is a generic framework dedicated to the development of Competency-Based Systems (CBS), *i.e.* specific People-Finder KMS. This framework is based on the following definition: " a *Competency*[1] is the effect of combining and implementing *Resources* in a specific *Context* (including physical, social, organizational, cultural and/or economical aspects) for reaching an *Objective* (or fulfilling a mission)". Three types of resources are distinguished: *Knowledge* which includes theoretical knowledge (*e.g.* knowing the second law of thermodynamics) and procedural knowledge (*e.g.* knowing the procedure for assembling a particular electronic card), *Skills* which include formalized know-how (*e.g.* the application of working procedures) and empirical know-how (*e.g.* tricks, abilities or talents) and *Behavioural aptitudes* which refer to the potential for performing an activity and correspond to the characteristics which underlie an individual's behaviour at work. This definition, which highlights the singular dimension of a competency, integrates the traditional view of KSA (Knowledge, Skills and Aptitudes). Indeed, in our approach, KSA are not competencies but only resources of competencies. Note that although "competency logic" is not a new approach in Human Resources Management, it has not been implemented yet in KMS in the sense that no operational competency-based systems are currently used in organizations. The main contribution of this paper is to show how a Competency-Based System, *i.e.* a system founded on a KBS constructed with CommOn and thus dedicated to competency management, can be of effective help for the managers involved in Human Resources Management.

Practically, CommOn is composed of three complementary tools which have been developed with the Protégé-2000 framework [4]. These tools, which are based on models defined through our conception of competency, allow one (i) to build competency reference systems related to particular domains, (ii) to identify the competencies and the Behavioural aptitudes a person has or a task (a job-position) requires and (iii) to compare competency profiles. Following the work of the HR-XML Consortium (http://www.hr-xml.org), these tools are defined within the Semantic Web context. Thus, the CommOn models (corresponding to Ontologies of Representation) and the knowledge bases constructed from these models (corresponding to Domain Ontologies) are represented as ontologies expressed in OWL, and the proposed tools are considered as Web Services.

CommOn is currently being experimented in the context of the BRIDGE research project which is funded both by the French Government (http://www.diplomatie.gouv.fr/en/) and by the research foundation of the South East European University (SEEU) of the Republic of Macedonia (http://www.see-university.com). BRIDGE aims at dealing with the problem of e-recruitment by considering a new approach based on competency management. The principle underlying BRIDGE consists in considering a CV (respectively a job offer and a training programme) as a synthetic view (expressed, in natural language, in terms of qualifications, work experiences and extracurricular activities for a CV) of a richer network

---

[1] We voluntarily use the expression *competency* (or *competence*) in order to avoid confusion with skill, ability or know-how.

of competencies. According to this principle, the first objective of the project is to allow the end-user (*i.e.* a job seeker, a recruiter and a training provider) to make all the competencies underlying its resources (*i.e.* a CV, a job offer and a training programme) explicit. The second objective is to formally represent these competencies in order to provide more powerful e-recruitment services: the content (expressed in terms of competencies) of CVs, job offers and training catalogues must be manageable by computers in order to provide automatic matching services and gap measurement services. These objectives require (1) the definition of a competency model and (2) the definition of a process dedicated to the management (*i.e.* identification, formal representation and exploitation in terms of gap measurement) of the competencies underlying a CV, a job offer or a training programme.

The rest of this paper is structured as follows. Section 2 presents the competency model underlying the CommOn framework. Section 3 presents the model of a competency reference system we advocate and the CommOn tool we have developed for building such a reference system for a particular domain D; this reference system corresponds to an ontology of the competencies underlying D. Section 4 presents the tools we propose to identify competencies profiles. Finally, section 5 illustrates, in the context of the BRIDGE project, the use of the CommOn tools and the benefits of our approach in the context of e-recruitment.

2   CommOn: The Competency Model

In our work, a competency is the effect of combining and bringing into play its Resources (*i.e.* knowledge, know-how, and behaviours) in a given Context to achieve an objective or fulfil a specified mission. The cognitive process of bringing-into-play a competency is not considered in this definition. Besides, the know-how is considered as a complete competency, which has little or no resources clearly identified. Finally, it is important to underline that our model only focuses on *individual competencies*; it does not deal with *collective competencies*, which is a problem out of the scope of our work.

In this context, the definition of a competency C_i is formally represented by the following quintuplet (justified in [2]): $C_i = (K, B, C, A, o)$ where

- K is a set of knowledge which is necessary for C_i. An element K_i of this set can be theoretical or procedural.
- B is a set of behaviours which are necessary for C_i.
- C is a set of basic competencies which are necessary for C_i. An element C_j of this set corresponds to a know-how (formalized or empirical) which, in our work, is considered as a complete competency.
- A is a set of aspects which define the context of C_i. Several types of aspects can be considered: social and organizational aspects, economical aspects, physical aspects that include machines and technologies, informational aspects, etc.
- o is an objective (it is not a set of objectives). This objective can correspond to a job position, a mission to carry out or to a task to achieve.

This quintuplet specifies that a competency is defined by a set of sets of resources (K, B and C) which is mobilized in a particular context A for reaching an objective o (cf. figure 1). When a competency is elementary (for instance, a know-how), the sets K, B and C can be empty. When the competency corresponds to an empirical know-how, the sets K, B and C can be indefinite. Finally, when the competency is universal, the set A can be empty.

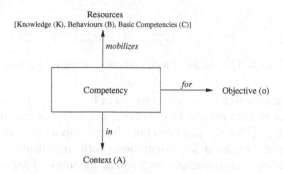

Resources
[Knowledge (K), Behaviours (B), Basic Competencies (C)]

mobilizes

Competency   *for*   Objective (o)

in

Context (A)

Fig. 1. The definition of a competency

3   Building Competency Reference Systems

3.1   The Model

The model we advocate provides all the concepts (structured according to the *Specialisation/Generalisation* relationship) and the relations which must be identified when defining a competency reference system for a specific domain such as Healthcare or Banking and Finance. As shown in figure 2, this model specifies that a competency reference system is defined by a set of tasks (a Task can be an Elementary Task or a Composite Task) which are respectively based on Resources (Knowledge, Skill or Aptitude) also structured hierarchically. Each resource can imply other resources or be specialised in more specific resources. For instance (cf figure 3), knowledge on `Active part of connection facilities` necessarily implies knowledge on `Connection facilities`; it can be specialised in knowledge on `Hub`, `Bridge` or `Router`.

3.2   The CommonReference Tool

CommonReference is the tool which implements the model presented above; it allows one to build a knowledge base characterising a specific competency reference system. Such a knowledge base includes a fine-grained description of all KSA required for the job-position (and their associated tasks) of the considered domain. For instance, in the context of the Information and Telecommunication domain, this knowledge base includes a description of all the KSA and tasks required for performing job-positions such as Database Administrator, Desktop Technician or System Analyst. From a technical point of view, CommonReference has been developed from Protégé-2000 [4] (http://protege.stanford.edu).

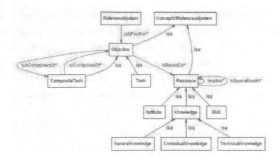

Fig. 2. The model of a competency reference system

The use of CommonReference is illustrated in figure 3 in the context of a competency reference system related to the domain of Information and Telecommunication Technology (ITT). It has been built from a report provided by the Cigref (http://www.cigref.fr), an independent/non-profit organisation which includes the major ITT French corporations such as Air France or France Télécom.

The extract of the knowledge base presented in figure 3 shows that the composite task Network & Telecommunications Technician (considered as a JobPosition of the Cigref) is composed of several elementary tasks such as Test network equipment or User support. Synonyms of this job-position are Telecommunications Technician or Network/Telecoms Technician. Performing this job-position requires Behavioural aptitudes such as Capacities for negotiation or Sense of relationship building. The elementary task Test network equipment is based

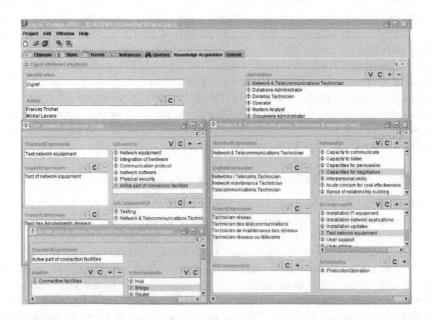

Fig. 3. Extract of the knowledge base corresponding to the Cigref

both on general knowledge such as `Physical security` and on technical knowledge such as `Communication protocol` or `Active part of connection facilities`. The latter necessarily implies knowledge on `Connection facilities`; it can be specialised in knowledge on `Hub`, `Bridge` or `Router`.

4 Building Competency Profiles

4.1 Identifying Behavioural Aptitudes with CommonAptitude

CommonAptitude is a tool which allows the end-user of a CBS to identify its personality traits and then to automatically match these traits with Behavioural aptitudes. CommonAptitude reuses a predefined tool called Performanse-Echo which allows the user to identify human traits; Performanse-Echo has been developed by Performanse (`http://www.performanse.com`), a French firm specialized in the development of software dedicated to the analysis of individual behaviours.

The approach we advocate for evaluating Behavioural aptitudes is based on a two-step process: (1) evaluation of human traits from answers to questions and (2) identification of Behavioural aptitudes from evaluated human traits.

The *questionnaire* used to perform the first step is composed of 75 closed questions such as "I think that any experience, pleasant or not, is an occasion (1) to discover something or (2) to verify something" or "To get interesting results, I prefer (1) to control my actions or (2) to adapt my actions". This questionnaire has been put together by the psychologist from Performanse. Its objective is to evaluate twenty human traits such as Self-assertion/Self-questioning, Extroversion/Introversion or Anxiety/Relaxation. These traits are related to a model corresponding to a refinement of the five-factor model (Openness to experience, Conscientiousness, Extroversion, Agreeableness and Neuroticism), more well-known as the Big Five dimensions of personality. Each question is dedicated to the evaluation of one of several human traits. A human trait can be evaluated from several questions; some questions can increase the weight of a trait whereas others can decrease this weight. Thus, answering the 75 questions leads to an individual assessment composed of the twenty human traits respectively characterised by a weight (expressed as a percentage). An extract of such an assessment can be expressed as follows: *Self-assertion: 23%, Extroversion: 88%, Anxiety:54%, ...*

The *expertise* used to perform the second step is composed of inference rules. These rules have been defined in collaboration with the psychologist from Performanse. Each rule defines a way to attest a Behavioural aptitude from a combination of human traits. Thus, the hypothesis of a rule is composed of a conjunction of human traits characterised by an interval and the conclusion of a rule is a linguistic expression characterising a Behavioural aptitude. An example of such a rule related to the aptitude called "Negotiation and Persuasion" is expressed as follows: *(Self-assertion $\in$ [60..70]) and (Anxiety $\in$ [40..60]) and (Combativeness $\geq$ 60) and (Extroversion $\in$ [33..50])* $\rightarrow$ *Negotiation and Persuasion*.

4.2 Identifying Competencies with CommonCompetency

Based on the use of the knowledge bases constructed with CommonReference and on the integration of the results produced by CommonAptitude, the first functionality of CommonCompetency is to facilitate the identification of competencies expressed in terms of *Resources* mobilized, combined and implemented in a *Context* for reaching an *Objective*. In the context of one competency, this task which is performed by the end-user (for instance a job seeker who wants to annotate its CV) consists in first searching (through all the tasks described in the given competency reference system) for the task which best characterises the intended *Objective* and then focusing on the *Resources* needed to reach this objective. For resources related to Aptitudes, the results provided by Common-Aptitude can be used directly. For resources related to Knowledge or Skills, the end-user can attest or refute the ones proposed by the system (because in the knowledge base they are associated with the selected task) and/or define new ones. For describing the *Context*, we plan to use existing domain ontology dedicated to the modeling of organisations such as Enterprise ontology [3]; this work has not yet been studied.

Figure 4 shows an extract of a prototype used to put our approach into practice. Annotating an electronic resource from a competency point of view (for instance the second professional experience of Mr Chettri identified by the URI http://www.sciences...chettri.html#ProfessionalExperience2) consists in attesting a set of competency instances (*e.g.* AnnotatingWithCigref_00120 ... AnnotatingWithCigref_00129) where each instance is described by using the three

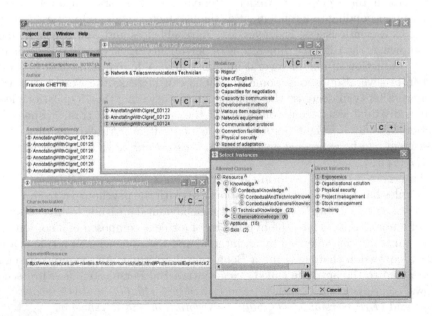

Fig. 4. Annotating electronic documents with CommonCompetency

relations involve in our definition: `Mobilizes(Competency,Resource)`, `For(Competency,Objective)`, `In(Competency,Context)`. Each instance of the `In` relation is related to an economical, social or technical aspect; this allows the user to describe a competency context including several dimensions. As specified by the signature of the `For` relation, the objective of a competency can only be a job-position (considered as a Composite Task in our model) or a task of a job-position described in the considered reference system. This approach seems to be relevant in a context of e-recruitment because when an applicant wants to describe an experience, he always think about the job or the tasks he has performed. For the relation `Mobilizes`, the end-user can attest all (or only a part of) the resources automatically proposed by the system because they are connected (by the relation `IsBasedOn`) to the selected `Objective` in the considered reference system. He can also add new resources.

5 Bridge: An Application in e-Recruitment

5.1 Objectives

The BRIDGE project, currently developed for the Career Centre of the SEEU (South East European University, Republic of Macedonia), aims at developing a web portal based on the principles underlying the CommOn framework. The goal is to deal with the problematics of e−recruitment by considering a new approach based on competency management. The idea consists of allowing a job seeker (respectively a recruiter and a training operator) to identify and formally represent the competencies underlying its Curriculum Vitae (respectively its job offer and training programme). These competencies, which allow to make explicit knowledge, skills, abilities, traits and motives acquired by a person (respectively required for a job and provided by a training programme), are then used to refine the matching process between "supply and demand". In other words, the objective of is to provide to the end-users of websites dedicated to e−recruitment new job-matching services based on competency management.

BRIDGE should benefit to all actors of the Employment Market and Training Market of the Republic of Macedonia. The interests for job seekers are: (1) availability of a platform ensuring a better standardized expression of their competencies; this platform will be compatible with the Europass CV Template[2] and (2) availability of a platform that will show the lacking skills and will propose links with relevant and training possibilities. The interests for companies are: (1) better definition of the candidate profile needed for a given position and (2) better management of the Human Resources policies. The interest for training operators is mainly the improvement of the business because, thanks to BRIDGE, job seekers and companies will be able to identify precisely lacking competencies and thanks to the links with training, operators will be able to show the best suited trainings, which could in return increase the number provided training sessions.

---

[2] Europass (http://europass.cedefop.eu.int/), which has been established by the European Parliament and the Council in 2004, aims at defining a single transparency framework for qualifications and competences.

5.2   Ontologies and e-Recruitment: A Scenario of Use

In the context of BRIDGE project, ontologies are crucial because they allow a recruiter, a job seeker and a training provider (i) to have a common understanding of the competencies and the tasks underlying a job-position and (ii) to share the same vocabulary for denoting theses notions. Moreover, an ontology can be used by a job seeker as a reference system for identifying its personal competencies. Indeed, when writing a CV, it is usually difficult to choose the best sentence (in natural language) for expressing the competencies acquired during a professional history. Sometimes, the adopted sentences are not very significant and do not include or precisely reflect all the competencies of a person. Therefore, having a reference of the tasks and competencies underlying a job-position can be an effective help when dealing with the identification of individual competencies. Such a reference can also be used by a job seeker to evaluate whenever its competencies are compatible with the one's required for a job-position; if it is not the case, he can plan a formation in order to acquire the missing competencies.

As introduced in section 3, the ontologies we consider include all the concepts that are necessary for representing the resources, the context and the objective of the competencies underlying a significant part of a CV; these concepts can be related to the tasks associated to a job-position, know and know-how underlying a diploma or a task, the organizations of enterprises, cultural or economical aspects denoting the considered context, etc.

Figure 5 illustrates, in the context of a CV, the annotating process (based on our competency model) we consider (the same process is applied to a job offer or a training program). The competency C_1 (which is one of the competencies underlying the second work experience of Mr CHETTRI) is related to a task (characterizing the objective of C_1) of the job position called "Database Administrator". This competency has been acquired in a particular context which is described by a technological aspect (*Oracle DBMS*), a physical aspect (*Mainframe*), an

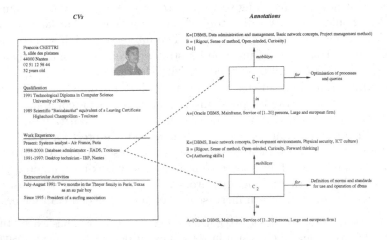

Fig. 5. Annotating CVs with competencies

organizational aspect (*Service of* [1..20] *persons*) and an economical aspect (*Large and European firm*). This scenario can be applied for a qualification (in this context, the domain ontologies can be related to a discipline or to a high school) or an extracurricular activity.

6 Conclusion

CommOn is a generic framework which aims at developing operational Competency Based Systems. Based on a fine-grained description of the competency concept and on a semantic web approach, this framework facilitates the construction of competency reference systems for particular domains and the exploitation of such reference systems for identifying and matching competency profiles. This work is currently in progress towards the definition of more powerful operators dedicated to matching of *required competency profiles* and *acquired competency profiles*. These operators will be based on the reasoning mechanisms provided by the semantic web languages.

Acknowledgements. For their valuable contributions for this work, we are grateful to Michel LECLERE (University of Montpellier), Michel BOURSE (Galatasaray University) and Mounira HARZALLAH (University of Nantes).

References

1. M. Alavi and D. Leidner. Knowledge management systems: issues, challenges and benefits. In *Communications of the Association for Information Systems*, volume 1(7), 1999.
2. M. Bourse, M. Harzallah, M. Leclère, and F. Trichet. Commoncv: modelling the competencies underlying a curriculum vitae. In *Proceedings of the 14th international conference on Software Engineering and Knowledge Engineering (SEKE'2002)*, pages 65–73. ACM Press, 2002.
3. M. Fox and M. Gruninger. Enterprise modeling. *AI Magazine*, 19(3):109–121, 1999.
4. R. W. Fergerson W. E. Grosso M. Crubezy H. Eriksson N. F. Noy S. W. Tu J. Gennari, M. A. Musen. The evolution of protege: An environment for knowledge-based systems development (http://protege.stanford.edu/). In *International Journal of Human-Computer Studies*, volume 58(1), pages 89–123, 2003.

Towards a Human Resource Development Ontology for Combining Competence Management and Technology-Enhanced Workplace Learning

Andreas Schmidt[1] and Christine Kunzmann[2]

[1] FZI Research Center for Information Technologies – Information Process Engineering
Haid-und-Neu-Straße 10-14, 76131 Karlsruhe, Germany
Andreas.Schmidt@fzi.de
[2] Kompetenzorientierte Personalentwicklung
Ankerstraße 47, 75203 Königsbach-Stein, Germany
kontakt@christine-kunzmann.de

Abstract. Competencies as abstractions of work-relevant human behaviour have emerged as a promising concept for making human skills, knowledge and abilities manageable and addressable. On the organizational level, competence management uses competencies for integrating the goal-oriented shaping of human assets into management practice. On the operational and technical level, technology-enhanced workplace learning uses competencies for fostering learning activities of individual employees. It should be obvious that these two perspectives belong together, but in practice, a common conceptualization of the domain is needed. In this paper, we want to present such a reference ontology that builds on existing approaches and experiences from two case studies.

1 Introduction

Competencies as abstractions of work-relevant human behaviour have emerged as a promising concept for making human skills, knowledge and abilities manageable and addressable. Although competencies are still an overly simplification of the "real" world, they are a more adequate approximation than the notion of "knowledge" in traditional knowledge management approaches as they can represent a *set* of skills, knowledge, and abilities that belongs together. Furthermore it seems to be common-sense that competencies of individuals have to be developed and that this development is a complex learning activity – in contrast to the language often used in knowledge-based approaches like "transferring knowledge" [1].

Current competency-driven approaches can be divided into two categories according to the perspective they take (organizational vs. individual):

- **Competence management** represents the organizational perspective and denotes a management approach providing processes and a methodological framework for developing the competencies of an organization by aligning human resource development activities (in a broad sense) with business goals. Proposed methods and

R. Meersman, Z. Tari, P. Herrero et al. (Eds.): OTM Workshops 2006, LNCS 4278, pp. 1078–1087, 2006.

activities have first focussed on identifying, securing and making use of competencies, but increasingly they are concerned with developing competencies by fostering learning processes of employees in manifold ways, e.g. by identifying potentials and by offering training activities [2].

– As a perspective focusing on the individual, **technology-enhanced workplace learning** has emerged as an approach bundling classical e-learning with knowledge management techniques for holistic workplace learning support covering both formal and informal learning. Its focus are learning activities integrated into work processes, merging e-learning, knowledge management, and performance support. Recent approaches like [3], [1] or [4] are all more or less competency-driven, i.e., they regard competencies as a major conceptualization for any technological enhancement in a business context.

It seems to be natural to combine the two perspectives. Technology-enhanced workplace learning needs the integration into the organizational environment, and current approaches show that there currently is a lack in the sustainability of this integration because usually changes are not adequately represented. On the other side, competence management in most cases still relies on a more traditional, formal way of human resource development and does not cover more intangible learning processes, e.g., result from informal teaching activities.

An important step towards this integration is a shared conceptualization of the two perspectives. In this paper we want to present a first step towards a reference ontology, which has been constructed based on ontologies and reference models developed in the project *Learning in Process* [1] on technology-enhanced learning and a competence management approach towards training needs planning in the healthcare domain [2], augmented by the consideration of existing ontology-based approaches. In section 2, we first want to summarize the requirements and purpose of such a reference ontology before briefly reviewing existing approaches in section 3. Section 4 and 5 will be devoted to describing and visualizing the key ideas of the reference ontology (the graphical notation is explained in fig. 5 in the appendix) before we will explain some implementation issues (section 6) and conclude the paper in section 7.

2   Requirements

Conceptualizations or models are always purpose-oriented. In first step, thus, it is important that we clearly state the purpose in the form of the requirements that this ontology should fulfill:

– *Alignment of human resource development with business processes and goals.* On a macro level, it is one of the benefits from competence management that it provides systematic alignment of development activities with business goals and processes. The conceptual model must provide the foundation for this alignment.

– *Automatability of learning micro management.* With the training and learning activities turning more and more individual and informal, the task of efficiently managing these activities becomes increasingly complex. Enhancements through technology in this context also mean that the micro management get automated as far as possible. The ontology needs to provide the basis for this.

- *Smooth transition to knowledge management activities.* Although competence management appears to be the successor of knowledge management, it should be acknowledged that we need to integrate the handling of explicit "knowledge" in knowledge management systems. The ontology must make visible where the links to traditional ontology-based KM approaches are.
- *Holistic view on human resource development.* Human resource development must be understood in a broad sense, incorporating formal training, self-directed learning, informal and collaborative learning activities. The ontology should avoid an overly bias towards one of these forms, although it is clear that formal training is much better understood than informal and collaborative leanrning activities which is still subject of major research activities.

One important distinguishing aspect of ontologies (in a narrower sense, i.e., with a formal semantics) in contrast to other methods of conceptualization is that these models are machine-processable and can be directly used to make applications more aware of the domain semantics. So what kind of algorithms do we want to support? The following two cases have emerged:

- *Profile matching with similarity measures.* The most frequently analyzed case is the matching of a individual's competency profile with a requirements profile, e.g. for applicant selection ([5], [6]) or for team staffing [6]. For this purpose, a framework for defining ontology-based similarity measures has already been developed by [7].
- *Finding learning opportunities with knowledge gap analysis and competency subsumption.* Whereas in the aforementioned case, the result is the degree how well a person fits to a requirement, another important use case is the identification of suitable learning opportunities that can even be proactively recommended. In order to realize this, a knowledge gap needs to be calculated by comparing the requirements profile with the current competency profile, yielding missing competencies [8]. One important aspects that needs to be taken into account here is the issue of competency subsumption, i.e., we cannot simply rely on direct comparison, but need to consider that a competency can be subsumed by another competency (e.g. higher competency level, generalization, composition).

3   Existing Approaches

So far, there has been no integrated approach that covers both the macro and the micro perspective as explained above. However, there is prior work we can build upon when creating a human resource development ontology. The most important for our goal are:

- In [9], an integrated approach to human resources management was developed that builds on ontology-based techniques. The developed ontology focuses on modeling of competency catalogs and job and employee profiles in order to apply similarity measures on profile matching.
- [10] developed a competency ontology framework, mainly for the use cases expert finder and team staffing. Its strength is the formal foundation.

- For describing learning objects and learning designs, several approaches exist, e.g. the ALOCoM ontology concentrates on describing learning content itself [11]; LOCO describes learning designs and proposes competency annotations [12]. The LIP ontology [1] was developed for competency-based context-aware recommendation of learning objects in work situations.
- A very limited step towards integrating competence management with learning paths is [13].

4 Defining and Assessing Competencies

For our reference ontology, competencies are defined as bundles of work-relevant skills, knowledge and abilities. Competencies are usually associated with competency levels to describe different degrees of an abstract competency type. Ordinal scales are typically used for that purpose like [14] or the reference levels for language proficiency [15]. In order to account for that, we introduce the distinction between competencies (having attached a competency level) and competency types (having attached a competency scale), where *Competency* is an instance of *CompetencyType*, introducing meta-modeling (i.e., treating concepts as instances, see section 7 for how to represent this in OWL-DL). This makes sense because we can talk about competency concepts as such (e.g., English language proficiency), for you can define a scale to measure it, and individual competencies at a certain level (e.g., English C2 Mastery).

Useful competency models usually consist of hundreds of different competencies, which are hard to handle. In order keep them manageable, competencies can be organized hierarchically, where usually competencies can have more than a single parent competency (poly-hierarchy). This hierarchic structure is often semantically undefined so that real world catologs use nesting both for generalization and composition. We propose to clearly differentiate between competency generalization (with an *is-a*-semantics) on the level of competency types (regardless of the competency level) and competency composition on the level of individual competencies (see 1, for a legend

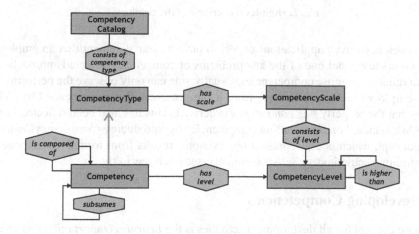

Fig. 1. Core part of the ontology: Modeling Competencies

5). One example for generalization could be a competency *Ontology Modeling* and a sub-competency *OWL Modeling*; generalization means that we can infer that an intermediate in *OWL Modeling* is also an intermediate in *Ontology Modeling*. Composition is more curriculum-like: the different levels of competencies are defined by enumerating the required elements, e.g. the competency OWL Modeling at intermediate requires that you have the competency of using a modeling tool at expert level and the competency of mastering a modeling methodology at beginner level.

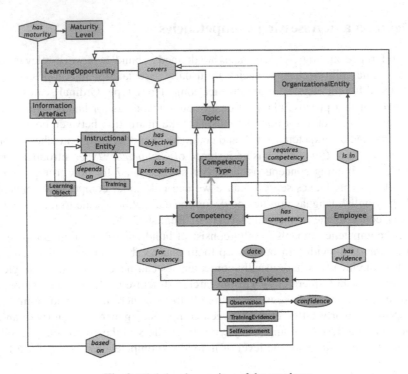

Fig. 2. High-level overview of the ontology

Competency-driven applications expect to have a clear statement that an employee has a competency, but one of the key problems of competency-oriented approaches is how to reliably diagnose competencies. Usually, one can only observe the performance of an employee and try to deduce from it the presence of a competence [16]. That means that the property *has-competency* is derived. This has also been reflected in the HR-XML standard on representing competencies by introducing *CompetencyEvidence* as a concept, which could represent observations, results from formal assessments (after training activities), or self-assessments (see overview in fig. 2).

5 Developing Competencies

The base concept for all development activities is the *LearningOpportunity*; it is an abstract representation of any form of (repeatable) activity that can contribute to competency development. In order to structure the "learning opportunity landscape", we classified them into maturing phases [17], ranging from emerging ideas via community formation and formalization to ad-hoc and formal training. Using this coarse model, we can identify the following subconcepts (from mature to immature):

– **InstructionalEntity.** An instructional entity is any entity that was designed for fostering individual learning processes. Subconcepts are, e.g., classical presence trainings, and learning objects or learning programs. For such entities, it can be assumed that they they have a well-defined learning objective. Although currently, this learning objective is rarely formalized, in our competency-based approach, we require that at least part of the learning object definition is the assignment of a target competency (see also [1]).

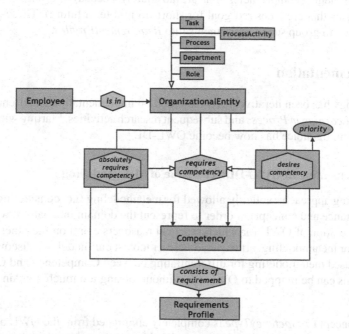

Fig. 3. The requirements part of the ontology

– **InformationArtefact.** In contrast to an InstructionalEntity, information artefacts were not didactically designed for learning activities. As a consequence, clear objectives cannot be formulated. Rather, these opportunities are about a subject or topic. To account for that, we introduce a semantically relaxed concept *Topic* and a relaxed property *covers*. By making *CompetencyTypes* a special kind of *Topic*, we can smoothly integrate knowledge area (i.e., topic) taxonomies with competence catalogs. Information artifacts do not have to classified according to competencies, but we can still view CompetencyTypes as a special topic so that there is no need of two taxonomies.

- **Employee.** Informal learning activities via inter-human communication form a major part of workplace learning [18]. Thus it is important to represent the colleague as a learning opportunity. Here, the *has-competency* property can be viewed as a specialization of the *covers* property, referring to competencies.

But how do we know which *LearningOpportunity* is appropriate for a certain situation? As business process-oriented knowledge management [19] shows, the business context provides some clues on which aspects of a work situation require which competencies. In competence management, requirement profiles are used that are typically attached to roles, or organizational units. In our ontology, we introduce the concept of an OrganizationalEntity that is connected to a Competency via a *requires-competency* property (see fig. 3). As our experience in [2] shows, we need to distinguish between hard requirements (competencies that are absolutely needed) and soft requirements (competencies that are a desired goal for short- to mid-term future). These properties can be reified to group such requirements into *RequirementProfiles*.

6   Implementation

This ontology has been iteratively refined based on implementation experiences within the project *Learning in Process* and subsequent research activities. Starting with RDF(S), the formalism of choice has now become OWL-DL.[1]

6.1   Implementing in OWL-DL: The Issue of Metamodelling

Our modeling approach explicitly allowed for metamodeling (i.e. considering concepts as both instance and concept) in order to represent the domain in a natural way. OWL-DL (as the edition of OWL for which practical reasoners exist) on the other side does not allow for metamodeling.[2] If we have a closer look at our model, we discover that we have only used metamodeling for differentiating between Competency and CompetencyType. This can be mapped to OWL-DL without loosing too much domain semantics by:

- The concept *CompetencyType* is completely eliminated from the OWL ontology.
- It is assumed that competencies are modeled in a concept hierarchy (under *Competency*) representing generalization on competency types.
- *CompetencyScales* are assigned to the relevant subconcepts of *Competency* via annotation properties.
- For classifying information artefacts, we use instance of a competency concept that do not have any competency level associated with it.

This mapping inevitably looses some domain semantics, but for algorithms operating on this ontology, this has not turned out to be problematic.

---

[1] The OWL-DL ontology is released under a CreativeCommons license under http://www.professional-learning.eu/competence_ontology.html
[2] A more natural implementation would be possible in the KAON RDFS extension with the concept of spanning instances [20].

6.2   Implementing Derived Properties

More severe is a problem that we have not considered yet. Many of the properties in the ontology are time-dependent and uncertain (which applies especially for the derived property *has-competency*).

For representing time-dependence, we could reify properties into concepts, of course, and add a validity period to them, but this would clutter the resulting ontology and thus reduce the usability drastically. We see the solution in having a database with the complete history below and feed the instance-level of the ontology with a snapshot view for a specific instant in time. The uncertainty resulting from deriving heuristically from other facts is addressed likewise by having a user context management layer (for technical details see [21]) below that stores all facts and aggregates them into *has-competency* statements. In order to account for the fact that competencies can be lost if they are not actively used, this user context management service provides configurable aging mechanisms for collected and inferred data.

Although originally foreseen, it has turned out that SWRL rules are not suitable for computing derived properties (apart from syntactical shortcuts). For the *has-competency* property, this has mainly to do with the uncertainty and temporal aspects. For the *subsumes* property, the complexity of the algorithm cannot be represented in SWRL rules in a reasonable way.

7   Conclusions and Outlook

We have presented the basic concepts of our reference ontology for human resource development in a technology-enhanced setting. This ontology brings together the different disciplines concerned with learning in organizations, see fig. 4):

- **Competence Management.** It incorporates as its core the competency catalog for describing and organizing competencies and provides concepts to align competencies with business entities by specifying requirements profiles. These requirement profiles can carry both short-term goals and mid-term development routes.
- **Knowledge Management.** Knowledge taxonomies can be integrated with competency modeling so that easily less mature information artefacts (sometimes called knowledge assets) can co-exist with more mature training material.
- **Business Process Management.** The ontology also provides the link to business processes, which are represented as a special *OrganizationalEntity* in the model.
- **Technology-enhanced workplace learning.** In addition to requirements, organizational entities can also be annotated with additional domain knowledge for adapting learning support based on the organizational context, e.g., for specific business processes it can be specified whether learning embedded in this process is possible at all or not (as for process activities with direct customer contact).

The next step on our agenda is the definition of reference processes that consider the dynamics of such a human resource development ecosystem. This includes processes for maintaining and developing competency catalogs and requirement profiles, processes for developing more mature training content.

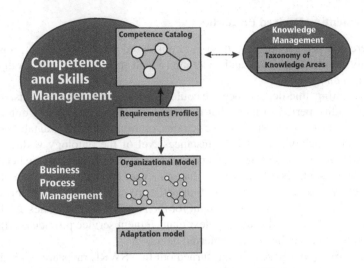

Fig. 4. The ontology and its relationship to different areas

References

1. Schmidt, A.: Bridging the gap between knowledge management and e-learning with context-aware corporate learning solutions. In: Professional Knowledge Management. Third Biennial Conference, WM 2005, Kaiserlautern, Germany, April 2005. Revised Selected Papers. Volume 3782 of Lecture Notes in Artificial Intelligence., Springer (2005) 203–213
2. Kunzmann, C., Schmidt, A.: Ontology-based competency management for healthcare training planning - a case study. In: 6th International Conference on Knowledge Management (I-KNOW 06), Graz. (2006)
3. Woelk, D.: E-learning, semantic web services and competency ontologies. In: World Conf. on Educational Multimedia, Hypermedia and Telecommunications (EDMEDIA). (2002)
4. Lindstaedt, S., Mayer, H.: A storyboard of the aposdle vision. In: 1st European Conference on Technology-Enhanced Learning (ECTEL 06), Crete. (2006)
5. Mochol, M., Paslaru, E., Simperl, B.: Practical guidelines for building semantic erecruitment applications. In: International Conference on Knowledge Management (IKNOW 06), Special Track: Advanced Semantic Technologies (AST'06), Graz, Austria. (2006)
6. Biesalski, E., Abecker, A.: Integrated processes and tools for personnel development. In: 1th International Conference on Concurrent Enterprising, University BW Munich, Germany, 20-22 June 2005. (2005)
7. Biesalski, E., Abecker, A.: Similarity measures for skill-profile matching in enterprise knowledge management. In: 8th International Conference on Enterprise Information Systems (ICEIS), 23 - 27, May 2006 Paphos - Cyprus. (2006)
8. Schmidt, A.: Context-steered learning: The Learning in Process approach. In: IEEE International Conference on Advanced Learning Technologies (ICALT '04), Joensuu, Finland, IEEE Computer Society (2004) 684–686
9. Biesalski, E.: Unterstützung der Personalentwicklung mit ontologiebasiertem Kompetenzmanagement. PhD thesis, University of Karlsruhe (2006)
10. Zelewski, S., Alan, Y.: Generische kompetenzontologie für computerbasierte kompetenzmanagementsysteme. In et al., S.Z., ed.: Ontologiebasierte Kompetenzmanagementsysteme – Grundlagen, Konzepte, Anwendungen. Logos (2005)

11. Verbert, K., Gasevic, D., Jovanovic, J., Duval, E.: Ontology-based learning content repurposing. In: 14th International World Wide Web Conference, Chiba, Japan. 1140–1141 (2005)
12. Knight, C., Gasevic, D., Richards, G.: Ontologies to integrate learning design and learning content. Journal of Interactive Media in Education **7** (2005)
13. Draganidis, F., Chamopoulou, P., Mentzas, G.: An ontology based tool for competency management and learning paths. In: 6th International Conference on Knowledge Management (I-KNOW 06), Special track on Integrating Working and Learning, 6th September 2006, Graz. (2006)
14. Dreyfus, H.L., Dreyfus, S.: Mind over Machine. The Power of Human Intuition and Expertise in the Era of the Computer. Basil Blackwell, New York (1986)
15. Council of Europe: The Common European Framework of Reference for Languages. Cambridge University Press (2001)
16. Ley, T.: Organizational Competence Management - A Competence Performance Approach. PhD thesis, University of Graz, Austria (2006)
17. Schmidt, A.: Knowledge maturing and the continuity of context as a unifying concept for knowledge management and e-learning. In: Proceedings of I-KNOW 05, Graz, Austria. (2005)
18. Braun, S., Schmidt, A.: Don't annoy the informal teacher: Context-aware mediation of communication for workplace learning. In: 6th International Conference on Knowledge Management (IKNOW '06). (2006)
19. Abecker, A.: Business process oriented knowledge management: concepts, methods, and tools. PhD thesis, Fakultät für Wirtschaftswissenschaften, Universität Karlsruhe (2004)
20. Maedche, A., Motik, B., Stojanovic, L.: Managing multiple and distributed ontologies in the semantic web. VLDB Journal **12** (2003) 286–302
21. Schmidt, A.: Ontology-based user context management: The challenges of dynamics and imperfection. In: Proc. of ODBASE 2006, On the Move Federated Conferences (OTM), Montpellier, France. LNCS, Springer (2006)

Appendix: Notation

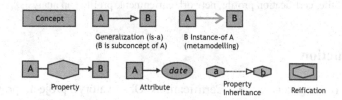

Fig. 5. Graphical notation for representing the ontology

The eCCO System:
An eCompetence Management Tool
Based on Semantic Networks

Barbara Pernici[1], Paolo Locatelli[2], and Clementina Marinoni[2]

[1] Dipartimento di Elettronica e Informazione, 20133 Milano, Italy
pernici@elet.polimi.it
[2] Fondazione Politecnico, Via Garofalo, 39, 20133 Milano, Italy
{marinoni, locatelli}@fondazionepolitecnico.it

Abstract. According to several national Institutions', ICT company associations' and the Italian Ministry of Innovation and Technology's requests for standardisation of ICT job profiles, an ICT job profiles model was defined. It is based on ontologies principle to describe "Knowledge Objects", "Skills", "Competences" and their relations. The model takes into account the several formalisations from national and company ICT job profiles frameworks and refers to the scientific literature about ontology and competences definitions. A software tool has been implemented on the basis of the model defined. It allows collecting individual users' job profiles and analysing the gaps against a set of ICT standard profiles. The semantic network behind gives the system flexibility. Furthermore, the system enables the dynamical enrichment of the semantic network by uploading new skills by users, who can also suggest linkages between the new nodes. The system administrator will later evaluate and accept them.

Keywords: ontology, semantic network, knowledge object, skill, competence, job profile, certification profile, network enrichment, profile gap analysis.

1 Introduction

The eCCO (eCompetences and Certifications Observatory) project, promoted by Italian industry associations (AICA and Federcomin) and the technical university of Milan (Fondazione Politecnico di Milano), under the aegis of the Italian Government, was born to satisfy the need of transparency, comparability, information and guidance expressed by the European Commission [1] and also claimed by several local players with regard to ICT competences[1] and job profiles.

In the last years many different ICT competences and job profiles models have been multiplied in Italy; at present, there are neither shared ICT languages nor common points of views on ICT job profiles. Moreover, tools available to help people

---

[1] In this paper, the term "competence" is used in a generic and broad sense. The term "competency" is only quoted when referred to specific technical works using it.

R. Meersman, Z. Tari, P. Herrero et al. (Eds.): OTM Workshops 2006, LNCS 4278, pp. 1088–1099, 2006.
© Springer-Verlag Berlin Heidelberg 2006

know their positioning in the labour market are still not recognized by the market itself; no common reference ICT certification systems have been developed yet; learning and training objectives are often unclear and not comparable. Accordingly, local Institutions and Government asked for an ICT competence management system, able to compare and integrate the different Italian and European approaches.

1.1   The Context Analysis

The eCCO project started with an analysis of the present national and transnational approaches to ICT competences and job profiles, in order to find common features as well as key factors to be considered and integrated within the system.

Several approaches such as IEEE [2] and HR-XML [3] were examined. IEEE is primarily focused on online and distributed learning and not on competences management; the HR-XML Consortium has defined a set of documents to provide a standard vocabulary on Human Resources. HR-XML specifications are organized by common use cases, which refer to main HR processes. In particular, the HR-XML Competency schema is used to communicate both unstructured competency data (such as that that may be captured from a resume or profile) or structured competency data from a taxonomy. The focus in this case is on measuring the competencies in order to provide a numerical evaluation. However, the dependencies between competency elements can only be expressed through a description attribute, which might be used to provide useful information about the relationship between parent and child competencies. On the other hand, in taxonomies used in e-learning and for certification, a deep nesting of component items is proposed, which might be confusing or misleading when the taxonomy is used within processes which are not related to certification, e.g. for user interaction.

Concerning certification-qualification frameworks and job profiles models, APO-AITTS [17], EUCIP [18], SFIA [19], eSkillsUK [20], Career Space [21], were analysed at a European level. At a local level the study focused on the ISFOL [22] (Istituto per lo Sviluppo Professionale dei Lavoratori, close to the Italian Ministries of Welfare and Education, University and Research) competence model, the IFTS [23] (Istruzione e Formazione Tecnica Superiore) ICT training programmes based on the concept of "Competency Unit", the Italia Lavoro [24] (The Ministry of Welfare's Agency for Employment, Social Inclusion and Labour Market Policies) Job Market Place, and other ICT competence frameworks from national companies associations. In spite of their mutual unhomogeneity, these frameworks were selected because of their relevance at a national and international level and this study aimed to detect the prevailing and most flexible approaches, in order to adopt and reasonably combine them within an integrated system.

1.2   The Use of Ontologies to Make the System Dynamic

As [4] state, an ontology defines a common vocabulary for researchers who need to share information in a domain. An important aspect is related to the knowledge of the processes in which the ontology is used, and therefore there is no single solution for an ontology in a given domain.

The goal of the use of ontologies to model competences of human resources proposed in this paper is twofold: to be able to recognize elementary components of competence, extracting them from a textual description on the basis of a given ontology and text similarity analysis, and to manage a HR ontology, with the capability of restructuring concepts, adding new concepts and new relations among them. The approach is generic, i.e. it is not linked to a specific ontology. Therefore, it can be applied to different taxonomic approaches to define competences and can be tailored to be used in a personalized way in each company, adopting the specific company's terminology.

Moreover, the approach allows a dynamic updating of the system by the users themselves. This aspect becomes even more relevant if we think of ICT innovation and development of competences [5]. The effective evolution of ICT competences is usually faster than its formal codification. So, bottom–up monitoring of competences would make it easier the recognition of new job profiles emerging from praxis: i.e., if several users suggest the same new competences and relations, a new set of performances or even a new job profile is likely present in practice.

2 Theoretical and Methodological Assumptions Behind eCCO

The key features emerging from the analysed competence frameworks are summarized in Table 1:

Table 1. Competence frameworks key features

Key Features	Italian models	APO – AITTS	Career Space	Eucip	SFIA, e-Skills UK
Competence definition	most approaches share that competences are knowledge (and skills) put into action within specific contexts of activities				
Competence identification	Top-down criteria (from job descriptions)	Top-down criteria (from business processes)	Top –down / bottom up criteria (from individuals and "best performers")	Top-down criteria (from business processes)	Top-down criteria (from business processes)
Competence representation	modular representation	holistic descriptions	holistic descriptions	modular representations	modular representations
Aims of competences representations	towards both performances and learning	towards learning	towards both performances and learning	towards learning	towards performances and learning

2.1 The eCCO Definitions of Knowledge, Skill, Competence, Towards a Common Language and Job Profile Flexibility

According to the competence definition coming out of the initial analysis, the eCCO basic definitions are:

- Knowledge ≡ the set of know-what, know-how and know-why
- Knowledge Object (KO) ≡ a "small enough", self consistent set of knowledge (with respect to specific areas of analysis, targets, objectives, etc.)
- Skill ≡ KO put into action, KO + Action Verb (AV): to be able to do something
- Competence ≡ a skill in a specific context (Cx) of activity, KO + AV + Cx: to be able to do something with respect to a specific context of activity
- Performance ≡ a set of observable behaviours producing an objective result
- Job profile ≡ a set of competences related to the concept of key performances, expected results

The detection of KOs, AVs and Cxs only requires a textual analysis. Hence, it can be applied to both top-down and bottom-up approaches to competence identification, starting from either a business process analysis [5] or the investigation of individual learning and working experiences [6], [7], [8].

According to definitions above, a skill differs from a competence because it is not related to a specific context of working or learning. On the contrary, when it is contextualised and defined in terms of autonomy and responsibility levels, it becomes a competence [9].

Moreover, competence definition above integrates the different trends in literature that consider competences as "subject's attributes" [10], [6], [7], versus "organisation's attributes" [5]. In fact, the individual and organisational dimensions are just linked together by descriptions of competences as individual "observable" behaviours towards objective results, *to be able to do something in a context*, exactly in the same way as performances [11]. On the contrary, the psychological components behind are left to learning and training.

Just with respect to this, the eCCO model considers *what* people should be able to do in specific contexts of activities but it says nothing about *how* people learn to shift from knowledge to action into a specific context (i.e., what is concerned with the *hidden* side of competences). Likewise, a KO is not synonymous with Learning Object, even though there are analogies between them, e.g. learning objects too can be defined as self-consistent sets; nonetheless they are concerned with learning units [12], [13].

Finally, a job profile is but an aggregate of competences that allow achieving key performances. Actually, in any work context, specific job profiles can be flexibly defined and continuously updated, by adding or replacing their set of competences.

Within this framework, language standardisation as well as comparisons between different ways of designing and describing profiles and competences is made possible at KOs and AVs levels. In the eCCO model KOs, AVs and Cxs are the vocabulary of competences and profiles. The representations of linkages between them are based on the concept of "semantic network". Conceptually, a semantic network is a diagraph made of nodes and arcs labelled by symbols. A node can represent a concept, a word, a set or an individual; an arc represents a binary correlation between the entities represented by the source and the target nodes [14], [15]. In the eCCO model the nodes are KOs, and KO + AVs, the arcs represent the "IS-A", "requirement" relations. See 3 and 4 paragraphs below.

2.2   Key Functionalities Provided for by the eCCO Model

The eCCO model has also defined the information system functionalities to satisfy the needs of flexibility and integration.

In particular, the eCCO model provides for the construction of different job profiles starting from the same network of knowledge, skills and competences. ICT profiles already codified inside the information system are called "standard profiles"; profiles built by the eCCO users during the assessment are called "individual profiles"; those ones defined by companies are called "company profiles".

Moreover, just in line with the approaches analysed, the eCCO model allows to build both qualification profiles, i.e., knowledge and skills a user has to learn, and professional profiles, i.e. a sequence of skills required by companies, - starting from the same semantic network. Hence, when available, users can asses what qualification and proficiency standard profiles are closest to their own ones.

During the assessment through the eCCO information system, users are allowed to choose whether writing their skills and competences freely or selecting them from predefined lists. When inputs to the system are free, the model provides for text recognition (e.g. a curriculum) by also using synonymous in different languages.

By assuming that competences are knowledge put into action in specific contexts of activities, users have to describe their contexts of experiences (work experiences, projects developments, formal, non formal, informal learning experiences, etc). Hence, competences stated by users will be recognised by the system only if they can be associated to contexts descriptions.

Furthermore, the eCCO model provides for different levels of network administration. On one hand administrators must be able to fuel the network with new KOs, AVs and linkages between them; on the other hand, company human resource managers are required to manage competences and job profiles.

Finally, in accordance with the competence approaches analysed, the eCCO model provides for both top-down and bottom-up approaches to new knowledge, skills and competences identification. That is, knowledge, skills and competences can be detected starting from business processes analysis by expert teams as well as from experiences declared by individual users of the system. They will be allowed to add into the network their skills and competences not found in the system and to make connections. The network administrators will further validate the items and linkages suggested by users. In that way, new competences already informally grown inside ICT communities of practice can get into the network stream.

3   The eCCO Model: Using a Semantic Network to Build Knowledge, Skills and Competences

3.1   Formalizing Concepts in the eCCO Model

The ontology used in eCCO is a semantic network which links the representation of knowledge objects, skills, and competences. The conceptual model at the basis of the semantic network is shown in Fig. 3.1., representing it using an Entity-Relationship model, which allows also to indicate cardinalities of relationships.

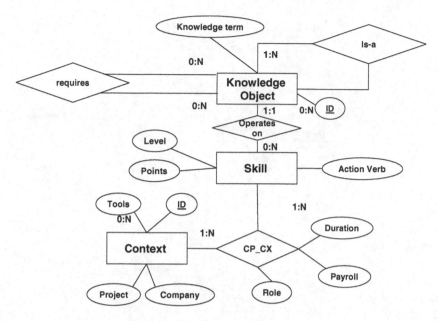

Fig. 1. Concepts in the eCCO ontology

The basic concept of Knowledge Object is represented as an entity, with a Knowledge Term and an Id attribute, and can be linked to other KO used either requires or is-a relationships. Synonym relationships can be defined among Knowledge Terms and representative terms are chosen (not indicated in the figure for simplicity). The instances of KOs form a semantic network like the one presented as an example in Fig. 3.2.

Skills associate action verbs to knowledge objects, such as, for instance, design, understand, plan, and so on.

A competence provides a context for a skill, indicating where the skill has been put in practice. In the current implementation some attributes are defined for skills, but a more detailed description could be provided using exchange languages such as the ones defined in HR-XML documents.

A professional profile can be constructed indicating which KOs and skill are included in the profile.

3.2   Querying and Reasoning Using the eCCO Model

Two types of queries can be performed using the above mentioned models. In the first case, the assumption is that the processes using the ontology are based on a free text interaction with the tool, for instance a user indicating "Design entity keys including FOREIGN KEY constraints". In the second case, reasoning is performed on the basis of the semantic network to assess the relevance of a given assertion to given concepts, such as How close are "use a procedural programming language" and "use C"?

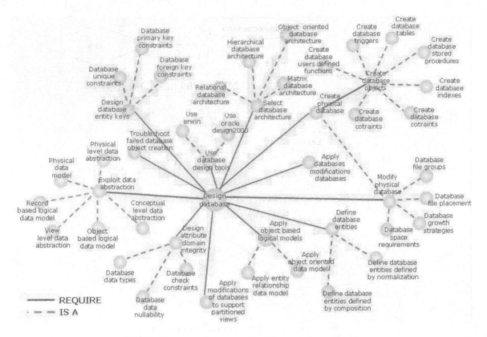

Fig. 2. A semantic network of knowledge objects

3.2.1 Term Similarity Using q-Grams

To evaluate similarity between strings the technique of positional q-grams is applied [16]. A positional q-gram on a string s is a couple of i, indicating the position of the q-gram in the string, and a substring of length q staring from position i. The basic idea behind positional q-grams is that if two strings have a large number of common q-grams they are semantically close. For instance John Smith and John A. Smith where q=3 yields 11 common q-grams out of 12 in the shorter string and 14 in the longer one.

A semantic distance k between strings can be defined using q-grams.

As shown in the following section, term similarity is used to identify Knowledge Objects during user interaction and map user's terms to the terms contained in the semantic network.

3.2.2 Reasoning on KOs

To apply this evaluation algorithm to the standard profiles by using the semantic network we have to consider the IS-A and REQUIRED links:

- IS-A: a certain node is satisfied proportionally to the highest of its subtypes and itself value;
- REQUIRED: a 100% percentage matching occurs when all the nodes required are completely satisfied. However, if all the required nodes are satisfied, we cannot assume that the master node is fully satisfied. In fact, the master node is a node which represents a specific knowledge (and experience) in itself, that we cannot neglect. So the requisites of a node are a part of its value, and they will be less important if they have a lower level of detail inside the network.

Applying the rules described, if the user X cannot program with C programming language, but he knows how to program in JAVA programming language, a hypothetical node "being able to program in a programming language" is satisfied with a percentage that is 100%. So if all the other nodes of the profile are required nodes, and the user has this ability, there will be a total matching between the user and the standard profile.

A mathematical expression to evaluate how much weight a node has got (that in an extreme case, looking at the semantic network, could eventually be a profile itself) with respect to a given profile is:

$$
Val(node) = \begin{cases} 1 & \text{if the user has the "node" knowledge} \\ Max\left(0, \{Val(isa_0), Val(isa_1), ..., Val(isa_n)\}, \dfrac{\sum_{i=0}^{m} Val(req_i)}{m+c}\right) & \text{otherwise} \end{cases} \tag{1}
$$

Where the constant c is used to assess that a complete knowledge of all required components is not fully equivalent to a stated knowledge on the node taken into consideration.

The above formula is applied recursively to all linked nodes.

4 The eCCO Information System (IS): Architecture and Rules

The eCCO IS is based on the concepts of knowledge object (KO), skill, competence and semantic networks introduced in the previous sections:

- a standard profile is a sequence of KOs and skills;
- the network links KOs and skills that belong to different profiles, independently from their level of detail;
- a dictionary makes the network stronger, with the possibility to choose both words and verbs, from not only synonyms, but also different languages.

The eCCO System architecture is based on the main blocks represented in the following image.

All data are organized in a MySQL 5 database. It contains information about user profiles, standard profiles, which are matched against user's knowledge, KOs and skills, the semantic network and synonyms used for natural language recognition and profile matching. The eCCO System data structure allows users to insert different levels of knowledge, so for each skill or KO, they can determine whether they know it as well as how much deeply.

The database is linked to an expert system (written in Java 5) which manages and uses the semantic network. This system works as a specialized application built above the relational database (used as persistent memory) to manage the links between KOs, skills and competences, but it also contains:

- the kernel of the inductive logic capable of evaluating the profile matching percentage between standard and personal profiles, or even between two standard profiles;
- the application logic of the term similarity using q-grams.

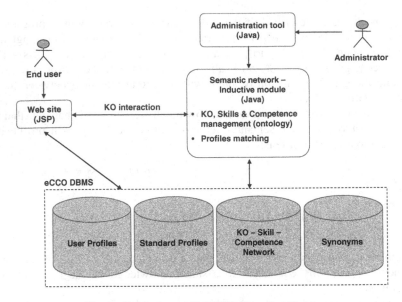

Fig. 3. Architecture of eCCO Information System

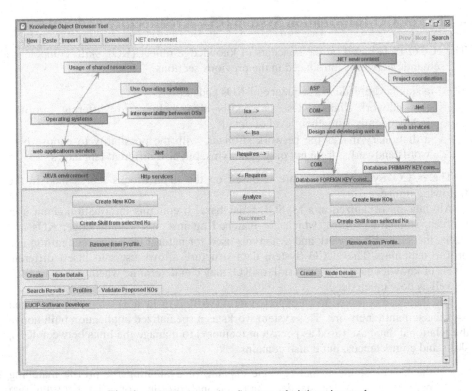

Fig. 4. eCCO Information System: administration tool

The administrator of the knowledge system can access the semantic network, and so the database, using an administration tool written in Java (and deployed with Java Web Start on the web), directly linked to the inductive module (see Figure 4). With this tool, an administrator can insert new standard profiles, navigate the network (with a graphical representation) and administer the elements of the network (KOs, skills and links between them).

Users get access the eCCO IS using a website, based also on Java technology using JSP 1.2 (on Apache Tomcat 5.5). On this website, users can register a new account, insert learning and work experiences, update their personal profiles (with KOs and skills) and evaluate the matching of their personal profiles against standard profiles.

The System helps users create a personal profile with a wizard. The first step of the wizard uses the free text elaboration using q-grams and the semantic network to evaluate terms similarity: users insert a free text in a text area and the system suggests the KOs that are more similar to the inserted text. Users can select one or more proposed KOs and the system suggests the related skills. In the last step, users can define a context (working and learning experiences defining competences) for each selected skill. Users can use the wizard one or more times; the System has an "Evaluation" area where users visualize the matching of their personal profiles against the professional and qualification standard profiles (see Figure 5).

In this area, users can evaluate the missing items for each standard profile and can add KOs or skills (this choice activates the wizard to define the skill contexts). The

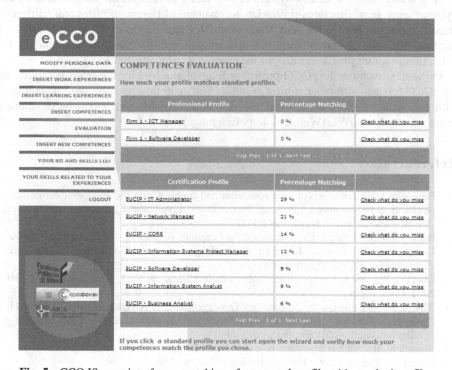

Fig. 5. eCCO IS: user interface – matching of a personal profile with standard profiles

iterative process drives users to complete their personal profiles and to define a final matching with standard profiles.

The system can also rapidly evolve by collecting up-to-date hints about competences and profiles from users who can directly propose new items and linkages. They will require an administrator's validation to be eventually inserted into the semantic network; however, a high statistical usage of the same insertion by different users can make them formally accepted.

5 Open Questions and Next Steps

At present, in the database are codified EUCIP profiles and also profiles coming from Europe (AITTS, SFIA, CIGREF), so it is possible to make comparisons between local and international frameworks.

The eCCO System has just started being used by companies for defining the mutual roles inside a project and to transparently decide what competences any partner (vendor and buyer) can make available, hence for evaluating suppliers' competences; selling own company competences to clients and determining an objective competence-based quotation of human resources at clients; understanding new emerging ICT job profiles. It can also be used to develop homogeneous ICT career paths and to facilitate internal mobility.

A new release of the eCCO System is now under development. This version of the System uses new functions in order to manage different profiles for different organizations, to apply different frameworks for the levels of KOs and skills, to improve the user iteration with the wizard part of the System, to manage the validation of a user profile for his/her manager in a company and so on.

In the next months, the eCCO project will develop a tool for the interoperability of the eCCO System with other similar systems. The main interoperability issue is linked with the standard representation of the semantic network and it can be developed using standards as OWL (Web Ontology Language).

References

1. European ministers of vocational education and training, and the European commission, Declaration on enhanced European cooperation in vocational education and training, Copenhagen (29 and 30 November 2002)
2. IEEE 1484.20.1/Draft 3, Draft Standard for Learning Technology – Standard for Reusable Competency Definitions, Learning Technology Standards Committee of the IEEE Computer Society (08 March 2006)
3. Chuck Allen (ed.), Competencies (Measurable Characteristics), Recommendation, HR-XML Consortium (Feb 2006)
4. Noy N. F., McGuinness D. L.: Ontology Development 101: A Guide to Creating Your First Ontology, Stanford University link http://protege.stanford.edu/publications/ontology_development/ontology101-noy-mcguinness.html
5. Mansfield, R.: What competence is really about Competency, v 6, n 4, (1999) 41-44
6. Hemel, G., Prahalad C.K.: Harvard Business Review (May-June 1990)
7. McClelland, D. C., Daily, C.: Improving officer selection for the foreign service, McBer and Co, Boston (1972)

8. McClelland, D.C.: Identifying competences with behavioural-event interviews, Psychological Science 9 (5) (1998) 331-339
9. Spencer L.M., Spencer S.M.: Competence at Work: Models for Superior Performance (Hardcover) (March 1993)
10. European Qualifications Framework (EQF) Grid of statements defining levels in the European Qualifications Framework, 130606
11. Boyatzis, R. E.: The Competent Manager: A Model for Effective Performance, John Wiley & Sons, New York (1982)
12. Cortellazzi, S., Pais, I.: Il posto della competenza, Franco Angeli (2001)
13. LTSC Learning technology standards committee website (2000) link http://ltsc. ieee.org/
14. Bransford, J. D., Brown, A.L. & Cocking, R.: How people learn:Brain, mind, experience and school. Washington, D.C., National Academy Press (1999)
15. Colombetti. M.: Appunti dalle lezioni di Ingegneria della conoscenza e sistemi esperti, Politecnico di Milano, (a.a. 2000/2001 – version of June 2001) Section IV, chapter 12
16. Quillian, M. R.: Semantic memory. In M. Minsky, ed., Semantic information processing, MIT Press, Cambridge Review (1968)
17. Gravano L., et al., Using q-grams in a DBMS for approximate string processing, IEEE Data Engineering Bulletin, 24(4), (2001) 28-34
18. http://www.apo-it.de/
19. http://www.eucip.it/
20. http://www.sfia.org.uk/
21. http://www.e-Skills.com/
22. http://www.career-space.com/
23. http://www.isfol.it/
24. http://www.bdp.it/ifts/
25. http://www.italialavoro.it/

Competency Model in a Semantic Context: Meaningful Competencies (Position Paper)

Stijn Christiaens[1], Jan De Bo[2], and Ruben Verlinden[1]

[1] Semantics Technology and Applications Research Laboratory
Vrije Universiteit Brussel
{stijn.christiaens, ruben.verlinden}@vub.ac.be
[2] Synergetics NV
Antwerpen
jdebo@synergetics.be

Abstract. In this paper, we will propose our ideas for a semantically ready competency model. The model will allow semantic enrichment on different levels, creating truly meaningful competencies. The aim of this model is to provide a flexible approach for (re)use, matching, interpretation, exchange and storage for competencies. Our competency model is based on the DOGMA ontology framework and the proposed IEEE standards RCD and SCRM. We will focus on the model itself and how semantics can be applied to it as these elements form the basis for any kind of processing on them.

Keywords: competence, competency, RCD, semantics, DOGMA, e-HRM, HRM, occupation, ontology, Semantic Web.

1 Introduction

On the highly volatile job market that we are living in at this moment, getting a good match between a CV and a job opening is a key problem. The main element in this matching process is shifting from monolythic function titles to functions built with minimalistic, descriptive and highly-reusable competency building blocks. Such a bunch of small information pieces put together allows for a far more detailed and closely fitting match. Both a person and a function can be seen as a grouping of competencies and fitting one with the other becomes a matter of comparing these collections of building blocks.

What is still missing in this picture, is the exact view of a competency and a group of competencies. What identifies a competency? How do you describe it? How can we identify the intended meaning of a competency? And how do you put competencies together in a meaningful and clear manner? These are the kind of questions that we try to answer in our model of meaningful competencies.

A short look at the current state-of-the-art with these questions in mind results only in partial answers. The HR-XML consortium[1] provides a schema[2] for competency description, however the main focus seems to be on the possibility to capture evidence

---

[1] www.hr-xml.org

[2] http://ns.hr-xml.org/2_4/HR-XML-2_4/CPO/Competencies.html

R. Meersman, Z. Tari, P. Herrero et al. (Eds.): OTM Workshops 2006, LNCS 4278, pp. 1100–1106, 2006.

and provide weighting. They provided an element to store semantics, but only limited to a taxonomy. Claude Ostyn[3] created the reusable competency definition (RCD) which is expected to be accepted as an IEEE standard [1] soon. This standard provides the minimal elements (id, title, description and a structured free-text definition) to describe a competency. A metadata field allows the introduction of semantics, however there is no further specification about how exactly semantics should be introduced and what they look like. Ostyn also proposed the Simple Reusable Competency Map (SRCM) standard [2]. This pending IEEE standard provides a way to capture possible parent-child/sibling relations between RCDs. This way different communities of practice can use the same RCDs, but group them together differently. The limitation of this approach is in the fact that the relation types are limited to parent-child or sibling. Our work is based on the current situation, but forms a model which allows rich semantics on different levels.

In this introduction we described the theory which served as the basis for our competency model. We give a brief overview of the DOGMA framework for ontology engineering in Section 2. Our model was inspired by this framework, and we also make use of it for formalizing semantics. In Section 3 we present our model and how meaning fits in this picture. Finally, in section 4, we summarize our further intentions.

2   The DOGMA Framework

DOGMA[4] is a research intitiative of VUB STARLab where various theories, methods, and tools for ontologies are studied and developed. A DOGMA inspired ontology is based on the classical model-theoretic perspective [3] and decomposes an ontology into a *lexon base* and a layer of *ontological commitments* [4,5]. This is called the principle of double articulation [6].

A lexon base holds (multiple) intuitive conceptualisation(s) of a particular domain. Each conceptualisation is simplified to a "representation-less" set of context-specific binary fact types called *lexons*. A lexon represents a *plausible binary fact-type* and is formally described as a 5-tuple <V, term1, role, co-role, term2>, where V is an abstract context identifier, lexically described by a string in some natural language, and is used to group lexons that are logically related to each other in the conceptualisation of the domain. Intuitively, a lexon may be read as: within the context V, term1 (also denoted as the header term) may have a relation with term2 (also denoted as the tail term) in which it plays a *role*, and conversely, in which term2 plays a corresponding *co-role*. Each (context, term)-pair then lexically identifies a unique *concept*. A lexon base can hence be described as a set of plausible elementary fact types that are considered as being true. The terms in the lexon combined with the context resulting in 2 concepts. By also conceptualizing the role/co-role, the lexon becomes a language- and context independent metalexon.

Any specific (application-dependent) interpretation is moved to a separate layer, i.e. the commitment layer. The commitment layer mediates between the lexon base and its applications. Each such ontological commitment defines a *partial semantic account*

---

[3] www.ostyn.com

[4] Developing Ontology-Grounded Methods for Applications.

of an intended conceptualisation [7]. It consists of a finite set of axioms that specify which lexons of the lexon base are interpreted and how they are visible in the committing application, and (domain) rules that semantically constrain this interpretation. Experience shows that it is much harder to reach an agreement on domain rules than one on conceptualisation [8]. E.g., the rule stating that each car has exactly one license plate number may hold in the Universe of Discourse (UoD) of some application, but may be too strong in the UoD of another application. A full formalisation of DOGMA can be found in De Leenheer, Meersman, and de Moor [9,10].

3 Meaningful Competencies

3.1 Competency Model

As we explained in the previous sections, the DOGMA architecture divides the complexity over three levels: lexonbase, commitment layer and application layer. We were inspired by this approach to construct our competency model. The total overview on the model can be seen in Figure 1. The lowest level is the RCD (or competency) repository, the middle level is the reusable competence layer and on top are the users of the competency data, the applications. We adopt the definition of competency as given by the HR-XML consortium: *A specific, identifiable, definable, and measurable knowledge, skill, ability and/or other deployment-related characteristic (e.g. attitude, behavior, physical ability) which a human resource may possess and which is necessary for, or material to, the performance of an activity within a specific business context*[5]. A competency is used as the smallest unit of capability in our model (a highly flexible, modular building block). A competence is a structured set of competencies. Note that in our model a competency can only be used to construct competences. We will give a more detailed description of every layer in the following subsections.

Competency Repository. The lowest level is a repository filled with RCDs. These RCDs can be obtained by automatic mining (e.g., from O*NET[6]), by human input or both. Any RCD present in the repository can be linked with an arbitrary relation to any other RCD. These relations have no interpreted meaning in the competency repository layer (other than the one in the mind of the human creator of the relation). We call them *plausible* relations, as they represent a fact that might (or might) not be true. As we do not restrict ourselves to the "is composed of" relation, we can build a more semantically rich set of competencies. For instance, an RCD "can drive" can be related with an RCD "can read road signs" using an "assumes"-relation instead of a "requires"-relation to indicate a softer constraint between the two RCDs.

The RCD is built using a dedicated web interface (still to be created) which will encourage the reusability of the competencies. For instance, if the repository already contains an RCD "can drive a car", and the user creates a new RCD "can drive a truck", the system will (1) inform the user of the existing RCD and (2) encourage him to group these related RCDs with a relevant relation. Reusability is a strong point to interoperability, as the use of the exact same objects (competencies) implies a shared understanding.

---

[5] http://ns.hr-xml.org/2_4/HR-XML-2_4/CPO/Competencies.html
[6] http://online.onetcenter.org/

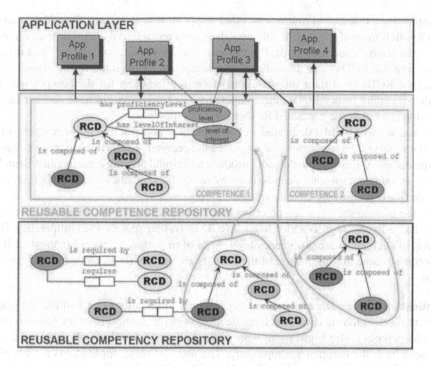

Fig. 1. Layered Competency Model

Furthermore, we will allow the user to semantically tag or *DOGtag*[7] the RCD with a part of the domain ontology. The system will propose concepts (and relations between them) from the ontology as semantic tags and the user can select the exact one (or multiple ones). In this way, an RCD can be annotated with semantics, ranging from one simple concept to complete semantic graphs. We will make use of the already entered fields of the RCD (title, description and definition) to apply some heuristic search for possibly related concepts in the ontology. This metadata can be stored in the metadata field of the RCD. We will make use of the most commonly known formats for such description, like RDF(S) [11] and OWL [12]. Next to this information we will also store standard Dublin Core metadata[8].

Competence Repository. The competence repository creates a committed view on the RCD repository. Applications can make a selection of the RCDs (and the plausible relations between them) and commit to them. This means that the application fixes this structured set of RCDs to be truthful for its own application context. At this point the application commits to using (exchanging, matching, ...) that specific competence (built from those specific RCDs and their relations). As such it also locks the interpretation of the plausible relations, and thus the relations are no longer simply plausible, but actually factual. The application can now provide an explicit formalization of the relation

---

[7] Short for DOGMA-tag. DOGMA is grounded in linguistic representation, and DOGMA engineered ontologies as well. This results in user-friendly possibilities for annotation.

[8] http://dublincore.org/documents/2006/05/29/dc-rdf/

meaning (e.g., if it has to match with other applications) or simply leave it as a term with implicit meaning (e.g., if it only uses the competence internally). The user can describe the competence with a title. For instance, she creates the competence "can drive" containing the RCDs "can drive a car"-(requires)-"can understand traffic signs". The contained RCDs (and their inter-relations) form the meaning for the competence. In another meaning (other RCDs) the competence "can drive" could have another interpretation (stored in the contained RCDs of that competence).

Again, we will build a dedicated web interface for constructing these competences. It will encourage the user in several ways (see the previous subsection) to reuse existing competences. At this layer we do not introduce additional tagging functionality. Searching for existing competences can be done by using the semantics inside (DOGtag) and outside (RCD relations) that are part of the competence.

As the picture shows, a competence is more than data from the competency repository. Extra fields are also added to each RCD to further specify the competency. Examples of such fields are proficiency level, level of importance, level of interest, ... It is important to note that the *values* of these fields are not yet fixed, as this would hinder reuse.

Application Layer. The application layer holds all applications that will use our competency model (and its data). Each application uses the same repository (competence and competency). The applications work with application profiles, collections of competences from the competence repository. The users of these applications are responsible for filling both repositories with relevant data. However, one type of application can be completely dedicated to adding data, while another only uses existing data. The application collects required competencies and populates the extra field values. It is also responsible for setting the expertise level of the competence. The expertise level specifies at what level the competence needs to be. With level we do not simply mean a number (e.g., on some further unspecified scale) or a symbol (e.g., good, bad, medium), but a real definition of the expertise level. Using semantic annotation (DOGtag) the expertise level can be linked to the domain ontology, and thus be expressed formally. We constrain this expertise level by stating that it can only make the competence more specific. For instance "can drive a car" can have an expertise level "can drive a car in the dark", but not "can drive a truck" as the first level is a specification of the competence, while the second is not if the used ontology does not state that "truck"-is a-"car" (or "truck" does not specify "car").

3.2 Semantic Levels

In the previous subsections we explained our model and how we added semantics in each layer of the competency model. We will now focus on these *semantic extension points* and explain how they can improve competency-related processes. We will use the matching process as an example to clarify this improvement.

The first semantic enrichment is attached to the RCD in the metadata field. Using ontologized tags the RCD is annotated with relevant formal domain knowledge. These annotations can be seen as a formalized semantic description of the RCD. This semantic description is the basis for RCD matching. Because concepts (with their relations[9]) can be used, matching takes place at the conceptual level, instead of at the lexical level (title, definition and description of the RCD). For instance, assume we have two RCDs: (1) "can drive", annotated with the concept "vehicle" and (2) "can drive a car", annotated with "car". RCD 1 and 2 can now be matched (and considered equivalent to a high degree) because in the ontology there is a relation "car"-(is a)-"vehicle".

The second semantic enrichment is the fact that we allow rich relations between RCDs. These indicate how RCDs can be grouped together and the specific details of their grouping are described by the relations. In our example we will assume that the meaning of a relation is implicit (but commonly understood like eg. the relation "is part of") and that the matcher does its work based on the term that symbolizes the relation.

The third semantic entry point can be found in the specification of the expertise level. These can be entered in plain text form (to provide a human-readable definition), but we will also foresee annotation possibilities in the interface (similar to those found in the creation of the RCD) so that the expertise level can be specified formally. In our matching example, the matcher can now use these semantics to further refine its search. Note that when the specificity constraint (see section 3.1) is violated, the results of the matching will be of inpredictable quality. For example, assume we have a competence "can drive" with an *illegal* expertise level "can fly a plane". A match with the competence "can fly a plane" will never be found, as the competence in the database is about driving, not flying a plane. The matcher ignores this competence as it does not give any hint about planes, except in the expertise level, which is only looked at if the competencies matches in the first place.

4   Conclusions and Future Work

Although our model is only in its first stage, we made sure that it solves the problems we identified in the state-of-the-art competency models. The rich semantic presence will enhance competency-related application processes (e.g., matching). The different levels on which we can introduce formal meaning provide extra levels of granularity. In the context of the Prolix project[10], we will build a competency registry and a semantic competency analyzer. We will capture domain knowledge using the DOGMA approach. We will build an DOGMA annotation tool that is linked to the competency registry. Test-bed partners will convert their current competency data to our model using tuned interfaces. As such the EU Prolix project will be our experiment, and we are confident that our model will hold and improve existing competency-related processes. This use-case will also allow us to further refine and finalize our model.

As many (larger) organizations already have a competency models, we can deliver extra work on finding efficient (semi-)automated ways to transform their data into our model. Smaller organizations lack this kind of data (because of the high cost). For their benefit, we can look for ways to obtain, analyze and convert publicly available data (eg. O*NET[11]). On the semantic side, we will look for ways to maximize the automated part

---

[9] Do not confuse the ontological relations between concepts with the relations between RCDs.

[10] http://www.prolixproject.org/

[11] http://online.onetcenter.org/

of semantic enrichment (e.g., by text mining) and thus minimize the human effort. We will also research how we can improve the annotation scope.

Acknowledgments. The research described in this paper was partially sponsored by the EU IP 027905 Prolix project and the IWT-Tetra 50115 PoCeHRMOM project. The authors would like to thank their colleagues, Luk Vervenne, Claude Ostyn and the people from L3S for their interesting feedback and discussions.

References

1. IEEE 1484.20.1/draft - draft standard for reusable competency definitions (RCD), november 2005. http://ieeeltsc.org/wg20Comp/wg20rcdfolder/IEEE_1484.20.1.D3.pdf.
2. Claude Ostyn. Proposal for a simple reusable competency map standard, 24/02/2006. http://www.ostyn.com/standardswork/competency/ReusableCompMapProp20051117.pdf.
3. R. Reiter. Towards a logical reconstruction of relational database theory. *In Brodie, M., Mylopoulos, J., Schmidt, J. (eds.), On Conceptual Modelling*, pages 191–233, 1984.
4. R. Meersman. The use of lexicons and other computer-linguistic tools in semantics, design and cooperation of database systems. In *In Zhang, Y., Rusinkiewicz, M., Kambayashi, Y. (eds.), Proceedings of the Conference on Cooperative Database Systems (CODAS 99)*, pages 1–14. Springer-Verlag, 1999.
5. R. Meersman. Ontologies and databases: More than a fleeting resemblance. In *In d'Atri, A., Missikoff, M. (eds.), OES/SEO 2001 Rome Workshop*. Luiss Publications, 2001.
6. P. Spyns, R. Meersman, and M. Jarrar. Data modelling verus ontology engineering. *SIGMOD Record: Special Issue on Semantic Web and Data Management 31(4)*, pages 12–17, 2002.
7. N. Guarino and P. Giaretta. Ontologies and knowledge bases: Towards a terminological clarification. In *In Mars, N. (ed.) Towards Very Large Knowledge Bases: Knowledge Building and Knowledge Sharing*, pages 25–32. IOS Press, 1995.
8. R. Meersman. Semantic web and ontologies: Playtime or business at the last frontier in computing? In *In NSF-EU Workshop on Database and Information Systems Research for Semantic Web and Enterprises*, pages 61–67, 2002.
9. P. De Leenheer and R. Meersman. Towards a formal foundation of dogma ontology: part i. Technical Report STAR-2005-06, VUB STARLab, Brussel, 2005.
10. P. De Leenheer, A. de Moor, and R. Meersman. Context dependency management in ontology engineering. Technical Report STAR-2006-03-01, VUB STARLab, Brussel, March 2006.
11. Eric Miller and Frank Manola. RDF primer. W3C recommendation, W3C, February 2004. http://www.w3.org/TR/2004/REC-rdf-primer-20040210/.
12. Frank van Harmelen and Deborah L. McGuinness. OWL web ontology language overview. W3C recommendation, W3C, February 2004. http://www.w3.org/TR/2004/REC-owl-features-20040210/.

Pruning Terminology Extracted from a Specialized Corpus for CV Ontology Acquisition

Mathieu Roche[1] and Yves Kodratoff[2]

[1] LIRMM - UMR 5506, Université Montpellier 2, 34392 Montpellier Cedex 5 - France
[2] LRI - UMR 8623, Université Paris-Sud, 91405 Orsay Cedex - France

Abstract. This paper presents an experimental study for extracting a terminology from a corpus made of Curriculum Vitae (CV). This terminology is to be used for ontology acquisition. The choice of the pruning rate of the terminology is crucial relative to the quality of the ontology acquired. In this paper, we investigate this pruning rate by using several evaluation measures (precision, recall, F-measure, and ROC curve).

1 Introduction

This paper presents the experimental study of an evaluation of the best rate of pruning for terminology extraction. Below, we describe our global method for terminology extraction and we define the pruning of a terminology.

The terms extracted from a specialized corpus are instances of the concepts that will become the frame of a domain ontology. In our work, the terms are extracted from a Curriculum Vitae (CV) corpus provided by the company VediorBis[1] (120000 words after various pretreatments described in [13]). This specialized corpus is written in French, it made of very short sentences and many enumerations. For example, in this field, "logiciel de gestion" (management software) is an instance of the concept called "Activité Informatique" (Computer Science Activity). The concept is defined by the expert of the field.

The first step of our terminology extraction approach is based on text normalization by using cleaning rules described in [13]. The next step provides grammatical labels for each word of the corpus, using a Part-Of-Speech tagger ETIQ [1]. ETIQ is an interactive system based on Brill's tagger [4] which improves the quality of the labeling of specialized corpora. Table 1 presents an example of tagged sentence from CV corpus.

We are then able to extract tagged collocations in CV corpus, such as Noun-Noun, Adjective-Noun, Noun-Adjective, Noun-Preposition-Noun collocations. For example in table 1, we can extract the Noun-Preposition-Noun collocation "logiciel de gestion" (management software).

The next step consists in selecting collocations more relevant according to the statistical measurements described in [13, 14]. Collocations are groups of words defined in [11, 17]. We call *terms*, collocations relevant to the field of interest.

---

[1] http://www.vediorbis.com/

R. Meersman, Z. Tari, P. Herrero et al. (Eds.): OTM Workshops 2006, LNCS 4278, pp. 1107–1116, 2006.
© Springer-Verlag Berlin Heidelberg 2006

Table 1. Part-Of-Speech tagged corpus (in French)

Développement/SBC:sg d'/PREP un/DTN:sg **logiciel/SBC:sg de/PREP** **gestion/SBC:sg** du/DTC:sg parc/SBC:sg informatique/ADJ:sg ...
SBC:sg → *Noun, singular*   PREP → *Preposition*   DTC:sg, DTN :sg → *Determiners, singular*   ADJ:sg → *Adjective, singular*

The binary terms (or ternary for the prepositional terms) extracted at each iteration are reintroduced in the corpus with hyphens. So, they are recognized like words. We can thus carry out a new terminology extraction from the corpus taking into account of terminology acquired at the preceding steps. Our iterative method which has similarities with [8] is described in [13, 15]. This approach enables to detect very specific terms (made of several words). For example using the term "logiciel de gestion" extracted at the first iteration of our approach, after several iterations we can extract the specific term "logiciel de gestion du parc informatique" (see table 1).

The choice of the pruning rate consists in determining the minimal number of times where relevant collocations are found in the corpus.

First, this paper presents briefly the state-of-the-art of terminology extraction methods (section 2). The presentation of the application of various pruning rates is described in section 3. After the presentation of the collocations expertise in section 4, the section 5 describes various evaluation measurements of the terminology based on the problems of the choice of the pruning rate. Finally, in section 6 we discuss future work.

2   The State-of-the-Art of Terminology Extraction Approaches

In order to extract and structure the terminology, several methods are developed. Here, we will not deal with the approaches of conceptual regrouping of terminology as they are described in [16, 2].

The methods of terminology extraction are based on statistical or syntactic approaches. The TERMINO system [6] is a precursory tool that uses a syntactic analysis in order to extract the nominal terms. This tool carries out a morphological analysis containing rules, followed by an analysis of nominal collocations using a grammar. The XTRACT system [17] is based on a statistical method. Initially XTRACT extracts binary collocations in a window of ten words which exceed a statistical significant rate. The following step consists in extracting more particular collocations (collocations of more than two words) containing the binary collocations extracted at the preceding step. ACABIT [5] carries out a linguistic analysis in order to transform nominal collocations into binary terms. They are ranked using statistical measurements. Contrary to ACABIT which is based on a statistical method, LEXTER [3] and SYNTEX [9] use syntactic analysis. This method extracts the longuest noun phrases. These phrases are transformed into "head" and "expansion" terms using grammatical rules. The terms are structured using syntactic criteria.

To discuss the choice of the pruning rate, we will rank collocations by using Occ_L measurement as described in [13]. This measurement which gives the best results [14] ranks collocations according to their number of occurrences (Occ). Collocations having the same number of occurrences are ranked by using the loglikelyhood (L) [7]. Thus, Occ_L is well adapted to discuss the choice of the pruning rate.

3   Pruning Rate of the Terminology

The principle of pruning the collocations consists in analyzing the collocations usefulness for ontology acquisition : their number has to be above a threshold of occurrences in the corpus. We can thus remove rare collocations which can appear as irrelevant for the field. Table 2 presents the various prunings we applied (first iteration of our terminology extraction approach). Table 2 shows that the elimination of collocations with one occurrence in the CV corpus allows us to remove more than 75% of the existng collocations.

Table 2. Pruning and proportions of pruning

	nb	pruning 2	pruning 3	pruning 4	pruning 5	pruning 6
Noun-Noun	1781	353 (80%)	162 (91%)	100 (94%)	69 (96%)	56 (97%)
Noun-Prep-Noun	3634	662 (82%)	307 (91%)	178 (95%)	113 (97%)	80 (98%)
Adjective-Noun	1291	259 (80%)	103 (92%)	63 (95%)	44 (97%)	34 (97%)
Noun-Adjective	3455	864 (75%)	448 (87%)	307 (91%)	222 (94%)	181 (95%)

4   Terminology Acquisition for Conceptual Classification

To build a conceptual classification, collocations evoking a concept of the field are extracted. Table 3 presents examples of French collocations associated to concepts met in the CV corpus.

In order to validate the collocations, several categories of relevance (or irrelevance) are possible:

- **Category 1:** Collocation is relevant for conceptual classification.
- **Category 2:** Collocation is relevant but very specific and not necessarily relevant for a domain conceptual classification.
- **Category 3:** Collocation is relevant but very general and not necessarily relevant for a conceptual classification specialized.
- **Category 4:** Collocation is irrelevant.
- **Category 5:** The expert cannot judge if collocation is relevant or not.

Table 3. Part of conceptual classification from CV corpus (in French)

Collocations	Concepts
aide comptable	Activité Gestion
gestion administrative	Activité Gestion
employé libre service	Activité Commerce
assistant marketing	Activité Commerce
chef de service	Activité Encadrement
direction générale	Activité Encadrement
BEP secrétariat	Compétence Secrétariat
BTS assistante de direction	Compétence Secrétariat
baccalauréat professionnel vente	Compétence Commerce
BTS commerce international	Compétence Commerce

5 Evaluation of the Terminology and Pruning Rate

An expert evaluates Noun-Adjective collocations extracted in CV corpus using all rate pruning.

5.1 Terminology Expertise

Table 4 gives the number of Noun-Adjective collocations associated with each category of expertise. Each category is described in the section 4 of this paper.

Table 4 shows the results of the expertise carried out according to various pruning rates. The most relevant collocations (category 1) are privileged by applying an large pruning rate. If all collocations are provided by the system (i.e. pruning at one), the proportion of relevant collocations is 56.3% and more than 80% with a pruning at four, five or six.

5.2 Precision, Recall, and F-Measure

Precision is an evaluation criterion adapted to the framework of an unsupervised approach. Precision calculates the proportion of relevant collocations extracted among extracted collocations. Using the notations of table 5, the precision is given by the formula $\frac{TP}{TP+FP}$. A 100% precision means that all the collocations extracted by the system are relevant.

Another typical measurement of the machine learning approach is recall which computes the proportion of relevant collocations extracted among relevant collocations. The recall is given by the formula $\frac{TP}{TP+FN}$. A 100% recall means that

Table 4. Number of collocations in each category

pruning	category 1	category 2 and 3	category 4	category 5	Total
1	1946 (56.3%)	919 (26.6%)	395 (11.4%)	195 (5.6%)	3455
2	631 (73.0%)	151 (17.5%)	58 (6.7%)	24 (2.8%)	864
3	348 (77.7%)	73 (16.3%)	17 (3.8%)	10 (2.2%)	448
4	256 (83.4%)	36 (11.7%)	8 (2.6%)	7 (2.3%)	307
5	185 (83.3%)	29 (13.1%)	3 (1.3%)	5 (2.2%)	222
6	152 (84.0%)	23 (12.7%)	2 (1.1%)	4 (2.2%)	181

all relevant collocations have been found. This measurement is adapted to the supervised machine learning methods where all positive examples (relevant collocations) are known.

Table 5. Contingency table at the base of evaluation measurements

	Relevant collocations	Irrelevant collocations
Collocations evaluated as relevant by the system	TP (True Positive)	FP (False Positive)
Collocations evaluated as irrelevant by the system	FN (False Negative)	TN (True Negative)

It is often important to determine a compromise between recall and precision. We can use a measurement taking into account these two evaluation criteria by calculating the F-measure [19] :

$$F - measure(\beta) = \frac{(\beta^2 + 1) \times Precision \times Recall}{(\beta^2 \times Precision) + Recall} \tag{1}$$

The parameter β of the formula (1) regulates the respective influence of precision and recall. It is often fixed at 1 to give the same weight to these two evaluation measurements.

The table 6 shows a large pruning and gives the highest precision. In this case, the recall is often small, i.e. few relevant collocations extracted. With $\beta = 1$, we can see in table 6 that the F-measure is highest without applying pruning. This is due to the high result of the recall without pruning. Indeed, as specified in table 2, a pruning at two prevents the extraction of 75% of Noun-Adjective collocations.

Table 7 shows varying β in order to give a more important weight to the precision ($\beta < 1$) gives a F-measure logically higher in the case of a large pruning. This underlines the limits of this evaluation criterion because the results of the F-measure can largely differ according to the value of β. Thus, the following section presents another evaluation criterion based on ROC curves.

Table 6. Precision, recall, and F-measure with $\beta = 1$

Pruning	Precision	Recall	F-measure
1	59.7%	100%	74.8%
2	75.1%	32.4%	45.3%
3	79.4%	17.9%	29.2%
4	85.3%	13.1%	22.8%
5	85.2%	9.5%	17.1%
6	85.9%	7.8%	14.3%

Table 7. F-measure according to various values of β (1, ..., 1/10) and various rates of pruning (1, ..., 6)

β	1	1/2	1/3	1/4	1/5	1/6	1/7	1/8	1/9	1/10
1	74.8%	64.9%	62.2%	61.1%	60.6%	60.4%	60.2%	60.1%	60.0%	59.9%
2	45.3%	59.5%	66.4%	69.7%	71.5%	72.5%	73.2%	73.6%	73.9%	74.1%
3	29.2%	47.0%	59.1%	66.1%	70.2%	72.7%	74.3%	75.4%	76.2%	76.8%
4	22.8%	40.7%	55.1%	64.5%	70.5%	74.3%	76.9%	78.7%	80.0%	80.9%
5	17.1%	32.9%	47.4%	58.0%	65.2%	70.1%	73.5%	75.9%	77.7%	79.0%
6	14.3%	28.6%	42.9%	54.1%	62.0%	67.6%	71.6%	74.4%	76.5%	78.1%

5.3   The ROC Curves

In this section ROC curves (Receiver Operating Characteristics) are presented (see also work of [10]). Initially the ROC curves come from the field of signal treatment. ROC curves are often used in the field of medicine to evaluate the validity of diagnostic tests. The ROC curves show in X-coordinate the rate of false positive (in our case, rate of irrelevant collocations) and in Y-coordinate the rate of true positive (rate of relevant collocations). The surface under the ROC curve (AUC - *Area Under the Curve*), can be seen as the effectiveness of a measurement of interest. The criterion relating to the surface under the curve is equivalent to the statistical test of Wilcoxon-Mann-Whitney (see work of [20]).

In the case of the collocations ranking in using statistical measurements, an perfect ROC curve corresponds to obtaining all relevant collocations at the beginning of the list and all irrelevant collocations at the end of the list. This situation corresponds to $AUC = 1$. The diagonal corresponds to the performance of a random system, progress of the rate of true positive being accompanied by an equivalent degradation of the rate of false positive. This situation corresponds to $AUC = 0.5$. If the collocations are ranked by decreasing interest (i.e. all relevant collocations are after the irrelevant ones) then $AUC = 0$. An effective measurement of interest to order collocations consists in obtain a AUC the highest possible value. This is strictly equivalent to minimizing the sum of the rank of the positive examples.

The advantage of the ROC curves comes from its resistance to imbalance (for example, an imbalance in number of positive and negative examples). We can illustrate this fact with the following example. Let us suppose that we have 100 examples (collocations). In the first case, we have an imbalance between the positive and negative examples with only 1 positive and 99 negative examples. In the second case, we have 50 positive and 50 negative examples. Let us suppose that for these two cases, the positive examples (relevant collocations) are presented at the top of the list ranked with statistical measurements.

In both cases, the ROC curves are strictly similar with $AUC = 1$ (see figures 1(a) and 1(c)). Thus, getting relevant collocations in the top of the list is emphasized by evaluating the ROC curves and the AUC. With calculation of F-measure (with $\beta = 1$), we obtain two extremely different curves (see figures 1(b)

Table 8. AUC with several prunings

Pruning	AUC	Pruning	AUC
1	0.4538	4	0.5012
2	0.5324	5	0.5432
3	**0.5905**	6	0.5447

and 1(d)). Thus, imbalances between positive and negative examples strongly influence F-measure contrary to the ROC curves.

From one pruning to another, the rate of relevant and irrelevant collocations can appear extremely different. It means that we are in presence of an imbalance between the classes. For example, applying a pruning at six, 84% of collocations are relevant against 56% whithout pruning (see table 4). The table 8 calculates the various AUC by choosing various pruning rates. Then, in this case, using ROC curves and AUC is particularly well adapted.

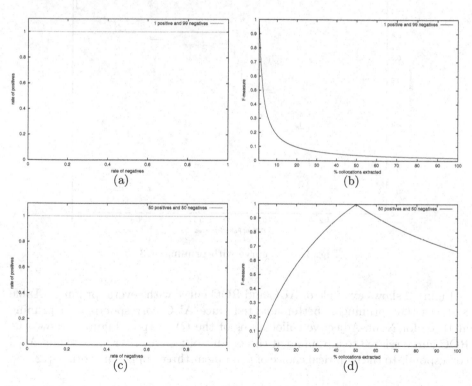

Fig. 1. ROC Curve (a) and F-measure (b) with 1 positive example placed at the top of the list and 99 negative examples placed at the end of the list. ROC Curve (c) and F-measure (d) with 50 positive examples at the top of list and 50 negative examples at the end of the list. For the calculation of the F-measure, $\beta = 1$.

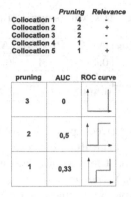

	Pruning	Relevance
Collocation 1	4	-
Collocation 2	2	+
Collocation 3	2	-
Collocation 4	1	-
Collocation 5	1	+

pruning	AUC	ROC curve
3	0	
2	0,5	
1	0,33	

Fig. 2. Example of several prunings

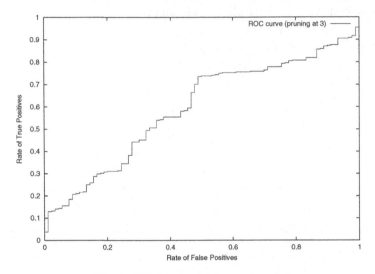

Fig. 3. ROC curve with pruning at 3

Figure 2 shows example of AUC and ROC curve with several prunings. Table 8 shows that pruning is better adapted since AUC corresponds to a pruning at three for Noun-Adjective collocations of the CV corpus. Figure 3 shows the ROC curve related to a pruning at three. This objective criterion based on AUC corresponds to the empirical choice of pruning at three applied in work of [12, 18].

6   Conclusion and Perspectives

The experimental study conducted in this paper enables the discussion of the choice of the pruning rate for terminology extraction in view of ontology acquisition. Various criteria of evaluation exist such as precision, recall, and F-measure which takes into account these two criteria. A defect of the F-measure is the choice not always obvious of a parameter best adapted to privilege precision or recall in the calculation. Thus, in this paper, we propose to use ROC curves and AUC to evaluate the choice of pruning. This criterion is not sensitive to imbalance between the classes (such as classes of relevant and irrelevant collocations).

In a future work, we will improve quality of normalization and we will add new CV to increase the number of collocations extracted. Our experiments on the CV corpus show that a pruning at three seems well adapted. In our future work, we propose to compare this result with the one for other specialized corpora. So, we will carry out a complete expertise of collocations of other fields. This will require non negligible expert work.

References

1. A. Amrani, Y. Kodratoff, and O. Matte-Tailliez. A semi-automatic system for tagging specialized corpora. In *Proceedings of PAKDD'04*, pages 670–681, 2004.
2. N. Aussenac-Gilles and D. Bourigault. Construction d'ontologies à partir de textes. In *Actes de TALN03*, volume 2, pages 27–47, 2003.
3. D. Bourigault and C. Jacquemin. Term extraction + term clustering: An integrated platform for computer-aided terminology. In *Proceedings of EACL'99, Bergen.*, pages 15–22, 1999.
4. E. Brill. Some advances in transformation-based part of speech tagging. In *AAAI, Vol. 1*, pages 722–727, 1994.
5. B. Daille. Study and Implementation of Combined Techniques for Automatic Extraction of Terminology. In *P. Resnik and J. Klavans (eds). The Balancing Act: Combining Symbolic and Statistical Approaches to Language, MIT Press*, pages 49–66, 1996.
6. S. David and P. Plante. De la nécessité d'une approche morpho syntaxique dans l'analyse de textes. In *Intelligence Artificielle et Sciences Cognitives au Quebec*, volume 3, pages 140–154, 1990.
7. Ted E. Dunning. Accurate methods for the statistics of surprise and coincidence. *Computational Linguistics*, 19(1):61–74, 1993.
8. D.A. Evans and C. Zhai. Noun-phrase analysis in unrestricted text for information retrieval. In *Proceedings of ACL*, pages 17–24, Santa Cruz, US, 1996.
9. C. Fabre and D. Bourigault. Linguistic clues for corpus-based acquisition of lexical dependencies. In *Corpus Linguistics, Lancaster*, pages 176–184, 2001.
10. C. Ferri, P. Flach, and J. Hernandez-Orallo. Learning decision trees using the area under the ROC curve. In *Proceedings of ICML'02*, pages 139–146, 2002.
11. M. A. K. Halliday. *System and Function in Language*. Oxford University Press, London, 1976.
12. C. Jacquemin. *Variation terminologique : Reconnaissance et acquisition automatiques de termes et de leurs variantes en corpus*. PhD thesis, Mémoire d'Habilitation à Diriger des Recherches en informatique fondamentale, Université de Nantes, 1997.
13. M. Roche. *Intégration de la construction de la terminologie de domaines spécialisés dans un processus global de fouille de textes*. PhD thesis, Université de Paris 11, Décembre 2004.
14. M. Roche, J. Azé, Y. Kodratoff, and M. Sebag. Learning interestingness measures in terminology extraction. A ROC-based approach. In *Proceedings of "ROC Analysis in AI" Workshop (ECAI 2004), Valencia, Spain*, pages 81–88, 2004.

15. M. Roche, T. Heitz, O. Matte-Tailliez, and Y. Kodratoff. EXIT: Un système itératif pour l'extraction de la terminologie du domaine à partir de corpus spécialisés. In *Proceedings of JADT'04*, volume 2, pages 946–956, 2004.
16. M. Shamsfard and A. A. Barforoush. The state of the art in ontology learning: a framework for comparison. *The Knowledge Engineering Review, Volume 18 , Issue 4 (December 2003)*, pages 293–316, 2003.
17. F. Smadja. Retrieving collocations from text: Xtract. *Computational Linguistics*, 19(1):143–177, 1993.
18. A. Thanopoulos, N. Fakotakis, and G. Kokkianakis. Comparative Evaluation of Collocation Extraction Metrics. In *Proceedings of LREC'02*, volume 2, pages 620–625, 2002.
19. C.J. Van-Risbergen. *Information Retrieval*. 2nd edition, London, Butterworths, 1979.
20. L. Yan, R.H. Dodier, M. Mozer, and R.H. Wolniewicz. Optimizing classifier performance via an approximation to the Wilcoxon-Mann-Whitney statistic. In *Proceedings of ICML'03*, pages 848–855, 2003.

ORM 2006 PC Co-chairs' Message

Following a successful workshop held in Cyprus in 2005, this is the second in a series of fact-oriented modeling workshops run in conjunction with the OTM conferences. Fact-oriented modeling is a conceptual approach to modeling and querying the information semantics of business domains in terms of the underlying facts of interest, where all facts and rules may be verbalized in language that is readily understandable by non-technical users of those business domains. Unlike entity-relationship (ER) modeling and UML class diagrams, fact-oriented modeling treats all facts as relationships (unary, binary, ternary etc.). How facts are grouped into structures (e.g., attribute-based entity types, classes, relation schemes, XML schemas) is considered a lower-level implementation issue that is irrelevant to the capturing essential business semantics. Avoiding attributes in the base model enhances semantic stability and populatability, as well as facilitating natural verbalization. For information modeling, fact-oriented graphical notations are typically far more expressive than those provided by other notations. Fact-oriented textual languages are based on formal subsets of native languages, so are easier to understand by business people than technical languages like OCL. Fact-oriented modeling includes procedures for mapping to attribute-based structures, so they may also be used to front-end other approaches.

Although less well known than ER and object-oriented approaches, fact-oriented modeling has been used successfully in industry for over 30 years, and is taught in universities around the world. The fact-oriented modeling approach comprises a family of closely related nd links to other relevant sites, and may be found at http://www.orm.net/.

This year we had 20 quality submissions from all over the globe. After an extensive review process by a distinguished international Program Committee, with each paper receiving three or more reviews, we accepted the 13 papers that appear in these proceedings. Congratulations to the successful authors!

Apart from the contribution by paper authors, the quality of this workshop depends in no small way on the generous contribution of time and effort by the Program Committee. Their work is greatly appreciated. We also express our sincere thanks to the OTM Organizing Committee, especially Pilar Herrero (Universidad Politenica de Madrid), and Peter Dimopoulos (Royal Melbourne Institute of Technology) for overseeing the workshop programs and the publication of the workshop proceedings.

Enjoy the workshop proceedings! We look forward to your continuing support of ORM.

August 2006   Terry Halpin, Neumont University, USA
                          Robert Meersman, Vrije Universiteit Brussel, Belgium

R. Meersman, Z. Tari, P. Herrero et al. (Eds.): OTM Workshops 2006, LNCS 4278, p. 1117, 2006.
© Springer-Verlag Berlin Heidelberg 2006

Part-Whole Relations in Object-Role Models

C. Maria Keet

KRDB Research Centre, Faculty of Computer Science,
Free University of Bozen-Bolzano, Italy
keet@inf.unibz.it

Abstract. Representing parthood relations in ORM has received little attention, despite its added-value of the semantics at the conceptual level. We introduce a high-level taxonomy of types of meronymic and mereological relations, use it to construct a decision procedure to determine which type of part-whole role is applicable, and incrementally add mandatory and uniqueness constraints. This enables the conceptual modeller to develop models that are closer to the real-world subject domain semantics, hence improve quality of the software.

1 Introduction

Of all roles one can model in ORM, it is obvious from the set-theoretic formal semantics that subsumption is a first-class citizen as constructor, which is reflected in its graphical representation with a subsumption arrow instead of a role-box. Giving such first-class citizen status to part-whole roles can be less obvious. The *partOf* relation between object types in ORM has received little attention, apart from Halpin's assessment [9] [10]. He concludes that it is doubtful if it adds any semantics at the conceptual level and that design considerations can 'sneak into' conceptual modelling, because it is said to involve modelling object life cycle semantics (propagating object creation & destruction in the software). So, why bother? First, this conclusion was reached based on the treatment of the aggregation relation in the UML specification v1.3, which is known to be inadequate for representing the semantics of part-whole relations (e.g. [7] [14]). Second, as will be come clear in this paper, part-whole roles *do* enable a modeller to represent the semantics of the subject domain more precisely; hence one can create software that better meets the user's requirements. Third, in the past several years, research into bringing the part-whole relation toward the application stage has gained momentum. The latter entails other advantages such as concept satisfiability checking [3] [5], inferring derived relations and ensuring semantically correct transitivity of relations [4] [5] [20], and achieve (semi-)automatic abstraction and expansion of large conceptual models [12].

We approach part-whole roles for ORM from the perspective of usability and focus on the modeler and user. Many formal ontological aspects of the part-whole role have been discussed (e.g. [1] [4] [6] [16] [17] [18] [19] [21] [22]) and extensions to conceptual modelling languages have been suggested, like [2] [7] [14] for UML. This this is summarised and improved in section 2. Unfortunately, none of the extensions are implemented, as the wide range of modelling options tend

R. Meersman, Z. Tari, P. Herrero et al. (Eds.): OTM Workshops 2006, LNCS 4278, pp. 1118–1127, 2006.
© Springer-Verlag Berlin Heidelberg 2006

to be off-putting. We propose stepwise 'incremental modelling' of part-whole roles, which can be integrated with the customary approach in ORM modelling, thereby structuring and easing the modelling of part-whole roles. This consists of the use of a) a decision procedure to facilitate eliminating the wrong types of part-whole and apply the right one, and b) additional question & answer sessions for uniqueness and mandatory constraints. This is presented in section 3 and applied to an example ORM model in section 4. Last, we draw conclusions and point to further research.

2   Parthood Relations and Aggregation

Mereology is the formal ontological investigation of the part-whole relation. It has an overlap with meronymy – which concerns part-whole relations in linguistics – but they are not the same, as there are meronymic relations that are not partonomic (see below). Varzi [18] provides an overview of the more and less constrained versions of mereology from the viewpoint of philosophy, and Guizzardi [7] provides a summary from the perspective of conceptual modelling. What mereology lacks, however, is the engineering usefulness for conceptual modelling by being at times more comprehensive (e.g. mereotopology) and limiting regarding other aspects, such as 'horizontal' relations between the parts and the inverse relation *hasPart*. First, we analyse the main aspects of part-whole relations and propose a top-level taxonomy of relations, and subsequently discuss and compare how its main characteristics have been translated to different conceptual modelling languages.

2.1   Mereology and Meronymy

The most basic constraints on the parthood relation in mereology, called *Ground Mereology*, are that a partial ordering is always reflexive (1), antisymmetric (2), and transitive (3). All other versions [7] [18] share at least these constraints. Taking *partOf* as primitive relation, i.e. it does not have a definition, then (1-3) enables one to define *proper* part as (4), from which asymmetry, and irreflexivity follows; thus, x is not part of itself, if x is part of y then y is not part of x, and if x is part of y and y part of z then x is part of z.

$$\forall x(partOf(x, x)) \tag{1}$$

$$\forall x((partOf(x, y) \land partOf(y, x)) \rightarrow x = y) \tag{2}$$

$$\forall x, y, z((partOf(x, y) \land partOf(y, z)) \rightarrow partOf(x, z)) \tag{3}$$

$$properPartOf(x, y) \triangleq (partOf(x, y) \land \neg(partOf(y, x))) \tag{4}$$

Contrary to these straightforward axioms, the transitivity of the *partOf* relation is regularly discussed and contested (e.g. [11] [16] [20]), including introducing 'types' of part-whole relations to ensure transitivity. On closer inspection, it appears that in case of different types of part-whole relations, different types of universals are related, and, provided one makes the required distinctions, transitivity still holds (see also [19]). For instance, it is common to relate a process to its part-processes as *involvedIn* to distinguish it from the *partOf* relation between endurants (object types). Each type of part-whole role then has to be extended with constraints on the participating object types, like

$$\forall x, y(involvedIn(x, y) \triangleq properPartOf(x, y) \wedge Process(x) \wedge Process(y)) \quad (5)$$

Other variants include relating object types spatially through the part-whole relation, denoted as *containedIn* [4], or *locatedIn* for relating spatial (geographical) objects. An important distinction exist between mereological *partOf* relations and meronymic part-whole relations, where the latter is not necessarily transitive. For instance, *memberOf*, also referred to as "member-bunch" [16], is an intransitive meronymic part-whole relation, like players are members of a rugby team, probably member of that team's club, but as player certainly not member of the rugby clubs federation. We illustrate (in-)transitivity of several mereological and meronymic part-whole relations in the following examples, where we have extended or modified the names of the relations in most examples to indicate their ontological type.

* ★ - Centimeter part of Decimeter
     - Decimeter part of Meter
     therefore Centimeter part of Meter
     - Meter part of SI
     but *not* Centimeter part of SI, because Meter is actually a *member of* the Système International d'Units.
* ★ - Vase constituted of Clay
     - Clay has structural part GrainOfSand
     but *not* Vase constituted of GrainOfSand
* ★ - CellMembrane structural part of Cell
     - Cell contained in Blood
     but *not* CellMembrane structural part of Blood
     - Lipid structural part of CellMembrane
     therefore Lipid structural part of Cell
* ★ - Politician member of PoliticalParty
     - PoliticalParty located in Bolzano
     therefore Politician located in Bolzano? But *not* Politician member of Bolzano
* ★ - ReceptorBindingSite regional part of Receptor
     - Receptor functional part of SecondMessengerSystem
     therefore ReceptorBindingSite functional part of SecondMessengerSystem?

To disambiguate these differences and ensure transitivity, efforts have gone into constructing a taxonomy of part-whole relations. The first proposal, motivated by linguistic use of 'part', i.e. meronymy, was made by Winston, Chaffin and Herrmann (WCH) [22] and several successive articles deal with analysing the WCH taxonomy and modelling considerations (e.g. [1] [6] [7] [16]). For instance, Gerstl and Pribbenow [6] prefer a "common-sense theory of part-whole relations" instead, to allow for "different views on the entities". They reduce the six types of part-whole relations of WCH into three: component-complex, element-collection, and quantity-mass. Conversely, this has been extended and improved upon by Guizzardi [7], who provides criteria for several types, although note that his *subCollectionOf* is actually a set-subset relation and therefore not included in the taxonomy in Fig.1. In concordance with foundational ontological notions [13], we categorise element-collection as a type of *membership*, which is a meronymic relation. In addition, quantity-mass has to do with object types generally denoted with mass nouns that are not countable, such as water or wine, but one can count *portions* of wine and slices of the pie; thus, a portion is of the same substance (amount of matter) as the whole. Odell's material-object "part-of" relation [16] ontologically corresponds to *constitution*, where a vase is *made of* clay or a bike *constituted of* steel (see also [13]). Taking into account the additional ontological distinctions, we devised a taxonomy of – for conceptual data modelling relevant – types of mereological *partOf* and meronymic relations, which is depicted in Fig.1. This, however, does not yet deal with other facets of parthood relations, such as existential and mandatory parts, the inverse relation *hasPart*, and if the parts together are *all* parts that make up the whole. These facets are relevant for conceptual data modelling and therefore addressed in §3 and 4.

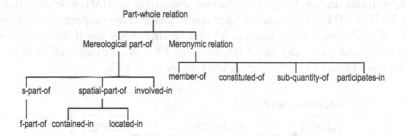

Fig. 1. Taxonomy of basic mereological and meronymic part-of relations. s-part-of = structural part-of; f-part-of = functional part-of.

2.2   ER, UML, ORM, and DL

ER, ORM and Description Logics (DL) do not have special constructors in the language to represent *partOf*, and few are in favour of giving it a first-class citizen status in ER [17] and DL [1] [4]. This does not mean that one is better off with UML. UML implements two modes of the *partOf* relation: composite and shared aggregation [15]. Composite aggregation, denoted with a filled diamond on the whole-side of the association (Fig.2-A), is defined as

> a strong form of aggregation that requires a part instance be included in at most one composite at a time. If a composite is deleted, all of its parts are normally deleted with it. Note that a part can (where allowed) be removed from a composite before the composite is deleted, and thus not be deleted as part of the composite. Compositions define transitive asymmetric relationships – their links form a directed, acyclic graph. [15]

This 'implementation behaviour' of creation/destruction of parts implicitly states that the parts are *existentially dependent* on the whole, and not that when a whole is destroyed its parts can exist independently and become part of another whole. Thus, UML's implementation behaviour is an implicit *ontological commitment at the conceptual level*. In addition, only binary associations can be aggregations [15], which is peculiar from an ontological perspective, because it suggests that a whole can be made up of one type of part only, except for extending the representation with a {complete} in the OCL (e.g. [14]). This difference is not addressed in the UML specification, i.e. it is a "semantic variation point" [15]. Likewise, shared aggregation, denoted with an open diamond on the whole-side, has it that "precise semantics ... varies by application area and modeler" [15], and presumably can be used for any of the *partOf* types described in Fig.1 and by [11] [14] [16] [22] etc. Unlike composite aggregation, shared aggregation has no constraint on multiplicity with respect to the whole it is part of; thus, the part may be *directly shared* by more than one whole at the same time. Overall, the ambiguous specification and modelling freedom in UML does not enable making implicit semantics explicit in the conceptual model, and rather fosters creation of unintended models.

Halpin's mapping from UML aggregation to its ORM representation [9], on the other hand, indirectly gives a formal semantics to UML's aggregation, as, unlike UML, ORM actually has a formal semantics. This mapping is depicted in Fig.2. Using Halpin's formalisation [8] and setting aside the difference between membership and parthood, the *Club-Team* fact has its corresponding first order logic representation as (6-9) and *Team-Person* as (10-11).

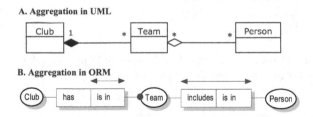

Fig. 2. Graphical representation of "aggregation" in UML and ORM. (Source: [9])

$$\forall x, y, z((isIn(x,y) \land isIn(x,z)) \rightarrow y = z) \tag{6}$$

$$\forall x, y(isIn(x,y) \rightarrow Team(x) \land Club(y)) \tag{7}$$

$$\forall x(Team(x) \rightarrow \exists y(isIn(x,y))) \tag{8}$$

$$\forall x_1, x_2(isIn(x_1,x_2) \equiv has(x_2,x_1)) \tag{9}$$

$$\forall x, y(isIn(x,y) \rightarrow Person(x) \land Team(y)) \tag{10}$$

$$\forall x_1, x_2(isIn(x_1,x_2) \equiv includes(x_2,x_1)) \tag{11}$$

The difference between ORM and UML intended semantics is that with composite aggregation in UML, part x *cannot* exist without that whole y, but ORM semantics of the suggested mapping [10] says that 'if there is a relation between part x and whole y, then x must participate exactly once'. Put differently, x may become part of some other whole y' after y ceases to exist, as long as there is *some* whole of type Y it is part of, but not necessarily *the same* whole. Hence, in contrast with UML, in ORM there is no strict existential dependency of the part on the whole. Both more [2] [7] [14] and less [3] comprehensive formalizations and extensions for aggregation in UML have been given. For ORM, richer representations of the semantics are possible already even without dressing up the ORM diagram with icons and labels.

3   Options to Represent Part-Whole Relations in ORM

Advantages to include different parthood relations are automated model verification, transitivity (derived relations), semi-automated abstraction operations, enforcing good modelling practices, and it positions ORM further ahead of other conceptual modelling languages. On the other hand, specifying everything into the finest detail may be too restrictive, results in cluttered diagrams, is confusing to model, and costs additional resources to include in ORM tools. That is, if we include all basic options in the syntax, with the formalization, particular graphical notation, and fixed-syntax sentences, there are at least 63 combinations. Gradual integration of modelling parthood relations will yield better results at this stage. Therefore, we introduce guidelines in the form of a decision procedure, and additional modelling questions to facilitate conceptual modelling process. The major advantages of this approach are its flexibility for both current use and future extensions, it reduces modelling mistakes, and with syntactic and textual analysis, it is still usable for aforementioned reasoning tasks.

The first, and main, step is to decide which role to use. Fig.3 presents a decision procedure, which first assesses – or rules out – all meronymic part-whole relations (up to *participatesIn*) and subsequently goes through the various mereological parthood relations. Although the order of the decision steps can be changed, ordering the two kinds in sequence serves conceptual clarity. Maintaining mereology in the second part of the decision procedure permits non-disruptive extensions to even finer-grained distinctions of parthood relations, if deemed desirable. There are several possibilities to implement the procedure. These options range from a 'no tech' cheat-sheet, 'low tech' drop-down box with the 9 types, to software-support for a decision procedure that asks questions and provides examples corresponding to each decision diamond.

The next step comprises ascertaining existential dependence, mandatoryness and shareability. In addition to the questions that are automatically generated in e.g. VisioModeler, we propose 5 additional questions specific for the parthood roles, which also consider the inverse roles. Looking ahead to the example ORM model in Fig.5, for the fact ShoulderHandle f-part of ConferenceBag / ConferenceBag has f-part ShoulderHandle the default questions generated for selecting 0:1, 0:n, 1, or 1:n are:

Each **ConferenceBag** has how many **f-part ShoulderHandle**?

How many instances of '**ShoulderHandle**' may be recorded for each instance of '**f-part of ConferenceBag**'?

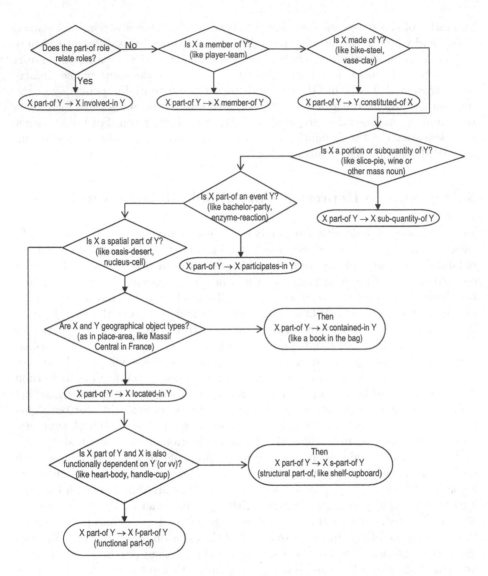

Fig. 3. Decision diagram to ascertain the appropriate parthood relation

We reformulate and extend the questions for the part-whole roles to emphasise the properties strict existential dependence, mandatory participation, and shareability. Generalizing for any case of *partOf* (A1-A3) and *hasPart* (B1, B2), where the part is of type P and whole of type W, we have:

A1. Can a **P** exist without some **W** it is **part of**?

A2. Can a **P** exist without the same **W** it is **part of**?

A3. Can a **P** be **part of** only one whole? (if not, then **P** can be shared among wholes)

B1. Can a **W** (continue to) exist when it does not **has part** some **P**?

B2. Can a **W** (continue to) exist when it does not **has part** the same **P**?

Fig.4 shows the resultant facts for each answered question; note the different effects of the "some" and "same" in the questions and representation. In a real model, P and W are replaced by their respective object types in the ORM model and part of and has part are replaced by the corresponding type of part-whole roles.

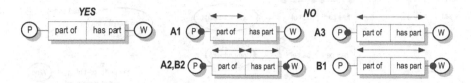

Fig. 4. Representations resulting from the answers to questions A1-B2, with one "yes" result and four distinct representations for "no"

4   Disambiguation of Part-Whole Roles: An Example

We demonstrate the results of applying the decision tree and additional questions with a sample ORM model. The top-half of Fig.5 has a model with underspecified part-whole facts, whereas the bottom-half contains the disambiguated version after going through the descision procedure for each role. For instance, Envelope is not involved-in, not a member-of, does not constitute, is not a sub-quantity of, does not participate-in, is not a geographical object, but instead is contained-in the ConferenceBag. Now, with the clear semantics of the part-whole roles, transitivity holds for the mereological relations: derived facts are automatically correct, like RegistrationReceipt contained-in ConferenceBag. Also intransitivity is clear, like that of Linen and ConferenceBag, because a conference bag is not wholly constituted of linen (the model does not say what the Flap is made of). The notion of completeness, i.e. that *all* parts make up the whole, is implied thanks to the closed-world assumption. For instance, ConferenceBag directly contains the ConfProceedings and Envelope *only*, and does not contain, say, the Flap. The structural parts of the whole ConferenceBag are Compartment and Flap. The composite has a functional part, has f-part of Shoulderhandle, which is neither an essential nor a mandatory part of the whole, yet it does not imply shareability either.

5   Conclusions and Further Research

We have introduced a taxonomy of types of meronymic and mereological relations, and used it to construct a decision procedure to determine which type of parthood relation is applicable. Incrementally, mandatory and uniqueness constraints can be added, which enable the conceptual modeller to develop models that are closer to the real-world semantics, hence improve quality of the software. When used more widely, it will be useful to add extensions to the language, e.g. as a separately loadable module in ORM tools for those analysts who need it, analogous to the Description Logics approach with a family of more and less expressive knowledge representation languages.

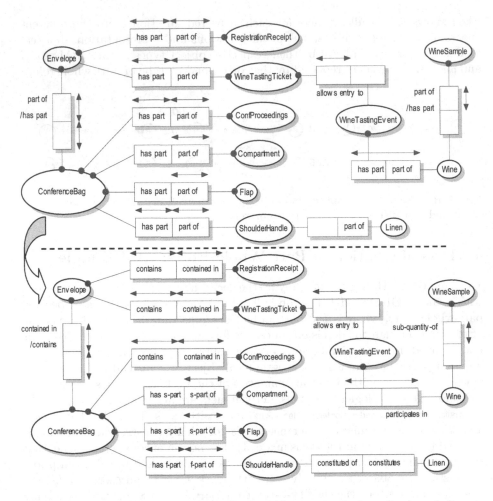

Fig. 5. Example ORM model with all part-of/has-part relations (top) and disambiguated mereological and meronymic parthood relations (bottom)

References

1. Artale, A., Franconi, E., Guarino, N., and Pazzi, L. (1996). Part-Whole Relations in Object-Centered Systems: an Overview. *Data & Knowledge Engineering*, 1996, 20(3):347-383.
2. Barbier, F., Henderson-Sellers, B., Le Parc-Lacayrelle, A., Bruel, J.-M.. Formalization of the whole-part relationship in the Unified Modelling Language. *IEEE Transactions on Software Engineering*, 2003, 29(5):459-470.
3. Berardi, D., Calvanese, D., De Giacomo, G. Reasoning on UML class diagrams. *Artificial Intelligence*, 2005, 168(1-2):70-118.
4. Bittner, T., Donnelly, M. Computational ontologies of parthood, componenthood, and containment, In: *Proceedings of the Nineteenth International Joint Conference on Artificial Intelligence 2005 (IJCAI05)*. Kaelbling, L. (ed.). pp382-387.

5. Franconi, E., Ng, G. The iCom tool for intelligent conceptual modelling. *7th Intl Workshop on Knowledge Representation meets Databases*. Berlin, Germany. 2000.
6. Gerstl, P., Pribbenow, S. Midwinters, end games, and body parts: a classification of part-whole relations. *Intl. Journal of Human-Computer Studies*, 1995, 43:865-889.
7. Guizzardi, G. *Ontological foundations for structural conceptual models*. PhD Thesis, Telematica Institute, Twente University, Enschede, the Netherlands. 2005.
8. Halpin, T.A. *A logical analysis of information systems: static aspects of the data-oriented perspective*. PhD Thesis, University of Queensland, Australia. 1989.
9. Halpin, T. UML Data Models from an ORM Perspective (Part 8). *Journal of Conceptual Modeling*, Issue 8, April 1999. http://www.inconcept.com/jcm.
10. Halpin, T. *Information Modeling and Relational Databases*. San Francisco: Morgan Kaufmann Publishers, 2001.
11. Johansson, I. On the transitivity of the parthood relation. In: *Relations and predicates*, Hochberg, H., Mulligan, K. (eds.). Ontos Verlag: Frankfurt, 2004. pp161-181.
12. Keet, C.M. Using abstractions to facilitate management of large ORM models and ontologies. *International Workshop on Object-Role Modeling (ORM'05)*. In: OTM Workshops 2005. Halpin, T., Meersman, R. (eds.), Lecture Notes in Computer Science 3762. Berlin: Springer-Verlag, 2005. pp603-612.
13. Masolo, C., Borgo, S., Gangemi, A., Guarino, N. and Oltramari, A. *Ontology Library*. WonderWeb Deliverable D18 (ver. 1.0, 31-12-2003). http://wonderweb. semanticweb.org. 2003.
14. Motschnig-Pitrik, R., Kaasbøll, J. Part-Whole Relationship Categories and Their Application in Object-Oriented Analysis. *IEEE Transactions on Knowledge and Data Engineering*, 1999, 11(5):779-797.
15. Object Management Group. *Unified Modeling Language: Superstructure*. v2.0. formal/05-07-04. http://www.omg.org/cgi-bin/doc?formal/05-07-04.
16. Odell, J.J. *Advanced Object-Oriented Analysis & Design using UML*. Cambridge: Cambridge University Press. 1998.
17. Shanks, G., Tansley, E., Weber, R. Representing composites in conceptual modeling. *Communications of the ACM*, 2004, 47(7): 77-80.
18. Varzi, A.C. Mereology. *The Stanford Encyclopedia of Philosophy*. (Fall 2004 Edition), Zalta, E.N. (ed.). http://plato.stanford.edu/archives/fall2004/entries/mereology/.
19. Varzi, A.C. The formal ontology of space: parts, wholes, and locations. In: *The Logic of Space*, Aiello, M., Pratt-Hartmann I., van Benthem J. (eds.). Dordrecht: Kluwer Academic Publishers. Chapter 1, 104p. draft http://www.columbia.edu/~av72/papers/Space_2006.pdf, date accessed: 16-5-2006.
20. Varzi, A.C. A Note on the Transitivity of Parthood. *Applied Ontology* (to appear).
21. Vieu, L., Aurnague, M. Part-of Relations, Functionality and Dependence. In: M. Aurnague, M. Hickmann, L. Vieu (eds.), *Categorization of Spatial Entities in Language and Cognition*. Amsterdam: John Benjamins. 2005.
22. Winston, M.E., Chaffin, R., Herrmann, D. A taxonomy of partwhole relations. *Cognitive Science*, 1987, 11(4):417-444.

Exploring Modelling Strategies in a Meta-modelling Context

P. van Bommel, S.J.B.A. Hoppenbrouwers, H.A. (Erik) Proper,
and Th.P. van der Weide

Institute for Computing and Information Sciences, Radboud University Nijmegen
Toernooiveld 1, 6525 ED Nijmegen, The Netherlands, EU
{P.vanBommel, E.Proper, S.Hoppenbrouwers, Th.P.vanderWeide}@cs.ru.nl

Abstract. We are concerned with a core aspect of the *processes* of obtaining conceptual models. We view such processes as information gathering dialogues, in which strategies may be followed (possibly, imposed) in order to achieve certain modelling goals. Many goals and strategies for modelling can be distinguished, but the current discussion concerns *meta-model driven* strategies, aiming to fulfil modelling goals or obligations that are the direct result of meta-model choices (i.e. the chosen modelling language). We provide a rule-based conceptual framework for capturing strategies for modelling, and give examples based on a simplified version of the Object Role Modelling (ORM) meta-model. We discuss strategy rules directly related to the meta-model, and additional procedural rules. We indicate how the strategies may be used to dynamically set a modelling agenda. Finally, we describe a generic conceptual structure for a *strategy catalog*.

1 Introduction

This paper reports on an intermediary result in an ongoing effort to analyse and eventually improve processes for conceptual modelling (domain modelling) in information and knowledge system development. In [6], we have argued that such modelling processes can be viewed as specialized information gathering dialogues in which knowledge of a domain expert is gradually made explicit and refined until the resulting representations conform to relevant aspects of the domain expert's conception and also to the demands on well-formedness posed by the modelling language (usually a formal or semi-formal one).

As argued at length in [8], not much research has been conducted concerning stages in, and aspects of, ways of working used in modelling efforts. The *how* behind the activity of creating models is still mostly art rather than science. A notable exception is work by Batra et al. for example [1, 3]. Though their work includes rules very much like the ones presented in section 3 of this paper (but for ER instead of ORM), they are not concerned with the rules as such, but in applying them in a knowledge-based system for conceptual modelling support. This is also a long-term goal for us, but we approach it from "within" the modelling process, whereas Batra et al. seem to rather "work their way in

R. Meersman, Z. Tari, P. Herrero et al. (Eds.): OTM Workshops 2006, LNCS 4278, pp. 1128–1137, 2006.

from the outside". Thus, there is a small overlap between their and our own work, but there is also a difference in approach and focus.

There are various reasons for improving our understanding of the details of the modelling process, and how to improve it. Some aspects of model quality (most in particular, validation) can be better achieved through a good modelling process rather than by just imposing requirements on the end product. Valid models are only attainable by viewing a model in context, and therefore in relation to the actors who have created and agreed with some model [7]. The process of modelling thus is a crucial link between the end product and its context. Another important reason for studying which course of action leads to good models concerns human resources. Generally, few experts are available who are capable of, or willing to, perform high-quality modelling. Anything that helps guide modelling behavior and support the process would be helpful. Eventually, we therefore hope to contribute to the creation of intelligent guiding systems that aid, and where required control, the modelling process. First, however, detailed study of (aspects of) the modelling process is required. One such aspect is dealt with in this paper.

2   Modelling as a Structured Dialogue

As briefly stated in the introduction, we view modelling processes as dialogues: the bringing forth of series of statements (including questions, propositions, etc.) by the participants in a modelling activity, together making up the step-by-step creation of a model (including rejection or revision of previous statements) [7, 4]. The main roles played by participants distinguished by us are:

Domain Expert (DE) – provides valid information about the domain modelled, and is capable of deciding which aspects of the domain are relevant to the model and which are not.

Model Builder (MB) – is responsible for choosing the modelling meta-concepts appropriate for the modelling task at hand; i.e. the concepts fit for correct modelling conform the chosen modelling paradigm.

Modelling Mediator (MM) – helps the DE to phrase and interpret statements concerning the domain that can be understood or are produced by the MB. The MM also helps to translate questions the MB might have for the DE, and vice-versa.

Let us consider in some detail six classes of modelling goals we have distinguished so far for modelling processes:

Over-all goals – The most general goals, the central ones of which are the *completeness*, and *consistentness* goals. Though there surely exist strategies that help achieve these goals, they are relatively straightforward.

Validation goals – These goals concern the level of knowledge sharing involved in the information exchange underlying a modelling effort [6].

Argumentation goals – Such goals make for the description of (some aspect of) the argumentation behind a particular modelling choice; in an increasing number of model types, such argumentation is included.

Meta-model oriented goals – Goals imposed by the modelling language, and the correctness of the statements made in it. If a modelling language is strictly defined (syntactically, semantically, or both), these goals are at the core of the strategies that lead to well-formed models in that language.

Abstraction goals – These goals are set in order to assure optimal choices in the level of abstraction applied in modelling. Though such choices may be partly engrained in the meta-model, choosing a good level of abstraction is crucial for good modelling.

Interpretation goals – Goals raising the question whether the meaning of concepts or statements used in the model but not further defined or formalized are sufficiently clear for all participants.

Currently we focus on the fourth type: meta-model oriented modelling goals.

Modelling languages (especially formal ones) impose requirements not only on model structure but as a consequence also on modelling processes. Typically, if a concept is introduced into the model, often some clearly defined co-concepts are also required, as well as particular relations between the concepts involved. For example, in the ORM modelling paradigm the central modelling concepts are Objects (*Game,Student*) and Roles (*plays*), that together constitute Fact Types (*Students play Games*). Thus, Objects and Roles are typical co-concepts.

Since we regard modelling as a process there is also a temporal aspect involved: certain concepts (of some type), or combinations thereof, are required or allowed to be added to the model in view of previously introduced concepts. The metaphor we suggest is that of slot filling. Each meta-concept has its place in the general slot structure for a (part of) the model under construction. The meta-concepts provide pull for information about the model conform the meta-model. In a way, they represent potential, abstract questions asked by the MB to the DE (possibly with the MM as intermediary) in order to achieve the meta-model oriented goals. Addition of a new concept may thus trigger a sequence of consecutive modelling actions. In this way, the meta-model (or modelling language) for a considerable part *drives the information gathering and creation process*, by setting detailed goals for the model's syntax and structure. By imposing constraints on the meta-structure (let us call them *meta-constraints*) it is possible to structure the questions generated by the meta-model over time. The meta-model, combined with the (meta-)constraints, constitutes a rule system that dynamically restricts the modelling possibilities as modelling progresses.

For example, fact types in ORM are usually complemented by constraints that are imposed on the population of these fact types. A number of different constraint types can be used, but the main ones are similar to existential and universal quantifiers in predicate logic. Thus, the constraints restrict allowed populations for the predicates. Concretely, if a fact type (*Students play Games*) has been added to the model, the question is raised what constraints hold for that fact type; a request along such lines is added to a *modelling agenda*. It is our purpose to *make explicit such a modelling agenda and the rules that generate it.* With respect to our constraints example, there are some choices to be made with respect to the precise meta-constraints on constraints:

- Are constraints (possibly of a specific sub-type) obligatory or not?
- Do certain constraints need to be added to a predicate directly after it is introduced, or can this be postponed?
- Do certain constraints have to be verifiably derived from a known (i.e. modelled) population, or not?

3 Strategies for Modelling

As discussed, a meta-model Way of Modelling has an immediate influence on the way of working used (or *to be* used) by some participant(s) in a modelling process. In addition, variations in meta-constraints can be used to compose procedural rules for different modelling strategies. In ORM practice, for example, the following main over-all strategies have been observed to co-exist (in part some styles are reflected in ORM-related textbooks, e.g. [9, 2, 5, not intended to be a comprehensive overview]:

```
"ObjectType Driven" Strategy
a. Provide ObjectTypes
b. Provide complete FactTypes (adding Roles to the ObjectTypes)
c. Possibly, provide Facts (including Objects) illustrating the FactTypes
d. Provide Constraints (possibly based on the collection of Facts)

"Fact Driven" Strategy
a. Provide Facts
b. Create FactTypes
    (c. Provide ObjectTypes)
    (d. Provide Roles)
e. Provide constraints (strictly based on the collection of facts)
```

Trivial though the differences between these over-all strategies may seem to the casual observer, they have given rise to considerable debate among experienced modelers. In addition, novice ORM modelers often feel uncertain about ways to proceed in modelling: where to start? Where to go from there? What to aim for? Below, we will provide a more detailed analysis of over-all modelling strategies and rephrase them as *meta-model based modelling (sub)strategies.* Though all examples are ORM related, we indeed believe our approach to be useful for many other modelling languages, both formal and semi-formal. We intend to explore strategies for various modelling languages (and parallels and differences between them) before long.

So far, we have discussed procedural choices and steps in modelling under the assumption that the meta-model involved is stable. However, it is not unthinkable that meta-concepts in a modelling language are progressively switched on, for example in case a static model is created first, after which temporal concepts are added [10]. This would result in a modelling procedure that spans several types of model, and allows for evolution of one model type to another. We have already worked out conceptual details of such an approach. We refrain from elaborate discussion of this direction in this paper.

Meta-model choices that have been set as part of the ORM paradigm can themselves be represented as a conceptual schema. In this paper, for illustration purposes only, we use a simplified version of the ORM meta-model, presented below in verbalized ORM form (as opposed to an ORM schema). For the additional procedural rules, we added some straightforward but admittedly ad hoc temporal terminology. Please note that this ORM meta-model is used for illustration purposes only, and in no way is intended to reflect the "ultimate ORM meta-model".

Tightening our definitions, meta-model related modelling strategies are linked to three sets of modelling choices to be made:

Meta-model choices: The entire set of potential "concept slots" that are to be filled; the "maximum meta-model".

Modeling procedure choices: The meta-model parameters (see above) can be set and reset both *before* and *during* the modelling process. Keeping to the slot filling metaphor, the parameters result in decisions whether or not particular slots related to the maximum meta-model actually need to be filled. In addition, rules are added that render an *order* in which slots are to be filled.

Rationale choices: In some cases, items in the model can be introduced for various different reasons, and based on various different sources.

For example (based on ORM):

- facts obligatory / facts optional [*meta-model choice*]
- constraints optional / constraints obligatory [*meta-model choice*]
- objects first / fact types first / roles first [*procedure choice*]
- constraints immediately after fact types
- facts first (driving elicitation) / facts later (completing elicitation) [*procedure choice combined with rationale choice*]
- facts for concept validation / facts for constraint derivation and validation [*rationale choice*]
- facts as example (made up) / facts as concrete link with domain [*rationale choice*]

Such choices once made, can be crystallized into *rules for modelling.*

Below we specify two related sets of rules that together provide a reasonably complete basis for meta-model based modelling goals and strategies, for the Strict Fact-based approach to ORM modelling. A generic advantage of declarative rules is that they can restrict the course of a modelling process as much as is needed, without the obligation to comprehensively specify all possible modelling sequences. Admittedly, the distinction between goals and strategies is somewhat blurred here. We choose fact-based approach to ORM because it is a relatively restrictive flavour of modelling which allows us to nicely demonstrate the operation of our restrictive rules. In the example, the first set of rules ("M-rules") simply reflect the ORM meta model. The rules are expressed here in a semi-natural, controlled language that is standard for ORM verbalizations and that can easily be formalized. The second set of rules also includes some terms for expressing procedural aspects; this is not standard ORM, but any sort of straightforward temporal modelling should be able to deal with them. In addition, we use the term "Action", meaning the objectified combination of a meta-model item (e.g. FactType, Object) and a mutation of the model (e.g. add, modify).

```
META-MODEL FOR STRICT FACT-BASED MODELLING
M1   Each ObjectType is populated by one or more Objects
M2   Each Object populates exactly one ObjectTypes
M3   Each ObjectType has exactly one Type
M4   Each Type is of one or more ObjectTypes
M5   Each ObjectType plays one or more Roles
M6   Each Role is played by exactly one ObjectType
M7   Each Object is of one or more Facts
M8   Each Fact has one or more Objects
M9   Each Fact has one or more Roles
M10  Each Role is of one or more Facts
M11  Each Role is of exactly one FactType
M12  Each FactType has one or more Roles
M13  Each Role has one or more constraints
M14  Each Constraint applies one or more Roles
M15  Each Constraint has exactly one ConstraintType
M16  Each ConstraintType is of zero or more Constraints
```

```
TEMPORAL CONSTRAINTS FOR STRICT FACT-BASED MODELLING
P1  an Action that involves Addition of an Object is immediately followed by an Action that
    involves Addition of an ObjectType that is populated by that Object
P2  an Action that involves Addition of an Object Type takes place later than an Action that
    involves Addition of a Fact that has a Role that is played by that same ObjectType
P3  an Action that involves Addition of a Role is immediately followed by an Action that
    involves Addition of an ObjectType that plays that Role
P4  no Action that involves Addition of an Object takes place before an Action that involves
    Addition of a Fact that has that same Object
P5  no Action that involves Addition of an ObjectType takes place before an Action that
    involves Addition of an Object that populates that same ObjectType
P6  no Action that involves Addition of a Role takes place before an Action that involves
    Addition of a Fact that has that same Role
P7  an action that involves Addition of a Constraint coincides with the Addition of a
    ConstraintType that is of that Constraint
```

Not all these rules are to be enforced absolutely and immediately. Some only set an agenda, while others allow for only one possible next step in the modelling process.

The initial agenda sets a first move. As can be derived from the rules (most prominently, P2,P4,P6), the only way to start modelling in Strict fact-Based Modelling is to introduce a Fact. Thus, in such a situation there is only one modelling action on the agenda: "add Fact". Note that the meta-model as such does not prevent the model from being empty. The rules merely determine that if an initial step is taken (starting either from an empty model or from another stable model), this *has* to be the addition of a Fact.

We assume for now that the agenda is merely set on the basis of slots that are actually filled in (i.e a concrete intermediate model version). In other words: no agenda points are inferred merely one the basis of existing agenda points. Once an initial action is performed (for example, the fact "John plays tennis" has been added), then various M-rules dictate the setting of the following agenda points:

```
M8: add one or more Objects that are of the Fact ''John Plays tennis''
M9: add one or more Roles that are of the Fact ''John Plays tennis''.
```

At this point, no P-rules enforce an order. Hence, either one or more Roles or one or more Objects may be added. Suppose an Object is added: "John". In relation to the meta-model, this implies that 'The Object "John" is of Fact "John Plays Tennis" '. This action de-activates rule M8 (the minimum of one object per fact has been reached); however, note that it is still *allowed* to add Objects to the

Fact. The addition of "John" also activates another rule. This results in the following new agenda points:

```
M2: add one ObjectType that is populated by Object ''John''.
```

In addition, a P-rule now becomes active:

```
P1: immediately add one ObjectType that is populated by Object ''John''.
```

There is another P-rule that is activated: P2. This rule requires that "an action that involves addition of an ObjectType takes place later than an action that involves addition of a Fact that has a Role that is played by that same ObjectType". In other words, we need the Fact's Role even before we get to the ObjectType. So:

```
P2: immediately add one or more Roles that are of the Fact ''John Plays tennis''
P1: immediately add one ObjectType that is populated by Object ''John''.
```

In response, first a Role is added to the fact "John plays Tennis"; this is "plays". Thus, 'The Role "plays" is of Fact "John plays tennis" '. This action activates rule M6; this results in a combination between P1 and M6 that adds a request for addition of a particular ObjectType. Also, another M-rule is activated: M13. So now we have the following agenda:

```
P1: immediately add one ObjectType that is populated by Object ''John''.
M6: add one ObjectType that plays Role ''plays''.
M13: add one Constraint that applies to Role ''plays''.
```

In response, ObjectType "Person" is added: 'The ObjectType "Person" is populated by Object "John" '. Also added: 'The ObjectType "Person" plays Role "plays". Two words from the Fact have now been qualified. Only the word "tennis" is yet unqualified. Indeed, in the current setup it is not obligatory to qualify all words in a Fact, yet a rule to this effect could well be added. Let us assume that the modeler, by her own initiative, first adds "tennis" as an Object (i.e. before the required constraint is tackled). Thus we get 'The Object "Tennis" is of Fact "John Plays Tennis" '. This triggers a few new agenda point, repeating a pattern already shown:

```
P2: immediately add one or more Roles that are of the Fact ''John Plays tennis''
P1: immediately add one ObjectType that is populated by Object ''Tennis''.
```

In response, we get 'The Role "is played by" is of Fact "John plays tennis'. This again triggers M6 and M13, so we now have:

```
P1: immediately add one ObjectType that is populated by Object ''Tennis''.
M6: add one ObjectType that plays Role ''is played by''.
M14: add one Constraint that applies to Role ''is played by''.
```

The response is 'The ObjectType "Sport" is populated by Object "Tennis" '. Now two agenda points are left:

```
M14: add one Constraint that applies to Role ''plays''.
M14: add one Constraint that applies to Role ''is played by''.
```

As mentioned, in this paper we only provide an example, without claiming to present some definite meta-model or set of rules. So, to wrap things up: Response: 'Constraint with ConstraintType "SharedUniqueness" is placed on Role "plays" '; 'Constraint with ConstraintType "SharedUniqueness" is placed on Role "is played by" '. This results in a Uniqueness Constraint being placed on the combined Roles "plays" and "is played by". No agenda points are left; a "stable model" has been reached. All meta-model oriented rules are satisfied until a further addition is made. We may or may not return to the "add Fact" agenda, depending on the Over All goals (see section 2), which are not discussed in detail here. This concludes our example.

4   Strategy Catalog

Our framework emphasizes meta-model driven modelling strategies. In order to facilitate the construction of these modelling strategies and the reasoning about strategies, we propose an underlying structure of strategies called a *strategy catalog*. The different parts of a strategy catalog are used to capture components of modelling agendas and modelling dialogues. These components, such as model mutations and phasing of modelling actions are considered basic building blocks for modelling strategies.

In a strategy catalog we will find *items* which are of a a particular *item kind*. Examples of items are: John, person, John works for the personnel department, and persons work for departments. The corresponding item kinds are: entity, entity type, fact, and fact type, respectively. Items are inherited from the application domain, whereas item kinds come from the meta-model of the technique used for modelling that domain.

The basic building blocks for modelling strategies are mutations and actions. As an example, consider mutations such as addition, modification, and deletion. A modelling action then is characterized as a mutation applied to an item kind. For example: addition of an entity type, addition of an entity, addition of a fact type, modification of an entity type, and the addition of a constraint. Clearly these modelling actions deal with item kinds rather than items. However, the execution of actions does indeed affect the items, for example by the addition of entity type *person*, and the addition of entity *John*.

At this stage, the modelling actions discussed above, are randomly ordered. In some situations this will be fine, but for most more restrictive modelling procedures we require a specific order. Modelling actions may be related to each other via *ordering* and *succession*. The first is used to express that a certain action should be performed after another action, whereas the second is used to require that an action is the *immediate* successor of another action. This allows for sequential as well as parallel actions. To capture more of the properties of modelling actions, our catalog records further properties such as *urgency* and *phasing*:

Urgency. Examples are: forbidden, required, optional, allowed.
Phasing. Examples are: first, last, middle.

Urgencies are used as a refinement of *must* and *can*, while the phasing of modelling actions is used as a shorthand for certain orderings. The intention of modelling actions and their properties is that modelling strategies can be defined in a flexible manner. Strategies may then be varying from a very strict application where modelling is a predefined path, to more liberal applications where modelling is more like a pathless land. Exact concepts for procedural rules will vary; we make no decision here, we just provide examples.

The execution of modelling actions yields specific items occurring in the application domain. These items may have certain properties related to the application environment. For example, we have a *purpose* and *reality value* as follows:

Purpose. Examples are: validation, constraint derivation, type introduction.
Reality value. Examples are: real, fictive, expected.

These aspects deal with rationale choices discussed in section 3. Summarizing, the purpose and reality value of items may be used in different ways, for example:

- Certain entities are real and are used for type introduction.
- Certain facts are real and are used for constraint derivation.
- Certain facts are fictive and are used for validation.

5   Next-Generation Studies of Modelling Strategies

In this paper we have presented a concise overview of our work in the area of meta-model related modelling strategies. Using modelling agendas with an underlying strategy catalog, we arrive at the situation where reasoning about (a) the construction of modelling strategies, and (b) the behaviour of modellers during strategy execution, becomes possible. For example, if the input of the modelling process is seen as some kind of informal specification coming from a domain I, and the output is a model expressed in a more formal language L, a strategy S has the following signature: $S : I \longrightarrow 2^L$

So for some input $i \in I$ a strategy S yields the models $S(i) \subseteq L$. Of course if the result of the modelling process is required to have certain predefined characteristics, a strategy should support this. A typical example is the production of models in a particular normal form. In order to deal with such postconditions, suppose P is a property of models, which can be defined as a predicate over L. A strategy supports this property if the property holds for all possible output models: $\forall_{i \in I, x \in S(i)} [P(x)]$

If the strategy does not fully support the postcondition, it often can be guaranteed by an additional requirement Q on the informal specification, expressing the appropriate precondition: $\forall_{i \in I} [Q(i) \Rightarrow \forall_{x \in S(i)} [P(x)]]$

In order to compare two strategies S_1 and S_2, we suppose $i \in I$ is a given informal specification. On the one hand, the strategies are *orthogonal* for specification i if they can not result in the same model: $S_1(i) \cap S_2(i) = \emptyset$

On the other hand, the different strategies S_1 and S_2 are *equivalent* if they result in exactly the same models. We then have $S_1(i) = S_2(i)$. In most cases we will be somewhere between these extremes, having overlap in $S_1(i)$ and $S_2(i)$. Note that this also allows us to study the effect of changing a given strategy. We then want to compare the strategies S_1 and $S_2 = r(S_1)$ where r is a reorganization operator.

The above sketch of the reasoning framework leaves open many parameters. Reasoning may have other purposes as well, for example a dual approach where two different input specifications are compared for the same strategy. Clearly much work is still to be done. The formalization of rationale choices in strategy rules need further attention. Deterministic strategies with $|S(i)| = 1$ may be studied. Moreover, automated simulation of non-deterministic modelling processes with $|S(i)| > 1$ allows for the characterization of different cognitive identities of system analysts.

References

1. S. Anthony, D. Batra, and R. Santhanam. The use of a knowledge–based system in conceptual data modeling. *Decision Support Systems*, 41:176–190, 2005.
2. G.P. Bakema, J.P.C. Zwart, and H. van der Lek. Fully Communication Oriented NIAM. In *Proceedings of NIAM–ISDM 2*, pages 1–35, August 1994.
3. D. Batra and S. Antony. Consulting support during conceptual database design in the presence of redundancy in requirements specifications: an empirical study. *IBM Journal of Research and Development*, 54:25–51, 2006.
4. P.J.M. Frederiks and Th.P. van der Weide. Information Modeling: the process and the required competencies of its participants. *Data & Knowledge Engineering*, 2005.
5. T.A. Halpin. *Information Modeling and Relational Databases, From Conceptual Analysis to Logical Design*. Morgan Kaufmann, San Mateo, California, USA, 2001.
6. S.J.B.A. Hoppenbrouwers, H.A. (Erik) Proper, and Th.P. van der Weide. A Fundamental View on the Process of Conceptual Modeling. In L. Delcambre, C. Kop, H.C. Mayr, J. M ylopoulos, and O. Pastor, editors, *ER 2005 – 24 International Conference on Conceptual Modeling, Klagenfurt, Austria, EU*, volume 3716 of *Lecture Notes in Computer Science*, pages 128–143. Springer, June 2005.
7. S.J.B.A. Hoppenbrouwers, H.A. (Erik) Proper, and Th.P. van der Weide. Formal Modelling as a Grounded Conversation. In G. Goldkuhl, M. Lind, and S. Haraldson, editors, *Proceedings of the 10th International Working Conference on t he Language Action Perspective on Communication Modelling (LAP'05)*, pages 139–155. Linköpings Universitet and Hogskolan I Boras, Sweden, EU, June 2005.
8. S.J.B.A. Hoppenbrouwers, H.A. (Erik) Proper, and Th.P. van der Weide. Understanding the Requirements on Modelling Techniques. In O. Pastor and J. Falcao e Cunha, editors, *17th International Conference on Advanced Information Systems Engineering, CAiSE 2005, Porto, Portugal, EU*, volume 3520 of *Lecture Notes in Computer Science*, pages 262–276. Springer, June 2005.
9. G.M. Nijssen. *Universele Informatiekunde*. PNA Publishing, The Netherlands, EU, 1993. In Dutch.
10. H.A. (Erik) Proper, S.J.B.A. Hoppenbrouwers, and Th.P. van der Weide. A Fact–Oriented Approach to Activity Modeling. In R. Meersman, Z. Tari, and P. Herrero, editors, *OTM Workshops – OTM Confederated International Workshops and Posters, Agia Napa, Cyprus, EU*, volume 3762 of *Lecture Notes in Computer Science*, pages 666–675. Springer, October/November 2005.

Giving Meaning to Enterprise Architectures: Architecture Principles with ORM and ORC

P. van Bommel, S.J.B.A. Hoppenbrouwers, H.A. (Erik) Proper,
and Th.P. van der Weide

Institute for Computing and Information Sciences, Radboud University Nijmegen
Toernooiveld 1, 6525 ED Nijmegen, The Netherlands, EU
{P.vanBommel, S.Hoppenbrouwers, E.Proper, Th.P.vanderWeide}@cs.ru.nl

Abstract. Formalization of architecture principles by means of ORM and Object Role Calculus (ORC) is explored. After a discussion on reasons for formalizing such principles, and of the perceived relationship between principles and (business) rules, two exploratory example formalizations are presented and discussed. They concern architecture principles taken from The Open Group's Architecture Framework (TOGAF). It is argued that when using ORM and ORC for formal modelling of architecture principles, the underlying logical principles of the techniques may lead to better insight into the rational structure of the principles. Thus, apart from achieving formalization, the quality of the principles as such can be improved.

1 Introduction

Model-driven system development is a major direction in information systems development today. Roughly speaking, it advocates the modelling of various aspects of enterprises as a basis for the design of both the detailed, operational organization of the enterprise (mostly process engineering) and the IT to support it. Model-driven IT development can be traditional (engaging human developers), but in an increasing number of cases fully automated creation (generation) of software from models is strived for [2].

Increasingly, organizations make use of enterprise architectures to direct the development of the enterprise as a whole and IT development in particular [8]. These developments are fuelled by requirements such as the Clinger-Cohan Act in the USA[1], which force government bodies to provide an IT architecture based on a set of architecture principles.

One of the key roles of enterprise architecture is to steer the over-all enterprise/system development within a large organization (enterprise). A more specific way of expressing this is to state that "Architecture serves the purpose of constraining design space"[2]. In most (enterprise) architecture approaches, this

---

[1] http://www.cio.gov/Documents/it_management_reform_act_Feb_1996.html
[2] See: http://www.xaf.nl

R. Meersman, Z. Tari, P. Herrero et al. (Eds.): OTM Workshops 2006, LNCS 4278, pp. 1138–1147, 2006.

constraining is done by means of so-called architecture principles [7, 10]. These principles usually take the form of informal statements such as (taken from [10]):

> *Users have access to the data necessary to perform their duties; therefore, data is shared across enterprise functions and organizations.*

According to the TOGAF architecture framework [10], "Principles are general rules and guidelines, intended to be enduring and seldom amended, that inform and support the way in which an organization sets about fulfilling its mission." Such principles typically address concerns of the key stakeholders within an organization. In this case, a stakeholder may be highly concerned about the organization's ability to flexibly deploy their workforce over different work locations.

When using architecture principles as the core element in enterprise architecture, informal statements as exemplified above arguably do not provide enough precision to concretely limit design space. Therefore, they have limited power as a steering instrument. The call can already be heard for SMART[3] treatment of architecture principles. Both in view of their formulation and their enforcement, formalizing principles in a rule-like fashion can be expected to bring the SMART objectives closer. What is more, if architecture and development are complex, and demands on quality, performance, and agility are high, formalization of such rules will enable their embedding in a fully rule-based modelling setup. This may include capabilities for simulation of alternative architectures and their impact, quantitative analysis, and formal verification of and reasoning about and with rules (for example, weeding out contradictions and inconsistencies, or deriving new facts). These and other advantages claimed by rule-based approaches (most prominently, the Business Rules Approach or BRA [12]) may thus also become available to system development under architecture.

It has been argued by some architects that architecture principles should never be formalized, since this would lead to them being too restrictive. They should "leave room for interpretation". We would argue, however, that sharp definition and careful, rational composition of rules should not be mistaken for overly detailed regulation. Even the sharpest formalization of a high-level principle merely sets constraints; if the principle is general enough, ample room is left for more details, at lower levels of design, within those constraints.

In this paper we do not discuss any further the question whether formalization of architecture principles in a rule-driven development setup is a good idea or not. Instead, we assume that it is at the least an idea worthwhile exploring. What we focus on is the idea that formalization, when properly and systematically performed, may also lead to better analysis of certain patterns of meaning underlying the principles, and thereby to improvement of the (formulation of) the principles as such –even of their informal formulations.

We base our account on the ORM and ORC (Object Role Calculus) approach because of its formal foundations, its close relation to the BRA, and its long

---

[3] Specific, Measurable, Achievable, Relevant, Time-bound; a common mnemonic used in project management.

running affiliation with cooperative domain modelling involving varied, often non-technical domain experts. The *Object-Role Calculus* [6] (ORC) is an evolved variant of RIDL [9]. Two earlier variants where Lisa-D [5], which provided a multi-sets based formalization of RIDL, and ConQuer [11, 1], which provides a more practical approach (that is, from an implementation point of view). The ORC aims to re-integrate the Lisa-D and ConQuer branches of RIDL.

2   Architecture Principles, Rules, and Formalization

In their Architecture Framework (TOGAF), the Open Group [10] lists five criteria that distinguish a good set of principles:

1. **Understandable:** The underlying tenets can be quickly grasped and understood by individuals throughout the organization. The intention of the principle is clear and unambiguous, so that violations, whether intentional or not, are minimized.
2. **Robust:** Enable good quality decisions about architectures and plans to be made, and enforceable policies and standards to be created. Each principle should be sufficiently definitive and precise to support consistent decision making in complex, potentially controversial, situations.
3. **Complete:** Every potentially important principle governing the management of information and technology for the organization is defined. The principles cover every situation perceived.
4. **Consistent:** Strict adherence to one principle may require a loose interpretation of another principle. The set of principles must be expressed in a way that allows a balance of interpretations. Principles should not be contradictory to the point where adhering to one principle would violate the spirit of another. Every word in a principle statement should be carefully chosen to allow consistent yet flexible interpretation.
5. **Stable:** Principles should be enduring, yet able to accommodate changes. An amendment process should be established for adding, removing, or altering principles after they are ratified initially.

We will use the following two example principles, also taken (rather arbitrarily) from TOGAF, throughout the remainder of this paper:

Data is Shared (TOGAF1): "Users have access to the data necessary to perform their duties; therefore, data is shared across enterprise functions and organizations."

Common Use Applications (TOGAF2): "Development of applications used across the enterprise is preferred over the development of duplicate applications which are only provided to a particular organization."

Now we suggest the reader briefly compare the criteria for good architecture principles with the following articles selected from the Business Rules Manifesto[12], describing the nature of business rules:

3.2 Terms express business concepts; facts make assertions about these concepts; rules constrain and support these facts.

3.3 Rules must be explicit. No rule is ever assumed about any concept or fact.

4.1 Rules should be expressed declaratively in natural-language sentences for the business audience.

5.1 Business rules should be expressed in such a way that they can be validated for correctness by business people.

5.2 Business rules should be expressed in such a way that they can be verified against each other for consistency.

5.3 Formal logics, such as predicate logic, are fundamental to well-formed expression of rules in business terms, as well as to the technologies that implement business rules.

7.1 Rules define the boundary between acceptable and unacceptable business activity.

8.4 More rules is not better. Usually fewer good rules is better.

8.5 An effective system can be based on a small number of rules. Additional, more discriminating rules can be subsequently added, so that over time the system becomes smarter.

We have no space here to discuss in detail the apparent match of the TOGAF "good principles" characterizations and the BRA in view of our exploration of the formalization of architecture principles, but trust the reader can observe for herself at least a clear similarity of the rationales behind principles and rules.

There is one striking difference between TOGAF principles and BRA rules. The Business Rule Approach aims to help create agile information systems. Rules should be easily changeable, and preferably automatically lead to system adaptations; this should greatly improve agility in business-IT alignment. This sharply contrasts the explicitly phrased Stability characteristic of Principles. However, obviously the possible agility that results of the BRA does not imply that rules have to change often; in fact, many business rules are extremely static.

Note that modality of rules plays an important part in dealing with rule formalization [4]. This is expected to hold also for architecture principles. However, we do not go into modality issues here.

There is one article in the Business Rule Manifesto that deserves some further discussion in view of our formalization goal:

3.1 Rules build on facts, and facts build on concepts as expressed by terms.

This statement, sometimes referred to as the "Business Rule Analysis Mantra", explicitly points towards the approach to formalization shown in the remainder of the paper. ORM is particularly well suited to deal with the formalization of facts (or rather, fact types; "level two") and constraints (i.e. rules: "level one"). It is no coincidence that in the BR Manifesto, facts are mentioned so explicitly: ORM is an important means of analysis and representation used in the business rules community [3]. The third level of analysis, term level, is the "ontological" level at which intensional and mostly lexical meaning is added to the predicate structures represented in ORM. A typical language/framework that includes means for modelling at this level in the BR community is "Semantic of Busines Vocabulary and Rules" or SBVR [13]. Unfortunately, mostly for reasons of space we could not include a full three-level analysis. Instead we use ORC and ORM to analyze levels one and two.

Level one analysis boils down to adding constraints to the basic ORM role/predicate structures. If constraints are not too complex, they can be expressed either as ORM graphical constraints (internal or external), or verbally by using Object Role Calculus or (ORM/ORC; see next section). More complex constraints typically are beyond graphical ORM and require verbal representation (ORM/ORC).

3   Stating Principles: ORM and ORC

In this section we scrutinize two sample architecture principles taken from [10]. Each time, the goal is to interpret the sample architecture principle as an ORM/ORC expression. Note that we set out to explore an approach, not to provide definitive formalizations of TOGAF principles.

The Object-Role Calculus (ORC) aims to re-integrate the Lisa-D and Con-Quer branches of RIDL. It therefore also has a configurable definition of its semantics in the sense that a distinction is made between four abstraction layers, and that at each layer specific choices can be made with regards to the semantic/syntactic richness of the language. The bottom level is a *counting layer* concerned with an algebra defining how the the occurrence frequency of results of ORC expressions should be combined. The next layer up, the *calculus layer*, defines logical predicates, connectives and an associated inference mechanism. The next layer, the *paths layer*, deals with paths through an ORM schema including connectives enabling the construction of non-linear paths. Finally, the fourth layer is the *presentation layer*. At this level, the path expressions from the paths layer are presented either graphically, or verbalized using a textual language. In this section we only show expressions at the presentation level. We will do this either graphically (corresponding to the traditional graphical constraints), or textually in a naturalized but fully formalized format that is a slightly enriched version of traditional Lisa-D. For details on layers 1-3 see [5, 6].

We will now stroll through the examples and provide some comments on issues raised during analysis of the principles. We provide an interpretation based on our own knowledge of architecture issues and, admittedly, on guesses. In a real modelling context, such guesses would of course have to be systematically validated by the relevant stakeholders. All graphical (ORM) information we provide is concentrated in Figure 1. Please note that none of the internal uniqueness and total role constraints in the diagram could be directly derived from the principles; they too are interpretations and therefore educated guesses that would have to be validated. The only constraints in the diagram that were more directly derived from the analysis of the principles are the *external* constraints in the 'TOGAF Principle 1' ORM model (the upper half of Figure 1).

We do not mean to suggest that our representations, either verbal or graphical, are fit to completely replace the original natural language phrasings of the principles. They are chiefly analytical devices still. However, those people phrasing the principles should at least agree that the ORM/OCR rephrasings acceptably reflect the intended meaning.

Data is Shared (TOGAF1): "Users have access to the data necessary to perform their duties; therefore, data is shared across enterprise functions and organizations."

Concerning TOGAF1: what is an enterprise function? TOGAF does not provide a definition. According to a (presumably related) ArchiMate [8] definition, a business-function "offers functionality that may be useful for one or more business processes". We presume that in the same vein, enterprise functions are production activities that are part of one or more of the enterprise's operations.

Another issue concerns the meaning of "therefore". It does not seem to be equivalent to a regular logical *imply*, but rather something like "p is enabled by q". We assume that because users need to perform their duties they have access to data, and that users are both part of organizations and support enterprise functions (see Figure 1; the paths in the diagram can be best traced by focusing on the capitalized words in the formulations below; these words correspond to object types in the diagram). We thus have two related rules, both implied by TOGAF1:

1.a Each Enterprise-function has access to Data which some User [that supports that Enterprise-function]
      needs for some Duties

1.b Each Organization has access to Data which some User [that belongs to that Organization]
      needs for some Duties

In this interpretation, we assume that in the TOGAF point of view, there are two ways to decompose an enterprise: into functions and into organizations. Either decomposition type now requires its own data access rules. Obviously, this apparent redundancy in the model could be avoided by making explicit that both organizations and enterprise functions are "enterprise parts" and then make one rule for enterprises parts. However, this might mean a considerable infringement of the domain model/language for sake of elegant modelling. The two issues may represent two related but separate concerns that require explicitly separate formulation in the eye of the stakeholders. Therefore, the newly suggested component-rules would have to be validated. For now, we would suggest to maintain the rule as a conjunction of 1.a and 1.b:

1.c Each (Enterprise-function and Organization) has access to Data needed by some User
      [that (supports or belongs to) that (Enterprise-function or Organization)] for some Duty

The TOGAF1 example has allowed us to show how a moderately complex architecture principle can be analyzed using ORM/ORC, through a reasonably straightforward interplay between analysis, questions, and propositions. TOGAF2 will show that more complex situations may occur, in which the ability to perform basic formal reasoning can be helpful (we will return to this briefly at the end of this section).

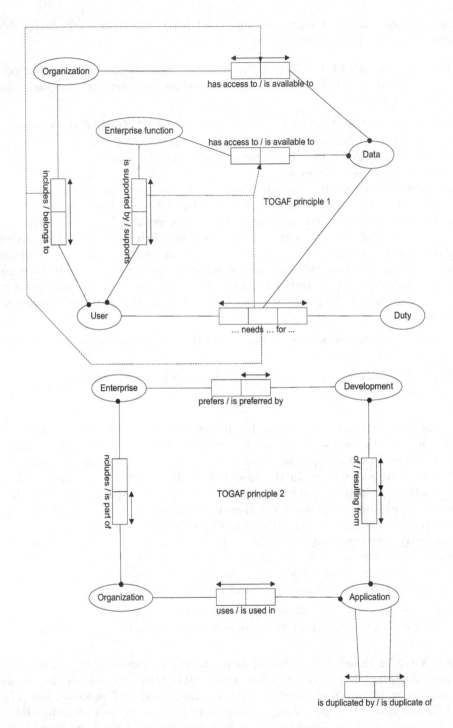

Fig. 1. ORM models underlying the TOGAF principles

Common Use Applications (TOGAF2): "Development of applications used across the enterprise is preferred over the development of duplicate applications which are only provided to a particular organization."

The TOGAF2 conceptual analysis is related to that of TOGAF1. We again assume that organizations are part of enterprises. We interpret "applications being used across the enterprise" as applications being used in two or more organizations. In addition, we model the notion of "duplication" as a distinct predicate. Lexically, it corresponds to some measure or judgement concerning great similarity in functionality of two applications. Another issue is the interpretation of the term "preferred". For simplicitie's sake we assume here, maybe naively, that a development is either preferred or not. However, in practice it seems more realistic to provide a rated interpretation, for example by counting the number of duplicates occurring (decreasing preference), or the number of times a single application is used in different organizations being 1 or larger (increasing preference as the count goes up). This would more actively encourage actual development of applications that are used in more than one organization.

In correspondence with Figure 1, we now have:

2. If an Application A [that is used in an Organization O] results from some Development, and
   this Application A is not a duplicate of another Application
   [that is used in another Organization than O], then that Development
   is preferred by the Enterprise that includes both Organizations and both Applications.

So this is our formalized interpretation of the original TOGAF2a rule. However, as we were performing the ORM analysis of TOGAF2, it became clear that "duplications" and "use across organizations" relate to essentially different concepts (the first to similarity in functionality between different applications, the second to distributed use of the same application). Consequently, we saw that logically, "Duplication" alone could do the job:

2.a If an Application results from some Development, and that Application is not a Duplicate of
    another Application, then that Development is preferred by the Enterprise.

This boils down to the simple informal rule "no duplicate applications". Rule 2.a is stronger than rule 2, which it subsumes (i.e. makes it redundant). Its extensional interpretation includes duplicates that occur *within one organization*. To make absolutely sure this is correct (obvious thought it may seem), we should therefore validate rule 2.b:

2.b If an Application A [that is used in some Organization] results from some Development,
    and that Application is not a duplicate of any other Application that is used in the same Organization,
    then that Development is preferred by the Enterprise that includes Application A.

2.a would make 2.b redundant (just as it subsumes 2). However, perhaps this logic-based assumption should not be embraced too rashly. It seems equally reasonable to assume that 2 was put forward (and not 2b) to emphasize the preferred status of "acrossness" in application development. However, even if this were the case, and therefore principle 2 (or rather, the natural language equivalent thereof) was maintained, then still we would like rule 2.a and rule 2.b to be explicitly validated to safeguard the correct interpretation of principle 2.

Note that some assumptions made in the discussion above could be, and to some extent would need to be, formally verified or proven. For example:

- Does (1.a AND 1.b) indeed amount to 1.c?
- Does 2.a indeed logically subsume 2? Also, does 2.a indeed logically subsume 2.b?
- Does 2.b indeed fail to be logically covered by 2?

Formal reasoning in order to answer such questions is possible with ORC, as we have demonstrated in [6] (we cannot include the actual formal exercise here, for reasons of both space and relevance). A sufficiently accessible way of performing such formal reasoning would, in our conviction, be a welcome contribution to a set of tools that aims to support the formalization of principles.

4   Conclusion

In this case paper, we demonstrated and discussed the formal analysis, using ORM and ORC, of architecture principles. We provided two example analyses based on principles taken from the TOGAF architecture framework. First, we discussed why it seems a good idea to, at the least, explore the possibilities for formalizing architecture principles as declarative rules, inspired on the Business Rules Approach. Next, we reported in some detail the experiences and results of analyzing the two principles.

We found not only that such analysis is quite possible, but more importantly that it can lead to better understanding of and even improvement of the principles as such, so apart from their formalization. Using ORM and ORC for principle analysis helps give clear and unambiguous meaning to those principles. In our example case, it led to reconsideration of formulations (both informal and formal) that did not occur when we first read the principles in their original natural language form. However, one has to take care not to discard formulations that make explicit some specific stakeholder concern, even if they lead to redundancy in the model resulting from formal analysis.

We have based the interpretations that inevitably underlie each analysis on assumptions that were educated guesses; in a real analysis process, every assumption should have been validated by relevant stakeholders. However, we have also seen that the approach used makes it very clear which precise assumptions (and formulations thereof) are to be validated. Also, ORC provides us with means, beyond mere intuition, for verifying whether presumed logical relations between propositions in fact hold true. Instead of demonstrating such proofs in detail in this paper (which we have already done elsewhere, for similar cases), we identified them and indicated how they would help back up and consolidate the analysis of principles.

We have not included a way to explicitly show relations between principles. However, it seems possible to do this on the basis of overlap between ORM models of different principles and of shared terminological definitions.

References

1. A.C. Bloesch and T.A. Halpin. ConQuer: A Conceptual Query Language. In B. Thalheim, editor, *Proceedings of the 15th International Conference on Conceptual Modeling (ER'96)*, volume 1157 of *Lecture Notes in Computer Science*, pages 121–133, Cottbus, Germany, EU, October 1996. Springer, Berlin, Germany, EU.
2. D.S. Frankel. *Model Driven Architecture: Applying MDA to Enterprise Computing.* Wiley, New York, New York, USA, 2003.
3. T.A. Halpin. Business Rules and Object Role Modeling. *Database Programming and Design*, 9(10):66–72, October 1996.
4. T.A. Halpin. Business Rule Modality. In T. Latour and M. Petit, editors, *Proceedings of the Workshop on Exploring Modeling Methods for Systems Analysis and Design (EMMSAD'06), held in conjunctiun with the 18th Conference on Advanced Information Systems 2006 (CAiSE 2006)*, pages 383–394, Luxemburg, Luxemburg, EU, June 2006. Namur University Press, Namur, Belgium, EU.
5. A.H.M. ter Hofstede, H.A. (Erik) Proper, and Th.P. van der Weide. Formal definition of a conceptual language for the description and manipulation of information models. *Information Systems*, 18(7):489–523, October 1993.
6. S.J.B.A. Hoppenbrouwers, H.A. (Erik) Proper, and Th.P. van der Weide. Fact Calculus: Using ORM and Lisa–D to Reason About Domains. In R. Meersman, Z. Tari, and P. Herrero, editors, *On the Move to Meaningful Internet Systems 2005: OTM Workshops – OTM Confederated International Workshops and Posters, AWeSOMe, CAMS, GADA, MIOS+INTEROP, ORM, PhDS, SeBGIS, SWWS, and WOSE 2005*, volume 3762 of *Lecture Notes in Computer Science*, pages 720–729, Agia Napa, Cyprus, EU, October/November 2005. Springer, Berlin, Germany, EU.
7. Recommended Practice for Architectural Description of Software Intensive Systems. Technical Report IEEE P1471-2000, The Architecture Working Group of the Software Engineering Committee, Standards Department, IEEE, Piscataway, New Jersey, USA, September 2000.
8. M.M. Lankhorst and others. *Enterprise Architecture at Work: Modelling, Communication and Analysis.* Springer, Berlin, Germany, EU, 2005.
9. R. Meersman. The RIDL Conceptual Language. Technical report, International Centre for Information Analysis Services, Control Data Belgium, Inc., Brussels, Belgium, EU, 1982.
10. The Open Group. *TOGAF – The Open Group Architectural Framework*, 2004.
11. H.A. (Erik) Proper. ConQuer–92 – The revised report on the conceptual query language LISA–D. Technical report, Asymetrix Research Laboratory, University of Queensland, Brisbane, Queensland, Australia, 1994.
12. R.G. Ross, editor. *Business Rules Manifesto.* Business Rules Group, November 2003. Version 2.0.
13. SBVR Team. Semantics of Business Vocabulary and Rules (SBVR). Technical Report dtc/06-03-02, March 2006.

Using ORM-Based Models as a Foundation for a Data Quality Firewall in an Advanced Generation Data Warehouse

Baba Piprani

SICOM, Canada
babap@attglobal.net

Abstract. Data Warehouses typically represent data being integrated from multiple source systems. There are inherent data quality problems when data is being consolidated in terms of data semantics, master data integration, cross functional business rule conflicts, data cleansing, etc. This paper demonstrates how multiple Object Role Models were successfully used in establishing a data quality firewall architecture to define an Advanced Generation Data Warehouse. The ORM models realized the 100% Principle in ISO TR9007 Report on Conceptual Schemas, and were transformed into attribute-based models to generate SQL DBMS schemas. These were subsequently used in RDBMS code generation for a 100% automated implementation for the data quality firewall checks based on the described architecture. This same Data Quality Firewall approach has also been successfully used in implementing multiple web based applications, characteristically yielding 35-40% savings in development costs.

1 Introduction

Data Warehouses typically integrate data from multiple source systems. The term data warehousing generally refers to combining the data from many different databases across an entire enterprise, into a data warehouse database. The effort to bring together data from heterogeneous sources requires significant time and resources. Creating a multi-subject, consolidated information store requires reconciling the different data models involved. Data quality is one of the most overlooked challenges.

Several approaches have been described for the development of data warehouses, from simple hastily assembled data marts, to un-modeled, denormalized collections of SQL tables requiring extensive navigation, and to attribute based data models resulting in highly normalized SQL tables. The success rate for data warehouses based on these approaches is dismal to mediocre. Data warehouse failure rates or limited acceptance rates have been in the range of 92% (back in late 1990s) to greater than 50% for 2007 [1]—a dismal record indeed. Just like any engineering initiative, improperly designed data warehouses tend to experience significant rework to keep up with the changing business needs.

In its simplest incarnation, the data warehouse incorporates a direct feed from multiple sources, often using surrogate keys regardless of the source. If there is no conceptual model, this dumping of the data produces reconciliation nightmares. Data

R. Meersman, Z. Tari, P. Herrero et al. (Eds.): OTM Workshops 2006, LNCS 4278, pp. 1148–1159, 2006.
© Springer-Verlag Berlin Heidelberg 2006

brought together from multiple sources is often inconsistent because of conflicting business rules across system models pertaining to the shared or overlapping data.

The situation is exacerbated when the source system data models are attribute-based, because, in general, a good portion of the business rules that are "routine" in ORM based models are simply non-existent in the attribute based data models. In the author's 28-year experience in implementing several dozens of NIAM/ORM data models, the declaration and conformance to a business rule set has been the most critical factor contributing to a successful implementation of an application.

The ISO TR9007:1987 Technical Report on Concepts and Terminology for the Conceptual Schema and the Information Base [2], was a landmark effort in formalizing the role and content of a metadata driven implementation, stressing the need to declare 100% of the rules of the Universe of Discourse. The Reference Model of Open Distributed Processing [3] took this a step further with multiple viewpoints that are involved in implementations for a distributed environment.

The process of combining databases in an integrated DW involves semantic integration of information from multiple sources, requiring one to not only bring together common data representations, but also address the data's meaning and its relationships to other data and information, including associated business rule propositions. In other words, there needs to be a conceptual schema for the data warehouse.

In pre-DBMS and early DBMS days, 100% of the business rules resided in the application. With a typical early DBMS (hierarchical, network, CODASYL era), only 20% or so of the business rules could be enforced in the DBMS. Today, with a strong ISO SQL [4] complement, 100% of the rules are enforceable by a fully conforming ISO SQL DBMS, although current RDBMSs support only a subset of the standard.

Our task was to define a consistent architecture for data integration that supports dynamic changes in the business environment. The result was an advanced generation data warehouse architecture, that has its fundamental data model defined using ORM, and navigates the information flows through a series of Data Quality Firewalls.

The implementation in an RDBMS environment is maximally automated using dynamic SQL for the modules handling the flow of application data. Since al the rules were declared and implemented in the SQL schema environment (with minimal support from coded modules in the form of triggers and user defined functions), the code for information flow interface applications was automatically generated.

The foundation for the Advanced Generation Data Warehouse Architecture consists of the 6 building blocks shown in Table 1. The data warehouse derives from an ORM model that is transformed to an attribute based data model, then defined in an SQL schema that includes all the business rules declared in ORM. The resulting data model contains a mix of normal forms (3rd, 4th, 5th and Boyce-Codd Normal Form).

The thrust here is to maximize the schema declaration statements and minimize the use of triggers and stored procedures. The relationships and business rules are mapped to appropriate primary key, unique constraint, foreign key, CHECK, and default column value constraints. Other remaining non-directly-mappable business rules are implemented via SQL stored procedures, user defined functions or triggers.

The data warehouse physical model may include additional tables, pre-formed queries or procedures and other constructs to support data cleansing and data scrubbing activities. Additional constructs may need to be added to the generated models (e.g. additional indexes, temporarily disabling constraints and the like).

Table 1. Building Blocks for an Advanced Generation Data Warehouse

Building Block	Description	How Achieved
Data Quality/ Data Validation	Inspect data for errors, inconsistencies, redundancies and incomplete information;	Declare a strong ORM based data model with business rules, transform to an attribute based SQL schema, establish Data Quality Firewall, and validate data for conformance to business rules
Data Correction	Correct, standardize and verify data	Declare an ORM based mapping and transformation schema to assist the data quality firewall, transform to an attribute based SQL schema and Initiate correction process to data where necessary, or improve/modify return content
Data Integration	Match, merge or link data from a variety of disparate sources	Declare an ORM based semantic data model, transform to an attribute based SQL schema and consolidate the different data across the various classes of data from multiple sources to a unified set ensuring data integrity through the data quality firewall
Data Augmentation	Enhance data using information from internal and external data sources where appropriate and necessary	Declare an ORM based interface data model with dynamic business rules for behavior, transform to an attribute based SQL schema, and establish event driven business processes triggered through schema instance populations
Data Composition	Data requirements change in response to external changes, trends in industry, or governance	Declare an ORM based data model with dynamic business rules for behavior, transform to an attribute based SQL schema, address changes via event driven business processes triggered through schema instance populations
Persistent Data Chronology	Collect history and control data integrity over time	Declare an ORM based temporal data model, transform to an attribute based SQL schema, and maintain a time series of data for history, and to track and maintain changes of returns over time

2 The Advanced Generation Data Warehouse Framework

Fig. 1 shows our Data Warehouse Framework. The source system data is extracted into a staging area that simply mirrors the data structures of the source applications. The data structures of the staging area should not contain any integrity constraints and may represent a full set or subset of the source base tables or source viewed tables from which the data is being extracted. The source-to-staging extract generally undergoes some data transformation or selection, making the data ready for integration.

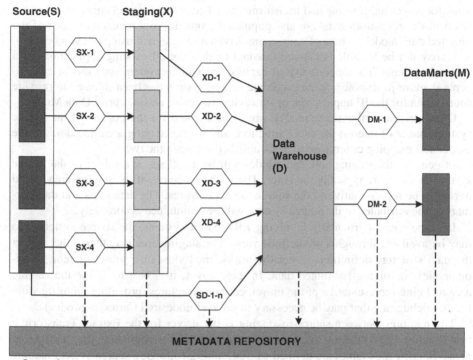

Fig. 1. Advanced generation data warehouse architecture

Legend: Mapping Schemas are shown as:
S - Source Systems   SXn: Source to Staging Area mapping for Source system n
X - Staging Area   XDn: Staging area to data warehouse mapping for Staged system n
D - Data Warehouse   DMn: Data Warehouse to Data Mart mapping for Data Mart n
M - Data Marts   SD1-n: Source to data warehouse mapping for Source Systems 1..n

Data then moves from the staging area to the data warehouse area, again with possible data transformation or selection, but this time the target data structures represent the normalized integrated data warehouse data model including a full set of integrity constraints resulting from ORM based business rules data model and analysis.

In selected cases, data can be extracted directly from the source area into the data warehouse area. The integrated data from the data warehouse is then extracted into data marts, again undergoing the necessary transformation and selection, to suit the Business Intelligence data requirements. No other extraction or transformation paths, either explicit or implicit, are permitted.

Considering there are several mappings involved amongst several components, the data warehouse framework needs to be adopted and implemented as shown. The advanced generation data warehouse architecture positions the various components of the data warehouse in relationship with the associated mappings.

The Meta Data repository has built-in mechanisms to provide several cross mappings between repository objects and data lineage. However, specific mappings need to be designed for cross model mapping via mapping schemas, including associated rules for selection, filtering and transformation. These mapping schema tables are defined in the repository database and populated from the row metadata values of the inputted data models. These of course, are driven and designed using ORM models.

It may not be feasible to capture the data models for all existing applications as a stand-alone task. The opportunity to capture the source system data model components is more justifiable when a candidate source system has been selected to provide source data for the BI application, or for review to derive an Enterprise Data Model.

ORM driven attribute data models are to be defined for the portion of the source system that is of interest for data extraction, and for the staging area. In addition, the associated mapping criteria are to be established between the two.

In general, the staging area data model will be a full set or a subset of the source system mode, more typically the latter. The table structures of the staging area would normally be representative of the source table structures. The data sizes and data formats of the attributes of the source system will be maintained accordingly.

In some cases, particularly involving ERP based systems, the source system data may be available through a pre-defined view. The staging area may then either reflect the data structure definitions as per the pre-defined view or a subset thereof, or another view involving pre-joined data. In these cases, it is best to define the staging area as being representative of the un-joined data structures, providing more freedom for any debugging that may be necessary to unravel undesired Cartesian products.

The mapping between source-to-staging is the driver for the Extract Transformation Loading (ETL) facility to extract data from source for populating into the staging areas. Staging area tables are defined as SQL tables, following source system naming conventions. This allows for these tables to be classified as external tables, and be treated as Foreign Tables as per SQL2003 in the future when these features are available in an SQL implementation. The source-to-staging area mappings are defined in the repository, with the staging area schema definitions declared in an SQL-schema.

The mapping between the staging area and the integrated data warehouse includes CAST definitions for data type transformations, cleansing algorithms, or any filtering criteria where applicable. The mapping schema should contain entries for the mapping between the source staging area and the target integrated data warehouse area.

The entries in the mapping schema should contain any CASTing rules i.e. transformation or conversion of data types in SQL2003 format, any filtering or merging/splitting criteria in SQL2003 syntax, to address the different mapping forms listed above. Data filtering, data transformation rules apply at all stages of transfer. Mappings between the DW and data mart models should also be maintained. The following information is relevant for Business Intelligence purposes and should be defined for each BI requirement: (1) business descriptions of target data elements, e.g. report and screen columns; (2) description of transformations from the data warehouse to data marts, e.g. algorithms, consolidation, aggregation; (3) description of data mart data load validation and control parameters e.g. control dates, min-max boundaries; (4) business descriptions of preformatted reports.

Data cleansing aims to ensure the integrity and quality of data, using rules for restructuring data elements, column value decoding and translation, supplying missing data element values, and applying rules for data integrity and consistency checking.

3 Data Warehouse Data Quality

Experience shows that an ORM driven attribute based data model is one of the most critical factors in the definition of data quality aspects for a data quality firewall. The advanced generation framework provides a stable platform to enable sustainable mechanisms for the establishment and maintenance of mappings. This same framework is now used to establish and position a data quality firewall as shown in Fig. 2. The Data Quality Firewall is a backbone for establishing data quality by the judicious use of two data areas: a holding area and the data collector area.

The holding area does not enforce any constraints. Data is simply transformed into the holding area from the staging area tables. The data collector area contains schema declarations for all integrity rules, using a 3NF database structure. The holding area acts as a transit point for the data to migrate from the staging area to the data collector area. Each row of data being loaded is first brought into the holding area tables from the staging area. Each row is given a unique row identity, and is tagged by a batch run identifier. No integrity checks other than data type checks are made at this time.

Any required transformations or selections or re-formatting to meet the data structuring requirements of the fully normalized data structures of the collector from the incoming source data structures as in the staging area, are done *en route* from the staging area into the holding area. Additional transformations may be conducted while the data is in the holding area for convenience as needed. A row in the holding area is prepared for a full data integrity check cycle at the data quality firewall.

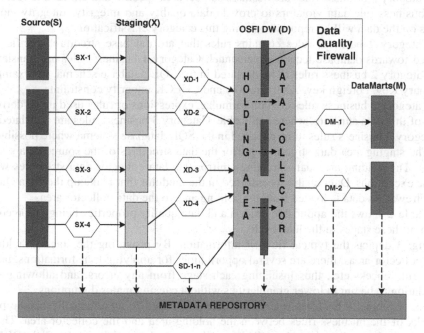

Fig. 2. Data quality firewall in the advanced generation data warehouse architecture

The Data Collector acts as a data collection point where business rules are enforced via SQL schema declarations (as derived from an ORM schema). The data collector area tables form the focal point for the integrity rule mechanisms. The modules of the data quality firewall selectively screen the data in the holding area for SQL constraint violations before transferring the data from the holding area to the data collector.

Business rules constrain the set of permissible values in a "data attribute" (as seen from the user's viewpoint). A business rule defines or constrains some aspect of the data belonging to an ORM fact type that maps to one or more attributes. Several business rules may pertain directly to the fact type or its relationship to other fact types.

Each ORM fact type must have at least one business rule associated with it. Data quality in the data warehouse depends on the degree to which the warehouse data conforms to the SQL integrity constraints which are derived from the consolidation of user requirements, business rules, and data models as derived from ORM modeling.

Audit and Control of data quality is driven directly by the declaration of the SQL integrity constraints that are named and declared in the SQL database schema.

To facilitate a user-driven pre-ORM modeling analysis phase, three categories of business rules were declared and a form was handed to the user whenever there was a requirement seen for a 'new data item' in the enterprise. The business rules were categorized into three types to assign responsibility, and to drive the constraint violation notification process in the implementation phase. For example Category 1 business rule notifications go to end-users, while category 2 and 3 notifications are funneled to data administrators for further action during operation.

Category 1 business rules are business subject area specific and are used to identify the business rule data violators to provide data quality and integrity. Integrity violations on the data will be reported on using this category classification.

Category 2 business rules contains rules that are database structure specific directed towards database technical personnel. Category 1 business rules are translated to Category 2 business rules to be declared in the SQL database schema, for example Primary Key, Foreign key, Alternate Key and CHECK integrity constraints.

Category 3 business rules contain formulae, expressions or rules used in the derivation of this data attribute, where applicable. Category 3 business rules are translated to Category 2 business rules to be declared in the SQL database schema where possible.

The staging area data structures mirror the data structures of the source data structures. The holding area data structures mirror the data collector data structures with some exceptions. Data quality is enforced in the modules that make up the Data Quality Firewall as data is loaded from the holding area to the data collector area.

Table 2 shows the applicable criteria and data quality properties being enforced at each of these stages in the load cycle.

Fig. 3 depicts the typical flow of information. By providing the staging, holding and collector areas, there are several opportunities for applying transformations, business rule checks etc., thus insulating each stage from any errors, and allowing any validation to be run in lower granularities without causing major disruptions.

For example, a business rule engine was developed to automatically handle prechecks of the business rules between the holding area and the collector area. These business rules declared in the ORM model are implemented via the SQL DBMS based business rule engine modules that can be selectively applied at different stages.

Table 2. Properties of Staging, Holding Area and Data Collector Tables

Property	Staging Area Tables	Holding Area Tables	Data Collector Tables
Data Structure	Same or sub-set/view of source	Same as Collector but without PK or FK	Full Third Normal Form (3NF) normalized
Table Naming Standards	Based on source + X (for external Tables)	Based on Data Collector + RPR (holding area for repair)	Local Table naming standard
Column Naming Standards	Same as source column	Same as Data Collector column	Local Column naming standard
Data type checks	Yes	Yes	Yes
Assign unique row id for each row	No	Yes	Carry over from Holding Area
Assign batch run id	Optional	Yes	Carry over from Holding Area
Primary Key	No key	Row IDENTITY	Natural Key
Unique Constraints	No	No	Yes
Foreign Keys	Optionally yes (for internal housekeeping batch run id)	No (except for internal housekeeping batch run id)	Yes
Data integrity checks	Optional (within same row only)	No	Yes
Data Validated	Optional (within same row only)	No	Yes
Usage during loading	Local incremental extract	Intermediary for transform & pre-check	Merge/Insert
Usage after loading	Archived upon acceptance of batch run	Emptied except for violator rows	Fully validated (except for Soft Inserts)

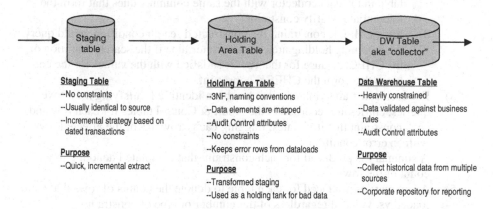

Staging Table
--No constraints
--Usually identical to source
--Incremental strategy based on dated transactions

Purpose
--Quick, incremental extract

Holding Area Table
--3NF, naming conventions
--Data elements are mapped
--Audit Control attributes
--No constraints
--Keeps error rows from dataloads

Purpose
--Transformed staging
--Used as a holding tank for bad data

Data Warehouse Table
--Heavily constrained
--Data validated against business rules
--Audit Control attributes

Purpose
--Collect historical data from multiple sources
--Corporate repository for reporting

Fig. 3. Process flow through the advanced generation DW architecture

The data quality firewall enforces data quality checks during the data load process for the data collector using 5 distinctly separable mechanisms as declared in the SQL schema in this order: Primary Key constraint; Uniqueness constraint; Foreign Key constraint; CHECK constraint; Trigger. Each constraint is named as per the local constraint naming standard and maps to a business rule declared in the ORM model.

Each of the data quality firewall enforcement modules except the trigger module is generic and is generated automatically. Except for triggers, each module consists of dynamic SQL statements with parameterized entries for the qualified table name. Trigger modules are individually scripted to address special and specific situations of integrity constraints, including inter-table assertions. Each module, except for the trigger module, essentially has the same processing set of operations. Each module, except for the trigger, receives the <table name> and a <run id> as input parameters.

The module performs the following operations:

1) Determine the applicable SQL integrity constraints by interrogating the extended Information Schema tables in the Audit Control schema.
2) Scan the corresponding holding area table populations with a dynamic query that is constructed from each of the applicable constraint type for the <table name> and <run id>. The constructed query interrogates the incoming rows to check the validity of the applicable constraint as noted below:
   a) For a primary key PK, the constructed search condition would query the incoming holding area rows to determine if there is a corresponding row in the data collector table with the same column values that form the Primary Key constraint.
   b) For a uniqueness constraint, the constructed search condition would query the incoming holding area rows to determine if there is a corresponding row in the data collector table with the same column values that form the uniqueness constraint.
   c) For a foreign key constraint, the constructed search condition would query the incoming holding area rows (forming the referencing column values) to determine if there is a corresponding row in the referenced table in the data collector with the same column values that form the referential integrity constraint.
   d) For a CHECK constraint, the constructed search condition would query the incoming holding area rows to determine if the search condition of the CHECK clause for that row is satisfied with the values for the columns that form the CHECK constraint.
3) For each constraint violation that has been identified satisfying the above queries, entries are recorded in the Audit & Control tables for each row and each constraint that it violates, flagging each <row id> of the affected row with an error condition.
4) A summary is produced for each constraint that is violated denoting the count of the rows
5) A summary is produced for each table to denote the counts of rows that were loaded vs. violated regardless of the number or type of constraints.
6) Load the data collector tables with only the rows that do not contain any violations as identified by the Audit & Control table for constraint violations

7) Delete the corresponding rows in the holding area that have been loaded in the data collector. A row cannot exist in both tables with the exception of a temporary 'soft insert' condition.

8) In a 'soft insert' condition, the violated row is to be loaded in the data collector notwithstanding the constraint violation. This is done by disabling the constraint on the data collector table, loading the row(s), and re-enabling the constraint with a NOCHECK to prevent the DBMS from determining any violations for existing rows. Note this can only be performed for CHECK constraint violations. Other constraint violations cannot be circumvented by a 'soft insert'. In the case of the 'soft insert' a corresponding row will exist in the holding area until the constraint violation condition has been removed.

Regardless of the number of tables, there is only one module for a given type of integrity constraint check, i.e. one each to handle a PK, Unique (AK), FK and CHECK constraint, in total 4 modules. The same module can address PK and AK constraints.

4 Data Warehouse Audit and Control

This section briefly addresses audit and control during data loading. The emphasis is on monitoring data integrity and data quality issues during the loading process over the stages as defined in the architecture. Audit and Control addresses two aspects to enable decision making in the loading process: detection of the occurrence of bad quality data; prevention of the occurrence of bad quality data.

Prevention is achieved mainly via non-automated means by the user analyst or designated personnel reviewing the results of the Audit and Control data and enabling decisions to proceed further in the loading process.

It is necessary to maintain an audit trail of the rows being loaded at each Extract-Transform-Load (ETL) process in the DW environment. The audit control data to be collected varies from simple number counts, to sanity counts, to validation counts, depending on the processes involved in the transformation or load cycle.

At a minimum, the basic audit control information required for each data load at any point in the load life cycle includes the number of occurrences loaded or rejected, as well as statistics such as start date-time of load run, end date-time of load run, identification of a load run, user identification of load operator, and type of run (incremental, full, periodic load, initial, test load etc.). Additional information is collected for data validation, or data cleansing runs, pre-BI aggregation or pre-join runs.

The metadata repository is used to define a supplemental support model in the extended Information Schema, which contains constructs to capture these additional metadata occurrences. This model is realized via an external SQL Server database.

An ORM based load control model (and transformed to SQL schema) is defined to support the required statistics and audit control information during the load process. The load control model is defined via the extended information schema of entities/tables that contains metadata describing the audit and control requirements. The extended information schema series of tables hold data for the audit and control, and are populated for every load operation in the data warehouse.

Statistics are collected for every load run for any given table, qualified by a given database, at every Audit Control Point (ACP). An Audit Control Point is established at every ETL run as shown in Fig. 4.

The attributes and statistics measured vary by ACP, starting from simple counts-in, counts-out, to more detailed data quality violations at each progressive ACP. These attributes and statistics are grouped into attribute groups as shown in Table 3. Attribute groups measure groups of applicable attributes depending on levels of data loadings and data quality availability over the load process.

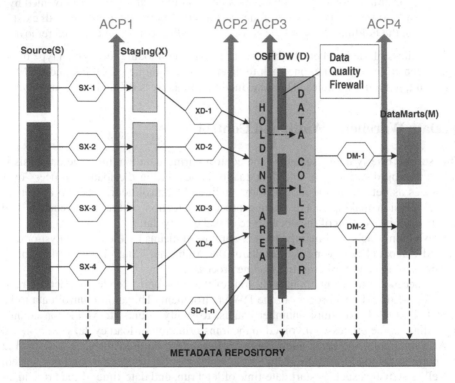

Fig. 4. Audit control points in the data warehouse framework

Table 3. Correlation of Audit Control Points and Required Attribute Groups

Audit Control Point	Required Attribute Group at ACP
ACP1	Basic Counts, Input Format Check, Go-Nogo Threshold Check
ACP2	Basic Counts, Go-Nogo Threshold Check
ACP3	Basic Counts, Enhanced Threshold Check, Sanity Check, Validation Counts, Integrity Violations By Row
ACP4	Basic Counts, Go-Nogo Threshold Check, Sanity Check, Validation Counts, Integrity Violations By Row

5 User Experiences

The ORM based advanced generation data warehouse and firewall approach has proven successful in developing very large data warehouses and web based applications. Previous incarnations of these applications minimally existed (or struggled to exist) and were developed on poorly defined attribute-based data models. The production environment of these applications was essentially a glorified prototype.

The use of ORM for the fundamental semantic models, and subsequent transformation to attribute based models using CASE tools, with final implementation based on strong ISO SQL adaptations of RDBMSs, resulted in a 100% success rate, including award winning implementations [5]. Typically, the data warehouses and applications developed using ORM were completed ahead of schedule, with measured savings of 35-40% realized over the entire project costs. More importantly, the implementation worked the first time around with a 95-98% correctness of the data model fit to user requirements, because of the discipline and rigor inherent in the ORM approach.

In the author's 36 years experience of systems development, and having reviewed 100s of data models, I have yet to come across an application designed with attribute based data modeling that has all the business rules readily defined **and** implemented! Here "all" uses an ORM yardstick of 100% rule set, because, most of the time the analysts and developers comment that they would never have even "thought" of the business rules that were discovered via ORM.

The data warehouse architecture and associated data quality firewall modules described in this paper were implemented 100% over the years from 1997 onwards. ORM was the foundation used in the development of the components and the stages constituting the design of the advanced generation data warehouse architecture itself.

An extended metamodel for the architecture was developed in ORM, with the accompanying Audit and Control Framework and Data Quality Firewall becoming a by-product of the business rule conformance set required for the realization of the ORM data warehouse data model. What would the world be without ORM?

References

1. Gartner Group Report: see Gartner Press Release, 24 Feb 2005, Gartner Website – Media relations http://www.gartner.com/press_releases/pr2005.html
2. ISO/IEC TR9007:1987 Technical Report on Concepts and Terminology for the Conceptual Schema and the Information Base: editor: Joost van Greutheuysen, International Standards Organization, Geneva.
3. ISO/IEC 10746-1, 2, 3, 4: Reference Model of Open Distributed Processing (RMODP), International Standards Organization, Geneva.
4. ISO/IEC 9075-1, 2, 3, 4, 9, 10, 11, 13, 14 Database Language SQL, 2003.
5. TC Express, a Transport Canada publication referencing Government of Canada Technology Week (GTEC) bronze medal awarded towards the implementation of a strategic information management application e-Directory at Transport Canada, 2002. See http://www.tc.gc.ca/TCExpress/20021112/en/fa05_e.htm.

Evolution of a Dynamic Multidimensional Denormalization Meta Model Using Object Role Modeling

Joe Hansen and Necito dela Cruz

4100 Hamline Ave N, St. Paul, MN USA 55112
Joe.Hansen@Guidant.com,
Necito.delaCruz@Guidant.com

Abstract. At Guidant, a Boston Scientific Company, systems that collect data in support of medical device clinical research trials must be capable of collecting large, dynamic sets of attributes that are often reused in later research activities. Their resultant design, based on conceptual analysis using Object Role Modeling (ORM), transforms each unique business fact into an instance in a highly normalized star schema structure with related dimensions. When it becomes necessary to generate focused denormalized reporting structures from this star schema, hereafter referred to as miniature data marts or simply "mini marts", the dynamic nature of these source attributes can present a maintenance challenge. Using ORM, we propose a meta model that supports the definition, creation, and population of these denormalized reporting structures sourced from a multidimensional fact table that also leverages a hierarchical taxonomic classification of the subject domain.

1 Introduction

The types of data collected at Guidant for medical device clinical research activities pose unique challenges to research managers, data analysts, developers, database administrators, and data modelers. In many cases, the set of business facts or attributes collected may vary from one research study to the next as different aspects or new features of devices are examined. In addition, these varying attributes may be grouped into hierarchical structures of attributes based on a classification of the clinical domain.

A significant complication of these environments occurs in the generation and maintenance of denormalized reporting structures. Due to the large number of attributes involved, there is a clear need to generate these mini marts in a manner that takes full advantage of their hierarchical nature.

Given these characteristics, the domain of database applications for clinical research data collection and analysis demands a metadata-driven solution. Fortunately, an analysis of the problem using ORM reveals a metadata approach that accurately models the various attributes gathered, leverages a structured classification of the domain, and supports the definition, generation, and population of these mini marts sourced from a multi-dimensional fact table.

R. Meersman, Z. Tari, P. Herrero et al. (Eds.): OTM Workshops 2006, LNCS 4278, pp. 1160–1169, 2006.
© Springer-Verlag Berlin Heidelberg 2006

2 Multi-dimensional Model

For the purposes of developing a universally understandable and non-proprietary example throughout the course of this paper, we will examine sales data collected by a hypothetical vehicle manufacturer. The manufacturer wishes to track a large number of business facts for each of its vehicle sales across its full product line. The actual attributes tracked will vary based on the type of vehicle sold; personal vehicles will have different attributes from commercial vehicles, cars will have different attributes from trucks, and so forth.

In order to organize the manufacturer's array of vehicle offerings, it has classified its product offerings into a product hierarchy. This hierarchy begins with a root vehicle node, to which all products belong. Next, it arranges the company's products into three core business units: personal, commercial, and industrial. The hierarchy then decomposes each business unit into a general vehicle type and finally vehicle model. By classifying their product lines in this way, the manufacturer has set the stage for capturing different sets of attributes for vehicles in different parts of the hierarchy. An abbreviated version of the taxonomy is shown in Figure 1.

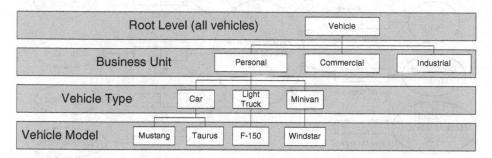

Fig. 1. Abbreviated Vehicle Manufacturer Product Hierarchy

The manufacturer wishes to have one data repository that will store all relevant attributes for all vehicle sales, including new attributes that may be required as the system matures or new product lines are introduced. To address this need, the vehicle manufacturer has set up a multi-dimensional database to track these attributes for each vehicle sale. At the core of this database is a fact table, each row of which represents an instance of a user defined dynamic attribute. Each row is also related to several common dimensions, allowing the manufacturer to track for each sale the date sold, the dealership recording the sale, and the vehicle's location in the product hierarchy ("F-150 Truck" or "Minivan", for example). Example rows from this table may be found in Table 1.

Table 1 implies that the manufacturer has a number of standard attributes, including Color and Warranty End Date, which may be tracked for all vehicles sold. In addition, there are a number of dynamic attributes that are specific to the type of vehicle sold. In this example, attribute Towing Capacity applies to the F-150 vehicle model and Top Type applies to the Mustang vehicle model. A model of the manufacturer's fact table can be found in Figure 2.

Table 1. Sample Vehicle Manufacturer's Dynamic Attribute Fact Table

Sur	Sale Sur	Date Sur	Dealer -ship Sur	Product Hier- archy Node Sur	Dynamic Attribute Name	Dynamic Attribute Data Type	Numeric Value	Date Value	Text Value
1	1	2	30	1 (F-150 Truck)	Color	Text			Blue
2	1	2	30	1 (F-150 Truck)	Warranty End Date	Date		2-Mar-2009	
3	1	2	30	1 (F-150 Truck)	Towing Capacity	Numeric	4000		
4	2	10	150	20 (Mustang)	Color	Text			Red
5	2	10	150	20 (Mustang)	Warranty End Date	Date		4-Mar-2008	
6	2	10	150	20 (Mustang)	Top Type	Text			Fabric

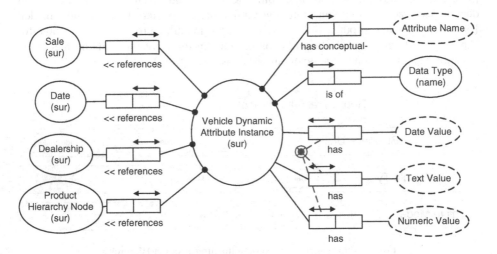

Fig. 2. Multi-Dimensional Fact Table Model

As the above model specifies, each Vehicle Dynamic Attribute Instance is identi-fied by a surrogate key. The actual attribute value is mapped to either a Numeric Value, Date Value, or Text Value based on the business fact "Vehicle Dynamic Attribute is of Data Type". In addition, each instance is associated to the common reporting dimensions: Sale, Date, Dealership, and Product Hierarchy Node.

3 Attribute Repository

An attribute repository may be created to store all of the metadata related to the dy-namic attributes and dimensions in the manufacturer's database. A model for this repository is shown in Figure 3. This model supports the storage of both the business-defined dynamic attributes and the attributes that come from the common dimensions of the source fact table. Both types of attribute are subtypes of a common attribute object, to which metadata is attached for the purpose of mini mart creation.

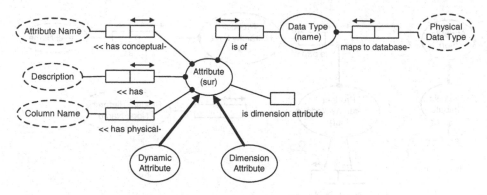

Fig. 3. Attribute Repository Model

Several sample dynamic attributes that the manufacturer wants to track can be seen in Table 2. Each attribute is defined with a name and description and is then assigned to a particular node in the product hierarchy. A product hierarchy node is any position in the manufacturer's dynamic hierarchy; sample nodes from Figure 1 include "Vehicle", "Commercial", "Light Truck", and "Mustang". Note that nodes inherit dynamic attributes from their parents in the hierarchy; an attribute attached to the "Light Truck" node is also relevant to that node's "F-150" child node.

Table 2. Sample Dynamic Attributes for the F-150 Truck Product Hierarchy Node

Dynamic Attribute Name	Vehicle Hierarchy Node	Description
Warranty End Date	Vehicle	The date that the vehicle's warranty expires
Engine Size	Vehicle	The size of the vehicle's engine, in liters
Color	Vehicle	The exterior color of the vehicle
Trade-in Value	Personal	The value, in USD, of a trade-in applied to this vehicle purchase
Suspension Capacity	Light Truck	The load limit of the truck's suspension, in kilograms
Towing Capacity	Light Truck	The maximum load the truck can tow, in kilograms
Seat Configuration	F-150	The arrangement of the seats inside the F-150's cab
Rear Window Type	F-150	The type (e.g., sliding, fixed) of rear window in the F-150's cab

A more detailed look at the dynamic attribute subtype is shown in Figure 4. This model defines the dynamic attribute's relationship to a node in the manufacturer's product hierarchy. Exemplifying this relationship is the Towing Capacity dynamic attribute, which is related to the Light Truck vehicle hierarchy node. When this mapping is done within the attribute repository, the Towing Capacity dynamic attribute becomes relevant for all vehicles of type Light Truck, including child nodes that may be added at a later date.

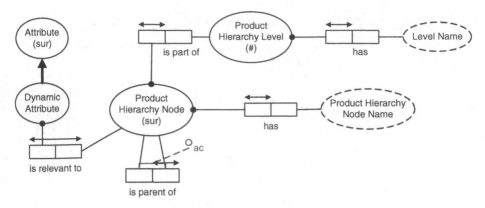

Fig. 4. Dynamic Attribute Model

The model above also provides for the dynamic definition of the product hierarchy itself via an acyclic ring relationship "is parent of" on the Product Hierarchy Node object. This structure allows for the dynamic construction of a taxonomic tree of indefinite depth, allowing the manufacturer's product hierarchy to evolve with its business.

Examining the dimension attribute subtype reveals its relationship to the dimensions of the manufacturer's fact table, as shown in Figure 5. This model allows the manufacturer to store metadata regarding the dimensions of its fact table. As an example, the dealership dimension may contain dimension attributes for dealership name, dealership phone number, and dealership manager. A unary "is identifying" fact on the dimension attribute assists with SQL generation by flagging the attribute or attributes that serve as a primary key for each dimension.

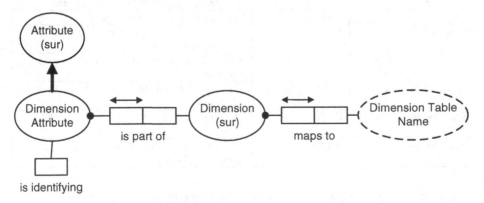

Fig. 5. Dimension Attribute Model

4   Denormalized Reporting Structure (Mini Mart)

A common reporting requirement for our vehicle manufacturer may be to generate separate reporting tables for different models of vehicles, each of which would bring together the various dynamic attributes associated with that model. An example of one such table is shown in Table 3, a mini mart constructed for the F-150 product hierarchy node.

Table 3. F-150 Truck Mini Mart

Sale Sur	Date	Dealership Name	Model	Color	Warranty End Date	Engine Size	Suspension Capacity	Towing Capacity
1	2-Mar-2006	Western Motors	F-150 Truck	Blue	2-Mar-2009	5800	750	4000
3	2-Mar-2006	Southern Motors	F-150 Truck	Red	2-Mar-2010	4600	500	3500
6	3-Mar-2006	Eastern Motors	F-150 Truck	Black	3-Mar-2009	5800	750	3500
9	6-Mar-2006	Southern Motors	F-150 Truck	Blue	6-Mar-2010	6800	750	4000

An analysis of the denormalized table shown above yields the model presented in Figure 6. This model displays the denormalized attributes as assigned to a data row concerning the sale of a vehicle of type F-150.

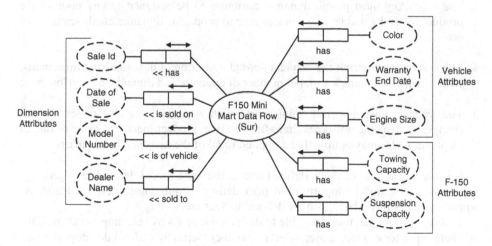

Fig. 6. F-150 Truck Sale Mini Mart Model

In addition to showing the attributes for a single denormalized data row, the model above also provides some insight into the grouping of attributes based on vehicle model. Suspension Capacity, for example, exists in this mini mart because it is relevant to sales of vehicles of type F-150 truck. If an attribute were to be added to the set of F-150 truck attributes, one could reasonably expect that it should be added to this mini mart as well. Color, on the other hand, belongs to a set of attributes relevant to all vehicle sales. Several other attributes, such as Dealer Name, are derived from the source fact table's dimensions.

Though the source fact table contains all of the information necessary to produce mini marts such as Table 3, the maintenance of numerous such structures can become problematic for two reasons. First, it is difficult to keep track of which dynamic attributes are relevant to a given product hierarchy node, especially because some of these attributes may be relevant for all vehicles sold or numerous classifications of vehicles. Secondly, it is difficult to properly adjust all affected tables when a dynamic attribute is added or changed.

5 Denormalized Reporting Structure Meta Model

Given the nature of the manufacturer's data and reporting needs, it can be seen that a suitable data analysis system in this environment must have the following characteristics:

1. The system must support the creation of a metadata repository for dynamic and dimensional attributes containing both a logical description and physical details.

2. The repository must support the logical classification of the manufacturer's product line into a dynamic hierarchy of varying depth.

3. The repository must permit dynamic attributes to be assigned to any node in the product hierarchy and leverage inheritance to propagate dynamic attributes to child nodes.

4. The system must permit the metadata-based definition of denormalized mini marts, each of which contains a variable number of dynamic and dimensional attributes.

5. The system must associate mini marts with product hierarchy nodes so that changes to dynamic attributes that affect a given product hierarchy node or one of its parent nodes may optionally be applied to all of the associated mini marts.

Mindful of the requirements defined above, the meta model defined in Figure 7 is proposed. This model supports mini mart definition utilizing dimensional and dynamic attributes from the repository defined in Section 3.

Through this model, users are able to define mini marts by selecting items from the attribute repository. Once a user selects a product hierarchy node to develop a reporting structure for, the system would be capable of providing a list of attributes relevant to that particular node.

This model also facilitates the construction of a mini mart repository. This repository would serve to list at a high-level the many available reporting structures, encouraging their re-use and providing a platform for further metadata enhancement. A sample of this repository for our hypothetical vehicle manufacturer is shown in Table 4.

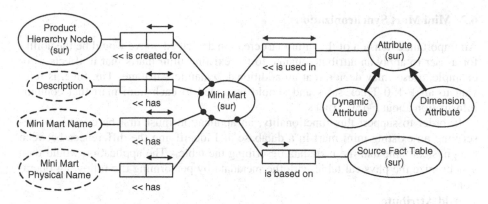

Fig. 7. Mini Mart Meta Model

Table 4. Mini Mart Repository

Mini Mart Sur	Mini Mart Name	Mini Mart Description	Vehicle Hierarchy Node	Attributes
1	F-150 Sales	All sales of F-150 light trucks	F-150	Dealership Name, Color, Engine Size, Towing Capacity...
2	Personal Sales	All sales of personal vehicles	Personal	Dealership Name, Color, Trade-in Value...
3	Car Sales	All car sales	Car	Dealership Name, Color, Transmission Type...

6 Physical Database Functionality

Once a repository of both attributes and mini marts has been established, a natural and valuable extension would be to support the creation, synchronization, and population of these reporting structures from the source fact tables. As mentioned above, this capability is supported by the addition of physical attributes in the meta model.

For the purposes of this paper, DDL scripts have been given in Oracle format. It is anticipated that an application implementing the model proposed in this paper would support the generation of such DDL scripts in formats acceptable to most common DBMS packages.

6.1 Mini Mart Creation

The first essential physical mini mart function would be the generation of empty database tables from the mini mart metadata. In this function, the repository would generate DDL scripts similar to the following:

```
CREATE TABLE <Mini Mart Physical Name> (

<Attribute n Column Name> <Attribute n Physical Type>);
```

6.2 Mini Mart Synchronization

An important extension of the mini mart creation described above would be the ability for a user to apply an attribute change to the existing mini marts that it affects. For example, a user may decide that an additional Dynamic Attribute, Tire Size, is relevant to all F-150 Truck sales and should be added to each mini mart that contains information about F-150 Trucks.

In order to support this functionality, an application must first be capable of describing an existing mini mart in a database and identifying the differences between the physical table and the metadata describing the table. The application would then synchronize the physical table with the metadata by performing the following operations:

- **Add Attribute**

```
ALTER TABLE <Mini Mart Physical Name> ADD <Attribute
Column Name> <Attribute Physical Type>;
```

- **Drop Attribute**

```
ALTER TABLE <Mini Mart Physical Name> DROP <Attribute
Column Name>;
```

6.3 Mini Mart Population

A final function of a system designed to manage research data collection and analysis would be the automated population of mini marts from the normalized fact tables. This function would also be possible by leveraging the mini mart meta model and the attribute repository.

Essential to the population of mini marts is a common key that can be used to tie the multiple fact table rows for a particular denormalized data row together. In the mini mart example in Table 3, the Sales Sur fulfills this role. This fact is tracked via the unary "is identifying" fact in the meta model of Figure 6. This supports the generation of SQL similar to the following:

```
INSERT INTO <Mini Mart Physical Name>

SELECT DISTINCT <Identifying Column Name>

FROM <Fact Table Name>;

UPDATE <Mini Mart Physical Name> INNER JOIN <Fact Table
Name> ON <Mini Mart Physical Name>.<Identifying Column
Name> = <Fact Table Name>.<Identifying Column Name>

SET <Mini Mart Physical Name>.<Column Name n> = <Fact
Table Name>.<Dynamic Attribute Text/Numeric/Date Value>

WHERE <Fact Table Name>.DynamicAttributeName = '<Dy-
namic Attribute n Name>';

UPDATE <Mini Mart Physical Name> INNER JOIN <Fact Table
Name> ON <Mini Mart Physical Name>.<Identifying Column
Name> = <Fact Table Name>.<Identifying Column Name>
INNER JOIN <Dimension Table Name> ON <Mini Mart
```

```
Physical Name>.<Dimension Identifying Column Name> =
<Dimension Table Name>.<Dimension Identifying Column
Name>

SET <Mini Mart Physical Name>.<Dimension Column Name n>
= <Dimension Table Name>.<Column Name>;
```

Note that the common case involves creation of mini marts at a reasonably granular level, such as a listing of vehicle sales. By inserting aggregate operations into the SQL above, an analysis application could generate summarized mini marts providing, for example, sales totals per dealership.

7 Conclusion

The types of data collected by clinical trials and other research activities can pose unique challenges for reporting environments. The hierarchical nature of attributes collected, the dynamic nature of these attributes, and the need to efficiently create, maintain, and populate a large number of denormalized reporting structures requires a metadata-driven solution. Using the ORM data modeling technique, it can be shown that such a solution is possible that supports these functions based on user-maintained metadata and allows organizations to leverage the investment made in the accurate classification of their business environment.

Fact-Oriented Modeling from a Programming Language Designer's Perspective

Betsy Pepels[1,3], Rinus Plasmeijer[1], and H.A. (Erik) Proper[2]

[1]Software Technology, [2]Information Retrieval and Information Systems
both of Radboud University Nijmegen, The Netherlands
[3]Informatics and Communication Academy,
HAN University of Applied Science, The Netherlands
{betsy, rinus, E.Proper}@cs.ru.nl

Abstract. We investigate how achievements of programming languages research can be used for designing and extending fact oriented modeling languages. Our core contribution is that we show how extending fact oriented modeling languages with the *single* concept of *algebraic data types* leads to a natural and straightforward modeling of complex information structures like unnamed collection types and higher order types.

1 Introduction

In this paper we consider modeling languages based on the fact-oriented paradigm [1]. The most well known are ORM [2] with its successor ORM2 [3], NIAM [4], FCO-IM [5], and PSM [6]. This group of closely related dialects we will call fact-oriented modeling (FOM) languages.

FOM has proven to be a powerful approach; yet for some information structures *easier or more intuitive* modeling facilities could be available. For instance types being types themselves (categorization types), unnamed collection types, and the crossing of levels/metalevels are difficult to model [7]. In [8] various modeling problems are addressed, like the identification of Dutch Cabinets, which we present in Section 4.

Throughout the above and related publications there is an on-going, but less structured and less explicit discussion about the *necessity* to introduce new modeling concepts. For instance, PSM extends the basic FOM expressive facilities with concepts like *Set* and *Sequence* to model unnamed sets.

In this paper, we take part in both discussions yet from a different angle: we treat FOM languages from the perspective of programming languages theory, and especially one of its sub-disciplines, type theory. Programming language theory makes a distinction between expressiveness being conceptually *essential* and expressiveness being *convenient*. Type theory provides the formal basis for the design, analysis and study of type systems. Type systems offer many powerful possibilities for modeling data structures.

Our aim is to demonstrate that achievements of programming languages theory can fruitfully be used for designing and extending FOM languages. As our

R. Meersman, Z. Tari, P. Herrero et al. (Eds.): OTM Workshops 2006, LNCS 4278, pp. 1170–1180, 2006.

core contribution we show in the Sections 3 and 4 that extending the *essential* expressiveness of FOM languages with the *single* concept of *algebraic data types* allows a natural and straightforward modeling of the aforementioned information structures and many others too.

We conclude with a brief sketch of some of the expected benefits and the research questions arising when FOM languages are extended following the programming languages approach.

2   Achievements of Programming Language Theory

In this subsection we give a short summary of the approach commonly accepted for the (formal) design of programming languages [9] and we introduce algebraic data types as well.

2.1   Formal Design of a Language

The expressive possibilities of languages are layered, as illustrated in Figure 1. The basis of formal languages is a *computational model*. Examples of computational models are the Turing machine, the lambda calculus, the relational algebra and Petri nets. The *aim* of a computational model is to establish a mathematical foundation for computations possible in a language. A computational model is a mathematical model and commonly has a simple and clear semantics.

With the computational model the essential computational *power* of the language is defined: every computation possible in the language has to be expressible in the computational model too.

On this mathematical foundation a core language is defined. The big difference between a computational model and a language is that the latter is meant to define programs in and that it can be executed on a suitable platform. Compared to the computational model, a core language does not have more *computational* power, only more con-

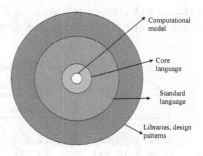

Fig. 1. Layering

venience. It offers additional constructs to support programming, for instance module structures. Every construct in the core language has either a direct counterpart in the computational model, or can be translated to it.

The core language is often extended with all kinds of syntactic constructs for convenient programming. An example is the (Java and C construct) i++ which is used for expressing a loop counter. This syntactically extended language is the *standard* language programmers work with. It is geared towards practicability and usability.

Most often a plethora of facilities enabling further ease of programming is available, like libraries, design patterns etc. All these facilities have in common that they are basically *programs* using the language defined by the lower layers.

Examples of languages defined this way are SQL (based on the relational algebra), workflow languages like YAWL [10] (based on Extended Workflow Nets which are again based on Petri nets), functional programming languages like Haskell [11] and Clean [12] (based on term rewriting systems which are again based on the lambda calculus) and the .NET framework [13].

It might be clear that no sharp distinction between the several layers can be made. Computational models are often layered themselves. Furthermore, some expressive feature of a language might be found either in the core language, in the standard language, or in libraries.

2.2 Algebraic Data Types

We briefly introduce algebraic data types. In the next section we will show how algebraic data types can be part of FOM models. An algebraic data type is a language construct known from the functional programming languages field. It can be regarded as a grammar with which new types can be defined. We explain this by a well-known example, the List data type:

:: List a = Cons a (List a) | Nil

For the notation we adopt the notation used in the functional programming language Clean. The :: is a keyword indicating the beginning of a type definition. The definition should be read as the type List (holding elements of any type *a*) is *either* (indicated by the symbol |) the Cons of an element of type *a* and a List or Nil (the empty list). Square brackets [] are often used as a shorthand notation for lists. Examples of lists can be found in Table 1.

Table 1. Example lists

Example list	Shorthand notation	Which list?
Nil	[]	the empty list
Cons 1 (Cons 2 Nil)	[1,2]	the list consisting of the integers 1 and 2
Cons 3.14 Nil	[3.14]	the list consisting of the real 3.14

This List data type is *recursive*: the constructor Cons holds sub-values of the type List. It is also *polymorphic*: a List can hold values of *any* type.

In algebraic data types there is a difference between *types* and *terms*. List Int is a type and the list Cons 1 (Cons 2 Nil) is a term.

Type systems and hence algebraic data types are commonly specified by grammars. In Figure 2 we give a grammar for the definition of an algebraic type using EBNF notation. This grammar is taken from [12]; we will use it also in the next sections. {q}+ means one or more appearances of q. Terminals are denoted in capitals, non-terminals in lower case. The underlined symbols are terminals as well, to make a distinction between similar symbols of the grammar itself. Note that the grammar also describes algebraic data types that are not well-formed.

One of the (many) well-formedness requirements is that a type variable used in the right hand side should be defined in the left hand side of the definition too.

3 Extending Fact-Oriented Modeling Languages

In this section we will demonstrate how, using the approach described in Section 2, FOM languages can be extended. Distinguishing between fundamental expressiveness and convenient expressiveness is applicable to FOM languages as well. There is however a difference with programming languages: FOM is not primarily meant to write programs in and is not expected to be *executed* (yet).

```
algebraicTypeDef = ∷ typeLhs = constructorDef {| constructorDef}
typeLhs = typeConstructorName {typeVariable}
constructorDef = constructorName {type}
type = typeVariable | TypeConstructorName | (type) | basicType
basicType = Int | Real | Char | Bool | String
typeConstructorName :== String
typeVariable :== String
```

Fig. 2. Grammar describing algebraic data types

3.1 A Grammar for Basic FOM Structures

As for the algebraic data types, we give in Figure 3 a grammar describing basic structures of fact oriented models. Our grammar describes what we consider to be a core FOM language. We limit ourselves considerably: we only describe a language for the *structure* of fact oriented models, not (yet) taking into account specialization and generalization, and leave out aspects like constraints as well. These restrictions however do not influence the generality of our discussion.

```
model = {namedtype}+
namedtype = facttype | objecttype
facttype = (NAME identifier, FT {role}+)
objecttype = (NAME identifier, OBJ identifier)
role = (PB roleplayer)
roleplayer = labeltype | identifier // identifier must be existing name
labeltype = LB identifier
identifier :== String
```

Fig. 3. Grammar describing FOM structures

We describe *the* basic characteristic of FOM structures: their basis in *facts*. Our grammar only provides for expressing fact types (in the grammar: FT), label types (in the grammar: LB) and objectification (in the grammar: OBJ). Roles are either played by (in the scheme: PB) label types or by items in the scheme that have a *name* (which is used to refer to them), the latter being either fact types or object types. In the next subsection we will explain how other constructs can be translated to the language defined by this grammar.

One of the well-formedness requirements for this grammar is that if a role is played by an identifier, this identifier must be the elsewhere defined name of a fact type or object type. Note furthermore that the grammar just produces fact oriented models in a mechanical manner: the *syntax* of the language. Its *semantics* have to be assigned separately. For FOM this is commonly done using set theory, for instance in [14]. Following the layered scheme of Section 2.1, we could designate set theory the *computational model*.

Example model. The same (well-formed) model defined by the grammar is expressed textually in Figure 4 and diagrammatically in Figure 5.

```
(NAME ft1, FT (PB (LB lb1)))
(NAME o1, OBJ ft1)
(NAME ft2, (PB o1) (PB o1))
(NAME o2, OBJ ft2)
(NAME ft3, FT (PB o2) (PB lb2))
```

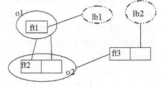

Fig. 4. Example scheme as text   **Fig. 5.** Example scheme as diagram

3.2   Mapping Non-basic Structures to Basic Structures

Our grammar defines a core language. FOM languages like FCO-IM, ORM and PSM allow more constructs than our grammar defines; for instance ORM and PSM have *Objects* which are not defined by our grammar. Following the layered scheme we introduced in Section 2.1, we will now point out how some particular constructs of these FOM languages can be mapped to the language defined by our grammar.

Mapping example 1. The structure of FCO-IM schemes is very much like those defined by our grammar. Each label and fact type in an FCO-IM scheme directly correspond to a similar label and fact type in our computational model. FCO-IM is fully communication oriented and hence every fact type (unary and higher) must be accompanied by a *sentence*. Such a sentence can be mapped to our language by objectifying the original fact type and adding a fact type expressing the sentence, as

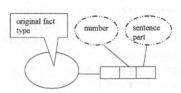

Fig. 6. Mapping of sentence

demonstrated in Figure 6. The fact type in the figure is to be read as "The fact type ⟨Fact type⟩ has as ⟨number⟩ th sentence part ⟨sentence part⟩.".

Mapping example 2. The ORM and ORM2 languages (and NIAM as well) have *Entity types*. These are not directly defined by our grammar, but can be translated to objectified unary fact types. ORM objects are required to have an identification, which is naturally accomplished this way.

Some constructs cannot be mapped to our core language:

Non-mapping example. PSM has the *Set* and *Sequence* type enabling the modeling of unnamed collections. With the *Set* type a fact type like "Trainer ⟨Name⟩ trains team ⟨Set of Player⟩." can be phrased. Such a structure fundamentally cannot be expressed in our core language.

The Set type is just one of the many examples of a *collection* type: a type encompassing a collection of members and having certain characteristics (like no duplicates for Set and an order for Sequence). Collection types are analyzed in [15].

FOM languages struggle with collection types, especially when they are unnamed. Many strategies to tackle this problem have been proposed, like introducing types for kinds of collections (in PSM), the extensional uniqueness constraint [16] thus avoiding complex semantics, higher order logic [17], and avoiding the problems at all by remodeling to a first-order scheme.

Our way to address this problem is by adding algebraic data types to the fundamental expressiveness of FOM languages.

3.3   Adding Algebraic Types to Fact Oriented Models

Our core idea is to allow that in FOM schemes *roles* can be played by algebraic data types as well. This we express by updating our grammar (see Figure 7).

```
roleplayer = labeltype | identifier | algebraictype
algebraictype = typeConstructorName roleplayer
```

Fig. 7. Updates to grammar for FOM structures

The definition of the algebraic data type itself is not part of the scheme, but is to be given *separately* as a kind of program text.

A graphical notation for an algebraic data type has to be chosen. As yet, we pick *just one* of the many diagrammatic possibilities: a rectangle with the name of the type in it. Independent of which representation is chosen, somehow in the scheme it should be referred to the algebraic data type.

Illustrating example. A ToDo list, identified by its name, holds a list of tasks, identified by their names. Using the List type defined earlier we can phrase the fact type "The ToDo list ⟨Name⟩ holds tasks ⟨List Task⟩". This is illustrated in Figure 8. A example fact is "The ToDo list *Urgent* holds tasks *[Finish research proposal, Mark recent exams]*."

The observant reader will notice that in fact types (algebraic) *types* are used, whereas facts use *terms*.

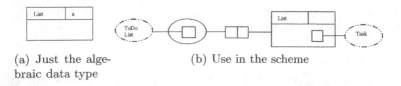

(a) Just the alge-   (b) Use in the scheme
braic data type

Fig. 8. Picturing algebraic data types

4   Modeling Examples

We now demonstrate with some examples how algebraic data types can be used for easy and straightforward modeling of complex information structures.

Unnamed list. For a medical survey, (only) the sex and birth dates of children of the involved families are recorded. Families are identified by a `FamilyId` (a number). Conceptually, per family an unnamed list of combinations of sex and birthdate is recorded. We define the following types:

```
:: ChildInfo = Info Sex Date
:: Sex = Male | Female
:: Date = D Year Month Day
```

Now the information recorded for a family is a `List` of `ChildInfo`, and for the information structure we phrase the fact type: "Family ⟨`FamilyId`⟩ has children's info ⟨`List ChildInfo`⟩." Some example facts are: "Family *23987* has children's info *[]*." and "Family *56342* has children's info *[Info Female (D 2001 12 5)]*." and "Family *34231* has children's info *[Info Male (D 2002 3 25), Info Male (D 2002 3 25), Info Female (D 2003 11 16)]*.", the last family having a male twin.

Identification of Dutch cabinets. The following example we borrow from [8]. The authors artfully solve this problem and others too by using generalization and by allowing null values in populations having a uniqueness constraint as well.

In the Netherlands a cabinet is named after its Prime Minister. For instance the Cabinet Den Uyl governed from 1973 to 1977. When a Prime Minister serves more than one term, the corresponding cabinets are named I, II, III, etc. For instance, the Cabinets Lubbers I, Lubbers II and Lubbers III were three successive cabinets governing from 1982 to 1994. To model this information structure, we define the following type:

```
:: CabinetName = OneTerm String | MoreTerms String RomanInt
:: RomanInt = ...
```

We now can phrase the fact type "The term of cabinet ⟨`CabinetName`⟩ started in the year ⟨`Year`⟩." Some example facts are: "The term of cabinet *(OneTerm Den Uyl)* started in *1973*." and "The term of cabinet *(MoreTerms Lubbers I)* started in *1982*.".

Set type. The well-known game of Quamsplash [5] is played by unnamed teams consisting of players identified by their name. Teams play matches against each other. To model this information structure, we define the algebraic data type:

```
:: Set a = E | S a (Set a) // E for Empty Set
```

Sets do not have duplicate members. Notice that such a property can not expressed with an algebraic data type, but should be implemented by access functions of the data type.

With the above `Set` type, and assuming that the type `PlayerName` is a string, a match is described by the fact type "⟨Set PlayerName⟩ plays against ⟨Set PlayerName⟩". An example fact is "Team *Set Guido E* plays against team *Set (Jan Pieter (Set Marko (Set Fazat E)))*.", or using the shorthand notation with curly brackets {} "Team {*Guido*} plays against team {*Jan Pieter, Marko, Fazat*}."

Higher order types. We present an information structure that is very much like the example in [7], which was again borrowed from [17].

ACME (A Company that Makes Everything) produces everything. Table 2 is a tiny part of the data available about ACME, presenting a list of its best selling products and some of their attributes. The third column specifies the colors in which a product is made by ACME. Some products can be enhanced with options, given in the fourth column. For example, for the *Portable hole* is made in two colors and optionally can be provided with an *Explosive* and/or a *Fence*. The last column indicates what attributes of the product are up to the costumer to be chosen. For instance, although the *Mojo* is manufactured in two colors, the customer cannot choose: the color is a surprise upon receipt.

Notice that Table 2 only gives information about ACME products, not about actual choices of customers.

Table 2. Best selling products of ACME

Prod.	Product name	Possible colors	Options	Customer chosen
101	Personal jetpack	{Green, Brown}	–	{Colors}
102	Inflatable submarine	{Yellow}	{Restroom}	{Options}
701	Portable hole	{Black, Grey}	{Explosive, Fence}	{Colors, Options}
1001	Mojo	{Pink, Purple}	–	{}

To elucidate the modeling problem, we quote from [7]: "First, it is in non-first normal form, allowing unnamed sets as entries (for instance Colors). ⟨snip⟩ Secondly, its final attribute (column) allows as entries unnamed sets whose instances appear to be attributes themselves, thus crossing levels/metalevels."

Using the standard FOM approach, this information structure either can be treated directly but then higher order logic is needed, or it is to be transformed to a first order scheme. Using algebraic data types, modeling can be done almost straightforwardly, because both metalevels and levels are just types. We define the following types (assuming that `ColorName` and `OptionName` are both strings):

```
:: Colors = Set ColorName
:: Options = Set OptionName
:: CustomerChoice = C Colors | O Options
:: CustomerChosen = Set CustumerChoice
```

Table 3 gives the fact types and example facts using the types defined above, where furthermore **no** is a number and **name** is a string.

Table 3. Fact types and example facts

Fact type (using types)	**Example fact** (using terms)
Product ⟨no⟩ has name ⟨name⟩.	Product *1001* has name *Mojo*.
Product ⟨no⟩ has possible colors ⟨Colors⟩.	Product *701* has possible colors {*Black, Grey*}.
Product ⟨no⟩ has options ⟨Options⟩.	Product *102* has options {*Restroom*}.
For product ⟨no⟩ may be chosen by customer ⟨CustomerChosen⟩.	For product *101* may be chosen by customer {*C Colors*}.

5   Reflection, Conclusion and Future Work

We showed how fact oriented models can be extended with algebraic data types, using the approach from the programming languages field. Thus we obtain natural and straightforward modeling of complex information structures like unnamed collection types and higher order types.

By introducing algebraic data types, we move from set theory and first order logic as formal foundation of FOM to type theory, the latter having its origins in the Principia Mathematica by Russell and Whitehead [18]. Set theory and type theory were both answers to paradoxes arising from naive set theory. Set theory together with classical logic is the standard foundation of modern mathematics, whereas type theory is one of the major pillars of computer science.

By regarding fact oriented models from the programming language perspective (by regarding them as types), a wealth of results from decades of programming language research might become applicable. We briefly mention the most interesting *research issues*:

Abstraction. Type theory provides for mechanisms for the definition of many more advanced types, like abstract data types and quantified types. Furthermore, type systems offer tremendously powerful abstraction mechanisms, which are one of the core features of functional programming languages. Abstraction is a heavily desired feature for fact oriented models, as many authors previously pointed out [19], [20], [21], [22].
Integration of functionality. With programming languages data structures are defined (using types) as well as algorithms manipulating these data structures. By having types as basis for fact oriented modeling languages we can integrate functionality very naturally into information models. An apparent example

are abstract data types, which define a specification of a set of data and the set of operations that are allowed on the data.

Implementation. With the definition of complex data types in fact oriented models, problems with mapping them to a target platform (for example relational tables) arise. This is a major research subject. A promising starting point is polytypic programming [23], using transformations working on types (models). Research for mapping types to relational tables can be based on this technology, together with the already existing orthogonal persistence of any type in files [24].

In our opinion it would be valuable to start a discussion in the fact oriented modeling community whether and how FOM languages could be designed and extended following the approach we sketched.

References

1. T.A. Halpin and M.E. Orlowska. Fact–oriented modelling for data analysis. *Journal of Information Systems*, 2(2):97–119, April 1992.
2. T. Halpin. Object-role modeling (ORM/NIAM). In P. Bernus, K. Mertins and G. Schmidt, editors, *Handbook on Architectures of Information Systems*. Springer Verlag, 1998.
3. Terry Halpin. ORM 2. In Robert Meersman, Zahir Tari, and Pilar Herrero, editors, *On the Move to Meaningful Internet Systems 2005: OTM 2005 Workshops*, volume 3762 of *LNCS*, pages 676–687, 2005.
4. G. M. Nijssen and Terry Halpin. *Conceptual Schema and Relational Database Design*. Prentice Hall, 1989.
5. G.P. Bakema, J.P.C. Zwart, and H. van der Lek. Fully communication oriented NIAM. In *NIAM-ISDM 1994 Conference, Working Papers*, pages L1–L35, 1994.
6. A.H.M. ter Hofstede and Th.P. van der Weide. Expressiveness in conceptual data modelling. *Data & Knowledge Engineering*, 10(1):65–100, February 1993.
7. Terry A. Halpin. Information modeling and higher-order types. In *CAiSE Workshops (1)*, pages 233–248, 2004.
8. Guido Bakema, Jan Pieter Zwart, and Harm van der Lek. *Volledig Communicatiegeorinteerde Informatiemodellering FCO-IM*. Academic Service, The Netherlands, 2005. Textbook in Dutch. The English version can be downloaded via http://www.casetalk.com/php/index.php?FCO-IM%20English%20Book.
9. Benjamin C. Pierce. *Types and programming languages*. MIT Press, Cambridge, MA, USA, 2002.
10. W.M.P. van der Aalst and A.H.M. ter Hofstede. YAWL: yet another workflow language. *Information Systems*, 30(4):245–275, 2005.
11. Simon Peyton Jones et al. *Haskell 98 Language and Libraries: the Revised Report*. Cambridge University Press, 2003.
12. Rinus Plasmeijer and Marko van Eekelen. *Concurrent CLEAN Language Report (version 2.0)*, December 2001. http://www.cs.ru.nl/~clean/.
13. http://www.microsoft.com/net/default.mspx. The .NET website.
14. Arthur H.M. ter Hofstede. *Information Modelling in Data Intensive Domains*. PhD thesis, University of Nijmegen, The Netherlands, 1993.
15. Terry Halpin. Modeling collections in UML and ORM.

16. A.H.M. ter Hofstede and Th.P. van der Weide. Deriving Identity from Extensionality. *International Journal of Software Engineering and Knowledge Engineering*, 8(2):189–221, June 1997.
17. Melvin Fitting. Databases and higher types. In *CL '00: Proceedings of the First International Conference on Computational Logic*, pages 41–52, London, UK, 2000. Springer-Verlag.
18. Bertrand Russell and Alfred North Whitehead. *Principia Mathematica*. Cambridge University Press, 1910–13.
19. L.J. Campbell, T.A. Halpin, and H.A. (Erik) Proper. Conceptual Schemas with Abstractions – Making flat conceptual schemas more comprehensible. *Data & Knowledge Engineering*, 20(1):39–85, 1996.
20. P.N. Creasy and H.A. (Erik) Proper. A Generic Model for 3–Dimensional Conceptual Modelling. *Data & Knowledge Engineering*, 20(2):119–162, 1996.
21. Mustafa Jarrar. Modularization and automatic composition of object-role modeling (ORM) schemes. In *OTM Workshops*, pages 613–625, 2005.
22. C. Maria Keet. Using abstractions to facilitate management of large ORM models and ontologies. In *OTM Workshops*, pages 603–612, 2005.
23. Ralf Hinze. Generics for the masses. In *ICFP '04: Proceedings of the ninth ACM SIGPLAN international conference on Functional programming*, pages 236–243, New York, NY, USA, 2004. ACM Press.
24. M.R.C. Pil. Dynamic types and type dependent functions. In Kevin Hammond, Tony Davie, and Chris Clack, editors, *Implementation of Functional Languages (IFL '98)*, volume 1595 of *LNCS*, pages 169–185. Springer Verlag, 1999.

Automated Verbalization for ORM 2

Terry Halpin and Matthew Curland

Neumont University, Utah, USA
{terry, Matthew.Curland}@neumont.edu

Abstract. In the analysis phase of information systems development, it is important to have the conceptual schema validated by the business domain expert, to ensure that the schema accurately models the relevant aspects of the business domain. An effective way to facilitate this validation is to verbalize the schema in language that is both unambiguous and easily understood by the domain expert, who may be non-technical. Such verbalization has long been a major aspect of the Object-Role Modeling (ORM) approach, and basic support for verbalization exists in some ORM tools. Second generation ORM (ORM 2) significantly extends the expressibility of ORM models (e.g. deontic modalities, role value constraints, etc.). This paper discusses the automated support for verbalization of ORM 2 models provided by NORMA (Neumont ORM Architect), an open-source software tool that facilitates entry, validation, and mapping of ORM 2 models. NORMA supports verbalization patterns that go well beyond previous verbalization work. The verbalization for individual elements in the core ORM model is generated using an XSLT transform applied to an XML file that succinctly identifies different verbalization patterns and describes how phrases are combined to produce a readable verbalization. This paper discusses the XML patterns used to describe ORM constraints and the tightly coupled facilities that enable end-users to easily adapt the verbalization phrases to cater for different domain experts and native languages.

1 Introduction

To help ensure that a conceptual schema accurately models the universe of discourse, the schema should be validated by a business domain expert. One effective way to facilitate this validation is to *verbalize* the schema in language that is both unambiguous and easily understood by the domain expert, who may be non-technical. Various proposals and tools exist to facilitate verbalization of business rules. The RuleSpeak sentence templates [19] provide basic rule verbalization patterns, but their informal nature obviates automatic transformation into executable code. The Object-oriented Systems Analysis (OSA) model [6] supports high level, informal rules as well as formal rules in a predicate calculus notation. Our approach instead uses a single language that is both formal and conceptual, so that it can serve for communication and validation with domain experts, as well as being executable. While its motivation is similar to that of Common Logic Controlled English (CLCE) [20], its syntax is higher level (e.g. pronouns are often used instead of variables), and it is designed for ease of localization into different native languages.

R. Meersman, Z. Tari, P. Herrero et al. (Eds.): OTM Workshops 2006, LNCS 4278, pp. 1181–1190, 2006.

In industry, the most popular high level information modeling approaches are the Entity-Relationship (ER) approach [5] and the Unified Modeling Language (UML) [18], with dialects of Object-Role Modeling (ORM) [e.g. 2, 8] arguably being in third place. The Barker ER approach [3] provides a discipline for relationship readings that enables internal uniqueness and mandatory constraints to be verbalized. The NaLER [1] approach extends this somewhat. However these approaches handle only a small fragment of ORM constraints, are restricted to binary relationships, and are unsuited to verbalizing fact instances. For textual expression of rules, UML advocates the use of the Object Constraint Language (OCL) [21], but the syntax of this language is too mathematical to enable reliable validation by non-technical business domain experts.

While many ORM languages exist for model specification, such as RIDL [16] and LISA-D [15], few tools support automatic verbalization of ORM models. In the 1990s, one of the authors specified automated support for verbalization in ORM [7], and later extended this for Microsoft's ORM source model solution [14]. More recently, we specified and implemented a substantially improved verbalization mechanism for Neumont ORM Architect (NORMA) [17], an open-source tool for entering second generation ORM (ORM 2) [10] models and transforming these to application code. In addition to catering for new features in ORM 2, such as deontic modality, role value and explicit subtyping constraints, we now support improved verbalization in both positive and negative forms, including verbalization of the set-based nature of spanning uniqueness constraints, and the absence of relevant constraints [9].

While preliminary versions of a few of our simpler verbalization patterns have appeared in popular journals [e.g. 11], this paper is the first to discuss the detailed specification and implementation of the verbalization patterns. Section 2 provides a brief overview of verbalization support in NORMA. Section 3 specifies some typical verbalization patterns. Section 4 details how the verbalization engine is implemented in NORMA, including reasons for certain design decisions. Section 5 summarizes the main results, suggests topics for further research, and lists references.

2 Overview of Verbalization in NORMA

Our verbalization language for ORM 2 was architected to meet five main design criteria: expressibility, clarity, flexibility, localizability, and formality [9]. For expressibility reasons, both alethic and deontic *modalities* are supported [12]. Localization concerns as well as support of natural verbalization for predicates of any arity dictated use of *mixfix* predicates (e.g. ... introduced ... to ... on ...). For clarity and flexibility reasons, constraint verbalizations may be presented in *positive or negative form* (showing how to satisfy or violate the constraint), and may use *relational or attribute style* (employing predicate readings or role names) or a mix of the two.

NORMA automatically verbalizes whatever part of the ORM model is currently selected. As a simple example, Fig. 1 displays a NORMA screen shot showing the automated verbalization in positive form of three fact types along with seven constraints (four alethic and three deontic). The mandatory and uniqueness constraints on the top binary fact type in Fig. 1 are verbalized in positive form thus: **Each** Person was born in **exactly one** Country.

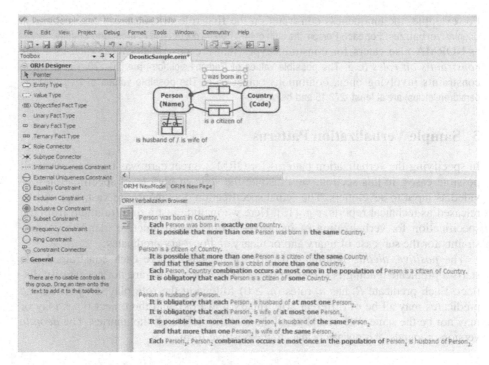

Fig. 1. Screenshot of positive verbalization in NORMA

The *absence of a uniqueness constraint* on the right-hand role is verbalized: **It is possible that more than one** Person was born in **the same** Country. Pressing the "–" button re-displays the constraints in negative form: **For each** Person, **it is impossible that that** Person was born in **more than one** Country; **It is impossible that any** Person was born in **no** Country.

The uniqueness constraint spanning both roles of the citizenship fact type specifies both that the association is many:many, and that its population must be a *set* rather than a bag of facts. These two aspects are verbalized separately: **It is possible that more than one** Person is a citizen of **the same** Country **and that the same** Person is a citizen of **more than one** Country; **Each** Person, Country **combination occurs at most once in the population of** Person is a citizen of Country. The constraints discussed so far are *alethic* (they are logical or physical necessities and hence cannot be violated).

Deontic constraints (marked graphically with "o") indicate rules that ought to be obeyed but may possibly be violated. As a simple example of deontic verbalization, the left deontic uniqueness constraint in Fig. 1 is verbalized in positive form thus: **It is obligatory that each** Person is a husband of **at most one** Person. In negative form, we have: **For each** Person$_1$, **it is forbidden that that** Person$_1$ is a husband of **more than one** Person$_2$.

Forward hyphen binding treats the word before the hyphen as an adjective (e.g. a uniqueness constraint on the first role of Person has first- GivenName verbalizes as "**Each** Person has **at most one** first GivenName."). As new features, NORMA also caters for *reverse hyphen binding* (e.g. Student has Preference -1 may be used instead of Student has first- Preference) and predicates with *front text* (text before the first object placeholder).

For example, the uniqueness constraint on the first role of the birth of Person occurred in Country verbalizes: **For each** Person, the birth of **that** Person occurred in **at most one** Country.

NORMA also caters for constraint types that are new in ORM 2, such as *value constraints on roles* (e.g. **The possible values of** Person.height(cm) **are** [20..270].) and value constraints involving open, continuous ranges (e.g. **The possible values of** NegativeTemperature(Celsius) **are at least** -273.15 **and below** 0.).

3 Sample Verbalization Patterns

In specifying the verbalization patterns for ORM 2, great care was taken to cover all possible cases. In this section, we illustrate the style of high level specification provided as input to developers. The actual specification documents are vast, and will be released as technical reports, e.g. [13]. Here we include just a tiny fragment from the specification for verbalization of inclusive-or (ior, i.e. disjunctive mandatory) constraints for the sub-case of unary and/or binary and/or n-ary predicates.

The *positive, alethic relational* pattern for the case where each constrained role starts a predicate reading is shown in Fig. 2. The object types are not necessarily distinct. Each predicate R_i has n_i roles ($n_i \geq 0$) following the role played by A. So the predicates may all be of different arity (unary upwards), and the object types may or may not be the same. We verbalize all the binaries before all the unaries. The *deontic* version prepends "**it is obligatory that**" to the positive form.

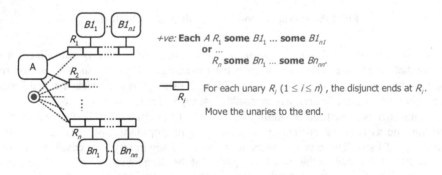

Fig. 2. Inclusive-or verbalization pattern when each constrained role starts a predicate reading

Examples: **Each** Partner became the husband of **some** Partner on **some** Date
or became the wife of **some** Partner on **some** Date.

It is obligatory that
each Vehicle was purchased from **some** BranchNr of **some** AutoRetailer **or** is rented.

If even one predicate in the previous case has *front text*, the pattern in Fig. 3 (some constrained roles do not start a predicate reading) is used instead. If any R_i predicate contains front text, this is included as part of the predicate reading. The *positive, alethic relational* pattern is shown. The object types are not necessarily distinct. If A plays more than one role in at least one of the R_i predicates, we subscript its instances to distinguish them. Each predicate R_i may have *ni* roles ($ni \geq 0$) plus the role played by A.

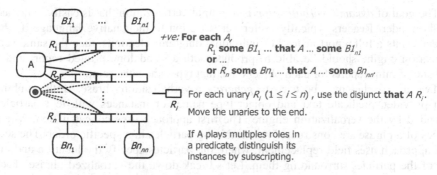

Fig. 3. Ior verbalization pattern when some constrained roles don't start a predicate reading

Examples: **For each** Partner₁,
                 on **some** Date **that** Partner₁ became the husband of **some** Partner₂
                 or on **some** Date **that** Partner₁ became the wife of **some** Partner₂.

It is obligatory that for each Vehicle,
         some BranchNr of **some** AutoRetailer sold **that** Vehicle
         or that Vehicle is rented.

4 Implementation in NORMA

This section briefly outlines how verbalization support is implemented in NORMA. Implementing a verbalization pattern needs care because the number of potential variations is very high. A conservative estimate is that a full ORM verbalization implementation coded by hand requires 10,000-15,000 lines of code, or about 6 person months. Incremental maintenance costs would also be extremely high due to the size of the code. To succeed both short term and long term, we decided to use a pattern-driven generative approach to implement the code whenever possible.

The rules for verbalization of a constraint pattern are constant, but the actual text used for different parts of the verbalization depends on environment-specific factors.

1. Although our reference implementation uses English, verbalization in other languages should incur only incremental implementation costs.

2. The same verbalization engine should be able to render different output formats. NORMA's verbalization window will display html, but we may want different html for a report view, and plain text in other views.

3. Personal verbalization preferences are also an environment factor. For example, by default we do not show the implied "It is necessary that" before positive alethic constraints. However, any skilled user should be able to choose to see the explicit form, or rephrase it (e.g. "The following condition is necessary: ").

4. A skilled user should be able to easily adapt the verbalization output to the current target audience (e.g. replace the default deontic "it is obligatory that" with "It ought to be that" or even a personalized '*CompanyName* policy requires that').

The goal of *dynamic verbalization* is to output verbalization that is easily validated by the reader. Readers typically prefer verbalization in their native language. If the reader wants a full report instead of individual diagram selections, then the same verbalization engine should be able to produce both a standalone printed report and a website of mini-reports for each object type, fact type, and constraint.

Two approaches may be used to *generate* a verbalization phrase. Both combine user-provided predicate text and object type names or instances with text particles provided by the verbalization engine. The first approach uses concatenation, where pieces of a phrase are constructed by combining particles in a specific order. The second approach uses field replacement, where the particles specify the location and order of the particles surrounding them. Let's break down the verbalized phrase "**Each** Person was born in **some** Country" using both approaches.

To use *concatenation* to verbalize this phrase requires seven strings to be combined in the correct order. Arbitrary predicate text requires arity+1 strings. In this case, the three predicate strings are {"", " was born in ", ""}. In addition to the predicate strings, the user-provides the object type names {"Person", "Country"}. The verbalization engine then provides the universal quantifier "**each** " and the existential quantifier "**some** ". The specified pattern (a simple mandatory constraint on a binary predicate where the mandatory role begins a predicate reading) is now built as follows. Though not shown here, each verbalization starts with a capital letter and ends in a period ".".

"" + "**each** " + "Person" + " was born in " + "**some** " + "Country" + ""

In practice, generating formatted text is significantly more complicated because each particle must include formatting specifications before and after the text, thus tripling the number of text particles necessary to complete the phrase.

The *field replacement* approach uses numbered replacement fields. We'll show these in the format required for the .NET System.String.Format function, which uses (regular expression) "\{\d+\}" to denote a zero-based replacement field in a format string. For example, "{0}" in a format string is the placeholder for the first replacement field. The Format function takes a format string as the first argument, followed by arguments for the replacement fields. For our current phrase, the predicate text is "{0} was born in {1}" and the quantifiers become "**each** {0}" and "**some** {0}". The equation now looks like:

REPLACE("{0} was born in {1}", REPLACE("**each** {0}", "Person"), REPLACE("**some** {0}", "Country"))

Note three immediate advantages to this approach. First, the model stores a single predicate text with replacement fields instead of arity+1 strings. Second, adding formatting specifications to verbalization-provided quantifiers does not increase the number of snippets or increase the algorithmic complexity. Third, order dependency is eliminated: "**each**" may come before "Person" in English, but other languages may have some quantifiers either after or around a given replacement field. Using the concatenation approach would require new code for each language or before/after specification for every phrase. The replacement approach removes all ordering and formatting considerations from the code, placing the onus for ordering on the snippets.

Using field replacement exclusively in the ORM2 verbalization engine allows all *snippets* to be specified as user-modifiable data. Concatenation is used only for list generation and incorporates user-specified list separators. Using field replacements simplifies the verbalization engine and enables data-driven snippet sets to be specified according to both language and user preferences. Snippets are considered dynamic data; how they are combined is specified statically for each verbalized model element.

Given the decision to employ field replacement, the next step was to identify components and determine which pieces should be generated and which ones hand coded. Two primary factors weighed in this decision: First, how often is the code reused? Code generation is generally cost effective only if the generator is applied to more than one piece of data. Second, how complex is the mapping from the verbalization specification to the generated code? The more complex the pattern, the more vital it is to concisely represent that pattern as data, allowing the resulting verbalization implementation to be indirectly modified by changing the input data to the generator.

The implementation was eventually broken down into the following components:

1) The *selection manager* determines which elements are to be verbalized, applies all phrase delimiters such as capitalization and punctuation of sentences, adds lines between selected elements, and indents verbalization phrases for aggregated elements. A good selection management routine allows individual elements to concentrate on self-verbalizing without worrying about the context in which they are verbalized. Selection management routines reference dynamic snippets for document header and footer information, punctuation, and white space, but are otherwise hand coded. The engine recognizes the IVerbalize interface implemented by individual elements.

2) The *snippet manager* determines which snippet variations are available on the user's machine. Snippets can be specified by the core model and any other extension model (the core is not given preferential treatment). User-authored XML files provide customization. The snippet manager presents the user with the available snippets (in the options page), then validates and loads the files. The reference implementation of each snippet set is coded into the application to protect the engine from rogue customizations. The snippet manager is hand-coded, while the snippet set implementation is generated. XML for the reference snippet set is installed but never loaded.

The selection and snippet management components provide the necessary framework for individual elements to verbalize themselves. From the selection manager perspective, an element can be verbalized if it implements the IVerbalize interface. This paper focuses on the XML patterns used to represent the complex patterns in the verbalization specification. Individual element verbalization is difficult and involves precise translation from specification to code. Representing the specification in XML provides a formal, unambiguous representation of the expected verbalization in a form that can be easily verified and modified. Given the XML, generating IVerbalize interface implementations is an XSLT exercise that is beyond the scope of this paper.

Various XML constructs are needed to fully reflect the verbalization specification. The Snippet element, referencing a snippet name, is the only obvious construct. The number of children inside a Snippet tag corresponds to the number of replacement fields expected. The XML schema then revolves around different ways to specify replacement fields, often recursively. The difficulty is to specify conditions to determine which snippet combinations to use. Conditions come in many different forms.

1) *Differences in modality* (alethic or deontic) *and sign* (positive and negative verbalization) are primarily handled by providing different snippets with the same name. Retrieving a snippet by {name, modality, sign} instead of just {name} takes care of the largest variability in specifying which snippet to use. It is possible to specify

radically different verbalizations for sign and modality, but the majority of the cases, especially with modality, have the same pattern with minor variations in the snippet. For the common case, no additional XML is required to switch modality and sign.

2) *Differences in the shape of constraints.* These differences revolve around the number and arrangement of roles and are represented by the *ConstrainedRoles* tag. Possible attributes of *ConstrainedRoles* include factArity (the number of roles in the fact being constrained, used for internal uniqueness and simple mandatory constraints), factCount (the number of fact types being constrained), maxFactArity and minFactArity (similar to factArity, but used for multi-fact constraints), and sign (set to either positive or negative, to use different patterns on sign).

3) *Differences in the availability of reading text* for a given lead role or reading order. ORM verbalization uses the most natural reading available, falling back on a more complicated form if the optimal reading is not available. The *ConditionalReading* tag, occurring directly inside *ConstrainedRoles*, contains *ReadingChoice* tags, each of which specifies a match attribute with reading conditions. Reading precedence corresponds to the order of the ReadingChoice tags. The last ReadingChoice tag can omit the match attribute, indicating the lowest priority fallback condition.

4) Once a pattern and reading are selected, decisions still need to be made based on *how a given role is used in the constraint.* The most common classification is whether a role in the FactType is *included* or *excluded* in the constraint. Additional classifications occur when roles are iterated (with the *IterateRoles* tag). Inside an iteration, a given role can be *included* (a constrained role), *excluded* (not a constrained role), *primary* (the current role in the set being iterated), and *secondary* (a role in the set being iterated that is not the current role). Specifying sets of roles in this fashion gives us a flexible, set-based algorithm that works for both single-role and multi-role sets.

The following sample, which is part of the MandatoryConstraint specification, illustrates uses of these tags and conditions. <!-- Comments --> are in the XML.

```
< !-- Specify the type of constraint. This will implement IVerbalize on the MandatoryConstraint class. -->
<Constraint type="MandatoryConstraint" patternGroup="SetConstraint">
<!-- Positive verbalization of a mandatory constraint on a unary fact type --><!-- Each A R -->
        <ConstrainedRoles constraintArity="1" factArity="1" sign="positive">
<!-- ImpliedModalNecessityOperator: '{0}' (positive alethic), 'it is obligatory that {0}' (positive deontic) -->
            <Snippet ref="ImpliedModalNecessityOperator">
<!-- UniversalQuantifier is 'each {0}' -->
                <Snippet ref="UniversalQuantifier">
<!-- Fill the default predicate text replacement fields with the role player names -->
                <Fact/></Snippet></Snippet></ConstrainedRoles>
<!-- A single-role simple mandatory constraint on a binary fact type --><!-- Each A R some B -->
        <ConstrainedRoles constraintArity="1" factArity="2">
<!-- The pattern will change based on the available predicate text -->
            <ConditionalReading>
<!-- A reading is available that begins with the constrained role -->
                <ReadingChoice match="RequireLeadReading">
                <Snippet ref="ImpliedModalNecessityOperator">
<!-- Populate the predicate text using the reading from the current context -->
                <Fact readingChoice="Context">
<!-- Qualify all roles included in the constraint with the UniversalQuantifier 'each {0}' -->
                    <PredicateReplacement match="included">
                    <Snippet ref="UniversalQuantifier"/></PredicateReplacement>
```

```
<!-- Qualify all remaining roles included in the constraint with the ExistentialQuantifier 'some {0}' -->
            <PredicateReplacement>
                <Snippet ref="ExistentialQuantifier"/>
            </PredicateReplacement></Fact></Snippet></ReadingChoice>
```

<!-- The negative form of the snippets changes 'each' to 'any' and 'some' to 'no'. Combining these two snippet variations with the ImpliedModalNecessityOperator changes 'Each A R some B' to 'It is impossible that any A R no B'. Given that the pattern change is limited to the snippet variations only, there is no reason to provide an alternate pattern for negative or deontic forms of the verbalization phrase -->

```
<!-- Move onto the fallback form (no lead reading is available) --><!-- For each A, some B S that A -->
            <ReadingChoice>
<!--The ForEachCompactQuantifier snippet has two replacement fields on the same line -->
                <Snippet ref="ForEachCompactQuantifier">
```

<!-- List all included roles. A listStyle is not needed here as the ConstrainedRoles conditions ensure there will only be one item in the set. Otherwise, listStyle could be SimpleList. The hyphenBind attribute indicates that any hyphen binding in the predicate text should also be applied when the roles are listed -->

```
                    <IterateRoles match="included" listStyle="null" hyphenBind="true"/>
```

<!-- The rest is similar to the previous case, except 'each A' becomes 'that A' -->

```
                    <Snippet ref="ImpliedModalNecessityOperator">
                        <Fact>
                            <PredicateReplacement match="included">
                                <Snippet ref="DefiniteArticle"/></PredicateReplacement>
                            <PredicateReplacement>
                                <Snippet ref="ExistentialQuantifier"/>
                            </PredicateReplacement></Fact>
</Snippet></Snippet></ReadingChoice></ConditionalReading></ConstrainedRoles></Constraint>
```

This style of XML is used to verify that we have an exact match with the specification, and forms the input to the code generator. There are other conditional constructs that are not shown. For example, *ConditionalSnippet* allows us to use the same replacement fields while varying the snippets and *ConditionalReplacement* allows us to use different replacement contents inside a single snippet. Additional conditional and iteration constructs are being added as needed to formalize the verbalization requirements. Including standard code to verify error conditions that is generated with all constraints, the sample XML above (~30 lines of data, comprising 2 of the 6 *ConstrainedRoles* elements on MandatoryConstraint) produces ~350 lines of code. In general, we're getting at least a 1/10 ratio between XML and generated code. In addition to being able to easily verify the implementation against the spec, we also have the advantage that a minor change in the code generator can produce widespread changes in the code base. For example, ~50 lines of new XSLT and some new hand-coded support functions added hyphen binding support to all constraint verbalizations.

5   Conclusion

This paper discussed the automated support for verbalization of ORM 2 models provided by the open source NORMA tool, which caters for verbalization patterns that go well beyond previous verbalization work in ORM, and uses a generation process based on application of XSLT transforms to an XML file that succinctly identifies different verbalization patterns and describes how phrases are combined to produce a readable verbalization. At the time of writing, most ORM constraint patterns have been specified and implemented. Future work will extend the verbalization to cover all aspects of ORM 2 models (schemas plus populations).

References

1. Atkins C. and Patrick J. P., 'NaLER: A natural language method for interpreting entity-relationship models', *Campus-Wide Information Systems* 17(3), 2000, pp. 85-93.
2. Bakema, G., Zwart, J. & van der Lek, H. 2000, *Fully Communication Oriented Information Modelling*, Ten Hagen Stam, The Netherlands.
3. Barker, R. 1990, *CASE*Method: Entity Relationship Modeling*, Addison-Wesley, Wokingham.
4. Bloesch, A. & Halpin, T. 1997, 'Conceptual queries using ConQuer-II', *Proc. ER'97: 16th Int. Conf. on conceptual modeling*, Springer LNCS, no. 1331, pp. 113-26.
5. Chen, P. P. 1976, 'The entity-relationship model—towards a unified view of data'. *ACM Transactions on Database Systems*, 1(1), pp. 9–36.
6. Embley, D. 1998, *Object Database Management*, Addison-Wesley, Reading, MA.
7. Halpin T. & Harding J. 1993, 'Automated support for verbalization of conceptual schemas', *Proc. 4th Workshop on Next Generation CASE Tools*, eds S. Brinkkemper & F. Harmsen, Univ. Twente Memoranda Informatica 93-32, Paris, pp. 151-161.
8. Halpin, T. 2001, *Information Modeling and Relational Databases*, Morgan Kaufmann, San Francisco.
9. Halpin, T. 2004, 'Business Rule Verbalization', *Information Systems Technology and its Applications*, Proc. ISTA-2004, (eds Doroshenko, A., Halpin, T., Liddle, S. & Mayr, H.), Salt Lake City, Lec. Notes in Informatics, vol. P-48, pp. 39-52.
10. Halpin T. 2005, 'ORM 2', *OTM 2005 Workshops*, eds R. Meersman, Z. Tari, P. Herrero et al., Springer LNCS 3762, Cyprus, 2005, pp. 676-87.
11. Halpin, T. 2006, 'Verbalizing Business Rules: Part 14', *Business Rules Journal*, Vol. 7, No. 4. URL: http://www.BRCommunity.com/a2006/b283.html.
12. Halpin, T. 2006, 'Business Rule Modality', *Proc. CAiSE'06 Workshops,* eds T, Latour & M. Petit, Namur University Press, pp. 383-94.
13. Halpin, T., Curland, M. & CS445 Class 2006, 'ORM 2 Constraint Verbalization: Part 1', *Technical Report ORM2-02*, Neumont University. Available online at http://www.orm.net/pdf/ORM2_TechReport2.pdf.
14. Halpin, T., Evans, K, Hallock, P. & MacLean, W. 2003, *Database Modeling with Microsoft® Visio for Enterprise Architects*, Morgan Kaufmann, San Francisco.
15. ter Hofstede, A. H. M., Proper, H. A. & Weide, th. P. van der 1993, 'Formal definition of a conceptual language for the description and manipulation of information models', *Information Systems*, vol. 18, no. 7, pp. 489-523.
16. Meersman, R. M. 1982, *The RIDL conceptual language*. Research report, Int. Centre for Information Analysis Services, Control Data Belgium, Brussels.
17. NORMA URL: https://sourceforge.net/projects/orm.
18. Object Management Group 2003, *UML 2.0 Superstructure Specification*. Online: www.omg.org/uml.
19. Ross, R., Lam, G. 2001, 'RuleSpeak Sentence Templates: Developing Rules Statements Using Sentence Patterns', Business Rule Solutions, Online at www.BRCommunity.com.
20. Sowa, J. F. 2004, 'Common Logic Controlled English', Draft available online at http://www.jfsowa.com/clce/specs.htm.
21. Warmer, J. & Kleppe, A. 2003, *The Object Constraint Language: Getting Your Models Ready for MDA, 2nd edn.*, Addison-Wesley.

T-Lex: A Role-Based Ontology Engineering Tool

Damien Trog, Jan Vereecken, Stijn Christiaens,
Pieter De Leenheer, and Robert Meersman

Semantics Technology and Applications Laboratory (STARLab)
Department of Computer Science
Vrije Universiteit Brussel
Pleinlaan 2, B-1050 BRUSSELS 5, Belgium
{dtrog, javereec, stichris, pdeleenh, meersman}@vub.ac.be

Abstract. In the DOGMA ontology engineering approach ontology construction starts from a (possibly very large) uninterpreted base of elementary fact types called lexons that are mined from linguistic descriptions (be it from existing schemas, a text corpus or formulated by domain experts). An ontological commitment to such "lexon base" means selecting/reusing from it a meaningful set of facts that approximates well the intended conceptualization, followed by the addition of a set of constraints, or rules, to this subset. The commitment process is inspired by the fact-based database modeling method NIAM/ORM2, which features a recently updated, extensive graphical support. However, for encouraging lexon reuse by ontology engineers a more scalable way of visually browsing a large Lexon Base is important. Existing techniques for similar semantic networks rather focus on graphical distance between concepts and not always consider the possibility that concepts might be (fact-) related to a large number of other concepts. In this paper we introduce an alternative approach to browsing large fact-based diagrams in general, which we apply to lexon base browsing and selecting for building ontological commitments in particular. We show that specific characteristics of DOGMA such as grouping by contexts and its "double articulation principle", viz. explicit separation between lexons and an application's commitment to them can increase the scalability of this approach. We illustrate with a real-world case study.

1 Introduction

Ontology engineering methodologies use some combination of ontology engineering processes. Equally important are powerful tools to support the knowledge engineer in applying these methodologies. Our main focus in this paper is how proper visualization can assist the engineer in his work. We do not discuss large-scale visualizations (e.g., a hyperbolic view), as we intend to research a more directed browsing approach instead of a large-scale search (e.g., to discover patterns on the entire data).

In the past years several tools supporting ontology building have been developed. An elaborate overview of such ontology tools can be found in several sources [1,2,3,4].

R. Meersman, Z. Tari, P. Herrero et al. (Eds.): OTM Workshops 2006, LNCS 4278, pp. 1191–1200, 2006.

Protégé [5] is an ontology development tool developed at Stanford University. The knowledge model supporting the tool is designed to use a frame-based formalism, but is flexible enough to be easily transported to other knowledge models [6]. In the Protégé project different visualization modules have been developed. The most active one is an integrated environment called Jambalaya [7], which facilitates the construction and exploration of ontologies. Practically this means an additional Jamabalaya tab is available for the user in the Protégé environment. The module uses a nested graph-based representation of hierarchical structures, together with nested interchangeable views. It supports a range of small to large-scale visualizations.

Variations of the spring embedder algorithm [8] are also widely used in tools. Examples are AIdminister [9], the work of Mutton and Golbeck [10], the OIModeller plug-in for the KAON server [11], and the visualization user interface in OntoEdit [12]. The ontology is considered as a graph whose vertices represent concepts and whose edges represent relationships. Vertices are positioned randomly as their initial position. Each vertex is considered to cause a repulsive force on the others, while edges represent an attracting force. When minimum energy is reached, the visualization is complete. The advantage is that high-level structure can be detected. The disadvantage is that the number of iterations and the initial positions can create a new representation on each call for a visualization.

Bosca, Bonino, and Pellegrino apply a hyperbolic view [13] in the OntoSphere ontology visualization tool. This is very powerful for displaying very large scale graphs.

In this paper, we discuss the T-Lex suite, which is a combination of tools we created and added to the DOGMA Studio Workbench to support the DOGMA approach on ontology engineering. We focus on visualization in the T-Lex suite, as we will use this to elicit and apply lexons.

Section 2 gives a brief introduction to the DOGMA approach. In Sect. 3 we propose the NORM tree, a visualization based on ORM. We illustrate how the tool works in a small real-world case study in Sect. 4. We end with a conclusion and possibilities for future work in Sect. 5.

2   DOGMA Framework

The DOGMA[1] approach has some distinguishing characteristics such as its groundings in the linguistic representations of knowledge, and the explicit separation of conceptualization and axiomatization. The DOGMA approach is supported by DOGMA Server, an ontology library system, that already features context-driven disambiguation of lexical labels into concept definitions [14].

DOGMA is an ontology approach and framework that is not restricted to a particular representation language. An important characteristic that makes it different from traditional ontology approaches is that it separates the specification of the *conceptualization* (i.e. lexical representation of concepts and their

---

[1] Acronym for Developing Ontology-Grounded Methods and Applications; A research initiative of VUB STARLab.

inter-relationships) from its *axiomatization* (i.e. semantic constraints). The goal of this separation, referred to as the *double articulation* principle [15], is to enhance the potential for re-use and design scalability.

This principle corresponds to an orthodox *model-theoretic* approach to ontology representation and development [15]. Consequently the DOGMA framework consists of two layers: a *lexon base* (conceptualization) and a *commitment layer* (axiomatization).

A lexon base holds (multiple) intuitive conceptualization(s) of a particular domain. Each conceptualization is simplified to a "representation-less" set of context-specific binary fact types called lexons. A lexon represents a plausible binary fact-type and is formally described as a 5-tuple $\langle \gamma, term_1, role, co-role, term_2 \rangle$, where γ is an abstract context identifier, lexically described by a string in some natural language, and is used to group lexons that are logically related to each other in the conceptualization of the domain.

Intuitively, a lexon may be read as: within the context γ, the $term_1$ (also denoted as the header term) may have a relation with $term_2$ (also denoted as the tail term) in which it plays a role, and conversely, in which $term_2$ plays a corresponding co-role. Each (context, term)-pair then lexically identifies a unique concept. A lexon base can hence be described as a set of plausible elementary fact types that are considered as being true. Any specific (application-dependent) interpretation is moved to a separate layer, i.e. the commitment layer.

The commitment layer mediates between the lexon base and its applications. Each such ontological commitment defines a partial semantic account of an intended conceptualization [16]. It consists of a finite set of axioms that specify which lexons of the lexon base are interpreted and how they are visible in the committing application, and (domain) rules that semantically constrain this interpretation. Experience shows that it is much harder to reach an agreement on domain rules than one on conceptualization [17]. E.g., the rule stating that each patient is a person who suffers from at least one disease may hold in the Universe of Discourse (UoD) of some application, but may be too strong in the UoD of another application. A full formalization of DOGMA is found in [18,19].

3 NORM Trees

When an ontology engineer is confronted with a lexon base it is paramount that the visual representation is both structured and scalable. Working his way through a lexon base the engineer creates paths, which can be remembered and stored for later use/reconstruction. This visualization process is highly interactive and enables the engineer to hide or display information at will. These requirements will allow the engineer (1) to browse easily through the vast amount of knowledge and (2) to efficiently select paths with which he can construct commitments.

ORM [20] is excellent for visualizing whole schema containing complex structures in a scalable manner. If the schema grows too large for a proper overview, it supports several abstraction mechanisms [21]. A potential downside is that it is possible that cyclic graphs occur, which are unsuitable when looking for paths.

Another consequence of cyclic graphs is the complexity for automatic layout algorithms when there is a high number of objects in the schema. We propose the NORM tree[2] to overcome these problems in visualization. It is based on the abstraction mechanism of local context.

We claim that our method is structured and scalable. It allows us to create paths intuitively and hides the complexity of the lexon base and the commitments. However, we have to make some assumptions: (1) we know the starting point which will be the root-term for our NORM tree, and (2) we have a general idea of the terms we want in our commitment. The first assumption is to avoid having to visualize the entire lexon base at once. Because a lexon base is meant to contain a huge amount of lexons, we would need visualization that can display everything and still provide a good overview. Such functionality is achieved in other work, for instance by Pretorius [22] or using a hyperbolic view [13]. Our focus is on a smaller amount of lexons (i.e., a single context). The second assumption is related to the first, as it also depends on the user knowing where to browse. Our target engineer is someone who knows for which domain or for which application he is modeling. He can quickly locate the relevant context, and the relevant terms inside that context that he needs. In another approach (e.g., for an knowledge engineer who is exploring), the engineer could start from the high complexity view (e.g., hyperbolic) and then focus on interesting patterns. Our NORM tree representation would allow him to dig deeper into a certain pattern without getting lost in irrelevant information (e.g., from another pattern).

A NORM tree is an undirected rooted tree. There is no meaning in being the root of the tree, except for the fact that this is the term that the engineer started with. Any term in a NORM tree can be the root. It is not the intention to show the whole tree to the knowledge engineer. Rather we let the engineer traverse the tree by expanding the parts he is interested in.

A variation on the NORM tree is the infinite NORM tree, where the tree can be infinitely expanded. This is done by always adding the reverse lexon.[3] We then add this reversed lexon to the current node. This creates duplicates, that are identified by coloring them gray. We believe that this duplication helps because it preserves the *complete* local context in a restricted area.

Consider a simplified example where the knowledge engineer is interested in the person that is the owner of a chateau. He does not know what label is given for this term, so he starts his search from the term 'Wine'. He locates the context 'Wine Ontology' in the lexon base and requests a (infinite) NORM tree with 'Wine' as root term. Figure 1 illustrates this process. We can identify three steps that the engineer followed; (1) the root-term 'Wine' is expanded and all its immediate neighbours are displayed, (2) 'Chateau' is expanded where the term 'Person' becomes visible, and (3) 'Person' is expanded to see with which other terms it is related.

---

[2] NORM is a recursive acronym which stands for "NORM Ontology Representation Method".

[3] To reverse a lexon, we switch the head-term with the tail-term and we switch the role and co-role.

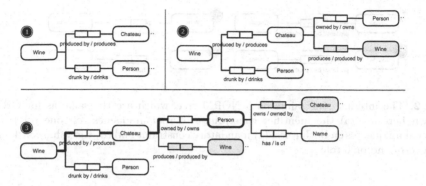

Fig. 1. Expansion of an Infinite NORM tree. The grayed-out parts of the tree indicate the redundancies through reversing of lexons. On (3) a path is marked from the currently selected term 'Person', over 'Chateau' ending in 'Wine'.

3.1 Semantic Rules on NORM Trees

NORM trees are based on ORM, so it is logical to also adapt the same constraints [20]. Because of our NORM tree representation, it is not always trivial to use a similar technique. We modified the representation for the external uniqueness and total union constraints over multiple roles. We did this because the same role or term can appear multiple times in our NORM tree. Adhering to the same notation for all constraints in ORM would rapidly clutter the diagram.

In this paper we limit ourselves to the uniqueness (including identifier), total union (including mandatory) and value constraints. We denote constraints that are applied to elements in the same lexon as *internal constraints*. Constraints that are applied to elements from different lexons, we refer to as *external constraints*.

3.2 Internal Constraints

The representation for the internal constraints remains equal to that in ORM. These constitute the internal uniqueness, mandatory and value constraints. Figure 2 gives an example of these constraints.

3.3 External Constraints

For the external constraints we propose an alternate representation to the one in ORM. We made this choice for two reasons. Firstly, a NORM tree has redundancy in terms and roles, which would lead to cluttering in the regular ORM notation. And secondly, not all roles may be visible that participate in a certain constraint. This leaves two choices: (1) only draw the constraint when all roles are visible, or (2) make all participating roles visible. The first choice would lead to confusion and the second to a rapidly cluttered diagram. Therefor, we propose to use the same symbols for the constraints, but not to connect them to the participating roles. Instead we use an index number to identify the constraints.

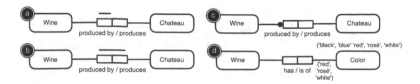

Fig. 2. The internal constraints on a NORM tree, which are the same as for ORM. Shown here are (a) the identifier constraint (internal uniqueness on one role), (b) internal uniqueness on both roles, (c) mandatory constraint and (d) the value constraint on a term and on a role.

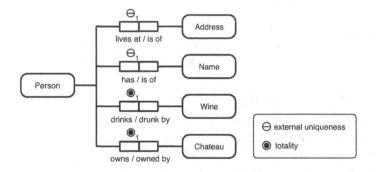

Fig. 3. The external constraints on a NORM tree. Here shown are the external uniqueness and total union constraints.

In Fig. 3 we show an example of an external uniqueness constraint and total union constraint. Here we indicate that a Person either needs to drink Wine, own a Chateau or both. Additionally we indicate that the combination of Address and Name is unique for a Person.

3.4 NORM Trees in DOGMA Studio

We have created two plugins in Eclipse[4] that form the T-Lex suite. The plugins are part of the DOGMA Studio Workbench, which supports the DOGMA ontology engineering approach. By combining the plugins from this Workbench (through Eclipse perspectives), different aspects of DOGMA are supported. DOGMA uses double articulation, viz. there is a lexon base and commitment, so we have two plugins: The T-Lex Browser for browsing the lexon base, and the T-Lex Committer for creating and editing ontological commitments.

The T-Lex Browser provides a view on the lexon base. Using another plugin from the Workbench, the user selects a term in a particular context. In the Browser a NORM tree is created with the selected term as the root-term. This tree contains all the lexons in the chosen context. A screenshot of the browser is depicted in Fig. 4.

---

[4] http://www.eclipse.org/

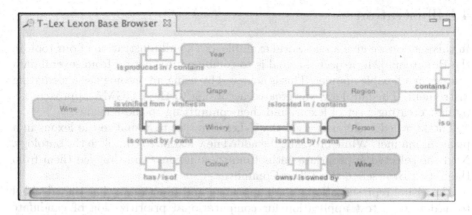

Fig. 4. A screenshot of the T-Lex Lexon Base Browser exploring 'Wine Ontology' context in a lexon base

In order to construct an ontological commitment, the knowledge engineer needs to select paths in the Browser. She starts by creating a new commitment in the Committer. She then selects paths in the Browser and drags and drops them onto this new commitment. Such a commitment can be created with lexons from different contexts. Once the necessary paths of lexons have been added to the Committer, semantic constraints can be applied on these paths. A screenshot of the editor is depicted in Fig. 5.

For the Browser we use infinite NORM trees, as we allow the user all freedom for browsing. By only showing lexons grouped in one context, we limit the size of the tree. However, in the Committer we use ordinary NORM trees, because the focus is not as much on browsing, but rather on editing and adding constraints.

Additionally the Committer is used for mapping the concepts in the commitment to application symbols, such as tables and attributes in a relational database. This is based on the work by Verheyden et al. on database mediation [23].

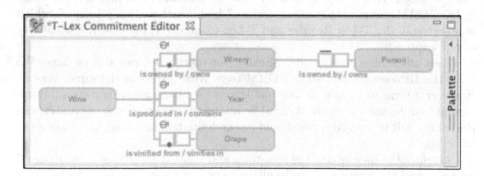

Fig. 5. A screenshot of the T-Lex Commitment Editor. Displayed is an example ontological commitment.

4 Illustration

In this section we give a real-world example as a small illustration of our tool. In the Bonatema [24] project the goal is to combine information from several data sources in a flexible manner. This is achieved by using an ontology as a mediating instrument. The ontology was created according to the DOGMA approach, i.e. by first creating a set of lexons and then committing to these lexons.

The knowledge engineer used the T-Lex Browser to visualize the lexons in a pleasant manner. While browsing, he added new lexons to complete the ontology. Next, he selected appropriate paths from these lexons, and dragged them from the T-Lex Browser to the T-Lex Committer.

The visual representation was so appealing and functional, that they decided to add it to a test application for computational prioritization of candidate disease genes, called Endeavour. In this application, they will use the NORM tree to browse through the conceptual model, while data for the selected path is shown, as well as relevant contextual information. This information is obtained by displaying data that maps to neighbouring nodes of the selected term.

Since the NORM tree representation is reused by an application in the Bonatema project, we can say it is no longer an obscure feature of just the T-Lex suite in DOGMA Studio. This shows it is a promising technique for managing complexity of visualizing ontologies. Due to space limitations we refer to the Bonatema project as an illustration [24].

5 Conclusion and Future Work

For directed browsing of a lexon base with small to medium sized sets of lexons in a context, T-Lex performs very well. However, for large scale visualizations we suggest different approaches such as found in Pretorius [22]. Also, other tools described in the introduction provide interesting views for large scale visualization. When we compare our approach to theirs, we can only conclude that our local context based NORM tree is ideal for small to medium scale directed browsing.

DOGMA's grouping by contexts and its "double articulation principle", which is reflected in the T-Lex Browser and T-Lex Committer, increase the scalability of our approach.

T-Lex offers nice functionality already, but more work can still be done. We limit the Browser to only show NORM trees with lexons in the same context. However a term can occur in multiple lexons in different contexts (possibly referring to different concepts). It could be interesting to browse across contexts in the same NORM tree. Also, we should research limitations for such cross-context browsing.

Currently the user selects the root-term and context from a list containing all contexts and their terms. More intuitive ways can be implemented to find this starting point. E.g., an option to search the terms in the lexon base, making use of the semantic knowledge to suggest related terms. Another possibility is to implement a large scale visualization plugin (possibly using a hyperbolic view) to provide an overview on the whole lexon base. Then, when the user has selected a term, this term (and its context) is used to create the NORM tree in the T-Lex Browser.

Only a limited set of constraints are available in the Committer. In the future we would like to have all ORM constraints available. We will also research other additional constraints (e.g., if-then-else condition).

By using an index to identify external constraints, we remove cluttering but lose an easy overview of which lexons participate in a particular constraint. To solve this we would present the user with the option to show the participating lexons of a constraint. This could be done by graying out all the lexons on screen, except for those participating in the selected constraint.

References

1. Gomez-Perez, A., Angele, J., Fernandez-Lopez, M., Christophides, V., Stutt, A., Sure, Y.: A survey on ontology tools. OntoWeb deliverable 1.3, Universidad Politecnia de Madrid (2002)
2. Duineveld, A.J., Stoter, R., Weiden, M.R., Kenepa, B., Benjamins, V.R.: Wondertools?: a comparative study of ontological engineering tools. Int. J. Hum.-Comput. Stud. **52**(6) (2000) 1111–1133
3. Lambrix, P., Edberg, A.: Evaluation of ontology merging tools in bioinformatics. In: Pacific Symposium on Biocomputing. (2003) 589–600
4. Gómez-Pérez, A., Corcho, O., Fernández-López, M.: Ontological Engineering. Springer-Verlag New York, LLC (2003)
5. Noy, N.F., McGuinness, D.L.: Ontology development 101: A guide to creating your first ontology. Technical Report KSL-01-05, Knowledge Systems Laboratory, Stanford University, Stanford, CA, 94305, USA (2001)
6. Gennari, J.H., Musen, M.A., Fergerson, R.W., Grosso, W.E., Crubézy, M., Eriksson, H., Noy, N.F., Tu, S.W.: The evolution of protégé: an environment for knowledge-based systems development. Int. J. Hum.-Comput. Stud. **58**(1) (2003) 89–123
7. Storey, M., Musen, M., Silva, J., Best, C., Ernst, N., Fergerson, R., Noy, N.: Jambalaya: Interactive visualization to enhance ontology authoring and knowledge acquisition in protege (2001)
8. Eades, P.: A heuristic for graph drawing. Congressus Numerantium 42 (1984) 149–160
9. Fluit, C., Sabou, M., van Harmelen, F.: Ontology-based information visualization. In Geroimenko, V., ed.: Visualizing the Semantic Web. Springer Verlag (2002) 36–48
10. Mutton, P., Golbeck, J.: Visualization of semantic metadata and ontologies. In: IV '03: Proceedings of the Seventh International Conference on Information Visualization, Washington, DC, USA, IEEE Computer Society (2003) 300
11. Gabel, T., Sure, Y., Völker, J.: Kaon – ontology management infrastructure. SEKT informal deliverable 3.1.1.a, Institute AIFB, University of Karlsruhe (2004)
12. Sure, Y., Erdmann, M., Angele, J., Staab, S., Studer, R., Wenke, D.: OntoEdit: Collaborative ontology development for the Semantic Web. j-LECT-NOTES-COMP-SCI **2342** (2002) 221–235

13. A. Bosca, D. Bonino, P.P.: Ontosphere: more than a 3d ontology visualization tool. In: SWAP 2005, the 2nd Italian Semantic Web Workshop. CEUR Workshop Proceedings. (December 14-16, 2005)
14. De Leenheer, P., de Moor, A.: Context-driven disambiguation in ontology elicitation. In Shvaiko, P., Euzenat, J., eds.: Context and Ontologies: Theory, Practice and Applications. Volume WS-05-01 of AAAI Technical Report., Pittsburg USA, AAAI Press (2005) 17–24
15. Spyns, P., Meersman, R., Jarrar, M.: Data modelling versus ontology engineering. SIGMOD Record Special Issue on Semantic Web, Database Management and Information Systems **31**(4) (2002) 12–17
16. Guarino, N., Giaretta, P.: Ontologies and knowledge bases: Towards a terminological clarification. In Mars, N.J.I., ed.: Towards Very Large Knowledge Bases. IOS Press (1995)
17. Meersman, R.: Web and ontologies: Playtime or business at the last frontier in computing? In: Proceedings of the NSF-EU Workshop on Database and Information Systems Research for Semantic Web and Enterprises (on-line). (2002) 61–67
18. De Leenheer, P., Meersman, R.: Towards a formal foundation of DOGMA ontology. part i: Lexon Base and Concept Definition Server. Technical Report STAR-2005-06, STARLab (2005)
19. De Leenheer, P., de Moor, A., Meersman, R.: Context dependency management in interorganizational ontology engineering. Technical Report STAR-2006-02, STAR-Lab, Brussel (2006)
20. Halpin, T.: ORM 2. In Meersman, R., Tari, Z., et al., P.H., eds.: OTM Workshops. Volume 3762., Berlin Heidelberg, Springer Verlag, LNCS (2005) 676–687
21. Halpin, T.: Information Modeling and Relational Databases: From Conceptual Analysis to Logical Design. Morgan Kaufmann, San Francisco, CA, USA (2001)
22. Pretorious, J.A.: Lexon visualization: Visualizing binary fact types in ontology bases. In: IV. (2004) 58–63
23. Verheyden, P., Bo, J.D., Meersman, R.: Semantically unlocking database content through ontology-based mediation. In: SWDB. (2004) 109–126
24. Coessens, B., Christiaens, S., Verlinden, R.: Ontology guided data integration for computational prioritisation of disease genes. Accepted in proceedings of KSinBIT, OTM 2006, Spring-Verlag, In press.

Modeling Dynamic Rules in ORM

Herman Balsters[1], Andy Carver[2], Terry Halpin[2], and Tony Morgan[2]

[1] University of Groningen, The Netherlands
H.Balsters@rug.nl
[2] Neumont University, Utah, USA
{andy, terry, tony.morgan}@neumont.edu

Abstract. This paper proposes an extension to the Object-Role Modeling approach to support formal declaration of dynamic rules. Dynamic rules differ from static rules by pertaining to properties of state transitions, rather than to the states themselves. In this paper, application of dynamic rules is restricted to so-called single-step transactions, with an old state (the input of the transaction) and a new state (the direct result of that transaction). Such restricted rules are easier to formulate (and enforce) than a constraint applying historically over all possible states. In our approach, dynamic rules specify an elementary transaction type indicating which kind of object or fact is being added, deleted or updated, and (optionally) pre-conditions relevant to the transaction, followed by a condition stating the properties of the new state, including the relation between the new state and the old state. These dynamic rules are formulated in a syntax designed to be easily validated by non-technical domain experts.

1 Introduction

Object-Role Modeling (ORM) is a fact-oriented approach for modeling, transforming, and querying information in terms of the underlying facts of interest, where facts and rules may be verbalized in language readily understandable by non-technical users of the business domain. In contrast to Entity-Relationship (ER) modeling [4] and Unified Modeling Language (UML) class diagrams [18], ORM models are attribute-free, treating all facts as relationships (unary, binary, ternary etc.). ORM includes procedures for mapping to attribute-based structures, such as those of ER or UML. We use the term "ORM" to include a number of closely related dialects, such as Natural language Information Analysis Method (NIAM) [27] and Fully-Communication Oriented Information Modeling (FCO-IM) [1]. For a basic introduction to ORM see [13], for a thorough treatment see [8]. For a comparison of ORM with UML see [10].

Business rules include constraints and derivation rules. *Static rules* apply to each state of the information system that models the business domain, and may be checked by examining each state individually (e.g. each person was born on at most one date). *Dynamic rules* reference at least two states, which may be either successive (e.g. no employee may be demoted in rank) or separated by some period (e.g. invoices ought to be paid within 30 days of being issued). While ORM provides richer graphic support for static rules than ER or UML provide, ORM as yet cannot match UML's support for dynamic rules.

R. Meersman, Z. Tari, P. Herrero et al. (Eds.): OTM Workshops 2006, LNCS 4278, pp. 1201–1210, 2006.
© Springer-Verlag Berlin Heidelberg 2006

Since the 1980s, many extensions to ORM have been proposed to model temporal aspects and processes. The TOP model [7] allows fact types to be qualified by a temporal dimension and granularity. TRIDL [3] includes time operators and action semantics, but not dynamic constraints. LISA-D [16] supports basic updates. Task structures and task transactions model various processes [15], with formal grounding in process algebra. EVORM [22] formalizes first and second order evolution of information systems. Some explorations have been made to address reaction rules [e.g. 14], and some proposals suggest deriving activity models from ORM models ([23]).

Some fact-based approaches that share similarities with ORM have developed deep support for modeling system dynamics. For example, the CRL language in TEM-PORA enables various constraints, derivations and actions to be formulated on Entity-Relationship-Time (ERT) models [24, 25], and the OSM method includes both graphical and textual specification of state nets and object interactions [6].

Various attribute-based methods such as UML and some extensions of ER incorporate dynamic modeling via diagrams (e.g. UML state charts and activity diagrams). For textual specification of dynamic rules, the most popular approach is the Object Constraint Language (OCL) [19, 26], but the OCL syntax is often too mathematical for validation by non-technical domain experts. Olivé suggests an extension to UML to specify temporal constraints, but this is limited to rules about creation of objects [20]. Substantial research has been carried out in providing logical formalizations for dynamic rules, typically using temporal logics or Event-Condition-Action (ECA) formalisms (e.g. de Brock [2], Lipeck [17], Chomicki [5], and Paton & Díaz [21]). Many works also describe how to implement dynamic rules in software systems.

However, to our knowledge, no one has yet provided a purely declarative means to formulate dynamic constraints in a textual syntax suitable for non-technical users. This paper provides a first step towards such support for dynamic rules in ORM by addressing *single-step transactions*, with an old state (the input of the transaction) and a new state (resulting from that transaction). Our dynamic rules specify an *elementary transaction type* indicating the kind of object or fact being added, deleted or updated, and (optionally) pre-conditions relevant to the transaction, followed by a condition on the new state, including its relation to the old state. These dynamic rules are formulated in a syntax designed for easy validation by non-technical domain experts. Our aim is to identify basic rule patterns rather than provide a complete, formal grammar.

The rest of this paper is structured as follows. Section 2 focuses on rules involving updates to a single role in a functional binary fact type. Section 3 extends the examples of Section 2 to show how history can be added. Section 4 examines rules involving the addition of instances of non-functional fact types. Section 5 discusses a more complex case involving derivation. Section 6 briefly discusses fact deletion. Section 7 summarizes the main results, suggests topics for further research, and lists references.

2   Updating Single-Valued Roles in a Functional Fact Type

Our first sub-case is a functional (n:1 or 1:1) binary fact type. Fig. 1 shows a functional fact type in ORM 2 notation [11], where role names may be displayed in square brackets and used to verbalize rules in attribute-style [9].

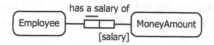

Fig. 1. In each state, each employee has at most one salary

Suppose a dynamic constraint requires that salaries of employees must not decrease. We show two alternative expressions for this constraint, using the reserved words **old** and **new** to refer to situations immediately before and after the transition.

(a) **Context**: Employee
new salary >= **old** salary

(b) **For each** Employee,
new salary >= **old** salary

Here the *context* of the constraint is the object type Employee, and the elementary transaction *updates* the salary of the employee. The presence of the **new** and/or **old** keywords signals that the prospective transaction is an update (rather than an addition or deletion); and this all implies that the rule is applicable only when there is in fact an "old" marital status (of the same student) to update. The constraint is violated if and only if it evaluates to false (like SQL check-clauses). So if the employee had no prior salary, the inequality evaluates to unknown and hence is not violated. In this case we record only a "snapshot" of the current salary (i.e. no salary history) which allows a simple constraint structure. A later example considers salary history.

Specification of Employee as the context is sufficient in this case because the fact type is n:1. While the rule may be specified in relational style, using a predicate reading, an attribute style formulation using a role name is often more convenient. Each transaction is always considered to be isolated (serializable).

Constraints of this kind are fairly common in business systems. Generalizing from the example above to any functional binary fact type of the form A R's B, with B's role name p (denoting the property or "attribute" of A being constrained), we obtain the constraint formulation pattern in Fig. 2, where Θ denotes the required relationship between the values of the property p after and before the transition.

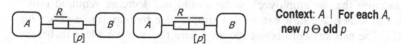

Context: A | For each A,
new $p \ominus$ old p

Fig. 2. General pattern for updating a named, single-valued role on n:1 and 1:1 relationships

Our dynamic-constraint language should also be able to handle constraints that involve a table of state-transitions. A simple example involves marital states:

From \ To	Single	Married	Widowed	Divorced
Single	0	1	0	0
Married	0	0	1	1
Widowed	0	1	0	0
Divorced	0	1	0	0

The matrix shows which updates to a given student's marital status are possible. There is no functional or deterministic relationship between an old state and a new state that can or cannot follow. One simple solution involves that sort of construct which, in programming languages, is commonly called a case or switch statement:

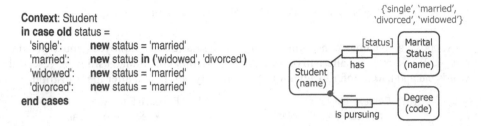

Context: Student
in case old status =
    'single':   **new** status = 'married'
    'married':   **new** status **in** ('widowed', 'divorced')
    'widowed':   **new** status = 'married'
    'divorced':   **new** status = 'married'
end cases

Fig. 3. Updating the marital status of a student

One may alternatively specify impossible transitions for any given case., e.g. the divorced case could be reworded as "**new** status **not in** ('single', 'divorced', 'widowed')". To say the **new** status must *not* equal some value, one uses <> instead of =.

We can generalize similar kinds of constraints in the manner shown in Fig. 4. In the constraint, *B1*, *B2*, *B3*, etc. represent possible *B*s that may play role *p*.

Context: A
in case old p =
    'B1':   **new** p **in** (B2, B3, ...)
    - - etc.
end cases

Fig. 4. General pattern for enumerated values

3 Examples of Historical Facts

Our earlier constraint that an employee's salary could not decrease required only a "snapshot" view of salary. We now extend this simple case by requiring a salary *history* (see Fig. 5). The **new** keyword is not required here because we add a fact rather than update an existing fact. We assume here the existence of a function **previous** that can return the existing salary most recently added for any specific employee.

Context: Employee
For each salary **added**
if before:
    Employee was awarded **some** salary on **some** Date
then after:
    salary >= **previous** salary

Fig. 5. Salary example with history

Returning to the specific example of recording a student's marital status, a similar extension to add a history of marital status values for each student is shown in Fig. 6.

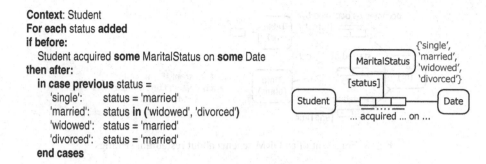

Context: Student
For each status **added**
if before:
    Student acquired **some** MaritalStatus on **some** Date
then after:
    in case previous status =
        'single':   status = 'married'
        'married':   status **in** ('widowed', 'divorced')
        'widowed': status = 'married'
        'divorced': status = 'married'
    end cases

Fig. 6. Marital status example with history

We generalize this example to a pattern for recording history of some kind of thing acquiring some property at some instant, as shown in Fig. 7.

Context: A
For each p **added**
if before:
    A acquired **some** B at **some** Tag
then after:
    in case previous p =
        B1: p **in** (B2, B3, ...)
        - - etc
    end cases

Fig. 7. General pattern for enumerated values with history

As before, *B1*, *B2*, etc. represent possible *B*s that may play role *p*. "Tag" represents some value that consistently increases (or perhaps decreases) for a given *A* as new facts are added. Tag values equipped with an ordering criterion are isomorphic to a linearly ordered time-stamping mechanism. Dates and times obviously fit this role, but so also do other kinds of sequenced identifiers such as "incident number", "version number" or other kinds of sequenced identifiers. We assume that the Tag history is complete for each *A* (we add a new fact to a history of all previous facts of the same type for that *A*, and never add a fact that is "earlier" than some existing fact).

The dynamic constraint above applies to a situation where new facts are added to an existing history. If we require a constraint on the addition of the first fact of this type for each object of type *A*, then we need a separate constraint without the "before" condition given above. For the first addition of a fact of this type, if we do not care about the role *p* added, then we do not need to specify the additional constraint.

4   Adding Instances of a Non-functional Fact Type

We now consider *adding fact instances* to a *non-functional fact type* (no single-role uniqueness constraint), such as the Seating occupies Table association in Fig. 8, which shows a model fragment extracted from a restaurant application.

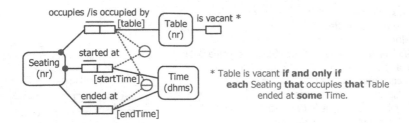

Fig. 8. Fragment of an ORM schema about restaurant seatings

A seating is the allocation of a party (of one or more customers) to one or more vacant tables. Each seating starts at some instant and eventually ends at some instant. The circled bars depict the external uniqueness constraints that when a seating starts or ends, any given table is assigned to at most one seating. The asterisked rule is a derivation rule for the snapshot fact type Table is vacant. Notice that the model maintains a *history* of seatings (e.g. for each table we record all the seatings it was previously allocated to). To ensure that no seatings that overlap in time occupy the same table, the following rather complex textual constraint could be added:

For each Seating₁, Seating₂:
    if Seating₁.startTime <= Seating₂.startTime
          and (Seating₂.startTime <= Seating₁.endTime **or not exists** Seating₁.endTime)
          then no Table **that** is occupied by Seating₁ is occupied by Seating₂

Instead of this static rule, if we ignore the possibility of people changing their tables during a seating, the user interface itself can ensure that only tables that are currently vacant may be selected for a seating (for multiple screens used in parallel, an appropriate locking mechanism is assumed). Fig. 9 shows the relevant schema fragment and the dynamic rule that a table may be assigned to a seating only if it is vacant *at that time*. The *context* for the constraint is the *fact type* Seating occupies Table. The elementary transaction *adds* an *instance* of this fact type. The reserved words **before** and **after** denote the states just before and after the transaction, **needed** indicates the precondition is necessary for the fact addition to take place (not just for this constraint), and **the** is scoped to the transaction instance.

Context: Seating is occupied by Table
For each fact added
needed before: the table is vacant
after: the table is **not** vacant

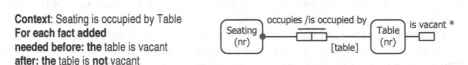

Fig. 9. A dynamic constraint for adding instances to the seating fact type

Note that the ability to specify a fact type for the context leads to a much more natural formulation than would be obtained if the context had to be specified as an object type or class, as is the case with OCL. Fig. 10 models the seating example in UML in less detail (e.g. UML has no graphic notation for uniqueness constraints on attributes).

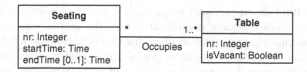

Fig. 10. A UML class diagram for the seating example

To specify in OCL the dynamic constraint that a table may be assigned to a seating only if it is vacant at that time, we could try to state this in the context of the Seating class using an operation addTable (taking a parameter *t* of type Table) thus:

```
context Seating::addTable(t:Table)
pre: (t.isVacant)
post: not(t.isVacant) and (table → includes(t))
```

This however is *incorrect* OCL, because it introduces a side effect: the update operation addTable(*t*: Table) updates not only an object from the class Seating, but also the value of the parameter *t*. If we use Table as the context, we may rephrase our constraint as "A seating can be allocated to a table only if that table is vacant", and introduce an update operation allocateSeating(s: Seating) within the class Table thus:

```
context Table::allocateSeating(s: Seating)
pre: isVacant
post: not isVacant and (seating → includes(s))
```

This constraint, though free of side effects from the point of view of the Table class, is still arguably not free of side effects as seen from the Seating class, since invocation of allocateSeating to some specific table t_0 and seating s_0 would result in the property "s_0.table → includes(t_0)" changing the value of s_0. These side effects result from trying to specify the addition of a complete fact within the context of one specific class. A possible resolution is to introduce an auxiliary class C (e.g. representing the full model), associated with both the Seating and Table classes, as shown in Fig. 11. Addition of the fact "s_0 occupies t_0" could then be represented within the context of class C. This rather roundabout and artificial solution is needed in order to add complete facts simply because OCL requires that any rule context must be a class.

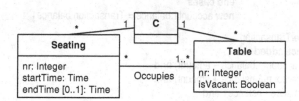

Fig. 11. Introducing an artificial class to provide the context for a side-effect free rule

5 A More Complex Case Involving Derivation

Let us now consider the case of a transaction dealing with operations on one or more accounts (see Fig. 12). Accounts can be augmented by having a deposit or interest added, or they can be diminished by a fee charge or withdrawal. Simple transactions refer to an operation on one account only, while transfer transactions deal with two accounts, where a money amount is transferred from the first account to a second account. We record historical information of all transactions, from which the current account balances may be derived. We assume that an account exists prior to any transaction on it, and that on the event that an account is opened, its balance is set to zero.

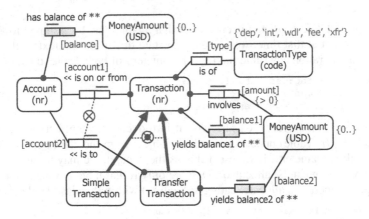

Each SimpleTransaction **is a** Transaction **that** is of TransactionType <> 'xfr'.
Each TransferTransaction **is a** Transaction **that** is of TransactionType 'xfr'.

Fig. 12. An example involving historical and derived snapshot data

We now use dynamic rules to describe a transition from an old state to a new state for both a simple and a transfer transaction. The order of the components is irrelevant.

Context: Account
For each instance added
balance = 0

Context: SimpleTransaction
For each instance added
in case type =
    'dep', 'int': Transaction.balance1 = (**old** account1.balance + amount)
    'wdl', 'fee': Transaction.balance1 = (**old** account1.balance - amount)
end cases
new account1.balance = Transaction.balance1

Context: TransferTransaction
For each instance added
balance1 = (**old** account1.balance – amount) **and**
balance2 = (**old** account2.balance + amount) **and**
new account1.balance= balance1 **and**
new account2.balance= balance2

6 Deleting Instances of a Non-functional Fact Type

So far, all our example rules apply to either state-updates or fact-additions; we now briefly consider an example that applies to fact-deletions. A common situation involves a constraint on the length of time that a certain history of events or entity states is kept. For example, a history of payments made to companies might need to be retained for at least 2 years. This constraint might be expressed as follows. We assume here the existence of functions such as **today** and various operations on date values.

Context: MoneyAmount is paid to Company on Date
For each fact deleted
needed before: the date < **today** – 2 years

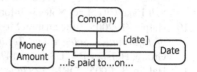

Fig. 13. A dynamic constraint for deleting instances from the payment fact type

7 Conclusion

This paper proposed an extension to ORM supporting purely declarative specification of dynamic rules restricted to single-step transactions, using syntax designed to be easily validated by non-technical domain experts. These dynamic rules specify an elementary transaction type indicating which kind of object or fact is being added, deleted or updated, any pre-conditions relevant to the transaction, and the relationship between the new state and the old state. By collaborating with other researchers in the ORM community, we intend to incorporate the identified rule patterns with enhancements to previous work on ORM textual languages to provide a formal grammar for a standard textual language for ORM, intended to express static and dynamic rules (constraints and derivations), as well as conceptual queries.

Other future research may be directed at adding actual operations to the ORM-language, explicitly modeling single-step transactions as well as other dynamic rules, which may be alethic or deontic [12]. We also plan to extend the NORMA tool to generate code from dynamic rules. In this context, we hope to provide translations of our dynamic rules to the UML/OCL framework, where our declaration of dynamic rules would be closer to the business level of modeling, and the resulting translation to UML/OCL would be closer to the specification level of the software engineer.

Acknowledgement. This paper benefited from discussion with Matt Curland.

References

1. Bakema, G., Zwart, J. & van der Lek, H. 2000, *Fully Communication Oriented Information Modelling*, Ten Hagen Stam, The Netherlands.
2. de Brock, E. O. 2000, 'A General Treatment of Dynamic Integrity Constraints'. *Data and Knowledge Engineering, 32*(3): 223-246.
3. Bruza, P. D. & van der Weide, Th. P 1989, 'The Semantics of TRIDL', Technical Report 89-17, Department of Information Systems, University of Nijmegen.
4. Chen, P. P. 1976, 'The entity-relationship model—towards a unified view of data'. *ACM Transactions on Database Systems*, 1(1), pp. 9–36.
5. Chomicki, J. 1992, 'History-less Checking of Dynamic Integrity Constraints', *ICDE 1992*: 557-64.
6. Embley. D. W. 1998, *Object Database Development*, Addison-Wesley.
7. Falkenberg, E. D. & van der Weide, Th. P. 1988, 'Formal Description of the TOP Model'. Technical Report 88-01, Department of Information Systems, University of Nijmegen.

8. Halpin, T. 2001, *Information Modeling and Relational Databases*, Morgan Kaufmann, San Francisco.

9. Halpin, T. 2004, 'Business Rule Verbalization', *Information Systems Technology and its Applications*, Proc. ISTA-2004, (eds Doroshenko, A., Halpin, T. Liddle, S. & Mayr, H), Salt Lake City, Lec. Notes in Informatics, vol. P-48, pp. 39-52.

10. Halpin, T. 2005, 'Information Modeling in UML and ORM: A Comparison', *Encyclopedia of Information Science and Technology*, vol. 3, ed. M. Khosrow-Pour, Idea Publishing Group, Hershey PA, USA, pp. 1471-5.

11. Halpin, T. 2005, 'ORM 2', *On the Move to Meaningful Internet Systems 2005: OTM 2005 Workshops*, eds R. Meersman, Z. Tari, et al., Cyprus. Springer LNCS 3762, pp 676-87.

12. Halpin, T. 2006, 'Business Rule Modality', *Proc. CAiSE'06 Workshops*, eds T, Latour & M. Petit, Namur University Press, pp. 383-94.

13. Halpin, T. 2006, 'ORM/NIAM Object-Role Modeling', *Handbook on Information Systems Architectures*, 2nd edn, eds P. Bernus, K. Mertins & G. Schmidt, Springer, Heidelberg, pp. 81-103.

14. Halpin, T. & Wagner, G. 2003, 'Modeling Reactive Behavior in ORM'. *Conceptual Modeling – ER2003*, Proc. 22nd ER Conference, Chicago, October 2003, Springer LNCS.

15. ter Hofstede, A. H. M. 1993, 'Information Modelling in Data Intensive Domains', PhD thesis, University of Nijmegen.

16. ter Hofstede, A. H. M., Proper, H. A. & Weide, th. P. van der 1993, 'Formal definition of a conceptual language for the description and manipulation of information models', *Information Systems*, vol. 18, no. 7, pp. 489-523.

17. Lipeck, U. W. 1990, 'Transformation of Dynamic Integrity Constraints into Transaction Specifications', *Theor. Comput. Sci.* 76(1): 115-142.

18. Object Management Group 2003, *UML 2.0 Superstructure Specification*. Online at: www.omg.org/uml.

19. Object Management Group 2005, *UML OCL 2.0 Specification*. Online at: http://www.omg.org/docs/ptc/05-06-06.pdf.

20. Olivé, A. 2003, 'Integrity Constraints Definition in Object-Oriented Conceptual Modeling Languages', *Proc. ER2003*, Springer LNCS, pp. 349-362.

21. Paton, N. W. & Díaz, O. 1999, 'Active Database Systems', *ACM Computing Surveys*, 31(1): 63-103.

22. Proper, H. A. 1994, 'A Theory for Conceptual Modeling of Evolving Application Domains', PhD thesis, University of Nijmegen.

23. Proper, H. A., Hoppenbrouwers, S. J. B. A., & Weide, th. P. van der 2005, 'A Fact-Oriented Approach to Activity Modeling', *On the Move to Meaningful Internet Systems 2005: OTM 2005 Workshops*, eds R. Meersman, Z. Tari, P. Herrero et al., Cyprus. Springer LNCS 3762, pp 666-75.

24. Theodoulidis C., Loucopoulos P. & Kopanas, V. 1992, 'A Rule Oriented Formalism for Active Temporal Databases', *Next Generation CASE Tools*, eds K. Lyytinen & V.-P Tahvanainen, IOS Press, Amsterdam.

25. Theodoulidis C., Wangler B., & Loucopoulos P. 1992, 'The Entity-Relationship-Time Model', *Conceptual Modelling, Databases, and CASE: An Integrated View of Information Systems Development*, ch. 4, pp. 87-115, John Wiley & Sons.

26. Warmer, J. & Kleppe, A. 2003, *The Object Constraint Language, 2nd Edition*, Addison-Wesley.

27. Wintraecken J. 1990, *The NIAM Information Analysis Method: Theory and Practice*, Kluwer, Deventer, The Netherlands.

Some Features of State Machines in ORM

Tony Morgan

Neumont University, Utah, USA
tony.morgan@neumont.edu

Abstract. ORM provides an excellent approach for information modeling, but to date has been limited mainly to descriptions of static information structures. This paper provides an outline of how ORM could be extended to add behavioral descriptions through the use of state machines. Most of the discussion is illustrated by an example of how a simple model could be extended in this way. Some suggestions are given for an outline process for adding state machine descriptions to ORM models and the developments required to integrate such descriptions into a comprehensive modeling environment.

1 Introduction

In modeling enterprise information systems we have to consider two main aspects: the nature and structure of the information, and the way that the information is produced, transformed and consumed by business activities. Management of the resulting complexity and its alignment with the evolution of the business is a continued challenge. ORM provides a systematic approach to modeling information structure, to the extent that some information system assets (such as database designs) can be generated from a model, but does not address the behavioral aspects needed for system full definition.

One approach to the definition of dynamic behavior is built around the concept of state machines. In simple terms, a state machine encapsulates some data storage and behavior within a notional container that can take responsibility for some specific activities within an information system. State machines typically interact with their external environment by receiving and transmitting messages. The operation of a complete information system can be visualized in terms of messages flowing between a large number of state machine instances. Although the number of instances may be large, the number of different *kinds* of state machines required to provide the desired functionality is normally much smaller. In terms of modeling this reduces the problem to more manageable proportions, since it is only necessary to model each different kind of state machine, not each instance.

The approach has been used successfully for many years, particularly in the design of real-time systems (for which it is arguably the standard approach). It does introduce an additional technical artifact into a conceptual model, but one that does not need to assume any specific implementation technology. A state machine description of behavior can be just as conceptual as the *object type* and *fact type* artifacts in a conventional ORM model. The benefit gained is the ability to describe desired behaviors in addition to describing the information structure that supports those behaviors.

R. Meersman, Z. Tari, P. Herrero et al. (Eds.): OTM Workshops 2006, LNCS 4278, pp. 1211–1220, 2006.
© Springer-Verlag Berlin Heidelberg 2006

2 A Simple Example

2.1 The Basic Model

Fig.1 shows a fragment of an ORM model relating to seminars that may be offered to students in some hypothetical university. The diagram uses ORM2 notation [1].

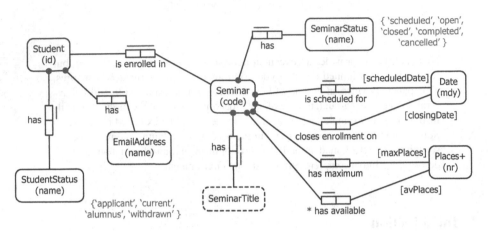

* Seminar.avPlaces = Seminar.maxPlaces - count(Seminar.student)

Fig. 1. A simple seminar model

Each specific seminar is identified by a code, and also has a unique title. Seminars are scheduled for a specific date, and have a maximum number of places available for students. Enrollment of students begins at some point convenient to the seminar administrators and remains open until a closing date, set to be some time before the scheduled date for the seminar. Enrollment may also be closed if there are no more places available on the seminar. The number of available places on a seminar can be derived by subtracting the number of students currently enrolled from the maximum number of places available. Each student (a potential enrollee for a seminar) is assumed to be given a unique identifier at the time of their application to the university, which is retained throughout their association with the university. Each student also has a status that reflects their current standing with the university and a unique email address, either of which could change over time.

There is no limit on seminar enrollments for current students. Applicants (prospective students) and alumni (past students) are allowed to be enrolled for up to one seminar. Students who have withdrawn are no longer eligible to attend seminars.

The model is deliberately simplified. In practice, many other fact types and object types would be likely, such as the name of the seminar presenter, the location of a seminar, student names and addresses, and so on. Also note that the only constraints used in this model are internal mandatory and uniqueness constraints. Some role names have been added for convenience.

Fig 2 shows an equivalent UML class model for the same example. This appears more compact model than Fig 1, but this is only at the price of losing some of the information exposed in the ORM model.

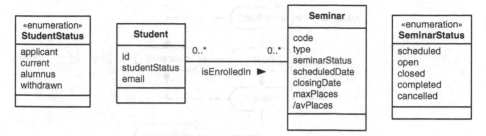

Fig. 2. An equivalent UML seminar model

2.2 Stateful Behavior

Focusing firstly on seminars, it's apparent that one of a few possible sets of conditions will apply to a seminar at any particular point in time. For our purposes we can take the following situations as significant.

scheduled – the seminar is defined and planned for a specific date

open – students can be enrolled for the seminar

closed – students can no longer be enrolled for the seminar

completed – the seminar has been held

cancelled – the previously scheduled seminar will no longer take place.

These conditions collectively capture the notion of the 'state' of a particular seminar. This particular notion of state differs from the more general notion sometimes used in an ORM context. For instance, a Conceptual Information Processor (CIP) for an ORM model will experience a change of state for any update, addition or removal of a fact in this most general sense (see [6]). On this scale we could say that the state of a seminar changes with *any* change to related facts, resulting in a potentially very large number of possible states. This is not particularly useful, and we need a more manageable way of defining behavior. In the remainder of this paper, 'state' is used to indicate one of a small set of possible situations (such as 'scheduled', 'open', etc.)

Even with the simple model above, we can see that desired behavior is influenced by state. For example, we would want to ensure that a new fact of the type Student is enrolled in Seminar can be added only if the seminar status is 'open'. Such an enrollment will not in itself change the state of the seminar (taking this more specific definition of state) providing that the number of students enrolled is less than the maximum number of places available.

Clearly, we need to identify the possible transitions between one state of a seminar and another. The most straightforward way of showing this is by a diagram with directed arcs between the labeled states, as shown in Fig. 3. The arcs between the states can be identified with actions or events causing the transitions, as explained in more detail shortly.

The diagram shows that each seminar begins in the 'scheduled' state, then can transition through the states 'open', 'closed' and 'completed' in succession. A change of circumstances may allow a seminar that has been closed to be re-opened. A seminar can be cancelled at any time while it is in the 'scheduled', 'open' or 'closed' states: it obviously makes no sense to cancel a seminar that had already been completed.

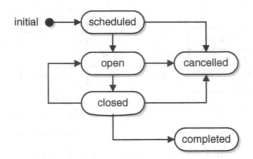

Fig. 3. State transition diagram for seminars

Information on seminars is assumed to be retained indefinitely, so there is no transition to an 'end' pseudo-state. Once scheduled, a seminar will ultimately end up as either 'cancelled' or 'completed', after which no further changes of state can occur.

States and transitions could be defined in various ways. One example would be a table with rows and columns representing 'from' and 'to' states, with the cells defining the actions or events causing the transition. Another might be a specialized small language for describing states and transitions. However, some form of graphical notation would probably be the most intuitive representation for the majority of modelers.

2.3 State Machine Definitions

Diagrams of this kind have been extended and formalized by Harel as 'statecharts' [2], and the ideas have been widely adopted, most notably as one of the diagram types available in the Unified Modeling Language (UML) [3]. These more elaborate statechart-based approaches allow for more complex constructs, such as nested states, and concurrent activities, but the simple transition diagram above is sufficient for the current discussion.

In general, then, we can use notations similar to Fig.3 to show the permitted transitions for any given state machine. Such diagrams are not currently defined for ORM, but there seems to be no reason why a statechart-like representation could not be used in conjunction with an information model similar to Fig.1. This makes it necessary to understand the relationship between these two representations. Putting this into simple terms: where is the state machine in Fig.1?

In order to answer this question we need to consider state machines from another perspective. There are two classic state machine models, named after their respective inventors [4]. Moore machines have outputs associated with states; Mealy machines have outputs associated with transitions as shown in Fig.4. Both models feature state memory to retain information pertaining to states and logic relating inputs and outputs to states and transitions. The models are equivalently powerful, and, indeed, one type can be converted systematically to the other.

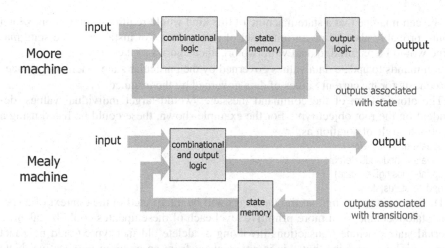

Fig. 4. Classical state machine models

From our perspective, the differences between these models are not particularly relevant: the crucial point they both make is that state machines require some form of state memory and some associated logic. In the context of an ORM model it should be clear that the state memory will correspond to one or more facts (i.e. instances of fact types), and that the logic will be defined by rules that operate with those facts. The inputs and outputs correspond to events in an information system. Again, these are not directly represented in ORM, but we can borrow some notions from other approaches to provide a sufficient outline.

2.4 Identifying State Machines

An ORM model will generally contain many object types. Any of these could potentially be a candidate as the focal point for a state machine. A large ORM model could conceivably include several state machines which could interact in an asynchronous way – a change of state in one state machine does not necessarily relate directly to a change of state in another state machine.

Returning to the simple model shown in Fig.1 we need to identify which fact types belong to which state machine. It's obvious that there will be a strong connection between the SeminarStatus and Seminar object types, since the former effectively provides an enumeration of the possible states of the latter. SeminarStatus is functionally dependent on Seminar – a seminar can be in only one state, but the same state could apply to several seminars. It's obvious from the diagram that there are several other functional dependencies covering the maximum and available number of places and the scheduled and closing dates for the seminar. Collectively, these dependencies point to a key role played by Seminar, and make it a prime candidate to be the focus for a state machine. Conceptually, we can consider a Seminar state machine that takes responsibility for maintaining information on its associated numbers of places and dates in response to messages received from its environment.

We can imagine that a state machine of this kind would require instantiation, which would probably also define an initial set of data values. An instance of the state machine would be required to deal with two broad categories of message:
- commands to update data values governed by the particular state machine instance
- requests for the current values of data governed by the instance.

The atomic form of the command messages would target individual values, dependent on the root object type. For the example shown, these could be listed using a functional style of notation as:

```
update-maxPlaces(nr)
update-scheduledDate(date)
update-closingDate(date)
update-status(status)
```

Here we are assuming that the messages will be interpreted in the context of a specific state machine. At a more primitive level each of these updates could be taken as internal state machine transactions involving a <delete old fact type>/<add new fact type> pair of operations, but this is not relevant from an external perspective. Note that there is no command message to update the number of available places, since we are assuming that this can be derived from other information.

In principle, a corresponding set of messages could be defined to retrieve the current data values, but it is not obvious from the model that this would be the best thing to do. In practice, it's likely to be more efficient to return multiple values in response to a single message. However, the conceptual model does not contain sufficient information to allow us to judge the best way of providing access to the information. Even for the small state machine in the example there are many possible combinations of data values, and the figure grows rapidly for more complex state machines. One possible default is to return all data relevant to the state machine instance in a single message, but this may also be inefficient if some of the returned information is only going to be discarded by the caller.

The missing element of guidance is a specification for the anticipated usage of the state machine, in terms of the data combinations required and the associated frequency of demand. This is not an intrinsic property of the information, and so is typically not represented in an information model. In fact, the relationship between an information model and its anticipated usage is not one-to-one. The same information model could have several different usage scenarios to meet different business conditions. For the moment it's convenient to assume the existence of some auxiliary information that would provide sufficient definition of usage.

It is less obvious, but similar comments apply to the 'update' commands. In the context of the seminar model it seems reasonable to suppose that any of the values could be updated independently, but this may not always be the case: we could imagine situations requiring updates to multiple values in different combinations, creating a similar situation to the information requests (and requiring a similar solution).

2.5 Other Fact Types

With the caveats above, the initial idea of imposing a state machine boundary around some of the object types and fact types in Fig.1 seems promising. However, there are other elements shown in the diagram that have not yet been considered.

The Seminar object type, plays two other roles. Firstly, each seminar has a unique SeminarTitle This plays no other role, and is unlikely to have its own dynamic behavior, so the best approach would be to incorporate it into the Seminar state machine.

The other role played by a seminar is in the relationship with students, in the fact type Student is enrolled in Seminar. This is a many-to-many relationship: a seminar is likely to have many students enrolled, and a student could enroll for several seminars. Since the relationship is symmetrical, it would appear to be just as sensible to include the fact type in a hypothetical Student state machine as in the Seminar state machine. We seem to have four possibilities for dealing with this fact type:

1. Make it a state machine in its own right
2. Incorporate it into the Seminar state machine
3. Incorporate it into a Student state machine
4. Allow both Seminar and Student state machines to hold copies of the fact type

The first option appears to be the cleanest because it maintains the integrity of the information structure ('normalized', in database terminology). We could give the state machine a name such as Enrollment and assume a similar style of activity as the tentative Seminar state machine already discussed, in terms of responding to messages from its environment. The only update commands to which it would need to respond would be to add or delete a fact of the one specific type. It's worth noting in passing that this option is not available in the UML model of Fig. 2. In UML, only classes can have stateful behavior, and so we would be forced to add an additional class to Fig. 2 to provide a container for anything that is 'between' the Student and Seminar classes.

It may seem an overkill to define a state machine to deal only with one simple fact type, and so we might consider the second or third options. In these cases we are implicitly assuming that the state machines will handle collections rather than individual facts: the Student state machine would need a list of seminars in which that student is enrolled or the Seminar state machine would need a list of enrolled students. This is similar to de-normalizing a database design, and may be appropriate to consider for similar reasons, largely based on performance (some other reasons are given below). As with the choice of message options discussed above, the choice of which state machine should 'own' the fact type for optimum performance requires additional information beyond the information structures, such as the relative numbers of students and seminars and the anticipated frequency of add/drop activities.

The fourth alternative might be relevant in cases where extreme responsiveness to queries is required, but the overhead of synchronizing changes to the Student and Seminar copies of the information might rule this option out in some situations.

2.6 State Machine Logic and Transactions

Most of the discussion so far has centered on fact types associated with a particular state machine, following partitioning concepts similar to those found in relational database design. Recall that as well as 'state memory', another essential ingredient of a state machine is the logic used to define the operations of the state machine. Another reason for preferring one clustering to another is therefore the ability of a state machine to apply the necessary constraints to its operations. We can examine some other issues by looking at the possible state transitions for Students, shown in Fig. 5.

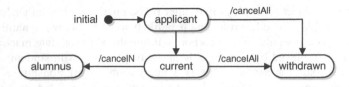

Fig. 5. Student state transitions

This state model has additional notation on some of the transitions to indicate actions, as explained shortly. As before, the information is assumed to be maintained indefinitely so there is no 'end' pseudo-state. Any student enrolled will ultimately end up in the one of state 'alumnus' or 'withdrawn'. The model as shown explicitly excludes the case of an alumnus becoming a current student again, but could easily be extended to add this possibility.

All states except 'current' have limitations on the number of seminars for which a student may enroll. We may therefore need to take some action to enforce this constraint if there is a change of status. Consider the case of a 'current' student enrolled for several outstanding seminars. The student graduates earlier than expected, and therefore changes status to 'alumnus'. The administration could adopt several possible policies, any of which could be a perfectly sensible response to this situation:

- apply status checks only for new enrollments (i.e. ignore changes in student status for existing enrollments)
- cancel all enrollments for this student, and ask them to re-enroll if they wish (in which case both Seminar and Student states will come into consideration)
- negotiate with the student to drop existing seminar enrollments until at most one remains.

We will assume here that the constraints are to be enforced on all state changes.

For students with no seminar enrollments, no action is required on change of state. A transition to the state 'withdrawn' will result in cancellation of all enrollments (there will be at most one if the previous state was 'applicant') through the cancelAll action. A transition to the state 'alumnus' may cancel several enrollments (but not necessarily all) through the cancelN action. The cancellation actions correspond to the deletion of instances of the fact type Student is enrolled in Seminar involving a particular student.

In order to maintain the information system in a consistent state, it is likely that several actions must be completed together (for example, change to student status, cancellation of several seminar enrollments, ...). It therefore seems reasonable to treat these together as a single transaction and automate them as such in implementation. However, this may not be desirable with the cancelN action if this involves negotiation with the student about which enrollments to drop. A more likely strategy in this case would be to define a compensating transaction.

Clearly, even the fairly straightforward logic of this example raises interesting issues. In practice, the logic associated with a state machine could be arbitrarily complex, depending on the application. State machines offer a potentially useful container for business rules [5] since bridge both static and dynamic views of information.

3   Relationship with Existing Approaches

Certain aspects of state modeling echo some features found in other fact-based approaches, such as DEMO [8], although space does not permit further discussion here. Also relevant are the realizations of ORM models in the form of databases (via RMap) and Object Oriented software designs (OOD).

RMap   The partitioning of an ORM model into state machines is strongly paralleled by the well known 'RMap' procedure for mapping an ORM model onto a relational database [6]. In the case of RMap, the partitioning decisions are made only on the basis of information structure. For state machine partitioning, other considerations come into play, and the boundaries between state machines may not be quite the same as the boundaries that RMap would have indicated for relational mapping.

OOD   In a similar vein, several Object Oriented Design (OOD) approaches advocate the use of state machine definitions for classes that have behaviors that can be defined in terms of states. This indeed has been the basis for entire methodologies, such as the Shlaer-Mellor approach, which has subsequently evolved into 'Executable UML' [7]. Typically, classes can define associated state machines, and the instances (objects) corresponding to those classes execute the defined behaviors. Although UML (and related approaches) provide a level of integration between definitions of information and behavior, information structure definitions in UML lack the precision available in ORM. There would seem to be no reason why ORM should not be augmented with the ability to define behavior the same way that classes can be supplemented by state machines in UML.

4   Conclusions

4.1   Tentative Design Guidelines

The following tentative guidelines offer some suggestions on the activities required to add state machine descriptions to ORM models. These steps are not intended to be taken in a strict sequence: in practice some iteration will be likely before reaching a satisfactory conclusion.

- Start from a conventional ORM model of the domain, giving a static view of all relevant information
- Use a modified RMap approach to identify potential state machines. Consider whether the object(s) within the boundaries do indeed have stateful behavior.
- Include a suitable object type in each identified state machine to contain its current state, with a value constraint to enumerate all of its possible states.
- For each state machine, produce a definition of its dynamic behavior using a statechart or some suitable alternative.

- For each state machine, produce a set of declarative rules that define the constraints on possible actions and transitions for each state.
- Add information on anticipated usage, to guide implementers in choosing the most appropriate realization of each state machine.

4.2 What's Required to Add State Machine Behavioral Descriptions to ORM?

Although it is possible to use various ad-hoc methods to augment ORM models with state machine descriptions, the full power of the approach can only be realized if there is a high degree of integration of static and dynamic views. The following points summarize some desirable extensions to support this agenda.

- Some additional notation is required to indicate state machine boundaries on an ORM diagram. This would not change the interpretation of any of the existing ORM notation and could be done by a simple 'lasso' style of graphical markup.
- An auxiliary notation is required to define states and their possible transitions. Some form of statechart diagram would probably be the most effective way of achieving this. This should include a means of defining the events and/or messages to which the state machine must respond (for example, by triggering state transitions). More work is needed to establish the precise form that this should take and the relationships between the various features of the state chart and the existing features of static ORM models.
- ORM has several alternative but informal notations for derivation rules. Defining the internal logic of a state machine would be greatly aided by single consistent rule definition notation. There is interest in this outside the context of state machines and some work on this is already under way as part of the ORM2 initiative.
- In order to guide the mapping of a state machine onto an implementation, some auxiliary information would be required to give at least an indication of anticipated usage. This could be provided by ad-hoc textual annotations, but, again, a more consistent and standardized approach would allow for better integration with other functions (such as code generation) in a comprehensive modeling environment.

References

1. Halpin, T. 2005, 'ORM 2', *On the Move to Meaningful Internet Systems 2005*: OTM 2005 Workshops, eds R. Meersman, Z. Tari, P. Herrero et al., Cyprus. Springer LNCS 3762, pp 676-87.
2. Harel, D and Gery E.: *Executable Object Modeling with Statecharts*, IEEE Computer, July 1997
3. UML: http://www.uml.org/
4. http://en.wikipedia.org/wiki/Moore_machine (links to Mealy machine)
5. Morgan, T.: *Business Rules and Information Systems*, Addison-Wesley (2002)
6. Halpin, T.: *Information Modeling and Relational Databases*, Morgan Kaufmann, (2001)
7. Mellor, S and Balcer, M.: *Executable UML*, Addison-Wesley (2002)
8. Dietz, J.L.G., T. Halpin, Using DEMO and ORM in Concert – a Case Study, in: K. Siau (ed.) *Advanced Topics in Database Research*, vol. 3, ch. XI, Idea Group Inc., 2004

Data Modeling Patterns Using
Fully Communication Oriented
Information Modeling (FCO-IM)

Fazat Nur Azizah and Guido Bakema

Research and Competence Group Data Architectures & Metadata Management
Informatics and Communication Academy, HAN University of Applied Science
Beverweerdlaan 3, 6825AE Arnhem, The Netherlands
Tel.: +31-26-3658271; Fax: +31-26-3658126
FN.Azizah@han.nl, Guido.Bakema@han.nl

Abstract. Data modeling patterns is an emerging field of research in the data modeling area. Its aims are to create a body of knowledge to help understand data modeling problems better and to create better data models. Current data modeling patterns are generally domain-specific patterns (only applicable in a specific domain, e.g. a business situation) and with an Entity Relationship Modeling (ERM) way of thinking. This paper discusses data modeling patterns using the expressive power of Fully Communication Oriented Information Modeling (FCO-IM), a Dutch Fact Oriented Modeling (FOM) method. We also consider more abstract data modeling patterns – the generic patterns – and describe a few basic generic data modeling patterns in brief as well as a generic pattern found in content versioning problems.

1 Introduction

The vast bulk of current work on patterns is carried out in the field of object oriented applications, but some notable work has been done in the field of data modeling as well [7, 12]. The importance of data modeling patterns is clear: although data modeling is a crucial part of the information systems development life cycle, data modeling is a rather expensive activity, and it is in general not easy to come up with a good data model. Patterns can help data modelers to do their job better and so reduce costs.

Most data modeling patterns are domain-specific ones; such patterns are applicable only to one particular domain, for example a given business case. It is interesting to investigate patterns from the structure level point of view of data modeling itself, instead of related to the domain of the content.

Current work on data modeling patterns generally employs Entity Relationship Modeling (ERM) for presenting patterns, not only as the means of describing the proposed data models, but also for discussing the way of thinking behind them. In the fact oriented data modeling community however, patterns are hardly discussed yet, although Fact Oriented Modeling (FOM) techniques provide a promising approach for dealing with data modeling patterns, because of their different way of thinking.

R. Meersman, Z. Tari, P. Herrero et al. (Eds.): OTM Workshops 2006, LNCS 4278, pp. 1221–1230, 2006.

2 Patterns

Generally speaking, people try to recognize patterns to understand the world better and to use these patterns to their advantage. The need of finding and codifying patterns arises in particular from the wish to reuse existing and proven solutions to particular recurring problems. This makes it an attractive subject, not only for researchers, but also for practitioners.

The goal of pattern finding is to create a body of knowledge that helps us to understand and to resolve recurring problems, by documenting insight and knowledge gained from problem solving experience and by putting these into a shared vocabulary that helps us to exchange these solutions and the lessons learned from them.

2.1 Definition

A widely accepted definition reveals a pattern as *a proven solution to a problem in a context* [2]. This definition is derived from one given by Christopher Alexander[1]: "each pattern is a three-part rule, which expresses a relation between a certain *context*, a *problem*, and a *solution*." [1]. Although others provide slightly different definitions, this one seems adequate.

So: a pattern is an instruction or a description of a solution to a (recurring) problem with its goals and constraints, which takes place in a certain context. But it does more than just *describe* a solution; it should also *explain* why the solution is adequate. For further discussions on this topic, see [2, 3].

2.2 Elements of Patterns

From the definition, the three basic elements of a pattern can already be seen: *context*, *problem*, *solution*. Several authors describe a few extra properties that should be present as well. For details on this subject, see [3]. Despite all differences in formats, the following essential elements are often mentioned [10]:
1. *Name*: a meaningful designation to refer to the pattern and the knowledge and structure it describes.
2. *Problem*: a statement that describes the intent of the pattern; i.e. the goals and objectives it wants to reach within the given context.
3. *Context*: the preconditions under which the problem and its solution seem to occur and for which the solution is desirable.
4. *Solution*: rules describing how to realize the desired outcome, often equivalent to giving instructions describing how to construct the necessary work products.
5. *Examples*: one or more sample applications which illustrate: a specific initial context; how the pattern is applied to it and transforms it, and the resulting context.

3 Data Modeling Patterns

Ever since the data modeling area was established by its founding fathers, such as Edward Codd, Peter Chen, Sjir Nijssen and others, data modeling has played a crucial

---

[1] Christopher Alexander, a physical architect, is known for his writings on patterns in urban planning and building architecture. His writings influenced people from other fields, including software engineers.

role in the development life cycle of software and information systems. Data modeling methods, such as ERM and FOM, were invented to master the vast amount of data owned by organizations and to derive physical data models to store, retrieve and manipulate these data efficiently. With the increasing number of data models created to solve various types of problems, data modelers started to think about patterns in these data models to reuse proven solutions.

The work of David Hay [7] is appreciated by researchers and practitioners in the software and information systems development area. He composed a collection of patterns of data models applicable in several business situations that is more or less accepted as a standard and used in practice. Other researchers refer to him for further study on patterns in data modeling. Other noteworthy work was done by Silverston [12], though this is more a collection of data models, rather than a collection of data model patterns. In [8], Ralph Kimball provides a useful and often consulted set of (dimensional) data models.

3.1   Levels of Data Modeling Patterns

The data modeling patterns mentioned above contain specific aspects that often occur in business applications, such as organization structure, product, manufacturing, and contract. The patterns are found in solutions to data modeling problems in businesses. Therefore, these patterns are only suitable for assisting the data modeling process in these business situations. If someone wants to create a data model for another type of application, then the patterns will probably not be useful anymore, or perhaps only a small portion of the patterns can be used for the new situation.

From the perspective of abstraction, such domain-specific data modeling patterns are at the lowest abstraction level. They have a particular domain of application, certain particular terminologies, and certain particular semantics of objects and relationships.

However, when the structure of these patterns is observed more carefully, it turns out that a higher abstraction level is sometimes present as well. Such a kind of pattern shows up in several domain-specific patterns. For example: the model of the hierarchy of *Geographic Location* in David Hay's *People and Organizations* pattern is essentially the same as the model of the hierarchy of *Activity* in his *Activities* pattern [7], and it is even similar to the way Martin Fowler modeled his *Organization Structure* object oriented pattern [6]. All these hierarchies have a common structure, which is simply a cyclic binary homogeneous relationship (i.e: the same entity type occurs at both ends of a binary relationship type, a structure that is sometimes incorrectly called recursive).

Such a generic pattern, showing up three times in different domain-specific patterns, can be used to build other domain-specific patterns. Therefore these patterns are related to a *class* of problems rather than to one domain problem. Hence, they belong to a higher abstraction level than the domain-specific patterns. Hypothetically, the generic patterns should be able to help solve a wider range of problems than the domain-specific ones.

In addition, above this generic pattern, there might be an even higher level of abstraction with respect to patterns: the meta generic pattern(s). The meta generic pattern(s) capture the entire idea of patterns and provide knowledge about patterns themselves. This constitutes the most interesting and also the most difficult topic of studying patterns, which we intend to study further in the near future. See figure 1.

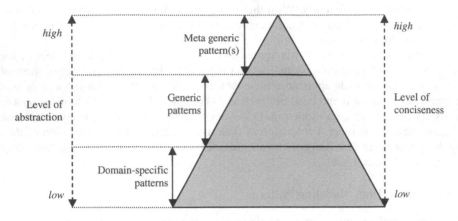

Fig. 1. The levels of patterns

Figure 1 also depicts the level of conciseness of data model patterns, which goes along the direction of the level of abstraction. This means that the higher the level of abstraction is, the more concise the pattern becomes, and vice versa. This conveys the principle of pattern generativity [3], which succinctly states: a more elaborated pattern (with low conciseness) is built from more concise patterns.

In the following sections of this article, the full emphasis is on the generic patterns.

3.2 Data Modeling Patterns in FOM

Although the primary focus of defining patterns is not so much on technology, but on creating the culture to document the patterns [3], with respect to data modeling patterns, it is important to choose the appropriate methodology of representation. The methodology is not about creating diagrams that describes how data is represented, but primarily a way of thinking in viewing a problem and a way of communicating ideas for problem solving among analysts and domain experts.

The ERM approach, the most popular approach to data modeling and describing data modeling patterns, considers the Universe of Discourse (UoD) as a collection of entities having relationships which each other. In a similar fashion, an Object Oriented Modeling (OOM) approach[2] sees the UoD as a collection of objects interacting with each other. FOM approaches consider the UoD to be described by a set of declarative facts. These different approaches provide different ways of looking at patterns.

In the FOM community, not much discussion has taken place till now about data modeling patterns. A FOM approach offers several valuable things for finding and describing patterns. Firstly, it provides a more detailed way, even at an atomic level, of

---

[2] Although formally the Object Oriented Modeling approach is not a data modeling technique, some parts of it are commonly used for data modeling; e.g. class diagrams in UML.

looking at things, because it analyzes *elementary* facts instead of grouped facts in the form of entities or objects. This provides an advantage in examining the problem from the most basic level. Secondly, a FOM approach has a higher level of conceptuality compared with the ERM or OOM approaches (see [5] for 100% conceptualization principle). It is closer to the user world by providing a better way of communication. Finally, some FOM methods, such as FCO-IM, offer the possibility of using powerful modeling constructs such as generalization and recursive identification [5], providing a broader opportunity for pattern application. In [4] a complex example of recursive identification is discussed. FCO-IM consistently presents all of the power of fact oriented data modeling mentioned above.

3.3 Quality of Data Modeling Patterns

Patterns in data modeling are found from perhaps hundreds of different solutions to a particular problem, designed by different data modelers. It is possible that all these solutions correctly capture the user requirements. Nevertheless, not all of these solutions have the quality to be considered as good data models. So, it is desirable to be able to select a qualitatively good solution to a particular problem given a certain context. After all, the goal of data modeling patterns is to help information modelers to create better data models. So, we have to define criteria for good data modeling patterns.

Some experts list which qualities should be present in a good pattern [3, 9]. However, it is Christopher Alexander who has described a stunning definition of quality that he called the 'Quality Without A Name' (QWAN). This quality imparts incommunicable beauty and immeasurable value to a structure. Alexander proposes the existence of an objective quality of aesthetic beauty that is universally recognizable [3].

Nevertheless it seems desirable to define more precisely which qualities a data modeling pattern should possess. No author has written about quality of data modeling patterns[3]. Not much has been written about the quality of data models either, apart from models (using ERM) produced by students in simple and contrived exercises.

Still, there are some useful works. Graeme Simsion provides ten quality factors for data models [13]. Some of these quality factors may be applicable to patterns as well; for example *non-redundancy*[4] (which is more or less automatically assured when a FOM method, like FCO-IM, is used). Another quality factor might be the key factor for determining the QWAN for data modeling patterns: *elegance*. The concept of elegance is associated with *consistency*, *conciseness* and *comprehensiveness*. A few criteria that hypothetically will be useful for measuring the elegance of a data model:

1. *Syntactic, semantic, and layout standards*
   A standard style of defining the data model leads to a more consistent data model, by consequently using standards of syntax and semantics and providing standard layout that helps understand the data model.
2. *Size of a data model*
   In general: the smaller the data model for a given UoD, the more concise it is. In FCO-IM terms: the fewer elementary fact types (either nominalized or not nominalized), the better the model; and for each fact type: the fewer roles, the better.

---

[3] In [5] David Hay speaks about drawing up a good data model, but he does not mention anything about the quality of data model patterns itself.

[4] FOM methods, when employed properly, guarantee 5NF data models.

3. *Abstraction level of a data model*

Conciseness of data models can be achieved by putting more general (higher level of abstraction) structures in the data model. General structures can also improve the level of comprehensiveness. More abstract data models might also be reuseable in broader contexts. But introducing abstraction must be done in a controlled way, because over-abstraction could lead to the contrary: loss of comprehensiveness, apart from difficulties with respect to the implementation.

4. *Completeness of a data model*

The data model must cover all aspects of the UoD that should be modeled. This should not be sacrificed for the sake of conciseness.

In the end, the pursuit of equilibrium among these aspects is the most important factor for defining the elegance of a data model as well as a data model pattern. Further investigation is required to determine exact scale to measure the elegance; therefore, this will not going to be considered further for the moment.

4   Generic Data Modeling Patterns

Finding a good pattern is a difficult task. However, the principle of generativity of patterns [3] gives us a clue on how to find patterns. This principle states that patterns are built from building blocks that are also patterns; a procedure which ends with the most basic building blocks. In the case of generic data modeling patterns, these basic building blocks can be determined from the smallest recurring structures that can be used to build larger building blocks. From the level of conciseness of the pattern point of view, this provides a bottom up approach in finding larger generic data modeling patterns.

However, since generic patterns can be found from the study of domain-specific patterns, a top down approach can also be employed by studying several domain-specific patterns, or even by studying cases in which no pattern has been defined before, that possess similar structures. These similar structures can be abstracted into the generic patterns.

4.1   Basic Generic Data Modeling Patterns

The basic generic data modeling patterns provide the highest level of abstraction of the generic data modeling patterns. From the point of view of conciseness, they could be the most concise patterns however. They provide the basic pattern structures that can be employed by other generic and domain-specific level patterns.

There are several basic constructs in FCO-IM that can serve as basic generic patterns. Some of them are:

1. Semantically Equivalent Transformation Patterns (e.g. object to fact type transformation, nominalization, and specialization/subtyping).
2. Generalization Patterns (e.g. generalization with synonymy, generalization with homonymy, and recursive identification).

The full description of all these constructs can be found in [5], including denormalization, handling exception cases, etc.

4.2 Example: A Generic Pattern in Content Versioning Problem

This section discusses a brief example of pattern documentation in cases with content versioning problems. It is an example of a generic pattern derived from domain-specific patterns and cases. The generic notion of the case is about the management of the content of documents that undergo versioning, i.e. the history of versions of the document must be recorded. This can occur in many fields, from legislation to manufacturing industry. Consequently, it is a useful pattern. Two cases have been studied:

Legislation[5]. This case reflects the management of revisions of laws. The case – coming from the principle that every citizen must have access to laws – asks for a repository for laws and their successive versions.

A volume of laws consists of several parts. These parts contain chapters and chapters contain sections. Each section consists of articles. Each of these elements can be subjected to revision. For example, revision may occur at the article level, in which case the version of the section (the next higher level) does not change, just the version of the article in question. But it can also occur that a whole law changes, which leads to a different version of the entire law.

Each version must be in one of the following states: draft, review, approved, or historical. The content of each version is stored in an XML file.

Bill of Materials[6]. The bill of materials case is related to the planning and assembling of products in manufacturing processes. Each product comprises several components (which are also products). When a product is ordered, it means that its components must be ordered. The components may be in-house products or must be ordered from outside party. Each of these components may consist of several other components which must be ordered as well then.

Versioning may take place at every level of hierarchy. Each version may be in one of at least two states: current or historical. For each level of the bill of materials, the quantity ordered is recorded, and some other attributes.

Both cases deal with versioning of objects. Each version may have several attributes; an attribute in common is the state of the version. Both cases deal with compound objects, i.e. objects that are composed of one or more elements. In the legislation case, it is the law document that possesses the hierarchical structure of a document; in the bill of materials case, it is the bill of materials that may consist of several levels of components.

The following description can be made for the pattern found in these content versioning cases:

1. *Name*: Content Versioning Pattern
2. *Problem*: Create a data model for a structure that deals with an object that may have several versions due to revision acts. The object may be a compound object i.e. an object that is composed of one or more elements that may be compound as well. In the case of a compound object, each of the elements may be subjected to revision.

---

[5] This case is a simplified version of a case used in an Enterprise Content Management course in the study program Master of Information Systems Development of HAN University.

[6] For a more detailed description of the bill of materials case, see for example http://www.ciras.iastate.edu/publications/CIRASNews/fall97/bom.html.

1228   F.N. Azizah and G. Bakema

3. *Context*: No particular context is required.
4. *Solution*: Data modelers can think of several ways of modeling this. The following proposed solution is (with some adaptation and simplification) based on a data model that was created in practice for the legislation case. We chose this data model because of its simplicity in solving a relatively complex problem. It models the compound objects as a single object type, showing a high level of abstraction in the understanding of the compound object.

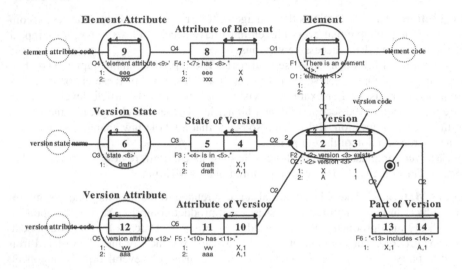

Fig. 2. General FCO-IM data model solution for the Content Versioning Pattern

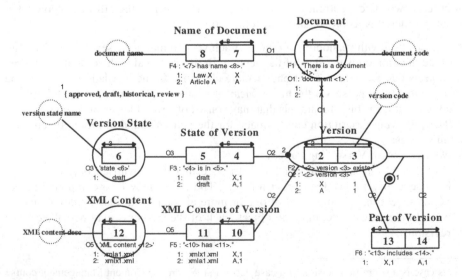

Fig. 3. Data model for legislation problem based on the Content Versioning Pattern

The general solution is shown in figure 2. 'Version' is an object type, i.e. a nominalized fact type, with two roles; one role played by 'version code', the other played by an object type 'Element'. The hierarchy is modeled by defining the parts of a 'Version' (which are also a 'Version'), shown by fact type 'Part of Version'. For example: in the law document, element X version 1 which is a volume of law can have element A version 1 as its part, which is a chapter.

Element and Version can have their own attributes, which are depicted as extra fact types – called 'Attributes of Element' and 'Attribute of Version' – played by the respective object types. These fact types can be further adapted depending on the situation in which the pattern is implemented. A common fact type for every content versioning problem is about the state of version, as depicted in fact type 'State of Version'.

5. *Example*: The application of the pattern for the legislation problem based on the content versioning pattern is shown in figure 3. To cut the discussion short, only the data model solution is given. In this model, the term 'Element' is modified into 'Document' to meet the terminology used in legislation problem. Some extra fact types are added as the attributes of both 'Version' and 'Document'.

5 Conclusion and Future Work

Although still in a very preliminary stage, the result of this study gives a promising prospect of finding more generic data modeling patterns. However, finding and writing a pattern is not an easy task and feedback from other parties is required.

The difficulty in defining generic data modeling patterns lies in two aspects:

- understanding deeply the underlying structure;
- choosing the best solution out of all existing proven solutions.

Even in the simple case of the content versioning pattern, these difficulties are present. Therefore, it is important to study quality criteria for data modeling patterns further and to find proper criteria and scale for measuring the quality of patterns. Nevertheless, in cases that have the same structure as the content versioning pattern, this solution can be reused, with little adaptations.

The use of a FOM method, such as FCO-IM, provides a more detailed and yet more conceptual view: the real structure of the solution of the pattern can be captured properly. It is not very difficult to adapt the described pattern to a new situation that contains the same type of structure. FCO-IM provides also the advantage of describing some basic generic patterns, such as generalization and recursive identification, that are proven to be powerful patterns [4, 11].

We would like to underline the concept of levels of patterns. With more data models created for a wide range of areas, it is essential to acquire a broader view on patterns. This does not mean that domain-specific patterns are not useful, but generic patterns will provide a more consistent way for describing data model. This will help to create a comprehensive body of knowledge of data modeling patterns.

Further study is needed to investigate the role of meta generic patterns, based on the hypothesis that meta generic patterns will provide a powerful way for defining the concept of pattern description.

Acknowledgement. Jan Pieter Zwart is gratefully acknowledged for reviewing the phrasing in this paper.

References

1. Alexander, C.: *The Timeless Way of Building*, Oxford University Press, USA, 1979.
2. *A Pattern Definition*, http://hillside.net/patternsdefinition.html, downloaded at 19/04/2006.
3. Appleton, B: *Pattern and Software: Essential Concepts and Terminology*, http://www.cmcrossroads.com/bradapp/docs/patterns-intro.html, downloaded at 19/04/2006.
4. Azizah, F.N: *A Case Study of Recursive Data Modeling*, Libyan First International Symposium on Information Systems Modeling and Development, working papers, Tripoli, Libya, 2006.
5. Bakema, G.; Zwart, J. P.; Lek, H. van der: *Fully Communication Oriented Information Modeling (FCO-IM)*, 2002. The book can be downloaded for free from http://www.casetalk.com/php/index.php?FCO-IM%20English%20Book.
6. Fowler, M.: *Patterns in Enterprise Software*, http://www.martinfowler.com/articles/enterprisePatterns.html, downloaded 19/04/2006.
7. Hay, D.C.: *Data Model Patterns*, Dorset House Publishing, New York, 1996.
8. Kimball, R., Ross, M.: *The Data Warehouse Toolkit: The Complete Guide to Dimensional Modeling*, John Wiley & Sons, 2nd Edition 2002.
9. Lea, D: Christopher Alexander: *An Introduction for Object-Oriented Designers*, http://g.oswego.edu/dl/ca/ca/ca.html, downloaded at 19/04/2006.
10. Lehti, L., Ruokonen, A.: *Foundation of the patterns*, http://www.cs.tut.fi/~kk/webstuff/Foundationofpatterns.pdf, downloaded at 06/07/2006.
11. Lek, H. van der: *On the structure of an Information Grammar* , NIAM-ISDM 1993 Conference, Working Papers, Utrecht (1993).
12. Silverston, L.: *The Data Model Resource Book: Revised Edition*, Volume 1 and 2, John Wiley & Sons, Inc., 2001.
13. Simsion, G: *Better Data Models – Today, Understanding Data Model Quality*, http://www.tdan.com/ i034ht01.htm, downloaded at 19/04/2006.

Using Fact-Orientation for Instructional Design

Peter Bollen

Department of Organization and Strategy
Faculty of Economics and Business Administration
University of Maastricht
6200 MD Maastricht, The Netherlands
p.bollen@os.unimaas.nl

Abstract. In this paper we will show how fact-orientation can be used as a knowledge structuring approach for verbalizable knowledge domains, e.g. knowledge that is contained in articles, text books and instruction manuals further to be referred to as 'subject matter'. This article will illustrate the application of the fact-oriented approach as a subject matter structuring tool for a small part of the sub-domains of operations management and marketing within the university subject of business administration. We will also show that the fact-oriented modeling constructs allow us to structure knowledge on the first five levels of Bloom's taxonomy of educational objectives and we will show how the fact-oriented approach complies to the 4C/ID model for instructional design. Moreover, we will derive a 'knowledge structure metrics' model that can be empirically estimated and that can be used to estimate the complexity metric of a subject matter.

Keywords: Fact-oriented information modeling, ORM, instructional design.

1 Introduction

In the body of literature on fact-oriented conceptual modeling, a number of publications define a hierarchy in knowledge elements for a specific knowledge domain [8, 9, 10]. This research has generalized the fact-oriented modeling constructs and CSDP into a knowledge reference model for subject matters, thereby applying fact-orientation on a much larger playing field than the field of schema design for relational databases.

In this paper we will illustrate the applicability of fact-orientation for the objective of structuring knowledge, by showing that a fact-oriented knowledge reference model (KRM) can also be used for determining the complexity of a given subject domain and subsequently for the instructional design of a course on a such a subject. We will illustrate this with examples in the field of university education on two generally accepted sub-domains within the business administration subject: operations management and marketing. Earlier work that discussed the application of a predecessor to this KRM on the field of logistics can be found in [4]. In that paper the following knowledge classes are distinguished: *sentence instances*, *sentence types* (including *associated constraints*) and *derivation rules*.

R. Meersman, Z. Tari, P. Herrero et al. (Eds.): OTM Workshops 2006, LNCS 4278, pp. 1231–1241, 2006.

A subject matter has its own intrinsic structure [10]. Educational programs on a subject matter therefore, need to enable students to access such a structure or 'conceptual schema'. Unfortunately, in many available descriptions of a subject matter, e.g. text books, lecture notes, manuals, the intrinsic structure is (at best) hidden among non-structural descriptions of such a subject matter. In analogy with the Conceptual Schema Design Procedure [5: 58-60] for application domains, that serves as a 'knowledge extractor' by structuring the explicit and eliciting the implicit knowledge of domain experts in a user-analyst dialogue, we can define a knowledge extracting procedure (KEP) [3] that can be applied on explicit subject knowledge that is documented in a web-document, a text book or an instruction manual.

2 Deriving the Intrinsic Structure of a Subject Domain

In most, if not all cases, a verbalizable knowledge source is a document that often is incomplete, informal, ambiguous, possibly redundant and possibly inconsistent. As a result of applying the fact-oriented knowledge extracting procedure (KEP) [3, 9], we will yield a document that only contains structured knowledge or a knowledge grammar which structures verbalizable knowledge into the following elements (*knowledge reference model(KRM)*):

1. Knowledge domain sentences
2. Definitions and naming conventions for concepts used in domain sentences
3. Knowledge domain fact types including sentence group templates
4. Population state (transition) constraints for the knowledge domain
5. Derivation rules that specify *how* specific domain sentences can be derived from other domain sentences.
6. Rules that specify *what* fact instances can be inserted, updated or deleted.
7. Event rules that specify *when* a fact is derived from other facts or when a fact must be inserted, updated or deleted.

A KRM of a complete text book would contain hundreds, possibly thousands of concept definitions, naming conventions, fact types, population constraints, derivation rules and event rules. The knowledge extracting procedure (KEP) specifies *how* we can transform an informal, mostly incomplete, mostly undetermined, possibly redundant and possibly inconsistent description of domain knowledge into the following classes: *informal comment, non-verbalizable knowledge* and *verbalizable knowledge* to be classified into types 1 through 7 of the KRM. We note that the sub-procedure that is needed to instantiate the elements 1 through 5 (of the KRM) in this knowledge extracting procedure is an extension of ORM's conceptual schema design procedure (CSDP) [5: 58-60]. In section 3 we will give a sample of the results of applying the knowledge extracting procedure on an operations management text book and a marketing text book. Our position is that the elements in a fact-oriented KRM can be used as a metric to determine the complexity of a 'standardized course unit' and therefore, as an indicator for the study load for such a course and possibly the required number of contact hours, semester hours or course credits (see section 5).

3   Application of the KEP on the Business Subject Matter

In this section we will show the KRMs, which are a result of the application of the fact-oriented KEP on the content of textbooks on the operations management and marketing subjects of business administration. Because of space limitations in this article we haven chosen to select a very small subset of concepts, fact types and constraints contained in these subjects.

3.1   The Operations Management Subject of the Economic Order Quantity

We have selected a widely-used text book on the field of operations and process management: Ritzman, Krajewski and Malhotra: Operations Management: Processes and Value Chains, 8th edition, Pearson/Prentice-Hall, 2007 [12]. We will now provide a self-contained sample of the KRM for this text book (see the list of definitions for operations management and the diagrammatic part of KRM elements 3, 4 and 5 expressed as a *knowledge structure diagram* in ORM-1 notation in figure 1).

List of definitions for operations management subject: Economic Order Quantity EOQ

Item	An individual product that has an identifying item code and is held in inventory somewhere along the value chain (p.524[1]). Synonym: Stock Keeping Unit
Item Code	An item code is a unique signification for an [Item] that enables us to identify a specific [Item] within the set of all [Item]s within the context of a business organization.
Lot	A lot is a quantity of [Item]s that are processed together (p.350).
Cost	A sacrifice or expenditure
Ordering Cost	The [Cost] of preparing a purchase order for a supplier or a production order for the shop. (p. 464). Synonym: Set Up cost (p.472)
Inventory Holding Cost	The sum of the [Cost] of capital and the variable [Cost]s of keeping [Item]s on hand, such as storage and handling, taxes, insurance and shrinking (p.463).
Cycle Inventory Cost	The portion of [Inventory Holding Cost] that varies directly with [Lot] size (p.465).
Economic Order Quantity	An economic order quantity is the quantity of a [Lot] that minimizes total annual [Cycle Inventory Cost] and [Ordering Cost] for a given [item]. (p.470).
Annual Demand	The yearly total demand for a given [Item] (p.472).
Units	A unique signification for an [Economic Order Quantity] or [Annual Demand] that enables us to identify a specific quantity within the set of all [Economic Order Quantitie]s or [Annual Demand]s.
Unit Holding Costs	The costs for holding one unit of a given [Item] in inventory for a year (p.472).
Dollar amount	A unique signification for a [Cost] that enables us to identify a specific [Cost] within the set of all [Cost]s.

---

[1] The referenced pages in the list of definitions refer to [12].

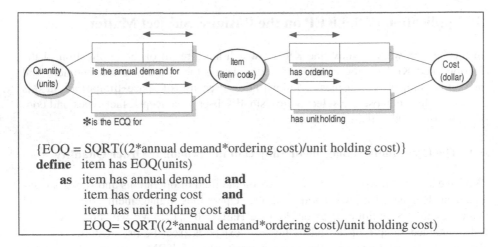

{EOQ = SQRT((2*annual demand*ordering cost)/unit holding cost)}
define   item has EOQ(units)
    as   item has annual demand   **and**
         item has ordering cost   **and**
         item has unit holding cost **and**
         EOQ= SQRT((2*annual demand*ordering cost)/unit holding cost)

Fig. 1. Knowledge structure diagram in ORM-(1) notation for EOQ from [12]

3.2   The Marketing Subject of Branding

We have chosen the following text book on the field of marketing: David Jobber, Principles and Practice of Marketing, 4th edition, McGraw-Hill, 2004 [7]. We will now provide a KRM for a sample from this text book in the list of definitions for marketing management and the diagrammatic part of KRM elements 3 and 4 (expressed as a *knowledge structure diagram* in ORM-1 notation) in figure 2.

List of definitions for marketing management subject: Branding

Product	Anything that is capable of satisfying customer needs (p. 260[2]).
Brand	A distinctive name, packaging and design for a [Product] (p.261).
Brand name	A brand name is a unique signification for an [Brand] that enables us to identify a specific [Brand] within the set of all [Brand]s within the context of a specific company.
Product line	A group of [Brand]s of a Company that are closely related in terms of their function and the benefits they provide (p.262)
Product line name	A product line name is a unique signification for a [Product Line] that enables us to identify a specific [Product Line] within the set of all [Product Line]s within a specific company.
Product mix	The total set of [Brand]s marketed in a company (p. 262) or the set of [Brand]s contained in all [Product Line]s offered by a specific company.
Brand name category	A set of [brand] names related via a criterion.
Category name	A Category name is a unique signification for an [Brand Name Category] that enables us to identify a specific [Brand name Category] within the set of all [Brand Name Categorie]s.

---

[2] The referenced pages in the list of definitions refer to [7].

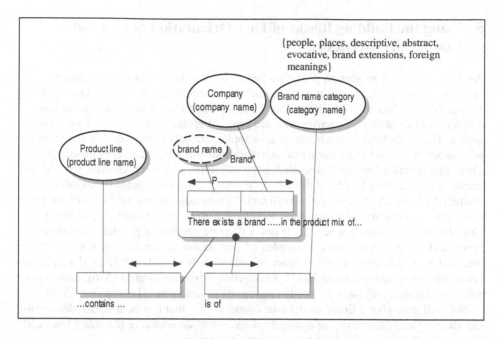

Fig. 2. Knowledge structure diagram in ORM-(1) notation for Branding from [7]

4 Using Fact-Orientation to Compare Subject Matters

When the relative amount of *informal comment* and *non-verbalizable knowledge* in such a knowledge field is large we can consider the knowledge field to be of the 'phenomenological' type. This normally points at knowledge fields that are beginning to develop and in which no clearly agreed upon relevant concepts and their definitions exist. When the relative amount of informal comment and non-verbalizable knowledge of the subject matter, on the other hand, is small, the knowledge domain can be considered relatively structured, this means that basic domain concepts are agreed upon and their definitions are known. Furthermore, semantic relationships between those concepts exist and are known to the extent that they can be verbalized. In the latter types of knowledge domains, it is possible that more complex rules, laws, derivation rules and event rules can be defined. The former analysis naturally applies, in those situations in which a text book is well-written from an educational point of view. In some cases the actual quality of writing can be insufficient, which can lead to a 'phenomenological' text book for a very well-structured knowledge domain or a text book in which the order of comprehension for the introduction and definition of concepts is practically random. In the next section we will postulate a model that can be used to estimate the size and complexity of a subject matter.

5 Using the Building Blocks of Fact-Orientation as Size and Complexity Metrics

As was illustrated in section 3 of this paper, for the text books on marketing and operations management, it is possible to apply the KRM and its accompanying KEP on the field of business administration. In many situations, educational programs at colleges and (professional) universities are built up around acknowledged subjects or topics. The study load for such a subject or topic is mostly determined by the number of contact hours and the *quantity* of literature that must be read and studied. In our view, this practice does not acknowledge the differences between knowledge fields in terms of the building blocks of the KRM. We will restrict the fields of knowledge of interest to 'structurally relevant verbalizable' knowledge domains. We will furthermore divide the fourth element of the Knowledge Reference Model: population state (transition) constraints (see section 2) into a discrete number of pre-defined constraint types and general constraints. Examples of population constraint types in the fact-oriented approach consist of a number of acknowledged and widely used graphical constraints: uniqueness constraints [5, 6] set-comparison constraints [5, 6], mandatory role constraints [5, 6], partial equality constraints [8] and general constraints [5, 6].

We will now give a linear model (see equation (1)) that can be used for determining the size and complexity of a subject domain and determining the study load and the educational design for a course on the subject matter.

$$SL=(a*DEF)+(b*FT)+(\Sigma(c_j*PSC_j))+(d*PTC)+(e*GC) + (f*DR) + (g*ER) . \quad (1)$$

Where SL is the study load (in hours) of a knowledge field or a 'size and complexity' metric that can be easily transformed into a study load equivalent and where a, b, c_j , d, e, f, g, respectively are weight factors for the number of definitions in the list of definitions, the number of fact types, the number of population constraints of type PSC_j , the number of state transition constraints, the number of general population constraints, the number of derivation rules , the number of event rules in the application knowledge structure (diagram). Finally, DEF, FT, PSC_j , PTC, GC, DR and ER are the total number of definitions, the total number of fact types, the total number of constraints, the total number of state transition constraints, the total number of general population constraints, the total number of derivation rules and the total number of event rules, respectively in the application knowledge structure.

This model can be empirically determined by estimating the weight factors: a, b, c_j, d, e, f, g after a large number of samples of knowledge fields (e.g. text books, instruction manuals) have been analyzed in terms of the knowledge reference model. For this future empirical research we need to define standardized test that enable us to determine to what extent students have sufficient knowledge of the relevant parts of the text book.

When we compare the two knowledge reference models for the *operations management* and the *marketing management* examples, we see that relative extent of concept definitions is about equal for both example fields, the number of constraints is bigger for the *operations management* example. The operations management example contains a derivation rule whereas the *marketing management* KRM does not have a derivation rule (see table 1).

Table 1. Sample data for linear model

Variable\subject	EOQ (operations man.)	Branding (marketing)
DEF	10	12
FT	4	2
PSC_1 (uniqueness)	4	1
PSC_2 (mandatory role)	0	1
PSC_2 (value)	0	1
DR	1	0

6 Application of Fact-Orientation in Instructional Design

In this section we will show how the fact-oriented analysis and abstraction of (a) subject matter(s) in combination with the determined weight factors from our study load estimation model in section 5 can be used for instructional design. The total study load can be determined using the linear model in section 5. The next decision that has to be made is to design the tasks, exercises, assignments, chapters to study and so forth in a way that optimizes the productivity of teachers and instructors and that also optimizes the required time for a student to fully understand the subject. The fact-oriented knowledge reference model (KRM), provides the blue-print for the creation of educational material and its accompanying instructional design and test-design. In [9] this is called *knowledge driven instructional design* which contains (amongst others) the step 'didactizing' which can lead to the following instance of an instructional design:

1)   In instructional design, the existing knowledge network of the prospective students will (partly) determine the sequence in which concepts should be introduced and it will determine the way in which competencies should be trained [9, 11]. In some cases available representations of subject matter, e.g. manuals, text-books do not provide the explicit structure to do this at all times [13: 633]. Fact-orientation can help structuring the subject matter by creating a list of definitions that can be anchored in the student's existing knowledge network and it can be sequenced in order of comprehension. Furthermore, a knowledge structure diagram that contains fact types, population constraints and derivation- and event-rules can be added (see figures 1and 2 and the accompanying lists of definitions).

2)   Let the students prepare a number of pages of the text book (preferably in the fact-oriented KRM format) that contain α concept definitions and β fact types and the accompanying population constraints, derivation rules and event rules.

3)   Design an instructional session in which the comprehension of the concepts, fact types and constraints is tested by providing 'sentence instances' or scaled down 'real-life' examples in such a way that in the beginning in each example, one rule is confirmed or violated (see figure 3a), leading to exercises in which multiple constraints are violated/confirmed at the same time (see figure 3b).

4)   A final set of exercises can be constructed in such a way that the comprehension of the concepts, fact types, constraints and derivation rules is tested by providing students with instances of fact types and values for parameters that are contained in one or more derivation rules. The students will subsequently be asked to apply the derivation and/or event rules (see figure 3c).

5)   On a program level it is recommended to provide integrated exercises that cover subject matter that has been covered in earlier courses on a specific subject.

Item	ordering cost
ab105	$ 43,--
ab106	$ 56,--
ab105	$ 66.--

Question: is this an allowed
        example of
        communication ?

(A)

Company	Brand	Brand category
Masterfoods	Mars	people
Masterfoods	Whiskas	--
Masterfoods	Mars	brand extension

Question: is this an allowed
        example of
        communication ?

(B)

The company Ajaxfan, produces all kinds of accessories for the Amsterdam football team Ajax ranging from shawls to coffee cups. For the stock keeping unit with item code a345 the annual demand is estimated at 12 000 units. There is a fairly constant demand throughout the year. The ordering cost with the chinese supplier for this item is Euro 234.--. The unit holding cost for this SKU at Ajaxfan is Euro 1.25/unit/year.

Question: calculate the EOQ for item a345

(C)

Fig. 3. Examples of exercises to be used for instruction

In addition we can use the same underlying KRM to design exams and test questions that can range from problems on an application instance level to problems on a meta level. The design of course evaluations, exams or tests goes hand in hand with the aforementioned instructional design. The test will exactly reflect the level of instruction, since the underlying test objectives have been clearly laid down in the KRM of the subject matter.

6.1   The Fact-Oriented KRM and Bloom's Taxonomy

In educational sciences, Bloom's taxonomy of educational objectives [2] is an accepted framework to divide objectives in the cognitive domain. Bloom's taxonomy can be considered a pyramid, in which every next-higher level includes the lower level as a subset. *Level 1* in Bloom's taxonomy: *knowledge*, is defined as the remembering or recall of previous learned material. *Level 2*: *comprehension* is defined as the understanding of the material or the ability to interpret the material. *Level 3* of Bloom's taxonomy: *application refers* to the ability to use the learning material in new situations. Bloom's *level 4* of educational objectives refers to the ability to break down material into component parts. *Level 5* in Bloom's taxonomy: synthesis, refers to the ability to put parts together.

We will now match the levels and elements from the KRM with the levels in Bloom's taxonomy. The availability of domain sentences without an accompanying list of definitions for the concepts can be considered to refer to the knowledge *level 1*. If we add the (relevant) concept definitions and naming conventions we will be able to communicate 'knowingly' about a subject domain (*level 2* of Bloom's taxonomy). For polytechnic and university level educations, we require the content of the courses to be on *at least level 3* of Bloom's framework which implies that students must at least be able to apply derivation rules to derive new sentences if 'knowledgeable' ingredient sentences (including a list of definitions) is provided in a practical case setting. Bloom's *level 4* of educational objectives refers to the meta-level of the KRM. This basically is the same KRM, albeit applied on a specific UoD, namely the UoD of creating a knowledge reference model [8, 9]. Level 5 refers to the ability to put parts together. Our claim is that this involves multi-disciplinary knowledge and therefore can only be achieved when knowledge for different domains is integrated and therefore, level 5 (and this implies level 6) can in general not be achieved by the educational objectives laid down in a single text book. Level 5, however can be achieved by integrating multiple relevant subjects. If we would consider the synthesis of two subjects that we have given in this article, we could for example derive the knowledge that the manufacturing of more brands would lead to more production set ups. Level 6 in Bloom's taxonomy: *evaluation,* is a level that is normally achieved after students have had experience in a specific field for a number of years, and thereby have achieved the ability to evaluate their way of working in the field.

6.2   The Fact-Oriented KRM and the 4C/ID-Model for Instructional Design

In this section we will show that the application of the fact-oriented approach for instructional design complies to the interrelated components of van Merriënboer's four-component instructional design model (the 4C/ID-model) for competence based education [14].

The first component of the 4C/ID model is *learning tasks.* In [1] task classes are given in which simple-to-complex categories of learning tasks are defined. In this section it was already illustrated how this can be done in the fact-oriented KRM.

The second component of the 4C/ID model is *supportive information.* This component deals with the availability of additional information that is coupled to tasks classes that may contain general knowledge and concrete cases that exemplify the 'theoretical' knowledge [1]. In terms of the fact-oriented approach it means that the example information on a UoD is provided, that allows learners to abstract from tangible examples and to test the presence/absence of constraints by inspecting the supplied case information in the taks.

The third component of the 4C/ID model is *Just-In-Time information* which refers to the specification of routines that are identical for many learning tasks [1]. In terms of fact-orientation we can consider the different steps in the 'knowledge extracting procedure' (KEP) to be the most important example(s) of this. This means that students must acquire these skills in order to be able to 'grasp' the content of the course in the fact-oriented format, but most of all acquiring these skills will allow the students to handle every future situation in which knowledge must be absorbed and applied.

The fourth component of the 4C/ID model is *part-task practice*. In this component provisions are made for additional learning of particular routine aspects that need a high degree of automaticity [1]. In the application of the fact-oriented approach on the field of instructional design, this part-task practice can be directed at meta-level cognitive skills (applying (parts of the) KEP) or on application-level skills (the application of derivation rules, e.g. a calculation of a EOQ).

We now have shown how the fact-oriented KRM enables us to fulfill educational objectives up to level 5 of Bloom's taxonomy and how the fact-oriented approach complies to the 4C/ID model for instructional design.

In the past 15 years, a large number of students on a polytechnical level in the field of computer science, business administration and law have been [9] trained using educational material expressed in a knowledge reference model format based upon standard text books on the subject matter. The time investment needed for the students in such an 'accelerated' learning program turned out to be substantially lower than in a 'conventional' educational setting [11:434-435].

7 Concluding Remarks

The fact-oriented approach has its roots in the conceptual modeling school for information systems development and database schema design. In this paper we have extended the 'playing field' of this approach as a knowledge structuring approach, illustrated by two samples of subjects within the academic field of business administration. Moreover, we have given a (linear) model that can be used for determining and predicting the size and complexity of a subject matter. The size and complexity of the implicit structure of a subject can range from structures that can be fully modeled by a small number of definitions, via models of implicit structures that contain a large number of definitions and fact types, to 'complex' knowledge reference models in which a large variety of population state (transition) constraints exist eventually having derivation rules, and event rules.

The conclusion and implications for the educational practice of the fact-oriented KRM are threefold. Firstly, the KRM for a text book will give us insights into the context of the knowledge domain in terms of relevant structural knowledge. Secondly, the fact-oriented KRM will allow us to estimate the study-load and contact hours for a specific course having a given text book/domain knowledge by using the complexity model that was given in section 5. Thirdly, the fact oriented approach can be applied as a methodology for instructional design that complies to Bloom's taxonomy of educational objectives and the 4C/ID model for instructional design.

As a proposition for future research we recommend to test the 'study-load' model that was provided in this article empirically in a large number of knowledge fields and determine the weight factors and the conditions under which they are valid for each of the coefficients in the model. Our belief is that the 'quantification' of knowledge that is proposed in this article will lead to a more productive and effective 'engineering' of educational systems in a broad sense and will provide a solid foundation for claims as 'better learn one rule than 20 facts'.

References

1. Bastiaens, T., van Merriënboer, J and Hoogveld, B.:A design methodology for Complex (E)-learning. Innovative session 2. AHRD conference, Honolulu Hawai (2002)
2. Bloom, B. and Krathwohl, D.: Taxonomy of educational objectives: the classification of educational goals- handbook I: cognitive domain, McKay, New-York (1956)
3. Bollen, P.: The Natural Language Modeling Procedure', In: Fifth Workshop on Next Generation Information Technologies and Systems (NGITS'2002), Lecture Notes in Computer Science 2382, Springer-Verlag, (2002) 123-146.
4. Bollen, P. and Nijssen, G.: Universal Learning as a tool for educational transformation and process control systems in problem-based programs', in: W,Gijselaers, D. Tempelaar, P. Keizer, J. Blommaert, E. Bernard & H. Kasper (eds.), *Educational innovation in economics and business administration: the case of problem-based learning*, (1995) 436- 443.
5. Halpin, T.: Information Modeling and Relational Databases, Morgan Kaufmann (2001)
6. Halpin, T., Evans, L., Hallock, P., macLean, B.: Database modeling with Microsoft visio for enterprise architects, Morgan Kaufmann (2003)
7. Jobber, D.: Principles and practice of marketing, 4th edition, McGraw-Hill (2004).
8. Nijssen, G.: Kenniskunde 1A, PNA Publishing, Heerlen, Netherlands (in dutch) (2001)
9. Nijssen, G. and Bijlsma, R.: Kennis-gebaseerd onderwijs ontwerpen" (Knowledge Driven Instructional Design), *OnderwijsInnovatie (Instructional Innovation) Nr 3*, Open Universiteit Nederland, September (2005) pp. 17-26. (in dutch)
10. Nijssen, G. and Bijlsma, R.: A Conceptual Structure of Knowledge as a Basis for Instructional Designs. The 6th IEEE International Conference on Advanced Learning Technologies, Theme: Advanced Technologies for Life-LongLearning", *ICALT*,(2006)
11. Nijssen, G. and Bollen, P.: Universal Learning: A science and methodology for education and training', in: W,Gijselaers, D. Tempelaar, P. Keizer, J. Blommaert, E. Bernard & H. Kasper (eds.), *Educational innovation in economics and business administration: the case of problem-based learning*, (1995) 428- 435
12. Ritzman, L., Krajewski, L. and Malhotra, M.: Operations Management: Processes and Value Chains, 8th edition, Pearson/Prentice-Hall. (2007).
13. Thomson, J., Greer, J. and Cooke, J.: Automatic generation of instructional hypermedia with APHID. Interacting with Computers 13 (2001) 631-654.
14. Van Merriënboer, J.: Training complex cognitive skills: A four-component instructional design model for technical training. Englewood Cliffs, NJ (1997)

Capturing Modeling Processes – Towards the MoDial Modeling Laboratory

S.J.B.A. (Stijn) Hoppenbrouwers, L. (Leonie) Lindeman, and H.A. (Erik) Proper

Institute for Computing and Information Sciences, Radboud University Nijmegen
Toernooiveld 1, 6525 ED Nijmegen, The Netherlands, EU
S.Hoppenbrouwers@cs.ru.nl, E.Proper@cs.ru.nl

Abstract. This paper is part of an ongoing research effort to better understand the process of conceptual modeling. As part of this effort, we are currently developing a modeling laboratory named MoDial (*Mo*deling *Dial*ogues). The main contribution of this paper is a conceptual meta-model of that part of Mo-Dial which aims to capture the elicitation aspects of the *modeling process* used in creating a model, rather than the model as such. The current meta-model is the result of a two-stage research process. The first stage involves theoretical input from literature and earlier results. The second stage is concerned with (modest) empirical validation in terms of interviews with modeling experts.

1 Introduction

Conceptual modeling is at the core of information systems engineering. In view of deliverables produced during information systems engineering, in [12] a distinction is made between *usage world*, *subject world*, *system world* and *development world*. Understanding each of these worlds requires considerable modeling efforts to define the requirements on the system and to produce the design of a system. The work reported in this paper is part of an ongoing effort by our group to better understand the act of conceptual modeling [6,] in the context of information system engineering. One of our longer term goals is to turn the *art* of modeling into a *science* of modeling.

As put forward during the panel session of the ORM 2005 workshop, one of the strategies of our research group is to be able to more explicitly capture conceptual modeling cases, where the aim is to not only include the resulting models, but also to capture the modeling process leading up to the model (and the strategies shaping it; [9]). To better understand modeling processes, and to also be in a position to gather direly needed empirical data on the details of modeling processes, we are developing a modeling laboratory called MoDial, which stands for *Mo*deling *Dial*ogues.

In line with our earlier results [8, 7] we regard modeling processes as involving two related dialogues: for *elicitation* and for *formalization*. The elicitation dialogue takes place between an informer (presumably a domain expert) and a model mediator (typically an information analyst). The formalization dialogue, on the other hand, takes place between the model mediator and the model builder (usually some tool

R. Meersman, Z. Tari, P. Herrero et al. (Eds.): OTM Workshops 2006, LNCS 4278, pp. 1242–1252, 2006.

used to capture and verify the actual model). In the past we have already provided a theoretical model for the formalization dialogue [6] based on preliminary work reported in [14]. This dialogue is characterized by the use of strict controlled language [3] which lends itself very well to a transformation towards a formal language. In the elicitation dialogue between an informer and the model mediator, however, the use of a strict controlled language for making initial statements is not very realistic. The properties of the dialogue language is dictated by the abilities of the informants to express themselves (and for model mediators to validate their understanding of the informants' statements) rather than by the needs of formalization.

The work reported in this paper is primarily concerned with the *elicitation* dialogue. Many important modeling decisions emerge, or are at least resolved, in this dialogue rather than in the formalization dialogue. We eventually want to capture modeling decisions and the processes in which they take place. Our aim here is therefore to derive a meta-model of the concepts needed to capture elicitation-related parts of the modeling processes for use in a modeling laboratory such as MoDial.

The current meta-model as reported in this paper is the result of an MSc research project [11], and has been created in two stages. In the first stage, an abstraction was made of three pre-existing conceptual modeling procedures described in literature. During the second stage, three experienced modelers were interviewed in order to validate the meta-model resulting from the first stage. In the remainder of this paper, we consecutively discuss these stages, followed by a discussion of the resulting model and planned follow-up research activities.

2 First Stage – Described Modeling Procedures

Several descriptions of conceptual modeling processes exist. Each of these documented procedures can be regarded as a guidebook for the creation of a specific kind of conceptual model. Such guidebooks are typically based on commonly used modeling practices. Below we will discuss three procedures, which will then be generalized. The three procedures compared are aimed at the creation of ORM diagrams [4], UML class diagrams [13] and ER diagrams [1], respectively.

2.1 ORM Diagrams

Object-Role Modeling (ORM) is a fact oriented method, which has initially been developed for modeling information systems at a conceptual level. ORM makes use of natural language statements by examining them in terms of elementary facts. In [4] a *Conceptual Schema Design Procedure* (CSDP) is provided, consisting of seven steps:

1. Transform familiar information examples into elementary facts, and apply quality checks.
2. Draw the fact types, and apply a population check.
3. Check for entity types that should be combined, and note any arithmetic derivations.

4. Add uniqueness constraints, and check arity of fact types.
5. Add mandatory role constraints, and check for logical derivations.
6. Add value, set comparison and sub-typing constraints.
7. Add other constraints and perform final checks.

2.2 UML Class Diagrams

The Unified Modeling Language (UML) is an object modeling and specification language that is designed to make object oriented analyses and designs for information systems. UML 2.0 defines thirteen types of diagrams, divided into three categories. The UML class diagram belongs to the category of "structure diagrams" [13]. The UML, being a language, does not provide a procedure for the creation of UML class diagram. However, procedures do exist for creation of a class diagram. We have used the procedure described in [15]. This procedure has the following outline:

1. Identify all possible candidate classes.
2. Select classes from the list of candidates.
3. Make a model dictionary.
4. Identify associations.
5. Identify attributes.
6. Identify operations.
7. Generalize with the help of inheritance.
8. Add business rules with Object Constraint Language (OCL).
9. Divide classes into packages.
10. Repeat over executed steps.

2.3 ER Diagrams

The Entity Relationship (ER) model was introduced in 1976 by Peter Chen [1]. There is no generally accepted standard for ER, but there are different corresponding components that exist in most of its variants. An ER diagram is the graphical result of the ER model and shows entities and the coherence between them [2]. Various guidelines exist for the creation of an ER diagram. We have used the guidelines as provided in [5]. Before this procedure can be followed, information has to be collected: functional requirements, forms, reports or existing models. The procedure starts from studying facts or sentences:

1. Identify possible entity types.
2. Identify possible relationship types between identified entity types.
3. Determine cardinalities of the relationship types.
4. Identify and associate attributes with entity types.
5. Identify and associate attributes with relationship types.
6. Determine domains of attributes.
7. Determine potential identifiers for every entity type.
8. Think about the use of specialization/ generalization (sub-types/ super-types).
9. Check the model on redundancy.
10. Validate the ER model.
11. Plan a review about the model with users.

2.4 Generalization of Modeling Procedures

In [11], the above procedures were scrutinized to infer what kind of information was handled in each of the involved steps, leading to an initial meta-model. This meta-model has been validated by populating it with a few examples of models and modeling sessions. Generalizing, we observed that each of the three modeling procedures essentially proceeds through six stages:

1. Identify requirements-on/goal-of the model to be produced.
2. Identify the modeling language to use.
3. Select and gather sources.
4. Scope the domain.
5. Engage in a question and answers process with an informer(s).
6. Conduct final quality checks.

Needless to say, iteration between these stages is likely to occur. We will now briefly discuss the stages, providing an indication of the kind of information that will be involved in capturing the part of the modeling process under concern.

Before a modeling process starts, a valid goal for the creation of the model should be identified [8] and the requirements on the model to be produced. Once the requirements on the model have been identified, it is important to choose the right kind of model. Every artifact has its own strengths and weaknesses, and every kind of model is only applicable in particular situations.

All three procedures require collection of information about the Universe of Discourse before actual modeling starts. There are different ways to do this, for example by gathering reports, forms, tables, diagrams, or texts. When a description of the problem is available, then this is also a useful source of information.

The next stage is to take decisions about the concepts that play a part in the domain, also known as scoping the domain. After scoping the domain, the determination of the relevant concepts occurs, e.g. by organizing modeling sessions. This is where we enter the elicitation dialogue between an informant and the model mediator [6, 7, 9]. This dialogue is dominated by a "game" of questioning and answering. The informant is a domain expert who harbors knowledge of some domain, and is presumed to know about the target domain (or can find out more if needed). It is assumed that domain experts can express and validate statements about the domain in a language which is suitable to *them* (probably disqualifying, for example, to the strict controlled language used during the formalization dialogue). Statements can take the form of free-hand drawing, (partial) diagrams, semi-formal expressions, texts, etc. The model mediator is not required to have any specific knowledge of the domain, but is assumed to know how to create a verifiably correct model [6].

The final stage of the modeling process is a quality check of the model. The question that needs to be answered here is whether the model produced fits the requirements/goals as stated in the first stage. The procedures discussed propose different checks for redundancy, derivations, consistency and completeness, and to validate the model. When a problem is found, the modeler can choose to update the model at that point, or to accept the model the way it is now. In some situations, a model is judged "good enough", and need not be perfect.

Our initial meta-model was refined on the basis of (modest) empirical validation, as described in the next section. We will not present the initial model, only the meta-model resulting after the round of interviews of modeling experts (see Section 4).

3 Second Stage – Experiences from Practitioners

Using as a starting point the meta-model derived from the first stage, interviews were conducted with three expert modelers. To ensure that these based their input on their own experiences, and not on company standards, independent consultants/architects where selected as interviewees. Each of them has ample experience in information and/or knowledge modeling:

1.   Mr. De Vries, Zetetic, http://www.zetetic.nl
2.   Mrs. Bleeker, Gemara-Consulting, http://www.gemara-consulting.nl
3.   Mr. Crompvoets, Bommeljé Crompvoets and partners, http://www.bcp-software.nl

3.1 Interview with Mr. de Vries

Mr. de Vries specializes in consultancy and architecting in the field of knowledge management and knowledge technology. In these assignments, he produces many models, for example of processes, information flows and information systems. In his experience, the first step of a modeling process is trying to clarify what it is he's hired for. This allows him to so he can identify the goal of the model. Next, Mr. de Vries chooses a suitable modeling technique. This selection depends on both the goal of the model and the techniques already used by the organization.

Mr. de Vries usually organizes workshops with people who are involved with some process, system, or specific domain. At the beginning of the modeling process these workshops are at an overall level and aim to discover which concepts matter. In later sessions the understanding of key concepts is deepened. To get the concepts clear, it is important to talk to the right stakeholders, so these have to be identified at the beginning of the modeling process.

When an issue arises during a workshop a few scenarios can be thought up which potentially resolve it. The issue is then 'put on hold' and the stakeholder commissioning the model is requested to select the desired scenario.

3.2 Interview with Mrs. Bleeker

Mrs. Bleeker is an independent information architect and requirements engineer, who uses models to clarify which information or business concepts play a part in a domain. She uses ORM, primarily as a way of structuring her thoughts. For documenting, however, UML and natural language are also used.

In modeling sessions, Mrs. Bleeker prefers interviews to workshops. In interviews Mrs. Bleeker frequently uses common interviewing techniques, such as summarizing and a drill-down style of questioning. Her general way of working is to take a top-down approach. She first determines the boundaries of the domain and sub-domains. This is followed by an elaboration on the identified sub-domains.

Mrs. Bleeker enquires with the commissioning party to discover promising informants. However, these are generally the busiest people around, so sometimes she has to make do with people who know less about the domain. Besides interviewing domain experts, she also discusses the key issues with the decision makers. This way she ensures commitment to the resulting model from these decision makers.

Before starting a modeling process, Mrs. Bleeker first determines the goals for producing the model. In addition, she determines beforehand the way in which the model will be documented. She has a number of standard ways of documenting that work well for her. However, some projects need a creative approach to documenting.

Mrs. Bleeker stops modeling when she has a clear overview of the domain. When there is little time available, she aims to achieve as much clarity about the domain as possible in the given time. In such cases, Mrs. Bleeker also speaks explicitly about the ambition level with regards to the depth and breadth of the resulting model. It is not always possible to produce the 'perfect' model in view of resources available. These constraints are added as disclaimers to the documentation accompanying the models.

3.3 Interview with Mr. Crompvoets

Mr. Crompvoets is consultant and uses various techniques to create models, but his choice of technique depends on the organization an situation in which the project takes place. He often uses modeling sessions to adjust concepts and to create a common view. Before starting a modeling session, he usually studies some documents, so he can steer a session as he sees fit.

A modeling session starts by shaping a picture of the strategy and the vision of the future of the company. After that, he focuses on the products and services of the company. He zooms in more and more, paying attention to the different views of the participants, so every concept becomes clear for every participant. Asking questions is very important to realize clarity. When a concept is not clear for everyone, discussions arise, unveiling different interpretations of a concept. Once a concept is clear for (enough) participants, the next concept is discussed.

4 Resulting Model

The resulting meta-model is presented as an ORM model, divided in three parts. The partial meta-model shown in Fig. 1 concerns the contextual aspects of a modeling process. A modeling process is presumed to be initiated by some stakeholder, aims to produce a model, at a certain level of ambition, in order to meet some goal that has a pre-determined quality check, making use of some modeling technique, limiting itself to some scope, and possibly using additional documentation. The model produced during a modeling process must indeed be a model that is allowed in the selected modeling technique. Note that the latter relationship is a derived one (see Fig. 3).

The partial meta-model depicted in Fig. 2 deals with actual modeling processes. A modeling process is regarded as consisting of a number of modeling sessions. Each modeling session involves a number of session involvements: the actual involvement of some actor in a particular modeling session. Currently we identify three kinds of involvement: *informing*, *mediating* and *deciding*[1]. The informing and mediating involvement kinds correspond to what has been stated in the introduction about the elicitation part of the modeling process. The deciding role has been added based on input from the interviewees. As it turns out, during a modeling session, several issues arise that cannot be answered within the session. An external party is needed to answer these questions. Usually the stakeholder initiating the modeling process needs to be consulted to resolve such issues.

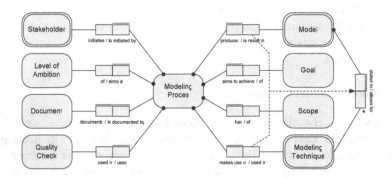

Fig. 1. Modeling context

The involvement of the actors in a modeling session leads to a number of questions, and statements answering these questions. In capturing modeling processes we are not only interested in questions put forward by the mediator, but also by questions put forward by the informers. We therefore allow all kinds of session involvements to be the originator of questions and answers.

Questions can not only be posed, but can be withdrawn as well. However, we would want to record withdrawals explicitly as they constitute interesting junctions in a modeling process. Statements are either made in response to questions, are a position statement, or are based on a decision made by a deciding involvement. Furthermore, each proposed statement can be accepted, rejected, or withdrawn during the modeling process.

The area enclosed by the rectangle adorned with a clock identifies that for the enclosed area a history needs to be maintained. For example, the order in which questions are put forward and answered is relevant to us.

The final partial model is depicted in Fig. 3. It concerns models, modeling techniques, and meta-models. The approach taken is this fragment aims to be neutral

---

[1] Note that the open circle at the base of the sub-type arrow signifies it to be a "self defining" sub-type. This can best be regarded as a graphical abbreviation.

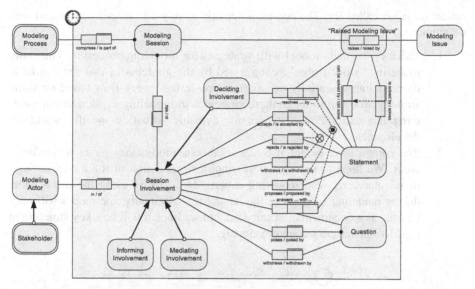

- Each Model Session has at least one Session Involvement which is a Mediating Involvement
- Each Model Session has at least one Session Involvement which is an Informing Involvement

Fig. 2. Modeling dialogue

with regard to specific modeling languages. A model is presumed to comply with a meta-model, while a modeling technique has an underlying meta-model. We assume meta-models to consist of a set of meta-types, while a model is presumed to consist of model elements (which can be decomposed). The model elements are tied to the meta-model by typing the elements in terms of meta-types.

The model elements, which are the building blocks of the models being produced, are implied by the statements produced in the elicitation dialogue. In the formalization dialogue, the relationship between these statements and the model elements can be made much more rigid [6, 7], and can to some extend even be derived automatically.

5   Conclusions and Further Research

We presented a first version of the part of MoDial's meta-model which deals with the elicitation dialogue between informers and model mediators. The main focus of the meta-model was the process of modeling rather the creation of the actual model in isolation.

The meta-model resulted from a two-stage development: a theory-based stage (literature) and a practice-based stage (modest empirical work in terms of interviews and discussions with practitioners). Further theoretical embedding and empirical validation is yet called for. The current schema is merely a first result. As a next step we aim to:

1. Enhance the meta-model with strategies for modeling processes. The many modeling "work-flows" as suggested by the guidebooks that are available on modeling essentially constitute a pre-defined work-flow based on some strategy. We aim to make these strategies in modeling explicit in our modeling laboratory. We also aim for dynamic, situation-specific workflow development.

2. The current meta-model also lacks elaborate motivations for modeling decisions. We hope to perform more empirical validation of the model through more interviews with modeling experts, but also by using the meta-model during modeling sessions in the laboratory. Minimally, the model will only be used as a documentation standard, but we hope it will be a key structure in the MoDial system we are developing.

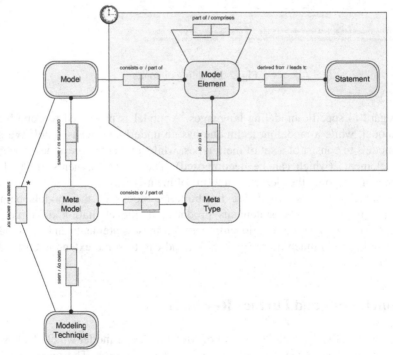

* A Model is stated in a Modeling Technique IFF
  that Model conforms to a Meta Model which is used by that Modeling Technique

· Each Model Element which is part of a Model Element which is part of a Model is also part of that Model
· The Meta Type of a Model Element which is part of a Model   is part of the Meta Model allowing that Mode

Fig. 3. Models, meta-models and modeling techniques

3. Currently, we focus on modeling dialogues where the informers are presumed to have a homogenous view on the domain to be modeled. This is, however, rather unrealistic from a practical point of view. Once we have conducted modeling experiments in a controlled homogenous setting, we aim to also cater for the negotiation processes in creating a unified model when dealing with heterogeneous views of different informers on the same domain.

References

1. P.P. Chen. The Entity-Relationship Model: Towards a Unified View of Data. *ACM Transactions on Database Systems*, 1(1):9-36, March 1976.
2. Kroenke D.M. *Databases, principles, design and implementation (Databases, beginselen, ontwerp en implementatie)*. Pearson Education Benelux, Amsterdam, The Netherlands, EU, 9th edition, 2004. In Dutch.
3. Norbert E. Fuchs, Uta Schwertel, and Rolf Schwitter. Attempto Controlled English - Not Just Another Logic Specification Language. *Lecture Notes in Computer Science*, 1559: 1-20, 1999.
4. T.A. Halpin. *Information Modeling and Relational Databases, From Conceptual Analysis to Logical Design*. Morgan Kaufmann, San Mateo, California, USA, 2001.
5. B. van Hoof, H. van Seters, and J.P. Zwart. *Lecture Notes on Proces and Data Modeling (Syllabus Proces- en Datamodellering)*. HAN University of Applied Science, Arnhem, The Netherlands, EU, 2002. In Dutch.
6. S.J.B.A. Hoppenbrouwers and H.A. (Erik) Proper. A Fundamental View on the Process of Conceptual Modeling. In *Conceptual Modeling - ER 2005 - 24 International Conference on Conceptual Modeling*, volume 3716 of *Lecture Notes in Computer Science*, pages 128-143, June 2005.
7. S.J.B.A. Hoppenbrouwers and H.A. (Erik) Proper. Formal Modelling as a Grounded Conversation. pages 139-155, June 2005.
8. S.J.B.A. Hoppenbrouwers, H.A. (Erik) Proper, and V.E. van Reijswoud. Navigating the Methodology Jungle - The communicative role of modelling techniques in information system development. *Computing Letters*, 1(3), 2005.
9. S.J.B.A. Hoppenbrouwers, H.A. (Erik) Proper, and Th.P. van der Weide. Towards explicit strategies for modeling. In T.A. Halpin, K. Siau, and J. Krogstie, editors, Proceedings of the Workshop on Evaluating Modeling Methods for Systems Analysis and Design (EMMSAD'05), held in conjunctiun with the 17th Conference on Advanced Information Systems 2005 (CAiSE 2005), pages 485-492, Porto, Portugal, EU, 2005. FEUP, Porto, Portugal, EU.
10. S.J.B.A. Hoppenbrouwers, H.A. (Erik) Proper, and Th.P. van der Weide. Understanding the Requirements on Modelling Techniques. In O. Pastor and J. Falcao e Cunha, editors, *17th International Conference on Advanced Information Systems Engineering, CAiSE 2005, Porto, Portugal, EU*, volume 3520 of *Lecture Notes in Computer Science*, pages 262-276, Berlin, Germany, EU, June 2005. Springer-Verlag.
11. L. Lindemans. Modeling Processes (Modelleerprocessen). Master's thesis, Institute for Computing and Information Sciences, Radboud University Nijmegen, Nijmegen, The Netherlands, EU, June 2006. In Dutch.

12. J. Mylopoulos. Techniques and Languages for the Description of Information Systems. In P. Bernus, K. Mertins, and G. Schmidt, editors, Handbook on Architectures of Information Systems, Berlin, Germany, EU. Springer, Berlin, Germany, EU, international handbooks on information systems edition, 1998.
13. OMG. UML 2.0 Superstructure Specification - Final Adopted Specification. Technical Report ptc/03-08-02, August 2003.
14. Patrick van Bommel, P.J.M. Frederiks, and Th.P. van der Weide. Object-Oriented Modeling based on Logbooks. *The Computer Journal*, 39(9):793-799, 1996.
15. J. Warmer and A. Kleppe. *Practical UML (Praktisch UML)*. Pearson Education Benelux, Amsterdam, The Netherlands, EU, 3 edition, 2004. In Dutch.

PerSys 2006 PC Co-chairs' Message

We welcome our workshop attendees to a very interesting collection of discussions. We received many papers and had to limit the acceptance rate to 40those papers submitted. The papers cover a range of topics from infrastructure, service discovery, personalization, environments, security, privacy, to wireless and sensor networks, showing the scope of interests and activities represented by the PerSys participants. We would like to thank everyone who submitted a paper and believe readers will all find the content of this volume stimulating and worthwhile. The reviewers of the papers did a terrific job in helping authors prepare better final papers and deserve special thanks for completing the job promptly. Last, we would like to thank the organizers of the conference for the hard work they put into providing us with the opportunity to gather, present, listen, and discuss our research.

August 2006   Skevos Evripidou, University of Cyprus, Cyprus
                 Roy Campbell, University of Illinois at Urbana-Champaign, USA

R. Meersman, Z. Tari, P. Herrero et al. (Eds.): OTM Workshops 2006, LNCS 4278, p. 1253, 2006.
© Springer-Verlag Berlin Heidelberg 2006

Live and Heterogeneous Migration of Execution Environments

Nicolas Geoffray, Gaël Thomas, and Bertil Folliot

Laboratoire d'Informatique de Paris 6
8 rue du Capitaine Scott, 75015 Paris France
firstname.lastname@lip6.fr

Abstract. Application migration and heterogeneity are inherent issues of pervasive systems. Each implementation of a pervasive system must provide its own migration framework which hides heterogeneity of the different resources. This leads to the development of many frameworks that perform the same functionality. We propose a minimal execution environment, the micro virtual machine, that factorizes process migration implementation and offers heterogeneity, transparency and performance. Systems implemented on top of this micro virtual machine, such as our own Java virtual machine, will therefore automatically inherit process migration capabilities.

1 Introduction

Process migration is the act of transferring a process from one system to another. When the two systems differ in hardware or operating system, migration is said to be heterogeneous. The main goals of process migration include [14]: accessing more processing power, exploitation of resource locality, resource sharing, fault resilience, system administration, and recently pervasive computing.

Most of the existing process migration implementations lack in heterogeneity. The base requirement of these systems is an homogeneous environment, which is unconceivable for a pervasive system. Furthermore, the use of static languages such as C or C++, and dynamic libraries of the operating system render the implementation of process migration difficult, allthough some seem to be operational but limited [4,25].

With the arrival of virtual machines such as the Java Virtual Machine (JVM) implementation of process migration in heterogeneous environment became easier. A JVM hides to applications the underlying operating system and hardware. Therefore, the execution environment of a process can be represented in a portable manner. Many different approaches have been developed for migrating threads in the JVM [21,28,18,3,32]. We think these approaches are in the right direction to achieve process migration in heterogeneous environments, but they by essence lack in genericity as they only target the JVM and the Java language.

In this paper, we propose a new execution environment that will enable process migration for every bytecode-targeted languages. This environment is a minimal

R. Meersman, Z. Tari, P. Herrero et al. (Eds.): OTM Workshops 2006, LNCS 4278, pp. 1254–1263, 2006.

virtual machine, called the *micro-virtual machine*, that contains the base of a virtual machine architecture. Virtual machines like JVM or .Net can thereafter be implemented on top of the micro-virtual machine and automatically benefit from process migration. We intend to apply process migration to our existing JVM implementation, JnJVM. The process migration system is an extension of the micro-virtual machine. The contributions of this paper are:

- A proposal for a minimal execution environment with process migration facilities. The environment is minimal enough to allow process migration for higher level virtual machines,
- An explanation of a standard algorithm for process migration,
- A reflexion on operating system migration on heterogeneous environments, when the operating system is implemented within a virtual machine.

Section 2 presents background and related work in the field of process migration. Section 3 presents the architecture of our minimal virtual machine and Section 4 explains how thread migration will be achieved in the micro-virtual machine. Section 5 presents perspectives, including our current ideas on how migrating an operating system provided that it is executed on a virtual machine. Operating system migration is a trend in ubiquitous computing, as it will allow users to migrate their entire working environment. Section 6 concludes the paper.

2   Related Work

Process migration is a popular field in systems research. Many implementations have been proposed. They differ in heterogeneity, performance, transparency and reusability. In this section, we give an overview of existing systems and compare them with respect to these four characteristics.

2.1   Binary Process Migration

In homogeneous systems: Binary process migration upon operating systems has long considered homogeneity to be the base requirement. Milojicic *et al.* [14] give a panel of process migration in operating systems. Process migration can be implemented either in the kernel, in system libraries (user-space), or in end-user applications. The three levels differ in complexity, transparency, performance and reusability. Kernel-space implementations typically regroup all these characteristics. User-space implementations are simpler than kernel-space implementations, but suffers from performance and transparency. Application-level implementations suffer from reusability, because modification of the application is most of the time required. Examples of kernel-level process migration are Locus [17], the V Kernel [26] or Amoeba [24]. Implementations in user-space include Condor [13] or MPVM [2]. Finally, Freedman [7] has implemented process migration in end-user applications.

In heterogeneous systems: Few attempts on process migration on heterogeneous systems have been accomplished. Most significant systems are Tui [23], SNOW [25] and recently MigThread [4].

The Tui system provides heterogeneous process migration by modifying the ACK (Amsterdam Compiler Kit). It generates an executable with process migration possibilities.

SNOW (Scalable Network Of Workstation) and MigThread consist of a pre-processor and a runtime system. The pre-processor performs a source-to-source transformation to provide an equivalent program with process migration facility. The program is compiled into all targeted architecture. When process migration is triggered, the runtime support of the three systems computes the type and value of each variable, the stack trace, the memory graph and the program counter. It represents them in an intermediate form and sends it to the destation host. The execution environment is then reconstructed at the destination host.

For these three systems, the program has to be written in a type-safe subset of standard languages (Ansi-C, Pascal and so on). Type safety is required because the runtime support must compute location of each objects manipulated, and the values and type of each variable of the program. Migration can not occur anytime during execution: the pre-processor or compiler inserts adaptation points that will poll migration status. This leads to decrease performance.

2.2   Process Migration Upon Virtual Machines

Virtual machines such as JVM or .Net hide the underlying execution environment. The code is compiled into an intermediate bytecode that is either interpreted during execution or compiled dynamicaly by a just in time compiler (JIT). A virtual machine is therefore a convenient architecture for program portability. However, they do not provide in their specification thread or process migration facility. The difficulties to implement thread migration upon virtual machines include derivating the type of variables present on stack, selecting the thread's reachable object graph and restoring the thread at the destination from where it was interrupted. Three appraoches were taken by the research community to add process migration for the JVM: source-level transformation, bytecode-level transformation and extended virtual machines.

Source-level transformation: Funfroken implemented process migration by mean of source transformation [8]. It uses a specific compiler in order to add thread-state capturing and restoring in methods of the program. Migration is triggered by the thread itself by raising a Java exception. This code addition in the program decreases performance when no migration is triggered.

Bytecode-level transformation: Brakes [28] and the system of Sakamoto *et al.* [18] perform bytecode transformation. The algorithms taken for thread migration are basically the same than source-level transformation. Bytecode-level transformation has the advantage of enabling migration to applications only available in bytecode format.

Extended virtual machines: MOBA [21] or the system of Bouchenak *et al.* [3] extend the Sun JVM to provide thread migration. Both systems consist of a thread API, and the use of the Java debugging interface. The debugging interface allows to compute type and values of variables, and the thread's execution environment. The main issue faced by using the debugging interface was performance: the JIT had to be disabled. To bypass this issue, MOBA implemented type inference of the thread's stack, however the system could face collision of references with integer. Bouchenak *et al.* implemented a second run-time stack, that stores the type of variables stored on the memory stack.

Jessica2 [32] is a distributed JVM that runs on a cluster of workstations. It gives the illusion to applications of a single system image. It uses a distributed shared memory, the Global Object Space (GOS). Thread migration has been implemented on top of Jessica2 [31]. It performs dynamic recompilation of currently executing methods in order to compute the bytecode program counter, the emplacements of the methdods variable (memory or registers) and their type. This execution environment is then stored in an intermediate form and sent to the destination node. This algorithm does not face object accessibility because it is based on a distributed shared memory. Furthermore, the virtual machine is note migrated, it must be executing on the destination node. Squawk [22] is a JVM that does not need an operating system. It considers applications as isolates and is able to migrate them between different Squawk instances. In this context, the virtual machine is not migrated, only the application.

2.3   Summary on Existing Systems

Table 1 compares all presented systems with respect to heterogeneity, performance, transparency and reusability.

Table 1. Comparison between different process migration systems

System	Heterogeneity	Performance	Transparency	Reusability
Locus, V Kernel, Amoeba	no	***	***	***
Condor, MPVM	no	**	**	***
Freedman's	no	**	*	*
Tui, Snow, MigTthread	yes	**	**	**
VM Source transformation	yes	*	***	*
VM Bytecode transformation	yes	*	***	*
Moba and Bouchenak's	yes	***	*	*
Jessica2, Squawk	yes	***	***	*

All these systems have limitations. Binary process migration targets mostly homogeneous network of workstations. The few systems that allow heterogeneity can not trigger migration anytime during execution. Furthermore, it needs the source code of the application and requires that the application is implemented in a subset of standard languages such as Ansi-C or Pascal to ensure type safety.

Process migration upon a virtual machine is another approach. Virtual machines are usally type-safe, and hides the hardware and the operating system to the application. Extended virtual machines have less limitations than bytecode or source-level transformation. They do not add extra computations when migration is not triggered. However, the existent systems such as Moba or the one from Bouchenak *et al.* do not provide transparency, because the application must use a specific thread API. Furthermore, they both suffer from using the Sun JVM: they bypass its restriction on stack capturing by using a non-standard approach and does not benefit from the JVM evolution. The Jessica2 thread migration performs transparent migration anytime during execution, and does not face object graph migration. We think the algorithm taken by Jessica2 is the one that has the best advantages, because it is directly integrated in the JVMs, uses its JIT compiler and does not require to modify the application, nor use a specific API. However, their implementation is eased by the distributed shared memory.

3   The Micro Virtual Machine

Achieving heterogeneity in process migration with virtual machines is more straightforward and convenient than with binaries. However the proliferation of virtual machines (Smalltalk, JVM, .Net, Ocaml and so on) requires to implement thread migration for each one. The goal of the micro-virtual machine (MVM) is to resolve this type of issue [6].

The micro virtual machine is a minimal execution environment that can be specialized dynamically by applications. Early projects include specializing the MVM for active networks, web caches [15], or Java [27]. In this paper we propose an implementation for thread migration that will enable migration for all systems implemented on top of the MVM, and especially Java. For example, the work done to achieve a functionnal JVM can be applied for a .Net virtual machine.

Figure 1 represents the micro-virtual machine, specialized to become a Java virtual machine called JnJVM. The MVM is structured with components. It is composed of standard virtual machine components such as a thread manager, a memory manager and a JIT compiler. To enable dynamic adaptation, it also contains a Lisp front-end, an extensible compiler and a component system. It uses aspect technology [12] to modify and extend the components. JnJVM extends the MVM by adding new components that alltogether implement a Java virtual machine.

4   Thread Migration in the Micro Virtual Machine

The algorithm of our thread migration is close to the algorithm of the thread migration system of Jessica2. Because the MVM does not use distributed shared memory by default, our algorithm has to compute the object graph reachable from the migrating thread.

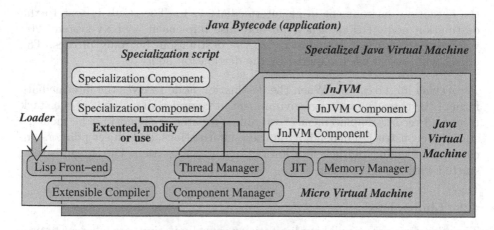

Fig. 1. Architecture of the MVM

4.1   Algorithm

The MVM components ease the implementation of our algorithm. It uses the just in time compiler to save the type of the variables on stack and the program counter relative to a MVM bytecode instruction. It uses the memory manager to locate the object graph of the thread.

Type information: The MVM reads by default a Lisp-like language. An application can however modify this language. The MVM compiles its input with a just in time compiler called the Virtual Processor Unit [16]. The VPU is a stack-based abstract machine that transforms a sequence of actions on a stack into an assembled form. Migration requires to know the type of each variable on the stack. Therefore the compiler makes a distinction between integers, float, and objects. After compiling, the VPU returns a method object. It contains the sequence of VPU actions, and the assembled code.

Recompilation: Migration is triggered by an external entity by using Posix signals. The thread interrupts and retrieves its stack trace. For each method on the stack, it analyses its sequence of VPU actions. This allows to found the frame pointer of each method, and the type of each variable on stack (register or memory). In order to compute the program counter and send it in a portable manner, the program counter must represent the start of a virtual instruction of the VPU. If it is not the case, execution is processed until it reaches the end of a virtual instruction.

Object Graph: Some variables on the execution stack are objects. These objects might reference other objects and the overall references give an object graph, all reachable from the thread. The memory manager allows to construct the graph and find the objects. A first naïve implementation would gather this graph with the execution environment in an intermediate form. The result is sent to the destination node. For efficiency, we may also implement a proxy system [20], where objects are not sent directly to the destination, but only proxies. The object will be sent when required by the destination node.

Recovering the execution: When the destination node receives the intermediate form of the thread's execution environment, it compiles all methods of the stack trace and records emplacement of variables (register or memory). The memory stack is reconstructed depending on these informations, and object pointers are changed depending on their location in the new workstation. The thread is then started with the given stack.

4.2   Limitations

The migration system will have limitations: some limitations are inherent to process migration, others are particular to our architecture. In the first case, process migration must face dependances with kernel structures such as open files, or sockets. In the second case, with our architecture, process migration can not occur while the process is compiling a method (due to the architecture-dependant code generation) or while it is collecting memory (because it manipulates structures dependant of the memory graph).

In order to allow migration allmost anytime during execution, the MVM can not rely on a C/C++ implementation as it does in the present. We will have to introduce a metacircular virtual machine, i.e. a virtual machine implemented in itself. It will enable migration of any of its methods. Recent metacircual virtual machine implementations such as Klein for the Self language [29] or Squawk for the Java language [22] show many interest of this approach. For example, it inherits features of the virtual machine such as possible type safety, garbage collection or exception handling. It also generally eases porting and debugging the virtual machine. Squawk executes without an operating system on top of small devices. It defines isolates which are basically applications, that can be migrated between different Squawk virtual machines. Our proposed architecture follows this direction, but enables the virtual machine to migrate as well, therefore the entire system itself.

5   Perspective: Heterogeneous OS Migration

Live OS migration has become realistic with the arrival of virtual machine monitors (VMM) such as Xen [1], or VMWare [30]. Virtual machine monitors enable execution of many operating systems simultaneously on the same hardware. In this context, a virtual machine is an operating system executing on top of the VMM. Clark *et al.* have implemented OS migration with Xen [5], and Sapuntzki *et al.* with VMWare [19]. Migration is based on memory page transfer. The base requirement for these systems is homogeneity: the processor has to be the same between nodes. The harware dependances are mostly dealt by the virtual machine monitor.

In order to reconcile OS migration with heterogeneity, we propose to combine our minimal virtual machine approach with emergent OS implemented in a virtual machine such as JVM. There are two main systems that propose OS abstractions in virtual machines. KaffeOS [9] is an extension of the Kaffe virtual machine, a free JVM. KaffeOS enables execution and protection of many processes inside one virtual machine. It requires to execute on an existing operating system. On the other hand, Jnode (Java New Operating system Desing Effort) [11], or JX [10] are complete operating systems implemented in Java that execute Java-only applications. They are composed of a nano-kernel for basic hardware communications, a JVM implemented in Java, and device drivers implemented in Java.

Combining the micro virtual machine with the concepts of KaffeOS would allow migration of processes and the virtual machine (therefore the OS, as seen by the KaffeOS authors). A wider perspective is to combine the Jnode operating system with the micro-virtual machine. The entire operating sytem could be migrated allmost anytime during execution, limitation being access to device drivers, compilation and garbage collection. Kernel structures can be migrated because they are implemented in Java. We can not however deal with local hardware access such as local files, but OS migration with virtual machine monitor faces the same issue.

6   Conclusion

In this paper we have presented a thread /process /OS migration architecture in heterogeneous environments. The architecture is a proposal and OS migration is more of a reflexion than a proposal. Much effort has to be provided to enable this architecture in the micro virtual machine framework. Moreover, the combination of a virtual machine oriented operating system and the micro virtual machine remains to be discussed.

Thread and process migration have long time proved their efficiency for load-balancing, mobile computing, resource sharing, fault resilience, etc. OS migration is recently in current investigation thanks to the arrival of virtual machine monitors. It inherits all advantages of process migration at coarse grain. One of the main benefit of OS migration presented by Clark et al. [5] is for cluster administration. System and hardware are clearly separated, and the removal of a node does not lead to loosing its operating system. Furthermore, mobile computing is allways an interesting target for migration; OS migration will allow a user to carry and use its operating system wether it is on a Portable Digital Assistant, a laptop or a personal computer.

References

1. P. Barham, B. Dragovic, K. Fraser, S. Hand, T. Harris, A. Ho, R. Neugebauer, I. Pratt, and A. Warfield. Xen and the Art of Virtualization. In *Proceedings of the Symposium on Operating Systems Principles*, pages 164–177, New-York, USA, October 2003.

2. A. Beguelin, J. Dongarra, A. Geist, R. Manchek, K. Moore, and V. Sunderam. PVM and HeNCE: Tools for Heterogeneous Network Computing. In J. S. Kowalik and L. Grandinetti, editors, *Software for Parallel Computation*, volume 106. Springer-Verlag, 1993.
3. S. Bouchenak and D. Hagimont. Zero Overhead Java Thread Migration. Technical Report 0261, INRIA, 2002.
4. V. Chaudhary and H. Jiang. Techniques for Migrating Computations on the Grid. *Engineering the Grid: Status and Perspective*, January 2006.
5. C. Clark, K. Fraser, S. Hand, J. Gorm Hansen, E. Jul, C. Limpach, I. Pratt, and A. Warfield. Live Migration of Virtual Machines. In *Proceedings of the Symposium on Networked Systems Design and Implementation*, Boston, USA, May 2005.
6. B. Folliot, I. Piumarta, and F. Riccardi. A Dynamically Configurable, Multi-Language Execution Platform. In *8th ACM SIGOPS European Workshop*, 1998.
7. D. Freedman. Experience Building a Process Migration Subsystem for UNIX. In *Proceedings of the Winter Usenix Conference*, pages 349–356, 1991.
8. S. Funfrocken. Transparent Migration of Java-Based Mobile Agents. In *Mobile Agents*, pages 26–37, 1998.
9. G. Back and W. H. Hsieh and J. Lepreau. Processes in KaffeOS: Isolation, Resource Management, and Sharing in Java. In *Proceedings of the Symposium on Operating Systems Design and Implementation*, San Diego, USA, October 2000.
10. M. Golm, M. Felsera, C. Wawersich, , and J. Kleinoeder. The JX Operating System. In *Proceedings of the Usenix Annual Technical Conference*, pages 45–58, Monterey, USA, June 2002.
11. JNode: Java New Operating System Design Effort. http://www.jnode.org.
12. G. Kiczales, J. Lamping, A. Menhdhekar, C. Maeda, C. Lopes, J-M. Loingtier, and J. Irwin. Aspect-Oriented Programming. In *Proceedings of the European Conference on Object-Oriented Programming*, pages 220–242, Jyväskylä, Finland, June 1997.
13. M. Litzkow. Remote UNIX. Turning Idle Workstations into Cycle Servers. In *Proceedings of the Summer Usenix Conference*, pages 381–384, June 1987.
14. D. S. Milojicic, F. Douglis, Y. Paindaveine, R. Wheeler, and S. Zhou. Process Migration. *ACM Computer Survey*, 32(3):241–299, 2000.
15. F. Ogel, S. Patarin, I. Piumarta, and B. Folliot. C/SPAN: A Self-Adapting Web Proxy Cache. In *Proceedings of the Autonomic Computing Workshop*, pages 178–186, Seattle, USA, June 2003.
16. I. Piumarta. The Virtual Processor: Fast, Architecture-Neutral Dynamic Code Generation. In *Proceedings of the Virtual Machine Research and Technology Symposium*, pages 97–110, San Jose, USA, May 2004.
17. G. Popek, B. Walker, J. Chow, D. Edwards, C. Kline, G. Rudisin, and G. Thiel. LOCUS a Network Transparent, High Reliability Distributed System. In *Proceedings of the Symposium on Operating Systems Principles*, pages 169–177, Pacific Grove, USA, December 1981.
18. T. Sakamoto, T. Sekiguchi, and A. Yonezawa. Bytecode transformation for portable thread migration in java. In *Proceedings of the International Symposium on Agent Systems and Applications/Mobile Agents*, pages 16–28, Zurich, Suisse, 2000.
19. C. P. Sapuntzakis, R. Chandra, B. Pfaff, J. Chow, M. S. Lam, and M.Rosenblum. Optimizing the Migration of Virtual Computers. In *Proceedings of the Symposium on Operating Systems Design and Implementation*, Boston, USA, December 2002.
20. M. Shapiro. Structure and Encapsulation in Distributed Systems: the Proxy Principle. In *Proceedings of the International Conference on Distributed Systems*, pages 198–204, Cambridge, USA, May 1986.

21. K. Shudo and Y. Muraoka. Asynchronous Migration of Execution Context in Java Virtual Machines. *Future Generation Computer Systems*, 18(2):225–233, October 2001.
22. D. Simon and C. Cifuentes. The Squawk Virtual Machine: Java on the Bare Metal. In *Proceedings of the Companion to the Object-Oriented Programming, Systems, Languages, and Applications Conference*, pages 150–151, San Diego, USA, October 2005.
23. P. Smith and N. Hutchinson. Heterogeneous Process Migration: The Tui System. *Software Practice and Experience*, 28(6):611–639, 1998.
24. C. Steketee, W. Zhu, and P. Moseley. Implementation of Process Migration in Amoeba. In *Proceedings of the International Conference on Distributed Computing Systems*, pages 194–201, June 1994.
25. X. Sun, V. Niak, and K. Chanchio. A Coordinated Approach for Process Migration in Heterogeneous Environments. In *Proceedings of the SIAM Parallel Processing Conference*, March 1999.
26. M. Theimer, K. Lantz, and D. Cheriton. Preemptable remote execution facilities for the V-system. In *Proceedings of the Symposium on Operating Systems Principles*, pages 2–12, Orcas Island, USA, December 1985.
27. G. Thomas, F. Ogel, A. Galland, B. Folliot, and I. Piumarta. Building a Flexible Java Runtime upon a Flexible Compiler. In Jean-Jacques Vandewalle David Simplot-Ryl and Gilles Grimaud, editors, *Special Issue on 'System & Networking for Smart Objects' of IASTED International Journal on Computers and Applications*, volume 27, pages 28–47. ACTA Press, 2005.
28. E. Truyen, B. Robben, B. Vanhaute, T. Coninx, W. Joosen, and P. Verbaeten. Portable Support for Transparent Thread Migration in Java. In *Proceedings of the International Symposium on Agent Systems and Applications/Mobile Agents*, pages 29–43, Zurich, Suisse, 2000.
29. D. Ungar, A. Spitz, and A. Ausch. Constructing a Metacircular Virtual Machine in an Exploratory Programming Environment. In *Proceedings of the Companion to the Object-Oriented Programming, Systems, Languages, and Applications Conference*, pages 11–20, San Diego, USA, October 2005.
30. VMWare, Inc. VMWare VirtualCenter Version 1.2 User's Manual, 2004.
31. W. Zhu, W. Fang, C. Wang, and F. Lau. A New Transparent Java Thread Migration System Using Just-in-Time Recompilation. In *Proceedings of the International Conference on Parallel and Distributed Computing and Systems*, pages 766–771, Cambridge, USA, November 2004.
32. W. Zhu, C. Wang, and F. Lau. JESSICA2: A Distributed Java Virtual Machine with Transparent Thread Migration Support. In *Proceedings of the International Conference on Cluster Computing*, Chicago, USA, September 2002.

A Comparative Study Between Soft System Bus and Traditional Middlewares

Mohammad Reza Selim, Takumi Endo, Yuichi Goto, and Jingde Cheng

Department of Information and Computer Sciences
Saitama University, Saitama, 338-8570, Japan
{selim, endo, gotoh, cheng}@aise.ics.saitama-u.ac.jp

Abstract. Although persistent availability is one of the basic requirements of the middlewares for pervasive computing systems to provide "anytime anywhere" services, very little work has been done on this issue. Soft System Bus (SSB) was proposed to provide "anytime anywhere" middleware platform support to large-scale reactive systems which run continuously and persistently. However, till now no SSB has been implemented. In this paper, we present a comparative study between the SSB and different types of traditional middlewares, e.g., synchronous Request/Reply, Message Oriented, Publish/Subscribe middlewares, etc, in order to find the implementation issues of an SSB. We show that although existing middlewares have some characteristics that are common in an SSB too, they lack some features which are unique and essential for an SSB. Finally, we present the implementation issues of an SSB to ensure persistent availability.

Keywords: Soft System Bus, Data/Instruction Station, Middleware.

1 Introduction

The ultimate goal of pervasive/ubiquitous computing is to provide users with the way of computing anytime and anywhere such that one can use computing systems without even thinking of them [5]. Obviously, a necessary condition to underlie pervasive computing is that the computing systems have to be functioning anytime (anytime functionality will also be termed as persistent running, persistent availability or everlasting availability in this paper) and be available throughout the physical world. Moreover, since in general we can not ensure the development of a computing system which will not fail, anytime and anywhere functionality entails that the computing system should also be maintained, upgraded and reconfigured anytime and anywhere. Therefore, anytime anywhere availability, maintainability, upgradeability and re-configurability of computing systems are indispensable to true pervasive computing [4], [5].

Motivated by the need to build such computing systems, Cheng first proposed a design methodology, called Soft System Bus based methodology [6], to build reactive systems that functions continuously all the time without stopping its interactions even when it is being maintained, upgraded or reconfigured, it has some trouble, or it is being attacked. A system built using this methodology is called Soft System Bus Based System (SSBBS). SSBBSs have two fundamental features; persistently continuous functioning, i.e., the systems can function continuously without stopping its reaction,

R. Meersman, Z. Tari, P. Herrero et al. (Eds.): OTM Workshops 2006, LNCS 4278, pp. 1264–1273, 2006.

and dynamically adaptive functioning, i.e., the systems can be dynamically maintained, upgraded or reconfigured during its continuous functioning and reacting [4], [5]. For example, Autonomous Evolutionary Information Systems and Anticipatory Reasoning Reactive Systems are two among several proposed SSBBSs [4].

An SSBBS (Figure 1) consists of a number of *components* and one or more *SSBs*. The components are connected to the SSB. An SSB is a communication channel used to provide hardware and platform independent middleware support to the components. It conveys the *data/instructions* (we use the term *message* also) from component to component, provides language independent *unified* interface to the components and *preserves* the data/instructions if the destination component is not connected to the SSB. An SSB consists of one or more nodes called *Data/Instruction Stations* (DISs).

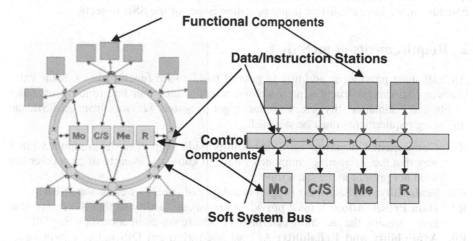

Fig. 1. Circular (left) and linear (right) SSBBS architectures

There are two types of components in an SSBBS: one or more general purpose permanent *Control Components* (CCs) and some application specific *Functional Components* (FCs). Based on runtime information, the CCs measure, monitor and control the FCs in some way. On the other hand, the FCs, which provide functionalities to the application scenario, are developed by the application developers. In an SSBBS, any two components are not allowed to communicate directly. They must use the (unified) interface of the SSB to interact with each other.

Our ultimate purpose is to build the general purpose part of SSBBSs, i.e., the SSB and CCs which is collectively called *SSB package*. The SSB package will be used to build large-scale long lasting reactive systems, e.g., air traffic control systems, operating systems, transportation/industrial control systems, etc. The application developers' responsibility is to develop the FCs and to attach them to the SSB. Thus, with minimum effort a long lasting reactive system can be built.

A communication layer that allows applications to interact across hardware and network environments is called a Middleware [1], [10]. Middlewares mask the heterogeneity of computer architectures, operating systems, programming languages, and networking technologies to facilitate application programming and management [10]. Both CORBA, Java RMI, MS DCOM based *synchronous middlewares* and *asynchronous* Message Oriented Middlewares (MOM) like IBM MQSeries, Siena, TSpaces, JavaSpaces, etc have these common functionalities [8]. In this sense the SSB is also a middleware. However, there are some basic differences between an SSB and the traditional middlewares. The purpose of this paper is to compare the SSB and existing middlewares in theoretical level and identify the implementation issues of the SSB. This paper presents a list of requirements of the SSB and then discusses those requirements against existing middleware solutions. This comparison reveals that some implementation issues are potentially solvable by the existing middleware technologies while others are either partially solvable or not at all. Finally, we present a list of implementation issues of the SSB categorized according to their solvability.

In the next section, we list the requirements of the SSB. In section 3, we compare the SSB and existing middlewares from the viewpoint of their requirements. Before conclusion, we have identified implementation issues of the SSB in section 4.

2 Requirements of an SSB

An SSB must provide, in addition to general middleware functionalities, some extra features like data/instruction preservation, reliable data transfer, runtime upgrade-ability and maintainability, etc. In order to get persistent services from an SSB, the following requirements must be satisfied:

R1. Component Coupling: An SSB has to provide support to the components in a way that the interacting components have to know the identity of each other but need not present at the same time.

R2. Scalability: An SSB must support scalability of itself as well as the SSBBS.

R3. Data Preservation: It must provide *preservation* facility so that if a component is not present, the incoming data/instructions are stored in corresponding DIS.

R4. Availability and Reliability: At least one (arbitrary) DIS must be running all the time. The states of a DIS must be recoverable in case of failure and an SSB must also be resilient to link failure.

R5. Dynamic Connectivity: An SSB must allow a component to select and connect to its currently associated DIS dynamically.

R6. Runtime Upgrade and Maintenance: There must have a way to upgrade and maintain an SSB (i.e., the DISs) at runtime in order to provide evolutionary changing services to the components.

R7. Runtime Adaptability/Re-configurability: Since an SSB is general purpose, it will evolve over time and it may operate in dynamic environments, runtime adaptability/re-configurability is an essential requirement for an SSB.

R8. Transmission Model: A one to one communication has to be used in a partially distributed architecture.

R9. Unified Interface: An SSB must provide a unified interface to the components.

R10. Reconfigurable Security: An SSB must ensure reconfigurable security so that they can be adjusted with the evolution of the SSBBSs.

3 SSB Versus Traditional Middlewares

The above list of requirements is sound and complete for an SSB. Our purpose is to find out the implementation issues that must be solved to satisfy those requirements.

One of the best ways to identify the issues is to compare the SSB with existing middlewares from the view points of those requirements. This comparison will isolate the requirements that can be fulfilled by using the technologies already used in existing middlewares from those that are unique in an SSB and therefore new methods have to be developed to satisfy those unique requirements. In this section we present this comparative study.

3.1 Component Coupling

Many types of middlewares have already been proposed [8]. Based on decoupling ability regarding *space*, *time* and *flow/synchronization*, middlewares have been classified into several categories. Some middlewares especially RPC/RMI, CORBA [16], [17] based middlewares are not decoupled in time and space, but provide partial or full flow decoupling [8]. Some other middlewares like TSpaces, JavaSpaces (Linda based) [11], [13], [15], Oracle Advanced Queuing [8] provide full space and time decoupling but partial flow decoupling. But in *publish/subscribe* based middlewares like Hermes [18], [19], TIBCO Rendezvous [22], Siena [3], Java Messaging Services (JMS) [12], etc offers a full space, time and flow decoupling ability. The first type of middlewares is regarded as *tightly coupled* and the last two *as loosely coupled* middlewares.

An SSB is a middleware that is neither tightly coupled nor loosely coupled. Although it does not provide space decoupling, it offers time and flow decoupling. An SSBBS is modeled by dividing it into lots of components (i.e., FCs). The components interact with each other not directly but only through the SSB. This implies that a component must know another component by its identity. Therefore, an SSB is coupled in space.

Space coupling is also given by some type of existing middlewares like RPC/RMI, Observer D pattern, etc. In these middlewares, a consumer explicitly keeps the addresses (usually the URLs or IP addresses) of all of the producers, and vice versa. This is one kind of direct interaction in distributed environment. However, an SSB suggests that a component accesses another component by its ID just like a local component, i.e., the communication detail is hidden from the components by the SSB.

In an SSBBS if a component is not present, the incoming data is stored into the DIS the component is tapped to. Since two interacting components need not present at the same time, an SSB is *decoupled in time*. An SSB also provide *flow decoupling*, i.e., a component is not blocked until a data reaches from another component. A component is notified automatically by the SSB when a data reached.

3.2 Scalability

An SSBBS is a large-scale (closed) reactive system [4]. Since numerous components are attached to an SSB, it is not unusual that within a short period of time some of the components are disconnected and some new components join the SSB. Besides, as an SSBBS evolves over time, the number of components will also increase. Therefore, an SSB should provide support to the increasing number of components as well as frequent arrival and departure of components. In order to support increasing number of components, new middleware nodes, i.e., DISs may also need to be added sometimes. Although the node arrival and departure is not frequent, there must have a way to add a node to or remove a node from an SSB at runtime.

Most of the middlewares, especially large Internet-scale middlewares, like Tuple spaces, MOM and publish/subscribe middlewares, are scaleable [8], [18], [19]. They support a large number of publishers and subscribers and their frequent arrival and departure do not affect the system performance largely. Besides, they also support cost-effective extending or shrinking of the middleware by adding a new node to or removing an old node from the middleware. On the other hand, the performance of the RPC/RMI based middlewares is affected largely as the number of consumers (clients) increases.

The scalability requirement of an SSB is in between Internet-scale middlewares and RPC/RMI based middlewares. An SSB must provide efficient support to the random arrival and departure of components as well as to the expansion of the SSBBS (by adding new components). Also the performance of an SSB should not be affected much after it is extended or shrunk by adding or removing DISs respectively. Since this expansion and shrinking of an SSB is not frequent, instant cost of adding and removing a DIS is acceptable to some extent.

3.3 Data Preservation

Data/instruction *preservation* is an essential requirement of an SSBBS [4], [6]. It means that if a component is not present, the incoming data is stored into the corresponding DIS. Several types of middlewares such as Tupple Spaces, Message Queuing (MOM) and all Publish/subscribe middlewares provide time decoupling facility like an SSB, i.e., the middleware stores the data until the consumer connects to the middleware.

However, what and how much information should be preserved in the middleware is still an issue in an SSB. In publish/subscribe based middlewares, only the data which is communicated through it is stored. However, in an SSBBS to provide fault tolerance to the components, an SSB may need to store some more information, e.g., the program states of the running components attached to it.

3.4 Availability and Reliability

In an SSBBS, since all interactions among components are performed only through the SSB, if all the DISs fail, the whole system will die because there is no way for the components to interact. Since persistent running is one of the fundamental requirements, at least one DIS must be running to maintain the interactions among components. Besides, another necessary condition is that an SSB must be fault tolerant enough to recover from node or link failure.

The above requirements for providing availability and reliability are also common in most of the middlewares especially in MOMs and publish/subscribe based middlewares [8], [18], [19]. Various measures are taken to improve the availability and reliability but, at present, no middleware can ensure them. However, in case of SSBBSs, an SSB must provide continuous services all the time to an SSBBS [4]. How to obtain such nonstop services is still a challenge, not only for an SSB but also for software engineering paradigm.

3.5 Dynamic Connectivity

For fault tolerance, one component may be tapped to one or more DISs statically. But this is not a satisfactory approach to improve reliability, because, if all the connected

DISs fail together, the components attached to them also fail. Therefore, an SSB must provide connectivity support in such a flexible way that a component can select and connect its associated DIS dynamically. It ensures that if one DIS fails, the components can be tapped to another one at runtime.

Overlay network based publish/subscribe (e.g., Hermes[18], [19], Siena[3]) oriented middlewares usually provides such dynamic connectivity to the publishers and subscribers to some extent. In this type of middlewares the subscription information of a subscriber is usually replicated into several nodes and if one fails the other replica can keep contact to that subscriber. However, if all the replicas fail then there is no way to keep the subscribers getting messages from the middleware. We envision a mechanism in which a component has the ability to connect to all the middleware nodes (i.e., DISs), may be one at a time, and get services as long as one node is alive.

3.6 Runtime Upgrade and Maintenance

Since an SSBBS runs for endless time, the components will evolve over time in order to adapt to the changing requirements. To provide middleware platform support to such evolving components, an SSB must also be upgradeable and maintainable. Since an SSBBS is not stopped, the SSB must provide such facilities at runtime. How a system can be upgraded or maintained at runtime is still a computer science issue. However, we adopt a slightly different definition of runtime upgradeability and maintainability. We consider that a part (e.g., a DIS) of the SSB is taken offline without affecting the system and updated and maintained while other part of the SSB is running and providing services. After completing upgrade and maintenance, the renovated part of the SSB is taken online and starts working with old part. In this way the whole SSB can be upgraded and maintained incrementally without affecting the services. However, this incremental upgradeability and maintainability has two prerequisites: a part (i.e., the DISs) of an SSB must be removable and addable at runtime and the renovated part must have the ability to work with the old part.

In most of the distributed peer to peer middlewares like Hermes, Siena [3], [18], [19], etc, nodes can be removed and added at runtime even the rate is very frequent. Although this is a very positive side of those middlewares, they do not consider runtime or incremental upgrade and maintenance of the middlewares as an essential requirement.

3.7 Runtime Adaptability/Re-configurability

In various situations an SSB may need to adapt itself. The same SSB and CCs will be deployed in different application arena to solve different problems. Since an SSBBS will evolve over time, an SSB may also need to reconfigure itself when the SSBBS is adapted to new requirements. Besides, the middleware may need to operate in dynamic environments, where the application requirements and the underlying network properties, such as resource availability and link connectivity, are constantly changing during the operation of an SSB. In all these situations, adaptability is essential [18].

Some existing middlewares (e.g., OpenORB[2], dynamicTAO[14]), called reflective middlewares, support runtime adaptability. Contrary to other traditional middlewares, which hide its state in order to give a high-level abstraction to applications, a reflective middleware exposes its state by means of meta-interfaces. Besides, current reflective middlewares are strongly influenced by synchronous request/reply communication as proposed by CORBA.

Since an SSBBS will run for unlimited time, adaptability feature is especially important for an SSB to cope with changes in the environment. Since an SSB is not synchronous, it should eliminate the drawback of existing reflective middlewares. Also for reliability and simplicity, an SSB should not expose its internal states to the components.

3.8 Transmission Models

An SSB uses a partially distributed model for data transfer among components. Unlike IBM MQSeries and Oracle Advanced Queuing [8], where messages are passed to a central entity and from this shared space messages are forwarded to the subscribers, an SSB uses some intermediate DISs to forward the messages. Some middlewares, like Gryphon [8], Siena [3], use this type of media architecture. They differ from the truly distributed media architectures in a way that, in later case the message forwarding responsibility goes to the publishers themselves (e.g., TIBCO Rendezvous [22]).

In publish/subscribe model communication is *many to many*. One publisher may publish data which can be consumed by many subscribers, whereas a single subscriber may receive from multiple publishers. Although MOMs (e.g., JMS, IBM WebSphere MQ, etc) are loosely coupled, like tightly coupled middlewares they also use a *one to one* communication paradigm. Likewise, an SSB uses a *one to one* communication. This is because one component of an SSBBS knows another component by its identity and like a component interacts with it by sending messages.

3.9 Unified Interface

Since an SSBBS has to ensure persistent running and runtime upgrade and maintenance, the component should be as independent as possible, i.e., if one component fails or disconnected for upgrade or maintenance the other components should be affected as low as possible. Therefore, components must not be allowed to interact directly, otherwise it may be very difficult to control the dependency among massive number of components. An SSB must provide a unified interface which is used by all the components connected to the SSB in order to communicate with each other. Another reason of this unified interface is to mange the complexity of interactions among this huge number of components.

Unified interface is also provided in traditional middlewares like MOM and publish/subscribe middlewares. However, the synchronous RPC/RMI middlewares do not support unified interface.

3.10 Reconfigurable Security

In SSBBSs, ensuring security is essential in order to provide reasonable and trusted services persistently and continuously. The general requirement is that data/instructions traveling through an SSB must be kept secured and any operation (e.g., adding or removing a component) must be authenticated. However, our main focus in achieving security is dynamic reconfiguration of security policies or mechanisms (e.g., protocols, algorithms, or models) with minimal effect on providing services, so that SSBBSs can perform evolutionary improvement of the security [7].

This is based on the recognition that almost all security mechanisms cannot prove and verify that it is secure forever. Since no system can be assured to be completely secured, we think that detection of and recovery from unexpected attacks are more important than prevention of them.

On the other hand, almost all traditional middlewares never emphasize the above-mentioned propositions. Besides, many works regarding security aspect of middlewares are positioned on low and technical level and therefore depend on computer architectures, operating systems, or network environments. However, some researches that focus their attention on security in publish/subscribe systems can be found in [9], [17], [20]. The main focus of these works is to implement trusted interaction among publishers/subscribers in a large-scale network environment where there are a number of publishers/subscribers some of which are partially trusted.

3.11 Summery

From the above comparative study between the SSB and traditional middlewares, we see that, although some of the features of the SSB are common in some middlewares, it has some unique requirements which can not be fulfilled by any existing middleware. For example, everlasting availability, dynamic connectivity, etc are the unique requirements of an SSB which are not satisfiable by using traditional middlewares.

4   Implementation Issues of SSB

In this section, we identify and list the implementation issues from the above comparative study. These issues have been classified into three categories: category I contains the issues which can not be solved using currently available technologies, Category II includes the issues which are not available in the existing middlewares but obtainable in some way. Finally Category III lists the issues which are available in the existing middlewares.

Category I Issues

I1-1. For everlasting availability at least one DIS must be running. But how can we ensure that all DISs will not fail at the same time? Current technology only can improve reliability and availability to some extent, but can not ensure them.

I1-2. In order for dynamic connectivity, a component must at least know the address of one running DIS. It can be known from a third party. However, continuous availability of the third party is still an issue.

Category II Issues

I2-1. Even if we assume that at least one DIS will be present all the time, to ensure availability of the preserved data, an SSB need to keep backup of the data in all the DISs. Although, this is achievable, certainly this technique is impractical.

I2-2. Currently available middlewares are either decoupled in both time and space or none. However, an SSB is decoupled in time but not in space. Although no existing middleware have this feature, it is not difficult to achieve such facility.

I2-3. Since runtime add or removal of a component is achievable, incremental upgrade and maintenance is also obtainable, although no existing middleware take special measures for it.

I2-4. In reflective middlewares, runtime adaptability is achievable in limited scale. How can an SSBBS achieve this runtime adaptability without exposing its internal states and alleviating synchronous nature of existing reflective middlewares?

I2-5. How can the SSB obtain reconfigurable security in an SSBBS?

Category III Issues

I3-1. To provide scalability, change in system states should be as low as possible when a component is added to or removed from an SSBBS.

I3-2. Unnecessary backup messages in a DIS should be deleted. How can a DIS know the appropriate time to delete it?

I3-3. An SSB need to implement a one to one communication model on a partially distributed architecture, i.e., the SSB takes the message transfer and delivery responsibility.

I3-4. The component should get the ordered message delivery. The destination DIS can take the responsibility or the SSB may need to adopt a method to maintain a strict linear order among the dependent messages.

I3-5. Like many other middlewares (e.g., publish/subscribe middlewares), it provides unified interface. It is the responsibility of components to transform and interpret the messages.

I3-6. How can an SSB distinguish valid components and malicious components? Some authentication mechanisms are indispensable.

5 Conclusion

Continuous and persistent running is not usually taken as an essential requirement for a system. Although *software/component bus* concept is not new, no one considers data preservation as a requirement. Even though some middlewares specially publish/subscribe middlewares provide data preservation facility, runtime upgrade and maintenance of the middlewares as well as the client programs is not taken specially [8], [18]. Besides, all general purpose programs can not be designed using publish/subscribe paradigm. IBM's autonomic computing aims to reduce the complexity of a system by providing some autonomic behavior to the elements of the system. Although some autonomy is needed in an SSBBS also, the main purpose of it is to provide system persistence. There are some other fundamental differences that can be found in [5].

Persist running is essential for any pervasive system. In this paper, based on a comparative study we have identified the issues that must be solved to build an SSB which is core to provide persistent running. We believe that due to its persistence and adaptable nature, in future, SSBs will be used in numerous pervasive computing systems. Our work is a starting point to build the middleware of such pervasive systems.

References

1. P. A. Bernstei: Middleware: A Model for Distributed System Services. Communications of ACM, 39(2): 86-98, 1996.
2. G. S. Blair, G. Coulson, A. Andersen, L. Blair, et al.: The Design and Implementation of Open ORB Version 2. IEEE Distributed Systems Online, 2(6), 2001.

3. Carzaniga, D.S. Rosenblum, and A.L. Wolf: Achieving scalability and expressiveness in an internet-scale event notification service. In Proc. of Nineteenth ACM Symposium on Principles of Distributed Computing, 2000.
4. J. Cheng: Persistent Computing Systems as Continuously Available, Reliable, and Secure Systems, In Proc. of 1st International Conference on Availability, Reliability and Security, pp. 631-638, IEEE-CS, 2006.
5. J. Cheng: Comparing Persistent Computing with Autonomic Computing. In Proc. of 11th IEEE-CS International Conference on Parallel and Distributed Systems, Vol. II, pp. 428-432, 2005.
6. J. Cheng: Connecting Components with Soft System Buses: A New Methodology for Design, Development, and Maintenance of Reconfigurable, Ubiquitous, and Persistent Reactive Systems. In Proc. of 19th International Conference on Advanced Information Networking and Applications, Vol. 1, pp. 667-672, IEEE-CS, 2005.
7. T. Endo, J. Miura, K. Nanashima, S. Morimoto, Y. Goto, and J. Cheng: Security in Persistently Reactive Systems, In T. Enokido, L. Yan, B. Xiao, D. Kim, Y. Dai, L. T. Yang (Eds.). Embedded and Ubiquitous Computing. EUC 2005 Workshops: UISW, NCUS, SecUbiq, USN, and TAUES, Japan, 2005, In Proc., LNCS, Vol. 3823, pp. 874-883, Springer-Verlag, 2005.
8. P. Th. Eugster, P. A. Felber, R. Guerraoui, A. M. Kermarrec: Many faces of Publish Subscribe. ACM Computing Surveys (CSUR), Vol. 35 Issue 2, 2003.
9. L. Fiege, A. Zeidler, A. Buchmann, R. K. Kehr and, G. Muhl: Security Aspects in Publish/Subscribe Systems. In Proc. of Distributed Event Based Systems, UK, 2004.
10. K. Geihs: Middleware Challenges Ahead. Computer 34(6): 24-31, IEEE Computer Society Press, 2001.
11. D. Gelernter: Generative communication in Linda. ACM Transactions on Programming Languages and Systems, 7:80–112, 1985.
12. M. Hapner, R. Burridge, R. Sharma, J. Fialli, and K. Stout: Java Message Service. Sun Microsystems Inc., 2002.
13. JavaSpaces Service Specification, http://www.sun.com/software/jini/specs/jini1.2html/js-title.html, 2002.
14. F. Kon, M. Roman, P. Liu, J. Mao, T. Yamane, L. C. Magalhaes, and R. H. Campbell: Monitoring, Security, and Dynamic Configuration with the dynamicTAO Reflective ORB. In Proc. of the IFIP/ACM International Conference on Middleware, LNCS vol. 1795, pp. 121–143, Springer-Verlag, 2000.
15. T.J. Lehman, S.W. Mac Laughry, and P. Wyckoff: Tspaces: The next wave. In Proc. of Hawaii International Conference on System Sciences, 1999.
16. The Common Object Request Broker: Core Specification. Version 3.0.3, OMG, 2004.
17. L. I.W. Pesonen and J. Bacon: Secure Event Types in Content-Based, Multi-Domain Publish/Subscribe Systems. In Proc. of the 5th international workshop on Software engineering and middleware, pp. 98 – 105, ACM Press, 2005
18. P. R. Pietzuch: Hermes: A scalable event-based Middleware. Technical Report, Cambridge University Computer Laboratory, 2004.
19. P. R. Pietzuch and J. M. Bacon: Hermes: A distributed Event-Based Middleware Architecture. In the Proc. of the 1st International Workshop on Distributed Event-Based Systems, 2002.
20. M. Srivatsa and L. Liu: Securing Publish-Subscribe Overlay Services with EventGuard. In Proc. of the 12th ACM conference on Computer and communications security, pp. 289-298, 2005.
21. Sun Java Remote Method Invocation Specification, 2000.
22. TIBCO. TIB/Rendezvous, White Paper, 1999.

A Semantic Location Service for Pervasive Grids

Antonio Coronato, Giuseppe De Pietro, and Massimo Esposito

ICAR-CNR, Via Castellino 111, 80131 Napoli, Italy
{antonio.coronato, massimo.esposito,
giuseppe.depietro}@na.icar.cnr.it

Abstract. Grid computing environments have recently been extended with Pervasive computing characteristics leading to a new paradigm, namely the Pervasive Grid Computing. In particular, QoS of existing Grid services is being augmented by means of location-awareness. This paper presents a location service that locates active mobile objects, such as Wi-Fi enabled devices and RFID tagged entities, in a real Pervasive Grid. The key feature of the service is the use of ontologies and rules to define a uniform, unambiguous and well-defined model for the location information, independently from the particular positioning system. Moreover, the location service performs logic and reasoning mechanisms both for providing physical and semantic locations of mobile objects and for inferring the finest granularity for location information in the case a mobile object is located by more than one positioning system. The service has been developed at the top of the standard OGSA architecture.

1 Introduction

During the last decade, new computing models have emerged and rapidly affirmed. In particular, terms like Grid Computing and Pervasive Computing have become of common use, not only in the scientific and academic world, but also in business fields.

The Grid Computing paradigm enables resource sharing and coordinated problem solving in dynamic multi-institutional organizations [1]. Grid denotes the virtualization of geographically distributed computing and data resources, such as processing, network bandwidth and storage capacity, to create a single system image, granting heterogeneous users and applications seamless access to vast IT capabilities.

Differently, the goal for Pervasive Computing is the development of environments where highly heterogeneous hardware and software components can seamlessly and spontaneously interoperate, in order to provide a variety of services to users independently of the specific characteristics of the environment and of the client devices [2].

These two worlds are now evolving towards a common paradigm, namely the Pervasive Grid Computing [3]. In particular, from the Grid Computing community point of view, it's now time to integrate mobile devices into the grid because they are becoming of common use for accessing to services in any distributed environment. In particular, a key feature of the Pervasive Computing, like the location-awareness, can proficiently enhance the QoS of existing Grid services, that is Pervasive Grid environments should customize services access depending on mobile users and objects locations.

R. Meersman, Z. Tari, P. Herrero et al. (Eds.): OTM Workshops 2006, LNCS 4278, pp. 1274–1284, 2006.
© Springer-Verlag Berlin Heidelberg 2006

In any kind of location-aware environment (pervasive environments, smart homes, pervasive grids, and so on), diverse types of wireless and wired positioning systems can be used to detect presence and proximity of people and mobile objects. The inter-working of more than one positioning system can undeniably provide a synergetic approach of localization, but it requires that such environments be supported by advanced location services able to integrate the location information coming from different sources. Indeed, each positioning system produces location data characterized by a specific representation and granularity.

In this paper, we propose a Semantic Location Service that localizes mobile entities in a Pervasive Grid environment; but, such a service can conveniently be integrated in any kind of environment as long as it is equipped with different positioning systems and wants to be able to handle both physical and semantic location information. The service exploits the inter-working of more than one positioning system, by utilizing the Semantic Web technologies [4]. Besides, we define a unique and unambiguous model for localization issues for integrating different positioning systems. In the case study, the defined model has been applied for integrating two specific types of positioning systems, respectively based on Wi-Fi and RFID technologies.

Moreover, the location service performs logic and reasoning mechanisms in order to generate semantic information from physical locations or to give the location information with the finest granularity when a mobile object is located by more than one positioning system.

The rest of the paper is organized as follows. Section 2 discusses some motivations and related work. Section 3 overviews a proposal of location model for a Pervasive Grid. Section 4 describes the location service and outlines the implementation details. In section 5 we present our Pervasive Grid environment and describe some applicative scenarios. Finally, section 6 concludes the paper.

2 Motivations and Related Work

2.1 Motivations

Several Pervasive Grid applications have recently be proposed in literature [8,9,10]. In many of such applications, services have to be location-aware; that is, they can proficiently enhanced by location information.

It is also worth to note that Pervasive Grids (as well as any classic Pervasive environment) can be equipped with a multitude of different positioning systems. Ideally, a positioning technology should provide both complete and accurate location information. In the absence of an ideal solution, multiple technologies are used and each of them can face specific requirements; i.e. a Wi-Fi based system can be used in order to locate mobile devices whereas an RFID based system can locate tagged users. Moreover, the emerging of new technologies doesn't necessary produce the replacement of the old ones; but, the integration of new and old systems is often required. As a result, this increases the complexity of the location-aware services, for the following reasons: i) the services should deal with many and different positioning systems and their low-level protocols; ii) they should know all the specific representations, defined and used by the positioning systems, for location information; besides, they should convert the location information from each specific representation to an internal one and this produces several different representations for each service; iii) additional location information, such as the semantic location (that is the meaning of a location) should be produced by the specific services.

2.2 Our Contribution

This paper proposes an enhanced location service able i) to localize mobile entities by using diverse types of positioning systems and localization techniques and ii) to integrate location information characterized by a specific format and granularity.

In detail, this work consists in the following issues:

Semantic integration of different positioning systems: The location service exploits the inter-working of more than one positioning system by hiding the format of location information coming from different positioning systems and by granting both syntactic and semantic interoperability between services and positioning systems.

Definition of a location model: A specific location model has been defined in order to provide a unique and uniform representation for location information, independently from the particular positioning system and to represent both physical and semantic location. The location model has been specified by using the Semantic Web technologies, and in particular the OWL [20] ontologies and SWRL [19] rules languages.

Logic and reasoning mechanisms: We have also defined and built logic and reasoning mechanisms that enable the location service to generate semantic information from physical positions or to give the location information with the finest granularity when a mobile object is located by more than one positioning system.

Integration with the Globus Toolkit: The location service has been developed at the top of the standard OGSA (Open Grid Services Architecture). and integrated with the Globus Toolkit [17].

2.3 Related Work

In the last few years location-aware computing and services have been of interest in several research areas, but the mobile devices, and consequently the issues related to localization, have been largely discriminated by Grid computing. Besides, no relevant experiments have been performed in Pervasive Grids. Differently, a number of pervasive computing systems can be described by the terms location or context-aware and in particular the approaches adopted in [6,7] are illustrated below.

In [6] the author presents a flexible platform for location-based services, which hides specific details of positioning systems and provides a uniform representation of both physical and semantic information. The corresponding infrastructure reflects a location domain model, which defines a semantic structure of the entire location space. This structure is composed of hierarchies that are built up of domains and logical links between domains. A domain represents a semantic location, whereas a link is the expression of a semantic relation between locations. On the other hand, our approach relies on the Semantic Web technologies, and so it grants both the syntactic as well as the semantic interoperability between services and the positioning systems.

Besides, the platform proposed in [6] doesn't provide a support for location reasoning, that is no logic mechanisms have been realized for obtaining semantic locations from physical ones or for determining the location information with the finest granularity when a mobile object is located by more than one positioning system.

CoBrA [7] is an architecture to support context-aware services in smart spaces. It locates mobile entities by using two types of positioning systems, respectively based on RFID and Bluetooth technologies. Besides, a set of ontologies has been defined for modelling context information. Semantic Web languages are used for representing them and for supporting context reasoning. Nevertheless, CoBrA doesn't aim at realizing a semantic integration of different types of positioning technologies. As a result, context ontologies don't model location information coming from positioning systems; but, they provide only a uniform and well-defined representation for the semantic locations which can characterize an environment. This choice is purely based on the type of context-aware applications to be supported in prototyping CoBrA.

3   The Semantic Approach

3.1   Our Proposal of a Location Model

The approach presented in this paper relies on a location model that we have defined to provide a unique and uniform representation for location information, indepe-ndently from the particular positioning system.

The model is based on the concepts of physical and semantic locations. These notions are not new in literature [11], but we have partially re-elaborated them. A physical location specifies the position of a mobile entity and is characterized by different granularities and scopes, depending on the particular positioning system. Instead, a semantic location specifies the meaning of a location and usually groups more physical locations. As an example, GPS coordinates are physical locations, whereas a semantic location can be a building, an office inside a building, a meeting room, an area in front of a wall-monitor and so on. In particular, our model describes the physical locations that can be specified by determining the proximity to well-known points, but it can also be easily extended by defining other types of physical locations.

The technique of proximity requires that the environment be equipped with sensors that reveal mobile users presence, or of particular devices to which mobile users can connect. So, in the figure, a physical location is not referred to physical coordinates (like in the case of a GPS system); but, identify the region, called sensed area, covered by a positioning system.

We have focused on two specific types of positioning systems, respectively based on Wi-Fi and RFID technologies, and so we have defined two types of sensed areas:

- Wi-Fi sensed area, which is identified by the physical location covered by a specific wireless Access Point (AP), i.e. a mobile entity is located by an AP when her mobile device becomes active into its area;
- RFID sensed area, which is identified by the physical location covered by a specific RFID reader, i.e. a mobile entity is located by an RFID reader when her RFID tag is sufficiently near it.

Moreover, we have defined some semantic locations for an environment, as building, room, corridor, and so on. Then, we have subdivided all these semantic locations in many atomic locations, that represent the minimal semantic locations in which a mobile entity can be localized. As an example, an atomic location can contain a desk, a pc, a table or it can be empty.

Figure 1 illustrates the relationships existing among semantic locations, atomic locations and sensed areas. Our model is general and, thus, can be applied for describing a large number of location-aware environments. The environment in Figure 1 is composed by semantic locations, such as laboratories, meeting rooms, office rooms, corridors. Each location is subdivided in atomic locations.

A sensed area maps one or more atomic location, and, in particular, an RFID sensed area matches just one atomic location, whereas a Wi-Fi sensed area groups more atomic locations. This choice has been motivated by technological issues; that is, the RFID based positioning system that we have adopted is a short range (30 cm) system and provides finer grain location information rather than the Wi-Fi based ones (this is not true in general). As a result, the relationship between a sensed area and one or more atomic locations allows to identify the atomic and also the semantic location of a mobile entity.

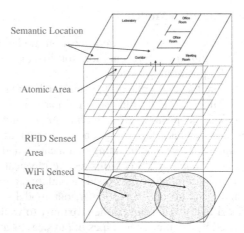

Fig. 1. Representation of the location model

3.2 Ontologies and Rules for the Location Model

The location model defines location information in a unique and uniform way, but these information must be represented in an unambiguous and well-defined formalism and expressed in a machine-readable format. Besides, it has to provide a support for granting both the syntactic and the semantic interoperability between the environment and positioning systems.

The Semantic Web technologies, which have been widely applied in many areas, can be used to face such needs because: i) ontologies and rules respectively enable the definition of domain vocabularies and allow declarative data processing, by providing a way to share knowledge without misunderstandings; ii) RDF [8], SWRL and OWL are semantic representation languages with high degree of expressiveness; iii) ontologies and rules can be reasoned by logic inference engines. We can use ontologies and rules coupled with subsets of first order logics to infer new knowledge and to ensure that the system is always in a consistent state.

Therefore, we have modeled three OWL ontologies and a set of SWRL rules related to location issues. In the following, a brief description for the defined ontologies and rules is reported.

The first ontology models all the concepts for defining semantic locations. Location is the root concept of this ontology and represents the generic location of an environment. Each location has a name and can contain or be contained in an other location. Room, Building, Floor and Corridor represent the particular semantic locations of such an environment. They are sub-concepts of the Location concept, and, as a result, each of them inherits the super-concept properties and adds new specialized features to them. For instance, a building is characterized by an address, a number of floors and is composed by corridors, floors and rooms (that is, these concepts are related to the Building concept by a whole-part relationship). We also define different types of rooms, as office-room, meeting-room and laboratory, by specializing the Room concept.

All these possible semantic locations are composed by atomic locations and so all the sub-concepts of Location are related to the Atomic Location concept by a whole-part relationship.

The graphical representation of this ontology is reported in Figure 2.

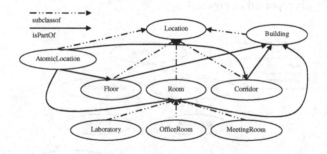

Fig. 2. Ontology for semantic locations

A second OWL ontology identifies, as shon in figure 3, the entities of the environment. Entity is the root concept and represents the generic entity of the environment. User and Device are sub-concepts of Entity and represent respectively users and devices that can be present in the environment. For instance, a user can be characterized by a name, a surname, an e-mail, a profile and so on.

A positioning system, an RFID Tag and a mobile Pc are particular devices and are described by specific properties. For example, a mobile Pc is characterized by a set of hardware and software properties, which describe memory capabilities, connection's bandwidth, cpu speed, available applications, and so on.

RFID Reader and Wi-Fi Access Point are sub-concepts of Positioning System and define the two positioning systems we have integrated and described in the model.

A mobile user can be equipped with an RFID Tag or can be the owner of a mobile PC. An RFID Tag can be sensed by an RFID Reader, whereas a mobile PC can be sensed by a Wi-Fi access point.

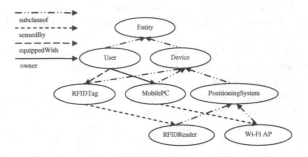

Fig. 3. Ontology for entities of a pervasive grid

The last ontology specifies all the concepts for describing the physical locations. SensedArea is the root concept of this ontology and represents a generic area covered by a positioning system. RFIDSensedArea and Wi-FiSensedArea are sub-concepts of SensedArea and. represent the regions respectively covered by an RFID Reader and Wi-Fi AP. The relationship between a sensed area and one or more atomic locations allows to identify the atomic and, as a result, the semantic location of a mobile user.

This ontology is reported in Figure 4.

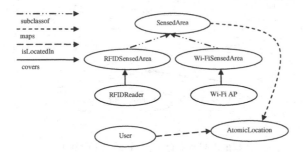

Fig. 4. Ontology for physical locations

Moreover, as an example, we describe two SWRL rules that we have realized to couple with the previous ontologies. In particular, such rules are used to select the location information with the finest granularity when an object is located by more positioning systems. In detail, the next rule makes the environment able to conclude that, if a mobile entity is sensed by an RFID reader, then it is located in the atomic location associated to the sensed area covered by that RFID reader.

sensedBy(entity, RFID reader) $\wedge$ covers(RFIDreader,RFIDSensed Area) $\wedge$ maps(RFIDSensedArea, AtomicLocation) $\Rightarrow$ isLocatedIn(entity,AtomicLocation)

Instead, by using the second rule, the environment can conclude that, if a mobile entity is sensed by a Wi-fi AP and is not sensed by an RFID reader, then it is located in the atomic location associated to the sensed area covered by that Wi-Fi AP.

sensedBy(entity,Wi-Fi AP) ∧ notSensedBy(entity,RFID reader) ∧ covers(Wi-Fi AP, Wi-Fi APSensedArea) ∧ maps(Wi-Fi APSensed Area, AtomicLocation) ⟹ isLocatedIn(entity, AtomicLocation)

If a mobile entity is sensed by both an RFID reader and a Wi-Fi AP, the environment obtains the atomic location with the finest granularity by utilizing both the rules shown above. As a matter of fact, there is a condition that is not verified in the second rule (the mobile entity is sensed by an RFID reader), only the first rules hits and thus we can conclude that the mobile entity is located only in the atomic location associated to the sensed area covered by the RFID reader.

4 The Semantic Location Service

Current implementation of our location service integrates two distinct positioning systems for locating active mobile objects, like Wi-Fi enabled devices and RFID tagged entities. It has been developed in a real Pervasive Grid environment.

It provides both location and locating functions. A location function is a mechanism for identifying objects active at a specific physical location, whereas a locating function is a mechanism for identifying the location of specific objects [14].

The location service has been realized as an OGSA-compliant Grid Service. It has been developed and integrated in the Globus Toolkit [18], extending the open source collection of OGSA-based Grid Services offered by it. The service architecture consists of the following components:

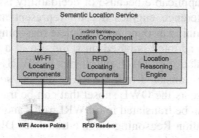

Fig. 5. The Location service architecture

Currently, we have developed two locating components that identify the location of mobile objects by using respectively the Wi-Fi and RFID based positioning systems. New locating components for other positioning technologies, such as the Bluetooth technology, can be realized and easily integrated in the service.

The *Wi-Fi Locating Component* is in charge of locating Wi-Fi enabled mobile devices, by periodically interrogating Wi-Fi APs. Indeed, each AP writes an event into a log file whenever a device becomes active into its area. By comparing such logs and by handling global states, it is possible to detect location changes. A similar approach has been realized in [15]. This technique can not be used to recognize when a device becomes inactive, because hand-offs are not reported in the log file. It is possible to adopt a strategy based on checkpoints, and in particular the environment can periodically detect each mobile device with a ping operation. After having issued a ping message, the environment waits for a response or for a timeout. A mobile device is declared inactive after having missed a certain number of consecutive ping messages. Current implementation uses 3Com Office Connect Wireless 11g Access Points.

The *RFID Locating Component* is in charge of locating RFID tagged entities, by periodically interrogating RFID readers. When an entity is sensed by a reader, we can obviously conclude that it is located in the atomic location covered by that reader. A similar approach has been described in [16]. Current implementation uses the passive, short-range (30 cm), Feig Electronic RFID, model ISC.MR 100/101.

The *Location Component* is in charge of handling global location states obtained by combining information coming from Locating components.

The *Location Reasoning Engine* is the core-component of the semantic location service and is in charge of managing the location ontologies and rules. First of all, it uses location ontologies and rules to specify location information in a uniform representation. As a result, it is able to grant both the syntactic as well as the semantic interoperability between the environment and any positioning system. Therefore, it uses a logic inference engine to perform reasoning mechanisms about the location information. In particular, our location ontologies and rules are submitted to the inference engine and reasoned by it in order to i) generate the semantic locations of mobile entities from their physical locations and ii) give the location information with the finest granularity when a mobile entity is located by more than one positioning system. Nevertheless, the Location Reasoning Engine cannot use SWRL rules and OWL ontologies in a unique inference engine, because a complete integration of them in a unique system is inapplicable because of decidability issues. Besides, a solution based on a stack of inference engines doesn't represent an efficient, simple, and scalable solution for obtaining a sound and complete reasoning process.

The solution we have adopted is based on i) the use of a unique inference engine for rules and ii) the translation of OWL ontologies in SWRL rules. But, OWL syntax constructs can not all be translated into SWRL rules, and so we have used the DLP OWL language. It represents the OWL subset that can be translated in SWRL, that is DLP OWL ontologies can be translated into SWRL rules and vice versa.

Definitively, the Location Reasoning Engine translates DLP OWL ontologies into SWRL rules and then it is able to use a unique rule engine to infer and reason in a complete and sound way. It is worth noting that DLP OWL is less expressive than either the ontology or rule languages, but, in many cases, the complete expressiveness of OWL is not needed and a restriction such as DLP OWL is enough.

5 Experimental Scenario

The experimental scenario consists of an intra-Grid, composed by diverse physical site located in a three floors building. The virtual environment uses two floors of the building.

Floor zero has a computing laboratory in which a cluster of 24 linux PCs, a 12 processors Silicon Graphics workstation, and a motion capture system are deployed. Such resources are collected in a wired grid built at the top of the Globus Toolkit 4.0 platform.

On floor two, wireless access to the grid is available. As a matter of fact, two 3Com Office Connect Wireless 11g Access Points identify two distinct locations. L1 is a laboratory where our students develop their activities and periodically perform E-Tests. It contains two multimedia displays and some desktop PCs. L2 is a meeting room equipped with a projector, an interactive monitor, and other multimedia devices. The floor two is subdivided in atomic locations, and each of them is equipped with a Feig Electronic RFID reader.

Some services are available:

- *RenderingService* – This service enables users to submit row motion data and to build 3D graphic applications. This service is exposed as a Grid Service and is available at every location (L1, L2);
- *ETestingService* – This service performs on-line evaluation tests for courseware activities. Evaluation tests are synchronized and students have a predefined period of time for completing each test section. This service is exposed as a Grid Service, but it must be available only in the laboratory (L1).

6 Conclusions

In this paper we presented a Semantic Location service locates active mobile objects, such as Wi-Fi enabled devices and RFID tagged entities, in Pervasive Grids. The key feature of the service is the use of ontologies and rules i) to define a uniform, unambiguous and well-defined model for the location information, independently from the particular positioning system; ii) to perform logic and reasoning mechanisms for providing physical and semantic locations of mobile objects and for giving the location information with the finest granularity when a mobile object is located by more than one positioning system. This facility provides the Pervasive Grid with support for customizing services depending on the user location, as well as enabling mobile users to get access.

Future work will aim to realize locating component for integrating new positioning technologies, such as Bluetooth. As a result, the location model will be extended by defining the concepts related to these new positioning systems, and in particular the new types of physical locations provided by them.

References

[1] I.Foster, C. Kesselman, S. Tuecke, "The Anatomy of the Grid: Enabling Scalable Virtual Organizations", International J. Supercomputer Applications, 2001
[2] D. Saha and A. Murkrjee, "Pervasive Computing: A Paradigm for the 21st Century", IEEE Computer, March 2003.
[3] V. Hingne, A. Joshi, T. Finin, H. Kargupta, E. Houstis, "Towards a Pervasive Grid", International Parallel and Distributed Processing Symposium, IPDPS 2003.

[4] "Semantic Web" web site, http://www.w3.org/2001/sw/.

[5] L. W. McKnight, J. Howinson, S. Bradner, "Wireless Grids", IEEE Internet Computing, July-August 2004.

[6] J.Roth, "Flexible Positioning for Location-based Services", IADIS Journal on WWW/Internet, Vol. I, Nr. 2, Dez. 2003, IADIS Press, 18-32

[7] Harry Chen, Filip Perich, Dipanjan Chakraborty, Tim Finin, Anupam Joshi, "Intelligent Agents Meet Semantic Web in a Smart Meeting Room", Department of Computer Science & Electrical Engineering, University of Maryland, Baltimore County

[8] B. Clarke and M. Humphrey, "Beyond the 'Device as Portal': Meeting the Requirements of Wireless and Mobile Devices in the Legion of Grid Computing System", International Parallel and Distributed Processing Symposium, IPDPS 2002.

[9] T. Phan, L. Huang and C. Dulan, "Challenge: Integrating Mobile Devices Into the Computational Grid", International Conference on Mobile Computing and Networking, MobiCom 2002.

[10] D. C. Chu and M. Humphrey, "Mobile OGSI.NET: Grid Computing on Mobile Devices", International Workshop on Grid Computing, GRID 2004.

[11] S.Pradhan, "Semantic locations", Personal Technologies, Vol. 4, No 4, 2000, 213-216.

[12] L. Ferreira, V. Berstis, J. Armstrong, M. Kendzierski, A. Neukoetter, M. Takagi, R. Bing-Wo, A. Amir, R. Murakawa, O. Hernandez, J. Magowan, N. Bieberstein, "Introduction to Grid Computing with Globus", IBM RedBooks, September, 2003.

[13] J. Joseph, M. Ernest, C. Fellenstein, "Evolution of grid computing architecture and grid adoption models", IBM Systems Journal, December, 2004.

[14] S. Fischmeister, G. Menkhaus and A. Stumpfl, "Location-Detection Strategies in Pervasive Computing Environments", in the proc. of the 1st international conference on Pervasive Computing, PERCOM03.

[15] S. G. M. Koo, C. Rosenberg, H. H. Chan, Y. C. Lee, A. Vilavaar, A. Wenzel, "Location-Based E-Campus Web Services: From Design to Deployment", in the proc. of The first IEEE International Conference on Pervasive Computing and Communications, PERCOM 2003.

[16] J. Hightower and G. Borriello, "Location Systems for Ubiquitous Computing", IEEE Computer, August 2001.

[17] Grosof B., Horrocks I., Volz R., and Decker S., "Description Logic Programs: Combining Logic Programs with Description Logic", In: Proc. 12th Intl. Conf. on the World Wide Web (WWW-2003), Budapest, Hungary, May 20-23, 2003.

[18] I.Foster, C. Kesselman, J. Nick, S. Tuecke, "The Physiology of the Grid: An Open Grid Services Architecture for Distributed Systems Integration", Open Grid Service Infrastructure WG, Global Grid Forum, June 22, 2002.

[19] Ian Horrocks, Peter F. Patel-Schneider, Harold Boley, Said Tabet, Benjamin Grosof, Mike Dean, "SWRL: A Semantic Web Rule Language Combining OWL and RuleML", W3C Member Submission 21 May 2004. Latest version is available at http://www.w3.org/Submission/2004/SWRL/.

[20] Peter F. Patel-Schneider, Pat Hayes and Ian Horrocks, "OWL Web Ontology Language Semantics and Abstract Syntax", W3C Recommendation 10 February 2004. Latest version is available at http://www.w3.org/TR/owl-semantics/.

[21] Graham Klyne, Jeremy J. Carroll, and Brian McBride, "Resource Description Framework (RDF) Concepts and Abstract Syntax.", W3C Recommendation 10 February 2004. Latest version is available at http://www.w3.org/TR/rdf-concepts/.

A Pragmatic and Pervasive Methodology to Web Service Discovery

Electra Tamani and Paraskevas Evripidou

University of Cyprus, Department of Computer Science
75 Kallipoleos St., T.K. 537, 1678 Nicosia, Cyprus

Abstract. Service-Oriented computing can be characterized as the motivating force for interoperable web applications. Businesses that embark on service-oriented technology are inclined to an effective interoperation with other businesses. This interoperation not only can expand businesses' markets but also allow the provision of quality services to citizens for carrying out their everyday transactions. However for an effective utilization of service-oriented computing a variety of other technologies must be involved namely semantics, pragmatics, effective search techniques, intelligent agents and pervasive services. In this paper we focus in one of the phases of service-oriented computing, the web service discovery, and propose an effective pragmatic and pervasive methodology that will enable potential business partners to discover the web services[1]/processes of their interest. We are particularly emphasizing on the importance of pragmatics and their application during web service discovery, because only a pragmatic consideration can provide complete and unambiguous meaning to web service usage.

1 Introduction

As the title implies, Service-Oriented Computing is a computing technology based on services. The underlying architecture in a Service-Oriented environment, known as SOA[2], expresses a perspective of a software architecture that facilitates services to support the requirements of software users. In a SOA environment, network resources are deployed as independent services, usually based on Web Services standards, that can be accessed without knowledge of their underlying platform implementation. Web Services have become the de facto standard for interoperability and the technology for building distributed web applications capable of achieving seamless business-to-business or enterprize application integration. Businesses that embark on service-oriented technology are inclined to an effective interoperation with other businesses which eventually will not only allow them to expand their markets but also provide quality services to citizens for carrying out their everyday transactions.

---

[1] The term web services, as in this paper, is used to refer to semantic web services.
[2] Service-Oriented Architecture.

R. Meersman, Z. Tari, P. Herrero et al. (Eds.): OTM Workshops 2006, LNCS 4278, pp. 1285–1294, 2006.

However in order for businesses to exploit the full potential of service-oriented technology, they must first be in place of discovering effectively each other's business services. Web service discovery, is one of the phases of service-oriented computing towards this direction. During this phase the closest[3] to the requestors' context services are retrieved. Latest research motives are emphasizing the need for semantic enhancements, through ontologies usage[4], to a web service life-cycle process in order to facilitate an efficient discovery of web services by prospective business partners. These ontologies however, as pragmatists' argue, should not, as they are, be exploited as fixed conceptualizations of some domains but rather as dynamic structures which co-evolve with their communities of use[4,10]. Business parties have to communicate and continuously negotiate about what they agree to be their shared background/context[4]. This communication is especially important across organizational boundaries where business parties from different professional, social, or cultural backgrounds need to understand each other in order to collaborate effectively. Therefore, semantics alone can be judged as insufficient in providing effective solutions for collaborative businesses[13].

In this paper, we recognize this limitation and propose a pragmatic approach/ methodology to web service discovery which captures the context of web services' usage by considering the context of the interacting business parties. We distinguish three types of business collaborators: 1) the *provider* or the business which provides the web services of some area, 2) the *requestor* or the business which requests for the discovery of some web services of a specific area, and 3) the *provider-requestor* or the business which both provides web services but also requests some others. We are considering pervasive solutions that facilitate mobile devices[5], by capturing the context of the interacting business parties in an effective way. We demonstrate the effectiveness of our methodology through an example.

The rest of the paper is organized as follows: Section 2 elaborates on the types/roles of business collaborators and their actions in web service discovery. Section 3 introduces the pragmatic methodology that captures the pragmatics (context) of web services' usage. In Section 4 we consider a pervasive approach which allows business collaborators to define their context. Section 5 presents a realistic example to prove the effectiveness of our methodology. Section 6 introduces related work. Finally, we conclude in Section 7.

2   The Collaborators

The types of the collaborators considered in this paper are grouped into three categories as follows:

- *Provider*: represents the business which provides the web services in order to facilitate collaboration with other businesses and expand its markets.

---

[3] The term closest is used to refer to those offered web services that have the higher matching degree with those requested.
[4] Knowledge repositories of meaningful and structured content.
[5] Laptop, handheld.

Table 1. Collaborators' Actions

Type/Role	Actions	Description
Provider	offer	provision of web service/s
Requestor	demand	request for web service/s
Provider-Requestor	offer,demand	provision and request of/for web service/s

- *Requestor*: represents the business which requests the discovery of web services to exploit them according to its organizational needs/interests.
- *Provider-Requestor*: represents the business which both provides and requests web services from other businesses in order to fulfil its organizational goals.

Potential interest for specific retrieved web services from the requestor suggests entering into a commitment with the provider and together they collaborate to achieve a mutual goal which will benefit both of them.

Collaborators enact their roles by taking the actions listed in Table 1. As indicated in the table, the role of each collaborator determines the action to be performed. Providers offer the web services the requestors demand. A provider can only offer web services or both offer and demand web services. Similarly a requestor can only demand web services or both demand and offer web services. Let us now see how these roles and actions of collaborators are utilized during web service discovery process.

3   The Pragmatic Methodology to Web Service Discovery

As already indicated, the semantics alone are judged as insufficient in providing effective solutions for collaborative service-oriented businesses[13]. This limitation is particularly evident in web service discovery phase where the most relevant web services (to the requestor context) are retrieved. To backup semantic's approach insufficiency, let us consider things from the beginning.

During web service discovery the question to be answered is whether the offered web service is suitable to fulfill the requested web service needs. Prior to semantic web evolution the offer and request service descriptions were purely message-based, a solution that allowed the usage of rather simplistic matching algorithms (keyword-based search, type-based matchers). The problems with this approach were:

- *Semantics clarity*: the functionality of a web service had to be guessed from the flow of information, a situation that complicated the automatic selection of web services
- *Strict message compatibility*: if messages between provider and requestor did not match, then the service could not be used

Once researchers have identified these limitations, they proposed semantic solutions to web service description. Particularly, OWL-S (Ontology Web Language for Services) group is developing the tools and the technology to enable automation of services on the semantic web. OWL-S is mainly an OWL-based web service ontology which binds operations, inputs, outputs, preconditions, and effects to the corresponding WSDL parts[8]. The OWL-S matchmaker facilitates a matchmaking algorithm for matching two descriptions (offer and request) and identifying the different relations between the two descriptions (match,no match). On the other hand, the WSDL-S (Web Service Semantics) group is suggesting extensions to the current web service description langauge by adding ontology (OWL) references to operations, inputs, and outputs[9]. The matcher facilitated in this case is a combination of two types of matching algorithms (element level and schema) which complement one another in order to find all possible mappings between WSDL and ontology concepts. Finally WSMO (Web Service Modeling Ontology)[6] group is developing a conceptual model for the description of semantic web services together with a family of underlying formal languages and an execution environment. Similar to OWL-S matchmaker, WSMO differentiates between different types of matches (exact-match, subsumes-match, plug-in-match and intersection match).

In all these semantic solutions, the semantic meaning resolution between the offer and request service descriptions is left completely to the matcher. Let us assume that a generic enough matcher that captures all possible paths to meaning resolution exists. Even if that was the case, our matcher would have dramatically failed when a web service, designed to be used for a completely different situation than that the requestor needed (assuming a successful meaning resolution at every aspect), is selected as compatible. In order for the semantic web to reach its full potential, collaborators must communicate and continuously negotiate about what they agree to be their shared background/context. For this reason ontologies should not be exploited as fixed conceptualizations of some domains, as they are, but rather as dynamic structures which co-evolve with their communities of use.

To overcome the problems of the semantic approach during the web service discovery, we propose a pragmatic methodology which captures the context of web services' usage. According to this methodology, the context of web services' usage can be determined by considering the context of collaborators themselves. We argue that the context of collaborators must be well defined at the time of offer/demand definition for web services.

The methodology we propose to model the context of collaborators is through the exchange of some standard XML-based message types that are to be interpreted identically by all collaborators. Each message, which may be thought of as an object (in the sense of object-oriented programming), has a performative (which may be thought of as the class of the message) and a number of context parameters (attribute/value pairs, which may be thought of as instance variables). The performatives are the permissible actions the collaborators can

---

[6] http://www.wsmo.org

Table 2. The structure of the messages exchanged

Performative	Context Parameters	Structure
offer	who, why, what	: offer(who, what, why)
demand	who, why, what	: demand(who, what, why)
offer-demand	who, why, what	: offer-demand(who, why, what)

perform as those have been defined in Section 2. The context parameters, on the other hand, are the content of these actions i.e what is being offered and requested respectively along with some other parameters regarding personal information of the collaborator i.e identity, background information, interests etc. The structure of the messages exchanged along with their context parameters and explanations are listed in Tables 2 and 3 respectively. In this paper we present only those context parameters required. In a later section, we will see how these messages are used through an example.

Table 3. Parameter format and meaning

Parameter	Sub-Parameters	Meaning
who	identity, role	identity and role of the initiator
why	purpose, goal	purpose(and/or interest/s) and goal/s of initiator
what	input/s, output/s	semantic web service input/s and output/s

The matching process that occurs between the request and the offer first matches the "what" (i.e the semantic input/output parameters) and then the "who" and "why" parameters respectively. This matching process complicates the existing semantic matching algorithms (the "what") by taking into consideration additional context parameters (the "who" and the "why") in order to achieve complete and unambiguous matching.

4   Capturing the Context of Collaborators

As already mentioned, pervasive solutions will be facilitated for capturing the context of the collaborators. These solutions will allow collaborators to define their (offer/demand) context through a web site that can be accessed from any internet-enabled desktop machine or mobile device. Due to portability constraints the web site will be kept as simple as possible with a user-friendly interface. In this paper instead of presenting the interface, which is rather simplistic and straightforward to conceive, we show the XML messages format/structure (shown below). We demonstrate examples of the XML messages when we consider our pragmatic scenario later on in this paper.

```
<?xml version="1.0" encoding="iso-8859-1"?>
<demand>
    <Who Identity="" Role=""/>
    <Why Purpose="" Goal=""/>
    <What>
        <Input="" Onto-uri=""/>*
        <Output="" Onto-uri=""/>*
    </What>
</demand>
```

5   A Pragmatic Scenario

Let us realize the effectiveness of the methodology we propose through an example. Assume that there exists a WYW=WTO (What You Want = What They Offer) broker service that is responsible for the searching and the matching. When a request is received, the broker service searches for web services that meet the request requirements and hands the results to the requestor. During this searching, the matching algorithms applied might also reference trusted ontologies[7] (if required) to resolve conflicts. Consider a scenario where a lo-

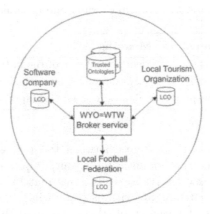

Fig. 1. A pragmatic scenario

cal government has assigned to a software company the development of a local travel guide in order to better assist tourists when visiting the country and thus increase tourists' interest for that country. The software company decides to invest in service-oriented technology in order allow easy integration with external/internal businesses. The company seeks to find web services that offer the functionality required for a travel guide to become a reality. Specifically the travel guide is aimed to provide services for accommodation and events lookup, map driving directions etc. Let us consider the accommodation provision for the sake of this example.

---

[7] Ontologies with good reputation values.

Assume that the software company initiates the following request r: "I want a web service that provides me with a hotel list $(or_1, or_{1_{uri}})$ given hotel search criteria $(ir_1, ir_{1_{uri}})$ to $(ir_n, ir_{n_{uri}})$" (where or = request output, ir = request input). Also assume that there exist a local tourism organization and local football federation that provide exactly the desired functionality (refer to Figure 1). In the first case all the hotels available to tourists that match the search criteria are retrieved but in the second case only those hotels that both match the search criteria and have special arrangements with the local football federation to host players are retrieved. Which of the two web services should the matcher/broker select? Unavoidable, automatic selection can be error-prone in this situation where the context of a web service usage is not determined beforehand.

The methodology we proposed in this paper solves this problem by considering the context of web service usage. This is accomplished by capturing the context of collaborators in an offer-request service exchange. Let us therefore revisit the above example by considering the context of collaborators as this is defined in Section 3. As table 4 shows the request for a web service that provides a hotel list given n hotel search criteria matches exactly two offers (URI is the semantic annotation of the WSDL part which references an ontology concept). In contrast to before the matcher/broker has additional information to check and therefore extract the offered service that best matches the request. In this case since the requestor targets the service for tourists' usage, it is clear that the local tourism organization offer is the one that best matches the request. Therefore the matcher automatically selects the web service offer of the local tourism organization. The XML messages exchanged during the web service discovery of our example, are are shown below.

```xml
<?xml version="1.0" encoding="iso-8859-1"?>
<demand>
    <Who Identity="X" Role="requestor,software company"/>
    <Why Purpose="fulfil government assignment"
        Goal="development of local travel guide for tourists)"/>
    <What>
        <Input="hotel search criteria" Onto-uri="X"/>
        <Output="hotel list" Onto-uri="Y"/>
    </What>
</demand>

<offer>
    <Who Identity="X" Role="provider, local tourism organization"/>
    <Why Purpose="tourists assistance" Goal="inform tourists about local hotels"/>
    <What>
        <Input="hotel search criteria" Onto-uri="X"/>
        <Output="hotel list" Onto-uri="Y"/>
    </What>
<offer>

<?xml version="1.0" encoding="iso-8859-1"?>
<offer>
    <Who Identity="X" Role="provider, local football federation"/>
    <Why Purpose="football teams assistance"
        Goal="inform football teams about hotels committed to host football players"/>
    <What>
        <Input="hotel search criteria" Onto-uri="X"/>
        <Output="hotel list" Onto-uri="Y"/>
    </What>
</offer>
```

Table 4. Offer and Request messages

Type	Message Content
offer:	*who* (identity: X, role: provider, local tourism organization),
	why (purpose: tourists assistance, goal: inform tourists about local hotels),
	what (input: (hotel search criteria, uri X), output: (hotel list, uri Y))
offer:	*who*(identity: X, role: provider, local football federation),
	why (purpose: football teams assistance, goal: inform football teams about hotels committed to host football players),
	what (input: (hotel search criteria, uri X), output: (hotel list, uri Y))
request:	*who* (identity: X, role: requestor, software company),
	why (purpose: fulfil government assignment, goal: development of local travel guide for tourists),
	what (input: (hotel search criteria, uri X), output: (hotel list, uri Y))

6   Related Work

The idea of this paper is inspired from Pragmatic Web principles as these have been defined in [4]. The Pragmatic Web is a new research direction which aims to extend the Semantic Web by capturing the context of ontologies' usage, from the participants' point of view, in a given communication process. Pragmatic Web research is still in its first stages and nobody knows the direction it will go yet. With the few knowledge we currently possess in that area, we think that the methodology we propose differentiates from Pragmatic Web's patterns in the fact that it captures the context of web services usage (pragmatics) instantly instead of acquiring it periodically (by continually interrupting the collaborators).

The methodology we propose to model the context of collaborators is an exchange of some standard XML-based message types which are interpreted identically by all collaborators. This methodology possess similarities with the Knowledge Query and Manipulation Language (KQML)[18] in the sense they are both message-based. They are both utilizing performatives and context parameter constructs but they differ in the language action perspective and purpose of use. KQML is a message-based langauge for agent communication in contrast to our methodology which is intended for capturing the context of collaborators during web service discovery.

Another similar approach with our methodology is the one that the CORBA (the predecessor of web service technology) Trader service facilitates. The Trader service, as in our case, provides location and discovery facilities to requestors. In contrast to our methodology, the CORBA Trader service: 1) maintains a repository where the offered objects are advertised instead of allowing each provider to maintain its own repository, 2) matches the objects against the service type and the characteristics instead of the semantic input/ouput parameters and the context, and 3) returns all possible matchings (in order) instead of the one with the highest value.

7   Conclusion

In this paper we have proposed a pragmatic methodology to web service discovery which captures the context of web services' usage by considering the context of the collaborators. We have identified three types of business collaborators and presented their roles and actions. Based on these actions we presented the methodology we used to model the context of collaborators and demonstrated its effectiveness through a realistic example. Finally we have shown how pervasive solutions can be facilitated in capturing the context.

Limitations of our approach currently lay in the specification of user-defined context, the context parameters list and the frequency of context capturing-matching. In the future we will consider approaches for deriving user context automatically, through the usage some sensor devices, in addition to the user-defined context approach proposed in this paper. Moreover we aim to consider more context parameters when capturing collaborators' context and possible transformation of our methodology into a full-blown language if that is judged necessary. Finally we will consider introducing multiple rounds of the (offer and request) context capturing-matching so that the maximum desired effect is achieved.

References

1. Alan Cruse : Meaning in Language: An introduction to Semantics and Pragmatics. 2000
2. R. McCool: Rethinking the Semantic Web, Part I. IEEE Internet Computing. 2005
3. A. De Moor: Making Doug's Dream Come True: Collaborations in Context. 2002
4. A. De Moor: Patterns for the Pragmatic Web (invited paper). 13th International Conference on Conceptual Structures (ICCS 2005). Kassel, Germany.July.2005.
5. Tom Gross and Roland Klemke: Context Modelling For Information Retrieval-Requirements and Approaches. 2003
6. K. Jaszczolt: Semantics and Pragmatics: Meaning in Language and Discourse.2002
7. Geoffrey Leech: Principles of Pragmatics.1983
8. David Martin and Massimo Paolucci and Sheila MacIlraith and Mark Burstein and Drew McDermott and Deborah McGuiness and Bijan Parsia and Terry Payne and Marta Sabou and Monika Solanki and Naveen Srinivasan and Katia Sycara: Bringing Semantics to Web Services: The OWL-S Approach.2004
9. Rama Miller and Joel Farrel and John Miller and Meenakshi Nagarajan and Marc-Thomas Schmidt and Amit Sheth and Kunal Verma: Web Service Semantics - WSDL-S. IBM and University of Georgia. April.2005
10. Jacob L. Mey:Pragmatics: an introduction.Blackwell.1993
11. Stuart Russel and Peter Norvig: Artificial Intelligence: A Modern Approach. Pretnice Hall.2003
12. Munindar P. Singh and Michael N. Huhns: Service-Oriented Computing. Willey. 2005.410–495
13. Munindar P. Singh:The Pragmatic Web: Pleliminary thoughts. NSF-OntoWeb Workshop on Database and Information Systems Research for Semantic Web and Enterprises.April. 2002. 82–90

14. Aida Jertila and Mareike Schoop: The Language-Action Perspective and the Semantic Web A Language-Action Approach to Electronic Contracts. The Language Action Perspective on Communication Modelling.2005
15. Amit Sheth and Kunal Verma and John Miller and Preeda Rajasekaran: Enhancing Web Service Descriptions using WSDL-S.2005
16. Electra Tamani and Paraskevas Evripidou: Applying Trust Mechanisms in an agent-based P2P Network of Service Providers and Requestors. Sixth IEEE International Symposium on Cluster Computing and the Grid Workshops (CC-GRIDW'06). 2006.13
17. Ken Turner: Semantics vs. Pragmatics.Handbook of Pragmatics.1997
18. Michael Wooldridge: MultiAgent Systems. Willey. 2005

Mobile User Personalization with Dynamic Profiles: Time and Activity

Christoforos Panayiotou and George Samaras

Department of Computer Science, University of Cyprus, CY-1678 Nicosia, Cyprus
{panchris, cssamara}@cs.ucy.ac.cy

Abstract. Mobile clients present a new and more demanding breed of users. Solutions provided for the desktop users are often found inadequate to support this new breed of users. Personalization is such a solution. The moving user differs from the desktop user in that his handheld device is truly personal. It roams with the user and allows him access to info and services at any given time from anywhere. As the moving user is not bound to a fixed place and to a given time period, factors such as time and current experience becomes increasingly important for him. His context and preferences are now a function of time and experience and the goal of personalization is to match the local services to this time-depended preferences. In this paper we exploit the importance of time and experience in personalization for the moving user and present a system that anticipates and compensates the time-dependant shifting of user interests. A prototype system is implemented and our initial evaluation results indicate performance improvements over traditional personalization schemes that range up to 173%.

1 Introduction

Today it is understood that wireless access is not about browsing the Web on your cell phone; it is about providing personalized services that are highly sensitive to the immediate environment and needs (i.e., context) of the moving user. The most recent efforts to support the mobile user focus to the ability to access **local** and the most relevant information and services. The solution of personalization and user profiling is often used to effectively aid this task. Solutions, however, that was well studied and provided for the desktop user proved to be inadequate for the moving user as these two types of users differ in quite fundamental aspects. The one is restricted in a fixed place, for a fixed period of time and his device (i.e. the desktop PC or even laptop) is not generally used as a *personal assistant*. On the other hand the moving user is quite mobile and at any time, place or situation turns to his mobile device (PDA or mobile phone), the *truly* personal device, for access to information and services that are relevant to his current needs. In essence, the moving user is a new breed of users and his handheld device is constantly complementing his current activities. Looking a bit deeper in the mobile user's environment one can clearly see that the new factors involved are **time** and current **activity**. In reality, the **user's needs**, and thus his

R. Meersman, Z. Tari, P. Herrero et al. (Eds.): OTM Workshops 2006, LNCS 4278, pp. 1295–1304, 2006.
© Springer-Verlag Berlin Heidelberg 2006

context, are a function of time and experience. His interests and needs change along with the time and the situation he's currently experiencing.

These are new factors to the personalization problem and are introduced mostly because the needs of the moving users are not any more limited to the time he is in front of his office PC, but around the clock, all year long, including weekends and vacations. Imagine the following scenario where a user cruises around at lunch time browsing his favorite content provider through a personalization system. Most likely, the system would provide only the local to him content. However, the provided content, while matching his interests, would not differentiate between restaurant services, bookstores or fax centers in any meaningful way. Thus, if our user was hungry he should first navigate through all the available services find the restaurant services and then invoke them to get the desired information. In this scenario the personalization system ignored a vital piece of information, namely the fact that it is "lunch time". If the system took the **time**, and what time represents into the users day cycle, into consideration it could alter the provided results to display first the restaurant services.

Another interesting, but not thus far utilized, concept is the so called "**user experience**". By "user experience" we mean the activity (or condition) the user is currently experiencing. For example, during normal working days the user experience could be described as "normal day", while when on vacation as the "vacation" experience. Obviously his needs during "normal days" are quite different than during "vacation". Even the day cycle of the user during the various experiences might be different. It is thus, imperative, for the personalization system, to take the changing of activities into consideration. We want to enable, for example, the system to effectively provide, at a specific time, a vacationing user with the nearest bar or pool, while when he's back to work with the nearest business center. Given an experience, time identifies the specific interests of the user during that activity at that particular time, e.g. during vacation at 8 PM, open bars and happy hours are of great interest to vacationers while during normal days, Pizza restaurants and rent-a-movie places might be of interest instead. The task of such a personalization system is to identify and match these dynamically changing interests to the local services.

The rest of the paper is organized as follows. Section 2 presents a general overview of the personalization problem and further elaborates on "time" and "user experience" concepts. Section 3 presents the needed design changes for a personalization system in order to incorporate time and experience in a personalization system. How to support time and experience based personalization for the moving user is discussed in section 4, while the next section presents an implemented prototype, metrics, experiments and performance analysis. Finally, some related work is presented in section 6 and section 7 concludes the paper.

2 The Personalization Problem

The problem of personalization is a complex one with many aspects and issues that need to be resolved [15]. Some of these issues become even more complicated once viewed from a moving user's perspective. Such issues include, but are not limited to, the following: *What content to present to the user, how to show the content to the use, how to ensure the user's privacy* and *how to create a global personalization scheme.* They could be summarized in the following phrase: *"What, how and for everything."* There are many approaches to personalization [1-14] and each one of them usually focuses on a specific area, whether this is profile creation, machine learning and pattern matching, data and web mining or personalized navigation. *Time* and *current activity*, however, as factors affecting personalization for the moving user are widely missed. Thus, the summarizing phrase for the personalization issues for this type of users (i.e., mobile and wireless) should actually be: *"When, what, how and for any activity,"* where "when" relates content and user preferences to time and current experience/activity.

2.1 Time Based Personalization

Beyond the exploitation of location *"timing"* and *"user experience"* factors seem to have significant importance. These are the. To understand the significance of these factors, one must consider the needs of the mobile user and the effect they may have if exploited. Undeniably his need for content is not limited to a specific time period. Instead the mobile user may browse for content 24 hours a day, 365 days per year. Hence it becomes a reality to have a user where his interests change in an extremely dynamic way (just consider the lunch time scenario where we see this dramatic shift in preferences). A shift that seems to be tied to the various time intervals governing the user's day-cycle becoming even greater when he switches between activities (e.g. taking a vacation after a tiresome business wcck).

In order to be able to tackle these shifts gracefully we need to know what the users preferences are at any given time. When using user profile for storing those preferences we can easily reach a situation where the user profile is too big to handle and thus useless. Especially when dealing with great continuum called "time". As a first step we can divide the day into several time-zones and store user's preferences per time-zone. These time zones represent the user's day cycle. Yet the problem still remains as there is too much information which must be handled, most of it just replicated. We circumvent this problem by associating each user's interest with a set of weights as they relate to a specific time-zone and experience. This allows the dynamic creation of the user profile based on the current time-zone and activity by applying the relevant weight set on his preferences. In this way time based personalization becomes possible and the benefits seem quite significant (see experimental results in section 5) despite the possibility of higher computational costs.

3 Incorporating Time Based Personalization

Having in place a personalization system that handles user's profiles, content description and application of the user's profiles on that content is the first step towards incorporating time in the personalization process. Most current personalization approaches (that are profile based) handle the following:

- Capture, maintain and adapt the user's preference profile, either implicitly or explicitly. Performed by a "user profile management" component.
- Capture the user's device profile. This could be part of the "user profile management" component.
- Describe the available content. Having a "content description" component suffices.
- Apply the user's preferences on the content description in order to select the desired one. A "content selection" component could implement this.
- Reform and deliver the selected content based on the user's device profile via a "content reform" component.

Beyond that, personalization systems that are focused on the mobile user just adapt the user's profile to the local content. Since these systems don't consider the concepts introduced by time and experience certain changes to their design are needed. *The necessary changes affect mainly the selection of the content to be displayed and the user's profile.*

The user profile must be enhanced in order to accommodate all the (newly) required/available metadata such time-zones preferences and user experiences. As a chained reaction the description of the available content may also need to be enhanced, e.g. from a simplistic keyword scheme to a sophisticated ontology scheme. We need better description of the content in order to be able to make more intelligent decisions. Another needed change, is related with the profile maintenance. We show that keeping the user's profile in sync with his interests' shifts in our case becomes more complicated and an even bigger necessity. Now there is also the need to compensate for user timing shifts (time-zone shifts) and thus, the monitoring of user's preferences mechanism should consider (and adapt) this as well.

4 Designing a Time Based Personalization System

4.1 Content Description Format

In order to have a good description of the provided content, ontologies were used. When using ontologies, in essence we define a vocabulary and a structure (using XML schema) for certain content domains. Having in place the vocabulary (which may or may not be common for all content providers) we define the structure of the content description. Two major distinctions are made: content categories/subcategories and content instances.

The content categories describe general characteristics of some content. We can categorize content on the type of the provided information e.g. restaurant content, pharmacies content etc. Of course we can continue this categorization with more levels, e.g. we can elaborate on the news content category by introducing the sports or political subcategory. Note that a content category does not describe any actual data generator (e.g. the "Paradise Hotel" content page) rather than it groups the characterizing attributes of similar content pages (e.g. all the pages that contain information on restaurants). On the other hand content instances provide actual values for content categories. This information is directly linked with a given content page.

Even though the content description format is not directly related with time-based personalization we need to have knowledge of both the category schema and category instance when we incorporate timing factors in the user's profile. We need to assign weights to both categories and instances of these categories. To understand this lets compare the keyword approach with this one. When using keywords we have a list of all possibly describing words associated with each node without making any distinction as to what they describe. Thus, for example, we cannot tell that the word "Chinese" could describe the restaurant type (content instance) while the word "Restaurant" could give the content category. On the other hand when using an ontology we know what the content category is (i.e. "Restaurant") and what the restaurant type of the described specific node is (i.e., *"Chinese"*). This is important as it allows prioritization based on both, the category and the instance of a content node. In this way timing and the user's experience can be used with both of these, thus leading to the case where they can effect the selection of an entire content category (e.g., display or not any restaurant), as well as, the selection of specific instances of a category (e.g., display *only Chinese* restaurants). Of course the timing and experience information will be stored in the user's profile.

4.2 User's Theme Profile Format: Time and Experience Factors

In order to be able to match the user's interests with the provided content his preferences must be captured in a similar format as the description of the content. Towards this goal we use an ontology that is very similar to the content description one. Thus, what we see as user's preferences are the same content categories and instances as the ones in the content description, and thus enabling the match between them. However, this merely enables us to know if a user is interested in something.

We need to assign a weight to each of the user's preferences to differentiate among them. Weights in effect, show how much a user likes or dislikes a specific content category and/or instance. Being able to differentiate among the user's preferences is crucial in time based personalization. To achieve time based personalization we need to know how the user's preferences change over the 24 hour day cycle.

To represent time we suggest dividing the day into different time-zones. This is possible if we study the daily routine of our users and then split it into time-zones based on the user's activities. By dividing the day in time-zones, we drastically reduce the possible combinations between time and user's preferences, keeping our design scaleable. Having the time-zones on one hand, and the preferences' weights on the other, enables us to capture the required information: *we just need to record how the weight of each preference changes over each time-zone*.

The same information (i.e. preference weights per time zone) can be recorded for the various content instances. Fig. 4.1 shows how time affects the user's restaurant preferences in relation with the restaurant type (i.e., cuisine). We, thus, know how the user preferences for a specific cuisine change according to a time zone. Note that in fig. 4.1 we show weights for both category and instance. In essence we define how much weight the characteristic 'cuisine' has on the user's preferences (1st line of fig. 4.1) and also define the weight of different values for that characteristic. Figure's 4.1 example means that finding a restaurant that has a desired cuisine is averagely important for the user (stated by the first line). However, when examining the cuisine of restaurants, our user states that between 9 and 12 'Kebab House' is preferred over 'Cypriot' cuisine.

User Experiences. Using this weighted system enables the user to declare what (and when) something is more important to him. We can repeat the weight association for each user's experience. In that way by just adding another set of weights we can record the user's preferences for a new experience. For example if the user goes on vacation then his experience would be vacation. What changes from his normal (or daily) experience is the composition of his day cycle. In effect, integrating the user's experience is like building a user's profile for each of his activities cycles. The difference, however, is that we may exploit the obtained knowledge and that we do not need to store a separate profile. Basically we replicate the weight structure of the normal daily cycle with different values, resulting a dynamically changing user profile that covers all user's activities in a continuous fashion.

```
<restaurantsTypeByTime categoryWeight="50">
    <timeZone time="0-3">
        <restaurantType name="Fast Food" weight="90"/>
    </timeZone>
    <timeZone time="3-6"></timeZone>
    <timeZone time="6-9"></timeZone>
    <timeZone time="9-12">
        <restaurantType name="Fast Food" weight="90"/>
        <restaurantType name="Greek" weight="70"/>
        <restaurantType name="Cypriot" weight="60"/>
        <restaurantType name="Kebab House" weight="95"/>
    </timeZone>
    <timeZone time="12-15">
        <restaurantType name="Pizzarias" weight="85"/>
    </timeZone>
    <timeZone time="15-18"></timeZone>
    <timeZone time="18-21">
        <restaurantType name="Chinese" weight="90"/>
        <restaurantType name="Italian" weight="80"/>
        <restaurantType name="Mexican" weight="75"/>
    </timeZone>
    <timeZone time="21-24"></timeZone>
</restaurantsTypeByTime>
```

Fig. 4.1. User's restaurants preferences based on time

4.3 Matching User Interests with the Content

Since the user profile and the content description are based on similar ontology we achieve improved effectiveness during the content selection. At matching, we compare each content information node (content service) description with the user's profile. The comparison is made on the characteristics between matching categories of the content description and the user's profile for the current time zone. We get the preference weight for each characteristic, from the user profile along with the weight for the given category. The weight set associated with the current user's experience is loaded. In essence we have a dynamic user profile which changes, literally, by the minute and current experience. The final step in the content selection is the averaging of the retrieved weights and assignment of it as a selection weight to each content node. The results are presented to the user sorted, based on this weight. Nodes with lower weight than a user selected threshold are completely omitted. The high level algorithm of this procedure would look like this:

1. Find the interesting content categories using the "How much I like a given category – e.g. Restaurants" weight.
2. Evaluate each characteristic of each content node in the given category that is present in the user's profile using the following formula: ("How important is this factor to me - e.g. Cuisine type" weight * "How much I like this value for this factor - e.g. Italian" weight) / 100.
3. Assign the average of the prev. evaluation as the selection rank of each node.

4.4 Manipulating the Time Based Profile

Initially the user is assigned a default (predetermined by experts) profile based on his social group. Social group can be used as a clustering factor as users tend to form their interests according to their group. However since this is not absolute, collaborative filtering (which may also include history analysis), along with direct user input, can be used to fine tune these default profiles. There might still be a difference between the actual user interests and his profile in terms of interests and weights. Through the use of the system, the user's profile is constantly adapted based on his selections thus leading to a convergence with his actual interests.

The system accepts weights in the range -1 to 100. Value -1 enables the system to completely disregard certain content categories and instances (the system can present disregarded content if the user asks for it explicitly). Updating of the user profiles is based on user selections. Each time a user selects to view a given content service the system tracks it and updates his profile. We need to consider (and thus adapt) all of the characteristics as we cannot single out the ones that led to the selection of the given content. We reduce the weight of unmatched characteristics in order to phase out of the profile preferences that might not be valid in the future. This result in a large number of updates, however, since all the updates are made on the already loaded profile the costs is negligible. The high level algorithm of this procedure would look like this: For the category of the user selected content node do:

1. For all characteristics that are present in both node description and the user's profile increase their weight in the user's profile by 1.
2. For all characteristics that are present only in the user's profile decrease their weight in the user's profile by 1.
3. Add all characteristics that are present only in the node description to the user's profile.

4.5 Keeping in Sync the Profile and User's Timing

As already stated, it is imperative to have the correct timing information in the user's profile. Thus the monitoring mechanism that watches over user's preferences must be extended to incorporate "time" as well. In our case, we monitor the click stream of the user in order to know when and what the user selected. In detail, we timestamp each user click to a service and save it in a log, much like a web log. Later on we analyze this log (when the user is offline or on a different machine) to detect anomalies in the timing. Such anomalies include the user consistently requesting a specific service during a time period that he is not expected (based on his current profile) to do so. A minimum consistency of the anomalies found should be met before considering them to be timing shifts in order to avoid having the casual fluke influencing the profile. One such fluke could be the user anticipating his lunch and thus making a reservation early in the morning. If that happens once in a while we do not want to shift his lunch time zone in the morning. However if it is common practice then we might add a new time zone in the morning that reflects on this specific behavior.

Having flagged all the anomalies in this log we can adapt (or even create new) the time zones that regard the service where the anomaly was noticed. The log analysis is clearly a costly operation and thus should be optimized as much as possible. One such optimization is to identify potential anomalies as they happen. Another optimization is that we keep two logs instead of one; the first holds all the click stream of each user and the second keeps only the identified potential anomalies. The first log can be used to discover previously unknown user preferences and their related time zones. Both logs are analyzed in order to adapt (or create new) the time zones of the user's preferences. However the analysis, which is periodic, for each log has a different frequency. The first log can be analyzed on a much slower pace than the second. In fact, the first log is mainly used to add new time zones and preferences in the user profile, while the second log is (mainly) used to urgently detect shifts in the user's timing. This is the reason that the analysis of the second log has a much higher frequency. The high level algorithm of this procedure would look like this:

1. Monitor and log the user's click stream.
2. Flag potential anomalies with various degrees of priorities and log them.
3. Analyze the anomalies log for timing shift and adapt the user profile. This is periodic with high frequency.
4. Analyze the click stream log to identify new time zones as well as timing shifts missed by the previous analysis. This is periodic with low frequency.

5 Prototype and Experimentation

Our prototype is derived from the mPERSONA [15] system. In our current version, we focused and experimented on the new factors (time and experience). Thus we modified only the content description, selection and profile management components.

Metrics: In order to show that time and user experience are important factors in the personalization process we need to define a way to measure its effect. We do so by comparing the results of personalization without using timing or user experience versus using them. To do this comparison, we need to measure the quality and quantity of the effect of personalization. Towards this end we define the "effective rate" as a quantitative metric and the "overall success factor" as the qualitative metric. The "effective rate" is the percentage of the times the system was successful in providing what the user wanted. A provided result is considered successful if the user finds what he wants within the first N provided choices. That is if the user chooses the nth element of a given result, then the provided result is considered successful if, and only if $n \leq N$. We denote n as the "actual success factor" and N as the "desired success factor". Having a high effective rate while keeping the desired success factor low indicates that the personalization process works well and that the users profile accurately presents his interests. The "overall success factor" S_{over} is denoted as the average of the "actual success factor" for all provided results. Lower values mean that the quality of the personalization results is high. The ratio between overall success factor and desired success factor (S_{over} / N) provides an indication if a personalization system meets the given quality restrictions. Furthermore, keeping N value fixed enables the comparison of the result quality of two (or more) personalization systems.

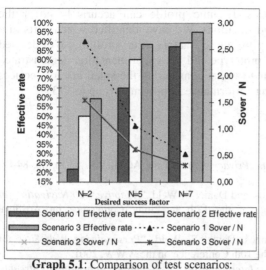

Graph 5.1: Comparison of test scenarios:
Scen.1: Ignoring time and experience, Scen.2: Exploiting
time/Ignoring experience, Scen.3: Exploiting time & experience

Experiments: Three different scenarios were tested. Under the 1st scenario, a set of users request a predefined set of services without exploiting time and experience. The service set is defined by random selection. Which services are selectable is determined according to the high-level user's interests (e.g. likes Chinese restaurants). The users' requests are made during the whole period of a week at 4 different time-zones per day. Scenario 2 is similar to the 1st with the difference that time is used (user's experience is still ignored). In the 3rd scenario we repeat the previous scenario but this time we include user's experience as well. The test bed used utilized 10 service categories with thirty instances each.

Graph 5.1 is a direct comparison of the scenarios. We repeated our measurements for the values 2, 5 and 7 as the desired success factor. Since the lower the desired success factor the higher the expectations from the systems our results look very promising. Looking at the graph one can see that the higher the expectations from the systems the more benefit we have from incorporating time and experience. Even though our initial results show only 8% to 173% gain (for N=2 scenario 3 is by 173% better than scenario 1 while for N=7 only 8%) we expect that having more services the gain will be significantly higher due to the number of available choices and the degree of differentiation. Considering the second measurement that shows ratio between the "overall success factor" (S_{over}) and the "desired success factor" (N) we can see that the 3rd scenario also performs better. Recall that lower values mean better quality results (scenario 3 gives 42% lower values than scenario 1). Clearly as the value of N is increasing the effect of time and experience decreases.

6 Conclusions

Mobile users are a new and more demanding breed of users and they differ significantly from the traditional desktop users. In this paper we have identified factors that until this day were overlooked in the design of personalization systems for this type of users. These factors are related to time. We presented two major factors, time and user's experience, showing their importance. We showed that exploiting time enables us to capture the shifts of user's interests based on the time of the day and adapt his preferences accordingly. User experience, takes the concepts introduced by timing one step further. It provides a means to effectively merge many different instance of the user's profile (one instance for each state of mind, e.g. vacation, work etc.) into one dynamic profile. This dynamic profile can accurately cover the preferences of a user at all times and situations. We have identified which parts of a personalization system is affected by these factors (i.e. profile). We devised appropriate metrics, implemented a prototype and via experimentation demonstrated the viability of our proposal. Our first results, considering the small size of services used, are quite encouraging indicating performance improvements up to 173%.

References

1. Eugene Volokh, *Personalization and Privacy,* Com. of the ACM, Vol. 43(8), pp. 84-88, August 2000.
2. Corin R. Anderson, Pedro Domingos, and Daniel S. Weld. *"Adaptive Web Navigation for Wireless Devices."* In Proceedings of the 17th Int. Joint Conference on Artificial Intelligence (IJCAI-01). 2001.
3. Corin R. Anderson, Pedro Domingos, Daniel S. Weld. *"Personalizing Web Sites for Mobile Users."* In Proceedings of the 10th Conference on the WWW, 2001.
4. Paul Maglio and Rob Barrett, *Intermediaries Personalize Information Streams,* Communications of the ACM, Vol. 43(8), pages 96-101, August 2000.
5. C. Thomas and G. Fischer. *Using agents to personalize the web.* In Proc. ACM IUI'97, pages 53--60, Orlando, Florida, USA, 1997.
6. Rucker, J., Marcos, J.P., Siteseer: Personalized Navigation for the Web, Communications of the ACM, pp. 73-75, Vol. 40, no. 3, March 1997.
7. Adomavicius, G. and Tuzhilin, A. "User profiling in personalization applications through rule discovery and validation." KDD-99, 1999.
8. E. Adar, D. Karger, and L. Stein. Haystack: Per-user information environments. In Proceedings of the 1999 Conf. on Inf. and Knowledge Management, CIKM, 1999.
9. Haym Hirsh, Chumki Basu, and Brian D. Davison. Learning to personalize. Communications of the ACM, 43(8), Aug 2000.
10. Kurt Bollacker, Steve Lawrence, and C. Lee Giles. A system for automatic personalized tracking of scientific literature on the web. In Digital Libraries 99 - The Fourth ACM Conference on Digital Libraries, pages 105--113, New York, 1999.
11. Sung Myaeng and Robert Korfhage. Towards an intelligent and personalized information retrieval system. Technical Report 86--CSE--10, Dept. of Computer Science and Engineering, Southern Methodist University, Dallas, Texas, March 1986.
12. M.M. Lankhorst, H. van Kranenburg, A. Salden, A.J.H. Peddemors, "Enabling technology for personalizing mobile services". Proceedings of the 35th Annual Hawaii Int. Conf. on System Sciences HICSS, p.1107 -1114, 7-10 January 2002
13. N. Bogonikolos, D. Fragoudis, S. Likothanassis, "ARCHIMIDES": an intelligent agent for adaptive-personalized navigation within a WEB server. Proc. of the 32nd Annual Hawaii Int. Conf. on System Sciences, HICSS-32. Vol:Track5, 5-8 Jan. 1999.
14. Doron Cohen, Michael Herscovici, Yael Petruschka, Yoëlle S. Maarek, Aya Soffer, "Personalized pocket directories for mobile devices". Proceedings of the eleventh international conference on World Wide Web, p. 627-638, isbn 1-58113-449-5, Honolulu, Hawaii, USA, 2002.
15. Christoforos Panayiotou, George Samaras, "mPERSONA: Personalized Portals for the Wireless User: An Agent Approach". Journal of ACM/Baltzer Mobile Networking and Applications (MONET), special issue on "Mobile and Pervasive Commerce".

Rethinking the Design of Enriched Environments

Felipe Aguilera[1], Andres Neyem[1], Rosa A. Alarcón[2],
Luis A. Guerrero[1], and Cesar A. Collazos[3]

[1] Department of Computer Science, Universidad de Chile,
P.O. Box 2777, Santiago, Chile
[2] Department of Computer Science, Pontificia Universidad Católica de Chile,
Av. Vicuña Mackenna 4860, 6904411, Santiago, Chile
[3] Systems Department FIET, Universidad del Cauca,
Campus Tulcan, Popayán-Colombia
{faguiler, aneyem, luguerre}@dcc.uchile.cl,
ralarcon@ing.puc.cl, ccollazo@unicauca.edu.co

Abstract. Most advances in pervasive computing focus strongly on technological issues (e.g. connectivity, portability, etc.); as technology becomes more complex and pervasive, design achieves a greater relevance. Inadequate design leads to unnatural interaction that may overload users, hampering the old aspiration of creating transparent artifacts. Transparency is a concept that describes technology that allows users to focus their attention on the main activity goals instead of on the technology itself. Transparency is strongly related with the relevance of individuals' goals, their knowledge, and conventions learned as social beings. This paper aims to provide a framework for the design of augmented artifacts that exploit users' knowledge about how things work in the world both in the syntactic and the semantic level.

1 Introduction

The goal of ubiquitous computing is to "to make a computer so imbedded, so fitting, and so natural, that we use it without even thinking about it" [21]. The challenge is faced through various approaches. For instance, context-aware computing aims to enrich the environment so that applications can recognize their situation and adapt itself in a proper way [1]; through tangible user interfaces people may manipulate the computational power through enriched physical devices [7, 9]. In mixed reality, physical objects in the environment are enriched with information and have a virtual representation in the virtual world [11]. In instrumented environments, computing power is embedded into everyday artifacts, augmenting their capabilities [16].

Initial efforts on these areas have focused mainly on technical issues ranging from communication and architectures to possible applications. The achieved improvement had generated new technologies so that computer disappearance is closer. Such disappearance could be physical (miniaturization and integration into everyday objects) and mental (enriched objects do not draw our focus of attention towards them) [15]. However, the latter issue is complex and not yet fully solved. Core issues are related to interaction design, environment sensing, context modeling, resource discovery, privacy and security as well as infrastructure [15, 1].

R. Meersman, Z. Tari, P. Herrero et al. (Eds.): OTM Workshops 2006, LNCS 4278, pp. 1305–1314, 2006.
© Springer-Verlag Berlin Heidelberg 2006

Design achieves a center stage for allowing a seamless interaction between people and the computational infrastructure, so that computers can mentally disappear or become "transparent". Transparency [21, 2, 15], claims that a well-designed artifact (such as a door) becomes transparent when used if it allows us to focus on the task at hand instead of on the artifact itself (e.g. a door allows us to focus on our plans when getting into the kitchen instead of on the door itself) [2]. In order to achieve such transparency an object must exhibit some properties that exploit the human cognitive system such as affordances, feedback, and user's knowledge [10].

Inadequate designs lead to unnatural interfaces, hard to understand, requiring an extra cognitive effort from users for learn how to manipulate them (syntax), and interpret the result of such manipulation (semantics). As a result, there is not a clear understanding of users' needs, restrictions, knowledge and assumptions in relation with the interface. How does the interaction between humans and these kinds of artifacts should be defined? What features of the settings and artifacts must be considered when designing? How can people discover and interact through the active elements of an augmented environment?

In this paper, we present a framework for guiding the design of enriched artifacts. Our approach follows a cognitive stance that aims to understand and exploit user's knowledge beyond artifacts mere manipulation. We recognize that users assign meaning to objects based on its context of use [2]. Particularly, Everyday Objects (EO) such as keys, doors, rooms, etc., has a meaning shared by a specific community. Users have expectations about them: a lawyer may expect to find his door office closed, while students may expect to find their room door opened.

The work presented here draws from previous experiences that allowed us to refine extensively our first approach. We also apply our framework for guiding the design of an enriched everyday object, which is a portrait. The rest of the paper is organized as follows: section 2 elaborates on the conceptual background and relates it to other approaches. Section 3 shows the proposed framework. In section 4 we apply the framework in a practical example, and finally, in section 5 we present some conclusions.

2   Related Work

Norman [10] provides a guide for understanding objects functioning from a cognitive point of view. He defines concepts such as affordances (things' properties determining its manipulation), constraints (thing's properties prohibiting some activities and encouraging others), feedback (thing' properties informing users about actions performed), etc. Norman's concepts describe object manipulation, but they are too general for enriched artifacts design where users' expectancies about manipulation may be completely diverse. In addition, they are mostly related to the objects' physical properties neglecting the cultural understanding about how objects are supposed to be manipulated and work, that is, the objects' context of use [4].

There is no consensual definition about what is context or what it comprises. In a broader sense, it can be understood as "the interrelated conditions in which an event, action or situation takes place" or as "a complex description of shared knowledge within which an action or event occurs". Context definitions seem to agree in two aspects: First, context comprehends everything that surrounds "something" (e.g., situation, an activity, an idea), but is not the thing itself. Second, context embraces a set of interrelated elements that maintain a coherent relationship, providing a particular meaning to the thing [2, 13].

The need of proper design can be also observed through the recent papers regarding evaluation of ubiquitous computing using ethnomethodology methods [5, 19], or analyzing the field development [1, 15]. Although insightful, such approaches are insufficient for supporting artifacts' design. Another approach followed by Hong et al. [8], propose a requirements elicitation methodology for supporting context-aware applications design in ubiquitous environments. The methodology have seven steps (identify target groups, estimate typical contexts involved, enlist requirements for each context, determine users' activities while using the system, identify context impact on such activities, detail the context-aware capabilities, compare capabilities with requirements) that allows a progressive analysis of the contexts that will occur when the application runs. Unfortunately they mainly consider physical context but include as well, few concerns about the context of use.

Finally, Theofanos et al. [17] grounds a framework for evaluation of UbiComp applications where they identify nine areas of evaluation. The framework considers cognitive (attention, conceptual models, interaction), social (adoption, trust, impact and side effects), aesthetics (appeal) and computational aspects (robustness) of applications. From those, we are mainly interested in the cognitive and social aspects and its impact when designing an application. Next section considers the revised concepts (Norman's concepts, context of use and evaluation) for defining a framework for the design of enriched artifacts in instrumented environments.

3 Framework for Enriched Artifacts Design: Syntax and Semantics

We define the context of use as the interrelated conditions in which an individual interact *purposely* with such object. Such conditions can be differentiated at least in two complexity levels: the manipulation or actions performed by users on the object (*syntax*) and the interpretation of its results (*semantics*).

Based on a previous work [3] as well as the work of Theofanos, Norman and Hong, we have defined a set of dimensions of analysis (DOA) for each category (syntax and semantics). Such dimensions allow us to describe an everyday artifact syntax and semantics, decide which of them will be changed and afterwards analyze the choices' impact when users interact through the artifact. Some dimensions belong to both the syntactic and semantic category, but in each one they have different meaning. Syntactic DOAs aims to understand an objects manipulation from various perspectives, while semantic DOAs allow designers to understand the users' higher goals when using the artifact. Table 1 provides a brief description of each DOA. DOAs themselves are composed of sets of dimensions.

Table 1. DOA Model. The table shows the detailed description of each DOA.

Category	DOA	Description
Syntax	Manipulation	Describes the object's physical manipulation, the attributes expected to change, and the caused changes. It includes the Usage, Feedback, Intention, Consequence, Action, and Opportunity dimensions.
	Attention	Describes users' attention pay to the object, and the physical features that generate focus change. The following dimensions compose this category: Focus, Interrupt, and Overhead.
	Accessibility	Describes the physical access to the object. The following dimensions compose this category: Access, Privacy, Control, Roles, Reach, and Transfer.
	Restriction	Describes the physical restriction of the object. The following dimensions compose this category: Dependence, Cost, Availability, Flexibility, Past History, and Scalability.
Semantic	Conceptual Model	Describes user's conceptual model about the object, the meaning assigned to the object by certain community. It includes the Opportunity, Intention, Consequence, Action, History, Relevance, Value, and Exclusivity dimensions.
	Accessibility	Similar to syntax's accessibility with an emphasis on the meaning of having access to the object. The following dimensions compose this category: Access and Privacy.
	Restrictions	Describe no tangible restrictions of the object. The following dimensions compose this category: Knowledge and Dependence.
	Attention	Similar to the syntax's attention, but with an emphasis on the meaning of paying attention to the object. The following dimensions compose this category: Focus, Interrupt, and Overhead.

3.1 Everyday Objects Syntax and Semantic Modeling

Our aim is to design physical environments that include everyday objects augmented with new features. Our first step is to determine which objects will be considered as

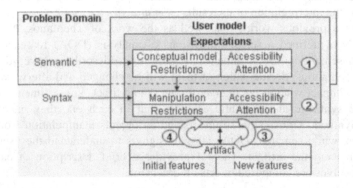

Fig. 1. An outline of the user model

part of the environment. One of the risks when augmenting objects with new functionality is that we distort objects' syntax and semantics in a way that we lose useful properties or change the object so much that users may need extra cognitive effort to use it. In order to avoid this, we model the object real syntax (manipulation) and semantics (interpretation) using the dimensions defined in Tables 1 (numbered circles 1 and 2 in fig, 1). In this way, we can perform later a controlled distortion. Is up to the designer to define how many times the analysis-distortion cycle will be performed. It will depend on the uncertainty of the wanted effects. Due to space limitation we will briefly describe the most important in Table 2, the others dimensions are self-explanatory.

Table 2. Description of the most important dimensions of the Syntax and Semantic Models

Syntax Model		
DOA	Dimension	Description
Manipulation	Usage	Describes the mechanism for manipulating an object. (Norman's affordance concept).
Attention	Focus (Gaze)	Provides information when a user needs to focus in the object.
Accessibility	Control	Describes the ability of users to manage who can use an object.
Restrictions	Scalability	Provides information about number of objects that is possible to have.
Semantic Model		
DOA	Dimension	Description
Conceptual Model	Opportunity	Describes when an object is used.
Accessibility	Access	Describes who can use the object.
Restrictions	Knowledge	Describes the necessary knowledge to use an object.
Attention	Overhead	Provides information about workload imposed on the user due to changing focus.

3.2 Augmented Objects

Previous phases, aims to identify the objects to augment, their physical restrictions and manipulation constraints as well as the expectations hold by each type of user in relation with each object. Now we can define the objects new features (numbered circle 3 in fig. 1). These features should be consistent with the syntax and semantics defined in the previous steps. A designer may choose to change some of them, but s/he will know in advance if users may need to learn to use these new features.

As well, a designer may choose to modify an object (numbered circle 3 in fig. 1). For instance, s/he could add leds, speakers, motors, etc. Again s/he should consider the impact of his/her choice on syntax and semantics. If the object is modified, then its physical constrains and manipulation could change. Furthermore, users may decide to change their shared policies in order to take advantage of objects new possibilities. In this case the cycle must be followed again (cyclic arrows numbered 4 in fig. 1).

Table 3. Syntactic and Semantic model for a portrait. A detailed analysis of most important dimension allows the understanding of its manipulation and the shared meaning.

		Syntax Model	
DOA	Dimension	Question	Answer (Portrait)
Manipulation	Usage	How do you handle a portrait?	Putting the photograph in the portrait. Locating the portrait on a visible place facing towards me.
	Feedback	How do you know it is working well?	Because the photograph fits to the portrait and I can see the picture.
	Intention	What do you intent when operating the portrait?	That it holds a picture and I can watch the picture later. That it remains where I put it on. That it faces me.
	Consequence	What is the direct consequence of using a portrait?	It remains in the last place I put it on. It shows the last picture placed there.
	Action	What do you do with a portrait?	Hold the portrait. Put pictures on it
	Opportunity	When is a portrait used?	When I want to see a picture. When I want to show a picture to other people.
Attention	Focus (Gaze)	When do you focus on the portrait?	When I look at it.
	Interruption	When are you interrupted by the object?	Never.
	Overhead	When do you need to put attention on the portrait?	Only when *I want* to see the picture.

		Semantic Model	
DOA	Dimension	Question	Answer (Portrait)
Conceptual Model	Opportunity	When is a portrait used?	When I want to remember "loved beings" or "unforgettable moments".
	Intention	What is the user intention when have a portrait?	Providing a constant reminder of the feelings and emotions associated with this person or moment.
	Consequence	What is the direct consequence of using a portrait?	Providing a constant reminder of the feelings and emotions associated to that particular time frame or circumstances.

		Syntax Model	
DOA	Dimension	Question	Answer (Portrait)
	Action	What do you do with a portrait?	Watch the picture hold by the portrait. Get close to the picture and grab it
	History	How do you know if a portrait was used?	When the picture or location has changed. When my emotions distort the picture.
	Relevance	What is the relevance with a portrait?	Emotional. It maintains bonds with people, animals, places, etc.
	Value	What kind of value has a portrait for me?	Emotional, personal.
	Exclusivity	Is the portrait able to be replaced?	Maybe, by a framed picture on the wall...

4 Applying the Model

In this section, we apply the proposed framework for augmenting an everyday object, namely a portrait. Photographs are an important part of many people's life; they arrange their personal pictures on their desks and around their homes. For example, photographs of "loved beings" or "unforgettable moments" are symbols of a personal bond and provide a constant reminder of the feelings and emotions associated to that particular time frame or circumstances. Emotions [6] and cultural expectations about handling a portrait are the basis of the syntactic and semantic models of Table 3.

4.1 Augmenting a Portrait

The previous analysis of portrait's syntax's and semantic dimensions shows that this particular everyday object is strongly related to emotions. Emotions are a social need, representing an important channel of communication with one-self and others (e.g. reminding someone, showing loved persons or situations to others). This kind of communication can be difficult at a distance, because of the limitation of physical access to the others' personal space. This analysis makes us wonder *whether by augmenting an everyday portrait with computational capabilities we could support the affective communication at distance*. Hence, we decided to create a physical augmented portrait maintaining some syntax and semantics but disregarding others. Table 4 presents some dimensions that changed base on our design choices.

Table 4. Design choices for an augmented portrait in both syntactic and semantic categories

		Syntax model	
DOA	Dimension	Question	Answer (Portrait)
Manipulation	Usage	How do you handle a portrait?	Connect the portrait to PC. Putting photographs that represent *each emotional state* of only one person in the portrait.
Attention	Interruption	When are you interrupted by the object?	When any emotional state is arriving and change the picture associated with the emotional state. When a light blinks, indicating that an emotion has been received
		Semantic model	
Conceptual Model	Opportunity	When is a portrait used?	When I *want to* communicate the feelings and emotions for the person related with the photograph contained in the portrait. When I *want to* see the current emotional state of the person related with the photograph contained in the portrait.
	Value	What kind of value has a portrait for me?	Have emotional awareness. Communicate several tokens of affection in a semi-transparent way. Interpersonal communication.

The described choices were considered for enriching an everyday portrait. A physical device and a GUI equivalent were developed. Figures 2 depict the device and the application respectively.

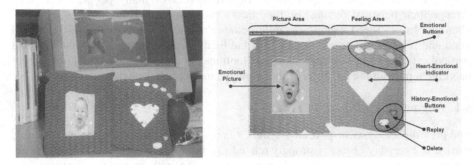

Fig. 2. The new chosen features are implemented in the portrait

Figure 2 describes the virtual features that we have chosen for augmenting a portrait in order to support affective communication. The augmented portrait has been designed to be used like an everyday picture frame, showing pictures of loved beings. It has two main parts: (a) a picture area, showing a picture representing an emotional state of a remote person, and (b) a feeling area, containing Emotional Buttons, a Heart-Emotional Indicator and History-Emotional Buttons. When the user wants to transmit some feeling, s/he has to press any Emotional Button. Each colored button represents some emotional state; they provide information about the local emotional state (e.g. blue color represents a melancholic emotional state) [12, 14, 18, 20].

When any emotional state arrives to the augmented portrait, it pop-ups a picture representing the emotional state received. The red light located around the Heart-Emotional Indicator, will blink, indicating that an emotion has been received. If a user wants to communicate the emotion "I'm thinking about you", s/he must touch the picture located in the Emotional Picture zone. Then, the augmenting portrait will shows a picture with green light blinking indicating that an emotion has been received. The user can stop the blinking of the Heart-Emotional Indicator, simply by touching the surface of the heart.

Additionally the user can block the reception of emotions by closing the portal of the Heart-Emotional Indicator, this action is never informed to the other user and all the emotional states that are received after such action are stored in the history database for a later optional recovery. The prototype developed, called Emoti-Picture Frame, allows anyone with Internet access to transmit their feelings as a way of communicating emotions and displays them on a Tangible User Interfaces (TUI) a Graphical User Interface (GUI) interface or both. The TUI and the GUI interfaces are shown in Fig, 2, left and right side respectively. The TUI version is designed as component Phidgets [7] and the GUI, developed in C#, is composed from the information generated by the Phidgets through APIs provided by the respective supplier.

5 Discussion and Conclusions

A common problem when designing new interfaces and tools in the pervasive computing field relies in the analysis stage. It is hardly questioned which interaction features are effectively supported and which ones will require users' to learn new styles of interaction. We face the problem, by providing an analysis framework that allows identifying several interaction aspects involved in the design of these new solutions. The framework embraces various dimensions in the syntactic (all the information about both object management and its physical features) and semantic (all the information about the meaning we give the object and its usage) levels.

An advantage of the proposed methodology is that it allows defining a priori the impact of augmenting an artifact with new features. Such impact could be stated both in the syntactic and semantic level. In addition, designers may choose to create radical ways of interaction that distort the artifact strongly. Our approach does not limit design forcing them into the traditional way an artifact is used, but provides a framework for understanding the consequences of the design choices.

For guiding the design, analysis dimensions have been categorized in several topics such as Manipulation, Restrictions, Conceptual Model, Access, and so on. Notice the differences on the impact produced when modifying the dimension form one category to another. For instance, modifying the Conceptual Model of some object can be much less desirable than modifying its Restrictions. This will help designers to make informed decisions for its deployment and also permit users adopting and taking benefits from the augmented object. A frequent problem is having objects that are unnatural in its use; the lack of the proposed analysis impedes the understanding of the user's mental model about the object.

The proposed methodology should be used together with other design procedures such as Hong's strategy in order to define which is the ultimate goal of the design, what kind of need will the artifacts satisfy, providing a complex spectrum in the development of augmented objects. A lot of effort is put on products evaluation, however, objects design must be immersed in a methodology that guarantees that the development of new tools is effective and include all the involved factors in the use of this kind of tools. A second stage of research will include the definition of formalism for design based on UML.

Further work is required in order to determine which are the best candidates for augmentation, which are the best techniques for augmenting some features but maintain the "naturalness" of use, which are the relationships among the dimensions described by the paper, and defining adequate evaluation mechanisms. We expect that the present work contribute with such goals.

References

1. Abowd, G., Mynatt, E., Rodden, T. The human experience. IEEE Pervasive Computing (2002) 48-57.
2. Alarcón, R., Guerrero, L., Ochoa, S.F., Pino, J.A.: Analysis and Design of Mobile Collaborative Applications using Contextual Elements. Accepted in Computing and Informatics (2006), in press.

3. Aguilera, F., Alarcón, R.A., Guerrero, L.A., Collazos, C.: A cognitive model of user interaction as a guideline for designing novel interfaces. LNCS.
4. Bannon L., Bødker S. Beyond the interface: Encountering artifacts in use. In: J.Carroll (ed.): Designing Interaction: Psychology at the Human-Computer Interface. Cambridge University Press (1991) 227-253.
5. Carter, S., Mankoff, J. Prototypes in the Wild: Lessons Learned from Evaluating Three UbiComp Systems. IEEE Pervasive Computing 4(4), (2005) 51-57.
6. Damasio A. R., Descarte's. Error: Emotion, Reason, and The Human Brain, New York, NY: Gosset/Putnam Press, (1994).
7. Greenberg, S., Fitchett, C., Phidgets: Easy development of physical interfaces through physical widgets. Proc. of the User Interface Software and Technology (UIST). Orlando-Florida USA, ACM Press, (2001) 209-218.
8. Hong, D., Chiu, D. K. W., Shen, V. Y. Requirements elicitation for the design of context-aware applications in a ubiquitous environment. Proc. of the 7th International Conference on Electronic Commerce (ICEC). ACM Press Vol. 113, (2005) 590 – 596.
9. Ishii, H., and Ulmer, B., Tangible bits: Towards seamless interfaces between people, bits and atoms. Proc. of the International Conference for Human-computer Interaction (CHI), ACM (1997) 234-241.
10. Norman, D. A. The Design of Everyday Things, London/New York: MIT Press, 2000.
11. Ohta, Y., Tamura, H. Mixed Reality–Merging Real and Virtual Worlds, Tokyo, (1999).
12. Picard, R. W., Affective Computing. M.I.T. Press, Cambridge, MA, (1997).
13. Rittenbruch, M.,: ATMOSPHERE: A Framework for Contextual Awareness.International Journal of Human-Computer Interaction 14(2), 159-180 (2002)
14. Scheirer, J., Picard, R., Affective Objects, MIT Media lab Technical Rep. No 524, (2000).
15. Streitz, N., Nixon, P. The disappearing computer. Commun. ACM 48(3), (2005) 32-35.
16. Strohbach, M., Gellersen, H., Kortuem, G., Kray, C. Cooperative Artefacts: Assessing Real World Situations with Embedded Technology. Proc. of the Sixth International Conference on Ubiquitous Computing (UbiComp), LNCS 3205, Springer-Verlag, Nottingham England, (2004) 250-267.
17. Theofanos, M.F., Scholtz, J. A Diner's Guide to Evaluating a Framework for Ubiquitous Computing Applications. Proc. of the 11th International Conference on Human-Computer Interaction (HCI), Nevada USA, (2005).
18. Thompson, E., Colour Vision: A Study in Cognitive Science and the Philosophy of Perception. London: Routledge Press, (1995).
19. Trevor J. and David M. Hilbert. A Comparative Prototype Research Methodology. Proc. of 4th International Conference on Ubiquitous Computing (UbiComp), LNCS 2498, Springer-Verlag, Göteborg Sweden, (2002).
20. Valdez, P., Mehrabian, A., Effects of color on emotions, Journal of Experimental Psychology: General, (1994) 394-409.
21. Weiser, M. The Computer for the Twenty-First Century, Scientific American, September (1991) 94-10.

The eHomeConfigurator Tool Suite

Ulrich Norbisrath, Christof Mosler, and Ibrahim Armac

Department of Computer Science 3, RWTH Aachen University,
Ahornstr. 55, 52074 Aachen, Germany
{uno, christof, armac}@i3.informatik.rwth-aachen.de

Abstract. In contrast to decreasing costs of electronic appliances enabling the realization of pervasive systems, the price of individual development of the software making up eHome systems is one of the major problems preventing their large-scale adoption. By introducing a specification, configuration, and deployment process, the environment-specific development effort is reduced. We support this process by our tool suite, the eHomeConfigurator which is introduced in this paper. It creates a configuration graph, capable of describing dependencies and contexts of components in the eHome field. The tool suite is used to configure and deploy various eHome services on different home environments. Compared to the classical development process, the effort for setting up eHome systems is reduced significantly and opens up the possibility to decrease the development costs for eHome systems.

1 Introduction

Appliances usable in pervasive computing environments, such as computer controlled lamps, cameras, or various sensors, are already affordable for most home-owners. Hence, from this point of view, the hardware for the realization of smart home environments is already available at reasonable costs. This is proven by various setups of such smart home environments. We call those environments eHomes or eHome systems [3,9,1]. All these implementations are either research or hobby projects. The question arising is: Why are eHomes not more wide spread? One of the main barriers blocking this is the price of such systems. Even if appliances are affordable, the software driving the eHome is rather expensive since it is mostly developed or adapted for every single eHome. A complete software development process per case is not affordable for everyone.

As software engineers, we are particularly interested in simplifying the software development process, arising when implementing a service for a specific home environment. Our vision: If the software for eHomes could be reused, and its adaptation and configuration could be automated, one of the price barriers for mass-market home automation would be broken. The key point of our research is the reduction of the effort for software development and adaption.

The classic development process for eHome systems is carried out in full for each new eHome environment. In our process, the development has only to be done once for all regarded environments. The repetitive portion is reduced to the level of mere specification of the environment and the services, as well as interactive configuration of the given service components into the eHome system with no coding overhead. Our goal

R. Meersman, Z. Tari, P. Herrero et al. (Eds.): OTM Workshops 2006, LNCS 4278, pp. 1315–1324, 2006.

is the support of composition and configuration of services for eHome systems. In this context, we introduce a special specification, configuration, and deployment process. We will refer to this as the eHome-SCD-process. This process is supported by our tool suite, the eHomeConfigurator, which will be presented in this paper.

2   Scenario

We assume the following scenario will be typical for establishing future eHome environments: First, an inhabitant has the wish to install an eHome service in his/her home environment. He/she is the *customer*. The customer will specify which functionality should be provided by his/her eHome system. He/she will do this by contacting a *provider* or using a tool which contacts the provider. The provider offers eHome hardware, software, and configuration support. In our case, the customer will consult a configuration tool delivered by the provider for selecting a service offering the desired functionality. The services are described and classified on an abstract level to make an intuitive selection possible. The tool will provide suggestions for appliances needed to enable the selected functionality and will take the environment's existing infrastructure into account. After the installation of the proposed appliances, the software will support the configuration process of the software and deploy it automatically.

We distinguish between basic and integrating services offered by components. *Integrating services* are services composed of various basic services which provide interfacing with single appliances. These integrating services usually represent the functionality the inhabitants are interested in.

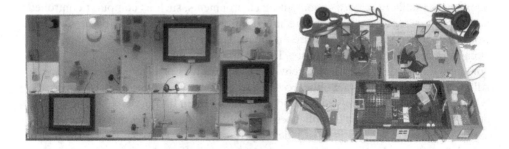

Fig. 1. eHome demonstrators

In our evaluation, we offer the following integrating eHome services: **LightingService:** This service offers simple functionality to turn on and off the illumination in specific areas in the home environment via manual switches or buttons. **LightMotionService:** This service offers the possibility to turn on and off the illumination via motion detection. **SecurityService:** If activated, the security service offers surveillance of a home via detecting intrusion and raising accordingly the alarm and informing an inhabitant and/or the police. **MusicFollowsPersonService:** Combining electronically controlled multimedia devices and person detection, this service lets a music stream associated with a specific person follow this person through his/her home. If one inhabitant switches on the music in the living room and goes to the kitchen, the music stops playing in the living room and continues in the kitchen. **AllOnService:** This service switches on all the lights in the whole house. For example: If an inhabitant is awoken by a noise in the middle of the night, he/she can switch everything on. **AllOffService:** This service ensures that all electronic appliances are deactivated, such as in the case, when all inhabitants have left the house.

We have tested our scenario in various environments: We have built two miniature demonstrators (see figure 1). The first one, on the left, (presented on a workshop in Tartu, Estonia [12]) is built from wood and equipped with available eHome appliances (X10 lamps, movement sensors, switch panels, speakers, and webcams [18]). Whereas for the second one (presented at UbiComp2005 [11]), we have used Lego and equipped it with self-built Lego lamps, switches, USB-webcams, and USB-audio systems. Our third test environment is a real house of our cooperation partner located in Duisburg (see section 5). It is equipped with European Installation Bus, Honeywell, and RFID sensors. This diversity of environments and technology standards used, forms a realistic scenario for evaluating the described eHome process. We use these results for proving and improving our concepts realized in the eHomeConfigurator tool suite [4].

3 Process

Current eHome systems are developed individually for each customer by a classic development process. The classic development process includes for every new environment the following steps: **Requirements Engineering:** The customer has to decide beforehand which services he/she wants in his/her house. **eHome system development:** The concrete realization in terms of appliances, communication infrastructure, and middleware must be worked out together with specialists from hard- and software providers. The implementation of the eHome system is the next step. Usually this will be a hand-coded and very environment specific solution. **Execution and Maintenance:** The software is installed and deployed by the provider. Later changes and extensions demand further coding and development time, as described in the previous step. **De-installation:** The software components are de-installed, and the contact between the customer and the provider ends.

3.1 The SCD-Process

The first step to the reduction of repetitive development is to shift the development away from the per case related development to an a-priori development of reusable components. What remains is a repetitive configuration process consisting of specification, configuration, and deployment. Still, the configuration is a challenging task when done manually. By introducing functionality composition, allowing automatic resolution of subservices, and corresponding appliances for given integrating services, the configuration process can be partly automated. We call this supported configuration process the SCD-process.

The idea of the SCD-process is to establish an iterative chain of procedural techniques to automate the creation of the eHome system as much as possible. This means that we are looking for ways to automate and support the process of specifying, configuring, and deploying an eHome system into the normal home – transforming the regular home into an eHome. This is achieved by means of tool support, reuse, and mere configuration of software components for providing eHome services. It is essential that the shift from a normal home to an eHome does not involve developing the software for that home but merely configuring and deploying it. As the result, the specification of the home environment, selection of the desired eHome services, and installation of necessary appliances are the only activities performed manually. Current configuration management research mainly deals with manual configuration management and software deployment [17,14]. Here, the configuration and deployment of the given components must also be done automatically and support functionality composition. Hence, we are focusing not on versioning aspects but rather on semantic support. The three phases of the SCD-process are described in the following:

Specification of the eHome Environment and Required Services. During this phase, the architectural information about the eHome is captured – how the rooms in the home are located and connected with the different location elements such as doors and windows. The existing appliances and their location in the home environment are described. The already existing eHome services are also identified – when modifying the configuration of the eHome, the already existing eHome services have to be specified. Whenever new eHome services are needed, they are selected and added to the specification. Only integrating services are selected. Along with the eHome environment, the services used later in the eHome environment, plus the required appliances and functionalities, need to be defined and specified beforehand, as well.

Automatic Configuration of the Selected Services. The services selected in the specification phase are automatically configured. This means that necessary appliances that are still missing in the eHome are added to the configuration, with the impact that the customer will have to buy them before deploying. Likewise, required sub-services that are missing in the specification are selected to meet the functional requirements of the selected services. For each location with active services, corresponding service objects are allocated. For example, if the lighting service needs at least one lamp per room and one switch to control the lamp, these appliances are added to the configuration. Furthermore, the corresponding driver component services for the lamp and switch controllers are added to the configuration. After finishing this traversal, the configuration graph includes all necessary information for the deployment.

Deployment of the Service Configuration Onto the Service Gateway in the eHome. The software components specified and configured during the first two phases are deployed automatically onto the service gateway residing in the eHome. The software components are also initialized properly and launched automatically. The third phase of the eHome-SCD-process concerns the deployment of the eHome configuration graph. Up to now, the deployer tool is only realized for the OSGi framework [5]. The implemented algorithm is very straight forward and should be easily transferable to other middlewares. The algorithm consists of five steps. First, the software components (in OSGi called bundles) are loaded. Second, the components are stated. Third, the references between the runtime model and the runtime components are built. Fourth, the software component are initialized in correspondence to their dependencies. And fifth, the service object interfaces in the software components corresponding to the integrating services are executed. Possible extensions of this deployment approach concern dynamic reconfiguration and the integration of different middlewares.

4   Tool Support

Our tool suite, the eHomeConfigurator, supports the eHome-SCD-process. In this subsection we describe how this tool can be used in practice.

Before the customer can use the tool suite, the provider or the software component developer has to provide a set of software components (in OSGi called bundles) and their service descriptions in a semantic context. To specify a service, all its semantic requirements and exports must be given. Its URL has to be given to locate the compiled component code. Furthermore, the service must be classified to be a top level (selectable by the eHome customer) service or not. An integrating service will be selectable by the customer. In figure 2, a security service is specified. It requires the functionalities for intrusion detection, alarm raising, and the alarm activation state. Some services, especially driver services, can control appliances. They also have to be specified including their describing attributes, such as address numbers for X10-lamps.

After launching the eHomeConfigurator at the customer's home, his/her environment has to be modeled. In our case (see the Lego demonstrator in figure 1) just kitchen, living room, bedroom, hall, and bathroom and their connections have to be modeled (see figure 3). Until now, no appliances have been specified; there are no software controllable appliances in the customer's environment. This means that all required appliances to fulfill the selected services will be recommended by the tool suite.

In the next step, the inhabitant has to select which services should be installed in his house (see figure 4). Each service will be assigned to desired locations. Already installed appliances can be taken into account while selecting the locations to fulfill the respective service. As in our example no appliance are installed, this step is not relevant. In our case, the inhabitant selects the first five services from the service list and configures the services in all rooms (he selects Select All Locations) and configures the services with the minimal set of needed appliances (he/she selects Necessary Devices Only).

In the next step, the inhabitant can fine tune the room-selection: Some services such as **AllOnService**, which turns on all the lights in the complete environment with one button, might only be accessed from special locations, such as the bedroom or the hall. They need not be accessible from every room.

After providing this information, the configuration tool can compute which software realizations of the selected top level services exist for the given parameters and environment. In our scenario, the inhabitant is offered the realization using drivers for the Lego demonstrator as well as alternatives for other drivers, resulting in other required hardware and software components, such as hardware used in another demonstrator. In the depicted scenario, also an X10-based realization [18] in one or all rooms is possible. The system notices that it can realize the illumination-functionality via an X10-controller service or a Lego Lamp Controller service (see figure 6).

When this selection is done, the configuration tool finishes the computation of necessary software components and appliances. The inhabitants can now buy the appliances

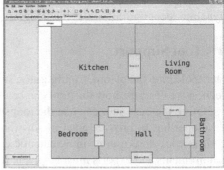

Fig. 2. eHomeConfigurator: service specification

Fig. 3. eHomeConfigurator: empty environment

and enter their hardware addresses and other parameters in our tool (see figure 7). These parameters could be the address numbers of the Lego lamps (i.e. 2 for the kitchen) or email addresses (i.e. uno@i3.informatik.rwth-aachen.de), and message texts (i.e. "intrusion detection in the kitchen") for the security service. In the figure, the parameters for the notification service of the security service are depicted.

As a first result, all appliances required to fulfill the selected services have been added to the environment (see figure 8). These have to be installed in the corresponding room before performing the actual deployment.

A further result is the deployable configuration graph, which can be brought to life by our deployment tool. This graph is not intended to be viewed or processed by the customer, but is used for the automatic deployment and as a visual entry point for debugging. In the context of our scenario, this graph contains nodes representing the service objects, appliances, and their attributes, associated with the different locations. In figure 9, we

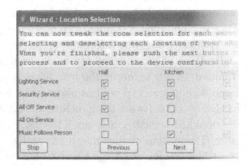

Fig. 4. eHomeConfigurator: service selection   **Fig. 5.** eHomeConfigurator: location selection

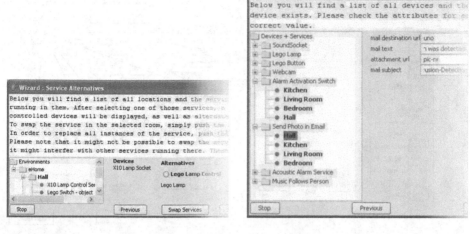

Fig. 6. eHomeConfigurator: alternatives of software components

Fig. 7. eHomeConfigurator: attribute editor

see a section of the configuration graph showing the **MusicFollowsPerson** service in the living room. It shows only the graph nodes related to the living room and the **MusicFollowsPerson** service. These nodes represent appliances (Sound Device, On/Off Switch, and Webcam), subservices (Person Detector, Motion Controller, and Switch), attributes (Destination, Camera Number), and states (`switch` and `person`). Furthermore, the graph edges represent the dependencies of software components (the Music Follows Person - object uses the SoundRouter - object), physical contain relations (the Sound Device is in the Living-room), responsibilities of runtime software components for environment elements (the Soundrouter - object is responsible for routing sound to the Living-room), and links to attributes (attr edges) and states (state edges).

5   Related Work

While a lot of research is being done in the field of ubiquitous and pervasive computing, the main focus is usually on the development and study of new types of applications. However, there are few related scientific projects which also have the simplification of the development process in the center of their interest. The following section aims at pointing out similarities and differences between the previously presented eHomeConfigurator and some of those projects.

A number of prototype eHome buildings are located in different parts of Germany. In the city of Duisburg, a building equipped with state of the art technology has been constructed by inHaus in close cooperation with The Fraunhofer Institute for Microelectronic Circuits and Systems (IMS) for the purpose of developing products and strategies in that segment and being able to perform tests in a real environment [3]. Similar to this building, a different project has been realized by T-Com and WeberHaus in Berlin, Germany. In contrast to the building in Duisburg, this eHome was built specifically using technology which is either already available or will be available within the next

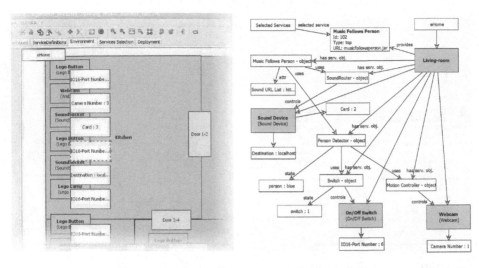

Fig. 8. eHomeConfigurator: environment with appliances

Fig. 9. Deployable configuration graph for the MusicFollowsPerson Service

few months [9] (similar to our wooden demonstrator). There is one common character trait for each of these eHomes. All of them have been developed and built individually, using custom software components which had to be realized through a vast amount of work being done by expensive experts. As a direct result, large investments have been necessary in order to realize those buildings.

SmartHome User Interface [15] has been developed by SIKT, HK\R and EnerSearch in Sweden. This tool provides a user interface to view and manipulate appliances over the internet. It is also capable of displaying the environment three-dimensionally to simplify access to those appliances. In contrast to the tool presented in this paper, *SmartHome User Interface* does not allow the user to model complex services or to configure them in an environment. Therefore, it provides no support during the eHome configuration process.

ECT [2] is a toolkit to support developing and deploying installations for ubiquitous computing. Its main focus is the interaction of heterogeneous soft- and hardware components. It establishes three distinct layers for different types of users. The lowest layer represents the core implementation of ECT which is only of interest for a certain kind of experienced developers. On a second layer, other programmers can develop new components in accordance to a component approach similar to Java Beans. On the highest level, unexperienced users can make use of the graphical user interface to assemble these components.

In contrast to the approach presented in this paper, this toolkit provides no means to model the environment in which the ubiquitious computing takes place. It only focuses on the creation of new services through component interaction and on how to make this process accessible to unexperienced users. When using the eHomeConfigurator, service modeling is not done by the end user, but by experts. End users only choose from existing services and configure them according to their taste. Consequently, the modeled services can be applied to an arbitrary number of environments, which is not the case for services created with ECT. A similar approach is the *CAMP* [10] project. It does not implement different abstraction layers, but rather focuses on the end user level. Extensive research on how end users with no technical experience perceive applications has been conducted. The *Open Services Gateway Initiative* (OSGi) [6] specifies a set of software application interfaces (APIs) for building open-service gateways. Central to the OSGi specification [5] is the *service framework* with a service registry. Components register their services at the service registry where other applications may retrieve and use them. Based on the concept of residential gateways [16,8], the open services gateway specification describes an approach that permits coexistence of and integration with multiple network and device access technologies. In addition, components may be added implementing new technologies as they emerge. Interaction is enabled via Java interfaces, without relying on proxy objects. While other systems (e.g Jini) are decentralized, the OSGi approach is a centralized system, which simplifies system maintenance to the disadvantage of distribution aspects. OSGi is our project's middleware.

6   Conclusion and Outlook

Automatic configuration of services and appliances is an important requirement for the acceptance of eHome systems. In this paper, we presented an approach for modeling specific eHome environments, comprising different services and appliances and performing automatic configuration of various eHome services corresponding to this environment. We have developed a tool suite called the eHomeConfigurator to support all steps of our SCD-process: specification, configuration, and deployment of eHome systems. The eHomeConfigurator calculates and proposes different combinations of appliances and drivers. The resulting configuration graph contains all the information needed for automatic deployment. In the classical development process, where intense requirement analysis, manual specification and formalization, and functionality and glue programming is required, we need multiple specialists for performing these tasks for every new environment. Our approach offers a convenient way to shift the need of specialists to the a-priori development phase specifying functionalities, appliances, and coding services. The remaining tasks can be carried out by most customers. Of course, aspects concerning the user interface can still be improved in future work; localization of appliances and detection of their attributes (for example with UPnP [13]) is ongoing work in the field of pervasive computing. Such extensions should be easily includable in our tool suite. Other future work related to our project concerns the improvements of the MDE-based software development process of our tool suite itself and the enhancement of the functionality description with more fine-grained parametric contracts [7].

References

1. Beisheim Holding GmbH.   FutureLife – Das Haus der Zukunft.   http://www.futurelife.ch/ (6.4.2005), 2005.
2. Humble J. Greenhalgh C., Izadi S., Mathrick J. and I. Taylor. ECT: A toolkit to support rapid construction of ubicomp environments. In *In Proceedings of the Sixth International Conference on Ubiquitous Computing (UBICOMP'04)*, September 2004.

3. inHaus Duisburg. Innovationszentrum Intelligentes Haus Duisburg. http://www.inhaus-duisburg.de (22.6.2004), 2005.
4. Ulrich Norbisrath, Priit Salumaa, and Adam Malik. eHomeConfigurator. http://sourceforge.net/projects/ehomeconfig, 2006.
5. Open Services Gateway Initiative. OSGi Service Platform Specification. http://www.osgi.org/osgi_technology/download_specs.asp (2.3.2005), 2002.
6. Open Services Gateway Initiative Alliance. OSGi Service Platform. http://www.osgi.org/osgi_technology/download_specs.asp#Release_3 (2.3.2005), April 2003. Release 3.
7. Ralf Reussner, Jens Happe, and Annegret Habel. Modelling parametric contracts and the state space of composite components by graph grammars. In *FASE*, pages 80–95. Springer-Verlag, 2005.
8. Takeshi Saito, Ichiro Tomoda, Yoshiaki Takabatake, Junko Ami, and Keiichi Teramoto. Home Gateway Architecture and Its Implementation. *IEEE Transactions on Consumer Electronics*, 46(4):1161–1166, November 2000.
9. T-Com. T-Com Haus. http://www.t-com-haus.de/ (26.9.2005), 2005.
10. Khai N. Truong, Elaine M. Huang, and Gregory D. Abowd. CAMP: A magnetic poetry interface for end-user programming of capture applications for the home. In *Ubicomp*, pages 143–160, 2004.
11. Ulrich Norbisrath, Priit Salumaa, Adam Malik. eHome Specification, Configuration, and Deployment. http://ubicomp.org/ubicomp2005/programs/demos.shtml, 2005. Demonstration Paper D15 on UbiComp2005.
12. Ulrich Norbisrath, Priit Salumaa, Adam Malik. Specification, Configuration, and Deployment in eHome Systems. http://math.ut.ee/~peeter_l/seminar/eelmised/05k/ehome.html, 2005.
13. UPnP-Forum. UPnP-Forum Homepage.
14. AndrT van der Hoek. Integrating Configuration Management and Software Deployment. In *Proceedings of the Working Conference on Complex and Dynamic Systems Architecture (CDSA 2001)*, 2001.
15. Rolf Raven Elmar van Dijk and Fredrik Ygge. Smarthome user interface: Controlling your home through the internet. *ISES*, 8, 1996.
16. Dave L. Waring, Kenneth J. Kerpez, and Steven G. Ungar. A newly emerging customer premises paradigm for delivery of network-based services. *Computer Networks*, 31(4):411–424, February 1999.
17. Bernhard Westfechtel and Reidar Conradi. Version Models for Software Configuration Management. *ACM Computing Surveys*, 30(2), June 1998.
18. X10. Protocol Specification. http://www.marmitek.com/en/basisimages/x10_protocol.PDF (30.5.2005), 2004.

Mobile Phone + RFID Technology = New Mobile Convergence Toward Ubiquitous Computing Environment

Taesu Cheong and Marie Kim

Electronics and Telecommunications Research Institute, 161 Gajeong-dong, Yuseong-gu,
Daejeon, 305-700, Republic of Korea
{qlink, mariekim}@etri.re.kr
http://www.etri.re.kr

Abstract. Radio Frequency Identification (RFID) is increasingly used to improve the efficiency of business processes by providing the capability of automatic identification and data capture and it is expected to extend its significant potential to daily life improvement. On the other hand, the convergence of the telecommunication, media and information technology industries has generated massive change in not just industries but also our daily lives, and none are more apparent than the mobile phone. Such convergence trend for mobile phone seems inevitable and the integration of RFID technology and mobile phone is regarded as one of promising technologies to accelerate such convergence trend toward the ubiquitous computing environment. In this paper, we discuss the benefits, business cases and system architectures emerging from the integration between RFID technology – especially, RFID reader – and mobile phone with existing wireless network infrastructure in terms of business and software perspectives. Moreover, we present the reference implementation for the RFID-based cellular network architecture incorporated with a mobile phone mounted with RFID reader in order to evaluate the technical feasibility of this convergence.

1 Introduction

Recent advances in the field of Radio Frequency Identification (RFID) technology have reached a state that will allow us within the next years to equip virtually every object in an environment with small, cheap tags [1]. Meanwhile, the convergence of the telecommunication, media and information technology industries has generated massive change in not just industries but also our daily lives, and none are more apparent than the mobile phone.

The two eminent technologies – RFID and mobile phone technology – are considered as the key drivers toward ubiquitous computing environment and it is natural to think that the integration of RFID with mobile devices as well as the existing cellular network brings new markets and research challenges to commercialize.

In this paper, we discuss the benefits, business cases and system architectures emerging from the integration between RFID technology – especially, RFID reader –

R. Meersman, Z. Tari, P. Herrero et al. (Eds.): OTM Workshops 2006, LNCS 4278, pp. 1325–1336, 2006.
© Springer-Verlag Berlin Heidelberg 2006

and mobile phone with existing wireless network infrastructure in terms of business and software perspectives. Moreover, we present the reference implementation for the RFID-based cellular network software architecture integrated with a mobile phone mounted with RFID reader in order to evaluate the technical feasibility of this convergence.

2 Motivation

When it comes to the integration between a mobile phone and RFID technology, there are two kinds of possible integration: one is the mobile phone which possesses a RFID tag in it and the other is the mobile phone mounted with RFID reader.

In case of a mobile phone with an embedded RFID tag, the RFID tag has personal information. When the mobile phone with the RFID tag is moved within the range of external RFID reader, the tag data is sent to the reader so that it enables the phone user to get personalized services. For example, it can be used for payment [2], entry control and identification with authentication.

The mobile phone mounted with RFID reader – which we call 'Mobile RFID Phone' in other words – can be carried anywhere and anytime as people carry their cellular phones. It can be utilized for providing end-users detailed information about the tagged object through accessing information server connected with the cellular network. According to the typical RFID-based business scenario, the RFID readers are static devices installed at fixed positions while RFID tags which are attached on items are moving through the readers' read range. On the other hand, in the case of mobile RFID phone, the RFID reader is moveable and it can collect information from fixed or mobile RFID tags. In this paper, we focus on the later one, mobile RFID phone-based RFID network services and their technologies.

As the price of RFID tags has been significantly decreased, RFID tags are expected to become pervasive as they are attached on everything such as foods and home appliances, and this implies that people get chances to utilize RFID tags in their everyday lives. This could be a big opportunity for mobile telecommunication companies because a mobile phone can be used as a hand-held RFID reader if a RFID reader can be equipped with mobile phone. In fact, mobile telecommunication companies in Korea have been trying to find other sources for making revenues other than voice communication. They view that mobile RFID phone technology is eligible for a driver to open a new opportunity for continuing market growth [3].

Recently, most people have cellular phones capable of wireless Internet [4]. In South Korea, about 78% population of Korea have cellular phones and 96.4% of their phones are capable of accessing wireless Internet and 40.2% of them use wireless Internet. Figure 1 shows wireless Internet access rate via mobile phone. Younger generations incline to high preference of wireless Internet comparing to old generation, whose tendency reflects that there exists a potential to boost the rate of wireless Internet access, which in turn lead to the growth of revenue for mobile telecommunication companies if new types of attractive service models are proposed.

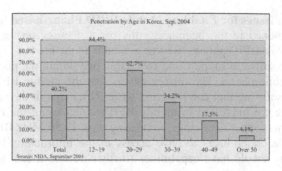

Fig. 1. Wireless Internet access by age in South Korea [5]

Korea has established one of the most advanced cellular telecommunication networks with the widespread of wireless Internet-accessible phones and the increase of demanding new types of service through wireless Internet over the cellular network. At the same time, the recent technical advance of RFID in this country demands the opening of such new business opportunities from the integration between the leading mobile phone technology in Korea and RFID. There is no doubt that a mobile phone will evolve into the most ubiquitous device in the world, integrating all other devices including a RFID reader into a single device and Korea has recognized that such convergence is expected to broaden the usage of RFID to the daily life. Currently, mobile RFID forum [6] in Korea has been established to boost such technology by developing diverse business cases and standards. As presented in this paper, we tried to develop a reference system to evaluate the technical feasibilities.

3   Technical Challenges and Business Opportunities

In this section, we discuss the technical expectations with some challenging issues as this convergence comes into the real life and several business applications are also introduced to see what kinds of business opportunities it will provide.

3.1   Technical Considerations and Challenges for Mobile RFID Solutions

To make this convergence possible, there are many technical challenges to overcome. In this subsection, we discuss the possible technical problems from three different standpoints: Hardware Challenges, Software Design Issues and Global Standards.

Hardware Challenges for the Integration between RFID Reader and Mobile Phone

Basically, the foremost technical challenge is how we can make the RFID reader small enough to be embedded in the mobile phone and developing a mobile RFID system-on-chip (SoC) for mobile devices [7] is desirable although there are many technical barriers to accomplish. At the same time, the power consumption of the reader should be controlled in a reasonable level because the only power source of a mobile phone is the battery mounted with the phone. Moreover, the interference between the antenna of a mobile phone and that of RFID reader should be minimized.

Software Design Issues for Enabling Mobile RFID Phone-based Service
As already mentioned in the beginning, this paper focuses on the software issues arising when mobile RFID phones become available in the market.

We divide the software support into two parts: one within the phone and the other external to a mobile phone. The former means that the mobile RFID phone should have embedded software that can read and write RFID tags in the read range. Moreover, because we are interested in mobile RFID reader using the frequency of 900 MHz which allows longer read range comparing with 13.56 MHz RFID that it seems proper for mobile phone users to have access to the information by sensing RFID tags, the software should have capabilities to filter out the redundant tag reads in a primitive level.

When it comes to the case external to a mobile phone, one of the benefits by the integration between RFID and cellular phone comes from the use of the cellular network: that is, the cellular network connection enables real-time data transfer between mobile phone and the information server managing the tag-related information with less location restriction. So, the embedded software can communicate to backend servers over the cellular network in order to transmit the collected tag reads to the servers and receive tag-related information and service.

Global Standards for the Interoperability
The absence of technical standards for mobile RFID platform seems evident that it can impede the proliferation of mobile RFID services in the market. Therefore, we need to develop or be compliant with sort of global or domestic RFID standard specifications including tag-reader air interface, data communication specifications between a mobile RFID reader and an information server over the cellular network and so on. Otherwise, the diversity of protocols and interfaces among the components in the mobile RFID platform must be taken care of by hardware or software. However, it is unlikely to support all market-available and nation-varying standards. In addition, the code structure and tag data format used for mobile RFID services should be determined.

3.2 Examples of Business Scenarios and Their Opportunities

The business applications vary from personal usage to enterprise services including supply chain management. This subsection presents a few examples by utilizing the mobile RFID platform. Examples herein contain basic idea of how this mobile RFID can be applied and show the potential of the integration.

Real-time Information Access
If all products have their own RFID tags, you can get the IDs of the products via mobile RFID phone and get the up-to-date information pertaining to the IDs in the Internet. For example, when you buy food materials to cook, you can obtain not only the recipe but also their distribution channel by simply reading tags attached on them.

Consumer Service, Real-time Information Collection and CRM
A mobile phone user approach mobile phone equipped with mobile RFID reader onto a poster promoting a new album and he/she can gain the information on the singer,

view the music-video clips and even place an order with the album or download MP3 files to the phone immediately. Moreover, such contents-access information along with personal and location information can be gathered and later such information can be utilized for the marketing.

Track and Trace
When you receive a package you ordered via web site, you can scan the tag attached on the package to check the history of trace from manufacturer to consumer right away and you can also check what products the package contains in order to make sure the right delivery. With help of some authentication process, you may confirm the delivery or reject it by looking into whole delivery process.

4 WIPI-Based Mobile RFID Network Platform over Cellular Network: System Design and Its Implementation

4.1 Overview of Mobile RFID Network Platform

As shown in figure 2, the main components in this mobile RFID network are as follows: *a tag* which is attached on the item and contains unique identifier, *a mobile phone mounted with RFID reader* which is controlled by mobile users and senses tags, *ODS*(Object Directory Service; ONS in other words) *server* [8] which performs RFID code resolutions and returns the access URI to information server storing tag-related information in return for RFID tag identifier, and *an information server* which manages and serves the detailed information of a tag or an item which the tag is attached on. The following describes the request sequences: a mobile RFID phone reads a tag, and mobile RFID software filters the redundant tag reads and asks ODS server for the access URI to the information server by sending RFID tag identifier as an input over the cellular network. Then, the mobile RFID software receives the URI of the information server and performs information or service request to the information server through the URI. Finally, the user can get any information or services related to the RFID tag identifier on the mobile phone screen. Depending on mobile applications, the user may further its service use.

In this section, we present each entities discussed above in terms of associated software systems architectures.

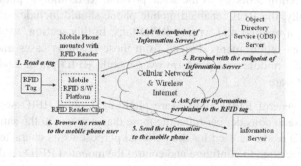

Fig. 2. Mobile RFID Network Configuration

4.2 WIPI, Wireless Internet Software Platform on Mobile Phone

Mobile platform implies a software system which opens a set of API (Application Programming Interface) applicable to mobile applications or related developing environments. WIPI (Wireless Internet Platform for Interoperability) is a mobile standard platform providing the environment for application programs loaded on the wireless devices [9] and this specification is made by KWISF (Korea Wireless Internet Standardization Forum) that consists of about 30 Korean telecommunication industries.

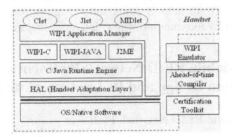

Fig. 3. Wireless Internet Platform for Interoperability (WIPI) Platform Architecture

Figure 3 shows the general WIPI architecture and additional WIPI-related tools. WIPI platform consists of four layers: Handset Adaptation Layer (HAL) for hiding the complexities of the underlying device operations, Runtime Engine Layer as the execution environment for WIPI applications, API Layer for providing rich libraries (WIPI-C/Java APIs) for developing WIPI applications (Clet, Jlet, MIDlet) and WIPI Application Manager for installing, deleting, listing and searching applications.

The main reason to choose WIPI platform as a fundamental mobile software platform for mobile RFID solution is that the Korean government has mandated the use of this domestic wireless Internet platform in handsets, WIPI, on domestically used cellular phones [10] so that we expect the rapid deployment of mobile RFID services in the market.

4.3 Software Requirements Derived from Business Case Analysis

The previous section 3 discusses the some possible RFID mobile phone-based applications. Basically, the RFID enabled mobile phone should include software platform that is capable of reading and writing RFID tags. In this section, we present several possible software requirements derived from those business cases and the comparisons between the middleware platform over mobile RFID phone and general RFID middleware software.

1) Unlike the general RFID middleware platform, mobile RFID software platform does not have to consider coordinating more than a reader at the same time because mobile RFID reader is used for the personal purpose as its characteristic in nature. That is, it is enough to configure and control the mounted RFID reader solely.

2) The raw stream of RFID tag reads is not appropriate for executing sensing-based business logic, so RFID middleware software is generally concerned about generating more meaningful semantic events after collecting tag reads coming from RFID readers. For example, a "smart shelf" application is interested in knowing about tags which are retrieved or stacked on the shelf while an "inventory monitoring" application wants to know the total number of distinct items in the stock area. On the other hand, mobile RFID software platform is only interested in the identification of tags in the field of mobile RFID reader and the semantic events like tags' field-in or field-out events seem less important of it.

3) Mobile RFID reader is power-sensitive because it uses the battery of mobile phone in order to read tags; on the other hand, networked RFID readers generally get a power supply in the stable manner and they – especially, passive RFID readers - can keep scanning the reading field of them to monitor the tags' movement. Therefore, in the mobile RFID platform case, it is reasonable to initiate tag reading by users whenever they want.

4) One of the expected benefits from tag sensing by mobile RFID phone is to provide users more convenient services by reducing key press so that it can lead to avoidance of human errors with less key-in and just one-click 'Read Tags' allowing machine-to-machine communications and automatic information retrievals.

5) The mobile RFID software should be equipped with the means to be integrated with other phone-support basic functionalities such as wireless Internet access over the cellular network, sending SMS, searching and recording the address book, alarming and so on.

4.4 Proposed WIPI-Based Software Architecture on Mobile Phone

According to the software requirements in section 4.3, the mobile RFID software loaded on handsets should have capabilities of controlling the RFID reader, manipulating tag reads from the reader, taking advantage of other software blocks on the phone and communicate with information server connected to the cellular network. In this subsection, we discuss WIPI platform-based software architecture spanning all functionalities mentioned right before on the mobile phone.

Before we move onto the discussion of mobile RFID software architecture along with WIPI platform, we first discuss the API design residing in WIPI C/Java API layer in the case of querying tag data collection from WIPI applications to WIPI platform. A RFID reader continuously scans for tags that are within the read range and reports each tag it senses at each time. This raw data stream seems inappropriate for the use on the business purpose because the stream contains redundant tag data, so it is required to process the raw stream into more meaningful information. In this sense, the purpose of such API design is to allow the application to make a high-level request for the ready-to-use RFID data through WIPI API while RFID-featured WIPI platform fulfills such requests so that it helps to reduce time to create mobile RFID applications.

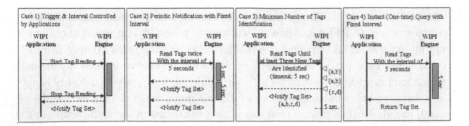

Fig. 4. WIPI API Model for the Interaction between WIPI Platform and RFID WIPI Application

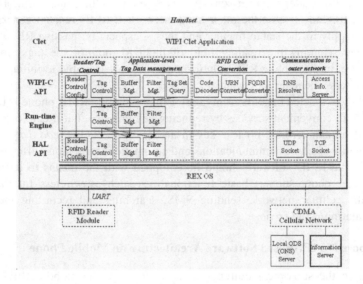

Fig. 5. WIPI-based Mobile RFID Software Platform Architecture

As presented in figure 4, we define four different types of requests for RFID data [11, 12]: (a) explicit request of start/stop of tag reading from user or WIPI applications, (b) request of periodic RFID data notification in the fixed length of interval, (c) request of tag reading until at least the specified number of new tags are identified and (d) one-time query of tag data for the specified length of interval. The delivery as a result of each request contains the distinct set of tag identifiers after uninterested tags are filtered out.

Including the APIs above, most major functions of mobile RFID software are described in the WIPI-C/Java layer. Figure 5 shows the extension of software building blocks for mobile RFID services on WIPI platform. As explained in the previous sections, WIPI platform is divided into three hierarchical layers: HAL as the abstraction of RFID reader hardware, WIPI API as exposure of high-level APIs for mobile applications and Run-time Engine as mediation of program executions. The detailed explanation for each block is presented in subsequent section.

4.5 Reference Implementation

In this subsection, the reference implementation of mobile RFID software network is presented. Our implementation spans from the extension of WIPI platform for supporting RFID functionalities to the prototype of the information server for offering RFID tag-initiated services to a mobile RFID phone user. Figure 6 shows the pictures of a mobile phone mounted with external RFID reader while providing mobile RFID service on the phone.

Fig. 6. Reference implementation of mobile RFID phone which provides information of a RFID tag to a mobile phone user

Reader Interface

'Reader Interface' is defined as the communication protocol between MCU (Micro Control Unit) and a RFID reader in a mobile phone and consists of three types of command types: Command, Response and Notification. Every command, which is expressed in 8 bit encoding, falls into one of six categories: Reader control/management, Tag Read/Write, Tag Lock/Unlock, Tag Revision and Additional Functions and the payload format is shown in figure 7.

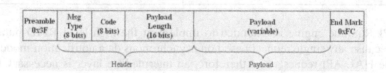

Fig. 7. Reader interface payload format

RFID Reader/Tag Management and Data Processing in WIPI

This layer is implemented by extending WIPI platform and primarily focuses on RFID reader management, the tag data filtering and collection, and delivery of RFID data to upper application layer on the mobile device. As illustrated in figure 5, the extended version of WIPI platform to support such functions consists of three distinct layers: HAL, Runtime engine and WIPI C API.

The interface with RFID reader is abstracted as HAL and it enables WIPI engines or WIPI API layer to have access to RFID reader through reader-dependent device driver in a standardized way. Functions of HAL include RFID reader control and configuration, RFID tag control (read/ write/lock tags), buffer control and primitive-level filtering via pattern matching. Table 1 shows some HAL APIs for RFID reader.

Table 1. Examples of WIPI HAL APIs [13]

Category	Function	Description
Reader Control Functions	MH_rfidPowerOn(Off)	Power on/off RFID reader
	MH_rfidOpen(Close)Reader	Open/Close the connection to RFID reader
	MH_rfidGet(Set)RFStrength	Get/Set the RF strength (power) of RFID reader
Tag Control Functions	MH_rfidReadUIIBlock	Read one read cycle of tags in the read zone
	MH_rfidReadUserDataBlock	Read data block in each tags given by tag identifiers
	MH_killTag	Kill tags given by tag identifiers
Buffer Management Functions	MH_rfidCreate/DestoryBuffer	Create/Destroy buffer storing tag data
	MH_rfidRead/DeleteBuffer	Read/Destroy tag data in buffer

WIPI API layer defines the specification for APIs of wireless Internet platform, described in both C and Java programming language, and its extension for mobile RFID application includes all functions of HAL and high-level RFID data query interface (refer to figure 4) [11, 12]. Examples of WIPI C APIs are shown in table 2.

Table 2. Examples of WIPI C APIs for RFID Applications [12]

Category	Function	Description
Tag Set Query with Call-back Functions	MC_rfidReqStart/StopTrigger	Start/stop the tag data collection
	MC_rfidReqPeriodicUIIBlocks	Request the periodic tag data notification
	MC_rfidReqMinIdentifiedNum	Request tag data collection till at least given number of new tags are identified
	RFIDGETUIIBlockListCB	Call-back function invoked after all three requests above
	MC_rfidPollUIIBlocks	Read tags during the interval of the given time
Reader Control Functions	MC_rfidPowerOn(Off)	Power on/off RFID reader
	MC_rfidOpen/Close/ResetReader	Open/Close the connection and reset the RFID reader
	MC_rfidisBusyReader	Check whether the reader is busy or not
Miscellaneous Functions	MC_rfidReportReaderStatus	Get the status information of RFID reader

WIPI Runtime engine is extended to implement the high-level RFID data query APIs because any single request based on asynchronous data notification model spans multiple HAL API requests and therefore, an intermediate layer is necessary to control such mediation.

Information Retrieval by Interacting between a Mobile Phone and Information Server over the CDMA Cellular Network

In order to offer RFID-based services to mobile users after capturing tags, HAL and WIPI API are extended in the aspect of RFID code conversion and communication with backend information servers. As briefly explained in section 4.1, raw hexadecimal string stored in a tag chip is in hand right after RFID reader identifies a tag. Our ultimate goal is to provide information initiated by the tag reading to mobile phone users, so the next steps must be taken into actions – that is, (a) obtaining URL of an information server which stores information pertaining to the tag and (b) having access to the information server via the URL.

Obtaining URL of an information server can be realized by inquiry to ODS (Object Directory Service) Server [8], which leverages DNS (Domain Name Server) to discover the network accessible service endpoint that contains the actual data pertaining to a RFID code. In order to use ODS to find the endpoint, the hexadecimal encoded RFID code string must be converted into a format that ODS can understand, so the hexadecimal string must pass through the ODS code resolution process. The extended WIPI API supports all the conversion process by code converter, URN converter and FQDN converter. After then, the mobile phone application issues DNS query to ODS server by invoking DNS resolver of WIPI C API layer. As a return of the request, the mobile phone application receives answer that contains URL of the information server pertaining to the RFID code.

The next step is to contact the information server found in the URL for the RFID code. The mobile phone application connects to the information server via URL by sending HTTP request and browses the tag data-related information on the mobile phone screen.

5 Conclusions with Qualitative Analysis

In this paper, the opportunity and feasibility of the combination of RFID and mobile phone technology are discussed, and the primary API design and software architectures are derived from the discussion. We have prototyped our system comprising of (a) commercial cellular phone and RFID reader modules, which are running on ARM 7 processor and interfacing each other through UART, (b) SK telecom's commercial cellular network, (c) local ONS server which works on Linux and (d) the information server implemented on Microsoft .NET platform. Moreover, we implemented the extended version of WIPI platform following the architecture of figure 5 and deployed the platform on the mobile phone. Although we observe the technical feasibility, we have found many challenging issues left as follows:

- The hardware problems still remain as mentioned in section 3 such as size of RFID reader which is supposed to be small enough to be embedded into a mobile phone and battery consumption problems. However, there are many efforts to make SoC for mobile RFID reader [7], so this problem will be tackled in the near future.
- Another hardware problem is the interference among mobile RFID readers when they are so closed to each other that the interference may impede the tag reading.
- We still suffer from the lack of global standards - including tag-reader protocol, reader-gateway protocol and so on - for mobile RFID communications which tend to prevent proliferation of this RFID services. Moreover, many countries adopt different policies for the use of frequencies and standards.
- We shape the basic network architecture for the immediate mobile RFID service deployment. Although we implement this networked RFID service architecture with the cooperation of SK telecom [14], the current RFID network architecture implies the exclusion of the key mobile telecommunication operators like SK Telecom. The ways for the companies to reap the benefits from this mobile RFID services and control the packets over the cellular network – such as, the broker

system residing in gateway of mobile telecommunication companies in order for the packet traffic control and pay-per-use measurement – are required for promotion of mobile RFID services. Besides, the methods to reduce the traffic of a vast amount of RFID data which is expected to be flowed into the cellular network must be devised with the perspectives of overall mobile RFID network stacks.

Despite some problems as discussed above, this introduction of the convergence between RFID and mobile phone technologies will bring the unique opportunity to easily bridge the physical and virtual world anytime and anywhere. It will surely be the win-win situation for all the participants – mobile telecommunication companies, phone manufacturers, third-party contents providers and customers by leveraging the RFID value, real-time information offer, to the everyday life in the ubiquitous computing world.

References

1. Klaus Finkenzeller: RFID Handboook: Radio-Frequency Identification Fundamentals and Applications. Wiley, New York (2000)
2. Tokyo Cabs to Try RFID Payments,
   "http://www.rfidjournal.com/article/articleview/1197/1/1/"
3. S. Oh, J. Chae, "Information Report on Mobile RFID in Korea", ISO/IEC JTC1 SC31 WG4, Report (2005)
4. Wireless Internet Access Climbs Nearly 30% In 2004,
   "http://www.ipsos-na.com/news/pressrelease.cfm?id=2598"
5. National Internet Development Agency of Korea (NIDA): "http://www.nida.or.kr"
6. Mobile RFID Forum: "http://www.mrf.or.kr"
7. ETRI Developed Mobile RFID SoC,
   "http://www.ddaily.co.kr/english/?fn=view&article_num=12024"
8. RFID Object Directory Service: "http://www.ods.or.kr/english/index.jsp"
9. WIPI Specification: "http://www.kwisforum.org"
10. KOREA: Korea, U.S. agree on Internet standard:
    "http://128.97.165.103/article-eastasia.asp?parentid=10578"
11. T. Cheong, M. Kim, K. Park, H. Yoon, "WIPI Java API Standard for Mobile RFID Reader", Mobile RFID Forum (2005)
12. M. Kim, T. Cheong, K. Park, H. Yoon, "WIPI C API Standard for Mobile RFID Reader", Mobile RFID Forum (2005)
13. K. Park, H. Yoon, M. Kim, T. Cheong, "WIPI HAL Standard for Mobile RFID Reader", Mobile RFID Forum (2005)
14. SK Telecom: "http://www.sktelecom.com/main.html"

Clicky: Input in Pervasive Systems

Andrew Weiler, Jeffrey Naisbitt, and Roy Campbell

andrew.weiler.uiuc@gmail.com, naisbitt@uiuc.edu, rhc@uiuc.edu

Abstract. Pervasive computing systems are physically bounded spaces of physical and digital devices such as desktop computers, laptops, handheld devices, and sensors. These systems attempt to integrate the information space of computers and the physical space of the real world. With multiple devices and heterogeneous inputs, seamless interaction with these systems remains a challenge. We have developed an input system that overcomes many obstacles facing users in pervasive systems. We provide support for multiple users to control multiple mice on the same display. We also provide an interface using a video stream, allowing the user to click on devices shown in the video to control other devices in the room. Finally, we demonstrate experimentally that these techniques are useful in a pervasive space and do not impose a significant overhead in our system. Using our system, users are able to seamlessly interact with pervasive systems through a single, universal input.

Keywords: pervasive systems, input systems, mice, multiple mice, video control.

1 Introduction

Pervasive computing systems, also referred to as ubiquitous computing environments, are physically bounded spaces of physical and digital devices such as desktop computers, laptops, handheld devices, and sensors. One goal of these systems is to integrate the information space of computers and the physical space of the real world. One such system for pervasive computing is the Gaia meta-operating system[1].

Our research elaborates on one important facet of a truly pervasive system: input. Pervasive computing environments are normally composed of many computers and other devices, each with their own input mechanisms. We have developed a protypical system called Clicky[2]. With Clicky, the user runs two programs, an endpoint and a redirector, on separate computers. The user controls the computer running the redirector. Any events the user initiates on the computer running the redirector are sent to the computer running the endpoint. The endpoint then performs the same action on its computer. This allows the user to remotely control a computer. Additionally, the redirector knows where all the endpoints are spatially, so it can redirect its input from one endpoint to another if moving the mouse would cause it to move off of a display and into another endpoint's region.

We identified two primary focal points to improve input mechanisms for pervasive computing:

R. Meersman, Z. Tari, P. Herrero et al. (Eds.): OTM Workshops 2006, LNCS 4278, pp. 1337–1346, 2006.

1. allowing multiple people each to use input devices to control the desktops of the same computer;
2. expanding the idea of the mouse to control any device in the physical space, not just computers.

These two directions are explained further below.

First, we implemented the mechanism allowing multiple mice on one screen. Multiple users are given their own mouse and window focus on a remote machine, allowing several people to use the same set of desktops and applications without conflicting with each other. This also opens up the possibility of user collaboration on any application.

Most of the support for multiple mice in the past has come in the form of groupware, as in the Pebbles project [4] and Ubit [5]. In both these systems, applications are written using a special API. Multiple users connect to the user running the custom application and acquire control of a mouse specific to that application. The multiple-mice support in Clicky does not require an application to be written specifically for multiple mice. Additionally, the mice are global to the computer, not to the application.

Finally, we expanded the mouse to be able to control any device in the room. Clicky was extended to include a clickable video stream from a webcam. This gives the user a view of the room, from which the user may click on a device and assume control of it. Keyboard and mouse actions are mapped through to the endpoint. The actions depend on the endpoint. For example, a left-click on a lamp may cause it to turn on and off.

The research projects that most resemble this work are Roomote [6] and Pebbles Universal Controller [7]. Both of these programs enable the user to control an arbitrary remote device, similar to Clicky. However, neither project allows the user to click on a device in a room to choose it. Also, both require the creation of complicated GUIs to drive devices, whereas Clicky simplifies it with a common interface.

Delay remains the most significant hindrance to a successful input mechanism. To this end, many of the evaluation experiments conducted measured the delay of various aspects of the system, such as the round-trip time and time required for overhead.

This research was implemented on Windows XP and over an Ethernet connection. However, the code is very portable to other systems. This is because all networking is handled via CORBA calls. Additionally, all data structures and math operations were performed using standard C++ library calls. The only thing platform-specific are commands to direct the mouse and set up windows. Most windowing systems have similar functionality, making it not an issue.

The rest of this paper is organized as follows: Section 2 describes how multiple mice can work in conjunction with each other. Section 3 discusses using a video stream to control arbitrary devices in the room. Finally, section 4 discusses implications for further research and section 5 concludes the paper.

2   Multiple Mice

Initially, we focused on providing a mechanism allowing multiple mice on one desktop. In typical redirection environments such as the original Clicky mentioned in the introduction, the redirection is one mouse to one computer. This, however, has many limitations. A one-mouse desktop means only one user may use that desktop at a time, necessitating user cooperation to ensure that two people do not use the same endpoint at once. Additionally, one of the goals of pervasive computing is to further enable collaboration among people in a common area. Collaboration is hindered if the collaborators are not able to use the same computer at the same time.

The motivating scenario for multiple mice consists of two students in a room collaborating on a paper for a conference. Someone has a suggestion on how to better word a piece of writing, and wants to make the edit without interfering with the other user. Traditional redirection systems will balk at such an input method, as each student would, at best, share control over the main cursor. The new system would give each student their own cursor to control, and the two may edit at will or point out things with their cursor. Another situation might occur where there is one computer with applications on it that multiple people want to use. Normally, only one person at a time could control the computer and therefore the applications on that computer, but with multiple mice, each user may run their application without interfering with the other users.

Clicky overcomes these obstacles by giving each user their own mouse on the desktop. The user moves a virtual mouse when the mouse is in motion. Keyboard events are sent to the last window clicked on. Mouse button events use the real mouse temporarily.

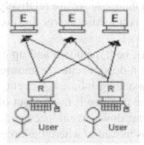

Fig. 1. Typical room configuration

Figure 1 shows a diagram of a typical room configuration. The lines represent the communication between the endpoints and redirectors and also the view that a particular redirector has of the room. A redirector is connected to one endpoint at a time. All communications between endpoint and redirector are performed over CORBA objects, making the solution very portable.

2.1 Design and Implementation

In the course of implementing multiple mice, two design objectives, over and above multiple mice, became apparent: low delay and seamlessness. Low delay refers to the time between an action being performed on the redirector to when it is realized on the endpoint. The goal during this stage of the project was to minimize this delay. Seamlessness refers to the degree of similarity in using single or multiple mice. The aim was to minimize the impact of multiple mice on normal usage.

The endpoints have a list of all redirectors that are currently redirecting to them. When a redirector wants to connect to the endpoint, it first sends the enter message, along with its unique identifier, to the endpoint. The endpoint then creates a mouse object to represent this redirector's input device, and adds it to the list of all redirectors currently redirecting to the system. An image of a mouse, henceforth referred to as a "fake" mouse, is associated with this object.

This mouse object stores data and operations that would normally be associated with a mouse pointer. It holds the x and y locations of the mouse pointer. It knows how to hide the mouse from the screen (normally by moving it to an extreme corner). It knows how to create and destroy the fake mouse associated with the object. It stores the handle of the last window clicked on with this mouse so that it can be brought to the foreground.

The actions performed during a mouse event depend on the nature of the event and the number of mice currently on-screen. If only one mouse is on-screen, the action is performed using the normal mouse. However, the actions performed get more complex when multiple mice are issuing commands, as typical mouse actions such as dragging windows and double-clicking need to be performed atomically so that users do not interfere by initiating an action in the middle of another user's action. This would leave either or both actions in an incomplete state.

The actions performed on a mouse move are relatively simple. If multiple mice are present, and the mouse event is a mouse move, the fake mouse is merely moved in place of the real mouse.

During mouse button events, both the down and up events are stored and executed atomically. On a mouse button-down event, the mouse object stores the location of the mouse. When the corresponding mouse up event is received, this sequence of events takes place: First, the fake mouse is moved out of the way. Second, the actual mouse is moved to where the down event occurred. Third, the down event is executed. Fourth, the mouse is moved to where the up event occurred; the up event is executed. Lastly, the window with the current window focus is set to this mouse object, thus allowing keyboard events to be sent to the proper window. The drawback to this approach is that, if the action was a dragging one, the item dragged is not moved until the end of the whole sequence.

These steps allow the mouse to operate similarly to how it would in a one-mouse scenario. The only differences between using the mouse when there is only one mouse and when there are several mice is that in a multiple-mice scenario, events that require multiple user input must be executed atomically. Therefore, the user might not see feedback for the event until every action to trigger that event has completed. An example of this is the drawback mentioned previously about dragging windows.

Additionally, these steps are all executed as an atomic unit, which prevents users from conflicting with each other. However, this atomicity is handled by an individual endpoint. This prevents mouse actions from spanning endpoints.

On a keyboard event, the window focus currently set for this mouse object is brought to the foreground, and the event is sent to that window.

2.2 Results

The most measurable result from this stage of Clicky is the degree to which multiple mice increase the latency from the creation of the event on the redirector to the realization of the event on the endpoint.

2.2.1 Latency Increase of Mice

Latency is the measured delay from the time an event is generated until the event is delivered. Too much latency results in the system becoming hard or impossible to use. Latency is measured by connecting increasing numbers of redirectors to an endpoint and noting how much this increases the delay.

The following experiment attempts to quantify this delay. We measured this delay by taking the system time immediately before the events are sent to the endpoint and again immediately after the endpoint returns. We simulated multiple redirectors connecting to a single endpoint by having the event hook in the redirector send the same event several times. We incrementally increased the number of times the event hook sent the same event. The variables in this experiment are the number of currently simulated redirectors and the particular event type being sent. Previous research by MacKenzie et al[3] has shown that a latency of greater than 75 milliseconds interferes with a user's accuracy, therefore 75 milliseconds is our target.

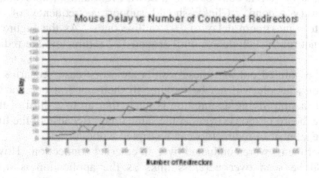

Fig. 2. Graph of Mouse Delay vs. Connected Redirectors

As shown in Figure 2, a clear linear progression of the delay can be seen with respect to the number of redirectors. At around 40 redirectors delays are greater than the target of less than 75 milliseconds. Past this point a user might experience degradation.

Comparing the keyboard delay yields a similar linear graph, as shown in Figure 3. One thing to note, however, is the increased randomness in the keyboard delay when compared to the mouse delay. Furthermore, the keyboard delay is much less than the

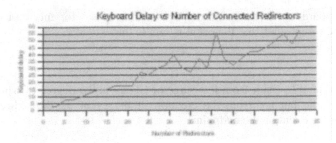

Fig. 3. Graph of Keyboard Delay vs . Connected Redirectors

corresponding mouse delay for a particular number of redirectors. This is likely because keyboard events are sent to an event queue and then the redirector can return it, whereas the mouse events must be executed before returning. This means that the endpoint computer may execute several keyboard commands at once, causing several redirectors to not be tasked in to return and thus be delayed. Because this behavior is relatively random in the operating system, it results in randomness in keyboard delay. This queuing also means that an endpoint can return from sending a keyboard event more quickly, thus resulting in the smaller overall delays.

User typing speeds determine how problematic this delay becomes. As a representative case, consider a paper with 11347 characters spread over 1915 words, giving us average of 5.9 characters per word. A user typing at 50 words per minute yields an average of 295 keystrokes-per-minute - or 4.9 keystrokes-per-second. Because each keystroke is composed of a down-event and an up-event, a user sends 9.8 events every second. Clicky should support a frequency of 9.8Hz, which corresponds to a maximum delay of 102 milliseconds. As the Figure 3 shows, the system does not reach such delays until around 122 redirectors are redirecting to the endpoint.

It should be pointed out that these results are worst-case scenarios. In most real world situations, people will not be moving all their mice at once or typing at the same time. If a simplifying assumption is made that up to a third of the redirectors are doing a keyboard or mouse event at the same time. Because of the linear nature of the graphs the number of redirectors can be tripled without issues.

These experiments were conducted over an ethernet connection. However, similar results should be seen over wireless links as the application is not bandwidth-intensive.

3 Video Control

Clicky's primary function is to bridge the conceptual gap between various display devices in a computationally-based room, which begs the question, why only display devices? Why not expand the idea to encompass any device in the room? The next stage of the research was designed to address this issue. Through the use of a video stream, coupled with applications that know their location in 3-D space, such control becomes possible.

The motivating example for this research is a room full of computer-driven devices, many without an easy-to-reach interface, such as light switches on opposite sides of the room. In such an instance, video control is useful in bridging the spatial gap between the user and the machine. By starting up the program and clicking on the light switch in the video stream, the user may turn the corresponding lamp on and off without getting up. Due to the users' view of the whole room, any other device in the room may be controlled. The mouse and keyboard jump from controlling the virtual environment of the desktop to controlling the real world, effectively making it a "space" mouse.

The contributions of this research are in presenting the user with a simplified interface to a device and allowing the user to click on devices in the room in 3-D space to control them.

3.1 Design and Implementation

In the course of designing video control, our two main goals were to reduce latency and to simplify the interface. Too much delay can make the system difficult to use. The problem is compounded in this stage of the project due to the overhead of grabbing frames from a camera and expensive, but necessary, OpenGL calls.

Interface issues were also of particular concern for this project. The user should just have to point at a device and go, without having to deal with a number of menus or learning a new, possibly complicated, interface for every device. Ideally, each device would have a standard keyboard/mouse interface with which to interact.

3.1.1 Endpoint

The endpoint program runs whatever device the programmer chooses. A user clicks on a device in a video stream associated with a program. All keyboard and mice events are then sent to this program, which drives the device in question. An example of such a situation is the user clicking on a lamp in the video stream to turn it on and off.

The new endpoint was rewritten as a framework. The previous endpoint's keyboard and mouse message functions were stubbed. A programmer creating an endpoint application would then fill out these stubs with appropriate code for the device being controlled. The programmer also must set up a representative bounding box for the device.

3.1.2 Redirector

Video control is performed through a Gaia component called the CameraController [8]. This controller provides a CORBA/IDL interface, allowing the redirector to remotely pan and tilt the camera, along with determining where the camera currently points.

The video window is composed of 3 components: the video feed from the camera, a cross hair that the user can use to point the camera, and a bounding box, if one is being placed. The cross hair is drawn on the video directly, while the bounding box is rendered on top of the video. The crosshair tells the user where the camera is pointing so it can aim the camera properly. It is not possible to allow the user to click on an arbitrary location, as the CameraController does not give the field-of-view of the camera. Without this it is not possible to figure out how many degrees correspond to a pixel.

Associating endpoint applications with devices in the room is performed in the redirector. The user brings up a list of all endpoints running in the room and chooses which one to set up. The redirector then asks the chosen endpoint for a representative bounding box for the object, by asking for the length, width, and height of the box. This triggers the video component to start drawing the bounding box. The user then places the box by rotating it around the camera, moved up and down, and pushed backwards and forwards.

To render the bounding box in the video stream, a quad textured with the video image is first placed in front of the camera at (0,0,0) and aimed at (0,0,-1). The scene is rotated to the angle in the cylinder mentioned above, minus the pan of the camera. This difference gives an offset that the box needs rotated to match where it should be in the video stream, creating the illusion of the box staying in the same location when the camera pans.

Upon pressing a key to set the box, a function is called to write the box's real work coordinates to a repository. To arrive at these coordinates, a rotation-translation matrix is calculated as if the box was going to be rendered on the screen, using the same techniques discussed in the previous paragraph. This matrix is then applied to every point on the bounding box, giving the real-world position of the box. After this is written to the repository, it is then available to any redirector wanting to control the device.

Once an endpoint is set up, the user may then take control of the device by panning and tilting the camera to line up the cross hair with the device. When the camera is aligned as the user wants, a button is pressed, effectively "clicking" on the device. To decide which device was clicked on, a ray is generated from the camera's current position to the position where it is aiming. Collision detection is performed between this ray and every box. If a box intersects, the redirector uses the device name and the Gaia space repository to get the endpoint associated with that device. The video screen is blacked out and any further mouse or keyboard events are sent to the endpoint. Pressing a key brings back the video stream so that the user may select another device.

3.2 Results

Most of the research in this stage of the project runs in constant time and is heavily GPU dependent. Two major exceptions, however, are the effect of the number of boxes in the scene has on the delay in selecting a device, and the delay sending an event to a device after it has been clicked. We devised the following experiment to measure the delay in selecting a device, as shown in Figure 4. The delay was measured by subtracting from the system time when the redirector enters the FindIntersect function from the system time when it exits the FindIntersect function. Only the number of devices can affect delay. Bounding box size has no effect because all boxes are composed of the same number of triangles. There is no target delay as the only effect of an excessive delay is an angry user.

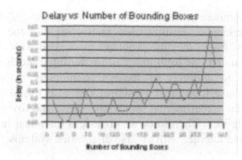

Fig. 4. Graph of the number of bounding boxes effect on delay

As can be seen, there is a general linear trend in the increasing delay. However, it does not climb very fast, enabling Clicky to easily scale to rooms with many devices in it.

The delay to send an event to a clicked on device was measured to be between 0-20 milliseconds. A more accurate measurement was not possible due to the time slice of the operating system. This is no slower than the redirector described in section 3, and therefore should not pose any degradation in system usage. Similarly to the multiple mice scenario, whether the connection is a wireless or Ethernet link should not increase this delay as it is not bandwidth-intensive. However, the associated video stream from the webcam may increase the delay to actually choose a device due to video taking much more bandwidth. The effect can be mitigated by choosing a camera capable of compressing the video stream.

4   Future Work

The goal of Clicky was to break down the input barriers between computers and other devices in the room. It largely succeeded in its goals. At the same time, new issues were raised, which could result in further investigation. A major future direction could involve the expansion of the redirector mechanisms away from a mouse/keyboard/monitor setup.

Generally, although a laptop forms an adequate input and selection mechanism with which to operate the video control, other input devices can be used, and open up interesting usage patterns. One such input device is a cell phone. Many current cell phones are equipped with a built-in camera and an LCD screen. If the cell phone was coupled with a mechanism to tell the redirector its pan and tilt and location in the space, it could function similar to the stationary camera used in section 4. The user could wave the camera around the room, treating it as a window to the world, and press a button to access any endpoints it is aligned with.

5   Conclusion

One of the major issues facing ubiquitous and pervasive computing is dealing with multiple devices in the room, each with its own method of input. We have developed mechanisms to allow mouse movement between computers. Additionally, we have addressed the issues related to multiple users interacting with the same computer. We provide a solution that overcomes the problems associated with obstructed machines. Finally, we have expanded our solution to allow the input mechanism to operate any device in the room in addition to standard computers. Our results are very encouraging, and we have found that a pointing device is useful in a pervasive space. Additionally, from an experimental point of view, the overhead from all our approaches was negligible. Therefore, we provide a universal input mechanism that allows us to control and interact with diverse distributed systems.

References

1. Manuel Roman, Christopher K. Hess, Renato Cerqueira, Anand Ranganathan, Roy H. Campbell, and Klara Nahrstedt, "GaiaOS: A middleware infrastructure to enable Active Spaces," *IEEE Pervasive Computing*, pp. 74-83, Oc-Dec 2002.
2. Andrews, C., Sampemane, G., Weiler, A., Campbell, R.: "Clicky: User-centric input for Active Spaces". UIUC Technical Report: UIUCDCS-R-2004-2469, UILU-ENG-2004-1770.
3. I. Scott MacKenzie and Colin Ware, "Lag as a determinant of human performance in interactive systems," in *Proceedings of the ACM Conference on Human Factors in Computing Systems*, 1993, pp. 488-493.
4. Brad A. Myers, Herb Stiel, and Robert Garguilo, "Collaboration using multiple PDAs connected to a PC," in *Proceedings of the 1998 ACM conference on computer supported cooperative work CSCW*, 1998, pp. 285-294.
5. Edward Tse and Saul Greenberg, "Rapidly prototyping single display groupware through the SDGToolkit," in *Proceedings of the Fifth Australasian User Interface Conference, volume 28 of CRPIT Conferences in Research and Practice in Information Technology Series*, 2004, pp 101-110.
6. Ryuji Wakikawa, Jonathan Trevor, Bill Schilit, and John Boreczky. "Roomotes: Ubiquitous room-based remote control over web phones," in *Proceedings of the SIGCHI conference on Human factors in computing systems*, 2001, pp. 239- 240.
7. Jeffrey Nichols, Brad A. Myers, Michael Higgins, Joe Hughes, Thomas K. Harris, Roni Rosenfeld, and Mathilde Pignol, "Generating remote control interfaces for complex appliances," in *CHI Letters: ACM Symposium on User Interface Software and Technology*, 2002, pp. 161-170.
8. Jeffrey Naisbitt, Jalal Al-Muhtadi, and Roy Campbell, "Active interaction: Live remote interaction through video feeds", UIUC, Urbana, Illinois, Technical Report, UIUCDCS-R-2005-2579, 2005.

A User-Centric Privacy Framework for Pervasive Environments

Susana Alcalde Bagüés[1,2], Andreas Zeidler[1],
Carlos Fernandez Valdivielso[2], and Ignacio R. Matias[2]

[1]Siemens AG, Corporate Technology
Munich, Germany
{susana.alcalde.ext, a.zeidler}@siemens.com
[2]Public University of Navarra
Department of Electrical and Electronic Engineering
Navarra, Spain
{carlos.fernandez, natxo}@unavarra.es

Abstract. One distinctive feature of pervasive computing environments is the common need to gather and process context information about real persons. Unfortunately, this unavoidably affects persons' privacy. Each time someone uses a cellular phone, a credit card, or surfs the web, he leaves a trace that is stored and processed. In a pervasive sensing environment, however, the amount of information collected is much larger than today and also might be used to reconstruct personal information with great accuracy. The question we address in this paper is how to *control* dissemination and flow of personal data across organizational, and personal boundaries, i.e., to potential addressees of privacy relevant information. This paper presents the *User-Centric Privacy Framework* (UCPF). It aims at protecting a user's privacy based on the enforcement of privacy preferences. They are expressed as a set of constraints over some set of context information. To achieve the goal of cross-boundary control, we introduce two novel abstractions, namely *Transformations* and *Foreign Constraints*, in order to extend the possibilities of a user to describe privacy protection criteria beyond the expressiveness usually found today. *Transformations* are understood as any process that the user may define over a specific piece of context. This is a main building block for obfuscating – or even plainly lying about – the context in question. *Foreign Constraints* are an important complementing extension because they allow for modeling conditions defined on external users that are *not* the tracked individual, but may influence disclosure of personal data to third parties. We are confident that these two easy-to-use abstractions together with the general privacy framework presented in this paper constitute a strong contribution to the protection of the personal privacy in pervasive computing environments.

1 Introduction

Pervasive computing involves merging technology into everyday life to such an extent that computer environments will be integrated into people's ongoing needs, practices, values, and goods. Technology becomes invisible and seamlessly interconnected. Users will be provided with services and information in an anywhere, anytime fashion. This

R. Meersman, Z. Tari, P. Herrero et al. (Eds.): OTM Workshops 2006, LNCS 4278, pp. 1347–1356, 2006.
© Springer-Verlag Berlin Heidelberg 2006

vision also entails a pervasive sensing of personal information, often in real time, such as identity, location, and activity (in the following simply called context information). Privacy issues are some of the main concerns about pervasive computing: the vision of Mark Weiser [20] ultimately can fail without explicit control by the individual what data is disclosed when, how, to whom, and under what constraints.

In this paper, we introduce a User-Centric Privacy Framework which aims at protecting a tracked individual's privacy. The respect of privacy preferences is not an easy issue, since they depend on a user's *wishes* which are variable by nature. Privacy preferences commonly are expressed as a set of constraints to control the flow of information from the sender to the recipient. So far, constraints only affect the tracked individual or/and a service's features [13] [10], e.g. time, service, activity, or location constraint. However, often one may wish to express not only constraints on one's own context but also on the context of the recipient or other *external* users, as in the following example: 'Bob wants to reveal his activities to his wife only if they are in the same city'. In this case not only the tracked individual's context has to be considered but also the recipient's context, a situation which cannot be catered for by today's privacy frameworks.

Our framework is based on the use of policies to define and to enforce user's privacy constraints. Another important feature in this approach is the possibility to enrich policies by transforming context information. So far, policy languages cannot be used to express the obligation of transforming data before publishing. Policies are widely classified in the literature [16] [4] [9] as either *authorization* or *obligation* policies. Authorization policies are used in the context of privacy to permit or deny the delivery of a piece of context information (absolute decisions). An obligation policy involves a future promise linked to the fact of disclosing information. There could be many situations in which to fulfill the user's privacy preferences includes the deliberate modification of a piece of context information, e.g., reducing the precision of a tuple of coordinates.

Policy-based privacy frameworks have been implemented in, e.g. [2] [11] [13] [17]. In general, such frameworks define policies in a non-semantically enriched language, which we consider to fall short in many cases. In order to be able to express the richness of the user's privacy preferences, we adopt and extend a semantic policy language, namely the *Rei declarative policy language* [9] [8], applied mainly to facilitate effective agent communication and access control. In order to cater situations in which we have to *transform* data from one data set into another, we introduce *SeT*, a policy language for creating *transformation policies*.

The remainder of this paper is structured as follows: We motivate our approach by introducing a simple application scenario in Section 2. Section 3 discusses relevant related work in some detail, followed by the introduction of our user-centric privacy framework and the complementing SeT policy language in Section 4 and 5, respectively. Finally, Section 6 concludes this paper and indicates the directions of future work.

2   Example Scenario

We want to illustrate the concept of *Foreign Constraints* and *Transformation* in privacy preferences by introducing the following example scenario.

Target	Context	Constraints	Transformation	Service
Ana	Location	- Working time - Authorized personnel	N/N	LBS Center
Ana	Location	- Working time - Unauthorized personnel	Spatial Obfuscation 500 meters	Other LBS
Ana	Location	- Identity anonymous	Identity abstraction in K	Traffic Information
Bob	Activity	- Id = Ana - Same city than Bob	N/N	Current activity

Fig. 1. Scenario Rules

Ana is an employee of a home health-care organization (the HHCO). As all the nurses in that company, Ana allows her employer to track her during working times. The HHCO wants to improve its service by informing the patients of the nurses' estimated time of arrival, a very much appreciated service. Additionally, Ana is subscribed to a traffic information service (TIS), which provides real-time information about the traffic conditions found en-route to the next patient. Also, another location-based service (LBS) is used whenever her car needs to be refilled at the nearest petrol station approved by her company.

On the other hand, privately Ana is used to synchronizing her calendar electronically with her husband Bob. Arguing that knowing about Bob's activity will help her to organize the daily life better, Bob agrees to give Ana additional information about his current activity, e.g, in a meeting, driving, etc, but only when both are in the same city.

Obviously, even in this simple scenario, various privacy issues are tackled. It is important for an organization like the HHCO to respect its customers' wish to keep the actual identity undisclosed to someone other than the HHCO. Therefore, the location of the customer visited by the nurses has to be obfuscated as much as possible. The problem of privacy disclosure occurs when Ana interacts with some *implicitly untrusted* service like the LBS for finding a petrol station. In the case of the TIS, we assume that the HHCO states that the nurse's identity is not revealed, since the location has to be disclosed. Hence, both interactions with an external service imply that the original coordinates are *transformed* into a different data set than the original one. In the first case to decrease the accuracy and in the second case to meet a parameter K in an *anonymity set* within K users. This concept is detailed in Section 3 below.

Summarizing, services that use context information in the above scenario are: the HHCO's LBS, the TIS, an LBS that informs of the nearest petrol station, and the Bob's activity service. The free distribution of the Ana's location and Bob's activity are restricted by a set of constraints as shown in the Figure 1. The delivery of a nurse's location to some external LBS or TIS includes the necessity to transform coordinates. The use of foreign constraints is illustrated in the situation in which Bob decides only to reveal his activities to his wife when both are in the same city, which means considering not only Bob's but also Ana's actual location before delivering any information.

3 Related Work

There are different methods to address privacy protection, mainly: policies, anonymization and obfuscation techniques. None of them achieve the goal of total protection of the user privacy integrity, thought. In order to interact meaningfully with a pervasive environment, it will always be necessary to give up some amount of privacy. The goal is to control how much privacy is disclosed for what reason.

According to [3], a privacy policy is an assertion that a certain amount of information may be released to a defined entity under a certain set of constraints. We classify privacy policies from the point of view of defining *service privacy practices* or *user privacy preferences*.

A well-know approach of privacy policies stems from the World Wide Web Consortium (W3C), which standardizes the *Platform for Privacy Preferences (P3P)* [2]. P3P enables web sites to express their privacy policies and compare them with the user's privacy preferences, which, in turn, can be specified by using *A P3P Preference Exchange Language (APPEL)* [12]. The policies are transferred to the user's browser and then matched to his personal preferences there. However, as stated in [3], P3P has not been tailored to the specific requirements of pervasive applications. *PawS*, a privacy awareness system for ubiquitous computing [11], extends P3P to cover aspects of pervasive applications. In PawS, when a user enters an environment in which services are collecting data, a *privacy beacon* announces privacy policies of each service. A user's *privacy proxy* then checks these policies against the user's privacy preferences. If the policies agree, the services can collect information and users can utilize the services. If the policies do not match, the system notifies the user, who then can choose not to use the service in question or, in some cases, simply physically can leave the area in which the collection of information occurs. Both define privacy practices for services which are not within the scope of this work.

While APPEL [12] provides a good starting point for expressing privacy preferences, it cannot support the richness of expressions necessary for the evaluation of user criteria in real-world application domains. In [13] such requirements are implemented as system components called *validators*. The features of validators are described without defining a concrete implementation language and they need a centralized location provider to enforce them. Another approach is the *Confab system* [7], where a complex data structure is elaborated to represent contextual information, the basic context atom called a *context tuple*, which is equivalent to a web page. Information is captured, stored, and processed on the end-user's computer. This gives end-users a great level of control and choice over what personal information is disclosed but fails in its flexibility in sharing context information.

Anonymization mechanisms technically hide the identity of a tracked user with respect to emitted context data so that she is not identifiable within a set of other tracked subjects, constituting the *anonymity set* [14]. We can distinguish between techniques of data and identifier abstraction. In a data abstraction, anonymity can be accomplished by cloaking data, e.g., by reducing temporal and/or spatial accuracy, so that data of different targets cannot be distinguished. In [6], cloaking is based on the formal model of k-anonymity [18]. For enforcing k-anonymity, a trusted context provider is needed, which has global knowledge about a group of targets. In identifier abstraction, pseudonyms are associated with context data. However, this approach suffers from the obvious problem that pseudonyms can be uncovered by statistical attacks. For this reason, in [1], pseudonyms are dynamically changed into *mix zones* to avoid linking different pseudonyms of a target together. In [5], a formal model for obfuscating location information is given. In contrast to anonymization techniques, which have the objective of hiding targets' identities, the identity is supposed to be known. Instead, position accuracy is reduced as far as application requirements can still be adhered to.

So far Transformations have been only considered by *Geopriv* in the draft proposal for expressing privacy preferences for location information [15]. In this approach transformations are part of authorization policies. The evaluation of the authorization policy is done by the location server which executes the transformation to ensure minimal disclosure of location information.

4 User-Centric Privacy Framework

In this section we present the User-Centric Privacy Framework (UCPF). We propose a user-centric approach to safeguard user privacy preferences. Several publications in the area of privacy protection, such as the well-known P3P [2], are concerned with how to define service-side privacy practices. The user is then limited to checking the service's privacy criteria and either accepting or rejecting the service. Our approach, like the Confab system [7], seeks to give as much control as possible to the tracked user, without assuming that the sensing technology is attached to the user's computing device. A privacy framework should give users explicit control over what data are disclosed when, how, to whom, and under what constraints.

We introduce two novel concepts, *Transformations* and *Foreign Constraints*, to allows users to better specify their privacy preferences. Basically, we define Transformations as any process that the tracked user may define over a specific piece of context information, and Foreign Constraints as the context information of *external* users which must be taken into account before forwarding privacy relevant information. An example is the current location of Ana determining whether information about Bob's activity is delivering to her.

The integration of these features in the UCPF has the following requirements: any transformation on a piece of context information should only be known by the tracked individual. Transformations should be automatically applied when the selected policy is enforced. The UCPF should act as the point of enforcement for Foreign Constraints; this implies that before delivering context information to a third party, Foreign Constraints must be retrieved, evaluated and the enclosed policy has to be enforced by the UCPF. If all constraints are satisfied, the UCPF should also act as the context provisioning proxy.

In order to address the requirements stated above we introduce *Sentry*. Sentry is a major architectural building block within the UCPF. An Sentry instance manages the context disclosure of a tracked entity to third parties. To do so, it gathers and filters collected data about an entity and - based on the set of Foreign Constraints and Transformations - disseminates suitable data to third party services as a context proxy.

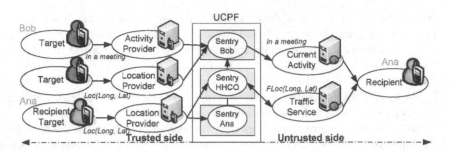

Fig. 2. Dataflow in the UCPF

4.1 Role Model

The data flow along the processing chain in a service that is fed with context information involves different autonomous entities like people, companies or organizations, which we refer to as actors, see [10]. In order to understand how the UCPF works in the processing chain, we distinguish the following roles: *Target* is the tracked individual, in the scenario Ana is the target for the HHCO's LBS and the TIS. Based on Ana's location *service providers* compile locations for users of this services, which are the *recipients* of the information (respectively the HHCO and Ana). An intermediate role is played by the *context provider*. In our guiding scenario this is the mobile provider as the location information provider, who is also responsible for collecting, caching and managing location information of Ana and disseminating it, accordingly.

The actors along the processing chain can be classified as *trusted* or *untrusted*. Trusted parties are those entities that have a contractual and usually legally binding relation governing the exchange of the target's context information, such as between the HHCO and its mobile provider. Untrusted parties, on the other hand, are third parties that are not under the control of the target, like the TIS.

Using policies entails including a policy distribution architecture [21], introducing the following four roles: the *policy repository*, the policy management tool, the *policy decision point* (PDP) and the *policy enforcement point* (PEP). From the point of view of the target's privacy, only trusted parties should act as the PEP, while untrusted parties should only receive context information from the PEP.

The most favorable solution, from the point of view of privacy, is that the context provider adopts the role of the PEP, since we assume that there is a contractual relationship between the HHCO and its location provider; this is also the solution followed in [13], [17]. However, this solution is not applied when a policy has Foreign Constraints to be enforced. For example, in our scenario, Bob's activity is disclosed only when Ana is in the same city. Since Ana's mobile provider, Bob's mobile provider and Bob's activity provider might be three different entities, Bob's activity provider is not able to enforce a policy constrained by the physical position of Bob and Ana. The use of Foreign Constraints poses the problem of introducing a separate entity to act in the role of a trusted PEP. As a solution we leverage our UCPF and introduce a special component called *Sentry*.

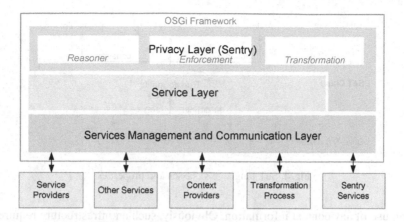

Fig. 3. Architecture Overview

The UCPF is located between trusted and untrusted entities and thus can act as a mediator, see Figure 2. Additionally, the Sentry component is part of the UCPF and acts in the role of a trusted PEP for the tracked target. The Sentry is attached to the target infrastructure. In this environment, context providers forward raw data to the *Sentry* where the data is filtered and/or transformed, see also section 4.2. The Sentry is provided with mechanisms to query and retrieve Foreign Constraints as needed. In our example scenario, Bob is requested to reveal his activity to Ana. In order to decide what to do, Bob's Sentry has to consider the Foreign Constraints regarding Ana. Therefore, it queries Ana's Sentry. This particular instance of a Sentry is registered as the Context Provisioning Service for Ana. Therefore, Bob's Sentry can obtain a reference via the UCPF's service registry. After querying the position of Ana, Bob's Sentry decides on a suitable course of action. In this model, each target has its own Sentry.

4.2 Architecture Overview

Figure 3 shows a sketch of the UCPF architecture. The uppermost layer is the Privacy Layer implementing all the functions of the policy distribution architecture as defined in [21] and additionally incorporating two functionalities: the capability of transforming context information and of being the central point of distribution for context information according to the target's privacy criteria. The *Sentry* is a component integrated into the Privacy Layer responsible for the PDP and the PET roles, cf. Section 4.1, and acts as the context provisioning proxy.

The UCPF architecture also provides the means to publish the Sentry as a service offering a target's context information in a UCPF's service registry. In order to respect the privacy preferences, all third party services (service providers, other sentry services, etc.) are required to retrieve a target's context only from the appropriate Sentry.

One of the key features of our framework is its ability to interact with a wide variety of service types. The UCPF then manages the different entities and mediates between them, accordingly. Entities can be service providers, context providers, transformation services, *Sentry* services (to retrieve Foreign Constraints), as well as other services not

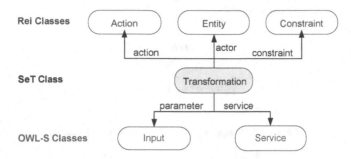

Fig. 4. SeT language's classes and properties

making use of any context information. Obviously, such an infrastructure requires the flexibility to add and remove services dynamically without interrupting the overall operation and the flow of data along the context processing chain. Therefore, a separate layer for the management and remote deployment of services was introduced into the UCPF architecture as already shown in Figure 2.

A first prototype of the UCPF is implemented on the top of the Open Service Gateway Initiative (OSGi) framework. OSGi provides a rich environment for multiple Java-based components to work on a single Java Virtual Machine (JVM). OSGi also adds the ability to manage the life-cycle of the software components from anywhere in the network.

The UCPF provides a secure environment to enforce authorization and transformation policies where the transformations used are only known to the target's Sentry. Moreover, any service can retrieve context information about a certain target whereby the pre-set privacy settings of a target are respected and enforced, automatically.

5   SeT Language / Transformation Policy

The language chosen to define policies in the UCPF is Rei [8]. Rei is a policy specification language in OWL-Lite that allows users to develop declarative policies over domain specific ontologies. Rei is used to describe positive and negative permissions and obligations of entities in the policy domain. In order to define transformation policies the Rei policy language had to be extended; we created the SeT language, therefore, mainly to define transformation policies. Figure 4 illustrates the most important classes and properties of SeT. We use the OWL-S [19] to describe transformations and the corresponding inputs. Accordingly, SeT imports Rei and OWL-S ontologies.

Each transformation available in the UCPF is specified and registered as a service in the OSGi framework. Transformations thus can be seen as services offered by the UCPF. We model transformations as processes with the *process ontology*, one of the three main parts of the OWL-S. The goal is to identify and automatically apply a transformation process whenever a transformation policy is enforced.

In our first prototype the scope of transformations is: spatial obfuscation, identity and data abstraction in K users, and the use of 'White Lies'. White lies involve enforcing transformations to calculate virtual context data which will be delivered instead of the actual context. Each transformation has a different set of inputs that are specified with SeT.

6   Conclusions and Outlook

In this paper, we presented our User-Centric Privacy Framework (UCPF) which aims at protecting a user's privacy based on the enforcement of privacy preferences. They are commonly expressed as a set of constraints over some set of context information. We introduced two novel abstractions, namely *Transformations* and *Foreign Constraints*, and showed how they can be used to extend the expressiveness of privacy policies. Transformations are an important tool for enforcing a certain kind of privacy preferences, like obfuscation and introducing uncertainty. Foreign Constraints on the other hand are a truly novel concept for formulating preferences, which include the actual context of the recipient or other *external* users, over some privacy relevant information.

Both concepts are founded on the generic UCPF framework and the *SeT language* for formulating and subsequent enforcement of privacy preferences. The UCPF provides a secure environment where Transformations will be only known by the user, allowing for the integration of obfuscation, anonymization, and *white lies* in the policy domain. So far, policies cannot be used to express the need for transforming data before accepting and releasing context information to a service. Currently, in parallel to the refinement of the concepts of Transformations and Foreign Constraints, we are working on the further extension of the SeT language.

We designed the UCPF in a way that *Sentry*, as part of the UCPF, can act as a context provisioning proxy for third party services. This way a user's context is accessible by external entities but only under the control of the tracked person's privacy preference.

Part of the ongoing and future work is to complete the implementation of our UCPF prototype, which currently is in an early stage. We are also planning to use the UCPF to present the concept of *white lies* as potential privacy mechanism. White lies involve Transformations which calculate virtual context data, which will be delivered *instead* of the real context data. In future work we plan to analyze the use of static transformations (for the same input, always the same output) and dynamic transformations that may generate different outputs for the same set of inputs, inhibiting the use of reverse-engineering techniques to a large degree. An important issue in further work will be to explore ways to provide policy conflict resolution in a hierarchy of sets of policies within the same and different instances of Sentries.

In summary, we believe that the approaches presented in this paper add significantly to the field of privacy protection of individuals in pervasive computing environments. Obviously, parts of the approaches presented here are work-in-progress and need further investigation, e.g. conflict-free formulation of policies for white lies. However, the foundations of Transformations and Foreign Constraints are sound and together with the generic UCPF build a strong foundation for personal privacy protection.

References

1. A. R. Beresford and F. Stajano. Location privacy in pervasive computing. *IEEE Pervasive Computing*, 2(1):46–55, 2003.
2. L. Cranor, M. Langheinrich, M. Marchiori, and J. Reagle. The platform for privacy preferences 1.0 (P3P1.0) specification. W3C Recommendation, Apr. 2002.

3. J. R. Cuellar. Location information privacy. In B. Sarikaya, editor, *Geographic Location in the Internet*, pages 179–212. Kluwer Academic Publishers, Norwell, MA, 2002.
4. N. Damianou, N. Dulay, E. Lupu, and M. Sloman. Ponder: A language for specifying security and management policies for distributed systems, 2000.
5. M. Duckham and L. Kulik. A formal model of obfuscation and negotiation for location privacy. In *Pervasive*, pages 152–170, 2005.
6. M. Gruteser and D. Grunwald. Anonymous Usage of Location-Based Services Through Spatial and Temporal Cloaking. In *Proceedings of the First International Conference on Mobile Systems, Applications, and Services*, May 2003.
7. J. I. Hong and J. A. Landay. An architecture for privacy-sensitive ubiquitous computing. In *MobiSYS 04: Proceedings of the 2nd international conference on Mobile systems, applications, and services*, pages 177–189. ACM Press, 2004.
8. L. Kagal. Rei ontology specifications, version 2.0. http://ebiquity.umbc.edu/resource/html/id/34/Rei-Specifications, July 2004.
9. L. Kagal, T. Finin, and A. Joshi. A policy language for a pervasive computing environment. In *Proceedings of the 4th International Workshop on Policies for Distributed Systems and Networks*, September 2003.
10. A. Küpper. *Location–based Services — Fundamentals and Operation*. John Wiley & Sons, Aug. 2005.
11. M. Langheinrich. A privacy awareness system for ubiquitous computing environments. In *Proceedings of the 4th International Conference on Ubiquitous Computing*, pages 237–245. LNCS No. 2498, Springer-Verlag, September 2002.
12. M. Langheinrich, L. Cranor, and M. Marchiori. Appel: A P3P Preference Exchange Language. W3C Working Draft, Apr. 2002.
13. G. Myles, A. Friday, and N. Davies. Preserving privacy in environments with location-based applications. *IEEE Pervasive Computing*, 2(1):56–64, 2003.
14. A. Pfitzmann and M. Köhntopp. Anonymity, unobservability, and pseudonymity - A proposal for terminology. In H. Federrath, editor, *Proceedings of the International Workshop on Design Issues in Anonymity and Unobservability, Berkeley, CA, USA*. Springer, 2001.
15. H. Schulzrinne, H. Tschofenig, J. Morris, J. Cuellar, and J. Polk. A document format for expressing privacy preferences for location information. http://www.ietf.org/html.charters/geopriv-charter.html, February 2006.
16. M. Sloman. Policy driven management for distributed systems. *Journal of Network and Systems Management*, 2:333–360, 1994.
17. E. Snekkenes. Concepts for personal location privacy policies. In *EC '01: Proceedings of the 3rd ACM conference on Electronic Commerce, Tampa, Florida, USA*, pages 48–57, New York, NY, USA, October 2001. ACM Press.
18. L. Sweeney. k-Anonymity: a model for protecting privacy. *International Journal on Uncertainty, Fuzziness and Knowledge-based Systems*, 10(5):557–570, 2002.
19. The OWL Services Coalition. OWL-S: Semantic markup for web services. http://www.daml.org/services/owl-s/1.0/owl-s.html, November 2004.
20. M. Weiser. The computer for the twenty-first century. Scientific American, pp. 94-10, September 1991.
21. R. Yavatkar, D. Pendarakis, and R. Guerin. RFC2753 - A framework for policy-based admission control, January 2000.

An XML-Based Security Architecture for Integrating Single Sign-On and Rule-Based Access Control in Mobile and Ubiquitous Web Environments

Jongil Jeong, Dongil Shin, and Dongkyoo Shin[*]

Department of Computer Science and Engineering, Sejong University
98 Kunja-Dong, Kwangjin-Ku, Seoul 143-747, Korea
jijeong@gce.sejong.ac.kr, {dshin, shindk}@sejong.ac.kr

Abstract. Since mobile and Web applications are integrated, the number of services, a typical mobile user can now access, has greatly increased. With a variety of services, a user will be frequently asked to provide his security information to a system. This iterative request is one critical problem which can cause frequent transmission of user's security information. Another serious problem is how an administrator controls access request of internal users who were authenticated. In order to establish effective security scheme for integrated environments, Single Sign-On and access control also need to be integrated. In this paper, we propose an XML-based architecture integrating authentication and access control policy in integrated environment to be extended to ubiquitous environment. To provide flexibility, extensibility, and interoperability between environments to be integrated, we have implemented an architecture based on SAML and XACML, which are standardized specifications. By specifying security policies in XML schema and exchanging security information according to that schema, the proposed architecture offers the opportunities to build standardized schemes for authentication and authorization. Additionally, the proposed architecture makes it possible to establish a fine-grained access control scheme by specifying the XML element unit as a target to be protected.

Keywords: single sign-on, SAML, access control, RBAC, XACML, mobile device.

1 Introduction

Since mobile and Web applications are integrated, the number of services a typical mobile user can now access has greatly increased. As a result, target services that a user wants to access become various. However, the user will be frequently asked to provide his security information to systems which manage target services. In relation to the integration of different environments, another serious problem is how an

---

[*] Correspondence author
This study was supported by a grant of the Korea Health 21 R&D Project, Ministry of Health & Welfare, Republic of Korea. (0412-MI01-0416-0002).

R. Meersman, Z. Tari, P. Herrero et al. (Eds.): OTM Workshops 2006, LNCS 4278, pp. 1357–1366, 2006.

administrator controls access request of internal users who were authenticated. Recently, the Open Web Application Security Project (OWASP) emphasized the importance of these issues by declaring 'Broken Access Control' as one of the top ten most critical Web application security vulnerabilities [1]. The same situation can be extended to ubiquitous service environments that consist of different kinds of personal equipment, wireless sensors, gateways, Web Servers, and services [2].

A key to the problem of the iterative request is to reduce the number of user authentication. Single Sign-On (SSO) can give the key. As a security feature, SSO allows a user to log into many different services offered by the distributed systems while the user needs to authenticate identification only once, and always in the same way [3]. In relation to the problem of a management of internal users' access request, Access control can be the key to solve it. Access control either permits or denies user access requests by checking whether the user has permission to access target resources. Therefore, it is strongly recommended that SSO and access control also need to be integrated for establishing effective security scheme in integrated environments. In this paper, we propose an XML-based architecture integrating authentication and access control policy to suggest actual guidelines for constructing secure Web Systems in a ubiquitous environment. The proposed architecture is based on two standard specifications which are ratified by Organization for Advancement of Structured Information Standards (OASIS) [4]: Security Assertion Markup Language (SAML) [5] and eXtensible Access Control Markup Language (XACML) [6].

This paper is composed of five sections. (Mention Section 1 also) Section 2 includes an overview of single sign-on, SAML, access control, and XACML. In Section 3, we introduce the principle of least privilege and define rules for testing RBAC policy and then express those rules in XACML. In Section 4, we propose architecture for integrating user authentication and access control for mobile and ubiquitous Web Services environments and describe the structure of Java-based SAML and XACML libraries that we have developed. Finally we conclude our discussion in Section 5.

2 Background

For successful integration between different environments, it is necessary to understand technologies in order to solve the complexity of user authentication and the vulnerable access control mechanism mentioned in the previous section. This section introduces single sign-on, access control, and the tendency of standardization for related technologies, such as SAML and XACML.

2.1 Single Sign-On

The basic idea of single sign-on (SSO) is to shift the complexity of the security architecture to the SSO service and release other parts of the system from certain security obligations.

The SSO service acts as the wrapper around the existing security infrastructure that exports various security features like authentication and authorization [7]. To support single sign-on, the system collects all the identification and user credentials at the time of primary sign-on. This information is then used by SSO Services within the primary domain to support the authentication of the user to each of the secondary domains with which the user may interact.

2.2 Role Based Access Control

Role-Based Access Control (RBAC) makes it simple to allocate and remove privileges for large numbers of users. To simplify such management of privileges for large numbers of users, the RBAC scheme is based on the user's roles [8]. These roles reflect organization structure. For instance, a user with a role of employee can access certain resources, and another user with a role of manager can access certain, perhaps very different, resources. The roles have the permission sets, not the users. A role can be created by inheriting one or more attributes from other roles like an object can inherit attributes from multiple objects in object-oriented programming.

2.3 The Tendency of Standardization for Related Technologies

To implement web-based single sign-on and access control by applying RBAC, OASIS has developed technologies related to each concept. At the same time, the organization has propelled the standardization of these technologies.

a. SAML (Security Assertion Markup Language)

SAML enables the exchange of authentication and authorization information about users, devices, or any identifiable entity called subjects. Using a subset of XML, SAML defines the request-response protocol by which systems accept or reject subjects based on assertions [5].

An assertion is a declaration of certain facts about a subject. SAML defines three types of assertions:

- Authentication: indicating that a subject was authenticated previously by some means (such as a password, hardware token, or X.509 public key).
- Authorization decision: indicating that a subject should be granted or denied resource access.
- Attribution: indicating that the subject is associated with attributes.

The existing SSO schemes, such as Kerberos, limit their applicable scope to a single security domain due to the lack of interoperability. SAML opens the possibility that SSO schemes can be passed between other domains via common XML schema.

b. Single Sign-On Browser/artifact Profile

SAML can be bound to multiple communication and transport protocols. It can be linked with Simple Object Access Protocol (SOAP) over HTTP [5]. SAML operates without cookies in a browser/artifact profile. Using browser/artifact, a SAML artifact is carried as part of a URL query string, as shown in Figure 1, where a SAML artifact is a pointer to an assertion.

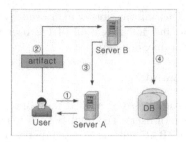

Fig. 1. A Browser/Artifact profile

The steps in Figure 1 are explained as follows.

(1) User of an authenticated browser on Server A requests access to a database on Server B. Server A generates a URL redirect, which contains a SAML artifact, to Server B.

(2) Browser redirects user to Server B, which receives an artifact pointing to the assertion on Server A.

(3) Server B sends artifact to Server A and gets a full assertion.

(4) Server B checks the assertion and either validates or rejects the user's request for access to the database.

c. XACML (eXtensible Access Control Markup Language)

XACML is used in conjunction with SAML and supplements lacking access control policy in SAML. XACML can specify various targets, such as resource, an entire document, a partial document, or multiple documents. It can even specify an XML element as the target to be protected. This aspect makes it possible to implement fine-grained access control. The sequence of data-flow for SAML and XACML is as follows: If Web Services receives a SAML assertion once, sends it to SAML PDP (Policy Decision Point); then the PDP requests XACML PRP (Policy Retrieval Point) to check XACML policies. This route shows the decision making to determine if access request should be granted to certain resources, based on rule sets or policies defined by the provider. Once the policy is evaluated and then returns the true or false, an SAML authorization decision assertion is made by SAML PDP and then returns it to SAML PEP (Policy Enforcement Point). Finally, SAML PEP grants or denies the access request according to the authorization decision assertion [5], [6].

3   The Principle of Least Privilege and the Expression of the Principle Using XACML

One of the most important ways to secure resources is to minimize privileges [8]. A privilege is simply a permission to do something that not everyone is allowed to do. The principle of least privilege means that a user cannot have any privilege except the privileges that he or she can perform [9]. Through RBAC, enforced minimum privileges for general system users can be easily achieved. To minimize privileges, it is necessary to do the following [9]:

- Identify user functions.
- Determine the minimum set of privileges required to perform the specific function.
- Restrict the user to a domain having relevant privileges.

XACML provides an XML-based RBAC profile for expression of authorization policies to build them into Web applications. We propose a practical model for transcribing the RBAC profile into XACML using some examples. The *Order.xml* file consists of three elements. *PaymentInfo* is an element including settlement information. *Items* is an element including information for goods that a user wants to buy. *CustomerInfo* is an element including information for the transaction owner. By describing RBAC in XACML, we can focus on an access control unit in each element within a file. Thanks to it, we can achieve the fine-grained access control we want.

```
<?xml version="1.0" encoding="UTF-8"?>
<Order No="3039484" xmlns="http://www.sjcredit.com/schemas/order.xsd"
    xmlns:xsi="http://www.w3.org/2001/XMLSchema-instance">
  <PaymentInfo>
    <CreditCard Limit='500,000' Currency='WON'>
      <Number>4000 2234 0222 5533</Number>
      <Issuer>Bank of the December</Issuer>
      <Expiration>05/09</Expiration>
      <Password>3098</Password>
    </CreditCard>
  </PaymentInfo>
  <Items>
    <Item No='uy-098-oci0021'>
      <Unit>3</Unit>
      <Price Currency="WON">30,000</price>
      <Destination>Kunja-dong 505, Kwangjin-gu, Seoul, Korea</Destination>
    </Item>
  </Items>
  <CustomerInfo>
    <Name>Jeong J</Name>
    <Email>jijeong@gce.sejong.ac.kr</Email>
    <Address>Kunja-dong 505, Kwangjin-gu, Seoul, Korea</Address>
  </CustomerInfo>
</Order>
```

Fig. 2. Order.xml

The following are rules for access control against the *Order.xml* file.

- Rule 1: A person, identified by his credit card number and password may read any record for which he is the designated customer.
- Rule 2: An administrator shall not be permitted to read or write to the *PaymentInfo* element of the Order element.

The above rules will reflect the goal that a least privilege policy is pursuing. In a document including a transaction particular to a customer, the *PaymentInfo* element must be opened only to the transaction owner because it holds crucial information, such as a credit card number and password. Rule 2 is a rule that makes an administrator unable to 'read' and 'write' the *PaymentInfo* element except with his own permission.

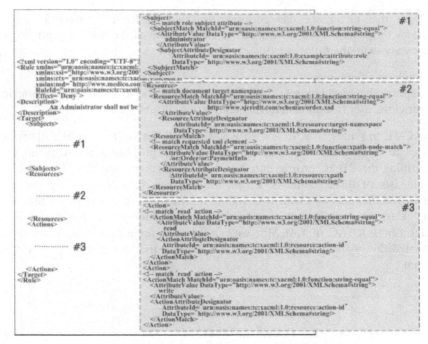

Fig. 3. Description of Rule 2 using XACML

Fig. 4. A rule restricting a user specific domain having relevant privileges

Figure 4 is a rule to meet the third requirement of least privilege. Rule 2 allows all users who have e-mail address ending with "sjcredit.com" to make out the *Items* element of *Order.xml*. Rule 1 is specifying that the user's e-mail address should correspond with the rfc822Name offered by the Rule. Rule 2 is specifying a resource that the relevant user can access. The subject has to be able to perform an 'action' for only the *Items* element of those elements corresponding with the target namespace within *Order.xml*.

4 Architecture for Integrating User Authentication and Access Control for Mobile and Ubiquitous Web Services Environments

In the transfer of the user's authentication information from a mobile environment to the authentication server of the wired service environment, the following considerations need to be taken into account [10]:

- The equipment, which can translate into an appropriate protocol to transfer the user's authentication information between mobile and wired service networks.
- Confidentiality and integrity, which should be guaranteed during the transfer of the user's authentication information.
- The framework aiming for a single sign-on implementation that transfers the user's authentication information should handle the user authentication mechanism defined in each domain.

One of the examples of a widely used framework, which connects mobile and wired service networks, is OMA's WAP (Wireless Application Protocol) gateway, also known as the WAP proxy [11]. The WAP gateway connects the mobile domain and the wired Internet and acts as a protocol gateway to encode and decode content.

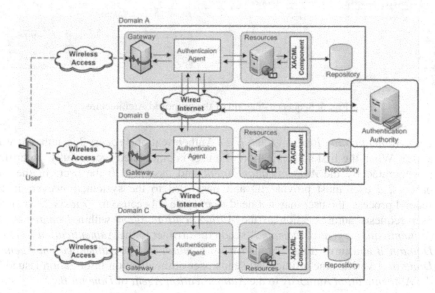

Fig. 5. Architecture for integrating user authentication and role-based access control

We propose an integrated architecture in which a mobile user offers his credential information to the wired service network to obtain user authentication and authorization and then access to another domain using this authentication and authorization, based on the SAML and XACML standard. Figure 5 shows the concept of this architecture. Each box in the diagram denotes an entity involved in the process. Figure 6 explains the messages between entities, applying a user's single sign-on and access control in three domains in which there is a mutual trust relationship.

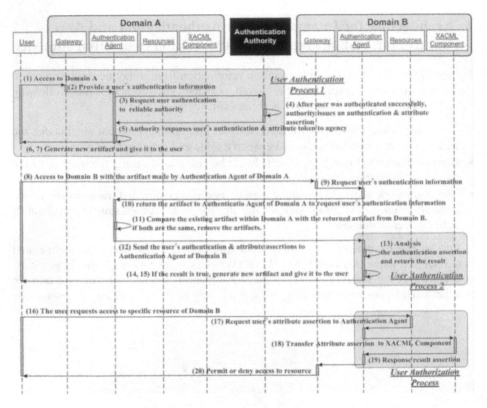

Fig. 6. Sequence diagram of the proposed Architecture

- *User Authentication Process 1* and *User* Authentication *Process 2* is authenticating a user. When the first authentication of a user is completed successfully, an artifact is generated by the *Authentication Agent* and assigned to the user. In the first process, a user must provide ID and password to the system; however, in the second process, the user may not need to provide it because in *Process 2*, when the user requests authentication to the *Authentication Agent* within *Domain B*, the *Authentication agent* of *Domain A* sends the artifact to the *Authentication Agent* of *Domain B* and turns it back around from *Domain B*. The *Authentication Agent* of *Domain A* verifies the artifact and sends user authentication information issued by the *Authentication Authority* to the *Authentication Agent* of *Domain B*.

- The *User Authorization Process* checks whether a user has permission to access specific resources. The *XACML Component* requests the user's attribute information for the *Authentication Agent* and further analysis. Then, the *XACML Component* determines whether the user's access request is permitted or denied.

```
<saml:Assertion AssertionID="00cda300-0d5de-8521-83c5-c2d9f6847b91"
    IssueInstant="2004-08-02T13:33:02Z" Issuer="gce.sejong.ac.kr"
    MajorVersion="1" MinorVersion="0">
    <saml:Conditions NotBefore="2004-08-02T13:33:02Z" NotOnOrAfter="2004-08-02T13:38:02Z"/>
        <saml:AuthenticationStatement AuthenticationMethod="password"
                                      AuthenticationInstant="2004-08-02T13:33:02Z">
            <saml:Subject>
                <saml:NameIdentifier NameQualifier="gce.sejong.ac.kr">jijeong</saml:NameIdentifier>
            </saml:Subject>
        </saml:AuthenticationStatement>
        <saml:AttributeStatement>
            <saml:Subject>
                <saml:NameIdentifier SecurityDomain="gce.sejong.ac.kr" Name="samler"/>
            </saml:Subject>
            <saml:Attribute AttributeName="jobattribute"
                            AttributeNamespace="http://www.sjcredit.com/schema/order.xsd">
                <saml:AttributeValue>
                    <Customer>
                        <company>sjcredit</company>
                        <email>uuu7@sjcredit.com</email>
                    </Customer>
                </saml:AttributeValue>
            </saml:Attribute>
        </saml:AttributeStatement>
</saml:Assertion>
```

Fig. 7. Assertion with Authentication and Attribute Statement

```
<saml:Assertion AssertionID="00cda300-0d5de-8521-83c5-c2d9f6847b91"
    IssueInstant="2004-08-02T13:33:02Z" Issuer="gce.sejong.ac.kr"
    MajorVersion="1" MinorVersion="0">
    <saml:Conditions NotBefore="2004-08-02T13:33:02Z" NotOnOrAfter="2004-08-02T13:38:02Z"/>
    <saml:AuthenticationStatement >
        .....................
    </saml:AuthenticationStatement>
    <saml:AttributeStatement>
        .....................
    </saml:AttributeStatement>
    <saml:AuthorizationDecisionStatement Decision="Permit" Resource="http://www.sjcredit.com/order.jsp">
        <saml:actions/>
        <saml:Subject>
            <saml:NameIdentifier SecurityDomain="www.sjcredit.com" Name="samler"/>
        </saml:Subject>
    </saml:AuthorizationDecisionStatement>
</saml:Assertion>
```

Fig. 8. Assertion with Authentication, Attribute, and Authorization Decision Statement

Figure 7 is an assertion statement issued by the *SAML Authority* (refers to Step (4) of Figure 6). Figure 8 is an assertion statement issued by the *XACML Component* (refers to Step (19) of Figure 6). These messages were verified by a simulation where two domains were constructed with a mutual trust relationship and the SAML and XACML libraries, which were built from previous work [10].

5 Conclusion

There have been a number of research studies on secure integration of authentication and authorization between distributed systems; however, such integrated models limited their applicable scope to a single security domain because the research projects could not have the interoperability for exchanging security information with other security domains. To provide flexibility, extensibility, and interoperability between environments to be integrated, we have implemented an architecture based on SAML and XACML, which are standardized specifications. By specifying security policies in XML schema and exchanging security information according to that schema, the proposed architecture offers the opportunities to build standardized schemes for authentication and authorization. Additionally, the proposed architecture makes it possible to establish a fine-grained access control scheme by specifying the XML element unit as a target to be protected.

In our future research, we will analyze security threats that can occur in the proposed architecture, and prepare countermeasures against them.

References

1. OWASP (Open Web Application Security Project): http://www.owasp.org/document/topten.html
2. He Q, Khosla P, Su Z.: A Practical Study on Security of Agent-Based Ubiquitous Computing, in Proc. AAMAS'02 Deception, Fraud, and Trust in Agent Societies workshop, 2002.
3. Parker, T.A.: Single sign-on systems-the technologies and the products, European Convention on Security and Detection, 16-18 May (1995) 151-155
4. http://www.open-oasis.org
5. Bindings and Profiles for the OASIS Security Assertion Markup Language (SAML) V1.1: http://www.oasis-open.org/committees/security/
6. eXtensible Access Control Markup Language (XACML) Version 1.0: http://www.oasis-open.org/committees/xacml/repository/
7. Pfitzmann, B., Waidner, B.: Token-based web Single Signon with Enabled Clients, IBM Research Report RZ 3458 (#93844), November (2002)
8. Barkley J, Cincotta A, Ferraiolo D, Gavrila S, and Kuhn R.: Role based access for the world wide web, In National Information Systems Security Conference, October 1997
9. http://csrc.nist.gov/rbac/NIST-ITL-RBAC-bulletin.html
10. Ferraiolo D, Barkley J, and Kuhn R.: A Role Based Access Control Model and Reference Implementation within a Corporate Intranet, ACM Transactions on Information Systems Security, Volume 1, Number 2, 1999
11. Jeong J, Shin D, Shin D, Oh H.: A Study on XML-based Single Sign-On System Supporting Mobile and Ubiquitous Service Environments, Lecture Notes in Computer Science 3207, (2004).
12. WAPWhite_Paper1.pdf: http://www.wapforum.org/what/WAPWhite_Paper1.pdf

Architecture Framework for Device Single Sign On in Personal Area Networks

Appadodharana Chandershekarapuram, Dimitrios Vogiatzis, Spyridon Vassilaras, and Gregory S. Yovanof

Athens Information Technology
{acha, dvog, svas, gyov}@ait.edu.gr

Abstract. This paper addresses the Single Sign On (SSO) issue in personal Area Networks (PANs) comprising of heterogeneous handheld devices. Architectures for service SSO solutions at the enterprise level are already in the market and some standards for such solutions exist. In this paper however we introduce the notion of device level SSO. By device SSO, we refer to the process of logging on to one device and then subsequently being authorized for other devices on a need only basis, without the user being prompted for his credentials or requiring any further manual interaction. Device SSO secures the authentication process in a PAN and alleviates the users from the burden of handling and managing the credentials of each device in the PAN. While borrowing elements from the enterprise level SSO standards, our architecture has been custom-tailored to the characteristics and inherent features of a PAN environment. Client server and peer-to-peer SSO schemes have been designed to fit both PAN star and mesh architectures. The proposed scheme is an application layer solution that is independent of the device platform and the underlying radio link. A sample prototype application has been developed as a proof of concept that runs on laptops and PDAs communicating over Bluetooth links.

1 Introduction

A Mobile Ad-hoc Network (MANET) consists of set of mobile nodes which form peer to peer connections in an automatic and distributed way when they come in close proximity to each other. MANETs do not demand an infrastructure or centralized controller for maintaining the network. In such a case the mobile nodes themselves can act as forwarding devices to establish communication between other nodes in the network. Over the years, a lot of research and development has been going on in this field. One of the major issues in the case of MANETs is the secure authentication of nodes entering the network. This is the first and necessary step that guarantees the identity of the user and provides for secure communications between the nodes.

A Personal Area Network (PAN) can be considered as a special type of MANET, formed by a set of mobile devices in close proximity that typically belong to a single person. Due to this reason, PANs are usually of limited size. The network itself is heterogeneous in nature, in the sense that it is composed of different devices, ranging from cell phones and PDAs to laptop and desktop PCs. Due to its nature, a PAN can

R. Meersman, Z. Tari, P. Herrero et al. (Eds.): OTM Workshops 2006, LNCS 4278, pp. 1367–1379, 2006.
© Springer-Verlag Berlin Heidelberg 2006

be used as a tool for synchronization of personal information among various devices, as well as data sharing and lightweight personal service provisioning.

As in the case of MANETs, the wire free aspect of a PAN poses difficulties in the authentication of the nodes. However, the fact that most of the time a PAN belongs to the same entity/user introduces an additional level of difficulty with respect to the network's security, set-up and maintenance. The owner of the PAN is required to maintain a different sets of credentials for each device in the PAN in order to decrease the possibility that an unauthorized user accesses multiple devices, once he compromises a single password. However, it is obvious that this leads to increased complexity and overhead in terms of network maintenance, since it involves the storage or memorizing of multiple passwords. It would be more efficient for the user to maintain a different set of credentials for each of the devices and then use one device to be responsible for the identification and authentication of the other devices that are in its close proximity. This scheme is known as Single Sign On (SSO).

A PAN SSO scheme has to take into account the network architecture of the PAN. PAN architectures usually follow either the client-server/star model or the peer-to-peer/mesh model. In the first case the authentication and communication between the nodes has to go through a primary device, called 'server'. In the latter case, every device can authenticate any other device that is signing in the network. We propose SSO solutions for both types of architectures. For the client-server model, the SSO scheme is based on a variation of the Kerberos authentication protocol, whereas for the peer-to-peer model, we base our solution on a variation of the Bluetooth authentication protocol. Apart from that, as it was mentioned earlier, a PAN consists of a set of devices which are heterogeneous both in hardware and software. Small personal handheld devices, having limited computing power, little or no memory at all and limited battery life, impose several power constraints and memory limitations to a PAN network, which are taken into account and dealt with properly within the proposed SSO scheme.

The rest of the paper is organized as follows: In Section 2 a brief overview of the problem is provided, along with the description of related work on the subject. Section 3 summarizes the operation of the Kerberos authentication protocol. In section 4 we present the proposed SSO scheme for a PAN, both for the client server and the peer-to-peer model. Section 5 describes our custom application and section 6 concludes the paper.

2 Single Sign On in PANs

Currently, the Single Sign On problem has been extensively studied and analyzed in the context of multiple users signing in different services across the Internet [1]. A user/employee in a big Enterprise or a user of the Internet while roaming between a great variety of offered services, always faces the problem of maintaining multiple identities and passwords for those identities. This is often problematic for both the service provider (SP) and the client availing the service, in the sense that the client is often inclined to use the same set of credentials over different services. Consequently such an event increases the threat of theft of sensitive information once the profile for one of the services is compromised. In case the user chooses to maintain a different password and identity for each service, the process of doing so is very cumbersome and should be done meticulously. Also, in the latter approach there is a higher chance that a user could forget his password and at times even his username. The SP therefore has to have a mechanism to provide a solution for this impasse. The usual solution is to provide a 'password reset' mechanism based on some predefined secret (e.g. answer to a predefined question) that the user and the SP have agreed upon at the time of user registration.

With the advance of short range wireless communications, the emergence of short range protocols, such as Bluetooth, ZigBee, UWB, etc. and the development of many new, innovative personal devices, Personal Area Networks are increasingly deployed for short range transactions and applications. In such networks it is evident that a different aspect of the Single Sign On problem emerges, which has to do with the "registration" and management of so many devices (most often owned by the same user) in a single network. In the common case, the owner of the PAN has to provide the login and password for each new device that requires to enter the network. However, such a solution increases the complexity and the overhead imposed, since the user has to memorize the passwords for each network device. At the other extreme, having a single password for all the devices, leads to increased probability of network compromise by the time the password is revealed once. Ideally, what we would like is that this login procedure is followed once at a single device and then all the other devices sign in the network in a transparent to the user way. The signing-in process could be initiated upon switching a device on and/or when it comes into the proximity of another device that has already signed in the PAN. The device that is chosen to lead this procedure, could be either the first device that logs in the network or the most powerful device in terms of power (or other resources) that is currently logged in the network. Alternatively, any other predefined and properly selected rule could be followed as well.

Therefore, generalizing and slightly modifying the definition given in [2] with respect to service SSO, we could say that the device Single Sign On problem refers to the process of logging on to one device and then consequently being authorized for other devices on a need only basis, without the user being prompted for his credentials or requiring any further manual interaction.

With respect to the service SSO, there are various SSO solutions available in the market that provide SSO services in different ways. Some of them are open standards while some are proprietary in nature. Some SSO solution schemes have been also implemented in hardware as well. The most known among them are the Kerberos protocol [14], the Liberty Alliance and SAML [4], the Microsoft .NET Passport [5], the SSO scheme using GSM/UMTS [6] and the SSO scheme proposed by the TCPA [7].

Although there certainly exist some common aspects between the service and device SSO instances, there are also some important differences that dictate the study and analysis of the PAN SSO on a separate basis. Some of these differences are presented below:

1. Existing service SSO solutions do not address the device SSO problem. They are basically designed to provide SSO across multiple services or applications as opposed to authenticating devices themselves. TCPA and the GSM/UMTS based SSO schemes could be used for device authentication as well, but still the primary

objective is to provide web service authentication. In this work, we propose a SSO scheme to authenticate the device itself.

2. Existing service SSO schemes aim at providing SSO for huge business organizations or web applications. This means that they demand the infrastructural resources that exist in such organizations. On the other hand a PAN SSO scheme should make use of primitives that just reside within the devices themselves.

3. Service SSO schemes assume that a PKI is in place. Since the services are provided by a trusted entity that is well known, it is reasonable to have a Public Key Infrastructure for its security infrastructure, which facilitates identity management as opposed to symmetric key primitives. However this is not the case for a PAN, where the lack of PKI forces the devices to rely entirely on their own resources to carry out the duty of logging in.

4. The service SSO solutions do not aim to provide mobility for the user or the verifier. In the case of a PAN SSO scheme though, the solution should also afford for a small amount of device mobility as well.

5. The models for Enterprise SSO are mostly based on the Client Server model. This is not directly applicable though in a PAN environment, which is mostly ad hoc based and the peer-to-peer model is intuitively more suitable for PANs.

6. Power management is not an issue for service SSO schemes. PANs though are made up of personal devices that impose severe power constraints due to their limited power budget. Thus, the design of a power aware device SSO scheme is of paramount importance for the case of PANs.

As we mentioned earlier, Liberty and SAML are working on the Single Sign On issue to make it available to the market for easy development of Single Sign On solutions. In addition, Shibboleth [8] is an internet2 initiative to provide federated identity management using the OpenSAML specifications. However, these are related to Single Sign On in a broader perspective, focusing mainly on web services or enterprise solutions. In [9] Jeong et al. propose a single sign-on scheme in which a mobile user offers his credential information to the home network to obtain user authentication and access to another domain based on the SAML standard. This approach resembles our approach in the way that it provides Single Sign On for a mobile environment with small devices. In [10] the authors discuss a distributed service for network authentication, allowing application servers to delegate client identity checking to combinations of authentication servers potentially residing in separate administrative domains. However, both [9] and [10] deal with the issue of providing SSO services for inter domain access and authentication and not for device sign on itself. The authors in [11] describe a scheme that enables two wireless devices to securely authenticate one another and agree on a shared data string. However this solution involves the manual interaction between the devices, which most of the time is not desirable and opposed to the single sign on concept and objectives.

3 Kerberos

Since the solution that we propose for the PAN SSO problem is partially based on the Kerberos protocol, in this section we provide a brief description of the Kerberos authentication protocol.

Kerberos is basically a Trusted Third Party Authentication Protocol. Kerberos is a distributed authentication service that allows a process (client) running on behalf of a principal (user) to prove its identity to a verifier (server) without sending data across the network that might allow an attacker or the verifier to subsequently impersonate the principal. RFC 1510 specifies the Kerberos 5 mechanism [14]. The basic working of Kerberos is outlined in Fig. 1.

Kerberos authentication System consists of four entities: A server s, a client c, a Key Distribution Service (KDC) and a Ticket Granting Service (TGS). The KDC and the TGS entities act as the SSO component. The KDC is the authority that issues tickets to the client and the server. Specifically, the KDC issues a Ticket Granting Ticket (TGT) to the client. The client having the TGT, requests a ticket from the Ticket Granting Server (TGS). The TGS sends back a ticket to the client containing the secret key that the client and the server are going to use for the session. The client then passes this key to the server securely. Once they both have a copy of the secret key they can start communication.

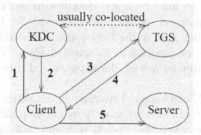

Fig. 1. Kerberos Setup

The first time a user comes in, he logs into the SSO component to get a TGT from the KDC server. The client retains this ticket till its validity expires. For each new service from a new server that the client demands, the protocol automatically uses the TGT that it has already acquired from the KDC, and asks for a ticket for the new service. The fact that the client side does not have always to authenticate for each new service makes this system a service SSO scheme. In case the validity period of the TGT has expired, the client has to re-authenticate to the KDC and get a new TGT.

However, in the context of device SSO provisioning within a PAN, the set up of the Kerberos system and the message exchange need to be tailored appropriately.

4 PAN SSO Architecture

As mentioned previously this paper addresses the problem of a user having to maintain a multiple set of passwords and log on to his set of devices in the case of a PAN. Fig. 2 gives an overview of the scenario.

The devices Dev_1, Dev_2 and Dev_3 belong to a single person. Let's assume that Dev_1 is the one that is currently logged in by the user. This means that the device is turned on, authenticated and is authorized for a specific user to use it. The challenge is to automatically log in to all the other devices that this user owns using the already logged in device. Let's suppose that a second device Dev_2 is within range of the device Dev_1. To successfully log on to Dev_2, it must be turned on and in the transmission range of Dev_1. Assuming this is the case, Dev_1 detects Dev_2, and logs into Dev_2 using the user name and password of the particular user for Dev_2. The whole mechanism of logging in should be secure enough and therefore proper security handshakes must be used. The same should happen with a third device Dev_3, in which case either Dev_1 or Dev_2 should be able to sign the new device in the PAN. After successful login each device would also maintain connection with the others so that they communicate securely on top of just being remotely logged in. This mechanism, though easy to visualize, is difficult to achieve.

The SSO model for a PAN should take into account issues such as who should be the initiator of the sign-in process, who should be the decision maker in the network, etc. It should also provide a properly designed middleware to abstract the heterogeneity of the underlying radio technology, so that the proposed scheme could work equally well and efficiently either with Bluetooth or ZigBee or any other short range wireless technology.

Since the devices range from high end desktops to mobile phones that are very limited in their computational power, the proposed SSO scheme uses security primitives that are portable even to the least capable device in the network. For this reason, symmetric key cryptography is selected. We further assume that the symmetric keys are distributed among the network and trust between the devices is established a priori.

The Sign On in a PAN can happen between devices which are only one hop away. This means that a device can sign on to only its one-hop neighbors. In case of Sign On for multi hop neighbors we have to deal with authentication, trusting and routing issues. We are not concerned with such a scenario here.

Since the SSO scheme is going to be deployed over a specific PAN architecture, it is essential that the designed SSO scheme adheres to the specific features of the architecture of the PAN network. For this purpose we propose two different PAN SSO schemes, namely the client server PAN SSO and the peer-to-peer (P2P) PAN SSO. The Client Server based model is usually designed for an environment where the user is logged into his Laptop or Desktop (typically at home or office). On the other hand, the Peer-to-Peer model is mostly valid for more dynamic environments where the user is on transit or highly mobile compared to a home environment.

4.1 The Client Server PAN SSO

The Client Server model is a very common model for PAN architectures. An illustration of the client server model is shown in Fig. 3.

In this case the server is the device in which the primary user login takes place and afterwards any other device in the network is authenticated and logged in by the server. Consider for example the case where a user uses his set of personal devices in his home or office. In this scenario, the device that is the most frequently used (in the sense that it is turned on and logged in most of the times) assumes the role of the server. Typically, such a device could be the desktop or the laptop of the owner of the PAN. Let's assume now that a new device (C_1 or C_2 as in Fig. 3), which is in the

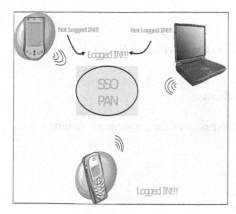

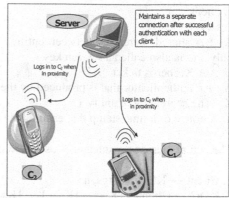

Fig. 2. Device SSO in a PAN   **Fig. 3.** Client Server SSO in a PAN

vicinity of the 'server' device that is already turned on, needs to be logged in. An example would be the user entering into his office (where his 'server' is already logged in) with his PDA, which is not turned on/logged on yet. At this point of time, what normally happens is that the user is prompted with a login screen in the server and/or client side to provide the appropriate logins and password for device mutual authentication. According to the device SSO scheme though, this communication between the server and the client device should happen in a transparent way.

For this purpose we propose an SSO scheme based on a service application that runs both at the server and at the client side as daemon application. While at the server side the service starts up after invocation by the server, on the client side it runs as part of the device boot up process. Upon discovery of the client device, the server performs a security handshake with the client to assure mutual authentication of the device. Once the mutual authentication part is carried out successfully, the server initiates the log on into the client device on behalf of the user. The client device is now formally logged in and part of the PAN. Authentication is thus established. Once signed on, the devices can communicate between each other securely, since mutual authentication is already done and a session key is established at the end of mutual authentication.

The crucial issue that the SSO scheme has to take care of, is to guarantee that the mutual authentication is performed in a way that is both secure and takes also into account the limitations posed by the personal devices and the client-server model.

For the security framework of the client server model we propose a Kerberos based SSO scheme. Assuming that the server has better and wealthier resources in terms of energy and computing power as compared to the clients in the network, we choose to put the burden of the authentication mechanism on the server side. For the authentication process we use the Kerberos protocol, which is hosted and executed by the server device. The SSO component consists of both the KDC and the TGS, running on the server machine. This can be in the form of two separate services running on the same system.

In the following we briefly outline the Kerberos based PAN SSO scheme for the client server model. Before that, a short description of the conventions is provided.

c: client
s: server
$K_{x,y}$: A shared secret key between entities x and y. It is normally used for a session only and is also called a session key
$T_{x,y}$: A Kerberos ticket
A_c: An authenticator that is produced by the client
K_x: The secret key of entity x
n: A nonce or a time stamp that ensures the freshness of the message transmitted.

The actual messages exchange is as follows:

1. Client $\rightarrow$ KDC: <c, tgs, n>
2. KDC $\rightarrow$ Client: <$\{K_{c,tgs}, n\}K_c$, $\{T_{c,tgs}\}K_{tgs}$>
3. Client $\rightarrow$ TGS: <$\{A_c\}K_{c,tgs}$, $\{T_{c,tgs}\}K_{tgs}$, s, n>
4. TGS $\rightarrow$ Client: <$\{K_{c,s}, n\}K_{c,tgs}$, $\{T_{c,s}\}K_s$>
5. Client $\rightarrow$ Server: <$\{A_c\}K_{c,s}$, $\{T_{c,s}\}K_s$>
where $\{\bullet\}K$ stands for the message $\bullet$ encrypted by the key K and
$T_{c,tgs} = $ <TGS, $\{c, v, K_{c,tgs}\}$> where v is the validity period of the ticket.

Initially the client communicates with the KDC service of the server to obtain a TGT. Along with the TGT, the KDC sends also the key that the client will use for the communication with the TGS. This key is sent to the client encrypted using the client's secret key. Note that the client has his secret key generated from a password that the client provides to the KDC only the first time after the validity period expires. The storage of the password, the generation of the client's secret key both at the client and the KDC side and the adjustment of the validity period, are all issues that our application takes care of. After the reception of message 2, the client has the decrypted key $K_{c,tgs}$. This key is then used to encrypt the Authenticator A_c. The Authenticator is of the form $A_{c,s}=\{c, t, key\}K_{c,s}$. Once the TGS confirms the authenticity of the request it issues to the client the actual ticket that the client could use to start communication with the server. The client then provides to the server an authenticator encrypted with the session key $K_{c,s}$ provided by the TGS along with the ticket. The server can authenticate the client by checking the Authenticator. If successful, the client can join the PAN.

The basic difference of the proposed Kerberos based SSO scheme with the initial Kerberos protocol is that the device SSO scheme does not require the existence of any PKI infrastructure. On the contrary, since the devices in a PAN most of the times belong to the same user, it is reasonable to assume that the role of the trusted third party authority can be undertaken by a device within the PAN, namely the server device. Even in the case that not all of the PAN devices belong to the same entity, it is also reasonable to consider that there is a fair amount of trust between the participating devices, since the corresponding users consent to join their personal devices to form a PAN. Both the KDC and the TGS components reside in the server and can operate as daemon services in the background of the machine.

Another advantage of the Kerberos based SSO scheme is that the synchronization requirement that is necessary in the Kerberos protocol can be better fulfilled in the context of a PAN, since personal devices within a PAN can be better and easier synchronized through the server device.

Additionally, the validity period of the TGT ticket issued by the KDC component can be much shorter in the device SSO scheme. It is a usual case in PANs that devices join and leave the network in a rather high frequency, so it would be safer to issue a brand new TGT ticket in more frequent, regular time intervals. Besides that it is a well known fact that many attacks on the Kerberos protocol exploit the vulnerability of long ticket lifetimes, by replaying old tickets within the lifetime of a valid ticket. A typical duration of a ticket lifetime could be as long as eight hours [12]. To deal with such an attack by storing old valid tickets is not always easy because of the excessive storage requirements at the server side. However this problem in PANs can be easily dealt with by issuing TGT tickets on a more frequent basis. By appointing the device that will undertake the task of the SSO to be a desktop PC or a laptop, along with the use of the symmetric key primitives of the Kerberos authentication protocol makes it obvious that the power and other processing constraints can be significantly alleviated.

4.2 The P2P Model

Now we discuss the SSO solution for a PAN network with peer-to-peer (P2P) model architecture. Since PANs are ad-hoc in nature, it makes more sense to deploy this type of architecture for a PAN, allowing thus for direct authentication and communication from any device to any other device in the network. For this reason the P2P architecture is the most popular and most widely used for PAN networks. An illustration of the P2P SSO is shown in Fig. 4.

In the case of a P2P scenario, any device can be logged in by the user. This device could be then used to log on to other devices. Therefore in a P2P SSO scheme, each device has equal responsibility and can undertake the task of signing in any new device in the PAN.

In the diagram shown in Fig. 4, P_1 is assumed to be logged in, while the devices P_2 and P_3 are not yet logged in. We assume that the first peer P_1 of the PAN is logged in by the user. This device has already authenticated the user/owner of the device. Assume that P_2 is the new device that comes to proximity of P_1.

Our device SSO solution dictates that a service application will be running in both P_1 and P_2. Unlike the case of the client server model, in this case both peers have to run this service at the boot up process, since it is not known in advance which of the peers is going to log on to which. P_2 being at the vicinity of P_1 detects P_2 and initiates mutual authentication for both the devices (action 1). If the authentication handshake is successful, the new device completes signing in the network (action 2). Now the states of both P_1 and P_2 are identical. This is because both of them have been logged in and are thus in the same state, behaving as two 'peers' of the PAN. In order to completely maintain a consistent view for the user, a connection is made back from the new device (P_2) to the already logged in device P_1 (action 3). Now there exists a bidirectional link between both the devices. Suppose now that a third device P_3 comes into the vicinity of both P_1 and P_2. P_3 now needs to be logged in by an already logged in device. This could be either P_1 or P_2. In the illustration P_1 is shown logging into the device P_3 (action 4). After the authentication mechanism is complete the new device logs in to its OS (action 5). The new device makes then a connection back to P_1 and establishes a bidirectional link with all the other logged in devices (actions 6, 7 and 8), which are mutually authenticated. Note that at the end of the whole sequence, a user would not be able to distinguish between which device was logged in first and which one was last thus making every device to be a peer of every other device in the network.

Unlike the client server model where the bulk of the work for authentication is done at the server side, in the P2P model both the devices take equal responsibility in the mutual authentication mechanism. For this purpose we chose not to use a Kerberos server running at each node and authenticate the incoming clients for one-way connection, since such a solution would demand a lot of computing power at each node. Instead, the solution that we adopted for the mutual authentication mechanism was similar to the one that is used for the authentication between two Bluetooth devices. This is a more tangible solution that also incorporates symmetric key primitives to make the overall authentication scheme lightweight and suitable for handheld devices. Fig. 5 provides an illustration of the modified Bluetooth basic authentication mechanism proposed for the P2P SSO architecture.

We assume that a pair of devices, A and B, shares a secret key K_{AB} before they actually start being part of the network. Although such an assumption is not always applicable, the limited size of a PAN makes it feasible. The duty of specifying, managing and updating the symmetric keys is carried out by the application itself. Let also MAC be the Message Authentication Code that is generated using the secret key, K_s the secret key for a session s, t a timestamp and K_{new} the authentication key for a new session. Both devices generate a random number R_A and R_B respectively. These are generated at the local system and cannot be reproduced by any other entity. The random numbers are then sent to the other node (action 2). The message contains the random number encrypted using the key K_{AB}. This key is used only for the first time that the two nodes communicate. A MAC is also provided to prove the integrity of the message. The key used for this MAC is the same as that of the key used for encryption. This is the case in order to reduce the number of keys associated with a node. It should be noted that the time stamp could either be the current time in the machine or a nonce which is incremented each time a communication is initiated. The latter is a simpler option since it does not involve timing and synchronization issues.

Upon receiving the MAC, each node checks the integrity of the message and if the integrity check is passed, the random number is decrypted (action 3). At this point both node A and node B obtain the random numbers R_B and R_A respectively. Now, the two nodes can independently calculate the key for their session by doing some kind of a scrambling operation (denoted in the figure as $\oplus$). This operation can be as simple as XOR-ing the two values or using an algorithm such as E_{21}. The new value of K_S will be $K_S = R_B \oplus R_A$ and this will be the session key for the current session (action 4). To further verify the use of this session key, both nodes encrypt and send to the other parties a random number using the new session key. Since the use of the same K_{AB} for encrypting the random number during each run is not safe enough, it would be better to use a new key, being a combination of the initial key K_{AB} and the previous session key, such as $K_{NEW} = K_{AB} \oplus K_S$.

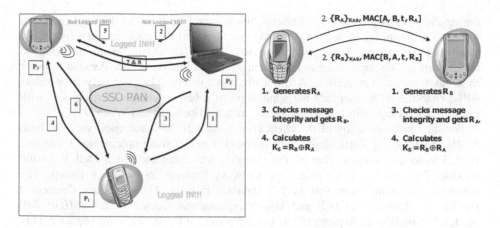

Fig. 4. Peer-to-Peer SSO in a PAN   **Fig. 5.** The proposed P2P Authentication protocol

Comparing the two SSO schemes, it is obvious that the SSO client server model is conceptually easy and its design and implementation are easier than the corresponding P2P SSO. Key management is also easy in the sense that all that the server has to bother is to have a key for each client of the system. At the same time, a client needs only one key to share with the server. Secure communication can be established between two clients (more than one hop) easily by using the client server model. Additionally, there are no issues regarding association in such a system since the server always acts as the master. However, it is obvious that in the client-server SSO model, a device assuming the role of the server must be in place beforehand so that the whole system is functional. In case of absence of the server device, two devices cannot perform the sign-on even if they are in the vicinity of each other. Furthermore, the design of the client-server SSO model is very static in nature, in the sense that the system is preconfigured with one server and all other as clients. If the server is not in range the client devices cannot sync. However, this is a limitation posed by the client server network architecture and not by the SSO scheme itself.

On the other hand, the P2P model implements SSO in the true sense, since any device can sign on to any other device. Any subset of devices can engage in SSO and join or form a PAN. This is not possible in the case of a client server model since a server should be appointed for managing SSO functions. The P2P SSO model however is more difficult to implement. Since currently there are not so many APIs built in for a peer-to-peer model, one should have a client server based model tuned to work as a peer-to-peer one. In addition, key management is an issue, since each peer must posses or negotiate beforehand a secret key with every other peer, hindering thus the scaling of the network.

5 Our Application

In order to test and evaluate the proposed device SSO schemes, we developed a custom application. This application was developed on top of Java to take advantage of the level of abstraction from hardware that it provides and use it as middleware for our application. Alternatively, another solution would be to build the application on top of Linux, running on a PDA or laptop and then port the necessary drivers for the radio link. However, Java provides a friendlier user environment, allowing to concentrate on the application development itself and this is why we decided to use it as a basis for our application. Additionally, Java offers a large variety of wireless APIs, enabling us to integrate the application in a heterogeneous environment with multiple short range wireless technologies, such as Bluetooth and Wi-Fi.

For the implementation of the client server and P2P SSO schemes, we used both J2ME and J2SE [3]. Particularly, the client server model was implemented using two USB Bluetooth Dongles. One of the Dongles was connected to a Dell Precision desktop PC and the other one on a Compaq Presario 2100 series laptop. The development environment was Java 2 Standard Edition. The necessary *Connected Device Configuration (CDC)* and *Mobile Information Device Profile (MIDP 2.0)* needed for the Bluetooth protocol stack, were provided by the software vendor Atinav [13]. For the P2P model additionally, the J2ME Wireless Toolkit 2.2 with MIDP 2.0 support was used to simulate the two mobile phones with Bluetooth Connectivity.

6 Conclusions

In this paper we discussed and investigated the issue of Device Single Sign On in Personal Area Networks. Device SSO can prove very helpful in order both to secure and reduce the overhead of managing a PAN during the authentication process. However, several issues have to be addressed in a rigorous manner when designing a device SSO scheme. These issues have to do mainly with the high level of heterogeneity that a PAN environment introduces. The use of Symmetric key primitives is recommended for such an environment since today's technology does not support high computational capabilities on handhelds which makes the use of PKIs impractical. We have developed two models for SSO on handheld networks, which are designed for specific scenarios, depending on the network model architecture that a PAN deploys. The Client-Server SSO is designed mostly for signing in a home/office environment where the client server model is more popular. The Peer-to-Peer SSO scheme provides signing in more dynamic environments, where the user is on transit and PANs are created dynamically and spontaneously. The security framework of the client server SSO is based on a variation of the Kerberos authentication protocol, whereas the corresponding one of the P2P SSO on Bluetooth authentication primitives. Both schemes perform mutual authentication using symmetric key cryptography to tackle the energy resource constraints of PANs. The two proposed PAN SSO schemes were implemented based on a custom prototype application.

References

[1] Michael Kelly, *"Is Single Sign on a Security Risk?"* Version 1.2e, © SANS Institute, June 2002, SANS Institute, GIAC Certified Student Practical
[2] Andreas Pashalidis and Chris J. Mitchell, *"A Taxonomy of single sign-on systems,"* Information Security and Privacy, 8th Australasian Conference, ACISP 2003, Wollongong, Australia, July 2003

[3] Enrique Ortiz, "A *Survey of J2ME Today,*" October 2004
[4] Liberty Alliance Specifications, www.projectliberty.org
[5] David P. Kormann and Aviel D. Rubin, "*Risks of the Passport Single Sign on Protocol,*" Computer Networks, Elsevier Science Press, volume 33, pages 51-58, 2000.
[6] Andreas Pashalidis and Chris Mitchell, "*Using GSM/UMTS for Single Sign-On,*" Proceedings of SympoTIC '03 Joint IST Workshop on Mobile Future Symposium on Trends in Communications, Bratislava, Slovakia, Oct. 2003, IEEE Press, pp. 138-145
[7] Andreas Pashalidis and Chris J. Mitchell, "*Single Sign-On using Trusted Platforms,*" Information Security, 6th International Conference, ISC 2003, Bristol, UK, October 2003
[8] http://shibboleth.internet2.edu/
[9] Jongil Jeong, Dongkyoo Shin and Dongil Shin, "*An XML-based Single Sign-On Scheme Supporting Mobile and Home Network Service Environments,*" IEEE Transactions on Consumer Electronics, Vol. 50, no. 4, pp. 1081-1086, Nov. 2004
[10] William Josephson, Emin Gun Sirer, Fred B. Schneider, "*Peer-to-Peer Authentication with a Distributed Single Sign-On Service,*" Peer-to-Peer Systems III: Lecture Notes in Computer Science 3279, pp. 250-258, 2004
[11] Christian Gehrmann, Kaisa Nyberg, Chris J. Mitchell "*Manual authentication for wireless devices,*" Cryptobytes, Vol. 7, no. 1, Spring, 2004, pp. 29-37
[12] Bruce Schneier, "Applied Cryptography: Protocols, Algorithms and Source Code in C", Second Edition, John Wiley & Sons, Inc.,1996
[13] www.atinav.com
[14] RFC 1510, The Kerberos Network Authentication Service (V5), www.ietf.org/rfc/rfc1510.txt

Applying the Effective Distance to Location-Dependent Data*

JeHyok Ryu and Uğur Çetintemel

Department of Computer Science, Brown University
Providence, RI 02912, USA
{jhryu, ugur}@cs.brown.edu

Abstract. In wireless mobile environments, we increasingly use data that depends on the location of mobile clients. However, requested geographical objects (GOs) do not exist in all areas with uniform distribution. More urbanized areas have greater population and greater GO density. Thus the results of queries may vary based on the perception of distance. We use urbanization as a criterion to analyze the density of GOs. We propose the Effective Distance (ED) measurement, which is not a physical distance but the perceived distance varying based on the extent of urbanization. We present the efficiency of supporting location-dependent data on GOs with proposed ED. We investigate several membership functions to establish this proposed ED based on the degree of urbanization. In our evaluation, we show that the z-shaped membership function can flexibly adjust the ED. Thus, we obtain improved performance to provide the location-dependent data because we can differentiate the ED for very densely clustered GOs in urbanized areas.

Keywords: Location-Dependent Data, Pervasive Computing.

1 Introduction

The current trend in workspace is a change from wired and stationary to wireless and mobile. The white paper from UMTS Forum argues that the trend has already happened and will continue [1]. Boosters of this trend are renovative portable computing devices such as smart phones or laptops, and enhanced wireless technologies such as PCS networks, GPS and wireless sensor nodes. These boosters are gradually extending the space of the applications of various wireless mobile workspace and sensing systems [2,3,4,5,6]. For instance, they allow mobile clients to access their desired data regardless of their place and time. However, the accessed data may become obsolete whenever mobile clients change their locations. This kind of data is called location-dependent data (LDD), which corresponds to the results of a query according to the location of a mobile client [7,8,9,10,11,12].

* This work is supported in part by the Korea Research Foundation (KRF-2005-214-D00147) and the National Science Foundation (IIS-0448284).

R. Meersman, Z. Tari, P. Herrero et al. (Eds.): OTM Workshops 2006, LNCS 4278, pp. 1380–1390, 2006.
© Springer-Verlag Berlin Heidelberg 2006

For example, let's consider a request: "Find a nearby police station." The result may be different according to the mobile client's location at which the query was issued. Moreover, "nearby" has fundamental uncertainty, so it is difficult to represent its value accurately. The degree of distance is felt differently in an urbanized region and its suburbs, because the closeness between geographical objects varies according to the degree of urbanization. Similar problems may appear for a shopper or a business traveller.

Urbanization, which means the growth in the proportion of a population living in urban areas, accelerates expansion of the infrastructure, such as educational facilities, accommodations, medical centers, roads, and offices. Therefore, mobile clients may get many more results in response to their queries in an urbanized area compared to what they would get in a suburb. As a result, when we consider many results of a query at the urbanized area, like mega-cities or urban agglomerations [13], query processing needs to be differentiated from that for a suburb environment. Since geographical objects are deployed differently according to the degree of urbanization, we need an appropriate evaluation of distance measurement in these queries. The distance may also be uncertain, like the "nearby" example in this section. In this paper, we compare and evaluate several membership functions (mfs) to find an appropriate data management model for query processing for location-dependent data.

The rest of the paper is organized as follows. Section 2 discusses related work. Section 3 shows several mfs quantifying a sense of urbanized distance for location-dependent mobile query processing. We present the analysis on applied membership functions applying proposed urbanized distance in Section 4. In Section 5, we evaluate several mfs of the Effective Distance for LDD requests and analyze performance changes by the variation of simulated systems and mfs parameters. Section 6 concludes the paper.

2 Related Work

We first define the terminology we use in the rest of the paper. A mobile query (MQ) is mobile client's queries. If we classify these MQs, they may be two classes. The first, the query of the example in Sect.1 is a location-dependent mobile query (LDMQ). The LDMQ is a query for fixed GOs (geographical objects) such as the police station mentioned in Sect.1. If the queried data are moving objects such as a car, we'll use the term moving object mobile query (MOMQ). In both of the two MQs, mobile clients can move or stay. In this paper, we focus on the LDMQ.

Most of the previous work in mobile environments has assumed that mobile clients access data in one region or one cell [14,15]. But the possibility of different MQs has become increasingly considered. Madria et al., [8] introduced the use of concept hierarchies based on location data. These hierarchies define mappings among different granularities of locations. In this work, the concept hierarchies were used for the level of cities and states only. But a useful symbolic model for the location may include smaller hierarchies such as roads, streets, boulevards, and avenues. There is no obvious difference among the terms road, street, boulevard or avenue. Since all of these terms are commonly used in most cities, concept hierarchies do not distinguish between them in terms of precision but simply classify them as a group at a similar precision level in the hierarchy.

Dunham and Kumar [7] introduced an approach to manage LDD that has their intrinsic characteristics. Previous approaches of managing data of GOs in wireless mobile environments did not usually consider the relationship between data objects and their geographical distance. They defined a spatial replication, which may have different correct data at any point in time. They also introduced the concept of data region to explain their view of the data. A data region is different from a cell of wireless mobile environments and identifies data of GOs. They showed an implementation architecture for LDD in which a requested query is routed to the appropriate data region to service the LDD correctly. Ryu et al., [16] also evaluated the LDMQ in two kinds of data regions: geographical data regions (GDRs), which have an initial set of data objects for GOs at its own geographical area, and proposed LDD regions (LDRs).

Xu and Lee [17] investigated issues for querying wireless location-dependent data (WLDD). This work identified five query types based on access to location information. A cell ID is used for location binding. Local queries such as "List the local hotels," search the database starting from the current BS to the root until the results are found. In Non-Local cases, a query, e.g. "Find the weather in Cell #8," is redirected to the corresponding cell, and then follows the same method as local queries. Geographically Clustered and Geographically Dispersed queries have to be processed in a cluster of cells and in every cell, respectively. Likewise, a nearest query is processed in the current cell and the nearest cell to the farthest cell until the query is satisfied. In our work, LDMQs are assumed to follow the processing in the same manner as [7,17,16] in terms of how the queries are routed.

In [18], the authors proposed the method of dynamic attributes whose values change continually as a function of time. From the point of view of the queried objects, they investigated moving objects for MOMQs. But our managed data objects correspond to the geographical objects that are not moving, such as restaurants, hotels, and airports.

The relationship between the location granularity and the precision of results causes tradeoffs in LDMQ processing. Location models [11] were summarized in two models. They depend on the system's underlying location identification technique. Two models for representing locations are the geometric model and the symbolic model. The geometric model has compatibility across heterogeneous systems. However, it can be costly and complex. For example, the geometric model includes the latitude-longitude pair returned by GPS (Geographical Positioning Systems) or a set of coordinates defining the area's bounding geometric shape, such as a polygon. In the symbolic model, logical and real-world entities describe the location space. Entities can be buildings, streets, cities, or system-defined elements such as wireless cells, and are uniquely identifiable by a hierarchical naming system. This model typically has coarser location granularity than

Fig. 1. Threshold mf for ED

the geometric model because it stresses the representation of relationships between logical entities rather than their precise coordinates. And converting locations among heterogeneous systems is difficult. But discrete and well-structured symbolic location information is easier to manage. In terms of the GOs, the process of urbanization was already very advanced in more developed regions, where 75 percent of the population lived in urban areas in 2000 [13,19]. This means that a number of GOs were already built in the urbanized areas. In these areas, the expansion rate of GOs is slower than the rates in other areas. In this context, to achieve efficient support for LDD in urbanized areas, it is necessary to incur the cost of LDD organization in advance. The LDD organization have been discussed in [16]. Since new GOs are not constructed frequently, frequent updates to LDD organization are not required. Thus, the degree of urbanization to which an area is urbanized should be considered together.

3   Quantifying Urbanized Sense of Distance

In processing the LDMQ, the location binding may be performed by two types, according to the expression of distance. The first type expresses explicit measured distance in a LDMQ. In the second type the LDMQs have uncertain distances. In the example of Sect.1, we looked into the second type, using the "nearby" term as a representative example. The "nearby" distance in an urbanized area makes us feel or expect shorter distances to GOs than expected in a less urbanized suburb. Usually, this arises from the fact that a number of geographical objects are densely deployed in an urbanized area, such as many stores and facilities on a busy street. In this context, we define a new urbanized distance as follows:

Definition 1. *Effective Distance (ED) is a perceived distance that reflects a human's feeling according to the degree of urbanization.*

For example, we expect that the distance from a mobile client's current location to a hotel in urban agglomerations is probably very near. But we also expect that the distance in a rural area may be relatively far away. We'll call this distance ED. In an urbanized area, the binding location based on the ED is relatively narrower than the ED for the suburb. But, there is no exact boundary between an urban area and the suburb. This requires a method to represent the degree of urbanization for the ED. Thus, we consider mfs for sophisticated binding of the

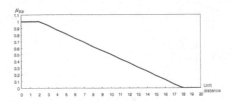

Fig. 2. Trapezoidal mf for ED

degree of ED because geographical objects are usually distributed more densely in urbanized areas. In the first case, the ED may be estimated by a threshold mf:

$$\mu_{thr}(x) = \begin{cases} 1, & 0 \leq x \leq a \\ 0, & a < x \end{cases} \tag{1}$$

If a given "near" corresponds to "a" for the ED in the mf μ_{thr} and the value of a is 2, the ED by the threshold mf can be shown as in Fig.1. The output value is either 1 or 0, depending on the criterion of ED for input value x. This threshold style may be applied in cell-based wireless networks. However, there is a shortcoming that definitely divides the boundary among the cells in a wireless region, though the boundary is indivisible. This is also the intrinsic limit of cell-based location management.

$$\mu_{tra}(x) = \begin{cases} 1, & 0 \leq x \leq a \\ \frac{s-x}{s-a}, & a < x < s \\ 0, & s \leq x \end{cases} \tag{2}$$

In the second consideration, a trapezoid mf may also be applied for the ED. When the value of 'a' and 's' is 2 and 18 in the mf μ_{tra}, respectively, the ED by the trapezoid mf can be presented as in Fig.2. The value of s may be set for the scale of a serviced area which is possible to request LDD. This trapezoid style makes up for the weak point in the threshold mf. But ED in trapezoid mf decreases regularly to the distance within the range of 'a' to 's' in μ_{tra}. Thus, it is difficult to differentiate the degree of ED for urbanization in which many geographical objects are densely deployed. Thus, the trapezoid style is not flexibly congruent with the concept of ED. Finally, we investigate the z-shaped mf:

$$\mu_z(x) = \begin{cases} 1, & 0 \leq x \leq a \\ \frac{1}{1+e^{b(x-c)}}, & a < x \end{cases} \tag{3}$$

If the given distance of 'near' is also 2 for the value of 'a' in mf μ_z, Fig.3 shows the z-shaped mf. Nearby locations after the distance 2 in Fig.3 have almost the same memberships but are slightly lower than the membership for the location of given distance 2 for 'a'. This may minutely represent that geographical objects in an urbanized area are deployed very close together. We can adjust the value of 'b' to the slope of this curve for the degree of ED, and 'c' extends the range of

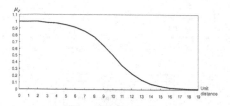

Fig. 3. z-shaped mf for ED

urbanized distance 'a' in the range from 0 to 1 the degree of membership. So, 'c' is the given 'a' plus a distance 'ext.' The distance ext can be adjusted if the scale of given urban area is extended. If we adjust the value of 'c' and 'b' in mf μ_z, it represents more subtly the membership degree of ED for clustered geographical objects located after given nearby distance 'a' in a more urbanized area. Thus, we expect that mf μ_z may resolve the problems in mf μ_{thr} and μ_{tra} and flexibly represent for the ED, especially the indefinite boundary between urbanized areas and suburbs.

For instance, the value 'a' may be considered as the radius of a data region. In μ_z, adjusting the values of 'c' and 'b' allows us to represent the degree of urbanization. We will consider the sensitivity between two variables to give us guidelines for our evaluation in the performance study.

4   Effective Distance in Data Region

4.1   Data Region with ED

A model constructing Data Region for the LDD, proposed in [16], was called the Location-dependent Data Region (LDR). We use the data region to apply proposed ED (refer to [16] for details). To make the paper self-contained, however, we will briefly discuss the LDR with the ED. A data region manages its own data for GOs. A data region may be differently constructed according to the applied mobile computing environments. For instance, if a cell-based location management model is applied, a data region may consist of a data set for GOs covered by one base station (BS) or more BSs. This data region is not clear because the data regions depend on the evaluation of the distance for the mobile client's request on the LDD. We consider that the membership degree of the ED stated in Sect.3 is reflected in constructing the data regions. When we construct the data regions, we apply the membership degree of the ED on the physical distance as well as the access locality of the location of the requested LDD, and the location of the data. We summarize organizing LDRs adapted ED as follows. We assume the knowledge of the physical location of GOs. Let the entire service field be F. The F consists of a set of regions $R = \{r_1, r_2, \ldots, r_u\}$. Let us also suppose that $D = \{d_1, d_2, \ldots, d_n\}$ is the serviced data of GOs in F, and $Q = \{q_1, q_2, \ldots, q_t\}$ is the set of LDD requests. First, one of the mfs for ED from (1), (2), and (3) is used for the degree of distance between LDD. That

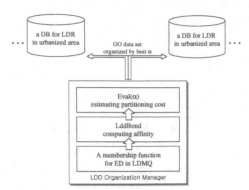

Fig. 4. Steps organizing LDRs

is data in set D. Second, the frequency and locality between two LDD accessed together is considered. In other words, organizing LDRs reflects the frequency at each location from where queries are issued and serviced data are accessed by the same request. We use these relationships between two LDDs by an affinity, called *LDDBond*. Figure 4 illustrates the model organizing LDRs. With this organization, we exploit mfs for proposed ED. The LDD Organization Manager (LOM) warms up organizational steps with a given number of LDD requests. This manager may work in the Location Service Center (LSC) and be linked to Mobile Support Stations (MSSs). An LOM covers LDRs in the serviced regions. We assume that each LDR is linked to a database for the GOs in its region. The *LddBond* represents the possibility that two data objects may be grouped in the same data region. It reflects the frequency of accessed data objects d_i and d_j at the regions from which queries are issued, and the degree of the ED for the distance not only between d_i and d_j, but also from the queries issued locations to each accessed data objects.

4.2   Adjusting the ED with mf μ_z

In the mfs, the threshold mf is a baseline to be compared with trapezoidal and Z-shaped mfs. We can expect μ_{tra} to give a more appropriate degree of ED than that of μ_{thr}, but it is difficult to differentiate the degree of the very densely located GOs in urban areas. In terms of that, μ_z gives two parameters to adjust the ED according to the level of urbanization. When we apply the membership function μ_z, the sensitive data set of geographical objects affected by ED corresponds to the objects located in the urban area after the given near distance. This expectation is due to the reason that the ED for urbanization differentiates minutely the membership degrees of distance for the GOs, which are closely clustered together. Thus, we need to analyze how sensitive the changes of two variables in μ_z affect the degree of ED so that it also changes the performance.

Let μ_z be $f(x; b, c)$, where x is the given input distance to be evaluated for ED. We can find how sensitive the output of f is to a change in the input at different values 'b' and 'c' by evaluating the partial derivatives, $\partial f/\partial c$ and $\partial f/\partial b$:

Table 1. Setting the parameters of the simulated environment with urbanization

Parameter	Description	Setting
$KndOfGO$	No. of kinds of serviced geographical objects	30
$NoMC$	No. of mobile clients	600
$NoLDR$	No. of LDRs	12×12
$NoSvcGO$	No. of serviced geographical objects	400
SKW	Skewness for the Zipf distribution	0.55 0.77, 0.99
MLQ	Distribution of mobile clients' locations issu- ing LDD requests	Zipf with SKW
$NrScp$	The scope of near sense (value 'a' in mfs)	2
Zb	The variable b of Z-shaped mf (4 values in $NrScp{<}\mathrm{b}{<}\mathrm{c}$)	2, 2.5, 3, 3.5
Zc	The variable c of Z-shaped mf' $(2{+}NrScp)$	4
$DgrUrbn$	Degree of urbanization	Zipf with SKW

$$\frac{\partial f}{\partial c} = \frac{\partial \frac{1}{1+e^{b(x-c)}}}{\partial c} = b(1+e^{b(x-c)})^{-2}e^{bx}e^{-bc} \tag{4}$$

$$\frac{\partial f}{\partial b} = \frac{\partial \frac{1}{1+e^{b(x-c)}}}{\partial b} = -(x-c)(1+e^{b(x-c)})^{-2}e^{b(x-c)} \tag{5}$$

To find the effect on outputs according to the changes of the variables, we take $|\partial f/\partial c|/|\partial f/\partial b|$, and have the result, $|b|/|c-x|$. We can recognize the sensitivity from $b/|c-x| < 1$ and $b/|c-x| > 1$ by c and b, respectively. Since b is greater than 0, we have the two ranges as follows:

$$c - b < x < c + b \quad if\ b > |c-x| \tag{6}$$
$$x < c - b,\ x > c + b \quad if\ b < |c-x| \tag{7}$$

From the above expressions, we can see that the degree of ED is more sensitive to a change in 'b' when 'b' is smaller than 'c', where the given distance 'x' for ED in a LDD request is less than $c-b$ or greater than $c+b$ from (7). As we can see from (6), the degree is more sensitive to a change in 'c' if the distance x to evaluate the degree of ED is $c - b < x < c + b$. In this paper, the region where $x < c - b$ ($x, c,$ and $b \geq 0$) is an important target area to finely differentiate the degree of ED where so many GOs are densely located, due to urbanization. We discuss this issue further with simulation results in Sect.5

5   Evaluation

We simulate the access number of data region by LDD requests in its LDRs by the ED and GDRs by the physical distance. We measure the improvement from the difference of the total access number at LDRs and GDRs. From the improvement, we compare the performance of the ED using the three mfs in Sect.3, especially the z-shaped mf based on the analysis in Sect.4.2. We set the parameters of our simulated environment as shown in Table 1.

We apply random distributions used in [20] for MLQ and $DgrUrbn$ in Table 1. The distribution of mobile clients' locations issuing queries (MLQ) is modeled

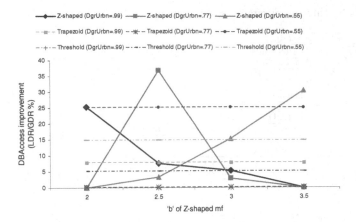

Fig. 5. Performance comparison by the ED in urban areas by three degree of urbanization

using a Zipf distribution, because we want to simulate LDD requests crowding on the urban area according to the anticipated urbanization. This means that the urbanized area corresponds to a small part of an entire service field. We simulate the degree of urbanization by a Zipf distribution of geographical objects in the serviced field ($DgrUrbn$). Thus, the higher skewness is (0.99 in Table 1), the smaller part of the serviced field is set to be concentrated most of all GOs, thereby simulating a very urbanized area. The $KndOfGO$ is the number of types of geographical objects (such as hotels, restaurants, shopping malls, bus stops, and police stations). We distribute the given geographical objects in a grid of 12 by 12 GDRs. We set the $NrScp$ for the given near sense by 2 distance units. The unit distance may be measured in meters, kilometers or miles according to the applied environments. We assume that the $NrScp$ as the half size of a data region. Each mobile client issues one request for LDD. An request accesses one or two LDD by mobile clients, and the number of issued requests per $KndOfGO$ is an average of 30 requests by the uniform distribution.

5.1 Simulation Results and Analysis

We apply three degrees of urbanization ($DgrUrbn$ in Table 1). As we described in Sect.4.2, the results of performance are mainly affected by quantifying the ED for urbanization. Especially, the $mf\mu_z$ makes effect on the results by variations of 'c' and 'b' with the degree of urbanization. Based on (6) and (7), the urban area where GOs are densely located is evaluated and affected by 'b' more than that by 'c.' So, we show the results in Fig.5, which gives more changes by the variation of 'b' in the ranges of $x < c - b$ in (7). For 'c', we fix the value to assume a urban area. If we would like to enlarge the size of the urban area, then we can adjust 'c' by 'ext' of Sect.3 correspondingly. We performed 600 LDD requests for each variation of 'b' for μ_z, and the other mfs based on three $DgrUrbn$. Figure 5 follows our analysis well in Sect.4.2. That is, the point of highest improvement in each 'b' of μ_z is moved to a lower value of 'b' close to the given $NrScp$ according to higher $DgrUrbn$. This means higher $DgrUrbn$ made densely located GOs and issued the LDD request, and the outputs are affected by 'b' when 'x' to be evaluated for ED is in $x < c - b$ of (7). So, in the case of the lower urbanized area and the range x from (6), the best improvement of results start to show in the range over $x < c - b$. In the results, μ_{thr} is a baseline to find minimum results. Furthermore, μ_{tra} relatively performed well but it does not flexibly represent the ED. So, from these results, we can recognize that μ_z differentiates the degree of ED well using flexible adjustments for different urbanized areas. It also effects the performance much more than the other mf.

6   Conclusions

Location-dependent queries may have results that are uncertain depending on the evaluation of distance. Due to the degree of urbanization, we may have a different sense of distance, called Effective Distance. We proposed a method to support LDD by the membership degree of Effective Distance based on urbanization. In our evaluation, we performed LDD requests based on LDRs by applying several membership functions for the Effective Distance from the degree of urbanization. Our experiments presented improved support for LDD and the analysis of the affects of the sensitivity of membership functions of ED on performance. The results reveal that a refined membership reflecting the characteristics of the environment, such as urbanization, introduces more possibilities of sophisticated pervasive computing services in next generation applied environments (such as advanced mobile environments and wireless sensor networks). In future work, we will investigate the sensitive relationship between urbanization and membership functions in more detail, and consider the pervasive applications with sensor nodes in the growth of urban areas.

References

1. Forum, U.: Mobile evolution shaping the future. White paper, UMTS Forum, http://www.umts-forum.org/ (2003)
2. Rao, B., Minakakis, L.: Evolution of mobile location-based services. Communications of the ACM **46**(12) (2003) 61–65
3. Imielinski, T., Badrinath, B.R.: Querying in highly mobile and distributed environments. In: Proceedings of International Conference on Very Large DataBase. (1992) 41–52
4. Woo, A., Madden, S., Govindan, R.: Networking support for query processing in sensor networks. Communications of the ACM **47** (2004) 47–52
5. Beaver, J., Sharaf, M.A., Labrinidis, A., Chrysanthis, P.K.: Location-aware routing for data aggregation in sensor networks. In: 1st Geo Sensor Networks Workshop. (2003) 1–18
6. Srivastava, M., Hansen, M., Burke, J., Parker, A., Reddy, S., Saurabh, G., Allman, M., Paxson, V., Estrin, D.: Wireless urban sensing systems. In No.65, C.T.R., ed.: University of California at Los Angeles. (2006) 199–210

7. Dunham, M.H., Kumar, V.: Location dependent data and its management in mobile databases. In: 9th International Workshop on Database and Expert Systems Applications. (1998) 414–419
8. Madria, S.K., Bhargava, B., Pitoura, E., Kumar, V.: Data organization issues for location-dependent queries in mobile computing. ADBIS-DASFAA, LNCS **1884** (2000) 142–156
9. Zheng, B., Lee, D.L.: Location-dependent queries in a multi-cell wireless environment. In: Proceedings of the 2nd ACM International Workshop on Data Engineering for Wireless and Mobile Access (MobiDE01). (2001) 54–65
10. Seydim, A.Y., Dunham, M.H., Kumar, V.: Location dependent query processing. In: MobiDE. (2001) 47–53
11. Lee, D.L., Xu, J., Zheng, B., Lee, W.C.: Data management in location-dependent information services. IEEE Pervasive computing (2002) 65–72
12. Gao, X., Hurson, A.R.: Location dependent query proxy. In: ACM Symposium on Applied Computing. (2005) 1120–1124
13. Division, U.N.P.: World urbanization prospects: The 2001 revision (2001)
14. Pitoura, E., Samaras, G.: Data Management for Mobile Computing. Kluwer Academic Publishers (1997)
15. Tan, K.L., Ooi, B.C.: Data Dissemination in Wireless Computing Environments. Kluwer Academic Publishers (2000)
16. Ryu, J., Song, M., Hwang, C.S.: Organizing the ldd in mobile environments. IEICE TRANS. INF. & SYST. **E86-D**(9) (2003) 1504–1512
17. Xu, J., Lee, D.L.: Querying location-dependent data in wireless cellular environment. In: WAP Forum/W3C Workshop on Position Dependent Information Services. (2000)
18. Wolfson, O., Xu, B., Chamberlain, S., Jiang, L.: Moving objects databases: Issues and solutions. In: Proceedings of International Conference on Scientific and Statistical Database Management (SSDBM '98). (1998) 111–122
19. Division, U.N.P.: Future world population growth to be concentrated in urban areas of world. Department of Economic and Social Affairs Press Release (http://www.un.org/esa/population/unpop.htm (2002)
20. Nascimento, M., Theodoridis, Y.: Benchmarking spatio-temporal databases: The gstd software. http://www.cti.gr/RD3/GSTD (1998)

Scalable Context Simulation for Mobile Applications

Y. Liu[1], M.J. O'Grady[2], and G.M.P. O'Hare[2]

[1] School of Computer Science & Informatics, University College Dublin (UCD), Belfield,
Dublin 4, Ireland
Yue.Liu@ucdconnect.ie
[2] Adaptive Information Cluster (AIC), School of Computer of Computer Science &
Informatics, University College Dublin (UCD), Belfield, Dublin 4, Ireland
{michael.j.ogrady, gregory.ohare}@ucd.ie

Abstract. Mobility, and, implicitly, context-awareness, offer significant opportunities to service providers to augment and differentiate their respective services. Though this potential has been long acknowledged, the dynamic nature of a mobile user's context can lead to various difficulties when engineering mobile, context-aware applications. Classic software engineering elements are well understood in the fixed computing domain. However, the mobile domain introduces further degrees of difficulty into the process. The testing phase of the software engineering cycle is a particular case in point as modelling the myriad of scenarios that mobile users may find themselves is practically impossible. In this paper, we describe a scalable framework that can be used both for initial prototyping and for the final testing of mobile context-aware applications. In particular, we focus on scenarios where the application is in essence a distributed multi-agent system, comprising a suite of agents running on both mobile devices and on fixed nodes on a wireless network.

1 Introduction

Advances in wireless communications and hardware miniaturization have combined to bring about an era of unparallel access to and availability of computing resources. This is particularly evident in the mobile computing domain with the demarcation between classic computing and traditional telephony becoming increasingly blurred. However, it has been observed for some time now that developments in hardware have not been matched with corresponding advances in software. Thus engineering applications and services for mobile users still remains more an art than a science.

Historically, models of use for various applications and services evolved, leading to a reasonably mature understanding of the design and engineering issues involved. The introduction of mobility, along with other aspects of the end-user's situation, or context, challenges some the assumptions underpinning the traditional software development cycle. Granted, the key stages remain the same but the tasks associated with each stage need further augmentation and refinement if they are to successfully address the challenge posed by the mobile computing paradigm. Prototyping and testing phases are particularly susceptible as it is impossible in all but the simplest cases to anticipate and effectively model the countless scenarios that the average

R. Meersman, Z. Tari, P. Herrero et al. (Eds.): OTM Workshops 2006, LNCS 4278, pp. 1391–1400, 2006.
© Springer-Verlag Berlin Heidelberg 2006

mobile user may encounter in the course of their everyday pursuits. Indeed, modeling these scenarios is an increasingly complex endeavor, and how best to do this remains an open question. One approach that has raised much interest is that Agent-Oriented Programming (AOP) where agents represent the core abstractions, as distinct from objects. Such an approach is perceived as being particularly suited to those domains where traditional approaches do not prove adequate. Domains characterized by inherent complexity and dynamism are cases in point; a pertinent example being the mobile computing domain.

This paper is structured as follows: Section 2 outlines some related work in this area. In Section 3, some issues for consideration during the software engineering lifecycle are elucidated. Section 4 presents the design and implementation of the framework for simulating context. Some reflections on the system and planned future work are presented in Section 5 after which the paper is concluded.

2 Related Research

A cursory examination of the research literature will illustrate quickly the significance that the research community attaches to the mobile computing paradigm. A number of what may be cautiously termed sub-disciplines including ubiquitous computing, pervasive computing, and more recently, ambient intelligence (AmI) [1], all seek to deliver services to mobile users; though the specifics of how this is achieved differ in each case. While significant progress has been documented in a number of relevant sub-domains, in particular hardware, development methodologies and support tools are, in contrast, notable by their scarcity. Given the relative newness of mobile computing, this is not surprising. However, some researchers have realized that the complexity and dynamicity of the mobile computing environment raises specific difficulties that traditional software engineering techniques do not adequately address.

UBIWISE [2] is described by its developers as a simulator for ubiquitous computing. From a software engineering perspective, it would likely be classified as a rapid prototyping toolkit. A model of the physical environment is maintained on a central server. Users can then connect to this server and, while maintaining a first-person view of the environment, proceed to interact with various devices in the environment using their desktop keyboard and mouse.

Morla [3] has developed a test and simulation environment for evaluating location-based applications. Web services form the core paradigm around which the system is designed. Interestingly, it also incorporates the well known NS network simulator, which allows the application in question be tested under various network configurations. Bylund and Espinoze [4] have demonstrated the potential of using 3D game engines as a basis for testing and prototyping context-aware services without a need for people or objects moving around the real world.

Given the broad range of mobile devices currently available, and their different specifications, a particular difficulty arises for network operators who must support a broad range of applications on such devices without compromising the integrity or stability of their networks. In an effort to address this, Ichiro Satoh, at the National Institute of Informatics in Japan, has developed a framework called the Flying Emulator [5][6]. The core constituent of this framework is a mobile agent that emulates mobile devices. As it is mobile, the agent can migrate to distant nodes and remote networks and test the software in situ. Should the application behave satisfactorily, the actual software itself can be deployed on a physical device without recompilation or modification.

The potential of intelligent agents for simulating various scenarios has been recognized by other researchers. Hou et al [7] describes an environment that utilizes multiple agents for testing web-based applications. Likewise, Narendra [8] also advocates the use of agents for large scale testing of pervasive computing systems.

3 Engineering Context-Aware Applications

Context is a dynamic construct [9]. It is this dynamism that introduces additional levels of difficulty into the software engineering process. As a brief illustration of just some of the issues involved, three aspects of an archetypical mobile user's context are now briefly considered.

1. Spatial Context: In essence, a person's spatial context refers to their physical location and orientation. This is normally interpreted as their geographical position and heading. A number of technologies facilitate the measurement of a person's spatial context. The Global Positioning System (GPS) is the de facto standard at present and measures a person's position to within 20 meters of their actual physical position. If Satellite Based Augmentation System (SBAS) technologies are used, for example the European Ground Navigation Overlay Service (EGNOS), positions can be determined to within 5 meters on average. The forthcoming European initiative - Galileo, will offer further possibilities, especially regarding the reliability of the broadcasted signal. However, a key limitation of satellite-based technologies concerns their ineffectiveness in indoor environments. While technologies exist that operate in indoor environments, for example UBISENSE [10], indoor solutions are almost inherently propriety in nature and are not as ubiquitous as GPS. Thus while position forms a critical aspect of a user's context, capturing and interpreting it in a meaningful manner requires careful consideration of the technologies used and their associated limitations.

2. Environment: For brevity, discussion is limited to the data communication's aspect of a person's environment, rather than reflecting on the broad spectrum of issues associated with the physical environment. The availability of wireless or data communications is dependent on a number of factors, but the nature of the available connection is of particular interest, when a subscriber's context is considered. If a basic second generation (2G) network is availed of, data communications speeds of less than 20 kb/s may be the norm. In contrast, a third generation (3G) connection may offer speeds of up to 2 Mb/s. In urban environments, the proliferation of WiFi hotspots offers a viable alternative to 3G. Thus data-rate is an important element of a mobile user's context. However, it is the nature of the mobile application that determines the attention that should be given to it in the design process. Should the application incorporate a significant multimedia component, high data-rates are required if the user experience is to be a positive one. For less data-intensive applications, the nature of the wireless connection may not be so important.

3. Device: In recent years, the range of mobile devices in the marketplace has grown significantly. However, the essential features of each model are becoming increasingly disparate. This is a well-known issue and makes the design of applications for mobile devices a difficult and time-consuming task. Devices may differ in several regards including supported network protocols, multimedia formats supported, processor and memory, and screen size. Again, the nature of the application in question will determine the importance the designer attributes to each of these characteristics.

4 Modeling Context in Software

Testing software applications is a difficult and time-consuming process. In the case of mobile users, the difficulties are exacerbated. It is just not practical for a developer to physically and repeatedly explore multiple environments while debugging their applications and services. A solution to this issue is the effective and realistic modeling of users' contexts in software. However, given the complexity of the scenarios that could be modeled, a conventional solution is inadequate. In practice, deriving and maintaining a dynamic model of a user's context demands that a degree of intelligence be exhibited. Thus, the intelligent agent paradigm has been identified as one that can encapsulate the necessary intelligence and around which individual context elements can be effectively modeled. A number of agent models exist [11], one of which is the Belief-Desire-Intention (BDI) [12] model. In this model, an agent can maintain a model of its environment via a set of beliefs. Its objectives, or reasons for existing, are maintained as a set of desires. Depending on its mental state, that is, the state of its environment, it may be in a position to satisfy some of its desires (objectives) at certain times. These desires that it can carry out are formulated as intentions which the agent proceeds to fulfill. It can be easily seen that these mentalistic notions of belief-desire-intention offer intuitive constructs around which context may be modeled and resultant user behavior determined.

Thus the context simulation framework is envisaged as a Multi-Agent System (MAS) in which a suite of agents collaborate so as to derive a model of a user's behavior based on certain contextual cues. This is a particularly apt solution for those cases where the mobile application is itself an MAS; a scenario that is increasingly realistic, as the recent porting of MAS runtime engines to portable devices testifies. Assuming the agents employ an Agent Communication Language (ACL) that conform to an international standard, for example, the Foundation for Intelligent Physical Agents (FIPA), issues concerning interoperability are reduced significantly.

Using the framework with other non-agent solutions is possible. However, this necessitates the development of a protocol translator for interfacing with the framework. In itself, this is not particularly difficult, but it does increase the workload of the designer and programmer somewhat. However, a simpler solution has been adopted using a blackboard metaphor. At present, a snapshot of the prevailing context during a simulation is regularly posted to a shared blackboard from where it can be queried by the application under test.

4.1 Design

The context simulation framework can be divided into two main parts, one part is Graphical User Interface (GUI) that facilitates interaction between the framework and the software engineer to display simulated end-user behaviors in a physical environment. The second part consists of those agents that model the individual context elements. The framework consists of the following components (Fig. 1):

- Scenario Agent – simulates the user movement based on policies specified by the software tester. For example, the speed at which the subject follows the selected path may be adjusted. Furthermore, the tester may zoom in around certain buildings and define very fine grained trajectories. In this way, the behavior of the system under examination can be scrutinized in areas where difficulties may be expected.
- GUI Manager – updates the display accordingly based on prompts from the Scenario Agent, allowing the tester track the position of the subject.
- IO Manager – manages input from the software tester regarding configuration of the framework.
- Message Router – passes messages to the application or service under test.
- Spatial Agent – Simulates spatial data for the current user position. In this case, standard data that in normal circumstances would be gleaned from GPS NMEA sentences, namely longitude, latitude and orientation, is produced.
- Context Agent – an agent template that can be extended by the tester to generate the required simulated context. The context simulated is of course application dependent. A simple m-commerce example might be that of an agent that maintains a model of the shops in a neighborhood and identifies the nearest one to

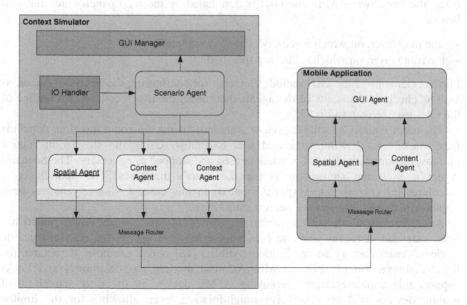

Fig. 1. Architecture of the Context Simulator

the shopper, possibly forming the basis of mobile shopping assistant type application. It is precisely this ease with which additional context simulating agents can be incorporated into the framework that makes it extensible.

Though mobile applications differ substantially in the services they offer, experience gained from designing agent-based mobile applications [15][16][17] suggests a core kernel of agents augmented with further agents as the particular application domain demands:

- GUI Agent – responsible for all I/O activities including display management and capturing user input.
- Content Agent – downloads appropriate content and collaborates with the Spatial Agent and GUI Agent to display the content at the appropriate tine, that is, when the Spatial Agent determines that the user is at the required position
- Spatial Agent – will usually interface with a GPS device, ascertain the current position, and inform other agents of the user's current spatial context.

4.2 Implementation

The entire framework is implemented in Java. All agents are implemented using Agent Factory [13][14]. The Agent Factory framework is a complete agent prototyping environment, providing a suite of facilities for the rapid prototyping of agent-based applications including: prototype agent designs; language interpreters and compilers; a fully functional IDE; and agent and platform viewers. An Agent Factory agent conforms to the BDI paradigm.

The GUI consists of a number of graphical components which are implemented using the Java Swing API. The GUI is dominated by the map panel which has two layers:

- the map layer, on which a geo-coded map is rendered;
- the route layer, on which routes are specified.

Further elements of the GUI include elements for configuring the Scenario Agent, as well as checking the status of the agents that model the user's context. An outline of the GUI may be seen in Fig. 2.

The tester initially sets the degree of granularity using the zoom function. A path is then marked out for the simulated user to follow. Using the simulation control buttons, the simulation can be started, paused and stopped as necessary. The Scenario Agent controls the simulation as per the tester's directives. The Spatial Agent calculates the corresponding spatial context. In this case, a Shop Agent has been implemented that identifies the nearest shop.

Agent Factory, along with a number of other agent development environments has been extended in recent years such that its agents can operate on standard mobile devices. Agent Factory Micro Edition (AFME) [18] is one example. It requires the lightweight version of Java - J2ME. As most modern mobile phones and PDAs support this implementation, deploying AFME agents on the next generation of mobile devices will be relatively straightforward, even allowing for the limited computational resources characteristic of such devices.

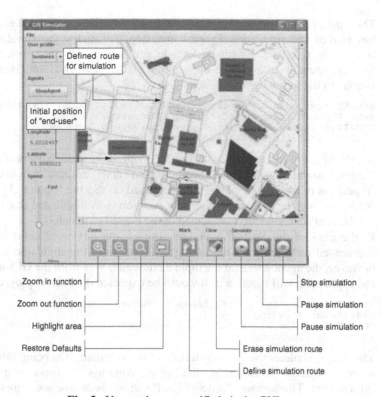

Fig. 2. User paths are specified via the GUI

4.3 Enabling Communication Between Simulator and Application

One distinguishing characteristic of intelligent agents is their social ability. All agents support an Agent Communication Language (ACL) of some variety, although most now seek to utilize an ACL that is FIPA compliant. Agent Factory has its own ACL implementation – AF-APL. However, support for an ACL alone is not sufficient. A mechanism for routing message between agents must also be supported. Agent Factory includes a Message Transport Service (MTS) that delivers this functionality. For messages between different physical platforms, the http protocol is used. For messages between agents residing on the same platform, a local MTS has been implemented. So for simulation purposes, the simulator itself can be hosted on one workstation and application for testing may be either hosted on the actual device or, more likely, on a emulator running on a local workstation. In the former case, however, it is essential that security issues are addressed, as in essence, the IP address will belong to the local network operator.

To establish communication between the simulator and the application, it is necessary to infuse a number of rules into the appropriate agents. For the purposes of this discussion, we consider the simple case of the Spatial Agent on the simulator sending simulated positional data to its namesake on the application.

1. The Spatial Agent on the Simulator, on being informed that the Scenario Agent has moved the simulation forward one step, calculates the simulated spatial context, in this case, longitude, latitude and heading. It must then inform the Spatial Agent on the mobile application of the new situation. Hence, a rule similar to the following will be activated:

```
BELIEF(newSimulatedPosition(?longitude, ?latitude, ?heading)) &
BELIEF(positionRequested(?agent, ?address)    =>
COMMIT(Self,Now,BELIEF(true),(inform(?agent,?address,
newPosition(?longitude, ?latitude, ?heading)))));
```

In AF-APL, tokens denoted with the "?" symbol are placeholders, for example "?agent" would have the value "Spatial Agent" and "?address" would contain the IP address of the device the agent is deployed on. So the "Spatial Agent @ <IP Address>" will be informed that a new position is available and that new values for the user's position are represented in the passed parameters.

2. In the case of the Spatial Agent running on the device, it must likewise be augmented with a rule for processing the input from the simulator. In this case, however, the agent will treat the input as though it was from the GPS device, and the application will function as it would be expected do when deployed.

```
BELIEF(fipaMessage(inform,?sender,newPosition(?longitude,
?latitude, ?heading))) =>
COMMIT(Self,Now,BELIEF(true),processNewPosition(?longitude,
?latitude, ?heading));
```

This rule completes the process started on the simulator. On being informed that a new position is available, the agent commits to processing this new information. The actuator "processNewPosition" is in essence a method in the agent class file that implements the logic for handling this scenario, perhaps by requesting the GUI Agent to update the display, should the application comprise a component that displays the user's position in real time.

In this example, it can be seen that the process of directing output from the simulator to the application under test is relatively straightforward. Moreover, the process for simulating additional contextual cues is identical. An agent is incorporated into the Simulator and infused with the necessary logic to realistically simulate the provision of the required aspect of the user's context. Hence the Simulator is inherently scalable, and the interplay between individual contextual parameters may be explored. In straightforward cases, there may be a peer-to-peer relationship between the agents on the simulator and those on the device, such as with the Spatial Agent case just outlined. However, this will not always be the case, as it may not prove feasible to implement a 1-to-1 relationship between individual agents and the context cues it monitors, due to the computational overhead involved.

5 Future Work

Given the wide variety of situations where mobile computing applications and services can be deployed, it can be seen that the more realistic the model of the user's context is, the more useful such a framework would be in the software development process. Therefore it is planned to augment the number of context elements further.

For example, the accurate simulation of a wireless connection is essential. In particular, the modeling of latency, as well as the variable and unpredictable data-rates such as one would normally encounter, would significantly added to the realism of the context model. Another issue concerns developing a more realistic model of spatial context. In the case of GPS, signal quality may vary and, particularly in so called urban canyons, the signal can be lost entire albeit temporally. Verifying the robustness of an application in such circumstances is of critical importance.

Though a user's movements can be modeled at present, there is significant scope and motivation for facilitated more realistic and sophisticated user behavior. In practice, people may stop at pedestrian crossings, do some window shopping and so on. They may also get lost! Thus modeling elements of variable and unpredictable behavior, would add a significant degree of realism to the context models.

Extensibility is of critical importance if third party software engineers wish to develop models of the context that is relevant to their individual applications. Though intelligent agents offer an intuitive mechanism by which this can be achieved, the process of incorporating third-party agents is currently somewhat unwieldy and difficult. Therefore it is planned to simplify this process considerable. As part of this, the specification of a basic ontology that developers could extend and enhance according to their individual needs will be considered.

6 Conclusion

Services and applications for mobile users will form a significant revenue generator for many software houses and consultancies over the coming years. Therefore, there will be an increasing demand for sophisticated toolkits and frameworks that support the modeling of user behaviors and the derivation of appropriate context elements. In this paper, we have described one such framework. Intelligent agents form the core entities around which the framework is constructed and offer interesting possibilities for modeling complex and dynamic user behavior. In developing this context modeling framework, we have demonstrated one viable approach by which the needs of a new generation of software engineers may be addressed.

Acknowledgements

This material is based upon works supported by the Science Foundation Ireland (SFI) under Grant No. 03/IN.3/1361.

References

1. Aarts, E, Marzano, S. (editors), The New Everyday: Views on Ambient Intelligence, 010 Publishers, Rotterdam, The Netherlands, 2003.
2. Barton, J., Vijayaraghavan, V., Ubiwise: A Ubiquitous Wireless Infrastructure Simulation Environment, tech. report HPL-2002- 303, HP Labs, 2002.
3. Morla, R., Davies, N., Evaluating a Location-based Application: A Hybrid Test and Simulation Environment, IEEE Pervasive Computing, 3(3), pp. 48-56, 2004.

4. Bylund, M. Espinoza, F., Testing and Demonstrating Context-aware Services with Quake III Arena, Communications of the ACM, 45 (1), 46-48, 2002.
5. Satoh, I., Software Testing for Wireless Mobile Computing, IEEE Wireless Communications, 11(5), pp. 58-64, October 2004.
6. Satoh, I., A Testing Framework for Mobile Computing Software, IEEE Transactions on Software Engineering, 29(12), pp. 1112-1121, December 2003.
7. Hou, Q., Zhu, H., Greenwood, S., A Multi-Agent Software Environment for Testing Web-based Applications. Proceedings of the 27th Annual International Computer Software and Applications Conference (COMPSAC'03), Dallas, Texas, 2003, pp. 10-15.
8. Narendra, N.C., Large Scale Testing of Pervasive Computing Systems Using Multi-Agent Simulation. Proceedings of the Third Workshop on Intelligent Solutions in Embedded Systems (WISES'05), Hamburg, Germany, 2005, pp. 27-38.
9. Greenberg, S. "Context as a Dynamic Construct," Human-Computer Interaction, Vol. 16, pp. 257-268, 2001.
10. Ubisense, http://www.ubisense.net/
11. Wooldridge, M., Jennings, N.R., Intelligent Agents: Theory and Practice, The Knowledge Engineering Review, vol.10, no.2, 1995, pp. 115-152.
12. Rao, A.S., Georgeff, M.P., Modelling Rational Agents within a BDI Architecture. In: Principles of Knowledge Representation. & Reasoning, San Mateo, CA. 1991.
13. Collier, R., O'Hare, G. M. P. Lowen, T. D., and Rooney, C. F. B., Beyond Prototyping in the Factory of Agents, In Proc. 3rd Int. Central and Eastern European Conference on Multi-Agent Systems (CEEMAS), Prague, Czech Republic, 2003.
14. O'Hare G.M.P., Agent Factory: An Environment for the Fabrication of Multi-Agent Systems, in Foundations of Distributed Artificial Intelligence (G.M.P. O'Hare and N. Jennings eds) pp. 449-484, John Wiley and Sons, Inc., 1996.
15. O'Grady, M.J., O'Hare, G.M.P., Just-in-Time Multimedia Distribution in a Mobile Computing Environment, IEEE Multimedia, vol. 11, no. 4, pp. 62-74, 2004.
16. Keegan, S, & O'Hare, G.M.P., EasiShop - Agent-Based Cross Merchant Product Comparison Shopping for the Mobile User, proceedings of ICTTA '04, Syria, 2004.
17. Strahan, R., O'Hare, G.M.P., Phelan, D., Muldoon, C., Collier, R., ACCESS: An Agent based Architecture for the Rapid Prototyping of Location Aware Services, 5th International Conference on Computational Science, Emory University Atlanta, 2005.
18. Muldoon, C., O'Hare, G. M. P., Collier, R. W., O'Grady, M. J., Agent Factory Micro Edition: A Framework for Ambient Applications, proceedings of the Intelligent Agents in Computing System Workshop, ICCS, Reading, UK, 2006.

OTM 2006 Academy Doctoral Consortium PC Co-chairs' Message

The OTM Academy Doctoral Consortium is the third edition of an event at the "On The Move Federated Conferences" that provides a platform for researchers at the beginning of their career. Promising doctoral students are encouraged to showcase their work on an international forum, where they are provided with an opportunity to gain feedback and guidance on future research directions from prominent professors.

For enabling this supportive setting, we want to thank the Dean of the OTM Academy, Jan L.G. Dietz, and the OTM General Chairs who strongly stimulated the participation of doctoral students to this event by offering them an internationally highly reputed publication channel, namely, the Springer LNCS proceedings of the OTM workshops, and an overall conference access at a much reduced rate. In particular, we appreciate the support by the accompanying professors, namely, Johann Eder from the University of Vienna, Austria, and Maria Orlowska, from the University of Queensland, Australia. Furthermore, we want to thank the additional reviewers Domenico Beneventano and Sonia Bergamaschi from the Universitá di Modena e Reggio Emilia, Italy, and Jaime Delgado, Universitat Pompeu Fabra, Spain, for giving valuable feedback on the submitted contributions.

We received 14 submissions by doctoral students from 6 different countries, whereby each paper was evaluated by three reviewers. Seven of these papers were accepted for presentation at the OTM Academy and for publication in the proceedings of the OTM workshops.

We invite the participants of the OTM conferences and workshops as well as the readers of these proceedings to discover the next generation of promising scientists in our research field and get acquainted with their research topics. One can hardly overestimate the importance of sharing a culture of scientific interrogation, discussion, reflection and stimulation between the members of our research community.

Best regards from the OTM Academy Doctoral Consortium Program Chairs!

August 2006   Antonia Albani, University of Augsburg, Germany
                Gábor Nagypál, Forschungszentrum Informatik - FZI, Germany
        Johannes Maria Zaha, Queensland University of Technology, Australia

R. Meersman, Z. Tari, P. Herrero et al. (Eds.): OTM Workshops 2006, LNCS 4278, p. 1401, 2006.

Multidimensional Effort Prediction
for ERP System Implementation

Torben Hansen

Institute for Information Systems at the
German Research Center for Artificial Intelligence,
Stuhlsatzenhausweg 3,
66123 Saarbruecken, Germany
torben.hansen@iwi.dfki.de

Abstract. The Ph.D. thesis builds upon the state-of-the-art in effort prediction for ERP-implementation projects. While current approaches use the complexity of the technical system as only indicator for estimation, a multidimensional key ratio scorecard is developed to enhance the quality of effort prediction. Key ratios from the technical dimension are extended towards service-oriented architectures as the upcoming, dominating architectural ERP concept. Within the organizational dimension, competencies of the project team are evaluated and quantified as key ratios. Key ratios from the situational dimension are used for approximating the expected degree of employee cooperation. As fuzzy key ratios cannot be manually derived from business requirements, an IT-based tool is designed, prototypically realized and empirically evaluated in order to be used for retrieval of defined key ratios in the scorecard.

Keywords: Enterprise Resource Planning, Effort Prediction, Key Ratios, Data Mining.

1 Motivation

Effort prediction is a key activity for determining necessary budget and resource allocations for project planning. In the field of software development, Lines-of-Code metrics as well as Function-Point based approaches have been widely used for this purpose [1, 2]. Application of these concepts for ERP implementation projects however is not possible as software implementation projects are not focussed primarily on code creation but on customization [3, 4]. Customization describes the process of tailoring already existing functionality to the specific demands of the customer. For effort prediction in software customization settings, similarity-based measures have found practical application. Efforts of upcoming projects are inferred based on past experience with comparable projects in size and complexity [5, 6].

The quality of similarity-based estimations depends on the selection of key ratios used for project description. Ideally, key ratios describe the entirety of effort-driving factors. Estimation errors necessarily take place, if success-critical factors are not covered with key ratios and information loss occurs [7].

R. Meersman, Z. Tari, P. Herrero et al. (Eds.): OTM Workshops 2006, LNCS 4278, pp. 1402–1408, 2006.

Approaches for effort prediction in ERP-Implementation projects use key ratios specifying details of the technical system structure [3, 8, 9]. This includes the number of clients, plants and company codes as well as the amount of customer-specific functions and programs to be implemented in the ERP installation. Major non-technical effort drivers as constantly identified in both constructive as well as empirical research from the field of ERP success factor literature [10, 11, 12] have so far been disregarded from effort prediction. They do not impact therefore the similarity measure used for identifying comparable projects. Examples for non-technical effort drivers include project team competence, the level of project acceptance or the degree of top-management support.

Summarizing, current effort prediction approaches share the underlying assumption that non-technical factors such as who implements and where the implementation takes place, have no impact on the implementation effort. This results in a misspecification of the effort prediction model and an inadequate support for resource allocation. Consequently, literature lists about 50-90% of all ERP-implementation projects as to be exceeding time and budget restrictions [13, 14].

2 Research Question

Research focuses on designing, implementing and empirically evaluating an IT-supported key ratio scorecard, which adequately represents multidimensional effort drivers for ERP-Implementation projects. By using this scorecard, project managers are enabled to potentially increase the quality of their effort predictions by identifying more similar project structures. In order to achieve this, the Ph.D. work addresses three research goals as laid out in Table 1:

Table 1. Overview of research goals of the Ph.D. thesis

Goal	Description	Approach
Identification of dimensions and corresponding key ratios for ERP-Implementation.	On a conceptual level, key ratios have to be identified from dimensions impacting project effort.	Analysis of ERP-implementation and success factor literature.
Method selection in order to obtain data input for defined key ratios.	Regarding design specification, methods have to be identified, that allow for measuring the defined ratios. A specific challenge is quantifying soft fuzzy ratios.	Interdisciplinary research within the fields of information systems, artificial intelligence and personal psychology.
Conceptualization and prototypical realization of IT-based tools partially necessary for key ratio identification	IT-based tools are partially needed to reason upon gathered information for fuzzy key ratios, which cannot be deduced from formal business requirements.	Information Systems Development cycle following the structure of [14]; empirical validation of the constructed tool in a real-life setting.

3 Research Methodology and Selected Results

The Ph.D. thesis consists of eight chapters. Following the introductory first chapter, the state of the art in effort prediction for ERP implementation is presented in chapter 2. The validity of current ERP effort prediction models that are based on key ratios from the technical system domain is questioned. Using an ERP-literature review, three dimensions with potential impact on effort prediction are identified as presented in Table 2. Hypotheses are generated, assuming the potential influence of factors from all three dimensions on effort prediction. Possibilities for testing the hypotheses are discussed. Empirical studies are selected based on defined requirements, such as study size, study creation date or methodological soundness. Analysis of the selected empirical studies confirms the hypotheses. The situational dimension is furthermore identified as being most difficult to work with and therefore requires special emphasis due to the broadness and fuzziness when approximating external human behavior. In order to determine key ratios for each of the three dimensions, meta effort drivers are deduced from the studies. Meta effort drivers describe factors, which cannot be directly measured as single numeric values without previous aggregation due to their complexity. As such, meta effort drivers need further detailing in order to be characterized using key ratios. Each meta effort driver can then be described using a multitude of key ratios.

Table 2. Overview of dimensions of the key ratio scorecard and identified meta effort drivers

Dimension	Description	Domain for key ratio definitions	Meta Effort Drivers
Technical	"What is being implemented?"	Information System Science	Technology Complexity
Situational	"Where is the implementation taking place?"	Organizational Analysis	Future Employee Behavior
Organizational	"Who implements?"	Human Resource Management	Team Competence

Chapter 3 focuses on the refinement of technical effort drivers. While approaches so far have suggested key ratios to be used for module-based ERP-architectures [3, 8], these ratios are not applicable with upcoming service-based enterprise architectures (SOA) and resulting technological implications [15]. Unlike traditional module-based structures, customizations of ERP-installations in the future need to be measured in regards to the service structure applied, the concept of services within the SOA or the amount and granularity of services and service layers implemented. This imposes an even greater challenge, as there is no standard SOA structure currently defined [16]. Instead vendors use the term of service orientation in terms of their ERP architectures differently. While the desired alignment of SOA with business processes enables a potentially higher flexibility in adjusting processes at a later point in time as illustrated in Fig.1, the initial set-up of such process-aligned service structures requires additional effort [15].

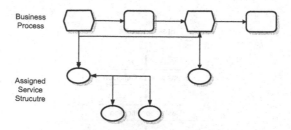

Fig. 1. Desired Alignment between Services and Business Functions

A framework to measure the implementation effort therefore needs to ensure the comparability of projects by defining ratios which on the one hand describe projects in sufficient detail, and on the other hand have a certain breadth to distinguish fundamental conceptual differences. Additionally, the amount of key ratios needs to be limited in order to secure practical applicability. Given these requirements, the methodology for identifying key ratios is discussed and using a two-tier approach, key ratios are selected following a through discussion of possible design specifications.

In Chapter 4, the selection of situational key ratios is in focus. The meta effort driver "future employee behavior" refers to actions of employees towards the change process initiated by the ERP-implementation, which impact project duration. In order to operationalize this measure at time of effort prediction, quantified estimates of expected future behavior need to be created using adequate methods. For describing the state-of-the-art of cross disciplinal, IT-based behavioral prediction in literature, the boundaries of behavior prediction need to be defined first. As such, behavior is decomposed into underlying causal states and events whose instances can possibly be used for prediction. Using a behavioral reference model from the field of personal psychology, approaches for predicting behavior across disciplines can then be classified regarding the inference source, such as motives, actions or judgmental evaluations. The reference model used was chosen due to its close match with behavioral instances identified to be of special interest in the literature review in ERP-settings within chapter 2. Other reference concepts such as Social Cognitive Theory [17, 18] also potentially serve the purpose but would require significant amounts of additional adaptation effort. Approaches from the field of acceptance [19], resistance [20] and deceit research [21] within Information Systems research are evaluated just as prediction system concepts from computer science [22] and psychological tests from the field of behavioral sciences [23]. As a result of the approach evaluation, no existing concept of behavioral prediction fully satisfies defined requirements for an ERP implementation project. However, analogies between behavioral predictions for ERP implementations and acceptance models [24, 25] from the IS-field allow for an orientation on existing conceptual structures. Key ratio collection is therefore not possible, unless a method is specified, that allows for behavior prediction in the context of ERP-implementations.

In Chapter 5, the prediction method is designed and is prototypically realized and empirically evaluated within an IT-based prediction tool for quantifying the meta effort driver of future employee behavior. The development cycle follows three major stages in analogy to the description of an information system (Fig.2):

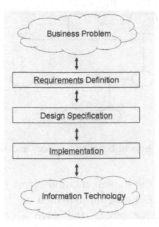

Fig. 2. Descriptive Levels of an Information System [26]

In conceptual design, the system architecture is presented and its components are detailed. Of specific interest is the inference component, which is used to create key ratios from data input streams. In order for an inference method to be selected, actual key ratios first need to be defined. Using the meta effort driver of employee behavior, it needs to be determined, which subordinate behavior or which set of subordinate behaviors is most relevant to be expressed as key ratios in context of an ERP effort prediction. This distinction is non-trivial as Information Systems literature suffers heavily from inconsistencies regarding terminology to describe states and actions [27]. Terms such as acceptance, resistance, cooperation, refusal, decline or satisfaction, need to be carefully given meaning in the ERP-context, before a selection can be made. After terminological clearing, the term resistance is selected as basis for the key ratios as being defined as the opposite behavioral instance. The evaluation takes place using an analogy to resistance theories from psychotherapeutic schools, in which resistance is an intensely researched construct. Within design specification phase of the tool development, methods are evaluated to transform the data input stream to discreet key ratio values. Methods for assigning singular data values to higher level constructs, such as neural networks and decision trees from the field of data mining or multivariate statistical measures such as factor analysis or structural equation modeling techniques are discussed in this context. The IT-based tool to generate key ratios of the situational dimension is prototypically realized and evaluated in a real-life setting.

Chapter 6 describes the organizational dimension and the quantification of the meta effort driver team competence. At first competence is defined. Competence can be considered to be a behavioral instance, so that the behavioral reference model from chapter 4 can be reused with differing behavioral instances. Competence Management is selected as a reference discipline. In order to determine suitable methods to quantify competence, the specifics of team structures in an ERP context need to be defined.

Chapter 7 summarizes the findings and discusses implications in terms of weighting key ratios, dealing with additional noise due to fuzziness and the applicability of the multidimensional framework with existing similarity measures. An outlook on chances and limitations concludes the Ph.D. work.

4 Ph.D. Project's Contribution to the Problem Domain

The Ph.D. project's contribution to the problem domain can be summarized within six major aspects:

1. Effort prediction approaches are extended beyond the technical dimension by quantifying fuzzy effort drivers of project team competence and employee resistance.
2. Key ratio definitions of traditional ERP effort prediction are updated regarding upcoming service-oriented architectures.
3. An IT-based Tool for identifying fuzzy key ratios is designed, prototypically realized and empirically evaluated. While the tool is designed to be used for effort prediction, it creates an additional benefit for change management purposes.
4. Currently unrelated IS research fields of acceptance, resistance and deceit research are bridged and a common understanding of these constructs in an IS implementation setting is established.
5. Currently scattered research within the academic disciplines of IS research, computer science, social sciences and cognitive psychology is merged.
6. Discussion of socio-technical factors in IS research is facilitated.

References

1. Fenton, N. E., Pfleeger, S. L.: Software Metrics: A Rigorous and Practical Approach. PWS Publishing, Boston (1998)
2. Shepperd, M., Schofield, C., Kitchenham, B.: Effort Estimation using Analogy. In: Proceedings of the 18th International Conference on Software Engineering. (1996) 170-178
3. Stensrud, E.: Alternative Approaches to Effort Prediction of ERP Projects. Information and Software Technology 43 (2001) 413-423
4. Stensrud, E., Myrtveit, I.: Identifying High-Performance ERP-Projects. IEEE Transactions on Software Engineering 29 (2003) 398-416
5. Walkerden, F., Jeffery, R.: An Empirical Study of Analogy-Based Software Effort Estimation. Empirical Software Engineering 4 (1999) 135-158
6. Loos, P.: Advanced Information Technology Application in ERP Systems. In: Proceedings of the 6th Americas Conference on Information Systems (2000) 635-640
7. Diamantopoulos, A., Siguaw, J. A.: Formative vs. Reflective Indicators in Measure Development: Does the choice of Indicators Matter? Cornell University Working Paper Series 05-21-02 (2002)
8. Francalanci, C.: Predicting the Implantation Effort of ERP Projects: Empirical Evidence on SAP R/3. Journal of Information Technology 16 (2001) 33-49
9. Parr, A., Shanks, G.: A Model of ERP Project Implementation. Journal of Information Technology 15 (2000) 289-303
10. Bradley, J.: Are All Critical Success Factors in ERP Implementation Created Equal? In: Proceedings of the 11th Americas Conf. on Information Systems 2005 (2005) 2152-2160

11. Somers, T. M., Nelson, K.: The Impact of Critical Success Factors across the Stages of Enterprise Resource Planning Implementations. In: Proceedings of the 34th Hawaii International Conference on System Sciences Volume 8 (2001) 8016-8027
12. Zhang, L., Lee, M. K. O., Zhang, Z., Banerjee, P.: Critical Success Factors of Enterprise Resource Planning Systems Implementation Success in China. In: Proceedings of the 36th Hawaii International Conference on System Science (2002) 10-21
13. Holland, C. P., Light, B.: A Critical Success Factors Model for ERP Implementation. IEEE Software 16 (1999) 30-36
14. Scheer, A.-W., Habermann, F.: Making ERP a Success. Co. of the ACM 43 (2000) 57-62
15. Erl, T.: Service-Oriented Architectures: A Field Guide to Integrating XML and Web-Services. Pearson Education, Upper Saddle River (2004)
16. Krafzig, D., Banke, K., Slama, D.: Enterprise SOA: Service-Oriented Architecture Best Practice. Prentice Hall Education, Upper Saddle River (2004)
17. Bandura, A.: Social Cognitive Theory: An Agentive Perspective. Annual Review of Psychology 52 (2001) 1-27
18. Bandura, A.: Social Foundations of Thought and Action. Prentice Hall, Englewood Cliffs (1986)
19. Amberg, M., Hirschmeier, M., Schobert, D.: DART - An Acceptance Model for the Analysis and Design of Innovative Technologies. In: Proceedings of the Seventh Conference on Synergetics, Cybernetics and Informatics (2003)
20. Mullany, M.: Using cognitive style measurements to forecast user resistance. In: Proceedings of the 14th Annual Conference of the NACCQ (2001) 95-100
21. Zhou, L., Burgoon, J. K., Nunamaker, J. F., Twitchell, D.: Automatic Linguistics-based Cues for Detecting Deception in Text-based Asynchronous Computer-mediated Communication. Group Decision and Negotiation 13 (2004) 81-107
22. McGrath, G. M., Dampney, C. N. G., More, E.: MP/L1: An Automated Model of Organisational Power and its Application as a Conflict Prediction Aid in Information Systems Strategy Implementation. In: Proceedings of the 11th Conference on Artificial Intelligence for Applications (1995) 56-65
23. Viney, L.: The Assessment of Psychological States through Content Analysis of Verbal Communications. Psychological Bulletin 94 (1983) 542-564
24. Davis, F. D.: A Technology Acceptance Model for Empirically Testing New End-User Information Systems. MIT Dissertationsreihe, Cambridge (1986)
25. Venkatesh, V., Morris, M. G., Davis, G. B., Davis, F. D.: User Acceptance of Information Technology: Towards a Unified View. MIS Quarterly 27 (2003) 425-479
26. Scheer, A.-W.: Business Process Engineering: Reference Models for Industrial Enterprises. Springer, Berlin (1994)
27. Lauer, T., Rajagopalan, B.: Examining the Relationship between Acceptance and Resistance in System Implementation. In: Proceedings of the Eighths Americas Conference on Information Systems 2002 (2002) 1297-1304

A Decision-Making Oriented Model for Corporate Mobile Business Applications

Daniel Simonovich

European School of Business, Reutlingen University,
Alteburgstrasse 150, D-72762 Reutlingen
daniel.simonovich@reutlingen-university.de

Abstract. Information and communication technology (ICT) has witnessed mobility as an important development over the last few years. So far the discussion about mobile information systems has largely been techno-centric and supplier oriented rather than business-centric and user oriented. The lack of available methods for business driven evaluation motivates the research question of effective decision making support. This paper summarizes the PhD research effort aimed at constructing a decision support model to enhance the awareness and understanding of mobile applications impact. It presents a formal approach and lays out in the underlying research methodology as well as the epistemological position. This contribution also highlights the recent and dynamic debate on suitable IS research standards, thereby inviting a discussion on appropriate artifact-based design research and the central question of validation to successfully complete the research project.

Keywords: Mobile business, conceptual modeling, business process modeling, ICT strategy, IS research.

1 Introduction

Mobile systems have received considerable attention over the last few years, extending the application boundaries of modern information and communication technology (ICT) [1]. The overwhelming majority of research publication in this field either addressed technological advances or aggregate market potential of these technologies [2]. However, it has become increasingly obvious that a technological push can hardly result in the full exploitation of value adding business applications unless the business impact of such technologies is better understood. Consequently, calls for the execution of serious research to be undertaken from a differentiated stakeholder perspective, including the business and user perspectives, were expressed [3]. This paper lays out the research effort represented by a corresponding PhD thesis, positioned for a better understanding of mobile technology impact in a corporate context.

2 From Research Domain to Research Question

Despite interdisciplinary research interest, the field of mobile technologies and applications has created an imbalance between a strong technological push and actual awareness and adoption by corporate users and decision-makers. This section lays out

R. Meersman, Z. Tari, P. Herrero et al. (Eds.): OTM Workshops 2006, LNCS 4278, pp. 1409–1418, 2006.
© Springer-Verlag Berlin Heidelberg 2006

the research gap within the context of mobile technology and business research and carefully defines the problem domain leading to the research question.

2.1 Research Domain

The availability and application potential of mobile technologies has created a sustained research interest, as witnessed by the evolution of dedicated conferences and workshops in this field (see Fig. 1).

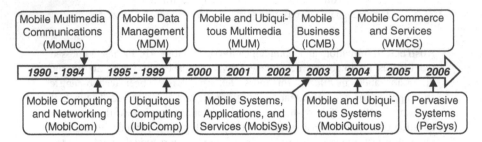

Fig. 1. Evolution of major international conferences and workshops related to mobile business

However, most research efforts reflected by these research communities have mainly been technology and systems oriented with little systematic orientation for a well informed corporate use. When one of the longest established conferences introduced business-centric contributions [4], it concluded realizing a tremendous understanding gap between business and computer science academics.

Actually, research into the application of mobile technologies is far from being limited to the computer science discipline. While computer science has certainly played an enabling role by advancing mobile communication protocols [5], quality of service [6], systems integration [7] and security aspects [8], economics and social sciences have joined in interdisciplinary research activities. These interdisciplinary contributions cover technology acceptance [9], overall market potential studies [2], or human-computer-interface design [10]. The market prospects of mobile business opportunities have also added the study of so called business models to the research spectrum [11]. However, these publications address the business opportunity question of providers of mobile services rather than exploiting application rationale from the corporate user's perspective. In essence, a major research gap remains in assisting corporate decision-makers in translating mobile business characteristics into tangible and communicable benefits. In response to a business-centric research agenda, originally laid out to elicit business-driven research contributions [3], the following subsection will translate the research gap into a concrete research question.

2.2 Problem Formulation and Research Question

It is widely accepted that information systems support value creating activities which in turn are targeted to achieve corporate goals dictated by an overall business strategy [12]. This implies that understanding the contribution of specific mobile applications depends on the comprehension of their business strategy and process activity support potential. To this present date, these are hardly explored connections. The current barriers represented by this research gap keep corporate decision makers from systematically analyzing the potential of available mobile business solutions. The situation is further complicated by the fact that electronic and mobile business publications have produced much inconsistent and self-contradicting vocabulary [12]. Consequently, any attempt to integrate required dimensions of business analysis depends on cleaned up definitions.

Before narrowing down the chosen research question, it is important to clearly define the boundaries of the problem domain: As motivated in the preceding sections, the focus is on the corporate user's perspective in an investment decision phase. To enable a linkage to business strategy research and practice, the strategic business unit is chosen as the established unit of analysis. Fig. 2 summarizes the problem domain leading to the research question.

Fig. 2. Problem domain and research question

The research question in Fig. 2 is broken down into three guiding sub questions:

1) Which dimensions of analysis are relevant in a corporate context while being understood by a management audience?
2) How can the prevalent and counterproductive lack of definition clarity concerning mobile applications be alleviated?
3) How can an integrative model capture these analytic dimensions and their interrelationships to support decision-making?

3 Research Approach

3.1 Chosen Research Methodology

Ultimately, the goal is to meaningfully integrate relevant analysis dimensions into a comprehensive conceptual model explaining the potential impact of the mobile business application class for a corporate decision-making audience. The research process is a step-by-step buildup. After substantiating the dimensions of analysis to be dealt with, a comprehensive definition set is crafted since any formal modeling attempt needs to be grounded on stable definitions. Formal model construction is executed using predicate calculus and relational algebra. This model is generic and instantiated using empirical insights from the analysis dimensions. This approach is deliberately designed in line with accepted design science research criteria [13]. The modeling technique builds on recent conceptual modeling research in the area of business process modeling [14]. As discussed below, model validation remains the essential discussion for thesis completion.

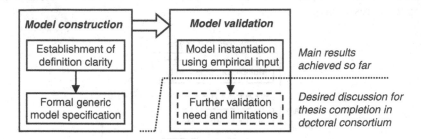

Fig. 3. Design science oriented research approach

3.2 Epistemological Position

Critical realism is a widespread position on truth in the natural and social sciences. Modeling artifacts for the design of systems and procedures, however, do not fit the hypothesis based search for objectivity [15] and therefore are better captured by a minor constructivist position [16] (see Fig. 4). Despite the lack of empirical research inclination in this field, the recent and unconcluded debate on model validation invites a careful combination of constructivist research with empirical elements [17]. Therefore, empirically gained sub models are preferred. However, empiricism in the construction phase does not replace validation of the resulting model. Validation remains the open discussion thesis issue.

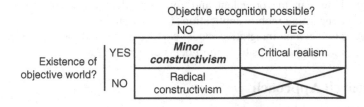

Fig. 4. Chosen epistemological position

4   Research Results Achieved so Far

4.1   Definition Clarity

As pointed out in the chosen methodology in Fig. 3, stable definitions are a prerequisite for complex model construction. Unfortunately, mobile business literature has neither produced a single definition nor avoided definitions which can be easily falsified. For example, any attempt to define mobile business as a mobile internet phenomenon unacceptably excludes established application categories using cellular communication standards, local wireless area networks (WLANs) or off-line-and-synchronization techniques. In addition, the terms "commerce" versus "business" are sometimes used synonymously and sometimes in subset relationships.

Let i, m, and t denote the properties of internet access, mobility and transaction execution. Then the application classes of e-business (A_{EB}), m-business (A_{MB}), e-commerce (A_{EC}) and m-commerce (A_{MC}) can be defined in regard of an overall IS application class A:

$$A_{EB} = \{a \in A \mid i(a)\} \quad \wedge \quad A_{MB} = \{a \in A \mid m(a)\} . \tag{1}$$

$$A_{EC} = \{a \in A_{EB} \mid t(a)\} \quad \wedge \quad A_{MC} = \{a \in A_{MB} \mid t(a)\} . \tag{2}$$

Fig. 5 demonstrates a differentiated view of these application subsets. It is important to note that for any subset obvious real world application examples exist.

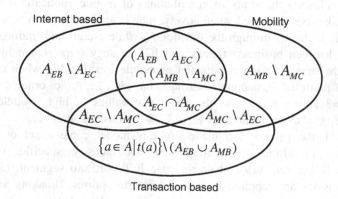

Fig. 5. Definition clarity for applications using mobile technology

The PhD thesis not only establishes definition clarity around the notion of mobile business applications but also outlines the choice of analysis dimensions required for corporate decision making: generic strategies [18], [19], ICT portfolio segments [20], and business processes [21], [22].

4.2 Generic Model Construction

The conceptual model suitable for integrating empirically motivated frameworks and data is shown in Fig. 6.

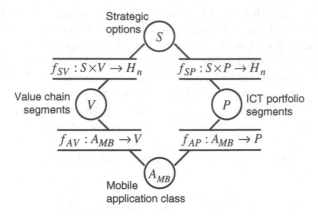

Fig. 6. Conceptual generic model

Through the function f_{AV} individual mobile applications $a \in A_{MB}$ are mapped onto business process or value chain activity segments V. Existing knowledge about how strategic options are reflected in specific activities can be captured using the function f_{SV}, thereby allowing the study of contributions of mobile applications to business strategies. Likewise or, indeed, alternatively, mobile applications can be attributed to ICT portfolio segments through the function f_{AP} while established findings about the relationship between business strategy and ICT strategy (represented by f_{SP}) helps estimating the strategic support potential of mobile functionality when added to an existing ICT portfolio. H_n denotes a scoring set h_0, h_1, ..., h_{n-1} of ordered values. For example, $n=3$ allows to express the qualitative values of high, middle and low, popularly depicted as the symbol set $\{\bigcirc, \rightmoon, \bullet\}$ in business practice.

Along with the generic formulation of this model come a set of underlying assumptions: (1) Mobile applications are not industry specific. (2) Mobile applications fit but one value chain and one ICT portfolio segment. (3) Strategic business decisions are captured by a set of generic options. Breaking any of these assumptions lends to the need of purpose-specific model extensions which are dealt with at the end of this section.

4.3 Model Instantiation Based on Existing Frameworks

To instantiate the generic model in a fashion that incorporates real-world experience, three empirically researched frameworks are chosen to fill out the abstract sets and their interrelationships (see Fig. 7).

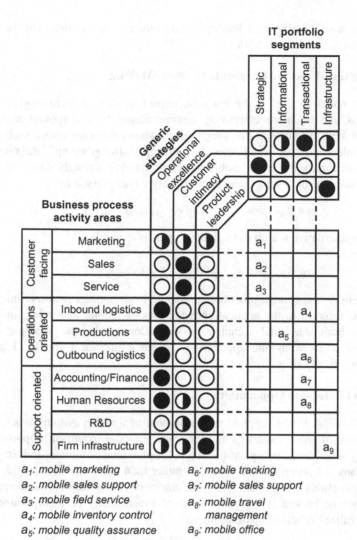

Fig. 7. Conceptual model instantiation

The first source is the value discipline framework which presents operational excellence, customer intimacy, and product leadership as generic strategy tradeoffs [19]. The second model classifies the nature of ICT benefits, such as better control for informational systems, or increased throughput for transactional systems, into distinct ICT portfolio segments [20]. Both frameworks were developed and validated using a large number of case studies and were also related to each other [23]. The third framework input was generated by the author of this paper in support of the plausibility for structuring mobile business applications along the corporate value chain [24], as was previously shown for electronic business applications [12]. Fig. 7

shows how a set of nine well known mobile business applications can be analyzed using the instantiated framework.

4.4 Using the Model for Corporate Decision-Making

Using the model in Fig. 7, the business impact of mobile technologies and their applications can be more effectively communicated to a corporate audience for decision-making. The usefulness is highlighted when asking questions, such as: which mobile applications are candidates for strategic strengthening? Relating to the formalism in Fig. 6, the set of mobile applications most strongly supporting a given strategy s through some value generation activity v is expressed by

$$\{a \in A_{MB} \mid \exists v \in V : f_{AV}(a) = v \wedge f_{SV}(s,v) = h_{n-1}\}, \tag{3}$$

whereas an alternative search through the IS portfolio yields

$$\{a \in A_{MB} \mid \exists p \in V : f_{AP}(a) = v \wedge f_{SP}(s,v) = h_{n-1}\}. \tag{4}$$

Using Fig. 7, a corporate practitioner wishing to strengthen customer intimacy, for example, is referred to the application categories of mobile marketing, mobile field support in both sales and technical service. Conversely, the strategic influence potential of a given mobile application can be expressed formally (Fig. 6) and searched practically (Fig. 7).

4.5 Model Extension Opportunity

The model of Fig. 6 was supplied with a number of limiting assumptions. Therefore, any breaking of these assumptions represents a model extension opportunity. The incorporation of industry-specific mobile applications requires industry-specific instantiations. To accommodate a general rather than functional relationship between mobile applications and segments of value chains or ICT portfolios, these applications might either be broken into smaller units of functionality or incorporated through more generalized relationship descriptions.

5 Evaluation of Results and Need for Discussion

5.1 Thesis Contribution

The PhD work presented in this paper is a response to an early mobile research agenda, calling for serious publications from a business perspective [3]. It has addressed the otherwise criticized lack of definition clarity in the mobile applications field and integrated previous business oriented contributions to assist corporate decision making, thereby motivating the natural consideration of such systems alongside traditional ICT applications. The model is limited by its assumptions including those from the underlying sub models.

5.2 Need for Open Discussion: To Validate or Not to Validate?

The work presented follows the design science practice in IS research [13]. Although this paradigm is far from sharing the empirical tradition of behavioristic research, the recent discussion about design science has raised the issue of artifact validation, including empiricism. While the generic model in Fig. 6 is accessible through logical argument and proper use of mathematical notation, the instantiated model in Fig. 7 offers potential for combining constructivism with empirical elements, as included through the sub models. However, basing model construction on empirical finings does not replace validation. Actually, there is a built-in validation mechanism thanks to a double path linking mobile applications to strategy (value chain and ICT portfolio). Model consistency is challenged whenever

$$\exists a \in A_{MB} \ \exists s \in S : f_{SV}(s, f_{AV}(a)) \neq f_{SP}(s, f_{AP}(a)) . \tag{5}$$

Should any validation, especially of empirical nature, be undertaken beyond this? Different research opinions point in different directions. Some claim that empirical research on new ideas is required to find out how good these ideas really are and how they can be improved. Others claim that empirical testing of modeling artifacts is methodologically unsound and counterproductive, requiring hard-to-get testing persons to become used to the model, consequently affecting the results. This is the author's aspired open discussion for the doctoral consortium audience.

References

1. Hu, W.C., Lee, C.W., Yeh J.H.: Mobile Commerce Systems. In: Shi, N.S. (ed.): Mobile Commerce Applications. Idea Group Publishing, Hershey London Melbourne Singapore (2004) 1-23
2. Samuelsson M., Dholakia, N.: Assessing the Market Potential of Network-Enabled 3G M-Business Services. In: Shi, N.S. (ed.): Wireless Communications and Mobile Commerce, IRM Press (2004) 23-48
3. Lehner, F., Watson, R.: From E-Commerce to M-Commerce: Research Directions.Working paper of the Chair of Business Informatics, University of Regensburg (2001)
4. Simonovich, D.: Business-Centric Analysis of Corporate Mobile Applications, 8th International Workshop on Mobile Multimedia Communications (2003) 269-273
5. Chlamtac, I: Editorial – Special Issue on Protocols and Software Paradigms of Mobile Networks, Mobile Networks and Applications, Vol. 3 (1998) 121-122
6. Markasin, A., Olariu, S., Todorova, P.: QoS Oriented Medium Access Control for All – IP/ATM Mobile Commerce Applications. In: Shi, N.S. (ed.): Mobile Commerce Applications. Idea Group Publishing, Hershey London Melbourne Singapore (2004) 303-331
7. Velasco, J., Castillo, S.: Mobile Agents for Web Service Composition. In: Bauknecht, K., Tjoa, A.M., Quirchmayr, G. (eds.): E-Commerce and Web Technologies. Proceedings of the 4th International Conference EC-Web, Springer, Berlin (2003)
8. Veiljalainen, J., Visa, A.: Security in Mobile Computing Environments. Mobile Networks and Applications, Vol. 8, 111-112

9. Ogertschnig, M., van der Heijden, H.: A Short Form Measure of Attitude Towards Using a Mobile Information Service. In: Proceedings of the 17th Bled Electronic Commerce Conference, Bled (2004)
10. Olsen, D.R.: Special issue on Human Computer Interaction with Mobile Systems, ACM Transactions on Computer-Human Integration, Vol. 7, No.3 (2000)
11. Kalakota, R. Robinson, M.: Mobile Business, the Race to Mobility. McGraw-Hill, New York (2002) 264-273
12. Porter, M.E.: Strategy and the Internet. In: Harvard Business Review, March (2001) 63-78
13. Hevner, A.R., March, S.T., Parc, J., Ram, S.: Design Science in IS Research. Information Systems Quarterly, Vol 28, No.1 (2004) 75-85
14. Neiger, D., Churilov, L.: Goal-Oriented Business Process Modeling with EPCs and Value-Focused Thinking. In: Proceedings of the Second International Conference, BPM 2004, Lecture Notes in Computer Science, Vol. 3080. Springer, Berlin Heidelberg New York (2004) 98-115
15. Buhl, H.U., Heinrich, B.: Empirical Research Strategies in Conceptual Modeling – Silver Bullet or Academic Toys? In: Wirtschaftsinformatik (Business Informatics), Vol. 47, No.2 (2004) 152
16. Becker, J.: Epistemological Perspectives on IS Development - A Consensus-Oriented Approach to Conceptual Modeling, in: Althoff, K.-D., Dengel, A., Bergmann, R., Nick, M., Roth-Berghofer, T. (eds.): Professional Knowledge Management, Lecture Notes in Artificial Intelligence, Vol. 3782. Springer, Berlin Heidelberg New York (2005) 635-646
17. Roseman M.: Just do it. In: Wirtschaftsinformatik (Business Informatics). Vol 47, No.2 (2004) 156-157
18. Porter, M.E.: Competitive Strategy – Techniques for Analyzing Industries and Competitors. Free Press, New York (1980) 34-46
19. Treacy, M., Wiersema, F.: The Discipline of Market Leaders. Addison-Wesley (1995)
20. Broadbent, M., Weill, P.: Management by Maxim: How business and IT managers can create IT infrastructures. Sloan Management Review, Spring 1997 (1997) 77-92
21. Davenport, T.H.: Process Innovation: Reengineering Work through Information Technology, Harvard Business School Press, Boston (1993) 5
22. Hammer, M.: Don't Automate, Obliterate. Harvard Business Review, July-August (1990) 104-112
23. Broadbent M., Weill, P.: Leveraging the New Infrastructure. Harvard Business School Press, Boston (1998) 132-135
24. Porter, M.E.: Competitive Advantage – Creating and Sustaining Superior Performance. Free Press, New York (1985) 33-61

Applying Architecture and Ontology to the Splitting and Allying of Enterprises: Problem Definition and Research Approach

Martin Op 't Land

Delft University of Technology, Netherlands
Capgemini, P.O. Box 2575, 3500 GN Utrecht, Netherlands
Martin.OptLand@capgemini.com

Abstract. Organizations increasingly split off parts and start cooperating with those parts, for instance in Shared Service Centers or by using in- or outsourcing. Our research aims to find the right spot and the way to split off those parts: "Application of which organization-construction rules to organizations with redundancy in processes and ICT leads to adequate splitting of enterprises"? Architecture and ontology play a role in the construction of any system. From organizational sciences we expect specific construction rules for splitting an enterprise, including criteria for "adequately" splitting an enterprise. We intend to find and test those construction rules by applying action research to real-life cases in which ontology and architecture are used.

Keywords: Splitting enterprises, Architecture, Ontology, Shared Service Center, BPO, action research, DEMO, Modern Sociotechnique.

1 Introduction

Organizations increasingly split off parts and start cooperating with those parts, for instance in Shared Service Centers (SSC) or by using in- or outsourcing. Hackett (2006) shows that for the Finance and Accounting business in 2006-2008, the use of outsourcing is expected to more than double. Reliance on shared service centers will increase slightly, and shared services is expected to remain the preferred sourcing alternative. The use of offshore shared services will double over the next 3 years.

Organizations want to be able to offer more complex products in a shorter time or to participate in complex product-offerings of another party. Splitting their organization in specialized parts makes those organizations more agile to recombine those parts time and again in the capability to deliver new products and to timely drop current products. Umar (2005) introduces the notion of Next Generation Enterprises (NGE), which conduct business by utilizing innovative new business models. He claims such a NGE (known by names like virtual enterprise, networked enterprise, real-time corporations etc.) will be the standard way of doing business, given its agility and ease of set up. Agility has become a business requirement in many lines of business, from the US army (schedules for combat systems from 8 years to 2 years)

R. Meersman, Z. Tari, P. Herrero et al. (Eds.): OTM Workshops 2006, LNCS 4278, pp. 1419–1428, 2006.

1420   M. Op 't Land

via the US car industry (from thought to finish for a new model in a few months instead of 6 years) to the Dutch banking industry (time to market for a new product
from 9-12 months to a few weeks (Arnold et al 2000)). Setting up new businesses has
become a matter of hours, including online purchasing and payment systems. Friedman (2005) states that businesses are being formed not based on the core competency
they have, but instead on their ability to provide services by clever combinations of
outsourcing and renting through service providers around the globe.

Internally, organizations want to reduce redundancy in processes and ICT in order
to save costs, simplify operations and make them more manageable. Splitting their
organizations in units with clear customer-supplier-responsibilities, clear competencies and geo-flexibility in operations and ICT improves those current operations,
stimulates entrepreneurship and gives those units a customer-oriented focus, with the
potential to broaden the customer base. According to Straten (2002), common motives
for Business Process Outsourcing (BPO) are (1) cost reductions, by increased efficiency and economies of scale; (2) focus on core competencies; (3) access to additional resources and capabilities; (4) creating incentives and stimulating entrepreneurship. Travis and Shepherd (2005) find comparable benefits for using shared services
and add to it (1) improved control and reduced regulatory compliance costs and (2)
faster time to upgrade processes, applications and technology.

When we say *splitting enterprises*, we mean the activity which results in assigning
roles and responsibilities to a separate organizational entity, which may (but does not
need to) be a separate legal entity. Typical results of splitting are a SSC, a BPO-party
or just a centralized department
in an organization. The roles and
responsibilities may concern any
business function, from "secondary" (like catering and housing)
via "primary back-office" (like
mortgage back-office processing)
to "primary front-office" (like
sales). Take for example Mario's
pizzeria, for which Fig. 1 shows
the DEMO Construction Diagram. Mario could outsource or
share the sales function with a
national call-centre. Together

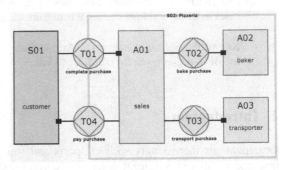

Fig. 1. Construction diagram pizzeria (DEMO-notation)

with his next-door neighbors, Giovanni's pizzeria and Antonio's pizzeria, he could
found a Shared Service Center Baking. And also the transportation could be out-
sourced to a logistics provider or shared with his neighbors.

The question *where to split the enterprise* is not easy to answer. Take for example
the sales function of pizzeria "Mario": should he outsource his sales function to a
national call-centre? To retain his personal contacts with customers may be he
shouldn't. On the other hand, the ability of handling payments of phone orders for his
anonymous customers could be attractive. In that case, would it be wise to outsource
only the payments-part of his ordering and not the ordering itself? For another example, would it be wise to found a Shared Service Center baking, enabling him to cooperate in the baking to make this more efficient, while competing in the frontage? If

so, should common purchasing and stock control be part of it, may be even including the financial administration? Already in this simple example we see motives of customer intimacy, efficiency, product uniqueness, broadening the product portfolio, cost control and equalizing capacity emerge. And even if the (functional) priorities chosen in those motives are clear, it is not immediately clear how this mix of priorities leads to choices in the construction of the enterprise. In real-life cases, like in banks, public or industry, this is even more complex.

According to our literature search, almost no research has been done in this area. Gulledge and Sommer (2004) make clear how the SAP Blueprinting methodology (ASAP) can be misleading if cross-functional business processes and organizational alignment are not considered part of the project scope. The costs of a wrong choice for splitting the enterprise, even if restricted to the software changes, can be huge.

Fig. 2 shows the added value of a competence for "right-splitting enterprises", summarizing the common motives for SSCs and BPO's mentioned before.

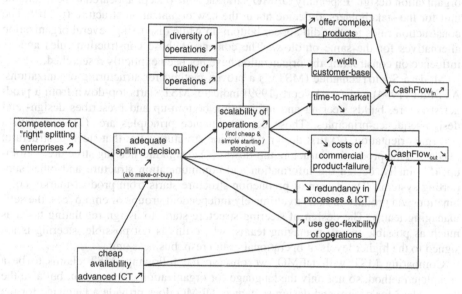

Fig. 2. Partial benefits logic for the competence of "right-splitting enterprises"

2 Currently Available Solutions

Splitting enterprises fits in the disciplines of organizational sciences and enterprise engineering.

Mulder (2006) gives a broad overview of organizational science schools and what they have to say about enterprise engineering. He concludes the Language Action Perspective (LAP-) school currently to be the most attractive option for enterprise engineering, given (1) the increased focus on external behavior of an organization; (2) the (dramatically) increased ability to work independently of location and time, enabled by ICT; (3) the need for constructional (instead of functional) guidelines for enterprise engineering; (4) the need for an integral design of business processes, information systems and ICT-infrastructures.

Dietz (2006) has transformed the LAP-vision into the DEMO-method. This method aims to deliver an Enterprise Ontology, which is a constructional model of an enterprise that is fully independent of its implementation; it is only dependent of the product (structure) the enterprise delivers. Dietz elaborates mainly how to derive this ontology from descriptions about already implemented organizations and procedures, but does not cover the "brand new creation" of an enterprise from market and customer demands (Dietz 2006 p 77), although he briefly shows how to derive an ontology from a product structure. Actually drafting an organization structure based on an enterprise ontology is not in his scope; DEMO itself does not contain criteria or construction rules for constructing an organization. Furthermore, he claims (p 184) an Enterprise Ontology to be a stable starting point for defining information systems.

In his ROOD-case Mulder (2006 pp 85-116) demonstrates how to apply DEMO on organization design. Especially DEMO's transaction concept appeared to be a suitable unit for the stakeholders to decide about the new organization structure (p 110). The construction rules for that did appear bottom-up while discussing several organization alternatives for the same ontology. The content of those construction rules and its influence on constructing the organization have not been explicitly researched.

Modern SocioTechnique (MST) is a proven method for structuring organizations. As Sitter (1994) and Amelsvoort (1999) indicate, MST starts top-down from a product structure, builds steering and information bottom-up and prescribes design- and design-sequence-principles. Those design-sequence principles are: (1) start with a strategic orientation; (2) first design production structure, after that steering structure; (3) design the production structure top-down; (4) design the steering structure bottom-up; (5) finally, design the information and communication structure and other supporting systems. The design of production structure starts from product-market combinations via product streams to ultimately independent groups of employees, the self-managing teams. The design of steering structure starts to assign regulating tasks as much as possible to self-managing teams; where this is not possible, steering is assigned to the higher levels of operational group resp. business unit.

Comparing MST with DEMO, we observe the following. MST claims to be a complete method, so not only the language for organization construction, but also the "principles" for design and design-sequence. DEMO does provide a language for the "parts" of an organization; however, DEMO does not provide the *criteria* and the method for enterprise engineering. DEMO starts explicitly with the product structure and derives from that the production structure, the Construction Model; MST starts with a production structure and derives business activities from that. MST bases its information requirements on the design of an implemented organization, while DEMO states that ontology is the stable basis for information requirements. Neither MST nor DEMO is explicitly interested in the issue of splitting enterprises.

Graaf (2006) is explicitly interested in the subject of splitting enterprises. He seeks however for generic principles, where we assume many principles and construction rules can be leading and we want to understand the impact of the choice of principles in drawing organizational borders. Also he uses a diversity of units for sharing/sourcing ("services" or "processes", sometimes "goals" and "products"), without underpinning this diversity. Graaf suggests that in order to decide for "outsourcable units", we should look not only at business coherence, but also to information coherence; we consider that an interesting hypothesis to test.

We conclude that currently available methods offer promising elements for the method we seek. MST could offer us construction rules and design sequence. DEMO could offer us a language to express the essence of an enterprise, which is also a stable starting point for gathering information requirements. In the construction rules and criteria, we might look to business coherence as well as information coherence.

We want to see how this all fits together in a method for splitting enterprises. And we want to see how that works in practice.

3   What Answer Are We Looking for?

We define *enterprise* as a goal-oriented cooperative of people and means. This leaves still open the decisions about what is external and what is internal. In the enterprise, we are interested in issues of *splitting*. When we discern areas of sharing, in- or outsourcing, we are conceptually making splits or cuts in the enterprise. In the enterprise, we are also interested in the issue of *allying* or *co-operating*. Splitting and allying enterprises are two sides of the same medal: the moment the work for an enterprise is split over parties, those parties have to ally in order stay that "goal-oriented cooperative of people and means".

We will treat *splitting enterprises* as a specific case of the Generic System Development Process (GSDP) from xAF (2006), which we will now briefly introduce, using Fig. 3. In every design process there are two systems involved, the *using system* (US) and the *object system* (OS). The OS is the system to be designed; the US is the system that will use the functions or services offered by the OS once it is operational.

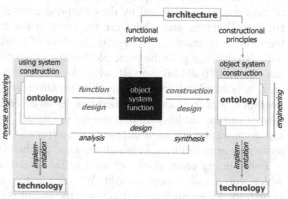

Fig. 3. Generic System Development Process (xAF 2006)

Function design, the first phase in the design of the OS, starts from the construction of the US and ends with the function of the OS. Function design delivers the requirements of the OS, so a black-box model of the OS. This function model of the OS does not contain any information about the construction of the OS. *Construction design*, the second phase in the design of the OS, starts with the specified function of the OS and it ends with the construction of the OS. Construction design bridges the mental gap between function and construction, which means establishing a correspondence between systems of different categories: the category of the US (where the function of the OS is defined) and the category of the OS. Construction design delivers an ontology, the highest level white-box model of the OS. By an *ontology* or ontological model of a system we understand a model of its construction that is completely independent of the way in which it is realized and implemented. The *engineering*[1] of a system is the process in which a number of white-box models are produced, such that every model is fully derivable from the previous one and the available specifications. Engineering starts from the ontological model, produces a set of subsequently more detailed white-box models and ends with the implementation model. By *implementation* is understood the assignment of technological means to the elements in the implementation model, so that the system can be put into operation. By *technology* we understand the technological means by which a system is implemented. A wide range of technological means is available, varying from human beings and organizational entities via ICT (e.g. phone, email, computer programs) to vacuum cleaners, cars, drilling machines and screw drivers. In general, the design freedom of designers is undesirable large. xAF (2006) therefore defines *architecture* conceptually as a normative restriction of design freedom. Operationally, architecture is a consistent and coherent set of design *principles* that embody general requirements. General requirements hold for a class of systems.

In terms of GSDP, we define splitting the enterprise as the first step in making an implementation model of the enterprise, namely assigning responsibilities to organizations and organizational units, so not to function profiles or individual people. Splitting is based on the enterprise ontology and, as part of the designing and engineering of the enterprise, restricted by the enterprise architecture. For example, the two bike-suppliers Batavus and Altera are the same in the essence of "supplying bikes" and therefore they share the *enterprise ontology* of a bike-supplier. Those bike-suppliers will also differ, e.g. in the principle "outsource all production". For example, Batavus has chosen to build bikes itself, while Altera has chosen to outsource that. This difference in principles from the *enterprise architecture* leads to a different pattern of cooperation with partners, and therefore to other organizations. Splitting is a special case of starting drafting an implementation model. Indeed, splitting is taking an existing organization, so an implemented enterprise, and reassigning the roles to one or more new organizations, in which the same product (family) remains to be delivered.

For splitting enterprises, we want to find *construction rules*, so the algorithm by which you decide where to split. We expect our construction rules to look like "if <condition> then preferably don't split the enterprise on that spot, because <reason>". For instance, "don't cut the enterprise on a spot with heavy information-exchange, because this will increase the error-rate". Also the construction rules may prescribe order of working, like "step 1 = distinguish areas with high internal information dependencies; step 2 = ...". The construction rules should tell us consequences of applying a decision rule too, like "when in this situation the enterprise is split, new roles will appear at the organization border, e.g. the role of service manager."

We expect construction rules from both *general systems development theory* (like expressed in GSDP) applied to enterprises as system type and *organization sciences* as far as it concerns designing and implementing organizations. Mulder (2006) demonstrated how enterprise ontology according to DEMO worked as a language for enterprise engineering, enabling conscious choices in splitting the enterprise. A theory

---

[1] Engineering is meant here in the narrow sense of the term, contrary to its general use in civic engineering, electrical engineering, mechanical engineering, etc.

about those construction rules, including the influence of architecture, is lacking. Organization sciences, on the other hand, will give us commonly used construction rules for enterprise engineering, like "split complex tasks", "keep similar tasks together", "split between primary and secondary business processes", "loose coupling" and "strong internal and weak external cohesion". The influence of architecture and ontology on that is currently not defined.

We want splitting of enterprises to be done *adequately*, which we define as being compliant with professional requirements, situational process-requirements and situational result-requirements. A professional requirement is broadly applicable and not situation-specific, e.g. "minimize need for tuning". It probably originates from general systems development theory and organization sciences. Situational process-requirements are specific for a specific process or project of splitting, e.g. project costs, timeliness, effectiveness and quality. Situational result-requirements are the goals to be reached by splitting the enterprise, including the constraints to be complied with. As mentioned in §1, the goals for splitting of enterprises can be quite diverse and include saving costs (location, people, tax), improving quality (right people with right qualifications in e.g. language, training and experience) and improving agility and flexibility. Constraints will typically originate from the ecosystem of the organization, like from (legal or branch-) supervisors, customers, suppliers and other network partners.

So in the construction rules we want to see the influence of architecture and ontology, together with professional and situational requirements, in the adequate splitting of enterprises. Researching all possible requirements will not be in scope.

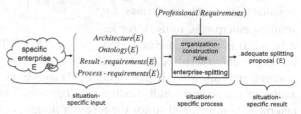

Fig. 4. Concepts for splitting enterprises

We further restrict our problem area by choosing as intended domain "enterprises, currently organized with redundancy in processes and ICT" of for short "organizations with redundancy in processes and ICT". The reason for this restriction is quite pragmatic. As we saw already in §1, for many organizations which presume to have redundancy in processes or ICT, this is an immediate cause for seeking optimizations like Shared Service Centers, BPO or centralized departments. That action confronts those organizations with the issue of adequately splitting their enterprise.

So our problem statement reads as follows: *Application of which organization-construction rules to organizations with redundancy in processes and ICT leads to adequate splitting of enterprises?*

4   Research Approach

In our research for organization-construction rules, we want to see especially (1) how architecture and ontology influence the splitting of an enterprise; (2) what is the "minimum size" of architecture and ontology to still let the organization-construction rules give the same result – thus discovering the "right size" of architecture and ontology in the splitting of an enterprise. Below we will argue an appropriate approach for the second result is action research and for the first result case studies.

We use a research approach in which in successive situations several enterprises are split. The use of organization-construction rules in *one* such a situation is studied according to the method of case study (see below why). Based on the experience of that one situation, new ideas about the construction rules will emerge and be reflected upon, which can be used in the subsequent situation. In that situation again a case study can be executed, etc. This cycle is commonly referred to as *action research*, defined by Avison (1999) as a repeating cycle of intervention, measuring, evaluation and improvement. Action research as research instrument is intended to apply a theory in practice and evaluate its value in the reality as changed by (the theory of) the researcher. Here the researcher selects or develops new concepts and tools, in our research program organization-construction rules for splitting enterprises, to use it (or let it be used) in new situations. Based on those characteristics of action

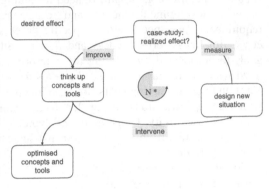

Fig. 5. The action research cycle

research and following (Babeliowsky 1997) and (Eijck 1996), we expect for the realization of the second result, finding the "right-size" of architecture and ontology in enterprise-splitting, and so for the research program as a whole, action research will be an adequate approach.

In a case-study, researchers take a position outside of the case and observe the case in its "natural" environment, without intervening or interfering (Yin 1994). Here, to achieve the first result, we concentrate on the correlation between architecture, ontology and requirements on one hand and the resulting split enterprise on the other hand, looking at the construction rules applied in a real-life environment. Information about that is only available in the specific situation itself. By using real-life experience of the researcher in his role as consultant, we expect to get access to sources nowhere else available. According to Yin (1994, p 13) and Babeliowsky (1997, p 18), a good research instrument in these circumstances is the case-study. Studying single cases can satisfy the standards of the natural science model of scientific research (Lee 1989). Therefore, for each single case we have set up a research design for that case study, following the notions of Yin (1994). Each case-study will therefore have its own sub problem, method, result and conclusions. The result of each case-study will have two levels (1) the splitting proposal for the enterprise and how adequate that splitting proposal was for that situation; (2) what that situation has learned us about the organization-construction rules.

We now split our over-all problem statement in 4 sub questions:

1. how do ontology & architecture of an enterprise look like in practice (in one case)?
2. how do architecture and ontology influence enterprise-splitting (in one case)? This should deliver a hypothesis on the value of architecture and ontology; the test on adequacy stays restricted to situational requirements;
3. what does organization science say about (a) professional criteria for adequacy of an organization (b) construction rules for splitting: what they are, how to measure?
4. what organization-construction rules work best (in one case) in enterprise splitting? We will now use additional construction rules from organization science; and the adequacy-test now includes professional requirements.

We looked for cases in which at least an architecture, an ontology and a splitting proposal is available. In those cases the researcher has a participating role, which satisfies the criteria for action research. We have selected case-material from two organizations, the Dutch-based bank-insurer ING and the public agency Rijkswaterstaat. ING is a large financial institution, operating internationally on many locations. ING is a result of mergers, which caused a significant redundancy in processes and ICT. Rijkswaterstaat is an agency of the Ministry of Transport, Public Works and Water Management, which constructs, manages, develops and maintains the Netherlands' main infrastructure networks. Especially by its strong regional autonomy in the past, Rijkswaterstaat faced large redundancy in processes and ICT.

When we compare this researched domain – Rijkswaterstaat and ING – with the intended domain – organizations with redundancy of processes and ICT –, we see the following. ING and Rijkswaterstaat differ considerably in sector (private-financial versus public) and over-all size (110,000 world-wide versus ± 10,000). Both are large, supra-local functioning organizations with redundancy in processes and ICT. From the 11 large sectors served by the consultancy-firm of the researcher in 2006, they are considered rather representative for two of them (Financial Services and Public Sector). So we expect reasonable generalizability in Financial Services and Public Sector.

Our approach to answer the 4 sub questions is as follows:

1. in a case study of Rijkswaterstaat, we will describe the architecture of Rijkswaterstaat as a whole and the ontology of Traffic Management;
2. in a case study of ING, we will describe the architecture and ontology of ING Securities and a proposal for the borders of ING's Shared Service Center Securities, including the measurement of situational adequacy;
3. the organization scientific reflection will be answered in a literature study;
4. in a case study of Rijkswaterstaat, we will describe several splitting alternatives, based on the architecture and ontology of Rijkswaterstaat, using additional construction rules from organization science and tested for situational and professional adequacy.

5 Expected Added Value

As main theoretical added value we expect to find explicit organization-construction rules and how those rules influence the splitting of enterprises. In (Dietz 2006) this influence has not been dealt with. In (Mulder 2006) those construction rules have not been explicitly addressed, but they appear bottom-up while discussing several organization alternatives for the same ontology.

As practical added value we expect an improved insight in the problem of reorganizing, sourcing and sharing. Especially we expect an improved manageability of this reorganizing, sourcing and sharing: what are professional "handles" for this problem? May be even more generic conclusions on the issue of organization structuring can be drawn. Mulder (2006) for instance applies ontology to an issue of organization structuring without splitting issues, so some of our construction rules might be useful as well. Finally we hope to find indications on the "minimum size" of an enterprise architecture and an enterprise ontology.

References

Amelsvoort Pierre van (1999) De moderne sociotechnische benadering – een overzicht van de socio-technische theorie. ST-Groep, Vlijmen

Arnold Bert, Engels Ariane, Op 't Land Martin (2000) FPS: another way of looking at components and architecture in the financial world. Congress paper for the Dutch National Architecture Congress 2000 (LAC2000), www.serc.nl/lac/LAC-2001/lac-2000/3-realisatie/fps.doc

Avison D, Lau F, Myers M, Nielsen PA (1999) Action research. Communications of the ACM 42:94-97

Babeliowsky Martijn (1997) Designing interorganizational logistic networks; A simulation based interdisciplinary approach. Doctoral dissertation, Delft University of Technology

DEMO (=Design & Engineering Methodology for Organizations)-website, www.demo.nl

Dietz Jan LG (2006) Enterprise Ontology – theory and methodology. Springer

Eijck Daniel TT van (1996) Designing Organizational Coordination. Doctoral dissertation, Delft University of Technology

Friedman Thomas L (2005) The World is Flat: A Brief History of the Twenty-first Century. Farrar, Straus and Giroux

Graaf Erwin van der (2006) Architectuurprincipes voor de afbakening van outsourcebare kavels. http://www.architecture-institute.nl/master-lab/pdf/ErwinVanDerGraaf.pdf

Gulledge TR and Sommer RA (2004) Splitting the sap instance: Lessons on scope and business processes. Journal of Computer Information Systems 44 (3): 109-115.

Hackett (2006) BPO-outlook for finance and accounting 2006-2008. The Hackett Group.

Lee Allen S (1989) A Scientific Methodology for MIS Case Studies. MIS Quarterly vol 13/1:33-50

Mulder Hans (2006) Rapid Enterprise Design. Dissertation Delft University of Technology.

Sitter LU de (1994) Synergetisch produceren; Human Resources Mobilisation in de produktie: een inleiding in structuurbouw. Van Gorcum, Assen

Straten Carolien van (2002) Disaggregating the firm by means of Business Process Outsourcing. Master thesis Erasmus University Rotterdam. http://www.strategie-vsb.nl/pdf/8.pdf

Travis Lance, Shepherd Jim (2005) Shared Services, Cost Savings, Compliance Relief and Prelude to Outsourcing. AMR-research

Umar A (2005) IT infrastructure to enable next generation enterprises. Information Systems Frontiers 7 (3): 217-256.

xAF (2006) Extensible Architecture Framework. Report of the xAF-working Group for NAF, offered on LAC2006. See http://www.xaf.nl

Yin Robert K (1994) Case study research, Design and Methods, 2nd edn. Newbury Park, Sage Publications

Profile-Based Online Data Delivery

Haggai Roitman

Technion - Israel Institute of Technology
Haifa 32000, Israel
haggair@tx.technion.ac.il

Abstract. This research is aimed at providing *theoretically rigorous, flexible, efficient,* and *scalable* methodologies for intelligent delivery of data in a dynamic and resource constrained environment. Our proposed solution utilizes a uniform client and server profilization for data delivery and describe the challenges in developing optimized hybrid data delivery schedules. We also present an approach that aims at constructing automatic adaptive policies for data delivery to overcome various modeling errors utilizing feedback.

1 Introduction

Web enabled application servers have had to increase the sophistication of their server capabilities in order to keep up with the increasing demand for client customization. Typical applications include news syndication, stock prices and auctions on the commercial Internet, and increasingly, access to Grid computational resources. Despite these advances, there still remains a fundamental trade-off between the scalability of both performance and ease of implementation on the server side, with respect to the multitude and diversity of clients, and the required customization to deliver the right service/data to the client at the desired time.

We begin with three motivating examples, demonstrating the necessity of a framework for data delivery that goes beyond existing standards.

Example 1 (News Syndication): As an example we consider RSS ([17]), which is growing in its popularity to deliver data on the Internet but currently faces scalability issues. The RSS 2.0 specification defines a mostly pull based protocol but supports a simple notification mechanism named "clouds" that can push notifications about RSS feed refreshment. Most RSS providers do not support the clouds mechanism since it requires bookkeeping about registered clients; this is not scalable for a popular RSS provider such as CNN. Current RSS consumers either poll the server periodically or pull according to authoring tags embedded within the RSS channel (*e.g.*, <ttl>). The pull based protocol of RSS also faces scalability issues; a recent survey in [10] of 100,000 RSS feeds, indexed by the popular RSS directory *syndic8.com*, showed that almost 90% of pull actions by RSS consumers, typically using software such as RSS Readers or Aggregators, did not capture any useful changes at the servers providing those RSS feeds.

R. Meersman, Z. Tari, P. Herrero et al. (Eds.): OTM Workshops 2006, LNCS 4278, pp. 1429–1438, 2006.

Example 2 (E-Commerce and E-Markets): Consider the commercial Internet where agents may be monitoring multiple information sources. An agent client may wish to be alerted upon a change in a stock price soon after a financial report is released. Individual servers for financial news and stock prices may push updates to the client but in order to implement the client's profile, one needs to reason about the server capabilities of two different servers. An agent who is handling such a complex profile would need to pull data from the stock market server soon after it receives an update from the financial report server. In this case, a single server supporting client's needs via push is insufficient and the combination of information push from one server and pulling another server is needed. Such a setting was also shown to be of interest in the digital libraries arena [3].

Example 3 (Grid): Consider a simplified scenario of a physicist client who wants to submit her application to a Linux Farm of several thousand nodes. The Linux Farm collects Node Status metadata for each node including attributes such as Machine Up Time, CPU Load, Memory Load, Disk Load, and Network Load; this data is updated every time a new job is submitted to the Linux Farm, and is periodically pushed to clients. She further determines that a remote dataset is needed and it can be retrieved from a number of replica sites. Network behavior metadata for these replica sites are available from either a GridFTP monitor or the Network Weather Service (NWS) monitor. Neither monitor pushes updates to clients. Current data delivery solutions provide few solutions to the physicist and she and other clients may have to poll the servers continuously; this may have a performance impact on these servers.

Current data delivery solutions can be classified as either *push* or *pull* solutions, each suffering from different drawbacks. Push (*e.g.*, [8]) is not scalable, and reaching a large numbers of potentially transient clients is typically expensive in terms of resource consumption. In some cases, where there is a mismatch with client needs, pushing information may overwhelm the client with unsolicited information. Pull (*e.g.*, [7]), on the other hand, can increase network and server workload and often cannot meet client needs. Several hybrid push-pull solutions have also been presented in the past (*e.g,* [5]). Examples of related work in push-based technologies include BlackBerry [8] and JMS messaging, push-based policies for static Web content (*e.g.*, [9]), and push-based consistency in the context of caching dynamic Web content (*e.g.*, [18]). Another related research area is that of publish/subscribe systems (*e.g.*, [1]). Pull-based freshness policies have been proposed in many contexts such as Web caching (*e.g.*, [7]) and synchronizing collections of objects, *e.g.*, Web crawlers (*e.g.*, [4]).

As demonstrated in the motivating examples, the problem we face is that of providing *theoretically rigorous, flexible, and efficient* methodologies for intelligent delivery of data in a dynamic and resource constrained environment that can efficiently *match* client *requirements* with server *capabilities* and generate a *scalable hybrid push-pull solution*.

The rest of the paper is organized as follows. In Section 2 we introduce our proposed model. We then present in Section 3 the different challenges of the proposed research. Section 4 describe our current research progress, and we conclude in Section 5.

2   Model for Online Data Delivery

We begin by presenting the general architecture of our proposed framework. We then introduce our model for data delivery based on the abstraction of *execution intervals*, followed by profile specification.

2.1   Architecture

The proposed framework aims at providing a scalable online data delivery solution. We identify three types of entities, namely *servers*, *clients*, and *brokers*. A server is any entity that manages resources and can provide services for querying them by means of pull (*e.g.*, HTTP GET messages) or push (*e.g.*, registration to an alerting service in digital libraries [3]). Each server has a set of *capabilities* for data delivery (*e.g.*, periodical push of notifications). A client is any entity that has an interest in some resources and has *data delivery requirements* in the form of *client profiles*. Given client requirements and server capabilities, a broker is responsible to *match* the client with suitable servers, and provide the client with the desired information of interest specified in the client profile. To do so, the broker may register to servers and as needed augment server notifications with pull actions. Each broker can further act as both a server or a client of other brokers, formatting a brokerage network as illustrated in Figure 1. The profile specification proposed in Section 2.3 allows a broker to *efficiently aggregate* client profiles, thus achieving scalability.

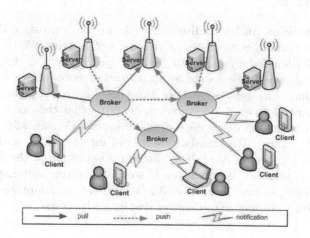

Fig. 1. Framework architecture

2.2 Model

Let $\mathcal{R} = \{R_1, R_2, ..., R_n\}$ be a set of n resources, where each resource R_i is described in some language (*e.g.*, RDF [13]) and has a set of properties, that can be queried. Utilizing a schema specification (*e.g.*, RDF Schema [14]) we further classify resources and describe properties in different granularity levels. We use $\mathbb{T}$ to denote a discrete timeline.

Execution intervals. Given a query Q which references resources from $\mathcal{R}$, we would like to formally define periods of time in $\mathbb{T}$ in which running query Q is useful for some client. Such periods of times are termed *execution intervals*. We further associate with each interval (denoted as I) the following properties.

Interval end points: Each interval has a start time $T_s \in \mathbb{T}$, and a time $T_f \in \mathbb{T}$, where $T_s \leq T_f$.
Query: A selection query over a subset of $\mathcal{R}$, denoted Q, that should be executed at some time $T_j \in I$.
Utility: A scalar vector of size $|I|$ that defines the utility of executing Q at any time $T_j \in I$. For the client, the utility models the benefit of getting a notification of Q during I, while for the server, the utility models the benefit of pushing data during I.
Label Function: Given the set of resources referenced by query Q (denoted $\mathcal{R}(Q)$), we define a labelling function $\mathcal{L}_I : \mathcal{R}(Q) \rightarrow \{\text{push}, \text{pull}, \text{none}\}$. push means that resource $R \in \mathcal{R}(Q)$ state (or values) is pushed during I by some server that stores R. pull means that the state of resource $R \in \mathcal{R}(Q)$ is pulled during I from some server that stores R. none means no action is taken during I.

Execution intervals are the basic elements of our model. We shall discuss their usage in Section 2.3.

Events, eventlines and timelines. Events in the context of data delivery identify possible changes to states of resources of interest. We define event e of resource R (denoted by $e(R)$) to be any update event or temporal (time based periodical) event. We denote by T_{e_k} the occurrence time of the k-th event on the eventline. An event occurrence time can be further defined to be the start or end time of an execution interval, denoting that the execution of query Q is conditional on the occurrence of some event (*e.g.*, an RSS channel was refreshed three times). We translate eventlines into timelines and use update models that rely on resource update histories observed from the data delivery process. Such models are usually given in stochastic terms and may suffer from different modeling errors. In Section 3.2 we present an adaptive scheme that aims at providing efficient data delivery despite such errors.

2.3 Profile Language Specification

We have a particular interest in semantic richness of profiles. Such richness allows reasoning about temporal evolution of resources, where profiles can be modified to add and remove resources of interest dynamically to express evolving interests. We aim at unique profile specification that can be used uniformly to describe client requirements and server capabilities in supporting such requirements. Profiles basically state four important aspects of data delivery, namely, *what are the resources of interest, when such interests exist and notifications should take place, what are the conditions upon notifications*, and *what is the value (utility) of each notification*. Examples for possible client and server profiles for the RSS domain are given in Figure 2 and Figure 3 respectively.

> *"Return the title and description of items published on the CNN Top Stories RSS feed, once three new updates to the feed channel have occurred. Notifications received within ten minutes after new three update events have occurred will have a utility value of 1. Notification outside this window has a value of 0. Notifications should take place in the two months following April 24th 2006, 10:00:00 GMT."*

Fig. 2. Example client profile for RSS domain

> *"CNN Top Stories RSS feed is refreshed every 5 minutes, starting from now."*

Fig. 3. Example server profile for RSS domain

Let $\mathbf{P}$ denote a profile language (or profile) class and let p be a profile. Let $\mathcal{R} = \{R_1, R_2, ..., R_n\}$ be a set of resources. Class $\mathbf{P}$ is a triplet $\mathbf{P} = \langle \Omega, \mathcal{N}, \mathcal{T} \rangle$, where $\Omega \subseteq \mathcal{R}$ is called *profile domain*. The profile domain contains a declarative description of the resources of interest associated with the profile (e.g., RDF), $\mathcal{N} = \{\eta_1, \eta_2, ..., \eta_m\}$ is a set of rules termed *notification rules*, and $\mathcal{T} = \{T_1, T_2, ..., T_N\}, \mathcal{T} \subset \mathbb{T}$ is a set of N chronons[1] termed *profile epoch*. Given an epoch $\mathcal{T}$ we define $\mathcal{I}_{\mathcal{T}} = \{[T_j, T_k] \,|T_j \leq T_k\}$. $\mathcal{I}_{\mathcal{T}}$ contains all possible intervals in $\mathcal{T}$.

Each notification rule η is a quadruple $\eta = \langle Q, \Gamma, \mathbf{T}, U \rangle$, where $Q \subseteq \Omega$ is termed *notification query*, $\Gamma \subseteq \mathcal{I}_{\mathcal{T}}$ is a set of *execution intervals*, $\mathbf{T} \subseteq \mathcal{T}$ is *notification scope*, and $U : \Gamma \to \mathbb{R}^m; m \in \mathbb{N}$ is a *utility function*.

This general class of profiles can be further classified, for example, to the class of languages that allow to refer to events on the eventline (using $\mathcal{T}_{e_k}$) or those which use deterministic timeline (*e.g.*, periodic time). As an example, Figures 4 and 5 contain the example RSS client and server profile specifications respectively.

---

[1] A chronon is defined as a discrete and indivisible "unit" of time.

1434   H. Roitman

$$\Omega(p_{client}) \leftarrow \{\texttt{http://rss.cnn.com/services/rss/cnn\_topstories.rss}\}$$
$$\mathcal{N}(p_{client}) := \{\eta\}$$
$$Q(\eta) := \sigma_{\texttt{title,description}}(\texttt{item})$$
$$e(\texttt{cnn\_topstories.rss}) := \texttt{"UPDATE TO channel"}$$
$$\Gamma(\eta) := \{[T_{e_{3k}}, T_{e_{3k}} + 10 \texttt{ minute}]; k \in \mathbb{N}\} \tag{1}$$
$$\mathbf{T}(\eta) := \texttt{"4/24/2006 10:00:00 GMT"} + 2 \texttt{ month}$$
$$\mathbf{U}(I) = \begin{cases} [1,1,...,1] & if\ I \in \Gamma(\eta) \\ [0,0,...,0] & otherwise \end{cases}$$

Fig. 4. Formal specification of the example client profile

$$\Omega(p_{server}) \leftarrow \{\texttt{http://rss.cnn.com/services/rss/cnn\_topstories.rss}\}$$
$$\mathcal{N}(p_{server}) := \{\eta\}$$
$$Q(\eta) := \sigma_{*}(\texttt{channel})$$
$$\Gamma(\eta) := \{[\texttt{now} + (5 \cdot (k-1) \texttt{ minute}), \texttt{now} + (5 \cdot k \texttt{ minute})]; k \in \mathbb{N}\} \tag{2}$$
$$\mathbf{T}(\eta) := \texttt{now}$$
$$\mathbf{U}(I) = [0,0,...,0]$$

Fig. 5. Formal specification of the example server profile

3 Challenges

We now introduce two main challenges. The first involves the provision of an optimized hybrid scheduling solution to the data delivery problem. The second challenge involves the provision of a mechanism for data delivery that can adaptively reason about events at servers despite update modeling errors, exploiting feedback gathered from the data delivery process. We now describe each challenge in details.

3.1 Optimized Hybrid Scheduling

Utilizing the unique profile specification for both client requirements for data delivery and server capabilities to support such needs, *we wish to construct efficient, flexible, and scalable hybrid data delivery schedules to satisfy a set of client profiles by exploiting server push as much as possible while augmenting with pull activities when needed.*

Profile satisfaction ([15]) means that clients are *guaranteed* to get notifications according to their profiles. Given a set of either client or server profiles $\mathcal{P} = \{p_1, p_2, ..., p_m\}$, we translate each profile into a set of client/server execution intervals respectively. For each client execution interval I and each resource R referenced by the interval associated query Q, a schedule S assigns a pair of values $\langle \mathcal{L}_I(R), T \rangle$ which denotes the type of action to be taken during I for resource R and the actual time $T \in I$ that such an action should take place. For example, if schedule S assigns $\langle pull, T \rangle$ than resource R should be pulled at time T. We denote by $\mathcal{S}$ the set of all possible schedules.

Any schedule that aims at satisfying a given client profile *must* assign either a **push** or **pull** action to each resource referenced by each client execution interval query. Using client profile *coverage*, formally defined in [16], we wish to efficiently find a *minimal* set of server execution intervals that *maximizes* the number of client execution intervals that can be covered by pushing data during the client execution intervals. Whenever we identify a set of candidate server intervals that can cover the same client execution interval, we shall further *rank* this set according to metrics such as server availability, commitment to push, and others.

We now describe three important aspects of data delivery that this research considers, namely, *constraint hybrid data delivery, scalability,* and *tradeoffs.*

Constraint hybrid data delivery. Data delivery becomes a constrained optimization problem when system resource usage is limited. Generally speaking, given a set of profiles $\mathcal{P}$ we define a target function $F(\mathcal{P})$ to be optimized, subject to a set of constraints on the data delivery schedule, $C(\mathcal{P}, \mathcal{S})$. Examples of possible constraints over pull actions are an upper bound on the total bandwidth, CPU, and memory that can be allocated per chronon (*e.g.*, [11]) or upper bound on the total number of probes allowed per the whole epoch, termed *politeness* in [6]. As for push related costs, each push may have an associated cost set by the server providing the push, thus a further upper bound on total payments can be set. Examples for target functions for the data delivery process are total gained utility, profile satisfaction, and system resources used to process $\mathcal{P}$.

Scalability. Both current pull and push based solutions face scalability problems. Using our suggested framework for data delivery, we shall accomplish better scalability. Client profiles will be *aggregated* and *optimized*, offering scalable profile processing. In the proposed system architecture, each broker will be responsible to track a set of servers and manage client profiles for several clients, and can further act as either a client or a server of other brokers. The hybrid approach can reduce server workloads and save network resources.

Data delivery tradeoffs. Data delivery tradeoffs can be captured by means of multi-objective optimization that involves a set of target functions $\mathcal{F} = \{F_1(\mathcal{P}), F_2(\mathcal{P}), ..., F_m(\mathcal{P})\}$ to be optimized. For example, the tradeoff between *data completeness* and *delay*[2] can be defined as a bi-objective optimization problem as follows.

$$\mathcal{F} = \{F_1(\mathcal{P}) = \text{``completeness''}, F_2(\mathcal{P}) = \text{``delay''}\}$$
$$maximize\ F_1(\mathcal{P})$$
$$minimize\ F_2(\mathcal{P}) \tag{3}$$
$$s.t.\ C(\mathcal{P}, \mathcal{S})$$

It is obvious that such target functions can be dependent as in Example 3, thus optimizing one function can come at the expense of the other. Such dependencies

---

[2] *Completeness* can be measured as the number of execution intervals correctly captured by any schedule, while *delay* can be measured as the time that elapses from the beginning of each such interval.

capture "tradeoffs" in data delivery. In multi-objective optimization problems we would like to find a set of non dominated solutions, also termed a *Pareto Set* in the literature, representing optimal tradeoffs and offering different alternatives to clients or servers during the data delivery process. In the general case, finding a Pareto set is an NP-Hard problem and we shall investigate approximated solutions instead ([12]).

3.2 Adaptive Policies for Data Delivery

Motivated with the work originated in [2] we shall investigate *adaptive policies* to overcome modeling errors and unexpected temporary changes ("bursts") to existing valid update models. Modeling errors generally occur due to two basic error types. First, the underlying update model that is assumed in the static calculation is stochastic in nature and therefore updates deviate from the estimated update times. Second, it is possible that the underlying update model is incorrect, and the real data stream behaves differently than expected. Bursts are kind of unpredicted noise in the underline update model and are hard to predict. This research will devise an *adaptive algebra* to create (automatic) adaptive policies for data delivery. The basic idea for such algebra is as follows. Given a profile p and some time $T \in \mathcal{T}$, we can associate two sets of execution intervals with each $\eta \in \mathcal{N}(p)$, denoted as $\Gamma_{t \leq T}(\eta)$ and $\Gamma_{t > T}(\eta)$. Lets assume that all actual execution intervals of η up to time T *are known* (*e.g.*, gathered from previous probes feedback). Thus $\Gamma_{t \leq T}(\eta)$ holds (maybe a subset of) those intervals. $\Gamma_{t > T}(\eta)$ still holds execution intervals that their actual alignment is known only in expected or probabilistic terms. An adaptive policy $\mathcal{A}$ takes as input the pair of sets $\langle \Gamma_{t \leq T}(\eta), \Gamma_{t > T}(\eta) \rangle$ and returns a set of execution intervals $\Gamma_{t > T}^*(\eta)$ as output, reflecting the adaptive policy implemented by $\mathcal{A}$. The output set $\Gamma_{t > T}^*(\eta)$ can include corrections to interval end points, alignments, additional intervals, or corrections to label assignments for the hybrid schedule. It is worth nothing that such adaptive policies can further take into consideration different constraints (*e.g.*, additional probes that the system can allocate to implement the policy), casting the adaptive task as an optimization problem.

4   Current Progress

Parts of the proposed research have already been accomplished. In [15] we have formally defined the notion of profile satisfiability and cast it as an optimization problem. We have developed an algorithm named SUP that guarantees to satisfy a set of profiles in expected terms, while minimizing the efforts of doing so. We also suggested an adaptive version for SUP, named fbSUP which is an example of an adaptive policy that uses feedback from previous probes and adds additional execution intervals as needed. Our study shows that we improved the data delivery accuracy with a reasonable increase in the amount of system resources that such adaptiveness requires.

In [16] we have suggested a generic hybrid scheduling algorithm named ProMo which utilizes profile coverage and aims at maximizing server capabilities usage while providing efficient augmentation of pull actions when needed. In `ProMo` we have dealt with 1 : 1 client-server relationships and provided a proxy based architecture. Future work with the brokerage architecture will use more general relationships focusing on providing expressive, yet scalable and efficient hybrid data delivery solution.

In our most recent work, we explore a problem termed the *Proxy Dilemma*, where a proxy is responsible to manage a set of client profiles and has the following problem: *"Maximize the set of client execution intervals that can be captured (and thus provide notifications to clients) while minimize the delay in notification to clients obtained by the proxy schedule, subject to an upper bound of resources that the proxy can monitor at each chronon."* We devise this problem formally as a bi-objective problem and present an approximation scheme that capture the different data delivery tradeoffs the proxy can consider. We further suggest a generic heuristic solution that offers fast alternative solutions to this problem.

5 Conclusions

In this paper we presented a novel framework for profile based online data delivery, including architecture, model, language, and algorithms for efficient, flexible, and scalable data delivery. We presented a unique profile specification based on execution intervals which can be used uniformly to describe both client requirements and server capabilities. We presented several challenges in supporting efficient data delivery using the proposed model, and discussed automatic adaptive policies for online data delivery.

Acknowledgments

I would like to thank my advisor, Dr. Avigdor Gal, who shares his time and expertise to guide me in this research. I thank Prof. Louiqa Raschid for her continuous collaboration in this research and for her fruitful thoughts and advises. Finally, I would like to thank Dr. Laura Bright who collaborated with us in the beginning of this research.

References

1. S. Bittner and A. Hinze. A detailed investigation of memory requirements for publish/subscribe filtering algorithms. In *Proceedings of On the International Conference on Cooperative Information Systems (CoopIS'2005)*, pages 148–165, 2005.
2. L. Bright, A. Gal, and L. Raschid. Adaptive pull-based policies for wide area data delivery. *ACM Transactions on Database Systems (TODS)*, 31(2):631–671, 2006.
3. G. Buchanan and A. Hinze. A generic alerting service for digital libraries. In *JCDL '05: Proceedings of the 5th ACM/IEEE-CS joint conference on Digital libraries*, pages 131–140, New York, NY, USA, 2005. ACM Press.

4. D. Carney, S. Lee, and S. Zdonik. Scalable application-aware data freshening. *Proceedings of the IEEE CS International Conference on Data Engineering*, pages 481–492, March 2003.

5. P. Deolasee, A. Katkar, P. Panchbudhe, K. Ramamritham, and P. Shenoy. Adaptive push-pull: Deisseminating dunamic web data. In *Proceedings of the International World Wide Web Conference (WWW)*, 2001.

6. J. Eckstein, A. Gal, and S. Reiner. Optimal information monitoring under a politeness constraint. Technical Report RRR 16-2005, RUTCOR, Rutgers University, 640 Bartholomew Road, Busch Campus Piscataway, NJ 08854 USA, May 2005.

7. J. Gwertzman and M. Seltzer. World Wide Web cache consistency. In *Proceedings of the USENIX Annual Technical Conference*, pages 141–152, San Diego, January 1996.

8. BlackBerry Wireless Handhelds. http://www.blackberry.com.

9. C. Liu and P. Cao. Maintaining strong cache consistency on the world wide web. In *Proceedings of the International Conference on Distributed Computing Systems (ICDCS)*, Baltimore, MD, 1997.

10. H. Liu, V. Ramasubramanian, and E.G. Sirer. Client and feed characteristics of rss, a publish-subscribe system for web micronews. In *Proceedings of Internet Measurement Conference (IMC)*, pages 360–371, Berkeley, California, October 2005.

11. S. Pandey, K. Dhamdhere, and C. Olston. WIC: A general-purpose algorithm for monitoring web information sources. In *Proceedings of the International conference on very Large Data Bases (VLDB)*, pages 360–371, Toronto, ON, Canada, September 2004.

12. C.H. Papadimitriou and M. Yannakakis. On the approximability of trade-offs and optimal access of web sources. In *FOCS*, pages 86–92, 2000.

13. RDF. http://www.w3.org/rdf.

14. RDFS. http://www.w3.org/tr/rdf-schema/.

15. H. Roitman, A. Gal, L. Bright, and L. Raschid. A dual framework and algorithms for targeted data delivery. Technical report, University of Maryland, College Park, 2005. Available from http://hdl.handle.net/1903/3012.

16. H. Roitman, A. Gal, and L. Raschid. Framework and algorithms for web resource monitoring and data delivery. Technical Report CS-TR-4806, UMIACS-TR-2006-26, University of Maryland, College Park, 2006.

17. RSS. http://www.rss-specifications.com.

18. J. Yin, L. Alvisi, M. Dahlin, and A. Iyengar. Engineering server-driven consistency for large scale dynamic web services. *Proceedings of the International World Wide Web Conference (WWW)*, pages 45–57, May 2001.

An Incremental Approach to Enhance the Accuracy of Internet Routing

Ines Feki[1]

[1] France Telecom R&D, 42 rue des coutures,
14066 Caen, France
ines.feki@orange-ft.com

Abstract. Internet is composed of a set of autonomous systems (AS) managed by an administrative authority. The Border Gateway Protocol (BGP) is the exterior routing protocol used to exchange network reachability between the border routers of each autonomous network. BGP allows the ASes to apply policies when they select the routes that their traffic will take. Policies are based on business relationships and traffic engineering constraints. It is currently assumed that the exchanged reachability information is correct. In other words, the ASes that originate a network prefix are supposed to be authorized to advertise it. It also means that the announced routing information is conformant with the routing policies of the ASes. This assumption is not true anymore. We review existing proposals aiming to solve internet routing security issues and present our contributions. First, we propose a system able to detect and to react to illegitimate advertisements. Then, we describe our current work that focuses on the specification of a collaborative framework between ASes aiming at cautiously select routes.

Keywords: Routing, BGP, security.

1 Introduction

The current trend in applications, networks and services is the use of Internet Protocol. While converging to this technology, we should also consider other features like security and not only its attractive low cost. The current philosophy behind security holds that systems inside the perimeter of a network must be protected from outside. Several mechanisms can be deployed to provide security functions and to ensure this protection. Nevertheless, in networks routing function is still vulnerable and more efforts should focus on this issue. Routing refers to selecting paths along which data will be sent. This function is important and should be well achieved in order to guarantee data delivery to its intended destination. In other words, with the current philosophy if networks were castles their security would rely almost entirely on building thicker walls and deeper moats. But if the roads between them were full of bandits, then commerce would collapse and the castles with it.

In Internet routing system castles are represented by the networks of Internet services providers and telecom operators. These networks -also called autonomous

R. Meersman, Z. Tari, P. Herrero et al. (Eds.): OTM Workshops 2006, LNCS 4278, pp. 1439–1449, 2006.

systems (ASes) - are interconnected in various ways. Routing function between these networks is achieved by the Border Gateway Protocol (BGP)[1]. This protocol is used to exchange between ASes network reachability. BGP messages contain a path composed of a sequence of ASes. Autonomous Systems pay each other to forward data to its destination. A BGP router receives several paths to a single destination and chooses the less expensive one. Data paths are then supposed to take the selected path to reach their destination. If the exchanged reachability information is incorrect then incorrect paths may be selected and traffic may be redirected or blackholed and it would not reach its destination. Data packets may contain voice, video and several applications. It is crucial for network providers and operators to have a guarantee on the correct delivery of their data. In this thesis, we have addressed these routing security issues. Firstly, we have studied the solutions that have been proposed to enhance security in the routing system. Secondly, we have studied security vulnerabilities that the routing system is facing. We have also assessed the risks related to these vulnerabilities. This analysis allowed us to identify requirements that a security solution should meet. These requirements are operational and security related. We distinguish two levels in security requirements. The first level is related to the security of the transport of the routing protocol messages. This means the verification of the integrity of BGP messages and their authentication. The second level of security requirements is related to the verification of the correctness of the exchanged routing. This means the conformance of the routing information with the topology, the routing policies and the network prefix ownership. Next, we proposed an approach to detect illegitimate routing information based on the analysis of the routing data received by the routers of an autonomous system and the public routing data received by route collectors. These collectors deployed in different locations in Internet. Our future plans are to evaluate the utilization of a collaborative recommendation system that enables autonomous systems to exchange the trust level they associate with a piece of routing information. This parameter is considered in the routes selection process in the autonomous system that collaborates in this framework.

In this paper we present an overview of the problem addressed in the thesis and overview of the proposed approach. The remainder of the paper is organized as follows. In section B, we formulate the problem addressed in the thesis that is related to routing security problem. In section C, we present the solutions proposed to enhance the security in the routing system. We analyze all these solutions and present their advantages and drawbacks. Section D describes the contributions that we have proposed and the methodology that we used to identify incorrect advertisements. Current work and future plans are described in the section E.

2 Problem Formulation: Internet Routing Security Issues

2.1 Introduction to Internet Routing System

Internet is composed of thousands of Autonomous Systems (ASes); those networks are owned and operated by a single administrative entity. These ASes are interconnected in various ways but not in a fully meshed way. In theory their interconnection should allow packets to be sent everywhere in the network. This interconnection may be modelled as a customer to provider relationship. Big ASes provide data transit service for the smallest one. Customer ASes can have multiple providers in this case it is multihomed.

Each AS is identified by an autonomous system number (ASN) and is reachable via an IP network prefix. These prefixes and ASNs are managed by the Internet Assigned Number Authority (IANA) which delegates them either directly to organizations or to Regional Internet Registries (RIR). In the latter case, RIRs allocates later these resources to organizations. As mentioned above, the exterior routing protocol used between ASes is BGP. It is used to exchange interdomain network reachability information between those ASes. BGP is a path vector routing protocol; its messages contain a path composed of a sequence or a set of ASes. This path should be used to reach the announced network prefixes. A BGP router does not have a global view on the Internet topology; it only knows the neighbour capable of reaching a destination. When the reachability changes it just sends updates to its neighbours which forward them to their neighbours and so on. BGP allows network administrators to apply routing policies used for different reasons (e.g. traffic engineering, load balancing, etc.). Business relationships play also an important role in defining those policies. It is possible, for example, for an organization to deny its traffic to traverse a competitor and to prefer another path, even longer. Moreover, providers often compete with one another for customers but must nonetheless cooperate to offer global connectivity to hundreds of millions of hosts. Routing policies are used to select which routes are advertised to which neighbours and which paths are used to send packets to any given destination.

2.2 Internet Routing Vulnerabilities

The Internet Routing System is vulnerable, the dynamic routes that are selected to forward data may be incorrect and the traffic may not be delivered to its destination. We have studied these vulnerabilities. They are related to the elements of the routing system introduced above. In this paragraph we present the vulnerabilities with the correspondent element.

Vulnerabilities related to autonomous systems
First, the number of ASes is increasing and it becomes inappropriate to trust every AS in the routing system. Thirty ASes join the routing system every week [2]. When ASes are directly interconnected their agreements may be considered as a trust relationship. But trust can not be transitive infinitely. In other words, if an AS A trusts its neighbouring AS B and B trust an AS C, A may trust C. But if C trusts an AS D that AS may not trust D. The trust level decreases as the number of hops and participants increases.

Next, the autonomy of ASes in the definition of their routing policies may introduce other vulnerabilities. In [3], Zhang et al analyzed selective dropping attacks that result from intentionally drop of incoming and outgoing Update messages. In [4], Feamster et al proved that certain received route rankings and announced route filters used by ASes may not ensure routing stability. They argue that AS's full autonomy and expressiveness of routing policies may have undesirable consequences on the routing system. Since BGP deployment some accidents have occurred. In 1997, AS7007 accidentally announced routes to most of the Internet and disrupted connectivity for over two hours [5]. Other incidents occurred and they are generally related to misconfiguration problems. Mahajan et al explored these misconfiguration problems in [6]. They identified two types of BGP misconfigurations: Origin misconfiguration where an AS injects prefixes it should not, and Export misconfiguration where the advertised path is in violation of the policies of one of the listed ASes. Origin misconfiguration is one of the illegitimate reasons for which some prefixes are announced by multiple origin ASes. According to RFC 1930 a prefix must be originated by a single AS. However, if we analyze public Internet routing information [7][8] many prefixes are frequently originated by multiple AS. Zhao et al analyzed these multiple origin AS conflicts (MOAS) in [9]. One of the legitimate reasons of these MOAS is related to prefixes associated to exchange points. These prefixes can be legitimately originated by all ASes participating in the exchange point. Multihoming is also a legitimate reason to see MOAS conflicts occur. Another legitimate reason is the aggregation achieved in transit ASes. Misconfigurations, prefix hijacking or even faulty aggregation can also be the reasons for MOAS conflicts occurrence. Since multihoming is not explicit in BGP, we cannot distinguish between legitimate and illegitimate conflicts. Different IP prefix hijacking attacks have occurred; the last one took place in January 2006 and led to a denial of services of a server provider because another ISP originated its prefixes [10].

Vulnerabilities related to registries
It is currently impossible to distinguish between valid MOAS and illegitimate ones. Registries that are responsible for the network resources delegation make available network resources databases. ASes are responsible for the maintenance of their data in these databases. But these ASes do not maintain up to date their data. Moreover, more efforts have to be made to enhance the security of the access to these databases. First, the access to data objects in the databases is not well secured. Next, the data model used in these databases does not map directly a network prefix to its legitimate autonomous system originator. Moreover, registries do not use the same data format in their databases. This introduces some difficulties when someone aims at the utilization of these data to find rapidly the correct information.

Vulnerabilities related to BGP
Internet Routing System vulnerabilities are also related the used routing protocol. In fact, BGP relies on TCP and is faced with TCP vulnerabilities. The TCP attack that has the most significant impact on BGP is TCP reset attack. In fact, BGP relies on a persistent TCP connection which is maintained between BGP peers. The connection reset implies the withdrawal of all the routes learned from the neighbour BGP router. It takes time to send all BGP messages and to rebuild routing tables. In order to protect BGP from spoofed TCP segments and specially TCP resets, an option has been added to BGP. It is based on an extension to TCP where every TCP segment contains an MD5 digest [11]. It provides connection oriented integrity and data origin authentication on a point to point basis. Another possibility is to use the Generalized TTL mechanism [12] where the TTL of BGP packets is set to the maximum value of 255. Any packets that do not have a TTL in the range of 255 – 254 are rejected [13].

Moreover, the exchange of routing information in BGP relies on the assumption that the participants are telling the truth when they exchange routing information. Routing data analysis shows that the autonomous systems participating in Internet routing system may not announce correct information. With BGP there is no way to verify that route advertisements are conformant with the network topology, with the routing policies. We have analyzed vulnerabilities related to BGP. The analysis was published in [14].

2.3 Internet Routing Security Risks

We have identified vulnerabilities related to each element participating to the Internet Routing System. If these vulnerabilities are exploited, the traffic that is forwarded in the Internet Routing System may be blackholed, subverted or redirected. In a blackholing attack an AS may be isolated from the entire Internet. Besides in a subversion or redirection attack, traffic in destination to an AS is forced to take another path [15]. Therefore routers may eavesdrop data packets.

It is crucial for ASes (organizations, operators, universities, and network services providers) to have a guarantee about the delivery of their traffic whether is contains voice, video or other data. So, it is important to work on the enhancements of the routing security and that is the goal of the thesis.

3 Related Work

In order to propose a solution, we have first analyzed the existing ones. In this paragraph we present taxonomy of the proposed solutions. Several solutions are based on cryptographic methods aiming at avoiding and preventing incorrect information propagation. One of these approaches is Secure BGP [16]. Its goal is to assure the integrity of BGP messages, the authorization of a router to originate and to announce a route. IPSec is used to provide messages integrity and peer authentication. A public key infrastructure is used to support the authentication of the ownership of address blocks and autonomous system identities, the given BGP router's identity and its right to represent the AS it claims. Certificates are issued as address blocks and autonomous systems numbers are allocated by Regional Internet Registries (RIR). Secure Origin BGP [17], a second solution using cryptographic methods, uses a public key infrastructure to authenticate the AS; RIRs are not involved as Certificate Authorities (CA) for their authentication. ASes issue certificates to authorize other ASes to announce their prefixes. Secure Origin BGP is based on the idea that ASes publish their policies which may be considered as a drawback since some ASes consider them confidential. Pretty Secure BGP [18] uses both centralized and distributed trust models used in SBGP and SoBGP. The first model is used for AS number authentication and the latter is used for IP prefix ownership and origination verification. The three solutions described above were presented in IETF Routing Protocols Security Working Group but there was no consensus on those solutions [19]. A new IETF working group focuses currently on Interdomain routing security [20]. Besides cryptographic solutions, other works focused on the MOAS conflicts. Wu et al worked on BGP anomalies and MOAS visualization tools [21][22]. Anomaly visualization is not efficient enough against anomalies, it would be more efficient to have a mechanism that detects and reacts to anomalies as the routing system is running or even a mechanism that prevent those attacks. Zhao et al proposed to create a list of multiple ASes who are entitled to originate a prefix and attach it to BGP community attribute in advertisements [23]. Another solution that validates advertisements is Interdomain Route Validation (IRV) [24]. It introduces a new protocol to validate routing information announced between ASes. IRV allows ASes to acquire and validate static (policies) and dynamic (advertisements) interdomain routing. The approach is based on an interdomain routing validator in each participant AS that receives validation requests from the other validators in the other ASes. The reasons that trigger the requests are not mentioned. It is left to the AS to choose its algorithm. This can be considered as an advantage and a drawback also since it gives flexibility to the AS but if the validation process is not frequent benefits will be reduced.

4   Contributions

4.1   Illegitimate Route Advertisement Detection Approach

The analysis of Internet routing system security issues presented above and the analysis of the related work allowed us to identify requirements that a solution should satisfy and several research work items. In this paragraph we present the requirements that we have defined and the first approach that we have proposed.

Requirements definition and work items identification
In this paragraph, we address all the requirements for a resilient interdomain routing system. The requirements that we have defined were published in [25]. The basic need of an AS is to be sure that its inbound and outbound connectivity is ensured. That means that a customer AS needs to be sure that its prefixes are announced correctly by their providers and that they will let it reach all networks. It also needs to be sure that its policies are applied. In the same way, a provider AS needs to be sure that not only its prefixes but also those of its customers ASes are correctly announced and that the traffic in their destination won't be subverted, redirected or blackholed. They also need to be sure that the traffic sent reaches its intended destination. So, when an AS border router receives BGP advertisements, it needs to

- Verify the transport security of the BGP message. In other words it needs to verify the integrity of the message. It also needs to authenticate the source of the message.
- Verify the correctness of the content of the message. This means that it needs to verify: Internet resources validity (public and allocated ASN and prefixes), AS legitimacy to originate the prefix, and the policy conformance of the path.

A security solution should not only meet the requirements mentioned above but also some operational requirements. One of the operational requirements is a low cost of the solution to be deployed. A second requirement is related to BGP convergence time which should not be heavily increased. Finally, the solution that will be adopted should be incrementally deployable.

We have also identified some work items related to the security requirements. First, related to the BGP messages transport security requirement, the authentication mechanism should be enhanced and provide more capabilities to routers to choose the supported methods and algorithms. Moreover, another work should focus on key distribution and management. Next, related to the information correctness requirement, registry databases security should be enhanced. Furthermore, an incentive mechanism should be deployed in order to let the ASes update their data in registries. Another possible work item is to contribute to the registries delegation policies. Another work item is the detection of anomalous advertisements based on the archived routing data. We have not investigated the transport security requirement, but we have focused on the second requirement related to the routing information correctness and conformance to the topology. This work is challenging since the topology of the Internet is not really well known. The reasons that are behind the routing protocol dynamics of are not known either. Our aim is to provide a method that detects incorrect routing information in order to avoid traffic delivery problems. In fact, it is likely to be some time before a centralized cryptographic mechanism for routing information authentication is deployed and have a significant security benefit. Our viewpoint is that in the meantime we need an intermediate solution that detects incorrect routing information. Routing system needs an "online" - runs while the routing is running- verification system which instantaneously distinguishes between suspicious and legitimate routes.

Statistical approach to detect illegitimate routes

We have designed a system able to detect and to react to anomalous advertisements. It can be deployed in every autonomous system participating to the Internet routing system. It is based on available network prefixes and AS numbers delegation information retrieved from Regional Registry databases, received routes, and archived public routing data. The first goal is to help the decision process when a route advertisement is received where the origin AS of the network prefix is different from the origin AS in the routing table and from the other advertisements received before. The idea is to associate with an AS a legitimacy level to originate a prefix. The conceptual model architecture of this system is composed of the following components:

- Origination legitimacy database: a legitimacy level to originate a prefix associated with an ASN is stored in this database.
- Data collection module: this module collects data from RIR databases. This data is used to initialize the values of the legitimacy level of an AS to originate a prefix. This legitimacy level is updated as received advertisements are processed. This module collects also advertisements from public routing data.
- Data processing module: collected data from the previous module is processed in this module. One of the functions of this module is to detect origin AS changes. A second function is to process received advertisements and public routing data and to infer legitimacy level.
- Decision module: This module is able to decide which action to carry out from the predefined set of possibilities. When an origin AS is detected the received advertisement may be filtered or dampened. The router may also de-aggregate its prefixes if it detects that they were originated by another unauthorized AS.

Legitimacy level inference algorithm

The legitimacy level is a real number between 0 and 1. It is the probability that an AS is a legitimate originator of a prefix. The legitimacy level is a weighted value computed as follows:

$$Leg\_Level(AS, P) = \alpha * Leg(Rtg\_Data) + (1-\alpha) * Leg(\text{Re} g\_Data)$$

Where Leg_Level(AS,P) is the legitimacy level of AS to originate P ; α is a weight factor; Leg(Rtg_Data) is the legitimacy level computed from received and archived routing data; Leg(Reg_Data) is the legitimacy level computed from registries data

These assumptions are considered in the computation of legitimacy values:

- The registered origin AS of a prefix in the registry database is the legitimate one.
- We consider that an AS A is a potential originator of a prefix P if its origin AS registered in the registry database exports this prefix to the AS A. The AS A must also import the prefix P from the origin AS. We also consider that the more the import/export relationship becomes indirect the less the AS is legitimate.
- If no origin AS is registered with the prefix then routing data is used. We consider that the more the prefix is announced by an AS at different times the more the AS is a legitimate origin AS. This assumption is based on the observation that multiple origin ASes corresponds to multihomed prefixes and that these advertisements are more long lasting than advertisements related to prefix hijacking.

We have analyzed the content of the registries databases and observed that the European registry has the most consistent database.

The analysis of the routing data has been achieved in three steps:

- The extraction of the necessary data from the raw BGP messages: prefixes, their origin ASes and the dates of the advertisements
- The construction of a database that contains prefixes originated by multiple ASes, the period between two advertisements with the same origin AS, their origin ASes registered in the registries databases, and export and import policies of the AS
- The legitimacy level computation

We extracted from RIS [8] archived routing data for the month of October 2005, and we observed daily MOAS reports. We focused on prefixes that are present more than 25 days in these reports. 65 % of these prefixes do not have a registered origin AS. The computation of the legitimacy level related to routing data of these tuples (AS, P) is based on the period during which the tuple has been seen. We also need to compute the legitimacy level related to the registries data. The 35% remainders have a registered origin AS. 70% of the registered ASes have published their routing policies in the registry database. The computation of the legitimacy level of the observed tuples (AS, P) is based on the routing policies of the registered origin AS. This requires the analysis of the routing policies of the ASes available in registries databases. We have also extracted and analyzed routing and network resources delegation data in order to evaluate the legitimacy level of the routing table of a European provider. 20% of the prefixes present in its routing table were delegated by IANA to the European registry and allocated by this registry to several organizations. The origin ASes of 90% of the prefixes in the routing table are registered and available. The algorithm that computes the legitimacy level from routing data was applied to the 10% remainder prefixes present in the routing table and originated by multiple ASes. The inference of the global legitimacy level will be possible as soon as the routing policies will be analyzed.

In the decision phase, a tuneable threshold can be used in the system. When a route advertisement is received, the legitimacy of the received origin AS is checked and compared to the list of the potential originators. If the legitimacy level is higher than the threshold then the route is accepted otherwise it discarded. If the received route contains prefixes that are owned by the AS that deploys the system, and if the observed origin AS was not authorized by the AS to originate the prefix, then the system allows the AS network administrators to deaggregate the affected prefixes. The deaggregation let the other ASes forward packets to the right destination. The deaggregation should last the period during which unauthorized prefixes origination.

If the legitimacy level of the received AS has not been yet evaluated, due to a lack of information in registries databases or because the announcement was sent for the first time, then the announcement will not be discarded but the selection will be delayed. The decision process will wait for more information to evaluate the legitimacy level.

Discussion

The deaggregation reaction may have some limitations since the length of the prefix, that was advertised by an unauthorized AS, may raise a problem. In fact, if the length of prefix is 16 then, advertising a prefix with a length of 17 may solve the problem. But if the prefix length is a 24, advertising a prefix with a length of 25 will not solve the problem since most of the ASes filter prefixes longer than 24. Moreover this reaction may be exploited by ASes that aim at redirecting the traffic. But, this should not be exploited by many ASes since the deaggregation is memory consumer. The router that deaggregates prefixes present in its routing table needs enough space to be able to support all the specific prefixes.

5 Current Work and Future Plans

As mentioned above our current work focuses on the analysis of the available routing policies of the ASes. This analysis aims at the classification of adjacencies between the ASes in order to evaluate the legitimacy level of tuples (AS, P). We aim at building a graph that represents the relationships between AS and the prefixes they export to each other and import from each other.

As we have mentioned in the requirements definition section, AS legitimacy to originate a prefix is one of the requirements of the routing correctness verification. Another requirement is the policy conformance of the received routing data. We plan to work also on this item. The routing policies analysis allows the inference of a policy conformance level of the received routing data.

We are also currently working on a collaborative framework that allows ASes to send to other ASes the legitimacy level they associate with routes. In this framework every AS deploys an agent responsible for the legitimacy evaluation. This agent sends the legitimacy level to the other agents deployed in the other ASes. Several constraints are considered in this framework specially the discovery of the agents and the parameters used by each agent to evaluate the routes legitimacy. We are also working on a specification of protocol that is used to negotiate these parameters and to disseminate on the overlay network the legitimacy values.

6 Current Work and Future Plans

The goal of our studies is to find out a solution able to identify incorrect advertisements when cryptographic solutions are not used. In brief, the question to which we try to answer is how an autonomous system can be sure that the received network prefixes are correct and that its traffic will take a correct path and reach its destination. Besides, how this autonomous system can be sure that the traffic supposed to reach its network traverses a correct path and reaches its network. Currently the route selection process considers only the cost of the routes. We believe that the route selection process should not consider only the cost of a route but also its reliability. In other words, one should verify that the route will correctly deliver the traffic. We also believe that another parameter should be considered. The route should be able to deliver all the traffic. This means that we should also consider the capacity and the quality of the route especially if the data traffic contains real time applications. This is also a research field that should be investigated.

References

1. Rekhter Y., Hares S., T. Li: the Border Gateway Protocol. RFC 4271 (2006)
2. www.potaroo.net/cidr
3. Zhang K., Zhao X., Felix Wu S.: An analysis on selective dropping attack in BGP. In Proceedings of IEEE International Conference on Performance, Computing, and Communications (2004)
4. Feamster N., Johari R., Balakrishnan H.: The Implications of Autonomy for Stable Policy Routing. In proceedings of ACM SIGCOMM (2005)
5. www.merit.edu/mail.archives/nanog/1997-04/msg00444.html
6. Mahajan R., Wetherall D., Anderson T.: Understanding BGP misconfigurations. In proceedings of ACM SIGCOMM (2002)
7. www.routeviews.org/
8. www.ripe.net/projects/ris/index.html
9. Zhao X., Pei D., Wang L., Massay D., Mankin A., Felix Wu S., Zhang L.: An Analysis of BGP Multiple Origin AS (MOAS) Conflicts. In Proceedings of the 1st ACM SIGCOMM Workshop on Internet Measurement (2001)
10. www.mail-archive.com/nanog@merit.edu/msg40003.html
11. Heffernan A.: Protection of BGP sessions via TCP MD5 signature option. RFC 2385 (1998)
12. www.nanog.org/mtg-0302/hack.html
13. Gill V., Heasley J., Meyer D.: The Generalized TTL Mechanism, RFC3682 (2004)
14. Feki I., Achemlal M., Serhouchni A.: Risques de sécurité lies à BGP. In Proceedings of the 4th conference on Security and Network Architecture (2005)
15. Nordström O., Dovrolis C.: Beware of BGP attacks. In ACM SIGCOMM Computer Communication Review, Volume 34, Issue 2 (2004)

16. Kent S., Lynn Ch., Seo K.: Secure Border Gateway Protocol. In IEEE Journal on Selected Areas in Communications, Vol. 18, No. 4, pp. 582-592 (2000)
17. R. White: Securing BGP through Secure Origin BGP. In Internet Protocol Journal, Cisco, Vol. 6 Num 3, p15-22 (2003)
18. Wan T.: Pretty Secure BGP. In proceedings of Network and Distributed System Security Symposium Conference (2005)
19. www.ietf.org/html.charters/rpsec-charter.html
20. www.ietf.org/html.charters/sidr-charter.html
21. Teoh, S.T.: Visual-based Anomaly Detection for BGP Origin AS Change (OASC) Events. In DSOM2003, 14th IFIP/IEEE International Workshop on Distributed Systems: Operations and Management (2003)
22. Teoh, S. T.: Combining visual and automated data mining for near-real-time anomaly detection and analysis in BGP, CCS Workshop on Visualization and Data Mining for Computer Security (2004)
23. Zhao X., Pei D., Wang L., Mankin A., Wu S., Zhang L.: Detection of Invalid Routing Announcement in the Internet. In Proceedings of International Conference on Dependable Systems and Networks (2002)
24. Goodell G., Aiello W., Griffin T., Ioannis J., McDaniel P., Rubin A.: Working Around BGP: An Incremental Approach to Improving Security and Accuracy of Interdomain Routing. In proceedings of Network and Distributed Systems Security (2003)
25. Feki, I., Achemlal M., Serhouchni A.: Internet Routing Security Issues and Requirements Definition. In proceedings of the International Conference on Telecommunications and Multimedia (2006)

Ontology-Based Change Management of Composite Services

Linda Terlouw[1,2]

[1] Delft University of Technology, Delft, The Netherlands
l.i.terlouw@tudelft.nl
[2] Ordina, System Development and Integration, Nieuwegein, The Netherlands

Abstract. As services in an SOA can be composed of lower level services, there will exist dependencies between services. Changing services can impact other services in the SOA and a lot of manual service management tasks are required. Our goal is to create a method for analyzing change effects of service adaptations within an SOA. More specific, we study: which services are affected when a certain service is adapted (dependencies), how the services are affected when a certain service is adapted (effects), and what is the best way to deal with this service adaptation (advice). We take an ontological approach to solve the problem and test this approach by building a prototype (tool).

1 Introduction

Service-Oriented Architecture (SOA) has gained popularity in industry as an *architectural style* for creating enterprise-wide and interorganizational application integration architectures. Researchers, consulting firms, and software suppliers promised organizations that SOA would result in better *business & IT alignment*, more *IT flexibility*, and *more IT reuse*. As with many new technologies the promises were too optimistic and this resulted in disappointments for the organizations that implemented SOA. As shown in figure 1, Gartner has now placed SOA in the disillusionment phase of its Emerging Technologies Hype Cycle, but Gartner expects support for SOA to grow and for it to mature as a technology within ten years. However, to reach the so called 'plateau of productivity' still a lot of problems have to be solved. Although the hype is over, the need for well founded research on the implementation and management of SOA is not over.

This article[1] presents our PhD research proposal. In section 2 it starts with explaining the relation between enterprise ontology and business services. Section 3 explains how these business services can be composed from other (lower level)

---

[1] This research is part of the CIAO!-program (http://www.ciao.tudelft.nl/). The CIAO!-program has a focus on two strongly related subject areas: collaboration within and between enterprises and interoperability between information systems [1]. Architecture and ontology are used as instruments for tackling the problems concerning collaboration and interoperability.

R. Meersman, Z. Tari, P. Herrero et al. (Eds.): OTM Workshops 2006, LNCS 4278, pp. 1450–1459, 2006.

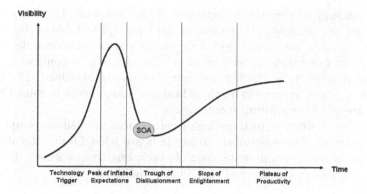

Fig. 1. Emerging Technology Hype Cycle 2005. Source: Gartner.

services. Section 4 provides an overview of problems related to SOA that still have to be solved. Section 5 explains the problem we are focusing on in our PhD research: dealing with change in service compositions. We state our goal and present our research methodology in section 6 and finally we present some related and alternative approaches to the problem in section 7.

2   Using Enterprise Ontology for Defining Business Services

Dietz [2] presents a methodology for producing *enterprise ontologies*[2]. The term ontology, originally a philosophical term meaning the study of existence, is defined in our context as follows:

> the *ontology of a system* is the understanding of the system's operation that is fully independent of the way in which it is or might be implemented.

The term system is used for something that has the following properties: *composition* (a set of elements of some category), *environment* (a set of elements of the same category disjoint with the composition), *production* (elements in composition produce things delivered to elements in environment), and *structure* (set of influence bonds among the elements in the composition, and between them and the elements in the environment). An enterprise is a system, since it conforms to all these properties. Therefore this methodology enables business modelers to create an understanding of the enterprise's operation without looking at its implementation.

The enterprise ontology provides a starting point for identifying *business components* [3], which are defined as the software components of an information

---

[2] When we speak of enterprises, we refer to commercial organizations, public organizations, as well as networks of these organizations (virtual organizations).

system that support directly the activities of an enterprise [4,5]. These business components can be identified by creating the Create/Use table of the enterprise ontology. Based on the grouping of the creation and use of object classes (e.g. a contract) and fact types (a result or effect of an act, e.g. 'a contract is offered') in specific process steps, the business components are identified. The mapping from process steps to services on these business components is gained from the action rules [2] of the enterprise ontology.

In this article we refer to these high level services of business components as *business services*. These business services indicate what IT functionality enterprises need in order to automate (part of) their business processes. So it really gives an overview of the *demand* for IT functionality.

3   Matching IT Demand and Supply in SOA

When we go down to the implementation level of enterprises, we find it is often not easy to match this demand of IT functionality to the supply of IT functionality, because software applications rarely directly support these business services. SOA is an *architectural style* that has a focus on matching supply and demand of IT functionality. The non-profit organization OASIS has constructed a reference model for SOA, in which SOA and service are defined as follows [6]:

- *SOA* is a paradigm for organizing and utilizing *distributed capabilities* that may be under the control of different *ownership domains*. It provides a uniform means to offer, discover, interact with and use capabilities to produce *desired effects* consistent with measurable preconditions and expectations.
- A *service* is a mechanism to enable *access to a set of one or more capabilities*, where the access is provided using a *prescribed interface* and is exercised consistent with *constraints and policies* as specified by the *service description*. In SOA services are the mechanism by which the needs and capabilities are brought together.

Thus the business services can be seen as the highest level of IT demand (the needs). These needs can be filled in by combining supply (capabilities) from lower level services. Figure 2 shows an overview of how business services can be composed from lower level services. Composition in this context does not mean that the lower level services are elements of the composite service, but that the composite service invokes the lower level services. We will use the following definitions for the lower level services:

- An *atomic service* (AS) is a term used from the *service provider point of view*. It indicates that the service *is not* composed of other services.
- A *composite service* (CS) is seen from the *service provider point of view*. It indicates that the service *is* composed of other (atomic, composite or elementary) services.
- An *elementary service* (ES) is seen from the *service consumer point of view*. It indicates that it is *not known* whether the service is composed of other services.

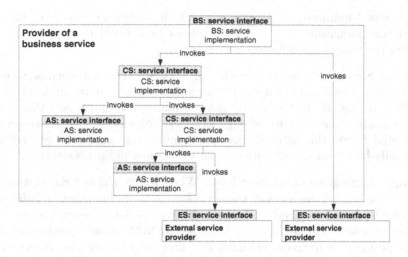

Fig. 2. Service compositions

A service provider can create new composite services by using its own (atomic and composite) services or by using the (elementary) services of other service providers as building blocks. In the last case the service provider for one service is a service consumer for another service. In order to find services offered by another service provider, one needs access to a service registry. This service registry can be private (only one organization or department has access to it), semi-public (a network of organizations has access to it), or public (everybody has access to it). In this article we will only consider private and semi-public registers, where exact scope of the register depends on the scope of the enterprise ontology.

A service provider and a service consumer have to make agreements on which services are offered, at what *Quality of Service* (QoS), at what price and for what duration. The service provider and consumer formalize these agreements in a *Service Level Agreement* (SLA).

4   Challenges of SOA

This section presents some of the challenges that will have to be solved in order to successfully use SOA.

Ownership of Services: When using 'normal' applications it is almost always clear who has ownership of a piece of IT functionality, because applications have clear boundaries. Ownership of services, however, is a more complex issue, because a service can use functionality from multiple applications having different owners. Who of these application owners gets to own the service and gets to make decisions about the service? This often is a politically complex problem.

Immature Technology: At this moment the technology for realizing SOA is still very immature. However, this will not be a problem in the long term, because the technology advances very rapidly.

Reusing Services: The real benefits of SOA are achieved when services are reused. A service consumer needs certain information in order to decide to use a service or not [6]. But to really achieve reuse, it is important that service providers are stimulated to offer generic services and service consumers are stimulated to use this services. Because stimuli in an enterprise are normally financially-based, an appropriate cost allocation method is necessary.

Change Management of Services: When the functional description of a service changes, all the users of the service have to be informed in order to be able to keep using the service. This can be very difficult, because some of the service consumers and providers may not belong to the same organization and it can be problematic to track dependencies (direct and indirect) between services.

5   Problem Description

In our PhD research we focus on the fourth problem: the change management of services. Changes in service definitions can occur in three situations:

1. the end date of an SLA is reached and the provider of an elementary service decides to apply changes to the service and no longer supports the old service which the provider of the composite service was using.
2. the provider of the composite service issues a Request for Change (RfC) to a provider of an elementary service and this request is granted (this is less problematic, because the provider of the composite service has control and knows what changes to expect).
3. a change request is requested or forced by management (more applicable within organizational boundaries than outside of organizational boundaries).

Figure 3 exhibits an example of a service change. A local IT department of a mortgage department of a bank, that handles private clients, acts as a service provider for the business service 'evaluatePotentialMortgageClient'. This service is composed of the services 'getMortgageApplicationInformation' and 'calculateRating'. The service 'evaluatePotentialMortgageClient' checks whether the client should be provided a mortgage based on his personal information (previous loans, job related information etc.) and the type of mortgage he requests. In the current situation the service 'getMortgageApplicationInformation' is an atomic service which uses a legacy mortgage application as backend system, which supplies the personal information of a client and information on the type of mortgage the client requests. The atomic service 'calculateRating' calculates the risk associated with the client for the selected mortgage and gives a positive or negative advice. Both atomic services are provided by the local IT department.

Because of cost savings the bank decides to centralize its customer information systems by introducing a CRM system which is managed by the central IT department. So the local IT department should now request the client information from the central IT department using a new service 'getClientInformation' and the service 'getMortgageApplicationInformation' becomes composite.

Now the following questions arise. Does the new 'getClientInformation' service provide all the client information that is needed to perform the service 'getMortgageApplicationInformation' or is an extra service from the mortgage system related to client information needed (e.g. for getting information about the client's mortgage history)? Can the service 'getMortgageInformation' be created automatically using the services 'getMortgageApplicationInformation' and 'getClientInformation'? How can the 'getMortgageApplicationInformation' be adapted in such a way that it combines the services 'getClientInformation' and 'getMortgageInformation'?

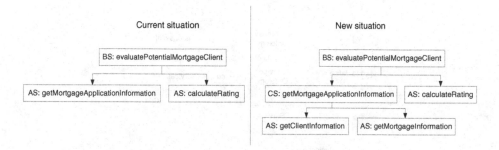

Fig. 3. Example of a service change

Replacing a backend system because of centralization is just one example of a change scenario. Other examples of service changes that can occur are: the bank decides to outsource part of its mortgage application to an external IT supplier or the business activities of the bank regarding to mortgages change and because of this the business services change (e.g. the bank starts offering mortgages for business clients).

6   Research Goal and Methodology

The goal of this PhD research is to create a method for analyzing change effects of service adaptations within an SOA. More specific, we study:

1. which services are affected when a certain service is adapted (dependencies)
2. how the services are affected when a certain service is adapted (effects)
3. what is the best way to deal with this service adaptation (advice)

To achieve our goal we follow an ontology-based approach. Figure 4 depicts the concepts we use within this approach, where diamonds depict an aggregation relationship and triangles depict a generalization/specialization relationship. The state model of the enterprise ontology [2] is the basis for the Common Information Model (CIM), which is sometimes referred to as a domain ontology. This CIM is more detailed than the state model, because it also describes information items on an implementation level which are derived from atomic and elementary services (this relation is not shown in the figure because of readability). The enterprise ontology is also used for defining business services. These services together with the composite, elementary, and atomic services are part of the service ontology. This service ontology among others captures the relationships between services and pre- and postconditions. The basis of this service ontology is also derived from the enterprise ontology. The services are specified using concepts from the CIM or a mapping between the service and the CIM exists in the service ontology. When a service changes, the service ontology and CIM are used to reason about the effects of this change on other services.

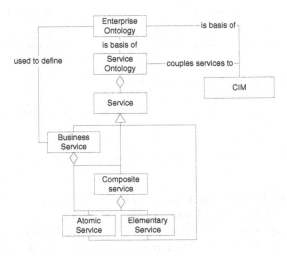

Fig. 4. Overview of concepts

We choose to follow an ontology-based approach, because:

- Other approaches (like *Petri nets* [7] and *state machines*) do not deal with the meaning of information items, but instead rely on a mapping of services based on syntax of messages and/or operations. This can result in wrong interpretations, because the meaning of an information item is not always clearly defined by its name. For example: different service providers can mean different things by the same description (same syntax, different semantics) or different service providers can mean the same thing by different descriptions (same semantics, different syntax). In our approach the meaning of the inputs and outputs are always clear, because either the concepts of the CIM are used directly, or a mapping exists between the inputs and outputs of a service and concepts of the CIM.

– We do not only want to analyze which other services are affected by a service adaptation, but we also want to give advice on how to adapt the other services. For some types of changes semantic knowledge is required in order to give an appropriate advice. For example, a company uses services from its suppliers to retrieve price information and it only has American suppliers. The company decides to buy goods from a new, Dutch supplier and wants to use its service for price information. Based on this information an advice can be given to incorporate an extra currency conversion service to convert the price information from euros to dollars. This information can not be extracted from syntactical information only.

Figure 5 depicts our research methodology. First of all, we study literature on enterprise ontology, ontological standards, semantic services, service-oriented architecture & design, and change management. Building upon this theory we will create selection criteria for standards for the CIM and service ontology, and select the best standards based on these criteria. Using mainly the theory on change management, service oriented design, and semantic services, we will select common change scenarios (e.g. new input or output information items are added to the service, two or more services are combined to one larger service, and the service is no longer available). Using this literature we will also create an overview of other change management methods and the suitability of (part of) these methods in a service-oriented environment.

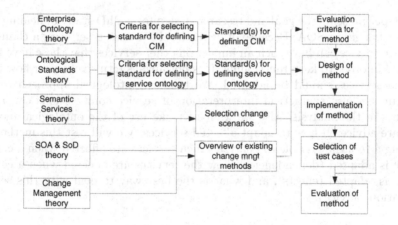

Fig. 5. Research methodology

The selected standards, change scenarios, and existing change management approaches act as an input for the design of our method for change management and the criteria we will use to evaluate our method. Example criteria for evaluation can be the percentage of correct change analyses and the percentage of generated advices that are correct. We will implement the design in a prototype (tool), select test cases, and finally evaluate the method.

7   State of Research

Currently we are in the first phase of the study, i.e. literature research and the definition of criteria for selecting a standard for defining a CIM and for selecting a standard for defining a service ontology.

We have studied literature of various authors on the creation and management of domain ontologies. Lee (Sunjae) et al. [8] for example provide a framework for creating and managing an ontology using a bottom-up approach. In this approach user's can evaluate the ontology, so the ontology users and not only the ontology administrator contributes to the ontology. Hau, Lee (William), and Newhause [9] present a framework for capturing the capability of services by annotating their programmatic interface using OWL in relation to domain concepts thereby allowing services to be semantically matched based on their ontological annotation.

The most promising standard for the CIM seems to be OWL. Currently we are examining if the ORM-based state model can be translated to OWL [10,11].

We have also studied literature of various authors on the creation of service ontologies [9,12,13,14] and on other popular, non-semantic approaches for specifying service compositions and reasoning about services, e.g. Petri nets [7,15] and state machines [16,17].

8   Conclusions

This paper presents the goal and research design for a PhD study of dealing with service changes in SOA. Because of dependencies between services, a change in a certain service can have such an impact on other services that these have to be changed in order to keep functioning. It is not always intuitively clear how these affected services should be adapted. We take an ontological approach to this problem, because syntactical interpretation of service compositions can result in errors in the analysis. Also we want to make use of the ontological models, to create advice on how to adapt affected services. We will test this method by building a tool that is able to analyze which services are affected when a certain service is adapted (dependencies), how the services are affected when a certain service is adapted (effects), and what is the best way to deal with this service adaptation (advice).

References

1. Albani, A., Dietz, J.: The benefit of enterprise ontology in identifying business components. In: WCC '06: Proceedings of the IFIP World Computer Congress, Santiago de Chile, Chile (2006)
2. Dietz, J.: Enterprise Ontology, Theory and Methodology. Springer, Berlin Heidelberg, Germany (2006)
3. Albani, A., Dietz, J., Zaha, J.: Identifying business components on the basis of an enterprise ontology. In: Interoperability of Enterprise Software and Applications, Geneva, Switzerland (2005) 335–347

4. Turowski, K., Zaha, J.: Methodological standard for service specification. International Journal of Services and Standards (2004) 98–111
5. Turowski, K.: Fachkomponenten: Komponentenbasierte betriebliche Anwendungssysteme. Shaker Verslag (2003)
6. OASIS: Reference model for service oriented architecture, committee draft 1.0. (2006) http://www.oasis-open.org/committees/download.php/16587/wd-soa-rm-cd1ED.pdf.
7. Hamadi, R., Benatallah, B.: A petri net-based model for web service composition. In: CRPITS '17: Proceedings of the Fourteenth Australasian database conference on Database technologies 2003, Adelaide, Australia, Australian Computer Society, Inc. (2003) 191–200
8. Lee, S., Seo, W., Kang, D., Kim, K., Lee, J.: A framework for supporting bottom-up ontology evolution for discovery and description of grid services. Expert Systems with Applications **In Press, Corrected Proof** (2006)
9. Hau, J., Lee, W., Newhouse, S.: Autonomic service adaptation in iceni using ontological annotation. In: GRID '03: Proceedings of 4th International Workshop on Grid Computing, Phoenix, Arizona, IEEE (2003) 10–17
10. Bollen, P.: A formal orm-to-uml mapping algorithm. Research Memoranda 015, Maastricht: METEOR, Maastricht Research School of Economics of Technology and Organization (2002) http://ideas.repec.org/p/dgr/umamet/2002015.html.
11. Jarrar, M., Demey, J., Meersman, R.: On using conceptual data modeling for ontology engineering. Journal on Data Semantics **2800** (2003) 185–207
12. Martin, D., et al.: Bringing semantics to web services: The owl-s approach. In: SWSWPC '04: Proceedings of the First International Workshop on Semantic Web Services and Web Process Composition. Volume 3387 of Lecture Notes in Computer Science., San Diego, CA, USA, Springer (2005) 26–42
13. Agarwal, V., Dasgupta, K., Karnik, N., Kumar, A., Kundu, A., Mittal, S., Srivastava, B.: A service creation environment based on end to end composition of web services. In: WWW '05: Proceedings of the 14th international conference on World Wide Web, Chiba, Japan, ACM Press (2005) 128–137
14. Lara, R., Roman, D., Polleres, A., Fensel, D.: A conceptual comparison of wsmo and owl-s. In: ECOWS '04: Proceedings of the 2004 European Conference on Web Services, Erfurt, Germany, Springer (2004) 254–269
15. Verbeek, H., van der Aalst, W.: Analyzing bpel processes using petri nets. In: PNCWB '05: Proceedings of the Second International Workshop on Applications of Petri Nets to Coordination, Workflow and Business Process Management, Miami, Florida, USA, Florida International University (2005) 59–78
16. Bultan, T., Fu, X., Hull, R., Su, J.: Conversation specification: a new approach to design and analysis of e-service composition. In: WWW '03: Proceedings of the 12th international conference on World Wide Web, Budapest, Hungary, ACM Press (2003) 403–410
17. Berardi, D., Giacomo, G.D., Lenzerini, M., Mecella, M., Calvanese, D.: Synthesis of underspecified composite e-services based on automated reasoning. In: ICSOC '04: Proceedings of the 2nd international conference on Service oriented computing, New York, NY, USA, ACM Press (2004) 105–114

Research on Ontology-Driven Information Retrieval

Stein L. Tomassen

Department of Computer and Information Science,
Norwegian University of Technology and Science,
NO-7491 Trondheim, Norway
stein.l.tomassen@idi.ntnu.no

Abstract. An increasing number of recent information retrieval systems make use of ontologies to help the users clarify their information needs and come up with semantic representations of documents. A particular concern here is the integration of these semantic approaches with traditional search technology. The research presented in this paper examines how ontologies can be efficiently applied to large-scale search systems for the web. We describe how these systems can be enriched with adapted ontologies to provide both an in-depth understanding of the user's needs as well as an easy integration with standard vector-space retrieval systems. The ontology concepts are adapted to the domain terminology by computing a feature vector for each concept. Later, the feature vectors are used to enrich a provided query. The whole retrieval system is under development as part of a larger Semantic Web standardization project for the Norwegian oil & gas sector.

1 Introduction

A problem with traditional information retrieval (IR) systems is that they typically retrieve information without an explicitly defined domain of interest to the user. Consequently, the system presents a lot of information that is of no relevance to the user. The research presented in this paper examines how ontologies can be efficiently utilized for traditional vector-space IR systems. The ontologies are adapted to the document space within multi-disciplinary domains where different terminology is used. The objective is to enhance the user-experience by improvement of search result quality for large-scale search systems.

One of the reasons for why IR systems do not have an explicitly defined domain of interest to the user is that most users tend to use very few terms (3 or less) in their search queries [1, 2]. As a result, the systems cannot *understand* the context of the user's query, which results in lower precision. By adding more relevant terms to the query, the domain of interest can, to some extent, be identified. However, adding both *correct* and *distinctive* terms is not always trivial, since the user needs knowledge about the terminology used in that particular domain to find those *correct* terms.

A novel and promising approach is concept-based search [3, 4, 5]. With this approach, the burden of knowing how the documents are written is taken off the user and hence the user can focus on searching on a conceptual level instead. One problem with this approach is to find good concepts. The approach described in [3, 5] finds

R. Meersman, Z. Tari, P. Herrero et al. (Eds.): OTM Workshops 2006, LNCS 4278, pp. 1460–1468, 2006.
© Springer-Verlag Berlin Heidelberg 2006

concepts based on the result set of the search, which then are used to refine the search. However, the relationships between the concepts are neglected.

Concepts and, in particular, relations between them can be specified in ontologies. Ontologies define concepts and the relationships among them [6]; therefore, they are often used to capture knowledge about domains. A growing number of IR systems make use of ontologies to help clarifying the information needs of the users, further described in section 3. However, a concern with these semantic approaches is the integration with traditional commercial search technologies.

In our approach [7], we propose a query enrichment approach that uses contextually enriched ontologies to bring the queries closer to the user's preferences and the characteristics of the document collection. The idea is to associate every concept (classes and instances) of the ontology with a feature vector (fv) to tailor these concepts to the specific document collection and terminology used. The structure of the ontology is taken into account during the construction of the feature vectors. The ontology and its associated feature vectors are later used for post-processing of the results provided by the search engine.

This paper is organized as follows. In section 2, we describe the context of this research. In section 3, related work is discussed. In section 4, we describe the approach including some research questions and the methodology used. Where in section 5, we present the current status of this research. Finally, section 6 concludes the paper.

2 Research Context

The context of this research is information retrieval utilizing ontologies. Furthermore, the work of this PhD is part of the Integrated Information Platform for reservoir and subsea production systems (IIP) project. The IIP project is funded by the Norwegian Research Council (NFR)[1]. The project started in 2004 and will end in 2007. The project employs two PhD students and one research scientist.

The IIP project is creating an ontology for all subsea equipment used by oil and gas industry. Unlike other initiatives, this project endeavors to integrate life-cycle data spanning several standards and disciplines. A goal of this project is to define an unambiguous terminology of the domain and build an ontology that will ease integration of systems between disciplines. A common terminology is assumed to reduce risks and improve the decision making process in the industry. The project will also make this ontology publicly available and standardized by the International Organization for Standardization (ISO)[2].

3 State-of-the-Art

Traditional information retrieval techniques (i.e., vector-space model) have an advantage of being fast and give a fair result. However, it is difficult to represent the content of the documents meaningfully using these techniques. That is, after the

---

[1] NFR project number 163457/S30.
[2] http://www.iso.org/

documents are indexed, they become a "bag of terms" and hence the semantics is partly lost in this process.

In order to increase quality of IR much effort has been put into annotating documents with semantic information [8, 9, 10, 11]. That is a tedious and labor-intensive task. Furthermore, hardly any search engines are using metadata when indexing the documents. AltaVista[3] is one of the last major search engines which dropped its support in 2002 [12]. The main reason for this is that the meta information can be and has been misused by the content providers in the purpose of giving the documents a misleading higher ranking than it should have had [12]. However, there is still a vision that for ontology based IR systems on Semantic Web, "it is necessary to annotate the web's content with terms defined in ontology" [13].

The related work to our approach comes from two main areas. Ontology based IR, in general, and approaches to query expansion, in particular. General approaches to ontology based IR can further be sub-divided into Knowledge Base (KB) and vector space model driven approaches. KB approaches use reasoning mechanism and ontological query languages to retrieve instances. Documents are treated either as instances or are annotated using ontology instances [13, 14, 15, 16]. These approaches focus on retrieving instances rather than documents. Some approaches are often combined with ontological filtering [17, 18, 19].

There are approaches combining both ontology based IR and vector space model. For instance, some start with semantic querying using ontology query languages and use resulting instances to retrieve relevant documents [16, 20]. [20] use weighted annotation when associating documents with ontology instances. The weights are based on the frequency of occurrence of the instances in each document. [21] combines ontology usage with vector-space model by extending a non-ontological query. There, ontology is used to disambiguate queries. Simple text search is run on the concepts' labels and users are asked to choose the proper term interpretation. A similar approach is described in [22] where documents are associated with concepts in the ontology. The concepts in the query are matched to the concepts of the ontology in order to retrieve terms and then used for calculation of document similarity.

[17] is using ontologies for retrieval and filtering of domain information across multiple domains. There each ontology concept is defined as a domain feature with detailed information relevant to the domain including relationships with other features. The relationships used are hypernyms (super class), hyponyms (sub class), and synonyms. Unfortunately, there are no details in [17] provided on how a domain feature is created.

Most query enrichment approaches are not using ontologies like [3, 4, 5]. Query expansion is typically done by extending provided query terms with synonyms or hyponyms (cf. [23]). Some approaches are focusing on using ontologies in the process of enriching queries [15, 17, 22]. However, ontology in such case typically serves as thesaurus containing synonyms, hypernyms/hyponyms, and do not consider the context of each term, i.e. every term is equally weighted.

[4] is using query expansion based on similarity thesaurus. Weighting of terms is used to reflect the domain knowledge. The query expansion is done by similarity measures. Similarly, [3] describes a conceptual query expansion. There, the query

---

[3] AltaVista, http://www.altavista.com/

concepts are created from a result set. Both approaches show an improvement compared to simple term based queries, especially for short queries.

The approaches presented in [5, 24] are most similar to ours. However, [5] is not using ontologies but is reliant on query concepts. Two techniques are used to create the feature vectors of the query concepts, i.e. based on document set and result set of a user query. While the approach presented in [24] is using ontologies for the representation of concepts. The concepts are extended with similar words using a combination of Latent Semantic Analysis (LSA) and WordNet[4]. Both approaches get promising results for short or poorly formulated queries.

To show the difference from the related work discussed above we emphasize on the main features of our approach as follows. Our approach relies on domain knowledge represented in ontology when constructing feature vectors, then traditional vector-space retrieval model is used for the information retrieval task, where feature vectors are used to enrich provided queries. The main advantage of our approach is that the concepts of an ontology is tailored to the terminology of the document collection, which can vary a lot even within the same domain.

4 Research Approach

The overall objective of this research is to enhance the user-experience by improving search result quality for large-scale search systems. This objective contains the following sub goals:

- Explore and analyze the usage of ontologies for large-scale search systems for the web.
- Contribute with a method for applying ontologies efficiently to large-scale search systems for the web.

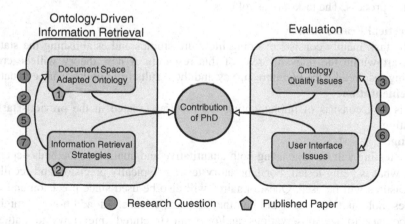

Fig. 1. Overview of research approach with the different main components and the relationship between them

---

[4] WordNet, http://wordnet.princeton.edu/

Fig. 1 depicts the overall approach of this research. The research is divided into two main areas, which are *Ontology-Driven Information Retrieval* and *Evaluation*. The former deals with aspects regarding ontologies in IR systems and different strategies of using ontologies and the latter deals with aspects regarding evaluation of ontology-driven IR systems, quality of IR ontologies, and user interface of ontology-driven IR systems. Fig. 1 also shows how the research questions, described in section 4.1, and relevant published papers, described in section 5.2, relates.

4.1 Research Questions

Research questions relevant to this work are as follows:

Q1: Can the retrieval effectiveness of large-scale search systems be improved by utilizing ontologies?

Q2: What components of large-scale search systems will benefit of using ontologies?

Q3: How can ontologies be used to help the user to improve the user experience of search systems?

Q4: What features of an ontology influence on the search quality?

Q5: How to provide the search system with more information of the user's intention of a query?

Q6: How to evaluate search systems where the user experience is taken into consideration?

Q7: How can ontologies be used to enhance search systems for web?

4.2 Research Method

This research will consist of several tasks being part of a cycle illustrated in Fig. 2. This cycle will be used for all the areas of research illustrated in Fig. 1 and will be an iterative process. The tasks are as follows:

Theoretical Framework:
– This task mainly consists of doing literature studies and establishing the state-of-the-art within the relevant areas of this research. A new theory will be created being inspired by the literature survey and the results from preliminary evaluations.

Implementation:
– This task consists of implementing the theories created in the previous task for testing.

Testing:
– The testing will be done using both quantitative and qualitative methods depending on what is being tested. For laboratory testing, typically precision and recall [25] measures will be used. Questionnaires will also be used since precision and recall does not take into account i.e. the user experience. In addition, it might be necessary to use observations and/or semi-structured interviews to gather all knowledge about the user experience of using the prototypes.
– Different test collections will be used depending on the ontologies. As part of the IIP project both some ontologies and text collections within the oil and gas domain

will be available. Wikipedia[5] will also be used as a text collection for testing usage of smaller ontologies both manually created and found on the Web. In addition, the API from Yahoo will be used for large-scale search testing.

Analysis:
– The results of the testing will be analyzed and compared with previously gathered results. Based on this analysis the theoretical framework will be revised or a new one will be created, which next will be implemented and tested, etc.

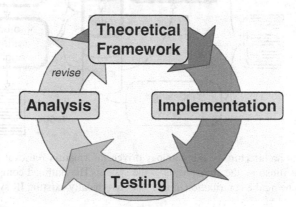

Fig. 2. Research tasks cycle. The cycle illustrates the tasks that are used for each individual aspect of the overall approach depicted in Fig. 1.

5 Approach and Research Status

In this section the proposed architecture and some preliminary results are presented.

5.1 Proposed Architecture

Fig. 3 illustrates the overall architecture of the ontology-driven information retrieval system. Next the individual components of the system are briefly described.

Feature vector miner: This component extracts the terms from the document collection and associates them with relevant concept(s) from the ontologies. The fv index is created offline equal to the *index* of the search engine.

Indexing engine: The main task of this component is to index the document collection. The indexing system is built on top of Lucene[6], which is a freely available and fully featured text search engine from Apache[7]. We will also do experiments using the index provided by Yahoo.

Query enrichment: This component handles the query specified by the user. The query can initially consist of concepts and/or ordinary terms (keywords). The concepts will be replaced by corresponding fvs. Each concept or term can be individually weighted. This component is further described in [7].

---

[5] Available for download from: http://download.wikimedia.org
[6] http://lucene.apache.org/
[7] http://www.apache.org/

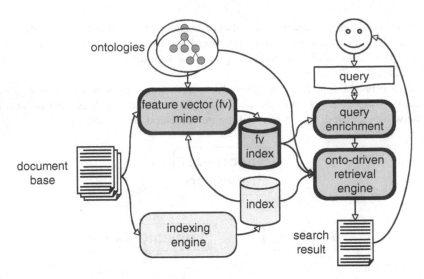

Fig. 3. The overall architecture of the ontology-driven information retrieval system. The no-transparent objects illustrate the components of the system. The outlined components illustrate those components being the contribution of this work to typically existing IR systems.

Onto-driven retrieval engine: This component performs the search and post-processing of the retrieved results. The ontologies and their corresponding *fv*s are used when post-processing the retrieved documents before presented to the user.

5.2 Preliminary Results

Some components of the proposed architecture shown in Fig. 3 are implemented and individually tested. These components are all related to the *Query enrichment* component that was presented in a paper [7] at the NLDB 2006 conference[8], depicted as paper 1 in Fig. 1. Main architectural components and techniques constituting the method were presented in that paper. The components implemented are built upon the full-text retrieval engine Lucene from Apache. As research reported here is still in progress, we have not been able to formally evaluate the approach. However, preliminary results indicate that the quality of the feature vectors is very important for the quality of the search result. Further, we have proposed that concepts and ordinary terms or keywords of the query should be handled differently since they have different roles identified by the user. This proposal is described in paper [26], depicted as paper 2 in Fig. 1.

6 Conclusion

In this PhD work we will explore and analyze methods for utilizing ontologies to improve the retrieval quality. The concepts in the ontology are associated with contextual definitions in terms of weighted feature vectors tailoring the ontology to

---

[8] http://www.nldb.org

the content of the document collection. Further, the feature vectors are used to enrich a provided query. Query enrichment by feature vectors provides means to bridge the gap between query terms and terminology used in a document set, and still employing the knowledge encoded in the ontology.

Acknowledgements. This research work is funded by the Integrated Information Platform for reservoir and subsea production systems (IIP) project, which is supported by the Norwegian Research Council (NFR). NFR project number 163457/S30. In addition, I would like to thank Jon Atle Gulla and Darijus Strasunskas for their support and help.

References

1. Gulla, J.A., Auran, P.G., Risvik, K.M.: *Linguistic Techniques in Large-Scale Search Engines*. Fast Search & Transfer (2002) 15
2. Spink, A., Wolfram, D., Jansen, M.B.J., Saracevic, T.: *Searching the Web: the public and their queries*. J. Am. Soc. Inf. Sci. Technol. 52 (2001) 226-234
3. Grootjen, F.A., van der Weide, T.P.: *Conceptual query expansion*. Data & Knowledge Engineering 56 (2006) 174-193
4. Qiu, Y., Frei, H.-P.: *Concept based query expansion*. Proceedings of the 16th annual international ACM SIGIR conference on Research and development in information retrieval. ACM Press, Pittsburgh, Pennsylvania, USA (1993) 160-169
5. Chang, Y., Ounis, I., Kim, M.: *Query reformulation using automatically generated query concepts from a document space*. Information Processing and Management 42 (2006) 453-468
6. Gruber, T.R.: *A translation approach to portable ontology specifications*. Knowledge Acquisition 5 (1993) 199-220
7. Tomassen, S.L., Gulla, J.A., Strasunskas, D.: *Document Space Adapted Ontology: Application in Query Enrichment*. 11th International Conference on Applications of Natural Language to Information Systems. Springer, Klagenfurt, Austria (2006)
8. Desmontils, E., Jacquin, C.: *Indexing a Web Site with a Terminology Oriented Ontology*. In I.F. Cruz, S. Decker, J. Euzenat and D.L. McGuinness (eds.) The Emerging Semantic Web. IOS Press, (2002) 181- 198
9. Motta, E., Shum, S.B., Domingue, J.: *Case Studies in Ontology-Driven Document Enrichment: Principles, Tools and Applications*. International Journal of Human-Computer Studies 6 (2000) 1071-1109
10. Popov, B., Kiryakov, A., Kirilov, A., Manov, D., Ognyanoff, D., Goranov, M.: *KIM - Semantic Annotation Platform*. In: Fensel, D., Sycara, K.P., Mylopoulos, J. (eds.): The Semantic Web - ISWC 2003, Second International Semantic Web Conference, Sanibel Island, FL, USA, October 20-23, 2003, Proceedings, Vol. 2870. Springer (2003) 834-849
11. Fensel, D., Harmelen, F.v., Klein, M., Akkermans, H., Broekstra, J., Fluit, C., Meer, J.v.d., Schnurr, H.-P., Studer, R., Hughes, J., Krohn, U., Davies, J., Engels, R., Bremdal, B., Ygge, F., Lau, T., Novotny, B., Reimer, U., Horrocks, I.: *On-To-Knowledge: Ontology-based Tools for Knowledge Management*. In Proceedings of the eBusiness and eWork 2000 (EMMSEC 2000) Conference, Madrid, Spain (2000)
12. Sullivan, D.: *Death of a Meta Tag*. Search Engine Watch (2002)

13. Song, J-F., Zhang, W-M., Xiao, W., Li, G-H., Xu, Z-N.: *Ontology-Based Information Retrieval Model for the Semantic Web*. Proceedings of EEE 2005. IEEE Computer Society (2005) 152-155
14. Rocha, C., Schwabe, D., de Aragao, M.P.: *A hybrid approach for searching in the semantic web*. Proceeding of WWW 2004, ACM (2004) 374-383
15. Ciorăscu, C., Ciorăscu, I., Stoffel, K.: *knOWLer - Ontological Support for Information Retrieval Systems*. In Proceedings of Sigir 2003 Conference, Workshop on Semantic Web, Toronto, Canada (2003)
16. Kiryakov, A., Popov, B, Terziev, I., Manov, D., and Ognyanoff, D.: *Semantic Annotation, Indexing, and Retrieval*. Journal of Web Semantics 2(1), Elsevier, (2005)
17. Braga, R.M.M., Werner, C.M.L., Mattoso, M.: *Using Ontologies for Domain Information Retrieval*. Proceedings of the 11th International Workshop on Database and Expert Systems Applications. IEEE Computer Society (2000) 836-840
18. Borghoff, U.M., Pareschi, R.: *Information Technology for Knowledge Management*. Journal of Universal Computer Science 3 (1997) 835-842
19. Shah, U., Finin, T., Joshi, A., Cost, R.S., Mayfield, J.: *Information Retrieval On The Semantic Web*. Proceedings of Conference on Information and Knowledge Management. ACM Press, McLean, Virginia, USA (2002) 461-468
20. Vallet, D, Fernández, M., Castells, P.: *An Ontology-Based Information Retrieval Model*. Gómez-Pérez, A., Euzenat, J. (Eds.): Proceedings of ESWC 2005, LNCS 3532, Springer-Verlag. (2005) 455-470.
21. Nagypal, G.: *Improving Information Retrieval Effectiveness by Using Domain Knowledge Stored in Ontologies*. OTM Workshops 2005, LNCS 3762, Springer-Verlag, (2005) 780-789
22. Paralic, J., Kostial, I.: *Ontology-based Information Retrieval*. Information and Intelligent Systems, Croatia (2003) 23-28
23. Chenggang, W., Wenpin, J., Qijia, T. et al.: *An information retrieval server based on ontology and multiagent*. Journal of computer research & development 38(6) (2001) 641-647.
24. Ozcan, R., Aslangdogan, Y.A.: *Concept Based Information Access Using Ontologies and Latent Semantic Analysis*. Technical Report CSE-2004-8. University of Texas at Arlington (2004) 16
25. Baeza-Yates, R., Ribeiro-Neto, B.: *Modern information retrieval*. ACM Press, New York (1999)
26. Tomassen, S.L., Strasunskas, D.: *Query Terms Abstraction Layers*. Submitted to Web Semantics (SWWS'06) in conjunction with OnTheMove Federated Conferences (OTM'06), Montpellier, France (2006)

RDDS 2006 PC Co-chairs' Message

Middleware has become a popular technology for building distributed systems from tiny sensor networks to large-scale peer-to-peer (P2P) networks. Support such as asynchronous and multipoint communication is well suited for constructing reactive distributed computing applications over wired and wireless networks environments. While the middleware infrastructures exhibit attractive features from an application development perspective (e.g., portability, interoperability, adaptability), they are often lacking in robustness and reliability.

This workshop focuses on reliable decentralized distributed systems. While decentralized architectures are gaining popularity in most application domains, there is still some reluctance in deploying them in systems with high dependability requirements. Due to their increasing size and complexity, such systems compound many reliability problems that necessitate different strategies and solutions. This has led, over the past few years, to several academic and industrial research efforts aimed at correcting this deficiency. The aim of the RDDS Workshop is to bring researchers and practitioners together, to further our insights into reliable decentralized architectures and to investigate collectively the challenges that remain.

The program for RDDS 2006 consisted of 11 research papers of very high quality, covering diverse topics. In total, 33 papers were submitted, and each paper was reviewed by a least 3 reviewers.

We are very grateful to the members of the RDDS 2006 Technical Program Committee for helping us to assemble such an outstanding program. We would like to express our deep appreciation to the authors for submitting publications of such high quality, and for sharing the results of their research work with the rest of the community.

August 2006   Eiko Yoneki, University of Cambridge, UK
                                Pascal Felber, Universite de Neuchatel, Switzerland

R. Meersman, Z. Tari, P. Herrero et al. (Eds.): OTM Workshops 2006, LNCS 4278, p. 1469, 2006.
© Springer-Verlag Berlin Heidelberg 2006

Core Persistence in Peer-to-Peer Systems: Relating Size to Lifetime

Vincent Gramoli, Anne-Marie Kermarrec,
Achour Mostefaoui, Michel Raynal, and Bruno Sericola

IRISA (Université de Rennes 1 and INRIA)
Campus de Beaulieu, 35042 Rennes, France
{vgramoli, akermarr, achour, raynal, bsericol}@irisa.fr

Abstract. Distributed systems are now both very large and highly dynamic. Peer to peer overlay networks have been proved efficient to cope with this new deal that traditional approaches can no longer accommodate. While the challenge of organizing peers in an overlay network has generated a lot of interest leading to a large number of solutions, maintaining critical data in such a network remains an open issue. In this paper, we are interested in defining the portion of nodes and frequency one has to probe, given the churn observed in the system, in order to achieve a given probability of maintaining the persistence of some critical data. More specifically, we provide a clear result relating the size and the frequency of the probing set along with its proof as well as an analysis of the way of leveraging such an information in a large scale dynamic distributed system.

Keywords: Churn, Core, Dynamic system, Peer to peer system, Persistence, Probabilistic guarantee, Quality of service, Survivability.

1 Introduction

Context of the paper. Persistence of critical data in distributed applications is a crucial problem. Although static systems have experienced many solutions, mostly relying on defining the right degree of replication, this remains an open issue in the context of dynamic systems.

Recently, peer to peer (P2P) systems became popular as they have been proved efficient to cope with the scale shift observed in distributed systems. A P2P system is a dynamic system that allow peers (nodes) to join or leave the system. In the meantime, a natural tendency to trade strong deterministic guarantees for probabilistic ones aimed at coping with both scale and dynamism. Yet, quantifying bounds of guarantee that can be achieved probabilistically is very important for the deployment of applications.

More specifically, a typical issue is to ensure that despite dynamism some critical data is not lost. The set of nodes owning a copy of the critical data is called a *core* (distinct cores can possibly co-exist, each associated with a particular data).

Provided that core nodes remain long enough in the system, a "data/state transfer" protocol can transmit the critical data from nodes to nodes. This ensures that a new core of nodes in the system will keep track of the data. Hence, such protocols provide data persistence despite the uncertainty of the system state involved by the dynamic evolution of its members.

R. Meersman, Z. Tari, P. Herrero et al. (Eds.): OTM Workshops 2006, LNCS 4278, pp. 1470–1479, 2006.

There is however an inherent tradeoff in the use of such protocols. If the policy that is used is too conservative, the data transfer protocol might be executed too often, thereby consuming resources and increasing the whole system overhead. Conversely, if the protocol is executed too rarely, all nodes owning a copy of the data may leave (or crash) before a new protocol execution, and the data would be lost. This fundamental tradeoff is the main problem addressed in this paper.

Content of the paper. Considering the previous context, we are interested in providing some probabilistic guarantees of maintaining a *core* in the system. More precisely, given the churn observed in the system, we aim at maintaining the persistence of some critical data. To this end, we are interested in defining the portion of nodes that must be probed, as well as the frequency to which this probe must occur to achieve this result with a given probability. This boils down to relating the size and the frequency of the probing set according to a target probability of success and the churn observed in the system.

The investigation of the previous tradeoff relies on critical parameters. One of them is naturally the size of the core. Two other parameters are the percentage of nodes that enter/leave the system per time unit, and the duration during which we observe the system. We first assume that, per time unit, the number of entering nodes is the same as the number of leaving nodes. In other words, the number of nodes remains constant.

Let S be the system at some time τ. It is composed of n nodes including a subset of q nodes defining a core Q for a given critical data. Let S' be the system at time $\tau + \delta$. Because of the system evolution, some nodes owning a copy of the critical data at time τ might have left the system at time $\tau + \delta$ (those nodes are in S and not in S'). So, an important question is the following: "Given a set Q' of q' nodes of S', what is the probability that Q and Q' do intersect?" We derive an explicit expression of this probability as a function of the parameters characterizing the dynamic system. This allows us to compute some of them when other ones are fixed. This provides distributed applications with the opportunity to set a tradeoff between a probabilistic guarantee of achieving a core and the overhead involved computed either as the number of nodes probed or the frequency at which the probing set needs to be refreshed.

Related work. As mentioned above, P2P systems have received a great deal of attention both in academia and industry for the past five years. More specifically, a lot of approaches have been proposed to create whether they are structured, such as Chord [18], CAN [15] or Pastry [16], or unstructured [5,6,9]. Maintenance of such overlay networks in the presence of high churns has also been studied as one of the major goal of P2P overlay networks [10]. The parameters impacting on connectivity and routing capabilities in P2P overlay networks are now well understood.

In structured P2P networks, routing tables contain critical information and refreshment must occur with some frequency depending on the churn observed in the network [2] to achieve routing capabilities. For instance in Pastry, the size of the leaf set (set of nodes whose identities are numerically the closest to current node identity) and its maintenance protocol can be tuned to achieve the routing within reasonable delay stretch and low overhead. Finally, there has been approaches evaluating the number of locations to which a data has to be replicated in the system in order to be successfully searched by flooding-based or random walk-based algorithms [4]. These approaches do not consider specifically churn in their analysis. In this paper churn is a primary concern. The result of this work can be applied to any P2P network, regardless of its structure, in order to maintain critical data by refreshment at sufficiently many locations.

The use of a base core to extend protocols designed for static systems to dynamic systems has been investigated in [14]. Persistent cores share some features with quorums (i.e., mutually intersecting sets). Quorums originated a long time ago with majority voting systems [7,19] introduced to ensure data consistency. More recently, quorum reconfiguration [11,3] have been proposed to face system dynamism while guaranteeing atomic consistency: this application outlines the strength of such dynamic quorums. Quorum-based protocols for searching objects in P2P systems are proposed in [13]. Probabilistic quorum systems have been introduced in [12]. They use randomization to relax the strict intersection property to a probabilistic one. They have been extended to dynamic systems in [1].

Roadmap. The paper is organized as follows. Section 2 defines the system model. Section 3 describes our dynamic system analysis and our probabilistic results. Section 4 interprets the previous formulas and shows how to use them to control the uncertainty of the key parameters of P2P applications. Finally, Section 5 concludes the paper.

2   System Model

The system model, sketched in the introduction is simple. The system consists of n nodes. It is dynamic in the following sense. For the sake of simplicity, let n be the size of the system. Every time unit, cn nodes leave the system and cn nodes enter the system, where c is the percentage of nodes that enter/leave the system per time unit; this can be seen as new nodes "replacing" leaving nodes. Although monitoring the leave and join rates of a large-scale dynamic system remains an open issue, it is reasonable to assume join and leave are tightly correlated in P2P systems. A more realistic model would take in account variation of the system size depending for instance, on night-time and day-time as observed in [17].

A node leaves the system either voluntarily or because it crashes. A node that leaves the system does not enter it later. (Practically, this means that, to re-enter the system, a node that has left must be considered as a new node; all its previous knowledge of the system state is lost.) For instance, initially (at time τ), assume there are n nodes (identified from 1 to n; let us take $n = 5$ to simplify). Let $c = 0.2$, which means that, every time unit, $nc = 1$ node changes (a node disappears and a new node replaces it). That is, at time $\tau + 1$, one node leaves the system and another one joins. From now on, observe that next leaving nodes are either nodes that were initially in the system or nodes that joined after time τ.

3   Relating the Key Parameters of the Dynamic System

This section answers the question posed in the introduction, namely, given a set $Q(\tau)$ of nodes at time τ (the core), and a set $Q(\tau')$ of nodes at time $\tau' = \tau + \delta$, what is the probability of the event "$Q(\tau) \cap Q(\tau') \neq \emptyset$". In the remaining of this paper, we assume that both $Q(\tau)$ and $Q(\tau')$ contain q nodes, since an interesting goal is to minimize both the number of nodes where the data is replicated and the number of nodes one has to probe to find the data. Let an *initial* node be a node that belongs to the system at time τ. Moreover, without loss of generality, let $\tau = 0$ (hence, $\tau' = \delta$).

Lemma 1. *Let C be the ratio of initial nodes that are replaced after δ time units. We have $C = 1 - (1 - c)^\delta$.*

Proof. We claim that the number of initial nodes that are still in the system after δ time units is $n(1-c)^\delta$. The proof is by induction on the time instants. Let us remind that c is the percentage of nodes that are replaced in one time unit. For the Base case, at time 1, $n - nc = n(1 - c)$ nodes have not been replaced. For the induction case, let us assume that at time $\delta - 1$, the number of initial nodes that have not been replaced is $n(1-c)^{\delta-1}$. Let us consider the time instant δ. The number of initial nodes that are not replaced after δ time units is $n(1 - c)^{\delta-1} - n(1 - c)^{\delta-1}c$, i.e., $n(1 - c)^\delta$, which proves the claim. It follows from the previous claim that the number of initial nodes that are replaced during δ time units is $n - n(1 - c)^\delta$. Hence, $C = (n - n(1 - c)^\delta)/n = 1 - (1 - c)^\delta$.

$$\square_{Lemma\ 1}$$

Given a core of q nodes at time τ (each having a copy of the critical data), the following theorem gives the probability that, at time $\tau' = \tau + \delta$, an arbitrary node cannot obtain the data when it queries q nodes arbitrarily chosen.

For this purpose, using result of Lemma 1 we take the number of elements that have left the system during the period δ as $\alpha = \lceil Cn \rceil = \lceil (1 - (1 - c)^\delta)n \rceil$. This number allows us to evaluate the aforementioned probability.

Theorem 1. *Let $x_1, ..., x_q$ be any node in the system at time $\tau' = \tau + \delta$. The probability that none of these nodes belong to the initial core is*

$$\frac{\sum_{k=a}^{b} \left[\binom{n+k-q}{q} \binom{q}{k} \binom{n-q}{\alpha-k} \right]}{\binom{n}{q} \binom{n}{\alpha}},$$

where $\alpha = \lceil (1 - (1 - c)^\delta)n \rceil$, $a = \max(0, \alpha - n + q)$, and $b = \min(\alpha, q)$.

Proof. The problem we have to solve can be represented in the following way:

The system is an urn containing n balls (nodes), such that, initially, q balls are green (they represent the initial core $Q(\tau)$ and are represented by the set Q in Figure 1), while the $n - q$ remaining balls are black.

We randomly draw $\alpha = \lceil Cn \rceil$ balls from the urn (according to a uniform distribution), and paint them red. These α balls represent the initial nodes that are replaced by new nodes after δ units of time (each of these balls was initially green or black). After it has been colored red, each of these balls is put back in the urn (so, the urn contains again n balls).

We then obtain the system as described in the right part of Figure 1 (which represents the system state at time $\tau' = \tau + \delta$). The set $\mathcal{A}$ is the set of balls that have been painted red. $\mathcal{Q}'$ is the core set $\mathcal{Q}$ after some of its balls have been painted red (these balls represent the nodes of the core that have left the system). This means the set $\mathcal{Q}' \setminus \mathcal{A}$, that we denote by $\mathcal{E}$, contains all the green balls and only them.

We denote by β the number of balls in the set $\mathcal{Q}' \cap \mathcal{A}$. It is well-known that β has a hypergeometric distribution, i.e., for $a \leq k \leq b$ where $a = \max(0, \alpha - n + q)$ and $b = \min(\alpha, q)$, we have

$$\Pr[\beta = k] = \frac{\dbinom{q}{k}\dbinom{n-q}{\alpha-k}}{\dbinom{n}{\alpha}}. \tag{1}$$

We finally draw randomly and successively q balls $x_1, ..., x_q$ from the urn (system at time τ') without replacing them. The problem consists in computing the probability of the event {none of the selected balls $x_1, ..., x_q$ are green}, which can be written as $\Pr[x_1 \notin \mathcal{E}, ..., x_q \notin \mathcal{E}]$.

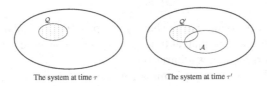

The system at time τ The system at time τ'

Fig. 1. The system at times τ and $\tau' = \tau + \delta$

As $\{x \in \mathcal{E}\} \Leftrightarrow \{x \in \mathcal{Q}'\} \cap \{x \notin \mathcal{Q}' \cap \mathcal{A}\}$, we have (taking the contrapositive) $\{x \notin \mathcal{E}\} \Leftrightarrow \{x \notin \mathcal{Q}'\} \cup \{x \in \mathcal{Q}' \cap \mathcal{A}\}$, from which we can conclude $\Pr[x \notin \mathcal{E}] = \Pr[\{x \notin \mathcal{Q}'\} \cup \{x \in \mathcal{Q}' \cap \mathcal{A}\}]$. As the events $\{x \notin \mathcal{Q}'\}$ and $\{x \in \mathcal{Q}' \cap \mathcal{A}\}$ are disjoints, we obtain $\Pr[x \notin \mathcal{E}] = \Pr[x \notin \mathcal{Q}'] + \Pr[x \in \mathcal{Q}' \cap \mathcal{A}]$. The system contains n balls. The number of balls in $\mathcal{Q}'$, $\mathcal{A}$ and $\mathcal{Q}' \cap \mathcal{A}$ is equal to q, α and β, respectively. Since there is no replacement, we get,

$$\Pr[x_1 \notin \mathcal{E}, ..., x_q \notin \mathcal{E} \mathbin{/} \beta = k] = \sum_{k=a}^{b} \prod_{i=1}^{q}\left(1 - \frac{q-k}{n-i+1}\right) = \sum_{k=a}^{b}\frac{\dbinom{n-q+k}{q}}{\dbinom{n}{q}}. \tag{2}$$

To uncondition the aforementioned result (2), we simply multiply it by (1), leading to

$$\Pr[x_1 \notin \mathcal{E}, ..., x_q \notin \mathcal{E}] = \frac{\sum_{k=a}^{b}\left[\dbinom{n+k-q}{q}\dbinom{q}{k}\dbinom{n-q}{\alpha-k}\right]}{\dbinom{n}{q}\dbinom{n}{\alpha}}.$$

$\square_{Theorem\ 1}$

4   From Formulas to Parameter Tuning

In the previous section, we have provided a set of formulas that can be leveraged and exploited by distributed applications in many ways. Typically, in a P2P system, the churn rate is not negotiated but observed[1]. Nevertheless, applications deployed on P2P overlays may need to choose the probabilistic guarantees that a node of the initial core is probed. Given such a probability, the application may fix either the size of the probing set of nodes or the frequency at which the core needs to be re-established from the current set of nodes (with the help of an appropriate data transfer protocol).

This section exploits the previous formula to relate these various elements. More precisely, we provide the various relations existing between the three factors that can be tuned by an application designer: the size of the probing set q, the frequency of the probing δ, and the probability of achieving a core characterized by $p = 1 - \epsilon$. (For the sake of clarity all along this section, a ratio C, or c, is sometimes expressed as a percentage. Floating point numbers on the y-axis are represented in their mantissa and exponent numbers.)

Relation linking c and δ.   The first parameter that we formalized is C, that can be interpreted as the rate of dynamism in the system. C depends both on the churn rate (c) observed in the system and the probing frequency ($1/\delta$). More specifically, we foresee here a scenario in which an application designer would consider tolerating a churn C in order to define the size of a core and thus ensure the persistence of some critical data. For example, an application may need to tolerate a churn rate of 10% in the system, meaning that the persistence of some critical data should be ensured as long as up to 10% of the nodes in the system change over time. Therefore, depending on the churn observed and monitored in the system, we are able to define the longest period δ before which the core should be re-instantiated on a set of the current nodes. One of the main interest of linking c and δ is that if c varies over time, δ can be adapted accordingly without compromising the initial requirements of the application.

More formally, Lemma 1 provides an explicit value of C (the ratio of initial nodes that are replaced) as a function of c (the replacement ratio per time unit) and δ (the number of time units). Figure 2 represents this function for several values of C. More explicitly, it depicts on a logarithmic scale the curve $c = 1 - \sqrt[\delta]{1 - C}$ (or equivalently, the curve $\delta = \frac{\log(1-C)}{\log(1-c)}$). As an example, the curve associated with $C = 10\%$ indicates that 10% of the initial nodes have been replaced after $\delta = 105$ time units (point A, Figure 2), when the replacement ratio is $c = 10^{-3}$ per time unit. Similarly, the same replacement ratio per time unit entails the replacement of 30% of the initial nodes when the duration we consider is $\delta = 356$ time units (point B, Figure 2). The system designer can benefit from these values to better appreciate the way the system evolves according to the assumed replacement ratio per time unit. To summarize, this result can be used as follows. In a system, aiming at tolerating a churn of $X\%$ of the nodes, our goal is to provide an application with the corresponding value of δ, knowing the churn c observed in the system. This gives the opportunity to adjust δ if c changes over time.

---

[1] Monitoring the churn rate of a system, although very interesting, is out of the scope of this paper.

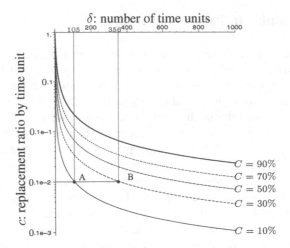

Fig. 2. Evolution of the pair (c, δ) for given values of C

Relation linking the core size q and ϵ. Now, given a value C set by an application developer, there are still two parameters that may influence either the overhead of maintaining a core in the system, or the probabilistic guarantee of having such a core. The overhead may be measured in a straightforward manner in this context as the number of nodes that need to be probed, namely q. Intuitively, for a given C, as q increases, the probability of probing a node of the initial core increases. In this section, we define how much these parameters are related.

Let us consider the value ϵ determined by Theorem 1. That value can be interpreted the following way: $p = 1 - \epsilon$ is the probability that, at time $\tau' = \tau + \delta$, one of the q queries issued (randomly) by a node hits a node of the core. An important question is then the following: How are ϵ and q related? Or equivalently, how increasing the size of q enable to decrease ϵ? This relation is depicted in Figure 3(a) where several curves are represented for $n = 10,000$ nodes.

Each curve corresponds to a percentage of the initial nodes that have been replaced. (As an example, the curve 30% corresponds to the case where $C = 30\%$ of the initial nodes have left the system; the way C, δ and c are related has been seen previously.) Let us consider $\epsilon = 10^{-3}$. The curves show that $q = 274$ is a sufficient core size for not bypassing that value of ϵ when up to 10% of the nodes are replaced (point A, Figure 3(a)). Differently, $q = 274$ is not sufficient when up to 50% of the nodes are replaced; in that case, the size $q = 369$ is required (point B, Figure 3(a)).

The curves of both Figure 2 and Figure 3(a) provide the system designer with realistic hints to set the value of δ (deadline before which a data transfer protocol establishing a new core has to be executed). Figure 3(b) is a zoom of Figure 3(a) focusing on the small values of ϵ. It shows that, when $10^{-3} \le \epsilon \le 10^{-2}$, the probability $p = 1 - \epsilon$ increases very rapidly towards 1, though the size of the core increases only very slightly. As an example, let us consider the curve associated with $C = 10\%$ in Figure 3(b). It shows that a core of $q = 224$ nodes ensures an intersection probability $= 1 - \epsilon = 0.99$, and a core of $q = 274$ nodes ensures an intersection probability $= 1 - \epsilon = 0.999$.

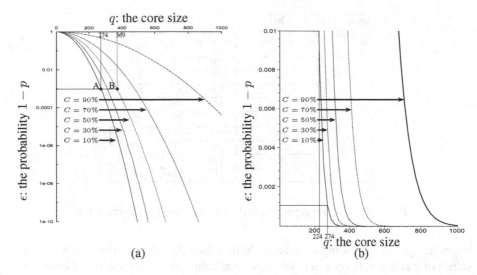

Fig. 3. Non-intersection probability over the core size

Interestingly, this phenomenon is similar to the *birthday paradox*[2] [8] that can be roughly summarized as follows. How many persons must be present in a room for two of them to have the same birthday with probability $p = 1 - \epsilon$? Actually, for that probability to be greater than $1/2$, it is sufficient that the number of persons in the room be equal (only) to 23! When, there are 50 persons in the room, the probability becomes 97%, and increases to 99.9996% for 100 persons. In our case, we observe a similar phenomenon: the probability $p = 1 - \epsilon$ increases very rapidly despite the fact that the frequency of the core size q increases slightly.

In our case, this means that the system designer can choose to slightly increase the size of the probing set q (and therefore only slightly increase the associated overhead) while significantly increasing the probability to access a node of the core.

Relation linking q and δ. So far, we have considered that an application may need to fix C and then define the size of the probing set to achieve a given probability p of success. There is another remaining trade-off that an application designer might want to decide upon: trading the size of the probing set with the probing frequency while fixing the probability $p = 1 - \epsilon$ of intersecting the initial core. This is precisely defined by relating q to $δ$ for a fixed ϵ.

In the following we investigate the way the size and lifetime of the core are related when the required intersection probability is 99% or 99.9%. We chose these values to better illustrate our purpose, as we believe they reflect what could be expected by an application designer. For both probabilities we present two different figures summarizing the required values of q.

Figure 4 focuses on the core size that is required in a static system and in a dynamic system (according to various values of the ratio C). The static system implies that no nodes leave or join the system while the dynamic system contains nodes that join and

---

[2] The paradox is with respect to intuition, not with respect to logics.

Intersection probability	Churn $C = 1 - (1-c)^\delta$	Core size $n = 10^3$	$n = 10^4$	$n = 10^5$
99%	static	66	213	677 *
	10%	70	224	714
	30%	79	255	809
	60%	105	337	1071
	80%	143	478	1516
99.9%	static	80 *	260	828 *
	10%	85	274	873 *
	30%	96	311	990 *
	60%	128	413 *	1311
	80%	182	584	1855

Fig. 4. The core size depending on the system sizes and the churn rate

leave the system depending on several churn values. For the sake of clarity we omit values of δ and simply present C taking several values from 10% to 80%. The analysis of the results depicted in the figure leads to two interesting observations.

First, when δ is big enough for 10% of the system nodes to be replaced, then the core size required is amazingly close to the static case (873 versus 828 when $n = 10^5$ and the probability is 0.999). Moreover, q has to be equal to 990 only when C increases up to 30%. Second, even when δ is sufficiently large to let 80% of the system nodes be replaced, the minimal number of nodes to probe remains low with respect to the system size. For instance, if δ is sufficiently large to let 6,000 nodes be replaced in a system with 10,000 nodes, then only 413 nodes must be randomly probed to obtain an intersection with probability $p = 0.999$.

To conclude, these results clearly show that a critical data in a highly dynamic system can persist in a scalable way: even though the delay between core re-establishments is reasonably large while the size of the core remains relatively low.

5   Conclusion

Maintenance of critical data in large-scale dynamic systems where nodes may join and leave dynamically is a critical issue. In this paper, we define the notion of persistent core of nodes that can maintain such critical data with a high probability regardless of the structure of the underlying P2P network. More specifically, we relate the parameters that can be tuned to achieve a high probability of defining a core, namely the size of the core, the frequency at which it has to be re-established, and the churn rate of the system.

Our results provide application designers with a set of guidelines to tune the system parameters depending on the expected guarantees and the churn rate variation. An interesting outcome of this paper is to show that slightly increasing the size of the core result in a significant probability increase of the guarantee.

This work opens up a number of very interesting research directions. An interesting question is related to the design and evaluation of efficient probing protocols, defining such a core in the system applicable to a large spectrum of peer to peer overlay networks. Monitoring the system in order to estimate the churn rate is another interesting issue.

References

1. I. Abraham and D. Malkhi. Probabilistic quorum for dynamic systems. *Distributed Computing*, 18(2):113–124, 2005.
2. M. Castro, M. Costa, and A. Rowstron. Performance and dependability of structured peer-to-peer overlays. In *Proc. Int'l IEEE Conference on Dependable Systems and Networks (DSN)*, pages 9–18, Florence (Italy), 2004.
3. G. Chockler, S. Gilbert, V. Gramoli, P. M. Musial, and A. A. Shvartsman. Reconfigurable distributed storage for dynamic networks. In *Proceedings of 9th International Conference on Principles of Distributed Systems (OPODIS)*, Dec. 2005.
4. E. Cohen and S. Shenker. Replication strategies in unstructured peer-to-peer networks. In *Proc. of ACM SIGCOMM*, pages 177–190. ACM Press, 2002.
5. P. T. Eugster, R. Guerraoui, S. B. Handurukande, A.-M. Kermarrec, and P. Kouznetsov. Lightweight probabilistic broadcast. *ACM Trans. on Comp. Systems*, 21(4):341–374, 2003.
6. A. J. Ganesh, A.-M. Kermarrec, and L. Massoulié. Peer-to-peer membership management for gossip-based protocols. *IEEE Trans. on Computers*, 52(2):139–149, February 2003.
7. D. K. Gifford. Weighted voting for replicated data. In *Proc. 7th Int'l ACM Symposium on Operating Systems Principles (SOSP)*, pages 150–162. ACM Press, 1979.
8. R. Isaac. *The pleasure of probabilities*. Springer Verlag, Reading in Mathematics, 1995.
9. M. Jelasity, R. Guerraoui, A.-M. Kermarrec, and M. van Steen. The peer sampling service: Experimental evaluation of unstructured gossip-based implementations. In H.-A. Jacobsen, editor, *Middleware 2004*, volume 3231 of *LNCS*, pages 79–98. Springer-Verlag, 2004.
10. D. Liben-Nowell, H. Balakrishnan, and D. Karger. Analysis of the evolution of peer-to-peer systems. In *Proceedings of the twenty-first annual symposium on Principles of distributed computing (PODC)*, pages 233–242, New York, NY, USA, 2002. ACM Press.
11. N. Lynch and A. Shvartsman. RAMBO: A reconfigurable atomic memory service for dynamic networks. In *Proc. of 16th International Symposium on Distributed Computing*, pages 173–190, 2002.
12. D. Malkhi, M. Reiter, A. Wool, and R. Wright. Probabilistic quorum systems. *Information and Computation*, 170(2):184–206, 2001.
13. K. Miura, T. Tagawa, and H. Kakugawa. A quorum-based protocol for searching objects in peer-to-peer networks. *IEEE Trans. on Parallel and Distributed Systems*, 17(1):25–37, January 2006.
14. A. Mostefaoui, M. Raynal, C. Travers, S. Peterson, A. E. Abbadi, and D. Agrawal. From static distributed systems to dynamic systems. In *Proc. 24th IEEE Symposium on Reliable Distributed Systems (SRDS)*, pages 109–119, 2005.
15. S. Ratnasamy, P. Francis, M. Handley, R. Karp, and S. Schenker. A scalable content-addressable network. In *Proc. of ACM SIGCOMM*, pages 161–172, San Diego, CA, 2001. ACM Press.
16. A. Rowstron and P. Druschel. Pastry: Scalable, distributed object location and routing for large-scale peer-to-peer systems. In R. Guerraoui, editor, *Middleware 2001*, volume 2218 of *LNCS*, pages 329–350. Springer-Verlag, 2001.
17. S. Saroiu, P. Gummadi, and S. Gribble. A measurement study of peer-to-peer file sharing systems. In *In Proceedings of Multimedia Computing and Networking*, 2002.
18. I. Stoica, R. Morris, D. Karger, M. F. Kaashoek, and H. Balakrishnan. Chord: A scalable peer-to-peer lookup service for internet applications. In *Proc. of ACM SIGCOMM*, pages 149–160, San Diego (CA), 2001. ACM Press.
19. R. H. Thomas. A majority consensus approach to concurrency control for multiple copy databases. *ACM Trans. on Database Systems*, 4(2):180–209, 1979.

Implementing Chord for HP2P Network*

Yang Cao, Zhenhua Duan, Jian-Jun Qi, Zhuo Peng, and Ertao Lv

Institute of Computing Theory and Technology,
School of Computer Science and Technology,
Xidian University, Xi'an, 710071, P.R. China
{zhhduan, etlv}@mail.xidian.edu.cn

Abstract. We propose a two-layer hybrid P2P network (HP2P), in which the upper layer is structured Chord network, and the lower layer is unstructured flooding network. HP2P benefits from the advantages of both structured and unstructured networks and significantly improves the performance such as stability, scalability and lookup latency of the network. In this paper, the Chord overlay algorithm is formalized. The data structure, node joining, node leaving, routing table stabilizing and lookup services are introduced in detail. Further the caching mechanism is employed to accelerate lookup services. In particular, the analysis shows that the stability of Chord overlay in HP2P network has been enhanced indeed.

1   Introduction

Along with the technical development of peer-to-peer (P2P), the distributed applications built on it have been used in file-sharing, instant message, distributed collaboration and other fields. P2P networks are favored for their adaptation, self-organization and decentralized control. It can be classified as either unstructured or structured.

Distributed Hash Table (DHT), which is the foundation of structured P2P network, is now an active research area. Several important proposals have been recently implemented for DHT protocol, including Chord [1], CAN [2], Pastry [3] and Tapestry [4]. Through DHT protocol the resources can be assigned and located with less peer hops and routing table entries. For example, Chord requires $O(\log N)$ peer hops and $O(\log N)$ routing table entries when there are N peers in the overlay [1].

The DHT can adapt the dynamic state to join or leave, and have the advantages of faster lookup, self-organization, load-balance and scalability. However, the applications based on DHT are not popular since DHT maintenance mechanism is complicated and the network churn caused by the frequent joining or leaving of peers can enormously increase DHT maintenance costs.

In contrast, the unstructured P2P using flooding [5] method is extremely stabile when peers joining and leaving the network. However, the current searching

---

* Supported by the NSFC Grant No. 60373103 and 60443010, and the SRFDP Grant 20030701015.

R. Meersman, Z. Tari, P. Herrero et al. (Eds.): OTM Workshops 2006, LNCS 4278, pp. 1480–1489, 2006.

mechanisms are unscalable and inefficient because flooding generates heavy loads on the network participants. To lookup a key, the query will be sent to all of peers over the whole network. This is a waste of bandwidths and may cause broadcasting storm.

Chord is a one-dimension and flat circular DHT network. In [6], we analyzes the above advantages and disadvantages of unstructured and structured P2P networks, and proposes a two-layer hybrid P2P system (HP2P) to improve the P2P network stability and underlying network proximity. The upper layer of HP2P system is a Chord overlay while the lower layer is a cluster overlay which is an unstructured flooding P2P network. HP2P establishes the Chord network with clusters instead of peers, where the cluster network is organized with peers of underlying network proximity. The information of the Chord overlay and the cluster overlay is maintained by supernodes which are the nodes with more power in terms of connectivity, bandwidth, processing, and non-NATed accessibility. Each cluster has an ID as the label of the Chord overlay node.

In this paper, we focus on the implementation of the Chord overlay in HP2P. The Chord overlay algorithm is formalized. The data structure, node joining, node leaving, routing table stabilizing and lookup services are introduced in detail. Further, the caching mechanism is employed to accelerate lookup services. To put the idea into practice, we have recently developed an file-sharing system based on HP2P in $C^\#$. All of relative protocols, algorithms, data structures etc. have been implemented. A friendly graphic user interface has also been developed. The analysis and the practice show that performance such as stability, scalability and lookup latency of the network has significantly been improved.

The paper is organized as follows. In the following section, HP2P framework is briefly described. The Chord overlay in HP2P network is discussed in Section 3. The analysis of performance of Chord overlay in HP2P network is given in Section 4. Finally, conclusion is drawn in Section 5.

2   HP2P Framework

In this section, the design of HP2P framework overlays is briefly described. In HP2P system, peers are organized by means of close underlying physical network. For convenience, some notations are given as follows:

Metadata: Recording the information of resources; they are identified by a hashed key ID.

CL: the cluster; it is the lower overlay network.

ODN: An ordinary node; the peer in cluster has only ordinary capability to lookup and publish resources.

SN: A supernode; the peer with more power in cluster, maintains the Chord overlay and cluster overlay routing information, and builds communication between clusters.

VN: A virtual node is actually a cluster. However, in Chord layer, the cluster appears as the virtual node.

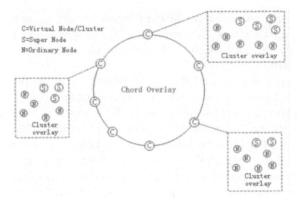

Fig. 1. The Two-layer Hybrid P2P Framework

The HP2P framework is shown in Figure 1. As you can see, the structure of the network is based on two overlays. The cluster overlay, which is an unstructured flooding P2P network, is organized by peers (ODNs and SNs) of underlying physical network proximity. Each cluster has a unique cluster ID (see naming system in Section 3.2(1)) and the ID key will not change any more once the cluster is established. On the Chord overlay, the Chord node is a VN, and its ID is VN ID (cluster ID). Further, the metadata are distributed stored on ODNs.

The size of a cluster denoted by M is predefined. When a peer is joining a cluster, the cluster's SN first checks that the number of online peers equals or is less than M. If it equals M then the cluster is full, otherwise the cluster is not full and peer can join the cluster. When a peer is joining a full cluster, the cluster checks that it has been split or not. If not it will cause the abruption of the cluster and the peer joins in a new cluster, otherwise the peer will join in the cluster that has already been split from the original cluster. The parameter M is determined by the capability of the cluster SNs in applications.

An SN is elected from ODNs, and is estimated as follows:

– Is under NAT/firewall or not (key one)
– Online time
– Bandwidth
– Speed of CPU
– The size of memory
– The number of TCP Connection supported

In these conditions the first is the most important one and a peer cannot be SN if it is under NAT/firewall. One can set weights to the other conditions and score ODNs. Then the CL elects ODNs with high score to be an SN.

The responsibilities of an SN are: (1) managing the cluster overlay; (2) managing the Chord overlay; (3) establishing relations between clusters; (4) affording the lookup services between peers and clusters.

Generally speaking, once a cluster is established, it will be stable in a long period, so the Chord overlay routing information will be not influenced by the frequent joining or leaving of peers and it will only impact several neighborhood peers in the same CL. Therefore the stability of whole network is enhanced. Further, with the using of "power" SNs, the peers with high bandwidth are effectively utilized.

3   Chord Overlay in HP2P

3.1   Original Chord Structure

Chord [1] maps a one dimensional hash space onto the unit circle. Its protocol supports just one operation: given a key, it maps the key onto a node. Depending on the application using Chord, that node might be responsible for storing a value associated with the key. In Chord, the key is the name of resource and the value is IP address where the resource is stored. Thus by lookup the (key, value) pair, a node can easily know where the resource required is located.

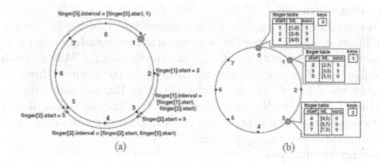

Fig. 2. Original Chord Structure

Figure 2[1] shows the Chord architecture. Messages are forwarded only in the clockwise direction in the circular ID space. The node is called the keys successor, whose identifier most closely follows the key. When a lookup message begins, the node checks its finger list and selects a node closest to the key. In an N-node Chord, each node maintains routing information for only about $O(\log N)$ other nodes. Routing efficiency depends on the finger list of $O(\log N)$ nodes spaced exponentially around the key space. The key lookup only need $O(\log N)$ hops. When a node joins or leaves, the routing information updating require $O(\log^2 N)$ messages [1].

In a Chord network with enormous nodes, the system will update routing information frequently according to the joining or leaving of nodes. This will reduce the system stability and the performance of lookup is also impacted because Chord does not consider underlying network proximity.

We use clusters instead of nodes on Chord overlay in HP2P system, and a cluster is actually a virtual node on this overlay. The cluster can exist for a long period, and it will not join or leave the Chord overlay frequently. Then the network stability can be enhanced.

3.2 Data Structure

In this section, we present data structure of the Chord overlay in HP2P network. First the naming system and metadata storage are described. Then the routing tables used in the lookup service are shown. At last, we present key and routing cache table list.

(1) Naming System

We identify cluster by consistent hash function [13]. When a cluster is established, it hashes the supernodes' IP address to be an m-bit identifier using hash function such as SHA-1 [14]. In a cluster, each peer holds several neighboring peers address information. The identifier of a peer is IP address. The main difference between HP2P Chord overlay and the original Chord is that the former identifies clusters rather than peers. The peer is only identified on the cluster overlay.

The resource key is hashed to be m-bit ID by the same hash function as cluster hashing. Then the relation between resource and cluster can be established.

(2) Metadata Storage

The resource information, including resource key, hashing ID, owner IP address and port at least, is recorded as metadata. The metadata are not stored on the Chord overlay, but in the peers on the cluster overlay. When resources are published by a peer, the metadata are made from the resource first. Then the peer lookup the "closest" cluster to the metadata ID, and sends the metadata to the cluster. Once an SN in the cluster receives the metadata, it distributes metadata copies to several peers in the cluster. Then the peers can maintain the metadata and offer the lookup service.

(3) Routing Mechanism

Each SN needs some routing information to maintain the HP2P network on the Chord overlay. It establishes an $O(\log N)$ space finger table to record cluster ID, and every item in finger table links to a supernode table to keep the cluster's SNs address information (see Figure 3(a)). If an SN is changed, the cluster's supernode table will be updated. In a supernode table, it must be assured that no less than one SN item is valid, then the cluster can be valid. Therefore the existence of several SNs in the supernode table enhances the stability of the routing table.

(4) Cache Table

To improve the speed of lookup, a key cache table is used to store the metadata ID and its maintainer IP address (see Figure 3(b)). The metadata are selected by the query times, and the cache table is stored in SNs.

Figure 3(c) shows the routing cache table. The routing cache table is used to store the clusters which are close to the current cluster in the underlying network.

3.3 Node Joining

There are two types of nodes: ODNs and VNs. ODNs join in the cluster, and VNs join in the Chord overlay network. If an ODN p wants to join in HP2P network, the steps of the joining are as follows:

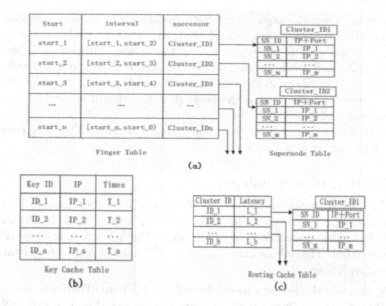

Fig. 3. Data structure: (a) Routing Table (Finger Table and Supernode Table), (b) Key Cache Table, (c) Routing Cache Table

1. p locates the "closest" cluster CL_i through a pre-known SN and gets the list of CL_i's SNs. Then p applies for joining the cluster.
2. SN_j is assigned to manage p and gives several ODNs information to p as its neighborhood peers.
3. p informs the neighborhood peers of its joining. Then p records its resources information to metadata and publishes them to network through SN_j.

When a new cluster is formed, it will join Chord overlay network as a VN. The cluster CL_j joining steps are as follows:

1. CL_j locates its position on the Chord overlay by its ID and gets the successor cluster information.
2. The finger table is first initialized (just like Chord [1]). Then each finger item's successor cluster is located and links to a supernode table which records the cluster's SNs information.
3. CL_j informs some existing CLs to update its finger table and the linked supernode table.
4. The metadata whose ID key is less than CL_j first item's successor cluster ID in this cluster are transferred to CL_j.

3.4 Node Leaving

The types of node leaving are different from node joining. Beside ODNs and VNs, the case of SN leaving will be considered. The operations of the different nodes leaving can be summarized as follows: First, the node informs the other nodes of its leaving. Then the node transfers the metadata to its neighborhood nodes (ODNS and SNs) or successor nodes (VNs). At last the node leaves the network. Note that when an ODN leaves, those of the nodes informed by it should be its cluster SNs and neighborhood ODNs. When an SN is leaving, it will inform other SNs to elect SN from the candidate SNs and get new candidate SN from ODNs. When the left SN joins the network again, it will be an ODN and wait for the election of candidate SNs.

The ODNs leaving will be the main form of leaving. This will reduce the influence to the whole network.

3.5   Routing Table Stabilizing

Every VN should check up the validity of other VNs in its routing table periodically to stabilize the routing table. If the VN in routing table is invalid (all of the SNs in linked supernode table are invalid), the VN information of this item will be updated. The VN_i is checking up its kth item (VN_k) in finger table, the process is as follows:

1. VN_i accesses the linked supernode table of kth item. Then VN_i connects all of the SNs in supernode table. If there are not less than two valid SNs, VN_i will check up the $(k+1)^{th}$ item and the process ends. Otherwise the process turns to the next step.
2. If all of SNs are invalid, the VN_k must be invalid. Otherwise the process turns to the next step. If VN_k is invalid, it will look up the correct successor VN and update the kth item and the process ends.
3. There is less than two valid SNs in supernode table but VN_k is valid. VN_i only needs to connect one of the valid SNs and asks for the other valid SNs in VN_k, then updates the supernode table.

3.6   Lookup Service

The lookup service is provided by the two overlays collaborations. Given a metadata key k, a peer p wants to determine the peer which is maintaining the metadata. The detailed operations are as follows:

1. p sends the lookup query message to one of its cluster's supernodes SN_i.
2. SN_i looks for its routing table. By the Chord lookup service, SN_i locates the "closest" cluster CL_j to k among all the clusters (it is ensured that SN_i can locate the "closest" cluster unless the network failure). Then the query message is sent to SN_j in CL_j.
3. SN_j sends query message to the peers in CL_j by flooding algorithm. If there are peers which hold the metadata, the peers return the metadata to p. Otherwise, SN_j returns the "no metadata" message to p.

As a file-sharing application example. Peer p wants to download a music named "canon.mp3" from our network. p first hashes the mp3 name into a key ID. If p can get the file's metadata through the above lookup process, it connects the peers by IP address recorded in metadata, and requests the mp3 resource. Then p can download the mp3 file from multi-peers.

3.7   Key Caching and Routing Caching

The key cache table is used to record the latest and the most query times of messages (see Section 3.2(4)). When a query message is sent to the cluster SN and looks for the metadata in the cluster, it can first lookup the cache table to check if the table has the metadata key ID or not. If the table keeps the information, the SN can get the metadata from the owner ODN directly instead of flooding the query message. After the query operation, SN will record the query results to the cache table by query's appearing times. The lookup latency between SNs and ODNs in the cluster can be reduced through the key cache table.

The routing cache table is used to record the nearest clusters with the lowest latency between SNs. Once a lookup prepared, the cluster gets the nearest clusters from the cache table and sends the query message to the cluster which is "closest" to the message key. Then this cluster gets the "closest" cluster from its cache table, and the operations will not stop until the destination cluster is located. The lookup latency and number of hops between clusters can be reduced through the routing cache table.

4   Performance Analysis

In this section, the analysis of the performance of the HP2P network will be given. In an N-cluster Chord overlay and M-peer cluster overlay, the capacity of peers in the HP2P network is $N \times M$. On the Chord overlay, the cluster is located with $O(\log N)$ hops the same as the Chord protocol. On the cluster overlay, the lookup needs $O(M)$ hops by the flooding method. As a result, the resource can be located with $O(\log N + M)$ hops in the whole system. Of course, the lookup hops can be reduced by caching mechanism above. When there are $N \times M$ peers on the Chord network, the lookup costs is $O(\log N + \log M)$. In contrast, the lookup latency in HP2P is longer than the Chord network. Eq.(1) shows that in the flooding network the lookup hops have the relationship with the degree of connectivity and the number of peers.

$$n_{hosts} \approx \sum_{i=1}^{n_{hops}} (d - 1)^i \tag{1}$$

Here n_{hosts} is the number of peers, n_{hops} is the number of hops and d is the average number of hosts reachable from each host (degree of connectivity). It can be calculated from the equation that a message can spread to all of peers in the cluster network within four hops in applications if the degree of connectivity is greater than four and M is not greater than one thousand. With this condition, the lookup costs of the HP2P network are almost as same as the original Chord.

An SN maintains two routing tables to provide the lookup services. We presume the size of supernode table is m. On Chord the space complexity of SN is $O(m) + O(\log N)$, and is the m times of the Chord routing table. An ODN is appeared on the cluster overlay and the degree of connectivity is denoted by d, its routing table only records the neighborhood ODNs. Therefore the space complexity is $O(d)$. It can be concluded that the routing table entries on the Chord overlay are bigger than the original Chord but in cluster the entries are much smaller.

The purpose of HP2P framework is mainly to improve the stability of the Chord network. We bartered little lookup latency and space complexity for stability in the framework.

5   Conclusion

In this paper, a two-layer hybrid P2P (HP2P) network framework which combines the advantages of structured Chord network and unstructured flooding network is briefly discussed. The Chord overlay in the HP2P network is mainly studied. In HP2P, the stability has been significantly improved, and the peers with high bandwidth can be utilized effectively. The lookup latency is longer than the Chord network but less than the flooding network. By the use of the cache mechanism, the lookup latency can be reduced effectively. The main benefits we can obtain is its stability. We can conclude that the HP2P network adds complexity to an implementation but offers significant benefits in real-world applications. However, in the paper, we have not exploited the algorithms and data structures regarding clusters in details. It will be investigated in the future. In addition, although a prototype of HP2P has been implemented, however, as an applicable system, there still is hard work to do. We are motivated to develop a robust real system which can be deployed on the Internet in the near future.

References

1. I. Stoica, R. Morris, D. Karger, M. Kaashoek, and H. Balakrishnan, Chord:A scalable peerto- peer lookup service for internet applications, In Proceedings of the 2001 ACM SIGCOMM Conference, 2001.
2. S. Ratnasamy, M. Handley, R. Karp, and S. Shenker, A scalable content-addressable network, in Proceedings of SIGCOMM 2001, Aug. 2001.
3. A. Rowstron and P. Druschel, Pastry: Scalable, distributed object location and routing for large-scale peer-to-peer systems, in IFIP/ACM International Conference on Distributed Systems Platforms (Middleware), (Heidelberg, Germany), pp. 329C350, November 2001.
4. B.Y. Zhao, J. Kubiatowicz, and A. D. Joseph, Tapestry: An infrastructure for fault-tolerant wide-area location and routing, Tech. Rep. UCB/CSD-01-1141, Computer Science Division, University of California, Berkeley, Apr 2001.
5. Q. Lv, P. Cao, E. Cohen, K. Li, and S. Shenker: Search and Replication in Unstructured Peer-to-Peer Networks, in Proc. Of the ACM ICS, 2002.
6. Z.Peng, Z.Duan, J. Qi, Y. Cao and E. Lv, HP2P: A Two-Layer Hybrid P2P Network. TR, No 2 Institute of Computing Theory and Technology, Xidian University, May, 2006 http://ictt.xidian.edu.cn.
7. J. Considine, Cluster-based Optimizations for Distributed Hash Tables, Tech. rep., Computer Science Department, Boston University, November 1, 2002.
8. P. Ganesan, K. Gummadi, H. Garcia-Molina, Canon in G Major: Designing DHTs with Hierarchical Structure, Proceedings of the 24th International Conference on Distributed Computing Systems (ICDCS04) 1063-6927/04 2004 IEEE

9. KaZaA. http://www.kazaa.com.
10. The KaZaA Overlay: A Measurement Study, http://cis.poly.edu/~ross/papers/KazaaOverlay.pdf.
11. B. Yang and H. Garcia-Molina. Designing a super-peer network[A]. 19th International Conference on Data Engineering, IEEE computer society[C]. March 5 CMarch 8, 2003 Bangalore, India. 3-6.
12. G. Doyen, E. Nataf, and O. Festor. A Hierarchical Architecture for a Distributed Management of P2P Networks and Services, IFIP International Federation for Information Processing 2005.
13. D. Karger, E. Lehman, T. Leighton, M. Levine, D. Lewin, R. Panigrahy. Consistent Hashing and Random Trees: Distributed Caching Protocols for Relieving Hot Spots on the World Wide Web, In Proceedings of the 29th Annual ACM Symposium on Theory of Computing, pp.654-663.
14. FIPS 180-1. Secure Hash Standard, U.S. Department of Commerce/NIST, National Technical Information Service, Springfield, VA, Apr. 1995.
15. S. Ratnasamy, S. Shenker, I. Stoica. Routing algorithms for DHTs: Some open questions. In: Druschel P, Kaashoek M, Rowstron A, eds. Proc. of the 1st Int'l Workshop on Peer-to-Peer Systems (IPTPS 2002). Berlin: Springer-Verlag, 2002. 174-179.

A Generic Self-repair Approach for Overlays

Barry Porter, Geoff Coulson, and François Taïani

Computing Department, Lancaster University, Lancaster, UK
{barry.porter, geoff, francois.taiani}@comp.lancs.ac.uk

Abstract. Self-repair is a key area of functionality in overlay networks, especially as overlays become increasingly widely deployed and relied upon. Today's common practice is for each overlay to implement its own self-repair mechanism. However, apart from leading to duplication of effort, this practice inhibits choice and flexibility in selecting from among multiple self-repair mechanisms that make different deployment-specific trade-offs between dependability and overhead. In this paper, we present an approach in which overlay networks provide functional behaviour only, and rely for their self-repair on a *generic self-repair service*. In our previously-published work in this area, we have focused on the distributed algorithms encapsulated within our self-repair service. In this paper we focus instead on API and integration issues. In particular, we show how overlay implementations can interact with our generic self-repair service using a small and simple API. We concretise the discussion by illustrating the use of this API from within an implementation of the popular Chord overlay. This involves minimal changes to the implementation while considerably increasing its available range of self-repair strategies.

1 Introduction

Overlay networks are quintessential examples of decentralized distributed systems. They consist of collections of software nodes, usually one per physical host, which form a logical topology and provide a mutually desired service. Many overlays require no managed infrastructure, and are therefore suitable to be deployed dynamically and on-demand in any physical network.

Self-repair is a key area of functionality in overlay networks, especially as overlays become increasingly widely deployed and relied upon. Today's common practice is for each overlay to implement its own self-repair mechanism. For example, Chord [1] is a popular distributed hash table (DHT) overlay that employs a self-repair mechanism in which each node maintains a list of the next M nodes following it in a ring structure, and this list is continuously refreshed so that if a node's immediate clockwise neighbour fails, the node becomes linked to the next live node in the list instead. Furthermore, this list can be additionally used to redundantly store a node's application-level data in case the node fails. As another example, Overcast [2] is a tree-based content dissemination overlay that employs a self-repair mechanism which attempts to ensure that a tree node always has a 'backup parent' in case its current parent fails. This is achieved by

R. Meersman, Z. Tari, P. Herrero et al. (Eds.): OTM Workshops 2006, LNCS 4278, pp. 1490–1499, 2006.
© Springer-Verlag Berlin Heidelberg 2006

having each node maintain a list of its ancestors, so it can choose a replacement parent from this list if its present parent fails.

But there are drawbacks to this 'per-overlay' approach to self repair. The obvious one is that it leads to duplication of effort. This is especially the case in situations where many overlay types within a 'class' (e.g. DHT overlays) ultimately use similar self-repair approaches with minor differences to suit the specifics of the particular overlay. But a more fundamental drawback is that the approach inhibits choice and flexibility in selecting from among alternative self-repair mechanisms that make different deployment-specific trade-offs between dependability and overhead. For example, where resources (e.g. free hosts) are plentiful, it may be appropriate to recover failed nodes by restoring them on other hosts. Alternatively, where resources are scarce it may be better to allow neighbouring nodes to take over the responsibilities of their failed peers.

Motivated by such considerations, we have developed an approach to self-repair in which overlay networks provide functional behaviour only, and rely for their self-repair on a *generic self-repair service*. Thanks to this separation of concerns, the application developer can be presented with two clear areas of *independent* choice: i) which overlay network to use, based on what that overlay is designed to do and how it achieves it, and ii) how that overlay should defend itself against node failure, based on the selection of an appropriate dependability/overhead trade-off, and expressed as easy-to-understand configuration options of the generic self-repair service.

In this paper we focus on API and integration issues of this approach. In particular, we show how overlay implementations interact with the generic self-repair service using a small and simple API. We concretise the discussion by illustrating the use of this API from within an implementation of the popular Chord overlay. This is shown to involve minimal changes while considerably increasing the range of self-repair strategies available to Chord.

In the rest of this paper, we first introduce in section 2 the overall architecture of our generic self-repair service and its APIs. Then in section 3 we present the above-mentioned Chord-based case study of the use of the service's API. Finally, section 4 discusses related work, and section 5 offers conclusions.

2   The Generic Self-repair Service and Its APIs

Our approach is based on the afore-mentioned separation of concerns, achieved by encapsulating all overlay self-repair concerns in a generic-but-tailorable *self-repair service*. Its design has been guided by the inherently decentralized nature of the overlays that it supports. Thus, an instance of the service runs on each applicable host (i.e. hosts that support overlay nodes that want to use the service), and the various service instances communicate in a peer-to-peer fashion to perform their respective functions.

The service comprises three distinct sub-services: i) a *distributed backup service* which takes key overlay state from a node and stores it in a 'safe' place (for example, at another overlay node) in case the node fails; ii) a *failure detection service* which checks neighbouring nodes for failure, and informs the recovery service when a failure occurs; and iii) *a recovery service* which uses previously backed-up data from the backup service to make appropriate repairs to the failed region of overlay. More detail on these is available in the literature [3, 4].

Between the self-repair service and the overlay there exists a two-way generic API; at one side is an API belonging to the service which permits exposition and guidance by the overlay with regard to its key state elements, and at the other side is an API allowing management of the overlay by the service.

The service does *not* therefore attempt to be fully transparent to the overlay. Rather, overlay nodes and self-repair service instances cooperate using explicit two-way interaction, whereby an overlay node calls methods on its local service instance, and a service instance calls methods on the overlay node it is support-ing. As will be seen, this 'dialogue' is crucial in allowing *overlay-specific needs* to be taken into consideration. While allowing this expressiveness, the API is designed to be as simple as possible, and the relevant interfaces and methods, discussed in detail below, are shown in figure 1.

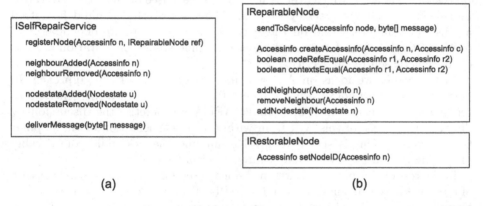

Fig. 1. The interfaces used in our architecture: (a) The self-repair service's main in-terface, and (b) Interfaces to be implemented by overlay nodes

Because of the 'two-way' nature of the API, we need overlay nodes to conform to a model and a semantic that is well-understood by the service. To this end, we require that overlay implementations structure their nodes in terms of two key abstractions: *accessinfos* and *nodestates*. Based on these abstractions, which are described below, the self-repair service can *inspect* the characteristics of each node in terms of both *topology* and *state*, and can also *adapt* the topology and state as required to carry out repairs. Figure 2 depicts the full 'model' of an overlay node and its interactions with the self-repair service. The below subsec-tions define and discuss accessinfos, nodestates and the interactions between the service and the overlay.

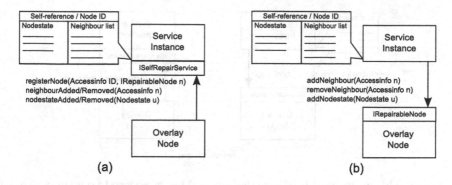

Fig. 2. API interactions: (a) An overlay node exposing its accessinfos and nodestates; and (b) The self-repair service inspecting and adapting these (e.g. at repair time)

Accessinfos. Accessinfos are used to expose the connectivity of the node with its 'neighbours' in the target overlay, and also to enable self-repair service instances to communicate with each other. This communication, which is useful for example to allow the service to send a backup of a node to another node, is achieved using the overlay's own topology. In terms of its representation, an accessinfo is a record that refers to an overlay node and encapsulates sufficient information to allow a message to be sent to that node. The internals of an accessinfo are entirely opaque to the self-repair service, and they are assumed to be 'serializable' so that they can be marshalled for transport and storage purposes.

When an overlay node first comes into existence, it is expected to provide its local self-repair service instance with an accessinfo that refers to itself, which is used to identify and associate various kinds of data with the node. This is achieved by calling *ISelfRepairService.registerNode(Accessinfo nodeRef, IRepairableNode n)*. This call also provides the self-repair service instance with a local object reference *n* on which the service can call overlay-side API methods.

Following this self-advertisement, each node is expected to keep its local self-repair service instance informed about changes to its 'local' topology—i.e. its connectivity to neighbouring nodes. This is achieved using *ISelfRepairService.neighbourAdded/Removed(Accessinfo n)*. With the information passed in these calls, the self-repair service instance is able to communicate with peer instances associated with the given neighbours by using *IRepairableNode.sendToService(Accessinfo n, byte[] message)*, illustrated in figure 3.

The above deals with basic topology management. However, in some cases this is not enough because it does not take into account the various topological 'roles' that might be played by certain nodes in certain overlays. For example, ring overlays may comprehend the roles of 'successor' and 'predecessor', while tree overlays may comprehend the roles of 'parent' and 'child'. To enable such semantic information to be expressed by the overlay, accessinfos can be 'tagged' by the overlay with arbitrary contextual information. As with accessinfos themselves, the nature of this information is opaque to the self-repair service.

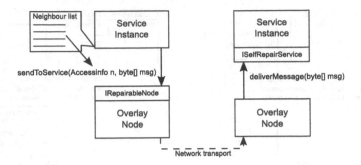

Fig. 3. Neighbours exposed by the overlay are used by the service to send data to other service instances

Nodestates. Nodestates are used to encapsulate state that an overlay node is interested in having restored when the node is recovered. They are optional and do not need to be used by overlays that don't need to maintain persistent state. Like accessinfos, nodestates are assumed to be 'serializable', and the internals of nodestates are opaque to the self-repair service.

Overlay nodes pass nodestates to the self-repair service using *ISelfRepairSer-vice.nodestateAdded/Removed(Nodestate u)*. The intention is that if there is a failure, *IRepairableNode.addNodestate(Nodestate u)* can be called by the self-repair service on an appropriate target node to restore the data encapsulated in these nodestates to the overlay (the issue of which node to select for this restoration is discussed in detail in [3]).

Like the contents of nodestates, the implementation of *addNodestate()* is entirely up to the overlay. For example, a DHT overlay node may expose each file stored locally as an individual nodestate unit, and implement *addNodestate()* to map to the DHT *store()* operation, thereby routing the data to the correct place in the overlay. Alternatively, a super-peer in a Gnutella-like overlay may store its resource index as a nodestate, and implement *addNodestate()* as a 'merge' operation to merge any existing local resource index with the provided one.

Repair Actions. We have demonstrated above how our service can modify the topology and re-distribute the state of an overlay using a common 'model' with the general IRepairableNode interface. Beyond this base API, we support additional repair strategies and overlay input though "progressive disclosure"; a set of optional interfaces available to the overlay developer wishing to have a greater understanding of, or level of control over, the service's operations. This is exemplified here through the *IRestorableNode* interface, as shown in figure 1.

This interface is designed to allow failed overlay nodes to be fully *restored* on alternate hosts, as opposed to compensatory topology modification. This strategy is useful in Grid-like deployments, where resources may be more plentiful. Restored nodes must be provided with the 'node ID' accessinfo of the failed node they are replacing (an accessinfo originally used with *registerNode()*), achieved with the *IRestorableNode.setNodeID()* method. Both of these repair types are generically applicable to a range of overlay networks; a discussion of this, and of the mechanics of a safe, decentralized repair approach, is provided in [3].

Following this example, different 'repair strategies' can be developed and used when appropriate, according to the current state of the overlay's deployment environment, provided any additional interfaces relating to specific repair strategies are implemented. Implementing such interfaces allows the overlay to configure which strategies it would like to support, and indeed further expansion of the overlay-side API can allow arbitrary overlay guidance on how a repair strategy is performed, achieved by the strategy querying the overlay before repair enactment. A discussion and evaluation of the benefits of dynamically selecting different repair strategies at the time of repair is available in [4].

3   Case Study

We now provide a detailed view of the overlay developer's task in making an overlay compatible with our self-repair service. We use Chord [1] as an example, as it is well-known and easy to understand without being trivial, though we have also modified TBCP [5] (an application-level multicast overlay) in a similar way. The presentation here is based on an actual modification of an existing Chord prototype [6] as used in our GridKit middleware. We assume some familiarity with Chord, as we do not have space to discuss it in detail here.

3.1   Instantiating the Abstractions

Chord has two main topological characteristics: (i) a ring structure, in which nodes are linked clockwise and anti-clockwise by 'successor' and 'predecessor' links respectively; and (ii) the use of per-node 'finger tables' that provide O(log N) routing for any key (as the ring alone would only provide O(N) routing).

For the purposes of this case study we decided to expose the ring structure in terms of accessinfos, but to model finger tables in terms of nodestates. This latter choice makes sense because we know that the finger table will be refreshed shortly after a repair anyway, and so use the finger table data only to speed up this process. However, it would also have been possible to expose finger tables in terms of accessinfos by calling *neighbourAdded/Removed()* as each finger link changes, with an appropriate 'finger' context (see below).

Having made this decision, the next step is to define an accessinfo class as shown in figure 4. The Chord implementation we modified uses Java RMI as its communication protocol, and so the *RemoteNode* reference is a wrapper around an RMI remote reference (and Chord node ID). Our accessinfo class also has a comparator method and a 'context' variable, which is used to tag the record with contextual data of 'successor', 'predecessor' or 'NodeID'. It is serializable for network transport and flat storage.

We next create a 'Chord nodestate' class to contain a node's finger table (simply an array of remote references). This completes our definition of Chord

```
class ChordAccessinfo implements java.io.Serializable {
    public static final int NODE_ID = 0, SUCCESSOR = 1, PREDECESSOR = 2;
    public RemoteNode nodeReference;
    public int context;

    public ChordAccessinfo(RemoteNode nodeReference, int context) { .... }

    public boolean equals(Object o) {
        if (o instanceof ChordAccessinfo) {
            ChordAccessinfo chk = (ChordAccessinfo) o;
            if ((chk.nodeReference.equals(nodeReference))
                && (chk.context == context))
                return true;
            else
                return false;
        }
        else return false;
    }
}
```

Fig. 4. Our `accessinfo` implementation for Chord

under the self-repair service's model. This is clearly both Chord-specific (with customized contexts), and implementation-specific (an RMI remote reference is used as our accessor detail). But again, we stress that our service does not have (or need) access to the contents of the above classes.

3.2 Using the API

To be repairable by our service, the Chord node implementation must implement seven methods, shown in figure 5. Our Java service implementation uses Java Objects to represent accessinfos and notestates, but to simplify the presentation here we have assumed 'implicit casting' to the ChordAccessinfo class (and corresponding nodestate class 'StoredFingerTable') in our code extracts.

Note the *receiveServiceMessage()* call, shown in figure 5, is a remote method call, from which the recipient overlay node calls *deliverMessage()* on its self-repair service instance to deliver the sent message (as in figure 3 in section 2).

In order to expose the overlay's topology and state to the service, the overlay node implementation also needs to call six methods on the self-repair service at various points during its execution. We call *registerNode()* on startup, then provide topology information as it becomes available or changes using *neighbourAdded/Removed()*. Successor changes occur within Chord's *stabilize()* method, of which we show an extract in figure 6.

Chord's *notify()* method was also modified in the same way to expose changes in the node's predecessor. In both cases, we decided not to internally store neighbour links as instances of our new ChordAccessinfo class, but instead to create them only when Chord interacts with our service. This decision was made because we were modifying an existing overlay, and therefore wished to make as few changes to it as possible.

Finally, when a Chord node updates its finger table, we again perform a similar procedure to that shown in figure 6, but this time using the methods

```
public void sendToService(ChordAccessinfo toNodeID, byte[] message) {
  ((ChordRef) toNode).nodeReference.receiveServiceMessage(message);
}

public ChordAccessinfo createAccessinfo(ChordAccessinfo toNode, ChordAccessinfo useContext) {
  return new ChordAccessinfo(toNode.nodeReference, useContext.context);
}

public boolean nodeRefsEqual(ChordAccessinfo r1, ChordAccessinfo r2) {
  return r1.nodeReference.equals(r2.nodeReference);
}

public boolean contextsEqual(ChordAccessinfo r1, ChordAccessinfo r2) {
  return r1.context == r2.context;
}

public void addNodestate(StoredFingerTable unit) {
  refreshFingerTable(unit.table);
}

public void addNeighbour(ChordAccessinfo neighbour) {
  //check what kind of neighbour it is
  if (neighbour.context == ChordAccessinfo.SUCCESSOR)
    setSuccessor(neighbour.nodeReference);
    else if (neighbour.context == ChordAccessinfo.PREDECESSOR)
    setPredecessor(neighbour.nodeReference);
}

public void removeNeighbour(ChordAccessinfo neighbour) {
  //check what kind of neighbour it is
  if (neighbour.context == ChordAccessinfo.SUCCESSOR)
    setSuccessor(null);
    else if (neighbour.context == ChordAccessinfo.PREDECESSOR)
    setPredecessor(null);
}
```

Fig. 5. Our implementation of the IRepairableNode interface for Chord

```
private void stabilize() {
  ...

  // Updating successor
  RemoteNode successor = getSuccessor();
  RemoteNode rn = successor.getPredecessor();
  // Check to see if the successor's predecessor is greater than Node ID
  if ((rn != null) && (ChordNodeID.inRange(rn.nodeID, myNodeID, successor.nodeID))) {
  // If it is, set node successor to the successor's predecessor
    dependabilityService.neighbourRemoved(new ChordAccessinfo(successor, ChordAccessinfo.SUCCESSOR));
    setSuccessor(rn);
    dependabilityService.neighbourAdded(new ChordAccessinfo(rn, ChordAccessinfo.SUCCESSOR));
  }
  ...
}
```

Fig. 6. Our modified implementation of the stabilize method in Chord

```
public ChordAccessinfo setNodeID(ChordAccessinfo nodeID) {
  setChordNodeID(nodeID.nodeReference.chordID);
  return new ChordAccessinfo(myRemoteReference, ChordAccessinfo.NODE_ID);
}
```

Fig. 7. Our implementation of *setNodeID()* for Chord

nodestateAdded/Removed(), where we remove the old finger table from persistent storage with the service, and add the new one, as nodestate.

3.3   Optional Additional Implementation

To allow the recovery service to choose at runtime between topology-modifying and node-restoring repair strategies, we implement the optional interface IRestorableNode, with its *setNodeID()* method as in figure 7.

We now have a version of Chord which can be maintained by our self-repair service, so that the service provides all aspects of redundancy, failure detection, and recovery. We believe that all overlay-side instrumentation is trivial for the overlay developer, as demonstrated by the code extracts above—in total, our modified version of Chord is 80 lines (10%) longer than the 'standard' version. We have not altered Chord's functional behaviour in any way, so it is fully compatible with existing applications.

Nevertheless, it is additionally possible for such applications, again with minor modifications, to themselves take advantage of the self-repair service to ensure that their data is safe across node failures. To achieve this, applications simply need to wrap their data as nodestates and call *addNodestate()* and *removeNodestate()* on the service as data is added to/removed from the local node.

4   Related Work

The notion of "progressive disclosure" has similarities with the "scope control" property advocated for reflective operating systems by Kiczales and Lamping in [7], though we also use it to help configure how the recovery service works.

The 'model' of an overlay as defined by our self-repair service can be seen as a kind of 'reflection' of an overlay, i.e. a causally-connected meta model of a running system. Previous work [8] has addressed 'domain-specific' reflection of a system for fault tolerance, but our model has much closer ties to the specific *application* (i.e. overlays), rather than general distributed systems.

Our approach could also be viewed as inserting 'probes' and 'actuators' into an overlay to monitor and modify it, in a similar way to an autonomic control loop [9], with our service as the decision-making module.

There has been some other interesting work on making overlay networks easier to develop, in a similar way to that in which we allow developers to ignore self-repair concerns. iOverlay [10] and MACEDON [11] both suggest frameworks in which to develop overlays; in the case of iOverlay, the developer expresses only the 'business logic' of the overlay, and communication and other concerns are handled by the framework. MACEDON aims to make overlay development easier by using a specialized language with which to design and evaluate overlays.

While both of these efforts may be valuable in the design process, we have deliberately aimed at an API which is very close to the way in which overlays operate today, which permits both minimal effort in modifying existing implementations, and a low 'learning curve' for new implementations, as we use standard object-oriented principles.

5   Conclusion

In this paper we have described how a generic repair approach can be integrated with overlay code in a very practical way. Although we had only space to discuss one concrete example, we hope the reader can see how the approach would apply equally to other overlays. The basic approach is to define some core abstractions (accessinfos and nodestates) and an API based on allowance for application-specific expressiveness and progressive disclosure. This potentially simplifies the implementation of new overlays, which no longer need concern themselves with failure and self-repair issues, and allows many of the wide range of overlay types that exist today to benefit from our self-repair service, without losing overlay-specific semantics. This integration opens up a much wider range of repair strategies than are typically available to off-the-shelf overlays.

By providing such a separation of *dependability* and *functionality*, two concerns often particularly closely tied in overlay networks, we enable design choice based on overlay functionality, and independent dependability property specification *as appropriate to the deployment* through a standard service.

References

1. Stoica, I., Morris, R., Karger, D., Kaashoek, M.F., Balakrishnan, H.: Chord: A scalable peer-to-peer lookup service for internet applications. In: Proceedings of the 2001 conference on applications, technologies, architectures, and protocols for computer communications, ACM Press (2001) 149–160
2. Jannotti, J., et al.: Overcast: Reliable multicasting with an overlay network. In: Proceedings of the Fourth Symposium on Operating System Design and Implementation (OSDI). (2000) 197–212
3. Porter, B., Taïani, F., Coulson, G.: Generalized repair for overlay networks. In: Proceedings of the Symposium on Reliable Distributed Sytems, Leeds, UK (2006)
4. Porter, B., Coulson, G., Hughes, D.: Intelligent dependability services for overlay networks. In: Proceedings of Distributed Applications and Interoperable Systems 2006 (DAIS'06). Volume 4025 of LNCS., Bologna, Italy (2006) 199–212
5. Mathy, L., Canonico, R., Hutchison, D.: An overlay tree building control protocol. Lecture Notes in Computer Science **2233** (2001) 76
6. https://sourceforge.net/projects/gridkit/: (Gridkit middleware public release)
7. Kiczales, G., Lamping, J.: Operating systems: Why object-oriented? In Hutchinson, L.F.C., Norman, eds.: the Third International Workshop on Object-Orientation in Operating Systems, Asheville, North Carolina (1993) 25–30
8. Killijian, M., Fabre, J., Ruiz-García, J., Shiba, S.: A metaobject protocol for fault-tolerant CORBA applications. In: 17th IEEE Symposium on Reliable Distributed Systems (SRDS-17), West Lafayette (USA) (1998) 127–134
9. Ganek, A., Corbi, T.: The dawning of the autonomic computing era. IBM Systems Journal **42:1** (2003) 5–19
10. Li, B., Guo, J., Wang, M.: iOverlay: A lightweight middleware infrastructure for overlay application implementations. In: Proceedings of IFIP/ACM/USENIX Middleware, Toronto, Canada (2004)
11. Rodriguez, A., et al.: Macedon: Methodology for automatically creating, evaluating, and designing overlay networks. In: Proceedings of the Symposium on Networked Systems Design and Implementation (NSDI), San Francisco, USA (2004)

Providing Reliable IPv6 Access Service Based on Overlay Network

Xiaoxiang Leng, Jun Bi, and Miao Zhang

Network Research Center, Tsinghua University
Beijing 100084, China

Abstract. During the transition from IPv4 to IPv6, it is necessary to provide IPv6 access service for IPv6 islands inside the native IPv4 network to access the native IPv6 network. The existing IPv4/IPv6 transition methods make IPv6-relay gateways maintained by IPv6 service providers become potential communication bottlenecks. In this paper, a new method PS6 is presented to reduce the reliance on these relay gateways by shifting the burden to edge gateways on each IPv6 island. In this method, direct tunnels are set up between IPv6 islands, and a overlay network is maintained between edge gateways of IPv6 islands to propagate information of tunnel end points. After describing the algorithm and overlay network design, we analyze the scalability of the algorithm. The simulation results and theoretical analysis show that the proposed method is reliable and scalable.

Keywords: IPv6 Access Service, Overlay Network, IPv4/IPv6 Transition.

1 Introduction

Mainly due to the fast expansion of the Internet and the lack of unallocated global IPv4 addresses, the transition from IPv4 to IPv6 [1] is now a reality and a growing trend while the Internet develops. Because of the sheer scale of the existing IPv4 network, the transition will need considerable time to complete. Some IPv4 subnets may, while having had their network infrastructure upgraded to support IPv6, still lack direct links to the native IPv6 network. That is, they will be isolated IPv6 islands inside the global IPv4 network. It is common for these IPv6 islands to use IPv6-in-IPv4 tunnels [2] via relay gateways maintained by IPv6 service providers in order to join the native IPv6 network. However, in these scenarios, all traffic from an IPv6 island to another IPv6 island will be forwarded via the IPv6-relay gateways from the source island to IPv6 network, and then be forwarded back from the IPv6 network to the destination island. While IPv6 is still emerging, a lot of IPv6 traffic may be transmitted between IPv6 islands. Therefore, these relay gateways maintained by IPv6 service providers can potentially become the communication bottlenecks.

A peer-to-peer (P2P) [3] based algorithm PS6 is proposed in this paper, in which direct tunnels are built between IPv6 islands to reduce the burden of IPv6-relay gateways maintained by IPv6 service providers. A P2P overlay network is set up among the gateways of IPv6 islands to propagate TEP (tunnel end point) information (<IPv6 prefixes, IPv4 address of edge gateway>). When an IPv6 island dual-stack

R. Meersman, Z. Tari, P. Herrero et al. (Eds.): OTM Workshops 2006, LNCS 4278, pp. 1500–1509, 2006.
© Springer-Verlag Berlin Heidelberg 2006

gateway receives a data packet sent to the IPv6 network, it firstly checks whether there is a direct tunnel to the destination address. For packets being transmitted, the shortcut tunnels between the source and destination islands are assigned higher route precedence than tunnels to relay gateways of service providers.

In P6P [4], P2P technology is also utilized to build the IPv6 backbone over the existing IPv4 network. It directly uses a DHT-based [5] P2P network to forward the IPv6 data packets. There are some drawbacks for this scheme. Firstly, DHT is usually used for exact matching, and is not suitable for the longest matching in packet forwarding. Secondly, there is problem in the performance of forwarding lookup on the distributed storage P2P network. In contrast to P6P, the PS6 algorithm only uses the P2P network for transferring control messages between edge gateways of IPv6 islands. Data packets are forwarded to the destination gateways by the source gateways of IPv6 islands directly after looking up their tunnel tables, allowing for better forwarding performance.

The rest of the paper is organized as follows. Section 2 shows the problem statement; Section 3 presents the PS6 algorithm; in Section 4, the design of the overlay network used in PS6 is introduced; In Section 5, the scalability of the proposed algorithm is discussed by theoretical analysis, and Section 6 summarizes this paper and proposes future work.

2 Problem Statement

In the course of the deployment of IPv6, native IPv6 networks - both IPv6-only and dual stacks - will connect with each other to eventually become an IPv6 continent. The upgrade of IPv4 networks to support IPv6, due to the huge existing investment in IPv4, will necessarily be a gradual process, and native IPv4 networks and native IPv6 networks will coexist for a long time. During this period of coexistence, there are two methods for dual stack hosts in an IPv4 continent to communicate with hosts in an IPv6 continent and to use IPv6 application. The first way is to directly set up an IPv6 tunnel - with the mechanisms ISATAP [6], Teredo [7], etc. - between a dual stack host and an IPv6-relay gateway provided by a service provider. The second way is to set up an IPv6 tunnel between an edge gateway of the local network and an IPv6-relay gateway. In this second method, the local network becomes an IPv6 island. When the internal information of local network needs to be protected, it is recommended that the second solution be used [8].

Existing methods for providing IPv6 access service for IPv6 islands include: 6to4 mechanism [9] in which 6to4 IPv6 addresses are used, and IPv6 configured tunnel [2] in which global IPv6 addresses are used. Without explicit tunnel setup, 6to4 technology is a simple solution for isolated IPv6 islands to communicate with each other and access the IPv6 continent with the help of 6to4 relays. The automatic tunnels between 6to4 networks can effectively mitigate the burden of 6to4 relays. This method does, however, pose significant management challenges for ISPs, and there are also security problems with 6to4 brought about by the automatic tunneling mechanism [10]. With IPv6 configured tunnels using global IPv6 addresses, the addresses of IPv6 islands are assigned by the providers of IPv6 access service. This manual configuration makes this kind of tunnel easy to control, and the security problems are greatly diminished when compared with 6to4. Furthermore, no extra route need be imported into the IPv6 network. The IPv6 islands can be treated as natural extensions of the IPv6 continent. For the purpose of decreasing the configuration overhead, a Tunnel Broker (TB) [11] is often used to manage the configured tunnels automatically.

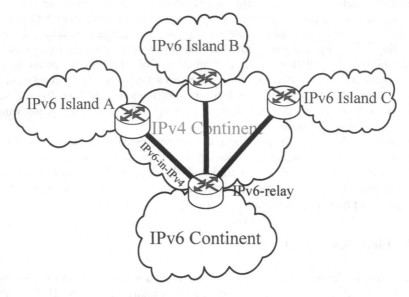

Fig. 1. Scenario of IPv6 islands

The mechanisms with global IPv6 addresses (such as IPv6 configured tunnel and Tunnel Broker) generally use IPv6-relay gateways to provide the IPv6 access service. As shown in Figure 1, all the traffic from IPv6 islands will be forwarded by the relay gateways, even if the traffic is between IPv6 islands. The relay gateways can potentially become communication bottlenecks. Since the existing optimization algorithms are mainly focusing on the service providers, the only way to increase overall performance is to increase the performance or the number of relay gateways, which could be a costly exercise.

3 The Algorithm

In this paper, we present an optimizing algorithm PS6 for the scenario above to provide high performance IPv6 access service. Besides the service providers, we also consider the customers - the edge gateways of IPv6 islands. When an IPv6 island gateway receives a data packet with a destination address in another IPv6 island, it directly forwards this packet to the destination island gateway through the IPv4 network. Otherwise, it sends the packet to the relay gateway of the service provider.

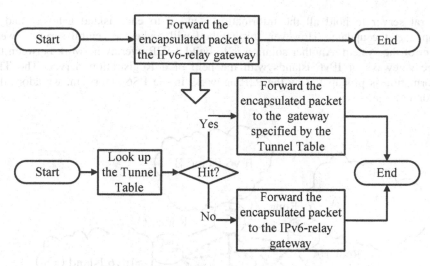

Fig. 2. Forwarding flow of IPv6 island gateway

As shown in Figure 2, in PS6, a lookup operation is inserted into the flow for packet forwarding of IPv6 island edge gateways. The steps of the proposed algorithm are described as follows:

(1) Form a Tunnel Table (as shown in Table 1) on each IPv6 island gateway by exchanging TEP information (<IPv6 prefixes, IPv4 address of edge gateway>) between the gateways.

(2) When an island gateway receives an IPv6 data packet, Firstly, it looks up the Tunnel Table to find out whether there is a direct tunnel to the destination. If yes, it then sends this packet directly to the IPv4 address specified by the Tunnel Table; Otherwise, it then forwards this packet to the IPv6-relay gateway of service provider

Table 1. Tunnel Table of IPv6 island gateway

IPv6 prefix	IPv4 address of gateway
2001:250:f001:f002:20a::/80	1.2.3.4
2001:250:f001:f002:28ba::/80	2.3.4.5
2001:250:f001:f002:fe30::/80	3.4.5.6

The PS6 algorithm is based on that for IPv6 configured tunnels, inheriting the advantages for control, management and security. In addition, as with 6to4, the direct tunnels between IPv6 islands can effectively reduce the burden on the IPv6 relay gateways.

In contrast to 6to4, the global IPv6 addresses of IPv6 islands make it impossible for the island gateways to get the TEP information from the destination IPv6 address of a data packet. How a gateway of IPv6 island gets the TEP information of all the other IPv6 islands is the key consideration in this algorithm. One solution is to set up a central server to hold all the information, send it to each island gateway and to propagate the updates. However, this method will make the central server a weak point of the system. Another solution is to build a P2P overlay network between the edge gateways of IPv6 islands with the help of a Registration Server. The TEP information is propagated by the P2P network. In the PS6 algorithm, we adopt this second option.

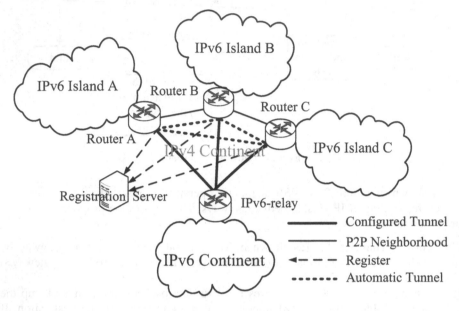

Fig. 3. The PS6 algorithm

The architecture of IPv6 overlay network is shown in Figure 3. Router A, Router B and Router C are edge gateways of three IPv6 islands. A P2P network is maintained by them to share TEP information. With the TEP information, shortcut tunnels are set up on each gateway for transferring data packets between IPv6 islands.

After presenting the PS6 algorithm, we describe the design of the overlay network and analyze the scalability of the proposed algorithm in the following parts.

4 Overlay Network Design

4.1 IPv6 Overlay Network

An IPv6 overlay network is set up to propagate TEP information among the IPv6 island gateways. Each IPv6 island edge gateway broadcasts its TEP information inside the overlay network and gets the other gateways' TEP information from its peers.

There are two classes of P2P overlay networks: Structured and Unstructured [12]. In the Structured P2P networks, a lot of overhead, either from network or computing, is introduced into the system in order to maintain the structure of the network. In contrast, in the Unstructured P2P network, there is no special global structure to be maintained. Instead, a partial view of the network is held for each node. The overheads for maintaining network topology can be much lower than those for the structured ones.

In the scenario proposed in this paper, the gateways of IPv6 islands are usually lightweight devices such as NAT Boxes which are not capable of maintaining large amounts of topology information. Therefore, in PS6, we have chosen to use an Unstructured P2P network in which each node chooses its neighbors randomly. Since there is no special structure to this P2P network, it is necessary to find a way to keep the nodes inside this P2P network connected with each other.

A Registration Server on which the IPv4 addresses of all nodes in the IPv6 overlay network are held is set up to help the gateways of IPv6 islands join the overlay network gradually. The Registration Server has to discover the changes of the overlay network, either from the removal or failure of nodes or from the changes of IPv4 addresses. Fortunately, these are already contained within the information spread inside the overlay network. We put the Registration Server into the P2P network as a normal node. Therefore, these changes are easily noticed by the update scheme of the IPv6 overlay network.

Similar to some routing protocols, such as OSPF [13], the flooding scheme is used to broadcast the TEP information inside the overlay network. When a node receives an update packet from one of its neighbors, it refreshes the related items in its local database, and then forwards the packet to all the other neighbors. Although flooding can be a waste of network resources, it's a reliable scheme to spread TEP information to all nodes in the IPv6 overlay network.

4.2 IPv6 Service Subscription

In PS6, a Registration Server is set up to help the IPv6 island gateways join the IPvt overlay network. When the Registration Server receives a subscription request from a newly arrived gateway, it randomly chooses 20 of all existing nodes and sends their IPv4 addresses to the new one. The new node then gets the TEP information of all the islands corresponding to the nodes specified by the received IPv4 addresses and forms a Tunnel Tables for data forwarding. The steps of a new subscription are shown in Figure 4 and described as follows:

(1) Register. The new arrived node registers at the Registration Server, and gets a list of IPv4 addresses for 20 existing nodes.
(2) Make overlay neighborhoods. The new node tries to make overlay neighborhoods with the nodes specified by the received IPv4 addresses.
(3) Exchange TEP information. The new node gets the TEP information of all other islands from its neighbors. Meanwhile, it spreads its TEP information inside the P2P network.
(4) Form a Tunnel Table. With the TEP information received, the new node sets up a Tunnel Table for data transmission.

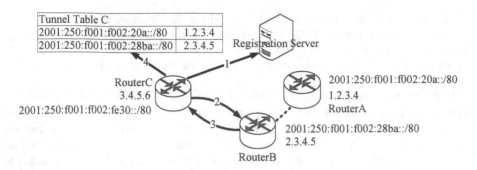

Fig. 4. New subscription

4.3 Failure Detection

It is common to hold the overlay neighborhoods of the IPv6 overlay network by sending keep-alive messages periodically. When a node detects that it hasn't received such keep-alive message from its neighbor for a certain time, it broadcasts the failure notice to the whole IPv6 overlay network through its live neighbors.

Furthermore, in order to increase the stability of the overlay network, we set the minimal degrees d for each node to be 5. When a node finds the count of its live neighbors is less than d, it randomly chooses some nodes from the TEP information stored locally and tries to make new overlay neighborhoods until the count of its live neighbors reaches d.

The simulation shows that when the node number is less than 10000, the IPv6 overlay network used in PS6 can keep connected as long as the minimal degree of each node d is equal to or more than 3. We can infer that when d is equal to or more than 3, the overlay network can always keep connected. Therefore, in the PS6 algorithm, d is set to 5. This should be enough to prevent disconnection of the IPv6 overlay network.

5 Scalability Study

During the transition from IPv4 to IPv6, isolated IPv6 islands will exist widely in the current IPv4 network. The PS6 algorithm must scale enough to support many IPv6 islands (i.e., 10,000).

On the data plane, the forwarding performance with such a huge number of tunnels on each gateway should be considered. There are already plenty of studies on the area of fast data forwarding. A trie-tree [14] structure is used to form the Tunnel Table and limit the overhead of prefix lookup.

On the control plane, the scalability of the IPv6 overlay network should be discussed. A flooding-based Unstructured P2P network (i.e., Gnutella [15]) may not be scalable because of the heavy flooding overhead cased by transient peers [15]. Fortunately, the edge gateways of IPv6 islands are much more stable, so the P2P network used in PS6 can support many more nodes. Since there is no consumed computing for each gateway upon receiving an update packet, the flooding overhead of the proposed P2P network scheme is mostly from the cost of network bandwidth.

Assume the duration time that each node (IPv6 island gateway) stays connected to the IPv6 overlay network independently has an exponential distribution with parameter λ. Within one second, a single node is destroyed with probability $1-e^{-\lambda}$. When the node number of the IPv6 overlay network is N, the number of nodes failed in one second is expected to be $N(1-e^{-\lambda})$. And the expected size S of each update packet flooding inside the IPv6 overlay network is $S_0N(1-e^{-\lambda})$, where S_0 indicates the size of each failure notice.

According to the founding process of the IPv6 overlay network with minimal degree d, the neighbor number of node i is expected to be:

$$E(n_i) = \begin{cases} d + \sum\limits_{l=d+2}^{N} \dfrac{d}{l-1}, 0 < i \leq d+1 \\ d + \sum\limits_{l=i+1}^{N} \dfrac{d}{l-1}, d+1 < i \leq N \end{cases} \tag{1}$$

From (1), we can see that the first $d+1$ nodes have the maximum neighbor number on average. These nodes may have more trouble with flooding. We consider the worst case that one of the first $d+1$ nodes receives the update packet from all its neighbors at the same time. Meanwhile, this node should forward the packet to all its neighbors after receiving it for the first time. In this case, the cost of network bandwidth of this node is expected to be:

$$C = 2S \max_{0<i\leq N}(E(n_i)) = 2dS_0N(1+ \sum_{l=d+2}^{N} \frac{1}{l-1})(1-e^{-\lambda}) \tag{2}$$

Suppose that the bandwidths of the nodes are independent, and each can most spend 10% of its total bandwidth B on flooding control packets, we have the restriction:

$$C \leq B \times 10\% \tag{3}$$

When $B = 10Mb/s$, $S_0 = 256bits$, $d = 5$, $\lambda = 1/1800$ (the duration time of each node is 0.5 hour on average), from (2) and (3), the max node number that the IPv6 overlay network can support in worst case is 6.5×10^4. This result shows that the P2P network used in PS6 scales enough to meet the scalability requirements during IPv6 transition.

6 Conclusion

In this paper, we present a peer-to-peer based method PS6 to provide IPv6 access service for isolated IPv6 islands. This algorithm distributes the traffic between IPv6 islands directly though IPv4 network and mitigates the burden of IPv6-relay gateways of service provider.

The scalability of the proposed algorithm i also analyzed. The simulation results show that the P2P network can keep connected with the Random Recovery Scheme; and the theoretical analysis indicates that the PS6 algorithm can meet the scalability requirements during IPv6 transition. In other words, the proposed algorithm is reliable and scalable.

The PS6 algorithm inherits the advantages of IPv6 configured tunnel in control, management and security, gets the high access performance and mitigates the burden of relay gateways like 6to4. The comparison to the existing tunneling mechanisms that can be used in the IPv6 island scenario is shown in Table 2. The PS6 algorithm has better qualities in access performance, reliability and scalability as well as lower investment cost for IPv6 ISPs to provide feasible IPv6 access service, especially along with the increasing number of isolated IPv6 islands.

Table 2. Comparison between PS6 and other tunneling mechanisms used for IPv6 islands
H = High, M = Moderate, L = Low

	Performance	Investment	Reliability	Scalability	Drawbacks
6to4	H	L	H	H	1. Special 6to4 prefix 2. Difficult control and management 3. Terrible security problems
Configured tunnel	L	H	L	L	1. Manual configure 2. That as TB
Tunnel Broker	L	H	L	L	1. Single point of failure 2.Communication bottleneck
P6P	L	M	H	M	1. Low performance on route lookup 2. Low performance on data transmission
PS6	H	L	H	H	

Up to now, the architecture and protocol details of PS6 has been designed already. A prototype system has also been developed. In future, we will do some further study on more security considerations of this algorithm. Since the edge gateways of IPv6 islands are sometimes lightweight devices and cannot support the heavy overhead of an end-to-end security scheme IPSec between each pair of TEPs [16], the SPM [17] technology can be deployed to provide a lightweight security guarantee for data transmission. Besides, the robustness of the registration scheme should also be increased. The failure of the Registration Server may make it impossible for a new node to join the P2P network. Some backup scheme, for example, using multiple records for the same domain name of Registration Server in DNS, should be introduced into this algorithm.

References

1. S. Deering, R. Hinden: Internet Protocol, version 6 (IPv6) specifications, RFC 2460, December 1998.
2. E. Nordmark, R. Gilligan: Basic Transition Mechanisms for IPv6 Hosts and Routers, RFC 4213, October 2005.

3. A. Oram: Peer-To-Peer: Harnessing the Power of Disruptive Technologies, O'Reilly Press, 2001.
4. Lidong Zhou, Robbert van Renesse: P6P: A Peer-to-Peer Approach to Internet Infrastructure, IPTPS'04, 2004.
5. Ion Stoica, Robert Morris et al: Chord: A Scalable Peer-to-peer Lookup Service for Internet Applications, SIGCOM'01, 2001.
6. F. Templin, T. Gleeson, M. Talwar, D. Thaler: Intra-Site Automatic Tunnel Addressing Protocol (ISATAP), draft-ietf-ngtrans-isatap-22, May, 2004
7. C. Huitema: Tunneling IPv6 over UDP through NATs(Teredo), draft-huitema-v6ops-teredo-05, April 5, 2005
8. E. Davies, S. Krishnan, P. Savola: IPv6 Transition/Co-existence Security Considerations, draft-ietf-v6ops-security-overview-03, October 2005.
9. B. Carpenter, K. Moore: Connection of IPv6 Domains via IPv4 Clouds, RFC 3056, February 2001.
10. P. Savola, C. Patel: Security Considerations for 6to4, RFC 3964, December 2004.
11. A. Durand, P. Fasano, D. Lento: IPv6 Tunnel Broker, RFC 3053, January 2001.
12. Eng Keong Lua, Jon Crowcroft, Marcelo Pias: A Survey and Comparison of Peer-to-peer Overlay Network Schemes, IEEE Communications Surveys & Tutorials, Second Quarter, 2005.
13. J. Moy: OSPF Version 2, RFC 2328, April 1998.
14. Miguel A.Ruiz-Sanchez et al.: Survey and taxonomy of IP address lookup algorithms, IEEE Network March/April 2001.
15. J. Guterman: Gnutella to the Rescue? Not so Fast, Napster fiends. Link to article at http://gnutella.wego.com, September 2000.
16. R. Graveman, M. Parthasarathy, P. Savola, H. Tschofenig: Using IPsec to Secure IPv6-in-IPv4 Tunnels, draft-ietf-v6ops-ipsec-tunnels-01, August 2005
17. A. Bermlerand, H. Levy: Spoofing Prevention Method, INFOCOM'05, 2005.

Adaptive Voting for Balancing Data Integrity with Availability

Johannes Osrael, Lorenz Froihofer, Matthias Gladt, and Karl M. Goeschka

Vienna University of Technology
Institute of Information Systems
Argentinierstrasse 8/184-1, 1040 Wien, Austria
{osrael, froihofer, gladt, goeschka}@tuwien.ac.at

Abstract. Data replication is a primary means to achieve fault tolerance in distributed systems. Data integrity is one of the correctness criteria of data-centric distributed systems. If data integrity needs to be strictly maintained even in the presence of network partitions, the system becomes (partially) unavailable since no potentially conflicting updates are allowed on replicas in different partitions. Availability can be enhanced if data integrity can be temporarily relaxed during degraded situations. Thus, data integrity can be balanced with availability.

In this paper, we contribute with a new replication protocol based on traditional quorum consensus (voting) that allows the configuration of this trade-off. The key idea of our Adaptive Voting protocol is to allow non-critical operations (that cannot violate critical constraints) even if no quorum exists. Since this might impose replica conflicts and data integrity violations, different reconciliation policies are needed to re-establish correctness at repair time. An availability analysis and an experimental evaluation show that Adaptive Voting provides better availability than traditional voting if (i) some data integrity constraints of the system are relaxable and (ii) reconciliation time is shorter than degradation time.

1 Introduction

Replication is one of the primary mechanisms to enhance availability of distributed systems. One correctness criterion for data-centric applications are data integrity constraints, such as value constraints, relationship constraints (cardinality, XOR), uniqueness constraints and other predicates. A system is *constraint consistent* if all data integrity constraints are satisfied.

If strict constraint consistency has to be ensured all the time - even in the presence of failures - the system becomes (at least partially[1]) unavailable in degraded scenarios (e.g., node or link failures) since neither potentially conflicting updates on replicas in different partitions nor updates that possibly violate data integrity constraints are allowed. On the other hand, some applications (e.g., [3, 4]) exist where consistency can be temporarily relaxed in order to achieve higher availability.

The DeDiSys [5] middleware extends state-of-the-art object-based middleware such es CORBA, EJB, or .NET with explicit management of data integrity constraints and

---

[1] Even if a majority partition or more generally - a quorum - exists [1, 2], significant parts of the system become unavailable.

R. Meersman, Z. Tari, P. Herrero et al. (Eds.): OTM Workshops 2006, LNCS 4278, pp. 1510–1519, 2006.
© Springer-Verlag Berlin Heidelberg 2006

provides novel adaptive replication protocols that enable the balancing between availability and consistency.

In this paper[2], we focus on the replication part of the DeDiSys middleware and contribute with a new replication protocol called *Adaptive Voting* (AV) that allows to configure the trade-off between availability and data integrity. AV is based on the traditional voting scheme [2] but allows non-critical operations even if no quorum exists. AV offers different policies to re-establish correctness when the failures are repaired.

Paper Overview. Our system model is presented in Sect. 2. Section 3 introduces the key idea of the new Adaptive Voting protocol. Section 4 describes the different modes of AV in detail. Section 5 presents the results of an experimental evaluation of the protocol. Our work is compared to related work in Sect. 6 before we conclude in Sect. 7.

2 System Model

We focus on tightly-coupled, data-centric, object-oriented distributed systems with up to about 30 server nodes and an arbitrary number of client nodes. Server nodes host objects which are replicated to other server nodes in order to achieve fault tolerance. We assume full replication, i.e., objects are replicated to all nodes. We consider both node and link failures (partitioning): The crash failure [6] model is assumed for nodes and links may fail by losing but not duplicating or corrupting messages.

We assume a partially synchronous system, where clocks are not synchronized, but message time is bound. A group membership service is assumed in our system, which provides a single view of the nodes within a partition, i.e., it is used to detect node and link failures. Furthermore, we assume the presence of a group communication service which provides multicast to groups with configurable delivery and ordering guarantees.

We assume the correctness of the system is expressed in the form of application-specific data integrity constraints, which are defined upon objects that encapsulate application data (e.g., Entity Beans in Enterprise Java Beans terminology). These objects do not contain business logic and typically correspond to a row in a table of a relational database.

Not all constraints of an application are of equal importance. Some have to be satisfied at any point in time while others might be relaxed temporarily when failures occur. To allow such flexibility, we provide two different constraint classes [7] with respect to the trading of constraint consistency for availability: *Non-tradeable constraints* must never be violated. Thus they cannot be traded for higher availability during degradation. *Tradeable constraints* can be temporarily relaxed during degraded situations. Read operations cannot affect data integrity constraints; thus they are non-critical with respect to data integrity. For write operations we distinguish *critical* and *non-critical* write operations. The former affect at least one non-tradeable while the latter affect only tradeable constraints.

---
[2] This work has been partially funded by the European Community under the FP6 IST project DeDiSys (Dependable Distributed Systems, contract number 004152, http://www.dedisys.org).

3 Adaptive Voting

3.1 Weighted Voting

In Weighted Voting [2], a generalization of Majority Voting [1], each replica is assigned some number of votes. Whenever a read or write operation shall be performed, at least RQ (read quorum) or WQ (write quorum) votes must be acquired. Let the total number of votes be V. The following conditions must be satisfied:

$$RQ + WQ > V \qquad (1) \qquad\qquad WQ > \frac{V}{2} \qquad (2)$$

$WQ, RQ, V \in \mathbb{N}$ and $WQ, RQ \leq V$ are assumed[3]. Condition (1) prevents read-write conflicts while condition (2) prevents write-write conflicts.

For the sake of simplicity we further assume in this paper that all replicas have equal votes (i.e., 1) and each node in the system hosts one replica. Thus, the total number of votes V becomes the total number of nodes in the system, denoted as N. We denote this simplification of weighted voting as *Traditional Voting*.

Quorum consensus techniques allow to balance the cost of read against write operations by adjusting the sizes of the read and write quorum appropriately. Furthermore, in static quorum schemes (as weighted voting), where the quorums are not reconfigured in response to failures, no intervention is necessary when network failures are repaired or nodes recover; i.e., failures are masked.

3.2 Key Concept of Adaptive Voting

Traditional voting blocks operations if the quorums cannot be built. However, as discussed in Sect. 1, some systems do not require strict data integrity all times, i.e., constraint consistency can be temporarily relaxed during degraded situations.

Thus, our key idea is to enhance availability of traditional voting by allowing non-critical operations even if no quorums exist, i.e., operations are allowed that may violate tradeable constraints but do not affect non-tradeable constraints. Furthermore, the new protocol called *Adaptive Voting* (AV) allows to re-adjust the quorums in degraded situations in order to support the tuning[4] of read against write operations. Since update conflicts and data integrity violations might be introduced, different policies are required to re-establish replica and constraint consistency after nodes rejoin. The replica consistency requirement for quorum consensus protocols is that a write quorum of replicas is consistent.

AV distinguishes three modes of operation: normal mode, degraded mode, and reconciliation mode. The latter can be further divided into two sub-modes: replica consistency reconciliation and constraint consistency reconciliation. The current mode of the replication protocol depends on the system state.

AV is in the *normal mode* when all nodes are reachable and all constraints are satisfied, i.e., no partitions are present and all repair activities (reconciliation) are finished.

---

[3] In this paper, we denote with $\mathbb{N}$ all positive natural numbers, i.e., zero is not included.
[4] The choice of the quorums depends on the read/write ratio and is not influenced by the data integrity constraints.

The replication protocol switches into the *degraded mode* when not all nodes are reachable. Since node and link failures cannot be distinguished [8], node failures are treated as network partitions until repair time.

AV enters *reconciliation mode* when two or more partitions rejoin. The objective of reconciliation is to re-establish replica and constraint consistency of the system. System-wide constraint consistency can only be guaranteed if all nodes are reachable (i.e., after the last rejoin of partitions). Thus, if partitions rejoin but the merged partition does not contain all nodes, only replica consistency is re-established. When the last partition rejoins[5], both replica and constraint consistency can be re-established.

4 Protocol Description

4.1 Normal Mode

In normal mode, AV behaves as the traditional voting protocol with the enhancement that constraints are checked in case of write operations.

4.2 Degraded Mode

In traditional voting, read operations are allowed if a read quorum can be acquired and write operations if a write quorum can be acquired.

AV enhances availability by allowing non-critical operations even if no quorum exists. Critical operations are treated as in the normal mode to ensure that non-tradeable constraints are never violated.

Partition Size. The behavior of AV in degraded mode depends on the size of the partition. The number of nodes within a partition is denoted as P. Thus the number of nodes outside the partition is $N - P$. We denote the quorum sizes of the healthy system (i.e., all nodes are reachable) as WQ_H and RQ_H. For the following considerations we assume that the quorums are not larger than necessary, i.e., $WQ_H + RQ_H = N + 1$, which further implies $RQ_H \leq WQ_H$.

Write and read quorum exist: If a write quorum exists in a partition, a read quorum exists as well. Outside the partition, no read or write quorum can exist.

$$N > P \geq WQ_H \geq RQ_H \qquad \Leftrightarrow \qquad N - P < RQ_H \leq WQ_H \qquad (3)$$

Both critical and non-critical operations are allowed. For critical operations, the behavior is as in the normal mode. We allow non-critical updates in other partitions even if no write quorum exists. Thus, the quorum conditions are no longer satisfied system-wide and write-write or read-write conflicts might arise. However, we avoid partition-internal conflicts by using a quorum scheme within the partition. The (partition-internal) quorums can be adjusted according to the size of the partition. We denote the reduced quorums in the partition as WQ_P and RQ_P.

---

[5] In our target application scenarios, nodes either eventually rejoin or are explicitly excluded from the system after a while, e.g., by a system administrator.

Since a read quorum RQ_H as defined in the healthy system exists, up-to-date copies of objects affected by non-tradeable constraints can be retrieved. For objects affected by tradeable constraints, the read quorum might have been reduced in the partition. Thus, performance of the read operation can be improved by reading from RQ_P. However, since updates on objects affected by tradeable constraints are allowed in all partitions, the read operation might return an object that is *possibly stale*.

Write quorum does not exist but read quorum exists: If a read quorum but no write quorum exists in the partition, outside the partition no write quorum can exist but a read quorum may exist:

$$WQ_H > P \geq RQ_H \qquad \Leftrightarrow \qquad WQ_H > N - P \geq RQ_H \qquad (4)$$

Only non-critical operations are allowed in this situation. As mentioned before, the quorum sizes can be reduced for non-critical operations since valid quorums are guaranteed only within the partition anyway.

Thus, the following steps are performed:

1. Check if one of the constraints affected by the operation is non-tradeable. If yes, the update is not allowed. Otherwise proceed.
2. Find write quorum WQ_P and apply operation.
3. Mark constraints for re-evaluation: All objects affected by tradeable constraints are possibly stale in degraded mode since updates are allowed in different partitions. Thus, the constraint check needs not to be performed since it has no significance in general. However, the constraint is marked for re-evaluation at reconciliation time.

An object is saved in a version history before it is changed in degraded mode. This allows detection of update conflicts and stepwise rollback during reconciliation in case of constraint consistency violations.

Read operations are treated as in case (3).

Write and read quorum do not exist: If no read and write quorum exist in the partition, both a read and write quorum may exist outside the partition:

$$RQ_H > P \geq 1 \qquad \Leftrightarrow \qquad N - P \geq WQ_H \geq RQ_H \qquad (5)$$

Write operations are treated as in case (4). Read operations can only be performed on a reduced read quorum RQ_P. Thus, all objects returned by a read operation are possibly stale. However, by applying the quorum conditions in the partition, it is guaranteed that subsequent read operations within a partition will return the same version.

Quorum Adjustment. AV allows updates in different partitions during degraded situations. However, within a partition, read-write and write-write conflicts shall be prevented and the tuning of read against write operations shall be supported. Thus, a quorum scheme adapted to the size of the partition is applied:

$$WQ_P + RQ_P > P \quad (6) \qquad\qquad WQ_P > \frac{P}{2} \quad (7)$$

$$WQ_P, RQ_P, P \in \mathbb{N} \quad (8) \qquad\qquad WQ_P, RQ_P \leq P \quad (9)$$

Different quorum adjustment policies can be distinguished:

Adjustment Policy 1: Maintaining read and write quorum The most obvious strategy is to maintain the quorum sizes as in the healthy system as long as possible. If the partition size P falls below WQ_H (RQ_H), the write (read) quorum is set to P:

$$WQ_P = \min(WQ_H, P) = \begin{cases} WQ_H & : \quad P \geq WQ_H \\ P & : \quad P < WQ_H \end{cases} \tag{10}$$

$$RQ_P = \min(RQ_H, P) = \begin{cases} RQ_H & : \quad P \geq RQ_H \\ P & : \quad P < RQ_H \end{cases} \tag{11}$$

Adjustment Policy 2: Proportional adjustment Adjustment policy 1 maintains the configuration of the healthy system as long as possible but with the cost that the quorums become larger than necessary. In order to maintain the read/write tuning of the healthy system, the read and write quorum in the partition can be adjusted proportional to the size of the partition. Since $RQ, WQ \in \mathbb{N}$, exact proportional adjustment is not always possible. However, to achieve "optimal" proportional adjustment,

$$\min_{RQ_P, WQ_P} \left| \frac{P}{N} - \frac{WQ_P}{WQ_H} \right| + \left| \frac{P}{N} - \frac{RQ_P}{RQ_H} \right| \tag{12}$$

needs to be solved, considering the above mentioned side conditions (6), (7), (8), (9), and $WQ_P + RQ_P = P + 1$ to minimize the quorum sizes. This discrete linear optimization problem can be solved e.g., by using the branch and bound algorithm [9].

Adjustment Policy 3: Arbitrary adjustment In principle, all adjustments are allowed, as long as the above mentioned conditions (6), (7), (8), and (9) are met.

Figure 1 gives examples for the presented quorum adjustment strategies. The horizontal axis denotes the size P of the partition, decreasing from the left side ($P = N$) to the right side ($P=1$). The vertical axis shows the sizes of the read and write quorums.

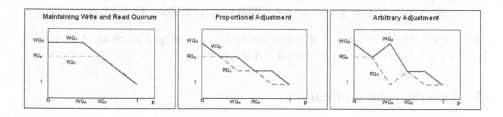

Fig. 1. Quorum adjustment policies

4.3 Reconciliation Mode

The overall goal of reconciliation is to re-establish constraint consistency. However, full constraint consistency can only be re-established if all nodes are available. Thus, if this is not the case, AV only re-establishes replica consistency in the merged partition.

Non-critical operations are not allowed in reconciliation mode, therefore availability is reduced in this mode. Thus, reconciliation should be as fast as possible. In order to avoid combinatorial explosion, we use simple (application-defined) heuristics in the reconciliation phase, e.g., to select a particular version in case of a write-write conflict. Reconciliation is performed in the following steps:

1. Re-adjustment of quorum sizes.
2. Re-establishment of replica consistency.
3. Re-establishment of constraint consistency if all nodes are available.

Re-adjustment of quorum sizes. The quorum sizes of the merged partition needs to be adjusted so that the appropriate quorum conditions are obeyed.

Re-establishment of replica consistency. AV allows non-critical updates in all partitions, even if no write quorum exists. Thus, write-write conflicts might arise. These conflicts can be detected by comparing the version lists of the partitions. If updates have occurred in only one partition, the version list of this partition is applied at a write quorum of the merged partition. In case of a conflict between the updates in the different partitions (we denote this as *replica conflict*), one of the replicas is chosen according to some pre-defined criterion (e.g., the larger partition wins). The version list of the losing partition is discarded. The version list of the winning partition is adopted by a write quorum of the merged partition.

Re-establishment of constraint consistency. System-wide constraint consistency can only be re-established if all nodes are available. If this is the case, all constraints that are marked for re-evaluation are checked again. If a constraint is violated, the following policies are defined to re-establish data integrity:

1. Constraint conflict policy 1: Stepwise rollback: Objects affected by the constraint are stepwise reverted to previous versions till the constraint is satisfied.
2. Constraint conflict policy 2: Compensation actions: In order to avoid rollbacks, application-specific compensation actions can be defined. For instance, a simple compensation action is to choose a default version in case of a conflict.

The chosen version is applied at a write quorum of the merged partition. All tentative versions are discarded, i.e., the version lists are cleaned.

5   Experimental Evaluation

Based on our availability analysis [10] we have concluded that AV yields better availability over time if reconciliation time is short in comparison to degradation time[6]. Thus, we have implemented AV in the Java-based Neko framework [11] and compare reconciliation time vs. degradation time for two different constraint conflict policies. In case of a replica conflict, the version of the partition where more updates have occurred is chosen.

---

[6] Degradation time is the period where node and/or link failures are present.

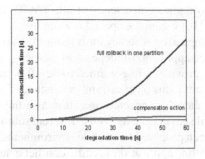

Fig. 2. Reconciliation time vs. degradation time

A simple inter-object constraint is assumed: The state of an object of class A/B is represented by an integer value a/b. For each pair of objects of class A and B, the constraint $a + b < constant$ must hold in the healthy system. The constraint is tradeable, i.e., it can be temporarily relaxed during degradation. An update operation can increment a/b by 1. The system consists of 20 nodes. The initial write quorum is 15 and the initial read quorum is 6. The system degrades into two partitions, both containing 10 nodes. The write/read quorums are adjusted to 8/3 in both partitions in order to balance read against write operations. On average, 150 invocations are started per second in each partition. a is updated in one partition and b in the other one. The total degradation time has been varied from 3 to 60 seconds. The measurements have been conducted in the Neko v0.9 simulation mode on a single machine (Pentium M, 795 MHz, 1 GB RAM, Windows XP SP2).

Figure 2 shows the lower bound of reconciliation time if a compensation action is applied and the upper bound if a roll-back strategy is applied in our example configuration. The fastest compensation action is to set default values in case of a constraint violation. If constraint consistency within the partitions is assured, the worst case for reconciliation is that a partition needs to be rolled-back completely.

The evaluation gives an indication that reconciliation time is shorter than degradation time in a configuration typical for our target applications. However, reconciliation time is highly application-specific (depending on the constraints, failure pattern, load during degradation, reconciliation policies, etc.), thus future work includes evaluation of the protocol in a real-world application scenario - the Experimental Physics and Industrial Control System (EPICS) [4].

6   Related Work

Various dynamic quorum schemes (e.g., [12, 13]) have been proposed which adapt to changes in the system due to failures. However, in contrast to our approach they are (i) pessimistic, i.e., they preserve replica consistency despite failures, and (ii) do not consider data integrity as correctness criterion.

Trading replica consistency for increased availability has been addressed in distributed object systems such as [14, 15]. However, these systems either guarantee strong replica consistency or no replica consistency at all. TACT (Tunable Availability and Consistency Trade-offs) [16] fills in the space between by providing a continuous consistency model based on logical consistency units (*conits*). The consistency level of each conit is defined using three application-independent metrics – numerical error, order error, and staleness. TACT provides a fine-grained trade-off between replica consistency and availability but does not focus on constraint consistency.

While our approach treats disconnected operation as a failure scenario, disconnections are inherent in mobile environments. Thus, different solutions for reconciliation of divergent replicas have been proposed for mobile environments: In Bayou [17], application developers need to define application-specific conflict detection and reconciliation policies. Replica consistency is re-established by an anti-entropy protocol with eventual consistency guarantees. Our approach offers the same flexibility as Bayou but offers pre-defined reconciliation policies in addition. Gray et al. [18] introduced the concept of tentative transactions: Transactions are tentatively committed on replicated data on mobile (disconnected) nodes and later applied at a master copy when the nodes rejoin. If the commit on the master copy fails, the originating node is informed why it failed. Application-specific semantics are used for conflict resolution in the mobile transaction management system presented in [19].

Besides the already mentioned differences to our approach, *all* of the above replication and reconciliation approaches and other optimistic replication systems [20] have one commonality: In contrast to our approach, they either do not address constraint consistency explicitly or presume strong data integrity.

7 Conclusion

We presented Adaptive Voting (AV), a new replication protocol based on traditional voting, that allows to balance data integrity against availability in degraded situations when node and link failures occur. The key idea of AV is to allow non-critical operations (that only affect non-critical data integrity constraints) even if the quorum conditions cannot be met. AV does not only provide adaptiveness by trading availability against constraint consistency, it also allows to re-adjust the quorum sizes in degraded situations in order to balance the cost of read against write operations within a partition. We have defined different reconciliation policies in order to re-establish replica and constraint consistency when nodes recover and network partitions rejoin.

Our availability analysis presented in [10] showed that AV provides better availability than traditional voting if (i) some of the data integrity constraints can be temporarily relaxed and (ii) reconciliation time is shorter than degradation time. Our experimental evaluation indicates that AV is beneficial in configurations typical for our target applications.

References

[1] R.H. Thomas. A majority consensus approach to concurrency control for multiple copy databases. *ACM Trans. Database Syst.*, 4(2), 1979.
[2] D.K. Gifford. Weighted voting for replicated data. In *SOSP '79: Proc. of the 7th ACM Symp. on Operating Systems Principles*, pages 150–162. ACM Press, 1979.

[3] R. Smeikal and K.M. Goeschka. Fault-tolerance in a distributed management system: a case study. In *Proc. 25th Int. Conf. on Software Engineering*, pages 478–483. IEEE, 2003.

[4] Epics - experimental physics and industrial control system. http://aps.anl.gov/epics/.

[5] J. Osrael, L. Froihofer, K.M. Goeschka, S. Beyer, P. Galdámez, and F. Muñoz. A system architecture for enhanced availability of tightly coupled distributed systems. In *Proc. of 1st Int. Conf. on Availability, Reliability, and Security*. IEEE, 2006.

[6] F. Cristian. Understanding fault-tolerant distributed systems. *Commun. ACM*, 34(2), 1991.

[7] L. Froihofer, J. Osrael, and K.M. Goeschka. Trading integrity for availability by means of explicit runtime constraints. In *Proc. 30th Int. Computer Software and Applications Conference*. IEEE, 2006.

[8] M.J. Fischer, N.A. Lynch, and M.S. Paterson. Impossibility of distributed consensus with one faulty process. *Journal of the ACM*, 32(2):374–382, 1985.

[9] S.L.K. Rountree and B.E. Gillet. Parametric integer linear programming: A synthesis of branch and bound with cutting planes. *European Journal of Operations Research*, 1982.

[10] J. Osrael, L. Froihofer, M. Gladt, and K.M. Goeschka. Availability of the adaptive voting replication protocol. Technical Report IR3.3-TUV-03, DeDiSys Consortium, 2006.

[11] P. Urban, X. Defago, and A. Schiper. Neko: a single environment to simulate and prototype distributed algorithms. In *Proc. 15th Int. Conf. on Information Networking*, pages 503–511. IEEE, 2001.

[12] S. Jajodia and D. Mutchler. Dynamic voting algorithms for maintaining the consistency of a replicated database. *ACM Trans. Database Syst.*, 15(2):230–280, 1990.

[13] J. Pâris. Voting with witnesses: A consistency scheme for replicated files. In *Proc. of the 6th Int. Conf. on Distributed Computing Systems*, pages 606–612. IEEE, 1986.

[14] P. Felber and P. Narasimhan. Reconciling replication and transactions for the end-to-end reliability of corba applications. In *Proc. of Confederated Int'l Conf. DOA, CoopIS and ODBASE 2002*, volume 2519 of *LNCS*, pages 737–754. Springer, 2002.

[15] Y. Ren, D.E. Bakken, T. Courtney, M. Cukier, D.A. Karr, P. Rubel, C. Sabnis, W.H. Sanders, R.E. Schantz, and M. Seri. Aqua: An adaptive architecture that provides dependable distributed objects. *IEEE Trans. on Computers*, 52(1):31–50, Jan. 2003.

[16] H. Yu and A. Vahdat. Design and evaluation of a conit-based continuous consistency model for replicated services. *ACM Trans. Comput. Syst.*, 20(3):239–282, 2002.

[17] D.B. Terry, M.M. Theimer, K. Petersen, A.J. Demers, M.J. Spreitzer, and C.H. Hauser. Managing update conflicts in bayou, a weakly connected replicated storage system. In *Proc. 15th ACM Symp. on Operating Systems Principles*, pages 172–182. ACM, 1995.

[18] J. Gray, P. Helland, P. O'Neil, and D. Shasha. The dangers of replication and a solution. In *Proc. Int. Conf. on Management of Data*, pages 173–182. ACM, 1996.

[19] N. Preguica, C. Baquero, F. Moura, J. Legatheaux Martins, R. Oliveira, H. Domingos, J. Pereira, and S. Duarte. Mobile transaction management in mobisap. In *Current Issues in Databases and Information Systems*, volume 1884 of *LNCS*, pages 379–386. Springer, 2000.

[20] Y. Saito and M. Shapiro. Optimistic replication. *ACM Comput. Surv.*, 37(1):42–81, 2005.

Efficient Epidemic Multicast in Heterogeneous Networks*

José Pereira[1], Rui Oliveira[1], and Luís Rodrigues[2]

[1] University of Minho
{jop, rco}@di.uminho.pt
[2] University of Lisbon
ler@di.fc.ul.pt

Abstract. The scalability and resilience of epidemic multicast, also called probabilistic or gossip-based multicast, rests on its symmetry: Each participant node contributes the same share of bandwidth thus spreading the load and allowing for redundancy. On the other hand, the symmetry of gossiping means that it does not avoid nodes or links with less capacity. Unfortunately, one cannot naively avoid such symmetry without also endangering scalability and resilience. In this paper we point out how to break out of this dilemma, by lazily deferring message transmission according to a configurable policy. An experimental proof-of-concept illustrates the approach.

1 Introduction

Epidemic multicast protocols, also known as probabilistic or gossip-based, have been proposed for information dissemination due to their scalability to large number of participants and high reliability [BHO+99, EGH+01, PRM+03]. They share at their core a simple procedure: Each item that is received by a node is relayed to a small random subset of other nodes. It can be shown that a message spreads exponentially fast and that the probability that all nodes are informed can be made as large as desired, although not 1, by adjusting configuration parameters [EGKM04]. The same approach has been used for other purposes such as aggregation and topology management [vRBV03, JB06, JKvS03].

The advantages of epidemic multicast stem from its symmetry: Each participant node contributes the same share of bandwidth thus spreading the load and allowing for large redundancy. On the other hand, the symmetry of gossiping means that it does not avoid nodes or links with less capacity, thus being hard to deploy in large and heterogeneous networks. Unfortunately, one cannot naively avoid such symmetry without also endangering scalability and resilience. Existing proposals address this by using explicit knowledge of topology to avoid redundancy on selected links [LM99] or create an additional structured overlay, restricting gossip to subsets of participants [GKG05].

In this paper we point out how to break out of this dilemma without abandoning the simple gossiping procedure. This is achieved by lazily deferring message transmission

---

* This work was partially supported by project "P-SON: Probabilistically Structured Overlay Networks" (POS_C/EIA/60941/2004).

R. Meersman, Z. Tari, P. Herrero et al. (Eds.): OTM Workshops 2006, LNCS 4278, pp. 1520–1529, 2006.

according to a configurable policy, which has a profound impact in resources used by different nodes and links. A prototype implementation allows the evaluation of several proof-of-concept policies, illustrating the approach.

The rest of this paper is organized as follows. In Section 2 we discuss different gossip strategies. In Section 3 we propose a multicast protocol that combines eager and lazy push gossip and speculate how this can be used to improve resource usage. Section 4 presents a proof-of-concept using the NeEM protocol implementation. Finally, Section 5 concludes the paper by discussing the conclusions and major open issues.

2   Background

Several variants of gossiping exist [KSSV00]. A first variant is *pull gossiping*. A node that wants to know something, contacts another node and asks for the news (e.g. "What's new?"). If the target node has learned something recently it, replies (e.g. "Italy won the world cup."). A straightforward optimization, called *two-phase pull* is to ask first news titles (e.g. "What's new?", "The world cup has a winner.") and then, selectively, pull each interesting item (e.g. "Tell me who it is."). The lazy variant is useful when the payload is large enough to offset the additional round-trip and control message overhead. This last option has been implemented in the USENET news protocol (NNTP) with the NEWNEWS and ARTICLE commands [KL86].

Alternatively, each node that knows new data contacts another node and tells it the news. Each node does this a limited number of times for each item. This is called *push gossiping*. An optimization of the push strategy, *lazy push*, is to defer the transmission of the payload. A node will therefore contact another node and identify the data (e.g. "I know who won the world cup."). If the data is unknown, full transmission is required (e.g. "Really? Tell me!"). The originator will then complete the transmission (e.g. "It was Italy."). Again, this is useful when the payload is large enough and it is likely that the data is already known. Both approaches have been implemented by NNTP [KL86]. Eager push is done with the POST command. Lazy push is done with the IHAVE command.

NNTP has however a very strict policy on which mechanism to use between each pair of hosts. First, for each connection it distinguishes between a server and a client, requiring that only the client issues commands. Namely, between two nodes, the client issues NEWNEWS and ARTICLE to download news and IHAVE to upload recent news. The POST command, and thus push, is reserved for user agent nodes, when uploading a message to a single server. This makes sense in the administratively configured, and mostly static, topology of NNTP.

3   Hybrid Push Gossip

We are now interested in combining the two push gossip strategies in an epidemic multicast protocol to improve its performance in heterogeneous networks. Specifically, during a gossip round, when forwarding a message we choose eager or lazy push independently for each target. Before introducing the algorithm, we discuss the expected impact on reliability and speculate about possible performance advantages.

3.1   Expected Impact on Reliability

The reliability of epidemic multicast is characterized by mathematical formulas that depend on gossip configuration and on fault probability [EGKM04]. Although the proposed changes don't have an impact on gossiping at an abstract level, lazy transmission impacts fault probability, as the additional round-trip and resulting increased latency, widens the window of vulnerability to network faults.

In detail, lazy transmission requires 3 individual packets exchanged in contrast with the single transmission required for eager push. Considering that each packet transmission, or eager push, is lost with a non-zero probability ϵ_e regardless of its size, and assuming that each transmission is an independent event, the probability of a lazy transmission being dropped is $\epsilon_l = 1 - (1 - \epsilon_e)^3$ and thus $\epsilon_e < \epsilon_l$. This should be accounted for when configuring protocol parameters, but has a very low impact for realistically small values of ϵ_e.

However, the probability of small control messages being lost might be smaller that the probability of loosing the entire payload. Furthermore, the probability of several messages being dropped between the same pair of nodes in a short period of time cannot be considered independent, as messages are dropped due to congestion or faulty links. Therefore it is likely that $\epsilon_l < 1 - (1 - \epsilon_e)^3$ by a fairly large margin, although $\epsilon_e < \epsilon_l$ should always hold. This is especially true in the NeEM protocol used in Section 4, due to its use of TCP/IP [PRM$^+$03], which will perform retransmission of spurious dropped packets.

3.2   Expected Impact on Performance

Intuitively lazy gossip is useful as it reduces the likelihood of transmitting the payload multiple times to the same target node. Considering the exponential nature of epidemic dissemination, which starts slowly, has a fast expansion phase and then terminates slowly again, eager gossip is less interesting during the last rounds, when a large share of target nodes have already received the message. Eager gossip is at the last rounds responsible for a large overhead, as each node receives multiple copies of the message. Likewise, lazy push is less useful during the first rounds when only a small share of target nodes has received the message and thus will certainly have to request transmission.

An obvious conclusion is that one should switch from an eager to a lazy strategy based on round number. This has been exploited in the original *pbcast* protocol [BHO$^+$99], although the preferred eager mechanism in *pbcast* is not gossip and the lazy mechanism is two-phase pull gossip. Based on identical arguments, it has been proposed that an eager push mechanism is used initially, and then switched to a pull mechanism [KSSV00].

In contrast, our proposal is based on independently configuring each transmission of a single gossip round: For each of the nodes chosen as targets for gossiping some message, one wants to query a configurable policy module for the appropriate strategy. Roughly, given a set of targets, the policy module partitions it in a lazy set and an eager set, basing its decision on some knowledge it possesses about the system and on the message itself.

```
 1  proc MULTICAST(d) do                    15  upon RECEIVE(MSG(i, d, r), s) do
 2     FORWARD(MKID(), d, 0)                 16     if i ∉ K then
                                             17        FORWARD(i, d, r)
 3  proc FORWARD(i, d, r) do
 4     DELIVER(d)                            18  upon RECEIVE(IHAVE(i), s) do
 5     K = K ∪ {i}                           19     if i ∉ K then
 6     W[i] = ∅                              20        W[i] = W[i] ∪ {s}
 7     if r < m do
 8        P = PEERSAMPLE(f)                  21  periodically, for some (i, s) : s ∈ W[i] do
 9        (E, L) = SPLIT(P, d, r)            22     SEND(IWANT(i), s)
10        for each p ∈ E do                  23     W[i] = W[i] \ {s}
11           SEND(MSG(i, d, r + 1), p)
12        C[i] = (d, r)                      24  upon RECEIVE(IWANT(i), s) do
13        for each p ∈ L do                  25     (d, r) = C[i]
14           SEND(IHAVE(i), p)               26     SEND(MSG(i, d, r + 1), p)
```

Fig. 1. Hybrid push gossip protocol

This approach has a more subtle impact on performance, which is not as easy to grasp. To help your intuition we make two assumptions, that we will not use later when evaluating the protocol. The first assumption is that the latency of a lazy round is much larger than the latency of an eager round.[1] If a source node s transmits a message m eagerly to a target t_1 and lazily to another target t_2, it is likely that t_2 ends up receiving m relayed eagerly through t_1 after several hops, instead of directly from s. This means that nodes such as t_2 will not request lazy transmission from s.

The second assumption is that message payload is so large that the overhead of lazy push, namely, the advertisement and request messages, is negligible.[2] Therefore, we conclude that traffic in the link from s to t_2 is negligible when compared to traffic in the link from s to t_1. Gossip strategy selection can therefore be used to divert the bulk of the traffic from lesser capable network links, as long as each node knows the cost of each link according to some interesting metric.

3.3 Algorithm

The algorithm to achieve this is presented in Figure 1. It uses the following variables in each node: a set K of known messages, initially empty; a map W of known source node sets for each message identifier, initially empty; a map C, holding the payload and round number for each message identifier, initially empty. It assumes also a peer sampling service providing an uniform sample of other nodes [JGKvS04]. A message m can be sent to a node p using the SEND(m, p) primitive and received by handling the RECEIVE(m, p) up-call. The strategy for each transmission is encapsulated in the SPLIT primitive described below.

---

[1] This is true to a certain extent, due to the additional round-trip required to request and perform the actual transmission plus some implementation dependent scheduling delay.

[2] This is most likely true in practice, although it depends on the application.

In detail, the algorithm works as follows. The application calls procedure MUL-TICAST(d) to multicast a message with payload d (line 1). This simply generates an unique identifier and forwards it (line 2). The identifier chosen must be unique with high probability, as conflicts will cause deliveries to be omitted. A simple way to implement this is to generate a random bit-string with sufficient length. Handling of messages received from other nodes is similar (line 15), although it is now necessary to check for and discard duplicates using the set of known identifiers K (line 16) before proceeding.

The forwarding procedure FORWARD(i, d, r) (line 3) uses the message identifier i, the payload d and the number of times, or rounds, the message has already been relayed r, which is initially 0. It starts by delivering the payload locally using the DELIVER(d) up-call. Then the message identifier is added to the set of previously known messages K (line 5) and the set of known sources $W[i]$ is cleared (line 6). These avoid multiple deliveries, as described before, and stop all retransmission requests.

Actual forwarding occurs only if the message has been forwarded less than m times (line 7) [Kol03]. Usually, using only an eager push mechanism, this would reduce to querying the peer sampling service to obtain a set of f target nodes and then sending the message, as in lines 8 and 11. Constants m and f are the usual gossip configuration parameters [EGKM04]. However, we use the SPLIT primitive (line 9) to partition the set P of node addresses in two, an eager set E and a lazy set L. Peers in set L will be sent only a message advertisement that does not contain the payload (line 14). Note that the only correctness requirement on the implementation of this primitive is that if $(E, L) = $ SPLIT(P, d, r), then $E \cup L = P$ and $E \cap L = \emptyset$. This ensures that each message is gossiped exactly f times, although some of them lazily.

Upon receiving a message advertisement for an unknown message, its source node is recorded (line 20). Periodically, a message identifier and source pair (i, s) is chosen (line 21) and a message requesting its transmission is sent (line 22). The source node is removed from $W[i]$, thus ensuring that it is used only once. Finally, when a node receives a retransmission request (line 24) it looks it up in the cache and transmits the payload (line 26). Note that a retransmission request can only be received as a consequence of a previous advertisement and thus the message is guaranteed to be locally known.

For simplicity, we do not show how identifiers are removed from set K or messages from C, preventing them from growing indefinitely. This problem has been studied before, and efficient solutions exist ensuring with high probability that no active messages are garbage collected [EGH$^+$01, Kol03].

4   Proof-of-Concept

To assess the viability of our proposal we built and experimentally evaluate a prototype. We start by lifting the assumptions used in the previous section, on latency and on size of payload, by using a homogeneous network and a relatively small message of 256 bytes. Experiments are then conducted with several selection strategies.

4.1   Experimental Setting

The protocol is built on an open source and lightweight implementation of the NeEM protocol [PRM$^+$03] that uses the java.nio API for scalability and performance [SP06].

Briefly, NeEM uses TCP/IP connections between nodes in order to avoid network congestion. When a connection blocks, messages are buffered in user space, which then uses a custom purging strategy to improve reliability. The result is a virtual connectionless layer that provides improved guarantees for gossiping.

This implementation was selected as NeEM 0.5 already supports eager and lazy push, although the later is selected only based on a message size and age threshold. Message identifiers are probabilistically unique 128 bit strings. The change required was to remove the hard-coded push strategy and query the strategy module during each gossip round.

The assumptions used in the previous section, on latency and on size of payload, are lifted by using a homogeneous network in which all nodes and links are equal, and a relatively small message payload of 256 bytes. To evaluate the impact of the proposed approach, we do however force nodes to behave as if they had diagnosed an heterogeneous network by implementing several strategies, which impose different static assumptions on network capacity:

ADSL Assume that half of the nodes have asymmetric connections with limited uplink bandwidth to all other nodes. These nodes use only lazy push. The other, assumed have symmetric connections, use only eager pushing.

"Reverse" ADSL Assume that half of the nodes have asymmetric connections with limited down-link bandwidth to all other nodes. Messages directed at these nodes always use lazy pushing. Messages to others are eagerly pushed.

Two ISPs Assume that each half of the nodes is in a different network, with a costly connection between them. Messages traversing to a different network are lazy pushed. Otherwise, within the network, are eagerly pushed.

We have also tested NeEM in its original configuration, which captures the obvious intuition that eager push should be used in the initial rounds. As a baseline, we have also configured the protocol to always do lazy push and always do eager push.

We then ran 200 protocol nodes in a machine with 2 AMD Opteron processors and 4GB RAM. The protocol was configured with gossip fanout of 11 and overlay fanout of 15. These correspond to a probability 0.995 of atomic delivery with 1% messages dropped, and a probability of 0.999 of connectedness when 15% of nodes fail [EGKM04]. Request for retransmissions are done with a uniform random interval between 0 and 200 ms. Each run consists of a 30 second warm-up period, while the overlay is formed and settles down, a 100 second test period, while 200 messages are transmitted with a 500ms interval, one by each node, and finally a 10 second cool-down period. All bytes transmitted, messages relayed and messages delivered during the 100 second period are recorded for later processing.

While tests run, there are at least 1500 TCP/IP sockets active, corresponding to 3000 open file descriptors. As each NeEM instance uses only one thread, there are 200 protocol threads plus 200 application threads running. We observe that this corresponds to approximately 50% processor load and about 1GB memory. This includes extensive logs performed on every I/O operation.

Results were confirmed by repeating them and running similar experiments in different hardware and software configurations with identical conclusions. Significance of the results is also improved by the size of the samples: Each run considers 40000 message deliveries, over 20000 TCP/IP connections, and close to half a million network packets transmitted.

4.2 Results

We collected several different metrics presented in Figure 2. All are presented as empirical cumulative distribution functions: The x-axis shows the metric and the y-axis shows the ratio of samples that were measured less or equal any specific value. A small variance is thus depicted as a close to vertical line and a multi-modal distribution as staircase function.

In detail, Figures 2(a) and 2(b) show the amount of network resources used by each message delivery, respectively, the average number of bytes sent and received. Given that each message carries 256 bytes payload, this clearly shows the amount of overhead. Figure 2(c) shows end-to-end delivery latency measured at the application level, considering all deliveries to all nodes. As a side effect, a large slant indicates high jitter. This provides a measurement of quality of service.

Figure 2(d) is computed as follows. For each delivered message, we take the path from sender to delivery. Then, we truncate the first and last nodes (which are invariably the sender and the target). We then count how many times each node appears in such paths that lead to delivery. The result for each node is divided by the number of messages that it has delivered. This gives us a measure of how much a node contributes to the effort required to spread messages. This should be compared with the amount of bytes transmitted, to determine whether a large amount of bytes is a large contribution or simply overhead.

We start by discussing the symmetric protocols: baseline eager and lazy push, as well as NeEM 0.5 default. These use the same strategy for all transmissions in a gossip round. The lazy push strategy achieves low network traffic at the expense of offering also the worst latency. In contrast, the eager push strategy results in a very large number of bytes transmitted, while achieving second best latency. Most interestingly, the relay count is close, showing that most of bytes transmitted are simply redundancy.

The NeEM 0.5 default is an interesting compromise, as it is the strategy that generates the lowest network traffic while providing good latency to half of deliveries, i.e. those that are served during the initial push gossip phase. It provides also extremely good fairness when distributing the load. Actually, the average number of bytes transmitted is very close to the absolute minimum of a single payload transmission (256 bytes) plus 11 headers (11×20 bytes). When compared with lazy push, half of the processes getting the entire payload earlier should also improve reliability.

The *Two ISPs* test shows how effective the technique can be: Compared with the eager push run, the overhead is cut in half with little impact in delivery latency. Better yet, the traffic on assumed inter-ISP links is severely reduced, even when compared to lazy push. This is shown in Table 1, which depicts the amount of data transmitted during the lifetime of a connection. Only the *Two ISPs* produces a statistically significant mean difference, as can easily be confirmed by running a test with a confidence level of 0.95.

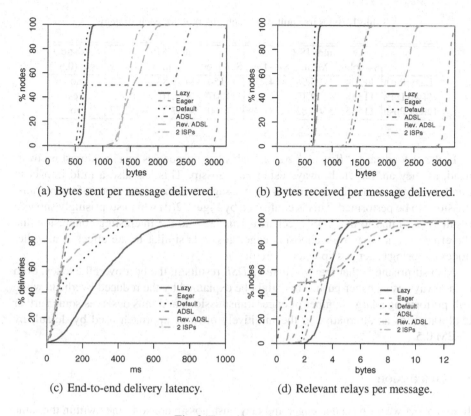

(a) Bytes sent per message delivered.

(b) Bytes received per message delivered.

(c) End-to-end delivery latency.

(d) Relevant relays per message.

Fig. 2. Experimental results

This happens as these links are seldom used to convey actual data, but only lazy push advertisements.

We now look at the *ADSL* and *"Reverse" ADSL* strategies. As expected, there is a sharp contrast between the two halves of nodes, but there are some unexpected results. In the first case, *ADSL*, half of the processes send a much lower amount of bytes, while the others produce a large amount of overhead. Actually the later use the exact same strategy as in the eager push experiment, but surprisingly, the amount of data transmitted is lower. The fact that some processes are using lazy push reduces the amount of data transmitted by the remaining processes that use always eager push.

This can be explained by deliveries occurring after a larger number of rounds, in average, as more hops through symmetric processes are required. This happens because asymmetric processes contribute later than they would in the eager push scenario, thus implicitly increasing the share of the remaining. A larger number of processes thus delivers messages in round m and does not gossip again, reducing network usage. A small number of processes has to wait for lazy transmissions, resulting in a longer tail in latency distribution. This is confirmed by Figure 2(d), where a number of processes does not contribute at all to deliveries, while others contribute a much larger share.

Table 1. Bytes transmitted in each link type for each strategy

	Intra-ISP			Inter-ISP			Statistical
	Samples	Mean	Std. Dev.	Samples	Mean	Std. Dev.	sign. (0.95)
Lazy Push	11264	1195.98	1147.79	11154	1192.83	1159.21	no
Two ISPs	11348	4119.17	3720.95	11207	859.10	908.83	yes
Eager Push	11545	5364.82	4781.49	11260	5337.21	4812.57	no

In the second case, *"Reverse" ADSL*, half of the processes receive almost no overhead, as they are targeted always using lazy gossip. This has also a mild impact in number of bytes transmitted, as receiving messages earlier causes more effective transmissions to be performed. This is confirmed by Figure 2(d) which surprisingly shows a result very similar to the ADSL scenario. This leads to the interesting conclusion that the effect of a node p itself choosing eager gossip is similar to the effect of all other nodes choosing eager gossip when targetting p.

Also surprising is that the *"Reverse" ADSL* results in the best overall latency, even than always using eager push. This might be explained by the reduced overhead while still performing a large number of eager transmissions and thus deserves some further exploration as an alternative to the intuitively obvious approach used by default by NeEM 0.5.

5 Discussion

In this paper we propose that eager and lazy push gossip are combined within the same round by encapsulating the choice in a configurable strategy module. This proposal is aimed at better matching resource usage with resource availability in epidemic multicast, thus improving performance in heterogeneous networks.

Although the presented experiments use simple policies, that build on static global knowledge of the network, they show that relevant results can be obtained (i.e. reduction of backbone traffic in the *Two ISPs* test) and that it is possible to control both the amount of data received and sent (i.e. the *ADSL* and *"Reverse" ADSL* tests). They also point out some surprising consequences of the approach, namely, how nodes are indirectly affected by other node's choices and how even a seemingly trivial policy produces a large impact in latency.

Note also that the proposed experimental framework, despite simple, is not the best case scenario. An heterogeneous network would help, for instance, by delaying lazy push on slower links thus further highlighting the impact of laziness. This is being addressed by testing on a realistic large scale network infrastructure.

Finally, what is the best policy and how to implement it deriving the required knowledge about the system in a scalable and efficient fashion, is still an open question. There are previous examples of how this can be achieved, namely, by building on local knowledge extracted from the network [PRPO04] and by using gossip itself to build global knowledge [RSP+03, JB06, MKG03, GKG05].

References

[BHO+99]   K. Birman, M. Hayden, O. Ozkasap, Z. Xiao, M. Budiu, and Y. Minsky. Bimodal multicast. *ACM Trans. Computer Systems*, 17(2), May 1999.

[EGH+01]   P. Eugster, R. Guerraoui, S. Handrukande, A.-M. Kermarrec, and P. Kouznetsov. Lightweight probabilistic broadcast. In *Proc. IEEE Intl. Conf. Dependable Systems and Networks (DSN)*, 2001.

[EGKM04]   P. Eugster, R. Guerraoui, A.-M. Kermarrec, and L. Massoulie. From epidemics to distributed computing. *IEEE Computer*, May 2004.

[GKG05]   I. Gupta, A.-M. Kermarrec, and A.J. Ganesh. Efficient and adaptive epidemic-style protocols for reliable and scalable multicast. *IEEE Trans. Parallel and Distributed Systems*, 2005.

[JB06]   M. Jelasity and O. Babaoglu. T-Man: Gossip-based overlay topology management. In *Proc. 3rd Intl. Ws. Engineering Self-Organising Applications (ESOA'05)*. Springer-Verlag, 2006.

[JGKvS04]   M. Jelasity, R. Guerraoui, A.-M. Kermarrec, and M. van Steen. The peer sampling service: Experimental evaluation of unstructured gossip-based implementations. In *Proc. 5th ACM/IFIP/USENIX Intl. Conf. Middleware*, 2004.

[JKvS03]   M. Jelasity, W. Kowalczyk, and M. van Steen. Newscast computing. Technical Report IR-CS-006.03, Vrije Universiteit Amsterdam, 2003.

[KL86]   B. Kantor and P. Lapsley. RFC 977: Network News Transfer Protocol. Internet Engineering Task Force, 1986.

[Kol03]   B. Koldehofe. Buffer management in probabilistic peer-to-peer communication protocols. In *Proc. IEEE Symp. Reliable Distributed Systems (SRDS)*, 2003.

[KSSV00]   R. Karp, C. Schindelhauer, S. Shenker, and B. Vocking. Randomized rumor spreading. In *IEEE Symp. Foundations of Computer Science*, 2000.

[LM99]   M.-J. Lin and K. Marzullo. Directional gossip: Gossip in a wide area network. In *Proc. European Dependable Computing Conf. (EDCC)*, 1999.

[MKG03]   L. Massoulié, A.-M. Kermarrec, and A. Ganesh. Network awareness and failure resilience in self-organising overlays networkss. In *Proc. IEEE Symp. Reliable Distributed Systems (SRDS'04)*, 2003.

[PRM+03]   J. Pereira, L. Rodrigues, M. J. Monteiro, R. Oliveira, and A.-M. Kermarrec. NeEM: Network-friendly epidemic multicast. In *Proc. IEEE Symp. Reliable Distributed Systems (SRDS)*, 2003.

[PRPO04]   J. Pereira, L. Rodrigues, A. Pinto, and R. Oliveira. Low-latency probabilistic broadcast in wide area networks. In *Proc. IEEE Symp. Reliable Distributed Systems (SRDS'04)*, October 2004.

[RSP+03]   L. Rodrigues, S.Handrukande, J. Pereira, R. Guerraoui, and A.-M. Kermarrec. Adaptive gossip-based broadcast. In *Proc. IEEE Intl. Conf. Distributed Systems and Networks (DSN)*, 2003.

[SP06]   P. Santos and J. Pereira. NeEM version 0.5. http://neem.sf.net, 2006.

[vRBV03]   R. van Renesse, K. Birman, and W. Vogels. Astrolabe: A robust and scalable technology for distributed system monitoring, management, and data mining. *ACM Trans. Computer Systems*, 21(2):164–206, May 2003.

Decentralized Resources Management for Grid

Thibault Bernard, Alain Bui, Olivier Flauzac, and Cyril Rabat

SysCom, CReSTIC
Université de Reims Champagne-Ardenne
BP1039, F-51687 Reims Cedex 2, France
{thibault.bernard, alain.bui, olivier.flauzac, cyril.rabat}@univ-reims.fr

Abstract. Among all components of a grid or peer-to-peer application, the resources management is unavoidable. Indeed, new resources like computational power or storage capacity must be quickly and efficiently integrated. This management can be achieved either by a fully centralized way (*BOINC*) or by a hierarchical way (*Globus, DIET*). In the latter case, there is a greater flexibility and a greater scalability. But the counterpart is the difficulty to design and to deploy such a solution, particularly if the resources are volatile.

In this article, we combine random walks and circulating word to derive a fully distributed solution to the resources management. Random walks have proved their efficiency in distributed computing and are well suited to dynamical networks like peer-to-peer or grid networks. There is no condition on nodes lifetime and we need only one application for each node.

1 Introduction

The aim of grid computing is to share resources for a global use. These resources can be in a local network or widely distributed over the Internet. Since few years, a lot of solutions have been proposed and each one is adapted to a specific grid application.

The authors of [1] have identified several kinds of grid applications. Among all of them, the *on-demand computing* needs a good cost-performance ratio rather than an absolute performance. At the opposite, the *distributed supercomputing* needs a lot of computing resources and generally this kind of grid gathers supercomputers. So, the resources management highly depends on the application that uses the grid and must be adapted in function.

In [2], the authors define the resources management as the localization and allocation of computational resources, process creation and resource preparation. They propose a complete architecture composed by resource brokers, resource co-allocators and resource managers. These components are integrated to the *Globus Toolkit* ([3]). So, the resources management is distributed and needs a hierarchy of components. For the middleware *DIET* ([4]), the authors choose to organize a hierarchy of servers called *agents*. Even if distributed methods are more scalable and flexible, the hierarchy of *Globus* and *DIET* can be hard to

R. Meersman, Z. Tari, P. Herrero et al. (Eds.): OTM Workshops 2006, LNCS 4278, pp. 1530–1539, 2006.

configure. How many components or agents we need and where they have to be installed?

A peer-to-peer approach has been proposed in [5] that lets the nodes in charge of the grid functions (resources management and scheduling). Another fully distributed method is proposed for the *CONFIIT* middleware ([6]): the nodes are gathered in a virtual ring and the topology management is assumed by a token circulation.

Our solution concerns wide volatile grids like desktop grids that are well suited to the on-demand computing. This kind of grid is composed of many computers that have a limited and heterogeneous computing power and a high volatility. No assumption is made on the nodes lifetime. The network has a low and variable bandwidth. So it is important to limit the number of exchanged messages. In these conditions, the random walk has already proved its efficiency. In [7], the authors use it in peer-to-peer networks for searching and building dynamical topology. Adaptation to dynamical environments is also a quality of the random walks: in [8], a solution for routing in ad-hoc networks is proposed. So, our resources management combines a random walk of a token and a circulating word to avoid the maintenance of virtual structures. It allows the detection of connection or lost of connection of resources and localization of specific resources corresponding to a request.

2 Preliminaries

A model for grid. In [9], we propose a model composed of 5 layers to analyze grid applications. The three lower layers concern the network, the routing and the messages exchange protocols. Layer 4 represents the resources management for the grid and the last one the other grid components (scheduling, monitoring, ...). Even if the solution we expose here is for Layer 4, a grid is built over three other layers and we have to take care of their impacts for the resources management. We show that we can model a grid by a *directed* graph $G = (V, E)$, where V is a set of active nodes of the grid with $|V| = n$ and E is the set of directed communication links. An active node is a resource or a node that uses resources. In the following, we use the terms "resource", "node" and "active node" interchangeably.

A communication link (i, j) exists if and only if j is a neighbor of i in the grid, i.e. i can directly send a message to j. Every node i can distinguish all its links of communication and maintains a set of neighbors denoted N_i. We consider that all resources of the grid have a distinct identity (IP address, for example or a complete description with a specific language like *RSL* [2], in that case an indexation is needed to have better performances).

As G is a communication graph, we assume it is strongly connected. Indeed, if the graph is not strongly connected at a time, there exists a sink subgraph $E(G)$: resources of $G \backslash E(G)$ cannot be reached from any node of $E(G)$. For a token circulation, it means that the token will stay in $E(G)$ and cannot reach nodes of $G \backslash E(G)$. With our method, we accept that the graph stays not strongly connected during a short time. If this transient state is too long, unreachable resources will be considered as disconnected.

Random walks. A random walk is a sequence of nodes visited by a token that starts at i and visits other resources according to the following transition rule: if the token is at i at time t then at time $t + 1$, it will be at one of the neighbors of i, chosen uniformly at random among N_i ([10,11]). Similarly to deterministic distributed algorithms, the time complexity of random walk based token circulation algorithms can be viewed as the number of "steps" it takes for the algorithm to achieve the network traversal. With only one walk at a time (which is the case we deal), it is also equal to the message complexity. The cover time C — the average time to visit all nodes in the system — and the hitting time denoted by h_{ij} — the average time to reach a node j for the first time starting from a given node i — are two important values that appear in the analysis of random walk-based distributed algorithms. Both of them are on average bounded by n^3. There are three properties about random walks: *percussion* – an arbitrary node is visited in a finite time, *coverage* – all nodes are visited in a finite time and *meeting* – several random walks will meet each other in a finite time. We have proposed a method to compute such values in [12].

3   Resources Management

We propose a fully distributed algorithm that maintains the set of grid resources and paths to reach them from any nodes of the grid. It is based on the token random moves. As it circulates perpetually, the set of grid resources and paths are maintained through a circulating word and are automatically updated.

3.1   Circulating Word Management

A *circulating word* is a token message collecting pieces of information along its moves through the grid. This concept has been introduced in [13]. The author presents the detection of all the communication graph cycles with the evaluation of the collected information of circulating words successively broadcasted by all nodes. Indeed, each node can build the path of received token thanks to the circulating word content.

We propose to use this concept in order to maintain a partial image of the grid communication graph. Such an image can be used to reach a resource corresponding to a specific request from a node. In [14], we address the problem of routing tables computation (i.e. maintain paths between each pair of nodes) but in an undirected environment. Because we focus on directed communications according to our model, we have to propose a new circulating word information management.

We note W_i the ith element of the circulating word W. Several functions are used to manage W. $size(W)$ returns the size of the word and $identities(W)$ returns the set of the distinct resources identities contained in the word. To add an element e at the first position (at left), we use the function $add(W, e)$.

$remove(W, i, j)$ deletes the subword $< W_i, ..., W_j >$. Finally, functions $left(W, k)$ and $right(W, k)$ return respectively the subwords $< W_1, ..., W_k >$ and $< W_k, ... , W_{size(W)} >$.

In order to collect the visited resources identities, each time the token moves, the current identity is added in the word at the first position (at the left). With the word content, a node can eventually compute a path from it to others resources. Particularly, it is possible to build from a specific position in the word paths from a specific resource to all others visited resources. The position of this element is called *minimal position*.

Definition 1. *The* minimal position *noted* pos_{min} *of word* W *satisfies:*

$$pos_{min} = \min \{i \in [1, size(W)] \, | \forall k \in identities(W), \exists j \le i, W_j = k\}$$

From pos_{min}, we can build a (partial) spanning tree rooted in $W_{pos_{min}}$. But it is insufficient to construct paths between each pair of nodes unless there exists a path from W_1 to $W_{pos_{min}}$. If there exists j such that $W_1 = W_j$ and $pos_{min} < j$, such a path exists. So, we have a cycle $< W_1, \ldots, W_{pos_{min}}, \ldots, W_j >$.

Definition 2. *Word* W *contains a cycle if there exists* $(i, j) \in \{1, \ldots, size(W)\}^2$, $i < j$ *and* $W_i = W_j$. *We note this cycle* $\mathcal{C}(i, j)$.

If all visited nodes identities are contained in a cycle $\mathcal{C}(i, j)$, we can construct a path between each visited node.

Definition 3. *A cycle noted* $\mathcal{C}(i, j)$ *in Word* W *is called constructive if:*

$$\forall k \in identities(W), \exists l \in \{i, \ldots, j\} | W_l = k$$

Remark 1. The first constructive cycle is reached when the token comes back to the first visited node.

Getting a constructive cycle is sufficient but not necessary to construct paths between visited nodes. For instance, the word $< 1, 2, 3, 1, 4, 3 >$ does not contain a constructive cycle, but we have paths between each pair of nodes. By combining two non-constructive cycles, we can build a constructive cycle: $< 3, 1, 4, 3 >$ is rotated and becomes $< 1, 4, 3, 1 >$ and with the cycle $< 1, 2, 3, 1 >$, the word becomes $< 1, 2, 3, 1, 4, 3, 1 >$ that contains a constructive cycle.

We decide to base our resources management on a constructive cycle maintenance inside the circulating word to reduce the complexity.

3.2   Constructive Cycle Maintenance

As the construction of all paths between resources does not require information beyond the constructive cycle, older information (at its right) can be deleted. But not the part at its left: it allows its evolution and thus to handle dynamicity.

Inside the constructive cycle, we can found useless information. But it is not possible to delete it easily. If we delete the subword $< W_i, \ldots, W_j >$, the link

(W_{i-1}, W_{j+1}) appears in the word and the node cannot verify if it exists in the communication graph of the grid. But, if W owns a cycle $\mathcal{C}(i,j)$, we can delete the subword $< W_{i+1}, \ldots, W_j >$ because the link (W_i, W_{j+1}) really exists. So, if information in $\mathcal{C}(i,j)$ is useless, we can delete this cycle called *non-constructive*.

Definition 4. *A cycle $\mathcal{C}(i,j)$ is called non-constructive if $\forall k, i < k < j, \exists (l > j) \vee (l < i) | W_k = W_l$*

In order to reduce all non-constructive cycles in the constructive cycle, we use Algorithm 1. For each identity of the word, the algorithm searches the same identity at the left. If it exists, the word contains a cycle. Then the algorithm checks if it is non-constructive. In fact, it has to search all identities of the cycle (the set $\mathcal{V}_C$) outside. To speed up this search, a set $\mathcal{V}$ is maintained that contains the identities at the right of the current identity.

Algorithm 1. Reduction of non-constructive cycles in a circulating word W

```
V ← ∅
pos ← size(W)
while pos > 2 do
   V ← V ∪ W_pos
   i ← pos - 1 /* We search a cycle C(i, pos) */
   V_C ← ∅
   while (i > 1) ∧ (W_i ≠ W_pos) do
      if W_i ∉ V then
         V_C ← V_C ∪ W_i
      i ← i - 1
   if W_i = W_pos then
      j ← i - 1 /* Cycle found : searching the elements of Vc at the left of i */
      while (j ≥ 1) ∧ (V_C ≠ ∅) do
         V_C ← V_C/W_j
         j ← j - 1
      if V_C = ∅ then
         remove(W, i + 1, pos) /* The cycle C(i, pos) is a non-constructive cycle */
         pos ← i
      else
         pos ← pos - 1
   else
      pos ← pos - 1
```

Lemma 1. *The size of the constructive cycle is bounded by $\frac{n^2}{4} + n$.*

Proof. We note i the identity which appears the most in the constructive cycle and k the number of occurrences of i. So, there are $k - 1$ cycles that are **not** non-constructive in the constructive cycle (else these cycles would have been reduced). So there are $k - 1$ identities that appear only one time in the constructive cycle and $n - (k - 1)$ identities that appear at most k times (by definition of k). The size of the word can be write in function of k: $T(k) = (k - 1) + (n - (k - 1)) * k = -k^2 + (n + 2)k - 1$. $T(k)$ has a maximum when $T'(k)$ equals 0: $T'(k) = 0 \Leftrightarrow k = \frac{n+2}{2}$. Then:

$$T_{max} = \begin{cases} \frac{n^2+4n}{4} & \text{if } n \text{ is even} \\ \frac{n^2+4n-1}{4} & \text{if } n \text{ is odd} \end{cases}$$

3.3   General Description of the Algorithm

The algorithm is divided in 3 different phases: the *initialization phase* consists in adding identities until obtaining a constructive cycle, the *maintenance phase* aims to maintain and let it evolve and the *collect phase* is an intermediary phase that consists in maintaining a maximal cycle that speeds up the construction of a constructive cycle when a new identity is discovered.

Initialization Phase. During this phase, information is collected in the word in order to build a constructive cycle. Then, the algorithm passes in the maintenance phase. At each move of the token, we reduce non-constructive cycles thanks to Algorithm 1 in order to limit the size of the token.

The percussion property of random walks ensures that the token will return on the first visited node. So, by Remark 1, a constructive cycle will be created and the algorithm will reach the maintenance phase. In fact Algorithm 1 can just be executed at this time.

Remark 2. The deletion of non-constructive cycles during this phase reduces the token size but some constructive information may be deleted. For instance, the word $< 3, 4, 1, 3, 1, 2, 1 >$ contains a non-constructive cycle $< 1, 3, 1 >$. If such a cycle is removed, it is no longer possible to build path between 3 and 4. But the set *identities*(W) is not modified and as described in the following, a constructive cycle finally appears.

Maintenance Phase. In this phase, the word contains a constructive cycle. The aim is to let it evolve in order to adapt it to topological changes (resource connection or disconnection). So, when the token comes in a node, its identity is added at the left of the constructive cycle (this part is called the *head*) until a new one is built. When i identities have been added, the word has the following structure:

$$< \underbrace{W_1, \ldots, W_i}_{head}, \underbrace{W_{i+1}, \ldots, W_{size(W)}}_{\mathcal{C}_C(i+1, size(W))} >$$

At each addition, either **the identity is a new one** so the constructive cycle is broken and the algorithm enters the collect phase or **the identity already appears in the word** and the algorithm verifies if a reduction is possible (a non-constructive cycle or a new constructive cycle).

Remark 3. The search of non-constructive cycles must be achieved only in the head else it could induce a loss of relevant information. For example, the word $< 4, 2, 1, 5, 2, 4, 2, 3, 1 >$ contains a constructive cycle $< 1, 5, 2, 4, 2, 3, 1 >$ and a non-constructive cycle $< 2, 4, 2 >$. If we remove this last one, Identity 4 disappears of the constructive cycle.

Property 1. If a word contains a constructive cycle $\mathcal{C}_C(i + 1, size(W))$, then all cycles $\mathcal{C}(j, k)$ with $j < k \le i + 1$ are non-constructive.

This property improves the search of non-constructive cycles. If we apply such a reduction, it ensures the only possible non-constructive cycle is $C(1, j)$ with $j \leq i + 1$. Moreover $size(left(W, i))$ becomes bounded by $n - 2$.

If a non-constructive cycle is found, then the constructive cycle is not modified. Else, we have to search if a new one appears.

Property 2. If a word contains a constructive cycle $C_C(i + 1, size(W))$, then the minimal position is inside $C_C(i + 1, size(W))$.

Property 3. Assume a word contains a constructive cycle $C_C(i + 1, size(W))$. If a new element is added to the word and if a new constructive cycle appears, its right bound is in $[pos_{min}, size(W)]$.

We have only to search W_j, the right bound of the new constructive cycle, in the part $< W_{pos_{min}}, \ldots, W_{size(W)} >$. In this subword, we cannot have any cycle and W_1 cannot appear (else a new constructive cycle is built). So, $right(W, pos_{min})$ is bounded by $n - 2$. Finally, the maintenance phase has only to analyze the subwords $< W_1, \ldots, W_i >$ and $< W_{pos_{min}}, \ldots, W_{size(W)} >$ then only n identities.

Collect Phase. To improve the construction of a new constructive cycle, we maintain a maximal cycle. So, we have the following structure:

$$W_1, \ldots, W_i, \ldots, W_k \text{ with } k = size(W) \text{ and } C(i, size(W)) \text{ the maintained cycle}$$

So, in this phase, we only add new identities until an identity already appears in this cycle. Then, we can easily rewrite the word:

$$W_1, \ldots, W_i, \ldots, W_j, \ldots, W_k, \ldots, W_j \text{ with } W_j = W_1$$

We have a new constructive cycle and the algorithm can return to the maintenance phase after reducing non-constructive cycles.

Main Algorithm. From the circulating word, the main algorithm can detect in which phase it is. This detection depends on the minimal position. If $pos_{min} = size(W)$, the algorithm is in the initialization phase. Else we search from W_1 a position i such $W_i = W_{size(W)}$. Then, $C(i, size(W))$ can be a maximal cycle or a constructive cycle. We verify if W_1 exists in this cycle then the algorithm is in the maintenance phase else the algorithm is in the collect phase.

3.4 Faults Management

Each fault that occurs in a grid must be managed to avoid unreachable resources. There are different kinds of faults that can be gathered in two main categories: topological changes and communication faults.

Topological Changes. As specified in Section 2, each node i manages its neighborhood denoted by N_i and if a network change occurs like a resource disconnection, N_i is updated and no other operation has to be done. Netherthelese a global topological information is stored in the token then a network change can produce erroneous paths. So, at the reception of the token, the node has to check locally the consistency between its neighborhood and the topological information contained in the word.

For instance, if a link (W_i, W_j) exists in the word and if Node W_j does not appear in N_{W_i}, Node W_i detects an inconsistence and has to correct the word. It removes the subword $< W_{k+1}, \ldots, W_j >$ where W_k is the first neighbor of Node W_i at its left. For instance, if Node 4 has $N_4 = \{1, 2\}$ and if the word is $< 1, 2, 3, 4, 2, 4 >$, there is an inconsistency and Node 4 reduces the word to $< 1, 2, 4, 2, 4 >$.

Remark 4. The correction of the word is done with local knowledge and some inconsistencies cannot be corrected. The circulation of the token will ensure that all concerned nodes apply this correction. Then all inconsistencies will be deleted.

Communication Faults. The first kind of communication faults concerns the *loss of a message*. To avoid the lack of token in the system, we place a timeout in each node, that is reseted on a token visit. On timeout triggering, the associated node produces a new empty token. The initial timeout value is very important. A good value is around $max_{(i,j) \in V^2} \{h(i,j)\}$ which is the average time to hit an arbitrary node.

Finally, we have to manage the *duplication of a message*. The timeout procedure described previously can produce a new token even if a token is already alive in the network. In order to reduce the bandwidth consumption the number of tokens should be reduced by keeping only one of them. To speed up the integration of new resources, the algorithm should also merge the topological information gathered by these tokens. The merge can be achieved easily if there is at least one constructive cycle in one of the tokens. If the merge can not be achieved, the two tokens continue their walks.

When the algorithm compares the two circulating words $W1$ and $W2$, it compares the sets *identities*$(W1)$ and *identities*$(W2)$ in order to build the largest (partial) image of the communication graph. So, if *identities*$(W1)$ is included inside *identities*$(W2)$, $W1$ can be dropped (all resources are already known by W_2). On the other hand, the algorithm merges the two words by inserting the constructive cycle of $W1$ inside $W2$. Because the token are on Node i, they share Identity i so such an insertion is always possible as soon as the element at the bound of a constructive cycle is the current node. If not, we can rotate it as described in Section 3.2.

4   Resources Localization

Resources management also consists in localization of a resource corresponding to a specific request. From the topological information of the circulating word, it is possible to build spanning structures. In particular, if the word contains a constructive cycle, we can build a spanning tree from each node. This construction is achieved by Algorithm 2.

Algorithm 2. Construction of a spanning tree $\mathcal{T}$ rooted on Node *root* from a circulating word W

```
set_root(T, root)
i ← 1
pos ← 1
while i < size(W) do
    while (i < size(W)) ∧ (Wᵢ ∉ T) do
        i ← i + 1 /* Node Wᵢ is not in the tree */
    if Wᵢ ∈ T then
        j ← i − 1 /* Adding the new branch rooted on i */
        while j ≥ pos do
            if Wⱼ ∉ T then
                add_tree(T, Wⱼ, Wⱼ₊₁)
            j ← j − 1
    i ← i + 1
    pos ← i
```

If a node needs to localize a specific resource of the grid, we can use the wave with feedback mechanism like *DIET*. It means that the request is sent along a spanning tree. The corresponding resource can reply along this same tree. But with our model, the grid is modeled as a directed graph and the spanning tree is not valid for the reply. So, we need two different trees: a diffusion tree $\mathcal{T}_D$ computed by Algorithm 2 and a feedback tree $\mathcal{T}_F$. Whereas $\mathcal{T}_D$ is directed from the request node to resources, $\mathcal{T}_F$ is directed from resources to the request node. The first identity of the circulating word is the request node one so, for construction of $\mathcal{T}_F$, each identity of the word is added as the son of its left identity.

If a node needs a specific resource, at the token reception, it builds $\mathcal{T}_D$ and $\mathcal{T}_F$. Then, it can send its request along $\mathcal{T}_D$ ($\mathcal{T}_F$ must be diffused in this request). Each node that receives this request can reply along $\mathcal{T}_F$. Then, the emitter can select among the set of the free corresponding resources.

5   Conclusion

We propose in this article, a resources management for wide and volatile grids. Contrary to many others resources managements, our solution is fully distributed. It is based on random walk and circulating word. No centralization on a node is needed and no hierarchy has to be deployed. So, it limits the waste of computational power. On the other hand, we take into account directed communications in order to maximize the resources localization and aggregation.

References

1. I. Foster and C. Kesselman, Eds., *The Grid: Blueprint for a Future Computing Infrastructure*. Morgan Kaufman Publishers, September 1999.
2. K. Czajkowski, I. Foster, N. Karonis, C. Kesselman, S. Martin, W. Smith, and S. Tuecke, "A Resource Management Architecture for Metacomputing Systems," in *The 4th Workshop on Job Scheduling Strategies for Parallel Processing*, ser. LNCS, vol. 1459. Springer-Verlag, 1998, pp. 62–82.

3. I. Foster and C. Kesselman, "Globus : a metacomputing infrastructure toolkit," in *Supercomputer Applications*, I. Press, Ed., vol. 11 (2), 1997, pp. 115–128.
4. E. Caron, F. Desprez, F. Lombard, J.-M. Nicod, M. Quinson, and F. Suter, "A Scalable Approach to Network Enabled Servers," in *Proceedings of the 8th International EuroPar Conference*, ser. LNCS, vol. 2400.   Springer-Verlag, 2002, pp. 907–910.
5. J. Cao, O. M. K. Kwong, X. Wang, and W. Cai, "A Peer-to-Peer Approach to Task Scheduling in Computation Grid." in *GCC (1)*, ser. LNCS, vol. 3032.   Springer-Verlag, 2004, pp. 316–323.
6. O. Flauzac, M. Krajecki, and J. Fugere, "CONFIIT : a middleware for peer to peer computing," in *ICCSA 2003*, ser. LNCS, vol. 2669.   Springer-Verlag, 2003, pp. 69–78.
7. C. Gkantsidis, M. Mihail, and A. Saberi, "Random Walks in Peer-to-Peer Networks," in *INFOCOM*, 2004.
8. W. Choi, S. Das, J. Cao, and A. Datta, "Randomized dynamic route maintenance for adaptive routing multihop mobile ad hoc networks," *Journal of Parallel and Distributed Computing*, vol. 65, pp. 107–123, 2005.
9. C. Rabat, A. Bui, and O. Flauzac, "A random walk topology management solution for grid," in *II2CS*, ser. LNCS, vol. 3908.   Springer-Verlag, 2006, pp. 91–104.
10. L. Lovasz, "Random walks on graphs: A survey," in *Combinatorics: Paul Erdos is Eighty (vol. 2)*.   Janos Bolyai Mathematical Society, 1993, pp. 353–398.
11. R. Aleliunas, R. Karp, R. Lipton, L. Lovasz, and C. Rackoff, "Random walks, universal traversal sequences and the complexity of maze problems," in *20th IEEE Annual Symposium on Foundations of Computer Science*, 1979, pp. 218–223.
12. T. Bernard, A. Bui, M. Bui, and D. Sohier, "A new method to automatically compute processing times for random walks based distributed algorithm," in *ISPDC 03*, vol. 2069.   IEEE Computer society Press, 2003, pp. 31–36.
13. I. Lavallée, *Algorithmique distribuée et parallèle*, Hermes, Ed.   Hermes, 1990.
14. O. Flauzac, "Random circulating word information management for tree construction and shortest path routing tables computation," in *On Principle Of DIstributed Systems*.   Studia Informatica Universalis, 2001, pp. 17–32.

Reliability Evaluation of Group Service Providers in Mobile Ad-Hoc Networks

Joos-Hendrik Böse and Andreas Thaler

Freie Universität Berlin, Institute for Computer Science
Takustr. 9, 14195 Berlin, Germany
{boese, thaler}@inf.fu-berlin.de

Abstract. A main challenge for applications in mobile ad-hoc networks (MANETs) is to survive link and node failures. One approach to overcome volatility of MANETs is to evaluate the reliability of communication peers allowing to choose the most reliable instances and to estimate the risk of failure before using a remote service. We present an approach that integrates discovery and reliability evaluation of group service providers. A group service provider is a node providing a service which is used by a group of nodes simultaneously.

1 Introduction

Mobile Ad-Hoc networks (MANETs) are selforganizing networks of mobile autonomous nodes that cooperatively form a network without relying on any infrastructure. Such networks are attractive in scenarios where an infrastructure cannot be established. Generally applications in MANETs face the challenge to survive node failures and blackouts of communication due to node movement or limited resources. However, in MANETs groups often carry out common tasks (e.g. a group of rescue workers searching for survivors). One important cooperation pattern is that all nodes of a group must use the same service, provided by a single node. E.g. for transactional commitment, a group must decide on the outcome of a distributed transaction using a commit coordination service. We define a group service as a service used by a group of nodes and provided by a single service instance. A failure of the group service provider affects the overall liveness of the common task. Hence, it is crucial to discover the most reliable node to provide this service. A group service provider is operational, if the provider node does not fail and a radio link to all group members is available for the whole service time.

Node reliability in MANETs is subject to numerous influences like node movement or environmental conditions interfering radio signals. The solutions presented here solve the problem of discovering a reliable service provider for a given group of user nodes. We present different methods to discover a potential set of service providers which can then be evaluated by different methods to determine the most reliable ones. For reliability computation we use multi criteria decision making (MCDM), fuzzy logic and an approach based on a failure probability model. We used experiments to measure the reliability of the providers

R. Meersman, Z. Tari, P. Herrero et al. (Eds.): OTM Workshops 2006, LNCS 4278, pp. 1540–1550, 2006.
© Springer-Verlag Berlin Heidelberg 2006

determined by the proposed methods and compare their message complexity. Message complexity is critical in MANETs due to high energy consumption of send operations. While the proposed methods can use all kinds of information for reliability computations, we solely consider energy resources, position and movement of nodes for evaluation by experiments.

1.1 System Model

In our system model mobile nodes randomly move and cooperate with other nodes in transmission range by providing and using services. A group of nodes called participants $T = \{T_0, \ldots, T_n\}$ is given by an application context e.g. a group of rescue worker searching for survivors. We assume that all nodes of T are in single-hop range. Coordination of common tasks of T requires group services which are provided by mobile nodes. The set of nodes providing such services is called $A = \{A_0, \ldots, A_m\}$, where a node in A can also be in T. A group T uses one group service provided by the most reliable node of A called A^*. The set A is restricted to nodes in single-hop distance of nodes in T, because evaluation methods favor nodes in single-hop distance and provider in multi-hop distance must be significantly more reliable to surpass provider in single-hop range. This is unlikely and the chance to find the most reliable povider in multi-hop distance is poor in proportion to the communication costs needed to include nodes in multi-hop distance in the discovery process. One node of T acts as initiator I, which initiates the evaluation process and the group service usage. Note, that I is also given by the application context. The evaluation process ranks all nodes in A according to their reliability. While using the group service all nodes in T must exchange messages with A^*, if messages cannot be exchanged the group service fails. While using the service two failures can occur: First, one or more nodes of T can fail being not able to exchange messages with A^*. Secondly, the provider A^* can fail completely, e.g. because of exhausted energy resources or only with respect to a subsection of T, e.g. because A^* moves out of transmission range of some nodes. In both cases we consider the service to be failed. As T is fixed, the only option is to choose A^* wisely to achieve a high probability of a successful service usage. Identifying A^* requires the following basic steps:

1. Discover the set A, which is the set of nodes providing the desired service, while each node in A must be in transmission range of all nodes in T.
2. Acquire context information of all nodes in A and of all nodes in T.
3. Rank the set of potential providers by computing a reliability value $R \in [0 \ldots 1]$ for each A_i and choose the most reliable ones.

By context in Step 2 we understand any information describing the current situation of a node affecting its availability. To model *context information* we define the following relations. A *context value* $x = C_{k_j}(N_i)$ with $x \in \mathbb{R}$ is a value of *context class* k_j characterizing node N_i. A context class describes a certain concept such as distance or movement direction. Hence the context information of a provider A_i is defined by a set of context values $K(A_i) = \{C_{k_0}(A_i), \ldots, C_{k_l}(A_i)\}$ each refering to a different context class. In Step 2 the context information of all nodes in A is acquired. We propose to embed this process into the discovery process of Step 1 to reduce message complexity. We present three different workflows to discover providers and gather their context information in Section 2.1. In Section 2.2 we propose different evaluation methods as required in Step 3 and prove their performance by experiments in Section 3. The next Section describes some related work for further motivation.

1.2   Related Work

Related work can be found in the domain of Quality of Service (QoS) and Service Discovery. In QoS aware computing applications demand for certain QoS guarantees on the transportation or server layer. Typical QoS guarantees at the transportation layer are high throughput or low latency, while on the server level availability or transaction differentiation are common demands. Research on QoS in MANETs is mainly driven by the demands of real-time and multimedia applications at the transportation level. Thus QoS in MANETs is mostly concerned with QoS aware routing protocols, where packages of certain applications or sessions are forwarded with higher priority, such as in [2, 11]. QoS demands at the service level gain less attention. The only approach we are aware of is [7], which considers service and host level attributes to compute reliability of service providers by enhancing the AdHocFS [3] system with context propagation. However, [7] does not consider group services and for evaluation completely disregards node mobility in MANETs. Another research topic related to our work is the domain of Service Discovery, which focuses on locating a service instance of a given type. For wired networks numerous service discovery systems like SLP, JINI and UPnP are in use but not directly applicable in volatile environments such as MANETs. For MANETs, [10] presents a modified version of SLP. In contrast to the concept of service awareness [14] our approach is motivated by the need to locate transaction commit coordinators in single-hop environments in the CoCoDa project [1], where commit service time is short (10s to 240s). Additionally existing service discovery systems following the service awareness paradigm do not provide up-to-date context information needed to evaluate the reliability of service providers.

Our work is unique, because we propose an integrated approach of reliability evaluation and acquiring of context information to rank providers reliability. We evaluate the reliability of a group service provider with regard to a user group T. Existing approaches generally only determine the availability of a bilateral service usage. The group services addressed in this work are especially of interest in MANET transaction processing, where transaction commit services are required by groups of mobile nodes. Related work for QoS aware transactions in MANETs can also be found in [5, 6].

2   System Design

In this section we describe the methods implemented in the CoCoDa middleware to discover and evaluate reliability of group service providers. We first describe different processes to discover nodes of A and simultaneously acquire their context information. Afterwards we describe different methods to evaluate the reliability of found providers.

2.1   Gathering Information and Computation Workflow

Because we do not assume a service discovery mechanism such as SLP to be available, a query message containing the service request must be spread to determine A, therefor all proposed processes use a single-hop broadcast message[1]. A single-hop broadcast distributes the query message only in single-hop range and is most effective in MANETs, because it counts only as one message on the message balance and as it is not forwarded by other nodes, a broadcast storm cannot emerge. We propose three different discovery processes. The first and second processes show a very moderate message consumption but are less efficient than the third as shown in Section 3. With small modifications we could increase the efficiency of the first and second process as described in Section 3. The design of the discovery process also depends on the reliability computation used, e.g. the MCDM method requires all context information $\{K(A_0), \dots, K(A_m)\}$ to be in one place, while other evaluation methods allow for a distributed calculation of R.

A: Multi Broadcast - Evaluation at Providers. The first process requires three message rounds to complete discovery and evaluation. The main idea is that A is the intersection of all nodes reached by all single-hop broadcasts issued by nodes in T. If these broadcast messages include context information of the participant issuing the broadcast and addresses of all in T, a potential provider can decide if it is part of A and with methods proposed in 2.2 compute its reliability R. Therefore the message flow is organized in three phases: 1. The initiator sends a *prepare* message to all participants as unicast message containing the addresses of all participants and the desired service. 2. A node receiving a *prepare* message creates a *determine* message, attaches local context information and addresses of all participants and issues a broadcast in single-hop range. 3. A node receiving a *determine* message checks if it provides the service. If the node provides an instance of the service, the context information are locally saved and after awaiting a timeout, the node checks if it received *determine* messages from all nodes in T. If this is true, then the node belongs to A, calculates its reliability R as described in Section 2.2 and sends a *provider-result* message containing R to I.

---

[1] The use of broadcast messages for node discovery can cause the phenomenon of gray zones as described in [8], which affects the presented approaches A and B and is not modelled by the emulator we use for evaluation. We belive that the negative effect is very small, because the gray zones are just small areas.

B: Multi Broadcast - Evaluation at Initiator. If the evaluation metric requires all context information to be in one place like MCDM in Section 2.2 the previous proposed message flow changes as follows: A node receiving a *prepare* message sends a *determine* message like in the previous section, but without attaching its context information. This context information is send in a separate *consumer result* message directly to I. A provider receiving *determine* messages from all nodes in T sends its context information also directly to I using a *provider result* message. Hence all context information of nodes in A and T is available at I.

C: Single Broadcast - Evaluation at Providers. While the previous two processes use multiple broadcasts to identify A, the idea of this process is that a single broadcast of the initiator reaches all nodes in A. All providers receiving this broadcast proactively check if they are in range of all nodes in T. Therefore the message flow is organized as follows. 1. The initiating node creates a *determine* message and broadcasts this message in single-hop distance. 2. Every node receiving the determine message checks if all participating nodes are in range, by sending a *ping* message to each node in T. 3. A node receiving a *ping* message answers by sending its context information using a *consumer result* message. 4. Every provider checks if it received *consumer result* messages from all participants. If this is true, the provider evaluates its reliability. 5. Every potential provider sends a *provider result* message to I containing its R value.

2.2   Evaluation Methods

A group service reliability evaluation method computes a value $R \in [0 \ldots 1]$ describing the availability of a service provider A_i for a given group of service users T and its context information $\{C_{k_0}(A_i), \ldots, C_{k_l}(A_i)\}$ describing the context values in relation to all participants T for context classes $k_0, \ldots, k_l$. Depending on the given context classes different computation methods are applicable. Because not every context class allows to compute a failure probability as proposed in the first method, we also propose a MCDM based method. As often the effect of context values on the reliability of A_i cannot be directly quantified, we also propose a Fuzzy Logic based approached for these classes.

P: Calculation of Failure Probabilities. Several context classes allow to apply methods to predict the time t_f a node will become unavailable, such as the Link Expiration Time (LET) [12], which is based on the context classes location, speed and direction. Another example of such methods is the calculation of the Battery Expiration Time (BET), where t_f is the time when the battery is completely drained. If the expected time the service usage is finished t_u is known, the availability can be approximated. Poor availability must be assumed if $t_f < t_u$. Because t_f and t_u are only approximations we model these values as random variables F and U and write $P_f = P(F < U) = P(Z < 0)$, where Z is a random variable with $Z = F - U$. The realizations of $F = f$ and $U = u$ are subject to numerous influences and hence are modelled as probability distributions, while the expectation of F is t_f as computed e.g. with LET or BET method. Assuming that F and U follow a normal distribution with parameters μ_F, σ_F and μ_U, σ_U we derive the cumulative distribution function F_Z of Formula (1) to calculate the probability of failure during service usage with one participant T_i.

$$P_{T_i} = F_Z(Z = 0) = \frac{1}{\sqrt{2\pi}} \int_{-\infty}^{0} e^{-\frac{1}{2}\left(\frac{t - \mu_Z}{\sigma_Z}\right)^2} dt \qquad (1)$$

Formula (1) requires input parameters $\mu_Z = E(Z) = \mu_F - \mu_U$ and σ_Z, which is derived by $\sigma_Z^2 = Var(Z) = \sigma_F^2 + \sigma_U^2$. The parameter μ_F, μ_U are given by e.g. LET or BET, while σ_U, σ_F must be statistically derived by observation, which is a main disadvantage of this approach. The reliability R of A_i for T is the product of the probabilities that a service usage with node T_i will not fail before t_u, which can be computed by $R = \prod_{i=1}^{n}(1 - P_{T_i}(Z = 0))$.

D: Multiple Criteria Decision Making. In reality not every node can detect context values like speed and direction for LET resp. for BET, hence evaluation methods that can deal with any set of context values are required. For such context information we use a multiple criteria decision making (MCDM) [15] based approach to rank available service providers. In MCDM a given set of providers $\{A_0, \ldots, A_m\}$ and their context $\{K(A_0), \ldots, K(A_m)\}$ is converted into an ordered list $o(A_i) < o(A_j), \ldots, < o(A_k)$, where $A_i = A^*$ is the most reliable provider in A. The MCDM approach first applies a linear normalization $n(C_{k_j}(A_i))$ to all context values $C_{k_j}(A_i)$, where positive or negative effects on the node reliability of each context class is considered and context values are made comparable, proportional to the maximum/minimum occuring of this value in A. For a detailed description of this normalization step as implemented in CoCoDa we refer to [13] and in general to [15]. In a second step, the normalized values for a service provider are combined into a single reliability value R using a function $o(A_i)$. In CoCoDa we choose the *simple additive weighting* (SAW) [15] method, where $o(A_i)$ is defined as $o(A_i) = \sum_{j=1}^{k} w_j \cdot n(C_{k_j}(A_i))$ and w_j is a weighting factor, which allows to modify the intensity of a context class on R.

In contrast to the probability based reliability evaluation, $R_i = o(A_i)$ as computed with this method is relative to the reliability of the other nodes in A. Hence, this method is only applicable if the most reliable provider is to be evaluated and not if the risk of the service usage to fail must be approximated. For this method all context information must be send to one place where the MCDM computations can take place, this implies that only process B can be used with MCDM.

F: Fuzzy Logic. Fuzzy Logic is an alternative to traditional notions of set membership and logic for representing crisp statements like "*node A_i is unreliable*". The basic idea is that membership of a set or correctness is not absolute, the grade of membership or correctness is indicated by a value in $[0 \ldots 1]$, where 0.0 represents absolute falseness and 1.0 absolute truth [4]. Hence, a fuzzy set $M = \{x, \mu(x) | x \in X\}$ is defined by a membership function $\mu(x)$ that maps x

to a membership grade (called fuzzification). In our approach all context values are fuzzificated to the crisp reliability sets *high, medium* and *low*. Derived membership grades are applied to a set of vague rules $U = \{U_0, \ldots, U_m\}$ such as $U_0 = $ *"If x_i high and x_j low then reliability is low"*, which translates into $U_0 = min\{\mu_{x_j}, \mu_{x_i}\}$. To consider the different numbers of rules fired for certain memberships we combine all grades for a level by taking the square root of the sum of all squares of membership grades. Finally the resulting output grades are defuzzificated using the *Center of Singleton* method.

The first approach is the most accurate as proved by experiments in Section 3. This is mainly because the service duration is directly considered. The main drawback is that knowledge about the deviations of context classes is required and context classes must describe a failure time. The other two methods can be applied to any context classes. For the fuzzy set based approach a set of informal rules is required, which must be derived by real world tests. The MCDM based approach can derive R based on any set of context values, if an appropriate normalization function is given. In the following section we will evaluate all three methods P, D and F in combination with the different processes A, B and C described in Section 2.1.

3   Evaluation

For evaluation we used the MarNET [9] emulator developed by University of Marburg. Emulation has the advantage over simulation, that CoCoDa components which are targeted at J2ME CDC enabled devices, can be directly executed in the emulation environment, while simulators such as ns2 require to reimplement logic for the given simulation model. For a detailed description of our emulation and deployment infrastructure we refer to our project website [1].

To represent the assumed system model of Section 1.1 we augment MarNET with an energy model. Decreasing energy levels and node failures due to exhausted resources are modelled using random initial capacity and consumption values for each node. The capacity is periodically decreased using the consumption value of the node which is assumed as normal distributed. A node failed due to exhausted energy resources cannot receive or send messages. It recovers after a defined period, representing recharge of the node's battery. Additionally we enhanced MarNET with a component, enabling a node to sense its location using

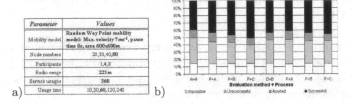

Fig. 1. a) Emulation parameters. b) Service usage results.

a faked GPS device. Hence we used the context classes battery capacity, energy consumption, radio range, movement direction, velocity and current position of nodes to evaluate the proposed methods.

To initiate reliability evaluations, we computed available links between nodes for every ten seconds of simulation duration and randomly choose T interconnected by links not exceeding a certain loss rate. To structure evaluation we first defined parameters for a fixed environment and compare the proposed approaches, in a second step we vary single parameters to learn about their influences. Figure 1a shows these parameters, where the bold are the fixed ones and the other their variations used in Step 2. Figure 1b shows the rate of successful service usages, while a combination is given by a message flow A, B or C as described in Section 2.1 and an evaluation method P, D or F from Section 2.2. Method R+R is a naive approach for comparison, which always chooses the initiator, without applying any reliability evaluation. If the initiator does not provide the desired service a node in T is chosen randomly.

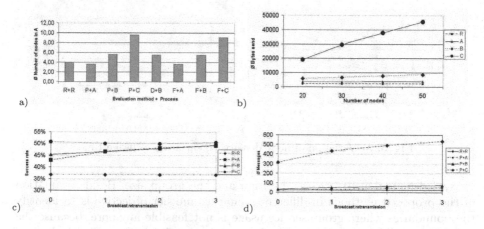

Fig. 2. a)Providers found. b)Bytes send to determine A. c)Broadcast repetition. d)Message complexity at broadcast recurrences.

Figure 1b shows the evaluation results of all combinations of message flows and reliability computations for the fixed scenario. For each combination we measured the rate of successful, unsuccessful, aborted and impossible service usages. A service usage is considered as successful, if the chosen A_i is operational and in radio range of all nodes in T, after the usage time lapsed. Otherwise the service usage is considered to be unsuccessful. Service usages count as aborted, if at least one participant was not operational at initiation time[2] or if no provider could be found. Additionally we count service usages, where movement of participants makes a successful services usage impossible and a service provider cannot even theoretically be found.

---

[2] Information about left energy resources are neglected for initiation, hence nodes chosen for T are possibly not operational because of exhausted battery.

The combination of C and P shows with 51% the highest rate of success-ful service usages in the fixed scenario, which is 12% more than achieved by R+R. Generally all combinations increase the rate of successful service usages compared with the naive R+R method. It can be observed, that the process significantly influences the performance of the provider evaluation. Independent from evaluation method, C always shows the highest success rates. The reason is, that message flow C identifies twice as much provider than A and B which is shown by Diagram 2a, hence A and B possibly miss more reliable provider.

To identify the set A, C transmits more messages than A and B as depicted in Diagram 2b. The high message complexity is caused by unicast messages used in C to check the reachability of participants. We could explain the poor results of A and B by high message loss of broadcasts used to discover A, hence only a fraction of the theoretically nodes in A receive a broadcast from all nodes in T. The difference in discovered potential provider of A and B is because the size of messages also effects their loss rate and in A context information increases the size of messages. To measure the influence of certain parameters,

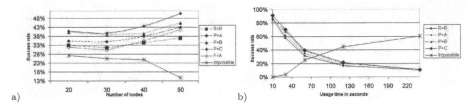

a)   b)

Fig. 3. a) Variation of node density. b)Variation of usage time.

we varied node density, service duration and the group size. Beside evaluation of the proposed methods in different scenarios another objective is to identify the boundaries where group service usage is not feasible anymore, because the rate of impossible service usages reach a certain threshold. To vary node density, we change the number of nodes from 20 to 50. Diagram 3a lists the rate of successful and impossible service usages. Below 40 nodes the success rate is generally below 38% while P+C achieves in average 10% more successful service usages than R+R. The F+A combination has a lower success rate than R+R for node numbers below 40, as message loss of broadcasts preponderates here. As expected at high node density the success rates increase, but on the other hand the message overhead rises as shown in Figure 2b. Especially message flow C utilizes disproportionately more messages compared to A and B.

To measure the influence of the usage time we varied this time from 10 to 240 seconds. We found that the process is the very dominant factor here, therefore we only plotted the success and impossible rate for the different processes with method P in Figure 3b. It can be observed, that success rates differ only slightly for all processes. For usage times greater than 120s the success rate falls below 20%, while between 10s and 30s usage time the success rate is generally above 50%. Hence service durations lasting longer than 120s must be generally assumed to be risky, because the rate of unsuccessful usages exceeds 80%, where 60% are impossible. After observing, that the reason for the lower performance of message flows A and B is the high loss of broadcast messages, we repeated transmissions of the *determine* messages up to three times. Figure 2c shows the interesting result that rebroadcasting the *determine* message is a most effective strategy to increase the size of *A* and therefore the success rate, at a resend rate of 3 the message flows A and B can compete with process C at a much lower message complexity as shown in Figure 2d. Because the size of *A* is crucial for the success of the evaluation method we identified process B with repetitive broadcasting of the determine message as the most efficient method.

4   Summary and Conclusion

We described the evaluation processes as implemented in the CoCoDa project to support a qualified selection of group service providers and presented their evaluation using experiments. The evaluation showed that proposed methods could increase the success rate of group service usages about 10% compared to the naive approach. We showed that completeness of *A* and hence the process of discovering *A* is crucial for the success of evaluation. Experiments showed that the evaluation based on probabilities (method P) is the most accurate of the three discussed methods. We also learned about the influence of certain parameters such as service usage time and node density and discovered according boundaries where a group service usage in our scenario is not feasible anymore.

References

1. Cooperation communication data project http://www.cocoda.de.
2. G. Ahn, A. Campbell, A. Veres, and L. Sun. Swan: Service differentiation in stateless wireless ad hoc networks, 2002.
3. M. Boulkenafed and V. Issarny. Adhocfs: Sharing files in wlans. In *Proceeding of the 2nd IEEE International Symposium on Network Computing and Applications*, Cambridge, MA, USA, April 2003.
4. E. Cox. Fuzzy fundamentals. *IEEE Spectrum*, 29:58–61, 1992.
5. L. Fife and L. Gruenwald. Trim: Tri-modal data communication in mobile ad-hoc networks. In *DEXA Workshops*. IEEE Computer Society, 2004.
6. L. Gruenwald and S. Banik. A power-aware technique to manage real-time database transactions in mobile ad-hoc networks. September 2001.
7. Jinshan Liu and Valérie Issarny. Qos-aware service location in mobile ad-hoc networks. In *Proceedings of the 2004 IEEE International Conference on Mobile Data Management (MDM'04)*. IEEE Computer Society, 2004.
8. Henrik Lundgren, Erik Nordstroem, and Christian Tschudin. Coping with communication gray zones in ieee 802.11b based ad hoc networks. 2002.
9. B. Freisleben M. Smith, S. Hanemann. Coupled simulation/emulation for cross-layer enabled mobile wireless computing. In *Proceedings of the Second International Conference on Embedded Software and Systems, Xian, China*, pages 375–383. Springer-Verlag, 2005.

10. Stefan Penz. Slp-based service management for dynamic ad-hoc networks. In *MPAC '05: Proceedings of the 3rd international workshop on Middleware for pervasive and ad-hoc computing*, pages 1–8, New York, NY, USA, 2005. ACM Press.
11. Samarth H. Shah, Kai Chen, and Klara Nahrstedt. Dynamic bandwidth management in single-hop ad hoc wireless networks. *Mob. Netw. Appl.*, 10(1-2):199–217, 2005.
12. William Su, Sung-Ju Lee, and Mario Gerla. Mobility prediction and routing in ad hoc wireless networks. *Int. J. Netw. Manag.*, 11(1):3–30, 2001.
13. Andreas Thaler. Reliability evaluation of service providers in mobile ad-hoc networks. Master's thesis, Freie Universität Berlin, 2006.
14. Jidong Wu and Martina Zitterbart. Service awareness and its challenges in mobile ad hoc networks. In *GI Jahrestagung (1)*, pages 551–557, 2001.
15. Chung-Hsing Yeh. A problem-based selection of multi-attribute decision-making methods. *International Transactions in Operational Research*, 9(2):169–181, 2002.

Traceability and Timeliness
in Messaging Middleware

Brian Shand and Jem Rashbass

Clinical and Biomedical Computing Unit, University of Cambridge
16 Mill Lane, Cambridge CB2 1SB, United Kingdom
{Brian.Shand, jem}@cbcu.cam.ac.uk

Abstract. Distributed messaging middleware can provide few delivery guarantees. Nevertheless, applications need to monitor timely delivery of important messages, both at the time and retrospectively, such as for reasons of safety and audit in a healthcare application. Timely, decentralised notification enables out-of-band resolution of problems beyond the messaging system's control. Instead of relying on applications to generate (and monitor) a proof of delivery message, which may itself be lost in transit, we instead propose a general-purpose service that provides local delivery logs, remote delivery confirmation, and automatic warning events about potentially undelivered messages, in a clean extension of the pub/sub paradigm. The service can also provide an audit trail across a chain of messages, by using message tokens to correlate the receipt and subsequent publication of otherwise apparently unrelated messages. This allows meaningful analysis of failures in a workflow, enabling reliable applications which recover gracefully from communication failures.

1   Introduction

Distributed messaging middleware systems can provide only minimal guarantees about timely message delivery. Nevertheless, this robust paradigm is well suited to developing large-scale, decentralised applications. In this position paper, we consider how to support applications' timeliness and audit requirements, with suitable distributed monitoring.

As an illustrative example, we consider a healthcare application which uses a common publish/subscribe messaging layer for various time-sensitive tasks. Fig. 1 shows some of the electronic messaging paths in a clinical environment: messages within a hospital, messages between hospitals for off-site pathology services, and messages sent for further analysis by a cancer registry. Additional communication paths outside the pub/sub system are shown as dotted lines, e.g. blood samples sent from Ward A to the Haematology department in Hospital 1, and printed copies of the blood results which are added to the patient notes.

Although the messaging system itself provides a homogeneous interface, different communication paths may have very different performance. In our example, we assume that messages within the hospital are routed over a fast local network, messages between hospitals go over a dedicated inter-hospital WAN, and messages to/from the cancer registry go once a month on a physical disk.

R. Meersman, Z. Tari, P. Herrero et al. (Eds.): OTM Workshops 2006, LNCS 4278, pp. 1551–1554, 2006.
© Springer-Verlag Berlin Heidelberg 2006

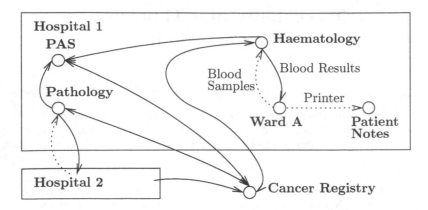

Fig. 1. Message paths in a clinical environment

Many of the communication channels have similar monitoring requirements, but with time granularity varying from minutes to months: the haematology department might want to be notified of any blood results that had apparently not been delivered to anyone within 20 minutes of sending[1]; similarly, the cancer registry might want to know if any hospital's data was more than two months out of date.

In both of these examples, knowing about a potential failure is essential for overall system reliability. It allows *out-of-band* resolution of problems beyond the messaging system's control, both at the physical level (such as by fixing a broken cable) and at the application level (by telephoning the ward if the delayed blood results were abnormal).

2   Related Work

This paper complements related work on extending pub/sub systems, to provide additional support for secure message delivery in multi-domain systems [1], and to monitor event patterns using composite event detection [2]. In pub/sub communication [3], *publishers* send notifications to *subscribers* indirectly, through the event service. Subscribers express their interest in particular events by *registering* for events on the associated topics. They are then *notified* whenever events are published on these topics.

This communication model is well suited to distributed systems, where unpredictable delays may occur in communication, and message publishers and subscribers might not know each other's identities in advance. However, it offers no explicit support for applications which need to be confident of timely message delivery, or for high-level monitoring of related messages. Work to date on reliable message-based middleware such as FT-CORBA has shown significant performance overheads, and increased application complexity [4].

---

[1] It may be that it was the receipt that was lost or delayed, not the original message.

Table 1. Additional message topics for monitoring message delivery

```
Topic: deliveryUnconfirmed              Topic: deliveryConfirmed
Attributes:                             Attributes:
   messageId, topic,                       messageId, topic,
   source, destination,                    source, destination
   timeout
```

3 Message Monitoring

In this section, we show how message delivery monitoring can be offered to applications as part of the general messaging interface, and outline the infrastructure and guarantees required to reliably provide this support in a distributed system.

For application developers, integrating monitoring with the existing pub/sub interface has the advantages of simplicity with minimal overhead, because no extra libraries are required, and because it integrates cleanly with existing event-based design. For middleware developers, the advantage is that monitoring can either be integrated tightly into the messaging system, or provided as a proxy service around an existing platform.

We introduce two additional message topics, `deliveryUnconfirmed` and `deliveryConfirmed`, which applications can use to monitor message delivery, outlined in Table 1. For example, the haematology department could ask for warning about delayed blood results with a subscription filter such as:

[`deliveryUnconfirmed(topic="Blood Results" AND source=Haematology AND timeout=20 minutes)`]

For security, subscribers would ordinarily only be allowed to monitor messages which they had been responsible for publishing, e.g. by proving that they knew the private key associated with the original publisher, or through more sophisticated automatic subscription restrictions such as those described in [1].

Behind the scenes, `deliveryUnconfirmed` messages could be provided over an existing middleware system in the following way:

1. On receipt of a `deliveryUnconfirmed` subscription request, set up a local subscriber for the corresponding `deliveryConfirmed` messages, and also for the original messages, e.g. blood results from haematology.

   This subscriber would reconcile the two message streams, and generate local notifications after an appropriate timeout, avoiding network delays. If a composite event detection service is available [2], this could be a composite event expression, $([E], [T_1 \subseteq \{D, T_1\}])_{T_1=20 \text{ mins}}$, where E and D would be parameterized expressions for the original messages and the corresponding `deliveryConfirmed` messages, and $[T_1 \subseteq \{D, T_1\}]$ means 'T_1 precedes D'.

2. On receipt of each message, a transparent proxy around the messaging interface would emit an appropriate `deliveryConfirmed` message, as well as passing the original message on to the subscriber.

   With appropriate source quenching, this adds minimal overhead for messages whose delivery is not monitored, and at most a linear increase with monitoring or without source quenching. Furthermore, it lets publishers switch on or off monitoring at will, with no special support from the message subscribers.

3. Finally, this approach requires *bounded delay on local messages* (between publishers and subscriber using the same broker), to ensure delivery of the `deliveryUnconfirmed` messages even in the presence of network failures. This and message filtering are the only particular middleware requirements.

The monitoring support described above is geared towards monitoring individual messages. But it can also be used to monitor sequences of messages in a workflow — with or without a Workflow Management System (WfMS) — by adding extra token meta-data to messages.

We assume that each ordinary notification in the pub/sub system can be given an associated token, and require each component to send a special notification for each token it receives, describing its destination.

For example, in a request/response interaction, the request and response messages are ordinarily independent and unconnected. But if a nonce-token is added to the request as it is received, it can then be correlated with the response message with the same token, or equally with the special `tokenAction` notification about the action performed. The reply can then be traced to its subscribers, based on the message identity, e.g. a secure hash of the message origin, timestamp and contents.

By following this chain of connections, the message workflow can be reconstructed. Where a WfMS is used, the tokens can instead correspond to workflow process identities. These token logs enable richer workflow reconstruction than conventional process logs [5] or message subscription analysis, by identifying actual workflow usage patterns, rather than only potential dependencies.

This token monitoring service integrates simply with single message monitoring, as it uses only `deliveryConfirmed` messages and ordinary message subscriptions to generate the logging data required for analysis. This analysis can be performed on the fly, or retrospectively from local logs of `deliveryConfirmed` and `tokenAction` messages and message publications.

Developers of reliable applications need tools which enable a resilient response to failures, and robust monitoring of performance. In this position paper, we have shown how this support is best integrated into the middleware messaging layer, to simplify the development and evolution of reliable distributed systems.

References

1. Bacon, J., Eyers, D.M., Moody, K., Pesonen, L.I.W.: Securing publish/subscribe for multi-domain systems. In: Middleware 2005. Volume 3790 of LNCS. (2005) 1–20
2. Pietzuch, P.R., Shand, B., Bacon, J.: Composite event detection as a generic middleware extension. IEEE Network **18**(1) (2004) 44–55
3. Eugster, P.T., Felber, P.A., Guerraoui, R., Kermarrec, A.M.: The Many Faces of Publish/Subscribe. ACM Computing Surveys **35**(2) (2003) 114–131
4. Felber, P., Narasimhan, P.: Experiences, strategies, and challenges in building fault-tolerant corba systems. IEEE Trans. Computers **53**(5) (2004) 497–511
5. Golani, M., Pinter, S.S.: Generating a process model from a process audit log. In: Business Process Management. (2003) 136–151

Transaction Manager Failover: A Case Study Using JBOSS Application Server

A.I. Kistijantoro, G. Morgan, and S.K. Shrivastava

School of Computing Science, Newcastle University, Newcastle upon Tyne, UK
{A.I.Kistijantoro, Graham.Morgan, S.K.Shrivastava}@ncl.ac.uk

Abstract. This paper describes, for the case of Enterprise Java Bean components and JBoss application server, how replication for availability can be supported to tolerate application server/transaction manager failures. Replicating the state associated with the progression of a transaction (i.e., which phase of two-phase commit is enacted and the transactional resources involved) provides an opportunity to continue a transaction using a backup transaction manager if the transaction manager of the primary fails. Existing application servers do not support this functionality. The paper discusses the technical issues involved and shows how a solution can be engineered.

Keywords: Availability, application servers, components, Enterprise Java Beans, fault tolerance, middleware, replication, transactions.

1 Introduction

Three-tier middleware architecture is commonly used for hosting large-scale distributed applications. Typically the application is decomposed into three layers: front-end, middle tier and back-end. Front-end ('Web server') is responsible for handling user interactions and acts as a client of the middle tier, while back-end provides storage facilities for applications. Middle tier ('Application Server') is usually the place where all computations are performed, so this layer provides middleware services for transactions, security and so forth. The benefit of this architecture is that it allows flexible configuration such as partitioning and clustering for improved performance and scalability. Furthermore, availability measures, such as replication, can be introduced in each tier in an application specific manner. In this paper we concentrate on application server (middle tier) replication. Data as well as object replication techniques have been studied extensively in the literature, so our task is not to invent new replication techniques, but to investigate how existing techniques can be migrated to middle tier.

One important concept related to availability measures is that of *exactly once transaction* or *exactly once execution* [1,2]. The concept is particularly relevant in web-based e-services where the system must guarantee exactly once execution of user requests despite system failures. Problems arise as the clients in such systems are usually not transactional, thus they are not part of the recovery guarantee provided by the underlying transaction processing systems that support the web-based e-services. When failures occur, clients often do not know whether their requests have been processed or not. Resubmitting the requests may result in duplication, and on the other hand it is also possible the requests have not been processed at all. This problem

R. Meersman, Z. Tari, P. Herrero et al. (Eds.): OTM Workshops 2006, LNCS 4278, pp. 1555–1564, 2006.
© Springer-Verlag Berlin Heidelberg 2006

can be handled by replicating the application server to achieve availability. As we discuss in the next section, while existing application servers for Enterprise Java Bean (EJB) components do use replication, they do not adequately support exactly once transaction capability. For this reason, there has been much recent research works on replication for supporting exactly once transactions over commonly used application servers. However, implementation work reported so far has dealt with transactions that update a single database only, so do not require two-phase commit.

In this paper we go a step further and present design, implementation and performance evaluation of a middle tier replication scheme for multi-database transactions using a widely deployed application server (JBoss). We describe how a backup transaction manager can complete two-phase commit for transactions that would otherwise be blocked. The paper discusses the technical issues involved and shows how a solution can be engineered. Our case study can be used by other designers intending to enhance application servers in a similar manner.

2 Related Work

The classic text [3] discusses replicated data management techniques that go hand in hand with transactions. Object replication using group communication, originally developed in the ISIS system [4], has been studied extensively [e.g., 5]. The interplay between replication and exactly once execution within the context of multi-tier architectures is examined in [6], whilst [7] describes how replication and transactions can be incorporated in three-tier CORBA architecture. The approach of using a backup transaction monitor was implemented as early as 1980 in the SDD-1 distributed database system [8]; another implementation is reported in [9]. A replicated transaction coordinator to provide non-blocking commit service has also been described in [10]. Our paper deals with the case of replicating transaction managers in the context of standards compliant Java application servers (J2EE servers).

There are several studies that deal with replication of application servers as a mechanism to improve availability [1,2,11,12]. In [2], the authors precisely describe the concept of exactly once transaction (*e-transaction*) and develop server replication mechanisms; their model assumes *stateless application servers* (no session state is maintained by servers) that can access multiple databases. Their algorithm handles the transaction commitment blocking problem by making the backup server take on the role of transaction coordinator. As their model limits the application servers to be stateless, the solution cannot be directly implemented on stateful server architectures such as J2EE servers.

The approach by Wu, Kemme et al in [12] specifically addressed the replication of J2EE application servers, where components may possess session state in addition to persistent state stored on a single database. The approach assumes that an active transaction is always aborted by the database whenever an application server crashes. Therefore, it uses a mechanism similar to testable transaction abstraction developed in [1], and on failover, the backup server uses this mechanism to find out the outcomes of transactions performed on the crashed primary. Our approach assumes the more general case of access to multiple databases; hence two phase commitment (2PC) is necessary. Application server failures that occur during the 2PC process do not always cause abortion of active transactions, since the backup transaction manager can complete the commit process.

JBoss clustering [13] uses session replication to enable failover of a component processing on one node to another. The approach targets load balancing among replicas and it allows each replica handles different client sessions. The state of a session is propagated to backup after the computation finish. When a server crashes, all sessions that it hosts can be migrated and continued on another server, regardless the outcome of formerly active transactions on the crashed server, which may lead to inconsistencies.

Exactly once transaction execution can also be implemented by making the client transactional, and on web-based e-services, this can be done by making the browser as a resource which can be controlled by the resource manager from the server side, as shown in [14,15]. One can also employ transactional queue [16]. In this way, user requests are kept in a queue that are protected by transactions, and clients submit requests and retrieve results from the queue as separate transactions. As the result, three transactions are required for processing each client requests and developers must construct their application so that no state is kept in the application servers between successive requests from clients. The approach presented in [17] guarantees exactly once execution on internet-based e-services by employing message logging. The authors describe which messages require logging, and how to do the recovery on the application servers. The approach addresses stateful application servers with single database processing without replicating the application servers. The table below summarizes the differences between the various approaches; concentrating on exactly once transactions as such approaches consider similar requirements to our work.

Table 1. Exactly once transaction solutions

Aspects	Transactional queue	Trans. client	Message logging [17]	e-transaction	Wu and Kemme	Our approach
App. server replication	No	No	No	Yes	Yes	Yes
Transactional client	Not required	Required	Not required	Not required	Not required	Not required
Stateful server	Supported	Supported	Supported	Not supported	Supported	Supported
Platform	TP monitors	Web	Web	Custom	J2EE	J2EE
Multi database	Supported	Supported	Not supported	Supported	Not supported	Supported

For the sake of completeness, we point out here that replication approaches for the third tier (back-end, database tier) that work with application servers have also been investigated by many researchers (see [18,19]).

3 Background

We assume the reader is familiar with EJB component model and how transactions are used through containers in J2EE servers (background details are available in the more detailed version of this paper [20]). We only provide a brief description of how services are integrated into JBoss via *interceptors, management beans* (MBeans) and *Java Management Extensions* JMX and then describe how this approach is used to implement transactions in JBoss middleware.

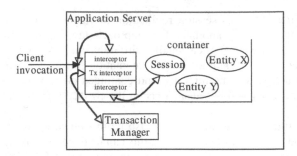

Fig. 1. Augmenting application server with transactions

In JBoss invocations pass through a series of interceptors within a container. These interceptors enable the integration of additional services into a container to support EJB execution (e.g., security, transactions), with the final interceptor in the incoming chain of interceptors handling method invocation on the actual EJB itself. Services may be added to JBoss via MBeans. An MBean exposes a management interface, attributes and operations while adhering to the JMX specification and may be made available for use via the standard object location services in JBoss (JNDI). JMX provides an API for management and monitoring of resources, including remote access, so a remote application can manage and monitor applications.

JBoss implements transactions with the aid of *tx interceptors* and the transaction manager (figure 1). The tx interceptor inspects an incoming invocation with the aid of the transaction manager and determines the appropriate settings for the transaction context before the receiving bean processes the invocation. A transaction context is used to identify a transaction and determines the transaction an invocation belongs to (in particular, the thread of execution associated to an invocation), allowing transactional mechanisms to be enacted in line with invocation processing on transactional objects (e.g., mark for rollback, throw exception, commit).

4 Model

Our approach to component replication is based on a passive replication scheme, in that a primary services all client requests with a backup assuming the responsibility of servicing client requests when a primary fails. Crash failures of servers are assumed. In a configuration of server machines where the failure of a server can be detected with accuracy, a minimum of f+1 replicas are needed to tolerate up to f server failures; such a scheme can be engineered for a well managed cluster of machines connected by a high bandwidth LAN. Configurations where accurate failure detection is not possible (e.g., the servers are widely distributed with arbitrary inter-communication delays), a minimum of 2f+1 replicas are needed. Performance evaluation that we present in section 6 are for a LAN configuration.

Recovery measures undertaken vary depending upon where the primary fails within a client session: (1) during non-transactional invocation phase, (2) during transactional phase. As entity beans access and change persistent state, the time taken to execute application logic via entity beans is longer than enacting the same logic using session beans. The reason for this is two fold: (1) the high cost of retrieving state on entity bean activation and writing state on entity bean deactivation; (2) the transactional management associated to persistent state updates. The structuring of an application to minimize the use of entity beans (and transactions) to speed up execution times is commonplace. This approach to development leads to scenarios in which a client enacts a "session" (a series of related invocations) on an application server, with the majority of invocations handled by session beans. Transactional manipulation of persistent state via entity beans is usually left to the last steps of processing in a client's session. The sequence diagram in figure 2 describes the style of interaction our model assumes. We are only showing application level logic invocations (as encoded in EJBs) in our diagram, therefore, we do not show the transaction manager and associated databases. The invocations that occur within a transaction are shown in the shaded area. As mentioned earlier, we assume a client is not part of the transaction.

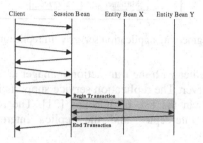

Fig. 2. Interactions between beans and client

We assume a single stateful session bean is used to present a single interface for a client during a session. The creation and destruction of a stateful session bean by a client delimits the start and end of a session (i.e., lifetime of stateful session bean). We assume the existence of a single transaction during the handling of the last client invocation and such a transaction is initiated by the stateful session bean and involves one or more entity beans. The transaction is container managed and is scoped by this last method invocation.

Failure of the primary during a session will result in a backup assuming responsibility for continuing the session. This may require the replaying of the last invocation sent by a client if state changes and return parameters associated to the last invocation were not recorded at backups. If state changes and parameters were recorded then the backup will reply with the appropriate parameters. During the transactional phase the transaction may be completed at the backup if the commit stage had been reached by the primary and computation has finished between the entity beans. The backup will be required to replay the transaction if failure occurs during transactional computation.

5 JBoss Implementation

Figure 3 shows the interceptors and associated services that implement our replication scheme in the JBoss application server. The interceptors perform the following tasks: *retry interceptor* – identifies if a client request is a duplicate and handles duplicates appropriately; *txinspector interceptor* – determines how to handle invocations that are associated to transactions; *txinterceptor* – interacts with transaction manager to enable transactional invocations (unaltered existing interceptor shown for completeness); *replica interceptor* – ensures state changes associated with a completed invocation are propagated to backups.

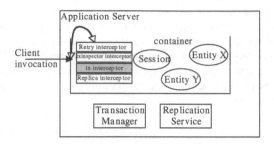

Fig. 3. Augmenting application server with replication service

The txinterceptor together with the transaction manager accommodates transactions within the application server. The replication service supports inter-replica consistency and consensus services via the use of JGroups [21]. The replication service, retry interceptor, txinspector interceptor and the replica interceptor, implements our replication scheme.

Replication logic at the server side makes use of four persistent logs that are maintained by the replication service: (i) current primary and backup configuration (group log), (ii) most recent state of session bean together with the last parameters sent back as a reply to a client invocation (bean log), (iii) invocation timestamp associated to most recent session bean state (timestamp log), (iv) state related to the progress of a transaction (transaction log). The replication service uses a single group via the JGroups service to ensure these logs are consistent across replicas.

We skip over the details of how a client side proxy has been enhanced with retry ability to backups as well as how session state checkpointing to backups is performed using group communication, as these techniques are well known (details can be found in [20]); instead we concentrate below on transaction failover management.

5.1 Transaction Failover Management

We assume container managed transaction demarcation. Via this approach to managing transactions the application developer specifies the transaction demarcation for each method via the transaction attribute in a bean deployment descriptor. Using this attribute a container decides how a transaction is to be handled. For example, if a new transaction has to be created for an invocation, or to process the invocation as part of an existing transaction (i.e., the transaction was started earlier in the execution chain). Based on this mechanism, a single invocation of a method can be: a single transaction unit (a transaction starts at the beginning of the invocation and ends at the end of the invocation), a part of a transaction unit originated from other invocation, or non transactional (e.g. the container can suspend a transaction prior to executing a method, and resume the transaction afterwards). We assume that the processing of an invocation may involve one or more beans (both session beans and entity beans) and may accesses one or more databases, requiring two phase commitment.

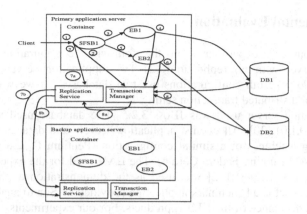

Fig. 4. A typical interaction for a transaction processing in EJB

Figure 4 illustrates the execution of a typical transaction (for brevity, we have not shown resource adaptors). We shall use this example as a comparison to highlight the enhancements we have provided to handle transaction failover (this example is represents the shaded area shown in figure 4). SFSB stands for a stateful session bean and EB stands for an entity bean. All methods on the beans have a *Required* tag as their transaction attribute, indicating to the container that they must be executed within a transaction. The invocation from the client initially does not contain a transaction context. At (1), a client invokes a method on a stateful session bean SFSB1. The container (e.g. the tx interceptor on JBoss app server) determines that the invocation requires a transaction and calls the transaction manager to create a transaction T1 for this invocation (2). The container proceeds to attach a transaction context for T1 to the invocation. The container does not have to create a new transaction for nested invocations (3) and (5). The invocation on EB1 requires access to a database DB1 (4) and at this point, the container registers DB1 to the transaction manager as a resource associated with T1. The same process happens at (6) where the container registers DB2 to be associated with T1. After the computation on SFSB1, EB1 and EB2 finishes, before returning the result to the client, the container completes the transaction by instructing the transaction manager to commit T1. The transaction manager then performs two phase commit with all resources associated with T1 (8) (not shown in detail here).

Our transaction failover mechanisms are performed at point (7) and (8). A multicast of the state update of all involved session beans together with the result parameter, the transaction id and information on all resources involved is made (7a) and (7b) to all backup replicas. If the primary fails after this point, a backup will try to finish the commit process. At point (8), a multicast of the decision taken by the transaction manager is made to all backup replica transaction managers via the replication service (8a) and (8b). If the primary fails after this point, a backup will try to finish the commit process according to the decision that has been taken by the failed primary.

A number of technical challenges needed to be overcome to provide an engineered solution. However, for brevity we do not go into such details here; the interested reader is referred to [20].

6 Experimental Evaluation

We carried out our experiments on the following configurations: (1) Single application server with no replication; (2) Two application server replicas with transaction failover. Both configurations use two databases, as we want to conduct experiments for distributed transaction setting.

The application server used was JBoss 3.2.5. The database used was Oracle 9i release 2 (9.2.0.1.0) [20]. All clients, application servers and database servers were deployed using machines of a similar configuration (Pentium IV 2.8 GHz PC with 2048MB of RAM running Fedora Core 4). The LAN used for the experiments was a 100 Mbit Ethernet. ECperf [22] was used as the demonstration application in our experiments. ECperf is a benchmark application provided by Sun to enable vendors to measure the performance of their J2EE products. For our experiments, we configured the ECperf application to use two databases instead of just a single database (as is the default configuration).

Two experiments are performed. First, we measure the overhead of our replication scheme introduces into application performance. The ECperf driver was configured to run each experiment with 10 different injection rates (1 though 10 inclusive). At each of these increments a record of the overall throughput (transactions per minute) for both order entry and manufacturing applications is taken. The injection rate relates to the order entry and manufacturer requests generated per second. Due to the complexity of the system the relationship between injection rate and resulted transactions is not straightforward. The second experiment measures how our replicated algorithm performs in the presence of failures. In this experiment we ran the ECperf benchmark for 20 minutes, and the throughput of the system every 30 seconds is recorded. After the first 12 minutes, we kill the primary server to force the system to failover to the backup server.

Figure 5 presents two graphs that describe the throughput and response time of the ECperf applications; figure 5(i) identifies the throughput for the entry order system, figure 5(ii) identifies the response time for the entry order system. On first inspection we see that our replication scheme lowers the overall throughput of the system. This is to be expected as additional processing resources are required to maintain state consistency across components on a backup server.

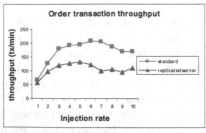
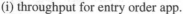
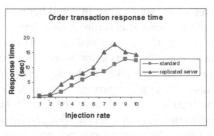

(i) throughput for entry order app.   (ii) response time for entry order app.

Fig. 5. Performance figures

Figure 6 presents a graph that describes the throughput of our system and the standard implementation over the time of the benchmark. After 720 seconds running (12 minutes), we crash the primary server. When no replication is present the failure of the application server results in throughput decreasing to zero, as there is no backup to continue the computation. When replication is present performance drops when failure of the primary is initiated. However, the backup assumes the role of the primary allowing for throughput to rise again. An interesting observation is that throughput on the new primary is higher than it was on the old primary. This may be explained by the fact that only one server exists and no replication is taking place. The initial peak in throughput may also be explained by the completion of transactions that started on the old primary but finish on the new primary. This adds an additional load above and beyond the regular load generated by injection rates.

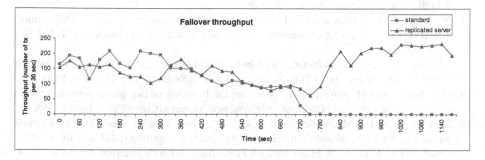

Fig. 6. Performance figures under a failure

The experiments show that our replication scheme does not incur high overhead compared to a non replicated system, and is able to perform quick failover when the primary crashes.

7 Concluding Remarks

We have presented a practical solution to the problem of incorporating availability through replication in application servers, specifically for the general case of multi-database transactions. Although our design and implementation have been for a specific component model (EJBs) and application server (JBoss), the ideas can be applied to other application servers. Thus our case study can be used by other designers intending to enhance application servers in a similar manner.

Acknowledgements

This work is funded by UK Engineering and Physical Sciences Research Council - Grant No. GR/S63199/01, "Trusted Coordination in Dynamic Virtual Organisations", and Platform Grant No. EP/D037743/1, "Networked Computing in Inter-organisation Settings"; Kistijantoro's work is funded by QUE Project Batch III, Institute Teknologi Bandung, Indonesia.

References

1. S. Frolund and R. Guerraoui, "A pragmatic implementation of e-transactions", 19th IEEE Symposium on Reliable Distributed Systems, SRDS 2000.
2. S. Frolund and R. Guerraoui, "e-transactions: End-to-end reliability for three-tier architectures", IEEE Transactions on Software Engineering 28(4): 378-395, 2002.
3. P.A. Bernstein et al, "Concurrency Control and Recovery in Database Systems", Addison-Wesley, 1987.
4. K. Birman , "The process group approach to reliable computing", CACM , 36, 12, pp. 37-53, December 1993.
5. P. Felber, R. Guerraoui, and A. Schiper, "The implementation of a CORBA object group service", Theory and Practice of Object Systems, 4(2), 1998, pp. 93-105.
6. B. Kemme, R. Jimenez-Peris et al, "Exactly once Interaction in a Multi-tier Architecture", VLDB Conf. Trondheim, Norway. Aug. 2005.
7. W. Zhao, et al., "Unification of Transactions and Replication in Three-tier Architectures Based on CORBA", IEEE transactions on Dependable and Secure Computing, Vol. 2, No. 1, 20- 33, 2005.
8. M. Hammer and D. Shipman, "Reliability mechanisms for SDD-1: A system for distributed databases" ACM Transactions on Database Systems 5(4): 431--466, 1980.
9. P.K. Reddy and M. Kitsuregawa, "Reducing the blocking in two-phase commit protocol employing backup sites", Cooperative Information Systems (CoopIS'98), August 1998.
10. Jiménez-Peris, R., M. Patiño-Martínez, et al, "A Low-Latency Non-blocking Commit Service", 15th International Conference on Distributed Computing (DISC), October 2001.
11. Ozalp Babaoglu et al, "A Framework for Prototyping J2EE Replication Algorithms", Int. Symposium on Distributed Objects and Applications (DOA), Agia Napa, October 2004.
12. H. Wu, B. Kemme, V. Maverick, "Eager Replication for Stateful J2EE Servers", Int. Symposium on Distributed Objects and Applications (DOA), Cyprus, October 2004.
13. S. Labourey and B. Burke, " JBoss Clustering 2nd Edition", 2002, www.jboss.org
14. M.C. Little and S K Shrivastava, "Integrating the Object Transaction Service with the Web", Enterprise Distributed Object Computing Workshop (EDOC'98), pp. 194 – 205, November 1998.
15. M.C. Little and S K Shrivastava, "Java Transactions for the Internet", Distributed Systems Engineering, 5 (4), December 1998, pp. 156-167.
16. P.A. Bernstein, M. Hsu, et al., "Implementing recoverable requests using queues", ACM SIGMOD international conference on Management of data, 1990, Atlantic City, New Jersey.
17. R. Barga, D. Lomet, et al. ,"Recovery guarantees for Internet applications", ACM Trans. on Internet Tech. 4(3): 289-328, 2004.
18. A. I. Kistijantoro, et. al, "Component Replication in Distributed Systems: a Case study using Enterprise Java Beans", 22nd IEEE Symposium on Reliable Distributed Systems, SRDS 2003
19. M. Patiño-Martínez, et. al, "Consistent Database Replication at the Middleware Level", ACM Transactions on Computer Systems (TOCS). Volume 23, No. 4, 2005, pp 1-49.
20. A. I. Kistijantoro, et. al., "Transaction Manager Failover: A Case Study Using JBOSS Application Server", Technical Report, School of Computing, Newcastle University, 2006.
21. B. Ban, "JavaGroups User's Guide" http://www.javagroups.com
22. S. Subramanyam, "JSR 4: ECperf Benchmark Specification Java Community Process" http://www.jcp.org/en/jsr/detail?id=4

SeBGIS 2006 PC Chair's Message

Many societal applications, for example, in domains such as health care, land use, disaster management, and environmental monitoring, increasingly rely on geographical information for their decision making. With the emergence of the World WideWeb this information is typically located in multiple, distributed, diverse, and autonomously maintained systems. Therefore, strategic decision making in these societal applications relies on the ability to enrich the semantics associated to geographical information in order to support a wide variety of tasks including data integration, interoperability, knowledge reuse, knowledge acquisition, knowledge management, spatial reasoning, and many others. While all research realized in the area of the Semantic Web provides a foundation for annotating information resources with machine-readable meaning, much work must still be done to elicit semantics of geographical information. Spatial information has embraced many recent technological developments in which semantics plays a crucial role. Data warehouses and OLAP systems constitute a fundamental component of today's diverse locations.

The aim of this workshop was to bring together researchers from academia and industry as well as practitioners to discuss views on how to integrate semantics into current geographic information systems, and how this will benefit the end users. The workshop was organized in a way to highly stimulate interaction among the participants.

Three or four experts from the same or a closely related discipline to the authors reviewed each of the 32 submissions. I would like to sincerely thank the Program Committee and the additional experts who realized an excellent work in carefully reviewing the papers: they made a strong contribution to the quality of the workshop. Fifteen high-quality papers were chosen, contributing to a successful and fruitful workshop.

The papers were presented in five sessions of three papers. Further, there was an additional session for the invited keynote speaker of the workshop. Session 1 (day 1) focused on GIS integration and GRID. Session 2 (day 1) was devoted to the topic of spatial data warehouses. Session 3 (day 1) hosted the invited speaker of the workshop, Jean Brodeur, who presented his work on semantic interoperability in geographic information at ISO/TC211, the technical committee for international standards in geographic information. Session 4 (day 1) coped with different aspects of spatio-temporal GIS. Session 1 on the following day (day 2) presented several approaches for coping with semantic similarity. Session 2 (day 2) covered the issue of enhancing usability. The workshop was concluded with Session 3 (day 2), which was devoted to an open discussion (round table) on the outcomes of this workshop and the future of Semantic-Based Geographic Information Systems.

August 2006   Esteban Zimány, Université Libre de Bruxelles, Belgium

R. Meersman, Z. Tari, P. Herrero et al. (Eds.): OTM Workshops 2006, LNCS 4278, p. 1565, 2006.
© Springer-Verlag Berlin Heidelberg 2006

Matching Schemas for Geographical Information Systems Using Semantic Information

Christoph Quix, Lemonia Ragia, Linlin Cai, and Tian Gan

Informatik V, RWTH Aachen University, Germany
{quix, ragia, cai, tian}@i5.informatik.rwth-aachen.de
http://www-i5.informatik.rwth-aachen.de/

Abstract. Integration and interoperability is a basic requirement for geographic information systems (GIS). The web provides access to geographic data in several ways: on the one hand, web-based interactive GIS applications provide maps and routing information to end users; on the other hand, the data of some GIS can be accessed in a programmatic way using a web service. Thereby, the data is made available for other GIS applications. However, integrating data from various sources is a tedious task which requires the mapping of the involved schemas as a first step. Schema matching analyzes and identifies similarities of two schemas, but all approaches can be only semi-automatic as human intervention is required to verify the result of a schema matching algorithm. In this paper, we present an approach that improves the matching result of existing solutions by using semantic information provided by the context of the geographic application. This reduces the effort for manually correcting the results which has been validated in several application examples.

1 Introduction

Integration and interoperability is a basic requirement for geographic information systems (GIS). The existence of a variety of geographical data is very important for geographic applications. A lot of phenomena can be explained using the knowledge extracted from data of past years. However, integrating data from various sources is a tedious task which requires the mapping of the involved schemas as a first step. There is sometimes insufficient description of the data, with no clear explanation of the entities, attributes etc. Standards like GML (Geography Markup Language, http://www.opengeospatial.org/) have been proposed but are not yet widely in use.

Since geographic data tends to be collected from various sources and archived locally, most geographic databases are heterogeneous, i.e., different types, different resolutions and different spatial properties under different formats. The problems that might arise due to *heterogeneity* of the data include *structural heterogeneity* (*schematic heterogeneity*) and *semantic heterogeneity* (*data heterogeneity*) [10]. The semantic conflicts occur when semantically similar information is represented by, for example, different data structures in different local databases.

Research in *schema matching* aims at providing automatic methods to identify relationships between different schemas [14]. The output of a schema matching system should be a mapping that enables the translation of data from one database to

R. Meersman, Z. Tari, P. Herrero et al. (Eds.): OTM Workshops 2006, LNCS 4278, pp. 1566–1575, 2006.

another database. Such a mapping can be expressed in form of a query which extracts the data from the source and transforms it into the schema of the target. Many aspects have to be considered during the process of matching, such as data values, element names, constraint information, structure information, domain knowledge, cardinality relationships, and so on. Several approaches have been proposed for schema matching [18,20]. There exist also a few matching prototypes such as Protoplasm [2] and Coma(++) [1,4]. They use mainly linguistic and structural schema matching techniques, sometimes in combination with external information such as thesauri to identify synonyms or similar terms.

Related to schema matching is ontology matching or ontology alignment [6]. An *ontology* provides a shared and common understanding of a domain that can be communicated between people with distributed or heterogeneous application systems [11]. In contrast to schemas which mainly describe the structure of data, ontologies rather define the semantics of data. While semantically rich modeling languages (such as EER or UML) are used at design time, the semantics is usually not becoming part of the database implementation (one reason might be performance). Thus, this semantic information is not available for schema matching.

We have made the experience that application of schema algorithms requires a detailed understanding of these algorithms to find the "right" algorithm and the "best" parameters. It also requires expertise in the domain of the schemas to be matched because no algorithm can deliver a perfect result; manual verification of the proposed mappings is always required. As this can become a tedious task for large schemas, our idea is to apply the knowledge that has been formalized as ontologies for a domain to the problem of schema matching. In particular, we use ontologies to identify incorrect mappings in a result of schema matching algorithm. In this paper, we show how this methodology can be applied to support schema matching in GIS. We propose to extend our generic schema matching system with a specific component for matching of GIS schemas which exploits the semantic information given in ontologies, type hierarchies, or taxonomies to improve the schema matching result.

In the following, we will first discuss related work in section 2. Section 3 then presents the main ideas of our method. In section 4, we will discuss the application of our system to GIS schemas. Section 5 concludes our paper and points out future work.

2 Related Work

There have been many approaches for schema matching. The main reason for the various approaches is that each schema matching problem has its own characteristics and might require a specific solution. In the following, we focus on the approaches which are relevant for our work; surveys about schema matching are given in [18,20].

The *Cupid* algorithm [14] is intended to be generic across data models and has been applied to XML and relational examples. Schemas are represented as tree structures; the main idea of the algorithm is that the similarity of leaf nodes (attributes) contributes also to the similarity of inner nodes (elements/relations). The initial similarity values are computed by a linguistic method, which might also use auxiliary information such as thesauri. A similar idea is followed by the *Similarity Flooding* algorithm [15]. Schemas are represented as directed labeled graphs. Based on the idea that if two nodes are similar then also their neighbors are similar, the similarity of two nodes in the graph is propagated to its neighbors. This procedure is repeated until a fix-point is reached. The initial input similarities can be computed by any kind of linguistic matching method. The algorithm can be applied to any kind of graph structure. The *COMA* schema matching system is a platform designed to combine multiple matchers in a flexible way [4]. It provides a large number of individual matchers, which contains both terminology approaches and structural approaches. COMA also allows users to reuse the previously obtained matching results. COMA++ [1] is an update of COMA and supports also ontologies as inputs and provides several matchers for ontology matching.

An early work on schema matching in GIS [16] is based on structural data description, finding similarities between the attributes and entities using various criteria. The aim was to identify a single schema to be used in land-use information systems. A matching system based on machine learning is proposed in [13]. The goal is to construct a mediated schema to allow uniform querying of multiple sources. Another approach provides the integration of spatial databases using different scales [5]. It involves schema matching process finding inter-schemas correspondences which are based on instance level relationships. In [17], a schema integration method is proposed, that consists of two steps: in a first step, the relationships between the source schemas are identified. Then, an integrated schema is generated and mappings between the integrated schema and the source schemas are established.

Other approaches focus on the semantic integration of geographic ontologies. For example, a formal concept analysis to integrate several geographic domain ontologies to one top-level ontology is used in [12]. Similar concepts are identified if they have similar characteristics or properties. A methodology for comparing categories among geographic ontologies is presented in [8]. Another aspect is addressed in [7], in which the authors use ontologies for the design of the system. They provide a formal framework for expressing the mappings between the ontologies used by the domain specialist and the models used by the information systems engineer.

3 Semantic Schema Matching

A common problem of schema matching algorithms is that they produce only approximate results, i.e. the similarity values are only one indicator for the similarity of two schema elements. Therefore, advanced matching systems such as COMA++ [1] and Protoplasm [2] follow a hybrid approach in which several matching techniques can be combined. However, also the combination of several matching algorithms cannot produce a result for which we can say with 100% confidence that two elements are or are not a match. Usually, one will consider only matching elements with a similarity value above a certain threshold. This might have the effect that too many matching elements (including incorrect matches) are detected if the threshold is too low. On the other hand, if the threshold is too high, only a few elements will be matched (and even this result might still contain incorrect matches). In any case, manual effort is necessary to verify the result, i.e. remove incorrect matches and insert matches that have not been detected.

Therefore, our approach tries to identify the wrongly matched elements to improve the result of a schema matching algorithm and thereby reducing the manual effort for the verification of the result. The idea is to use a logical formalism to represent the schemas, their constraints and the relationships between them. Then, we use this logical representation to validate the detected mappings between the schemas.

The main problem of this idea is to have information that can be used to identify incorrect mappings. In our system, we use ontologies for that purpose. An ontology defines a set of concepts and properties, which are connected by different types of relationships (e.g. specialization, generalization, synonyms) for a specific domain. Recently, ontologies have been formalized and standardized in the semantic web area in form of the Web Ontology Language (OWL). In this context, ontologies are defined as a set of formulas in description logics which may contain constraints and rich semantic relationships (subClassOf, cardinality constraints, disjunction, etc.).

The use of ontologies has several advantages. Firstly, ontologies contain the semantic information in form of logical formulas which is required to identify incorrect mappings. Detecting inconsistencies in an ontology is a very common task in this domain. Secondly, ontologies have usually a broader context than schemas. Ontologies model the knowledge of a domain whereas a schema is often limited to a specific application. Therefore, ontologies can be used to bridge the "gap" between two schemas. Finally, there are currently many efforts to develop standardized ontologies (expressed in OWL) for several domains. As we will explain in section 4, we are currently implementing a component that can make use of the semantic information expressed in weaker formalisms such as taxonomies or type hierarchies.

In the following, we will first explain in more detail the basic idea and the individual steps of our methodology and then discuss implementation issues.

3.1 Methodology

The outline of our solution is sketched in Fig. 1. First, the schemas are matched with an ontology. This matching results in a mapping between the elements of the schemas and the concepts of the ontology. Then, the two schemas are matched. All the discovered mappings are then integrated into an extended ontology which will be checked for inconsistencies.

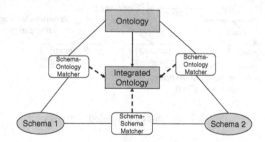

Fig. 1. Outline of the Semantic Schema Matching Algorithm

Step 1: Matching Schemas with the Ontology
The first step is to match the schemas with the ontology. This matching step requires high precision, because the result has high impact on the following steps. As the elements in schemas and ontologies are usually organized in different structures, the

elements will be matched using only linguistic information. We assume that the terms used in the ontology and the schemas are at least similar. If this is not the case, also auxiliary information such as dictionaries and thesauri could be used to find matches between schema and ontology elements. It is also possible to use general purpose ontologies such as SUMO.

The result of this step is a mapping between schema elements and the elements of the ontology. The schema elements are inserted into the ontology as artificial "concepts", related by "equivalent" statements to the original ontology elements.

Step 2: Matching Schemas
To match the schemas, any kind of matching algorithm can be used. The result is a list of mappings between the elements of the two schemas. In our system, we can use a simplified version of Cupid [14] or and Similarity Flooding [15].

As mentioned before, one advantage of our approach is that we are able to identify incorrect mappings (if this can be derived from the semantic information that is available). Therefore, it is possible to lower the threshold for the initial matching methods so that more matching elements are found.

Step 3: Extend Ontology with Mappings
In the third step, the equivalences implied by the detected mappings are inserted into the ontology. As we have already inserted "artificial" elements representing the schema elements, we just need to relate these elements with some additional "equivalent" statements.

Fig. 2 shows a fragment of an extended ontology. The original ontology contains classes such as "Country", "City", and "Continent". The corresponding elements of the schemas have been defined as "equivalentClasses" of the original classes (e.g. "Schema1Continent", "Schema2City"); these mappings have been identified by the schema-ontology matcher.

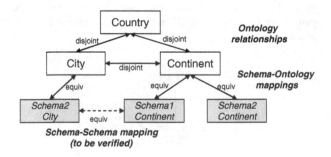

Fig. 2. Fragment of extended ontology

Step 4: Validate the Mappings
The extended ontology can now be sent to the reasoning system to detect the inconsistencies. This is done separately for each identified match. For example, the schema matching system has detected a match between the schema element describing the "name" of a city and the element describing the "name" of a continent. We would then insert into the ontology a statement saying that the corresponding

properties of the classes are equivalent. This implies that the classes representing the domains of these properties are not disjoint (unless they are empty). If the ontology contains a statement that the classes (or some other equivalent or super classes) are disjoint, then this leads to an inconsistency in the ontology. Therefore, we can derive that the current mapping is not correct.

The example of Fig. 2 does not contain any definition of properties; for reasons of simplicity, we have added an equivalence between the corresponding concepts ("Schema1Continent" and "Schema2City"). Now, it is easy to verify that this mapping implies an inconsistency as "Schema2City" as equivalent to "City" and "Schema1Continent" is equivalent to "Continent", but "City" and "Continent" are disjoint concepts.

3.2 System Architecture and Implementation

Our prototype has been implemented using the Microsoft .NET Framework 1.1 and C# as programming language. The whole process can be controlled from a GUI component which also displays the mapping results. The core of the system is the matching framework Protoplasm [2], a library that simplifies the implementation of matching algorithms. It contains several data structures (graphs, matrices) and operators which are often used in schema matching algorithms. These operators include several lexical matchers (such as tokenizers, n-gram-matchers) and also methods to iterate and navigate over the graph structure. We have extended Protoplasm with an import operator for ontologies and a specific schema-ontology matcher. We use the Racer system [www.racer-systems.com] as reasoning server which supports reasoning on OWL ontologies. The ontologies to be verified are sent to the Racer server separately, if Racer reports an inconsistency, the proposed mapping will be discarded.

3.3 Evaluation

We evaluated our system with some schemas from different domains. The first example is MONDIAL [http://www.dbis.informatik.uni-goettingen.de/Mondial/], a data set of geographical web data sources with information about cities, countries, etc. The second example is taken from GeneX [http://www.ncgr.org/genex/] database, a

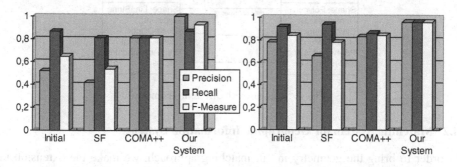

Fig. 3. Experimental Results for the MONDIAL (left) and GeneX (right) examples

database (and application) for the management of gene expressions. The ontologies for these examples have been created manually for an integration scenario, i.e., the ontologies were not tuned for the schema matching scenario.

The results of the evaluation are shown in Fig. 3, compared to Similarity Flooding (SF) and COMA++. In both cases, we used a simplified Cupid algorithm to produce initial schema matching result. As our system is only able to identify incorrect mappings and is not able to derive new mappings, only the precision of the result (the ratio between correct and incorrect mappings detected) could be improved compared to the initial results of the schema-schema matching algorithm. The performance of our system is comparable to other systems; the additional time for the semantic verification of the mappings is about 15-25% of the total time.

4 Semantic Schema Matching in Geographic Applications

4.1 Characteristics of Geographic Data

Geographic data include traditional geometric and thematic data. A typical GIS schema contains elements that (i) describe the geometry of the object, e.g. lines, shapes, polylines, etc.; (ii) describe other properties of the object (thematic data), e.g. surface of a road, population, data of the environment; and (iii) are used internally in the GIS such as identifiers, (foreign) keys. To achieve a high quality mapping between GIS schemas, we need to distinguish between these different types of elements. The idea is to apply specific matching techniques for each element type. Such a distinction fits nicely into our semantic approach, as specific ontologies for each element type can be applied separately.

Fig. 4 illustrates simple examples to show typical characteristics of of GIS schemas. The names of the elements (Road) are in this case the same, but there is the geometry of the objects does not match (Polygon vs. LineString). Although the names of the elements and some attributes are the same, the elements are characterized to be different. On the other hand, the similarity of the geometry might contribute to the overall similarity of the elements.

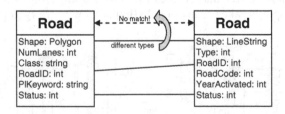

Fig. 4. Schemas with different geometry

4.2 Matching System for Geographic Information Systems

In order to bring the geometry in our matching approach, we make the extension in our system using the *Geography Markup Language* (GML). GML is an XML based encoding standard for geographic information developed by the *Open Geospatial*

Consortium (OGC, http://www.opengeospatial.org/). The main elements of the GML modeling structure are geographic features which represent real world geographical objects. Their geometric properties are modeled by a uniform geometric definition using two-dimensional coordinates. GML 2.0 is defined in XML Schema (XSD) and is divided into three parts: geometry schema, feature schema, and XLinks schema to provide support for linking the geographical data with other sources and to allow referencing on GML documents. The current version 3.1 of GML [3] also supports now also 3D geometry and complex values of features.

While the form of the geometrical description is defined very detailed, the form of the actual features is not. Instead GML offers a structural framework to fit the scenario it is meant to describe. Every model is made up of features. These features have properties. The properties have a name, a type and a value. The structure of the feature, hence the number and types of the properties, is defined by its type.

To identify semantic similarity of geometry types, we use the type hierarchy of GML geometry types [3]. For example, based on the hierarchy we can assume that 'Surface' and 'Polygon' are similar because they have the same direct super class. On the other hand, 'Polygon' and 'Curve' are not directly related in this hierarchy; thus, we can infer that these concepts are not similar. Of course, this is a very simplistic view of similarity of classes which has to be implemented using well-defined measures. Our implementation uses several different measures to compute the similarity of types (as defined in type hierarchies) or classes (as defined in ontologies). Type hierarchies and ontologies often do not contain the semantic information (explicit statements about disjointness or equivalence of concepts) which is required for our approach to detect logical inconsistencies. Therefore, we use the computed similarity values to enrich the ontologies with semantic information required. Examples for such measures are the linguistic similarity of class names and their synonyms, the properties of a class, and the similarity of semantically related classes. Such measures have been already defined in the context of ontology alignment [6,19]. More specific procedures for the geographic domain, that could be applied in this context, have also been described [8,12].

To analyze such relationships in geographic schemas, we have extended our schema matching system with *GeoMatcher* component. The *GeoMatcher* treats geometric information such as data types, value ranges and relationship types. It is also based on ontologies, and is therefore an extension of the ontological reasoning component of the core system. Please note that according to our discussion above, the similarity of geometry types might contribute to the similarity of the entities in which these geometry types are used. Because of this, the *GeoMatcher* might also add new mappings and not only delete mappings as the semantic matching component in the core system. A similar idea to derive indirect mappings has already been proposed earlier [21], but we use the knowledge contained in ontologies more explicitly.

The type hierarchy of GML is only one source for semantic information about geographic entities. In addition, we plan to use additional classifications and categorizations such as CORINE LC Classes [http://nfp-lv.eionet.eu.int/clc_db/en/classes/class_ndx.htm] or the ontology for the ISO standard Geographic Information – Metadata (ISO 19115:2003, http://loki.cae.drexel.edu/~wbs/ontology/iso-19115.htm). As discussed above, a problem here is that these ontologies often do not contain the required semantic information to detect logical inconsistencies. Therefore, a similarity value for two classes is computed (using the measures described above) if no explicit information is given.

5 Conclusion

Integration of data is a task that is especially required for geographical information systems as certain phenomena can be only explained by looking at several data sources at the same time. Schema matching methods have been proposed in the recent years to support the task of information integration in a semi-automatic way. Still, schema matching requires manual intervention as the methods are not able to deliver perfect solutions.

In this paper, we have presented an approach that improves schema matching results by exploiting semantic information that has been formalized in ontologies. Ontologies represent the knowledge of a particular domain. By introducing this knowledge into the schema matching process, we reduce the manual effort that is required for schema matching significantly as we are now able to detect most of the incorrect mappings automatically. Therefore, an information systems engineer needs to spend less time on the verification of the results of a schema matching algorithm. Our approach can be used as an extension to any schema matching algorithm as it is independent of the previous steps; it just requires a list of mappings as input.

The application of our basic matching system to GIS schemas was also promising, but our analysis of geographic data has shown that more specialized matchers for GIS schemas are necessary. Therefore, we extended our matching system with a *GeoMatcher* component which takes into account the specific features of GIS schemas. As the ontologies in the GIS domain do not contain the required explicit knowledge about disjointness or equivalence of concepts, an important feature of the *GeoMatcher* is computation of similarity values of concepts based on the (limited) information given in the knowledge. An initial evaluation of the core part of the system showed very good results; however, more evaluation results in the area of GIS schemas are required to verify and optimize the *GeoMatcher* component.

Future work will concentrate on providing optimized matching methods for the different parts of a GIS schema. In particular, our focus is on using more semantic information for matching, even if it cannot be used to prove inconsistencies in a strict logical sense. We plan to use our generic metamodel *GeRoMe* [9] to ease the matching of models from different modeling languages (e.g., OWL, XML Schema, SQL). Using such techniques, we can provide further extensions and improvements for schema matching results which are not limited only to the GIS domain.

References

[1] D. Aumüller, H.H. Do, S. Massmann, E. Rahm: Schema and Ontology Matching with COMA++. *Proc. Intl. Conf. on Management of Data (SIGMOD)*, 2005.

[2] P.A. Bernstein, S. Melnik, M. Petropoulos, C. Quix: Industrial-strength schema matching. *SIGMOD Record*, 33(4):38-43, 2004.

[3] S. Cox, P. Daisey, R. Lake, C. Portele, A. Whiteside: OpenGIS Geography Markup Language (GML) Implementation Specification. Version 3.1.0, 2004.

[4] H.H.Do, E.Rahm. COMA: a system for flexible combination of schema matching approaches. *Proc. Conf. on Very Large Data Bases (VLDB)*, pp. 610–621, 2001.

[5] T. Devogele, C. Parent, S. Spaccapietra: On Spatial Database Integration. *Intl. Journal of Geographical Information Science*, 12(4):335-352, 1998.

[6]   J. Euzenat (Ed.): State of the art in ontology alignment. *Deliverable 2.2.3, Knowledge Web Project*, http://knowledgeweb.semanticweb.org/, 2004.

[7] F. Fonseca, C. Davis, G. Camara: Bridging ontologies and conceptual schemas in geographic information integration. *Geoinformatica*, 7(4):355–378, 2003.

[8] M. Kavouras, M. Kokla, E. Tomai: Comparing categories among geographic ontologies. *Computers & Geosciences*, Vol. 31, no. 2, pp. 145-154, 2005.

[9] D. Kensche, C. Quix, M.A. Chatti, M. Jarke: GeRoMe – A Generic Role Based Metamodel for Model Management. *Proc. 4th Intl. Conf. on Ontologies, DataBases, and Applications of Semantics (ODBASE)*, Agia Napa, Cyprus, 2005.

[10] W. Kim, J. Seo: Classifying Schematic and Data Heterogeneity in Multi-database Systems. *IEEE Computer*, 24(12):12-18, 1991.

[11] M. Klein, D. Fensel, F. Harmelen, I. Horrocks: The Relation between Ontology and Schema-languages: Translating OIL-specifications in XML-Schema. *Proc. ECAI Workshop on Applications of Ontologies and Problem-Solving Methods*, Berlin, 2000.

[12] M. Kokla, M. Kavouras: Fusion of top-level and geographic domain ontologies based on context formation and complementarity. *Intl. Journal of Geographical Information Science*, 15(7):679-687, 2001.

[13] S. Manoah, O. Boucelma, Y. Lassoued : Schema Matching in GIS. *Proc. 11th Intl. Conf. on Artificial Intelligence: Methodology, Systems and Applications (AIMSA)*, Varna, Bulgaria, 2004.

[14] J. Madhavan, P.A. Bernstein, E. Rahm: Generic schema matching with Cupid. *Proc. Conf. on Very Large Data Bases (VLDB)*, pp. 49–58, Rome, Italy, 2001.

[15] S.Melnik, H. Garcia-Molina, E. Rahm: Similarity Flooding: A Versatile Graph Matching Algorithm. *Proc. 18th International Conference on Data Engineering (ICDE)*, pp. 117-128, San Jose, CA, 2002.

[16] L.T. Nyerges: Schema integration analysis for the development of GIS databases. *Intl. Journal of Geographical Information Systems*, 3(2):153-183, 1989.

[17] J. Park: Schema Integration Methodology and Toolkit for Heterogeneous and Distributed Geographic Databases. *Working Paper, University of Minnesota*, http://misrc.umn.edu/workingpapers/abstracts/0131.aspx, 2001.

[18] E. Rahm, P.A. Bernstein: A survey of approaches to automatic schema matching. *VLDB Journal*, 10(4):334–350, 2001.

[19] M.A. Rodríguez, M.J. Egenhofer. Determining Semantic Similarity Among Entity Classes from Different Ontologies. *IEEE Transactions on Knowledge and Data Engineering* 15(2):442-456, 2003.

[20] P. Shvaiko, J. Euzenat: A Survey of Schema-based Matching Approaches. *Journal on Data Semantics IV*, LNCS 3730, pp. 146-171, Springer, 2005.

[21] L. Xu, D.W. Embley: Using domain ontologies to discover direct and indirect matches for schema elements. *Proc. Workshop on Semantic Integration at ISWC 2003*, Sanibel Island, FL, 2003.

Towards a Context Ontology for Geospatial Data Integration

Damires Souza[1,2], Ana Carolina Salgado[1], and Patricia Tedesco[1]

[1] Centro de Informática, Universidade Federal de Pernambuco, Brazil
C.P. 7851, Recife, PE, Brasil – CEP 50732-970
{dysf, acs, pcart}@cin.ufpe.br
[2] Centro Federal de Educação Tecnológica da Paraíba – CEFET/PB, Brazil

Abstract. Recently, Geospatial data and Geographic Information Systems (GIS) have been increasingly used. As a result, the integration of geospatial data has become a crucial task for decision makers. Since GIS and geospatial databases are designed by different organizations using different representation models and there are diverse levels of detail for the spatial features, it is much more complex to achieve data integration in geospatial databases. To help matters, context information may be employed to improve two fundamental aspects in Geospatial Data Integration: (1) schema mapping generation and (2) query answering. However, a relevant issue when using context is how to better represent context information. Ontologies are an interesting approach to represent context, since they enable sharing and reusability and help reasoning. In this paper, we propose a context ontology to formally represent context in geospatial data integration. We also present an example where this context ontology is used to improve query processing.

Keywords: Geospatial Data Integration, Context, Ontologies.

1 Introduction

As the Geographic Information System (GIS) community grows and geospatial data increases in importance, many public and private organizations need to disseminate and access the latest data as fast as possible and at a minimum cost [1]. Most GIS data is usually stored in geographic databases, although some is still stored in proprietary archive systems. To allow data dissemination, GIS and their geographic database schemas have to be, at least, interoperable. However, over time, GIS have been developed independently to meet specific requirements. As a result, interoperability is hampered by the difficulty to reconcile and integrate geospatial data from the many heterogeneous GIS and their data sets. Amongst all the issues in interoperability, semantic heterogeneity is the hardest to reconcile and still remains open.

To overcome this difficulty, recent works have considered the use of ontologies [2, 3] as a way of providing a domain reference to improve geospatial schema and data integration. In this work, we use context information, i.e. the circumstantial information that makes a situation unique and comprehensible [4,5], as well as domain ontologies, as a way to enrich the geospatial data integration process. In this

R. Meersman, Z. Tari, P. Herrero et al. (Eds.): OTM Workshops 2006, LNCS 4278, pp. 1576–1585, 2006.

light, context information is used to ease schema mapping discovery, helping to determine the correct meaning of an entity. It is also used to improve query processing capabilities, providing users with "meaningful", i.e., more relevant results. Thus, context information (explicitly or implicitly gathered) and domain ontology are used to handle heterogeneity and, consequently, provide users with more complete answers according to their current context of work.

To illustrate the importance of context usage, consider two geospatial data sources which store the entity *"River"*. In data source A, *"River"* is called *"StreamofWater"* and is represented as a single line. In source B, *"River"* is represented as a compound line. When a user poses a query like *"select r.name, r.length from river r;"*, s/he is looking for all the rivers' names and their correspondent lengths. To answer that query, all context information around its formulation should be considered. Firstly a mapping such as *A.StreamofWater ⇔ B.River* (which has already been generated) is observed. This means that both entities are semantically equivalent. As a result, query execution retrieves all the rivers found in both sources. Furthermore, to produce the final result, the system takes into account the user application scale, which is the best representation to be depicted (line or compound line) and the user preferences. All these information are contextual and depend on query formulation moment.

An important issue in reasoning about context is how to represent its information [4,6,7]. Nevertheless, a challenge to be faced is the fact that there is not still a standard model for representing it. Context ontologies have been considered an interesting approach because they enable sharing and reusability and may be used by different reasoning mechanisms [6,7].

In this paper, we present an ontology to represent contextual information in geospatial data integration. The idea is to identify which information pertinent to the geospatial realm can be classified as context and which kinds of context should be considered to improve data integration. Through this model, it is possible to compose inference rules that enable the discovery of high-level implicit context from low-level explicit context. To clarify matters, we present a scenario illustrating how this context ontology can be used to improve query processing in geospatial data integration.

This paper is organized as follows: Section 2 introduces some concepts related to context and context representation; Section 3 presents context in the light of geospatial data integration; Section 4 describes our proposal and an example of its use. Finally, Section 5 draws some conclusions and points out some future work.

2   Context and Context Representation

Almost every statement we make is imprecise and hence meaningful only if understood with reference to an underlying context which embodies a number of hidden assumptions [8]. In this sense, context is any information that can be used to characterize the situation of an entity [5]. This entity may be an application user or a computational object, such as a device, a data source or a relation in a relational database schema. An application that gathers and uses context information in order to adapt its behavior accordingly is called a context-aware system.

As an illustration, imagine a geospatial database which stores the following: *Street('Epitacio Pessoa', 3000, 'Good')*. How can these values be interpreted? When trying to figure out the sentence's meaning, some possibilities may be considered: (1) *Street(name, length, conservation level)* or (2) *Street(name, width, cleanliness level)*. The point is that each database maintains its own assumptions about the data it stores in an autonomous and independent way. Thus, context information is used to specify the assumptions made in database design to understand the underlying semantics. In the database domain, context may be used in several ways to capture the relevant semantics related to an object and its relationships to other objects [9]. Metadata, for instance, are examples of information that can be dealt as context.

To allow context usage, it is crucial to define how context information will be represented. Some issues should be considered when evaluating techniques to represent context: (1) the model must be portable, (2) it should have validation tools for edition, type checking and conversion between formats, (3) formality is welcome since it eases definition, reasoning and reusability and (4) it must provide reasoning.

Current research has worked with a considerable number of context representation techniques, such as Contextual Graphs [4], Topic Maps [10] and Ontologies [6,7]. A contextual graph is an acyclic directed graph and allows a context-based representation for operational processes by taking into account the working environment [4]. Topic maps are an attempt to connect pieces of data into a graph which represent the relationship between them while providing a lightweight way of navigating the information [10]. Ontologies are commonly referred as the shared understanding of some domains, often conceived as a set of entities, relations, functions, axioms and instances [6]. Thus, shared ontologies are fundamental for reusing knowledge, serving as a means for integrating problem-solving, domain representation and knowledge acquisition modules [11].

According to the issues pointed out above, ontologies seem to be one of the best options for context representation. In other words, there are several advantages for developing ontology-based context models [6,7], namely: to provide knowledge sharing (services are supposed to deal with the same set of concepts), to enable information reuse, to define semantics independently from data representation, and finally to enable the use of existing inference engines.

3   Context in Geospatial Data Integration

Geospatial data integration solutions attempt to provide users with a uniform interface to access and retrieve information from distributed data sources (e.g. GIS or geographic databases) that are usually heterogeneous, autonomous and dynamic. The most important advantage of these systems is that they enable users to specify what they want without thinking about how to obtain the answers [12].

One of the main problems in geospatial data integration systems, which adopt a virtual approach [13], is query reformulation. When a user poses a query, it is decomposed into sub-queries to be evaluated and executed on the remote data sources. To this end, the system requires a complete understanding of the semantics of these sources. Thus, the description of a data source must include its metadata (schema), contents, completeness and its query capabilities, mostly in the geospatial realm, since not all data sources will be able to execute the required spatial operations. Besides, the complexity of the process of query reformulation depends on mappings defined between the related schemas.

Due to heterogeneity, schematic and semantic conflicts appear either at the schema level or the instance level. As geospatial data are often described according to multiple perceptions, using different terms with different levels of detail, heterogeneity becomes more accentuated. In this sense, geospatial data conflicts are concerned with all about general data conflicts, such as domain incompatibility (different data types, precision and measure units), incompatibility among entities (names, keys), generalization and aggregation, and so forth. Specific geospatial data conflicts are: different scales, different coordinate systems, different geometric data types and multi-representation, vector/raster storage models and specific geographical composition (e.g. a street in a source may be represented as a unique line; in another source the same street may be seen as a composition of various line segments).

To ease conflict resolution and improve query reformulation, context information can be used. Some of the metadata used to describe the data sources contents becomes contextual information (e.g. available spatial operators). Other contextual information is perceived or inferred dynamically during query processing (e.g. the application scale in use). Applying context reasoning in query processing enriches the complete process as well as provides what has been called *context-aware queries* - those whose results depend on the context at the time of their submission [14].

In the geospatial realm, specific data conflicts arise mostly when sub-queries answers are assembled to produce a final result. Context information such as user preferences, scale and coordinate system in use, multi-representation factors, intended level of detail and spatial relationships should be taken into account to determine the best scale, format and data representations to be presented to the user.

In summary, reasoning over context information can help us to improve geospatial data integration in various aspects, namely: (1) context may ease inter-schema mapping generation, since it helps to determine the meaning of the terms, in addition to domain ontology that is used as a semantic reference; (2) query answering becomes more relevant; and (3) specific geospatial conflicts are better solved according to query formulation context, necessary spatial operations and intended level of detail. In this paper, we present a geospatial context ontology and its usage. We focus on using context to better resolve data conflicts to produce more relevant query answers.

4 A Context Ontology for GeoSpatial Data Integration

In this section, we present our first steps towards the construction of an ontology for representing context according to geospatial data integration issues. The ontology has been developed using the Protégé 3.2 tool[1]. In order to motivate its construction, we firstly introduce a geospatial data integration example. Then, we explain the main concepts defined in the ontology and provide more examples to demonstrate its usage.

4.1 An Integration Example

Our motivating example is related to the integration of two geospatial data sources, A and B which store data about the Brazilian Hydrographic System. Source A is at scale

---

[1] http://protege.stanford.edu/

of 1:1'000'000, while source B is more detailed and is at scale of 1:250'000. Figure 1 shows a UML diagram[2] for both data sources.

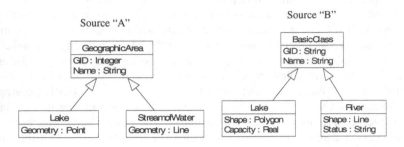

Fig. 1. "A" Data Source Schema and "B" Data Source Schema

Data Source "A" contains two classes – *Lake* and *StreamofWater* which inherit some characteristics from their superclass – *GeographicArea*. Both classes have a geometry attribute. Data source "B" contains *Lake* and *River* which are subclasses of *BasicClass*. Both have a shape attribute. In this example the semantic conflicts related to schema level are: (1) different entity names – *GeographicArea* vs. *BasicClass* and *StreamofWater* vs. *River*; (2) different attribute names – *geometry* vs. *shape*; and different data types – *integer* vs. *string* (*GID*) and *point* vs. *polygon* (*lake*).

Other relevant conflicts are the instance level ones. Here we have different scales *1:1'000'000* (source A) vs. *1:250'000* (source B) and the multi-representation problem, since lake is represented by a point in source A and by a polygon in source B. Finally, both data sources are considered to be vector, but, in fact, real data sets may be vector or raster, which raises complexity and may entail format conversions.

4.2 The Context Ontology

The context ontology for GeoSpatial Data Integration is depicted in Figure 2. For the sake of space, we have converted it to the UML notation. Firstly, an upper ontology has been defined (in gray with borders in bold) with meta-concepts that can be used in a broad range of domains. Then, concepts from data integration have been specified (in gray) in a middle ontology that can be used in data integration solutions. Finally, concepts from the geospatial realm have been added to produce the specific ontology for geospatial data integration. The context ontology concepts are explained below.

Context Information: this is the ontology root. It is divided into four sub-concepts: *UserContext, DataContext, AssociationContext* and *ProcedureContext*.

UserContext: contains information about the user, his/her *profile*, identification (*UserID*) and location (*UserLocation*). The user may define his/her preferences about the way a query result should be presented.

DataContext: refers to all context information related to data. *Geospatial Entity* constitutes the main concept in geospatial data integration. It has several slots: *dataID, entityLocation, scale, data source, geometric representation* (e.g. point, line

---

[2] http://www.uml.org/

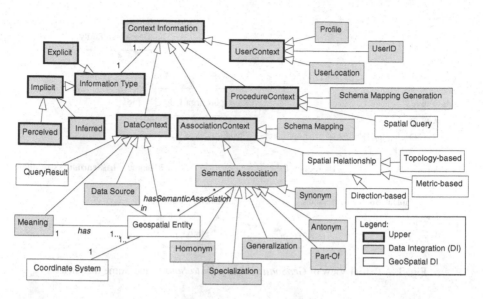

Fig. 2. Context Ontology for Geospatial Data Integration

or polygon), *coordinate system* and *meaning* (discovered when identifying its correspondent concept in the domain ontology). In Figure 3, we present a partial view of *Geospatial Entity* and *Data Source* with instances and relationships in the light of our motivating example. The example is in OntoViz (Protégé plug-in) notation[3], so instances are associated with their concepts through the *io* (instance of) relationship. Subtypes are associated with their supertypes through the *isa* relationship.

AssociationContext: is concerned with the relationships that may happen in geospatial data integration, such as *semantic associations, spatial relationships* and *schema mappings*. These are examples of inferred context information since they are derived according to a set of rules and conditions. *Semantic associations* represent relationships that really happen in real world and they are used to determine the similarity degree an entity (or an attribute) has to another. *Spatial relationships* may be derived through objects location analysis and they are classified into topological, directional or metrical. *Schema mappings* are the result of the schema mapping generation process and they are used to improve query reformulation.

ProcedureContext: a procedure is an ordered collection of actions [4]. The idea is to provide the contextualization of the steps that are executed in order to solve a problem. Each step is executed in a surrounding set of circumstances that compose the context of the execution and provide reaction accordingly. Therefore a procedure may be the complete *mapping generation* process or a particular *spatial query*.

All context information is also concerned with an information type that may be explicit or implicit. An explicit context information is obtained from static sources, such as a profile or an archive. An implicit one is perceived in the surrounding dynamic environment or it is derived through some reasoning process. For example, a spatial relationship is inferred through the analysis of two objects location. Still, a user's working scale may be identified through his/her application parameters.

---

[3] http://protege.cim3.net/cgi-bin/wiki.pl?OntoViz#nid6CS

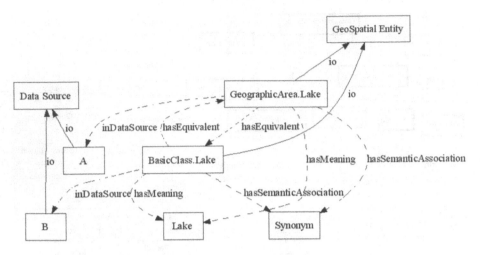

Fig. 3. A Partial View of *GeoSpatial Entity, Data Source* and Some Instances

4.3 Context Reasoning

The context ontology is used to represent and provide ways to maintain the contextual information used for the semantic interpretation of data sources elements as well as for the actual geospatial data integration. One of the advantages of using an ontology mechanism is inferring new complex information from existing basic context [7]. Hence, context may be used to ease mappings generation as well as improving query processing. In our example, we assume that those inter-schema mappings have already been generated, so we are able to focus on query reformulation.

We intend to use context to improve query processing and provide users with meaningful and more complete answers. In this sense, we consider *geospatial context-aware queries* as queries whose processing depends on the context at the time of their submission. This means that not only user preferences, scale, intended level of detail are to be considered but also the existent mappings between the sources that will be able to answer the query must be taken into account. Thus, all the surrounding query context must be used for reasoning.

Suppose that a user poses the following spatial query SQ1: *"SELECT Lake.name FROM Lake, Country WHERE INSIDE (Lake, Country) and Country.name like 'Brazil';"*. At query formulation time, there are some context information that have already been gathered while there are others that are perceived or inferred. For example, existent mappings between the entities must be observed. As *Lake* is one of the necessary entities to answer the query, we present some context values for its instances in Figure 4, using the OntoViz notation. The system infers that both entities are equivalent, but are represented differently and are stored in different scales.

In fact, the spatial query has its own context values, as we can see in Figure 5, also in the OntoViz notation. Since the query is about the "INSIDE" operation, the system can decide which data sources are able to execute it. Thus, *SQ1* is decomposed taking into consideration such information.

GeographicArea.Lake	
inDataSource =	A
hasSemanticAssociation =	Synonym
Scale =	1:1000'000
hasEquivalent =	BasicClass.Lake
GeometricRepresentation =	Point
hasMeaning =	Lake
hasType =	Explicit
ID =	114
hasName =	GeographicArea.Lake

BasicClass.Lake	
DescriptiveAttribute =	Capacity
inDataSource =	B
hasSemanticAssociation =	Synonym
Scale =	1:250'000
hasEquivalent =	GeographicArea.Lake
GeometricRepresentation =	Polygon
hasMeaning =	Lake
hasType =	Explicit
ID =	112
hasName =	BasicClass.Lake

Fig. 4. Context Values for Lake's Instances

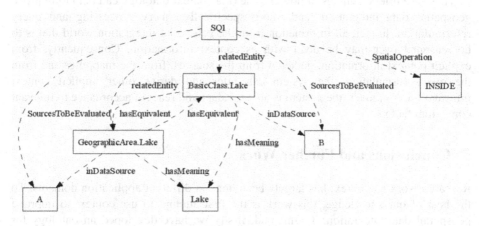

Fig. 5. Context Values for Spatial Query SQ1

When the sub-queries results are supposed to be assembled to produce the final answer, we have to consider other context information such as multi-representation and scales difference. Since the formulating scale is about 1:300'000, this means that the user is working with a more detailed view of the themes. Thus the graphical result will be taken from data source B whose scale of origin is closer and whose object representation (polygon) is more adequate to that level of detail. Sometimes, the final result may be produced from several sources if they return complementary information, for example, when some attributes are present in one source but are absent in another.

Representing context information using an ontology brings various benefits. It provides concept subsumption, concept consistency and instance checking (including object properties checking). A context ontology also allows defining constraints and reasoning rules that may be used to derive other implicit context information. For example, in Table 1, we present some properties that may be used to infer spatial relationships. Thus, knowing that *Brazil* is part of *South America*, we can provide users with the extra information that *Brazil* is also part of *America*. Also, if a user poses a query that needs the operation "INSIDE" but there is no available data source which realizes it, the system can search one that executes "CONTAINS", since from one we can derive the other and vice-versa.

Table 1. Some Property Rule Examples

Property	Rule	Instantiation
Part-of	If A isPartOf B and B isPartof C Then A isPartOf C;	If "Brazil" isPartOf "SouthAmerica" and "SouthAmerica" isPartOf "America" Then "Brazil" isPartOf "America";
Contains-Inside	If A contains B Then B isInside A;	If "Brazil" contains "São Paulo" Then "São Paulo" isInside "Brazil";

These are brief examples of how the use of a context ontology can help to improve geospatial data integration, and, more specifically, query processing and query reformulation. In fact, all information from the geospatial integration world that is to be reasoned over may be dealt with as context information. Consequently, from explicit context information, gathered from the sources, from the mappings and from the query formulation, the system can infer and derive other implicit context information. Moreover, the system is able to adapt and react in accordance to relevant contextual factors.

5   Conclusions and Further Work

Research work on context has largely been done in different application domains. To the best of our knowledge, this work is the first attempt to use context to improve geospatial data integration. To this end, firstly we have developed an ontology for context representation. Our ontology is a conjunction of three: an upper, a middle and a specific ontology.

To illustrate our ontology usage, we have presented a few examples according to a given geospatial data integration problem. Moreover, we have pointed out the importance context has when trying to provide users with more meaningful answers. This is extremely relevant in geospatial data integration systems.

We expect that this ontology will be used by developers of geospatial data integration solutions to identify, model and represent context information in their applications. In fact, the ontology can also be used by intelligent GIS agents to manage and infer all kinds of information that can be reasoned over.

We are currently developing additional scenarios which may allow us to work with other instances, constraints, queries and rules as well as with larger datasets. We intend to address the problem of query reformulation in a more complete sense, using the ontology to provide context reasoning over all the necessary steps.

References

1. Essid M., Boucelma O., Colonna F., Lassoued Y.: Query Processing in a Geographic Mediation System. Proceedings of the 12th annual ACM international workshop on Geographic Information Systems. ACM Press New York, 2004, pp: 101 – 108.
2. Wache H., Voegele T., Visser U., Stuckenschmidt H.: Ontology-based Integration of Information – A Survey of Existing Approaches. IJCAI-01 Workshop: Ontologies and Information Sharing, 2001, pp: 108 – 117.
3. Fonseca F., Davis C., Câmara G.: Bridging Ontologies and Conceptual Schemas in Geographic Applications Development. GeoInformatica: 7(4), 2003, pp: 355-378.
4. Brézillon P.: Context Dynamic and Explanation in Contextual Graphs. Proceedings of the 4th International and Interdisciplinary Conference, CONTEXT (2003), USA, pp: 94-106.
5. Dey A.: Understanding and Using Context. Personal and Ubiquitous Computing Journal, Volume 5, 2001, pp. 4-7.
6. Wang X., Zhang D., Gu T., Pung H.: Ontology Based Context Modeling and Reasoning using OWL. Second IEEE Annual Conference on Pervasive Computing and Communications Workshops, 2004, pp.18-22.
7. Vieira, V., Salgado, A.,Tedesco, P.: Towards an Ontology for Context Representation in Groupware. Proceedings of the 11th International Workshop, CRIWG 2005, Brazil, pp: 367-375.
8. Goh, C.: Representing and Reasoning about Semantic Conflicts in Heterogeneous Information Systems. Ph.D. Thesis, MIT Sloan School of Management, 1996.
9. Kashyap, V., Sheth, A.: Semantic and Schematic Similarities Between Database Objects: A Context-Based Approach. VLDB Journal 5, no. 4, 1996, pp: 276-304.
10. Power, R.: Topic Maps for Context Management. In International Symposium on Information and Communication Technologies (ISICT 2003), pp. 199-204.
11. Brézillon P.: Context in Problem Solving: A Survey. The Knowledge Engineering Review, 14(1), 1999, pp: 1-34.
12. Levy A.: Combining Artificial Intelligence and Databases for Data Integration. Artificial Intelligence Today, 1999, pp. 249-268.
13. Widerhold G. Mediators in the Architecture of Future Information Systems. IEEE Computer, 1992, pp: 38-49.
14. Stefanidis K., Pitoura E., Vassiliadis P.:On Supporting Context-Aware Preferences in Relational Database Systems. In Proc. of the first International Workshop on Managing Context Information in Mobile and Pervasive Environments (MCMP'2005), in conjunction with MDM 2005, Cyprus.

Spatial Data Access Patterns in Semantic Grid Environment

Vikram Sorathia and Anutosh Maitra

Dhirubhai Ambani Institute of Information and Communication Technology
(DA-IICT),
Gandhinagar - 382 007, Gujarat, India
{vikram_sorathia, anutosh_maitra}@daiict.ac.in
http://www.daiict.ac.in

Abstract. Starting from the era of stove-piped Geographical Information Systems up to interesting mash-ups involving Internet based mapping services, the approaches of handling Geographical Information (GI) have changed significantly. This paper briefly concentrates up on the distinctive features and current implementations of Spatial Data Access Patterns. Considering the information requirements of the users in Emergency Operations Center, this paper identifies the issues and challenges in handling GI in dynamically changing environments. Two new patterns based on appropriate integration of Semantics and Grid technology are introduced, that may satisfy the identified requirements. Necessary alterations in current practices for handling GI is discussed with detail considerations for realization of these patterns on open environments.

1 Introduction

The primary goal of GI Science is to provide right information to right person at right time[1] on a geo-spatial platform. The task involved in achieving this goal are: monitoring, representing, processing, handling and delivering the content to the user[2]. These tasks can be modified and executed in specific manners to match the user information requirements. Such distinctive approaches are identified and categorized as Spatial Data Access Patterns(SDAPs) to reveal the unique features, benefits and issues exhibited by them. As these methods were evolving to meet more complex user needs, the parallel developments in *Semantic Web* technology and *Grid Computing* environment also took place. These technologies introduced benefits of inter-organizational interoperability and non-trivial quality of service in dynamic environments. Current approaches to achieve the objectives of the GI Science is reconsidered in the light of novel application requirements. This paper mainly tries to explore how to exploit semantic grid environment using spatial information in order to change the way information needs are identified, collected, represented, processed, managed and published to meet organizational goals.

R. Meersman, Z. Tari, P. Herrero et al. (Eds.): OTM Workshops 2006, LNCS 4278, pp. 1586–1595, 2006.

2   GI Access Patterns

Spatial Access Methods covered in literature provides detail overview of various methods at data structure and algorithm point of view. One can choose appropriate methods from the available pool of space-driven or data-driven structures[2] to suit the application needs. The access pattern being discussed here, deals at different level including general strategies in collection, representation, handling and access to spatial data. This section very briefly summaries the evolution in SDAP from a general viewpoint which is not restricted only to representation structure of the data, but considers various other attributes observed during the life-cycle of GI. The attributes considered for the categorization of patters include: sources of information; spatial, semantic and temporal granularity of the content; navigation style; source update style; number of users in workspace; access privileges to workspace; and data update style.

2.1   Monolithic Access Pattern

The monolithic access patterns in GI Systems is depicted in Figure 1. Here the data is collected by the publisher and distributed on the secondary storage media. Most conventional Remote Sensing and GIS applications falls in to this category.

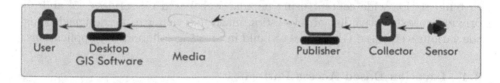

Fig. 1. The Conventional Monolithic Access Pattern

The figure shows monolithic single user, off line, data access pattern that provides fixed set of thematic information collected mainly from remote sensing satellites, or created as a result of ground survey. Some of the issues here are the propagation of updated information, limited set of observables with fixed spatial and temporal resolution, and the requirement of the expertise, software and hardware capabilities to manage the GI.

2.2   Web Services Based Access Pattern

Addressing the shortcomings of monolithic patterns, the standardization efforts[3] under the auspices of OGC[1] made it possible to allow the users access to GI and various geo processing services over the Internet. The end-user generally utilizes spaghetti model[2] to access the information by overlapping the layers containing

---

[1] The Open Geospatial Consortium, Inc. : http://www.opengeospatial.org

point, line or polygon features. User can discover and communicate with multiple servers to retrieve the thematic layers from multiple sources and render it simultaneously in the client applications like uDig[2]. With this pattern, client can not only have instantaneous access to updated information, but also crate content that can be accessible by other clients.

Fig. 2. Interactive Access to OGC Services

2.3   Collaboration Based Access Pattern

This pattern allows multi-user, online, read-write access to shared workspace. The users can manage their spatial content and allow access to others in shared environment. It enables the users to act as sources of information in a manner that many of the users can contribute the content to prepare a theme. One such experiment [4] demonstrated a collaborative effort of health professionals to build nation wide content using popular web based GI services. [5] and [6] provide an exhaustive list of interesting mash-ups that can be designed using the various web based GI services to build interesting collaborative applications.

2.4   Location Based Access Pattern

This technology enables GI access in pervasive environment where user can retrieve GI according to the dynamically changing coordinates. The issue of constantly adjusting navigation control as the coordinates are changed is tackled by keeping track of user movements using GPS, and sending the constantly updating position as navigation reference for GI retrieval. Applications like route planning, tracking, travel guides, and other interesting applications in [7],[8] provide successful implementation of this pattern.

2.5   Syndication Based Access Pattern

Patterns discussed so far are based on GI access in interactive manner. It may not be possible for users to constantly poll the servers to check for update. Syndication have been widely used by content management systems, where user can subscribe to the feeds of interest and using a feed reader user can poll the source URL for updates. The same strategy was identified[9] as suitable solution for GI access. The GI Sources may publish RSS feed with Geographically

---

[2] User-friendly Desktop Internet GIS: http://udig.refractions.net

Encoded Objects, and when feeds are received by client, the feed reader client application is modified to extract the spatial reference and render it on a map. This pattern allow single user, single/multi source, read-only access to syndicated GI content. The space, time and semantic granularity of the content is fixed by the content provider.

2.6 Semantics Based Access Pattern

Having addressed the syntactic heterogeneity issues, the recent focus of standardization[3] and research[10] community is now being diverted towards semantics of GI. In this approach, the domain knowledge captured and represented as *Ontology* is integrated at various steps involved in the GI. The experiments have demonstrated the effectiveness of semantics in improving the searching[11], navigation[1] and visualization[12]and portal based access [13]. Need for integration of semantic rule languages in GI is identified [14], for extending the existing web based GI services for future geo-spatial semantic web applications.

2.7 Event Based Access Pattern

This data access pattern allow single user, single/multi source, online, event driven read-only access to information based on the subscription conditions managed by the provider. A typical example of this pattern is implemented in location based service in which a person is notified the presence of a friend in particular proximity[8]. Event driven access to sensor data is also discussed in[15]. Location and time based access of information explained in [16] applied event based systems to provide tourism information. Following the *Slice* and *Dice* concept from business intelligence applications, [17]discussed integration of eventing information in space-time cube with map based interface.

3 Grid Based Access Pattern

The basic issue of providing scalable and reliable access to computing and data resources to perform geo-spatial data management operations have been addressed in this pattern. When multiple Virtual Organizations(VO) collaborate to manage GI content, they require more control over resources to ensure the availability in dynamically changing environment. Grid is claimed[18] to bring required features; specially in the case of Spatial Data Infrastructure (SDI). A common approach in introducing grid technology is to enable current standard based services[3] in grid environment. Catalog service in [19] and Web Map Services in[20] explains this approach. Beyond the efforts of hosting such services in Grid Environment, few attempts have been reported[21] to integrate GI processing models with grid features.

4 Requirement Scenario

The GI requirements in the planning phase are quite deterministic. Applications that deal with dynamic nature of systems where uncertainty is quite high include: Command and Control, Battlefield Management and Disaster Management. With uncertainly in availability of information sources, processing and storage resources and the end users in a dynamically altering environment, the methods of collecting, handling and publishing information needs modification. The SDAPs in such applications poses critical requirements that must be addressed. The following section identifies some issues in identifying the requirements and SDAPs that enable the required information flow.

4.1   Information Requirements of EOC

Determination of information requirement of an EOC is primarily based on the planning procedures that are reflected in their respective Operation Management Plans. The emergency operations with response activities in case of a disaster management scenario includes rehabilitation camps and handling medical, hygiene, food, sanitation, disposal etc that need reliable communication services. The information systems therefore provide theme based access to GI like medical camps, casualties, active respondents, critical services etc. In other words, depending upon the event and the planning of response activity, what information is to be collected and published in GI is identified. The critical issue here is that it is not pre-determined that who will be part of EOC, hence the detail planning steps can only be decided only after the event. This means that information requirements can only be determined only as the events unfold. Semantic Web Technology can play a critical role by selecting the rules to determine the information needs on the fly.

4.2   Relevant Spatial Data Access Patterns

Observations in recent disaster events has clearly indicated that respondents are mostly able to provide updates about the situation with the help of either personally owned or donated communication and computation devices. The argument is that careful integration of semantics in designing rule based eventing system for respondents and resource virtualization across EOC can provide basis to realize an EOC-scale GI management that will in-turn eliminate the trouble of information chaos. To support this argument two novel SDAPs are offered.

(a) **Rule Driven Event Based Access Pattern.** This pattern is based on multi-user, read-write access to collaborative workspace and allows semantics driven eventing. It addresses the problem of collecting missing information that is required at specified granularity for the situation awareness. Information collection is triggered by rules specifying required additional themes at specific space, time and concept granularity. It must support both synchronous and asynchronous communication among collaborating users based on explicit requests or implicit interest derived from their concurrent role in the VO.

(b) **Role Driven Collaboration Based Access Pattern.** This pattern is based on multi-user, read-write access to collaborative workspace and allows

Role Driven Access to virtualized resources of EOC Grid. It addresses the issue of determining delegation of rights for the incumbent members for appropriate access to the *grid resources*. These authorized users can then utilize grid services to ensure reliable access to GI across EOC.

5   Prospective Approaches Towards Solution

Figure 3 illustrates seven proposed key features in methods for handling data that will lead us towards achieving the identified SDAPs.

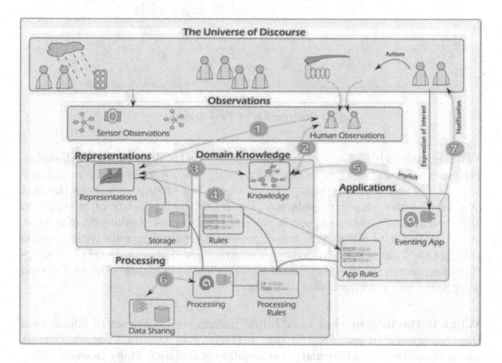

Fig. 3. Meeting EOC Information Requirements

5.1   Considerations for Modeling the World

How many themes? The information requirements for disaster applications are somewhat different as compared to planning applications where snap-shot of natural and man-made features in the area of interest are primarily considered. For GI in disaster management scenario the set of desired observables also contains the respondent-actions, the instantaneous changes in resources etc. As discussed earlier, all the related concepts are represented and shared as Ontology. Thus the additional themes that will be required after disaster events can be inferred from the such Ontologies as indicated with arrow 2 in Figure 3.

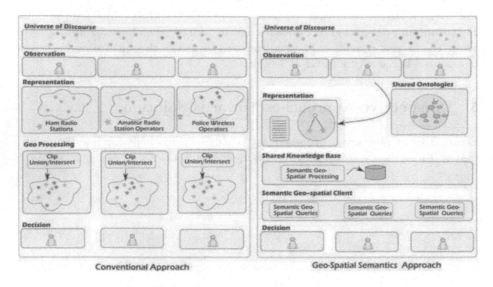

Fig. 4. Comparison of Two Approaches

What granularity? Granularity refers to the level of details at with the information is represented. Granularity of information is governed by the role, scope of activities and area of interest. The geometric resolution that defines the area of coverage, the temporal resolution that refers to the update of information and thematic access of most specific concepts that represents the area of interest most detailed level possible. Navigating to such required granularity is possible only if Ontologies are integrated with geographical representation. Thus adoption of semantics in representation of GI as indicated in Figure 4 can be followed as opposed to the conventional methods.

What is the information need? Information need is the set of information that is required by an actor to take decisions and plan necessary action. It assumes availability of information at required granularity. Many valuable pieces of information may come only when asked for. Such information can only be collected if the need is identified and then the sources of information are polled at required time interval. The time interval and sources of information can only be decided by the policy. Hence there must be some mechanism that will allow conversion of such policy in to formal rules[see arrow 2 in Figure 3], that can be executed on detection of the event to determine the information need.

What words to choose? The observations of the first respondents or victims that report the occurrence of the event for the first time are critical source of information. These verbal reports are to be converted to formal assertions to the systems with respect to some ontological representation[see arrow 3 in Figure 3]. The reasoner will in turn calculate membership of the asserted instances to possible classes represented in the ontology. This process is to be carried out by a non-expert receiving the calls at EOC. Hence, it is very essential for the system to allow search for proper concepts that will be used in representation. Ontological mapping[see arrow 1 in Figure 3] that integrates the concepts used by the user will help solve the problem.

Which ontologies? With identification of the fact that to be able to provide discovery and navigation to meaningful information, not only words that are used by the users and domain experts needs to be mapped, but also it becomes essential to co-relate the concepts used in applications that will handle the information to maintain the proper information flow. Thus the application specific concepts must also be part of the ontology mapping efforts[see arrow 4 in Figure 3]. For example, if the disaster response policy suggest that if a request is not addressed by a legally responsible person for specific period of time, then volunteer must be identified and notification should be sent. To realize this requirement, the eventing system must go beyond the definition of a *Subscriber* and identify the hierarchy of the concepts that will match the policies of the EOC. We advocate the requirement to consider the application rules in representation[see arrow 5 in Figure 3]. Having identified the requirement of integration of ontologies that defines the Domain, Organization, and application concept needs to be mapped. A few formal approaches for instance EU-ORCHESTRA [3] are investigating on integration of Ontologies for smiliar objectives.

5.2   Considerations for Managing Grid Resources

Managing the Processed Information. The snapshots providing the situation awareness or predictive analysis created by the experts can be used to allow event driven access to end users. Hence collection of such processed information, must be managed effectively. The *Grid Middleware* for data management [OGSA-DAI[4]] provides services facilitating management of multiple data structure and representation, the lineage of data, modes of working, and other requirements during the life-cycle of scientific data. The utility of such services is envisaged in managing data sources and resources in EOC Grid that will enable role based access to collaborative workspace[see arrow 6 in Figure 3]. According to user's role in EOC, the Grid security infrastructure can effectively utilize to assign the users specific roles in the VO to carry out operations for data management, computing resources management, task scheduling and other services offered by current *Grid Computing* environments.

Managing User Communication. It is argued that in order to achieve the desired access patterns, the behavior of the GI system must be *reactive* and in case of disaster management application the goal should be to achieve *pro-active*

---

[3] Orchestra Consortium: http://www.eu-orchestra.org/
[4] http://www.ogsadai.org.uk/about/ogsa-dai/

behavior. The concept of reactivity and proactivity can be archived first by appropriate representation of rules followed by integration of rules in appropriate communication among users. Up on arrival of a new fact, a series of rules can be triggered to enable collection, handling and notification of information. This requires tight integration of rules with synchronous or asynchronous communication with users exhibiting specific roles. Hence, is the requirement of integration of rule-driven approach in user communication to be archived to realize desired pattern[see arrow 7 in Figure 3].

6   Sample Use Case

This paper identified requirements for the development of GI System to support proposed SDAPs in Semantic Grid environment. This section very briefly introduces a sample use case, details on the realization of which are beyond the scope of this paper. We discuss a scenario in which proposed SDAPs will be used by the respondents of a series of fire alarms after a disastrous event. Upon receipt of an emergency call, appropriate fire fighting and rescue team should be assigned for the response. This decision requires city or town level information. The information requirement of a fire fighter entering the building includes the information at building level with highest level of granularity in the details of the structure. A rescuer requires details about the occupants in the building. The emergency medical team will require frequently updated information about the availability of beds in the hospitals where the rescued victims are routed. Hence, the logical pool of respondents belonging to various departments, having a specific role to play in given situation is to be incorporated in GI, which will be taken as base for taking instantaneous decisions. The decision to poll the respondents that report detail information about the situation justifies the SDAP that govern rule based information collection. The collection and management of information received from respondents to create snap-shots of situation taken at specific time intervals, management and sharing among users justifies the SDAP that governs the role based access such data resources in ensuring reliable access to multi-granularity information to users and to the public at large.

7   Discussion

This paper provided a brief account of evolution in Spatial Data Access Patterns to its current state. The emergence of semantic Grid technology have brought change the way the spatial data is accessed. It is noted that trivial use of semantics to extend meta-data capabilities and methods of managing data in grid environment will not suffice in harnessing the full potential of these technologies. To support this argument, various issues that must be resolved to meet the information need of Emergency Operations Center are discussed. Two novel SDAPs are identified that can help realize the goal to meet the information needs of multiple users in EOC. Subsequently the paper proposed the changes in using Semantics and Grid technology in GI Science to meet the challenging needs.

References

1. Smart, P.R., Shadbolt, N.R., Carr, L.A., c. Schraefel, M.: Knowledge-based information fusion for improved situational awareness. In: The 8th International Conference on Information Fusion. (2005)
2. Rigaux, P., Scholl, M., Voisard, A.: Spatial Databases. Morgan Kaufmann (2001)
3. Percivall, G.: Overview of geographic information standards development. In: Geoscience and Remote Sensing Symposium. Volume 5. (2000) 2096–2098
4. Boulos, M.N.K.: Web gis in practice iii: Creating a simple interactive map of england's strategic health authorities using google maps api, google earth kml, and msn virtual earth. Int. Journal of Health Geographics 4 (2005) 22
5. Erle, S., Gibson, R., Walsh, J.: Mapping Hacks. O'Reilly (2005)
6. Gibson, R., Erle, S.: Google Maps Hacks. O'Reilly (2006)
7. Karimi, H.: Telegeoinformatics. Taylor & Francis (2004)
8. Schiller, J., Voisard, A.: Location-Based Services. Morgan Kaufmann (2004)
9. Singh, R.: Geoblogging: collaborative, peer-to-peer geographic information sharing. In: URISA Public Participation in GIS 3rd Annual Conference. (2004)
10. Pires, P.: Geospatial conceptualisation: A Cross-Cultural Analysis on Portuguese and American Geographical Categorisations. Volume 3534. (2005)
11. Hbner, S., Spittel, R., Visser, U., Vgele, T.J.: Ontology-based search for interactive digital maps. IEEE Intelligent Systems 19(3) (2004) 80–86
12. Voudouris, V., Wood, J., Fisher, P.F.: Collaborative geoVisualization: Object-Field Representations with Semantic and Uncertainty Information. Volume 3762. (2005)
13. Nikolaos, A., Kostas, K., Michail, V., Nikolaos, S.: The Emerge of Semantic Geoportals. Volume 3762. (2005)
14. Chen, H., Fellah, S., Bishr, Y.A.: Rules for geospatial semantic web applications. In: Rule Languages for Interoperability, W3C (2005)
15. Joshi, A., Wytzisk, A.: Exploiting an event-based communication infrastructure for rule based alerting in sensor webs. dexa 00 (2005) 485–489
16. Hinze, A., Voisard, A.: Locations- and time-based information delivery in tourism. In Hadzilacos, T., Manolopoulos, Y., Roddick, J.F., Theodoridis, Y., eds.: SSTD. Volume 2750 of Lecture Notes in Computer Science., Springer (2003) 489–507
17. Gatalsky, P., Andrienko, N.V., Andrienko, G.L.: Interactive analysis of event data using space-time cube. In: IV, IEEE Computer Society (2004) 145–152
18. Ghimire, D.R., Simonis, I., Wytzisk, A.: Integration of grid approaches into the geographic web service domain. In: From Pharaohs to Geoinformatics, FIG Working Week 2005 and GSDI-8,Cairo, Egypt. April 16-21,. (2005)
19. Wei, Y., Di, L., Zhao, B., Liao, G., Chen, A., Bai, Y., Liu, Y.: The design and implementation of a grid-enabled catalogue service. In: Geoscience and Remote Sensing Symposium, 2005. IGARSS '05. Proceedings. 2005 IEEE International. Volume 6. (2005) 4224–4227
20. Aloisio, G., Cafaro, M., Conte, D., Fiore, S., Epicoco, I., Marra, G.P., Quarta, G.: A grid-enabled web map server. itcc 1 (2005) 298–303
21. Di, L.: Customizable virtual geospatial products at web/grid service environment. In: Geoscience and Remote Sensing Symposium, 2005. IGARSS '05. Proceedings. 2005 IEEE International. Volume 6. (2005) 4215–4218

GeWOlap: A Web Based Spatial OLAP Proposal

Sandro Bimonte, Pascal Wehrle, Anne Tchounikine, and Maryvonne Miquel

LIRIS (Laboratoire d'InfoRmatique en Images et Systèmes d'information) UMR CNRS 5205
INSA, 7 avenue Capelle, 69621 Villeurbanne Cedex, France
Name.Surname@insa-lyon.fr

Abstract. Data warehouses and OLAP systems help to interactively analyze huge volumes of data. Spatial OLAP refers to the integration of spatial data in multidimensional applications at the physical, logical and conceptual level. In order to include spatial information as a result of the decision-making process, we propose to define spatial measures as geographical objects in the multidimensional data model. This raises problems regarding aggregation operations and cube navigation in both semantic and implementation aspects. This paper presents a *GeWOlap*, a web based, integrated and extensible GIS-OLAP prototype, able to support geographical measures. Our approach is illustrated by its application in a project for the CORILA consortium (Consortium for Coordination of Research Activities concerning the Venice Lagoon System).

Keywords: Spatial OLAP, Spatial Decision Support, Spatial Data warehouse.

1 Introduction

Data warehousing combined with OLAP (On Line Analytical Processing) technologies provides an innovative support for business intelligence and knowledge discovery. It has now become a leading topic in the commercial world as well as the research community. The main motivation is to benefit from the enormous amount of data available in distributed and heterogeneous databases in order to enhance data analysis and decision making. Most OLAP applications focus on textual dimensions and numeric measures although many studies have come to the conclusion that about 80% of all data integrates spatial information. It is obvious that this meaningful information is worth being integrated into the decision making process as a first class knowledge, leading to the concept of Spatial On Line Analytical Processing (SOLAP). SOLAP is defined as a visual platform especially built to support rapid and easy spatio-temporal analysis and exploration of data following a multidimensional approach. It allows including aggregation levels available in cartographic displays as well as tabular and diagram displays [19]. Different SOLAP tools have been developed, all with different advanced characteristics. In [19] the fundamental features of a SOLAP tool are listed from different points of view: *visualization of data* (i.e. synchronized cartographic and non-cartographic displays, representation of one or more numeric measures and visualization of context data), *exploration of data* (i.e. multidimensional navigation by all display types, both cartographic and non-cartographic, calculated measures and

R. Meersman, Z. Tari, P. Herrero et al. (Eds.): OTM Workshops 2006, LNCS 4278, pp. 1596–1605, 2006.

filtering on dimension members) and *structure of data* (i.e. support for many geometric and mixed spatial dimensions and support for storage of historical geometric data).

In a previous work, we have defined a multidimensional model and algebra, GeoCube, which allow for the support of geographical measures and dimensions. In this model, the geographical measures are described by descriptive and geometric attributes and can be aggregated using inter-dependent aggregation functions. In this paper we will focus on *GeWOlap*, a web based, integrated and extensible GIS-OLAP prototype that implements the GeoCube model. An environmental application is used to illustrate the proposal. The rest of this paper is organized as follows: Section 2 describes main OLAP concepts; section 3 presents SOLAP concepts, an overview of the GeoCube model and related works on SOLAP tools. In section 4 the *GeWOlap* proposal is described ; we conclude section 5 with a discussion and future work.

2 OLAP and Data Warehousing

A data warehouse is "a subject-oriented, integrated, non-volatile and time-variant collection of data stored in a single site repository and collected from multiple sources" [11]. Information in the data warehouse is organized around major subjects and is modeled in order to allow pre-computation and fast access to summarized data in support of management's decisions. OLAP tools implement analysis techniques used to explore the data warehouse. Data warehouse models are called multidimensional models or hypercubes. They are designed to represent measurable *facts* or *indicators* and the various *dimensions* that characterize the facts and that represent analysis axes. As an example in a retail area, typical facts are the price and the amount of a purchase; dimensions are Product, Location, Time and Customer. A dimension is usually organized according to a *hierarchy*, for example the Location dimension aggregated in City, State, and Country, allowing analysis at different levels of details.

Multi-tier architectures are usually adopted for OLAP applications:
1. The first tier is a warehouse server, often implemented using a relational DBMS. Data of interest must be extracted from operational legacy databases, cleaned and transformed before being loaded into the warehouse. This step guaranties that the warehouse contains high quality, historical and homogeneous data.
2. The second tier is the OLAP server. It calculates and optimizes the hypercube i.e. the set of fact values for all combinations of instances of dimensions (also called members) in order to optimize accesses to detailed and aggregated data.
3. The third tier is an OLAP client, providing a user interface with reporting tools and OLAP operators that allow interactive queries and analysis. Common operators include roll-up, drill-down, slice and dice, rotate.

As a conclusion, one can say that data warehousing intends to provide a guarantee for the quality and comparability of data, a fast access to summarized data an interactive and user-friendly navigation through data at different levels of detail.

3 Spatial OLAP

3.1 Spatial Dimensions and Spatial Measures

One can integrate spatial information in a multidimensional decisional application as an analysis axis i.e. as a dimension. Spatial data in OLAP dimensions leads to the definition of a spatial dimension. As defined in [1] a spatial dimension can either be a spatial non geometric dimension (i.e. text only members), a spatial geometric dimension (i.e. members with a cartographic representation) or a mixed spatial dimension (i.e. combining cartographic and textual members). Adding a cartographic representation to the textual descriptions of the dimension members enhance the relevance of the multidimensional analysis allowing the user to visualize facts on maps and discover geographical correlations.

An example of a SOLAP application with a spatial dimension is shown Fig. 1 using the conceptual model proposed in [15]. This application concerns the environmental supervision of the Venice lagoon [4]. We have realized this work in the context of an international project regarding modelling, analysis and visualization for environmental data in the CORILA consortium[1] (Consortium for Coordination of Research Activities concerning the Venice Lagoon). We define one spatial geometric dimension (location) representing waterways ("fiume" in italian) and a numeric fact representing the measurement of pollution. The aggregation operations performed on the measure are AVERAGE, MIN and MAX.

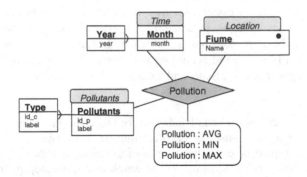

Fig. 1. CORILA SOLAP application with a Spatial Dimension

Several works investigate spatial dimensions from a theoretical point of view. In [15] a conceptual model for spatial OLAP is presented, based on the integration of the MultiDimER and MADS models. Ferri et al. [6] provide a unique formal framework that integrates a spatial database and a multidimensional database, exploiting the full-containment relation between hierarchy levels. Finally [8] proposes a multidimensional formal model that introduces a partial containment relation in order to handle spatially overlapping hierarchies.

---

[1] http://www.corila.it

The concept of spatial measure must be introduced when the subject of the decision process is the spatial information itself. The spatial measure can be analyzed through non spatial and/or spatial dimensions. Different definitions for the spatial measure can be found in literature: the measure is sometimes represented as a collection of references to spatial objects [23], [19], as objects resulting from topological (e.g. union or intersection) or metric (e.g. distance) operations [19], [15], or as measure associated to a spatial dimension [16]. In all these definitions the spatial measure is reduced to its geometric and/or metric part. The latter can be derived directly from the geometry. However, GIS models usually defines a geographic object through a geometric attribute (e.g. the polygon representing a region) in addition to thematic or descriptive attributes (e.g. the name, the socio-economic class of the region, etc.) which are necessary to conduct a real and effective spatial analysis [18]. In [7] the authors present a logical framework which supports geographical measures. They extend the classical star-schema modeling geographical measure as a spatial dimension. From a formal point of view in [5], the authors present a multidimensional model whose main characteristic is the representation of spatial measures at multiple level of geometric granularity.

3.2 Overview of the GeoCube Model

We present in [2] and [3] a formal multidimensional model called GeoCube that aims to support measures and dimensions defined as geographical objects i.e. as real world entities described by descriptive and geometric attributes. The objective is to enhance decision-making providing a model able to support geographical data according to its particular nature. GeoCube allows the usage of a set of spatial and/or alphanumeric attributes as one single complex measure, and defines inter-dependent aggregation functions for each attributes of the complex object representing the aggregated measure. GeoCube also provide an algebra that redefines common OLAP operators (*VROLLUP*, *VDRILLDOWN*, *VSLICE* and *VDICE*). The uniform object definition for dimension and measure consents their symmetrical treatment. Indeed the user can interactively "push" a measure to become a dimension and vice-versa. Using GeoCube we can model the multidimensional application of Fig. 2. The idea is to use the "unità barenale" as measure. A "unità barenale" is a part of the lagoon that emerges from water for long periods at low tide. Each "unità barenale" is characterized by several biological values as an index of salinity, types of plants, etc... From a conceptual point of view the multidimensional application presents four dimensions: Depth, Pollutants, Incidence, Time, and one measure Unità Barenale. Depth indicates the depth where the values of pollutants have been measured. Incidence represents a range value for the measured pollutants (i.e. [0.05-0.07 ng/l]). Attributes of the Unità Barenale are the geometry, name, the index of salinity, the list of plants and area. This model allows responding to the following type of query: *return the entire zone, its plants and index of salinity where "zinc" measured at depth "bottom" has a value of [0.05-0.07ng/l] ?*

GeoCube model requests the specification of an aggregation operator for the set of attributes of the complex measure. In this example, we select the geometric union for the geometry, the sum for the area, a range for the index of salinity given by the minimum and the maximum (i.e. [24-25]), a merge operator for the list of plants and no aggregation for the name. This leads to the definition of a geographical object that is no more a "unità barenale", but which represents the aggregation of some "unità barenali".

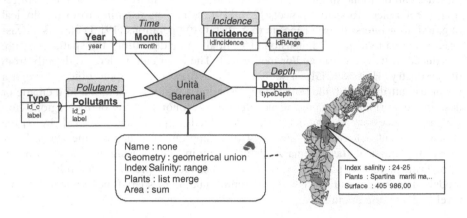

Fig. 2. Venice Lagoon SOLAP application with Geographical Measure

3.3 Spatial OLAP Tools

Several Spatial OLAP tools have been developed. A first classification can be made for these tools based on handled *data structure*. Most SOLAP solutions take into account only spatial dimensions (i.e. [10], [12], [21]). Some other tools [9], [16], [20],[22] provide management of spatial measures. In [20] the authors describe an SOLAP client tool which supports a tabular data representation, 7 different types of diagrams and maps, composed by visual variables and maps superimposed with graphical diagrams. Moreover, some particular SOLAP operators on spatial dimensions (spatial drill down or thematic roll up) have been realized. The system supports spatial measures as a set of all geometries representing the spatial objects corresponding to a particular combination of spatial dimension members (as defined in [23]). Shekhar et al. [22] develop a map cube operator extending the concepts of data cube and aggregation to spatial data but do not consent user-defined aggregations. In [9] Han et al present GeoMiner, a tool for spatial data mining which uses a SOLAP component in order to support on-line analytical mining (OLAM) on a spatial data warehouse.

From an implementation point of view, SOLAP technical solutions usually rely on coupling OLAP and GIS features. In [20] these solutions are categorized in 3 different classes: *OLAP dominant*, *GIS dominant* and *integrated OLAP-GIS solutions*. In [10], the authors describe CommonGIS, a powerful SOLAP tool which supports advanced methods of spatial analysis (e.g. multicriteria) and visualization. GIS functionalities as shown in [10] are necessary and complementary to the multidimensional view of the spatial data and OLAP dominant tools are incomplete solutions. On the other side, in GIS dominant solutions the OLAP server is simulated through a relational database allowing only a subset of OLAP functionalities (i.e. pivot of dimensions), limiting multidimensional analysis capabilities. These limitations can be avoided by integrating OLAP solutions (both server and client) and GIS functionalities. Thus GIS-OLAP integrated solutions appear to be the most adequate solution for a real multidimensional spatial analysis. Examples of GIS-OLAP integrated solution are [10], [12], [16], [20] [21]. To best of our knowledge, none GIS-OLAP integrated tool supports geographical measures.

4 The GeWOlap Proposal

In this section we describe the *GeWOlap* system whose main characteristic is the support for geographical measures in a GIS-OLAP integrated solution. *GeWOlap* allows interactive navigation in a hypercube designed following the GeoCube model. We present the architecture of our prototype, the main characteristics of each tier and finally the application of *GeWOlap* to the spatial multidimensional application described in the previous section.

4.1 Architecture of *GeWOlap*

GeWOlap is based on a three tier architecture consisting of an Object-Relational DBMS supporting spatial data, an OLAP Server, a front-end client based on an OLAP web client and a GIS web client (Fig. 3).

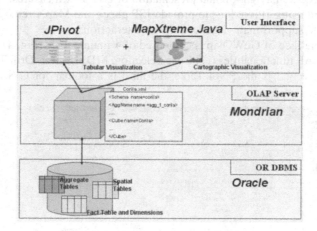

Fig. 3. *GeWOlap* Architecture

4.2 The Warehouse Tier

In most GIS, distinct storage systems are used to store and manage spatial and non-spatial data respectively. This approach is called a loosely coupled approach [18]. The warehouse tier of our proposal is implemented using ORACLE. Moving GIS data from proprietary databases to the data warehouse provides integration of spatial data with core business data, standard-based access to spatial information and GIS applications taking advantage of the security, resilience and scalability of a data warehouse. Consequently the primary reason for choosing ORACLE over a loosely coupled approach is its support for spatial data. Moreover, user-defined aggregation functions and user-defined types can be easily implemented in an OR DBMS.

4.3 The OLAP Server Tier

Mondrian [17] provides a full featured OLAP server based on a relational database backend. We extend its functionalities in order to support aggregation of complex objects using our own PL/SQL aggregation functions in ORACLE. With this method, the aggregation process and the definition of aggregation functions for geometric, alphanumeric and numeric attributes are delegated to the ORDBMS. All advanced OLAP functionalities in *GeWOlap* such as multiple hierarchies, user-defined functions and calculated members are provided by the Mondrian OLAP server. We add aggregation of geographical measures through a custom aggregate table mechanism which offers identifier-to-aggregate mappings. This tight coupling of Mondrian and ORACLE with an adequate modeling of the spatial data warehouse as described in [7], allows *GeWOlap* to effectively support geographical measures.

4.4 The Client Tier: The User Interface

Like the data management tiers, the client tier introduces some particular characteristics for an adequate navigation and presentation of complex measures. The client tier is implemented using JPivot [13] to provide JSP pages and MapXtreme Java (the trial version) [14] to support map visualization and interaction.

The user interface of GeWOlap is composed of 4 main panels (Fig. 4). The first is a toolbar for OLAP functionalities (i.e. Cube Selection, MDX Editor, Drill Through, Roll-up etc...), the second is the Pivot Table, the third is a toolbar for GIS functionalities

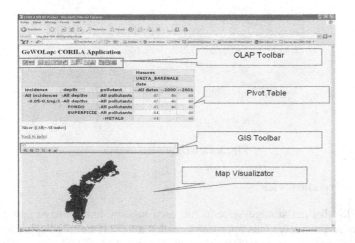

Fig. 4. *GeWOlap* User Interface

(Zoom in, Zoom out, Pan, Ruler, Info, Layer Control) and the fourth is the panel for map visualization. The Pivot Table incorporates multidimensional concepts into its structure and generates a set of small displays. It allows easy comparison of numerical data and visually encapsulates the structure of the analysis process. In *GeWOlap* the cells' values in the Pivot Table are the identifiers of (aggregated) geographical measures (Fig. 5b). In the context of information exploration, maps and graphics are active instruments in the end user's thinking process. For geographical measures as for spatial dimensions, the mere use of a Pivot Table appears insufficient to analyze spatio-temporal data and a cartographic component is mandatory for a SOLAP tool. This component will show a map representing the set of all measures and (contrary to spatial dimensions) a map whose elements are geographical measures dynamically chosen by the user.

The choice of the measures to visualize is done using the GIS toolbar. Let us describe an example of utilization of *GeWOlap*. To answer the query of section 3.2, the user chooses the "Cube Selection" utility in the OLAP tool bar and selects the dimensions, measures and a slice filter "bottom" ("FONDO" - see Fig. 5a).

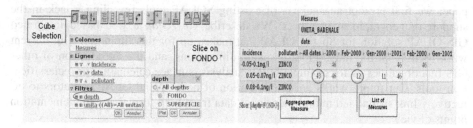

Fig. 5. a) Cube Selection: SLICE, b) Pivot Table

The pivot table obtained is shown in Fig. 5b. We can notice the identifier of the aggregated measures (i.e. 43) and of the lists of unità barenali (i.e. L2) (identifiers starting with the character L). The identifier 43 represents the aggregation of several unità barenali. 43 is the measure value for incidence "0.05-0.07ng/1", pollutant ZINCO, depth FONDO and date "all dates". The user can visualize one or more measures in the map visualization panel. Indeed this panel shows the geographical object and all the "unita barenali" on two different layers. Then the INFO utility in the GIS tool bar shows the index of salinity of the zone, the list of plants and the surface (Fig. 6a and 6b).

The user frequently wishes to analyze measures at the most detailed level. So he would visualize L2, which is the list measure for incidence "0.05-0.07ng/1", pollutant ZINCO, depth FONDO and date "Feb-2000". Simply showing geographical measures is not sufficient for spatio-temporal analysis: once the layer representing the chosen measures is created, the user can apply GIS functionalities to best analyze spatial data, as for example add another layer in order to visualize the context of data, using the add layer wizard of the layer control button.

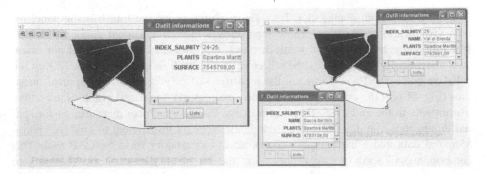

Fig. 6. Visualization of a) aggregated measure b) measures

5 Conclusions and Future Work

Introducing geographical measures in Spatial OLAP as defined in [2] raises several different problems from the theoretical and implementation points of view. In this paper we first present an analysis of existing SOLAP tools revealing a lack in the support of geographical measures. We describe *GeWOlap* a web based integrated GIS-OLAP solution for Spatial OLAP that makes up for this limitation. Our current work focuses on the integration of spatial dimensions, and the introduction of other GIS functionalities as for example buffer analysis, surface calculation or reclassification tools. Our future works are the definition of new Spatial OLAP operators to effectively link spatial and multidimensional data from both formal and implementation points of view.

References

1. Bédard, Y., Merrett, T., Han, J.: Fundaments of Spatial Data Warehousing for Geographic Knowledge Discovery. Geographic Data Mining and Knowledge Discovery. Taylor and Francis, London (2001) 53-73
2. Bimonte, S., Tchounikine, A., Miquel, M.: Towards a Spatial Multidimensional Model. In: Proceedings of the 8th International Workshop on Data Warehousing and OLAP (DOLAP 2005). ACM Press, New York, USA (2005) 39-46
3. Bimonte, S., Tchounikine, A., Miquel, M.: GeoCube, a Multidimensional Model and Navigation Operators Handling Complex Measures: Application in Spatial OLAP. In: Proceedings of the 4th Biennial International Conference Advances in Information Systems, Izmir, Turkey (2006)
4. Bimonte, S., Tchounikine, A., Miquel, M., Ahmed T., Laurini, R: Spatial On line Analytical Processing for Environmental Data. Quinta riunione Annuale, Programma di Ricerca 2004-2006, Venice, Italy, (2006)
5. Damiani, M.L., Spaccapietra, S.: Spatial Data Warehouse Modelling. Processing and Managing Complex Data for Decision Support. Idea Group Publishing (2006) 21-27
6. Ferri, F., Pourabbas, E., Rafanelli, M., Ricci, F.L.: Extending Geographic Databases for a Query Language to Support Queries Involving Statistical Data. In: Proc. 12th international conference on scientific and statistical database management. IEEE, Washington, USA (2000) 220-230

7. Fidalgo, R.N., Times, V.C., Silva, J., Souza, F.F.: GeoDWFrame: A Framework for Guiding the Design of Geographical Dimensional Schemas. In: Proceedings of Int. Conf. on Data Warehousing and Knowledge Discovery. Springer, Berlin Heidelberg (2004) 26-37

8. Jensen C., Klygis, A., Pedersen, T. and Timko, I. Multidimensional data modelling for location-based services. VLDB Journal, 13, 1. Springer-Verlag, New York (2004) 1-21

9. Han, J., Koperski, K., Stefanovic, N.: GeoMiner: A System Prototype for Spatial Data Mining. In: ACM-SIGMOD Int. Conference on Management and Knowoledge Discovery. ACM Press, Tucson Arizona (1997)

10. Hernandez, V. Voss A. Göhring, W. Hopmann, C.: Sustainable decision support by the use of multi-level and multi-criteria spatial analysis on the Nicaragua Development Gateway. In: From pharaohs to geoinformatics Proceedings of FIG Working Week 2005 and 8th International Conference on the Global Spatial Data Infrastructure, Cairo, Egypt, (2005)

11. Inmon, W. H.: The data warehouse and data mining. Communications of ACM, Vol 39, 11. ACM Press, New York, USA (1996) 49-50

12. JMap, http://www.kheops-tech.com/en/jmap/solap.jsp as of 10/07/2006

13. Jpivot, http://jpivot.sourceforge.net/ as of 10/07/2006

14. MapXtreme Java, http://extranet.mapinfo.com/products/Overview.cfm?productid=1162 as of 10/07/2006

15. Malinowski, E., Zimányi, E.: Representing spatiality in a conceptual multidimensional model. In: Proceedings of the 12th annual ACM International workshop on Geographic information systems. ACM Press, New York, USA (2004) 12-22

16. Marchand, P., Brisebois, A., Bédard, Y., Edwards G.: Implementation and evaluation of a hypercubebased method for spatio-temporal exploration and analysis. Journal of the International Society of Photogrammetry and Remote Sensing, Vol. 59.Elsevier (2004) 6-20

17. Mondrian, http://mondrian.sourceforge.net/, as of 10/07/2006

18. Rigaux, P., Scholl, M., Voisard, A.: Spatial databases with application to GIS. Morgan Kaufmann Publishers Inc., San Francisco, CA, (2002)

19. Rivest, S., Bédard Y., Marchand P.: Toward Better Support for Spatial Decision Making: Defining the Characteristics of Spatial On-Line Analytical Processing (SOLAP). Geomatica, Vol. 55, 4 (2001) 539-555

20. Rivest, S., Bédard, Y., Proulx, M.-J., Nadeau, M., Hubert F., Pastor, J.: SOLAP: Merging Business Intelligence with Geospatial Technology for Interactive Spatio-Temporal Exploration and Analysis of Data. Journal of International Society for Photogrammetry and Remote Sensing, Vol. 60, 1. Elsevier (2005) 17-33

21. Scotch, M., Parmanto, B.: SOVAT: Spatial OLAP Visualization and Analysis Tool. In: Proceedings of 38th Hawaii International Conference on System Sciences. IEEE (2005) 142-149

22. Shekhar, S., Lu, C.T., Tan, X., Chawla, S.: Map Cube: A Visualization Tool for Spatial Data Warehouses. In: Geographic Data Mining and Knowledge Discovery. Taylor and Francis, London (2001) 74-109

23. Stefanovic, N., Han, J., Koperski K.: Object-Based Selective Materialization for Efficient Implementation of Spatial Data Cubes. IEEE Transactions on Knowledge and Data Engineering, Vol 12, 6 (2000) 938-95

Affordable Web-Based Spatio-temporal Applications for Ad-Hoc Decisions

Vera Hernández Ernst

Fraunhofer Institute AIS, Schloss Birlinghoven,
53754 Sankt Augustin, Germany
vera.hernandez@ais.fraunhofer.de

Abstract. This paper outlines a framework to support the demand-driven analysis of spatio-temporal data. It will support decision making involving complex, multidimensional data and addresses the following challenges: (1) the demand-driven acquisition of context data, (2) the combination of context and user data, (3) the consideration of different aspects and levels of detail on the analysis and (4) the storage and integration of analysis results for further use. The framework will provide web-services based on open standards to populate and explore multidimensional spatio-temporal structures interactively. Online Analitical Procesing (OLAP) concepts will serve as model for storing and querying the data. Roaming-services will be used to update contents coming from different Spatial Data Infrastructures. Semantical descriptions will allow switching analysis operations at different levels of detail. Research questions and challenges related to the underlying model and implementation aspects will be discussed.

Keywords: spatial OLAP, semantic web services, roamable services, spatio-temporal decision support.

1 Introduction

The analysis of data related to space and time has gained importance in new application fields through concepts from geo-marketing and spatial data infrastructures (SDI) and through the increasing presence of mobile devices and (satellite) maps in day-to-day utilities. A hurdle to overcome for many decision makers is, firstly, data acquisition, taking into account the short lifetime and the high costs of current (commercial) spatial data. Secondly, the purchasable data does not always match the analysis requirements precisely enough and must be pre-processed. Thirdly, software for multidimensional analysis is expensive and its development is time consuming. Commercial software is limited by its use of proprietary data and/or predefined analysis methods. Specific expertise for collecting, maintaining and analyzing data with such software is required, but may be missing on SMEs (small and midsized enterprises). Moreover, commercial software for multidimensional analysis does not yet meet several functional requirements: (1) **federated data sources**: the data has to be collected from distributed data sources at different levels of detail and in different formats; (2) **multi-level analysis**: the data must be accessible quickly at different

R. Meersman, Z. Tari, P. Herrero et al. (Eds.): OTM Workshops 2006, LNCS 4278, pp. 1606–1615, 2006.

levels of detail according to spatial, temporal or any other item grouping aspect; (3) **extensible structure**: the data structure can be extended during the analysis by adding new data whose structure was previously unknown; (4) **consumable information**: data and results must be represented properly and be reusable for further purposes; (5) **transparent clearing**: data and functionality should be priced according to the user demands for each analysis.

This paper proposes a web-based outline for the dynamical creation and use of multidimensional structures to support SMEs in ad-hoc decision making and where prices are quoted transparently according to the requested services. After a brief introduction and an application scenario for motivation, section 2 will discuss challenges in modelling and implementing the multidimensional structures. Section 3 will outline the model and section 4 a solution approach based on semantic web services. Finally, section 5 will summarize the state of our work and the future research directions.

1.1 Application Scenario

In order to stay on track through this paper, let us choose a specific situation about a real application demand for a small enterprise. For the planning of a GIS congress event, potential locations should be analyzed considering the following aspects:

⇨ event locations (e.g. congress centres) and their scheduling, prices and descriptions like terrace, catering, it-infrastructure, number of rooms, etc.;

⇨ attractiveness of the location places grouped by the criteria culture, nature, history, sport;

⇨ commodities near the event location grouped by hotel category;

⇨ regional population (socio-demographic data) nearby the location places;

⇨ distances to the location of potential visitors (specific branches) grouped by categories like private enterprises, research institutions, education institutions and administrative bodies. These categories may be subdivided, e.g. private enterprises into data providers, software houses, consulting companies, etc.;

⇨ accessibility as distance to next important train station, airport, traffic ways,

⇨ distances to other places with related events grouped by themes like IT, geography, environment and traffic,

⇨ and data about the locations of former conferences of the same type, to avoid repeating locations.

The result of the search may be analyzed under different aspects. In a top-down analysis suitable regions or coarse time periods may be scanned before more details for specific options are evaluated. In order to collect all needed information, the user may choose data sources from different public and private SDI providers, according to price, quality and thematic relevance. Internal data should be loaded as another data source. To find the best location the user will navigate through the data considering temporal, spatial and thematic aspects at different levels. He may create some maps and charts to explore potential locations interactively. Computations, e.g. catchment areas, may be inserted into the data structure.

2 Requirements for the Ad-Hoc Analysis: Outline and Challenges

Supporting ad-hoc decision making differs from the process of constructing systems for a predefined tasks. While the latter comprises appropriate data modelling based on existing data sources and the definition of user interfaces according to specific demands on the system functionalities, ad-hoc support should be conceived much more flexible. This section describes the main characteristics of the solution and evaluates relevant existing approaches.

2.1 Open Technology

This research aims at define structures (models, operations, processes and methods) for the demand-driven analysis of multidimensional and hierarchically structured spatio-temporal data. The structures will be described generically, without commitments to a specific system, platform or technology. Nonetheless, practical applicability is also a major goal, since we believe that the demand-driven extraction of knowledge from data sources will be a trend for the next years. For SME's up-to-date data for their decision processes is vital, even if they can not afford to set up and maintain complex software systems. For a proof of concept we have chosen semantic web services (SMS) [11] as implementation technology. They use XML [21] as system-independent information transfer language, are self-contained, self-describing, discoverable, compoundable and executable over the web. Thus, our implementation will be interoperable, platform independent and accessible through the web. The practical result of our research will be a framework to build up an interoperable infrastructure for ad-hoc spatio-temporal analysis. In this context, the term (web) infrastructure refers to hardware and software yielding a bundle of semantic web services for a specific purpose; e.g. spatial data infrastructures (SDIs) offer content services for spatial data. The implementation solution will consider existing standard protocols for content data as the OGC[14] specifications for spatial data and XML for Analysis (XMLA)[22] for multidimensional data. Existing integration approaches, e.g. integrating OGC's GML and Hyperion's XMLA protocols [7,20], and optimization techniques for federated data sources [17] will be evaluated against modelling requirements and performance aspects.

2.2 Federated Context Data

Standardisation initiatives (e.g. OGC[1], GSDI[2], INSPIRE[3]) and an enhanced awareness of spatially related information has increased the amount of available digital public and private (spatial) data on the web. Through standardised user oriented services for spatial information (e.g. OGC services like WMS, WFS and WCS [14]) up-to-date data can be requested when it is really needed. On the other hand it is still a challenge to discover where the data can be found. Although SDI's metadata may be discovered through catalogues, they often are limited to spatial region or a specific theme.

---

[1] http://www.opengeospatial.org/
[2] http//www/gsdi.og
[3] http://inspire.jrc.it/, http://eu-geoportal.jrc.it

For the user is desirable to define certain aspects for data exploration, such that during an analysis, the currently examined values for one or more aspects can vary. One would like to have pattern that may be moved e.g. across space, time or a specific theme, setting the focus with each movement to different extents of the aspect. Once the focus has been positioned, all relevant data is harvested from different sources and presented to the user. Fitting to this metaphor is the concept of roaming process in the telecommunication sector, which is mostly applied to mobile phones and other mobile devices. As a user of a mobile phones is travelling, he is automatically transferred to a partner's network when he leaves the zone of his provider. The partner's network offers him similar services as his own provider. In this way a "roamable" infrastructure, which offer services supplied by the best matching partner's data infrastructure is an innovative approach to help customers access spatial contents. However, the implementation of roaming processes for spatio-temporal data brings up consolidation problems. The integration of data collected from different sources demands a harmonization of terms, the handling of data quality, missing data and the combination of data at different levels of detail. These issues should be solved on building the "roamable infrastructure". As the metaphor implies, the meaning of the data structures and the necessary translations should be defined semantically in agreements between the providers of roamable infrastructure and the content providers. The harmonization process will not be treated in depth on this research; the focus will be kept on the handling of different levels of granularity.

2.3 Multi-level Analysis

To handle, analyse and present data at different granularity and under different aspects requires a hierarchical, multidimensional model. Modelling multidimensional temporal data is a well treated issue since the 1990s, breeding technologies like Data Warehouse (DW) and Online Analytical Processing (OLAP) [6,10]. While DW and OLAP have achieved a wide popularity for business analysis, a comfortable integration of spatial data and operations has not yet been achieved in commercial systems. With the definition of Spatial OLAP (SOLAP)[19] analysis models have been extend to include spatial data and operations for server and client functionality. In the following we will adopt some OLAP terminology: A (hyper-)**cube**, is a complete view over observations (**facts**), which are composed by numerical and summarizable data (**measures**) and are described by independent characteristics (**dimensions**). The dimensions have an ordered structure (**hierarchy**), allowing the aggregation of measures at different granularities (levels).

Our data structure will be comparable to OLAP cubes. At the beginning of the analysis the dimensions and dimension values can be defined using metadata from a catalogue. The dimensions will contain descriptive attributes that represent the information the user wants to analyze at different levels of detail. These attributes can be numerical, categorical, temporal or spatial. At this point we differ from the OLAP concept of "measure", with just numerical values and use the term "observation" instead. Observations may exist at any level of detail. Aggregations and specialization operations for observations are needed, some of which may imply a change of the data type (e.g. from textual to boolean in case of applying a "has"-operation, from textual to a set of distribution indexes, etc.) [8].

A big challenge for complex operations on "observations", like statistical functions, data mining algorithms or visualisation methods is the handling of changes induced by changes of granularity. Aggregation or specialization functions may imply a drastic change of the input data like having a new data type, having a selection of functions to be used for computing the new values or having new borders for the content domain. The data model needs to provide a semantic description of possible responses in such situations, firstly using the underlying aggregation semantics and secondly taking into account previous user actions. User actions should guide the selection of parameters for the new computation.

2.4 Integration of Space-and Time Varying Data

The decision process may involve specific data from the user's own sources or produced by computations based on the context data. Specific data can as well refer to one or more dimensions on the model and their attributes can also be used as dimension attributes and as observations. In order not to increase the complexity of the approach we will assume that the data represents one dimension, is self describing and can refer to existing dimension levels or at least be easily computed to the lowest level of the referenced dimension. For instance, if some data attributes refer to a spatial location, the location should be found as a value at the defined spatial hierarchy levels. Otherwise a world coordinate (or an address) should be given, that can easily be computed to any higher spatial aggregation level.

Computation results should be integrated on the same way. Spatial analysis methods often imply the production of new spatial entities. This is the case for spatial clustering algorithms, network computations and propagation predictions, among others. Such computation methods will be observed as a dimension, with the result as an attribute (or observation). The model should then allow to define how this dimension should be aggregated using in this case spatial operators to transfer the results to other hierarchical levels, If this is not possible, the operation should be re-invoked at the other levels, using the values of new observations aggregated to these levels. Although aggregation will increase the level of uncertainty, as the degree of reliability of an expression, coarse but fast overviews of the behaviour of an analysis method at an aggregated level may be useful. The computation can be reproduced, if for a specific level a higher degree of certainty is needed. For this reason a reliability index should describe any observation.

2.5 Deducibility

The reduction of analysis costs in relation to the acquisition of standard tools and context data is a key requirement. It implies that operations should be chained to a calculation process. The model should provide structures for calculating the integrated data and methods. For the implementation it means that deducible attributes like analysis time, storage space used or service requested should be counted in order to compute the price for the analysis. The lack of existing pricing models for spatial web services is often an obstacle for content providers, especially for public institutions, to allow the commercial use of their data. Specifications for authentication, authorization and payment services (Web Pricing and Ordering Services WPOS, OGC discussion paper [14]), could help to solve this gap.

3 Characterising the Multidimensional Model

Existing extended multidimensional models, e.g. concerning evolving data [5,18], conceptual models [15], multiple representations [3,4,12] and flexible hierarchies [13, 15] will be analysed according to the requirements derived from the application demands. The requirements for a model allowing ad-hoc construction, flexible querying and intelligent visualisation are:

(1) **Flexible hierarchies:** The model should enable to define hierarchical structures that may not always be filled with values at all levels. After changing the underlying data source or the observation focus some levels may not be available any more. For instance, in the spatial dimension an administrative level may not exist at a particular region. Also the lowest level of detail can vary for a dimension according to the data source or the specific value.

(2) **Multi-hierarchies:** A dimension can have different hierarchies, but at the same time a level element can be contained in several hierarchies, allowing different aggregations for one single level. For instance on the temporal level, weeks can be contained on a month-oriented calendar hierarchy (year => month => week => day of month) or on a weeks-oriented calendar hierarchy (year => week => day of week).

(3) **Treatment of dimensions attributes as measures:** The model should allow a flexible definition of "measures" at analysis time. The analysis subjects are based always on existing (or constructed) dimension attributes of every data type.

(4) **Support for hierarchical semantics:** A semantic description of aggregations and specialization operations should be possible. Since not all data sources have the same lowest level of detail, it must be possible to define specialization operations to distribute the data to a lower granulation. This implies that imprecision in the data sources (the quality of a query) should be carried over to the model, to inform or warn the user when accessing computed data. A semantic description is needed to recognize explicit hierarchies on the data sources (time, spatial, etc) and to maintain consistent query answers when navigating through different hierarchies existent in a dimension, e.g. avoiding the use of values more than once, handling missing data, etc.

(5) **Flexible storage of analysis results:** The model and pre-computed aggregations should be reusable for further computations. When data change or the model is extended with new dimensions, existing aggregated data that is not affected by the changes should be recognised. Materialization operations should include existing preprocessed data.

(6) **Model extension for space and time dependent data:** space dependent and time dependent data should be incorporate into existing models so that they can be used as analysis observations.

(7) **Support for transferring user intentions:** The model should capture user actions in order to recognise intentions. This is necessary to seamlessly navigate through levels contained in different hierarchies. The path most applicable to the previous actions should be used. The user's intention should also be captured when computations

at a specific level have to be reflected at a new granularity to keep the computed analysis results "similar".

4 Implementation Approach

Suitable research approaches and standardization activities will be evaluated, integrated and, if reasonable extended, into a services-based approach. The idea is to achieve interoperability by exchanging data and requests via standard XML formats and also store some temporal data or additional data in those format, for instance for uploaded user data, aggregation and specification results. It should be possible to chain the services in order to define a particular analytical process. The services can coarsely be structured into these categories:

Conceptual modelling services (CMS): definition and modification of the conceptual model by setting the hypercube structures through implementing construction operations

Content Discovering Services (CDisS): Catalog Services and harvesting services to find particular content services and to request metadata information

Data linking services (DLS): Services to allow linking existent data to model structures by realizing ETL operations. Different data sources can also be joined into one concept and user data can be uploaded und transformed to be used as a data source. Other services like geocode, geoparse, gazetteer and coordinate transformation service can be implemented into this group, since they offer methods to support the ETL process.

Multidimensional services (MDS): Services performning typical OLAP operations like data loading, cube materialization, cube querying and multidimensional result presentation,

Data processing services (DPS): Services to realize analysis computations on the basis of a data structures described by the conceptual model. Here analysis methods like data mining, geostatistical and multicriteria computations can be implemented.

Content access services and transport protocols (CAS): Roamable services to query data from a data source by a client. The query services implement query operators as filter functions on the data structure. WFS and WCS services are access services as well.

Portrayal services (PS): they apply presentation operations to query results to be shown by a client. Styles are defined by Styled Layer Description (SLD) files. WMS is a service of this group.

Security and payment services (WPOS): Services for authentication, authorization and payment.

Fig. 1 represents a process chain using a spatial data warehouse (SDW) infrastructure. At the beginning of the analysis, available data related to the user specific demands can be discovered (1). Therefore catalogues offer metadata describing sources of content providers that have agreements with the infrastructure for data exchange and pricing models. The agreements my be cascading, providing a transparent access to different remote data sources. The infrastructure presents the metadata in form of content coverage, attributes, quality and access price to the user. The user chooses the sources and methods to construct the conceptual model (2). Additionally, the user may link his own data by loading documents into the infrastructure (3). Once the model is defined MDS operations can be used (4) to materialize the cube, performing aggregation and integrating the data sources' content, accessed via CAS, into the cube structure. This materialization will be temporarily stored in the infrastructure and all involved non-free services (represented by striped fill forms) will be logged in the WPOS temporary structures. Analysis services (5) can also be charged according to the applied method, data or computational time. The query or analysis results will be presented to the user using portrayal services (6) and can again be used as new data source to extend the existing model. At any moment a bill for the performed analysis can be obtained.

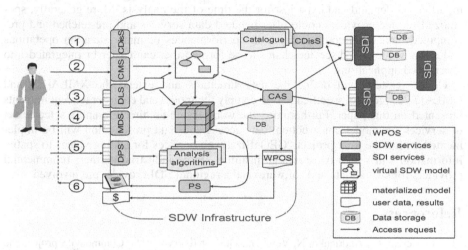

Fig. 1. Process chain and services involved on a SDW infrastructure

5 State of the Work

A first testbed has been created by joining CommonGIS [1], an interactive tool for spatio-temporal analysis, and SpOC, a Spatial OLAP client, that implements the JO-LAP[9] model for discovering OLAP structures and performing OLAP queries Within CommonGIS, independent variables can be declared as parameters. A wrapper for the CommonGIS structures allows the interpretation of the dimensions as parameters and the dynamic presentation of the query results on the maps. The implemented connectors for OLAP servers use the XMLA[22] protocol to enquire and access data from a Microsoft SQLServer Analysis Service. To support spatial data or dimensions, we take the GIS oriented approach, loading the spatial data into CommonGIS and then joining spatial referenced cube dimension levels such as addresses, postal codes and regions over a common attribute with the spatial data. By doing this, the data visualizations were updated simultaneously as though navigating through the cubes.

Task support should be offered by adding semantic information to the data processing services. Currently we are extracting analysis methods from CommonGIS to develop decision supporting visualization and analysis services. These may be composed to build workflows of analysis tasks. A Service catalogue should allow applications to offer alternative visualisations for analogous methods for other data types. In this context, we are developing an abstract language for describing spatial/multidimensional analysis tasks that allows domain-specific analysis steps [2].

5.1 Conclusion and Future Work

This paper presented some first ideas for a concept and implementational framework based on web services to support complex ad-hoc multidimensional and multilevel analysis using open public and private data infrastructures. A main aspect to consider during the implementation will be how to guide the user through the building of models and through the data access. For the scenario the underlying cube will be built and modified on demand and exist just for the time of the analysis. More generally, specialized service providers could offer bundled data services and pre-fetched and pre-computed data. This could improve the performances of materialization operations and allow value added service-chains to be formed that can easier br integrated into specialized applications.

Our next steps will define the data structures and extend the XMLA[22] and GMLA[7,20] protocol specifications to comply the model and data storage requirements presented on this paper. Furthermore, the web service architecture and a selected set of services for model construction, data access and data presentation will be implemented within the joint project "GEOeBizz, web services for adding values to spatial information", in which two research institutes, three industrial partners (commercial providers for spatial data and software) and a regional SDI provider are involved.

References

1. Andrienko, G., Andrienko, N, Voss, H..: GIS for Everyone: the CommonGIS project and beyond. In: M.Peterson (ed.) Maps and the Internet Elsevier Science, (2003)
2. Andrienko, N., Andrienko, G.: Exploratory Analysis of Spatial and Temporal Data A Systematic Approach. Springer-Verlag, (2005)
3. Andrienko, N., Andrienko, G.: Intelligent Visualisation and Information Presentation for Civil Crisis Management. In: Suares, J., Markus, B. (eds.), AGILE 2006, 9th AGILE Conference on Geographical Information Science, Proceedings, College of Geoinformatics, Unversity of West Hungary, (2006) 291-298
4. Bédard, Y., Bernier, E.,: Supporting Multiple Representations with Spatial View Management and the Concept of "VUEL"., Joint Workshop on Multi-Scale Representations of Spatial Data, International Society for Photogrammetry and Remote Sensing, (2003)
5. Body, M., Miquel, M., Bedard, Y., Tchounikine, A.,: Handling Evolutions in Multidimensional Structures, 19th International Conference on Data Engineering (ICDE'03), (2003)
6. Codd, E. F.: Providing OLAP (on-line analytical processing) to user anaysits: An IT mandate. Technical Report, E.F.Codd and Associates, (1993)
7. Fidalgo, R. N., Silva. J., Times, V. C., Souza, F.F., Barros, R. S. M.: GMLA: A XML Schema for Integration and Exchange of Mulitidimensional-Geographical Data. In: V Brazilian Symposium on GeoInformatics, Campos do Jordão (2003)
8. Hernández, V., Göhring, W., Voss, A. Hopmann, C. Sustainable Decision Support by the Use of Multi-Level and Multi-Criteria Spatial Analysis on the Nicaragua Development Gateway. In: FIG Working Week 2005 and 8th International Conference on the Global spatial Data Infrastructure, Proceedings, 18-21 April 2005, Cairo, Egypt, (2005)

9. JOLAP Expert Group. Java OLAP interface (JOLAP) – proposed final draft, JSR-000069, Technical report, Sun Microsystems Inc., (2003).
10. Kimball, R.: The Data Warehouse Toolkit. Wiley Computer Publishing, (1996)
11. McIlraith, S. A., Son, T. C., Zeng, H.:.Semantic Web Services, IEEE Intelligent System. Special Issue on Semantic Web March/April 2001, (2001)
12. Malinowski, E.: Concepts and methodological framework for spatio-temporal data warehouse design, Dissertation Thesis, Université Libre de Bruxelles, Belgium, (2003).
13. Malinowski, E., Zimányi, E.: Hierarchies in a Multidimensional Model: From Conceptual Modeling to Logical Representation. In Data & Knowledge Engineering, (2006). To appear.
14. OGC: The Open Geospatial Consortium, Online at http://opengeospatial.org
15. Parent, C., Spaccapietra S., Zimányi E.: Conceptual Modeling for Traditional and Spatio-Temporal Applications. The MADS approach. Springer-Verlag, Berlin Heidelberg New York, (2006)
16. Pedersen, D., Riis, K., Pedersen, T. B.: Query optimization for OLAP-XML federations. In Proceedings of the 5th ACM international Workshop on Data Warehousing and OLAP. DOLAP '02. ACM Press, New York, NY,.(2002) 57-64
17. Pedersen T. B.: Aspects of data modeling and query processing for complex multidimensional data. Ph.D. Thesis, Aalborg University, Aalborg st, Denmark, (2000)
18. Pestana, G., Silva, M., Bédard, Y.: Spatial OLAP Modeling: An Overview Base on Spatial Objects Changing over Time, IEEE 3rd International Conference on Computational Cybernetics, (2005).
19. Rivest, S., et al: SOLAP: Merging Business Intelligence with Geospatial Technology for Interactive Spatio-Temporal Exploration and Analysis of Data, Journal of International Society for Photogrammetry and Remote Sensing (ISPRS) "Advances in spatio-temporal analysis and representation, Vol. 60, No. 1, (2005). 17-33
20. Silva, J., Times, V. Fidalgo R. Barros, R.: Towards a Web Service for Geographic and Multidimensional Processing, In Brazilian Symposium on GeoInformatics, Campos do Jordão (2004)
21. W3C. Extensible Markup Language (XML) 1.0 (Third Edition). www.w3.org/TR/2004/REC-xml-20040204/, February 2004, last access August 2006
22. XMLA Consortium. XMLA documents. Online at http://www.xmla.org/docs_pub.asp (last access 06/29/2006).

Requirements Specification and Conceptual Modeling for Spatial Data Warehouses*

E. Malinowski** and E. Zimányi

Department of Informatics and Networks
Université Libre de Bruxelles
emalinow@ulb.ac.be, ezimanyi@ulb.ac.be

Abstract. Development of a spatial data warehouse (SDW) is a complex task, which if assisted with the methodological framework could facilitate its realization. In particular, the requirements specification phase, being one of the earliest steps of system development, should attract attention since it may entail significant problems if faulty or incomplete. However, a lack of methodology for the SDW design and the presence of two actors in specifying data requirements, i.e., users and source systems, complicates more the development process. In this paper, we propose three different approaches for requirements specifications that lead to the creation of conceptual schemas for SDW applications.

1 Introduction

The conventional DWs are designed based on the multidimensional view of data. It consists of fact and dimension tables. A fact table contains numeric data called measures while dimension tables include attributes that allow to explore measures from different perspectives. These attributes can form a hierarchy allowing to see measures at different levels of detail.

Since it is estimated that about 80% of data stored in databases (DBs) has a spatial or location component, the location dimension has been widely integrated in DW systems. Nevertheless, this dimension is usually represented in an alphanumeric, non-cartographic manner (i.e., using solely the place name) since these systems are neither able to store nor to manipulate spatial data.

On the other hand, spatial databases (SDBs) have been used for several decades for storing and managing spatial data. Therefore, bringing together DWs and SDBs, leading to spatial DWs (SDWs), allows to keep the intrinsic concepts of a DW and additionally provide support for managing spatial data.

However, SDWs as a new research field raise several issues [11, 12, 13]. For example, even though, in conventional DWs the advantages of using a multidimensional model for expressing users' requirements are well known, in SDWs this model is seldom used. Therefore, in order to exploit these advantages for

---

* The work of E. Malinowski was funded by a scholarship of the Cooperation Department of the Université Libre de Bruxelles.
** Currently on leave from the Universidad de Costa Rica.

R. Meersman, Z. Tari, P. Herrero et al. (Eds.): OTM Workshops 2006, LNCS 4278, pp. 1616–1625, 2006.
© Springer-Verlag Berlin Heidelberg 2006

SDWs, in [12, 13], we propose a conceptual multidimensional model that allows to include spatial support in different elements of a DW.

On the other hand, since there is still a lack of methodology for the DW design, SDW implementers incur to problems not only related to the DW design but also to the inclusion of spatial data in DWs. In particular, requirements specification is a difficult task since it must consider not only users' requirements but also data in source systems that are used to feed SDWs.

In [11] we propose a methodology for the DW design that is in line with the traditional DB methodology, i.e., it includes the requirements specification, conceptual, logical, and physical design phases. Considering users, source systems, and both, we extend this methodology by three different approaches for requirements specifications. In this paper, based on the methodology described in [11], we propose different approaches for the requirements specification and conceptual modeling phases that allow to include spatial support for different elements of multidimensional models.

This paper is organized as follows. Section 2 refers to works related to requirements specifications in conventional DWs. Section 3 describes spatial support that may be included in multidimensional models. Section 4 presents our proposal for different approaches for the requirements specification phase and the creation of conceptual schemas for SDWs. Section 5 concludes this paper.

2   Related Work

To our knowledge, there are not works related to the methodology for the SDW design. For the conventional DWs, several approaches exist for requirements specification and conceptual modeling. In [11] we classify them in order to make them easier to understand. Next, we briefly refer to this classification.

User-driven approach. This approach considers that users play a fundamental role during the requirements analysis and must be actively involved in the elucidation of relevant facts and dimensions [5, 10]. Users from different levels of organization are selected. Then, different techniques, such as interviews or facilitated sessions are used to specify the information requirements [5].

Business-driven approach[1]. This approach considers that the derivation of DW structures should start from analysis of either business requirements or business processes [2, 6, 9]. Business requirements specification provides a description of users' needs considering business goals, thus starting from the highest level of the organization. Then, users from lower organization levels may participate; their requirements are aligned with the previously-established business goals. The process of refining business goals is conduced until identifying the necessary multidimensional elements.

On the other hand, the analysis of business processes requires to specify different business services or activities that ensure to produce a particular output. Since different elements participate in these activities, they may be considered

---

[1] It is also called process-, goal-, or requirements-driven.

as dimensions. Further, decision makers need metrics to evaluate business activities, which may be considered as measures in the DW schema.

Data-driven approach. In order to obtain the DW schema, the underlying source systems are analyzed [1, 6, 7, 14]. These source schemas should exhibit a good degree of normalization [6] to facilitate the extraction of facts, measures, dimensions, and hierarchies. In general, the participation of users is not explicitly required [8]; however, in some techniques users should either analyze the obtained schema to confirm the correctness of the derived structures [1] or identify facts and measures as a starting point for the design of multidimensional schemas [7, 14]. After schema creation, users can specify their information requirements by selecting items of interest.

Demand/supply-driven approach[2]. This approach is the combination of business- or user-driven and data-driven approaches [3]. Demand indicates business or user data requirements while supply refers to the availability of data in source systems. In the ideal situation these two parts should be equal, i.e., all information that users (business) require for analysis purposes should be supplied by the data included in source systems.

3   Spatial Support for Elements of Multidimensional Models

Requirements specification determines, among others, what data should be available and how it is organized. This specification for DWs should lead to discover the essential elements of the multidimensional model, i.e., facts with associated measures, dimensions, and hierarchies [2, 4, 14], which are required to facilitate future data manipulations.

Similar approach should be applied for SDWs. However, it is necessary to know whether multidimensional models can be used for representing spatial data. In [12, 13] we proposed a spatial extension for the conceptual multidimensional model called MultiDimER. To describe our model, we use an example for the analysis of highway maintenance costs as shown in Figure 1[3]. To better understand the constructs of the MutiDimER model, we first ignore spatial support, i.e., the symbols of different geometries and topological relationships.

The schema in Figure 1 contains dimensions, hierarchies, a fact relationship, and measures. A dimension is an abstract concept for grouping data that shares a common semantic meaning within the domain being modeled. It represents either a level or one or more hierarchies. Levels correspond to entity types in the ER model. Hierarchies contain several related levels. They can express different structures according to an analysis criterion, e.g., geographical location.

Figure 1 includes Road Coating and Time as the one-level dimensions. The County[4] and Highway segment dimensions contain hierarchies. The Geo location

---

[2] It is also called top-down/bottom-up analysis.
[3] A formal definition of the model can be found in [11].
[4] We call a dimension using the name of the level that is attached to the fact relationship.

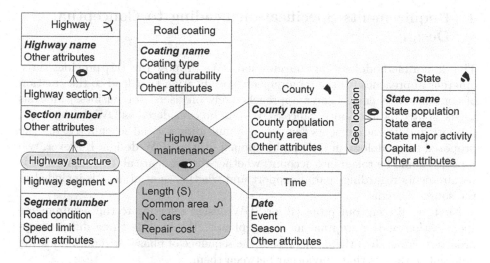

Fig. 1. An example of a multidimensional schema with spatial elements

hierarchy comprises the County and State levels while the Highway structure hierarchy includes the Highway segment, Highway section, and Highway levels.

A fact relationship, e.g., Highway maintenance in the figure, represents an n-ary relationship between dimensions. It may contain numeric measures that are used for aggregations, e.g., No.cars or Repair cost.

The spatially-extended MultiDimER model allows to include spatial support for levels, levels' attributes, fact relationships, and measures. Spatial levels are levels, for which the application needs to keep their spatial characteristics. This is captured by its geometry, which is represented using pictograms indicating spatial data types such as point, line, surface, or a collection of these data types. A level may have spatial attributes independently of the fact that it is spatial or not. In Figure 1 the spatial level State contains a spatial attribute Capital.

Two consecutive spatial levels forming a hierarchy are related through topological relationships. The latter is required for determining the complexity of procedures for measure aggregation [13]. Figure 1 shows two spatial levels, County and State, related through the intersect topological relationship (⬤).

A spatial fact relationship relates two or more spatial dimensions. It requires the inclusion of spatial predicate for the spatial join operations, e.g., in the figure an intersection topological relationship; it indicates that users require to focus their analysis on those highway segments that intersect counties.

The (spatial) fact relationship may include spatial measures. They can be represented by geometry or calculated using spatial operators, such as distance, area, etc. To indicate that measure is calculated using spatial operators, we use the symbol (S). The schema in Figure 1 contains two spatial measures: Length and Common area. Length is a number representing the length of the part of a highway segment that belongs to a county. Common area is a spatial data representing the geometry of the common part.

4 Requirements Specification Leading to Conceptual Design

The design methodology for conventional DWs proposed in [11] provides three different approaches for the requirements specification that lead to the creation of conceptual schemas. These approaches rely on users' (or business) analysis needs, source data, or both. Since SDWs can be considered as DWs with spatial support in different elements composing a multidimensional schema [12, 13], the proposed methodology in [11] can be applied for the SDW design. However, two aspects should be taken into account: whether the users are able to express their requirements regarding spatial support and whether spatial data is included in the source systems.

Next, we present our proposal for SDW design referring to the requirements specification and conceptual modeling phases. We include three different approaches. For each of them, we present the sequence of phases without indicating different iterations that may occur between them.

4.1 Demand-Driven Approach

In this approach business or user requirements are the driving force for developing a conceptual schema. For the SDW design, two different possibilities exist as shown in Figure 2. The upper line is used when users either are not familiar with spatial data management or have knowledge about spatial data, but they (or designers) prefer first to express their needs related to non-spatial elements and afterwards, include spatial support.

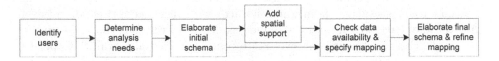

Fig. 2. General phases in the demand-driven approach for the SDW design

The first three phases are developed as for the conventional DWs. In the first phase, in order to ensure that requirements will express the organization-wide goals that a DW is expected to address, users on different management levels are identified. Executives, managers, professionals, and also an enterprise plan will help a developer team to understand the purpose of having a DW and to determine analysis needs (the second phase in the figure). For example, they may express the interest of analyzing highway maintenance cost in different counties and states considering different periods of time and road coating. The gathered information serves as basis in the elaboration of the initial DW schema (the third phase in the figure), e.g.,. of the schema as present in Figure 1 without spatial elements. During the next phase, i.e., add spatial support in Figure 2, this initial DW schema is analyzed to include spatial support.

As explained in Section 3, different multidimensional elements are examined. For one-level dimensions users may choose whether a level, its attributes, or both should be represented spatially. Then, every hierarchy level is analyzed in a similar way, e.g., users may require the spatial representation for states and capitals (Figure 1). If a hierarchy includes two or more consecutive spatial levels, e.g., County and State in Figure 1, the topological relationship between them is specified (the intersection relationship in Figure 1). If there are more than two spatial dimensions, e.g., Highway segment and County in Figure 1, designers can help the users to determine whether some topological relationships between dimensions may be of users' interest. In the affirmative case, a specific topological relationship should be included in the fact relationship to indicate a predicate for the spatial join operations (the intersection relationship in the figure). Finally, the inclusion of spatial measures is considered, e.g., Common area in Figure 1.

The next phase of checking data availability and specifying mapping determines whether data required by users is available in source systems. The mapping includes a general description of the correspondences between all elements of a multidimensional schema that match with data in source systems. This description refers also to the required transformations, if necessary. For example, for the attribute Road condition in the Highway segment level (Figure 1) this description could indicate the name of corresponding attribute in operational DBs and the transformation of numeric values to character representation, e.g., that 5 indicates very good, 4 is good, etc. This is necessary before the development of logical and physical schemas. Since spatial data may not be present in the source systems, users may require the access to external sources. Notice that adding spatial support may require additional iterations to include new users, to precise requirements needs, etc.

In the case of lacking some data items in operational DBs or external sources, a modification of schema should be made (the last phase in Figure 2). Modifications to the schema may lead to changes in the mappings.

The lower line in Figure 2 refers to the situation when the users are familiar with concepts related to spatial data. All phases, except adding spatial support, are the same as the ones described above; however, since from the beginning of the requirements gathering process the users are able to express the analysis needs referring them to spatial data, the elaborated initial schema already includes spatial elements.

4.2 Supply-Driven Approach

This approach relies on the data in source systems. It aims at identifying all candidate multidimensional schemas that can be realistically implemented on the top of the available operational DBs.

Similar to the previous demand-driven approach, we refer to two different situations. Since operational DBs are the driving force for this approach, we consider whether these DBs are spatial.

If spatial data is not included in the source systems, the first four phases of the supply-driven approach are the same as specified for the conventional DWs

Fig. 3. General phases in the supply-driven approach for the SDW design

[11]. The identification of source systems (the first phase in the figure) aims in determining existing operational systems that can serve as a data provider for a DW. The external sources are not considered in this stage. These DBs are analyzed in an exhaustive manner to discover the elements of multidimensional schemas (the second phase in the figure). For conventional DW design, different techniques can be used [1, 3, 4, 7, 14]. All these techniques require that operational DBs are represented using the ER model or relational tables.

In general, in the first step the facts and measures are determined. This can be done analyzing the existing documentation [1, 4, 14] or the DB structures [7]. Facts and measures are elements that correspond to events occurring dynamically in the organization, i.e., that are frequently updated, e.g., an attribute indicating a highway repair cost in different periods of time. An alternative option may be the inclusion of users that understand the operational systems and can help to determine which data can be considered as measures.

Different procedures can be applied for deriving dimensions and hierarchies. They can be automatic [3, 7], semi-automatic [1], or manual [4, 14]. The process of discovering a one-level dimension or a leaf level of a hierarchy usually starts from identifying in operational DBs the static (not frequently updatable) elements (e.g., an element that corresponds to the County level in Figure 1) that are related to the facts. Then, starting with this element every one-to-many relationship is revised to find other hierarchy levels (e.g., the State level in Figure 1).

Since facts with measures, dimensions, and hierarchies are already specified, the elaboration of an initial DW schema is straightforward (the third phase in Figure 3). In this phase the specification of mappings between source systems and the proposed schema should be also elaborated.

Until now the participation of the users was minimal responding only to the specific designer's inquiries. In the next phase, i.e., determine user interest in Figure 3, a user input is required in identifying which facts are important since the initial schema may contain more elements than those required by the users.

After determining users' interest related to the conventional DW schema, a new phase of adding the spatial support is realized. Notice that this support is only considered for the previously-chosen elements of the multidimensional schema. The analysis which elements should be spatially represented can be conduced in a similar way as explained for the demand-driven approach above.

Users' recommendations about changes will be reflected in the final schema (the last phase in the figure). Since spatial support does not form a part of the underlying operational systems, external sources should be considered to deliver required spatial data. The modifications in the schema and new data sources may require the changes in mappings.

In another situation when source systems include spatial data, the phases as for the conventional DW design can be used (the lower line in Figure 3). However, a special derivation process should be applied to create an initial schema with spatial elements. Currently this derivation process should be conduced manually, since to our knowledge semi-automatic or automatic procedures for SDWs as the ones developed for conventional DWs do not yet exist.

The phases indicated by the upper line in Figure 3 can also be used when the source systems include spatial data but the derivation process is complex.

4.3 Demand/Supply-Driven Approach

This approach combines both previously-described approaches that may be used in parallel. Therefore, two chains of activities can be distinguished. The first one corresponds to the demand-driven approach and creates a multidimensional schema as it emerges from business requirements. Another chain corresponds to the supply-driven approach and delivers a multidimensional schema that can be extracted from the existing operational DBs.

Similar to the previous approaches, we propose two different solutions considering whether source systems include spatial data and whether users are familiar with the concepts related to spatial data.

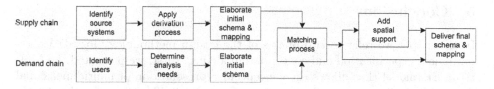

Fig. 4. General phases in the demand/supply-driven approach for the SDW design

If source systems do not include spatial data or users are not familiar with the concepts related to them, all steps until the matching process of schemas from demand and supply chains are the same as for conventional DWs already explained for the demand-driven and the supply-driven approaches above.

After the initial schemas are elaborated using both approaches, the comparison between them is realized. The comparison or integration process is not an easy task. Different aspects should be considered, such as used terminology, degree of similarity between the two solutions for each multidimensional element, e.g., between dimensions, between dimension attributes, or between hierarchy levels. Several solutions already exist for conventional DWs, e.g., [3, 6, 5].

During the matching phase user demands may be covered by data in operational systems and there may be no other data to expand the analysis spectrum, i.e., both schemas cover the same aspects of analysis. This is the ideal situation. Nevertheless, in real-world applications it is difficult to find that both schemas will cover the same analysis aspects. Indeed, the matching process can reveal that either business demands exceed the data availability or operational DBs provide more analysis scenarios that users did not consider before. In both situations, some actions must be taken to determine the direction of changes in one of the schemas. For example, another iteration in the demand and the supply chains might be required. In this iteration either new users could be involved who are interested in the new solutions provided by source systems or a new initial schema could be elaborated eliminating from the analysis some fact relationships and associated dimensions.

In the next phase, the resulting multidimensional schema is analyzed for inclusion of spatial support (the upper line in the figure). Notice that similar to the previous approaches, external sources may be considered in this stage for obtaining spatial data. Modification to the initial schema leads to elaboration of final schema and the changes in mappings, if required.

If source systems include spatial data and users have knowledge about it, the first three phases are realized as explained above for the demand-driven and the supply-driven approaches considering the spatial support from the first phase in both chains. Then, the matching process must also refer to spatial data that is included in both schemas, i.e., obtained from the demand and the supply chains. If the result of this matching process is satisfactory, the final schema is delivered (the lower line in Figure 4). In other case, additional iterations as explained above may be necessary.

5   Conclusions

In this paper we refer to two phases of the design methodology for SDWs: requirements specification and conceptual modeling. First, we presented the MultiDimER model that allows the conceptual representation of multidimensional data with spatial support. Then, we proposed three different approaches for requirements specification that lead to the creation of conceptual schemas. These approaches take into account whether the data requirements for SDW application are based on users' specification, available data in source systems, or both. For each approach we also considered the situation whether users have knowledge about spatial data or whether spatial data is included in source systems.

Proposed approaches provide different options for implementers during the first phases of the SDW development. They can choose an approach that fits better according to users' needs and particularities of the SDW project.

References

1. M. Böehnlein and A. U. vom Ende. Deriving initial data warehouses structures from the conceptual data models of the underlying operational information systems. In *Proc. of the 2nd ACM Int. Workshop on Data Warehousing and OLAP*, pages 15–21, 1999.
2. M. Böehnlein and A. U. vom Ende. Business process oriented development of data warehouse structures. In *Proc. of Data Warehousing 2000, Physica-Verlag*, pages 3–22, 2000.

3. A. Bonifati, F. Cattaneo, S. Ceri, A. Fuggetta, and S. Paraboschi. Designing data marts for data warehouses. *ACM Transactions on Software Engineering and Methodology*, 10(4):452–483, 2001.
4. L. Cabbibo and R. Torlone. The design and development of a logical system for OLAP. In *Proc. the 2nd Int. Conf. on Data Warehousing and Knowledge Discovery*, pages 1–10, 2000.
5. G. Freitas, A. Laender, and M. Campos. MD2 - getting users involved in the development of data warehouse application. In *Proc. of the 4th Int. Workshop on Design and Management of Data Warehouses*, pages 3–12, 2002.
6. P. Giorgini, S. Rizzi, and M. Garzetti. Goal-oriented requirements analysis for data warehouse desing. In *Proc. of the 8th ACM Int. Workshop on Data Warehousing and OLAP*, pages 47–56, 2005.
7. M. Golfarelli, D. Maio, and S. Rizzi. Conceptual design of data warehouses from E/R schemes. In *Proc. of the 31st Hawaii Int. Conf. on System Sciences*, page 334, 1998.
8. B. List, R. Bruckner, K. Machaczek, and J. Shiefer. Comparison of data warehouse development methodologies. case study of the process warehouse. In *Proc. of the 13th Int. Conf. on Database and Expert Systems*, pages 6–1–6–11, 2002.
9. B. List, J. Shiefer, and A. Tjoa. Process-oriented requirement analysis supporting the data warehouse design process - a use case driven approach. In *Proc. of the 11th Int. Conf. on Database and Expert Systems*, pages 593–603, 2000.
10. S. Luján-Mora and J. Trujillo. A comprehensive method for data warehouse design. In *Proc. of the 5th Int. Workshop on Design and Management of Data Warehouses*, 2003.
11. E. Malinowski. *Designing Conventional, Spatial and Temporal Data Warehouses: Concepts and Methodological Framework*. PhD thesis, Université Libre de Bruxelles, 2006.
12. E. Malinowski and E. Zimányi. Representing spatiality in a conceptual multidimensional model. In *Proc. of the 12th ACM Symposium on Advances in Geographic Information Systems*, pages 12–21, 2004.
13. E. Malinowski and E. Zimányi. Spatial hierarchies and topological relationships in the Spatial MultiDimER model. In *Proc. of the 22nd British Nat. Conf. on Databases*, pages 17–28, 2005.
14. D. Moody and M. Kortink. From enterprise models to dimensional models: a methodology for data warehouse and data mart design. In *Proc. of the Int. Workshop on Design and Management of Data Warehouses*, page 5, 2000.

A Classification of Spatio-temporal Entities Based on Their Location in Space-Time

Thomas Bittner[1,2,3,4] and Maureen Donnelly[1,3]

[1]Department of Philosophy, [2]Department of Geography
[3]New York State Center of Excellence in Bioinformatics and Life Sciences
[4]National Center for Geographic Information and Analysis
State University of New York at Buffalo

Abstract. We present an axiomatic theory of spatio-temporal entities based on the primitives *spatial-region, part-of,* and *is-an-instance-of.* We provide a classification of spatio-temporal entities according to the number and kinds of regions at which they are located in spacetime and according to whether they instantiate or are instantiated at those regions. The focus on location and instantiation at a location as the central notions of this theory makes it particularly appropriate for serving as a foundational ontology for geography and geographic information science.

1 Introduction

In geographic information science, there is a need for formal ontologies which provide semantic foundations for the terminology used in scientific theories as well as in data standards, data sets, and geographic information systems [2,1,7,4]. These formal ontologies should specify the semantics of for terminology that enables the user to describe how geographic objects persist through time, change over time, and instantiate geographic categories at certain locations in space and time.

In this paper, we present an axiomatic theory which is based upon a mereology [11] of spatio-temporal regions, a distinction between (3D) spatial regions and (4D) temporal regions, and an instantiation relation holding between a particular entity, a category (or *universal*), and a spatio-temporal region where the particular instantiates the universal. We distinguish spatio-temporal entities that instantiate at the regions at which they are located (particulars) from entities that are instantiated at the regions at which they are located (universals). For example, I am a particular, an instance of the universal human being wherever I am located. My life is a particular which instantiates the universal human life at the spacetime region it occupies.

Particulars are further distinguished according to the number (a single region vs. multiple regions) and the kinds of regions (spatial regions vs. temporal regions) at which they are located. *Endurants* (objects like you, your car, planet Earth, etc.) are located at multiple spatial regions (different 3D regions at different times). *Perdurants* (processes like your life, global warming, the blood

R. Meersman, Z. Tari, P. Herrero et al. (Eds.): OTM Workshops 2006, LNCS 4278, pp. 1626–1635, 2006.

flow in my body, etc.) are located at unique temporal (4D) regions. *Stages* are located at unique spatial regions and are instantaneous parts of perdurants [10].

Universals are distinguished into universals that are instantiated by endurants, universals that are instantiated by perdurants, and universals that are instantiated by stages. An overview of the basic categories is given in Figure 1. (See also [11] and [9].)

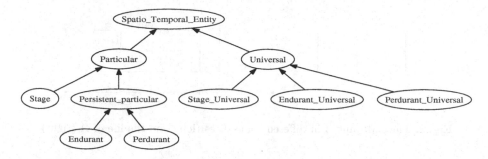

Fig. 1. A classification of spatio-temporal entities with respect to their location in space-time

An important feature of our theory is that it describes time-dependent properties and relations (e.g. instantiation of a given universal) in terms of location in spacetime. This makes our theory particularly appropriate as an ontological foundation for geography, geographic information science, and spatio-temporal information processing. (See [5] who discuss why a formal ontology for geography and GIScience should be based on the notion of location.) The theory presented in this paper is an extension of the theory of endurants and perdurants developed in our [3].

2 Example

Consider Figure 2. Instead of considering a four-dimensional model of spacetime, we use the subset of points of the plane which is specified by the coordinates t and s that satisfy the constraint $0 \leq t \leq t_4$ & $0 \leq s \leq 4$. In set-theoretic terms we write $\mathbf{ST} = \{(s,t) \mid 0 \leq t \leq t_4$ & $0 \leq s \leq 4\}$. The horizontal dimension in the figure is interpreted as temporal and the vertical dimension is interpreted as spatial.

The left part of Figure 2 shows an endurant, the line-shaped entity A, at times t_1, t_2, and t_3. The life of the endurant A is visualized as the solid two-dimensional region, $LifeOf\_A$, depicted in the right part of the figure. It shows that A comes into existence at t_1 and that it continues to exist until t_4. The lives of C, B and D are proper parts of the life of A and are respectively located at the spacetime regions $loc\_lf\_C = \{(s,t) \mid t_1 \leq t \leq t_4$ & $1 \leq s \leq 2\}$, $loc\_lf\_B = \{(s,t) \mid t_1 \leq t \leq t_5$ & $2 \leq s \leq 3\}$, and $loc\_lf\_D = \{(s,t) \mid t_6 \leq t_4$ & $2 \leq s \leq 3\}$ shown in the right part of Figure 2. The life of A, $LifeOf\_A$, is located at the region loc_lf_A, which is the union of the regions loc_lf_B, loc_lf_C, and loc_lf_D. We also include in our model the following stages of the lives of the endurants A, C, B and D: A^{t_1}, A^{t_2}, A^{t_3}, C^{t_1}, C^{t_2}, C^{t_3}, B^{t_1}, and D^{t_3}. For example, A^{t_1} is the instantaneous slice of A's life at t_1, A^{t_2} is the instantaneous slice of A's life at t_2, and so on.

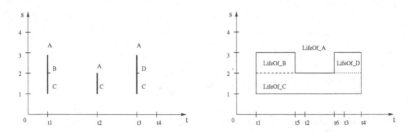

Fig. 2. The endurant A in different time-slices (left) and the life of A (right)

At a given moment during its life an endurant is exactly co-located with the stage of its life at that moment. For example, the location of A at t_1 is the location of the stage A^{t_1}: the region $loc\_A\_t_1 = \{(s,t) \mid t = t_1 \,\&\, 1 \leq s \leq 3\}$. The stages C^{t_1} and B^{t_1} are located at the regions $loc\_C\_t_1 = \{(s,t) \mid t = t_1 \,\&\, 1 \leq s \leq 2\}$ and $loc\_B\_t_1 = \{(s,t) \mid t = t_1 \,\&\, 2 \leq s \leq 3\}$. The stages A^{t_2} and C^{t_2} are both located at the region $loc\_A\_t_2 = loc\_C\_t_2 = \{(s,t) \mid t = t_2 \,\&\, 1 \leq s \leq 2)$. And so on.

At every region at which endurant A is located, A instantiates the universal LINE(-segment). For example A instantiates the universal LINE at $loc\_A\_t_1$, $loc\_A\_t_2$, etc. Similarly, endurant C instantiates LINE at $loc\_C\_t_1$, $loc\_C\_t_2$, etc. The universal LINE is located wherever it is instantiated by one of its instances. Thus LINE is located at $loc\_A\_t_1$, $loc\_A\_t_2$, $loc\_C\_t_1$, $loc\_C\_t_2$, etc. Similarly, the universal LIFE-OF-A-LINE is instantiated at regions loc_lf_A, loc_lf_B, loc_lf_C, and loc_lf_D by the perdurants $LifeOf\_A$, $LifeOf\_B$, $LifeOf\_C$, and $LifeOf\_D$ respectively. Hence, LIFE-OF-A-LINE is located at all those regions. Consider the universal (momentary) STAGE-IN-THE-LIFE-OF-A-LINE. This universal is instantiated for example by A^{t_1}, A^{t_2}, A^{t_3}, C^{t_1}, C^{t_2}, C^{t_3}, B^{t_1}, and D^{t_3} at their respective locations.

3   Space-Time Regions

In this section we briefly review our formal theory of space-time regions which was originally developed in [3]. We present the formal theory in a sorted first-order predicate logic with identity. All quantification is restricted to a single sort. Restrictions on quantification will be understood by conventions on variable usage. We use u, v, and w as variables ranging over regions and (in the second part of the paper) x, y, and z as variables ranging over entities.

Regional parthood. We start by introducing the binary predicate P, where $P\ uv$ is interpreted as 'the region u is a part of the region v'. We introduce the binary predicates PP for proper parthood (D_{PP}) and O for overlap (D_O).

$$D_{PP}\ \ PP\ uv \equiv P\ uv \wedge u \neq v \qquad D_O\ \ O\ uv \equiv (\exists w)(P\ wu \wedge P\ wv)$$

We require: P antisymmetric (AR2); P is transitive (AR3); if everything that overlaps u also overlaps v then u is a part of v (AR4); P is reflexive(AR1); and there exists a region which has all regions as parts (AR5).

$$AR2\ \ P\ uv \wedge P\ vu \rightarrow u = v$$
$$AR3\ \ P\ uv \wedge P\ vw \rightarrow P\ uw \qquad AR1\ \ P\ uu$$
$$AR4\ \ (w)(O\ wu \rightarrow O\ wv) \rightarrow P\ uv \qquad AR5\ \ (\exists u)(v)P\ vu$$

We then define spacetime as a predicate which holds for a region which has all regions as parts (D_{ST}). It follows that there is a unique spacetime (TR1 + AR5). We use the symbol $\mathcal{ST}$ to refer to this region.

$$D_{ST}\ \ ST\ u \equiv (v)P\ vu \qquad TR1\ \ ST\ u \wedge ST\ v \rightarrow u = v$$

On the intended interpretation in our example domain, spacetime is the set **ST**. Region variables range over all subsets of **ST**, and P is the subset relation, $\subseteq$.

Spatial regions and time-slices. We add as a new primitive the unary predicate SR. On the intended interpretation $SR\ u$ means: region u is a spatial region. Spatial regions are parts of spacetime which are either not extended at all in time or, in case of discrete time, do not extend beyond a minimal time unit. In the example model, $loc\_A\_t_1$, $loc\_B\_t_1$, and $loc\_C\_t_1$ are all spatial regions. More generally, any subset of **ST** consisting of points with a fixed time coordinate is a spatial region.

   Time-slices are maximal spatial regions. In other words, a time-slice is a spatial region u such that u overlaps a spatial region v only if v is part of u (D_{TS}).

$$D_{TS}\ \ TS\ u \equiv SR\ u \wedge (v)(SR\ v \wedge O\ uv \rightarrow P\ vu)$$

We add axioms requiring that any part of a spatial region is a spatial region (AR6), every region overlaps some time-slice (AR7), and spacetime is not a spatial region (AR8).[1]

$$AR6\ \ SR\ u \wedge P\ vu \rightarrow SR\ v$$
$$AR7\ \ (\exists u)(TS\ u \wedge O\ uv) \qquad AR8\ \ \neg SR\ ST$$

We can prove: distinct time-slices do not overlap (i.e., each region is part of at most one time-slice) (TR2); u is a spatial region if and only if u is part of some time-slice (TR3); spacetime, $\mathcal{ST}$, is the sum of all time-slices (i.e., any region overlaps $\mathcal{ST}$ if and only if it overlaps some time-slice) (TR4).

---

[1] If desired a linear ordering on the subdomain of time-slices can be added to the theory. With such an ordering we can say that one region temporally precedes another, succeeds another, and so on.

$TR2$ $TS\,u \wedge TS\,v \wedge O\,uv \rightarrow u = v$

$TR3$ $SR\,u \leftrightarrow (\exists v)(TS\,v \wedge P\,uv)$ $TR4$ $O\,uST \leftrightarrow (\exists w)(TS\,w \wedge O\,uw)$

Temporal regions. We define a *temporal region* to be any region that is not a spatial region (D_{TR}). Hence, spacetime is a temporal region. We can prove that u is a temporal region if and only if it overlaps more than one time-slice (TR5).

$$D_{TR}\ TR\,u \equiv \neg SR\,u$$
$$TR5\ TR\,u \leftrightarrow (\exists v)(\exists w)(TS\,v \wedge TS\,w \wedge v \neq w \wedge O\,uv \wedge O\,uw)$$

In our example model, *loc_lf_A*, *loc_lf_B*, *loc_lf_C*, *loc_lf_D*, and **ST** are all temporal regions. Note that a temporal region need not be extended in space. In the example model, $\{(1, t) \mid t_1 < t < t_3\}$ is a one-dimensional temporal region.

Simultaneous regions. Two regions are *simultaneous* if and only if they are parts of the same time-slice (D_{SIMU}).

$$D_{SIMU}\ SIMU\,uv \equiv (\exists w)(TS\,w \wedge P\,uw \wedge P\,vw)$$

It immediately follows that *SIMU* an equivalence relation (reflexive, symmetric, transitive) on the sub-domain of spatial regions. Notice that *SIMU uv* is always false if u or v is a temporal region.

4   Instantiation at Regions of Space-Time

The second sort in our formal theory is *spatio-temporal entities* (*entities* for short). Recall that variables x, y, and z are used for entities.

We introduce a ternary relation *Inst* between two entities and a region and interpret *Inst xyu* as y is *instantiated by* x at region u (or, equivalently, x *instantiates* y at region u or x is an *instance* of y at region u). For example, I am an instance of human being wherever I am located. Consider Figure 2. Wherever the entites A, B, C, and D are located they instantiate the entity LINE (a universal). Wherever the entites *LifeOf_A*, *LifeOf_B*, *LifeOf_C*, and *LifeOf_D* are located they instantiate the entity LIFE-OF-A-LINE (a universal).

We define: entity x is *located* at region u if and only if there exists an entity y such that x instantiates y at u or x is instantiated by y at u (D_L); entity x is a *particular* if and only if x instantiates wherever x is located (D_{Part}); entity x is an *universal* if and only if x is instantiated wherever x is located (D_{Uni}); entity x is *uniquely located* if and only if x is located at a single region (D_{UL}).

$$D_L\quad L\,xu \equiv (\exists y)(Inst\,xyu \vee Inst\,yxu)$$
$$D_{Part}\ Part\,x \equiv (u)(L\,xu \rightarrow (\exists y)(Inst\,xyu))$$
$$D_{Uni}\ Uni\,x \equiv (u)(L\,xu \rightarrow (\exists y)(Inst\,yxu))$$
$$D_{UL}\ UL\,x \equiv (u)(v)(L\,xu \wedge L\,xv \rightarrow u = v)$$

Since spatio-temporal entities and regions are disjoint sorts L is asymmetric and irreflexive. On the intended interpretation $L\,xu$ means: spatio-temporal entity x

is *exactly located* at region u [6]. In other words, x takes up the whole region u but does not extend beyond u. In our example model, the entity A is exactly located at the regions $loc\_A\_t_1$, $loc\_A\_t_2$, and $loc\_A\_t_3$. The entity $LifeOf\_A$ is exactly located at the region loc_lf_A. The entities A^{t_1}, A^{t_2}, A^{t_3}, C^{t_1}, C^{t_2}, C^{t_3}, B^{t_1}, D^{t_3}, $LifeOf\_A$, $LifeOf\_B$, $LifeOf\_C$, $LifeOf\_D$, A, B, C, and D are particulars. The entities LINE and LIFE-OF-A-LINE are universals.

We require: if x instantiates y at u then no z is an instance of x at some u (AE1); every spatio-temporal entity is located at some region (AE2); every entity is located only at spatial regions or only at temporal regions (AE3); if x instantiates y at a temporal region u then x uniquely located (AE4); if x is a particular and x is located at simultaneous regions u and v then u and v are identical (AE5); if y is instantiated by a uniquely located entity then each entity that instantiates y is uniquely located (AE6); if x instantiates y at u then there exist an entity z and a region v such that z instantiates y at v and x is distinct from z and u is distinct from v (AE7).

$$AE1\ Inst\ xyu \rightarrow \neg(\exists z)(\exists v)(Inst\ zxv)$$
$$AE2\ (\exists u)(L\ xu)$$
$$AE3\ [(u)(L\ xu \rightarrow SR\ u) \vee (u)(L\ xu \rightarrow TR\ u)]$$
$$AE4\ Inst\ xyu \wedge TR\ u \rightarrow UL\ x$$
$$AE5\ Part\ x \rightarrow (u)(v)(L\ xu \wedge L\ xv \wedge SIMU\ uv \rightarrow u = v)$$
$$AE6\ Inst\ xyu \wedge UL\ x \rightarrow (z)(v)(Inst\ zyv \rightarrow UL\ z)$$
$$AE7\ Inst\ xyu \rightarrow (\exists z)(\exists v)(Inst\ zyv \wedge z \neq x \wedge u \neq v)$$

Axiom (AE1) guarantees that there is a distinction between entities that instantiate and entities that are instantiated. We can prove that if x instantiates y at u then x is a particular and y is a universal (TE1). From (AE1) and (AE2) it follows: if x is a particular then x is not a universal (TE2) and every entity is either a particular or a universal (TE3); x is a particular if and only if x instantiates somewhere (TE4) and that x is a universal if an only if x is instantiated somewhere (TE5).

$$TE1\ Inst\ xyu \rightarrow (Part\ x \wedge Uni\ y)$$
$$TE2\ (Part\ x \rightarrow \neg Uni\ x)$$
$$TE3\ (Part\ x \vee Uni\ x)$$
$$TE4\ Part\ x \leftrightarrow (\exists y)(\exists u)(Inst\ xyu)$$
$$TE5\ Uni\ x \leftrightarrow (\exists y)(\exists u)(Inst\ yxu)$$

Theorems TE2 and TE3 tell us that the sub-domains of universals and particulars partition the domain of entities.

We can also prove: wherever a particular x is located there is a co-located universal that is instantiated by x (TE6); wherever a universal y is located there is a co-located particular x which instantiates y (TE7).

$$TE6\ Part\ x \wedge L\ xu \rightarrow (\exists y)(Uni\ y \wedge Inst\ xyu)$$
$$TE7\ Uni\ x \wedge L\ xu \rightarrow (\exists y)(Part\ y \wedge Inst\ yxu)$$

Notice that particulars can instantiate multiple universals at the same region. For example, at my current location I instantiate (among others) the universals human being and animal. Moreover, an individual x may instantiate the universal y at region u and fail to instantiate y at region v. For example, at my current location I instantiate the universal adult. There are, however, regions at which I instantiated the universal child.

From (AE2) and (D_L) it follows that on the sub-domain of uniquely located entities the location relation L is a function. It also follows that if x instantiates y at u then x and y are located at u. Note, that the converse does not hold: there are situations in which two entities are located at the same region without one being an instance of the other. For example the City of Vienna and the Austrian Federal State of Vienna are located at the same spatial region in many time-slices, but neither is an instance of the other at any region.

Axiom (AE3) requires that entities cannot be located at different kinds of regions. The implications for instantiation are made explicit in the following theorems: if x instantiates y at a spatial region then everything that has x as an instance or instantiates y is located only at spatial regions (TE8). Similarly, if x instantiates y at a temporal region then everything that has x as an instance or instantiates y is located only at temporal regions (TE9).

$TE8$ $Inst\ xyu \wedge SR\ u \rightarrow (z)(v)[(Inst\ xzv \vee Inst\ zyv) \rightarrow (w)(L\ zw \rightarrow SR\ w)]$

$TE9$ $Inst\ xyu \wedge TR\ u \rightarrow (z)(v)[(Inst\ xzv \vee Inst\ zyv) \rightarrow (w)(L\ zw \rightarrow TR\ w)]$

Axioms (AE4) and (AE5) provide additional constraints on how particulars can be located in space time. Particulars are located at no more than one temporal region, i.e., particulars that are located at temporal regions are uniquely located at those regions (TE10).

$$TE10\ Part\ x \wedge L\ xu \wedge TR\ u \rightarrow (v)(L\ xv \rightarrow u = v)$$

Moreover particulars are located at no more than one spatial region per time-slice, i.e., particulars are not located at distinct simultaneous regions.

Note that there are no such constraints for universals in our theory: universals may be located at multiple spatial regions per time-slice or at multiple temporal regions. For example, in this time-slice (at this moment in time) the universal building is located at every spatial region exactly occupied by a building. The universal erosion process is located at every temporal region where an erosion process is located.

Axioms (AE6 and AE7) enforce additional constraints on how universals are instantiated: no universal is instantiated by uniquely located and non-uniquely located particulars; every universal has at least two instances that are located at distinct regions.

5   Basic Categories of Particulars

As specified so far, location is a relation which can hold between a single entity and multiple regions. In our example model, particular A is exactly located at multiple spatial regions including $loc\_A\_t_1$, $loc\_A\_t_2$, and $loc\_A\_t_3$. On the other hand, the particular *LifeOf_A* is located at the single temporal region *loc_lf_A*. In this section we discuss ways of distinguishing particulars according to the number and the kinds of regions at which they can be located.

Stages and persistent particulars. A particular is a *stage* if and only if it is located at a single region and that region is a spatial region (D_{Stg}). Consequently, stages are instantaneous spatial particulars in the sense that they are confined to a single time-slice.

$$D_{Stg}\ Stg\ x \equiv Part\ x \land (u)(v)(L\ xu \land L\ xv \to (SR\ u \land u = v))$$

A particular is *persistent* iff it is not confined to a single time-slice (D_{Pst}).

$$D_{Pst}\ Pst\ x \equiv Part\ x \land (\exists u)(\exists v)(L\ xu \land L\ xv \land \neg SIMUuv)$$

In our example model the entities A^{t_1}, A^{t_2}, A^{t_3}, C^{t_1}, C^{t_2}, C^{t_3}, B^{t_1}, and D^{t_3} are stages and the entities A, B, C, D, *LifeOf_A*, *LifeOf_B*, *LifeOf_C*, *LifeOf_D* are persistent particulars. Other examples of stages include: every momentary slice of my life, every momentary stage of an erosion process, every momentary stage of the development of a geo-political entity (including the time-slice at which the geo-political entity was brought into existence by some administrative act). Persistent entities include myself, my life, planet Earth, the process of global warming on Earth, etc.

We can prove: stages are uniquely located (TI1); no stage is persistent (TI2); every particular is either a stage or a persistent entity (TI3). It follows from (TI2 and TI3) that the subdomains of stages and persistent entities partition the sub-domain of particulars.

$$TI1\ Stg\ x \to UL\ x$$
$$TI2\ Stg\ x \to \neg Pst\ x \qquad\qquad TI3\ Part\ x \leftrightarrow (Stg\ x \lor Pst\ x)$$

Kinds of persistent particulars. Persistent particulars are distinguished into endurants and perdurants. Entity x is an *endurant* iff x is a persistent particular and x is located at some spatial region (D_{Ed}). On the other hand, x is a *perdurant* iff it is a particular and x is located at some temporal region (D_{Pd}).

$$D_{Ed}\ Ed\ x \equiv Pst\ x \land (\exists u)(L\ xu \land SR\ u)$$
$$D_{Pd}\ Pd\ x \equiv Part\ x \land (\exists u)(L\ xu \land TR\ u)$$

In our example model the entities *LifeOf_A*, *LifeOf_B*, *LifeOf_C*, and *LifeOf_D* are perdurants and the entities A, B, C, and D are endurants.

We can prove: perdurants are uniquely located (TI4); perdurants are persistent entities (TI5); endurants are not uniquely located (TI6); nothing is both an endurant and a perdurant (TI7) ; x is a particular if and only if x is an endurant or a perdurant or a stage (TI8).

$$TI4\ Pd\ x \to UL\ x$$
$$TI5\ Pd\ x \to Pst\ x \qquad\qquad TI7\ Ed\ x \to \neg Pd\ x$$
$$TI6\ Ed\ x \to \neg UL\ x \qquad\qquad TI8\ Part\ x \leftrightarrow (Ed\ x \lor Pd\ x \lor Stg\ x)$$

It follows from TI2, TI3, TI7, and TI8 that the subdomains of stages, endurants, and perdurants partition the sub-domain of particulars.

6   Kinds of Universals

Corresponding to the three kinds of particulars we distinguish universals whose instances are endurants (*universals of endurants*), universals whose instances are perdurants (*universals of perdurants*), and universals whose instances are stages (*universals of stages*).

$$D_{UniEd}\ UniEd\ x \equiv Uni\ x \land (y)(u)(Inst\ yxu \to Ed\ y)$$
$$D_{UniPd}\ UniPd\ x \equiv Uni\ x \land (y)(u)(Inst\ yxu \to Pd\ y)$$
$$D_{UniStg}\ UniStg\ x \equiv Uni\ x \land (y)(u)(Inst\ yxu \to Stg\ y)$$

For example: Human being, city, lake, building, etc. are universals of endurants; Human life, erosion process, administrative process, etc. are universals of perdurants; Momentary stages of human lives are instances of the universal human-life-stage. Other examples of universals of stages include classes of momentary events such as the becoming effective of a law, the establishment of political subdivisions, etc. In our example model, the entity LINE is a universal of endurants, LIFE-OF-A-LINE is a universal of perdurants, and STAGE-IN-THE-LIFE-OF-A-LINE is a universal of stages.

We then can prove that universals of endurants, universals of perdurants, and universals of stages are disjoint kinds of universals (TU1-TU3). We can also prove that x is a universal if and only if x is either a universal of endurants, a universal of perurants, or a universal of stages (TU4).

$$TU1\ UniEd\ x \to \neg(UniPd\ x \lor UniStg)$$
$$TU2\ UniPd\ x \to \neg(UniEd\ x \lor UniStg)$$
$$TU3\ UniStg\ x \to \neg(UniEd\ x \lor UniPd)$$
$$TU4\ Uni\ x \leftrightarrow (UniEd\ x \lor UniPd\ x \lor UniStg\ x)$$

7   Conclusions

We developed an axiomatic theory of spatio-temporal entities based on the primitives *spatial-region*, *part-of*, and *is-an-instance-of* and provided a classification of those entities according to the number and kinds of regions at which they are located in spacetime and according to whether they instantiate or are instantiated at those regions. The various categories and their implication hierarchy are depicted in Figure 1. The arrows correspond to axioms and theorems of our theory. The categorization is exhaustive in the sense that every spatio-temporal entity falls in *exactly one* category at the level of leaf nodes of the depicted tree.

There are a number of top-level ontologies that distinguish spatio-temporal entities into universals and particulars and particulars into edurants, perdurants and stages [11,8,9]. None of these ontologies, however, develop those distinction based on the relation of location. The focus on location as one of the central notions of this theory makes it particularly appropriate for serving as a foundational ontology for geography and geographic information science. Also, in our theory we treat time in a way that is analogous to the way we treat space.

Another important feature of our theory is that it describes time-dependent properties and relations (e.g. instantiation of a given universal) without making assumptions about the structure of time. Thus we are not forced to make commitments on the specific structure of time (e.g., assume that time is continuous, rather than discrete). For example, our theory can have coarse grained models in which the minimal time unit is a calendar year and each stage in the development of a geographic process (e.g., climate change or the development of a nation) corresponds to a different year.

References

1. Alia I. Abdelmoty, Philip D. Smart, Christopher B. Jones, Gaihua Fu, and David Finch. A critical evaluation of ontology languages for geographic information retrieval on the internet. *Journal of Visual Languages & Computing*, 16(4):331–358, 2005.
2. P. Agarwal. Ontological considerations in giscience. *International Journal of Geographical Information Science*, 19(5):501–536, 2005.
3. T. Bittner and M. Donnelly. The mereology of stages and persistent entities. In R. Lopez de Mantaras and L. Saitta, editors, *Proceedings of the 16th European Conference on Artificial Intelligence*, pages 283–287. IOS Press, 2004.
4. T. Bittner, M. Donnelly, and S. Winter. Ontology and semantic interoperability. In D. Prosperi and S. Zlatanova, editors, *Large-scale 3D data integration: Problems and challenges*, pages 139–160. CRCpress (Taylor & Francis), 2005.
5. R. Casati, B. Smith, and A.C. Varzi. Ontological tools for geographic representation. In Nicola Guarino, editor, *Formal Ontology and Information Systems, (FOIS'98)*, pages 77–85. IOS Press, 1998.
6. R. Casati and A. C. Varzi. *Parts and Places*. Cambridge, MA: MIT Press., 1999.
7. F. Fonseca, M. Egenhofer, P. Agouris, and G. Câmara. Using ontologies for integrated geographic information systems. *Transactions in GIS*, 6(3):231–257, 2002
8. A. Gangemi, N. Guarino, C. Masolo, A. Oltramari, and L. Schneider. Sweetening ontologies with DOLCE. *AI Magazine*, 23(3):13–24, 2003.
9. P. Grenon and B. Smith. SNAP and SPAN: Towards dynamic spatial ontology. *Spatial Cognition and Computation*, 4(1):69–103, 2004.
10. T. Sider. *Four–Dimensionalism*. Clarendon Press, Oxford, 2001.
11. P. Simons. *Parts, A Study in Ontology*. Clarendon Press, Oxford, 1987.

Efficient Storage of Interactions Between Multiple Moving Point Objects

Nico Van de Weghe[1], Frank Witlox[1], Anthony G. Cohn[2],
Tijs Neutens[1], and Philippe De Maeyer[1]

[1] Department of Geography, Ghent University, Krijgslaan 281 (S8), B-9000 Ghent, Belgium
{nico.vandeweghe, frank.witlox, tijs.neutens,
philippe.demaeyer}@ugent.be
[2] School of Computing, University of Leeds, Leeds LS2 9JT, United Kingdom
a.g.cohn@leeds.ac.uk

Abstract. The quintessence of the Qualitative Trajectory Calculus – Double-Cross (QTC_C) is to describe the interaction between two moving objects adequately. Its naturalness has been studied before, both theoretically and by means of illustrative examples. Using QTC_C, this paper extends the fundamental approach to interactions of configurations of multiple moving objects. In order to be able to optimally store and analyse trajectories of moving objects within QTC_C, a transformation from traditional quantitative information to QTC_C information is needed. This process is explained and illustrated by means of an example. It is shown that once this transformation process is done, the storage and analysis of real world moving objects from the point of view of QTC_C, enables querying of moving objects.

1 Introduction

The use of spatio-temporal relations to define the motion of objects is an important issue in many domains. Besides traditional research areas such as geography, geology, archaeology, and different socio-economic disciplines (e.g. criminology and transportation), research domains in computer science such as, spatial databases, video retrieval and robotics extensively use this type of spatio-temporal data. In most spatial software packages, the absolute positions of spatial entities are represented by sets of coordinates in a Euclidean space, and information is extracted by means of arithmetic computations. In particular, numerical representations may be well suited where precise spatial information of a definite situation is available, and if the output required from the system is itself primarily numerical [1]. However, quantitative information tends to be less available and more expensive than its qualitative counterpart [2]. Additionally, quantitative information is often too precise for the given spatial context. For example, if we want to show a person the way to get to the train station, we do not need to be more precise than, just indicating the streets he has to follow. It has also been recognised that a qualitative approach is more appropriate for the representation of spatio-temporal human cognition than a quantitative one [3]; certainly, since the major goal of many reasoning processes is being able to take a decision be it rather qualitative than quantitative [2].

R. Meersman, Z. Tari, P. Herrero et al. (Eds.): OTM Workshops 2006, LNCS 4278, pp. 1636–1647, 2006.
© Springer-Verlag Berlin Heidelberg 2006

In the last two decades, qualitative formalisms suited to express qualitative temporal or spatial relations between entities have gained wide acceptance as a useful way of abstracting from the real world. Temporal (e.g. [4, 5]) and spatial (e.g. [6, 7]) calculi have been proposed. Despite extensive research during the past decade, both from the area of spatio-temporal reasoning (e.g. [8, 9]) and databases (e.g. [10, 11, 12), there are still many unresolved issues in the representation of and reasoning about space-time. One important remaining question is how to adequately describe motion, and more specifically, the interaction between moving objects, within a qualitative calculus. Apart from some limiting cases such as the reconstruction of a car accident and a predator catching a prey where moving objects *meet*, mobile objects such as traffic flows, and movements of people and animals are represented by use of the relation *disconnected from* in the widely used RCC- Calculus [6] and 9-Intersection Model [7]. It is clear that this approach ignores some important aspects of reasoning about continuously moving physical objects. For example, given two trains on a railroad or two planes in the air, it is important to know their movement with respect to each other in order to avoid potential collision. In other words, a challenging research question is: 'how to represent and handle changes in movement between moving objects, if there is no change in their topological relationship?' Answering this question implies developing a new formalism. This shortcoming is adressed in [13], where the Qualitative Trajectory Calculus (QTC) is advanced. QTC is a theory for representing and reasoning about movements of objects in a qualitative framework, differentiating groups of disconnected objects. Depending on the level of detail and the number of spatial dimensions, different types of QTC have been defined, all belonging to two variants: QTC - Basic (QTC_B) or QTC - Double Cross (QTC_C). Several issues of QTC have been studied before: [14, 15, 16]. In the current paper, we want to go into further detail on two specific topics concerning QTC_C. In Section 2, we extend the fundamentals of QTC_C where only two objects are moving to cases where there is an interaction between more than two objects. In Section 3, we discuss the need to transform quantitative intervals to QTC_C intervals. This issue is becoming more and more important due to the increased development of Moving Object Databases. We work out the methodology in detail by means of an illustrative example.

2 The Qualitative Trajectory Calculus – Double-Cross (QTC_C)

2.1 Fundamentals of QTC_C

In this section, QTC_C is briefly presented. For further reading, we refer to [13]. Continuous time for QTC_C is assumed. QTC_C is partly based on the Double-Cross Calculus introduced by Freksa and Zimmermann [2, 17]. QTC_C examines the movement of 2 point objects k and l with respect to each other. The movements of both point objects k and l are represented by a vector (Fig. 1(a)), degenerated to a point if an object is not moving (Fig. 1(b)). Through the origins of these vectors, the reference line (RL) is defined. Also through these origins and perpendicular to RL, RL⊥1 and RL⊥2 are defined. RL, RL⊥1, and RL⊥2 form the double-cross, being the reference frame for

QTC$_C$. Two dichotomies form the basis of the reference frame: towards/away-from and left/right. The first results in the first character (char1) and char2 of the QTC$_C$ label. The second dichotomy also results in 2 characters: char3 and char4. By reducing the continuum to the qualitative values –, 0 and +, the underlying continuous system can be described in a qualitative way. Hence, a 2D movement is presented in QTC$_C$ using the following four conditions (C1, C2, C3, and C4).

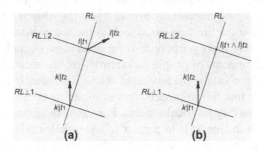

Fig. 1. Reference frame for QTCC: (a) two objects moving; (b) one object moving

We introduce the following notations for QTC$_C$:

objects k and l,
RL$_{kl}$ denotes the directed reference line from k to l,
$x|t$ denotes the position of an object x at time t,
$d(u,v)$ denotes the distance between two positions u and v,
$v_x|t$ denotes the speed of x at time t,
$t_1 \prec t_2$ denotes that t_1 is temporally before t_2.

C1 deals with the movement of k wrt RL$\perp$1 at t (distance constraint):

–: k is moving towards l: $\exists t_1 (t_1 \prec t \wedge \forall t^- (t_1 \prec t^- \prec t \rightarrow d(k|t^-, l|t) > d(k|t, l|t))) \wedge$

$\exists t_2 (t \prec t_2 \wedge \forall t^+ (t \prec t^+ \prec t_2 \rightarrow d(k|t, l|t) > d(k|t^+, l|t)))$

+: k is moving away from l: $\exists t_1 (t_1 \prec t \wedge \forall t^- (t_1 \prec t^- \prec t \rightarrow d(k|t^-, l|t) < d(k|t, l|t))) \wedge$

$\exists t_2 (t \prec t_2 \wedge \forall t^+ (t \prec t^+ \prec t_2 \rightarrow d(k|t, l|t) < d(k|t^+, l|t)))$

0: k is stable with respect to l: all other cases.
C2 deals with the movement of l wrt RL$\perp$2 at t (cf. C1, but with k and l interchanged).
C3 has to do with the movement of k wrt RL$_{kl}$ at t (side constraint). More formally,
–: k is moving to the left side of RL$_{kl}$: $\exists t_1 (t_1 < t \wedge \forall t^- (t_1 < t^- < t \rightarrow k$ is on the right side of RL$_{kl}$ at $t)) \wedge \exists t_2 (t < t_2 \wedge \forall t^+ (t < t^+ < t_2 \rightarrow k$ is on the left side of RL$_{kl}$ at $t))$
+: k is moving to the right side of RL$_{kl}$: $\exists t_1 (t_1 < t \wedge \forall t^- (t_1 < t^- < t \rightarrow k$ is on the left side of RL$_{kl}$ at $t)) \wedge \exists t_2 (t < t_2 \wedge \forall t^+ (t < t^+ < t_2 \rightarrow k$ is on the right side of RL$_{kl}$ at $t))$
0: k is moving along RL$_{kl}$: all other cases.
C4 describes the movement of l wrt the RL$_{lk}$ at t (cf. C3, but with k and l interchanged).

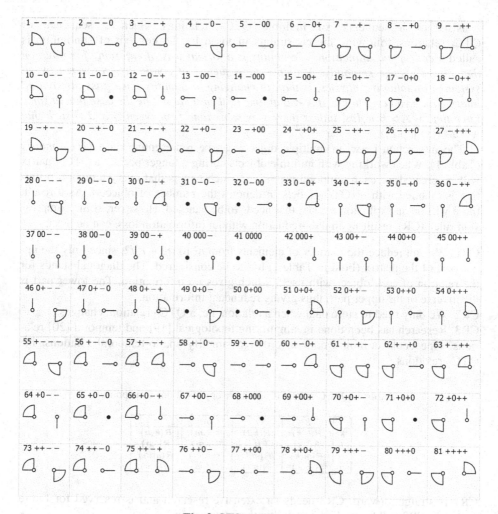

Fig. 2. QTC$_C$ relation icons

We can now represent a QTC$_C$ relation by a label consisting of 4 characters. Each of the 81 relations can be represented by a relation icon (Fig. 2). The left and right dot of a relation icon respectivelly represents the position of k and l. A dot is filled if the object can be stationary, and open if the object cannot be stationary. The disk quarters are, topologically speaking, open; for relation $(- - - 0)$ in Fig. 2: the movement of k can be from k to every point on the curved part of the quarter part excluding the horizontal and the vertical line segment, the movement of l can only be from l straight to k, which is along the line drawn from the open right dot.

2.2 QTC$_C$ for Multiple Temporal Primitives and Multiple Spatial Entities

There are two *temporal primitives* over which QTC$_C$ relations may hold: intervals (i_i) and instantaneous time points (t_i). A study period containing real world events mostly consists of a sequence of multiple QTC_C relations. Such a sequence of QTC_C relations, following the constraints imposed by the concept of continuity, is called a *conceptual animation*. '*Continuity is a formal way of enforcing the intuition that things change smoothly. A simple consequence of continuity, respected by all systems of qualitative physics, is that, in changing, a quantity must pass through all intermediate values. That is, if A < B at time t_1, then it cannot be the case that at some later time t_2 A > B holds, unless there was some time t_3 between t_1 and t_2 such that A = B'* ([18], p.25).

The interaction between multiple objects can be represented via a *QTC_C matrix* (Table 1). When working with multiple objects during a longer period, a QTC_C matrix will be created for each temporal primitive, which means that every temporal primitive is labelled with n^2 QTC_C labels (n denotes the number of objects). As a result, there will be an explosion of data that needs to be handled. However, some compression rules (CR), resulting in data-reduction without information loss, can be used:

CR1. We can reduce the number of elements from n^2 to $(n^2 - n)/2$, since only the upper part of the matrix (bold in Table 1) has to be considered. The diagonal stands for the relation of each object with itself, which gives no information. The lower part is the inverse of the upper part, thus giving redundant information.

CR2. We only need to store data when a relation, i.e. a QTC_C relation, changes.

CR3. Research has been done in simplifying topological [19] and temporal [20] relations. One could combine both in order to simplify spatio-temporal relations, i.e. QTC_C relations.

Table 1. QTCC matrix for multiple objects at one time point

	k	l	m	n
k	$R(k,k)$	$R(k,l)$	$R(k,m)$	$R(k,n)$
l	$R(l,k)$	$R(l,l)$	$R(l,m)$	$R(l,n)$
m	$R(m,k)$	$R(m,l)$	$R(m,m)$	$R(m,n)$
n	$R(n,k)$	$R(n,l)$	$R(n,m)$	$R(n,n)$

CR1 is straightforward. CR3 needs an extensive research and is reserved for future research. CR2 will be studied in detail in the next section.

3 Conversion Between Data Stored Using Current (Quantitative) Techniques and QTC_C

3.1 The Need to Transform Quantitative Intervals into QTC_C Intervals

A motion can be represented by a trajectory, which is a connected nonbranching continuous line having a certain shape and direction [21]. However, due to the sampling procedure of the tracking device and the need to translate the motion in a form suitable for storage and analysis in information systems, the essential characteristics of an observed track have to be represented in a discrete form [22]. Mostly, current observation-based systems capture data in an ordered sequence at regular intervals. The movement in-between these time stamps, is considered as having constant speed and direction, meaning that an intermediary time stamp can be represented via linear interpolation techniques, or in other words that the trajectories are represented by straight polylines.

Since Moving Object Databases soon will be ubiquitous, the need for conceptual models and management systems about continuously time-varying location data are vital [23]. It has been proved that humans' interaction with real life as well as humans' interaction with information systems benefits from qualitative approaches. It is thus worthwhile to find out whether it is possible to transform from quantitative data (x, y, t) into QTC_C relations. Ones this has been elaborated, it becomes straightforward to store and analyse moving objects by means of QTC_C. Thus, in order to be able to answer to CR2, the potential for conversion between data stored using quantitative techniques and QTC_C needs to be further studied. In other words, in order to store data of moving objects in QTC_C, we need a transformation of the data from (x, y, t) into QTC_C relations. How this is accomplished is explained by means of an example in the next section.

3.2 Transformation of Quantitative Spatio-temporal Data into QTC_C Relations

In this section, transformation of quantitative spatio-temporal data into QTC_C intervals[1] is shown for an example representing the movement of 4 point objects $(k, l, m,$ and $n)$ during a study period of 30 seconds. At regular intervals $(t_{0s}$ = time point after 0 seconds, $t_{10s}, t_{20s}, $ and $t_{30s})$, the coordinates of these objects were registered in a local reference system (Table 2). We assume that the movement inbetween these time points (i.e. during the *storage intervals*) may be considered as having constant speed and constant direction (Fig. 3). In order to have full QTC_C *detail*, we need to check

Table 2. (x,y)-coordinates multiple point objects moving in 2D

	t_0	t_{10}	t_{20}	t_{30}
k	(48.0;30.0)	(48.0;30.0)	(28.0;18.0)	(18.0;12.0)
l	(58.0;36.0)	(50.0;10.0)	(26.0;2.0)	(16.0;2.0)
m	(54.0;38.0)	(42.0;34.0)	(18.0;26.0)	(14.0;16.5)
n	(30.0;38.0)	(12.0;36.0)	(6.0;22.0)	(2.0;12.5)

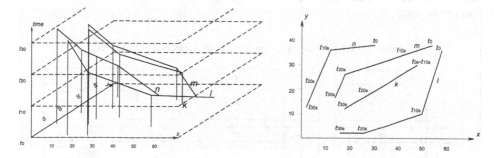

Fig. 3. Multiple objects moving in 2D: (a) space-time cube; (b) 2D representation

---

[1] A QTC_C *interval* is an interval consisting of one QTC_C relation, which would always get multiple QTC_C relations after extending the interval.

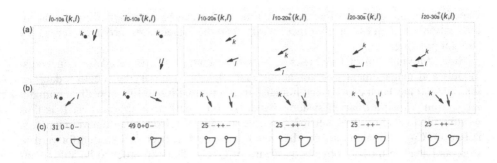

Fig. 4. Extraction of QTCC relations

whether every storage interval consists of just one QTC_C relation, and whether the whole evolution for each object pair fulfils the constraints imposed by continuity.

A first indication can be obtained by comparing, for each storage interval (i), whether its beginning (i^-) and end (i^+) have the same QTC_C relation. If not, this means that there has to be at least one change in QTC_C relation at a moment during this storage interval. Let us start by zooming in on the relative movement between k and l at the beginning and end of every storage interval. Fig. 4(a) shows the movements of k and l and how they were presented in the overall view of movements (Fig. 3). Fig. 4(b) shows an *oriented zoom* on each specific movement, oriented in a way that it becomes straightforward to find the QTC_C relations between objects k and l (Fig. 4(c)). One can see changes between $i_{0\text{-}10s}^-$ and $i_{0\text{-}10s}^+$, and between $i_{0\text{-}10s}^+$ and $i_{10\text{-}20s}^-$: $i_{0\text{-}10s}^-(k,l)(0-0-)$; $i_{0\text{-}10s}^+(k,l)(0+0-)$; $i_{10\text{-}20s}^-(k,l)(-+ +-)$; $i_{10\text{-}20s}^+(k,l)(-+ +-)$; $i_{20\text{-}30s}^-(k,l)(-+ +-)$; $i_{20\text{-}30s}^+(k,l)(-+ +-)$.

Studying the object pairs $((k, m), (k,n), (l,m), (l,n), (m,n))$ gives the QTC_C matrices presented in Table 3, resulting in the changes for:

(k,m): between $i_{0\text{-}10s}^-$ and $i_{0\text{-}10s}^+$, between $i_{0\text{-}10s}^+$ and $i_{10\text{-}20s}^-$, and between $i_{10\text{-}20s}^+$ and $i_{20\text{-}30s}^-$;
(k,n): between $i_{0\text{-}10s}^+$ and $i_{10\text{-}20s}^-$;
(l,m): between $i_{0\text{-}10s}^+$ and $i_{10\text{-}20s}^-$, and between $i_{10\text{-}20s}^+$ and $i_{20\text{-}30s}^-$;
(l,n): between $i_{0\text{-}10s}^-$ and $i_{0\text{-}10s}^+$, and between $i_{0\text{-}10s}^+$ and $i_{10\text{-}20s}^-$;
(m,n): nothing.

Table 3. QTC_C-relations for multiple point objects moving in 2D

$i_{0\text{-}10s}^-$	l	m	n
k	0-0-	0-0+	0+0+
l		++-+	-+-+
m			-+-+

$i_{0\text{-}10s}^+$	l	m	n
k	0+0-	0+0+	0+0+
l		+0-+	++-+
m			-+-+

$i_{10\text{-}20s}^-$	l	m	n
k	-++-	0+0+	-+-+
l		00-+	---+
m			-+-+

$i_{10\text{-}20s}^+$	l	m	n
k	-++-	-+-+	-+-+
l		00-+	---+
m			-+-+

$i_{20\text{-}30s}^-$	l	m	n
k	-++-	---+	-+-+
l		---+	---+
m			-+-+

$i_{20\text{-}30s}^+$	l	m	n
k	-++-	---+	-+-+
l		---+	---+
m			-+-+

There are two major categories (Cat) of changes that can be detected. A difference between:

- the relation at the end of the previous and the beginning of the next interval (Cat1)
$i_{0\text{-}10s}{}^{+}(k,l)(0 + 0 -)$ to $i_{10\text{-}20s}{}^{-}(k,l)(- + + -)$; $i_{0\text{-}10s}{}^{+}(k,m)(0 + 0 +)$ to $i_{10\text{-}20s}{}^{-}(k,m)(- + - +)$;
$i_{10\text{-}20s}{}^{+}(k,m)(- + - +)$ to $i_{20\text{-}30s}{}^{-}(k,m)(- - - +)$; $i_{0\text{-}10s}{}^{+}(k,n)(0 + 0 +)$ to $i_{10\text{-}20s}{}^{-}(k,n)(- + - +)$;
$i_{0\text{-}10s}{}^{+}(l,m)(+ + - +)$ to $i_{10\text{-}20s}{}^{-}(l,m)(0\ 0 - +)$; $i_{10\text{-}20s}{}^{+}(l,m)(0\ 0 - +)$ to $i_{20\text{-}30s}{}^{-}(l,m)(- - - +)$;
$i_{0\text{-}10s}{}^{+}(l,n)(+ + - +)$ to $i_{10\text{-}20s}{}^{-}(l,n)(- - - +)$.
- the relation at the beginning of the current and the end of the current interval (Cat2)
$i_{0\text{-}10s}{}^{-}(k,l)(0 - 0 -)$ to $i_{0\text{-}10s}{}^{+}(k,l)(0 + 0 -)$; $i_{0\text{-}10s}{}^{-}(k,m)(0 - 0 +)$ to $i_{0\text{-}10s}{}^{+}(k,m)(0 + 0 +)$;
$i_{0\text{-}10s}{}^{-}(l,n)(- + - +)$ to $i_{0\text{-}10s}{}^{+}(l,n)(+ + - +)$.

According to the theory of dominance [24]) an interval-like qualitative value (+ or – in QTC$_C$) will reach a landmark value (0 in QTC$_C$) at a time instant. Now, let us analyse the example1 of Cat1: from $i_{0\text{-}10s}{}^{+}(k,l)(0 + 0 -)$ to $i_{10\text{-}20s}{}^{-}(k,l)(- + + -)$; char1 changes from 0 to – and char3 changes from 0 to +. This means that at the time point where both intervals meet (t_{10s}), the char1 and char3 need to be 0, resulting in $t_{10s}(k,l)(0 + 0 -)$. Analogous reasoning applies to:

$i_{0\text{-}10s}{}^{+}(k,m)(0 + 0 +)$ to $i_{10\text{-}20s}{}^{-}(k,m)(- + - +)$ gives $t_{10s}(k,m)(0 + 0 +)$;
$i_{0\text{-}10s}{}^{+}(k,n)(0 + 0 +)$ to $i_{10\text{-}20s}{}^{-}(k,n)(- + - +)$ gives $t_{10s}(k,n)(0 + 0 +)$;
$i_{0\text{-}10s}{}^{+}(l,m)(+ + - +)$ to $i_{10\text{-}20s}{}^{-}(l,m)(0\ 0 - +)$ gives $t_{10s}(l,m)(0\ 0 - +)$;
$i_{10\text{-}20s}{}^{+}(l,m)(0\ 0 - +)$ to $i_{20\text{-}30s}{}^{-}(l,m)(- - - +)$ gives $t_{10s}(l,m)(0\ 0 - +)$.

Because continuity constrains the kinds of changes that are possible, a direct change from – to + and vice versa is impossible, since such a change must pass the qualitative value 0. This landmark value 0 only needs to hold for an instant [24]. Now, let us consider the remaining cases of the first category of changes. Let us analyse: from $i_{10\text{-}20s}{}^{+}(k,m)(- + - +)$ to $i_{20\text{-}30s}{}^{-}(k,m)(- - - +)$. Char2 changes from + to –. This means that at the time point where both intervals meet (t_{20s}), char2 needs to be 0, resulting in: $t_{20s}(k,l)(- 0 - +)$. Analogous reasoning: $i_{0\text{-}10s}{}^{+}(l,n)(+ + - +)$ to $i_{10\text{-}20s}{}^{-}(l,n)(- - - +)$ gives $i_{10s}(l,n)(0\ 0 - +)$.

After analysing the first category of changes, one can generate the QTC$_C$ matrices for all the time stamps t_{0s}, t_{10s}, t_{20s}, and t_{30s} (Table 4).

Table 4. QTC$_C$ relations for multiple point objects moving in 2D

t_{0s}	l	m	n	t_{10s}	l	m	n	t_{20s}	l	m	n	t_{30s}	l	m	n
k	0-0-	0-0+	0+0+	k	0+0-	0+0+	0+0+	k	-++-	-0-+	-+-+	k	-++-	---+	-+-+
l		++-+	-+-+	l		00-+	00-+	l		00-+	---+	l		---+	---+
m			-+-+	m			-+-+	m			-+-+	m			-+-+

In the second category of changes, new time points need to be inserted to present QTC$_C$ events. The only interval of the example that needs a further subdivision is $i_{0\text{-}10s}$. Three cases need to be studied in order to see where the further subdivision needs to be time snapped: (k,l), (k,m) and (l,n). The situations are analysed in Fig. 5. Let us start with situation 1: $i_{0\text{-}10s}(k,l)$. Comparing char2 of $i_{0\text{-}10s}{}^{-}(k,l)(0 - 0 -)$ and $i_{0\text{-}10s}{}^{+}(k,l)(0 + 0 -)$, implies that the interval needs a subdivision. Alternatively, based on the double-cross dichotomy, the movement of $lli_{0\text{-}10s}^-$ with respect to $lkli_{0\text{-}10s}^-$ is front-left, and the movement of $lli_{0\text{-}10s}^+$ with respect to $lkli_{0\text{-}10s}^+$ is back-left. Since a landmark needs to be passed in order to have a continuous evolution, the storage interval needs further subdivision, i.e., the velocity vector l needs to pass left. The question now is where this landmark is situated. The division process for $i_{0\text{-}10s}(k,l)$ is as follows (Fig. 5(a)):

Step 1: draw the movements of k and l during $i_{0\text{-}10s}$, together with $lkli_{0\text{-}10s}^-$ and $lkli_{0\text{-}10s}^+$
Step 2: draw lk at the middle of $i_{0\text{-}10s}$, which is $lklt_{5s}$.
   The movement of llt_{5s} with respect to $lklt_{5s}$ is back-left.
   Thus, the change occurs between $i_{0\text{-}10s}^-$ and t_{5s}. So: new interval is $i_{0\text{-}5s}$
Step 3:
   Repeat Step 1 and Step 2 for the new interval until the movement of l with respect to lk is 90° (or until the difference between the movement of l with respect to lk and 90° is less than a specified threshold). In the presented case, we need to iterate until step 7, where this point is reached at 32% of $i_{0\text{-}10s}$ giving the landmark value at $t_{3.2s}$.

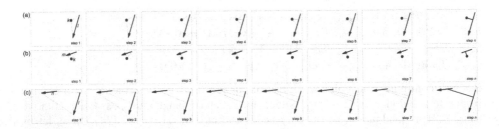

Fig. 5. Subdivision of QTC intervals: (a) i0-10s(k,l); (b) i0-10s(k,m); (c) i0-10s(l,n)

One can also generate the division process for $i_{0\text{-}10s}(k,m)$ (Fig. 5(b)) resulting in a change after 65% of $i_{0\text{-}10s}$ giving a landmark value at $t_{6.5s}$ and the division process for $i_{0\text{-}10s}(l,n)$ (Fig. 5(c)) giving a change after 32% of $i_{0\text{-}10s}$, being simultaneous to the change of (k,l). Thus $i_{0\text{-}10s}$ will be subdivided in: $i_{0\text{-}3.2s}$, $t_{3.2}$, $i_{3.2\text{-}6.5s}$, $i_{6.5}$, and $i_{6.5\text{-}10s}$. Since the other object pairs do not change during $i_{0\text{-}10s}$, the following changes are the only ones that need to be studied in order to get QTC_C matrices for $i_{0\text{-}3.2s}$, $t_{3.2}$, $i_{3.2\text{-}6.5s}$, $i_{6.5}$, and $i_{6.5\text{-}10s}$:

$i_{0\text{-}10s}^-(k,l)(0-0-)$ thus $i_{0\text{-}3.2s}(k,l)(0-0-)$, and $i_{0\text{-}10s}^+(k,l)(0+0-)$ thus $i_{3.2\text{-}10s}(l,k)(0+0-)$. Thus (cf. category 2 changes) $t_{3.2}(k,l)(0\,0\,0-)$.
$i_{0\text{-}10s}^-(k,m)(0-0+)$thus $i_{0\text{-}6.5s}(k,m)(0-0+)$,and $i_{0\text{-}10s}^+(k,m)(0+0+)$thus $i_{6.5\text{-}10s}(k,m)(0+0+)$. Thus (cf. category 2 changes) $t_{6.5}(k,m)(0\,0\,0+)$.
$i_{0\text{-}10s}^-(l,n)(-+-+)$ thus $i_{0\text{-}3.2s}(l,n)(-+-+)$, and $i_{0\text{-}10s}^+(l,n)(++-+)$ thus $i_{3.2\text{-}10s}(l,n)(++-+)$. Thus (cf. category 2 changes) $t_{3.2}(l,n)(0+-+)$.

Finally, one gets the whole configuration of the interactions between the 4 objects during the period of 30 seconds; Fig. 6 and Table 5 give a general overview. A compressed version (no information loss + redundant information deleted) can be written as follows:

(k,l): $t_{0s}(0-0-)$, $t_{3.2s}(0\ 0\ 0\ -)$, $i_{3.2-6.5s}(0+0-)$, $i_{10-20s}(-++-)$, $t_{30s}(-++-)$;

(k,m): $t_{0s}(0-0+)$, $t_{6.5s}(0\ 0\ 0\ +)$, $i_{10-20s}(-+-+)$, $t_{20s}(-0-+)$, $i_{20-30s}(---+)$, $t_{30s}(---+)$;

(k,n): $t_{0s}(0+0+)$, $i_{10-20s}(-+-+)$, $t_{30s}(-+-+)$;

(l,m): $t_{0s}(++-+)$, $i_{6.5-10s}(0+0+)$, $t_{10s}(0\ 0-+)$, $i_{20-30s}(---+)$, $t_{30s}(---+)$;

(l,n): $t_{0s}(-+-+)$, $t_{3.2s}(0+-+)$, $i_{3.2-6.5s}(++-+)$, $t_{10s}(0\ 0-+)$, $i_{10-20s}(---+)$, $t_{30s}(---+)$;

(m,n): $t_{0s}(-+-+)$, $t_{30s}(-+-+)$.

Table 5. QTCC relations for multiple point objects moving in 2D

t_{0s}	l	m	n
k	0−0−	0−0+	0+0+
l		++−+	−+−+
m			−+−+

$i_{0-3.2s}$	l	m	n
k	0−0−	0−0+	0+0+
l		++−+	−+−+
m			−+−+

$t_{3.2}$	l	m	n
k	000−	0−0+	0+0+
l		++−+	0+−+
m			−+−+

$i_{3.2-6.5s}$	l	m	n
k	0+0−	0−0+	0+0+
l		++−+	++−+
m			−+−+

$t_{6.5s}$	l	m	n
k	0+0−	000+	0+0+
l		++−+	++−+
m			−+−+

$i_{6.5-10s}$	l	m	n
k	0+0−	0+0+	0+0+
l		++−+	++−+
m			−+−+

t_{10s}	l	m	n
k	0+0−	0+0+	0+0+
l		00−+	00−+
m			−+−+

i_{10-20s}	l	m	n
k	−++−	−+−+	−+−+
l		00−+	---+
m			−+−+

t_{20s}	l	m	n
k	−++−	−0−+	−+−+
l		00−+	---+
m			−+−+

t_{20-30s}	l	m	n
k	−++	---+	−+−+
l		---+	---+
m			−+−+

t_{30s}	l	m	n
k	−++	---+	−+−+
l		---+	---+
m			−+−+

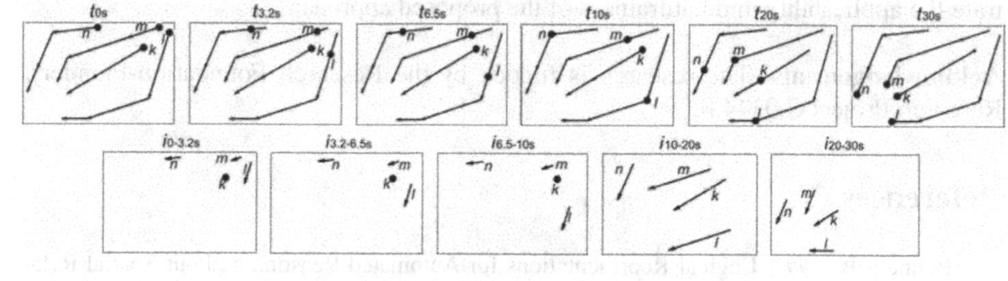

t_{0s} $t_{3.2s}$ $t_{6.5s}$ t_{10s} t_{20s} t_{30s}

$i_{0-3.2s}$ $i_{3.2-6.5s}$ $i_{6.5-10s}$ i_{10-20s} i_{20-30s}

Fig. 6. Multiple point objects moving in 2D

4 Outlook

At first sight, the amount of QTC_C data that needs to be stored is huge. However, one can see that the storage for quantitative data needs 2 real numbers (respectively for the x- and y-coordinate) for each temporal primitive that changes, being 4 bytes = 32 bit per number when taking single-precision floating-point.[2] The storage for QTC_C only needs 3 possible (qualitative) values that can be stored in a 2-bit word, per character. Each QTC_C relation needs 7 bits. The amount of data that needs to be stored when working in QTC_C is thus not significantly or exponentially more than if one works with quantitative data.

The presented work builds on the basis for an intelligent temporal GIS, being able to answer complex spatio-temporal queries concerning moving objects, i.e. analysing of and reasoning with complex relations between moving objects. In the near future, the different sorts of spatio-temporal queries (different types of spatio-temporal queries

---

[2] Single-precision floating-point standing for numbers between -3.402823E3 and -1.40129E-45 for negative values, and 1.40129E-45 and 3.40282E38 for positive values.

are studied in [23]) need to be studied in order to find out which sorts of queries prefer a quantitative strategy and which ones prefer a qualitative strategy (at level 1 or level 2). Be aware that if storing the information in QTC_C it is not possible to go back to (x, y, z). More important of course is that interesting spatio-temporal queries concerning moving objects and their interactions can be queried to the system without the need to do additional calculations. One could therefore question whether both the quantitative and the qualitative system are complementary and whether therefore the most interesting way to store this kind of data is in a hybrid system.

In [13], QTC_C has been extended to a second level by adding char5 and char6; char5 standing for the relative speed and char6 giving a qualitative measure for the relative direction of the velocity vector with respect to the reference line between k and l. At this second level, the speed and the angular constraints also can be considered. The subdivision process based on these characters will be studied in further research. This will result in a more profound subdivision from quantitative to QTC_C information.

On the one hand, further fundamental research has to be done in finding out the complexity, the update possibilities, and the simulation possibilities of the approach. On the other hand, more meaningful examples need to be worked out in order to illustrate the applicability and naturalness of the proposed approach.

Acknowledgements. The research is funded by the Research Foundation-Flanders, Research Project G.0344.05.

References

1. Bennett, B., 1997, Logical Representations for Automated Reasoning about Spatial Relationships, PhD Thesis, UK, University of Leeds
2. Freksa, C., 1992, Using orientation information for qualitative spatial reasoning, Int. Conf. on Theories and Methods of Spatio-Temporal Reasoning in Geographic Space, LNCS 639, 162-178
3. Sharma, J., 1996, Integrated Spatial Reasoning in Geographic Information Systems: Combining Topology and Direction, PhD Thesis, USA, University of Maine
4. Allen, J.F., 1983, Maintaining knowledge about temporal intervals, Comm. of the ACM, 26(11), 832-843
5. Freksa, C., 1992, Temporal reasoning based on semi-intervals, AI, (54), 199-227
6. Randell, D., Cui, Z., and Cohn, A.G., 1992, A spatial logic based on regions and connection, Int. Conf. on Knowledge Representation and Reasoning (KR), 165-176
7. Egenhofer, M. and Franzosa, R., 1991, Point set topological spatial relations, IJGIS,5(2),161-174
8. Claramunt, C. and Jiang, B., 2001, An integrated representation of spatial and temporal relationships between evolving regions, Geographical Systems, 3(4), 411-428
9. Hornsby, K. and Egenhofer, M., 2002, Modelling moving objects over multiple granularities, Annals of Mathematics and Artificial Intelligence, 36(12), 177-194
10. Wolfson, O., Xu, B., Chamberlain, S., and Jiang, L., 1998, Moving object databases: issues and solutions, Int. Conf. on Scientific and Statistical Database Management (SSDBM), 111-122

11. Erwig, M., Güting, R.H., Schneider, M., and Vazirgiannis, M., 1999, Spatio-temporal data types: an approach to modelling objects in databases, Geoinformatica, 3(3), 269-296
12. Nabil, M., Ngu A., and Shepherd A.J., 2001, Modelling and retrieval of moving objects, Multimedia Tools and Applications, 13(1), 35-71
13. Van de Weghe, N., 2004, Representing and Reasoning about Moving Objects: A Qualitative Approach, PhD Thesis, Belgium, Ghent University
14. Van de Weghe, N., Cohn, A.G., Bogaert, P., and De Maeyer, Ph.., 2004, Representation of moving objects along a road network, Geoinformatics, 187-197
15. Van de Weghe, N., Cohn, A.G., De Maeyer, Ph., and Witlox, F., 2005, Representing moving objects in computer based expert systems, Expert Systems with Applications, 29(4), 977-983
16. Van de Weghe, N., Kuijpers, B., Bogaert, P., and De Maeyer, Ph., 2005, A qualitative trajectory calculus and the composition of its relations,Conf. on Geospatial Semantics, LNCS 3799,p.60-76
17. Zimmermann, K. and Freksa, C., 1996, Qualitative spatial reasoning using orientation, distance, and path knowledge, Applied Intelligence, 6(1), 49-58
18. Forbus, D., 1990, Qualitative physics: past, present, and future, Readings in Qualitative Reasoning about Physical Systems, Morgan Kaufmann, 11-39
19. Rodriguez, A., Egenhofer, M., and Blaser A., 2003, Query pre-processing of topological constraints, SSTD, LNCS 2750, 362-379
20. Rodriguez, A., Van de Weghe, N., and De Maeyer, Ph., 2004, Simplifying sets of events by selecting temporal relations, GIScience, LNCS 3234, 269-284
21. Eschenbach, C., Habel, C., and Kulik, L., 1999, Representing simple trajectories as oriented curves, naïve geography, Int. Artificial Intelligence Research Society Conference 431-436
22. Laube, P., Imfeld, S., and Weibel, R., 2005, Discovering relative motion patterns in groups of moving point objects, IJGIS, 19(6), 639–668
23. Pelekis, N, Theodoulidis, B., Kopanakis, I., and Theodoridis, 2005, Literature review of spatio-temporal database models, The Knowledge Engineering Review journal, 19(3), 235-274
24. Galton, A.G., 1995, Towards a qualitative theory of movement, COSIT, LNCS, (988), 377-396

Implementing Conceptual Spatio-temporal Schemas in Object-Relational DBMSs

Esteban Zimányi and Mohammed Minout

Department of Computer and Decision Engineering (CoDE), CP 165/15,
Université Libre de Bruxelles,
50 av. F.D. Roosevelt, 1050 Brussels, Belgium
{ezimanyi, mminout}@ulb.ac.be

Abstract. Several spatio-temporal conceptual models have been proposed in the literature. Some of these models have associated CASE tools assisting the user from the creation of the conceptual schema until the generation of a physical schema for a target DBMS or GIS. However, such CASE tools only consider the translation of information structures (i.e. attributes). Since current DBMSs or GISs provide limited support for temporal and spatio-temporal information, when translating conceptual schemas it is necessary to automatically generate the functions and procedures allowing to manipulate spatio-temporal information in the target platform. In this paper we describe how to realize this generation in an object-relational DBMSs.

1 Introduction

Spatio-temporal databases have been the focus of considerable research activity over the last years. Many spatio-temporal models have been proposed in the literature (e.g., [8,4,10,2]). Spatial and temporal data types provide the building blocks for developing such models. While the definition of standard spatial data types [9] has reached a good level of consensus, there is no such agreement for temporal data types.

Currently there exists very few systems providing effective support for tracking changes of spatial and non-spatial data over time. Therefore, while users may use a conceptual spatio-temporal model for developing their applications, such specifications must be translated into the operational model of current DBMS or GIS, and this usually induces a reduction of expression power. In addition, when the resulting schema needs to be queried users must address the physical schema of their application and must use the data manipulation language of the target platform (e.g., SQL) for expressing the queries.

One solution for these problems is to express both the data definition and the data manipulation requirements at the conceptual level. These specifications can be then be translated by CASE tools into the particular languages provided by current implementation platforms (DBMS or GIS). However, typical CASE tools only consider the translation of information structures (i.e. attributes). In this paper we advocate that when translating conceptual schemas it is also necessary

R. Meersman, Z. Tari, P. Herrero et al. (Eds.): OTM Workshops 2006, LNCS 4278, pp. 1648–1657, 2006.

to automatically generate the functions and procedures allowing to query and manipulate spatio-temporal information in the target platform.

This paper is structured as follows. Sect. 2 briefly presents the MADS model. Sect. 3 explains with an example the translation of conceptual MADS schemas. Sect. 4 shows some spatio-temporal data types provided in MADS while Sect. 5 shows how to implement these types and their associated methods into Oracle 10g. Finally, Sect. 6 concludes and points to directions for future research.

2   The MADS Model

MADS [7] is a conceptual spatio-temporal model. It provides a set of spatial data types organized in a generalization hierarchy including generic (**Geo**), simple (e.g., **Point**, **Line**), and complex types (e.g., **PointBag**, **LineBag**). Similarly, there is a set of temporal data types, which are also organized in a hierarchy. Spatial and temporal data types have an associated set of methods to handle the instances of the type.

Spatiality and temporality can be associated both to types and to attributes. Spatial object or relationship types have an associated geometry. Temporal object or relationship types keep the lifecycle of their instances: objects or relationships are created, can be temporarily suspended, then reactivated, and finally disabled. The lifecycle is described by a particular attribute that can take one of four values: **scheduled**, **active**, **suspended**, or **disabled**. Further, spatial and temporal attributes can be attached to object or relationship types, independently of whether they are spatial/temporal or not.

Continuous fields are described with the concept of *varying attributes*, i.e., attributes whose values are defined by a function. Attributes may vary over space and/or time. For example, a space-varying attribute can be used for representing the depth of a lake while a space- and time-varying attribute can be used for representing moving objects.

Constrained relationship types are relationship types conveying spatial and temporal constraints on the objects they link. Topological relationships define a spatial constraint between the geometry of the related objects. MADS proposes a range of topological relationships [3] such as disjoint, adjacent, intersects, etc. Similarly, synchronization relationships allow specifying constraints on the lifecycle of the participating objects. Their semantics is based on Allen's [1] operators, e.g., before, equals, meets, etc., extended to complex temporal types.

Fig. 1 shows the MADS schema for a risks management application in mountain areas. The spatial and temporal characteristics are visually represented by icons. The temporal icon on the left-hand side of the object/relationship types expresses that the lifecycle information is to be kept. Spatial icons are shown on the right-hand side. Spatial and temporal attributes are represented by the corresponding icon, as for attribute protectStruct of AvalancheZone. Varying attributes are represented by the f( ) notation, as for the space-varying attribute elevation of LandslideZone. Located and Observes are relationship types defined, respectively, with the topological and synchronization intersects semantics. Finally,

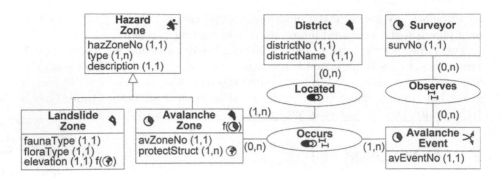

Fig. 1. Example of a MADS schema

Occurs is both a topological and synchronization relationship constraining both the lifecycle and the geometries of the related object types.

3   Translation of MADS Conceptual Schemas

We have developed a schema translator tool [5] that transforms a conceptual MADS schema into an equivalent logical schema that only employs the concepts provided by the target system. Fig. 2 shows the object-relational logical schema obtained by translating the conceptual schema in Fig. 1. We explain next some of these transformations.

Relationships are translated according to their type and the cardinalities of the roles. For example, the many-to-many relationship Observes is transformed by creating multivalued reference attributes avEventRef and survRef in the object types Surveyor and AvalancheEvent linked by the relationship.

For target systems supporting spatial attributes but not spatial object or relationship types (e.g., Oracle 10g), a spatial object or relationship type is transformed by creating a geometry attribute. Further, for systems providing only a generic spatial type (e.g., Oracle 10g), specialized spatial data types (for example, surface for District in Fig. 1) are transformed into the generic type Geo.

Varying attributes are replaced by a complex multivalued attribute encoding its defining function. Thus, the attribute is composed of spatial and/or temporal extents (depending on how many dimensions the attribute varies) and a value. Fig. 2 shows this transformation for the space-varying attribute elevation.

Temporal object types, such as Surveyor and AvalancheEvent in Fig. 1, are transformed by creating a monovalued time-varying attribute, called lifecycle. A second transformation replaces this time-varying attribute by a multivalued complex attribute composed of a temporal data type (e.g., an interval) and a value. Since most systems only provide a domain of the instant type (for example the DATE type), a last rule transforms an interval into a complex attribute whose components (starts and ends) are of type instant (cf. Fig. 2).

For each target DBMS and GIS there is a wrapper that rewrites the logical schema generated by the translator and produces a physical schema expressed in

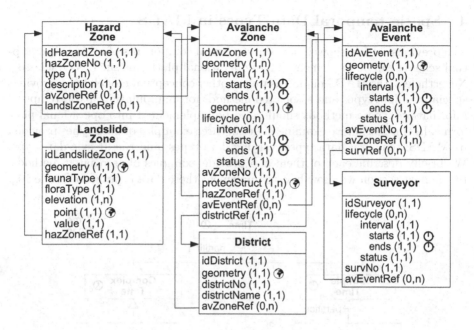

Fig. 2. Logical schema of Fig. 1 for Oracle 10g (object-relational model)

the language of the target system (e.g., SQL). In the case of Oracle, object types generate object tables and multivalued domains generate either nested tables or VARRAY types. Links are replaced by REF types that are logical pointers to row objects. An excerpt of the SQL script for the schema in Fig. 2 is as follows (only the type AvalancheZone and AvalancheEvent are shown):

```
create or replace type DId as object (idValue integer);
create or replace type DGeometrySet as table of mdsys.sdo_geometry;
create or replace type DAvEventSetRef as table of ref DAvalancheEvent;
create or replace type DAvZoneSetRef as table of ref DAvalancheZone;
create or replace type DSurvSetRef as table of ref DSurveyor;
create or replace type DAvalancheZone as object (idAvZone DId,
    geometry DTVGeometry, lifecycle DLifecycle, avZoneNo integer,
    protecStruct DGeometrySet, hazZoneRef ref DHazardZone,
    avEventRef DAvEventSetRef, districtRef DDistrictSetRef);
create table AvalancheZone of DAvalancheZone
    nested table geometry store as AvZoneGeometryNT
    nested table lifecycle store as AvZoneLifecycleNT
    nested table protectStruct store as AvZoneProtectStructNT;
    nested table avEventRef store as AvZoneAvEventRefNT
    nested table districtRef store as AvZoneDistrictRefNT;
```

DTVGeometry and DLifecycle are types for defining time-varying geometries and lifecycles, respectively. These types are defined in next sections.

4 Spatio-temporal Data Types in MADS

The previous section showed how the structural components of a MADS conceptual schema can be implemented into operational platforms such as Oracle 10g. Nevertheless, the MADS model (as well as other conceptual models) also provides specialized data types and associated methods for manipulating spatio-temporal information. Those methods should also be implemented into operational platforms. In this section we examine in detail three examples of data types provided by MADS: temporal data types, varying data types, and the lifecyle data type. We briefly describe each of them and provide examples of associated methods. In the next section we show how to implement these data types into Oracle 10g.

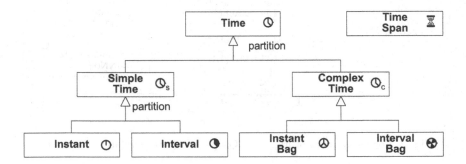

Fig. 3. MADS hierarchy of temporal data types

Temporal Data Types. Fig. 3 shows the hierachy of Temporal Data Types provided in MADS. Time, the root of the hierarchy, defines a set of attributes, methods, and operators common to all subtypes. Some of these are as follows:

- dimension() returning the dimension (0 or 1) of the temporal value,
- envelope() returning the minimum bounding interval of the temporal value,
- duration() returning the total time span of the temporal value,
- temporal predicates intersects(Time t), meets(Time t), overlaps(Time t), ... generalizing Allen's predicates [1] to complex temporal types.
- intersection(Time t), union(Time t), difference(Time t), computing the corresponding operator for temporal values.

Time is an abstract type, i.e., it is not instantiable. Further some of its methods are abstract, since the result of the method depends on the specific subtype. The subtypes of Time define additional attributes and methods. For example, Interval defines two attributes starts and ends defining the bounds of the interval, as well are redefines methods such as dimension inherited from Time.

Varying Data Types. These types allow to represent data that vary on space and/or on time. Varying data types are defined by a function whose domain is any spatial and/or temporal extent and whose range is a set of values. Some of the methods defined for varying types are as follows.

- defSpace(), defTime() returning the spatial and temporal extent on which the function is defined.
- rangeValues() returning the set of values taken by the function (its range).
- atLocation(Geo g) and atTime(Time t) returning the portion of the function that is defined for the spatial/temporal extent given as parameter.

Lifecyle data type. This type is used for capturing the lifecycle of object and relationship types. It is composed of a time-varying attribute status that keeps track of the status of the instance and two temporal attributes dob and dod that keep track, respectively, of the date of first activation ("date of birth") and the date of deactivation ("date of death") of the instances. In addition the type defines a set of methods such as the following ones.

- lifeSpan() returning the temporal extent during which the instance existed.
- activeSpan() returning the temporal extent during which the lifecyle is active.
- status(Intant t) returning the status value at the instant given as parameter.

5   Implementing Spatio-temporal Types in OR DBMSs

Traditional DBMSs provide limited support for temporal and spatio-temporal information. Therefore, when translating MADS conceptual schemas, all associated methods and operators must be implemented in the target DBMS. Our translator automatically generates these methods and operators. We explain next how this generation is realized in Oracle 10g.

Temporal Data Types. We have implemented these types in a package that will be used by any MADS database, i.e., it is independent of the schema. The inheritance model in Oracle 10g did not allow us to implement the hierarchy of types as shown in Fig. 3. For example, it is not possible to define an object type DTime having a method such as envelope returning a value of type DInterval (i.e., a subtype of DTime); this is called a non-ref mutually-dependent cycle in Oracle's terminology. Therefore, we implemented only the lower-level types of the hierarchy (DInstant, DInterval, etc.) and defined all temporal functions in each temporal type. The definitions of these types are sketched next. Please refer to the previous section for the meaning of the different methods.

```
create or replace type DInstant as object ( instant Date,
    member function Tdimension return number,
    member function envelope return DInterval,
    member function intersection(t DInterval) return DInterval,
    member function Tintersects(t DInterval) return integer,...
) instantiable final
create or replace type DInterval as object( starts Date, ends Date,
    /* ... the same set of member functions as above ... */
) instantiable final
```

The implementation of type DInterval and some of its methods are given next.

```
create or replace type body DInterval as
   member function envelope return DInterval as
   begin
      return DInterval(self.starts,self.ends);
   end;
   member function intersection(t DInterval) return DInterval as
   begin
      if (self.Tintersects(t))
         then return DInterval(maxDate(self.starts,t.starts),minDate(self.ends,t.ends));
         else return null;
      end if;
   end;
   member function Tintersects(t in DInterval) return integer as
   begin
      if (self.starts<t.ends and t.starts<self.ends)
         then returns 1;
         else returns 0;
      end if;
   end; ...
end;
```

Functions minDate and maxDate above return, respectively, the minimum and maximum of the two dates passed as parameters.

Time-Varying Data Types. As Oracle does not allow parameterized types, an object type definition is needed for each time-varying data type. We show next the definition of a time-varying geometry.

```
create or replace type GeometrySet as table of mdsys.sdo_geometry;
create or replace type TVGeometryValue as object (
   interval DInterval, geometry mdsys.sdo_geometry);
create or replace type TVGeometryValues as table of TVGeometryValue;
create or replace type TVGeometry as object ( tv_geometry TVGeometryValues,
   member function defTime return DInstant,
   member function defTime return DInterval,
   member function rangeValues return GeometrySet,
   member function atTime(t DInstant) return TVGeometry,
   member function atTime(t DInterval) return TVGeometry, ... )
```

We give next the implementation of the atTime function.

```
member function atTime(t DInterval) return TVGeometry is
   v1 TVGeometryValues:=TVGeometryValues();
   cursor c_TVGeometryValues is
      select v.interval,v.geometry from table(self.tv_geometry) v;
begin
   for v2 in c_TVGeometryValues loop
      if (v2.interval.Tintersects(t)=1)
         then v1.extend;
         v1(v1.last):= TVGeometryValue(v2.interval.intersection(t),v2.geometry);
```

```
        end if;
    end loop;
    return TVGeometry(v1);
end;
```

The atTime function starts by initializing the result variable v1 as an empty set. Then it uses a cursor for iterating in v2 the couples (interval,geometry) of the time-varying attribute. If the interval intersects with the temporal value t given as parameter it adds the result (interval',geometry) to the result set v1 where interval' is the temporal intersection of v2 and t.

Lifecycle. The type DLifecycle is defined as follows

```
create or replace type DIntervalBag as table of DInterval;
create or replace type TVStatusValue as object (
    interval DInterval, status varchar2(9));
create or replace type TVStatusValues as table of TVStatusValue;
create or replace type DLifecycle as object (
    tv_status TVStatusValues, dob Date, dod Date,
    member function lifespan return DInterval,
    member function activespan return DInterval,
    member function status(d in Date) return varchar2(9), ... )
```

We give next the implementation of functions activespan and status.

```
member function activeSpan return DIntervalBag is
    v1 DIntervalBag := DIntervalBag();
    cursor c_TVStatusValues is
        select s.interval,s.status from table(self.tv_status) s;
begin
    for v2 in c_TVStatusValues loop
        if (v2.status='active')
        then v1.extend;
            v1(v1.last)= DInterval(v2.interval);
        end if;
    end loop;
    return v1;
end;
member function status(t DInterval) return varchar2(9) is
    v varchar2(9);
begin
    select s.status into v from table(self.tv_status) s
    where s.interval.contains(t)
    return v;
end;
```

Function activeSpan first initializes the result variable v1 as an empty interval bag. Then it uses a cursor for iterating in v2 the couples (interval,status) of the time-varying status and keep only those couples with value equal to active. Function atTime returns the status of the couple (interval,status) containing the instant t given as parameter. Notice that this function presupposes that the intervals in the time-varying status are disjoint. This must be ensured by an integrity constraint expressed by a trigger as explained in [6].

6   Temporal Queries and Integrity Constraints

The MADS algebra [7] allows to use all methods and operators provided by the spatial and temporal data types when formulating queries. For example, the query "find the geometry of avalanche zones between 01/05/2004 and 08/12/2005" is expressed in the MADS algebra as follows:

```
select [ geometry.atTime([01/05/2004, 08/12/2005]) ] AvalancheZone
```

The translation of this query must take into account not only how the conceptual schema was transformed into the logical schema, but also the transformation of the spatial/temporal methods and operators. Using the implementation of these methods described in the previous sections, the above query can be written as follows:

```
select a.geometry.atTime(DInterval(01/05/2004,08/12/2005))
from AvalancheZone a
```

The query "find the identifiers of districts in which are located active avalanche zones whose geometry did not change between 22/05/2002 and 01/06/2006" can be written in SQL as follows:

```
select d.idDistrict
from district d, table(AvalancheZoneRef) refAv, table(refAv.column_value.lifecycle) l
where Tcontains(l.activespan(),sysdate) and
   ( select count(a.geometry.atTime(DInterval(22/05/2002,01/06/2006))
     from AvalancheZone a
     where refAv.column_value.idAvZone=a.idAvZone ) =< 1
```

In the above query, the method activespan() returns the temporal extent in which the lifecycle is active. Further, Tcontains(l.activespan(),sysdate) checks if the current date is included in the activespan of the lifecycle.

We can also use the implementation of these methods for expressing integrity constraints. For instance, one trigger will raise an error upon insertion of avalanche zone instances if two intervals of the lifecycle overlap.

```
create or replace trigger AvalancheZoneLCOverlappingIntervals
before insert on AvalancheZone for each row
begin
   if exists ( select * from table(:new.lifecycle) l1, table(:new.lifecycle) l2
          where l2.Toverlaps(DInterval(l1.stats,l1.ends))
   then raise_application_error(-20300, 'Overlapping intervals in lifecycle')
   end if;
end
```

7   Conclusion and Future Works

Many spatio-temporal models have been proposed in the literature. They allow users to design their applications at a conceptual level. However, since operational DBMSs or GISs provide little support for spatio-temporal data management, such conceptual specifications must be translated into the operational model provided by such implementation platforms. In addition, users must express their queries using the physical schema of the application.

Traditionally, the transformation from conceptual to physical schemas realized by CASE tools only copes with information structures (i.e., attributes). This paper advocates that it is necessary to include in the translation process the generation of functions and procedures that allow the manipulation of spatio-temporal information. We showed that this generation can be realized automatically and showed an example using Oracle 10g, an object-relational DBMS.

In the future we will continue to study the implementation of temporal and spatio-temporal queries and updates, and how a CASE tool can support this process. Although we have validated our strategy using Oracle 10g, we also plan to support other platforms.

References

1. J.F. Allen. Maintaining knowledge about temporal intervals. *Communications of the ACM*, 26(11):832–843, 1983.
2. E. Camossi, M. Bertolotto, E. Bertino, and G. Guerrini. A multigranular spatiotemporal data model. In *Proc. of the 11th ACM Int. Symp. on Advances in Geographic Information Systems, ACM GIS 2003*, pages 94–101, 2003.
3. M.J. Egenhofer, E. Clementini, and P. Di Felice. Topological relations between regions with holes. *Int. Journal of Geographic Information Systems*, 8(2):129–142, 1994.
4. V. Khatri, S. Ram, and R.T. Snodgrass. ST USM: Bridging the semantic gap with a spatio-temporal conceptual model. TimeCenter Research Report TR-64, 2001.
5. M. Minout, C. Parent, and E. Zimányi. A tool for transforming conceptual schemas of spatio-temporal databases with multiple representations. In *Proc. of the IASTED Int. Conf. on Database Applications, DBA'04*, pages 1–6, 2004.
6. E. Zimányi and M. Minout. Preserving Semantics when Transforming Conceptual Spatio-Temporal Schemas. *Proc. of the On the Move to Federated Conferences and Workshops, OTM 2005*, pages 1037–1046. LNCS 3762, Springer, 2005.
7. C. Parent, S. Spaccapietra, and E. Zimányi. *Conceptual Modeling for Traditional and Spatio-Temporal Applications: The MADS Approach*. Springer, 2006.
8. R. Price, N. Tryfona, and C.S. Jensen. Extended spatio-temporal UML: Motivations, requirements, and constructs. *Journal of Database Management*, 11(4): 14–27, 2000.
9. P. Rigaux, M. Scholl, and A. Voisard. *Introduction to Spatial Databases: Applications to GIS*. Morgan Kaufmann, 2000.
10. N. Tryfona and C.S. Jensen. Conceptual data modeling for spatiotemporal applications. *GeoInformatica*, 3(3):245–268, 1999.

A Semantic Similarity Model for Mapping Between Evolving Geospatial Data Cubes

Mohamed Bakillah, Mir Abolfazl Mostafavi, and Yvan Bédard

Chaire Industrielle CRSNG en bases de données géospatiales décisionnelles
Centre de Recherche en Géomatique, 0611 Pavillon Casault, Département des Sciences
Géomatiques Université Laval, Québec, Canada, G1K 7P4
Mohamed.bakillah.1@ulaval.ca
Mir-Abolfazl.Mostafavi@scg.ulaval.ca
Yvan.Bédard@scg.ulaval.ca

Abstract. In a decision-making context, multidimensional geospatial databases are very important. They often represent data coming from heterogeneous and evolving sources. Evolution of multidimensional structures makes difficult, even impossible answering to temporal queries, because of the lack of relationships between different versions of spatial cubes created at different time. This paper proposes a semantic similarity model redefined from a model applied in the ontological field to establish semantic relations between data cubes. The proposed model integrates several types of similarity components adapted to different hierarchical levels of dimensions in multidimensional databases and also integrates similarity between features of concepts. The proposed model has been applied to a set of specifications from different inventory in Montmorency Forest in Canada. Results show that the proposed model improves precision and recall compared to the original model. Finally, further investigation is suggested in order to integrate the proposed model to SOLAP tools as future works.

Keywords: Semantic similarity models, ontology, mapping between ontologies, geospatial data cubes.

1 Introduction

OLAP tools and their spatial extension SOLAP, which are based on multidimensional structures, were introduced to support analysis in a decision-making context and to allow users to easily access and explore the data according to various perspectives [1]. Multidimensional structures are composed of dimensions, measures and facts. Dimensions are the analysis themes and can be spatial, typically having levels described by geometric objects, such as polygons, for cartographic representations. Measures are the numerical attributes analyzed against different dimensions. Facts express the value of measures with respect to a specific combination of dimensions members for different aggregation levels. For example, the multidimensional structure can be made of the spatial dimension geography, formed of levels *city < area < country*, and measure *birth rate*. Multidimensional structure is brought to undergo evolution, affecting facts but also structure of dimensions [2], which are usually considered as static. Dimension

R. Meersman, Z. Tari, P. Herrero et al. (Eds.): OTM Workshops 2006, LNCS 4278, pp. 1658–1669, 2006.
© Springer-Verlag Berlin Heidelberg 2006

members can also be affected by semantic evolutions. An example of such is a modification resulting from the changes to a regulation affecting the management of a given territory. Such evolution of multidimensional structures affects temporal queries, and may lead to false results, when result there is [3] [2] [4]. Existing approaches suggested to manage the evolution in multidimensional data cubes [5] [2] [6] [7] do not explicitly consider semantic evolution as they manage only the case of explicit data evolution, i.e. when evolution is realized by evolution operators (add, delete, merge members of schema of instances of dimension, etc.) Evolution can also happen when several multidimensional databases represent the same reality for different epochs, for example when the data are collected independently for the same territory every 10 years as in forestry in Quebec. In this case, relations between the seemingly similar databases are difficult to establish and the evolution problem is more complex to solve since we need to restore these relations to answer temporal queries. In order to answer this latter problem, this paper proposes a new approach of semantic mapping between data cubes. The proposed approach is based on an ontological approach for the assessment of semantic relations between members of different data cubes. Multidimensional structures of a same area and their metadata can be seen as an evolving ontology and thus a semantic similarity model can be used as a mapping function. This similarity model is adapted to complex data and is flexible enough to support several data types. It defines a specific measure of similarity for the aggregated levels of a dimension hierarchy. Follow up on this work will show how the developed mapping function can support temporal queries processing in data cubes.

The reminder of this paper is as follows: section 2 presents a state of the art on ontology mapping and semantic similarity models. Section 3 describes the proposed approach and the similarity model used as a mapping function between data cubes. Section 4 shows the application and evaluation of the proposed approach in a forestry context. In section 5, we conclude this article.

2 State of Art on Ontology and Semantic Similarity Models

A suitable approach to overcome problems of semantic heterogeneity and evolution lies in ontologies, which are specifically designed to represent semantics and knowledge about data. In AI (Artificial Intelligence), ontology is defined as an explicit specification of a conceptualization [8]. In other words, an ontology is the outcome of a conceptual modeling process. Generally, the taxonomic structure of an ontology forms a graph where nodes represent concepts and arcs represent relations between them. An ontology thus constitutes an interesting framework for the discovery of semantic relationships between concepts, upon which we have founded our approach, i.e. a multidimensional structure with metadata can be regarded as an ontology. Moreover, just like the multidimensional structure, ontologies evolve, following modifications of specifications, standards, definitions of concepts, etc. [9] [10] [11].Ontology mapping aims at establishing relationships between ontologies while preserving their own structure. Among the approaches of ontology mapping, some use a semantic similarity model to relate concepts [12] [13] [14]. Similarity models can be classified according to the representation of the concepts they use: graphs, features of concepts, information content-based models, vector space models or a combination of different types of models (hybrid models).

Similarity models using ontology graphs are based on the assumption that a hierarchy of concepts is organized according to semantic similarity lines. Consequently, concepts are similar if the distance which separates them in the graph is short, the distance being given by the shortest path along the arcs to join both concepts [15]. The distance between two nodes is not necessarily uniform, thus other models take into account local density of nodes, depth of concepts in the graph, total depth of the graph and the force of the relations [16] [17] [18]. Models using features of concepts, based on set theory, are founded on the comparison of sets of features describing concepts. The ratio model [19], also used in other approaches [20] [21], compares the intersection set (common features) to the sets of exclusive features of each concept.

Models based on information content stipulate that the similarity between two concepts is getting higher as the shared information content increases. Information content of a concept is a logarithmic function of the probability of its components to appear in the ontology. Similarity between two concepts is given by the information content they share, i.e. by the information content of the first common parent in taxonomy [22]. According to another approach, information content of a concept is a function of the number of hyponyms and of the number of concepts in taxonomy [23]. Vector space models use the analogy where semantic proximity between concepts is represented by proximity in a vector space. This model is mainly used in information systems to represent documents, although it is also used for concepts in geometrical similarity models [24] [25], where those are represented by points or regions in a multidimensional conceptual space. The semantic distance between concepts is given by a metric, such as the Minkowski distance or cosine [26] in information systems.

Finally, hybrid models, such as the Matching Distance model, merge properties of several models into one [20] [27] [25]. Matching Distance model [20] is based on the ratio model [19], integrates context and distance in ontology graph and was designed to associate spatial entity classes from different ontologies. In Matching Distance Model, global similarity is a weighted sum of similarity between the different types of features (attributes, parts and roles) of concepts, lexical similarity (name of concepts) and neighborhood similarity in the graphs of ontologies:

$$S_g(c_1,c_2) = \omega_l S_l(c_1,c_2) + \omega_c(\omega_a S_a(c_1,c_2) + \omega_p S_p(c_1,c_2) + \omega_f S_f(c_1,c_2)) + \omega_n S_n(c_1,c_2) \qquad (1)$$

where the different similarities are given by an adaptation of the ratio model (shown in next section) and neighborhood similarity by :

$$S_n(c_1,c_2) = \frac{N_1 \cap N_2}{N_1 \cap N_2 + \alpha(c_1,c_2) * \delta(c_1, N_1 \cap N_2) + (1 - \alpha(c_1,c_2)) * \delta(c_2, N_1 \cap N_2)} \qquad (2)$$

N1 and N2 are entities forming the neighborhood of concepts in the ontology graph, α is the distance between concepts in graph and δ is the difference function between neighborhoods of concepts. This model has the advantage of being complete and to take into account the maximum of information contained in ontology, compared to other models. However, it only considers features as words. This can be insufficient since spatial entity may be defined by more complex features such as domain values or texts. Also, it does not consider the degree of similarity between features of concepts, nor the specificity of concepts from aggregated levels of graph. Based on this model, in this article we propose a new semantic similarity model that overcomes these limitations and that can be used as a mapping function between members of the schema of instances of dimension.

3 Proposed Approach

The multidimensional structure and its metadata are considered as the ontology of the databases in order to evaluate semantic similarity between members of the schema of instances of dimensions in different cubes. First, the user defines the context which represents a set of concepts that share a feature of interest (for example *ecological zone*) and will be used to compute weights for different similarities. Similarity is then evaluated on three levels: between features of concepts, between concepts of the detailed level (finest level of granularity in the schema of instances of dimension) and between concepts of aggregated levels. The global similarity allows computing the matrices of mapping which relate concepts from two levels of hierarchy of different cube versions. The proposed approach is shown on figure 1.

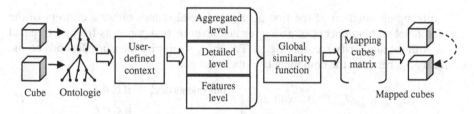

Fig. 1. Global approach for semantic mapping between evolving data cubes

Weights for the different similarities are defined by computing relevance of each type of features using the principles of commonality or variability. Relevance following the commonality principle (P_t^{comm}) is defined as the sum of the number of occurrences o_i of each feature i of type t in the concepts definitions, divided by the number n of features in the context, while relevance computed with using the variability principle (P_t^{var}) is defined as the converse of commonality principle. Weights are defined as following:

$$\omega_t = \frac{P_t}{\sum_i P_i} \quad i=\text{type of feature} \quad \text{where } P_t^{comm} = \frac{1}{n}\sum_{i=1}^{n} o_i \quad \text{or} \quad P_t^{var} = 1-\frac{1}{n}\sum_{i=1}^{n} o_i \tag{3}$$

3.1 Theoretical Framework

This section introduces basic definitions of our approach. First, we define the ontology and concepts, and then the mapping function and matrix of semantic mapping that relate concepts of different versions of the ontology. The mapping function is based on the similarity model that will be defined in the next section.

Definition of Concepts. A concept c of a version O^i is defined such as $c = \{id\_c,$ name_c, P, D, L_D, O^i, t$\}$, where id_c is the concept identifier, name_c is its name, P is a set of features (attributes, parts and functions) of the concept, D and L_D are respectively the dimension and the hierarchical level to which the concept belongs and t is a valid time interval for concept c. The set of features P may contain features which domain values are text or intervals given by specifications on concepts.

Mapping Function. This ontology-like representation of the multidimensional structure forms a framework for discovering semantic relations between members of the different cubes. Semantic relations are established by a mapping function which quantifies, by means of a semantic similarity measure, a similarity relation between two concepts. This mapping function takes two forms, depending on whether concepts belong to the detailed level or an aggregated level of a hierarchy. The mapping function for the detailed level relates concepts c_1^i and c_2^j of the detailed levels $L_d^{\ i}$ and $L_d^{\ j}$ of two versions i and j of ontology with the similarity measure S_{gd} :

$$f_d : S_{gd}(c_1^i, c_2^j) \text{ with } c_1^i \in L_d^i \text{ et } c_2^j \in L_d^j \tag{4}$$

The mapping function of the first aggregated level relates either a concept of the detailed level with a concept of an aggregated level or two concepts from aggregated levels with the similarity measure S_{g_agg}. The S_{g_agg} similarity measure depends on the similarity S_{gd} between the components of the concepts:

$$f_{agg1} : S_{g\_agg}(S_{gd}(P_1^i, P_2^j)) \text{ with } P_1^i = \begin{cases} \text{components of } c_1^i & \text{if } c_1^i \in L_{agg}^i \\ c_1^i & \text{if } c_1^i \in L_d^i \end{cases} \tag{5}$$

Components of a concept are children in the hierarchy. We can generalize the mapping function for arbitrary aggregated level n using the recursive principle:

$$f_{agg\_n} : S_{g\_agg\_n}(S_{g\_agg\_n-1}(S_{g\_agg\_n-2}(...(S_{gd}(P_1^i, P_2^j))))) \tag{6}$$

Matrix of Semantic Mapping. The mapping function allows computing the elements of the matrix of semantic mapping which relate concepts from two levels of two versions O^i and O^j of the ontology. We define a matrix of mapping for each combination of level of the two versions. Let $H(D, O^i) = \{c_1^i, c_2^i ..., c_k^i ... c_n^i\}$ be the set of n concepts forming the level L_1 of dimension D of the version O^i and $H(D, O^j) = \{c_1^j, c_2^j ..., c_l^j ... c_m^j\}$ be the set of m concepts forming level L_2 of dimension D of the version O^j. The matrix of semantic mapping M as dimension card($H(D, O^i)$)×card($H(D, O^j)$), where card() represents the number of element in a set. Each of its elements is defined by $M(D,O^i,O^j)_{kl} = f(c_k^i, c_l^j)$ where f is the mapping function for the detailed level f_d if L_1 and L_2 are detailed levels and f_{agg} if L_1 or L_2 is an aggregated level. Searching a semantic relation between all possible levels is necessary in order to identify concepts that may have changed level.

3.2 Redefined Semantic Similarity Model

The model described in this section improves the model Matching Distance (MD) by allowing us to measure similarity between the features of concepts and presents a new similarity measure for concepts of aggregated levels. Similarity is computed in a three step recursive process: (1) between features of compared concepts, (2) between concepts of the detailed level and (3) between concepts of aggregated levels of the schema of instance of dimensions, using the similarity values of detailed level concepts. Features can be complex and we include measures of similarity for texts and domain values (intervals).

3.2.1 Features Level Similarity
Matching Distance model (MD model) is based on the ratio model [19] which suggests that similarity is a function of the sets of common features and sets of exclusive features:

$$S(c_1, c_2) = \frac{f(C_1 \cap C_2)}{f(C_1 \cap C_2) + \alpha f(C_1 - C_2) + \beta f(C_2 - C_1)} \tag{7}$$

where is C_1 the set of features of c_1 and C_2 is the set of features of c_2, f is a monotonous increasing function and $\alpha \geq 0$, $\beta \geq 0$ are parameters which give relative importance to the sets of exclusive features. In MD model, f is the set cardinality and for a feature, being part of the set of common features is a binary function, i.e. a feature is or is not part of this set, but it cannot be included in the set in a partial way. Matching Distance model thus underestimates the similarity of two concepts, because it does not consider the degree of similarity of the features. However, we consider that, just as concepts, features may share some degree of similarity, so the contribution of a pair of features to the set of common features must be related to their percentage of similarity, so the first step of similarity assessment is to compute similarity between features. Similarity measures employed for text and intervals features are as follows:

Similarity Measure for Text. The similarity model employed to compare texts is generally used in information systems. Segmentation and indexing processes are resumed in figure 2. Result of indexing is a set of informative segments forming the lexicon.

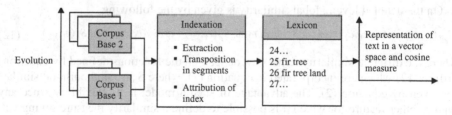

Fig. 2. Text similarity evaluation

Similarity is given by cosine measure [26], where each text is represented by a vector whose components $v_1, v_2, \ldots v_l$ are frequencies of informative segments of the lexicon :

$$sim(A_i, B_j) = \sum_{k=1}^{l} v_{ki} v_{kj} \Big/ \sqrt{\sum_{k=1}^{l} v_{ki}^2 \sum_{k=1}^{l} v_{kj}^2} \tag{8}$$

Similarity Measure for Intervals. Replacing summation with integration in the cosine measure (equation (8)) produces a vector space similarity measure adapted for the case of continuous data, i.e. where the number of dimensions in the vector space is infinite [28]. Frequency of terms, which usually quantifies the components of vectors representing the concepts, becomes a continuous function of density $\rho(r)$ that indicates distribution of values in a continuous range:

$$\text{sim}(c_1, c_2) = \frac{I(c_1, c_2)}{\sqrt{I(c_1, c_1) I(c_2, c_2)}} \quad \text{where } I(c_1, c_2) = \int \rho_1(r) \rho_2(r) dr \qquad (9)$$

This similarity measure can be applied to compare intervals since they are infinite sets of values. Then, the functions of density $\rho_1(r)$ and $\rho_2(r)$ indicates the distribution of the values in the compared intervals and $I(c_1, c_2)$ represent the intersection function between both intervals. Result is a similarity value that lies between 0 and 1. These similarity measures for text and intervals are included in equation (10).

3.2.2 Detailed Level Similarity

According to the principle that the contribution of a pair of features to the set of common features must be related to their percentage of similarity and considering that $C_{1t} = \{A_1, A_2 \ldots A_i \ldots, A_n\}$ and $C_{2t} = \{B_1, B_2 \ldots B_i \ldots, B_m\}$ are the respective sets of feature of type t of concepts C_1 and C_2 (t=attributes, parts, or role) function of the intersection f defined in equation (7) can be defined in the following way:

$$f(C_{1t} \cap C_{2t}) = \sum_{i=1}^{n} \sum_{j=1}^{m} \text{sim}(A_i, B_j) \qquad (10)$$

where $sim(A_i, B_j)$ evaluate similarity between features and depends on the data type of the feature A_i and B_j. The difference between the two sets of exclusive features is defined by:

$$f(C_{1t} - C_{2t}) = card(C_{1t}) - f(C_{1t} \cap C_{2t}) \text{ and } f(C_{2t} - C_{1t}) = card(C_{2t}) - f(C_{1t} \cap C_{2t}) \qquad (11)$$

On the detailed level, global similarity is given by the following,

$$S_{gd}(c_1, c_2) = \omega_l S_l(c_1, c_2) + \omega_c (\omega_a S_a(c_1, c_2) + \omega_p S_p(c_1, c_2) + \omega_f S_f(c_1, c_2)) + \omega_n S_n(c_1, c_2) \qquad (12)$$

where the different similarity terms now depend on the functions defined by equations (10) to (12) which are incorporated in equation (7), where S_n is neighborhood similarity given by equation (2). The advantage of such a model is its flexibility since any type of other feature for which it is possible to define a similarity measure giving values between 0 and 1 can be incorporated in equation (10).

3.2.3 Aggregated Level Similarity

Concepts from aggregated levels are formed by the underlying concepts in the hierarchy, i.e. their subordinated concepts (the components). In some cases, MD model may be insufficient to assess similarity between concepts of aggregated level which may have no intrinsic feature. For example, when concept are spatial zones, concepts of aggregated levels are an aggregation of concepts of detailed level which are related to them by part-of relations, and thus have no features except parts. Names of concepts of spatial zones may be unmeaning for lexical similarity: for example, even if the concept *forestry station* shares no lexical commonality with the concept *landscape unit*, they represent a very close reality in forestry. Following this last remark, parts of concepts of aggregated levels may be impossible to compare directly only by their names; it is necessary to assess their features similarity in order to know to which level parts are similar. In these cases, global similarity of MD model reduces to neighborhood similarity, thus not taking into account similarity between components of concepts. To extend the MD model to these cases, the following model for similarity assessment between concepts of aggregated level is proposed. Similarity assessment for aggregated levels is a recursive process, i.e. the comparison of the sets of components of each concept is also a similarity assessment. Consider that $P_1 = \{p_{11}, p_{12} \cdots p_{1i} \cdots, p_{1n}\}$ and $P_2 = \{p_{21}, p_{22} \cdots p_{2i} \cdots, p_{2m}\}$ are the sets of components of concepts c_1 and c_2 respectively. The similarity for aggregated levels between the concept c_1 and c_2 is given by:

$$S_{agg}(c_1, c_2) = \frac{f(P_1, P_2)}{f(P_1, P_2) + \alpha(c_1, c_2)D(P_1 - P_2) + \beta(c_1, c_2))D(P_2 - P_1)} \tag{13}$$

The function f represents the set of common components to concepts c_1 and c_2 and is evaluated by summing the similarities between the most similar concepts:

$$f(P_1, P_2) = \begin{cases} \sum_{k=1}^{card(P_1)} \max\left[S_{gd}(p_{1k}, p_{2i})\right] & \text{if } card(P_1) \le card(P_2),\ i \in \left[1, card(P_2)\right] \\ \sum_{k=1}^{card(P_2)} \max\left[S_{gd}(p_{1i}, p_{2k})\right] & \text{if } card(P_1) \succ card(P_2),\ i \in \left[1, card(P_1)\right] \end{cases} \tag{14}$$

Image of function f is constrained by the cardinality of the smallest set of components, because the cardinality of intersection set must be smaller or equal to the cardinality of the smallest set: $f:[0,1] \times [0,1] \rightarrow [0, \min\{card(P_1), card(P_2)\}]$. Differences between sets of exclusives components are given by the cardinality of components sets from which we substract the intersection function f:

$$D(P_1 - P_2) = card(P_1) - f(P_1, P_2) \quad \text{and} \quad D(P_2 - P_1) = card(P_2) - f(P_1, P_2) \tag{15}$$

Global similarity for aggregated levels is given by the following, where ω_p is the weight for similarity of aggregated level, since this last one evaluates similarity between parts (component) in hierarchy:

$$S_{g\_agg} = \omega_l S_l(c_1, c_2) + \omega_c(\omega_a S_a(c_1, c_2) + \omega_p S_{agg}(c_1, c_2) + \omega_f S_f(c_1, c_2)) + \omega_n S_n(c_1, c_2) \tag{16}$$

4 Evaluation of the Proposed Approach

The evaluation of our model has been done using a Java application with forestry spatial data and illustrates the accuracy of this redefined model as well as the increased performance of that model compared to the MD model. The data came from four different inventories (1973 to 2002) of Montmorency experimental forest of Laval University. Each inventory is associated to a data cube. A forest inventory consists in partitioning space in zones characterized by homogeneous properties of term of density, species, height, etc.(table 1), resulting in a set of basic spatial entities. Basic spatial entities are aggregated in higher level spatial entities, forming the hierarchy of the data cube spatial dimensions. For research, regulatory and environmental reasons, the specifications of theses spatial zones have changed from one inventory to another.

Table 1. Example of evolving basic spatial entities (from Montmorency forest specifications)

Year in-ventory	Attributes				Parts	Roles
	Age	Height	Density	...	Species	Zone type
1992	[20,40] years	[7,12] m	[61,81]%	...	Mixed zone where leafy tree represent over 50 % of ...	Ecological
2002	[30,45] years	[10,12] m	[55,81]%	...	Mixed zone where white-birches take over 45% of...	Ecological

At first, a simulation was carried out to validate the redefined semantic similarity model. Behaviour of the model was evaluated according to a sample of concepts for which the percentage of common features with a reference concept follows a linearly increasing function. Figure 3 shows that the model follows the predicted behaviour compared to the variability of the concepts.

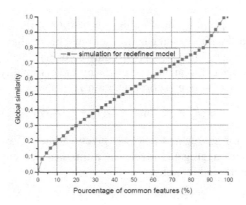

Fig. 3. Behaviour of the redefined model

Results of similarity obtained with the MD model and our redefined model were also compared, showing that for different classes of similarity, the MD model underestimates the value of the similarity because it rejects the features which are partially similar, whereas the redefined model gives values of similarity closer to the reality (table 2).

Table 2. Comparison of some values obtained for the redefined model and the MD model

Zone number	MD model	Redefined model	Expected range of values
23-3	0.3712	0.5874	Average similarity
11-3	0.1650	0.3990	Low similarity
2-40	0.1433	0.3784	Low similarity
12-54	0.0206	0.1639	Very low similarity

The efficiency of both models was compared by evaluating precision and recall, which are metrics currently used in information system:

$$\text{Precision} = \frac{\text{number of correct mapping}}{\text{number of detected mapping}} \text{ and Recall} = \frac{\text{number of correct mapping}}{\text{number of reference mapping}} \quad (17)$$

Expected mapping were manually evaluated using specifications and cartographic data for the compared spatial entities. The evaluation was carried out with 25 zones identified in the 1984 inventory and 77 zones identified in the 1992 inventory, since in 1992 the same surface was divided in smaller entities than in 1984. Results of precision-recall curves are shown on figure 4.

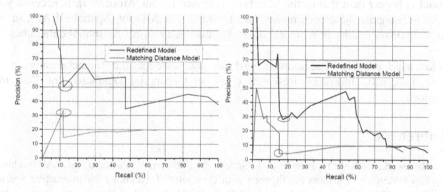

Fig. 4. Precision-recall curves for aggregated levels (left) and detailed level (right)

Values were obtained by successively applying decreasing threshold values, threshold indicating that beyond this value pairs of entities could be considered similar and part to the set of detected mapping. Set of correct mapping is a subset of the set of detect mapping and corresponds to the pairs of entities that are also part of the set of reference mapping. Results show that performance of the redefined model is higher than performance of MD model in any point, in particular, the difference between both models being more significant in the case of the aggregated level similarity, showing the need for a similarity model specifically designed for aggregated levels, particularly in the case where concepts are related by part-of relations and only defined by their subordinated concepts. Indeed, in this case, the similarity of the MD model is reduced to the graph neighborhood similarity and lexical similarity, whereas with the similarity for aggregated levels (redefined model), similarity between features is implicitly considered in the recursive function. In addition, figure 4 shows that the curves have significant variations (as shown on graphs), reflecting the clustering of the similarity values between spatial zones. Distribution of the similarity values is not uniform but form clusters because variability of the features of spatial zones (in term of density, species, height, etc.) remains limited. Consequently, this results in high sensitivity of the recall and precision to weak variations of threshold during the test.

5 Conclusion and Perspectives

Our article presented a general approach of semantic mapping between different versions of geospatial data cube, which is different from other existing approaches in multidimensional structures evolution as it considers the case where relations between different structure versions are not identified a priori and are affected by semantic evolution. The suggested similarity model improves the precision of the semantic similarity assessment by evaluating similarity not only between concepts, but also between their features. The model is flexible and generic and can incorporate any type of feature (sound, image, various languages, etc.) for which it is possible to define a similarity measure. Then, it can be used in a variety of cases as it allows the integration of various types of data. Results showed that the effectiveness of the redefined model is higher than that of the Matching Distance model. More work is necessary in order to integrate these preliminary results to the SOLAP tool (Spatial OLAP), in order to improve quality of temporal queries results in evolving geospatial data cubes.

Acknowledgements. The authors wish to acknowledge the financial support of Canada NSERC Industrial Research Chair in Geospatial Databases for Decision Support.

References

1. Rivest, S., Bédard, Y., Proulx, M-J, Nadeau, M., Hubert, F., Pastor, J.: SOLAP Technology : Merging Business Intelligence with Geospatial Technology for Interactive Spatio-Temporal Exploration and Analysis of Data, ISPRS Journal of Photogrammetry and Remote Sensing 60: (2005) 17-33
2. Body, M., Miquel, M., Bédard, Y., Tchounikine, A.: A Multidimensional and Multiversion Structure for OLAP Applications. In Procceedings of the 5th ACM international workshop on Data Warehousing and OLAP (2002)
3. Thurnheer, A : Les Changements dans les Bases de Données Analytiques. In: Information als Erfolgsfactor, Teubner, Stuttgart (2000)
4. Eder, J., Koncilia, C., Mitsche, D.: Automatic Detection of Structural Changes in Data Warehouses. Lecture Notes in Computer Science Vol. 2737 (2003) 119-128
5. Mendelzon, A.O., Vaisman, A.A. (2000) Temporal Queries in OLAP. Proceedings of the 26th VLDB Conference, Cairo, Egypt
6. Eder, J., Koncilia, C., Morzy, T.: The COMET Metamodel for Temporal Data Warehouses. In Proc. of the 14th Int. Conference on Advanced Information Systems Engineering (CAISE'02), Toronto, Canada (2002)
7. Morzy, T., Wrembel, R.: On querying Versions of Multiversion Data Warehouse. DOLAP'04, Washington, DC, USA (2004).

8. Gruber, T.R.: Toward Principles for the Design of Ontologies used for Knowledge Sharing. International Journal of Human–Computer Studies,Vol. 43 (1995) 907–928
9. Klein, M.: Combining and Relating Ontologies: an Analysis of Problems and Solution. In IJCAI-2001 Workshop on Ontologies and Information Sharing, Seattle, WA (2001) 53-62
10. Eder, J., Koncilia, C.: Modelling Changes in Ontologies. OTM Workshops 2004, LNCS, 3292 (2004) 662-673.
11. Sure, Y., Staab, S., et Studer, R.. On-To-Knowledge Methodology (OTKM). In S. Staab et R. Studer (Eds.), Handbook on Ontologies, Springer Verlag (2004) 117-132
12. Ehrig, M., Sure, Y.: Ontology Mapping – An Integrated Approach. Proceeding of the First European Semantic Web Symposium, ESWS 2004 Heraklion, Crete, Greece (2004).
13. Su, X., Gulla, J.A.: Semantic Enrichment for Ontology Mapping. F.Meziane, E. Metais (Eds.) : NLDB 2004, LNCS 3136 (2004) 217-228
14. Euzenat, J., Valtchev, P.: Similarity-Based Ontology Alignment in OWL-Lite. In the 16th European Conference on Artificial Intelligence, Valencia, Spain (2004)
15. Rada, R., Mili, H., Bicknell, E., Blettner, M.: Developement and Application of a Metric on Semantic Nets. IEEE Transactions on Systems, Man and Cybernetics 19(1) (1989) 17-30
16. Wu, Z., Palmer, M.: Verb Semantic and Lexical Selection. In Proceedings of the 32nd Annual Meeting of the Association for Computational Linguistic, Las Cruses, New Mexico (1994)
17. Jiang, J.J., Conrath, D.W.: Semantic Similarity Based on Corpus Statistics and Lexical Taxonomy. In Proceedings of the International Conference on Research in Computational Linguistic, Taiwan (1998)
18. Hirst, G., St-Onge, D.: Lexical Chains as Representations of Context for the Detection and Correction of Malapropisms. In Christiane Fellbaum (editor), WordNet: An Electronic Lexical Database, Cambridge, MA: The MIT Press (1998)
19. Tversky, A.: Features of Similarity. Psychological Review 84(4) (1977) 327-352
20. Rodriguez, M.A.: Assessing Semantic Similarity Among Entity Classes. Thèse de doctorat, University of Maine (2000)
21. Zurita, V.: Semantic-Based Approach to Spatial Data Sources Integration. PhD Thesis, Universitat Politecnica de Catalunya (2004)
22. Resnick, P.: Semantic Similarity in a Taxonomy: An Information-Based Measure and its Application to Problems of Ambiguity in Natural Language. Journal of Artificial Intelligence Research 11 (1999) 95-130
23. Seco, N., Veale, T.,Hayes, J.: An Intrinsic Information Content Metric for Semantic Similarity in WordNet. In Proceedings of ECAI 2004, the 16th European Conference on Artificial Intelligence (2004)
24. Gärdenfors, P.: Conceptual Spaces: The Geometry of Thought.Cambridge, MA, MIT Press (2000)
25. Schwering, A.: Hybrid Model for Semantic Similarity Measurement. OTM Conferences (2) (2005) 1449-1465
26. Salton, G., Buckley, C.: Improving Retrieval Performance by Relevance Feed-Back. Journal of the American Society for Information Science, Volume 14, Issue 4 (1990) 288-297
27. Knappe, R., Bulskov, H., Andreasen, T.: On Similarity Measures for Content-Based Querying. In O. Kaynak, editor, Proceedings of the 10th International Fuzzy Systems Association World Congress (IFSA'03), Instanbul, Turkey (2003) 400–403
28. Carbo-Dorca, R., Besalu. E.: A General Survey of Molecular Quantum Similarity. J. Mol. Struct-Theochem 451(1-2) (1998) 11-23

Query Approximation by Semantic Similarity in GeoPQL

Fernando Ferri[1], Anna Formica[2], Patrizia Grifoni[1], and Maurizio Rafanelli[2]

[1] IRPPS-CNR, via Nizza 128, 00198 Rome, Italy
fernando.ferri@irpps.cnr.it, patrizia.grifoni@irpps.cnr.it
[2] IASI-CNR, viale Manzoni 30, 00185 Rome, Italy
formica@iasi.cnr.it, rafanelli@iasi.cnr.it

Abstract. This paper proposes a method for query approximation in Geographical Information Systems. In our approach, queries are expressed by the Geographical Pictorial Query Language (GeoPQL), and query approximation is performed using *WordNet,* a lexical database for the English language available on the Internet. Due to the focus on geographical context, we address WordNet *partition taxonomies.* If a concept contained in a query has no match in the database, the query is approximated using the immediate superconcepts and subconcepts in the WordNet taxonomy, and their related degrees of similarity. Semantic similarity is evaluated using the *information content* approach, which shows a higher correlation with human judgment than the traditional similarity measures.

1 Introduction

A pictorial query on a geographical database allows the user to describe the configuration of the geographical objects of interest. When a query search condition does not match with those in the database, users would rather receive approximate answers by relaxing some constraints than no information at all. It would therefore be useful to obtain as answers not only configurations exactly matching the sketch representing the pictorial query, but also similar configurations obtained by relaxing some of the constraints in the pictorial query.

The most common approach for relaxing constraints is to measure the distance from the drawn query using criteria defined for the specific domain. Criteria for constraint selection generally involve the definition of weights assigned to the different types of constraints and, within these, to the specific constraint expressed in the query. This approach does not permit the selection or adaptation of criteria for relaxing constraints during query formulation, but the weights assigned to such constraints are defined *a priori*. In the case of pictorial queries on a geographical database, constraints can be classified as three main types: spatial, structural, and semantic. In this paper spatial constraints refer to the spatial relationships existing between geographical objects, structural constraints refer to the internal characteristics of geographical objects and semantic constraints refer to the concepts represented by the geographical objects. These types of constraints and how to relax them have been discussed in various papers in literature.

R. Meersman, Z. Tari, P. Herrero et al. (Eds.): OTM Workshops 2006, LNCS 4278, pp. 1670–1680, 2006.
© Springer-Verlag Berlin Heidelberg 2006

With reference to relaxing spatial constraints, in [1], [2] a computational model is defined for the similarity of the spatial relations by which to transform the pictorial query. This query, drawn by a sketch, can be represented as a semantic network of objects and the binary relations among them, where each object corresponds to one node. The oriented edges between two nodes correspond to the binary spatial relations. These papers consider five types of spatial relations: base topological binary, detailed topological binary, metric refining, base cardinal directions, and detailed cardinal directions. A weight for the possible relaxation of each relation is considered. The similarity between topological relations is described by the conceptual similarity graph, which links the most similar relations, defining the weight of each relaxation. The answers to queries made using a sketch are assigned a total score calculated by the computational model. Obviously, the user cannot restrict the spatial constraints to be relaxed.

Structural constraints can be relaxed by evaluating the similarity between geographical objects. As they are described by a set of attributes, a measure of the structural similarity of two geographical objects can be obtained by considering the similarity of their attributes, types and values [3]. This approach is frequently used to measure similarity starting from the attributes which describe the concept, and similarity of XML documents, whose structure is described by a tree.

Finally, the semantic constraint can be relaxed. This means that even if a concept expressed in the pictorial query is missing in the geographical database, it can be substituted with a similar concept which is present. We address this issue in this paper. In Geographical Information Systems (GISs) there is growing interest in semantic similarity, especially for the retrieval of geospatial data within heterogeneous databases, digital libraries and the World Wide Web [1]. A semantic similarity model facilitates the identification of objects that are conceptually close but not identical, and therefore supports information retrieval and integration. The goal of a similarity model is to obtain better and more flexible matches between user-expected and system-retrieved information. This paper proposes a method for query approximation in GISs. In our approach, queries are expressed by the Geographical Pictorial Query Language (GeoPQL) [4], and queries are approximated using the WordNet lexical database for the English language [5]. Due to the focus on geographical context, we address WordNet partition taxonomies. If a concept contained in a query has no match in the database, the query is approximated by providing the immediate superconcepts and subconcepts in the WordNet taxonomy, and their related degrees of similarity. The user can browse the taxonomy having access to the network of concepts. Others Ontologies closer than Wordnet to the database could be chosen by users in order to consider particular applications (application Ontologies), however for brevity sake they are not considered in this paper.

The semantic similarity of taxonomically related concepts has been widely investigated in the literature [2]. From the various proposals, we followed the probabilistic approach of [6], based on the notion of information content, which overcomes the drawbacks of the traditional edge-counting approach [13]. Note that the information content approach, originally introduced by Resnik [7][8], was conceived to compare concepts within Is-a hierarchies. The information content of a concept c quantifies as informativeness decreases when probability of the c concept increases [7].

Here, we propose to apply this method to *partition* hierarchies, due to the semantics of the meronymic relationship within the geographic context, referred to as "place-area" [9]. It essentially concerns parts which are similar to the whole and cannot be separated.

The paper is organized as follows: Section 2 examines some results from the Literature. Section 3 briefly introduces the pictorial query language GeoPQL and its algebra, and Section 4 discusses the evaluation of similarity when using GeoPQL to query geographical databases. Section 5 gives some examples of query approximation. Finally, Section 6 concludes and briefly describes our future research.

2 Related Works

Approximate queries were introduced to provide fast, approximate answers to complex aggregate queries in large data warehousing environments. There are several contexts in which an exact answer may not be required and a user prefers a fast, approximate answer, or the exact answer is not possible due to the unavailability of a concept involved in the query. In any case approximate query answers can be used to provide users with *sorting* mechanisms for answers. The problem was first studied to investigate techniques and strategies to reduce information in order to optimize access time and storage spaces, while continuing to give sufficiently meaningful answers.

The interest in approximate queries arises from both the need to optimize storage space and the need to provide answers for queries which involve unavailable information. In this paper, we consider the second issue, and discuss how users can relax constraints in order to obtain approximate answers. Literature papers have concentrated on processing issues for approximate queries. Barbará et al. [10] and Han and Kamber [11] have surveyed the various techniques and discussed their efficiency. The need to consider queries involving unavailable information requires the evaluation of similarity. When a query search condition cannot be matched in the database because a concept is missing (e.g. region), users would rather receive approximate answers through use of a similar concept (e.g. district) than no information at all.

Similarity is an important and widely used concept. Semantic similarity plays a significant role in GISs, as it supports the identification of objects that are conceptually close, but not equal. In particular in GISs Similarity spatial, temporal and structural dimension has to be considered in addition to the semantic one. For brevity sake this paper discusses semantic Similarity only. Spatial similarity referring to the spatial relationships existing between geographical objects has been presented in [12]. The problem of how to evaluate semantic similarity has been addressed by various authors at different times and from different points of view.

A natural way to compute semantic similarity in a taxonomy is to calculate the distance between the nodes corresponding to the items being compared (the shorter the path from one node to another, the more similar they are). For example, in [13] and in [14] the authors suggest that similarity in semantic networks can be thought of as involving just taxonomic (Is-a) links, to the exclusion of other link types. Distance-based measures of concept similarity assume that the domain is represented in a network, but such measures are not applicable if a collection of documents is not represented as a network. However, a known problem related to this approach is that in real taxonomies links do not generally represent uniform distances. For this reason in [6], [7], [8] measurement of semantic similarity in an Is-a taxonomy is based on the notion of information content. [7], [8] propose algorithms that take advantage of taxonomic similarity in resolving syntactic and semantic ambiguity. For instance, in [8] the author affirms that "semantic similarity represents a special case of semantic relatedness: for example, cars and gasoline would seem to be more closely related than, say, cars and bicycles, but the latter pair are certainly more similar." He also affirms that links such as Part-of can also be viewed as attributes that contribute to similarity (see also [15], [16]). In [6] the author investigates an information-theoretical definition of similarity that is applicable as a probabilistic model. The similarity measure is not directly stated as in earlier definitions; rather, it is derived from a set of assumptions, in the sense that if one accepts the assumptions, the similarity measure necessarily follows. He shows how his definition can be used to measure similarity in a number of different domains. He also demonstrates that this proposal can be used to derive a measure of semantic similarity between topics in an Is-a taxonomy. He briefly discusses these different points of view in relation to particular applications or domain models.

In [2] the authors present an approach to computing semantic similarity that relaxes the requirement of a single ontology and accounts for differences in the levels of explicitness and formalization of the different ontology specifications. A similarity function determines similar entity classes. Experimental results with different ontologies indicate that the model gives good results when ontologies have complete and detailed representations of entity classes. In [1] the same authors define the Matching-Distance Similarity Measure to determine semantic similarity among spatial entity classes, taking into account their distinguishing features (parts, functions, and attributes) and semantic interrelations (Is-a and Part-whole relations). Also from a spatial point of view, in [17] the authors discuss the need for semantic integration and present a prototype information source integration tool which focuses on schema integration of spatial databases. This tool recognizes the similarities and differences between the entities to be integrated. A domain-dependent ontology is created from the Federal Geographic Data Committee and domain-independent ontologies (Cyc and WordNet). The authors use a ratio model (ontology node distance) to assess similarities and differences between terms.

In [18] the authors distinguish between "tree-based similarity" and "graph-based similarity". The former starts from the idea that the information content of a class or topic t (or a concept c) is defined as -log p(t) (the probabilistic model as above), that is, as the probability of a concept increases, its informativeness decreases - therefore the more abstract a concept, the lower its information content, as also affirmed in [19]. The latter generalizes the tree-based similarity measure to exploit both the hierarchical and non-hierarchical components of an ontology. The proposed graph-based semantic similarity measure was applied to the Open Directory Project ontology. The described methodology to evaluate ranking algorithms based on semantic similarity can be applied to arbitrary combinations of ranking functions stemming from text analysis.

In [20] the author combines link and content analysis to estimate semantic similarity. The paper reports on the first attempt to approximate semantic associations by mining content and link information from billions of pairs on Web pages.

Other proposals are made in [21], where Dice and Cosine coefficients are proposed (even if they are applicable only when the objects are represented as numerical feature vectors), and in [22], where the authors investigate the idea of finding semantic similarity between search engine queries based on their temporal correlation and develop a method for efficiently finding the highest correlated queries for a given input query which uses far less space and time than the naïve approach.

3 GeoPQL

The Geographical Pictorial Query Language (GeoPQL), [4] allows the user to specify queries using *symbolic graphical objects (SGO)* that have the appearance of the three classic types of shapes: point, polyline and polygon. The user can assign each SGO with a semantic linked to the different kinds of information in the geographical database. Constraints can be imposed on both the attributes of the geographical data and their topological position and the query's target information (a specified layer or a set of layers) can be specified. Queries can thus be formulated by simply drawing a spatial representation of the SGO without the need to know a complex syntax or the database's structure. The GeoPQL algebra consists of 12 operators: Geo-union, Geo-difference, Geo-disjunction, Geo-touching, Geo-inclusion, Geo-crossing, Geo-pass-through, Geo-overlapping, Geo-equality, Geo-distance, Geo-any and Geo-alias. Geo-touching is equivalent to the *meet* operator, Geo-crossing refers to the crossing of two polylines, Geo-pass-through refers to a polyline which passes through a polygon, Geo-alias allows the same SGO to be duplicated in order to express the OR operator, and, finally, Geo-any permits any relationship between a pair of SGO to be considered valid, i.e. there is no constraint between the two SGO. This operator allows an unambiguous visual query to be obtained. For example, Figure 1 shows the following pictorial queries, Q1 and Q2:

Q1 "Find all the *Provinces* which are PASSED THROUGH by a *River*"
Q2 "Find all the *Regions* which are PASSED THROUGH by a *River* AND which OVERLAP a *Forest*".

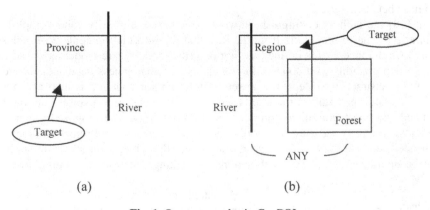

(a)   (b)

Fig. 1. Query examples in GeoPQL

4 Evaluating Similarity

Concept similarity in a taxonomy is evaluated according to the *information content* approach [6], originally introduced by Resnik [7]. This method has been already proposed within the geographic context in [3], to measure the similarity of GML elements. Note that this approach has been chosen because various results in the literature demonstrate that it has a higher correlation with human judgment than the traditional *edge counting* approach [13] [14]. The method's starting assumption is the association of weights with the taxonomy's concepts, which correspond to the probability that any instance belongs to the given concepts along the hierarchy. As already mentioned, in this paper we focus on *partition* taxonomies, as usually performed in the geographic context. The association of probabilities with the partition taxonomy allows us to introduce the notion of a *weighted partition taxonomy*. For instance, consider the subdivision of a *Location* into administrative boundaries such as *Countries*, and in turn, the subdivision of a *Country* into *Regions*, *States* or *Departments*, and so on. A fragment of this partition hierarchy as defined in the WordNet 2.1 lexical database for the English language [5] is shown in Figure 2. Probabilities have been evaluated according to the *frequencies* of concepts. For example, the concepts *Country*, *Region*, and *Province* are defined below, with their relative frequencies given in parentheses:

(276) Country -- the territory occupied by a nation;
(67)   Region -- the extended spatial location of something;
(4)   Province -- the territory occupied by one of the constituent administrative districts of a nation.

A concept's probability is calculated as its frequency divided by the total number of concepts in the taxonomy, which in the case of WordNet is 50,000. In this way we obtain the weighted partition taxonomy shown in Figure 2. Note that for concepts followed by the symbol *, a probability of 0.00001 has been assumed as the related frequencies are not specified in WordNet. A weighted partition taxonomy contains the most general concept, namely *Top*, whose probability is equal to 1.

In a weighted partition taxonomy, the information content of a concept c is defined as $-log\ p(c)$, that is, as the probability of a concept increases, its informativeness decreases, therefore the more abstract a concept, the lower its information content [19].

For instance, in Figure 2, *Region* is a more abstract concept than *Province*, and therefore has a higher probability (0.00134) than the latter (0.00008). As a result, the information content of *Region* ($log(0.00134) = 9.54$) is less than that of *Province* ($log(0.00008) = 13.61$).

According to [8], the similarity of concepts is given by the maximum information content they share; that is, the more information two concepts share, the more similar they are. Of course, if the taxonomy includes the least upper bound of the concepts, it provides the maximum information content that they share. Therefore, according to [6], the *information content similarity* (*ics*) is essentially defined as the maximum information content shared by the concepts divided by the information content of the compared concepts. For instance, consider the concepts *Province* and *County*. According to the probabilities shown in Figure 2, the following holds:

$$ics\ (Province,County) = 2\ logp(State)\,/\,(logp(Province) + logp(County)) =$$
$$2 * 7.52\,/\,(13.61 + 10.52) = 0.62.$$

Since *State* provides the maximum information content shared by *Province* and *County*, that is also their least upper bound in the taxonomy.

Note that according to the pure Resnik's approach, only the maximum information content shared by the concepts is addressed. For instance, the similarity between *Region* and *Department* coincides with that between *Region* and *State*, as both these pairs of concepts share the same maximum information content, that is provided by *Country*.

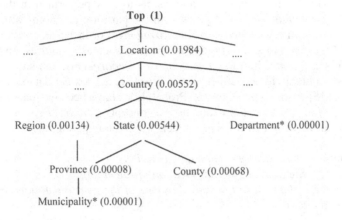

Fig. 2. Fragment of the weighted partition taxonomy of WordNet

Finally, consider the concepts *Province*, *Region* and *Municipality*. The following holds:

$$ics\ (Province,Region) = 2\ logp(Region)\,/\,(logp(Region) + logp(Province)) =$$
$$2 * 9.54\,/\,(9.54 + 13.61) = 0.82.$$

as *Region* is the maximum information content shared by *Region* and *Province*, and also their least upper bound in the taxonomy, and analogously:

$$ics\ (Province,Municipality) = 2\ logp(Province)\,/\,(logp(Municipality) +$$
$$logp(Province)) = 2 * 13.61\,/\,(16.61 + 13.61) = 0.90$$

as *Province* is the least upper bound of *Province* and *Municipality* in the taxonomy of Figure 2.

5   Query Approximation

As discussed in Section 3, the Geographical Pictorial Query Language (GeoPQL, [4]) allows the user to specify queries using *Symbolic Graphical Objects (SGOs)* that have the appearance of the three classic types of shapes: point, polyline and polygon. Each

SGO represents a specific concept in the geographical domain. A query in GeoPQL is represented by a set of SGOs, in which each SGO is described by a set of attributes defining its properties, and has a set of spatial relationships with each other SGO in the query. When a query cannot be matched within the database due to the absence of a concept represented by an SGO, approximate queries can be obtained by removing the constraint requiring the presence of the missing concept and considering queries in which the missing concept is replaced by a similar one as acceptable.

In GeoPQL a semantic slider is defined to select the concept closest to the missing concept and verify the query result. The semantic slider allows the concept taxonomy in Figure 2 to be navigated, highlighting the similarity between concepts. In this manner the user can evaluate different queries and choose the most appropriate.

For example suppose that GeoPQL is used to draw query Q1 in Section 3, i.e.:

Q1 "Find all the *Provinces* which are PASSED THROUGH by a *River*"

and suppose that the concept of Province is missing in the geographical database.

The semantic slider offers the possibility of approximating this query by accessing the hierarchy of Figure 2. In particular, by taking into account that the similarities (*ics*) between the concepts *Province* and *Region,* and *Province* and *Municipality* are respectively 0.82 and 0.90 (see Section 4), the previous query Q1 can be transformed into one of the following two queries Q3 and Q4:

Q3 "Find all the *Regions* which are PASSED THROUGH by a *River*"

Q4 "Find all the *Municipalities* which are PASSED THROUGH by a *River*"

In this manner, the missing concept is replaced by one of the two concepts which are immediately above and below it in the hierarchy and are present in the database.

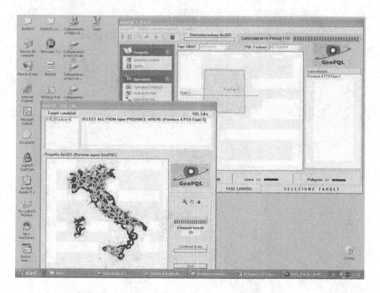

Fig. 3. Query result with the concept Province

The range of values of Q1 can also be evaluated using both Q3 and Q4, considering that "Region – Province – Municipality" is a partition hierarchy. In fact, the number of configurations satisfying Q1 is in the range of values of Q3 and Q4.

For example, consider a geographical database in which all three concepts are present. The "exact" answer to Q1 is "55", while the answers to the "approximate" queries Q3 and Q4 are respectively "14" and "699".

In this way, rather than giving no answer at all, GeoPQL provides a range of values which includes the correct answer. Figures 3, 4, and 5 show the above queries.

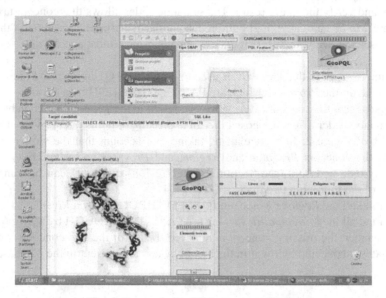

Fig. 4. Query result with the concept Region

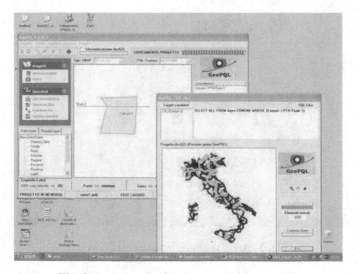

Fig. 5. Query result with the concept Municipality

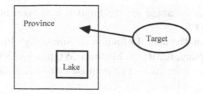

Fig. 6. The query Find all the *Provinces* which INCLUDE a *Lake*

Let us consider the query:
   Q5 "Find all the *Provinces* which INCLUDE a *Lake*" (Figure 6)
   Using the same procedure, i.e. changing from Province to Region and Municipality, the following queries Q6 and Q7 are provided:
   Q6 "Find all the *Regions* which INCLUDE a *Lake*"
   Q7 "Find all the *Municipalities* which INCLUDE a *Lake*".
In this case the results are 4 configurations for the query Q6, 0 for the query Q7, and 3 for the original query Q5.

6   Conclusion

This paper proposed an approach to relaxation of constraints to enable the approximation of query answers in Geographical Information Systems. It uses the similarity between concepts according to the WordNet hierarchy for geographic concepts. When a query involves information on a missing concept, the system provides approximate answers by using this hierarchy to select neighboring concepts. This approach enables the user to obtain both: 1) the number of objects giving an approximate answer, by considering similar concepts to the one missing in the hierarchy, and 2) a set of answers, from which the user can select the most relevant. We are now developing a new method for calculating the concept most similar to a missing concept, which involves the number of results for approximate queries on neighboring concepts in the WordNet hierarchy.

References

1. M.A.Rodriguez, M.J.Egenhofer "Comparing Geospatial Entity Classes: an Asymmetric and Content-Dependent Similarity Measure" International Journal of Geographical Information Science 18(3), pp. 229-256, 2004.
2. M.A.Rodriguez, M.J.Egenhofer "Determining Semantic Similarity among Entity Classes from Different Ontologies" IEEE Transactions on Knowledge and Data Engineering, Vol.15, n.2, pp. 442-456, 2003
3. F.Ferri, A. Formica, P. Grifoni, M.Rafanelli "Evaluating Semantic Similarity Using GML in Geographical Information Systems" OTM 2005 Workshops, Springer-Verlag Publ., LNCS n. 3762, pp.1009-1019, 2005
4. F.Ferri, M.Rafanelli "GeoPQL: a Geographical Pictorial Query Language that resolves ambiguities in query interpretation" Journal of Data Semantics, Springer-Verlag Publ., LNCS n. 3534, pp.50-80, 2005

5. WordNet 2.1: A lexical database for the English language; http://www.cogsci.princeton. edu/cgi-bin/webwn, 2005.
6. D.Lin "An Information-Theoretic Definition of Similarity" Proceed. 15th Intern. Conference on Machine Learning, ICML'98, Madison, WI, pp. 296-304, 1998
7. P.Resnik "Using information content to evaluate semantic similarity in a taxonomy" Proceed. IJCAI 1995
8. P.Resnik "Semantic similarity in a taxonomy: an information-based measure and its application to problems of ambiguity in natural language" Journal of Artificial Intelligence Research, Vol.11, pp. 95-130, 1999
9. V.C.Storey "Understanding Semantic Relationships" Very Large Data Bases Journal, Vol.2, pp. 455-488, 1993
10. Barbara, D., Faloutsos, C., DuMouchel, W., Haas, Hellerstein, P. J., J. M., Ioannidis, Y. E., Jagadish, H. V., Johnson, T., Ng, R. T., Poosala, V., Ross, K. A. and Sevcik, K. C., 1997, The New Jersey Data Reduction Report, IEEE Data Engineering Bulletin (1997), 20(4): 3-45.
11. Han, J., Kamber, M., 2001, Data Mining: concepts and techniques, Academic Press.
12. D'Ulizia, F. Ferri, P. Grifoni, M. Rafanelli, "Relaxing constraints on GeoPQL operators for improving query answering" 17th Intern. Conference on Data Base and Expert System Applications - DEXA '06, Springer-Verlag Publ., 2006.
13. J.H.Lee, M.H.Kim, Y.J.Lee "Information retrieval based on conceptual distance in is-a hierarchies" Journal of Documentation, Vol.49, n.2, pp.188-207, 1989
14. R.Rada, H.Mili, E.Bicknell, M.Blettner "Development and application of a metric on semantic nets" IEEE Transaction on Systems, Man, and Cybernetics, Vol.19, n.1, pp. 17-30, 1989
15. M.Sussna "Word sense disambiguation for free-text indexing using a massive semantic network" Proceed. Second Intern. Conference on Information and Knowledge Management (CIKM 93), Arlington, Virginia, 1993
16. R.Richardson, A.F.Smeaton, J.Murphy "Using WordNet as a knowledge base for measuring semantic similarity between words. Working paper CA-1294, Dublin City University, School of Computer Applications, Dublin, Ireland, 1994
17. V.Morocho, L.Perez-Vidal, F.Saltor "Semantic integration on spatial databases SIT-SD prototype" Proceed. Of VIII Jornadas de Ingenieria del Software y Bases de Datos, Alicante, Spain, pp. 603-612, Nov. 2003
18. A.G.Maguitman, F.Menczer, H.Roinestad, A.Vespignani "Algorithmic detection of semantic similarity", Intern. World Wide Web Conference Committee (IW3C2), WWW'05, Chiba, Japan, pp. 107-116, May 10-14, 2005
19. S.Ross. "A First Course in Probability. Macmillan", 1976.
20. F.Menczer "Combining link and content analysis to estimate semantic similarity" Intern. World Wide Web Conference, WWW'04, New York, USA, May 17-22, pp. 452-453, 2004
21. W.B.Frakes, R.Baeza-Yates Ed.s "Information Retrieval, Data Structure and Algorithms" Prentice Hall, 1992.
22. S.Chien, N.Immorlica "Semantic Similarity between Search Engine Queries using Temporal Correlation" Intern. World Wide Web Conference Committee (IW3C2), WWW'05, Chiba, Japan, pp. 2-11, May 10-14, 2005

Sim-DL: Towards a Semantic Similarity Measurement Theory for the Description Logic $\mathcal{ALCNR}$ in Geographic Information Retrieval

Krzysztof Janowicz

Institute for Geoinformatics
University of Muenster, Germany
janowicz@uni-muenster.de

Abstract. Similarity measurement theories play an increasing role in GIScience and especially in information retrieval and integration. Existing feature and geometric models have proven useful in detecting close but not identical concepts and entities. However, until now none of these theories are able to handle the expressivity of description logics for various reasons and therefore are not applicable to the kind of ontologies usually developed for geographic information systems or the upcoming geospatial semantic web. To close the resulting gap between available similarity theories on the one side and existing ontologies on the other, this paper presents ongoing work to develop a context-aware similarity theory for concepts specified in expressive description logics such as $\mathcal{ALCNR}$.

1 Introduction and Motivation

Within semantic-based geographic information systems and the upcoming geospatial semantic web, ontologies will play a crucial role in semi-automatic information retrieval, integration and concept matching. Two approaches turned out to be useful to support these tasks: subsumption reasoning and similarity measurement.

The idea behind subsumption-based retrieval as described by Lutz & Klien [1] is to rearrange a queried application ontology taking a search concept into account and to return a new taxonomy in which all subconcepts of the injected search phrase satisfy the user's requirements. However, using subsumption reasoning to query knowledge bases forces the user to ensure that the search concept is specified in a way that it is neither too generic and therefore at a top level of the new hierarchy nor too specific to get a sufficient result set. In fact the search concept is a formal description of the minimum characteristics all retrieved concepts need to share. Moreover no measurement structure is provided answering the question *which* of the returned concepts fits best. Yet this is not necessarily a critical point within this approach because all subconcepts at least share the demanded properties. In contrast, similarity computes the degree of overlap between search and compared-to concept and as measurement structure provides a (weak) order. Both characteristics turn out to be useful for information retrieval and matching scenarios: on the one hand the determination of conceptual overlap simplifies

R. Meersman, Z. Tari, P. Herrero et al. (Eds.): OTM Workshops 2006, LNCS 4278, pp. 1681–1692, 2006.

phrasing an adequate search concept and on the other hand the results are ordered by their degree of similarity to the *searched* concept. Similarity-based retrieval does not necessarily imply a subsumption relation between search and compared-to concept; in some cases even disjoint concepts may be similar to each other (e.g. Mother, Father). In opposite to subsumption-based retrieval, the search phrase typed into the system is not an artificial construct, but the concept the user is really looking for in the external ontology. The result set describes the measured overlap between compared concept descriptions without presuming that they share a specific property.

In other words the benefits similarity offers during the information retrieval phase, i.e. to deliver a flexible degree of conceptual overlap to a searched concept, stand against shortcomings during the usage of the retrieved information, namely that the results not *necessarily* fit the user's requirements. To make the difference between both approaches more evident (see figure 1), one could imagine a search phrase specified using a shared vocabulary to retrieve all concepts which's instances *overlap* with waterways. In contrast to the subsumption-based approach, similarity measurement will additionally deliver concepts which's instances are located *inside* or *adjacent* to waterways and indicate through a lesser degree of similarity that these concepts are close to, but not identical with the user's intended concept.

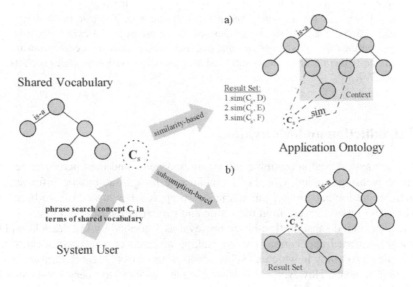

Fig. 1. Similarity (a) and subsumption (b) - based retrieval using a shared vocabulary

Similarity measurement has a long tradition in cognitive science and meanwhile also in computer science and has been applied to various information retrieval scenarios within GIScience for the last years [2-5]. An overview about existing similarity theories, their application areas and characteristics, is out of the scope of this paper and recently presented in [6, 7]. Instead we focus on briefly discussing why yet another similarity theory is necessary. Following the above argumentation, similarity supports users and software agents during information retrieval; however this presumes that the chosen similarity measure does not only satisfy the user's requirements, but also supports the representation language of the inspected ontology. It turns out that, besides the fact that several similarity theories make fundamentally different assumptions about how and *what* is measured (e.g. feature versus geometric model [6]), most of them come with their own proprietary knowledge representation format. In contrast, the majority of ontologies is specified using standardized or commonly agreed logic-based knowledge representation languages and especially various kinds of description logics. Without claiming that logic-based representation is *the* adequate tool for conceptualization and reasoning, we observe a gap between available similarity theories and existing ontologies which opposes a wider application of similarity measures as part of GIS or semantic-enabled web services in general.

In addition, several proprietary knowledge representation formats brought along with existing similarity theories lack of a formal semantic and language constructs proven to be useful for conceptualization, such as disjunction, negation, value and existential restrictions, number restrictions (cardinalities) and roles (binary predicates) in general. This is a crucial point because, at least in computer science, the concepts between which similarity is measured are *representations*[1] of the concepts in our minds. Consequently, the lack of a precise and expressive representation language has impact on the quality of the resulting similarity assessments as discussed in [8] for the lightweight ontology underlying the feature-based MDSM theory [4]. The same arguments hold for geometric approaches to similarity, based on Gärdenfors' [9] idea of conceptual spaces. To integrate relations and hence improve the expressivity of conceptual spaces for similarity measures, Schwering [10] for instance combines the geometric approach with classical network models.

In comparison to independently developed similarity theories for logic-based knowledge representation, such as discussed in [11] for similarity between web services or an approach to measure maximum dissimilarity between concepts represented in $\mathcal{ALC}$ [12], the theory introduced within this paper measures the overall similarity for the high expressive description logic $\mathcal{ALCNR}$. Moreover it supports a (basic) notion of context and conceptual neighborhood models, which are necessary to handle spatial and temporal relations. However, as will be discussed in the future work section, to capture the full extent of geospatial knowledge, even more expressive description logics are necessary [13]. For further work concerning similarity measures between logic-based representations see also [14, 15].

2 Syntax and Semantics of $\mathcal{ALCNR}$

This section gives a brief insight into syntax and semantics of the description logic used as concept representation language within this paper. $\mathcal{ALCNR}$ is an expressive description logic that supports intersection, union, full existential quantification, value restriction, full negation and number restrictions to inductively construct complex concept descriptions out of primitive concepts and roles (binary predicates). In the following sections the letters A and B are used to represent atomic concepts, R and S

---

[1] This is, at the same time, one of the reasons why we do not claim that the presented similarity theory is necessarily cognitive adequate; however due to lack of space this is not discussed here in detail.

for roles and C and D for complex (composed) concepts, while X and Y denote that a given formula can be applied to all of them. Additional background information about $\mathcal{ALCNR}$ and related description logics is discussed in [16].

Before similarity can be computed, the compared (complex) concepts have to be rephrased to the following $\mathcal{ALCNR}$ disjunctive normal form [17]: A concept description C is in normal form *iff* $C = \top$, $C = \bot$ or $C = C_1 \sqcup ... \sqcup C_n$ and each C_i (i= 1,...n) is of the form:

$$C_i := \prod_{A \in \mathrm{primitive}(C_i)} A \sqcap \prod_{R \in N_R} \left(\prod_{C' \in \mathrm{exists}_R(C_i)} (\exists R.C') \sqcap \forall R.\mathrm{forall}_R(C_i) \sqcap (\geq \min_R(C_i)R) \sqcap (\leq \max_R(C_i)R) \right)$$

The set *primitive(C)* represents all (negated) primitives (and absurdity) at the top-level of C. N_R is the set of available roles, and $exists_R(C)$ denotes the set of all C' for which there exists $\exists R.C'$ on the top-level of C. $forall_R(C)$ denotes the intersection of concepts $(C_1 \sqcap ... \sqcap C_n)$ derived by merging all value restriction for the role R ($\forall R.C_i$) on the top level of C. $min_R(C)$ and $max_R(C)$ represent the minimum and maximum cardinalities for the role R on the top-level of C. Complex roles are in conjunctive normal form ($R = R_1 \sqcap ... \sqcap R_n$) where each R_i is primitive. Note that the concepts $forall_R(C_i)$ and C' are again in $\mathcal{ALCNR}$ normal form.

Table 1. Syntax and semantics of $\mathcal{ALCNR}$ [16, 17]

Syntax	Semantics	Description
A	$A^{\mathcal{I}} \subseteq \Delta^{\mathcal{I}}$	atomic concept
R	$R^{\mathcal{I}} \subseteq \Delta^{\mathcal{I}} \times \Delta^{\mathcal{I}}$	atomic role
$\top$	$\Delta^{\mathcal{I}}$	Totality
$\bot$	$\varnothing$	Absurdity
$\neg C$	$\Delta^{\mathcal{I}} \setminus C^{\mathcal{I}}$	full negation
$C \sqcap D$	$C^{\mathcal{I}} \cap D^{\mathcal{I}}$	conjunction (intersection)
$C \sqcup D$	$C^{\mathcal{I}} \cup D^{\mathcal{I}}$	disjunction (union)
$\forall R(C)$	$\{ x \in \Delta^{\mathcal{I}} \mid \forall y. (x, y) \in R^{\mathcal{I}} \rightarrow y \in C^{\mathcal{I}} \}$	value restriction
$\exists R(C)$	$\{ x \in \Delta^{\mathcal{I}} \mid \exists y. (x, y) \in R^{\mathcal{I}} \wedge y \in C^{\mathcal{I}} \}$	existential quantification
$(\leq n\,R)$	$\{ x \in \Delta^{\mathcal{I}} \mid |\{y : (x, y) \in R^{\mathcal{I}} \}| \leq n \}$	number restrictions
$(\geq n\,R)$	$\{ x \in \Delta^{\mathcal{I}} \mid |\{y : (x, y) \in R^{\mathcal{I}} \}| \geq n \}$	$(n \in \mathbb{N})$
$R \sqcap S$	$R^{\mathcal{I}} \cap S^{\mathcal{I}}$	role conjunction

To ensure that the semantic similarity measure is not influenced by syntactic form, rewriting rules as discussed in [17, 18] have to be applied in order to get a canonical representation of the compared concepts. On the one hand these rewriting rules map between equivalent expressions such as $\forall R(\bot)$ and $(\leq 0\ R)$; on the other hand they make sure that only such descriptions are used within concept specifications that (by definition) have impact on the cardinality of the regarded sets.

3 Scenario

This section describes a simplified concept matching scenario to which SIM-DL is applied afterwards. Both the presented scenario and the introduced conceptualizations are intended to briefly demonstrate the abilities *and* shortcomings of the theory instead of trying to develop a meaningful and sound application ontology.

We assume that a European lodging portal on the internet is providing information about accommodations in touristy attractive cities. To avoid maintenance costs, the service provider does not store the information in a local database but dynamically connects to external (geo) web services. However to offer a consistent interface and vocabulary to the portal users, the service provides an own categorization. To do so, the types of accommodations distinguished in the external services have to be mapped to the local terminology. One of the external services, delivering information about accommodations in Amsterdam, provides separate conceptualizations for houseboats and botels[2] while the local knowledge base does not make this distinction.

The task of similarity measurement within this scenario is to propose whether botels should be displayed as hotels or houseboats within the local terminology presented to the system users. The service provider therefore runs a similarity query using the external Botel conceptualization as search phrase (C_s) and Housing as context (C_{lcs}) (see section 4).

Table 2. Conceptualizations for the accommodation service scenario

User defined context (C_{lcs}) and search concept (C_s)
$C_{lcs} \equiv$ Housing
$C_s \equiv$ Boat $\sqcap$ Hotel (E) $\sqcap \exists$inside(Waterway) $\sqcap \forall$inside(Waterway) $\sqcap (\leq 1$ inside)
Concepts/roles defined within the scenario
House $\equiv$ Building $\sqcap$ Housing
Hotel (E)$\equiv$ Housing $\sqcap \exists$offer(Room) $\sqcap \exists$serviceType(Service)
Hotel $\equiv$ House $\sqcap \exists$offer(Room) $\sqcap \exists$ serviceType (Service)
Youth_Hostel $\equiv$ Building $\sqcap$ Housing $\sqcap \exists$serviceType (Service $\sqcup$ SelfService) $\sqcap \exists$offer(Room)
Botel (E) $\equiv$ Boat $\sqcap$ Hotel (E) $\sqcap \exists$inside(Waterway) $\sqcap \forall$inside(Waterway) $\sqcap (\leq 1$ inside)
Houseboat $\equiv$ Boat $\sqcap$ Housing $\sqcap \exists$inside(Waterway) $\sqcap \exists$serviceType(SelfService) $\sqcap \forall$inside(Waterway) $\sqcap (\leq 1$ inside)
Cargo_Ship $\equiv$ Boat $\sqcap$ Storage $\sqcap \exists$inside(Waterway) $\sqcap (\leq 1$ inside)

To avoid debating fundamental difficulties in ontology matching[3], we assume that all services share a common base vocabulary for their primitives (such as described in [1] and depicted in figure 1). Note that the accessory (E) in table 2 denotes concepts from the external service. Moreover for reasons of readability and simplification, the concepts in table 2 are not expanded to their full normal form and those only appearing on the right hand side are assumed to be primitives.

---

[2] For instance: Hotel Amstel Botel Amsterdam: http://www.amstelbotel.nl/
[3] However we claim that also complex ontology matching tasks benefit from the idea of similarity measurement as demonstrated in [15].

4 SIM-DL

This section stepwise defines a context-aware and directed similarity measure for DL concepts applicable to information retrieval and matching scenarios. As the presented theory combines ideas from feature and network (distance) -based similarity models, conceptual commonalities and differences to existing approaches are pointed out.

In SIM-DL, similarity between concepts in normal form is measured by comparing their $\mathcal{ALCNR}$ descriptions for overlap, where a high level of overlap indicates high similarity and vice versa. As in description logics, (complex) concepts are specified out of primitive concepts and roles using given language constructors (see table 1), similarity is defined as polymorph, binary and real-valued function $\mathbf{X} \times \mathbf{Y} \rightarrow \mathbf{R}[0,1]$ providing implementations for all language constructs offered by the used description logic. The overall similarity between concepts is just the normalized (and weighted) sum of the single similarities calculated for all parts of the concept descriptions. A similarity value of 1 indicates that compared concept descriptions are equal whereas 0 implies total dissimilarity. In the following σ denotes the normalization factor while ω is used to represent weightings. Note however, that for reasons of readability and clarity of the presented equations only the weighting on disjunction level is discussed here in more detail[4]. Additional weightings, responsible for the balance between roles and fillers (range-concepts) or between several kinds of restrictions, are discussed in the further work section.

First of all, to measure similarity it has to be determined which parts of the concept descriptions (specified by the same language constructor) are compared to each other. To do so, the similarity for each element from the Cartesian product $X \times Y$ (for a certain constructor on the same level of the normal form) is measured. From the resulting set of tuples, those with the highest similarity value are chosen for further computation; where each X respectively Y is only selected once. In other words, for *each* part of the search concept's description, a counterpart from the compared-to concept's description is chosen in a way that the most similar parts are compared and each expression is only examined once. In the following the set of selected pairs is marked by the letter S followed by an abbreviation for the considered constructor.

The presented similarity theory is directed, i.e. asymmetric [4], in a sense that the resulting overall similarity depends on the search direction. Therefore sim(X, Y) is not necessarily equal to sim(Y, X). While each part of the search concept's description is compared to a counterpart from the compared-to concept, some parts of the latter may not be taken into account for comparison. This is always the case if the compared-to concept is specified by more expressions than the search concept. The similarity for these remaining parts is 0 while they do not increase the normalization factor σ. If however the search concept is described by more elements than can be compared, the similarity for these parts is also 0, but σ is increased by 1 for each remaining part. As result the overall similarity is decreased. In other words, if the examined concept in the application ontology is more specific than requested by the user

---

[4] This weighting is mandatory in a sense that leaving it aside would violate the idea of disjunction; however we do not claim that it is more important for overall similarity than the additional weightings discussed in the further work section.

(via the search concept) this has no impact on the measured overall similarity[5]. On the other side similarity decreases if the user's search concept is more specific than its counterpart in the queried ontology (see also [7]). Defining similarity as ratio between common and available (i.e. shared and distinguishing) parts of considered concept descriptions makes the presented approach comparable to the feature-based MDSM approach [4] and also the Lin's similarity theorem [19]. Note however that in fact SIM-DL compares formal set restrictions, not features (see section 5).

In the previous sections (see also figure 1) context was described as component of similarity-based retrieval. The idea underlying context (first integrated into geospatial similarity measures by Rodríguez & Egenhofer [4]) is on the one hand to determine which parts from the application ontology have to be compared to the search concept and on the other hand to influence the measured similarity making it situation-aware. Within SIM-DL, context is used to *combine* the benefits of subsumption reasoning and similarity-based retrieval (see section 1). Context is defined as a set of concepts from the application ontology that, after reclassification (comparable to the Lutz & Klien approach [1]), are subconcepts of C_{lcs}[6]: (Context = {C| C $\sqsubseteq$ C_{lcs}}). C_{lcs} itself is specified by the user together with the search concept (C_s) in terms of the shared vocabulary. In other words, context determines the universe of discourse (called application domain in [4]). In the presented accommodation scenario C_{lcs} ensures that all concepts proposed to be similar to Botel at least act as accommodations (subconcepts of Housing). Therefore similarity to cargo ships would not be measured, although they are kinds of boats as well (see table 2).

To compute overall similarity (sim_u) between two concepts C and D in $\mathcal{ALCNR}$ normal form, the similarity between the disjunctions $C_1 \sqcup ... \sqcup C_n$ and $D_1 \sqcup ... \sqcup D_m$ has to be measured according to equation 1. Simplifying one may argue that this is the maximum similarity occurring during the cross comparison of involved C_i to D_j, which is not the case, because this measure would reflect the maximum possible similarity occurring between certain individuals, but not the overall tendency. Instead, similarity is calculated for each element of SI (the set of tuples (C_i, D_j) chosen for comparison) and weighted (ω) according to their probability. Note that each C_i and D_j is formed by intersection (see $\mathcal{ALCNR}$ normal form) and their similarity is therefore measured by sim_i and described below (see equation 2).

$$sim_u(C, D) = \sum_{(C_i, D_j) \in SI} \omega_{ij} * sim_i(C_i, D_j) \qquad (1)$$

The weighting ω on disjunction level becomes necessary because, in contrast to intersection, each individual that is member of a concept formed by disjunction can be member of all its single concepts or only of some of them. Consequently overall similarity cannot simply be the sum of the similarities between compared C_i and D_j and hence ω acts as adjustable factor for their relative importance. Note that the sum of all ω is always 1. Depending on application area and search strategy, ω can be computed out of the set cardinality (A-Box) of all involved concept on disjunction level, using

---

[5] Note however, that while directed similarity fits the requirements of information retrieval [7], other tasks may benefit from default similarity [6] which can be achieved by setting the normalization factor (independently of the direction) to the number of selected pairs.

[6] The abbreviation was chosen to refer to the idea of the least common subsumer in DL [16].

probability assumptions (A&T-Box), or from the structure of the examined ontology (T-Box) (see [16] about A-Box and T-Box). The weighted similarities can then be amalgamated the same way as for the intersection constructor.

$$\mathrm{sim}_i(C, D) =$$

$$\frac{1}{\sigma}\left(\sum_{(A,B)\in SP} \mathrm{sim}_p(A, B) + \sum_{(R,S)\in SE} \mathrm{sim}_e(\mathrm{exists}_R(C), \mathrm{exists}_S(D)) + \sum_{(R,S)\in SF} \mathrm{sim}_f(\mathrm{forall}_R(C), \mathrm{forall}_S(D)) \right.$$

$$\left. + \sum_{(R,S)\in SMIN} \mathrm{sim}_m(\mathrm{min}_R(C), \mathrm{min}_S(D_j)) + \sum_{(R,S)\in SMAX} \mathrm{sim}_m(\mathrm{max}_R(C), \mathrm{max}_S(D))\right) \qquad (2)$$

On the level of intersection, similarity between two (complex) concepts is the sum of similarities derived from mutually comparing their primitive concepts as well as those formed by existential, value and number restrictions/quantification (see equation 2). In addition to the symbols introduced before, the normalization factor σ is defined as the sum of cardinalities derived from the sets of compared tuples (SP, SE, SF, SMIN and SMAX). Consequently the possible results of sim_i range between 0 and 1.

$$\mathrm{sim}_p(A, B) = \frac{|\{C \,|\, (C \sqsubseteq A) \sqcap (C \sqsubseteq B)\}|}{|\{C \,|\, (C \sqsubseteq A) \sqcup (C \sqsubseteq B)\}|} \qquad (3)$$

As for primitive concepts[7], similarity cannot be computed as degree of overlap between their descriptions, it has to be determined according to equation 3. SIM-DL considers primitives the more similar, the more common defined concepts both subsume. To be more precise, similarity between primitives is expressed as the ratio between the number of subconcepts of both primitives and the number of subconcepts of one or both of them determined in a given context. However this approach resembles Tversky's ratio model [20] and MDSM [4], it is not asymmetric because this would require a subconcept relationship between A and B or to a common superconcept which is per definition not the case for primitives. Moreover not features in the sense of attributes, functions or parts [4], but subconcepts are compared.

$$\mathrm{sim}_e(\mathrm{exists}_R(C), \mathrm{exists}_S(D)) = \mathrm{sim}_r(R, S) * \sum_{(C'_i, D'_j)\in SE} \mathrm{sim}_u(C'_i, D'_j) \qquad (4)$$

$$\mathrm{sim}_f(\mathrm{forall}_R(C), \mathrm{forall}_S(D)) = \mathrm{sim}_r(R, S) * \mathrm{sim}_u(\mathrm{forall}_R(C), \mathrm{forall}_S(D)) \qquad (5)$$

$$\mathrm{sim}_m(m_R(C), m_S(D)) = \mathrm{sim}_r(R, S) * \left(1 - \frac{|m_R(C) - m_S(D)|}{m_{RS}(\mathrm{total})}\right) \qquad (6)$$

Equation 4, 5 and 6 show how similarity is measured between restrictions and between quantifications. To determine the overlap both parts, the involved roles and the involved fillers (respectively cardinalities) have to be taken into account. Note that $forall_R(C_i)$ and C' are again in normal form (see section 2) while $m_R(C)$ and $m_S(D)$ are numbers restricting the max/min occurrence or the roles R respectively S. In addition to already introduced symbols, sim_r denotes the similarity between roles while m acts as abbreviation for *min* respectively *max*, indicating that the same equation is applied

---

[7] Per definition primitive concepts (also called base symbols) are those which *only* occur on the right hand side of axioms.

for both cases. m_{RS}(total) denotes the highest maximum (respectively minimum) cardinality for the roles R or S in the user defined context. In other words, similarity between number restrictions depends on their relative distance, where m_{RS}(total) reflects the notion of universe in statistics. While the similarity sim_r for primitive roles can be measured following the ideas introduced for primitive concepts (see equation 3), similarity between roles formed by intersection or situated in conceptual neighborhoods is computed according to equation 7 and 8.

$$sim_{ri}(R,S) = \frac{1}{\sigma} \sum_{(R',S') \in SRI} sim_r(R',S')$$ (7)

$$nsw(R,S) = \frac{max\_distance - edge\_distance(R,S)}{max\_distance}$$ (8)

$\mathcal{ALCNR}$ supports the composition of roles by intersection, consequently every (complex) role can be expanded to an intersection of primitive roles and hence similarity can be understood as the sum of the similarities for mutually compared (SRI) primitive roles from R and S (sim_{ri}; equation 7). The normalization factor σ becomes necessary to ensure that the derived inter-role similarity ranges between 0 and 1 and can be integrated as part for the similarity measures introduced for restrictions and quantifications.

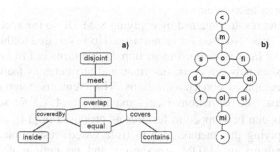

Fig. 2. a) Topological neighborhood [21] b) Temporal-(C) neighborhood [22][8]

Conceptual neighborhoods, such as the topological and temporal depicted in figure 2, are of major importance within GIScience. Per definition one of the benefits of neighborhood models is that they come with an own, straightforward notion of similarity which can be directly integrated as so-called network approach (see also [2, 10]) into SIM-DL. The neighborhood similarity weighting (nsw; equation 8) is defined in terms of edge distance between compared roles (shortest path) and maximum distance within the graph. This approach is comparable to the distance measure by Rada et al. [23]. The edge weightings used for determining distance depend on the neighborhood and even do not need to be symmetric. However they are assumed to be constantly 1 here. Within SIM-DL, nsw can be applied in place of or jointly with sim_{ri} (sim_r). For complex similarity measures between spatial scenes see [21, 24].

---

[8] [20] introduces three different graphs (A, B and C) for temporal neighborhood, which is not discussed here in detail.

5 Discussion and Further Work

Applying SIM-DL to the accommodation scenario in section 3 yields that Botel is more similar to Houseboat than to Hotel or Youth_Hotel (see table 3) and therefore the service provider can also display botels on the web portal whenever users are searching for houseboats in Amsterdam. Note that in contrast to subsumption-based retrieval the resulting similarities cannot be used to align the concept Botel within the local knowledge base. For instance the definition of Botel is also similar to the local Hotel concept; however a botel is not a building and therefore not a special case (i.e. a subconcept) of a hotel.

Table 3. Measured similarities for the concepts compared in the accommodation scenario

sim(C$_s$, Hotel)	sim(C$_s$, Houseboat)	sim(C$_s$, Youth_Hostel)
0.5	0.66	0.41

Moreover it has to be emphasized again that similarity in computer science measures overlap between representations. An application ontology about vessels would focus on other aspects then the accommodation ontology and hence the resulting similarities would be different. This is not a shortcoming of the presented theory, but an indicator for the situated nature of conceptualization [25] and hence the importance of context for similarity assessments.

In addition to the results obtained by applying SIM-DL to the accommodation scenario, MDSM[4][9] was also used for comparison. However, due to the different representation languages (and as claimed in section 1) this turns out to be a difficult task. MDSM distinguishes between parts, functions and attributes as features (i.e. characteristics) of the compared conceptualizations. The elements compared by SIM-DL however are formal set restrictions (see semantics of $\mathcal{ALCNR}$; section 2). While primitive concepts can be mapped to features as proposed in [14], the author is very skeptic about applying this method also to (role based) restrictions and quantifications, because features in MSDM are synsets and no notion of fillers or partial matches is defined (see [8]). Specifying the feature *inside* within a concept description in MDSM means that all its instances are inside something, which is not the case for $\forall inside(\top)$ or $\forall inside(\text{Waterway})$. Moreover basing on Tversky's ratio model, MDSM regards concepts as bags of features and therefore it is no clear how to integrate disjunction ($\sqcup$) into this approach.

Nevertheless the comparison between SIM-DL and MDSM points out an interesting aspect of the presented approach: If several constructors (for the same role) are necessary to restrict an intended set (such as for *inside* in table 2) this has multiple impact on the measured similarity[10]. This is not problematic from a set theoretic point of view, but not the way humans think about similarity (see also remark in section 1).

Although by integrating measures for role-based constructors, role intersection and neighborhoods, SIM-DL meets the demands claimed for modern inter-concept

---

[9] The same remarks also count for Tversky's ratio model.

[10] Note however that the redundant definitions for *inside* in table 2 are captured by the rewriting rules for the canonical normal form.

similarity theories [4, 7, 8], the presented approach is still in progress and a lot of work remains to be done: In addition to the weighting introduced on disjunction level, further weightings should be integrated into SIM-DL to balance the importance between roles and fillers for existential quantification (or value restrictions). However, defining sim_e as weighted sum of role and filler similarity raises the question how such weightings should be derived and whether the role or filler part of an existential quantification is more or less important for sim_e (and therefore overall similarity). Additional weightings should also determine the relative importance of language constructs. In terms of the presented scenario, the level of information about botels provided by ∃inside(Waterway) is higher than (≤ 1 inside), because the last mentioned expression only stats that a botel is at most inside (2D) one thing. Further work has to examine whether these weightings can be (semi)-automatically derived from the context, the kind of chosen description logic and canonical form. The integration of *Inference based Information Value* [11] and other information-theoretic approaches [19] into SIM-DL seems to be a promising approach.

Moreover, until now SIM-DL does not support cyclic concept definitions. To overcome this shortage, techniques such as fixpoint semantics have to be integrated into the theory. Additional work is necessary to develop similarity theories for even more expressive description logics (such as $\mathcal{ALCRP(D)}$ [13]), especially focusing on full qualifying number restrictions and concrete domains. In terms of the presented scenario this would allow to express *how* near something is to a waterway instead of merely distinguishing between inside, meet and overlap. Finally computation time is a critical aspect (especially for the Cartesian products) to be examined in more detail.

References

1. Lutz, M. and E. Klien, *Ontology-Based Retrieval of Geographic Information.* International Journal of Geographical Information Science, 2006. **20**(3): p. 233-260.
2. Janowicz, K., *Towards a Similarity-Based Identity Assumption Service for Historical Places*, in *Geographic Information Science - Fourth International Conference, GIScience 2006.Lecture Notes in Computer Science 4197*, M. Raubal, et al., Editors. forthcoming 2006, Springer: Berlin, Germany.
3. Raubal, M., *Formalizing Conceptual Spaces*, in *Formal Ontology in Information Systems, Proceedings of the Third International Conference (FOIS 2004)*, A. Varzi and L. Vieu, Editors. 2004, IOS Press: Amsterdam, NL. p. 153-164.
4. Rodríguez, A.M. and M.J. Egenhofer, *Comparing Geospatial Entity Classes: An Asymmetric and Context-Dependent Similarity Measure.* International Journal of Geographical Information Science, 2004. **18**(3): p. 229-256.
5. Schwering, A. and M. Raubal, *Measuring Semantic Similarity between Geospatial Conceptual Regions*, in *First International Conference on GeoSpatial Semantics, GeoS 2005, Mexico City, Mexico.* 2005, Springer-Verlag: Berlin. p. 90-106.
6. Goldstone, R. and J. Son, *Similarity*, in *Cambridge Handbook of Thinking and Reasoning*, K. Holyoak and R. Morrison, Editors. 2004, Cambridge University Press: Cambridge.
7. Schwering, A., *Semantic Similarity Measurement including Spatial Relations for Semantic Information Retrieval of Geo-Spatial Data.* (submitted 2006): Institute for Geoinformatics, University of Münster, Germany, PhD Thesis.

8. Janowicz, K., *Extending Semantic Similarity Measurement by Thematic Roles*, in *First International Conference on GeoSpatial Semantics, GeoS 2005, Mexico City, Mexico*. 2005, Springer Verlag: Berlin. p. 137-152.

9. Gärdenfors, P., *Conceptual Spaces - The Geometry of Thought*. 2000, Cambridge, MA: Bradford Books, MIT Press. 307.

10. Schwering, A. *Hybrid Model for Semantic Similarity Measurement*. in *4th International Conference on Ontologies, DataBases, and Applications of Semantics (ODBASE05)*. 2005. Agia Napa, Cyprus: Springer.

11. Hau, J., W. Lee, and J. Darlington. *A Semantic Similarity Measure for Semantic Web Services*. in *Web Service Semantics Workshop 2005 at WWW2005*. 2005. Chiba, Japan.

12. d'Amato, C., N. Fanizzi, and F. Esposito. *A Semantic Dissimilarity Measure for Concept Descriptions in Ontological Knowledge Bases* in *The Second International Workshop on Knowledge Discovery and Ontologies*. 2005. Porto, Portugal.

13. Möller, R., *Expressive Description Logics: Foundations for Practical Applications*. Habilitation Thesis. 2001, University of Hamburg, Computer Science Department, Germany.

14. Borgida, A., T.J. Walsh, and H. Hirsh. *Towards Measuring Similarity in Description Logics*. in *International Workshop on Description Logics (DL2005)*. 2005. Edinburgh, Scotland.

15. Ehrig, M., et al. *Similarity for Ontologies - A Comprehensive Framework*. in *13th European Conference on Information Systems*. 2005. Regensburg, Germany.

16. Baader, F. and W. Nutt, *Basic Description Logics*, in *The Description Logic Handbook*, D.C. F. Baader, D.L. McGuinness, D. Nardi, P.F. Patel-Schneider, Editor. 2002, Cambridge University Press: Cambridge p. 47-100.

17. Brandt, S., R. Küsters, and A.Y. Turhan, *Approximating ALCN-Concept Descriptions*, in *Proceedings of the 2002 International Workshop on Description Logics*. 2002.

18. Molitor, R., *Structural Subsumption for ALN. LTCS-Report 98-03, LuFG Theoretical Computer Science, RWTH Aachen, Germany*. 1998.

19. Lin, D., *An information-theoretic definition of similarity*, in *Proceedings of the Fifteenth International Conference on Machine Learning*. 1998, Morgan Kaufmann, San Francisco, CA. p. 296-304.

20. Tversky, A., *Features of Similarity*. Psychological Review, 1977. **84**(4): p. 327-352.

21. Bruns, T.H. and M.J. Egenhofer, *Similarity of Spatial Scenes*, in *Seventh International Symposium on Spatial Data Handling (SDH '96)*, M.-J. Kraak and M. Molenaar, Editors. 1996: Delft, Netherlands. p. 31-42.

22. Freksa, C., *Temporal Reasoning Based on Semi-Intervals*. Artificial Intelligence, 1992. **54**(1): p. 199-227.

23. Rada, R., et al., *Development and Application of a Metric on Semantic Nets*. IEEE Transaction on Systems, Man, and Cybernetics, 1989. **19**(1): p. 17-30.

24. Li, B. and F.T. Fonseca, *TDD - A Comprehensive Model for Qualitative Spatial Similarity Assessment*. Spatial Cognition and Computation, 2006. **6**(1): p. 31-62.

25. Barsalou, L., *Situated simulation in the human conceptual system*. Language and Cognitive Processes, 2003. **5**(6): p. 513-562.

A Primer of Geographic Databases Based on Chorems

Robert Laurini, Françoise Milleret-Raffort, and Karla Lopez

LIRIS, INSA de Lyon, F-69621 Villeurbanne
Robert.Laurini@insa-lyon.fr, Francoise.Raffort@insa-lyon.fr,
Karla.Lopez@insa-lyon.fr

Abstract. The goal of this paper is not to present outcomes of research, but rather present a new research plan in the use of chorems in geographic information systems. Created by R. Brunet, chorems are a schematic representation of a territory. Presently, geographic decision-makers are not totally satisfied by conventional cartography, essentially because they want to know where and what are the problems. And so chorems appear as an interesting approach to unveil geographic problems, and so to help decision makers understand their territory, their structure and their evolution. After having given the definition and presented some applications of chorems, we show how chorems can be discovered by spatial data mining, can help decision making, and also how chorem maps can be a novel approach to visually entry a geographic database or datawarehouse. Comparing with the Ben Shneiderman's approach, chorems can give an overview of the territory; then by zooming and filtering, and sub-chorem maps can be generated for smaller territories. Finally a list of barriers to overcome is given as main landmarks for a new research program in order to design new kind of geographic information systems or spatial decision support systems.

Keywords: chorems, spatial data mining, geographic databases, geographic datawarehouses, geographic knowledge, GIS, visual entry system, research plan.

1 Objectives and Organisation of the Paper

Chorems were created in 1980 by Pr. Roger Brunet, a French geographer. They are a schematic representation of a territory. This word comes from the Greek chôra which means space, territory. It is not a raw simplification of the reality, but rather aims at representing the whole complexity with simple geometric shapes. Even if it looks a simplification, the chorem tries to represent the structure and the evolution of a territory with a rigorous manner.

The basis of a chorem is in general a geometric shape in which some other shapes symbolize the past and current mechanisms. Brunet has proposed a table of 28 elementary chorems, each of them representing an elementary spatial configuration, and so allowing them to represent various spatial phenomena at different scales. According to Brunet, chorems are a tool among other to model the reality, but it is a very precious tool not only as a visual system, but also as a spatial analysis tool.

R. Meersman, Z. Tari, P. Herrero et al. (Eds.): OTM Workshops 2006, LNCS 4278, pp. 1693–1702, 2006.
© Springer-Verlag Berlin Heidelberg 2006

As an introductive example, let us mention the water problem in Brazil[1] as depicted in Figure 1. In Figure 1a, there is a conventional map of rivers in Brazil; as usual, at this scale only the main rivers are mapped, and this map will not be very useful for decision making. However, nothing indicates what and where the problems are. However, Figure 1b gives a chorem map of the situation according to the caption given Figure 1c. We can see more accurately where the humid and dry zones are, where water is missing, where dykes are located, where water is more demanded and so on. As a conclusion, this kind of drawing is much more informational to any decision-maker than the conventional river map.

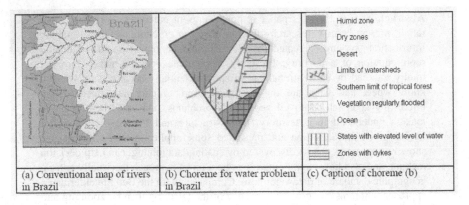

| (a) Conventional map of rivers in Brazil | (b) Choreme for water problem in Brazil | (c) Caption of choreme (b) |

Fig. 1. Comparing a conventional map of rivers in Brazil and a chorem map emphasizing the water problem in this country

The objective of this paper is to give the first outlook of a research program on using s for geographic decision-making. After a more accurate definition of chorems, we will describe how chorem map can assist decision-makers, and more important, we will describe the links with spatial data mining.

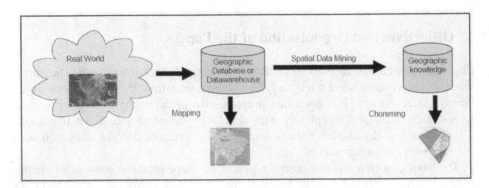

Fig. 2. Main steps of the proposed methodology

---

[1] This example is drawn from the web site http://histoire-geographie.ac-bordeaux.fr/espaceeleve/bresil/eau/eau.htm

Then, we will present how chorem map can help create a novel progressive entry system for geographic databases following Ben Shneiderman's mantra. We will finish this paper by emphasizing the barriers to be overcome to reach these objectives. The ultimate goal will be to create the main concepts in order to implement a decision support system which can be schematized as follows (Figure 2): starting from the real world, a geographic database or datawarehouse will be constructed and populated. Them by applying appropriate spatial data mining and filtering techniques, geographic knowledge will be discovered and then visualized as chorems (Lopez, 2006).

2 What Are Chorems? How Can They Help Decision-Making?

2.1 Elementary Chorems

As initially told, a table of 28 chorems were created by Roger Brunet (1986), Figure 3 gives this table (in French) representing the basic chorem vocabulary.

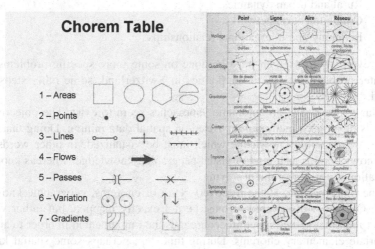

Fig. 3. Table of Brunet's chorems (in French)

Finally chorems can be defined as a visual vocabulary allowing the description of salient characteristics and problems of a territory. From our point of view, chorems are a nice basis for decision making, because they emphasize the more significant aspects, leaving apart secondary problems. Let us say that when it is necessary to understand the structure of a territory, a one-to-one map is not useful, whereas a small schema can be more useful. So chorem maps are a key-tool to schematize a territory, and then after, decision-makers or politicians can get a clearer view of the situation. Among applications, let us mention the schematic visualization for:

- salient political, economic and demographic problems,
- salient features in environment and climatology,
- main evolution in epidemiology,

- natural and technological risks or disasters,
- etc.

Regarding other applications, let us mention a very interesting approach to use chorems for way finding (Klippel et al. 2005).

2.2 Approaches, Manual Versus Automatic?

In the state of the art review, it appears that there are only manual approaches of discovering chorems. By analyzing the examples of Bolivia (Arreghini, 1995) given Figure 4, and Zaire (Bruneau-Simon, 1991), for a whole country, the typical manual approach for a global diagnostic can be as follows:

- Relief and climatology,
- Ecosystems, environment,
- History, population and demography,
- Rural and urban dynamics,
- Communication networks,
- Economy and international relationships.

However, when research must be done on some more specific problems, such as the water problem for Brazil, or politics in Switzerland, some other steps must be defined.

As far as we know, no automatic approaches seem to exist. The objective of this project is to set up a methodology based on spatial data mining. Doing that, chorems appear as geographic knowledge which must be visualized. In other words, we can define now chorems as a kind of visual geographic knowledge, whereas knowledge is information useful for problem solving.

To be more precise, at the discovery level of chorems, geographic knowledge is chased. Once it is discovered, it must be not exactly mapped, but rather visualized. That is to say that some layout procedure must be implemented in order to arrange the appropriate elementary chorems. During this step, perhaps some spatial knowledge must be used to perform the layout, for instance by using non-overlaps, spatial organization of elementary diagrams, etc.

Spatial data mining could be an interesting approach to discover chorems. Data mining can be defined as a systematic way of analyzing data stored in databases or in datawarehouses and of extracting patterns, i.e. useful information for decision makers. And spatial data mining (Ester et al. 1997) is the extension to the study of spatial data.

According to Pech-Palacio (2005), there are several kinds of spatial data mining or knowledge discovery techniques, such as aggregation, clustering, classification, trend detection, etc.; and he has proposed a new way based on graphs. Since geographic knowledge is hidden by coordinates, a way is to transform the geographic database content (perhaps limited to the territory under consideration) into a huge graph which is mined by the SUBDUE algorithm (http://cygnus.uta.edu/subdue/) developed by the University of Texas at Arlington (Holder-Cook, 2005).

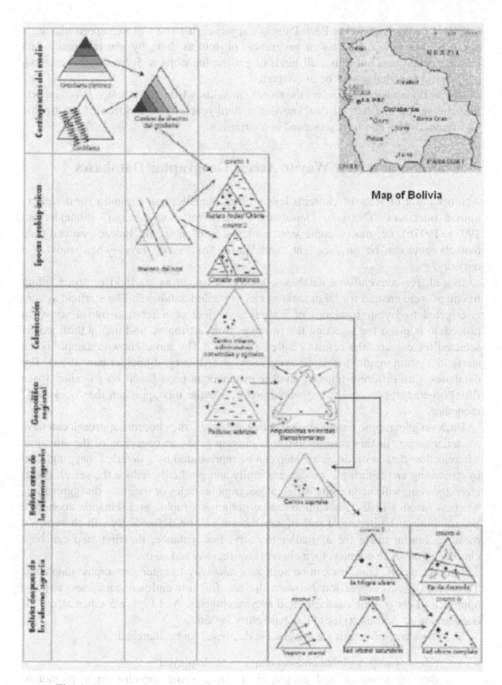

Fig. 4. Example of approach for designing chorems for Bolivia (Arreghini, 1995)

The big advantage of the Pech-Palacio's approach is to be a global approach, i.e., it considers not only one class of geographic objects as done by several spatial data mining techniques, but rather all kinds of geographic objects. By using this method, geographic knowledge will be discovered.

The next step will be to select the more salient knowledge. For that, a list of criteria must be set up to filter all that knowledge until reaching to a dozen of geographic knowledge which can be represented as chorems.

3   Chorems as a New Way to Access Geographic Databases

Another point of view of chorems lays on Ben Shneiderman's mantra for designing human interfaces *"Overview, zoom and filter, details on demand"* (Shneiderman 1997a, 1997b), i.e. macroscopic versus microscopic approach. Indeed, we can state that chorems can be an excellent candidate at "overview" level when studying a territory.

Indeed, for conventional databases, approaches such as starfield or space filling treemaps were created for relational or object-oriented databases. The starfield system is targeted to layout instances of a database object or a relation into a screen: a procedure is given for selecting the two axes from attributes, and then a third axis is selected for colours; the result is called a starfield. The more known example is the starfield system made for Hollywood movies (Ahlberg, Shneiderman 1994). For databases with different objects, another metaphor is used based on so-called space filling treemaps; personally, we would prefer to name this approach the "bookshelf" metaphor.

Back on geographic databases and datawarehouses, the chorems approach can have a similar target. In this case the territory chorem gives an overview of the situation, whereas the "details on demand" step can be represented by a detailed mapping. And by "zooming and filtering", we can gracefully and gradually reduce the search space. Here zooming will mean using different geographic scales or thematic disaggregation, whereas filtering reflects conditions and criteria (geographic and semantic zooming). By zooming and filtering, a sort of sub-chorem can be defined. By sub-chorem, we mean a chorem made for a smaller territory. For instance, the first step can be a chorem for a whole country, then chorems for regions and so on.

In other words, chorems can be seen as a new way to enter geographic databases. Table 1 gives a comparison between the use for conventional databases, and the approach to geographic databases and datawarehouses. And Figure 5 schematized the comparison of various styles of database entry systems.

So, a new way of entering a geographic database can be sketched:

1 – at the opening, a global chorem map can be displayed
2 – then by semantic and geographic filtering some sub-chorem maps can be visualized
3 – finally, the final query answer (map or table) can be displayed.

Table 1. Comparing accesses to conventional and geographic databases

Ben Shneiderman's mantra	Conventional databases	Chorem-based approach
Starting point	Relational or object-oriented database of an organization	Any kind of data which can be useful
1 – Overview	Generally the "overview" is visually presented by means of starfield or space filling treemaps; they are both structure- and content-oriented.	The territory-level chorem can give an overview, perhaps more linked to problems than to data contents.
2 – Zoom and filter	Criteria can be used to reduce the search space.	The territory can perhaps be split in different zones, each of them with a sub-chorem (geographic zoom). A second way can be to reduce the number of topics (semantic zoom)
3 – Details on demand	The final step delivers what could be necessary for the user, usually as a table.	Here both tables and maps can be the final steps, depending on the user's needs.

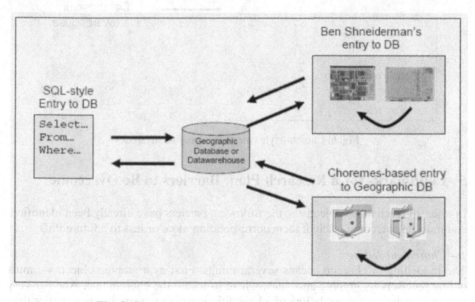

Fig. 5. Comparing various styles of database entry systems

4   Chorems as Visual Representation of Geographic Knowledge

It seems useful to distinguish spatial knowledge from geographic knowledge. "Spatial Knowledge" corresponds to relations which are common in any kind of space (whether 2D, 3D, etc.) such as Egenhofer topological relationships and their mathematical consequence; for us spatial knowledge is quite similar to geometric knowledge. Whereas by "Geographic Knowledge" we mean knowledge located in the earth; for instance a pattern such as "when there is a lake and a road leading to the lake, there is a restaurant" can be consider as geographic knowledge.

Finally, we can now define chorem as a visual representation of geographic knowledge. Until now, geographic and spatial knowledge were essentially represented verbally or by using some mathematic tools such as descriptive logics; now a new possibility is emerging based on chorems.

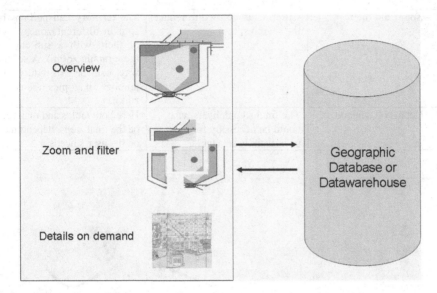

Fig. 6. Chorem-style entry to geographic databases

5 Landmarks for a Research Plan: Barriers to Be Overcome

In order to reach those objectives, the following barriers have already been identified, and must be overcome, each of them corresponding more or less to a future PhD.

1 – Chorem modelling
The modelling of chorems means several things. First as a graphic object, we must define precisely its graphic attributes, where to locate the chorem, etc. Another very important aspect is the modelling of all conditions which govern the chorem. For that, not only conditions must be modelled, perhaps by using descriptive logics, but also a definition language must be defined.

2 – Discovery of salient features
Let us consider the first elementary chorem corresponding to the more important points. What are important points? Maybe there are major cities from a political or an

economic point of view. Do we have to select one, two, five points? What are the limits?

In other words, among all features, we have to discover the more important, that is to say we have to define "importance". Suppose we have got 20 important features. Is it too much or too less? A second problem is the limitation. Too much will lead to some impossibility to understand, too less, the result can be biased by criteria weights.

In other words, once the geographic knowledge is discovered by spatial data mining, a methodology must be created to select the more important geographic knowledge.

3 – Spatial arrangement
Once the more salient features are discovered, the next step is the chorem map. By that, we must organize them spatially not only without overlaps, but also a nice spatial distribution to cover the whole territory, and color selection. Remember that geographic shapes must be generalized (Buttenfield et al. 1991), so implying to store those simplified shapes into the database, or to reconstitute them when necessary. This barrier appears to be overcome by using different agents, each of them using different spatial knowledge.

4 – From chorem map to sub-chorem maps
In connection with the zoom-and-filter phase, the generation of sub-chorem maps must be studied. Two solutions are possible, either to re-begin the chorem phase for a smaller territory, or to reuse the already discovered geographic knowledge to generate the sub-chorem map. Since it is well known that data mining is very consuming, the second approach looks more interesting.

5 – From chorem discovery to chorem-based access
Whereas chorem discovery in a territory can be seen as one task, the use of chorems to access a database is a little bit different. To accelerate the access of the geographic databases or the datawarehouses, chorems and sub-chorems can be stored and used when necessary as a visual entry system. For that an appropriate GUI must be created by following Ben Shneiderman's mantra.

6 – Interoperability
Once the system is made, it must work for any geographic database. Two solutions can be envisioned: the first one is to transform manually the whole content of the existing geographic database to match the structure and the names used in the chorem system; an alternative can be the definition of views as in relational databases. The second solution is to provide an interface to allow interoperability between any geographic database and the chorem system. Here an approach such as a geographic ontology can be a good candidate.

7 – Cognitive aspects
Once a first prototype is made, it will be important to study several kinds of users to test their reactions, their behaviours with such a novel approach, their understanding of the system, their performance, their acceptability, and so on.

6 Final Remarks

The goal of this paper was not to present any result, but rather present some landmarks for a research plan in geographic decision-making based on chorems. Two main aspects were emphasized:

- chorems can be a way to represent geographic knowledge, as a visual outcome of spatial data mining,
- chorems can be a new way to enter geographic databases as a global vision.

Anyhow, this research plan must be detailed, concepts must be clarified, and experimentations must be made through several prototypes.

References

AHLBERG, C., SHNEIDERMAN B. (1994) *"Visual Information Seeking: Tight coupling of dynamic query filters with starfield displays"*, Proc. of ACM CHI94 Conference (April 1994), 313-317.

ARREGHINI L. (1995) *"La modélisation graphique dans la réalisation des atlas pour le développement"*. Journées Géographiques de l'ORSTOM, 11-12/09/1995, Maison de la Géographie, Montpellier, France.

BERTIN J. (1973). *"Sémiologie graphique"*, Mouton/Gauthier-Villars, 2ème édition, 1973.

BRUNEAU J.-C., SIMON T. (1991) *"Zaïre, l'espace écartelé"*. Mappemonde 4/91.

BRUNET R. (1986) *"La carte-modèle et les chorèmes"*, Mappemonde 86/4 pp. 4-6.

BRUNET R. (1993), *"Les fondements scientifiques de la chorématique"*, in "La démarche chorématique", Centre d'Études Géographiques de l'Université de Picardie Jules Verne.

BUTTENFIELD B., McMASTER R., (1991) *"Map Generalization: Making Rules for Knowledge Representation"*, Longman, London, 1991.

ESTER M., KRIEGEL H.-P., SANDER J. (1997) *"Spatial Data Mining: A Database Approach"*. Proc. of the Fifth Int. Symposium on Large Spatial Databases (SSD '97), Berlin, Germany, Lecture Notes in Computer Science Vol. 1262, Springer, 1997, pp 47-66.

HOLDER L.B., COOK D. J., (2005) *"Graph-based Data Mining"*, J. Wang (ed.), Encyclopedia of Data Warehousing and Mining, Idea Group Publishing, 2005.

KLIPPEL A., RICHTER K.-F., HANSEN S., (2005) *"Wayfinding Choreme Maps"*. In Proceedings of 8th International Conference, VISUAL 2005, June 2005 Edited by S. Bres and R. Laurini *"Visual Information and Information Systems"*. Springer, Berlin. Lecture Notes in Computer Sciences 3736, pp. 94-108.

LOPEZ K. (2006) *"Génération Automatique de Cartes Chorématiques"*, Master Thesis in Computing, INSA of Lyon, June 2006.

PECH PALACIO M. (2005) *"Spatial Data Modeling and Mining using a Graph-based Representation"*. PhD in Computing, jointly awarded December 12, 2005 by INSA de Lyon, France, and Universidad de las Américas de Puebla, Mexico.

SHNEIDERMAN B. (1997a) *"Information visualization: Dynamic queries, Starfield Dis-plays, and LifeLines"* White paper: http://www.cs.umd.edu/hcil/members/bshneiderman/ivwp.html

SHNEIDERMAN B. (1997b) *"Designing the User Interface."* Third edition. Addison-Wesley Publishing Company. 600pp.

ZEITOUNI K. YEH L., (2000) *"Le data mining spatial et les bases de données spatiales"*, Revue internationale de Géomatique, Editions Hermès, Vol. 9, 4 (99), pp 389-423, Avril 2000.

A Service to Customize the Structure
of a Geographic Dataset

Sandrine Balley[1], Bénédicte Bucher[1], and Thérèse Libourel[2]

[1] Laboratoire COGIT - IGN, Saint Mandé, France
{sandrine.balley, benedicte.bucher}@ign.fr
[2] LIRMM - CNRS - Université Montpellier 2, Montpellier, France
libourel@lirmm.fr

Abstract. This paper deals with the usability of vector geographic data structures. We define usability of a geographic representation as the ability to fit the user's view, the user application and the user platform, plus the ability to be derived from a data producer dataset and to be maintained in the future if needed. Specifying the structure of a usable representation and deriving the corresponding data require specific tools and expertness. We propose to assist users in this process by means of a Web-based system able to assist users in specifying and performing a dataset restructuration process. The first step is to help users to set their requirements. To achieve this goal, we propose a graphical interface to specify differences between an existing data structure and a target data structure. The second step is to help users to commit these requirements into a transformation process applied to an existing dataset. We propose mechanisms to plan and execute this process and to check its result. The system relies on knowledge of existing data structures, platforms grammar rules and typical application schemas. The first part of this paper analyses the notion of a data structure and how to specify it. The second part describes our proposal.

1 Introduction

There is no best way to represent a portion of geographic space in a vector geographic database. Various users and applications, both of which are growing in number, have different best-fitted representations of geographic space. As they cannot design and create their own 'custom-made' dataset, users have to acquire them from an institutional data producer, but they wish to be provided with the amount and representation of information required by their application. For a national data provider such as IGN, enabling users to specify on the Web real world representations that are relevant to their application and providing them with the corresponding data is a great stake. By such a service users would keep benefiting from the data producer services to manage the dataset (quality checking and update), which is not the case if they adapt the data by themselves.

This paper introduces a service letting users specify their representation requirements starting from a representation proposed by the producer. These specifications are processed by the system to generate a transformation chain to actually derive the data. We do not address the whole issue of deriving a best fitted representation but

R. Meersman, Z. Tari, P. Herrero et al. (Eds.): OTM Workshops 2006, LNCS 4278, pp. 1703–1711, 2006.

concentrate on the structural aspects of the representation. Moreover, we insist on setting the path for an easier maintenance of the user dataset.

The first part analyses the notion of a data structure and how to specify it. The second part presents our proposal to assist users in getting data with a usable structure.

2 How to Formally Describe a Data Structure?

This part analyses what a data structure is and which languages are existing to describe it. Introduced concepts are summarized on figure 1.

The process of representing the real world in vector databases, i.e. abstracting real world entities into database objects, has been theoretically described [1] and practically documented [2]. The results of a representation process are the data, plus the framework to describe and encode this data. We called this framework the data structure. As shown in figure 1, designing a geographic data structure implies several steps: categorization, selection, modeling and implementation choices. These steps are successively defined below, together with existing solutions to document them.

The categorization step consists in defining categories of objects to be observed in the real world and somehow represented in the database, like 'road', 'forest', 'lake', 'building'. This step amounts to defining the ontology (or thesaurus) dedicated to the application domain of the representation designer.

The selection step consists in deciding which entities of these categories have to be represented in the database. A selection is usually expressed as filters, like 'roads that are dead-ends and that are shorter than 400 meters must not be represented in the database'.

The modeling step consists in deciding how to represent selected real world entities as objects. For instance, roads might be represented by linear objects of the ROAD class, figuring their centerlines, with indications about their driving sense and administrative number. These objects must compose a network. The accessed amenities (such as tollgates and service stations) shall be explicitly attached through the PROVIDE ACCESS TO relationship. This step amounts to specifying the dataset conceptual schema plus some rules for data capture and consistency.

Rather advanced object types can be used in a conceptual schema (e.g. types with temporal primitives or multiple representations), depending on the used data model. For example the UML profile based on the OGC General Feature Model [3], the UML+PVL model used by the Perceptory CASE tool [4] and the MADS model [5] are extremely rich. As explained below, this is not the case for data schemas at a lower abstraction level, i.e. logical and physical schemas. That is why conceptual schemas cannot be derived from logical or physical ones.

Unfortunately, formalized conceptual data schemas are rarely provided to users. Defined by the data producer, they do not take part in the data transfer. It is notably the case for OGC WFS and WMS diffusion services.

The implementation step consists in specifying how the objects designed at the previous step can be represented in a machine-readable form. This step amounts to defining two data schemas. The first one is a platform-dependant logical schema. It describes how users actually manipulate data in the used platform, e.g. through tables and columns. The second one is a physical schema describing how data are stored. For example, it might be decided that roads are represented in a single file and that road numbers are encoded by strings up to 10 characters.

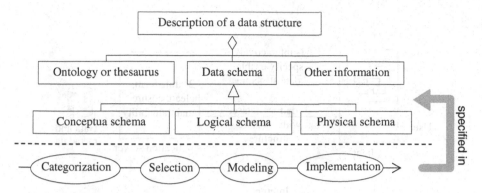

Fig. 1. Design steps to produce a structure to represent a portion of geographic space are displayed in the lower part. The upper part represents elements in which this design can be described.

Unlike in conceptual schemas, only the object types that are allowed by the used platform grammar rules can appear in logical and physical schemas. An example grammar rule of the PostGIS DBMS is that topological primitives are not supported. Grammar rules have no standalone description, even in platform documentations. They are implicitly enclosed in data translators (transforming a logical schema into another) and in CASE tools (deriving a logical schema from a conceptual schema).

The design steps of a data structure and their possible documentation are summarized in figure 1. It can be noticed that the entirety of a data structure can not be expressed by means of ontologies and data schemas. They appear as 'other information' in the figure. This is the case for the selection rules of real world entities, the capture conditions and the inner consistency rules defined at the modeling step. Most of the time this information is expressed through natural language statements in data specification documents. Different models tend to represent it more formally: among others, [1] proposes relations between an ontology of real world categories and a data schema. [6] proposes a spatial extension of the OCL formal language. [7] proposes a specification model including consistency constraints as an aspect of data quality.

This part has analyzed the notion of a data structure. It is a complex notion whose facets are unequally and independently described. As a consequence, it is difficult for a user to understand or to specify it at a glance. Our approach to assist users in specifying a usable data structure and deriving usable data consequently is presented below.

3   Helping Users to Restructure Existing Datasets into Datasets with a Usable Structure

This part describes our proposal to assist users in deriving datasets with a usable structure in their context. The first difficulty experienced by users in this process is to identify their requirements concerning the structure of these datasets. This is addressed in section 3.1. The second difficulty is the very transformation of existing datasets into usable datasets meeting the requirements. This is addressed in section 3.2.

We propose to handle these difficulties by means of a service helping users to get on-demand datasets. As shown on figure 2, the user first specifies its requirements on

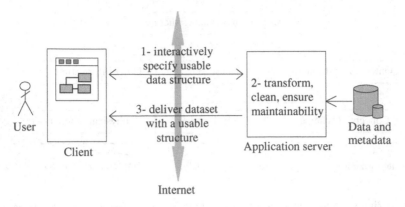

Fig. 2. Proposed data restructuration process

a graphical interface driven by an existing data structure. Relying on these requirements and some internal knowledge of constraints relative to data and data structures, the system automatically generates a suitable transformation chain. It last delivers usable data to the user.

This approach may be compared to existing tools for modeling (CASE tools), translating (e.g. the Safe Software FME translator), restructuring (e.g. the Safe Software FME workbench), or checking (e.g. the Laser Scan Radius studio) geographic data. Some of these functionalities are also emerging on the Web [8]. These tools are specialized and powerful, be it to represent platform constraints or to transform data. However they do not provide any knowledge on data structures constraints, esp. at the conceptual level, which is the main characteristic of our approach.

3.1 What Is a Usable Data Structure?

To define a usable data structure, we greatly rely on [9] description of geographical data usability: usability is considered as a ternary relationship between users and their needs, data and their characteristics, applications and their requirements.

We add two aspects to this definition in order to take into account the necessary relationship between the user and the data producer. This is represented on figure 3. In our work, a usable representation is:

- a representation that can be derived from an existing representation, for instance from an IGN data product (first requirement on figure 3),
- a representation that fulfills users requirements (second, third and fourth requirements on figure 3).
- a representation that can be maintained (fifth requirement of figure 3).

3.2 Assisting Users in Specifying Their Requirements for a Usable Data Structure

In our approach, requirements for a usable data structure are not expressed as a mere structure definition. As detailed hereafter, they are listed after to the five aspects considered in our definition of data usability (figure 3).

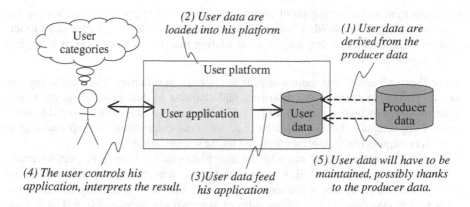

Fig. 3. Usable data representation must fulfill requirements of several processes

Firstly, a usable dataset must be derivable from some existing data. We propose to let users specify their structure requirements by stating differences between the needed structure and existing structures of data products diffused by a data producer like IGN. In our proposal, a two frame graphical interface (figure 5) provides a view of an existing data structure at the conceptual level, thanks to an object-oriented class diagram. This structure is stored in the system as a metadata. A user-defined data structure is designed by selecting and manipulating elements from the initial one. Design tools are used that provide functionalities such as renaming, splitting a class, dropping an attribute, etc.

Secondly, in a usable dataset, real world categories that are meaningful to the user must figure in the data structure. Depending on the producer dataset structure, they may not be represented by explicit classes in the conceptual schema. For example, in some IGN database, the 'bridge' category does not take part to the conceptual schema. To fulfill this requirement, we propose to enrich conceptual schemas with derivable implicit object types figuring a-priori meaningful categories. For example, the service provider could enrich the description of its conceptual schema with the implicit BRIDGE object type that can be derived from LINEAR CONSTRUCT and ROAD SECTION by means of predefined restructuration operations. Users can also define derived classes: by reading the structure description, they must assess if the required information is actually enclosed in the dataset. Then they must match implicit and existing object types by means of the design tools described previously.

Thirdly, a usable dataset must fulfill the requirements of the user application. Requirements on the inputs and outputs of an application are called pre-conditions and post-conditions. Here are listed the most frequent pre-conditions:

- Definition of the application schema, i.e. the conceptual data schema the most suitable for the application. For example, the application schema of any routing application is composed of ROAD and NODE object types explicitly linked by a topologic relationship.
- Platform constraints affecting the physical or logical schema: e.g. 'the service only reads GML data files',

– Information about setting input parameters affecting the process: e.g. 'setting parameters (e.g. a threshold, a tolerance value, etc.) can be set to zero for short itineraries', 'the used algorithm for route calculation may provide bad results if applied to very sinuous features'.

All of these pre-conditions cannot appear in application schemas. They are being further formalized to promote the discovery and chaining of data processing, especially those deployed as Web services [10] [11]. For our part, we only want to provide some general application schema templates (e.g. for route calculation or map making) to help users express the requirements issued by their application.

Fourthly, a usable dataset must fit the user platform, i.e. it must respect its grammar rules. Just as current CASE tools, we propose to prevent users from dealing with this technical issue. A first assistance we provide consists in generating suitable logical data schemas thanks to grammar rules of standard platforms published in our application. A second assistance consists in propagating conceptual schema evolutions to the logical level thanks to the stored links between these schema elements.

Fifthly, a usable dataset must be maintainable. To fulfill this requirement, we propose to trace transformations and to maintain correspondence links between initial objects, that are kept by the data producer, and the transformed ones. It enables to replay the restructuration process, to trace data errors and to propagate potential updates from the initial dataset to the user one.

In this section we have presented the main lines of our proposal to assist users in specifying requirements for a usable data structure. Users only express 'applicative' requirements. They are provided with existing conceptual schemas and some typical usable application schemas. Requirements on the logical and physical facets of data structures are automatically inferred by the system.

3.3 Assisting Users in Performing the Transformation Process

This section describes how our system assists users in performing the transformation process to derive a dataset compliant with the requirements specified above.

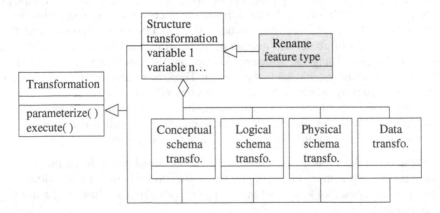

Fig. 4. The internal transformation model and an example of structure transformation (shaded class)

Applying Schema Transformations

As seen in the section before, users apply design tools that manipulate elements from an existing conceptual schema to specify their required structure. Our internal transformation model is shown on figure 4. Each design tool, e.g. 'rename feature type', is associated to a class extending the 'Structure transformation' class. A 'structure transformation' is an elementary step of a transformation process. It affects the whole data structure. It is composed of a 'conceptual transformation' (renaming a class of the conceptual schema), a 'logical transformation' (renaming a table), a 'physical transformation' (renaming a file) and a 'data transformation' (not affecting data in our example). Any 'Transformation' class has specific variables (e.g. 'oldName' and 'newName' for 'rename feature type'). It also has two methods : a parameterization method to allocate values to variables, and an execution method to execute the transformation.

Applying a design tool automatically triggers the creation of an instance of the underlying structure transformation class. The system automatically invokes the parameterization method of this structure transformation. This applies and propagates variables assessment from the conceptual level to the lower levels. This propagation relies on stored links between schema elements, and on an internal knowledge of used platform grammar rules. The system then invokes the execution method of the 'conceptual transformation' to transform the conceptual schema visualised by the user. The other transformation instances are inserted into a transformation plan for a later execution.

Planning and Tracing the Restructuration Process

When the user commits all his requirements and asks for the compliant data derivation, the system goes through its transformation plan and invokes the execution methods of successive transformations. Correspondences between the initial and transformed objects identifiers are stored.

During this transformation process, the system launches some additional expert mechanisms. As a matter of fact, the transformation process may lead to violate some general integrity rules (e.g., the existence of an association is conditioned by the existence of its member classes) or some specific ones stated in the data structure description (e.g., the road network is sectioned according to changes in the road attributes values). They trigger the parameterization of other transformations (e.g., some ROAD SECTION instances must be aggregated after the deletion of an attribute whose value was causing their separation).

3.4 Implementation

A prototype of our application has been implemented whithin the GeOxygene open Java framework[1]. In GeOxygene, spatial data classes extending the OGC concept of Feature are mapped to a relational database via an object-relational bridge. In the current prototype, GeOxygene is also considered as the default user platform.

The description we propose for data structures is based on:

- the ISO 19109 General Feature Model, based on Feature Types, for the conceptual or application schemas,

---

[1] http://oxygene-project.sourceforge.net/

- the "Class" and "Field" classes for describing the logical data schema in the Java platform
- the "Table", "Column" and "Key" classes for describing the logical schema in the relational storage platform

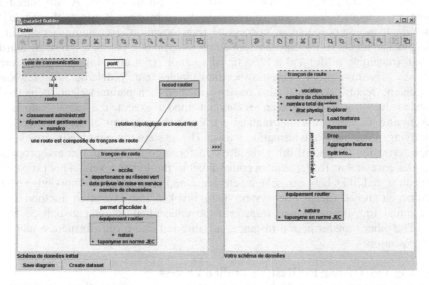

Fig. 5. The user interface: the user data structure (on the right) is specified based on elements selected from an existing data structure (on the left). Design tools are proposed in a contextual menu. An implicit object type is displayed as a transparent class on the left.

The user interacts with the system through a client implemented as a Java Web Start application. This client displays a conceptual schema in a UML-like form based on the JGraph library. It interacts with our server through Web Services.

System Evaluation

No user test has been carried out so far. An evaluation session is planned within the COGIT lab with a pre-defined use-case : the restructuration of a dataset for a map-making purpose. Of course, the COGIT users are more comfortable with geographic data structures than the users targeted by our system. A real condition evaluation is necessary to assess the usability of our system.

4 Conclusion and Perspectives

In this paper, the usability of a geographic representation is defined as its ability to suit the user's view, to fit into the user platform and application, to be derivable from an existing dataset and to be maintainable.

We propose to assist users in acquiring geographic data with a usable structure on the Web. Our approach aims to spare users from technical considerations and to let them focus on the application level. Starting from an existing data structure, a target data structure is interactively specified at the conceptual level. A complete transformation plan, including logical schema restructuration and data cleaning operations, is automatically designed by the system. This plan is executed on the initial data before they are sent to the user. The restructuration plan is stored, as well as links between initial and restructured datasets.

The main drawback of our system is that it requires formal descriptions of data structures, including an explicit mapping between schema elements at different abstraction levels. This issue is easily tackled in our case as the GeOxygene platform manages a data dictionary, a Java API and related tables in the same time thanks to mapping files. However, to reuse our approach on datasets that are not stored in GeOxygene, a solution must be found to acquire and manage such extensive metadata.

Our approach also requires the description of platform grammar rules and well known application schemas. Further work [Abd-el-Kader, 2006] should explore the mechanisms to acquire these descriptions.

References

[1] Gesbert, N.: Formalisation of Geographical Database Specifications. In: Proceedings of the ADBIS Conference on Advances in Databases and Information Systems (2004) 202-211.

[2] Environmental Systems Research Institute, Inc.: Modeling our World, the ESRI guide to geodatabase design. ISBN 1-879102-62-5 (1999)

[3] ISO TC21: ISO 19109 Geographic Information - Rules for Application Schema (International standard)(2005)

[4] Bédard, Y., Visual modelling of spatial databases: Towards spatial PVL and UML. Geomatica, 53(2) (1999) 169-186

[5] Parent, C., Spaccapietra, S., Zimányi, E.: Conceptual modeling for traditional and spatio-temporal applications. The MADS approach. Springer Verlag (2006)

[6] Pinet, F., Kang, M.A, Vigier, F.: Spatial Constraint Modelling with a GIS Extension of UML and OCL: Application to Agricultural Information Systems. In: Proceedings of the Metainformatics International Symposium (2004)

[7] Friis-Christensen, A., Christensen, J.V, Jensen, C.S : A Framework for Conceptual Modeling of Geographic Data Quality. In: P. Fisher (ed.): Proceeding of the 11th international Symposium on Spatial Data Handling (2004) 605-616

[8] Leite, F.L., De Sousa, A.G., De Souza Baptista, C., Nunes, C.P, Da Silva, E.R, De Almeida, D.R, De Paiva, A.C: Migratool: Towards a Web-Based Spatial Database Migration Tool. In: Proceedings of the 16th DEXA conference (2005) 480-48.

[9] Josselin, D.: Spatial data exploratory analysis and usability. Data Science Journal (Spatial Data Usability Section), 2(26) (2003)

[10] Abd-el-Kader, Y., Bucher, B.: Cataloguing GI Functions provided by NonWeb Services Software Resources Within IGN. In Proceedings of the 9th AGILE International Conference on Geographic Information Science, appendum (2006)

[11] Lemmens, R., Granell, C., Wytzisk, A., de By, R., Gould, M., van Oosterom, P.: Semantic and syntactic service descriptions at work in geo-service chaining,. In: Proceedings of the 9th AGILE Conference on Geographic Information Science (2006) 51-61

Using a Semantic Approach for a Cataloguing Service

Paul Boisson[2], Stéphane Clerc[1,2], Jean-Christophe Desconnets[1],
and Thérèse Libourel[2]

[1] IRD (Institut de Recherche pour le Développement),
34394 Montpellier Cedex 5, France
jcd@teledetection.fr, clerc@teledetection.fr
[2] LIRMM (Laboratoire d'Informatique, de Robotique et de Microélectronique de
Montpellier) UMR 5506, Université de Montpellier II, CNRS,
34392 Montpellier Cedex 5, France
libourel@lirmm.fr, boisson@lirmm.fr, clerc@lirmm.fr

Abstract. Environmental applications (support for territorial diagnostics, monitoring of practices, integrated management, etc.) have strengthened the case for efforts in the establishment of sharing and mutualisation infrastructures for georeferenced information. Within the framework of these initiatives, our work has led us to design and create a tool for cataloguing resources for environmental applications. This tool can be used to catalogue different types of resources (digital maps, vector layers, geographical databases, documents, etc.) by using the ISO 19115 standard, and offers a search engine for these resources. The goal of this proposition is to improve the relevance of search engines by relying on semantic knowledge (thematic and spatial) of the concerned domains. In the first stage, the proposition consists of helping the user in his search by offering mechanisms to expand on or to filter his query. In the second stage, we use the results obtained and the underlying semantics for a global presentation of the results.

1 Introduction

Environmental applications (support for territorial diagnostics, monitoring of practices, integrated management, etc.) have strengthened the case for efforts in the establishment of sharing and mutualisation infrastructures for georeferenced information[1]. Within the framework of these initiatives, our work has led us to design and create a tool for cataloguing resources, a fundamental and indispensable requirement for data infrastructure. The goal now is to make this tool's search engine more relevant by drawing on the semantics of the concerned domains.

Section 2 presents other works on the same subject. Section 3 of this article presents the context within which our work is placed and lists our motivations. In

---

[1] http://inspire.jrc.it/

R. Meersman, Z. Tari, P. Herrero et al. (Eds.): OTM Workshops 2006, LNCS 4278, pp. 1712–1722, 2006.

section 4, we recall the main features of the MDweb cataloguing tool by describing its original characteristics (genericity, use of a thesaurus and a reference base of geographical objects to control thematic and spatial descriptors). In fact, it is by the use of thematic and spatial reference bases that we propose to improve the relevance of the tool. In sections 5 and 6 we present the basic approach of our work. It involves the concept of expansion of a search based on spatial and thematic semantics and on the distribution of semantic relationships contained in the resources found. Section 7 discusses the future perspectives opened up by this work.

2 State of the Art

Since our intention was to improve the relevance of the MDweb resources search engine (see section 3), both at the level of the search itself and in the exploitation of its results, we looked for similar approaches in existing work done in this field.

Some cataloguing tools based on the use of metadata standards in the geographic information domain currently exist, for example, GéoConnexions (Canadian geospatial data infrastructure), Geospatial Metadata tools[2], M3Cat[3], EU Geo-Portal, GeoNetwork (FAO), GEoNorge, etc.

Some cataloguing services with a semantic-Web approach, in any field, have already enhanced their functionalities by drawing on the use of thesauri or ontologies. We can mention, for example, the French project Cismef (Catalogue and Index of French-language Medical Sites) [9] which has developed an intelligent system for the search of information based on a set of metadata elements describing resources in the medical domain. This system uses a medical ontology that makes inferences to provide results that are more user relevant. In this framework, ontology offers the possibility to the underlying search engine of automatizing reasoning, on the basis of the user's initial query, with the aim of providing better results. The mechanism consists of reformulating the initial query so that it returns additional results or, on the other hand, of filtering it to retain only the most relevant results. The use of ontologies depends on their type. In the context of geographic information, the process of query reformulation can be based on the thematic aspect by using the relationships between the search keywords (as in the Cismef project [9] or even [3]). We can also draw on the spatial aspect for using spatial relationships, as is done in the European project SPIRIT [4]. Other improvements in the relevance of information search results have been proposed; they rely on techniques based on the statistical co-occurrence of terms or even on the use of the user's profile [2].

The semantic use of the results depends on the formalisms proposed for knowledge representation. Even though there already exist formalisms such as those of conceptual graphs of Sowa [10], or RDF of Guha (1987), or Topics Maps, based on research by the Davenport Group in the 1990s, applications that allow graphical

---

[2] http://www.fgdc.gov/metadata/geospatial-metadata-tools
[3] http://www.intelec.ca/francais.html

visualization of knowledge are few and far between. The OKS[4] (Ontopia Knowledge Suite) project of Ontopia includes several ontology management modules using Topic Maps formalisms, of which one (Omnigator[5]) graphically displays the Topic Map. Similarly, the KAON[6] (Karlsruhe Ontology Management Infrastructure) programme also manages ontologies by using its own formalism. It allows graphical viewing of the ontology on which one is working. Amongst information-search tools, most present results traditionally: the query results are in the form of a list. We can, however, note some efforts towards visual representation, such as the Kartoo[7] metasearch engine which displays the results in cartographic form. Information is displayed in the form of "semantic" graphs, nodes corresponding to resource results, with arcs connecting nearby nodes semantically.

Drawing inspiration from this body of work, we shall now explain, in the following sections, our ideas for improving the relevance of the MDweb tool.

3   Context

This research was conducted by a group of multidisciplinary scientists bringing together information-technology and thematics specialists. The varied applications and interests of these scientists have, as a common point, the mutualisation and sharing of data, processes and knowledge. Their combined efforts led to the design and creation of a cataloguing tool, MDweb, which has been used in several projects and activities linking diverse communities (Coastal zone integrated management Syscolag [1], National Environmental Information System of Cape Verde[8], Network of Long Term Ecological Observatories ROSELT[9] [5], Programme DeSurvey: a surveillance system for assessing and monitoring of Desertification[10]).

The tool was designed to provide the concerned communities with a way of managing their internal resources and to distribute, over the Web, the knowledge necessary to locate these resources. Incorporating the dimension of *searching for information on the Web* requires tackling the inherent problems associated with information searches on the Web. Existing search engines are no longer capable of easily locating the concerned resources because the traditional Web collects heterogeneous information that is, for the most part, unstructured and which can only be processed by humans. To alleviate this shortcoming, the proposed tool uses metadata to annotate resources. Since the resources are georeferenced, the annotation conforms to the ISO standard: ISO 19115. While the structuring proposed by this standard (as by all other metadata standards) is only a first

---

[4] http://www.ontopia.net/
[5] http://www.ontopia.net/omnigator/models/index.jsp
[6] http://kaon.semanticweb.org/
[7] http://www.kartoo.com
[8] http://www.sia.cv/
[9] http://mdweb.roselt-oss.org/
[10] http://www.desurvey.net/

step towards automatized searches, the use of domain semantics is still in its infancy. In the general context of the Web, the final stage will be, as proposed by Tim Berners-Lee, the construction of a semantic web [11] whose contents will be comprehensible both by humans and machines, implying intelligent automatized searches of information.

The construction of ontologies thus becomes necessary to complement resource annotation. We have progressed in this direction by incorporating a shared representation of the knowledge domain. This will permit the annotation from a controlled vocabulary and it is on this explicit knowledge that we shall rely to enrich the search process and the results presentation.

4 The MDweb Tool

4.1 Principles and Genericity

Principles. In view of the variety of possible applications in the diverse communities that use georeferenced information, MDweb was designed as a generic, multi-lingual, multi-standard tool for cataloguing and searching georeferenced information[11]. Some informations about MDweb (MetaData on the web) are available on http://www.mdweb-project.org/. It can be used to create, manage and search one or more catalogues via the Web. MDweb is a server-side application. It has been designed so that it can be independently deployed on Windows or Linux operating systems. To ensure interoperability with other cataloguing applications, MDweb implements, most notably, the international standard for geographical information metadata, ISO 19115 [7], as far as metadata structuring is concerned, and the Catalog Service specifications of the OpenGIS Consortium [8] to ensure interoperability of the cataloguing service by implementing the protocol z3950-ISO 23950 [6].

Genericity. The tool's genericity is based on its core, which is a generic database (metabase) whose relational schema can be broken up into four subschemas:

- S1: storage schema for the standard's dictionary,
- S2: storage schema for the metadata template structures and their parameters inherited from a standard,
- S3: storage schema for metadata,
- S4: storage schema for the contents of the user interfaces (labels, user parameters).

This core thus ensures (S1) the storage of elements and structures of diverse metadata standards (ISO 19115, FGDC, Dublin core). The use of the storage schema of the standard's dictionary allows, by calculation, to arrive at new, varied structures, adapted to the needs of a community (templates or metadata

---

[11] It was designed and developed by our multi-disciplinary group that included members from IRD, LIRMM and Cemagref.

profile) without modifying the relational metadata storage schema (S3) and the user interfaces. The values stored in (S4) and (S2) allow the creation and customization of user interfaces as also of diverse parameters or values necessary for the entry of metadata. Metadata capture is done by the web, but given that is a laborious task, some complementary tools are developed to allow automatic retrieval of metadata (for instance from metadata of ArcCatalog).

4.2 Originality

Its genericity apart, the originality of the proposed service can be perceived from two different angles.

Firstly, conscious of the fact that headings included in metadata structures are insufficient for the annotation, we have complemented them by introducing the semantics of the concerned domains. Two reference bases have been added to the tool: a thematic reference base and a spatial reference base. The thematic reference base describes the semantics by the intermediary of explicit models. These models are described by an established and shareable vocabulary (the very basis of the concept of ontology) within the thesaurus.

The second characteristic, important in our view, and one that we have included in the tool, consists of helping the user in all his tasks. The input and search stages in a metadata service can very rapidly become restrictive and even disillusion users. MDweb therefore offers a set of user aids, the most important one being, as far as our work is concerned, the linking of the search engine's multi-criteria search interface with the semantic aspects of the two reference bases. Normally, a multi-criteria search is constructed by the combination of four criteria: **What** resource type? To **what subject** does the resource apply? **Where** is it located? and **When** was it created?

Nevertheless, as for any search engine, the response may be "silent" or, on the other hand, "too verbose". Our first aim therefore is to improve the search engine's behaviour in such situations. Subsequently, we hope that the results of any search can be best used (beyond a mere listing) by bringing out the implicit knowledge that they contain.

5 Improving Searches

The first idea is to improve the relevance and number of results returned as a response to a user's query by relying on the semantic addition to the tool (cf. section 4). Towards this end, we propose to adapt the *query expansion* mechanism to our context. Query expansion can be defined as a process that modifies the initial user query to better respond to his query. If the system remains *silent* to the user's search, expansion will take the form of enrichment by widening the search scope. If, on the other hand, the system responds *verbosely*, i.e., it returns too many results, the process filters the query to refine the response to the user. Different automatic and interactive expansion mechanisms have thus been developed.

5.1   Thematic Expansion

Thematic expansion of the search is based on a modification of the initial query (enrichment or filtering) using the thesaurus that the metadata service relies on. The search engine complements or refines the query using thesaurus keywords. These keywords are selected because they are in semantic relationships with those of the user. We recall here that terms in the thesaurus are organized in a hierarchy and are connected between themselves by different relationships such as synonym links, associated-terms links, etc. (details of possible relationships are presented in Table 1).

Table 1. Relationships in the thesaurus

> **BT:** "Broader term" relationship
> **NT:** "Narrower term" relationship
> **UF:** "Used for" relationship, i.e., equivalent terms or synonyms
> **RT:** "Related to" relationship, i.e., terms connected in the domain under consideration
> **SN:** "Scope note", i.e., note on the use of a term or its definition

The main thematic expansion algorithm (cf. Algorithm 1) uses two (parametrable) thresholds to decide the strategy to adopt.

Algorithm 1: Global algorithm for thematic expansion of the query

---

Data: the user query reqInitial, the thesaurus, threshold_low, threshold_high
reqModified;
if $numResults(reqInitial) \leq threshold\_low$ **then**
    reqModified = expansionThema (reqInitial, thesaurus, "UF");
    if $numResults(reqModified) \leq threshold\_low$ **then**
        reqModified = expansionThema (reqModified, thesaurus, "NT");
        if $numResults(reqModified) \leq threshold\_low$ **then**
            reqModified = expansionThema (reqModified, thesaurus, "BT");
        end
    end
    expansionInteractive(reqModified, thesaurus);
end
else if $numResults(reqInitial) \geq threshold\_high$ **then**
    reqModified = filteringThema (reqInitial, thesaurus, "NT");
end
execute (reqModified);

If the number of results obtained by the user's search is smaller than *threshold_low*, i.e., when we consider the number of results as insufficient, successive calls are made to an automatic expansion algorithm until a sufficient number of results are obtained (subject to a limit of 3 calls). This algorithm is called for a specific link type in the thesaurus (synonym, narrower term, broader term).

The algorithm searches for all keywords of the initial query that are found in the thesaurus, and then looks for additional keywords in the thesaurus that match the specified relationship type with them. The keywords found are added to the query and it is re-executed. In case the number of results returned is greater than *threshold_high*, a filtering algorithm is called. This algorithm is interactive and, after consulting the thesaurus, offers keywords that are more specific than those of the user. The user can then choose or reject one or more of the proposed terms and relaunch his query with the new keywords. For example, if the user provides *trawling* as search keyword and if the system does not return any result, the expansion algorithm will find that there exists a synonym relationship between the terms *trawling* and *trawl fishing*. A new query will then be executed with the keyword *trawl fishing*. If, on the other hand, the user selects a keyword that is too general such as *method of fishing*, which returns numerous results, the system can offer him terms to help narrow his query, such as *line fishing*, *net fishing*, *trawl fishing*, etc.

5.2   Spatial Expansion

Another type of query expansion seemed interesting enough to us to implement in the context of georeferenced data. This expansion method relies on data's spatial aspect. Here it is a filtering algorithm that intervenes when the user searches with a known geographical location as a search criterion and is faced with too many responses.

A spatial search can be conducted by drawing a *minimum bounding rectangle* around the search zone on the cartographic interface, either by providing the rectangle's geographical coordinates or by choosing a geographical object (which also possesses a corresponding minimum bounding rectangle). In either case, the expansion method is based on this concept of minimum bounding rectangle and the use of topological relationships between rectangles.

In case of a search with spatial criterion, the obtained results are documents whose associated containing rectangle is in intersection with or touches that of the search zone. If too many results are obtained, the system proposes to the user, based on topological relationships, to restrict the search to documents whose containing rectangle is strictly included in the search zone. Of course, it would be possible to use this algorithm with an other topological relationship, for example to expand the query.

5.3   Combined Expansion: Thematic and Spatial

Finally, a combined expansion mechanism was developed by combining the use of the thematic reference base and of the spatial reference base. If the user enters a spatial concept as a keyword, i.e., a keyword attached to a geographic layer of the spatial database, then the expansion – or rather the filtering – can use the choice of a specific object on the geographic layer as a way of refining the search.

For example, if the initial query includes a keyword such as the spatial concept *lagoon*, the system offers the user the opportunity of selecting one *lagoon* in particular from a displayed cartographical interface. This expansion is interactive; the user can very well choose to retain all initial responses.

Another improvement in the cataloguing service that seems interesting to us is to better exploit search results by using the representation of knowledge connected to these results.

6   Semantic Presentation of Results

Our idea is based on a *strong hypothesis:* the keywords present in the search results should allow the implicit knowledge to be extracted once a semantic network is established. This network will be constructed from the comparison of the keywords present in the result metadata records with the domain's ontological knowledge. In fact, it makes sense that the terms selected for annotating a record should represent concepts having, amongst themselves, a significant relationship. It is these links that we will try to retrieve from the structure of the domain's semantic representation (thesaurus, ontology, etc.) to be able to put together the semantic knowledge network existing between them. This network should allow domain specialists to verify the consistency of the expression of their knowledge (missing links or errors in link types in the thesaurus) or suggest semantically close words to the user so that he can refine his search.

Algorithm 2: Flooding initialization algorithm

Data: all the keywords extracted from the results
Result: the global variable H contains all the paths of the semantic
        network
for *all m ∈ keywords* **do**
    | *target ← keywords − m*;
    | create the PATH graph reduced to a single node m;
    | flooding(m,target,PATH);
end

In MDweb, the result of a query is, as in most search engines, supplied in the form of a list where each record fulfilling the criteria is summarized (title, date of record creation, catalogue where it is to be found, etc.). An initial task consisted of retrieving all the concepts (keywords) used to describe these records. For example, a query for "trawl fishing" gave all the keywords describing the result records: "marine fisheries", "trawling", "hakes". While this set of keywords constitutes a first summary of knowledge, the lack of a structure between them impairs interpretation. We therefore propose an algorithm that relies on the semantic reference base to find different "paths" between these words and thus to better extract the knowledge stored therein (see Fig. 1).

It is worth considering covering *all* the possible paths (especially if the reference base is of reasonable size) from different keywords present in the result to ascertain which amongst them arrives at another of these terms. The successive

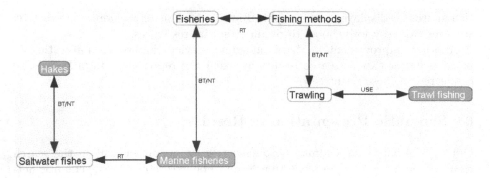

Fig. 1. Network of extracted knowledge (with the Prefuse visualization toolkit, http://prefuse.org/)

calls to the recursive algorithm 3 called by the algorithm 2 allows all the paths from one of these keywords (origin keyword) to be covered, and to store those that arrive at another of these keywords (destination keyword amongst the other keywords). We thus obtain the complete network with all the paths linking the keywords extracted from the result. Figure 2 shows one exploration stage of our example. Having started from the origin term "Marine fisheries", the algorithm arrives at "Trawling". On the figure, the greyed sub-graph represents the path already covered (the algorithm's PATH variable); the other nodes (in white) represent potential candidates for continuing the exploration (the successors of the "Trawling" node not yet processed). For each of these candidates, the associated node and the arc connecting it to PATH are added to PATH, and thus the exploration continues. When we process one of the search keywords ("Trawl

---

Algorithm 3: Greedy flooding algorithm

Data: the current node c, the set of destination nodes d, the PATH graph of the path already covered since the first call

Result: at the end of recursive calls, the global variable H contains the graph made up of all the paths between node c and one of the nodes d, plus PATH

if $c \in d$ then
  | save PATH in H;
else
  | for *all nodes v successor of c in the thesaurus* do
    | if *v does not belong to PATH* then
      | add the node v and arc (c,v) to PATH;
      | flooding(v,d,PATH);
      | delete arc (c,v) and node v from PATH;
    | end
  | end
end

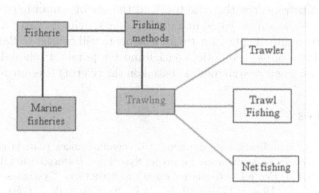

Fig. 2. Starting from "Marine fisheries", the algorithm processes "Trawling"

fishing" in the example), the nodes and the arcs of PATH which are not already present are added to the global variable H, and the exploration stops (the paths originating from this other keyword will be processed in a different exploration.

It soon becomes obvious that, due to its complexity, this solution is not viable for larger structures. A first method, already implemented, for optimizing the response time consists in limiting the path lengths by specifying a criterion of maximum path length covered, and thus abandoning terms too far away. An improvement over this method would be to find heuristics that would limit the exploration of the structure but would cover a sufficient number of significant semantic paths to construct a useful network. An idea is to follow only certain link types (for example, not to pursue SN (scope note) links of the thesaurus, see table 1), or to consider only certain link types either by selecting them in advance (for a specific search) or by relying on the immediate neighbourhood of each term. However, these heuristics, albeit necessary for an acceptable response time, do return partially truncated information (we can see this on the example: if we do not follow RT links (see Table 1), the network of Figure 1 will not be found).

7 Conclusion

The use of cataloguing services in environmental applications is becoming indispensable. Nevertheless, these services will only have an impact on the communities concerned when they lead to semi-automatic input and, additionally, if search engines results become more relevant than they currently are. The propositions described in this article aim for this latter objective. The contribution of the semantic aspect as we have proposed it within the MDweb metadata service, by incorporating thematic and spatial reference bases to the ISO 19115 standard, is significant. Our ideas of query expansion as well as those of extracting knowledge implicit in the results could only be tested on a limited number of metadata records but show promise. The way ahead is to pursue the integration of the semantic aspect within the tool and the use of semantic co-constructions (enriching the thesaurus stored in a database by moving towards a shared ontology). For the results display, future improvments will consist to flag the different types of relationships (semantic, spatial and temporal). It should be used as a foundation for a new search module based on the refering thesaurus total display.

References

1. Barde, J.: Mutualisation de données et de connaissances pour la gestion intégrée des zones cotières. Application au projet Syscolag. Mastersthesis (2005) Université Montpellier II, Ecole Doctorale Information, Structures, Systèmes
2. Bottraud, J.C., Bisson, G., Bruandet, M.F.: Expansion de requêtes par apprentissage automatique dans un assistant pour la recherche d'information. CORIA (2004) 89–108
3. Bourigault, D., Lame, G.: Analyse distributionnelle et structuration de la terminologie, application à la construction d'une ontologie documentaire du Droit Traitement Automatique de la Langue **43-1** (2002)
4. Fu, G., Jones, C.B., Abdelmoty, A.I.: Ontology-Based Spatial Query Expansion in Information Retrieval. OTM Conferences **2** (2005) 1466–1482
5. Desconnets, J.C., Moyroud, N., Libourel, T.: Méthodologie de mise en place d'observatoires virtuels via les métadonnées. INFORSID actes du XXIeme congres (2003) 253-267
6. ISO23950:1998: Information and documentation – Information retrieval (Z39.50) Application service definition and protocol specifications, ISO 23950. International Organization for Standardization (ISO) (1998)
7. ISO19115:2003: Geographical Information Metadata, ISO 19115. International Organization for Standardization (ISO) (2003)
8. OGC: Catalog Service Specification. Open Geospatial Consortium Inc (2005)
9. Soualmia, L.F., Darmoni, S.J.: Projection de requêtes pour une recherche d'information intelligente sur le Web. RJCIA (2003) 59–72
10. Sowa, J.F.: Conceptual Graphs for a Data Base Interface. IBM Journal of Research and Development **20** (1976) 336–357
11. Berners-Lee, T., Hendler, J., Lassila, O.: The Semantic Web. Scientific American **284** (2001) 35–43

SWWS 2006 PC Co-chairs' Message

Welcome to the proceedings of the 2nd IFIP WG 2.12 and WG 12.4 International Workshop on Web Semantics (SWWS 2006). These proceedings reflect the issues raised and presented during the SWWS workshop which proved to be an interdisciplinary forum for subject matters involving the theory and practice of Web semantics. This year three special tracks were organized as part of the main workshop, namely: security, trust and reputation systems, fuzzy models and systems and regulatory ontologies. The focus of such special tracks is to allow researchers of different backgrounds (such as business, formal models, trust, security, law, ontologies, fuzzy sets, artificial intelligence and philosophy) to meet and exchange ideas.

This year, a total of 34 papers were submitted to SWWS. Each submission was reviewed by at least three experts. The papers were judged according to their originality, validity, significance to theory and practice, readability and organization, and relevancy to the workshop topics and beyond. This resulted in the selection of 16 papers for presentation at the workshop and publication in this proceedings volume. We feel that these proceedings will inspire further research and create an intense following. The Program Committee comprised: Aldo Gangemi, Amit Sheth, Avigdor Gal, Carlos Sierra, Carole Goble, Chris Bussler, David Bell, Elisa Bertino, Elizabeth Chang, Ernesto Damiani, Ling Feng, Frank van Harmelen, Grigoris Antoniou, Hai Zhuge, Jaiwei Han, John Debenham, John Mylopoulos, Katia Sycara, Kokou Yetongnon, Kyu-Young Whang, Ling Liu, Lizhu Zhou, Lotfi Zadeh, Manfred Hauswirth, Masood Nikvesh, Mihaela Ulieru, Mohand-Said Hacid, Mukesh Mohania, Mustafa Jarrar, Neda Laurac, Nicola Guarino, Peter Spyns, Pieree Yves Schobbens, Qing Li, Ramasamy Uthurusamy, Robert Meersman, Robert Tolksdorf, Stefan Decker, Susan Urban, Tharam S. Dillon, Usuama Fayed, Wil van der Aalst, York Sure, Zahir Tari .

We would like to express our deepest appreciation to the authors of the submitted papers and thank all the workshop attendees and the Program Committee members for their dedication and assistance in creating our program and turning the workshop into a success. Producing this volume would not have been possible without the much-appreciated contribution of Peter Dimopoulos.

Thank you and we hope you will enjoy the papers as much as we do.

August 2006   Katia Sycara, Carnegie Mellon University, USA
                      Elizabeth Chang, Curtin University of Technology, Australia
                            (SWWS 2006 Program Committee Co-chairs)
                                Ernesto Damiani, Milan University, Italy
                        Mustafa Jarrar, Vrije Universiteit Brussel, Belgium
                            (SWWS 2006 Program Committee Vice-Chairs)
                    Tharam Dillon, University of Technology Sydney, Australia
                            (SWWS 2006 IFIP WG 2.12/ 12.4 Chair)

R. Meersman, Z. Tari, P. Herrero et al. (Eds.): OTM Workshops 2006, LNCS 4278, p. 1723, 2006.
© Springer-Verlag Berlin Heidelberg 2006

Reputation Ontology for Reputation Systems

Elizabeth Chang[1], Farookh Khadeer Hussain[1], and Tharam Dillon[2]

[1] Centre for Extended Enterprise and Business Intelligence and
School of Information Systems
Curtin University of Technology
Western Australia 6845
{Elizabeth.Chang, Farookh.Hussain}@cbs.curtin.edu.au
[2] Faculty of Information Technology, University of Technology, Sydney
Broadway, Australia
tharam@it.uts.edu.au

Abstract. The growing development of web-based reputation systems in the 21st century will have a powerful social and economic impact on both business entities and individual customers, because it makes transparent quality assessment on products and services to achieve customer assurance in the distributed web-based Reputation Systems. The web-based reputation systems will be the foundation for web intelligence in the future. Trust and Reputation help capture business intelligence through establishing customer trust relationships, learning consumer behavior, capturing market reaction on products and services, disseminating customer feedback, buyers' opinions and end-user recommendations. It also reveals dishonest services, unfair trading, biased assessment, discriminatory actions, fraudulent behaviors, and un-true advertising. The continuing development of these technologies will help in the improvement of professional business behavior, sales, reputation of sellers, providers, products and services. Given the importance of reputation in this paper, we propose ontology for reputation. In the business world we can consider the reputation of a product or the reputation of a service or the reputation of an agent. In this paper we propose ontology for these entities that can help us unravel the components and conceptualize the components of reputation of each of the entities.

1 Introduction

In this paper we propose two distinct definitions of reputation. The basic definition gives a simplistic view of reputation, and based on this simplistic view of reputation we propose ontology for reputation called the *Basic Reputation Ontology*. The basic definition and the basic reputation ontology are presented in Section 2.

The sophisticated definition of reputation gives a complete picture of reputation. We call this sophisticated definition of reputation an advanced definition of reputation, and based on this definition we define ontology for reputation termed as *Advanced Reputation Ontology*. The advanced definition and the advanced reputation ontology are presented in Section 3.

Reputation by itself is a generic term. In a service oriented or a business environment we may in fact refer to the reputation of a trusted agent, or the reputation of a product or service. Due to this we will have a specified and a specialized definition of

R. Meersman, Z. Tari, P. Herrero et al. (Eds.): OTM Workshops 2006, LNCS 4278, pp. 1724–1733, 2006.

the reputation of a product, service or trusted agent. Based on the specialized definitions of reputation of product, reputation of service and the reputation of a trusted agent, in this paper we will propose reputation ontology for each of these business entities. The ontology for reputation of a trusted agent is presented in Section 4. The ontology for reputation of a service and the ontology for the reputation of a product are presented in Section 5 and Section 6 respectively.

In Section 7 we present ontology for the trustworthiness about an *opinion communicated by a recommender*. Finally Section 8 concludes the paper.

From existing literature we note that there has been no effort to define ontology for reputation based on the finer granularity of defining reputation (Rahman et al 2003, Aberer et al 2003, Cornelli et al 2003, Xiong et al 2003, Yu et al 2002).

2 Basic Reputation Ontology

Reputation is about developing the measure of trustworthiness from Third Party Agent's recommendations, not by the Trusting Agents themselves. This is because the Trusted Agent is unknown to the Trusting Agent.

2.1 Basic Reputation Ontology

The Reputation of a Trusted *Agent is an aggregated Reputation Value that is recommended by all of the Third Party Recommendation Agents*.

The Reputation Value is known as the Reputation of the Trusted Agent. It is an aggregated Trust Value obtained from all of the Recommendation Agents who responded to a Reputation Query.

There are several methods used to aggregate the feedback. Discussing them would be out side the scope of the paper; however, the premise in calculating the basic reputation of a Trusted Agent is outlined below:

Basic Reputation of the Trusted Agent = $\bigcup$ (Recommendation Value)

where we define $\bigcup$ as an operator for combining the Recommendation Value.

A graphical view of the Basic Reputation Ontology is shown in the following diagram though the use of UML-OCL notation.

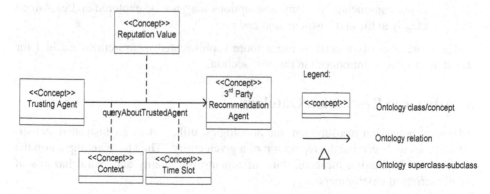

Fig. 1. Ontology for Basic Reputation of the Trusted Agent

In the above ontology diagram (Figure 1), boxes represent ontological concept, up-Arrow represent super class and sub class of concepts. Note that in ontology, there is no need to explicitly define what kind of relationship the super class (upper class) has with sub-class. The most important thing in Ontology is to build a relationship between the concepts, whether it is super-sub class hierarchy relationship or direct association (non-hierarchy). A line with an arrow represents that one concept is closely related to another. A Dotted line represents navigation to association concept. Association classes are used for associations that themselves participate in an association with another class.

Below is a formula table for the Basic Reputation Ontology:

Table 1. Formal Axiom Table of the Basic Reputation Ontology

Formula Name	Formula of Basic Reputation Value
Concept	Reputation Value
Inferred Attribute	Basic Value
Formula	Basic Value = U(Recommendation Value)
Description	Basic Reputation Value of the Trusted Agent
Variable	Recommendation Value
Ad hoc binary relation	QueryAboutTrustedAgent

With the simple (or Basic) Reputation Measure, there could be three problems created:

a) It may end up with out a normal distribution in statistical analysis, such as 99% of Third Party Recommendation Agents giving 'positive' or 'trustworthy' ratings to 99% of Agents (see e-Bay example in Figure 9.8).

b) It may create doubt on the accuracy and adequacy of the Reputation Measure itself, such as the truthfulness of the Reputation Rating and the depth of the criteria addressed in the reputation.

c) It may lack addressing the dynamic nature of Trust and Reputation, as Trust and Reputation will change over time. A simple 'one value for the lifetime' is not convincing, as many assumptions may not be explored and explained clearly to the end customer and end user.

Therefore, there is a need to use a more sophisticated measurement method for Reputation. This is introduced in the next section.

3   Advanced Reputation Ontology

Advanced reputation measurement methodologies, utilize more sophisticated statistical methods to determine the reputation of a given entity. They have an impact on the accuracy of Reputation measure, thus influencing the quality and moral hazards of service-oriented environments.

3.1 Advanced Reputation Ontology

The Reputation of a Trusted Agent is *an aggregated Reputation Value that is recommended by all of the Third Party Recommendation Agents. The aggregation is weighted by the Trustworthiness of the Recommendation Agent, the Trustworthiness of the opinion and the ranking of the 1st, 2nd and 3rd hand opinions.*

Mathematically the afore mentioned definition of reputation can be represented as:

Advanced Reputation of the Trusted Agent = $\bigcup$ (Recommendation Value * Trustworthiness of opinion * Perceived 1st. 2nd and 3rd hand opinion * Time elapsed factor).

Where we define $\bigcup$ is an operator for combining and taking into account the Trustworthiness of the Recommendation Agent's opinion, ratio of 1st hand, 2nd hand and 3rd hand opinion, and time factors. This advanced aggregation formula will enable the system to eliminate recommendations that are not trustworthy, self-recommendations, and those that are malicious.

A graphical view of the Advanced Reputation Ontology is shown in the following diagram through the use of UML-OCL notation.

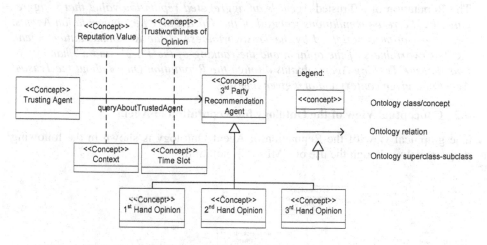

Fig. 2. Ontology for Advanced Reputation of the Trusted Agent

In the above ontology diagram (Figure 2) boxes represent ontological concept, up-Arrow represent super class and sub class of concepts, and a line with an arrow shows that one concept is closely related to another. Dotted line represents navigation to association concept. Association classes are used for associations that themselves participate in an association with another class.

Below is a formula table for the Advanced Reputation Ontology:

Table 2. Formal Axiom Table of the Advanced Reputation Ontology

Formula Name	Formula of Advanced Reputation Value
Concepts	Reputation Value, Trustworthiness of Opinion, Timeslot, 1st Hand Opinion, 2nd Hand Opinion, 3rd Hand Opinion
Inferred Attribute	Advanced Value
Formula	Advanced Value = U(Recommendation Value*Trustworthiness Value*{1st Hand Opinion Value, 2nd Hand Opinion Value, 3rd Hand Opinion Value}*Time Elapsed Factor)
Description	Advanced Reputation Value of the Trusted Agent
Variables	Recommendation Value, Trustworthiness Value, 1st Hand Opinion Value, 2nd Hand Opinion Value, 3rd Hand Opinion Value, Time Elapses Factor
Ad hoc binary relation	QueryAboutTrustedAgent

4   Ontology for Reputation of Agent

4.1   Ontology for Reputation of Agent

The Reputation of a Trusted *Agent is an aggregated reputation value that is aggregated by the recommendations from all of the Third Party Recommendation Agents. The aggregation is weighted by the Trustworthiness of the Recommendation Agent, the Trustworthiness of the opinion and the ranking of the 1st, 2nd and 3rd hand opinions that the Trusting Agent obtains through the Reputation Query about the Trusted Agent in a given context and at a given timeslot.*

4.2   Conceptual View of the Ontology for Reputation of Agent

The graphical view of the Reputation of Agent Ontology is shown in the following diagram below though the use of UML-OCL notation.

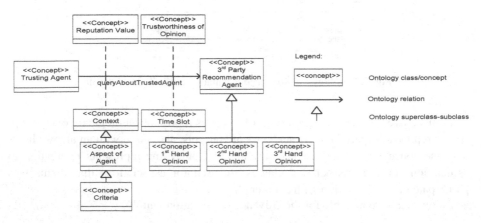

Fig. 3. Ontology for Reputation of Agent

In the above ontology diagram (Figure 3), boxes represent ontological concept, up-arrow represent super class and sub class of concepts. A line with an arrow represents that one concept is closely related to another. A Dotted line represents navigation to association concept. Association classes are used for associations that themselves participate in an association with another class.

5 Ontology for Reputation of Service

The ontology for the Reputation of Services has potential implications for the large growing number of service providers to join e-services. In this section we discuss the use of ontology for the Reputation and the Quality of Service.

5.1 Ontology for Reputation of Service

The Reputation of the quality of a *Service is an aggregated reputation value that is aggregated by the recommendations from all of the Third Party Recommendation Agents. The aggregation is weighted by the Trustworthiness of the Recommendation Agent, the Trustworthiness of the opinion and the ranking of the 1st, 2nd and 3rd hand opinions that the Trusting Agent obtains though the Reputation Query about the Trusted Agen, in a given context and at a given timeslot.*

5.2 Conceptual View of the Ontology for Reputation of Service

The graphical view of the Reputation of Service Ontology is shown in the following diagram though the use of UML-OCL notation.

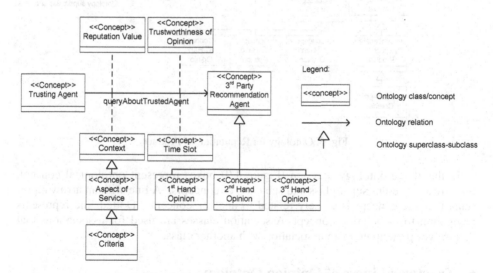

Fig. 4. Ontology for Reputation of Service

In the above ontology diagram (Figure 9.13), boxes represent ontological concept, up-Arrow represent super class and sub class of concepts. A line with an arrow represents that one concept is closely related another. A dotted line represents navigation to association concept. Association classes are used for associations that themselves participate in an association with another class.

5.3 Ontology for Reputation of Product

The Reputation of the quality of a Product *is an aggregated reputation value that is aggregated by the recommendations from all of the Third Party Recommendation Agents. The aggregation is weighted by the Trustworthiness of the Recommendation Agent, the Trustworthiness of the opinion and the ranking of the 1st, 2nd and 3rd hand opinions that the Trusting Agent obtains through the Reputation Query about the Trusted Agen, in a given context and timeslot.*

5.4 Conceptual View of the Ontology for Reputation of Product

The graphical view of the Reputation of Product Ontology is shown in the following diagram though the use of UML-OCL notation.

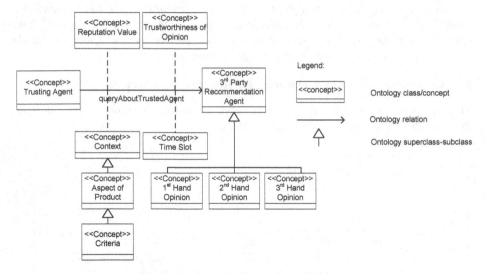

Fig. 5. Ontology for Reputation of Product

In the above ontology diagram (Figure 4.9) boxes represent ontological concept, up-Arrow represent super class and sub class of concepts. A line with an arrow represents that the concept is closely related to another concept. Dotted line represents navigation to association concept. Association classes are used for associations that themselves participate in an association with another class.

6   Trustworthiness of Opinion Ontology

6.1 Opinions in Reputation

The most crucial factor for reputation measurement (of a trusted agent or a service or a product) is the validation of trustworthiness of the opinion or the recommendation

provided by the Third Party Recommendation Agents. The trusting entity after soliciting recommendation from the third party recommendation Agents needs to have an
idea of the extent to which it regards each of the recommendations communicated by
each of the third party recommendation Agents as being correct. In other words it
needs to make known the trustworthiness of the opinion communicated by the third
party agent so that the communicated recommendation can be properly weighted.
Discussing the mathematical framework for determining the trustworthiness of the
opinion is outside the scope of this paper. Further discussion along with detailed
examples of how to determine the trustworthiness of the opinion can be found in
(Chang, Dillon and Hussain, 2005). In this paper we will provide a ontology for the
trustworthiness of the opinion.

6.2 Ontology for Trustworthiness of Opinion

We define the Opinion Trust Ontology as the following Trust Tuple:

*Review Trust [Receiver, Reviewer, Review or Feedback, Assessment Criteria,
Timeslot, and Trustworthiness of each assessment criterion)*

The graphical view of the Trustworthiness of Opinion Ontology is shown in the
following diagram though the use of UML-OCL notation

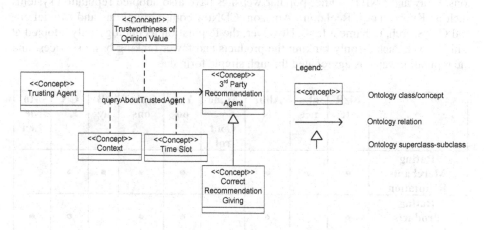

Fig. 6. Ontology for the Trustworthiness of Opinion

In the above ontology diagram (Figure 6), boxes represent ontological concept, up-
Arrow represent super class and sub class of concepts. A line with arrow represents
that the concept is closely related to another concept. Dotted line represents navigation to association concept. Association classes are used for associations that themselves participate in an association with another class.

Below is a table for the Trustworthiness of Opinion Ontology:

Table 3. Formal Axiom Table of the Trustworthiness of Opinion Ontology

Formula Name	Formula of Trustworthiness of Opinion Value
Concepts	Trustworthiness of Opinion Value, Correct Recommendation Giving
Inferred Attribute	Trustworthiness Value
Formula	Trustworthiness Value = Actual Trust Value Found On Interaction - Recommendation Value
Description	Trust Value of Recommendation Agent in giving correct opinion
Variables	Actual Trust Value Found On Interaction, Recommendation Value
Ad hoc binary relation	QueryAboutTrustedAgent

7   Application of Reputation Ontology and Technology

Reputation Systems address the quality of goods and services, sellers or service providers, network agents or reviewers, which is based on a number of criteria. Currently, some well known e-commerce portals already start using the reputation systems, such as BizRate, Slashdot, Elance, BBC, Alibris, MoneyControl, Yahoo, Epinions, eBay and CNET. Other popular websites have also adopted reputation systems such as KuroHin.org, Reel.com, Amazon, CDNow.com, GroupLens and MovieLens and CitySearch, to name a few. However, the Reputation technology only adopted at a high level, such as only ranking the products and fewer ranking basic services, and the reputation value is aggregated through simple formulae.

	BizRate	eLance	Alibris	MoneyControl	Yahoo	Epinions	eBay	CNET	MovieLens
Rating Merchants Reputation	•	•	•		•	•	•	•	
Rating Products Reputation	•		•		•	•		•	•
Rating Customers Reputation		•					•		
Rating Reviews Reputation				•					
Rating Reviewers Reputation				•					
Recommendation Systems									•

The above table gives a high-level view of the technology adoption (the black-dots) of the listed companies (see horizontal bar) for their business intelligence. Due to the space constraints of this paper, we will not introduce their site; however, readers are encouraged to visit website themselves.

8 Conclusions

In this paper we propose a basic and an advanced definition of reputation, and based on this definition we proposed the basic reputation ontology and the advanced reputation ontology respectively. Additionally, we proposed specialized reputation ontology for the reputation of a product, the reputation of a service or the reputation of the trusted agent. Finally we proposed ontology for the trustworthiness of the opinion of a recommendation.

References

Chang, E., Dillon T, Hussain, F "Trust and Reputation for Service Oriented Environment". John Wiley and Sons, 2005

Abdul-Rahman, A., & Hailes, S., (2003), *Relying On Trust To Find Reliable Information*, Available: http://www.cs.ucl.ac.uk/staff/F.AbdulRahman/docs/dwacos99.pdf (7/08/2003).

Aberer, K. & Despotovic, Z., (2003), *Managing Trust in a Peer-2-Peer Information System*, Available: http://citeseer.nj.nec.com/aberer01managing.html (11/9/2003).

Ba, S., and Pavlou, P., (2002). "Evidence of the Effect of Trust Building Technology in Electronic Markets: Price Premiums and Buyer Behavior". *MIS Quarterly*, 26 (3).

Bakos, Y., and Dellarocas, C., (2002) "Cooperation without Enforcement?-A comparative Analysis of Litigation and Online Reputation as Quality Assurance Mechanism". *Proceedings of the 23rd International Conference on Information Systems* (ICIS 2002), Barcelona, Spain.

Cornelli, F., Damiani, E., Vimercati, S., De Capitani di Vimercati, Paraboschi, S. & Samarati, P., (2003), *Choosing Reputable Servents in a P2P Network*, Available: http://citeseer.nj.nec.com/cache/papers/cs/26951/http:zSzzSzseclab.crema.unimi.itzSzPapers zSzwww02.pdf/choosing-reputable-servents-in.pdf (20/9/2003).

Dellarocas C., (2003) "The Digitization of Word-of-mouth: Promise and Challenges of Online Feedback Mechanisms" *Working Paper*, March 2003, Massachusetts Institute of Technology, http://ssrm.com

Xiong, L. & Liu, L., (2003), A *Reputation-Based Trust Model for Peer-to-Peer eCommerce Communities*, Available: http://citeseer.nj.nec.com/xiong03reputationbased.html (9/10/2003).

Yu, B., Singh, M. P., (2002). 'Distributed Reputation Management for Electronic Commerce.' Computation Intelligence 18 (4) : 535-549.

Rule-Based Access Control for Social Networks

Barbara Carminati, Elena Ferrari, and Andrea Perego

DICOM, Università degli Studi dell'Insubria, Varese, Italy
{barbara.carminati, elena.ferrari, andrea.perego}@uninsubria.it

Abstract. Web-based social networks (WBSNs) are online communities where participants can establish relationships and share resources across the Web with other users. In recent years, several WBSNs have been adopting Semantic Web technologies, such as FOAF, for representing users' data and relationships, making it possible to enforce information interchange across multiple WBSNs. Despite its advantages in terms of information diffusion, this raised the need of giving content owners more control on the distribution of their resources, which may be accessed by a community far wider than they expected.

In this paper, we present an access control model for WBSNs, where policies are expressed as constraints on the type, depth, and trust level of existing relationships. Relevant features of our model are the use of certificates for granting relationships' authenticity, and the *client-side* enforcement of access control according to a rule-based approach, where a subject requesting to access an object must demonstrate that it has the rights of doing that.

1 Introduction

Web-based social networks (WBSNs) [1] are online communities which allow Web users to publish resources (e.g., blogs) and to establish relationships with other users, possibly of different type ("friend", "colleague", etc.), for purposes which may concern, e.g., entertainment, religion, dating, or business. One of the recent trends in WBSNs is the adoption of Semantic Web technologies, in particular FOAF [2,3], to represent users' personal data and relationships [4]. Thanks to this and to the adoption of decentralized authentication systems such as OpenID [5], it has been made simpler to access and disseminate information across multiple WBSNs. If this has been quite a relevant improvement with respect to the previous situation, it is now necessary that resource owners have more control over information sharing. In fact, differently from 'traditional' social networks, where usually each user knows the others, WBSNs are quite larger, and each node (i.e., user) has direct relationships with only a subgraph of the network. As a consequence, it may be not appropriate to make available any information to all the users of one or more WBSNs. So far, this issue has been addressed by some of the available Social Network Management Systems (SNMSs) by allowing users to state whether a specific information (e.g., personal data and resources) should be public or accessible only by the users with whom the owner of such information has a direct relationship. Such simple access control strategies have the advantage of being straightforward, but, on one hand, they may grant access to non-authorized users, and, on the other hand, they are not flexible enough in denoting authorized users. In

R. Meersman, Z. Tari, P. Herrero et al. (Eds.): OTM Workshops 2006, LNCS 4278, pp. 1734–1744, 2006.

fact, they do not take into account the 'type' of relationship existing between users and, consequently, it is not possible to state that only, say, my "friends" can access a given information. Moreover, they do not allow to grant access to users who have an indirect relationship with the resource owner (e.g., the "friends of my friends").

We think that more sophisticated access control mechanisms can be enforced in the current WBSNs, dealing with such issues. Besides relationships, some other information can be used for this purpose. In fact, the graph of a WBSN allows us to exploit the notion of *depth* of a relationship, which corresponds to the length of the shortest path between two nodes. The depth of a relationship may be a useful parameter, which allows us to control the propagation of access rules in the network. Moreover, in some WB-SNs, users can specify how much they trust other users, by assigning them a *trust level*. Such information is currently exploited for purposes which encompass the primary objectives of a WBSN, e.g., as a basis for recommender systems, but it can be used as well to denote the subjects authorized to access a resource in terms of their trustworthiness. Note that the notion of trust applies also to users with an *indirect* relationship—i.e., a relationship with depth greater than 1—, and thus we can combine the usage of depth and trust in access policies.

In this paper, we propose a rule-based access control model for WBSNs, which allows the specification of access rules for online resources where authorized subjects are denoted in terms of the relationship type, depth, and trust level existing between users in the network. To the best of our knowledge, this is the first proposal of an access control model for social networks. The different tasks to be carried out to enforce access control are shared among three distinguished actors—namely, the owner of the requested resource, the subject which requested it, and the SNMS. More precisely, we adopt the approach outlined by Tim Berners-Lee & al. in [6], where access control is enforced client-side, since access to resources is granted if the requestor is able to demonstrate that he/she satisfies given requirements. For this purpose, users' relationships are represented by a specific OWL vocabulary we designed, REL-X [7], whereas access rules are expressed in Notation 3 Logic (N3) [8], and then evaluated by the Cwm reasoner [9] against the existing relationships in order to generate a proof.

The remainder of this paper is organized as follows. Section 2 discusses access control requirements of social networks. Section 3 summarizes the main features of our approach, whereas Sect. 4 illustrates the proposed access control model. Then, Sect. 5 describes the system architecture of the prototype being implemented. Moreover, a running example of how access control is enforced is provided in Sect. 6. Finally, Sect. 7 concludes the paper and outlines future research directions.

2   Access Control in Web-Based Social Networks

In this section, we discuss which are the basic requirements that an access control mechanism for WBSNs should satisfy. However, before discussing access control issues in social networks, we need to briefly introduce what a social network is and how we represent it.

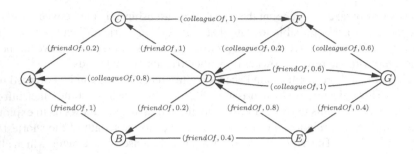

Fig. 1. A simple social network. Labels associated with edges denote, respectively, the type and trust level of the corresponding relationship.

2.1 The Social Network Model

A common way to represent a network is by means of a graph. This representation can be adopted also in the context of social networks, where each node denotes a user in the network, whereas edges represent the existing relationships between users (see Fig. 1 for an example). However, since users of the same community could establish among each others relationships of different nature, the graph representation of a social network must be extended to support the *type* of a relationship. Moreover, we have to take into account that not all relationships are mutual—consider, for instance, the "parent of" relationship. Thus, rather than a simple graph, we have to consider a direct graph, where the direction of the edges denotes, respectively, which user has specified the relationship and the user for whom a relationship has been specified: the former corresponds to the terminal node of the edge, whereas the latter to the initial one. According to this interpretation, we can read the graph in Fig. 1, as follows: A(lice) specified a relationship with both B(ob) and C(arl), denoting them as friends; Bob and Carl specified the same type of relationship with D(avid), and so on.

Relationships can be grouped into two different classes, i.e., *direct* and *indirect* relationships. A direct relationship of type rt between user b and user a is represented by a direct edge exiting from the node representing b and entering into the node representing a. As an example, let us consider the social network depicted in Fig. 1, where Bob has a direct relationship of type "friend of" with Alice, F(rank) has a direct relationship of type "colleague of" with David, etc. By contrast, an indirect relationship of type rt between user b and user a is represented as a path connecting b to a, consisting of all the edges representing relationships of type rt. Examples of indirect relationships are provided in Fig. 1, where E(ve) and Alice are not directly connected, but they are related in that Eve is friend of Bob, and Bob is friend of Alice. Thus, we say that Eve has an indirect relationship with Alice of type "friend of".

Besides their type, relationships are characterized by a *trust level* t (see [1] for an interesting discussion on trust in social networks). Given an in/direct relationship *rel* between user b and user a, the trust level denotes how much user a considers trustworthy user b wrt relationship *rel*. We do not enter here in the details of the formulas used to calculate the trust level, which may vary depending on the social network. However, we need to remark that, regardless of the algorithm used to compute the trust level t

of a relationship of type rt between user b and user a, such calculation needs to take into account the trust levels of all the edges belonging to paths corresponding to all the possible in/direct relationships of type rt between b and a. As will be explained in the next section, this aspect is quite relevant in our architecture.

It is important to remark that our notion of trust level is slightly different with respect to that defined in [1], where a trust level is associated with users, and not with a specific relationship involving them. Moreover, two types of trust are distinguished, namely, *topical* trust (i.e., how much a user consider trustworthy the opinions of another user about a given topic—e.g., movies) and *absolute* trust (i.e., how much a user consider trustworthy the opinions of another user independently from the topic). Our notion of trust is more similar to the latter, with the difference that we allow users to express different trust levels depending on the type of relationship. As will be mentioned in Sect. 7, we plan to extend our model in order to support also topical trust.

A further relationship's property is its *depth*. The depth of a relationship of type rt between user b and user a corresponds to the length of the shortest among the paths representing all possible in/direct relationships of type rt between user b and user a. For instance, from G(reg) to Alice, three paths exist of type "friend of": $GEBA$ (length 3), $GEDBA$, and $GEDCA$ (both of length 4). Consequently, the depth of the relationship existing between Greg and Alice is equal to 3.

Our notion of relationship can then be represented as a tuple, where its components denote the users participating in it, along with the type, depth, and trust level of the relationship itself. Thus, since a relationship is an entity with a set of attributes (i.e., type, depth, and trust level), we cannot represent it in RDF as a property. Consequently, we cannot adopt either the FOAF vocabulary or its extensions (such as the RELA-TIONSHIP vocabulary [10] and the Trust Ontology [11]), where relationships, along with their types and trust levels are represented as distinct properties of users. For this reason, we designed an OWL vocabulary, namely, REL-X [7], where a relationship is modelled as an instance of the `relx:Relationship` OWL class, characterized by a set of properties which allow us to associate with a relationship the users participating in it, its type, depth, and trust level.

2.2 Access Control Requirements in WBSNs

Devising an access control model for WBSNs requires to face up with a dynamic environment, where a user in the social network wishes to share his/her data with other users of the same network, on the basis of in/direct relationships existing between them, that may dynamically change. Therefore, a first requirement that we must address is supporting access control on the basis of users' relationships. Let us consider again the social network depicted in Fig. 1, and assume that Alice wishes to share her resources with her direct friends, and some of her indirect friends. More precisely, she wants to grant access to Bob and Carl, since they are direct friends of hers. She wants to allow also Eve to access resources, even if Alice does not know her, because she is a direct friend of Bob. Nonetheless, Alice may be not sure whether Greg is trustworthy or not, since she cannot know how Eve chooses his friends. Thus, Alice could decide to prevent him from accessing her resources. This example points out that the length of the path connecting two nodes is a relevant information for access control, since the longer is a path, the lower is the level of trust existing between its ends. For instance, if Alice states that a given resource r_A can be accessed by "a friend" with depth equal at most to 2 ($1 \leq d \leq 2$), users authorized to access r_A are Bob, Carl ($d = 1$), David, and Eve ($d = 2$). The depth of a relationship is thus a useful parameter, which gives owners more control on the distribution of their resources.

A further relevant aspect, that should be considered in devising an access control model for WBSNs, is the trust level of a relationship. Obviously, the notion of trust gains importance in the context of access control, since it is a further discriminant that can be exploited by users to decide whether a resource can be released or not. Thus, an access control policy for WBSNs should make a user able to state which type of relationship should exist between him/her and the requesting user, along with the maximum depth and the minimum trust level of the relationship.

From the side of access control enforcement, traditionally, this task is performed by an access control mechanism (referred to as *reference monitor*), that is, a trusted software module that intercepts each access request submitted to the system and, on the basis of the specified policies, determines whether the access should be partially or totally authorized, or it should be denied. To adopt this strategy in WBSNs, there is the need of a trusted place where the reference monitor should be safely hosted. A naïve solution is thus to assume that the SNMS hosts the reference monitor. Nonetheless, since the number of participants of a WBSN may be quite big, a centralized reference monitor would be a bottleneck. For this reason, we prefer to investigate an alternative strategy, where the owner him/herself is the only administrator of his/her data. Thus, he/she states the access control policies according to him/her preferences, and for each access request he/she locally determines whether the access should be authorized or not. Obviously, this solution ensures the user a total control over his/her data, but it requires software and hardware resources more powerful than those typically available to social network participants. In order to overcome this drawback, we have decided to take over the view outlined by Tim Berners-Lee & al. in [6], for enforcing access control in the Semantic Web. The main novelty of such approach is that, differently from traditional access control, the task of verifying whether a given user is authorized to access a given object is in charge of the requesting user, who must prove to the resource owner that it satisfies the requirements expressed by access control policies.

3   Overall of the Proposed Approach

As pointed out in Sect. 2.2, we here decided to customize in the context of WBSNs the client-side and decentralized access control outlined in [6]. This solution implies that when a user (hereafter, the *requestor*) requests a resource to another user (hereafter, the *resource owner*), the former receives from the latter a set of *access rules* regulating the release of the requested resource. These rules basically state which type of relationship should exist between the resource owner and the requestor, and the maximum depth and minimum trust level allowed. The requestor has to provide the resource owner with a *proof* showing that between them there exists the required relationship, and that this relationship has the required depth and trust level. Proofs are generated by exploiting a reasoner (see Sect. 5 for details). Thus, the resource owner provided with this proof is able to locally verify whether the resource has to be released or not. More precisely, in our system, access rules are expressed using N3, and evaluated by the Cwm reasoner. The adoption of N3 instead of Semantic Web rule languages, such as RuleML [12] or SWRL [13], is determined by the fact that N3 allows a compact representation of RDF statements, which can be easily delivered via HTTP headers.

Since in a WBSN scenario the access rules are defined against relationships, the requestor has to provide the reasoner with assertions on the existing relationships between him/her and the resource owner. This requires solving the following issue: how can a resource owner be ensured that assertions created by the requestor are correct and trustworthy? For instance, how the resource owner can be ensured that the requestor has not maliciously forged a new relationship? Thus, we need a mechanism which prevents a malicious user from submitting to the reasoner assertions on fake relationships.

To cope with these problems, we propose a solution exploiting the notion of *certificates*. According to this solution, whenever Alice establishes a new relationship with Bob, they both create and sign a certificate stating that between Bob and Alice there exists a direct relationship with a certain trust. By means of certificates, it is possible to verify the correctness of assertions on that relationship. More in general, the correctness of an assertion related to an in/direct relationship between users *a* and *b* can be verified by retrieving the chain of certificates confirming the existence of a path between them. By contrast, proving the assertion on the relationship's trust needs a more complex strategy, since the trust level between two nodes is computed taking into account all the possible paths connecting them [1]. Moreover, the requestor should provide the resource owner with all the corresponding chains of certificates in order to let him/her verify the correctness of the assertion wrt the trust level. Besides its inefficiency, this solution is liable to security attacks, in that the resource owner cannot be sure that the requestor has actually provided all the possible chains of certificates, or he/she has intentionally omitted a chain with a low trust level.

To overcome this drawback, we have investigated a slightly different architecture wrt the one outlined by Tim Berners-Lee & al. in [6]. Indeed, we propose a *semidecentralized* architecture, according to which a given trusted node in the network, referred to as *central node CN*, is in charge of managing certificates, and of computing the trust levels of relationships. Thus, whenever a requestor receives from the resource owner the access rules regulating the release of his/her resources, the former requests to *CN* the certificate chains proving the existence of a given relationship, as well as its trust level. The certificate chain, if any, is generated by *CN* by consulting the certificate repository, and, before being returned to the requestor, the corresponding trust level is signed by *CN*. Then, the requestor exploits the received certificate chain to generate the assertion for the reasoner. If the reasoner generates a proof, the requestor sends it to the resource owner, together with the certificate chain corresponding to the assertion, and the signed trust level. The main benefit of such semi-decentralized solution is that it fits well with the architecture of current WBSNs. Indeed, in such architectures, users' personal data (i.e., the data provided by users during the registration to a WBSN) and relationships are stored by the SNMS in a central repository, accessible via Web, whereas no information is stored by users on client-side. The central node corresponds then to the SNMS, which usually relies on hardware resources more powerful than those available on client-side. Thus, in the semi-decentralized approach, the central node is in charge of the tasks usually carried out by the SNMS, whereas the other nodes are in charge of enforcing access control for the resources they own. As a last remark, it is important to note that the central node is not in charge of storing users' data, but only relationship certificates. Thanks to this, we can ensure users' data confidentiality wrt the central node.

4 The Proposed Access Control Model

In order to enforce access control in WBSN environments, we defined a rule-based model where policies are specified by resource owners, and they denote implicitly the 'profile' of authorized users by means of one or more *access conditions*, i.e. constraints on the type, depth, and trust level of the relationships they have with other users in the network.

In what follows, we denote by V_{SN}, E_{SN}, RT_{SN}, T_{SN} the sets of nodes, edges, relationship types, and trust levels, respectively, of a social network *SN*. The notion of access condition is formally defined as follows.

Definition 1 (Access Condition). *Given a social network SN, an access condition cond against SN is a tuple* $(v, rt, \mathrm{D\,max}, t\,\mathrm{min})$*, where* $v \in V_{SN} \cup \{*\}$ *is the node with which the requestor must have a relationship,* $rt \in RT_{SN} \cup \{*\}$ *is a relationship type, whereas* $\mathrm{D\,max} \in \mathbb{N} \cup \{*\}$ *and* $t\,\mathrm{min} \in T_{SN} \cup \{*\}$ *are, respectively, the maximum depth and the minimum trust level that the relationship must have. If* $v = *$ *and/or* $rt = *$, *v corresponds to any user in* V_{SN} *and/or rt corresponds to any relationship in* RT_{SN}, *whereas if* $\mathrm{D\,max} = *$ *and/or* $t\,\mathrm{min} = *$, *there is no constraint concerning the depth and/or trust level, respectively.*

Access control requirements of a given object can then be expressed by a set of conditions. More precisely, given an object *obj* owned by v_o, the set of access conditions applying to *obj* are expressed by an *access rule* specified by v_o. Such notion is formally defined as follows.

Definition 2 (Access Rule). *An access rule rul is a tuple* $(oid, cset)$*, where oid is the identifier of object obj, whereas cset is a set of conditions* $\{cond_1, \ldots, cond_n\}$*, expressing the requirements a node must satisfy in order to be allowed to access object obj.*

It is important to note that the conditions in *cset* do not denote a set of alternative requirements, but *all* the requirements to be satisfied. In other words, the semantics of a set of conditions $\{cond_1, \ldots, cond_n\}$ can be expressed as $cond_1 \wedge \cdots \wedge cond_n$. It may be also the case that more than one rule is specified for a given object. For instance, let us suppose that object *obj* is associated with two rules *rul*, *rul'*. In such a case, we consider the corresponding two sets of conditions $\{cond_1, \ldots, cond_n\}$ and $\{cond'_1, \ldots, cond'_m\}$ as sets of alternative access control requirements—i.e., $(cond_1 \wedge \cdots \wedge cond_n) \vee (cond'_1 \wedge \cdots \wedge cond'_m)$.

As illustrated in Sect. 3, in general, a requestor is authorized to access an object if he/she provides the resource owner with a proof of the fact that he/she satisfies at least one of the corresponding access rules. To make the task of generating proofs easier, we translate relationships, conditions, and access rules into equivalent logical formulas. In particular, a relationship *rel* of type *rt*, depth D, and trust level *t*, between users *b* and *a*, can be expressed by the following assertion:

$$hasSubj(rel, b) \wedge hasObj(rel, a) \wedge hasType(rel, rt) \wedge hasDepth(rel, \text{D}) \wedge hasTrust(rel, t)$$

where *hasSubj, hasObj, hasType, hasDepth*, and *hasTrust* are predicates returning "true" if the corresponding relation is satisfied. Similarly, a condition $cond = (v, rt, \text{D max}, t \text{min})$ can be translated into an equivalent formula *p*, denoted as follows:

$$hasSubj(?rel, ?x) \wedge hasObj(?rel, v) \wedge hasType(?rel, rt) \wedge hasDepth(?rel, ?\text{D}) \wedge \leq$$
$$(?\text{D}, \text{D max}) \wedge hasTrust(?rel, ?t) \wedge \geq (?t, t \text{min})$$

where variable ?*x* represents the requesting user. Finally, according to the semantics of a set of conditions, an access rule $(oid, \{cond_1, \ldots, cond_n\})$ corresponds to a Horn-like clause $(p_1 \wedge \cdots \wedge p_n) \rightarrow canAccess(?x, oid)$, where the predicate *canAccess* states that the user represented by variable ?*x* is authorized to access the object with identifier *oid*. A proof is then obtained by using as arguments the set of existing relationships and access rules. If more than one rule applies to the same object, they are verified one by one, until a valid proof, if any, is obtained.

5 System Architecture

The architecture of the system we are currently implementing consists of two main services: the *central node CN*, corresponding to the SNMS, and a set of *periferal nodes*, corresponding to the nodes in the network. Figure 2 depicts the main components of such services, and an example of interaction between two periferal nodes, where the labelled arrows correspond to the steps of the access control procedure illustrated in Sect. 6. Our system exploits the OpenID framework, and thus users are identified by OpenID addresses. Moreover, we consider as a resource any information accessible via the Web, which is then identified by means of a URI.

The central node is a service run by the SNMS, and it consists of the certificate directory, storing all the certificates generated by the users in the network, and of two main modules: the *certificate manager* and the *certificate retrieval module*. The certificate manager is in charge of receiving the certificates sent by the users in the network, verifying their validity, and performing insert, update, and revoke operations. In our system, users can decide whether the relationships they are establishing (and thus the corresponding certificates) must be public or private. Private relationships can be used only by the users participating in them in order to perform access control. The certificate retrieval module is in charge of replying to requests asking for the chains of certificates existing between two nodes in the network. Such module is also in charge of computing the trust level of a relationship, derived from the information stored into the corresponding chains of certificates.

Periferal nodes are services which must be run by a server machine (either any server in the Internet or the end user's machine itself), and they consist of four main components: the certificate manager, the rule manager, and the access control and access

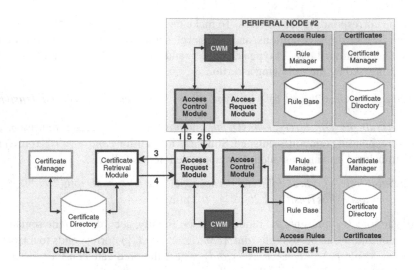

Fig. 2. System architecture

request modules. The certificate manager is in charge of managing and storing the certificates generated by the corresponding user, whereas the access rule manager stores and manages all the access rules specified by the user for the resources he/she owns. The access control module (ACM) replies to the access requests submitted by users in the network. More precisely, the ACM is in charge of a) sending the rules concerning the requested object, b) verifying the corresponding proofs, and c) delivering the requested object. For the first task, the ACM exploits an N3 translator, which transforms the rules stored into the access rule base. The second task is performed by the Cwm reasoner, which verifies the validity of the proof. In addition, the access control module may check the correctness of relationship assertions used as arguments in the proof, by verifying if they match with those obtained from the chains of certificates sent along with the proof by the requesting user. By contrast, the access request module (ARM) is in charge of a) submitting access requests, b) retrieving the chains of certificates from the central node and generating the relationship assertions to be used in a proof, and c) computing the proof itself. As the ACM, for these purposes the ARM exploits the N3 translator and the Cwm reasoner.

It is interesting to note that the ARM is a quite independent component of a periferal node, since it communicates only with the central node and with the ACMs of other periferal nodes. For this reason, we plan to implement periferal nodes in two different applications: the former will be a server application consisting of the ACM, the access rule base, and the certificate directory. By contrast, the latter will be a client application, to be built as a browser extension, implementing the ARM and providing a rule and certificate editor, allowing users to specify access rules and establish relationships without the need of connecting directly to their periferal nodes. Thanks to this, users who do not want to publish resources, or do not have the possibility to run a server application, can use only the browser extension.

6   Running Example

Let us consider the social network in Fig. 1. Suppose that Alice is the owner of an object with identifier obj1, and that she wishes to make it available to users who are direct friends of hers, provided that their trust level is not less than 0.5. Moreover, she wishes to grant access also to all her indirect friends, provided that they are also colleagues and that their trust level is not less than 0.5. Such policy can be expressed by the following access rules:

1. $(\mathtt{obj1},\{(\mathtt{Alice},\mathtt{friendOf},1,0.5)\})$
2. $(\mathtt{obj1},\{(\mathtt{Alice},\mathtt{friendOf},*,*),(\mathtt{Alice},\mathtt{colleagueOf},1,0.5)\})$

Let us now suppose that David submits a request to access obj1. David must then prove that he satisfies the requirements expressed by at least one of the two access rules applying to obj1, which can be transformed into the following Horn-like clauses:

1. $(hasSubj(?r,?x) \wedge hasObj(?r,\mathtt{Alice}) \wedge hasType(?r,\mathtt{friendOf}) \wedge hasDepth(?r,?\mathrm{D}) \wedge \leq (?\mathrm{D},1) \wedge hasTrust(?r,?t) \wedge \geq (?t,0.5)) \rightarrow canAccess(?x,\mathtt{obj1})$
2. $(hasSubj(?r,?x) \wedge hasObj(?r,\mathtt{Alice}) \wedge hasType(?r,\mathtt{friendOf}) \wedge hasSubj(?r',?x) \wedge hasObj(?r',\mathtt{Alice}) \wedge hasType(?r',\mathtt{colleagueOf}) \wedge hasDepth(?r',?\mathrm{D}') \wedge \leq (?\mathrm{D}',1) \wedge hasTrust(?r',?t') \wedge \geq (?t',0.5)) \rightarrow canAccess(?x,\mathtt{obj1})$

According to such rules, the relationships to be proved and evaluated are those existing between David and Alice (see Fig. 1), which are expressed by the following assertions:

A. $hasSubj(\mathtt{r1},\mathtt{David}) \wedge hasObj(\mathtt{r1},\mathtt{Alice}) \wedge hasType(\mathtt{r1},\mathtt{friendOf}) \wedge hasDepth(\mathtt{r1},2) \wedge hasTrust(\mathtt{r1},0.2)$
B. $hasSubj(\mathtt{r2},\mathtt{David}) \wedge hasObj(\mathtt{r2},\mathtt{Alice}) \wedge hasType(\mathtt{r2},\mathtt{colleagueOf}) \wedge hasDepth(\mathtt{r2},1) \wedge hasTrust(\mathtt{r2},0.8)$

Note that the trust level in relationship A corresponds to the one actually associated with edge *DA*, whereas the trust level in relationship B is an average of the trust levels associated with the edges in paths *DBA* and *DCA*, computed by using a given algorithm. Relationships A and B alone satisfy neither rule 1 nor rule 2, whereas relationships A and B together satisfy rule 2, since David is both a friend of Alice and a colleague of hers, with trust level equal to 0.8 (and thus ≥ 0.5).

The system components in charge of carrying out the tasks concerning access control enforcement are shown in Fig. 2. Let us suppose that periferal node #1 corresponds to David, whereas periferal node #2 to Alice. David's ARM sends the access request for obj1 (step 1), and Alice's ACM replies with the set of access rules to be satisfied (step 2). David's ARM then asks to the central node the chain of certificates concerning the existing relationship between him and Alice, and the corresponding trust level (steps 3-4); after having processed them, David's ARM obtains a set of assertions which are delivered to Cwm, along with the access rules sent by Alice's ACM. If a proof is returned, David's ARM sends it to Alice's ACM along with the corresponding certificate chain (step 5). After having verified the validity of the proof, Alice's ACM returns the requested object (step 6).

7   Conclusions and Future Work

In this paper, we presented an access control model for WBSNs, where policies are specified in terms of constraints on the type, depth, and trust level of relationships existing between users. Relevant features of our model are the use of certificates for granting relationships' authenticity, and the client-side enforcement of access control according to a rule-based approach, where a subject requesting to access an object must demonstrate that it has the rights of doing that by means of a proof. We have also proposed a decentralized system architecture on support of access control enforcement, based on the interaction of two agents: the central node of the network, which stores and manages certificates specified by users, and a set of periferal nodes, in charge of storing access rules and performing access control. Future work includes two main research directions, namely, the support for topical trust and the usage of access rules also for certificate protection.

References

1. Golbeck, J.A.: Computing and Applying Trust in Web-based Social Networks. PhD thesis, Graduate School of the University of Maryland, College Park (2005) http://trust.mindswap.org/papers/GolbeckDissertation.pdf.
2. Brickley, D., Miller, L.: FOAF vocabulary specification. RDF Vocabulary Specification (2005) http://xmlns.com/foaf/0.1.
3. Ding, L., Zhou, L., Finin, T.W., Joshi, A.: How the Semantic Web is being used: An analysis of FOAF documents. In: HICSS 2005 Proc. (2005)
4. Finin, T.W., Ding, L., Zhou, L., Joshi, A.: Social networking on the Semantic Web. The Learning Organization 12(5) (2005) 418–435
5. Fitzpatrick, B.: OpenID 1.1. Technical Specification, OpenID (2005) http://www.openid.net/specs.bml.
6. Weitzner, D.J., Hendler, J., Berners-Lee, T., Connolly, D.: Creating a policy-aware Web: Discretionary, rule-based access for the World Wide Web. In Ferrari, E., Thuraisingham, B., eds.: Web & Information Security. IDEA Group (2006) 1–31
7. Carminati, B., Ferrari, E., Perego, A.: The REL-X vocabulary. OWL Vocabulary (2006) http://www.dicom.uninsubria.it/~andrea.perego/vocs/relx.owl.
8. Berners-Lee, T.: Notation 3 logic: An RDF language for the Semantic Web. W3C Draft, W3C (2005) http://www.w3.org/DesignIssues/N3Logic.
9. Berners-Lee, T.: Cwm – A general purpose data processor for the Semantic Web. Project Web site, W3C (2006) http://www.w3.org/2000/10/swap/doc/cwm.html.
10. Davis, I., Vitiello Jr, E.: RELATIONSHIP: A vocabulary for describing relationships between people. RDF Vocabulary Specification (2005) http://purl.org/vocab/relationship.
11. Golbeck, J.A.: The trust ontology. OWL Vocabulary (2006) http://trust.mindswap.org/ont/trust.owl.
12. REI: The rule markup initiative. Project Web site (2006) http://www.ruleml.org.
13. Horrocks, I., Patel-Schneider, P.F., Boley, H., Tabet, S., Grosof, B., Dean, M.: SWRL: A Semantic Web rule language combining OWL and RuleML. W3C Member Submission, W3C (2004) http://www.w3.org/Submission/SWRL.

An OWL Copyright Ontology for
Semantic Digital Rights Management

Roberto García and Rosa Gil

Universitat de Lleida
Jaume II 69, E-25001 Lleida, Spain
roberto@griho.net
rgil@diei.udl.es

Abstract. Digitalisation and the Internet have caused a content reproduction and distribution revolution with clear implications for copyright management. There are many Digital Rights Management (DRM) efforts that facilitate copyright management in closed domains but they find great difficulties when they are forced to interoperate in an open domain like the World Wide Web. In order to facilitate interoperation and automation, DRM systems can be enriched with domain formalisations like the Copyright Ontology. This ontology is implemented using the Description Logic variant of the Web Ontology Language (OWL-DL). This approach facilitates the implementation of efficient usages against licenses checking, which is reduced to description logics classification.

1 Introduction

Recently, there have been great changes in the copyright market motivated by the digital and Internet revolutions. First, these revolutions have introduced new risks in the classical market, which was basically based on the distribution of physical instances of content. Second, they have opened opportunities to create new markets based on digital creations and the Internet distribution medium.

In order to manage this new situation, the main approach is to take profit from the new technological opportunities in order to develop systems to manage and protect digital works. This is referred to as Digital Rights Management, or DRM. A DRM system (DRMS) is build from IT components and services along with the corresponding law, policies and business models.

Due to the globalisation of the digital content market, different DRMSs are being forced to interoperate. One of the main initiatives for DRM interoperability is the ISO/IEC MPEG-21 [1] standardisation effort. The main interoperability facilitation component is the Rights Expression Language (REL), which is based on a XML grammar. Therefore, it is syntax-based. There is also the MPEG-21 Rights Data Dictionary (RDD) that captures the semantics of the terms employed in the REL [2]. However, it does so without defining a formal semantics [3].

The limitations of a purely syntactic approach and the lack of formal semantics can be overcome using a formal semantics approach based on ontologies. They have been used, for instance, to validate and correct inconsistencies in MPEG-21 RDD [4,5].

R. Meersman, Z. Tari, P. Herrero et al. (Eds.): OTM Workshops 2006, LNCS 4278, pp. 1745–1754, 2006.
© Springer-Verlag Berlin Heidelberg 2006

Another MPEG-21 RDD formalisation is OREL [6]. In any case, these initiatives focus on the RDD semantics, which are too specific to facilitate interoperability.

To the best of our knowledge, there is just another ontological framework for DRM, OntologyX [7]. However, it is a commercial product for which there is little publicly available information. Moreover, OntologyX concentrates on the kind of actions that can be performed on governed content; it does not take into account the underlying legal framework.

In order to build a generic ontological framework that facilitates interoperability, the focus must be placed on the underlying legal, commercial and technical copyright aspects. This is the approach for the Copyright Ontology [8], detailed in Section 2, which produces a general conceptualisation. Therefore, it can be used as an interoperability facilitator for the main DRM standards like MPEG-21 or the Open Digital Rights Language (ODRL) [9].

Moreover, the ontology is implemented as an OWL Web ontology based on the Description Logic (DL) variant, i.e. OWL-DL. This implementation facilitates DRMS development as license checking is implemented using a DL reasoner. The OWL-DL implementation is detailed in Section 3. Finally, the conclusions and the future work are presented in Section 4.

2 Copyright Ontology

The copyright domain is a very complex one and conceptualising it is a very challenging task. In order to facilitate this, the Copyright Ontology conceptualisation task has been divided in three parts. Each part concentrates on a portion of the problem. However, each part is not independent from the rest; there are many interrelations among them.

The conceptualisation starts from building a model for the more primitive part, the Creation Model. This model is the basis for building the conceptual models of the rest of the parts. The following step is to build the Rights Model, and then the Action Model is built on the roots of the two previous ones. This section presents the main points of these three models. There are more details in [10].

The Creation Model defines the different forms a creation can take, which are classified depending on three points of view:

- **Abstract**: Work.
- **Object**: Manifestation, Fixation and Instance.
- **Process**: Performance and Communication.

The Rights Model follows the World Intellectual Property Organisation (WIPO) [11] recommendations in order to define the rights hierarchy. It includes economic plus moral rights, as promoted by WIPO, and copyright related rights. The most relevant rights in the DRM context are economic rights as they are related to productive and commercial aspects of copyright. Reproduction, Distribution, Public Performance, Fixation, Communication and Transformation Right are economic rights.

Finally, the Action Model corresponds to the primitive actions that can be performed on the concepts defined in the Creation Model and which are regulated by the rights in the Right Model. For the economic rights, these are the governed actions:

- **Reproduction Right**: *reproduce*, commonly speaking *copy*.
- **Distribution Right**: *distribute*. More specifically *sell*, *rent* and *lend*.
- **Public Performance Right**: *perform*; it is regulated by copyright when it is a public performance and not a private one.
- **Fixation Right**: *fix*, or *record*.
- **Communication Right**: *communicate* when the subject is an object or *retransmit* when communicating a performance or previous communication, e.g. a re-broadcast. Other related actions, which depend on the intended audience, are *broadcast* or *make available*.
- **Transformation Right**: *derive*. Some specialisations are *adapt* or *translate*.

The action concepts are complemented with a set of relations that link them to the action participants. This set is adopted from the linguistics field and it is based on case roles [12,13].

Table 1, it is shown on the top the generic case roles and on the right the kinds of verbs they are related to. These kinds of verbs define verbs facets, not disjoint classes of verbs, and concretise the general thematic roles as shown in each row. Therefore, the same verb can present one or more of these facets. For instance, the play verb can show the action, temporal and spatial facets in a particular sentence.

Table 1. Case roles

	initiator	resource	goal	essence
Action	agent, effector	instrument	result, recipient	patient, theme
Process	agent, origin	matter	result, recipient	patient, theme
Transfer	agent, origin	instrument, medium	experiencer, recipient	theme
Spatial	origin	path	destination	location
Temporal	start	duration	completion	pointInTime
Ambient	reason	manner	aim, consequence	condition

The previously introduced pool of primitive actions can be combined in order to build different value chains in the copyright domain. Each of the value chains steps can be detailed using the specific action concept and the corresponding case roles.

In order to illustrate one of the numerous possibilities, Fig. 1 shows a model for all copy actions in a Peer to Peer network performed by agent "granted" who copies "content01" from "PeerA" to two peers from the set "PeerB, PeerC, PeerD" at any time point six months after "2006-01-01".

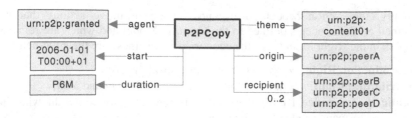

Fig. 1. Model for a copy action in the P2P diffusion scenario

This kind of action patterns can be used to model licenses. There are two additional licensing actions: *Agree* and *Disagree*. They are the building block of any license. Fig. 2 shows a license for the *Copy* action previously shown in Fig. 1. As it is shown, the *condition* case role is used in order to introduce a compensation for the agent that grants the copy action, a 3€ transfer from the granted agent.

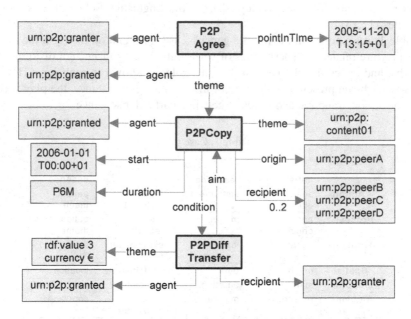

Fig. 2. Model for an agreement on a copy action pattern plus a condition

As it is going to be detailed in the next section, deontic operators are implicit in the agreement model. The agreement *theme* corresponds to an implicit permission, i.e. the theme of an agreement is permitted. The *condition* on the agreement theme correspond to an obligation, i.e. in order to fulfil the theme action it is necessary to satisfy the pattern defined by the condition property object. Finally, it is also possible to model prohibitions. This can be done in two ways, by agreeing on a negated pattern or by using the *Disagree* action.

3   OWL Implementation

The main objective has been to provide a straightforward and efficient implementation geared towards an extensive use of DL (Description Logic) reasoners. They are used to automatically check copyright-governed events against the authorised action patterns specified in the licenses. These patterns, the *theme* of an *Agree* or a *Disagree*, are modelled as classes. This facilitates checking if a particular action, once modelled as an instance, is allowed or not.

DL classifiers can be directly reused so there is no need to develop ad-hoc applications to perform this function. The more complex behaviours that cannot by captured using OWL-DL can be modelled using Semantic Web rules.

Licenses are modelled as OWL Classes and copyrighted content intended uses are modelled as instances. Then, in order to check if a usage (instance) is authorised by a set of licenses (classes) a DL reasoner is used to classify the instance in the available classes. If the instance is classified into a class that models an agreement, the *Agree* class as specified in the Copyright Ontology, the usage is authorised.

In order to model the licenses usage patterns, OWL classes and the "owl:Restriction" primitive are used. The restrictions are modelled as necessary and sufficient conditions in order to "trigger" the classification as authorisation mechanism. Each pattern property that is restricted is associated to the corresponding "owl:Restriction" through its "owl:onProperty" relation.

The restricted values for the property are specified with "owl:allValuesFrom" or "owl:someValuesFrom" when the range is a class and "owl:hasValue" when the range is limited to a specific instance. Therefore, it is possible to build patterns that define a concrete instance as the range of one of its case roles, e.g. a concrete user or a specific location. Therefore, very concrete events can also be modelled as classes and used afterwards as patterns or models for the actual action a user is trying to perform.

3.1.1   OWL-DL Implementation of a License Action Pattern

Suppose we want to implement the action pattern in Fig. 1. Table 2 shows the corresponding OWL class. The pattern is for *Copy* actions, so it is a subclass of *Copy*, and it is equivalent to the class resulting from the intersection of four OWL restrictions, which constitute the necessary and sufficient conditions that would trigger the classification of authorised usage instances.

Table 2. Class pattern for the actions authorised by the example license

Pattern $\sqsubseteq$	Copy	(1)
Pattern $\equiv$	$\forall$pointInTime.$\geq$ 2006-01-01T00:00:00, $\leq$ 2006-06-30T23:59:59 $\sqcap$	(2)
	$\exists$agent.{granted} $\sqcap$ $\exists$origin.{peerA} $\sqcap$ $\exists$theme.{content01} $\sqcap$	(3)
	($\leq$ 2 recipient) $\sqcap$	(4)
	$\forall$recipient.{peerC, peerD, peerB}	(5)

3.2 Overcoming Open World Assumption

The main problem of the OWL-DL implementation presented in the previous section is that of the Open World Assumption (OWA). This problem arises when the DL reasoners is trying to classify a given usage instance into the existing classes for usage patterns. It can be said that the reasoner is very "conservative" as, although the necessary and sufficient conditions are met, it will not classify an instance into a class if new facts can make it retract from this decision.

In other words, OWL-DL reasoners follow the open world assumption. In some cases this is the desired behavior but this is not the case for this license checking implementation. The intention is to make a local close world assumption and make a decision on the currently available facts as the outcome is to decide if the current action should be authorized or not just right now.

There are some OWL-DL restriction primitives that lead to OWA problems:

- **maxCardinality** ($\leq$ n): the reasoner is conservative with this restriction as, although the cardinality restriction might be satisfied at a given time, new facts can make the cardinality greater than n, i.e. ($>$ n). The cardinality restriction is also affected as it is the conjunction of a maxCardinality with a minCardinality.

- **allValuesFrom** ($\forall$R.C): the situation in this case is that, although at the current time all the values for the R property are in the C class, in the future, there might be new facts that involve R with a value not in C, i.e. R.($\neg$C).

On the other hand, other OWL-DL restrictions, or their combination, are not affected by the OWA and thus do not affect the license checking implementation. Some of them are:

- **minCardinality** ($\geq$ n): there is no OWA problem here as once the reasoner can check that the cardinality is equal or greater than n, i.e. ($\geq$ n), new facts cannot make this inference false, i.e. ($<$ n).

- **someValuesFrom** ($\exists$R.C): once there is some R whose value is in C, new facts cannot make that there does no exist some R with a C value, i.e. $\neg$($\exists$R.C). Therefore, there is not a OWA problem here.

- **allValuesFrom** ($\forall$R.C) and **FunctionalProperty** R: the combination of the allValuesFrom, a OWA sensible construct, with the FunctionalProperty in some cases, the combination of a OWA problematic construct with other

There are many ways to overcome OWL-DL's OWA through epistemic operators [14] and non-monotonic OWL extensions [15]. However, in these cases it is necessary to get outside standard OWL and, what is even more inconvenient, these approaches are basically theoretical and there are not complete implementations of them right now.

In order to implement the OWL-DL based license checker, we have adopted a more pragmatic approach, which does not require additional language constructs neither a reasoner different from the existing OWL-DL enabled ones.

Fig. 3 illustrates this approach. As it can be observed, a maxCardinality restriction defines a set of accepted cardinality values, e.g. from zero to two. However, as new facts are known under an OWA, instances previously classified into this restriction can "get out" of the corresponding set.

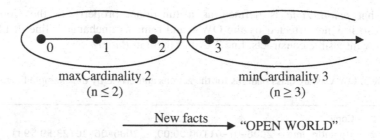

maxCardinality 2   minCardinality 3
(n ≤ 2)   (n ≥ 3)

New facts ──→ "OPEN WORLD"

Fig. 3. Oppose OWA-sensible maxCardinality to OWA-insensible minCardinality

On the other hand, it can be observed that a maxCardinality restriction ($\leq$ n) has an opposite set corresponding to the minCardinality restriction ($\geq$ n+1). As it has been shown, the minCardinality construct is not affected by OWA. Therefore, the idea is to take profit from this fact and make the reasoner look for the opposite set, the OWA-insensible one, and check that it is not satisfied. This implies that the reverse is satisfied by the current set of facts at hand, overcoming the OWA assumption that makes the reasoner not able to infer that.

Therefore, the approach is to negate the restriction and to undo this at the metalevel, it is to check outside the DL reasoner that the negated restriction is not satisfied and thus it can be inferred that the original one does. The negation is modelled at the metalevel introducing the *Disagree* class, which is the opposite of the *Agree* class.

Therefore, the allValuesFrom restriction on the *theme* class of an *Agree*, i.e. $\forall$**R.C**, is converted into a someValueFrom restriction on the *theme* class of a *Disagree*, i.e. $\exists$**R.¬C**. On the other hand, the maxCardinality restriction on the *theme* class of an *Agree*, i.e. ($\leq$ **n R**), is converted into a minCardinality restriction on the *theme* class of a *Disagree*, i.e. **Disagree theme ($\geq$ n+1 R)**.

To summarise, all the OWA-sensible constructs are moved to a new class pattern which is disagreed, i.e. unauthorised, in order to model the metalevel negation. This new class results from the disjunction of all the transformed restrictions and is intersected with the original pattern, which is now composed by just the OWA-insensible restrictions and is what remains as the subject of the *Agree*.

In order to check if a given usage instance is authorised, it is classified in the available license class patterns, both agreed and disagreed ones. If the instance is classified into an agreed class pattern, it is also checked if it has not been classified into the corresponding disagreed class pattern for the OWA-sensible restrictions. If it is so, the usage is authorised. Otherwise, it is not classified in the agreed pattern or it is classified in the disagreed pattern, the usage in not authorised. The following example illustrates this mechanism.

3.2.1 OWA-Insensible Implementation Example

Table 3 shows the class patterns that overcome the OWA and result from the previous transformation on the Table 2 OWA-sensible constructs. From lines 4 to 6 there is the *Pattern''* that contains the transformed OWL constructs.

Note that *pointInTime* is defined as a functional property in the Copyright Ontology so it is not affected by the OWA and remains unchanged, line 2, like the other OWA-insensible constructs, line 3. All of them in *Pattern'*.

Table 3. OWA-aware class patterns for the actions authorised by the example license

Pattern' ⊑	Copy	(1)
Pattern' ≡	∀pointInTime.≥ 2006–01–01T00:00:00, ≤ 2006–06–30T23:59:59 ⊓	(2)
	∃agent.{granted} ⊓ ∃origin.{peerA} ⊓ ∃theme.{content01}	(3)
Pattern" ≡	Pattern' ⊓	(4)
	((≥ 3 recipient) ⊔	(5)
	∃recipient.(¬ {peerC, peerD, peerB}))	(6)

The overall methodology is exemplified in Fig. 4. It shows three usage instances that are checked against the license patterns presented in Table 3. The first one is classified into *Copy* because the *theme* is "fragment02" and so it cannot be classified into *Pattern'*. Therefore, it is not authorised by the involved license.

The second one is classified into *Pattern'*, but not into *Pattern''*. Consequently, it is in an agreed class pattern and not in the corresponding disagreed pattern so it is authorised.

Finally, the third instance is classified into *Pattern''*, and correspondingly into *Pattern'*, because it satisfies both of its restrictions. There are three or more recipients, i.e. recipient cardinality is ≥ 3, and one of them is not in the authorised set of peers, i.e. there is some recipient which is the set of the unauthorised peer. Therefore, this usage instance is not authorised. Note that, as the transformed patterns

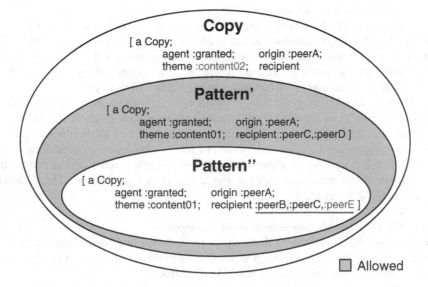

Fig. 4. Examples of the license checking methodology to overcome OWA

in *Pattern''* are disjointed, if any of them is satisfied the usage instance would be unauthorised, as it is the intended behaviour.

3.3 Building a Semantic DRMS

The Semantic DRMS [16] puts the Copyright Ontology into practice in order to build a semantics-oriented DRM system. It is implemented at two levels. The ground level is about OWL-DL classes and instances, the ones used to model licenses and usages, and it implements if instances are classified into class patterns. This level can be implemented with a common Description Logic reasoner. Pellet [17] has been selected because it can reason over custom data types and this has been very useful to check licensing time ranges.

Additionally, prior to loading license class patterns into the DL reasoner, it is necessary to perform the required transformations to make the class patterns OWA-insensible. This is done programmatically with Java through the Pellet's OWL API.

However, this is just the implementation at the ground level. All this must be complemented with a metalevel that implements the deontic aspects that are implicit in the conceptual model. The metalevel guides how the DL checks are performed and captures the semantics of the implicit obligations, permissions and prohibitions. Particularly, it implements the metalevel negation that has been employed to overcome the OWA.

The metalevel has been implemented programmatically. However, the most natural option would be to model the metalevel semantics using the Semantic Web Rule Language (SWRL) [18] and implement it using an appropriate rule engine, for instance SweetRules [19].

4 Conclusions and Future Work

As it has been shown, the Copyright Ontology constitutes a complete framework for representing copyright value chains and the associated flow of rights situations, agreements, offers, etc. It is build from the key concepts in the copyright domain so it constitutes an ontology for DRM interoperability.

Moreover, it has been implemented using OWL-DL, which has allowed reducing license checking to DL classification. DL reasoning is very efficient but it is based on a Open World Assumption (OWA). License checks are performed at usage time and must take a local Close World Assumption (CWA).

In order to provide that, this paper contributes a generic methodology that makes OWL-DL follow a CWA when required. It is based on negating OWL constructs that lead to an OWA and transforming to the reverse ones, which are not affected by the OWA. This negation is then undone at a metalevel. Altogether, this methodology does not introduce any significant overhead as it just requires an additional DL classification per license check and the transformation is performed at modelling time.

The future work concentrates now in building a complete Semantic DRM system based on the Copyright Ontology and its OWL-DL implementation. Moreover, the objective is to take profit from this generic ontology in order to map MPEG-21 REL expressions to the Copyright Ontology and make the Semantic DRMS MPEG-21 aware.

In order to achieve this, an ontology for MPEG-21 REL has been generated automatically from the XML Schemas that define this standard using the XML Semantics Reuse Methodology [20] and the ReDeFer [21] XSD2OWL tool. These ontologies provide the hook points for integrating MPEG-21 REL expressions into the SemDRMS ontological framework.

References

1. de Walle, R.V.; Burnett, I.: "The MPEG-21 Book". John Wiley & Sons, UK, 2005
2. Wang, X.; DeMartini, T.; Wragg, B.; Paramasivam, M.; Barlas, C.: "The MPEG-21 rights expression language and rights data dictionary". IEEE Transactions on Multimedia, Vol. 7, No. 3, pp. 408-417, 2005
3. García, R.; Delgado, J.: "An Ontological Approach for the Management of Rights Data Dictionaries". In Moens, M. & Spyns, P. (ed.): "Legal Knowledge and Information Systems". IOS Press, Frontiers in Artificial Intelligence and Applications Vol. 134, 2005
4. García, R.; Delgado, J.; Rodríguez, E.: Ontological Analysis of the MPEG-21 Rights Data Dictionary (RDD). Input document M12495, ISO/IEC JTC1 SC29 WG11 Meeting, Nice, France, 2005
5. Barlas, C.; Rust, G.: Rights Data Dictionary, Technical Corrigendum 1. ISO/IEC JTC1 SC29 WG11, 2005
6. Qu Y.; Zhang, X; Li, H.: OREL: an ontology-based rights expression language. In Proceedings of the 13th international World Wide Web Conference. ACM Press, pp. 324-325, 2004
7. OntologyX, http://www.ontologyx.com
8. Copyright Ontology, http://rhizomik.net/ontologies/copyrightonto
9. García, R.; Gil, R.; Delgado, J.: "A Web Ontologies Framework for Digital Rights Management". In press, Journal of Artificial Intelligence and Law, Springer, 2006
10. García, R.: "A Semantic Web Approach to Digital Rights Management". PhD Thesis, Technologies Department, Universitat Pompeu Fabra, Barcelona, ES, 2006. http://rhizomik.net/~roberto/thesis
11. WIPO, http://www.wipo.int
12. Sowa, J.F.: "Knowledge Representation. Logical, philosophical and computational foundations". Brooks Cole Publishing Co., 2000
13. Dick, J.P.: "A conceptual, case-relation representation of text for intelligent retrieval". University of Toronto, Canada, 1991
14. Grimm, S.; Motik, B.: "Closed World Reasoning in the Semantic Web through Epistemic Operators". OWL: Experiences and Direction Workshop, 2005
15. Katz, Y.; Parsia, B.: "Towards a Nonmonotonic Extension to OWL". OWL: Experiences and Direction Workshop, 2005
16. Semantic Digital Rights Management System, http://rhizomik.net/semdrms
17. Pellet OWL Reasoner, http://www.mindswap.org/2003/pellet
18. Horrocks, I.; Patel-Schneider, P.F.; Boley, H.; Tabet, S.; Grosof, B.; Dean, M: "SWRL: A Semantic Web Rule Language Combining OWL and RuleML". World Wide Web Consortium Member Submission, 2004
19. SweetRules, http://sweetrules.projects.semwebcentral.org
20. García, R.: "Chapter 7: XML Semantics Reuse". In "A Semantic Web Approach to Digital Rights Management". PhD Thesis, Universitat Pompeu Fabra, Barcelona, ES, 2006. http://rhizomik.net/~roberto/thesis/html/Methodology.html#XMLSemanticsReuse
21. ReDeFer, http://rhizomik.net/redefer

A Legal Ontology to Support Privacy Preservation in Location-Based Services

Hugo A. Mitre, Ana Isabel González-Tablas, Benjamín Ramos, and Arturo Ribagorda

Computer Science Department, Carlos III Technical University of Madrid
28911 Leganes, Madrid
100059676@alumnos.uc3m.es, {aigonzal, benja1, arturo}@inf.uc3m.es

Abstract. During the last years many laws have been promulgated in diverse countries to protect citizens' privacy. This fact is due to the increase of privacy threats caused by the tendency of using information technologies in all scopes. Location Based Services (LBS) compose a situation where this privacy can be harmed. Even there exist mechanisms to protect this right in LBS, generally this services have not been developed over regulatory norms or if so, it has been in a partial way or interpreting those norms in a particular form. This situation could be a consequence of the lack of a common knowledge base representing the actual legislation in matters of privacy. In this paper an ontology of the main Spanish privacy norm is presented as well as the method used to construct it. The ontology is specifically aimed and applied to the preservation of privacy in LBS.

Keywords: Ontology, regulation, privacy, location-based services.

1 Introduction

Nowadays, the use and expansion of digital information technologies to most fields have caused an increase in the number of threats to the citizens' privacy. The evolution of mobile and positioning technologies has allowed the recent development of Location Based Services (LBS). LBS offer value-added services based on the geographic position of mobile devices. In [1] an extensive classification of LBS applications can be found. Some examples of their applications are emergency, security and medical services; navigation and information services; m-commerce; fleets management; proximity and entertainment services. Concrete scenarios of LBS are a taxi company that drives the requested taxis to the place the clients have called from (clients' position is obtained during the call), a user that wants to locate a friend, and a provider of local information that personalizes it depending on the position of the requesting user (e.g., the weather).

Although LBS can provide great benefits, implications for users' privacy arise because of their utilization of user's location information. Location can be considered private from regulation's point of view when this information is associated with any identified or identifiable natural person. Furthermore, the monitoring and position

R. Meersman, Z. Tari, P. Herrero et al. (Eds.): OTM Workshops 2006, LNCS 4278, pp. 1755–1764, 2006.
© Springer-Verlag Berlin Heidelberg 2006

tracking of individuals allows the construction of locations profiles, making possible to recognize consumption habits, preferences, private costumes, and behavior of an individual. Alastair and Stajano define location privacy in [5] as the ability to prevent other parties from learning one's current or past location. Nowadays regulations of several countries include specific laws to protect citizens' privacy (e.g., most EU countries [19] and Japan [20]). Location privacy is a specific case also addressed by existing privacy regulations, either implicitly or explicitly. Therefore, it is necessary to provide in LBS enough guarantees to protect individuals' location privacy as required by regulations at the same time that the evolution of LBS is not limited [14].

Problem Description and Goal. Designing and integrating mechanisms that guarantee LBS's compliance with privacy regulation is a hard work, as some authors point out in [10]. On the one hand, designers should become experts in privacy legislation in order to interpret their precepts. On the other hand, they should know which security mechanisms are best for protecting location privacy, adapt them if necessary or design new ones in order to make LBS compliant with existing regulations. Although several researchers have proposed different location privacy mechanisms [2, 3, 4, 5, 6, 7, 9, 10, 11], they have not been developed using as base any regulatory norm or, if so, it has been in a partial way or interpreting the norms from a particular point of view. This situation can be a consequence of the lack of a common knowledge base that represents the current legislation in matters of privacy.

Christopher Welty and Nicola Guarino pointed out an important difference between an ontology and a data model. A conceptual model is an implementation that has to satisfy the engineering trade-offs of a running application, while The design of an onlotogy is to specify the conceptualization of the world underlaying such application [23]. In our case the conceptualization of the world can be represented by a specific domain. Ontologies can be used to reason about the objects in that domain and their relations. Ontology languages, such as OWL (Web Ontology Language [21]), allow the encoding of ontologies. Ontologies have been already used to represent several law domains such as in the TRACS system [15], and the E-POWER and E-COURT projects [17, 18]. An ontology for the privacy legislation domain will provide a common knowledge base that can be used to support privacy legislation interpretation and LBSs compliant with privacy regulations. In this paper a first approach to the development of an ontology for the privacy legislation domain is presented. In particular, the proposed ontology is based on the main Spanish norm for data privacy protection [13].

Organization of the paper. Next, in Section 2, some related works are analyzed. In Section 3, the construction method is presented and, in Section 4, the proposed ontology is described. Section 5 comprises the conclusions and future works.

2 Related Works

There exist several proposals that aim to solve location privacy problem. They can be classified in three groups according to the main security mechanism they are based on. A first group is composed by location privacy mechanisms based on attribute certificates [4, 9]. An attribute certificate is a digital token that binds privileges or specific information (group membership, role, category, etc.) to entities. Proposals in [4, 9] use attribute certificates to authorize users several actions such as location information obtaining, storage, processing or third-party communication. The second group of location privacy mechanisms is based in policy systems [2, 3, 7-11]. Policies can be defined as a set of rules that specify the behaviour of a system. This kind of location privacy mechanisms use the policies to define which actions are allowed to whom, which obligations are derived, etc. The third group dissociates the user's identity from the information related to them [5, 6], for example using a pseudonym instead or controlling the granularity of the revealed information.

Privacy legislation are huge and complex, making quite difficult its interpretation by non-experts. On one hand, proposals in [2, 3, 7, 11] have been developed taking into account privacy norms or the precepts inferred from them. However, the resulting location privacy mechanisms are partially compliant with privacy regulatory norms. From the point of view of the authors of this paper this fact is due to that the legislation has been interpreted in a simplified way and following personal criterion. On the other hand, proposals in [4, 9] do not consider legislation at all. Finally, proposals in [5, 6] are compliant with current privacy regulations as dissociating the identity from data is excluded of the norm scope.

3 The Construction Method

The ontology construction method is based in the four main activities of the TERMINAE method [12]: corpus constitution, linguistic study, normalization and formalization. This process is described following.

The *documental corpus* is the main Spanish law for privacy protection [13], comprising 12 pages. Its main goal is to guarantee and protect personal data processing, public liberties and fundamental rights of physical persons, taking special care of their honour and personal and familiar intimacy.

A *linguistic study* was made on the lecture of the document:

- The candidate terms were extracted without considering if they were concepts, relations or instances.
- From the candidate terms plus the documental corpus, the main terms were extracted, that is, the concepts. It was made by using comprehensive lecture of repeated terms and inference of the concept.
- From the candidate terms, relations between main concepts were extracted considering the specific cases that make sense in legislation.

Each concept's *semantic is normalized*, searching again in the documental corpus to extract structure properties (e.g., date, position, number) and functional properties (e.g., enacted by).

Last, the ontology was *formalized* and refined using LRI-Core [16]. LRI-Core is a core ontology that covers the main concepts that are common to all legal domains. New concepts were aggregated according to necessities of a legal domain. The concept of mental-world was excluded as it is not necessary to model human thinking, wish or motivation but only a representation of the facts happening during LBS scenarios. As well, quality concept was also discarded as energy, strength or substance concepts are not used. The ontology resulting from this step is based in roles, processes, physical concepts, abstract concepts and occurrences. It is described in next Section.

4 Description

LegLOPD (The Legal Ontology Domain) is compound by five top concepts extracted from the LRI-Core. They are: physical concept, occurrence, process, role, and abstract concept. To formalize the LegLOPD an useful subset of classes (Fig. 1) were taken from LRI-Core which defines a core ontology covering all legal domains.

Fig. 1. Class Hierarchy from LRI-Core taken as base for our legal ontology

In [16], the physical world evolves two main classes: physical objects and processes. Objects have mass, extension. Processes can change objects and consume energy. Energy is a current concept that could be interpreted as a metaphor, as the process of burning is a kind of energy. The same energy can be saved inside objects (batteries, petrol, etc.). In our ontology is not conceived any kind of energy, nor any kind of objects containing or consuming this energy, because is not necessary to represent simple facts.

Our approach will be explained related to LRI-Core (fig. 1) in next paragraphs of this section.

The objects render the physical world stable and observable. Inside the term **physical concept** we find time and space, both can be part of a process where any object can participate. Concepts added under the branch of physical concept (Concepto_Físico) in the figure 2 are explained in next sentences. Artefact (Artefacto) class represents all physical objects that treat digital information. Physical medium (Medio_Físico) represents the physical part of services (could be a LBS), giving also information treatment. We decide to add physical support (Soporte_físico) in order to save information into files (Fichero) or repositories (Repositorio). The concept natural object represents physical persons (Persona_física) and groups (Grupo). A group of persons could be an Organization, Administrative organ, etc.

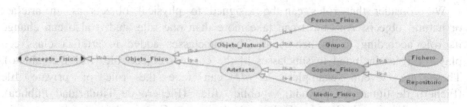

Fig. 2. Classes added to the physical concept of LRI-Core (Concepto_Físico)

The **abstract concept** is the clearest concept in common sense. A few mathematical concepts are known such as collections, sequences, and count numbers. Manipulating quantities or data structures is not common in the legislation.

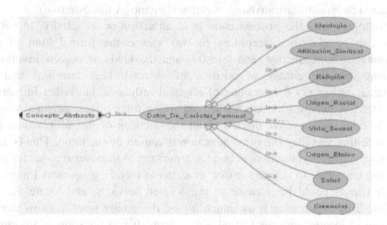

Fig. 3. Classes added to the Abstract concept of LRI-Core (Concepto_Abstracto)

The abstract concept sets numbers and structures to make up references associated to files, dates, repositories, etc. We added the concepts private data (Datos_De_Carácter_Personal)(fig 3), which is the essential structure to be protected. Sexual life (Vida_sexual), ideology (Ideología), health (Salud), syndical affiliation

(Afiliación_Sindical), racial origin (Origen_Racial), beliefs (Creencias), religion (Religión), and ethnic origin (Origen Etnico) are considered private data structures.

Roles in [16] are concepts that can be played by entities. It happens when the entity fits the role behavior, where instances are players. In addition, roles are properties and have dynamic properties. E. g. a role can be played by several entities, simultaneously or in different times. An entity can change its role or play multiple roles. Let's suppose that a physical person is responsible for private files treatment, being outside European territory. The responsible person has the obligation to asign a representative like an administrative organization. At the same time, this administrative organization could be responsible for other privacy file. This example shows two roles played by the same administrative organization, being at the same time representative and responsible of distinct private files.

We consider that roles can be assigned to physical objects as an artefact or natural objects. An object can take more than one role, and it also can change its role according to its behaviour. The subclasses added to artefact class can play the roles included in subclasses of the concept object role (Rol_Del_objeto). These are several examples: a *file* can take the role of private file (Fichero_de_titularidad_privada), public file (Fichero_de_Titularidad_Pública), forces and safety body file (Fichero_de_fuerzas_y_Cuerpo_de_seguridad), etc.; a *repository* (Repositorio) can play the role of the data protection general register (Registro_General_De_protección_De_Datos); and the *physical medium* as data treatment medium (Medio_de_Tratamiento_de_Datos). Furthermore, physical persons and groups, subclasses of natural objects playing roles such as legal roles or actors, e. g.: a person could be an actor (Actor) playing the role of affected (Afectado); a group could be an administrative organization (Organo_Administrativo).

Our ontology uses the **process** concept as an action or an activity. In LRI-Core, process can be classified according to two views: the formal kind of change (transformation, transduction, and transfer) and the kinds of objects involved (e.g. movements are the change of position of objects). [22] mentions that action communication has not the meaning of physical influence, but rather influenced by mental state. A person transfers his/her intentions for motives, personal plans, and beliefs to other persons. We discuss about the decision of this affirmation, and we conclude telling that they infer that an action is caused by intention. This is useful to find person culpability, but in our case, the aim is not to discover reasons for personal intentions, but rather to take the reason as a simple fact. E. g. personal intentions to eat with friends could be a cause to use located services, and locate the nearest restaurant. This information is too much for us, if we only want to know that a user makes use of located services to find a restaurant. It is a question of informing the user of the rights and obligations that imply the type of LBS that offers the service, and not to find guilts.

Actions can be provoked or caused by actors. These are some examples: the action of Reclaim (Reclamación) could be provoked by the affected (Afectado); Inscription can be caused by a representative.

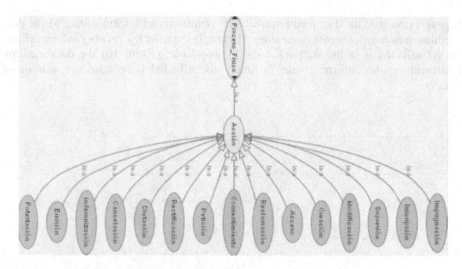

Fig. 4. Classes added to the process concept of LRI-Core (Proceso)

Occurrences capture all these aspects related to the execution of the scenes, and cover objects and processes. In a scene there may be events, states, situations, space and time references, and moments.

Events and States are occurrences. Both have a moment of execution in time. An event is caused by some physical object, and could happen after and before a situation (e.g. a service *transmits* inform). The state for us is, when an object is kept in some activity until any object provokes an event (e.g. a service keep in *treatment* information). The situations are caused by the actions of the actors on objects in a moment, and among the situations events can pass before and after this situation (e.g. between *verifies* register and *transmit* inform events is a information collection situation).

Occurrence concept is the most important concept to us, because it can help to represent the execution of a scene. The legal domain ontology LegLOPD is being constructed to represents scenarios. In the next figure, we describe a teorical scenario in order to understand the occurrence world in LBS. At the left side there are the physical objects and its roles: physical person as affected, and other physical person as interested; file as private file; and physical medium as data treatment medium. This scenario shows two actors, the interested that tries to collect privacy information of the affected by data treatment medium (e.g. an LBS). The physical medium makes use of the privacy file.

The order of execution is the following one: (Event 1) the interested makes a *request* register; (State 1) the interested is then in *data transferring* state; (State 2) the data medium treatment is in *treatment in recording* state; (Event 2) the private file is also an automated file (role) and *generates* an inform; (Event 3) the data medium treatment *transmits* inform; (State 3) the data medium treatment is in *treatment notification* state; (Event 4) the interested *consents* a treatment; (Event 5) the private file *registers* data; (Event 6) the interested makes a data *request*; (State 4) the data medium treatment, staying in *consulting data*; (Event 7) the private file *verifies* the register; (event 8) the data medium treatment *transmits* an inform; (State 5) the data medium treatment *consents requesting*; (Event 9) the affected *revokes* inform; (State 6) the affected is in the state *treatment in blockade*; (Event 10) the data medium treatment *revokes* inform; (State 7) finally the affected is in state *not authorized access*.

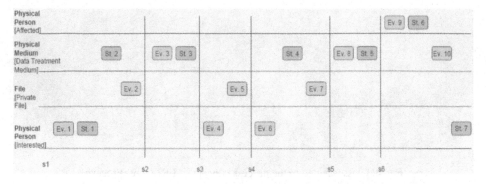

Fig. 5. This example shows a scene representing the occurrence world

To give an automatic reasoning of the legal domain can be necessary to be based on the occurrences. In [22] an approximation that allows an automatic analysis of cases described in terms of ontology. The proposed system is known as DIRECT. This system has to find casual and intentional relations in order to enable automatic analysis. This approach could be considered for our legal ontology, but oriented to causal relations.

5 Conclusions and Further Work

Nowadays, the use and expansion of digital information technologies to most fields have caused an increase in the number of threats to the citizens' privacy. Therefore, regulations of several countries have included specific laws to protect citizens' privacy. The evolution of mobile and positioning technologies has allowed the recent development of Location Based Services (LBS). Although LBS can provide great benefits, implications for users' privacy arise because of their utilization of user's location information.

Although several researchers have proposed different location privacy mechanisms [2, 3, 4, 5, 6, 7, 9, 10, 11], they have not been developed using as base any regulatory norm or, if so, it has been in a partial way or interpreting the norms from a particular point of view. This situation can be a consequence of the lack of a common knowledge base that represents the current legislation in matters of privacy.

In this paper a first approach to the development of an ontology for the Spanish main privacy law [13] has been presented and the method used in its construction (based on the TERMINAE method [12]). The proposed ontology has been developed using as base LRI-Core.

Future plans include finishing the legal domain ontology LegLOPD, and investigating other techniques for automated analysis in order to build an agent. Location-based systems and location services will be able to collaborate with the agent on the requests of the user in order to fulfil the law on protection of personal data for both parts.

References

[1] G. M. Giaglis, P. Kourouthanassis, and A. Tsamakos.: Towards a Clasification Framework for mobile location services, pages 67-85. Idea Group Publishing.

[2] Ana Isabel González-Tablas Ferreres.: Arquitectura de servicios de acreditación y sellado espacio-temporal .PhD thesis, Universidad Carlos III de Madrid, 2005.

[3] M. Langheinrich.: A privacy awareness system for ubiquitouscomputing enviroments. In the proceedings of 4th International Conference on Ubiquitous Computing (Ubicomp'02), pages 237-245, 2002.

[4] C. Hauser and M. Kabatnik.: Towards privacy support in a global location service. In the proceedings of the IFIP Workshop on IP and ATM Traffic Management (WATM/EUNICE 2001), 2001.

[5] A. R. Beresford and F. Stajano.: Location privacy in pervasive computing. IEEE Pervasive Computing, 2003.

[6] M. Gruteser and D. Grunwald.: Anonymous usage of location-based services through spatial and temporal cloaking. In the Proceedings of ACM/USENIX International conference on Mobile Systems, Applications, and Services (MobiSys), 2003.

[7] A. I. Gozález-Tablas, L. M. Salas, B. Ramos and A. Ribagorda.: Providing personalization and automation to spatial- temporal stamping services. In the Proceedings of the 16th Internacional Workshop on Database and Expert Systems Applications (DEXA'05), 2005.

[8] E. Snekkenes.: Concepts for personal location privacy policies. In the proceedings of the 3rd ACM conference on Electronic Commerce. ACM Press, 2001.

[9] U. Hengarther and P. Steenkiste.: Implementing access control to people location information. In the Proceedings of the Ninth ACM Symposium on Access Control Models and Technologies (SACMET'04), 2004.

[10] G. Myles, A. Friday, and N. Davies.: Preserving privacy in enviroments with location-based applications. IEEE Pervasive Computing, 2003.

[11] A. Gajparia, C. J. Mitchell and C. Y. Yeun.: Information Preference Authority: Suppoting user privacy in location based services. In the proceedings of the 9th Nordic Workshop on Secure IT-Systems (NordSec 2004), 2004.

[12] Sylvie Despres, Sylvie Szulman.: Construction of a legal Ontology from a European Community Legislative Tex., In T. Gordon (ed.), Legal Knowñedge and Information Systems. Jurix 2004: The Seventeenth Annual Conference. Amsterdam: IOS Press, 2004, pp. 79-88.

[13] Ley Orgánica 15/1999, de 13 de diciembre, de Protección de Datos de Carácter Personal.

[14] Dr. Robert P. Minch.: Privacy Issues in Location-Aware Mobile Devices. Proceedings of the 37th Hawaii International Conference on System Sciences, 2004.

[15] Joost Breuker and Radboud Winkels.: Use and reuse of legal ontologies in knowledge engineering and information management. ICAIL 2003 Workshop on Legal Ontologies & Web Based Legal Information Management, April 2003.

[16] Joost Breuker.: Constructing a legal core ontology: LRI-Core. University of Amsterdam, 2004.

[17] Joost Breuker, Abdullatif Elhag, Emil Petkov, and Radboud Winkels.: IT Support for the Judiciary: Use of Ontologies in the e-Court Project, 2002.

[18] Boer, R. Hoekstra, R. Winkels, and T. van Engers.: ^{META}lex: Jurisdiction and Language. In Monica Palmirani, Tom van Engers, and Maria A. Wimmer, editors, Proceedings of the E-Government Workshop in conjunction with JURIX 2003, pages 54-66. Universitätsverlag Rudolf Trauner, December 2003.

[19] European Union (EU) Data Protection Directive of 1995, Rebecca Herold, CISM, CISSP, CISA, FLMI, May 2002.

[20] Japanese Personal Information Protection Law, Tokyo Aoyama Aoki Law Office,Baker & McKenzie, Attorney at Foreign Law Office, Registered Associated Offices, June 17, 2004.

[21] OWL Web Ontology Language Overview. W3C Recommendation 10 Feb 2004.

[22] Joost Breuker and Rinke Hoekstra.: 'DIRECT: Ontology-based Discovery of Responsibility and Causability in Legal Case Descriptions' in T. Gordon (ed.), Legal knowledge and Information Systems. Jurix 2004: The Seventeenth Annual Conference.Amsterdan: IOS Press, 2004, pp. 59-68.

[23] C. Welty et N. Guarino.: Supporting Ontological Analysis of Taxonomic Relationships. Data and Knowledge Engineering, 2001. Également : LADSEB-CNR Int. Rep. 08/2001.

A Fuzzy Approach to Risk Based Decision Making

Omar Khadeer Hussain[1], Elizabeth Chang[1], Farookh Khadeer Hussain[1],
and Tharam S. Dillon[2]

[1] School of Information Systems, Curtin University of Technology, Perth, Australia
{Omar.Hussain, Elizabeth.Chang,
Farookh.Hussain}@cbs.curtin.edu.au
[2] Faculty of Information Technology, University of Technology, Sydney, Australia
tharam@it.uts.edu.au

Abstract. Decision making is a tough process. It involves dealing with a lot of uncertainty and projecting what the final outcome might be. Depending on the projection of the uncertain outcome, a decision has to be taken. In a peer-to-peer financial interaction, the trusting agent in order to analyze the Risk has to consider the possible likelihood of failure of the interaction and the possible consequences of failure to its resources involved in the interaction before concluding whether to interact with the probable trusted agent or not. Further it might also have to choose and decide on an agent to interact with from a set of probable trusted agents. In this paper we propose a Fuzzy Risk based decision making system that would assist the trusting agent to ease its decision making process.

1 Introduction

The trusting agent can make an informed decision of whether to interact with a probable trusted agent or not, by analyzing beforehand the possible level of Risk that could be present in interacting with it. The Australian and New Zealand Standard on Risk Management, AS/NZS 4360:2004 states that Risk Identification is the heart of Risk Management [1]. Hence, Risk should be identified in order to analyze and manage it better. Risk is important in the study of behavior in e-commerce, because there is a whole body of literature based in rational economics that argues that the decision to buy is based on Risk-adjusted cost-benefit analysis [11]. Thus, it commands a central role in any discussion of e-commerce that is related to a transaction.

The definitions of Risk in the literature highlight and emphasize the possible loss in an interaction. To mention some such definitions; March et al. define Risk more by the magnitude of the value of the outcome rather than by its likelihood [2]. Luhmann defines Risk in a transaction as where the possible damage might be more than the advantage sought [3]. Mayer et al. conclude that Risk is present in the transaction only if the negative outcome outweighs the positive outcome [4]. In contrast to this definition Rousseau et al. measure Risk as the potential negative consequence and probability of failure [5]. Sztompka defines Risk as the probability of the loss of the resources invested [6]. Grazoli et al. view Risk as the consumers'

R. Meersman, Z. Tari, P. Herrero et al. (Eds.): OTM Workshops 2006, LNCS 4278, pp. 1765–1775, 2006.
© Springer-Verlag Berlin Heidelberg 2006

perception of ucertainty and adverse consequences of engaging in an activity [7]. Cheung et al. define Risk as having two dimensions; one related to the uncertainty or probability of loss notion and the other related to a consequence of the importance of the notion of loss [8]. Hussain et al [9] define Risk in the context of peer-to-peer business interaction as the likelihood that the trusted agent might not act as expected according to the trusting agent's expectations in a given context and at a particular time once the interaction begins, resulting in financial loss of the resources involved in the interaction. Risk is seen as a combination of:

a) The possibility of failure in achieving the outcome; and

b) The cost of the outcome when it occurs, usually the loss incurred, which is related to Risk.

Risk evaluation involves the trusting agent having to determine beforehand the possibility of failure of the interaction and the subsequent possible consequences of failure to its resources involved in the interaction. This is different from trust evaluation. Trust evaluation measures the belief that the trusting agent has in a probable trusted agent in attaining its desired outcomes if it interacts with the probable trusted agent.

In a decentralized interaction carried out in service oriented architecture, the trusting agent should first analyze the possible level of Risk that could be involved in dealing with a probable trusted agent. Doing so would help the trusting agent to decide whether to interact with the probable trusted agent or not, or to choose an agent to interact with, from a set of probable trusted agents. But decision making is a tough process. It involves in dealing with a lot of uncertainty and projecting what the outcome might be. Depending on the projection of the final outcome a decision has to be taken. So in order to ease the decision making process for the trusting agent, or to further strengthen its previous belief of proceeding in an interaction with a probable trusted agent or not, we propose the utilization of a fuzzy system in decision making. The trusting agent can ease its decision making process by utilizing a fuzzy approach to Risk based decision making. The proposed fuzzy model combines the possibility of failure of the interaction and the possible consequences of failure in interacting with a probable trusted agent and gives an output to the trusting agent. Fuzzy logic is used to model uncertainty, and similarly the decision making process deals with predicting the possible uncertain outcome and deciding the future course of action based on the predicted uncertain outcome.

In this paper, we propose and define a fuzzy Risk based decision making system. The trusting agent inputs the aspects of Risk related to the probable trusted agent to the fuzzy system and based on that it gets an output whether to proceed or not in the interaction with the probable trusted agent. The proposed system is explained in the next sections. This paper is organized in 7 sections. In Section 2 we discuss our previous work of determining the different constituents for analyzing the possible Risk in an interaction. In section 3, we propose the fuzzy Risk based decision making system. In section 4 and section 5, we define the rules and the membership functions for our fuzzy model. In section 6, we demonstrate with an example the fuzzy Risk based decision making system and finally in section 7 we conclude the paper.

2 Analyzing the Possible Risk in an Interaction

As discussed earlier, the trusting agent can make an informed decision whether to interact or not with the probable trusted agent by analyzing the possible Risk that could be present in their interaction. Risk analysis by the trusting agent in its future interaction with the probable trusted agent can be done by:

- Determining the possibility of failure of the interaction; and
- Determining the possible consequences of failure of the interaction.

Hence, the trusting agent should consider these two factors for each probable agent in order to determine the possible Risk associated in interacting with each agent. Based on the analysis, the trusting agent can make an informed decision of whether to interact or not with a particular trusted agent.

2.1 Determining the Possibility of Failure of the Interaction

The possibility of failure of an interaction is the extent to which the trusting agent thinks that it might not achieve its desired outcomes in interacting with a probable trusted agent. The trusting agent can determine the possibility of failure in interacting with a probable trusted agent by analyzing its capacity of not completing the interaction according to how it wants. Further, the trusting agent should analyze the possibility of failure in interacting with a probable trusted agent according to the context and criteria of its future interaction with it. The trusting agent's interaction with the probable trusted agent is in the future state of time. Hence it has to analyze the possibility of failure in interacting with a probable trusted agent in two stages. They are:

1. Pre-Interaction start time phase
2. Post-Interaction start time phase

Pre-Interaction start time phase refers to the period of time before the trusting agent starts its interaction with the probable trusted agent, whereas Post-Interaction start time phase is the period of time after the trusting agent starts its interaction with the probable trusted agent. The possible interaction of the trusting agent with a probable trusted agent will be in the future state of time i.e. in the post-interaction start time phase and, hence the possibility of failure of the interaction must be determined in that phase. But in order for the trusting agent to determine the possibility of failure of a probable trusted agent in the post interaction start time phase, it should know its possibility of failure according to the specific context and criteria as that of its future interaction, till the pre-interaction start time phase. Based on the values achieved for the probable trusted agent till the pre-interaction start time phase, the trusting agent can determine the possibility of failure in the post-interaction start time phase.

In order for the trusting agent to determine the possibility of failure in interacting with a probable trusted agent we defined the term 'Riskiness' in Hussain et al [9]. Riskiness is a numerical value that is assigned to the trusted agent from the Riskiness scale. The Riskiness value shows the level of possibility of failure on the Riskiness scale. The Riskiness scale (as shown in figure 1) ranges from (0, 5) with the value 0 representing the highest level of possibility of failure and the value 5 denoting the

Riskiness Levels	Magnitude of Failure	Riskiness Value	Possibility of Failure Levels	Star Rating
Unknown Risk	.	- 1	Unknown	Not Displayed
Totally Risky	91 - 100 % Possibility of Failure	0	Definite Total Failure	Not Displayed
Extremely Risky	71 – 90 % Possibility of Failure	1	Extremely High	From ⭐ to ⭐
Largely Risky	51 – 70 % Possibility of Failure	2	Largely High	From ⭐⭐ to ⭐⭐
Risky	26 – 50 % Possibility of Failure	3	High	From ⭐⭐⭐ to ⭐⭐⭐
Largely UnRisky	11- 25 % Possibility of Failure	4	Significantly Low	From ⭐⭐⭐⭐ to ⭐⭐⭐⭐
UnRisky	0 – 10 % Possibility of Failure	5	Extremely Low	From ⭐⭐⭐⭐⭐ to ⭐⭐⭐⭐⭐

Fig. 1. Riskiness scale

lowest level of possibility of failure. The Riskiness value for a probable trusted agent in an interaction is assigned to it after determining its capacity to complete the interaction according to the expectations of the trusting agent. Each Riskiness value on the Riskiness scale has a corresponding level of possibility of failure associated with it.

Possibility of failure in interacting with a probable trusted agent in pre-interaction time phase can be determined by the trusting agent by considering the past interaction history or soliciting recommendations from other agents. As mentioned by Carter and Ghorbani [10] reputation of a peer can be relied upon in case of total ignorance.

We have developed a methodology by which the trusting agent determines the possibility of failure in interacting with a probable trusted agent and assigns it with a Riskiness value in both the pre and post interaction start time phase in Hussain et al [9]. Due to space limitation we will not be discussing it here.

2.2 Determining the Possible Consequences of Failure of an Interaction

Another aspect of Risk is the possible loss that could be incurred in an interaction. The trusting agent in order to measure the possible Risk in an interaction should also determine the possible consequences of failure to its resources in interacting with the probable trusted agent apart from determining the possibility of failure in interacting with that particular probable trusted agent. In a peer-to-peer financial interaction, the possible loss that could incur to the trusting agent is usually the financial loss in its resources that are involved in the interaction.

The consequences of failure of an interaction will be modelled over a scale of 0-100% representing the loss incurred. The possible consequences of failure in an interaction is determined only in the post-interaction start time phase, as this is the period in which the trusting agent interacts with the probable trusted agent and its resources are at stake. We have developed a methodology in Hussain et al [9] by which the trusting agent can determine the possible consequences in its resources involved in the interaction while interacting with a probable trusted agent.

Once the trusting agent determines the possibility of failure and the possible consequences of failure of an interaction it should combine those to determine the possible Risk in order to assist decision making. But as mentioned earlier decision making is a tough process. It involves in dealing with a lot of un-certainty. The trusting agent, in spite of determining the possibility of failure in interacting with a probable trusted agent, the possible loss in its resources, might still be uncertain or undecided whether to interact or not with the particular trusted agent. To alleviate this problem, we propose the utilization of a fuzzy system which will help the trusting agent in its decision making process. We will propose the fuzzy system in the next section.

3 Developing a Fuzzy Risk Based Decision Making System

Once the possibility of failure and the consequences of failure have been determined we need a systematic approach to synthesize these two constituents of Risk into a given Risk value for making an informed decision. We propose the use of a fuzzy approach to do this. The main aim of the fuzzy decision making system is to assist the trusting agent with the decision making process. In order to achieve that, we propose that the trusting agent inputs the relative values of the probable trusted agent to the fuzzy system, which in turn evaluates them according to the pre-defined rules. Based on the evaluations of the rules, an output is given to the trusting agent. The output of the fuzzy system will be in the form of 'Proceed (x)' or 'Don't Proceed (x)', where the value 'x' quantifies the strength to which the output qualifies.

The inpput from the universe of discourse (UOD) to the fuzzy system must in fuzzy variables. Fuzzy variables are linguistic objects or words rather than numbers. Hence the inputs (namely *Pre-Interaction: Possibility of failure, Post-Interaction: Possibility of failure* and *Consequences*) of the probable trusted agent must be in linguistic terms to the fuzzy system. In order to do this each of the inputs uses the following fuzzy sets to space their inputs values.

{Low, Medium and High}

Further in this paper, we will represent the inputs to the fuzzy system by their acronyms.

- Pre-Interaction: Possibility of failure is represented as *Pre-I: PoF;*
- Post-Interaction: Possibility of failure is represented as *Post-I: PoF;* and
- Consequences as *Consequences.*

4 Defining Rules for the Fuzzy Logic System

According to the Mamdani approach in order for the fuzzy system to conclude at an output, it needs some rules to process the inputs. Linguistic rules in the fuzzy system consists of two parts, an antecedent (between the IF and THEN) and consequent (following THEN). There are 3 inputs to our fuzzy system and there are 3 fuzzy sets. Hence the total number of rules is: $3^3 = 27$. The rules are:

1. If Pre-I:PoF= **L**, and Post-I:PoF= **L**, and Consequences = **L**, then Output = **P**
2. If Pre-I:PoF= **L**, and Post-I:PoF= **M**, and Consequences = **L**, then Output = **P**
3. If Pre-I:PoF= **L**, and Post-I:PoF= **H**, and Consequences = **L**, then Output = **DP**
4. If Pre-I:PoF= **M**, and Post-I:PoF= **M**, and Consequences = **L**, then Output = **P**
5. If Pre-I:PoF= **M**, and Post-I:PoF= **L**, and Consequences = **L**, then Output = **P**
6. If Pre-I:PoF= **M**, and Post-I:PoF= **H**, and Consequences = **L**, then Output = **DP**
7. If Pre-I:PoF= **H**, and Post-I:PoF= **L**, and Consequences = **L**, then Output = **DP**
8. If Pre-I:PoF= **H**, and Post-I:PoF= **H**, and Consequences = **L**, then Output = **DP**
9. If Pre-I:PoF= **H**, and Post-I:PoF= **M**, and Consequences = **L**, then Output = **DP**
10. If Pre-I:PoF= **L**, and Post-I:PoF= **L**, and Consequences = **H**, then Output = **DP**
11. If Pre-I:PoF= **L**, and Post-I:PoF= **M**, and Consequences = **H**, then Output = **DP**
12. If Pre-I:PoF= **L**, and Post-I:PoF= **H**, and Consequences = **H**, then Output = **DP**
13. If Pre-I:PoF= **M**, and Post-I:PoF= **M**, and Consequences = **H**, then Output=**DP**
14. If Pre-I:PoF= **M**, and Post-I:PoF= **L**, and Consequences = **H**, then Output = **DP**
15. If Pre-I:PoF= **M**, and Post-I:PoF= **H**, and Consequences = **H**, then Output =**DP**
16. If Pre-I:PoF= **H**, and Post-I:PoF= **L**, and Consequences = **H**, then Output = **DP**
17. If Pre-I:PoF= **H**, and Post-I:PoF= **H**, and Consequences = **H**, then Output = **DP**
18. If Pre-I:PoF= **H**, and Post-I:PoF= **M**, and Consequences = **H**, then Output = **DP**
19. If Pre-I:PoF= **L**, and Post-I:PoF= **L**, and Consequences = **M**, then Output = **P**
20. If Pre-I:PoF= **L**, and Post-I:PoF= **M**, and Consequences = **M**, then Output = **P**
21. If Pre-I:PoF= **L**, and Post-I:PoF= **H**, and Consequences = **M**, then Output = **DP**
22. If Pre-I:PoF= **M**, and Post-I:PoF= **M**, and Consequences = **M**, then Output = **DP**
23. If Pre-I:PoF= **M**, and Post-I:PoF= **L**, and Consequences = **M**, then Output = **P**
24. If Pre-I:PoF= **M**, and Post-I:PoF= **H**, and Consequences = **M**, then Output = **DP**
25. If Pre-I:PoF= **H**, and Post-I:PoF= **L**, and Consequences = **M**, then Output = **DP**
26. If Pre-I:PoF= **H**, and Post-I:PoF= **H**, and Consequences = **M**, then Output = **DP**
27. If Pre-I:PoF= **H**, and Post-I:PoF= **M**, and Consequences = **M**, then Output = **DP**

5 Membership Functions

Membership functions are a graphical representation, represented by different shapes in order to determine the magnitude of participation of each input. No matter by what shape any input or output is represented, the height or magnitude of the shape is usually normalized to 1. The width of the shape represents the base of the function. In our fuzzy system the range of two inputs i.e. *Pre-I: PoF* and *Post-I: PoF* is within [0, 5] and that of *consequence* is within [0-100%]. We represent the *gbell* shape to determine the strength of the inputs and the *triangle* shape to determine the strength of the output in our system. The membership functions for the inputs and outputs to the fuzzy system are shown in the figures below.

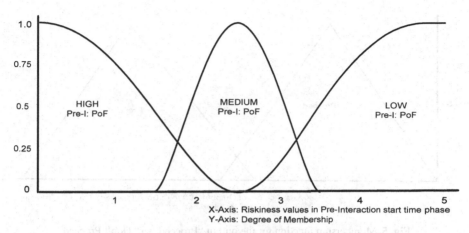

X-Axis: Riskiness values in Pre-Interaction start time phase
Y-Axis: Degree of Membership

Fig. 2. Membership function for the input "Pre-I: PoF"

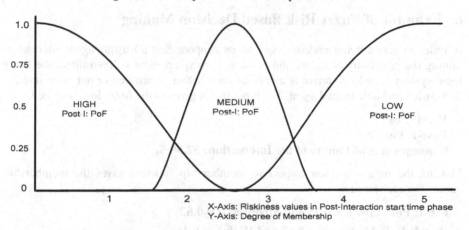

X-Axis: Riskiness values in Post-Interaction start time phase
Y-Axis: Degree of Membership

Fig. 3. Membership function for the input "Post-I: PoF"

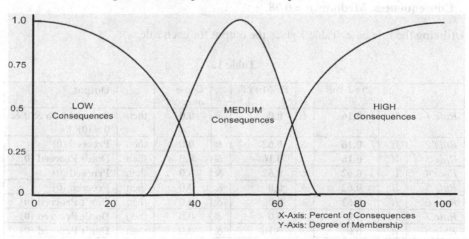

X-Axis: Percent of Consequences
Y-Axis: Degree of Membership

Fig. 4. Membership function for the input "Consequences"

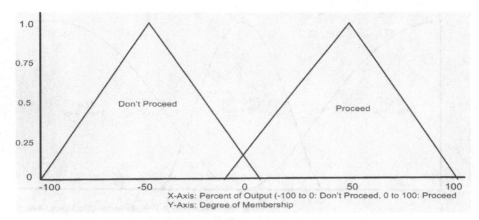

Fig. 5. Membership function for the output "Proceed" or "Don't Proceed"

6 Example of Fuzzy Risk Based Decision Making

In order to gain a better understanding let us suppose that a trusting agent after determining the possibility of failure and possible consequences of failure utilizes the fuzzy logic system in order to arrive at a conclusion whether to proceed or not in an interaction with a probable trusted agent. The input that it gives to the fuzzy logic engine is:

Pre-I: PoF: 3
Post-I: PoF: 2
Consequences of Failure of the Interaction: 52.90 %

Plotting the inputs on their respective membership function gives the membership values for each input.

Pre-I: PoF, Low μ = 0.16 and Medium μ = 0.62
Post-I: PoF, Medium μ = 0.62 and High μ = 0.16
Consequences, Medium μ = 0.98

Utilizing the rule base, Table 1 gives the output for each rule

Table 1.

		Pre-I:PoF		Post-I:PoF		Conse-quences		Output
Rule 1	If	0.16	&	0.0	&	0.0	then	Proceed 0.16 & 0 & 0 = (0)
Rule 2	If	0.16	&	0.62	&	0.0	then	Proceed (0)
Rule 3	If	0.16	&	0.16	&	0.0	then	Don't Proceed (0)
Rule 4	If	0.62	&	0.62	&	0.0	then	Proceed (0)
Rule 5	If	0.62	&	0.0	&	0.0	then	Proceed (0)
Rule 6	If	0.62	&	0.0	&	0.0	then	Don't Proceed (0)
Rule 7	If	0.0	&	0.0	&	0.0	then	Don't Proceed (0)
Rule 8	If	0.0	&	0.16	&	0.0	then	Don't Proceed (0)
Rule 9	If	0.0	&	0.62	&	0.0	then	Don't Proceed (0)

Table 1. (*continued*)

Rule 10	If	0.16	&	0.0	&	0.0	then	Don't Proceed (0)
Rule 11	If	0.16	&	0.62	&	0.0	then	Don't Proceed (0)
Rule 12	If	0.16	&	0.16	&	0.0	then	Don't Proceed (0)
Rule 13	If	0.62	&	0.62	&	0.0	then	Don't Proceed (0)
Rule 14	If	0.62	&	0.0	&	0.0	then	Don't Proceed (0)
Rule 15	If	0.62	&	0.16	&	0.0	then	Don't Proceed (0)
Rule 16	If	0.0	&	0.0	&	0.0	then	Don't Proceed (0)
Rule 17	If	0.0	&	0.16	&	0.0	then	Don't Proceed (0)
Rule 18	If	0.0	&	0.62	&	0.0	then	Don't Proceed (0)
Rule 19	If	0.16	&	0.0	&	0.98	then	Proceed (0)
Rule 20	If	0.16	&	0.62	&	0.98	then	Proceed (0.16)
Rule 21	If	0.16	&	0.62	&	0.98	then	Don't Proceed (0.16)
Rule 22	If	0.62	&	0.62	&	0.98	then	Don't Proceed (0.62)
Rule 23	If	0.62	&	0.0	&	0.98	then	Proceed (0)
Rule 24	If	0.62	&	0.16	&	0.98	then	Don't Proceed (0.16)
Rule 25	If	0.0	&	0.0	&	0.98	then	Don't Proceed (0)
Rule 26	If	0.0	&	0.16	&	0.98	then	Don't Proceed (0)
Rule 27	If	0.0	&	0.62	&	0.98	then	Don't Proceed (0)

The logical sum of the rules must be inferred first according to the possible output memberships before being defuzzified to produce a crisp output. We infer the logical sum of the rules by the Root-Sum-Square (RSS) method. The RSS method combines the effect of all applicable rules, scales the functions at their respective magnitude and computes the fuzzy centroid of the composite area. As compared to the other methods of inferring, the RSS gives the best weighted influence to all firing rules. Hence it was chosen in this example as it includes all contributing rules. Other methods of defuzzification can also be utilized to defuzzify the logical sums of the rules.

For the ongoing example, an input of 3, 2 and 52.90% which denotes the pre-interaction time start possibility of failure, the post-interaction time start possibility of failure and the possible consequences of failure respectively, the output membership function strengths from the defined rules are:

$$\text{"Proceed"} = \sqrt{\sum (proceed)^2} = \sqrt{0.0256} = 0.16$$

$$\text{"Don't Proceed"} = \sqrt{\sum (Don'tproceed)^2} = \sqrt{0.4356} = 0.66$$

Once the output membership function strength for each output has been determined, the data must be defuzzified to obtain a crisp output. The defuzzification is accomplished by combining the results of the inference process and computing the fuzzy centroid of the output area. The weighted strengths of each output member function is multiplied by its respective output membership function center points and summed. Finally, this area is divided by the sum of the weighted member function strengths and the result is taken as the crisp output.

1774   O.K. Hussain et al.

Determining the crisp output:

$$\frac{(\text{Dont proceed\_centre} * \text{Dont proceed\_strenght} + \text{Proceed\_centre} * \text{Proceed\_strenght})}{(\text{Dont proceed\_strenght} + \text{Proceed\_strenght})}$$

Substituting the respective values from above continuing example:

$$\frac{-100*0.66+100*0.16}{0.66+0.16} = -60.97$$

The output value of -60.97 % (60.97 %, Don't Proceed) seems logical since the particular input conditions (Pre-Interaction Possibility of Failure=3, Post-Interaction Possibility of Failure =2 and Consequences=52.90 %) indicate that the possible Risk associated in the interaction might by high. The minus (-) sign suggest that the output is in the 'Don't proceed' output member function.

7 Conclusion

It has been proven in the literature that Fuzzy logic models uncertainty and gives an output based on the vague inputs given. In this paper we developed a methodology which incorporates a fuzzy system that assists in Risk based decision making process. The fuzzy system assists the trusting agent to decide whether to proceed or not in an interaction with a particular trusted agent based on the inputs given. The inputs given to the fuzzy system are the values related to the trusting agent's future interaction with the probable trusted agent. Based on the output from the fuzzy system the trusting agent can either decide whether to interact or not with the trusted agent or affirm its previous decision.

References

1. Cooper, D.F.: The Australian and New Zealand Standard on Risk Management, AS/NZS 4360:2004', Tutorial Notes: Broadleaf Capital International Pty Ltd. (2004) Available: http://www.broadleaf.com.au/tutorials/Tut_Standard.pdf
2. March, G. J. and Shapira, Z.: Managerial perspective on risk and risk taking, Management Science, vol. 33, no. 11, (1987), 1404-1418.
3. Luhmann, N.: Familiarity, confidence, trust: Problems and alternatives, Making and Breaking Cooperative Relations, Basil Blackwell, New York, USA (1994).
4. Mayer, R.C., Davis, J.H., and Schoorman, F.D.: An interactive model for organizational trust, Academy of Management Review, vol. 20, no. 3, 709-734.
5. Rousseau, D.M., Sitkin, S.B., Burt, R.S., and Camerer, C.: Not so different after all: A cross-discipline view of trust, Academy of Management Review, vol. 23, no. 3, 391-404.
6. Sztompka, P.: Trust: A sociological theory, Cambridge University Press, Cambridge, U.K. (1999).
7. Grazioli, S. and Wang, A.: Looking without seeing: Understanding unsophisticated consumers success and failure to detect Internet deception, Proceedings of the International Conference on Information Systems, New Orleans, USA, (2001), 193-204.

8. Cheung, C. and Lee, M.K.O.: Trust in Internet shopping: A proposed model and measurement instrument, Proceedings of the 2000 Americas Conference on Information Systems, Long Beach, CA, (2000), 681-689.
9. Hussain, O.K., Chang, E., Hussain, F.K., and Dillon, T.S.: A Methodology for Risk Based Decision Making in a Service Oriented Environment", Proceedings of the IEEE International Conference on Sensor Networks, Ubiquitous, and Trustworthy Computing -Vol 1, Taichung, Taiwan, (2006), 506-513.
10. Carter, J. and Ghorbani, A.A.: Towards a formalization of value-centric trust in agent societies, Web Intelligence and Agent Systems, Vol. 2, No. 3 (2004), 167-183.
11. Greenland, S.: Bounding analysis as an inadequately specified methodology, Risk Analysis vol. 24, no. 5 (2004), 1085-1092.

Header Metadata Extraction from Semi-structured Documents Using Template Matching*

Zewu Huang, Hai Jin, Pingpeng Yuan, and Zongfen Han

Cluster and Grid Computing Lab
Huazhong University of Science and Technology, Wuhan, 430074, China
hjin@hust.edu.cn

Abstract. With the recent proliferation of documents, automatic metadata extraction from document becomes an important task. In this paper, we propose a novel template matching based method for header metadata extraction form semi-structured documents stored in PDF. In our approach, templates are defined, and the document is considered as strings with format. Templates are used to guide *finite state automaton* (FSA) to extract header metadata of papers. The testing results indicate that our approach can effectively extract metadata, without any training cost and available to some special situation. This approach can effectively assist the automatic index creation in lots of fields such as digital libraries, information retrieval, and data mining.

1 Introduction

Compared with hard copy documents, it is easy to keep and spread digital scientific documents, thus the digital scientific documents are widely accepted as the main document type in libraries and other places. Whether documents are digital or hard-copy ones, it is important to extract metadata of documents since it is impossible to retrieve documents without metadata of documents. Metadata is data about data, used to describe other information based on some rules or policies. Metadata of documents is used in many document processing fields such as search, browsing, and filtering [1].

Providing metadata is the responsibility of each data provider with the quality of the metadata. Many data providers [2] have had significant harvesting problems with XML syntax and encoding issues, even leading to unavailability of service [3]. Therefore, how to automatically extract metadata from documents turns out to be an indispensable research issue. However, because format of digital scientific documents varies according to publication type, e.g., books, journals, conference papers, research reports, and technical reports, it is difficult to automatically extract metadata. Therefore, it is very important to design tools to do that.

In this paper, we take a template matching based approach to extract metadata, including title, author(s), affiliation(s), abstract, and keywords, from semi-structured

---

* This paper is supported by the National 973 Key Basic Research Program under grant No.2003CB317003, and the Cultivation Fund of the Key Scientific and Technical Innovation Project, Ministry of Education of China under grant No.705034.

R. Meersman, Z. Tari, P. Herrero et al. (Eds.): OTM Workshops 2006, LNCS 4278, pp. 1776–1785, 2006.

scientific literature. Experimental results discussed below indicate that our approach is efficient for header metadata extraction from semi-structured documents. Our approach can be effectively used in a variety of situations such as: (1) automatic creation of indices for digital libraries, (2) conversion of documents to semantically richer representation, (3) metadata mining and, (4) the search engines base on metadata.

The rest of the paper is organized as follows. In section 2, we describe our method of header metadata extraction. Section 3 gives our experimental results. In section 4, we introduce related work. We make concluding remarks in section 5.

2 Header Metadata Extraction Method

2.1 Document Outline

In many circumstances, it is fundamental to disaggregate a paper into its basic components [4]. We propose a layout information based approach to document disaggregation. Our approach is based on exploiting the layout information while reading a document. Some layout information is listed as follows:

- The section properties, such as number of columns, section break type, position of page number.
- The paragraph properties, such as flush left, flush right, flush centre, left indent, right indent, and first indent in the first line.
- The font properties, such as size, style, color, bold, underline, Italic, and xy position information.
- The document properties such as page width, page height, left margin, right margin, bottom margin, top margin, starting page number.

In a PDF file, the typical word boundary based structure of a document is broken down into fragments [5]. However, it remains all spatial and font-related data contained in the input PDF file. The styles of documents vary greatly. There are various scientific paper layouts. Fig. 1 shows four typical layouts.

In general, within a document category, a certain visual layout can be identified for all documents within that category. Concretely, the layout information for each metadata is different. The characteristics of header metadata are listed as follow:

Title. Location is always on the upper portion of the first page; Font size is always the largest. Position is always in the middle of the line and flush centre. Font style is always bold. Section break symbol among metadata is always "enter".

Authors. Location is always immediately under the title; Font size is always smaller than title font. Font is always the same for all authors. Break symbols are always " ", "," or "and". Authors may or may not be listed in separated lines and flush centre. Author(s) and affiliation(s) may be listed on one column or more. Authors and affiliations may or may not always have superscripts.

Affiliations. Location is always immediately under the authors' list and before abstract. Characteristic words are always "university", "department", "@", "{", "}", etc. Font is always the same for all affiliations. Only one affiliation appears when all authors are associated with it, or affiliations mapping to authors are listed separately.

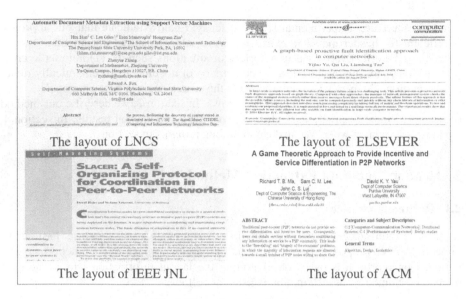

Fig. 1. Examples of typical layout

Abstract. Location is always immediately under the affiliations' list. Special word to start is always bold such as "abstract" etc. Abstract always lies behind the affiliation(s) and before the keywords if keywords exist or the introduction if keywords do not exist. First indent in the first line is always zero and left indent; Abstract and keywords may be listed on one column or two columns. The abstract is optional.

Keywords. Location is always immediately under abstract and before introduction. Special words to start are always bold such as "keywords" etc. First indent in the first line is always zero. Left indent is always zero. Font style is always the same for abstract and keywords except some words in abstract. The keywords are optional.

In section 2.2, we will discuss how to define template according to these layout information shown above. In section 2.3, we will discuss how to match template to extract metadata.

2.2 Template Define

Sharing of data, knowledge and analytical methodology becomes a reality using the layout template concept [6]. The layout templates, like interface--one that is similar in its structure to a Dublin Core template, are sets of operations implementing predefined analysis routines used for integrated analysis and is targeted towards a given analysis. More importantly, the integrated knowledge template approach provides a common framework for decision support. Layout template collection is derived from the layout of kinds of publication and can supply the overall arrangement of metadata.

In order to reach the stable status, the templates are active models which interact with variant properties such as position, page, style, and font. Therefore, the templates provide an evolution process for these parameters to be changed gradually into best-fit. We build a variety of template for each metadata regarding to different layout information. For each paper, the template schema is composed of 5 templates corresponding to each metadata. Our approach uses XML Schema to formulize templates. The structure of a template schema is shown in Fig. 2. The attributes and relation of a template for header metadata is shown in Fig. 3.

```
<xsd:element name="template schema">
    <xsd:complexType>
    <xsd:sequence>
        <xsd:element name="title template"/>
        <xsd:element name="authors template"/>
        <xsd:element name="affiliations template"/>
        <xsd:element name="abstract template"/>
        <xsd:element name="keywords template"/>
    </xsd:sequence>
    </xsd:complexType >
</xsd:element>
```

Fig. 2. The structure of a template schema

```
<xsd:element name="template">
<xsd:complexType>
<xsd:all>
<xsd:element name=" Page">
  <xsd:complexType>
  <xs: attribute name="height" type="xsd:int" />
  <xs: attribute name="width" type="xsd:int" />
  <xs: attribute name="column" type="xsd:int" />
  <xs: attribute name="paragraph" type =
  "xsd:string" />
  </xsd:complexType>
</element>
<xsd:element name=" Font">
  <xsd:complexType>
  <xs: attribute name="name" type="xsd:string"/>
  <xs: attribute name="size" type="xsd:float" />
   <xs: maxInclusive ref="title. font"/>
  </xsd:complexType>
</element>
<xsd:element name=" Style">
  <xsd:complexType>
  <xs: attribute name="bold" type="xsd:boolean" />
  <xs: attribute name="underline" type=
  "xsd:boolean" />
```

```
<xs: attribute name="Italic" type="xsd:boolean "
/>
<xs: attribute name="number of rows"
type ="xsd:int "/>
<xs: attribute name="array" type="xsd:string" />
</xsd:complexType>
</element>
<xsd:element name="Position">
  <xsd:complexType>
  <xs: attribute name="x1" type="xsd:float"/>
   <xs: minInclusive ref="title.x1"/>
   <xs: maxInclusive ref="keyword.X1"/>
  <xs: attribute name="y1" type="xsd:float " />
  <xs: attribute name="x2" type="xsd:float"/>
   <xs: minInclusive ref="title.s2"/>
   <xs: maxInclusive ref="keyword.x2"/>
  <xs: attribute name="y2" type="xsd:float " />
  <xs: attribute name="Text" type="xsd:string" />
  </xsd:complexType>
</element>
</xsd:complexType>
</xsd:all>
</xsd:element>
```

Fig. 3. The attributes and restriction of a template for each metadata

2.3 Template Matching Model

We develop a template generation system to transform known semi-structured strings into sequences of data stream with layout information discussed above. These sequences are then saved as templates in template collection manually. A new semi-structured document is also translated into a sequence of data stream. We match for the most similar template to the new sequence of data stream from the template collection constructed. We then parse metadata of the document according to the template.

Following is the model for matching templates. First, a data stream sequence V with all metadata including title, author(s), affiliation(s), abstract, keywords is defined. Second, we define template collection T for each metadata. Next, we define template schema for metadata sequence M compounding with T. Then we define the weight of T_i, in template schema Φ_i. At last, we define a formula to compute the similarity between a particular paper and template schema Φ_i. The formalization expression is listed as follow:

data stream sequence $V=v_1v_2...v_n$, v_i ($1\leq i\leq n$) delegates a sequence of data stream including different metadata such as title, author(s), affiliation(s), abstract, keywords and some arbitrary strings.

Template collection $T_j=\{T_{j1}, T_{j2}, T_{j3},..., T_{jm}\}$, T_{ji} ($1\leq j\leq 5$, $1\leq i\leq m$) is a template for each metadata, T_{ji} has a weight about importance W_{ji} ($0<W_{ji}<1$). Generally speaking the weight of authors' template is the highest.

Layout Template schema $L=\{\Phi_1, \Phi_2,..., \Phi_u\}$, $\Phi_x=T_{1t}T_{2n}...T_{5k}$, ($1\leq x\leq u$), ($1\leq t$, n, $k\leq m$).

$f_i=f(T_{ji}, \Phi_x)$ delegates the weight of template T_{ji} in template schema Φ_x. $f_j = W_{ji}$ If $T_{ji}\in \Phi_x$, otherwise, $f_i=0$.

$$f(T_{ji},\Phi_x) = \begin{cases} W_{ji} & T_{ji} \in \Phi_x \\ 0 & T_{ji} \notin \Phi_x \end{cases} \qquad (1)$$

$sim(R, \Phi_j)$ delegates the similarity between the header metadata of a particular paper and template schema. $sim(R, \Phi_j)$ is the sum of all f_i.

$$sim(R,\Phi_j) = \sum_1^5 f_i \qquad (2)$$

In order to match template, we construct a finite state automation with stochastic state transitions and data stream emissions. The automation models a probabilistic generative process whereby a data stream is produced by starting in some states and match template, transitioning to a new state, emitting a data stream selected by that state and matching the template, transitioning again, emitting another data stream and matching again until a designated final state is reached. There is a prior state distribution *start* and the end state *end*. There is also a state distribution *any* when the data stream does not match any template. Associated with each of a set of states, $S=\{$ *start, title, authors, affiliations, abstract, keywords, any, end* $\}$ is a probability distribution over the data stream in the emission data stream $D=\{m_1,...,m_k\}$.

The finite state automation is used for template matching by formulating a model in the following way: each state is associated with a metadata we want to extract. For a sequence of data stream R translated from document, we take out template schema Φ_x from S. If the layout information of data stream m_i can match the template T_{ji} in template schema Φ_x, the data stream m_i is one of metadata, we can get the f_i. Then, we get the next data stream m_{t+1} and translate repeatedly. If the layout information of data stream m_i can not match any template in template schema Φ_x, the data stream m_i is not any metadata, then get the next data stream m_t and translate repeatedly. The condition of state transition is listed as follow:

Cti: the layout information of the next data stream can match template T_{ij} in template collection T_{ij} of template schema Φ_x ($1\leq i\leq 5$).

C0: the layout information of the next data stream can not match any template.

Cm: the next data stream is null.

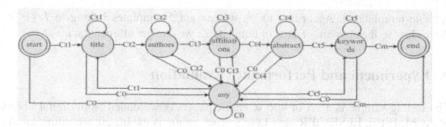

Fig. 4. Flow of template matching

The flow of template matching is shown in Fig. 4.

By matching templates, we can get $sim(R, \Phi_x)$ by adding f_i for the sequence of data stream s_k. We get $sim(R, \Phi_h)$ for each template schema of L. We can also get the appropriate template Φ_j for header metadata R when the value of $sim(R, \Phi_j)$ is the maximal. Then we use special rules corresponding to the template Φ_j. If the maximal value of $sim(R, \Phi_j)$ is under certain value, and there is no available template, we extract the layout information and make new templates manually.

The next issue is how to judge whether a data stream matches a template. In order to explain this, we give an example. The layout of authors is the most diverse. Therefore, we show an example how to extract author(s) by template matching in the section. The example layout of authors is shown in Fig. 5.

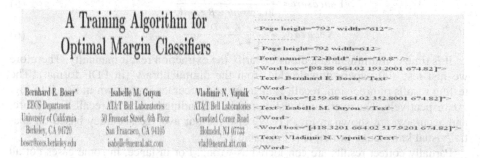

Fig. 5. An example of authors layout   **Fig. 6.** A fragment of layout about authors

By transforming the document into sequences of data stream, we can get a data stream and its layout information represented in XML shown in Fig. 6. From the box item of position (box="[98.88 664.02 193.2001 674.82]", box="[259.68 664.02 352.8001 674.82]", box="[418.3201 664.02 517.9201 674.82]") and page item (height="792" width="612"), we can deduce: column="3", partition="centre", number of rows="1". From the font item (Font name="T2-Bold" size="10.8"), we can deduce: bold=true, underline=false, Italic=false. Then we search template in author template collection T_2. At last, we can find a template T_{2k}. For template schema Φ_x, we can find the value of attributes in template T_{2k} is the same as this data stream, then we can say this data stream matches the template T_{2k}.

According to the above principle, we can get all data stream and match all templates for each template schema. For a sequence of data stream, we can get the most suitable template Φ_j. According to Φ_j, we can get 5 templates belong to T_j ($1\leq j\leq 5$). According to the element of *Text* of template T_j, we can get all metadata.

3 Experiment and Performance Evaluation

The testing sample is a set of 400 scientific papers downloaded from digital libraries of ACM, IEEE, ELSEVIER, and LNCS. The sample is evaluated according to precision, recall, F-measure, and accuracy. Precision is the fraction of the right metadata in the number of metadata correctly extracted; recall is the fraction of the true metadata in the number of metadata which is considered correct; F-measure is a synthesis index of precision and recall; accuracy is the fraction of the true metadata in the number of all extracted metadata.

If we define A as the number of true positive samples predicted as positive, B as the number of true positive samples predicted as negative, C as the number of true negative samples predicted as positive and D as the number of true negative samples predicted as negative, then precision, recall, F-measure, and accuracy can be expressed as follows:

$$\mathrm{Pr}\,ecision = \frac{A}{A+C} \tag{3}$$

$$\mathrm{Re}\,call = \frac{A}{A+B} \tag{4}$$

$$\text{F-}measure = \frac{2\,\mathrm{Pr}\,ecision * \mathrm{Re}\,call}{\mathrm{Pr}\,ecision + R\,e\,call} \tag{5}$$

$$\mathrm{A}\,ccuracy = \frac{A+D}{A+B+C+D} \tag{6}$$

It is time consuming and tedious to verify the extraction result manually. Therefore we just test 400 papers downloaded from the digital library (in PDF format). The testing results of precision, recall, F-measure and accuracy are shown in Fig. 7 to Fig. 10, respectively. The average of testing results, including precision, recall, F-measure, and accuracy, are shown in Fig. 11. We also list our average accuracy based on spatial/visual knowledge principle [5] in Table 1.

Partially correct results are considered as wrong. For instance, in some cases not all authors are properly identified which yields to a negative score in our performance estimation. "Title" is the most accurate findings due to their simple structural description.

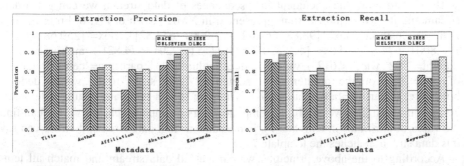

Fig. 7. Precision of metadata extraction   **Fig. 8.** Recall of metadata extraction

The accuracy of author(s) and affiliation(s) extraction is the lowest. There are many different cases in judging the affiliation(s), mapping the author(s) and affiliation(s), dividing the authors which are conjunctively listed. The reason that the accuracy of extraction keywords is higher than that of extraction abstract is that the abstract is always joined with some irrespective information such as copyright, publisher. Further more, most of the papers used in our test are never seen before, that is, we may not even have considered that specific situation during the design of our templates.

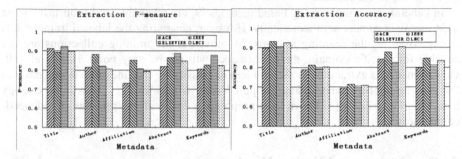

Fig. 9. F-measure of metadata extraction   **Fig. 10.** Accuracy of metadata extraction

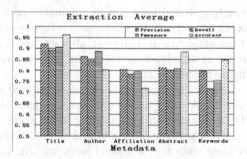

Fig. 11. Performance of metadata extraction

Table 1. Comparison on the accuracy (%) of metadata extraction based on spatial/visual knowledge principle and based on template

Metadata	spatial/visual	template
Title	92	96.3
Author	87	80.2
Affiliation	75	71.9
Abstract	/	88.4
Keywords	/	84.7

4 Related Work

Several methods have been used for automatic metadata extraction from documents. The main methods fall into two categories: rule based approach and machine learning based approach.

Rule based systems do not require any training and are straightforward to implement. However, they are not independence of the application domain, and need the help of expertise to set the rules or regular expression, all these limit their usage. Giuffrida et al. [6] developed a rule based system for automatic metadata extraction from research documents in Postscript. Liddy et al. [7] performed metadata extraction from educational materials using natural language processing technologies. Mao et al. [8] also conducted automatic metadata extraction by exploiting formatting information of research documents.

In general, machine learning based methods [9] are adaptable and robust. It can be used to any document set theoretically. However, generating the labeled training data is expensive for the learning systems. Moreover, if the training collections are not suitable for specific domain, the performance will not be very good. Han et al. [10] viewed metadata extraction as the problem of classifying the lines in a document into the categories of metadata using Support Vector Machines [11]. Maximum entropy based Markov models [12] have been proposed to deal with the problem of independent features.

5 Conclusions and Future Work

A novel template matching based approach to automatic metadata extraction from scientific literature is introduced and its performance is demonstrated. We can retrieve information on the title, author(s), affiliation(s), abstract, and keywords of scientific literature. This approach is also incorporated in the architecture of active digital libraries and search engine base on metadata.

New templates about new layout information can be defined and added to process certain types of documents. A wider variety of document types can also be considered in addition to the PDF documents such as handle patents, technical reports, dissertations, and broadcast news possibly in different formats (e.g., HTML, PS, PPT, DOC).

The system needs some temp files to extract metadata. The temp files waste some space and need extra resource to convert. Consequently it is necessary for our system to take some measures to optimize the conversions. We also plan to extract some other metadata such as reference. These newly extracted metadata as well as previously extracted metadata can be mined in order to discover useful knowledge.

References

1. Murphy, L. D. Digital document metadata in organizations: roles, analytical approaches, and future research directions. In *Proceedings of the 31st Annual Hawaii International Conference on System Sciences* (1998) 267-276
2. Brody, T. Celestial - Open Archives Gateway. http://celestial.eprints.org
3. Liu, X. Federating. Heterogeneous Digital Libraries by metadata harvesting. Ph.D. Dissertation, Old Dominion University (2002)
4. Bishop, A. P. Digital libraries and knowledge disaggregation: The use of journal article components. In *Proceedings of the 3rd ACM International Conference on Digital Libraries* (1998) 29-39

5. Giuffrida, G., Shek, E. C., and Yang, J. Knowledge-based metadata extraction from Post-Script files. In *Proceedings of the 5th ACM Conference on Digital Libraries* (2000) 77-84.
6. Nevill-Manning, C. G., Reed, T., and Witten, I. H. Extracting text from postscript. Technical report, Comp. Science Dept., University of Waikato, New Zealand (1997)
7. Liddy, E. D., Sutton, S., Allen, E., Harwell, S., Corieri, S., Yilmazel, O., Ozgencil, N. E., Diekema, A., McCracken, N., and Silverstein, J. Automatic Metadata generation & evaluation. In *Proceedings of the 25th Annual International ACM SIGIR Conference on Research and Development in Information Retrieval* (2002) 401-402
8. Mao, S., Kim, J. W., and Thoma, G. R. A dynamic feature generation system for automated metadata extraction in preservation of digital materials. In *Proceedings of the 1st International Workshop on Document Image Analysis for Libraries* (2004) 225-232
9. Hu, Y., Li H., Cao Y., Meyerzon D., and Zheng Q. Automatic extraction of titles from general documents using machine learning. In *Proceedings of the 5th ACM/IEEE-CS Joint Conference on Digital Libraries* (2005)
10. Han, H., Giles, C. L., Manavoglu, E., Zha, H., Zhang, Z., and Fox, E. A. Automatic document metadata extraction using support vector machines. In *Proceedings of the 3rd ACM/IEEE-CS Joint Conference on Digital Libraries* (2003) 37-48
11. Joachims, T. A statistical learning model of text classification with Support Vector Machines. In *Proceedings of the 24th ACM International Conference on Research and Development in Information Retrieval* (2001) 128–136
12. McCallum, A., Freitag, D., and Pereira, F. Maximum entropy Markov models for information extraction and segmentation. In *Proceedings of the 17th International Conf. on Machine Learning* (2000) 591–598

Query Terms Abstraction Layers

Stein L. Tomassen and Darijus Strasunskas

Department of Computer and Information Science,
Norwegian University of Technology and Science,
Sem Saelandsvei 7-9, NO-7491 Trondheim, Norway
{stein.l.tomassen, darijus.strasunskas}@idi.ntnu.no

Abstract. A problem with traditional information retrieval systems is that they typically retrieve information without an explicitly defined domain of interest to the user. Consequently, the system presents a lot of information that is of little relevance to the user. Ideally, the queries' *real intentions* should be exposed and reflected in the way the underlying retrieval machinery can deal with them. In this paper we propose using abstraction layers to differentiate on the query terms. We explain why we believe this differentiation of query terms is necessary and the potentials of this approach. The whole retrieval system is under development as part of a Semantic Web standardization project for the Norwegian oil and gas industry.

1 Introduction

Query interpretation is the first phase of an information retrieval (IR) session and the only part of the session that receives clear inputs from the user. Traditional vector space retrieval systems view the queries from a syntactic perspective and calculate document similarities from counting frequencies of meaningless strings. They typically retrieve information without explicitly defined domain of interest to the user. As a result, the system presents a lot of information that are of little relevance to the user. Consequently, the retrieval and ranking process is very important, though the result crucially hinges on the user's ability to specify unambiguously his/her information needs. Ideally, the queries' *real intentions* should be exposed and reflected in the way the underlying retrieval machinery can deal with them. In this paper we propose using abstraction layers to differentiate on the terms specified in a query to better grasp the *real intention* of the query.

Users tend to use very few terms (3 or less) in their search queries [1, 2]. As a result, the system cannot *understand* the context of the user's query, which results in lower precision. By adding more relevant terms to the query the domain of interest can to some extend be identified. However, adding the *correct* terms is not always trivial, since the user needs knowledge about the terminology used in that particular domain to find those *correct* terms. For an explorative search the process of finding those *correct* terms can be satisfactory. However, that is not the case when precise information is needed.

According to Gulla [1], there are only about 10% of the users, which are using the advanced features of a search engine found on the Web. In addition, an internal study

R. Meersman, Z. Tari, P. Herrero et al. (Eds.): OTM Workshops 2006, LNCS 4278, pp. 1786–1795, 2006.
© Springer-Verlag Berlin Heidelberg 2006

at FAST[1] show that 48% of the retrieved documents viewed are the three top ranked documents before they do a new search [1]. This makes it similarly difficult to state what kind of documents might be of interest to the user.

Another problem with current search engines is that they do not *understand* the content of the documents and consequently cannot filter out those documents not being relevant. Most search engines found on the Web do use many traditional information retrieval techniques when indexing the documents, like stemming, removal of stopwords, etc. In this process, they do not try to *understand* the content of the documents but primarily make them as easily available for retrieval as possible. This often means that the documents are *normalized* and it becomes even harder to differentiate on the documents.

A reason for why IR systems have major problems of *understanding* the intention of either queries or documents is how we humans use concepts. Typically, humans think of words as concepts, e.g. a word like 'sports' covers all kinds of sports like soccer, skiing, golf, etc. However, we also interpret the concepts differently depending on each persons background, for example some does not regard golf as a real sport. IR systems work in word-space while we humans deal with information in concept-space [3, 4]. Sine typical IR systems work in word-space to retrieve documents written by humans thinking in concept-space the result is often not satisfying.

A novel and promising approach is concept-based search [5, 6, 7]. With this approach, the burden of knowing how the documents are written is taken off the user and hence the user can focus on searching on a conceptual level instead. One problem with this approach is to find good concepts. Some promising approaches described in [5, 7] find concepts based on the result set of each search, which next is used to refine the search. However, the relationships between the concepts are neglected.

Ontologies can define concepts and the relationships among them from any domain of interest [8] and are therefore suitable to define domains. In our approach [9], we use ontologies to define concepts in a particular domain. We use a query enrichment approach that uses contextually enriched ontologies to bring the queries closer to the user's preferences and the characteristics of the document collection. The idea is to associate every concept (classes and instances) of the ontology with a feature vector (fv) to tailor these concepts to the specific terminology used in the document collection. Synonyms and conjugations would naturally go into such a vector, but we would also like to include related terms that tend to be used in connection with the concept and to provide a contextual definition of it. Afterward, the fvs are used to enrich the query provided by the user. In addition, we exploit the relationships between the concepts defined in the ontology when post processing the result set of the search for filtering and presentation.

Preliminary results of our approach looks promising compared to traditional IR approaches. Though, we have acknowledged the need to differentiate on the query terms to increase precision of search. For an explorative search, using only concepts when defining the query gives satisfactory results. However, for more precise search, using only concepts does not give the same acceptable results. Consequently, the user should be able to use a mixed approach being able to use both terms and concepts. In

---

[1] Fast Search & Transfer ASA, http://www.fastsearch.com/

our approach all the concepts are related to the domain specified by the ontology, this should also be the case with the other query terms. This proposed differentiation of the query terms is further described in section 3.

This research is part of the Integrated Information Platform for reservoir and subsea production systems (IIP) project supported by the Norwegian Research Council (NFR)[2] that funds this work. The IIP project is creating an ontology for all subsea equipment used by oil and gas industry. The project will make this ontology publicly available and standardized by the International Organization for Standardization (ISO)[3].

This paper is organized as follows. In section 2, related work is discussed. In section 3, the proposed layers of abstraction of query terms are presented. In section 4, we describe an approach of how feature vectors can be constructed. Finally, in section 5 we discuss the potentials of this approach and conclude the paper.

2 Related Work

Traditional information retrieval techniques (i.e., vector-space model) have an advantage of being fast and give a fair result. However, it is difficult to represent the content of the documents meaningfully using these techniques. That is, after the documents are indexed, they become a "bag of terms" and hence the semantics is partly lost in this process.

The related work to our approach comes from two main areas. Ontology based IR, in general, and approaches to query expansion, in particular. General approaches to ontology based IR can further be sub-divided into Knowledge Base (KB) and vector space model driven approaches. KB approaches use reasoning mechanism and ontological query languages to retrieve instances. Documents are treated either as instances or are annotated using ontology instances [10, 11, 12, 13]. These approaches focus on retrieving instances rather than documents. Some approaches are often combined with ontological filtering [14, 15, 16].

There are approaches combining both ontology based IR and vector space model. For instance, some start with semantic querying using ontology query languages and use resulting instances to retrieve relevant documents [13, 17]. [17] use weighted annotation when associating documents with ontology instances. The weights are based on the frequency of occurrence of the instances in each document. [18] combines ontology usage with vector-space model by extending a non-ontological query. There, ontology is used to disambiguate queries. Simple text search is run on the concepts' labels and users are asked to choose the proper term interpretation. A similar approach is described in [19] where documents are associated with concepts in the ontology. The concepts in the query are matched to the concepts of the ontology in order to retrieve terms and then used for calculation of document similarity.

[14] is using ontologies for retrieval and filtering of domain information across multiple domains. There each ontology concept is defined as a domain feature with detailed information relevant to the domain including relationships with other

---

[2] The Research Council of Norway, http://www.forskningsradet.no
[3] ISO, http://www.iso.org/

features. The relationships used are hypernyms (super class), hyponyms (sub class), and synonyms. Unfortunately, there are no details in [14] provided on how a domain feature is created.

Most query enrichment approaches are not using ontologies like [4, 5, 6, 7, 20]. Query expansion is typically done by extending provided query terms with synonyms or hyponyms (cf. [21]). Some approaches are focusing on using ontologies in the process of enriching queries [12, 14, 19]. However, ontology in such case typically serves as thesaurus containing synonyms, hypernyms/hyponyms, and do not consider the context of each term, i.e. every term is equally weighted.

[6] is using query expansion based on similarity thesaurus. Weighting of terms is used to reflect the domain knowledge. The query expansion is done by similarity measures. Similarly, [5] describes a conceptual query expansion. There, the query concepts are created from a result set. Both approaches show an improvement compared to simple term based queries, especially for short queries.

[20] is a commercial search engine which provide three basic search strategies, word, concept and superconcept search respectively. A concept is represented as a set of words, while a superconcept is a combination of several closely related concepts. The user may mix strategies when searching. Unfortunately, there are not enough details available in [20] to state how this work.

In [4] each document and query is represented by concept lattices and are not using ontologies. The concept lattice for a document can learn and be improved by relevance feedback. Testing done shows significant increase in efficiency as the system learns from experience. They have also recognized the need for a hybrid approach where both concepts and keyword matching is done.

The approaches presented in [3, 7] are most similar to ours. However, [7] is not using ontologies but is reliant on query concepts. Two techniques are used to create the feature vectors of the query concepts, i.e. based on document set and result set of a user query. While the approach presented in [3] is using ontologies for the representation of concepts. The concepts are extended with similar words using a combination pf Latent Semantic Analysis (LSA) and WordNet[4]. Both approaches get promising results for short or poorly formulated queries. The approach presented in [20] does differentiate on query terms by providing different search strategies. However, how equal this approach is to ours or how this is done is hard to tell since little details are provided.

3 Layers of Abstraction

As mentioned, one of the major problems for traditional IR systems is to *understand* the intended meaning of the queries as well as the content of the documents in order to provide high retrieval effectiveness. A reason for this is that IR systems work in word-space while we humans deal with information in concept-space [3, 4]. In addition, humans are in general good in figuring out from relatively few words what is the correct context. The reason for this is the enormous amount of common knowledge that we possess. Researchers of artificial intelligence (AI) have

---

[4] WordNet, http://wordnet.princeton.edu/

acknowledged this and are therefore trying to grasp this common knowledge into enormous knowledge bases (e.g. CYC[5], Open Mind[6]). This common knowledge that we possess is by practical means not available for typically IR systems to use.

For the IR systems to get better *understanding* of the user query the user needs to provide more information than is traditionally given. We believe that by specifying in the query what is a concept and what is a term and to what domain they relate the IR systems can better *understand* the *intended meaning* of the user. If the IR system can get a better understanding of the real intention of the user query then the retrieval effectiveness can be considerably improved.

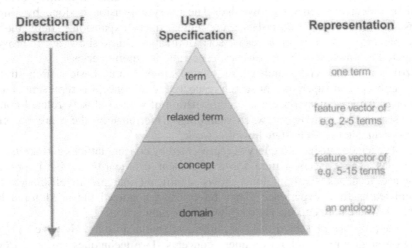

Fig. 1. Query terms abstraction layers. The user can specify any of the levels in the pyramid, but domain must always be specified to take full advantage of this approach. Further, *term*, *relaxed term*, and *concept* must also have some kind of a relation to the specified *domain*.

Fig. 1 depicts our proposal of how the different terms of a query can be grouped into different abstraction layers depending on their intended role. The idea is that every *term*, *relaxed term*, and *concept* has a relation to a *domain*. Where a *domain* is specified in an ontology consisting of classes and instances and the relationships among them. A *concept* is defined in a *domain* and is consequently either a class or an instance defined in an ontology. Further, each *concept* has a feature vector consisting of e.g. 5-15 terms from the document collection that has been associated with each *concept*. Synonyms and conjugations would naturally go into such a vector, but also related terms that tend to be used in connection with the concept are included. A *concept* can be defined for several *domains* but the corresponding *fv*s will most likely be different. A *relaxed term* is also defined in a *domain* and is proposed to have a shorter *fv* than a typical *concept*. An *fv* for a *relaxed term* contains normally synonyms that are closer to the original term than typically for a *concept* (e.g.

---

[5] Cycorp, Inc., http://www.cyc.com/
[6] Open Mind Initiative, http://www.openmind.org/

Volkswagen=<vw, folksvagen>). Note, that there is no restriction in this proposal that e.g. "Volkswagen" can be both a concept and a relaxed term where both can be defined in the same domain. In section 5, the process of how an *fvs* for both *relaxed terms* and *concepts* can be build is described, an example of *fvs* are depicted in Fig. 3. Finally, a *term* is equal to a query term in a traditional IR system. A *term* does not necessarily have to be defined in a *domain*, that is being a class or concept defined in an ontology, but is always indirectly related to a domain. A simple example of a *term* is "rabbit" which is used in many different contexts. However, if it were said to have a relation to a *domain* describing "cars" we would probably find that there is a car called, e.g. "Volkswagen Rabbit".

4 Feature Vector Construction

Fig. 2 gives an overall view of the steps involved in the feature vector construction process. Before the process can start, the user needs to identify both the ontology and the document collection to use, where the latter is indicated in Fig. 2 as *index* and *document collection*. Next, we will explain in more detail the different steps of this process.

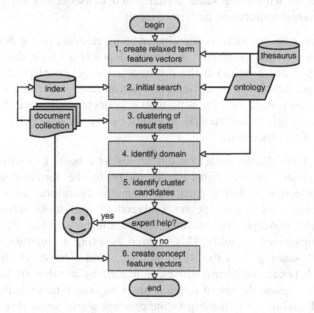

Fig. 2. The feature vector construction process. The dotted line from the document collection to the index indicates that the index is based on the document collection.

Step 1. Since we endeavor to create feature vectors for every concept in an ontology, the algorithm starts with traversing the ontology and creates a *fv* for each *relaxed term*. The *fvs* are based on a thesaurus like e.g. WordNet.

Step 2. The *fv*s for the *relaxed terms* are used when retrieving documents for each of the concepts in the ontology. This retrieval session is keyword-based (for instance, see concept "Christmas tree" in the ontology fragment illustrated in upper part of Fig. 3).

Step 3. The result set for each concept is further processed by clustering techniques in order to identify (discriminate) different domains within the document collection. Because, at this stage of the process the ontology concepts are treated as ordinary terms and can therefore be used in many different domains. Clustering allows finding different domains. However, we endeavor enriching concepts only by the terms from the domain relevant to the ontology at hand. That is done in next steps as follows.

Step 4. A problem at this stage is to identify the relevant domain. Therefore, we compute similarity between the clusters of the neighborhood concepts. Commonality (i.e. high similarity) here identifies the document sets (clusters) being relevant to the domain of our interest. The hypothesis is that individual clusters having high similarity across ontology concepts are with high probability of the same domain. This hypothesis is backed up with observed patterns of collocated terms within the same domain, and consequently different domains will have different collocation pattern of terms.

Step 5. In this step, we identify the cluster being relevant to the domain for each concept. However, the similarity of clusters depends a lot on the quality of the ontology, especially how much the different concepts overlap. If the degree of overlap is high, then it can be difficult to discriminate the clusters while choosing the most representative one for a particular concept. Therefore, to resolve this ambiguity we might need manual intervention by an expert to identify these candidates before proceeding.

Step 6. The final cluster for a concept serves as a basis to construct a feature vector, i.e. relate concept from the ontology to the terminology used in a document collection within a particular domain. Therefore, all the documents from each cluster of a concept are analyzed to find those terms being most relevant to that concept (for instance, see middle part of Fig. 3, where related terms are emphasized in bold). This is done by using a combination of Natural Language Processing (NLP), text mining, and statistical methods. The relationship between the terms will be indicated by a value from range [0, 1], where 1 is the highest degree of relationship. Only those terms being key phrases or terms and having a relationship to the concept above some threshold is being considered, all other terms are rejected. The relationship values will be used as the weight for each term of the feature vector (see bottom part of Fig. 3, there a feature vector is composed from the terms related to "Christmas tree" and found in the document collection).

Fig. 3 shows an explanatory example of this process for the concept "christmas tree".

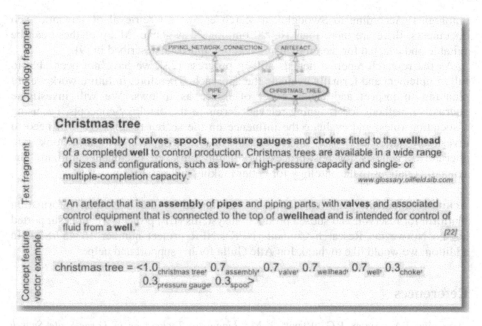

Fig. 3. An explanatory example to illustrate parts of the process of constructing a feature vector for the concept "christmas tree"

5 Discussion and Conclusion

In this paper we have proposed the usage of abstraction layers to differentiate on the query terms to better grasp the users *real intention* of a query. Results from concept-based approaches presented in section 2 show an improvement where short or badly formulated queries are used compared to traditional IR methods. However, for longer more specific queries results show a slight decrease in effectiveness. This indicates that only keyword- or concept-based approaches are not sufficient. Therefore, by differentiating on the query terms (a mixed approach) and also relating all the query terms to a domain, we believe that IR systems can better *understand* the *real intention* and hence improve retrieval effectiveness considerably.

However, this approach has to be accepted by the end users or else it will fail. As mentioned, only about 10% of the users are using the advanced features of a search engine found on the Web. A reason for this is probably that most users does not see the big increases in retrieval effectiveness in using the advanced feature dialog or know these features by heart and hence uses them directly instead. Nevertheless, for the approach presented here the users have to add some more information in comparison to what they might be used to. E.g. for a simple search the user must identify the correct *domain* for a *concept* or else the approach will be equal to typically IR systems existing today. But we believe that the user might be willing to do that if (s)he sees an improvement in search result quality, which we believe there will be. However, this will also very much depend on how easy it is for the user to specify this extra information. Another important issue is the availability of ontologies. According to Swoogle[7], a search engine for retrieval of semantic web documents, there are more than 10.000 ontologies available. Many of these can be suitable and adapted for search by using e.g. our approach described in [9].

As the research reported here is still in progress [23], we have not been able to fully implement and formally evaluate the approach. Therefore, in future work we are planning to inspect and tackle a set of issues as follows. We will investigate alternative methods for assigning relevant terms to the ontology concepts, i.e. using association rules, and evaluate the influence on the search results. We will need to investigate alternative user interfaces for this system. We will also look into alternative methods for post-processing of the retrieved documents utilizing the semantic relations in the ontology for better ranking and navigation.

Acknowledgements. This research work is funded by the Integrated Information Platform for reservoir and subsea production systems (IIP) project, which is supported by the Norwegian Research Council (NFR). NFR project number 163457/S30. In addition, we would like to thank Jon Atle Gulla for his support and help.

References

1. Gulla, J.A., Auran, P.G., Risvik, K.M.: *Linguistic Techniques in Large-Scale Search Engines*. Fast Search & Transfer (2002) 15 p.
2. Spink, A., Wolfram, D., Jansen, M.B.J., Saracevic, T.: *Searching the Web: the public and their queries*. J. Am. Soc. Inf. Sci. Technol. 52 (2001) 226-234
3. Ozcan, R., Aslangdogan, Y.A.: *Concept Based Information Access Using Ontologies and Latent Semantic Analysis*. Technical Report CSE-2004-8. University of Texas at Arlington (2004) 16
4. Rajapakse, R.K., Denham, M.: *Text retrieval with more realistic concept matching and reinforcement learning*. Information Processing & Management 42 (2006) 1260-1275
5. Grootjen, F.A., van der Weide, T.P.: *Conceptual query expansion*. Data & Knowledge Engineering 56 (2006) 174-193
6. Qiu, Y., Frei, H.-P.: *Concept based query expansion*. Proceedings of the 16th annual international ACM SIGIR conference on Research and development in information retrieval. ACM Press, Pittsburgh, Pennsylvania, USA (1993) 160-169
7. Chang, Y., Ounis, I., Kim, M.: *Query reformulation using automatically generated query concepts from a document space*. Information Processing and Management 42 (2006) 453-468
8. Gruber, T.R.: *A translation approach to portable ontology specifications*. Knowledge Acquisition 5 (1993) 199-220
9. Tomassen, S.L., Gulla, J.A., Strasunskas, D.: *Document Space Adapted Ontology: Application in Query Enrichment*. In: Kop, C., Fliedl, G., Mayer, H.C., Métais, E. (eds.): 11th International Conference on Applications of Natural Language to Information Systems (NLDB 2006), Vol. 3999. Springer-Verlag, Klagenfurt, Austria (2006) 46-57
10. Song, J-F., Zhang, W-M., Xiao, W., Li, G-H., Xu, Z-N.: *Ontology-Based Information Retrieval Model for the Semantic Web*. Proceedings of EEE 2005. IEEE Computer Society (2005) 152-155

---

[7] Swoogle, http://swoogle.umbc.edu

11. Rocha, C., Schwabe, D., de Aragao, M.P.: *A hybrid approach for searching in the semantic web*. Proceeding of WWW 2004, ACM (2004) 374-383
12. Ciorăscu, C., Ciorăscu, I., Stoffel, K.: *knOWLer - Ontological Support for Information Retrieval Systems*. In Proceedings of Sigir 2003 Conference, Workshop on Semantic Web, Toronto, Canada (2003)
13. Kiryakov, A., Popov, B, Terziev, I., Manov, D., and Ognyanoff, D.: *Semantic Annotation, Indexing, and Retrieval*. Journal of Web Semantics 2(1), Elsevier, (2005)
14. Braga, R.M.M., Werner, C.M.L., Mattoso, M.: *Using Ontologies for Domain Information Retrieval*. Proceedings of the 11th International Workshop on Database and Expert Systems Applications. IEEE Computer Society (2000) 836-840
15. Borghoff, U.M., Pareschi, R.: *Information Technology for Knowledge Management*. Journal of Universal Computer Science 3 (1997) 835-842
16. Shah, U., Finin, T., Joshi, A., Cost, R.S., Mayfield, J.: *Information Retrieval On The Semantic Web*. Proceedings of Conference on Information and Knowledge Management. ACM Press, McLean, Virginia, USA (2002) 461-468
17. Vallet, D, Fernández, M., Castells, P.: *An Ontology-Based Information Retrieval Model*. Gómez-Pérez, A., Euzenat, J. (Eds.): Proceedings of ESWC 2005, LNCS 3532, Springer-Verlag. (2005) 455-470.
18. Nagypal, G.: *Improving Information Retrieval Effectiveness by Using Domain Knowledge Stored in Ontologies*. OTM Workshops 2005, LNCS 3762, Springer-Verlag, (2005) 780-789
19. Paralic, J., Kostial, I.: *Ontology-based Information Retrieval*. Information and Intelligent Systems, Croatia (2003) 23-28
20. Adi, T., Ewell, O.K., Adi, P.: *High Selectivity and Accuracy with READWARE's Automated System of Knowledge Organization*. Management Information Technologies, Inc. (MITi) (1999)
21. Chenggang, W., Wenpin, J., Qijia, T. et al.: *An information retrieval server based on ontology and multiagent*. Journal of computer research & development 38(6) (2001) 641-647.
22. Det Norske Veritas: *Tyrihans Terminology for Subsea Equipment and Subsea Production Data*. Det Norske Veritas (DNV) (2005) 60 p.
23. Tomassen, S.L.: *Research on Ontology-Driven Information Retrieval*. In: Meersman, R., Tari, Z., Herrero, P., al., e. (eds.): OTM 2006 Workshops. Springer-Verlag, Montpellier, France (2006)

VQS - An Ontology-Based Query System for the SemanticLIFE Digital Memory Project⋆

Hanh Huu Hoang, Amin Andjomshoaa, and A Min Tjoa

Institute of Software Technology and Interactive Systems
Vienna University of Technology
Favoritenstraße 9-11/188, 1040 Vienna, Austria
{hanh, andjomshoaa, amin}@ifs.tuwien.ac.at

Abstract. Ever increasing capacities of contemporary storage devices inspire the vision to accumulate (personal) information without the need of deleting old data over a long time-span. Hence the target of the SemanticLIFE project is to create a Personal Information Management system for a human lifetime data. One of the most important characteristics of the system is its dedication to retrieve information in a very efficient way. By adopting user demands regarding the reduction of ambiguities, our approach aims at a user-oriented and yet powerful enough system with a satisfactory query performance. In this paper, we introduce the query system of SemanticLIFE, the Virtual Query System, which uses emerging Semantic Web technologies to fulfill users' requirements.

1 Introduction

Towards the goals of personal information storage and retrieval of all one's data throughout a lifetime, researchers consider continuous archival and retrieval of all media relating to personal experiences including emails, contacts, appointments, web browsing, documents, phone calls, etc. The challenging issues are how to extract useful knowledge from this rich library of information; and how to use this knowledge effectively [6]. The SemanticLIFE project [1] is an effort to come a step closer to a solution for mentioned issues and Vanevar Bush's vision of Memex [3] by providing a general semantic Personal Information Management (PIM) system. The SemanticLIFE user is supported in issuing imprecise queries to retrieve the rich semantic information from his/her historical personal data.

Most often when developing similar PIM systems, researches focus on back-end issues, i.e. capturing all data sources, integrate and then store them in huge repositories. For this purpose it is necessary to map the ontologies of the various data sources into a common ontology of the system. However, users are confronted with the lack of knowledge concerning the stored information inside the system, and they would formulate ambiguous requests, so that many barriers have to be overcome before the system could deliver the demanded results.

⋆ This work has been generously supported by ASEA-UNINET and the Austrian National Bank within the framework of the project Application of Semantic-Web-Concepts for Business Intelligence Information Systems - Project No. 11284.

R. Meersman, Z. Tari, P. Herrero et al. (Eds.): OTM Workshops 2006, LNCS 4278, pp. 1796–1805, 2006.

This paper is aiming at a design of the innovative features of our "Virtual Query System" design. This query system is based on a front-end approach allowing the user to retrieve information from huge ontology-based repositories in an efficient way. The conception of this query system which is primarily based on the reduction of semantic ambiguities of user query specifications at the very early stage of the retrieving process; and continually guide the user in query process using a set of query templates. This approach integrates many research efforts from the area of the Semantic Web, query refinement, semantic query caching for RDF data, inference, ontology mapping, and user interaction.

The remainder of this paper is organized as follows: a range of projects is currently addressing similar issues are briefly presented in Section 2. Section 3 presents a overview of the SemanticLIFE framework and the relevant query issues of the SemanticLIFE framework. Details of the Virtual Query System design are pointed out in sections 4. Section 5 presents the query language for the VQS. The paper is concluded with a sketch of the intended future work.

2   Related Work

There are several approaches to reduce the difficulty in creating queries from user-side in Semantic Web applications. One of these trends is going to design the friendly and interactive query user interfaces to guide users in generating the queries. The typical examples of this trend are GRQL [2] and SEWASIE [4].

GRQL - Graphical RQL - relies on the full power of the RDF/S data model for constructing on the fly queries expressed in RQL. More precisely, a user can navigate graphically through the individual RDF/S class and property definitions and generate transparently the RQL path expressions required to access the resources of interest. These expressions capture accurately the meaning of its navigation steps through the class (or property) subsumption and/or associations. Additionally, users can enrich the generated queries with filtering conditions on the attributes of the currently visited class while they can easily specify the resource's class(es) appearing in the query result. GRQL is the first application-independent GUI being to generate a unique RQL query which captures the cumulative effect of an entire user navigation session.

Another graphical query generation interface, SEWASIE, is described in [4]. Here, the user is given some pre-prepared domain-specific patterns to choose from as a starting point, which he can then extend and customize. The refinements to the query can either be additional property constraints to the classes or a replacement of another compatible class in the pattern such as a sub or superclass. This is performed through a click-able graphic visualization of the ontology neighborhood of the currently selected class.

Our approach, the VQS, supports the user in generating unambiguous requests by providing a "virtual data" layer to improve the user's awareness of the stored information in the system. This virtual data is also used for answering simple tasks from the user. VQS also has an effective and lighter weight query language, to assist the users generate queries in a simple manner.

3   The SemanticLIFE Framework

3.1   A Brief Overview

The SemanticLIFE framework is developed on a highly modular architecture provides the basic components for the VQS modules that will be discussed in later sections. SemanticLIFE stores, manages and retrieves the lifetime's information entities of individuals. It enables the acquisition and storage of data while giving annotations to emails, browsed webpages, phone calls, images, contacts, life events and other resources. It also provides intuitive and effective search mechanism based upon the stored semantics.

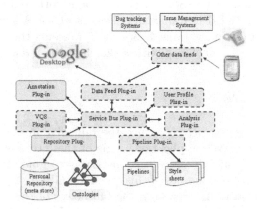

Fig. 1. The SemanticLIFE Framework Architecture

An overview of the system architecture is depicted in Fig. 1. The whole SemanticLIFE system has been designed as a set of interactive plug-ins that fit into the main application and this guarantees flexibility and extensibility of the SemanticLIFE platform. Communication within the system is based on a service-oriented design with the advantage of its loosely coupled characteristics. To compose complex solutions and scenarios from atomic services from SemanticLIFE plug-ins, the Service Oriented Pipeline Architecture (SOPA)[1] has been introduced. SOPA provides a paradigm to describe the system-wide service compositions and also external web services as pipelines. SOPA provides some mechanisms for orchestration of services and transformation of results.

Data with user annotation is fed into the system using a number of dedicated plug-ins from variety of data sources like Google Desktop[2] captured data, communication logs, and other application's metadata. The data objects are passed on by the message handler to the analysis plug-in. This plug-in contains a number of specific analysis plug-ins providing semantic mark-up by applying a bunch of feature extraction methods and indexing techniques in a cascaded

---

[1] JAX Innovation Award 2006 Proposal, http://www.jax-award.com/.
[2] Google Desktop, http://desktop.google.com/.

manner. The semi-structured and semantically enriched information objects are forwarded to the repository plug-in for an ontologically structured storage, so-called the metastore. A set of query processing and information visualization tools provides the means for information exploration and report generation. The analysis module and metadata extraction capabilities make associations among the lifetime items and lifetime events based on user annotation, user profile and the system ontologies.

3.2 Information Retrieval in the SemanticLIFE Framework

In SemanticLIFE, it is uneasy to define highly structured queries when a multitude of information systems are addressed or the information is only semi-structured. Hence the system must be capable to support user-queries which are formulated with an "imprecise search" terminology by automatically transforming them into more specific queries.

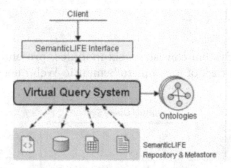

Fig. 2. The VQS in the SemanticLIFE context

In the SemanticLIFE metastore, the data is already stored in a semantically enriched manner, it provides more powerful imprecise searches. Here, the term "imprecise" has two meanings: firstly, the query processing system has to satisfy imprecisely defined user information needs. Secondly, the target of the user-query is well specified but there are ambiguities in processing the query because of the heterogeneity of the different data sources. Therefore, the system solves these problems during query generation by exploring the system database and ontology. A part of the query module uses system metadata and ontology to provide the user a better awareness of stored data.

The querying process in SemanticLIFE depicted in Fig. 2 is supported by our Virtual Query System. This mediator system is not only capable to deal with the discussed issues above but also reduces the imprecision of the user's requests by offering the user an overview of the relevant stored information. As a result, the user will significantly specify more precise queries on information and data stored in the system.

4   The Virtual Query System (VQS)

4.1   VQS Goals

Formulating unambiguous queries is always a demanding task to users as they do not have the overview on the semantics of stored data. The principle of the Virtual Query System (VQS) is to provide an ontology-based virtual information view of the system data. Hereby, the "virtual information" are the metadata extracted from the metastore and delivered to the the user after a well-organizing process. The user can clearly specify queries on the "real" data in the repositories when he/she can "be aware of" what is inside of the system.

The VQS also provides predefined query patterns which will be matched with users' query space and the matched ones then will be recommended to the users. In addition, based on a common ontology and the internal analysis (inference, detecting ambiguity and fuzziness of user queries), the VQS refines the user's queries and generates "real" queries against data sources in the metastore.

4.2   VQS Design

The Virtual Query System consists of six modules, presented in Fig. 3, to deal with the challenging task of a complete Semantic Web query system.

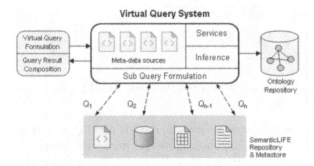

Fig. 3. The Components of the Virtual Query System

Virtual Data Component: Metadata Storage Sources. This VQS's crucial part contains the metadata of storage sources. This module acts as a "virtual" data source to be offered to the user. It enables the user to be aware of the semantics of the data sources stored and to specify more precise queries. The VQS collects metadata from data sources in the metadata repository of the SemanticLIFE system. An analysis process and statistical computation are carried out on these meta-data sources to get the semantic information. Then the processed information is stored in this module as a "context ontology" and will be delivered. The features of VQS are very similar to those of a recommender system. Furthermore, this part is also referred as an "image" of the system database in further query processing, so-called the context-based querying. A query languages has been developed for querying the virtual data from this component (Section 5 and more details in [7]).

This component is the main different point of our system in compared with mentioned systems. The behind idea is that when the user is aware of his/her data then he/she could generate more unambiguous requests. This ultimately leads to the reduction of the query refinement process complexity. Additionally, this virtual data component plays as a *context ontology*. This makes the SemanticLIFE system very flexible because the system can adapt a new scenario by simply changing the context ontology.

This component also enhances the query process by the "context-based" querying feature, i.e. the query patterns will be proposed by the system based-on the context where the user is in. For example, the context ontology being applied is about *project management*. The query context could be about Person, Location, Web search engines. In this case, a match of context ontology in the virtual data component and query context will be made and the query patterns such as *"finding a person I have contacted in Vienna in a related project found by a search engine"* will be proposed.

The Ontology Repository. The second part of the system is the ontology repository which builds up the core of the VQS. The repository contains the ontologies used in the VQS system such as the global ontology or inference ontology. Following [5] an ontology-driven approach to data integration relies on the alignment of the concepts of a global ontology that describe the domain, with the concepts of the ontologies that describe the data in the local databases. Once the alignment between the global ontology and each of the local ontologies is established, users can potentially query hundreds of databases using a single query that hides the underlying heterogeneities.

Sub-Query Formulation. Sub-queries formulation is another essential part of the VQS. From the user's initial virtual query, this part parses it into the sub queries (Q_i in the Fig. 3) based on the global ontology for specific data sources. This module does not only transform the virtual query to sub-queries for specific data sources but additionally perform inference on the user's request in order to create more possible sub-queries afterward. After this process, the 'real' queries (RDF queries) for each of the data sources will be generated.

The VQS Services
Ontology Mapping. Mapping service is a mechanism to map local ontologies into a global one. This service deals with new data sources added with their respective ontologies, so that these ontologies are mapped or integrated to the global ontology. In our approach, we do not reinvest to develop a new ontology mapping framework. We use the MAFRA framework [8] for our mapping tasks.

Query Caching. This service improves the performance of the VQS by caching the queries in a period of time. We distinguish two kinds of caching mechanisms: query caching and result caching. The first addresses the process of generating sub-queries; and the second covers the caching of query results. Both caching types will use the semantic query caching methodology proposed in [10].

Ontolgy-based Inference. The inference service provides a basis for the deduction process on the relationships (rules) of concepts of the ontologies specified. Inference tasks are performed on the foundation of the ontologies and the data described by them. This service helps the system to analyze and evaluate the user's virtual queries in the process of generating sub-queries based-on the inference ontology.

Query Refinement. Query refinement is another important service for our query processing. This is the interactive way for the VQS dealing with user's ambiguous queries, which is based on incrementally and interactively (step-by-step) tailoring a query to the current information needs of a user [9]. This query refinement service of the VQS is a semi-automated process: in the refinement process, the user is provided with a ranked list of refinements, which leads to a decrease of some of these ambiguities. In another hand, by exploiting the user's profile, the ontology background, and as well as user's annotation on data, this VQS service supports finding "similar" results.

The Virtual Query User Interface (VQUI). The VQUI delivers the virtual data to the user and helps the user to define virtual queries. A set of query patterns is offered to the user. If these patterns do not match the demands, the user can use a query-by-example tool alternatively to write the virtual queries. The VQUI also acts as query results composition which performs the integration and aggregation of the sub-query results and show to the user.

4.3   The Virtual Query System Workflow

The workflow of the VQS is illustrated in the Fig. 4. The dashed arrows denote the internal activities; normal arrows are used for the interaction between the user and the VQS. The external query queue is used for receiving queries from the user and to return the results. Inside of the system, an internal query queue will be used to receive processed sub-queries and to deliver results.

The following steps are performed in a chronological order: At the very early stage when the VQS is installed into the whole system of SemanticLIFE, action (1) will be performed. This action collects meta-data of the data sources from the meta-store, performs necessary statistical computation and stores the results into the Meta-data sources. Parallel, the global ontology is mapped from local ontologies using the VQS ontology mapping service.

As also depicted in Fig. 2, the user directly retrieves the information by specifying his/her queries to the VQS with help of the query interface. The VQS gets user input through the virtual queries. Using this interface, the user can

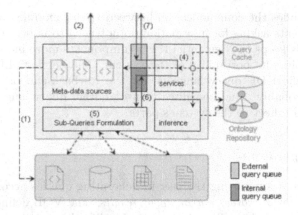

Fig. 4. The Workflow of the Virtual Query System components

be confronted with intentional information of the meta-data sources, so that we can avoid to a certain degree ambiguous requests (2).

In the next step, the formulated query, so-called virtual query, is sent to the VQS (3) and from this stage, the virtual query is evaluated on the foundation of the ontology-based services of the VQS (4). The VQS query caching service is now in charge of the subsequent processing of the virtual query: firstly, it looks up in to the query cache, if there is a match, the result is quickly returned to the user. In the second case if the virtual query does not match, an analysis and evaluation process will be undertaken (4) and the virtual query with the analyzed information will be sent to the Sub-queries formulation (5). As a result, sub-queries for each specific real data source will be generated. Finally, query results will be passed to the user ((6) and (7)). They are aggregated in the Query Result Composition part before the delivery to him/her in a suitable form.

5   The Virtual Query Language for the VQS

5.1   VQL Aims

Virtual Query Language (VQL) [7] is designed for the "Virtual Data Component". The VQL is used to model the query patterns and generate the virtual queries. The VQL is intended to be a simple query language which supports "semantic" manner from the user's queries. In context of the VQS and SemanticLIFE system:

- VQL helps clients making queries without knowledge of RDF query languages.
- VQL assists users in navigating the system via semantic links or associations, categorized context queries provided in the powerful query operators based-on ontologies.

- VQL simplifies the communication between Query module and other parts as the components asking for information do not need to issues the RDF query statement. This keeps the SemanticLIFE's components more independent.
- VQL enables the portability of the system. The SemanticLIFE and VQS choose a specific RDF query language for the its back-end database. In the future, they probably could be shifted to use another query language, and this change does not affect to the system's parts.

5.2 VQL Operators

The VQL aims at supporting the user in generating queries according to their nature: *minimum of words, maximum of results*. The VQL defines the virtual query operators and they allow the user to simplify the complex queries[3]:

- *GetInstances Operator* retrieves the appropriate information according to the criteria described in the parameters, sources and constraints of the query.
- *GetInstanceMetadata Operator* assists the user easily retrieve all metadata properties and correspondent result instances.
- *GetRelatedData Operator* provides the accessible related information to the current found information, i.e. finding relevant or associated information.
- *GetLinks Operator* operates using the system's ontology and RDF graph pattern to find out the associations/links between the instances and the objects.

```
<query type="data">
 <params>
  <param show="0" name="p1:emailTo">hta@gmx.at</param>
  <param show="1" name="p2:RELATED-WITH"/>
 </params>
 <sources>
  <source name="email">Email</source>
  <source name="contact">Contact</source>
 </sources>
 <relations>
  <relation id="1" param="p1" source="email"/>
 </relations>
 <resultformat>xml</resultformat>
</query>
```

Fig. 5. An example of a VQL query

For example, as depicted in Fig. 5, the *GetInstanceMetadata* query retrieves the information from **Email** and **Contact** data sources related to the email address **hta@gmx.at**.

By providing these operators, VQL offers a powerful feature of navigating the system by browsing data source by data source, instances by instances based on found semantic associations.

---

[3] The VQL samples, http://www.ifs.tuwien.ac.at/~hhhanh/VQL/samples/

6   Conclusion and Future Work

In this paper we have presented the Virtual Query System, an approach of building a complete Semantic Web query system based on a front-end approach. Besides applying current Semantic Web technologies known in the area such as ontology mapping, user annotation and semantic query caching for RDF data, we have designed a query system which aims at a significant complexity reduction in formulating semantic meaningful queries and at the same time aims at a considerable reduction of the number of ambiguous user queries.

The VQS is work in progress. Prototypes have been developed to test the various aspects and design alternatives and we have achieved many appreciate results. The most important parts are developed to obtain a proof of concept of the architecture described. As the next step, the issues of realizing a virtual query language such as semantic query caching, ontology-based query refinement, query optimization and user modeling will be discussed consequently in the details in context of the VQS.

References

1. M. Ahmed, H. H. Hoang, S. Karim, S. Khusro, M. Lanzenberger, K. Latif, E. Michlmayr, K. Mustofa, T. H. Nguyen, A. Rauber, A. Schatten, T. M. Nguyen, and A. M. Tjoa. Semanticlife - a framework for managing information of a human lifetime. In *Proceedings of the 6th International Conference on Information Integration and Web-based Applications and Services*, September 2004.
2. N. Athanasis, V. Christophides, and D. Kotzinos. Generating on the fly queries for the semantic web: The ics-forth graphical rql interface (grql). In *Proceedings of the 3rd International Semantic Web Conference*, pages 486–501, 2004.
3. V. Bush. As we may think. *The Atlantic*, 176(1):101–108, July 1945.
4. T. Catarci, P. Dongilli, T. D. Mascio, E. Franconi, G. Santucci, and S. Tessaris. An ontology based visual tool for query formulation support. In *Proceedings of the 16th European Conference on Artificial Intelligence*, pages 308–312, 2004.
5. I. F. Cruz, W. Sunna, and A. Chaudhry. Ontology alignment for real-world applications. In *Proceedings of The National Conference on Digital Government - DG.O 2004.*
6. A. Fitzgibbon and E. Reiter. Memories for life - managing information over a human lifetime. Technical report, Grand Challenges in Computing Workshop, UK Computing Research Committee, May 2003.
7. H. H. Hoang and A. M. Tjoa. The virtual query language for information retrieval in the semanticlife framework. In *Proceedings of the International Workshop on Web Information Systems Modeling - CAiSE 06*, pages 1062–1076, June 2006.
8. A. Maedche, B. Motik, N. Silva, and R. Volz. Mafra - an ontology mapping framework in the semantic web. In *Proceedings of the 12th International Workshop on Knowledge Transformation*, July 2002.
9. N. Stojanovic, R. Studer, and L. Stojanovic. An approach for step-by-step query refinement in the ontology-based information retrieval. In *Prococeedings of the IEEE International Conference on Web Intelligence (WI'04)*, pages 36–43, 2004.
10. H. Stuckenschmidt. Similarity-based query caching. In *Proceedings of the 6th International Confonference on Flexible Query Answering Systems*, 2004.

Software Design Process Ontology Development

P. Wongthongtham[1], E. Chang[1], and T. Dillon[2]

[1] Curtin Business School, Curtin University of Technology, Australia
[2] Faculty of Information Technology, University of Technology Sydney, Australia
{Pornpit.Wongthongtham, Elizabeth.Chang}@cbs.curtin.edu.au
tharam@it.uts.edu.au

Abstract. Software design process has been followed and widely used to describe logical organisation of software using different types of models. However, when it comes to remote communication over software design, it is prone to miscommunication, misunderstanding or misinterpretation especially with ambiguous terms or people having different backgrounds and knowledge of the software design process. This motivates the use of unified knowledge representation of software design process i.e. software design process ontology for communications and coordination. The knowledge representation introduced here in the form of software design process ontology is based on a formal description of the software design process using the web ontology language OWL. Software design process knowledge is defined or captured in a formal and machine processable fashion. The software design process knowledge is then open and facilitates the sharing of software design among software engineers. We discuss software design process ontology development in this paper.

Keywords: Ontology, ontology development, software design process ontology.

1 Introduction

Software design process has been followed and widely used to describe logical organisation of software using different types of models [1]. However, when it comes to remote communication or discussion over the software design, it is prone to miscommunication, misunderstanding and misinterpretation especially with ambiguous terms or people having different backgrounds and knowledge of the software design process.

It is obvious that software engineering is practiced by software engineers. There is a debate over who a software engineer is. In many large information technology organisations or large IT teams, some software engineers state they have never studied a subject called software engineering, however, they are software engineers. Also, some members claim this expertise, where in fact it does not apply. There are currently no widely accepted criteria for distinguishing one who is a software engineer from one who is not a software engineer. Moreover, the industry is in the midst of a complex debate on the licensing of practicing software engineers.

R. Meersman, Z. Tari, P. Herrero et al. (Eds.): OTM Workshops 2006, LNCS 4278, pp. 1806–1813, 2006.

Also software engineering training and practice vary markedly between cities and countries. Some universities courses in computer science and engineering do not have a subject on software engineering or software engineering methodologies, such as object oriented analysis and design in UML. It can be difficult to communicate between teams and among team members if strict software engineering principles and discipline is not understood and followed. The inconsistency in presentation, documentation, design and diagrams could exclude other teams or members. Sometimes they ignore them because they do not understand it (such as a diagram using non-standard notation) and they do not bother to clarify.

Despite that, software engineering has a commonly understood body of knowledge and is an easily learned subject with some of the latest technologies and methodologies, such as UML, which are easily adopted. However, different teams could have different information sources on software engineering. Some team use reference books with the title of software engineering but are mainly on Java whilst others do not mention software engineering such as 'Code Complete'. Other team members utilise Object Oriented and other use IT project management as software engineering references. All of which use them independently as their own guide and when they communicate. Many times the issues raised or argued are related to inconsistency in understanding of software engineering theories and practice. As Davenport and Prusak [2] mentioned, people cannot share knowledge if they do not speak a common language. Representing software design process knowledge in the form of ontology is helping to clear up ambiguities in the terms used in the context of software design process.

In the next section, we discuss ontology. We elaborate on present software design process ontology in section 3. In section 4, we provide conclusions and suggest future work.

2 Ontology

In order to explore the software design process ontology development, we need to explain what an ontology is and its elements, how many languages are available, which language we choose and what strategies are used to develop one.

2.1 Ontology Definitions

The term 'Ontology' is derived from usage in philosophy where it means the study of being existence as well as the basic categories [3]. Therefore, it is used in referring to what exists in a system model.

Definition 1. An ontology, in the area of computer science, is the effort to formulate an exhaustive and rigorous conceptual schema within a given domain, typically a hierarchical data structure containing all the relevant elements and their relationships and rules (regulations) within the domain [4].

Definition 2. An ontology, in the field of artificial intelligence study, is an explicit specification of a conceptualisation [5, 6]. In such an ontology, definitions associate the names of concepts in the universe of discourse e.g. classes, relations, functions, with describing what the concepts mean and formal axioms that constrain the interpretation and well-formed used of these terms [7].

For example, by default all computer programs have a fundamental ontology consisting of a standard library in a programming language or files in accessible file systems, or some other list of 'what exists'. However, the representations are poor for some certain problem domains, more specialised schema must be created to make the information useful and that is what ontology is for.

2.2 Ontology Languages

There are several ontology languages available such as Resource Description Framework (RDF) [8], Web Ontology Language (OWL) [9], DARPA Agent Markup Language (DAML) [10], Ontology Interchange Language (OIL) [11], DAML+OIL [12], Simple HTML Ontology Extensions (SHOE) [13], for capturing knowledge of interest. Different ontology languages have different facilities. The most recent development in standard ontology languages is OWL from the World Wide Web Consortium (W3C) (http://www.w3.org/). Henceforth, we use OWL to capture software design process knowledge for the software design process ontology.

2.3 Ontology Elements

OWL ontology consists of classes, properties and individuals. Classes or concepts are abstract groups, sets or collections of objects containing individuals, other classes or a combination of both. Importantly, a class can subsume or be subsumed by other classes. Anything that is a member of the subclass is a member of the superclass. Properties are binary relations on individuals. Individuals or instances are concrete objects in the domain of interest. Literally, ontology need not include any individuals but one of the general purposes of ontology is to provide a means of classifying individuals, even if those individuals are not explicitly part of the ontology. In this study, the software design process ontology includes individuals representing software design for a particular project.

2.4 Ontology Development

Our experiences of ontology development have revealed and concluded that the processes should include the set of tasks as following:

- To build concept hierarchy to classify and clarify concepts respectively;
- To build ad-hoc binary relations to identify ad-hoc relationships between 'concepts and concepts', so called object properties, and 'concepts and data type value', so called data type properties;
- To define formal axioms to be used for constraint checking and for inferring values for properties;
- To define instances. It is not necessary that ontology contains the instances. In this study, instances represent actual data or the software design of a particular project.

The tasks as shown in Fig. 1 are not linear even though some order shall be followed to ensure consistency and completeness of the representation. The ontologist can return to any previous tasks at any stage. In this paper, the above processes act upon the ontology development.

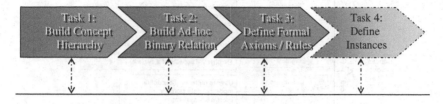

Fig. 1. Activity tasks of the design processes

3 Software Design Process Ontology

In this paper, to model software design process ontology, we use modelling notations developed in Wongthongtham's thesis [14]. We obtain knowledge of software design process presented in this paper from a book of software engineering by Ian Sommerville [1] and the Software Engineering Body of Knowledge (SWEBOK) [15]. Note that the objective of this paper is neither to introduce software design process nor to provide a framework of software design process understanding. Instead it aims to present an ontology model of the software design process to represent its knowledge.

Software design processes are categorised into structural design view and behavioural design view. In the structural view, nine models are relevant, as illustrated in Fig. 2(a), whereas in the behavioural view, eight models are considered as illustrated in Fig. 2(b), all together seventeen major models in software design process are addressed.

We provide two ontology models as examples: entity-relationship diagrams and statechart diagrams.

An entity-relationship diagram represents conceptual models of data stored in information systems [15]. Figure 3 shows an ontology model of entity-relationship diagrams. There are three main basic components in the entity-relationship diagrams which are entities, attributes, and relationships.

Attributes can be classified as being simple, composite or derived. A simple attribute is composed of a single component and a composite attribute is composed of multiple components. In the ontology model, cardinality restriction in relation *has_Subdivided_Attribute* defines attributes as being either being simple or composite. Derived attribute is based on another attribute(s) referred to relation *has_Derived_Attribute* restricting that at least one relation links to ontology class *EntitiyAttribute*. A key can be defined as a super key, alternate key, primary key or candidate key. This refers to relation *Entity_Attribute_Key* in the ontology model. Attribute can have single or multiple values. In the ontology model, cardinality restriction from relation *Entity_Attribute_Value* defines having a single or more than one value.

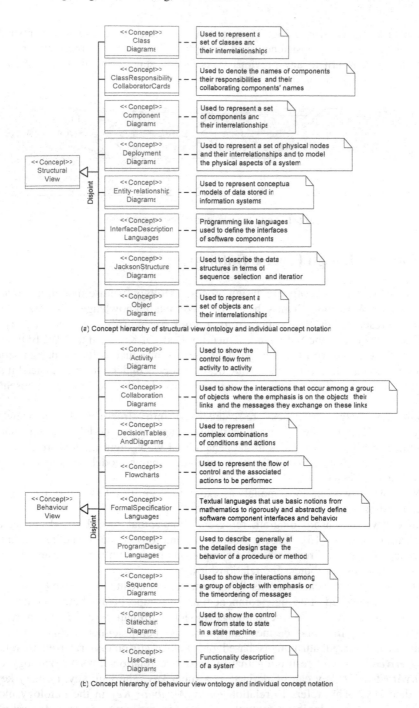

(a) Concept hierarchy of structural view ontology and individual concept notation

(b) Concept hierarchy of behaviour view ontology and individual concept notation

Fig. 2. Software design process ontology hierarchy

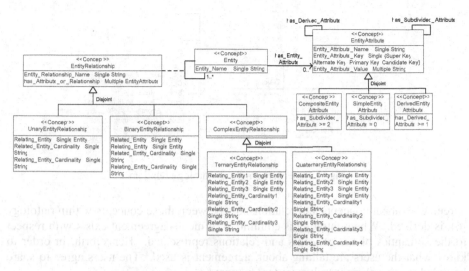

Fig. 3. Entity-relationship diagrams ontology relations

There are three main degrees of relationships which are unary, binary, and complex. The complex relationship can be divided into two cases which are quaternary and ternary. In the ontology model, cardinality restriction constraints number of entities that participate in a relationship. For example, unary relationship represents a relationship of one entity or precisely said that entity is self-linked. This, in the ontology view, refers to only one *Entity* in the relation *Retating_Entity* and no *Entity* in the relation *Related_Entity*. In entity relationships, cardinality can be specified as a string which can be string of1 (one and only one), * (zero or more), 1..* (one or more), 0..1 (zero or one), etc. as shown in the ontology model. Attributes can also be assigned to relationships referring to relation *has_Attribute_on_Relationships* in the ontology model.

A statechart diagram shows the control flow from state to state in a state machine [15]. Commonly statechart diagrams contain states and transitions. Figure 4 shows ontology model of statechart diagrams. A state refers to ontology class *State* can have details like an entry action, exit action and simple action referring respectively to relations *Entry* or *Entry_Class* or *Entry_Event*, *Exit* or *Exit_Class* or *Exit_Event*, and *Do* or *Do_Class* or *Do_Event*. A transition referring to ontology class *Transition* is categorised into three types. Firstly, state transition refers to ontology subclass *StateTransition*. Secondly, initial transition refers to ontology subclass *StartTransition*. Lastly, final transition refers to ontology subclass *StopTransition*. The event that triggers state transition refers to relation *Event*. The action that results from state transition refers to relation *Action*. The guard condition that allows a state transition, only if the condition is true, refers to relation *Guard_Condition*.

There is an agreement between users of ontology so that the meaning of the terms is used in a consistent way. In order for the domain knowledge to be shared amongst users or applications, agreement must exist on the topics about which information is being communicated. Issue of ontological commitment, which is described as the

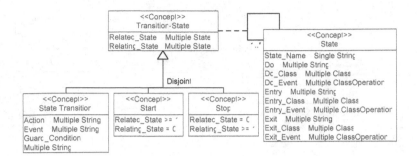

Fig. 4. Statechart diagrams ontology relations

agreements about concepts and relationships between those concepts within ontology [6], is derived. When ontology is committed, it means agreement exists with respect to the semantics of the concepts and relations represented. Henceforth, in order to know what the users are talking about, agreement is used. The users agree to share knowledge in a coherent and consistent manner.

For example, activity diagrams and statechart diagrams are related, hence, sometimes people get confused. While a statechart diagram focuses attention on an object undergoing a process (or on a process as an object), an activity diagram focuses on the flow of activities involved in a single process. The activity diagram shows how those activities depend on one another. Conclusively, determining what concept of information is captured (statechart diagrams or activity diagrams) or where that information resides (statechart diagrams or activity diagrams) is assumed that is determined by users who specify what the information is really meant in the context.

4 Conclusion

We have discussed the software design process ontology development. We have proposed the use of unified knowledge representation of software design process for communications and coordination. In future work, we aim to extend ontology development to have completed software design ontology and elaborate on software requirements, software construction, software testing, software method and tool and more.

References

1. Sommerville, I., 2004, 7th ed, *Software engineering*, Pearson Education Limited.
2. Davenport, T.H. & Prusak, L., 1998, *Working knowledge: How organisations manage what they know*, Boston, MA, Harvard Business School Press.
3. Witmer, G., 2004, *Dictionary of philosophy of mind - ontology*. [cited May 11, 2004]; Available from: http://www.artsci.wustl.edu/~philos/MindDict/ontology.html.
4. Wikipedia. *Ontology (computer science) From Wikipedia, the free encyclopedia*. 2006 [cited 8 June 2006]; Available from: http://en.wikipedia.org/wiki/Ontology_ %28computer_ science%29.

5. Gruber, T.R., 1993, *A translation approach to portable ontology specification.* in *Knowledge Acquisition.*
6. Gruber, T.R., 1993, 'Toward principles for the design of ontologies used for knowledge sharing', *Proceedings of the International Workshop on Formal Ontology in Conceptual Analysis and Knowledge Representation*, Padova, Italy: Kluwer Academic Publishers, Deventer, The Netherlands.
7. Beuster, G., 2002, *Ontologies Talk given at Czech Academy of Sciences.* [cited; Available from: http://www.uni-koblenz.de/~gb/papers/2002_intro_talk_ontology_bang/agent_ontologies.pdf
8. Klyne, G. & Carroll, J.J., 2004, *Resource Description Framework (RDF): Concepts and Abstract Syntax* [cited; Available from: http://www.w3.org/TR/rdf-concepts/.
9. McGuinness, D.L. & Harmelen, F.V., 2004, *OWL Web Ontology Language Overview.* [cited; Available from: http://www.w3.org/TR/owl-features/.
10. Finin, T., et al., 2003, 'Automatically generated DAML markup for semistructured documents'. *Proceedings of the 2003 AAAI Spring Symposium on Agent-Mediated Knowledge Management (AMKM).*
11. Fensel, D., et al., 2001, 'OIL: An ontology infrastructure for the semantic web',. *IEEE Intelligent Systems*, March/April 2001.
12. Horrocks, I. & Harmelen, F.V., 2001, *Reference Description of the DAML+OIL Ontology Markup Language.*
13. Luke, S. & Heflin, J., 2000, *SHOE 1.01 Proposed specification.* SHOE Project.
14. Wongthongtham, P., 2006, *A methodology for multi-site distributed software development*, in *School of Information Systems*, Curtin University of Technology: Perth.
15. Bourque, P., et al., 2004, *Guide to the software engineering body of knowledge.*

Ontology Views: A Theoretical Perspective

Rajugan, R.[1], Elizabeth Chang[2], and Tharam S. Dillon[1]

[1] eXel Lab, Faculty of IT, University of Technology, Sydney, Australia
{rajugan, tharam}@it.uts.edu.au
http://exel.it.uts.edu.au
[2] School of Information Systems, Curtin University of Technology, Australia
Elizabeth.Chang@cbs.cutin.edu.au

Abstract. Ontologies are the foundation of the Semantic Web (SW) and one of the keys necessary to its success. Conversely, ontology views hold the promise of; (a) provide a manageable portion of a larger ontology for the localized applications and users, (b) enable precise extraction of sub-onlogies of a larger ontology that commits to the main ontology, (c) enable localized customization and usage of the portion of a larger ontology and (d) enable interoperability between large ontology bases and applications. Therefore, it is interesting to look at ontology views and their desired properties, as there exists no agreed upon standard, methodology or formalism to specify, define and materialize ontology views. Thus, in this paper, we elaborate on our own research direction towards proposing a meaningful ontology view formalism and its associated semantics.

Keywords: Semantic Web (SW), ontology, ontology views.

1 Introduction

The Semantic Web, envisioned by Berners-Lee [1], promised to make the web a meaningful experience. SW enables users to define and represent information structures using widely accepted metadata standards to annotate new vocabularies that are independent of any language or syntax used to implement it. These accepted metadata standards are formulated into an *ontology*, a notion which is the foundation of the SW. That is, the success of SW depends on successful formulation of ontology bases [2] and the interoperability of such vast vocabularies shared over the SW.

An ontology is the notion of *shared conceptualization* [3]. It can also be stated as a specification of a conceptualization of a problem domain [4, 5] or may be viewed as a *shared conceptualization* of a domain that is commonly agreed to by all parties [6]. Formally, an ontology may be stated as "a specification of a conceptualization" [3]. Here, "conceptualization" refers to the understanding of the *concepts* and the *relationships* between the concepts that may exist or do exist in a specific domain or a community [6]. Also, a specification of the conceptualization refers to the notion or the representation of the commonly agreed, domain specific shared knowledge.

Thus, in the context of SW, theoretically, the entire world is modeled as one super-ontology [4, 5], providing great compatibility and consistency across all sub-domains. This illustrates the known characteristics of an ontology, where, in any application

R. Meersman, Z. Tari, P. Herrero et al. (Eds.): OTM Workshops 2006, LNCS 4278, pp. 1814–1824, 2006.
© Springer-Verlag Berlin Heidelberg 2006

domain, an ontology tends to grow larger than its original size, introducing problems such as: (i) being too large to be utilized in its original scale by potential applications; and (ii) capable of being understood by the community due to its size. In addition, in ontology engineering [4, 7, 2] it is also possible to have instance level data and logical level schemata descriptors to inter-mix, which may present a type of mixed sorts, which is not the case in traditional structured data (and also common in XML) data models. Also, ontology bases (and related concepts) should provide support for *intensional* and *extensional* queries executed over the base and view ontologies.

As described before, an ontology base tends to grow larger with usage. Therefore, there exists an interest to extract a portion (i.e. sub-section or *sub-ontology*) of the larger ontology that is of interest to the user for a given task. This would have benefited users from both over-utilizing valuable computing resources and time in carrying out their tasks. In addition, in doing so, it would have provided other benefits such as privacy, security, local customization and efficient access. Another reason for localized sub-ontology is the processing time involved executing semantic queries over large-scale ontology bases (for example, medical ontology UMLS[1]). In recent years, many academic and industrial research directions have been focused on these issues and some of the notable works include [8-12, 2].

For example, if we take the human disease classification (HDC) [11] ontology base or UMLS) at a given point in time, only a sub-section of the vast ontological structure is required by a medical analyst (or doctor) to complete his/her task. But due to its size, HDC (or UMLS) in its entirety, is a drawback as it presents one with a vast amount of un-wanted vocabularies for a given task, thus slowing or preventing the user from making time-critical decisions. Also, given the vast amount of classified data (such as medication, patient history etc.) in the HDC, providing privacy, security and access to all the information present in the HDC for number of users, is an unmanageable task. But, given a sub-ontology [13, 2] extracted from the base ontology for a given user profile, it is a manageable task. A sub-ontology is not just a portion of the existing ontology [2]. Rather, it is a *view* which may involve keeping the required nodes and concatenations of the relationships though nodes have been removed.

However, there exist many issues that need addressing in the case of ontology views (i.e. sub-ontologies); (a) First, unlike database or semi-structured views [2, 14], sub-ontologies are not just an extracted portion of the main ontology base, but a collection of concepts, relationships and concerns that itself is a new interpretation of the base ontology, (b) Second is the meaningful representation of such sub-ontologies that are easily understood by humans as well as easily transformed to machine (or user-application) readable notations that are at a level of abstraction that is capable of interpreting, querying and processing of concepts, relationships and constraints, (c) Third, are the complementary issues associated with sub-ontologies [3, 8, 14], such as view maintenance, versioning and materialization, that are synonymous with database views, but deserve detailed studies of their own in the context of ontologies, (d) Fourth is the issue of meaningful, yet efficient extraction of sub-ontologies from distributed base ontologies [2].

There are many ways of expressing sub-ontologies or views, but such simplified definitions may incorrectly lead to oversimplification of the ontology concept, i.e.

---

[1] http://umlsinfo.nlm.nih.gov/

ontology is a collection of words, definitions and concepts, a similar notion of knowledge bases in the classical artificial intelligence communities. Therefore, it should be noted that an ontology is more than a knowledge base and not merely a collection of distributed metadata repositories or annotated traditional databases. This is because ontology bases are metadata repositories described using metadata representation languages such as Resource Description Framework (RDF) [15], OWL [16], RDF-S [17], etc., and queried for metadata and vocabularies and the relationships (as opposed to data instances or tuples). However, the underlying representation model for the SW languages are usually XML based (i.e. they are XML documents) and exhibits XML characteristics, such as well-formness and validation. Therefore, to allow database-like features for ontology bases (e.g. querying, views, etc.), it requires more than just the adaptation of the concepts (e.g. view, query, etc.). Therefore in this paper we provide a theoretical framework for specifying *ontology views*.

The rest of this paper is organized as follows. In section 2 we present a survey of exiting ontology view formalisms. This is followed by section 3, which presents our own work including some of the desired properties of an ontology view formalism and its formal semantics. Section 4 concludes the paper with some discussion on our future research directions.

2 Related Work

We can group the existing view models into four categories, namely; (a) classical (or relational) views, (b) Object-Oriented (OO) view models, (c) semi-structured (namely XML) view models and (d) view models for SW [18]. A comprehensive discussion on these view models can be found in [13, 18]. Here, we briefly look at view models for SW. The existing ontology view research ranges from low-level, implementation specific interpretations to high-level semantic aware view formalisms, such as in [2]. These view researches are constrained by: (a) available ontology representation language or notation; (b) the lack of standardized storage model (and structure) for storing and querying ontology bases; and (c) the lack of standardized query languages. However, for ease of understanding, here, we broadly grouped the ontology view research into two categories based on the type of storage structure and/or data model adapted to store and represent the "stored" (or base) ontology. They are: (a) ontology views that are defined over ontology bases in a purpose built repositories for storing and querying ontologies. For example, the works that fall into this category includes, the MOVE view system [5], User Oriented Hybrid Ontology Development Environments [19], etc., and (b) ontology views that are defined over ontology bases in Object-Oriented (OO), relational or extended OO/relational environments. Here, the works include, the CLOVE project [20] and the KAON project [21]. Now we will present some of this research in detail.

One of the first works that explored the notion of RDF views was in [9]. It is a low-level, yet very practical approach combining RDF technologies and relational databases. It is a view formalism for RDF based documents with support for RDF schema (RDF-S) [17] using RDF schema supported query language called RQL [22]. This is one of the early works that focused purely on the RDF/SW paradigm and has sufficient support for logical modelling of RDF views. A working prototype was developed and the extension (and ongoing research) of this work (and other related projects) can be found at [21].

Another area that is currently under development is the view formalism for SW meta languages such as OWL. In some SW communities OWL is considered to be a conceptual level modelling language for representing ontologies, while some others consider it to be a crossover language with rich conceptual semantics and RDF like schema structures [5, 2]. It is outside the scope of this paper to provide argument for or against OWL being a conceptual modelling language. Here, we highlight only one of view formalism that is under development for OWL, namely views for OWL in the "User Oriented Hybrid Ontology Development Environments" (HyOntUse) [19] project. The project proposed to use its core knowledge and expertise in developing domain specific, e-Science related ontologies in developing ontology bases that are simpler representations with the power of expressive ontology formalisms with ease of use.

Though still in development, one of the interesting points in this project is the proposed approach taken towards the notion of ontology views and the level of abstraction to consider. Here, the OWL (ontology) representations are considered analogously to "assembly languages", while the ontology views are analogous to the "high level programming languages". That is, the views are considered as an "Intermediate Representation" [19]. This notion of ontology, in the context of abstraction levels, comes close to our notion of views considered in this research and that of ontology views considered in [2]. However, the HyOntUse is still a proposal and no specific information is available to evaluate the project further.

In a related area of research, the authors of the work Materialized Ontology View Extractor (MOVE) system [5, 2] proposed an ontology view formalism for ontology extraction, with limited conceptual semantics and logical extensions, where materialized ontology views are formulated from stored ontologies. Though the main work focuses on view-driven ontology extraction, this provides formal definitions and concept representations using high-level OO modelling languages, such as OMG's UML, XSemantic nets, etc. The work proposes a *restricted* ontology (and ontology view) definition, where high-level conceptual operators [14] are proposed to define ontology view representations with limited conceptual semantics. Later, these view definitions transformed to the MOVE specific algorithms to extract quality, optimized sub-ontologies.

3 Our Work: A Layered View Model (LVM) for Ontologies

In our work, we proposed a Layered View Model (LVM) for ontologies [13], where views are considered to be a special kind of transformation, namely the 3 E's [13, 14]: Extraction, Elaboration and Extension. Thus, an ontology view may be considered as a generic partitioning of any transformation into the 3 Es. That is: (a) Extraction can informally be defined as taking a part of the original, so without any modifications, (b) Elaboration is providing such an extracted part with additional levels of detail and (c) Extension can be considered as the addition of completely new elements (i.e. they were not present in any shape or form in the original). In the LVM, since the view specification and the definitions are done at the highest level of abstraction (i.e. the conceptual level), support for the three Es are provided by a collection of *conceptual operators* [13] and the view definitions are transferable (using transformations) across the required level of abstraction (i.e. conceptual, logical or document levels) without loss of semantics. In the next sections we outline some of the envisioned properties of ontology views in our LVM followed by its formal semantics.

3.1 Envisioned Properties of an Ontology View

In this section, based on the above discussions on ontology views and using our own experience and knowledge gained from the LVM for XML [13] and ontologies [14], we propose a set of *desired* properties for an ontology view formalism. In our work with views for XML, we found that it is imperative to maintain the quality of the view (data) generated and without loss of semantics. This is one of the core requirements for ontology views as the ontology view (or the sub-ontology extracted from the main ontology base(s)) is complete, cohesive and consistent and satisfies the user requirement [5]. In addition, ontology views should be useable as a standalone base ontology for the user and/or application by itself, independent of the parent/main ontology base, as opposed to data (or XML) views. Also, unlike database views, given an ontology view, users and applications should be able to further customize it locally to suit his/her within the scope of the ontology standards and annotations.

Thus, we identified some key *characteristics* that ought to be present in an *ontology view* formalism They are: (i) Ontology view definitions should be based on strong (generic) theoretical foundations than are bound to a query and/or language specific syntax. This is a challenging task, as unlike data views, theoretical foundations for SW and ontologies are not yet strong enough to accommodate view definition and specifications. Though many research directions are focused on this area, adopting a generic theoretical framework work for ontology view definition is still an open challenge, (ii) View specification and definition should be done (preferably) visually (e.g. such as view definitions using Query-by-Example frameworks developed for relational database models), at a higher level of abstraction due to the complexities involved in defining ontologies a lower level construct. Again, visualization of ontology bases are still in their infancy due to the complexities involved of doing such a computationally demanding task. This is mainly due to the scale (or size) and the complex inner structures (and the structural relationships) that are present in a typical ontology base, (iii) Ontology views should provide facilities to be modelled in top-down (and preferably bottom-up as well) to conceptualize the sub-models and concepts. Providing such facilities enables the ontology engineer to design views with rich semantics and constraints. Some work has been done in this direction to model ontology bases (and in some cases views) using proven software engineering modeling techniques, such as Object-Oriented (OO) techniques using notations such as UML [23, 5], ORM [4, 24] or XSemantic nets [25]. However, high level modelling, design and querying techniques still prove to be a challenging task for SW paradigm as, ontology definitions and querying are more complex in nature than traditional modeling notations can model/represent, (iv) Since SW models, namely ontologies, are defined and queried at a higher level of abstraction than at the data or instance level [9, 5], the ontology view model should be specified using an abstract notation that is easily transferable to any language or platform-specific syntax, (v) Since a given ontology view definition may be deployed in a variety of execution platforms, the view specification and definition must be portable. Also, an ontology view specification should be generic enough to be adaptable to new and emerging SW standards and annotations as the SW paradigm is still evolving with new languages, tools and platforms, (vi) The ontology view derivation process should be optimized as future query execution schemes against the ontology view should provide optimal performance, (vii) Given a main ontology which may contain distributed, inter-connected domains, ontology views should be able to distinguish between common concepts that may occur and do present in one or more inter-connected sub-domains. This is one of the major challenges faced in sub-ontology extraction, (viii) Since an ontology view may substitute itself as a base for users and/or applications, it should provide facilities to be materialized [5] and extraction of further views (or sub sub-ontologies) and (ix) Given a *specific* ontology view, it should be able to be *commit* to the base (and the generic) ontology and reflect schematic changes as they occur.

Given such properties, it is envisaged that ontology view formalism would; (a) manage large ontology bases with meaningful extraction of sub-ontologies [2] and interoperability between distributed ontology bases, (b) support localized customization of sub-ontologies (or views), (c) provide security and privacy, (d) enabled SW applications [26] and techniques such as privacy, trust, reputation etc. SW environments [12, 6], (e) provide performance and persistence sub-ontologies for SW applications in the form of materialized views [2], (f) provide ontology visualization [27] and (g) provide ontology management and maintenance such as version control [8], access control, etc.

3.2 Formal Semantics of Views in the LVM for Ontologies

Given below is a brief discussion on some of the formal semantics to specify and define ontology views in the LVM [13, 18]. It should be noted here that, there exists few definitions that are specific to one or more SW languages. This is because ontology bases are metadata repositories described using metadata representation languages such as Resource Description Framework (RDF) [15], OWL [16], RDF-S [17], etc., and queried for metadata and vocabularies and the relationships (as opposed to data instances or tuples). However, the underlying representation model for the SW languages are usually XML based (i.e. they are XML documents) and exhibits XML characteristics, such as well-formness and validation. As stated in [9], SW enables access to distributed content using a standardized semi-structured data model, at a higher level of abstraction than traditional data.

In our research we adapt, elaborate and extend the definitions provided by Wouters et al. in [3, 2], since this is one of the very few early works that provides some form of conceptual abstraction in modelling and defining ontology bases and ontology views. In this work, we our primary focus is on providing formal semantics associated with ontologies and ontology views that are synonymous with the LVM for XML in [13], as most SW meta languages are based on XML data model. Therefore, since the proposed model is based on the LVM for XML and the associated concepts, some of the concepts and definitions are extensions and/or elaboration of the concepts and definitions presented in the above mentioned works. It should also be noted that our intentions here are neither to propose new definitions for existing ontology standards nor to propose formal semantics for existing standards.

First we define the notion of Universe of Discourse. Universe of Discourse (UoD) is a familiar concept in logic, linguistics, and mathematics and computational theory. UoD develops an abstraction of the real world that captures relevant properties, characteristics, relationships, constraints and knowledge. Further, UoD is the set of all objects presumed or hypothesized to exist for some specific purpose. Objects may be concrete or abstract. Objects may be primitive or composite. Also, all the sets of entities defined in the UoD are capable of being represented in some declarative language or other formal systems. For the purpose of this research, let us denote the UoD as UoD. Also, let O_{bject} be a set of descriptors that uniquely identify *objects* in the real world, $A_{ttribute}$ be a set of descriptors that uniquely identify *attributes* of these objects in the real world, $R_{elationship}$ be a set of descriptors that uniquely identify *relationships* between a set of objects in the real world and $C_{onstraint}$ be a set of descriptors that uniquely identify constraints associated with O_{bject}, $A_{ttribute}$ and $R_{elationship}$ in the real world.

Definition 1. Ontology The Universe of Discourse UoD is a set of descriptors uniquely identifying objects O_{bject}, attributes $A_{ttribute}$, methods M_{ethod}, relationships $R_{elationship}$ and constraints $C_{onstraint}$ in the real world. Thus;

$$UoD = \{ O_{bject} \cup A_{ttribute} \cup R_{elationship} \cup C_{onstraint} \} \qquad (1)$$

Now we define the notion of a general ontology, given in [3]:

Definition 2. Ontology is an explicit specification of a conceptualization that corresponds to the *Universe of Discourse* (UoD) of the given domain.

Let an *agent* as an entity such that:

Postulate 1. An agent is a *participating* entity such as users, agents and software modules or applications in a Semantic Web environment.

As stated in [13, 14], a *context* refers to the portion of the domain that is of interest. Thus, in the case of ontologies, analogous to the definition of in the LVM, we elaborate and state a context as;

Postulate 2. The term *ontological context* $o\zeta_{ontext}$ refers to a portion of the conceptual specification of a given domain (i.e. UoD) that is of interest to one or more agents. Thus we can derive that;

$$o\zeta_{ontext} \in UoD \qquad (2)$$

Also from [13, 18], we can define an ontological context as:

Definition 3. An *ontological context* $O\zeta_{ontext}$ is a 4-ary tuple of $O\zeta_{name}, O\zeta_{obj}, O\zeta_{rel}$ and $O\zeta_{onstraint}$, where $O\zeta_{name}$ is the name of the context $O\zeta_{ontext}$, $O\zeta_{obj}$ is a set of objects in $O\zeta_{ontext}$, $O\zeta_{rel}$ is a set of object relationships in $O\zeta_{ontext}$, and $O\zeta_{onstraint}$ is a set of constraints associated with $O\zeta_{obj}$ and $O\zeta_{rel}$ in $O\zeta_{ontext}$.

$$O\zeta_{ontext} = (O\zeta_{name}, O\zeta_{obj}, O\zeta_{rel}, O\zeta_{constraints}) \tag{3}$$

Here, in definition 3 above, we denote the ontology terminology such that: (i)The set of objects in ontological context $O\zeta_{ontext}$ represents the notion of a set of concepts, as defined, (ii) The set of objects in ontological context $O\zeta_{ontext}$ are finite; that is, the number of concepts in an ontological context is finite, (iii) The set of objects in ontological context $O\zeta_{ontext}$ are a non-empty set, (iv) The properties (or elements) of $O\zeta_{obj}$ corresponds to the set of all possible attributes $O\zeta_{attribute}$ for the given concept, (v) The set of properties for a given context is always finite, (vi) As in the case with the LVM, the $O\zeta_{rel}$ corresponds to the set of all possible *binary* relationships between one or more concepts and/or their attributes in a given ontological context $O\zeta_{ontext}$, and (viii) The $O\zeta_{onstraint}$ corresponds to a set of all possible constraints associated with the concepts, attributes and relationships for a given ontological context $O\zeta_{ontext}$.

However, in defining the terms above, here, we make some implicit assumptions about the restrictions that are placed in defining an ontology definition, similar to the restrictions applied [2], in the case of the Internal Ontology Conceptualization (IOC) as defined in [2]. Let we denote $\Re$ as a restriction that is applied on a basic ontology definition.

Definition 4. An *ontological context* $O\zeta_{ontext}^{X}$ is said to be a valid ontology if and only if, it is a context with the restrictions $\Re$ are applied, such that:

$$O\zeta_{ontext}^{X} = (\forall O\zeta_{ontext}^{X}) \mid O\zeta_{ontext}^{X} \in O\zeta_{ontext} \wedge \Re(O\zeta_{ontext}^{X}) \tag{4}$$

Let $O_{ntology}^{X}$ denotes an ontology.

Definition 5. An ontology $O_{ntology}^{X}$ is said be a sub-ontology of a valid ontological context $O\zeta_{ontext}^{X}$, if and only if:

$$O_{ntology}^{X} = (\forall O_{ntology}^{X}) \mid O_{ntology}^{X} \in O\zeta_{ontex}^{X} \wedge O_{ntology}^{X} \subset O\zeta_{ontex}^{X} \tag{5}$$

From equation 4, it can be shown that, for $o_{ntology}^{X}$ to be a valid sub-ontology, it implies that:

$$o_{ntology}^{X} \Rightarrow o_{ntology}^{X} \in o\zeta_{ontext} \wedge \Re(o_{ntology}^{X}) \tag{6}$$

We denote the sub-ontology as $\subset\subset$, thus:

$$o_{ntology}^{X} \subset\subset o\zeta_{ontex}^{X} \tag{7}$$

Postulate 3. A *conceptual ontology view* refers to a certain portion or sub-set of a given ontological context that is of interest to participating agents in the SW environment, at a given point in time.

Definition 6. A *conceptual ontology view* oV_{iew}^{c} is a 4-ary tuple of $oV_{name}^{c}, oV_{obj}^{c}, oV_{rel}^{c}$ and $oV_{constraints}^{c}$, where oV_{name}^{c} is the name of the conceptual ontology view oV_{iew}^{c}, oV_{obj}^{c} is a set of objects in oV_{iew}^{c}, oV_{rel}^{c} is a set of object relationships in oV_{iew}^{c}, and $oV_{constraints}^{c}$ is a set of constraints associated with oV_{obj}^{c} and oV_{rel}^{c} in oV_{iew}^{c}.

$$oV_{iew}^{c} = (oV_{name}^{c}, oV_{obj}^{c}, oV_{rel}^{c}, oV_{constraints}^{c}) \tag{8}$$

Let λ be a set of conceptual operators, as defined in [13].

Definition 7. A *conceptual ontology view* oV_{iew}^{c} is called a *valid* conceptual ontology view of the ontological context $o\zeta_{ontext}^{X}$, if and only if the following conditions (i), (ii), (iii) (iv) and (v) are satisfied: (i) A valid sub-ontology such that, $oV_{iew}^{c} \subset\subset o\zeta_{ontext}$, (ii) For any object $\forall o_{obj}^{v} \in oV_{iew}^{c}$, there exist objects $\exists o_{obj}^{c1},..o_{obj}^{ci},..o_{obj}^{cn} \in o\zeta_{obj}$, such that, $o_{obj}^{v} = \lambda_{1},.., \lambda_{m}(o_{obj}^{c1},..o_{obj}^{ci},..o_{obj}^{cn})$ where $\lambda_{1}\lambda_{2},..., \lambda_{m} \in \lambda$. That is, o_{obj}^{v} is a newly derived object from existing objects $o_{obj}^{c1}, o_{obj}^{c2},.......o_{obj}^{cn}$ in the ontological context via a series of conceptual operators $\lambda_{1}\lambda_{2},..., \lambda_{m}.$, (iii) For any constraint $\forall c_{onstraint}^{v} \in oV_{constraints}^{c}$, there exists a constraint $\exists c_{onstraint}^{v'} \in o\zeta_{constraint}$ or a new constraint $c_{onstraint}^{v''}$ constraints associated with V_{obj}^{c} and V_{rel}^{c}, (iv) For any hierarchical relationship $\forall rel_{h} \in oV_{rel}^{c}$, there *does not exist* a relationship between one or more V_{obj}^{c} and ζ_{obj}, (v) For any binary association relationship/dependency relationships $\forall rel_{a} \in oV_{rel}^{c}$, there *may exist* a relationship between one or more oV_{obj}^{c} and $o\zeta_{obj}$.

It should be noted here that, due to page limitations, we did not present a detailed discussion on logical and document level ontology view semantics, as it largely dependent on the underlying metadata description and/or representation language such as RDF, RDF-S, OWL, etc. In regards to mapping our LVM ontology views to MOVE system, a detailed discussion can be found in [13, 2, 14]. However, for other language specific transformations (i.e. RDF, OWL, etc.), we intend to address this issue in the near future and at present we use other semantics and transformation methodologies proposed to carry out this task of mapping conceptual ontology views to logical and/or document views. Such transformations we consider include UML-to-OWL [23, 28] transformation and ORM-to-OWL [24].

4 Conclusion and Future Work

In this paper, we described ontologies, sub-ontologies and a proposal for ontology views. Also, based on our research findings, we proposed as set of desired properties for ontology views. For future work, some further issues deserve investigation. First, the investigation of a formal mapping approach for transforming LVM ontology views to one or more SW language (such as RDF and OWL schema) including view constraints. Second, the automation of the mapping process between conceptual operators to various SW (high-level) query language expressions (e.g. RDQL, XQuery, etc.) with emphasis on performance and materialization.

References

1. T. Berners-Lee, "Weaving the web," Harper, San Francisco, 1999.
2. C. Wouters, "A Formalization and Application of Ontology Extraction," School of Engineering and Mathematical Sciences Faculty of Sciences, Technology and Engineering, La Trobe University, Melbourne, Australia, Melbourne, Doctor of Philosophy (Ph.D) thesis, 2006. pp. 460.
3. T. R. Gruber, "A Translation Approach to Portable Ontologies," *Knowledge Acquisition*, vol. 5, pp. 199-220, 1993.
4. P. Spyns, R. Meersman, and J. Mustafa, "Data Modeling Versus Ontology Engineering," SIGMOD, 2002.
5. C. Wouters, T. S. Dillon, J. W. Rahayu, E. Chang, and R. Meersman, "A Practical Approach to the Derivation of a Materialized Ontology View," in *Web Information Systems*, D. Taniar and W. Rahayu, Eds. USA: Idea Group Publishing, 2004.
6. E. Chang, T. S. Dillon, and F. K. Hussain, *Trust and Reputation for Service Oriented Environments: Technologies for Building Business Intelligence and Consumer Confidence.* UK.: John Wiley and Sons, 2006.
7. A. Gâomez-Pâerez, M. Fernâandez-Lâopez, and O. Corcho, *Ontological engineering : with examples from the areas of knowledge management, e-commerce and the semantic Web.* London ; New York: Springer-Verlag, 2003.
8. N. Noy and M. Musen, "Promptdiff: a fixed-point algorithm for comparing ontology versions," Proceedings of the Eighteenth National Conf. on Artificial Intelligence, 2002.
9. R. Volz, D. Oberle, and R. Studer, "Views for light-weight Web ontologies," Proceedings of the ACM Symposium on Applied Computing (SAC '03), USA, 2003.

10. H. H. Do and E. Rahm, "Flexible integration of molecular-biological annotation data: The genmapper approach," Proceedings of the 9th Int. Conf. on Extending Database Technology (EDBT '04), Heraklion, Crete, Greece, 2004.
11. M. Hadzic and E. Chang, "Role of the Ontologies in the Context of Grid Computing and Application for the Human Disease Studies," Semantics for Grid Databases, First Int. IFIP Conf. on Semantics of a Networked World (ICSNW '04), Paris, France, 2004.
12. P. Ceravolo, E. Damiani, G. Elia, and M. Viviani, "Bottom-up Extraction and Maintenance of Ontology-based Metadata," in *Fuzzy Logic and the Semantic Web*: Elsevier, 2006.
13. R.Rajugan, "A Layered View Model for XML with Conceptual and Logical Extension, and its Applications," Faculty of Information Technology, University of Technology, Sydney (UTS), Australia, Sydney, PhD thesis, 2006. pp. 460.
14. C. Wouters, R.Rajugan, T. S. Dillon, and J. W. Rahayu, "Ontology Extraction Using Views for Semantic Web," in *Web Semantics and Ontology*, D. Taniar and W. Rahayu, Eds. USA: Idea Group Publishing, 2006, pp. 01 - 40.
15. W3C-RDF, "Resource Description Framework (RDF), (http://www.w3.org/RDF/)," 3 ed: The World Wide Web Consortium (W3C), 2004.
16. W3C-OWL, "OWL: Web Ontology Language 1.0 reference (http://www.w3.org/2004/OWL/)," W3C, 2004.
17. W3C-RDFS, "RDF-Schema (RDF-S), (http://www.w3.org/TR/rdf-schema/)," 3 ed: The World Wide Web Consortium (W3C), 2004.
18. R.Rajugan, E. Chang, T. S. Dillon, and C. Wouters, "Sub-Ontologies and Ontology Views: A Theoretical Perspective," *Int. Journal of Metadata, Semantics and Ontologies (IJMSO)*, vol. - to appear, 2006.
19. HyOntUse, "User Oriented Hybrid Ontology Development Environments, (http:// www.cs.man.ac.uk/mig/projects/current/hyontuse/)," 2003.
20. R. Uceda-Sosa, C. X. Chen, and K. T. Claypool, "CLOVE: A Framework to Design Ontology Views," Int. Conf. on Conceptual Modeling (ER '04), Shanghai, China, 2004.
21. KAON, "KAON Project (http://kaon.semanticweb.org/Members/rvo/Folder.2002-08-22.1409/Module.2002-08-22.1426/view)," vol. 2005, 2004.
22. W3C-RDQL, "RDQL - A Query Language for RDF, (http://www.w3.org/Submission/2004/SUBM-RDQL-20040109/)," W3C, 2004.
23. D. Gašević, D. Djuric, V. Devedzic, and V. Damjanovic, "Converting UML to OWL Ontologies," Proceedings of the 13 th Int. World Wide Web Conf., NY, USA, 2004.
24. M. Jarrar, J. Demey, and R. Meersman, "On Using Conceptual Data Modeling for Ontology Engineering," *Journal on Data Semantics*, vol. LNCS 2800, pp. 185-207, 2003.
25. R.Rajugan, E. Chang, L. Feng, and T. S. Dillon, "Modeling Views for Semantic Web," First IFIP WG 2.12 & WG 12.4 Int. Workshop on Web Semantics (SWWS '05), In conjunction with On The Move Federated Conf. (OTM '05), Agia Napa, Cyprus, 2005.
26. P. Wongthamtham, E. Chang, T. S. Dillon, J. Davis, and N. Jayaratna, "Ontology Based Solution for Software Development," Int. Conf. on Software Engineering and Applications (ICSSEA '03), Paris, France, 2003.
27. C. Wouters, T. S. Dillon, J. W. Rahayu, and E. Chang, "Large scale ontology visualisation using ontology extraction," *Int. Journal of Web and Grid Services*, vol. 1(1), pp. 113 - 135, 2005.
28. D. Gašević, D. Djuric, V. Devedžic, and V. Damjanovic, "UML for Read-To-Use OWL Ontologies," Proceedings of the IEEE Int. Conf. Intelligent Systems, Vrana, Bulgaria, 2004.

OntoExtractor:
A Fuzzy-Based Approach to Content and Structure-Based Metadata Extraction

Paolo Ceravolo, Ernesto Damiani, Marcello Leida, and Marco Viviani

Università degli studi di Milano,
Dipartimento di Tecnologie dell'Informazione, via Bramante, 65
26013 Crema (CR), Italy
{ceravolo, damiani, leida, viviani}@dti.unimi.it
http://ra.crema.unimi.it/kiwi

Abstract. This paper describes OntoExtractor a tool for extracting metadata from heterogeneous sources of information, producing a "quick-and-dirty" hierarchy of knowledge. This tool is specifically tailored for a quick classification of semi-structured data. By this feature, OntoExtractor is convenient for dealing with a web-based data source.

1 Introduction

Typically, knowledge management techniques use metadata in order to specify content, quality, type, creation, and context of a data item. A number of specialized formats for the creation of metadata exist. A typical example is the Resource Description Framework (RDF). But metadata can be stored in any format such as free text, Extensible Markup Language (XML), or database entries. All of these formats must relay on a vocabulary that can have different degree of formality. If this vocabulary is compliant to a set of logical axioms it is called an ontology.

There are a number of well-known advantages in using information extracted from data instead of data themselves. On one hand, because of their small size compared to the data they describe, metadata are more easily shareable than data. Thanks to metadata sharing, information about data becomes readily available to anyone seeking it. Thus, metadata make data discovery easier and reduces data duplication. But on the other hand some important drawbacks are restraining the diffusion of metadata format. First of all, building a knowledge-base is an onerous process. The domain analysis involves different activities often difficult to integrate, because they are usually performed by different professional roles. In addition, the high cost of knowledge-base building is in contradiction to important characteristics of knowledge management principles. Any knowledge management activity need to be configured for a given domain. But every domain evolves and the knowledge-bases related to it have to evolve as well. If the domain is evolving rapidly, a dis-alignment may result between the actual domain's

R. Meersman, Z. Tari, P. Herrero et al. (Eds.): OTM Workshops 2006, LNCS 4278, pp. 1825–1834, 2006.

state of affairs and the knowledge-base. In addition, classical knowledge extraction technologies are not tailored for web-based data. These techniques were largely experimented with successful results. Anyhow they present some limitations. First, they need a high number of documents (typically, many thousands) to work properly. Secondly, they hardly take into account document structure and are therefore unsuitable for semi-structured document formats used on the Web.

In this paper we present OntoExtractor a tool supporting knowledge extraction activities in a web-based environment. OntoExtractor was designed to be inserted in a more general system aimed at managing the whole Ontology Life Cycle [5]. The classification produced as output is transformed in a standard metadata format and proposed to a community of used. Feedbacks from the community are collected in order to refine the classification, discarding metadata expressing not relevant classes or misclassified documents [4]. In order to support continuos domain evolutions, OntoExtractor is designed for quickly producing a preliminary classification of a knowledge base. This tool supports heterogeneous source of information, including semi-strucutred data. A fuzzy representation of document vectors allows to segment documents according to their structural topology, assigning different relevance values to each segment. Another important feature of OntoExtractor is to produce different classifications organizing the classes of documents according to different degree of cohesion. This feature allows the user to quickly discard a classification not coherent to his vision of the domain.

The paper is organized as follows: Section 2, introduces the tool, Section 3 describes the format adopted for document representation, Section 4 explains the techniques used in the structural classification of documents, Section 5 explains the techniques used in the content classification, while Section 6 goes to the conclusions.

2   OntoExtractor

OntoExtractor is a tool, developed in the context of the KIWI project [1], which extracts metadata from heterogeneous sources of information, producing a "quick-and-dirty" hierarchy of knowledge. The construction of the hierarchy occurs in a bottom-up fashion: starting from the heterogeneous document set a clustering process groups documents in meaningful clusters. These clusters identify the backbone hierarchy of the ontology. Construction of the hierarchy is a three-step process, composed of the following phases:

1. Normalize the incoming documents into XML format [9].
2. Clustering the documents according to their structure using a Fuzzy Bag representation of the XML tree [3] [6].

[1] This work was partly funded by the Italian Ministry of Research Fund for Basic Research (FIRB) under projects RBAU01CLNB_001 "Knowledge Management for the Web Infrastructure" (KIWI).

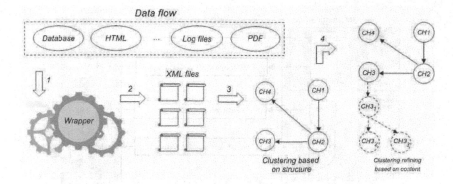

Fig. 1. Overview of the OntoExtractor process

3. Refine the structural clustering analyzing the content of the document, producing a semantic clustering of the documents.

3   Normalize the Knowledge Base

This first step in our process is choosing a common representation format for the information to be managed. Data may come from different and heterogeneous sources: including unstructured, semi-structured or structured information, such as textual documents, HTML files, XML files or records in a database. In order to conciliate these different data sources we developed a set of wrapper applications transforming most used document formats in a XML target representation. The wrapping process is shown in Figure 2: for semi-structured and structured sources the wrapper does not have much to do. All it has to perform is applying a mapping between the original data and elements in the target XML tree. Unstructured sources of information need additional processing aimed to extracting the hidden structure of the documents. This phase uses well-known text-segmentation techniques [9] in order to find relations among parts of a text. This is an iterative process that takes as input a text blob (which is a continuous flow of characters, representing the whole content of a document) and gives as output a set of text-segments identified by the text segmentation process. The process stops when no text blob can be segmented further. At this point, a post-processing phase analyzes the resulting tree structure and generates the corresponding XML document. In the current version of the OntoExtractor software, a Regular Expressions matching approach is also available in order to discover regular patterns like titles of sections in the documents, helping controlling the text segmentation process. This is a preliminary approach that compares each row of the document with the regular expression (i.e. $[0-9] + (([.]?)|([.]?[0-9]+)) * (\s + \w+)+$ we used this expression to match chapter, sections and paragraph headlines, which are usually proceeded by numbers separated by a ".".).

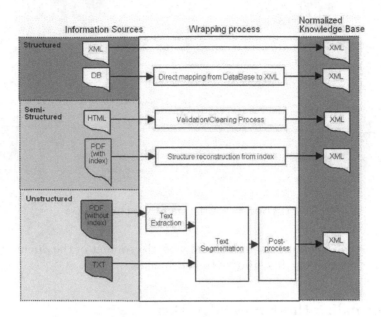

Fig. 2. Wrapping process

4   Clustering by Structure

The OntoExtractor tool uses a flat encoding for the internal representation of XML documents for processing and analysis purposes. Documents are represented as Fuzzy Bags, i.e. a collection of elements which may contain duplicates. Due to the fact that the importance of tags can differ, it is possible to assign a different weight (in the range form 0 to 1) to each tag in the document. In other words, for each element in the XML document d, the Fuzzy Bag encoding d contains a Fuzzy Element whose membership value is determined by the position of the tag in the document's structure or by other topological properties. OntoExtractor tool currently provides two different algorithms to calculate the membership function of a Fuzzy Element:

1. *Nesting*: this is a "lossy" representation of the original document's topology, because this membership value does not keep track of which is the parent tag of the current tag, as shown in Figure 3. Giving a vocabulary $V = \{R/1, a/0.9, b/0.8, d/0.6, e/0.4\}$, applying the nesting weighting function to a generic XML document, such as *A.xml* or *B.xml*, we obtain the fuzzy bag $A = B = \{R/1, a/0.3, a/0.225, b/0.2, d/0.3, e/0.2\}$. The membership value for each element is: $M = V_e/L$.
   Where:
   – M: membership value;
   – V_e: weight of the tag in the vocabulary;
   – L: nesting level of the tag with $L_{root} = 0$.

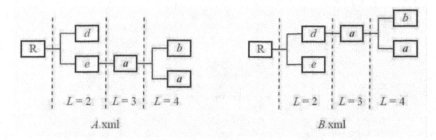

Fig. 3. Two generic XML documents A.XML and B.XML

2. MV: this is an experimental algorithm introduced by our group, which keeps memory of the parent tag. The membership value for each element is: $M = (V_e + M_p)/L$.

   Where:
   - M: membership value;
   - M_p: membership value of the parent tag with $M_{root} = 0$;
   - V_e: weight of the tag in the vocabulary;
   - L: nesting level of the tag with $L_{root} = 0$.

   The MV membership value helps, in certain cases, to keep memory of the tree structure of the original document, referring to figure 3: using the same vocabulary V, applying the MV weighting function to the tree representation of the two XML documents $A.xml$ and $B.xml$ we obtain $A = \{R/1, a/0.53, a/0.36, b/0.33, d/0.8, e/0.7\}$ and $B = \{R/1, a/0.56, a/0.37, b/0.34, d/0.8, e/0.7\}$ which are different. Figure 4 shows the differences in processing an XML document coming from Amazon, alternatively by *Nesting* and *MV* algorithms.

In order to compare the XML documents modeled as fuzzy bags well known similarity measures studied in [1] [2]. We privileged measures giving higher similarity weight to the bags where elements (tags) belonging to the intersection are less nested. This is motivated by the fact that, if a tag is near to the root it seems reasonable to assume that it has a higher semantic value. In OntoExtractor the comparison between two Fuzzy Bags is computed using Jaccard norm:

$$S(B1, B2) = Approx\left(\frac{|Bag1 \cap Bag2|}{|Bag1 \cup Bag2|}\right)$$

Where:

- **B1** and **B2** are the input fuzzy bags;
- $\cap$ is the intersection operator;
- $\cup$ is the union operator;
- $\|$ is the cardinality operator;
- **Approx()** is the approximation operator;
- **S** is the similarity value between B1 and B2.

Fig. 4. Fuzzy Bags generated by Nesting and MV algorithms. And the XML representation of the document.

For more theoretical information about this norm and how the union, intersection, approximation and cardinality operations are expressed, please refer to [3] and [6]. Using this norm the tool can perform a partitioned clustering technique that is an hybrid version between *K-means* and *K-NN* clustering algorithms. OntoExtractor uses an *alpha-cut* value as a threshold for the clustering process, in order to avoid to suggest the initial number of clusters (k) and skipping this way some clustering problems related to the *k-means* algorithm. The clustering algorithm compares all the documents with the centroid of each cluster, considering only the bigger resemblance value. If this value is bigger than the given *alpha* the document is inserted in the cluster, otherwise a new empty cluster is generated and the document is inserted in it.

OntoExtractor tool offers two different ways to calculate the centroid of each cluster: one method chooses the document that has the smaller representative Fuzzy Bag. In this method the centroid always corresponds to a real document. The other method generates a new Fuzzy Bag as the union of all the Fuzzy Bags in the cluster. This way the generated Fuzzy Bag does not have a compulsory correspondence in a real document.

5   Clustering by Content

The second clustering process that we propose is based on the content connected to leaf nodes. Content-based clustering is independent for each structural cluster selected so on it is possible to give different clustering criteria for each structural cluster generated, as shown in Figure 5. Note that users can select which clustering process to perform; for instance, if there is no need of structural clustering then only content-based clustering is performed. Is important to remember that

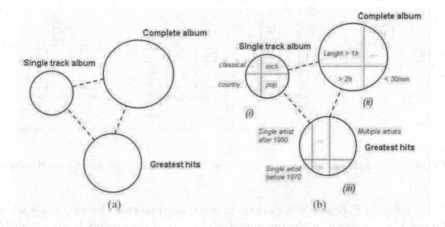

Fig. 5. Domain class subdivision based on structure (a) and refinement based on content (b)

our clustering technique works on XML documents that are somehow structured. Therefore we compute content-based similarity at tag level, comparing content of the same tag between different documents. Then we compute content-based similarity at document level by aggregating tag level similarity values. Referring

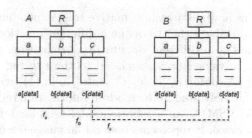

Fig. 6. Tag-Level ccomparison between data belonging to the same tag in different documents

to Figure 6 it is necessary to choose two different functions: a function f to compare data belonging to tags with the same name in different documents:

$$f_a(a[data]_A; a[data]_B); f_b(b[data]_A; b[data]_B); f_c(c[data]_A; c[data]_B) \quad (1)$$

and a function F to aggregate the individual fs: $F(f_a, f_b, f_c)$. We have two possibilities for choosing the F function:

- F is a *t-norm*: conjunction of the single values ($f_a \wedge f_b \wedge f_c$);
- F is a *t-conorm*: disjunction of the single values ($f_a \vee f_b \vee f_c$).

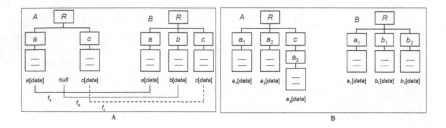

Fig. 7. A: comparison in case of null values. B: comparison in case of nested values.

Referring to Figure 7 it is evident that we need to consider also cases where the tag is not present in the document and cases of documents having multiple instances of the same tag at different nesting levels. So in the first case we have:

$$f_b(null; b[data]_B) = 0; \tag{2}$$

and in the second case we evaluate the distance between the tags using the formula:

$$f_x = \max_{p,k} \frac{1}{1 + \Delta_{p,k}} f_{x_{p,k}}(x_p[data]_A; x_k[data]_B); \tag{3}$$

$$\Delta = |\mu(x_p) - \mu(x_k)|. \tag{4}$$

Occurrences of terms have distinct informative roles depending on the tags they belong to. So, it is possible either to define a different function f for each group of data of the same tag in different documents, or choosing a function considering the membership value $\mu(x_i)$ associated to the i-th tag. We represent the content of each tag ($A_n[data], B_n[data,]C_n[data], ...$ in (1)) with the well-known *Vector Space Model*, widely used in the modern information retrieval system. The vector space model (VSM) is an algebraic model used for information filtering and information retrieval. It represents natural language documents in a formal manner by the use of vectors in a multi-dimensional space. The vector space model usually builds a documents-terms matrix and processes it to generate the document-terms vectors. Our approach is similar but we generate one matrix for each tag in the document; correspondingly, we generate a tag-terms vector. There are several methods to generate the tag-terms vector, such as *LSA* (Latent Semantic Analysis [7]) or *SVD* (Singular Value Decomposition), a well-known method of matrix reduction that adds latent semantic meaning to the vectors. In OntoExtractor, generating the tag-terms vectors is a three-step process:

- *Generating the tags-terms matrix*: for each tag in the document, a documents-terms matrix is produced. It is important to remember that we do not consider the document as a unique text-blob, but we build the documents-terms matrix at the tag level. If a tag is not present in a document, a row of zeros is added to the matrix. Each entry in the matrix can be computed in several ways as well, by choosing one of the weighting methods implemented in the tool. At now it is possible to choose among: $tf - idf$, $tf - df$, tf and *term_occurrency*.
- *Transforming the matrix*: once the matrix has been generated we process it by some matrix tranformations. We allow to choose between keeping the original matrix or transform it *LSA* by *SVD*. This method relies on the assumption that any $m * n$ matrix A (with $(m \geq n)$) can be written as the product of an $m * n$ column-orthogonal matrix U, an $n * n$ diagonal matrix with positive or zero elements(Σ), and the transpose of an $n * n$ orthogonal matrix V. Suppose M is an $m * n$ matrix whose entries come from the field K, which is either the field of real numbers or the field of complex numbers. Then there exists a factorization of the form: $M = U\Sigma V^*$; where U is an $m*m$ unitary matrix over K, the matrix S is $m*n$ with non-negative numbers on the diagonal and zeros off the diagonal, and $V*$ denotes the conjugate transpose of V, an $n * n$ unitary matrix over K. Such a factorization is called a singular-value decomposition of M. The matrix V thus contains a set of orthogonal "input" or "analysing" base-vector directions for M. The matrix U contains a set of orthogonal "output" base-vector directions for M. The matrix S contains the singular values, which can be thought of as scalar "gain controls" by which each corresponding input is multiplied to give a corresponding output. After the matrix decomposition we generate a new $n * m$ matrix using an r-reduction of the original SVD decomposition: $M = U_r \Sigma_r V_r^*$.
  Only the r column vectors of U and r row vectors of V^* corresponding to the non-zero singular values S_r are calculated. The resulting new matrix is not a sparse matrix anymore but it is densely populated by values, with hidden semantic meaning.
- *Storing the vectors*: each row in the matrix is stored in the associated tag in the document model as a new Fuzzy Bag with the terms as the element and the entry in the vector as membership value. Now tags' contents are represented by Fuzzy Bags and we can compare them by mean of different distances measures: we can use traditional *Euclidean distances* such as the *Cosine distance*.

6   Conclusions and Further Work

In order to avoid the siononimy and polisemy problem in the next versions of OntoExtractor will be added new processors using external ontologies to identify concept. Anyway this approach introduces other problems that have to be considered. One of this is the *Word Sense Disambiguation* (WSD). The validity of this tool must be evaluated in the complete system it inserted on. Further works will provide a report on evaluations of the KIWI system.

References

1. B. Bouchon-Meunier, M. Rifqi, S. Bothorel: "Towards general measures of comparison of objects". Fuzzy Sets and Systems, volume 84, pages 143-153, 1996.
2. P. Bosc, E. Damiani: "Fuzzy Service Selection in a Distributed Object-Oriented Environment". IEEE Transactions on Fussy Systems, volume 9, no. 5, pages 682-698, 2001.
3. P. Ceravolo, M.C. Nocerino, M. Viviani: "Knowledge extraction from semi-structured data based on fuzzy techniques". Knowledge-Based Intelligent Information and Engineering Systems, Proceedings of the 8th International Conference, KES 2004, Part III, pages 328-334, 2004.
4. P. Ceravolo, E. Damiani, M. Viviani: "Adding a Peer-to-Peer Trust Layer to Metadata Generators". Lecture Notes in Computer Science, Volume 3762, pages 809 - 815, 2005.
5. P. Ceravolo, A. Corallo, E. Damiani, G. Elia, M. Viviani, and A. Zilli: "Bottom-up extraction and maintenance of ontology-based metadata". Fuzzy Logic and the Semantic Web, Computer Intelligence, Elsevier, 2006.
6. E. Damiani, M.C. Nocerino, M. Viviani: "Knowledge extraction from an XML data flow: building a taxonomy based on clustering technique". Current Issues in Data and Knowledge Engineering, Proceedings of EUROFUSE 2004: 8th Meeting of the EURO Working Group on Fuzzy Sets, pages 133-142, 2004.
7. T. K. Landauer, P. W. Foltz, & D. Laham: "Introduction to Latent Semantic Analysis". Discourse Processes, 25, pages 259-284, 1998.
8. G. Salton. and C. Buckley: "Term Weighting Approaches in Automatic Text Retrieval". Technical Report. UMI Order Number: TR87-881., Cornell University. 1987,
9. G. Salton, A. Singhal, C. Buckley and M. Mitra: "Automatic Text Decomposition Using Text Segments and Text Themes". Conference on Hypertext, pages 53-65, 1996.

Towards Semantic Interoperability of Protein Data Sources

Amandeep S. Sidhu[1], Tharam S. Dillon[1], and Elizabeth Chang[2]

[1] Faculty of Information Technology, University of Technology, Sydney, Australia
{asidhu, tharam}@it.uts.edu.au
[2] School of Information Systems, Curtin University of Technical University, Perth, Australia
Elizabeth.Chang@cbs.curtin.edu.au

Abstract. Several approaches for data interoperation identified by Karp have been implemented for biological databases. We extend Karp's approach for interoperation not only to protein databases but also to knowledge bases and other information sources. This paper outlines algebra for protein data source composition based on our existing work of Protein Ontology (PO). In this paper we consider the case of establishing correspondence between various protein data sources using semantic relationships over the conceptual framework of PO. Here we provide specific set of relationships over PO framework to cover data semantics for integrating data information from diverse protein data sources. These relationships help in defining semantic query algebra for PO to efficiently reason and query the instance store.

1 Introduction

Structural Bioinformatics represents the subset that deals, directly or indirectly, with structure of macromolecules. Structural Bioinformatics includes study of structures of DNA, RNA and Proteins. Knowledge of protein structures gives us a bird's-eye view of protein fold space, and is helpful to understand the evolutionary principles behind structure, which architectures and topologies are observed (and why), which topologies are prevalent or avoided, and how structure of protein affects its function. It can be useful to organize protein resources in structural bioinformatics along the following lines. The structural information about protein molecules – the 3D atomic coordinates of structures – is the core from which all other details are derived; it is a primary resource of structural data and is central to everything else. The files containing atomic coordinates are uninformative to the majority of structural biologists; thus, there are algorithmic tools (applications) that transform, classify, analyse, and model this primary data. The results of the data analysis are often (but not always) stored in other databases, considered to be secondary resources, since they contain value-added information.

Several approaches for data interoperation identified by Karp (Karp, 1996) have been implemented for biological databases. We extend Karp's approach for interoperation not only to protein databases but also to knowledge bases and other information sources. This paper outlines algebra for protein data source composition

R. Meersman, Z. Tari, P. Herrero et al. (Eds.): OTM Workshops 2006, LNCS 4278, pp. 1835–1843, 2006.

based on our existing work of Protein Ontology (Sidhu et al., 2006c, Sidhu et al., 2006a, Sidhu et al., 2006b, Sidhu et al., 2005a, Sidhu et al., 2005b, Sidhu et al., 2004). Protein Ontology (PO) provides integration of heterogeneous protein and biological data sources. PO converts the enormous amounts of data collected by geneticists and molecular biologists into information that scientists, physicians and other health care professionals and researchers can use to easily understand the mapping of relationships inside protein molecules, interaction between two protein molecules and interactions between protein and other macromolecules at cellular level. In this paper we consider the case of establishing correspondence between various protein data sources using semantic relationships over the conceptual framework of PO. The proposed approach enables semi-automatic interoperation among heterogeneous protein data sources. We establish application-specific rules - rules that establish correspondence between concepts in different data sources using structured vocabulary of ontology semi-automatically. The contributions of this work are: (1) Articulation is provided using a pre-defined set of Semantic Relationships, and (2) Query optimisation is enabled based on query algebra.

The rest of the paper is organized as follows. After discussing problem of heterogeneity in Section 2, we discuss related works in Section 3. In Section 4 we describe PO common conceptual model that we use for resolving heterogeneity in protein data sources. In Section 5 we discuss PO Algebra for query composition. Section 6 concludes the paper.

2 Problem of Heterogeneity

Most biological resources available today on the web provide a good number of cross-links to other resources with relevant information. However, in our opinion, what is still lacking is an integrated view that provides complete coverage of information through single entry point. The main problems lie in interpreting biological nomenclature because the underlying data sources are inconsistent.

Creators of biological data sources use data descriptors with specific intended meanings in their own contexts. We will refer to this meaning as semantics of data descriptors throughout the chapter. Semantic Heterogeneity arises because different biological data sources have different vocabularies and semantics. Different creators use the same term with different meanings. Thus, the semantics of information from different data sources is different. Very often, two different data sources use the same term but associate different meanings to it, while different terms are used in two protein data sources to mean the same thing. Often, creators of protein data sources differ on how to classify objects. Creator of a protein data source structures the information in the source such that the interests of the creator and the immediate community are best satisfied. The creator is less concerned about the use of the protein data source by a secondary system or community that uses the information since catering to the needs of such a system or community is outside the scope of the creator's responsibilities.

Often, the authors of protein data sources use the same term to denote multiple meanings. Even if not entirely different, the scope of the intended meaning of a term differs. For example, the term *gene in* SWISS-PROT refers to gene name of specifying origin of the protein; whereas *gene in* Online Mendelian Inheritance in Man (McKusick, 1998) refers to a gene name, or to an isoform (i.e. similar gene name). In order for a researcher to compose information obtained from the SWISS-PROT and that obtained from the OMIM, one has to be cognizant of the differences of scope of the term gene as used by the two different protein data sources. The composer needs to know the exact specification of the semantics of the terms used in the different protein data sources used by different organizations to differentiate between the overlapping semantics of terms and avoid mismatch-related inconsistencies.

3 Related Work

In this section we will discuss various biomedical ontology works related to Protein Ontology. Gene Ontology (Ashburner et al., 2001) defines a hierarchy of terms related to genome annotation. GO is a structured network consisting of defined terms and relationships that describe Molecular Functions, Biological Processes, and Cellular Components of Genes. GO is clearly defined and modelled for numerous other biological ontology projects (Lewis, 2004). So far GO has been used to describe the genes of several model organisms *(Saccharomyces cerevisiae, Drosophila melanogaster, Mus musculus and others)*.

RiboWEB (Altman et al., 1999) is an online data resource for Ribosome, a vital cellular apparatus. It contains a large knowledge base of relevant published data and computational modules that can process this data to test hypotheses about ribosome's structure. The system is built around the concept of ontology. Diverse types of data taken principally from published journal articles is represented using a set of templates in the knowledge base, and the data is linked to each other with numerous connections.

Protein Data Bank (PDB) has recently released versions of the PDB Exchange Dictionary and the PDB archival files in XML format collectively named PDBML (Westbrook et al., 2005). The representation of PDB data in XML builds from content of PDB Exchange Dictionary, both for assignment of data item names and defining data organization. PDB Exchange and XML Representations use same logical data organization. A side effect of maintaining a logical correspondence with PDB Exchange representation is that PDBML lack the hierarchical structure characteristic of XML data.

PRONTO (Mani et al., 2004) is a directed acyclic graph (DAG) based ontology induction tool that constructs a protein ontology including protein names found in MEDLINE abstracts and in UNIPROT. It is a typical example typical example of text mining the literature and the data sources. It can't be classified as protein ontology as it only represents relationship between protein literatures and does not formalize knowledge about protein synthesis process. Ontology for Protein Domain must contain terms or concepts relevant to protein synthesis, describing Protein Sequence, Structure and Function and relationships between them. While defining PO we made an effort to emulate the protein synthesis and describe concepts and relationships describing it.

There is a still a need for more agreed-upon semantical standard to describe protein data. PO addresses this issue by providing clear and unambiguous definitions of all major biological concepts of protein synthesis process and relationship between them. PO provides a unified controlled vocabulary both for annotation data types and for annotation data.

4 PO Common Conceptual Model

We need to resolve the heterogeneity among protein data sources to enable meaningful data exchange or interoperation among them. The two major sources of heterogeneity among the sources are as follows: First, different sources use different conceptual models and modelling languages to represent their data and meta-data. Second, sources using the same conceptual model differ in their semantics. The proposed system uses a common PO format, which we have described in (Sidhu et al., 2006c). The proposed system first converts all external protein data sources to common PO format and then resolves the semantic heterogeneity among the protein data sources that we seek to articulate. (Melnik, 2000) have shown how to convert information sources and different classes of conceptual models into those using one common format.

Information sources were, are, and will be modelled using different conceptual models. We do not foresee the creation of a de facto standard conceptual model that will be used by all protein data sources. On the other hand, we need use a common PO format for our internal representation. PO format uses all relevant protein data sources. The sources include new proteome information resources like PDB (Bernstein et al., 1977, Weissig and Bourne, 2002, Wesbrook et al., 2002), SCOP (Murzin et al., 1995), and RESID (Garavelli, 2003) as well as classical sources of information where information is maintained in a knowledge base of scientific text files like OMIM (McKusick, 1998) and from various published scientific literature in various journals.

4.1 Graph Oriented Model

Our common conceptual model for the internal representation of PO is based on the work done by (Gyssens et al., 1990). In its core, we represent protein ontology as a graph. Formally, an ontology $O = (G, R)$ is represented as a directed labelled graph G and a set of rules R. The graph $G = (N, E)$ comprises a finite set of nodes N and a finite set of edges E. The label of a node is given by a non-null string. In the context of protein ontology, the label is often represents a concept defined in protein ontology. The label of an edge is the name of a semantic relationship among the concepts in protein ontology and can be null if the relationship is not known. The set of logical rules R, associated with protein ontology, are rules expressed in a logic-based language used to derive data from existing protein data and information sources.

4.2 Semantic Relationships

Semantics in protein data is normally not interpreted by annotating systems, since they are not aware of the specific structural, chemical and cellular interactions of protein complexes. Protein Ontology Framework provides specific set of rules to cover these application specific semantics. The rules use only the relationships whose semantics are predefined to establish correspondence among terms in PO. The set of relationships with predefined semantics is: *{SubClassOf, PartOf, AttributeOf, InstanceOf, and ValueOf}*. Some of these relationships (like SubClassOf, InstanceOf) are somewhat similar to those in RDF Schema. The following is a description of the set of pre-defined semantic relationships in our common PO conceptual model.

✓ **SubClassOf:** The relationship is used to indicate that one concept is a subclass of another concept, for instance: *SourceCell SubClassOf FunctionalDomains*. That is any instance of *SourceCell* class is also instance of *FunctionalDomains* class. All attributes of *FunctionalDomains* class *(_FuncDomain_Family, _FuncDomain_SuperFamily)* are also the attributes of *SourceCell* class. The relationship SubClassOf is transitive.

✓ **AttrributeOf:** This relationship indicates that a concept is an attribute of another concept, for instance: *_FuncDomain_Family AttributeOf Family*. This relationship also referred as *PropertyOf*, has same semantics as in object-relational databases.

✓ **PartOf:** This relationship indicates that a concept is a part of another concept, for instance: *Chain PartOf ATOMSequence* indicates that *Chain* concept describing various residue sequences in a protein is a part of definition of concept *ATOMSequence* for that protein.

✓ **InstanceOf:** This relationship indicates that an object is an instance of the class, for instance: *ATOMSequenceInstance_10 InstanceOf ATOMSequence* indicates that *ATOMSequenceInstance_10* is an instance of class *ATOMSequence*.

✓ **ValueOf:** This relationship is used to indicate the value of an attribute of an object, for instance: *"Homo Sapiens" ValueOf OrganismScientific*. The concept, in turn has an edge, for instance: *OrganismScientific AttributeOf Molecule*, from the object *(Molecule)* it describes.

4.3 Sequences

By itself semantic relationships described above, does not impose concept hierarchy or order in Protein Ontology. In applications using Protein Sequences, the ability of expressing the order is paramount. Generally Protein Sequences are a collection of chains of sequence of residues, and that is the format Protein Sequences have been represented until now using various data representations and data mining techniques for bioinformatics. In PO a special semantic relationship: *Sequence(s)* is used to describe order. Complex concepts are defined as Sequences of simpler generic concepts defined in PO. Simple concepts are defined as Sequences of object and data type properties defining them. The following sections provide a description of the set of sequences defined in PO conceptual framework.

Sequences defining PO Structure Concepts
PO defines a complex concept of *ATOMSequence* describing three dimensional structure of protein complex as a combination of simple concepts of *Chains, Residues, and Atoms* as: *ATOMSequence Sequence (Chains Sequence (Residues Sequence (Atoms)))*. Simple concepts defining ATOMSequence are defined as: *Chains Sequence (ChainID, ChainName, ChainProperty); Residues Sequence (ResidueID, ResidueName, ResidueProperty); and Atoms Sequence (AtomID, Atom, ATOMResSeqNum, X, Y, Z, Occupancy, TempratureFactor, Element)*.

Sequences defining PO Structural Domain Concepts
PO defines three complex concepts that describe the structural folds and domains of Helices, Sheets and Turns in a protein complex. Helices of a Protein Complex are defined using relationship of Sequence as: *Helices Sequence (Helix Sequence*

(HelixStrucure)). The concepts of Helix and HelixStructure are defined as: *Helix Sequence (HelixID, HelixNumber, HelixClass, HelixLength); and HelixStructure Sequence (HelixChain, IntialResidue, IntialReqSeqNum, EndResidue, EndReqSeqNum).* HelixChain, IntialResidue, and EndResidue are object properties of concepts Chains and Residues defined earlier. Similarly the Complex Concepts of Sheets and Turns in a protein complex are defined as: *Sheets Sequence (Sheet Sequence (Strands)); and Turns Sequence (Turn Sequence (TurnStructure)).*

Sequences defining PO Structural Domain Concepts

PO defines complex concepts of DisulphideBond, CISPeptide, HydrogenBond, ResidueLink, and SaltBridge describing chemical bonds in a protein complex. Chemical Bonds that have Binding Residue use the generic concept of Bind while defining chemical bonds using Sequence relationship, for instance: *DisulphideBond Sequence (BindChain1, BindResidue1, BindResSeqNum1, BindChain2, BindResidue2, and BindResSeqNum2).* Similarly the Chemical Bonds that have Binding Atoms use the generic concept of AtomicBind, for instance: *HydrogenBond Sequence (AtomicBindChain1, AtomicBindResidue1, AtomicBindResSeqNum1, AtomicBindAtom1, AtomicBindChain2, AtomicBindResidue2, AtomicBin-dResSeqNum2, and AtomicBindAtom2).* BindChain, AtomicBindChain, BindResidue, AtomicBindResidue, and AtomicBindAtom are object properties of concepts Chains, Residues, and Atoms defined earlier.

The PO common conceptual model is used to bring protein data sources to a common PO format – so that semantic interoperability can be established for effective query composition and optimization. PO common conceptual model helps in translating data descriptors of diverse protein data source formats. Using PO common conceptual model described here, data descriptors in one protein data model are matched with data descriptors in other data models carrying similar semantic messages. We will resolve heterogeneity with respect to existing protein data models and modelling languages by building wrappers that convert data formats using PO common conceptual to our PO format. In next section we propose protein ontology algebra that allows effective query performance and analysis.

5 Protein Ontology Algebra

The key to scalability of PO conceptual model is the systematic and effective composition of data and information. In this section, we present PO ontology algebra that allows composition of multiple levels of information stored in the ontology for information retrieval. By retaining a log of composition process, we can also, with minimal adaptations, replay the composition whenever any of the underlying data sources that PO integrates change. The algebra has one unary operator: *Select, and three binary operations: Intersection, Union and Difference.* More comprehensive generic definitions of unary and binary can be found in (R., Rajugan, 2006, Wouters et al., 2006).

5.1 Select Operator

The Select Operator allows us to highlight and select portions of the PO that are relevant to query at hand. Given the PO structure and a concept to be selected, the select operator selects the sub tree rooted at that concept. Given the PO structure and a set of concepts, the select operator selects only those edges in the PO that connect nodes in a given set. Select Operator is defined as:

$OS = \sigma(NS, ES, RS)$ where
$NS = Nodes\ (condition = true)$
$ES = Edges\ (\forall N \in NS)$

5.2 Intersection Operation

Intersection is the most important and interesting binary operation. Let $O1 = (N1, E1, R1)$, and $O2 = (N2, E2, R2)$ be the two parts of PO whose composition will provide answer to the query submitted by the user. Here N is the set of nodes or concepts of PO, E is the set of edges or the PO hierarchy, and R is set of Semantic Relationships (defined in Section 4). The intersection of two parts of PO with respect to semantic relationships (SR) of PO (defined in Section 4.2) is:

$OI\ (1, 2) = O1\ \cap_{SR} O2 = (NI, EI, RI)$, where
$NI = Nodes\ (SR\ (O1, O2))$,
$EI = Edges\ (E1, NI \cap N1) + Edges\ (E2, NI \cap N2) + Edges\ (SR\ (O1, O2))$, and
$RI = Relationships\ (O1, NI \cap N1) + Relationships\ (O2, NI \cap N2) + SR\ (O1, O2) - Edges\ (SR\ (O1, O2))$.

Note that SR is different from R, as it does not include sequences. The nodes in the intersection ontology are those nodes that appear in the semantic relationships, SR. The edges in the intersection ontology are the edges among nodes that are either present in the source parts of the ontology or have been established as a semantic relationship, SR. Relationships in the intersection ontology are the relationships that have not been already been modelled as edges and those relationships present in source parts of the ontology that use only concepts that occur in intersection ontology.

5.3 Union Operation

The union of two parts of PO, $O1 = (N1, E1, R1)$, and $O2 = (N2, E2, R2)$ with respect to semantic relationships (SR) of PO (SR in Section 4.2) is expressed as:

$OI\ (1, 2) = O1\ \cup_{SR} O2 = (NU, EU, RU)$, where,
$NU = N1\ \cup N2\ \cup NI\ (1, 2)$,
$EU = E1\ \cup E2\ \cup EI\ (1, 2)$, and
$RU = R1\ \cup R2\ \cup RI\ (1, 2)$, where,
$OI\ (1, 2) = O1\ \cap_{SR} O2 = (NI\ (1, 2), EI\ (1, 2), RI\ (1, 2))$ is the intersection of two ontologies.

The union operation combines two parts of the ontology retaining only one copy of the concepts in the intersection.

5.4 Difference Operation

The difference of two parts of PO, O1 and O2, written as $O1 - O2$, includes portions of the first part that are not common to the second part. The difference can be rewritten as $O1 - (O1\ \cap_{SR} O2)$. The nodes, edges and relationships that are not in intersection but are present in the first part comprise the difference. One of the objectives of computing the difference is to optimise the maintenance of PO. As the PO instance store is huge and so many people add instances to it, difference will suggest that instances are not entered properly or there is change in underlying data sources that PO integrates. Change suggested by difference is forwarded to the administrator. If the change happens to be in difference between structures of parts considered, then it does not occur in intersection and is not related to any semantic relationships that establish bridged between the parts of the ontology. Therefore Semantic Relationships do not need to be changed. If the changes is because of changes happened to underlying data sources that PO integrates, then set of concepts and semantic relationships need to be checked for any changes required to remove the difference.

6 Concluding Remarks

In this paper first we present an overview of common conceptual representation of PO that is needed to resolve the heterogeneity among protein data sources to enable meaningful data exchange or interoperation among them. Next we discussed semantic relationships in protein data that interprets semantics that is normally not interpreted by annotating systems, since they are not aware of the specific structural, chemical and cellular interactions of protein complexes. We also discussed sequence relationships that impose order among the children of the nodes. We also covered in the paper PO ontology algebra that allows composition of multiple levels of information stored in the ontology for information retrieval. The PO approach supports precise composition of information from multiple diverse sources providing semantic relationships between among such sources. This approach allows reliable exploitation of protein information sources without any imposition on sources themselves. PO algebra based on semantic relationships allows systematic composition, which unlike integration is more scalable.

References

ALTMAN, R. B., BADA, M., CHAI, X. J., CARILLO, M. W., CHEN, R. O. & ABERNETHY, N. F. (1999) RiboWeb: An Ontology-Based System for Collaborative Molecular Biology. *IEEE Intelligent Systems,* 14, 68-76.

ASHBURNER, M., BALL, C. A., BLAKE, J. A., BUTLER, H., CHERRY, J. C., CORRADI, J. & DOLINSKI, K. (2001) Creating the Gene Ontology Resource: Design and Implementation. *Genome Research,* 11, 1425-1433.

BAIROCH, A. & APWEILER, R. (1997) The SWISS-PROT protein sequence data bank and its supplement TrEMBL. *Nucleic Acids Research,* 25, 31-36.

BERNSTEIN, F. C., KOETZLE, T. F., WILLIAMS, G. J., MEYER, E. F., BRICE, M. D., RODGERS, J. R., KENNARD, O., SHIMANOUCHI, T. & TASUMI, M. (1977) The Protein Data Bank: a computer-based archival file for macromolecular structures. *Journal of Molecular Biology,* 112, 535-542.

BOECKMANN, B., BAIROCH, A., R., A., BLATTER, M., ESTREICHER, A., GASTEIGER, E., MARTIN, M. J., MICHOUD, K., DONOVAN, C., PHAN, I., PILBOUT, S. & SCHNEIDER, M. (2003) The SWISS-PROT protein knowledgebase and its supplement TrEMBL in 2003. *Nucleic Acids Research,* 31, 365-370.

GARAVELLI, J. S. (2003) The RESID Database of Protein Modifications: 2003 developments. *Nucleic Acids Research,* 31, 499-501.

GYSSENS, M., PAREDAENS, P. & GUCHT, D. (1990) A graph-oriented object database model. *9th ACM SIGACT-SIGMOD-SIGART symposium on Principles of database systems.* Nashville, Tennessee, ACM Press.

KARP, P. D. (1996) A strategy for database interoperation. *Journal of Computational Biology,* 2, 573-583.

LEWIS, S. E. (2004) Gene Ontology: looking backwards and forwards. *Genome Biology,* 6, 103.1-103.4.

MANI, I., HU, Z. & HU, W. (2004) PRONTO: A Large-scale Machine-induced Protein Ontology. *2nd Standards and Ontologies for Functional Genomics Conference (SOFG 2004).* UK.

MCKUSICK, V. A. (1998) *Mendelian Inheritance in Man. A Catalog of Human Genes and Genetic Disorders,* Baltimore, Johns Hopkins University Press.

MELNIK, S. (2000) Declarative mediation in distributed systems. *19th International Conference on Conceptual Modeling (ER 2000).* Salt Lake City, Utah, Springer.

MURZIN, A. G., BRENNER, S. E., HUBBARD, T. & CHOTHIA, C. (1995) SCOP: A Structural Classification of Proteins Database for the Investigation of Sequences and Structures. *Journal of Molecular Biology,* 247, 536-540.

R., RAJUGAN (2006) "A Layered View Model for XML with Conceptual and Logical Extension, and its Applications," Faculty of Information Technology, University of Technology, Sydney (UTS), Australia, Sydney, PhD thesis. pp. 460.

SIDHU, A. S., DILLON, T. S. & CHANG, E. (2005a) Ontological Foundation for Protein Data Models. *1st IFIP WG 2.12 & WG 12.4 International Workshop on Web Semantics (SWWS 2005), In conjunction with On The Move Federated Conferences (OTM 2005).* Agia Napa, Cyprus, Springer.

SIDHU, A. S., DILLON, T. S. & CHANG, E. (2005b) An Ontology for Protein Data Models. *27th Annual International Conference of the IEEE Engineering in Medicine and Biology Society 2005 (IEEE EMBC 2005).* Shanghai, China, IEEE Press.

SIDHU, A. S., DILLON, T. S. & CHANG, E. (2006a) Advances in Protein Ontology Project. *19th IEEE International Symposium on Computer-Based Medical Systems (CBMS 2006).* Salt Lake City, Utah, IEEE CS Press.

SIDHU, A. S., DILLON, T. S. & CHANG, E. (2006b) Integration of Protein Data Sources through PO. *17th International Conference on Database and Expert Systems Applications (DEXA 2006).* Poland, Spinger.

SIDHU, A. S., DILLON, T. S. & CHANG, E. (2006c) Protein Ontology: Data Integration using Protein Ontology. IN MA, Z. & CHEN, J. Y. (Eds.) *Database Modeling in Biology: Practices and Challenges.* New York, Springer.

SIDHU, A. S., DILLON, T. S., SIDHU, B. S. & SETIAWAN, H. (2004) A Unified Representation of Protein Structure Databases. IN REDDY, M. S. & KHANNA, S. (Eds.) *Biotechnological Approaches for Sustainable Development.* India, Allied Publishers.

WEISSIG, H. & BOURNE, P. E. (2002) Protein structure resources. *Biological Crystallography,* D58, 908-915.

WESBROOK, J., FENG, Z., JAIN, S., BHAT, T. N., THANKI, N., RAVICHANDRAN, V., GILLILAND, G. L., BLUHM, W. F., WEISSIG, H., GREER, D. S., BOURNE, P. E. & BERMAN, H. M. (2002) The Protein Data Bank: unifying the archive. *Nucleic Acids Research,* 30, 245-248.

WESTBROOK, J., ITO, N., NAKAMURA, H., HENRICK, K. & BERMAN, H. M. (2005) PDBML: the representation of archival macromolecular structure data in XML. *Bioinformatics,* 21, 988-992.

WOUTERS, C., RAJUGAN, R., DILLON, T. S. and RAHAYU, J. W. (2006) "Ontology Extraction Using Views for Semantic Web," in Web Semantics and Ontology, D. Taniar and W. Rahayu, Eds. USA: Idea Group Publishing, 2006, pp. 01 - 40.

QP-T: Query Pattern-Based RDB-to-XML Translation*

Jinhyung Kim[1], Dongwon Jeong[2], Yixin Jing[1], and Doo-Kwon Baik[1]

Dept. of Computer Science and Engineering, Korea University,
1, 5 ga, Anam dong, Sungbuk gu, Seoul, Republic of Korea
{koolmania, jing, baik}@software.korea.ac.kr
Dept. of Informatics and Statistics, Kunsan National University
San 68, Miryong dong, Kunsan, Jollabuk do, Republic of Korea
djeong@kunsan.ac.kr

Abstract. This paper proposes a new query pattern-based relational schema-to-XML schema translation (QP-T) algorithm to resolve implicit referential integrity issue. Various translation methods have been introduced on structural aspects and/or semantic aspects. However, most of conventional methods consider only explicit referential integrities specified in relational schema. It causes several problems such as incorrect transformation, abnormal relational model transition, and so on. The QP-T algorithm analyzes query pattern and extract implicit referential integrities through equi-join between columns. The QP-T algorithm is based on a concept that columns related to equi-join in relational schema can have referential integrity. The most distinct contribution of QP-T algorithm is to enhance extraction of referential integrity relation information for translation. Therefore, the QP-T algorithm reflects not only explicit referential integrities but also implicit referential integrities during RDB-to-XML translation. The QP-T algorithm also prevents XML documents from incorrect conversion and increase translation accuracy.

Keywords: Relational Schema Model, Query Pattern, XML Shema Model, Referential Integrity Relation Information.

1 Introduction

With XML emerging as the data format of the Internet era, there is a considerable increase in the amount of data encoded in XML [1, 2]. However, the majority of data is still stored and maintained in relational database [3]. Therefore, we need to translate such relational data into XML document. In RDB-to-XML translation, there is a problem which is particularly complex when old, ill-designed and poorly documented applications are addressed.

Various translation algorithms have been developed on structural aspects and/or semantic aspects. Generally, we can classify conventional algorithms into 3 categories; Manual structural algorithm, automatic structural algorithm, and semantic algorithm. FT, NeT, CoT, and ConvRel algorithm is typical algorithms for RDB-to-XML translation [5, 12, 13, 18]. However, conventional algorithms just consider syntax part

---

* This research is supported by BK(Brain Korea)21.

R. Meersman, Z. Tari, P. Herrero et al. (Eds.): OTM Workshops 2006, LNCS 4278, pp. 1844–1853, 2006.
© Springer-Verlag Berlin Heidelberg 2006

or restricted semantic part during translation. To solve this problem, the implicit referential integrity issue should be considered over the conversion.

Researches about syntactic/semantic structure reconstruction also have been introduced in reverse-engineering part [20, 21, 22]. The CASE tool [20] can help analysis of structure for database reconstructing. A [21] proposes a method for extracting an entity relationship schema by using node rules, link rules, and refinement rules. However, because there are too many rules for reconstruction, these methods are not effective to RDB-to-XML translation.

In this paper, we propose a new RDB-to-XML translation algorithm considering the implicit referential integrity relations. The QP-T algorithm analyzes user query pattern stored in DBMS and extracts implicit referential integrity relations by using equi-join property [4].

2   Translation Models

In this section, we define models to describe translation from a relational schema to a XML schema.

Definition 1 (Initial Relational Database Schema Model). A initial relational schema model is denoted by 5-tuple $R_{input} = (T, C, P, RI_{exp}, Q_p K)$, where

> ➤   T is a finite set of table names
> ➤   C is a function which represents a set of column names in each table
> ➤   P is a function which represents properties of each column and the result of P consists of 3-tuples:
>> ✓   t represents data type of column such as integer, string, etc
>> ✓   u represents unique or not of column value by u(unique, ~u(not unique)
>> ✓   n represents nullable or not of values of colunn by n(nullable), !n(not nullable)
> ➤ RI_{exp} represents explicit referential integrities information
> ➤ Q_p represents query pattern of users
> ➤   K is a function which represents primary key information

The output relation schema model is mid-output of QP-T algorithm.

Definition 2 (Output Relational Schema Model). A relational schema model with implicit referential integrity relations are denoted by a 6-tuples $R_{output} = (R, C, P, RI_{exp}, RI_{imp-Q}, K)$, where

> ➤ RI_{imp-Q} represents implicit referential integrities information extracted by the QP-T algorithm

The XML schema model is used as the output of the QP-T algorithm.

Definition 3 (XML Schema Model). A XML schema model is denoted by 4-tuples $X_{schema} = (R_{input}, R_{output}, OP_{generation}, X_{doc})$, where

> ➤ $OP_{generation}$ is a set of operations to create XML data with structure and explicit semantic constraints used by conventional translation methods including the extracted implicit relations.
> ➤ X_{doc} is the final result, XML data set translated by the QP-T algorithm

3 Translation Procedure

3.1 QP-T Algorithm

The QP-T algorithm consists of four steps. The first step is syntactic/semantic error checking step. We check queries received from DBMS by using SQL parsing rules. If there is some error in quires, we can request quires to DBMS again. The second step

Table 1. QP-T Algorithm

Input: An array of quires (QueryList). Array of query list is represented as $Q_L[]$. Array of tokenized query list is represented as $Q_T[]$. Array of where clause is represented as $Q_{WH}[]$.   **Mid Output**: An array of candidate for implicit referential integrities extracted by QP-T algorithm ($RI_{can-Q}[]$)   **Output**: An array of implicit referential integrities extracted by QP-T algorithm ($RI_{imp-Q}[]$)
Procedure :   1. **Initialize** a=1, b=1, c=1, d=1, g=1, n=1, m=1, j=1   2. **Do while** $b<b_{(max)}$ 3. $Q_L[a]$ = **GetQueryList**(b)   4.   **increment** a,b   5. **For** c=1 to $c_{(max)}$ 6.   **For** d=1 to $d_{(max)}$ 7. $Q_T[c][d]$ = **GetToken** ($Q_L[c]$, d)   8.   **Next** d   9. **Next** c   10. **For** c=1 to $c_{(max)}$ 11.   **For** d=1 to $d_{(max)}$ 12.   **if** ($Q_T[c][d]$ = 'where')   13.   **For** n=1 to $n_{(max)}$ 14. $Q_{WH}[c][n]$ = $Q_T[c][d+n]$ 15.   **Next** n   16.   **Next** d   17. **Next** c   18. **For** g=1 to $g_{(max)}$ 19.   **For** j=1 to $j_{(max)}$ 20.   **if** ($Q_{WH}[g][j]$ = '=')   21.   **For** m=1 to $m_{(max)}$ 22. $RI_{can-Q}[m]$ = ($Q_{WH}[g][j-3]$. $Q_{WH}[g][j-1]$,$Q_{WH}[g][j+1]$. $Q_{WH}[g][j+3]$)   23.   **Next** m   24.   **Next** j   25. **Next** g   26. **Initialize** k=2, t=1   27. RI[1] = $RI_{can-Q}[1]$ 28. **Do while** $k<k_{(max)}$ 29.   **For** t=1 to $t_{(max)}$ 30.   **if** $RI_{imp-Q}[k]$ = $RI_{can-Q}[t]$ 31.   **Increment** p   32.   **else** RI[k] = $RI_{can-Q}[t]$ 33.   **End if**   34. **Increment** k   35. **Loop**   **End procedure**

is new resource generation step. We extract 'where' clause from each query and use these as new resource for query analysis. The third step is query analysis step. We analyze new resources and extract columns related to equi-join. The fourth step is refinement step. Finally, we refine column list extracted at the third step and select implicit referential integrity relation.

3.2 Translation Procedure

In this chapter, we describe translation procedure from RDB to XML schema model through relational database example. This relational database consists of Student (SID, Sname, PID, Cname), Professor (Pname, Office), Class (Cname, Room, Time), and Project (Projname, SID, PID). Each student can take one or more classes and each professor can teach one or more students. The office column of the professor table can null value. Each project is related to one or more students and professors.

First of all, we translate RDB into the initial relational schema model. A Fig. 1 shows the initial relational schema model.

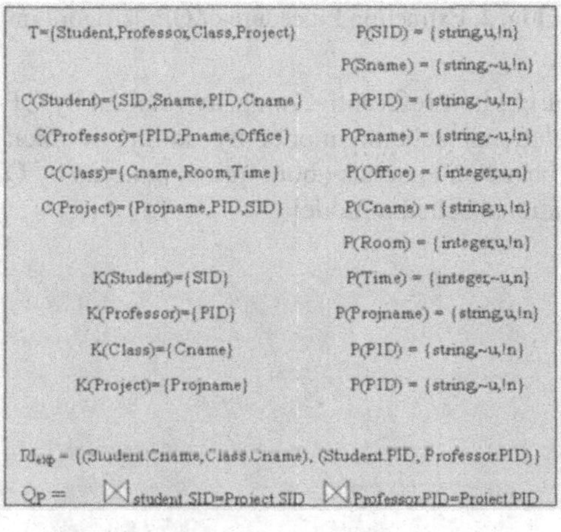

Fig. 1. Initial Relational Schema Model

Because the initial relational database schema model does not include implicit referential integrity relation information, we must extract by QP-T algorithm. Fig. 2 represents extraction procedure of the QP-T algorithm. First, we get query list from the shared SQL area in DBMS and store queries in query stack (array). Second, we extract 'where' clause from queries and store them in where clause stack (array). We create new resource for analysis of user query patter through the second step. Third, we analyzes where clause stack (array) and extract columns related to equi-join. Finally, we select implicit referential integrity relation as pair form from join stack (array). According to general properties of equi-join, if some columns are related to equi-join, those columns have close relationship such as foreign key constraint.

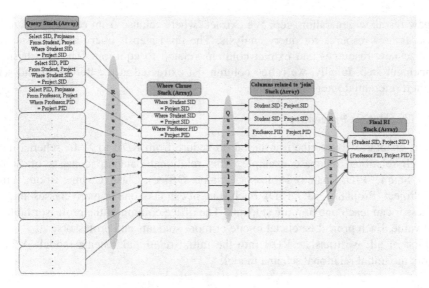

Fig. 2. Extraction Procedure of QP-T Algorithm

After extraction of implicit referential integrity relation by QP-T algorithm, we can create the output relational schema model by adding implicit referential integrity relation information based on analysis about quires patterns by QP-T algorithm. Fig. 3 shows the output relational schema model.

T={Student,Professor,Class,Project}	P(SID) = {string,u,!n}
	P(Sname) = {string,~u,!n}
C(Student)={SID,Sname,PID,Cname}	P(PID) = {string,~u,!n}
C(Professor)={PID,Pname,Office}	P(Pname) = {string,~u,!n}
C(Class)={Cname,Room,Time}	P(Office) = {integer,u,n}
C(Project)={Projname,PID,SID}	P(Cname) = {string,u,!n}
	P(Room) = {integer,u,!n}
K(Student)={SID}	P(Time) = {integer,~u,n}
K(Professor)={PID}	P(Projname) = {string,u,!n}
K(Class)={Cname}	P(PID) = {string,~u,!n}
K(Project)={Projname}	P(PID) = {string,~u,!n}

RI$_{exp}$ = {(Student.Cname,Class.Cname), (Student.PID, Professor.PID)}}
RI$_{imp-Q}$ = {(Student.SID, Project.SID), (Professor.PID, Project.PID)}

Fig. 3. Output Relational Schema Model

We translate the output relational schema model by referring explicit referential integrity relation information and implicit referential integrity relation information into XML document. We create a XML document by element information of the translation model. The final XML document includes not only explicit referential integrity relation information but also implicit referential integrity relation information. Fig. 4 shows the XML document as a final result of translation.

```
<!ELEMENT Student (SID, Sname)>
<!ATTLIST Student ID_Student ID>
<!ATTLIST Student Ref_Class IDREF>
<! ELEMENT Professor (PID, Pname, Office?, Student*, Project*)>
<!ELEMENT Class (Cname, Room, Time)>
<!ATTLIST Class ID_Class ID>
<!ELEMENT Project (Projname)>
<!ATTLIST Project Ref_Student IDREF>
```

Fig. 4. XML Document

4   Comparison Evaluation

4.1 Translated XML Documents

The NeT algorithm can remove redundancy by using nesting operators such as '*', '+'[11]. However, the NeT algorithm does not consider referential integrity relation and the translated XML document by the NeT algorithm cannot reflect semantic information of initial relational database exactly. The CoT algorithm can reflect explicit referential integrity relation information. The translated XML document by the CoT algorithm considers referential integrity relation information defined at the RI_{exp}. Thus, the CoT algorithm cannot guarantee referential integrity relation information defined implicitly. The translated XML document by the QP-T algorithm reflects not only explicit referential integrity relation information but also implicit referential

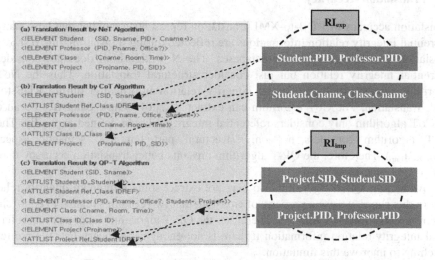

Fig. 5. Translated XML Documents by Various Algorithms

integrity relation information. Because we can extract referential integrity relation information defined implicitly by analysis of query patterns and reflect all information of initial relational database to XML document during RDB-to-XML translation. Translated XML documents by NeT, CoT, and the QP-T algorithm are as in Fig. 5.

4.2 Experimental Data

For performance evaluation of the QP-T algorithm, we use a MS Access Northwind Sample Database, a TPC-H sample schema v1.2.0 [19], and Oracle Business Database Sample Schema. The MS Access Northwind Sample Database consists of 9 tables, 87 columns, and 7 foreign key constraints. The TPC-h sample schema v.1.2.0 consists of 8 table, 59 columns, and 8 foreign key constraints. These 2 sample database is simple and small database for scholar experiment but Oracle Business Database Sample Schema is practical database which consists of 24 tables, 122 columns, and 37 referential integrities about goods selling, order, and human resource management.

Table 2. Experimental Data

Sample \ Item	T	C	RI_{all}	RI_{exp}	RI_{imp}	RI_{query}
MS Access NorthWind	9	87	7	2	5	3
TPC-H Sample Schema	8	59	8	2	6	4
Oracle Business Sample Schema	24	122	37	24	13	11

T: Table, C: Column, RI_{all}: All RI relation, RI_{exp}: Explicit RI relation, RI_{imp}: Implicit RI relation, RI_{query}: Implicit RI relation which we can extract by query pattern analysis

4.3 Translation Accuracy

Translation accuracy of RDB-to-XML translation represents a number that how many referential integrity relation informations are reflected during translation. Fig. 6 shows translation accuracy of 3 sample databases. The NeT algorithm does not consider referential integrity relation but just consider structural translation. Thus the NeT algorithm cannot extract referential integrity relation information during RDB-to-XML translation. The CoT algorithm can extract RI_{exp} of sample databases because the CoT algorithm only considers referential integrity relation defined explicitly. The QP-T algorithm considers not only structural part but also semantic aspect ($RI_{exp}+RI_{imp}$). Therefore, the QP-T algorithm presents better translation accuracy than NeT or CoT algorithms.

However, the QP-T algorithm also may not extract some referential integrity relation. In this paper, we use a property of equi-join that two columns related to equi-join have referential integrity relation. Therefore, the QP-T algorithm cannot extract referential integrity relation information if there is not enough user query list. We are researching to improve this limitation.

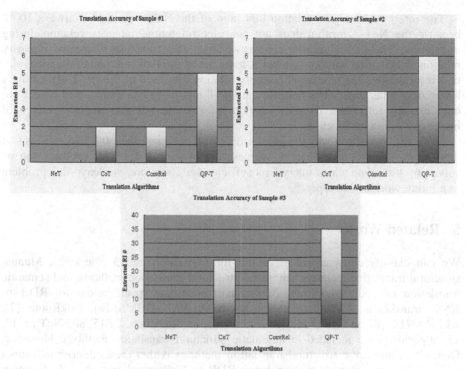

Fig. 6. Translation Accuracy of 3 Sample Databases

4.4 Referential Integrity Relation Loss Ratio

Referential integrity relation information loss ratio during RDB-to-XML is as in Fig. 7. Loss ratio presents a rate that how much referential integrity relation information is not extracted and lost during translation.

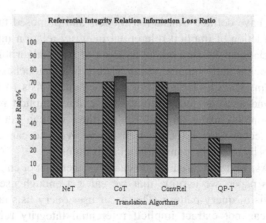

Fig. 7. Referential Integrity Relation Information Loss Ratio

The referential integrity relation loss ratio of the NeT algorithm is always 100% because the NeT algorithm does not consider referential integrity relation during translation. The CoT algorithm can extract and reflect explicit referential integrity relation information without loss but it loses all of implicit referential integrity relation information. The referential integrity relation loss ratio of the QP-T algorithm is lower than other algorithms because the QP-T algorithm can extract and reflect not only explicit referential integrity relation information but also implicit referential integrity relation information.

However, the reason why the proposed algorithm cannot have 0% loss ratio is that there is not enough query lists as we describe in section 4.3. This problem can be solved by providing added query lists sufficiently. Therefore, we leave this problem as a future work in this paper.

5   Related Works

We can classify conventional algorithm for translation into 3 categories; Manual structural translation methods, automatic structural translation methods, and semantic translation methods. Algorithms of first part need user specifications for RDB-to-XML translation. XML Extender from IBM, XML-DBMS [6], SilkRoute [7], XPERANTO [8], and DB2XML [9] are included in this group. FT [5] and NeT [5, 12, 13] algorithms are included in automatic structural translation methods. However, Demerit of automatic structural translation methods is that these algorithms cannot reflect referential integrity relation during RDB-to-XML translation. A CoT algorithm [12, 13] and the ConvRel algorithm [18] are included in semantic translation methods. However, these algorithms can only reflect explicit referential integrity relation. If implicit referential integrity relation is exists, the CoT and ConvRel algorithm cannot create exact XML document.

6   Conclusion and Future Works

In this paper, we have defined translation models and proposed the QP-T algorithm for automatic extraction of implicit referential integrity relation information. We defined the initial relational schema model as input of QP-T algorithm, the output relational schema model as mid-output, and the XML schema model as final output of our proposed algorithm. The QP-T algorithm get user query lists from DBMS through JDBC interface and analyze query pattern and extract implicit referential integrity relation information. By using the QP-T algorithm, we can get more exact XML documents and execute more effective translation. We also can avoid the insertion and deletion errors by using the conventional algorithms.

For future works, we must research the case that there is not enough user query list in DBMS. In this paper, we assume that we can get enough user query lists from DBMS for analysis of query pattern. That is, if user query lists are not enough, the QP-T algorithm can not extract implicit referential integrity relation information. Therefore, we need to research to solve this problem.

References

[1] T. Bray et al., Extensible Markup Language (XML) 1.0, 2nd Edition, W3C Recommendation, October 2000.

[2] ISO / IEC JTC 1 SC 34, ISO / IEC 8839:1986: Information processing -- Text and office systems -- Standard Generalized Markup Language (SGML), August 2001.

[3] R. Elmasri et al., and S. Navathe, Fundamental of Database Systems, 4th Edition, Addison-Wesley, 2003.

[4] W. Fan et al., "Integrity Constraints for XML," ACM PODS, Dallas, TX, May 2000.

[5] D. Lee et al., "Nesting-based Relational-to-XML Schema Translation," Int'l Workshop on the Web and Databases (WebDB), Santa Barbara, CA, May 2001.

[6] J. Naughton et al., "The Niagara Internet Query System," IEEE Data Engineering Bulletin, Vol. 24, No. 2, pp. 27-33, 2001.

[7] M. Fernandez et al., "SilkRoute: Trading between Relations and XML," Int'l World Wide Web Conf. (WWW), Amsterdam, Netherlands, May 2000.

[8] M. Carey et al., "XPERANTO: Publishing Orbject-Relational Data as XML," Int'l Workshop on the Web and Databases (WebDB), Dallas, TX, May 2000.

[9] V.Turau. "Making Legacy Data Accessible for XML Applications," 1999. http://www.informatik.fhwiesbaden.de/~tarau/veroeff.html.

[10] C. Kurt et al., Beginning XML, 2nd Edition, John Wiley & Sons Inc, 2001.

[11] G. Jaeschke et al., "Remarks on the Algebra of Non First Normal Form Relations," ACM PODS, Los Angeles, CA, Vol. 5, pp. 124-138, Los Angeles, March 1982.

[12] D. Lee et al., "Effective Schema Conversions between XML and Relational Models," European Conference on Artificial Intelligence (ECAI), Knowledge Transformation Workshop (ECAI-OT), Lyon, France, July 2002.

[13] D. Lee et al., "NeT&CoT: Translating Relational Schemas to XML Schemas using Semantic Constraints," 11th ACM Int'l Conference on Information and Knowledge Management (CIKM). McLean, VA, USA, November 2002.

[14] J. Goodson, "Using XML with Existing Data Access Standards," Enterprise application Integration Knowledge Base (EAI) Journal, pp. 43-45, March 2002.

[15] J. Widom, "Data Management for XML: Research Directions," IEEE Data Engineering Bulletin, pp. 44-52. September 1999.

[16] L. Seligman et al., "XML's Impact on Databases and Data Sharing. IEEE Computer, Vol. 34, No. 6, pp. 59-67, June 2001.

[17] A. Witkowski et al., "Advanced SQL Modeling in RDBMS," ACM Transactions on Database Systems," Vol. 30, No. 1, pp. 83–121, March 2005.

[18] A. C. Duta et al., "ConvRel: Relationship Conversion to XML Nested Structures," SAC '04, Nicosia, Cyprus, March 14-17, 2004.

[19] Transaction Processing Performance Councill, Http://www.tpc.org/tpch/spec/h130.pdf

[20] J. Hainaut et al., "Structure Elicitation in Database Reverse Engineering," IEEE, the 3rd Working Conference on Reverse Engineering (WCRE 96), pp. 131-140, Monterey, CA, USA, November 1996.

[21] M. Anderson, "Extracting an Entity Relationship Schema from a Relational Database through Reverse Engineering," the 13th Int. Conf. on ERA, Springer-Verlag, LNCS 881, pp. 387-401, December 1994.

[22] J. Hainaut et al., "Transformation of Requirement Specifications Expressed in Natural Language into an EER Model", the 12th Int. Conf. on ERA, EIR Institute and Springer-Verlag, LNCS 823, pp. 206-217, Arlington, Texas, USA, December, 1993.

A Study on the Use of Multicast Protocol Traffic Overload for QCBT

Won-Hyuck Choi and Young-Ho Song

R & D Departments, Hanback Electronics Company, Republic of Korea
rbooo@korea.com, yhsong@hanback.co.kr

Abstract. Multicast requires reliability in peer-to-peer or multiple-to-multiple communication services and such demand for reliability becomes more and more an important factor to manage the whole network. Communication method for multicast is a way of communication for a transmitter that provides multicast data to every registered member in the transmitter's group, and it can be classified into the traditional and the reliable communication methods in general. The traditional communication method is very fast in connection but quality of service is poor. In contrast, the reliable communication method provides good quality in service but its speed is somewhat poor. Thus to enhance such demerits, this paper proposes communication method of multicast by using QCBT (Quality of Service Core Based Tree) method. In this paper, a fair and practical bandwidth is used for data packet transmission along with the use of QCBT. The bandwidth and data processing capability filters out the transmitted data from an QCBT router through transmission packet and upgrades multimedia data packet more effectively. Therefore, recipients in various levels receive the effective data packet and based on these facts, the study actualizes and evaluates efficiency of a router, which is able to transmit the fair bandwidth from QCBT router in a simulation.

1 Introduction

Recently, multimedia work station, distributed system, and high speed communication have been developing in a great way. The combination of these technologies has accelerates dispersion multimedia system, and it enables us to transmit-receive more than text, such as voice, view, audio, image, graphic, etc. not only in work stations but in personal computers.

Moreover, demanding characteristic of service becomes various as users' expectation of system and capability of network get high, and each characteristic cooperates to bring great satisfaction to users. In order to provide various multimedia services to users, multicast communication method is introduced.

Multicast communication method is a way of communication for a transmitter that provides multicast data to every registered member in the transmitter's group, and it can be classified into the traditional and the reliable communication methods in general. The traditional communication method is very fast in connection but quality of service is poor. In contrast, the reliable communication method provides good quality

R. Meersman, Z. Tari, P. Herrero et al. (Eds.): OTM Workshops 2006, LNCS 4278, pp. 1854–1862, 2006.

in service but its speed is somewhat poor. Thus to enhance such demerits, this thesis proposes communication method of multicast by using QCBT method.

The QCBT method changes the concept that the routers of existing network are used only for the routing of packet. It is a network for users to select desired router and change any function of it for their own purpose. Change of router means nodes of network alters the included content in the packet that goes through itself and eventually enables it to apply program that has special purpose by using information of the packet.

In the study, various packet information of QCBT router is transmitted to users once the packet information is assigned as a multicast group. It is because the packet information can be known as the information of general packet and capsulated QCBT packet through QCBT router, thus each data packet is transmitted after filtering; therefore, various recipients in diverse level can transmit more effective multimedia data packet by utilizing a fair and a practical bandwidth.

For experiments of the thesis, we actualize and evaluate efficiency with CBT that is the traditional multicast protocol and multicast method that uses QCBT in simulation. In addition, chapter 2 analyzes CBT protocol and QCBT among traditional multicast, chapter 3 proposes characteristic of multicast that utilizes QCBT, and chapter 4 analyses and concludes result of the experiment and efficiency of simulation about the suggested method.

2 Background

2.1 Characteristic of Existing Multicast

Multicast protocol is classified into two kinds; Source based tree method and Shared tree method. SBT(Source Based Tree) is called as SDT(Source Distribution Tree), or SPT(Shortest Path Tree) because it is based on shortest path algorism and when express tree of SBT, (S, G) is used to indicate S(Source). If number of source is S and number of group is G, then the actual size of tree is calculated as $O(S* G)$ so it requires large amount of buffer memory for the management of tree.

The second Shared Tree (ShT) is expressed as $(*, G)$. Here * means every source and G means group. It is shared tree so the actual size of tree has $O(|G|)$ regardless of source's number. The cost for constitution of tree is economical; however it may cause serious delay in traffic if number of source is increased. ShT is appropriate when it applies multicast service in network that deals with traffic of relatively small bandwidth and has multiple numbers of transmitters.

2.2 CBT

CBT (Core Based Tree) protocol is recently suggested multicast routing method and its members share one tree together. CBT uses method that has expansion to constitute a unique bidirectional tree regardless of transmitter. Multicast traffic that is sent to each group receives through the same path without regard to transmitter.

Shared tree is connected around Core Router, and the core router is selected by hash function that does mapping on the multicast address and the core router. Each router has same hash function so only one core can be selected for each group. Because of this fact, the routing path of whole tree is formed around core router and the multicast packet is transmitted through the core; therefore, it causes increment in cost of link.

As figure 1shows, it has possibility to have a bottleneck in the core link because of traffic's convergence in core. To say this in other works, bottleneck arises through the demanding speed of link that exceeds bandwidth of core link and if such condition becomes much serious then it leads to blending in the core link, which may cause discontinuation of multicast service.

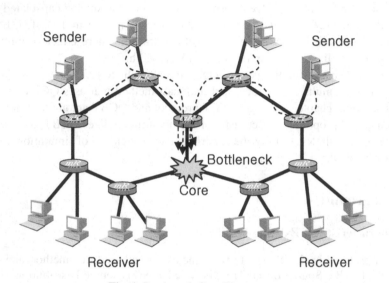

Fig. 1. Bottleneck Core Phenomenon

2.3 Characteristics of QCBT Server

The constituting elements of QCBT are formed through additional defining of packet part, which can be managed in QCBT router, to existing packet part in network and the QCBT server forms the QCBT packet. The transmitted QCBT packet does filtering for packet's prior rank and its specific part by the QCBT router and sends the filtered out data to various recipients. If a router, which takes care of information in the midpoint of network, is not an QCBT router, then the capsulated packet in QCBT packet transmits information in a simple IP packet to other nodes. [4][5]

2.4 QCBT Packet

There are two main methods for panning of QCBT packet. The first method is defining a new header for an QCBT packet called QEF (QCBT Encapsulation Protocol) to classify the QCBT packet with the existing packet and the second method is defining IP frame of the existing packet as a specified form through QCBT packet.

The first method, QEF, uses option of various characteristics to header. Kinds of options are certification, non-defect, etc. Packet received QCBT router transmits data fast and effectively according to the characteristics of data packet. At this time if QCBT packet is not used, then the existing packet with initial setting will be used.

The second method uses options of specified QCBT packet to a present IP packet to maintain compatibility with the existing IP packet for the process of special data or the measurement of network security and process speed. Thus, it is suitable for types of general data packet and the QCBT packet of differentiated special data packet.

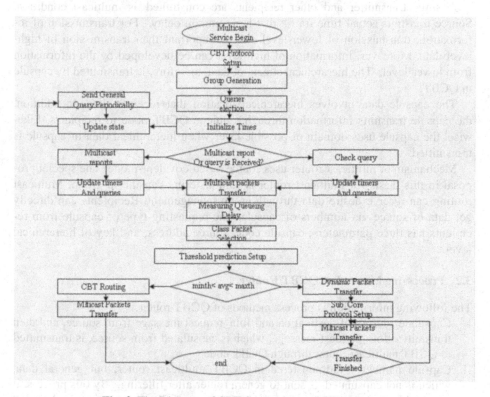

Fig. 2. The Diagram of CBT Conversion to QCBT Method

2.5 QCBT Router

QCBT router has to consider two different characteristics of hardware and software simultaneously in order to manage QCBT packet with various characteristics than the existing packets, for example like various packet scheduling techniques, packet classification, etc. In buffer scheduling, services like packet transmission base on characteristics of data and assignment of source have to be considered depends on condition for application. Not like the existing packet constitution, QCBT packet has to deals with capsulated option parts and controls every source management under one process condition. [4][5]

3 QCBT Utilized Multicast

3.1 Method of Multicast That Utilizes QCBT

The session of multicast routing that utilizes QCBT shows multicast domain within network. Schema that administers congestion of data is suggested by utilizing data from QCBT to multicast routing. Also, bandwidth of data is made between resources in order to eliminate congestion of data.

A singe transmitter and other recipients are constituted as multicast condition. Source transmits actual time traffic that has common delay. For transmission of information, transmission of lower-level data is important than transmission of high-level data. Moreover, information of high-level can be developed by the information from lower-level. The hierarchical stream of data, therefore, is transmitted by capsule in QCBT.

The capsule data involves hierarchical location that receives data. In addition, the capsule transmits information through a unique QCBT node to recipients. Likewise, the capsule uses domain of possible layer when hierarchical data of capsule is transmitted.

Mechanism of multicast router uses source based covalent-mode. The special proposal in this thesis for multicast router is administering capsule in group. Multicast routing can receive desire data through group management. Recipients can directly get data of source via numbers of capsule. The requesting type of capsule from recipients has three parameters; capsule code, source address, and key of hierarchical level.

3.2 Processing Method of QCBT Router

The following information is process methods of QCBT router.
I.   Capsulate address of destination and Join_request message from source, and then transmitted Join_request message, which is capsulated from source, is transmitted to QCBT multicast router through QCBT node.
II. Capsule number is administered in QCBT multicast router, but general data, which is not capsulated, is sent to genera router after filtering. By this process, it is possible to centralize traffic of data because of filtering of capsule data and genera data.
III. Join_request message's response in QCBT multicast router becomes Join_ack message. The data packet transmission is completed after Join_ack message is transmitted to source. If there is not any desired key in the capsule group of QCBT multicast router, transmit Join_ack message from the capsule group of router to other recipients.
IV. If response of Join_ack message is over the time of RRT, send disconnect message. The disconnect message is set to disconnect itself after send a quit message for the last time once lower-node sends Quit_ack message to source.
V. If other recipients ask to a same router at the same time, group of each transmitters transmits Abt_intt message.

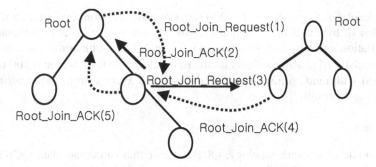

Fig. 3. Processing methods of QCBT router

4 Simulation and Result

4.1 Simulation Condition

In this thesis, evaluation of multicast router's efficiency that utilized QCBT is compared and analyzed with the exiting multicast based CBT. In the experiment, 10 transmitters and 6 groups were provided in order to vary the numbers of transmitters and groups, and each group has maximum 3 recipients to correspond with various numbers of group members.

Each multicast link has fixed bandwidth of 1.5Mbps and transmission delay of 10ms. Input rate of incoming packet to router forms Poisson. Arrival time of packet and service time are set by componential distribution and Queueing model M/M/1 is used, but limitation of Queueing capacity that depends on router's buffer is not considered.

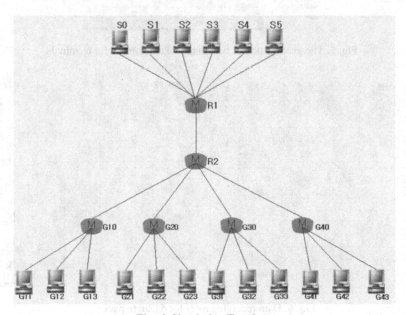

Fig. 4. Simulation Topology

The simulation is performed for 200 seconds and reception rate is measured based on number of byte in data. The characteristic of data packet is set by simulation and the simulation topology uses structure like figure 4. For simulation device, ns-2 (Network Simulator- II), which reflects multicast condition well, is used and 100 times are performed with random number to reliability. The average from the experiments is selected for the result.

4.2 Result

In the middle of network topology, QCBT server that can create data QCBT packet was set. General and QCBT routers were set separately for their covalent to construct more practical network structure. In the experiment 1, it compares each data packet according to increment of recipient entry in multicast protocol CBT and each transmitter of QCBT and transmitted packet amount when there is increment in each traffic.

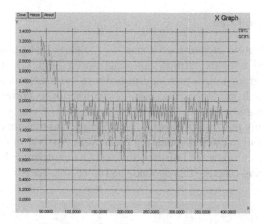

Fig. 5. The average delays between packets number for terminals

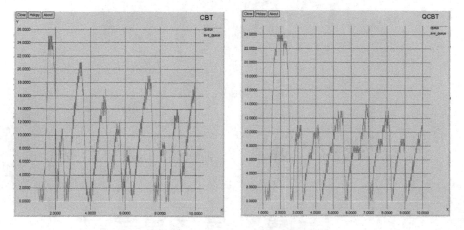

Fig. 6. Data receiving rates for 512byte packets

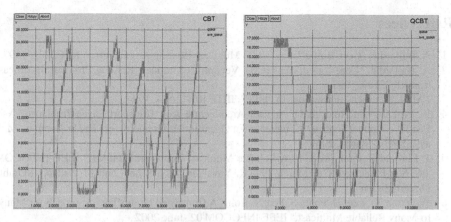

Fig. 7. Data receiving rates for 1024byte packets

As it is shown in figure 5, QCBT used multicast method transmits much more packets than CBT method in a same time and it proves better efficiency of QCBT used multicast method in transmission delay of traffic.

In the experiment 2, it shows process rate when general packet and capsulated packet from QCBT server are transmitted simultaneously in case of transmitting a packet to a recipient from source.

In figure 6, data packet's speed of transmission to recipient increases 12.45% in process rate than the existing multicast router when QCBT is applied and in the figure 7, process rate of QCBT router is increased to 21.42% by the hierarchical characteristic of multimedia data when QCBT is applied according to increment of recipient.

5 Conclusion

In order to support multimedia application that is arising issue nowadays, it is necessary to have link of broadband network, actual time transmission, and more effective characteristics of data. Capsulated QCBT packet, therefore, is used to effectively constitute characteristics of data. QCBT packet classifies packets into general and capsulated one according to characteristic of data and manages the process through QCBT multicast router, thus it is possible for QCBT packet to predict and control bandwidth and transmission delay. It increases reliable distribution of traffic and process rate of router.

The experiment 1 in the study proves that QCBT used multicast method superior to the existing CBT method in transmission delay of traffic and the experiment 2 confirms increased data process rate of router when there is also increment of recipient.

For the future study, it is necessary to expand the concept of utilizing possible bandwidth through interaction between QCBT router and general router, and study for controlling network traffic requires further consideration when broadband network is set.

References

1. A. Ballardie, "Core Based Trees (CBT) Multicast Routing Architecture," RFC2201, 1997.
2. A. Ballardie, "Core Based Trees (CBT Version 2) Multicast Routing Protocol Specificastion RFC2189, 1997.
3. J.Moy, "Multicast Extensions to OSPF", IETF RFC 1584, 1994.
4. K. Ettikan, "An Analysis Of Anycast Architecture And Transport Layer Problems," Asia Pacific Regional Internet Conference on Operational Technologies, Kuala Lumpur, Malaysia, Feb.,-March, 2001.
5. J. Lin and S. Paul, "RMTP: A Reliable Multicast Transport Protocol," IEEE INFOCOM '96, San Francisco, CA, March 1996.R. Yavatkar, J. Griffioen, and M. Sudan, "Reliable Dissemination
6. W. Yoon, D. Lee, H.Youn, S. Lee, S. Koh, "A Combined Group/Tree Approach for Many-to-Many Reliable Multicast," IEEE INFOCOM'02, June 2002
7. "The Network Simulator: ns-2," http://www.isi.edu/nsnam/ns/
8. D. Estrin, D. Farinacci, A. Helmy, D. Thaler, S. Deering, M. Handley, V. Jacobson, C. Liu, P. Sharma and L. Wei," Protocol Independent Multicast-Sparse Mode (PIM-SM): Protocol Specification"Internet Engineering Task Force (IETF), RFC 2362, June 1998
9. D. Meyer and B. Fenner, "Multicast source discovery protocol (MSDP)," Internet Engineering Task Force (IETF), RFC 3618, October 2003.
10. D. Kim, Verio, D. Meyer, H. Kilmer and D. Farinacci, "Anycast Rendevous Point (RP) mechanism using Protocol Independent Multicast (PIM) and Multicast Source Discovery Protocol (MSDP)," Internet Engineering Task Force (IETF), RFC 3446, January 2003
11. P. Sharma, E. Perry, and R. Malpani, "IP multicast operational network management: design, challenges, and experiences," IEEE Network, vol. 17, pp. 49{55, March/April 2003.

Semantic Granularity for the Semantic Web

Riccardo Albertoni, Elena Camossi, Monica De Martino,
Franca Giannini, and Marina Monti

IMATI-CNR,
Via De Marini, 6 – Torre di Francia - 16149 Genova, Italy
{riccardo.albertoni, elena.camossi, monica.demartino,
franca.giannini, marina.monti}@ge.imati.cnr.it

Abstract. In this paper we describe a framework for the application of semantic granularities to the Semantic Web. Given a data *source* and an ontology formalizing *qualities* which describe the source, we define a dynamic granularity system for the navigation of the repository according to different levels of detail, i.e., granularities. Semantic granularities summarize the degree of informativeness of the qualities, taking into account both the individuals populating the repository, which concur in the definition of the implicit semantics, and the ontology schema, which gives the formal semantics. The method adapts and extends to ontologies existing natural language processing techniques for topics generalization.

1 Introduction

Semantic Web is rising as an extension of the current Web to provide sophisticated and powerful inferences improving the accessibility to web content. In the traditional web, the huge amount of results returned by a search completely overwhelms the user's capability to exploit the represented information. The difficulties pertaining to information access are mainly due to a poor overlap between the information model employed by the user (i.e., the Cognitive Space) and the model defined by the information provider the information (i.e., the Information Space) [1]. Techniques of semantic searching as those proposed in [2] can be useful to improve the retrieval mechanism. However, in order to increase the aforementioned overlapping, every search activity has to be characterized by a highly interactive process [3]: the seeker refines the selection criteria according to the results he/she obtains alternating querying and browsing activities.

To reduce the consequences of information overload and the effects of the zero-hit problem, granularities may provide a valid help. Granularities allow exploring data according to different levels of detail, enhancing the flexibility in the information representation and retrieval. In the area of Information Systems, granularities have been already studied for both the temporal and the spatial domains [4,5,6]. However, in this field, granularities are static and embedded in the data model or in the database schema. The recent research has focused mainly on cognitive issues pertaining to the perception of vagueness, indeterminacy, imperfection, roughness, etc. [7]. Moreover, some attempts to define semantic granularities have been made with respect to terminologies by Fonseca et al. [8]. They introduced the term semantic granularity exploiting the casting

R. Meersman, Z. Tari, P. Herrero et al. (Eds.): OTM Workshops 2006, LNCS 4278, pp. 1863–1872, 2006.

mechanism employed in the object-oriented paradigm to represent ontology instances at different levels of detail.

In this work we inspect how ontologies can be adopted to define *semantic granularities* aiming at browsing. Ontologies are fated to play a central role in the Semantic Web. However, to build them is a costly and time consuming activity. Thus we consider a complete exploitation of such a precious artifact as a primary research issue. This work is conceived as a step in this direction: ontologies representing *qualities* which describe information *sources* and the relations among them provide the starting point from which to build the granularity system. The user is expected to access the repository by using increasing granularities, which correspond to increasing detailed qualities. The resources are grouped according to the granularity chosen.

Automatic techniques such as clustering and classification can be employed to organize repositories and to ease their browsing. The clustering only relies on the model emerging from the Information Space, whereas the classification relies on a set of classes which are expected to be meaningful as belonging to the user's Cognitive Space. On the contrary, the semantic granularity takes into account both the spaces. It considers part of the Cognitive Space represented in the ontology as well as the Information Space by balancing the sources at a given granularity according to their occurrence. In this work semantic granularities are defined dynamically, according to the data model (represented by an ontology schema) as well as to data (represented as ontology instances).

The method proposed follows a two-phase process. In the first phase, namely *quality filtering*, each quality is evaluated with respect to its capability of abstracting sources. This evaluation is given taking into account both the relations in which the quality is involved, and the sources defined for it. Then, the qualities which provide a satisfactory facility to abstract sources become *granules* of some granularity. The second phase, namely *granularity building*, distributes the granules returned by the filtering phase among different granularities. This phase returns the set of granularities to employ for the repository navigation.

The contribution of the paper is twofold. First, we propose semantic granularities as a mean to browse the Semantic Web content at different levels of detail. Secondly, we provide an approach to automatically define semantic granularities extending to ontologies and repository navigation previous research results presented for topics identification [9] and automatic discourse structuring [10].

In the following, we consider the browsing of a repository of papers to exemplify the proposed methodology and its objectives. Scientific papers are considered as the sources to be navigated, whereas their topics are the quality of interest.

The paper is organized as follows. In Section 2 we formalize semantic granularities. In Section 3 and 4 we discuss how semantic granules and granularities are built, describing quality filtering and granularity building phases. In Section 5 we provide an example of repository navigation. Finally, Section 6 concludes the paper, outlining future research directions.

2 Semantic Granularities

Semantic granularities aim at structuring a repository at different levels of detail taking into account both its conceptual structure and its content. Assuming the following entities are available:

S, the set of sources subject of the user exploration;

Q, a quality represented as set of nominal values according to which the sources are organized;

O, an ontology providing a data schema, where the sources and the quality are represented in terms of ontology entities;

the framework generates a *sequence* of granularities $G = <G_1, G_2, ..., G_n>$, such that each granularity G_i groups the sources the repository contains at increasing levels of detail, i.e., G_{i+1} gives a finer view on the sources in **S** than G_i (G_{i+1} is said to be *finer than G_i*). A granularity G_i is defined as a set of granules which provide a discrete view of the quality. A generic granule in G_i is denoted by g^{Gi}_j, and is described by a unique textual label $l^{Gi}_j \in$ **Q**. The granule labels are expected to be semantically meaningful for the user.

Let g^{Gi}_j be a granule at granularity G_i, the sources in **S** defined for g^{Gi}_j are denoted with s^{Gi}_j, whereas the sources defined for all the granules of granularity G_i are denoted with s^{Gi}. Let's consider for example a granularity G_i identifying scientific fields, such that the labels of its granules are $l^{Gi}_1 =$ "*Computer Science*", $l^{Gi}_2 =$ "*Mathematics*", $l^{Gi}_3 =$ "*Philosophy*", etc., and a repository **S** of scientific papers classified with respect to their topics. Then, s^{Gi}_1 denotes the set of papers on Computer Science, s^{Gi}_2 the set of papers on Mathematics, and so on. Given two granules of the same granularity G_i we do not require that the corresponding sets of sources are disjoint. For instance, $s^{Gi}_1 \cap s^{Gi}_2$ gives the set of papers on topics shared by Mathematics and Computer Science.

The approach we propose assumes the repository is organized according to an ontology which recalls the pattern depicted in Fig. 1. In Fig. 1, IO is the relation Instance-Of; Is-A and Part-Whole are partial order relations; entities with capital initials are classes; s_1, s_2, s_3, q_1, q_2, .., q_n are instances; F_1, F_2, A_1, A_2 are other class properties, which might be employed to further characterize the sources and the qualities. In particular, we assume the existence of a class grouping all the sources **S** the user is going to browse (**Source** in Fig. 1); a class representing the quality **Q** with respect to structuring the repository (**Quality** in Fig. 1); and a relation, which joins the sources s_1, s_2, s_3, etc. to the instances q_1, q_2, .., q_n representing the quality values (rel in Fig. 1). Given for instance the granularity G_i representing scientific fields we defined above, and the set **S** of scientific papers on those fields, the papers in **S** are sources to browse, which will be reorganized according to a quality *topics* (i.e., the granules in G_i). The **Quality** *Topic* is defined for the **Source** *Paper* through the relation *hasTopic*.

Futhermore, we assume a hierarchy H^Q is induced by the relations Is-A and Part-Whole relating the qualities $Q_1, Q_2, ..., Q_n$ in Fig. 1.

Part-Whole and similar relations among parts and wholes have been widely investigated by the scientific literatures (e.g., [11,12,13]). The literature demonstrates that distinct parthood relations can be identified depending on how the parts differently contribute to the structure of the whole. A complete treatment of the issues concerning parts and wholes is beyond the scope of this work, thus we restrict the possible interpretations of the relation Part-Whole assuming the parthood among the qualities in **Q** adheres to the following properties defined in [11]:

- *transitivity*, i.e., parts of parts are parts of the whole;
- *reflexivity*, i.e., every part is part of itself;
- *antisymmetricy*, i.e., nothing is a part of its parts;
- *homeomericity*, i.e., parts are of the same kind of things as their wholes.

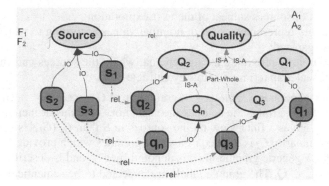

Fig. 1. The Ontology reference schema

The first three properties induce the partial order needed to preserve the hierarchical structure of the qualities. The fourth property instead ensures the parts in the hierarchy are still a quality as their whole (e.g., a topic can be part of another topic).

We observe that the entities in Fig. 1 can be represented differently according to the ontology design choices. The solution adopted mainly depends on the expressiveness of the ontology language employed and the needs pertaining to the reasoning. For simplicity, the paper assumes classes in the hierarchy can not be used as relation values, i.e., the relations have only instance values. Similar assumptions have been made also by OWL-DL[1], one of the ontology language most adopted. As consequence of the latter assumption, the qualities are represented both as classes and instances, and each class Q_n has exactly one instance q_n. We introduce these restrictions to simplify the presentation of our method, but the approach could be easily adapted to different ontology designs.

Given the ontology schema in Fig. 1, the qualities in **Q** are related by a partial order $\leq_Q$ induced by H^Q according to both Is-A and Part-Whole. Since the granule labels correspond to qualities in **Q**, $\leq_Q$ is defined also on labels. Note that not all the values in **Q** become granule labels for some G_i in **G**, but only those resulting from the phase of quality filtering described in Section 3. Given a quality Q in **Q**, the set of sources s^Q are the instances of **S** associated via rel to Q, while the set of sources s^{Q*} are the instances of **S** associated via rel to Q and to each quality Q' such that $Q' \leq_Q Q$. For example, considering the quality Q_2 in Fig. 1, s^{Q2} corresponds to $\{s_1\}$, whereas s^{Q2*} corresponds to the set of instances $\{s_1, s_2, s_3\}$.

Given the granule g^{Gi}_j at granularity G_i, such that $Q = l^{Gi}_j$, note that s^{Gi}_j is equivalent to s^{Q*}. Let G_1 and G_2 be two granularities belonging to **G**, such that G_2 is finer than G_1. Given g^{G1}_j a valid granule of G_1, we denote with $G_2(g^{G1}_j)$ the set of granules of G_2 which labels are related to l^{G1}_j through $\leq_Q$, i.e., $\{g^{G2}_k \mid l^{G2}_k \leq_Q l^{G1}_j\}$. Analogously, given g^{G2}_k a valid granule of G_2, we denote with $G_1(g^{G2}_k)$ the set of granules of G_1 $\{g^{G1}_j \mid l^{G2}_k \leq_Q l^{G1}_j\}$. Through this notation, we can move from a granularity to a different one. For instance, let's consider G_i the granularity for scientific fields defined above, g^{Gi}_1 the

---

[1] http://www.w3.org/2004/OWL/ (Accessed in July 2006).

granule for Computer Science, and G_{i+1} a granularity finer than G_i; $G_{i+1}(g^{Gi}_1)$ results in all the granules representing the sub-fields in which Computer Science can be expanded into (e.g., Database, Artificial Intelligence, Computer Graphics, etc.)

In the following sections, we will detail how granularities to browse the sources are built starting from information sources defined with respect to a set of qualities. Firstly, the phase *quality filtering* (described in Section 3) evaluates which qualities can be employed as granule labels. Then, in the phase *granularity building* (described in Section 4), granules representing qualities are assigned to different granularities.

3 Quality Filtering: Selection of Semantic Granules

The filtering selects the quality values to be adopted as granule labels. In the proposed approach, a quality value is considered as a granule label whenever it ensures a good level of abstraction or it is involved in Part-Whole.

The idea we adopt to evaluate the abstraction capability of qualities is borrowed from existing techniques applied in the area of Natural Language Processing for topic identification and generalization [9,10]. Lin [9] introduced the notion of degree of informativeness and summarization of a concept C in a lexical taxonomy as a measure of the capability of C to generalize its specializations, i.e., the children in the taxonomy, according to the terms occurrence in a corpus. According to Lin, the more the children of C have a similar number of occurrences, the more the concept C is a good generalization. The Lin algorithm is based on the assumption that the occurrences of the corpus are associated only to the leaves in the noun taxonomy.

Pike and Gahegan [10] extend the Lin's approach to identify and to abstract arguments of a discourse allowing the intermediate concepts of the taxonomy to have their own occurrences associated. Both works consider only the relation Is-A for structuring concepts, and ignore the occurrence of the concept C in the corpus for the evaluation of its degree of informativeness.

Given the schema of Fig. 1, to evaluate the degree of informativeness of a quality Q aiming at the definition of *semantic granularities*, we consider each source related through rel to Q as an occurrence of Q. We extend the method proposed by Pike and Gahegan to Part-Whole structures, taking into account also the influence of the occurrences of each quality under evaluation. Consider for instance the situation in Fig. 2, where we report a portion of a possible classification of the topics pertaining to the Data Mining research field. The values reported have been retrieved by querying the ACM digital library[2] and considering qualities as paper keywords.

In Fig. 2, Clustering has four unbalanced sub-topics, i.e., Document Clustering, K-Nearest Neighbors Based, K-Mean, and Hierarchical Clustering. According to both Lin-Pike's approach, Clustering does not provide a high level of generalization of its sub-topics. However, we observe that for Clustering a considerable amount of instances has been retrieved (14923), and this value is much bigger than the values reported for its sub-topics. In this situation, we would expect that this concept is eligible to be included among the most meaningful topics the repository refers to.

---

[2] http://portal.acm.org/ (accessed in March 2006).

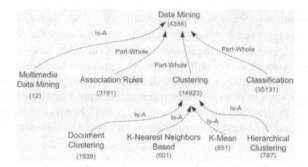

Fig. 2. Data Mining topics classification

Given the aforementioned observations, we say that a quality Q is a *good abstraction* for its direct sub-qualities (including, as we specify above, both the qualities reachable through Is-A and Part-Whole) if the ratio R_Q between the maximum numbers of occurrences in the repository defined for its sub-qualities and the recursive number of occurrences defined for Q in the repository (i.e., including both its own occurrences and the recursive occurrence of its immediate sub-qualities) is less then a given a threshold R_t. R_Q is defined in (1) and its value ranges in [0,1]. Leafs in the hierarchy have R_Q equal to 0. We denote with $\prec_Q$ the non-reflexive and non-transitive relation induced by H^Q (e.g., referring to Fig. 2, Multimedia Data Mining $\prec_Q$ Data Mining, Association Rules $\prec_Q$ Data Mining, K-mean $\prec_Q$ Clustering). R_Q is defined as follows:

$$R_Q = \frac{\max_{\{Q'|Q'\prec_Q Q\}} |s^{Q'*}|}{\sum_{\{Q'|Q'\prec_Q Q\}} |s^{Q'*}| + s^Q} \tag{1}$$

Let us consider in Fig 2 the topics Association Rule, Classification and Clustering, which are related to Data Mining through the relation Part-Whole. Conversely to Is-A, we consider Part-Whole as a landmark for granule identification, because it intrinsically discriminates two separate levels of abstraction. Thus whenever two qualities are directly related by Part-Whole they are considered as granules of distinct granularities.

In the next section, we adopt the predicate *isGranule(Q,R_t)* to determine if the quality Q is promoted to be a granule according to the quality filtering phase. The predicate *isGranule(Q,R_t)* is true whenever Q is involved in a Part-Whole, or it is a good abstraction, i.e. $R_Q \leq R_t$ where R_Q is defined according to (1).

4 Granularity Building: Distribution of Granules in Granularities

The granularity building phase aims at determining the distribution of the granules resulting from quality among the semantic granularities in **G**.

The partial order $\leq_Q$ induced by the relations Is-A and Part-Whole leads such a distribution. In particular, considering two distinct granule labels *a* and *b,* the principles we follow are:

(1) if $b \leq_Q a$, then the two granules have to belong to distinct granularities,

(2) if $b \leq_Q a$, b Part-Whole a holds and the whole granule with label a belongs to the granularity G_i, then the part granule with label b has to belong to the granularity G_{i+1}, such that G_{i+1} is finer than G_i.

Given for instance the hierarchy of Fig. 2, if Data Mining, Clustering and Document Clustering satisfy the predicate *isGranule* for a given value of R_t, and Data Mining belongs to granularity G_i, Clustering must belong to granularity G_{i+1}, while Document Clustering must belong to a granularity G_j, with $j > i+1$.

The granularity building phase is performed according to the algorithm in Fig. 3. The algorithm returns the sequences of granularities G. It performs a breath first visit of H^Q, inserting the granules in distinct granularities according to the principles stated in (1) (2). It terminates whenever the visit has reached all the H^Q leaves.

In Fig. 3, ds is the starting level (from the root) in H^Q; R_t is the ratio threshold for the evaluation of the degree of informativeness of qualities; next(Q) returns the child of Q in H^Q; node(1) returns the qualities laying at the level 1 in the hierarchy; $+$ and $-$ are the set operators for union and difference.

```
i = 0; G_i = {};
NodeToConsider = Node(ds);
While (! empty(NodeToConsider)){
  For each Q belonging to NodeToConsider {
    If  isGranule(Q, R_t) G_i += { Q };
    else If Q is not leaf NodeToConsider += next(Q);
    NodeToConsider -= { Q };
  }
  i++; G_i = {};
  For each Q belonging to G_{i-1} {
    For j=1 to i-1 {   // check for multi-inheritance
      For each Q_i belonging to G_j
        If ((Q_i part-whole Q) or (Q_i is-a Q)){
          G_j -= { Q_i }; G_i += { Q_i };
        }
      If Q is not leaf
        NodeToConsider += next(Q);
    }
  }
}
```

Fig. 3. Granularity building algorithm

5   Example: Semantic Granularity Extraction for Scientific Papers

In this section we refer to the repository of scientific papers provided by the ACM Digital Library, considering papers as the information sources to be browsed and the associated keywords as sources qualities. In the ACM Digital Library each paper is classified according to the ACM Computing Classification System[3], which is a taxonomy depicting the broadest research fields in the computer science. To provide an

---

[3] http://www.acm.org/class/1998/

example of semantic granularities extracted through its application, we extend the ACM taxonomy deepening the fields we are familiar with. A portion of this taxonomy has been already shown in Fig. 2. The classes in the resulting taxonomy are mainly related through the relation Is-A. Moreover, the relation Part-Whole has been adopted whenever a research field is classified with respect to its important sub-parts, like techniques applied in the field (e.g., Clustering and Data Mining in Fig. 2).

In Table 1 a meaningful portion of the quality hierarchy we consider and the results we obtained are shown. The first column of the table reports the quality values (the indentation resembles the H_Q structure); the second gives the number of papers referring to each quality in the ACM repository; the third column reports the degree of informativeness obtained by applying an approach based on what proposed in [9,10], while the fourth reports the values we obtain according to the evaluation we presented in Section 3; finally, the last column gives the granules distribution according to the phase granularity building we described in Section 4.

The threshold R_t we apply in this example is 0.50. With this evaluation of R_t the qualities Database Management, General, Logical Design, Transaction processing, Database

Table 1. Method evaluation with $R_t = 0.50$

Qualities-Research Topics	# Occurences	LPG-Based	R_q	Gi (Rt=0.50)
Database Management	6320	0.7869	0.7572	
General	1162	1.0000	0.9888	
Security, Integrity, and Protection	1664	0.0000	0.0000	G1
Logical Design	1899	0.7355	0.5238	
Data models	3382	0.0000	0.0000	G1
Normal forms	197	0.0000	0.0000	G1
Schema and subschema	1019	0.0000	0.0000	G1
Physical Design	499	0.6918	0.4879	G1
Access methods	326	0.0000	0.0000	G2
Deadlock avoidance	158	0.0000	0.0000	G2
Recovery and restart	210	0.0000	0.0000	G2
Languages	1438	0.6887	0.4027	G1
Transaction processing	1194	0.0000	0.0000	
Heterogeneous Databases	163	0.6838	0.2957	G1
Database Administration	745	0.9736	0.4557	G1
Database Applications	2639	0.9407	0.9292	
Image databases	660	0.0000	0.0000	G1
Scientific databases	956	0.0000	0.0000	G1
Statistical databases	229	0.0000	0.0000	G1
Data mining	4336	0.9612	0.9244	G1
Multimedia data mining	12	0.8922	0.9697	
Sound Analysis	90	0.0000	0.0000	G2
Video Analysis	414	0.0000	0.0000	G2
Spatio-Temporal Data Mining	27	0.8922	0.8432	
Temporal Data Mining	47	0.0000	0.0000	G2
Spatial Data Mining	138	0.0000	0.0000	G2
Text Mining	409	0.0000	0.0000	G2
Association Rules **(Part-Whole)**	3181	0.0000	0.0000	G2
Classification **(Part-Whole)**	35131	0.0000	0.0000	G2
Clustering **(Part-Whole)**	14923	0.9718	0.1012	G2
Document Clustering	1939	0.0000	0.0000	G3
k-Nearest Neighbors Based	601	0.0000	0.0000	G3
k-Mean	851	0.0000	0.0000	G3
Hierarchical Clustering	787	0.9000	0.0025	G3
Visual Data Exploration	3066	0.9909	0.1075	G2
Information Visualization	403	0.0000	0.0000	G3
Visual Reasoning	279	0.0000	0.0000	G3
Spatial databases, GIS	1499	0.2931	0.3466	G1

application, Multimedia Data Mining and Spatio-Temporal Data Mining are not considered as granules because their degree of informativeness is greater than the threshold. Note that the granularities preserve the partial order given by the hierarchy among qualities related by Is-A and Part-Whole, but not the general order as stated by the hierarchy. In particular, qualities at the same level in the hierarchy can be labels for granules that belong to different granularities.

Let's suppose a user wants to navigate the sources in the repository. At the first step, the labels of the granules at granularity G_1 give him/her a broad idea of the most meaningful arguments represented in the repository ($l^{G_1}{}_1$ is the label for the quality "Security, Integrity and Protection", $l^{G_1}{}_2$ is the label for "Data Models", etc). Let's suppose the user chooses to navigate the resources related to Data Mining. The labels of granules at granularity G_2 such that $G_2(g^{G_1}{}_{12})$, where $g^{G_1}{}_{12}$ is the granule with label "Data Mining", are retrieved. As we formally defined in Section 2, the conversion is based on the partial order induced by the hierarchy H^Q. Thus, the set of labels $l^{G_2}{}_5$= "Sound Analysis", $l^{G_2}{}_6$= "Video Analysis", $l^{G_2}{}_7$= "Temporal Data Mining", $l^{G_2}{}_8$= "Spatial Data Mining", $l^{G_2}{}_9$= "Text Mining", $l^{G_2}{}_{10}$ = "Association Rules", $l^{G_2}{}_{11}$ = "Classification", $l^{G_2}{}_{12}$ = "Clustering", and $l^{G_2}{}_{13}$ = "Visual Data Exploration" is retrieved. The same happens for all the levels for which a granularity has been built, according to the algorithm we described in Section 4. Once the user chooses the set of instances is interested in by the browsing of labels, the corresponding set of sources is retrieved. Let the user be interested in Document Clustering, represented by the granule $g^{G_3}{}_1$. Then, the set of sources $s^{G_3}{}_1$ is returned to be processed by applying, for instance, existing navigation techniques (e.g., see the information visualization tools surveyed in [14]).

6 Conclusions

In this paper we present a framework for the dynamic definition of semantic granularities aiming at the effective representation of a huge semantic web repository at different levels of detail. The method is inspired by existing work on topic identification for discourse structuring. With respect to existing methods in the literature, we extend them to the browsing of any kind of information sources described with respect to a set of qualities represented in ontologies. We encompass the generalization performed according to a taxonomy, dealing also with qualities related by Part-Whole, towards a full ontology support. Furthermore, we provide a definition of semantic granularity which is dynamic, providing a bridge among the conceptual model of the user (i.e., the Cognitive Space) and the model structuring the repository (i.e., the Information Space).

Semantic granularities provide a way of supporting the user in the Semantic Web browsing at different levels of detail. For each granularity only the meaningful granule labels for the specific repository are represented. Thus, the sources having qualities the user is not interested in can be discarded since the very first steps of the browsing. Semantic granularity is defined with respect to ontologies, aiming at fully exploiting the information this formal conceptualization can provide. A crucial extension is related to the inclusion of properties of ontology classes and their values in the evaluation of the degree of informativeness of qualities. We are also planning an experimental evaluation performed on multimedia sources (text, shape, etc.). Finally, we are going to integrate the method with traditional techniques of resource browsing (e.g., information visualization).

Acknowledgement

This work is partially supported by the AIM@SHAPE Network of Excellence (AIM@SHAPE) funded by the European Commission under the Contract IST 506766.

References

1. Newby, G. B.: Cognitive space and information space. Journal of the American Society for Information Science and Technology. Vol. 52 Issue 12 (2001) 1026-1048
2. Guha, R., McCool, R., and Miller, E.: Semantic search. Proc. of the 12th Int'l Conference on World Wide Web. ACM Press (2003) 700-709
3. Belkin, N. J., Oddy, N. R., and Brooks, M. H.: ASK for Information Retrieval: Part I. Backgrownd and Theory. Journal of Documentation. Vol. 38 Issue 2 (1982) 61-71
4. Bettini, C., Jajodia, S., and Wang, Sean X.: Time Granularities in Databases, Data Mining, and Temporal Reasoning. Springer-Verlag (2000)
5. Stell, J. G. and Worboys, M.: Stratified Map Spaces: A Fomal Basis for Multi-Resolution Spatial Databases. Proc. of 8th Int'l Symposium on Spatial Data Handling. (1998) 180-189
6. Camossi, E., Bertino, E., and Bertolotto, M.: A multigranular object-oriented framework supporting spatio-temporal granularity conversions. Int'l Journal of Geographical Information Science. Vol. 20 Issue 5 (2006) 511-534
7. Bittner, T. and Stell, J. G.: Stratified Rough Sets and Vagueness. LNCS Vol. 2825 Springer-Verlag (2003) 270-286
8. Fonseca, F. T., Egenhofer, M. J., Davis, C. A., and Camara, G.: Semantic Granularity in Ontology-Driven Geographic Information Systems. Annals of Mathematics and Artificial Intelligence, Special Issue on Spatial and Temporal Granularity. Vol. 36 Issue 1-2 (2002) 121-151
9. Lin, C. Y.: Knowledge-based automatic topic identification. Proc. of the 33rd Annual Meeting on Association for Computational Linguistics. Association for Computational Linguistics (1995) 308-310
10. Pike, W. and Gahegan, M.: Constructing Semantically Scalable Cognitive Spaces. LNCS Vol. 2825 Springer-Verlag (2003) 332-348
11. Winston, M. E., Chaffin, R., and Herrmann, D.: A Taxonomy of Part-Whole Relations. Cognitive Science. Vol. 11 (1987) 417-444
12. Varzi, A. C.: Parts, Wholes, and Part-Whole Relations: The Prospects of Mereotopology. Data & Knowledge Engineering. Vol. 20 (1996) 259-286
13. Artale, A., Franconi, E., Guarino, N., and Pazzi, L.: Part-Whole Relations in Object-Centered Systems: An Overview. Data & Knowledge Engineering. Vol. 20 (1996) 347-383
14. Albertoni, R., Bertone, A., and De Martino, M.: Information Search: The Challenge of Integrating Information Visualization and Semantic Web. Proc. of the 16th Int'l Workshop on Database and Expert Systems Applications. IEEE (2005) 529-533

Maximum Rooted Spanning Trees for the Web

Wookey Lee[1] and Seungkil Lim[2]

[1] Dept. of Industrial Engineering, Inha University,
Incheon-city, Korea
`wookeylee@gamil.com`
[2] Division of e-business IT, Sungkyul University,
Anyang-city, Kyunggi-Do, Korea
`seungkil@sungkyul.edu`

Abstract. This paper focuses on finding maximum rooted spanning trees (MRSTs) for structured web search including hop constraints. We describe the meaning of structured web search and develop two binary integer linear programming models to find the best MRST. New methods for measuring the relevance among web objects are devised and used for structured web search. Some case studies are performed with real web sites and results are reported.

1 Introduction

Web browsers allow users to access in substantial numbers of web objects, the explosively growing number of web objects makes it difficult for users to find contents they want. Search engines of most portal sites are developed for the purpose of helping users find relevant web objects for their search queries. The more the web objects increase, the more an effective web search method will be necessary.

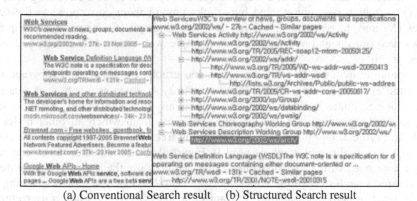

(a) Conventional Search result   (b) Structured Search result

Fig. 1. Typical two web search results

This paper focuses on web searches that use semantics that are implicitly contained in the hierarchical structure of the web. We call this type of web search as structured

R. Meersman, Z. Tari, P. Herrero et al. (Eds.): OTM Workshops 2006, LNCS 4278, pp. 1873–1882, 2006.
© Springer-Verlag Berlin Heidelberg 2006

web search. More specifically, we develop a search mechanism that generates the structured search tree when a user submits a search query. Here, structured search tree have a web object as a root of the search tree and hierarchically structured (or linked) web objects connected in tree form to the root rather than simply listing web objects in the decreasing order of computed ranks in the traditional web search.

On the other hand, in structured web search environments, a user can use a structured search tree when he or she enters a web site by selecting a URL from the list given by a search engine. Since the structured search tree has the selected web object (i.e., selected URL) as a root and hierarchically structured (or linked) web objects connected as a tree format to the root, the user can search web objects more effectively and efficiently. Figure 1 shows the comparison between the traditional web search and the structured web search.

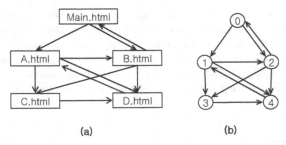

(a)   (b)

Fig. 2. (a) web objects and hyperlinks, (b) the corresponding directed graph

In this paper, we develop two models that can be used to realize the structured web search. In order to find the structured search tree for a web object, we first need to represent web objects of a web site as a structured form. In this research, we use a graph representation of a web site for the purpose. Since web objects in a web site are interconnected via hyperlinks, a web site can be represented as a directed graph, $G = (N, A)$, in which web objects and hyperlinks among them correspond to the set of nodes (N) and the set of arcs (A) of the directed graph (G), respectively. Figure 2 shows web objects and hyperlinks of an example web site and its corresponding directed graph.

A spanning tree, $G'=(N', A')$, for a directed graph $G = (N, A)$ is a subgraph of G that satisfies the following: 1) $N'=N$ and $A' \subseteq A$; 2) A' contains a subset of arcs in A, with which all nodes in N are connected without any directed circuits. A rooted spanning tree is a spanning tree that has one root node from which all other nodes can reach. In Figure 3, four possible rooted spanning trees are given for the same example web site and its directed graph as used in Figure 2. Since all other nodes can reach from a root node with a rooted spanning tree, we may use the rooted spanning tree as a structured search tree for the structured web search. That is, a rooted spanning tree can be used to help the user find relevant contents effectively when a user enters a web site by clicking a URL from the list given by a search engine. (Here, the web object the user selected from the list of URLs becomes the root node of the rooted spanning tree.)

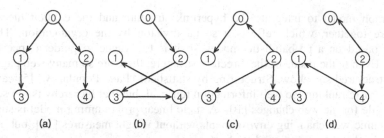

Fig. 3. (a) and (b) trees with node "0" as root, (c) and (d) trees with node "2" as root

In order to use a rooted spanning tree for the structured web search, we should answer to the following questions: 1) which rooted spanning tree is the best one if there are several rooted spanning trees existing with the same root node; 2) how the best rooted spanning tree can be found. In this paper, we use arc weights to give an answer to the first question and we make two assumptions for the arc weights. First, we assume that we can obtain some weights (for the arc weight of the two nodes) that represent the degree of relevance between two nodes (that is, between two web objects in a web site). Second, we assume that a rooted spanning tree with a larger sum of arc weights is better one if there are several rooted spanning trees with the same root node. With these assumptions, we can develop a binary integer linear program to find the best rooted spanning tree with the objective of maximizing the sum of arc weights. We call this problem of finding maximum rooted spanning tree as MRST problem.

This paper is organized as follows. After discussing the related works in section 2, we describe two binary integer linear programming models to find the best rooted spanning tree with arc weights. Next section gives some methods for determining arc weights used to find rooted spanning trees. Results of case studies follow. Finally we summarize research results with some concluding remarks.

2 Related Works

The web-as-a-graph has been rather useful to estimate the overall size of the web [1, 2], and it is acknowledged that the average number of hyperlinks and nodes statistically follow a power-law [4]. However, the web graph per se is still confusing for the specific web search, since the web is too complex to store or evaluate the individual changes within the web graph. Because of this, it is recommended that web searching by simple breadth first search can satisfactorily be done only up to a certain level of depths from the default node of a web site, instead of the whole web site [7, 13].

As an arc analysis, HITS has been a fundamental algorithm that extracts authorities and hubs from a given subgraph of the web with efficient iterative calculation [8]. The algorithm has widely been accepted to finding community networks, technical networks, classifications and clustering, patent citations, web spam proofing, etc [2, 9, 12]. The algorithm, however, intentionally excludes the navigation links that can be valuable to derive a structure. The PageRank measures the rank of the pages in terms of hyperlink structure which can modified for employing arc weights. There are works on exploiting the hierarchical structure of the web. Eiron et al. [3] described a web graph model to integrate the hyperlink structure and the explicit hierarchical structure together, which reflects a social division by the organization. They are mostly based on a probabilistic model, so it is too vague to guide a specific web search. Even in the inside of the directory structure, there are so many web pages need to be structured somehow. Structuring by statistical "Page Popularity" [5] can be an answer for re-ranking the web information retrieval, but that hierarchy is too sensitive and fragile for the web changes [10]. A static linear programming model is suggested for dynamic web changing environments without weight measures [11], but an exten sion with a hop constraint needs to be devised.

3 Mahematical Model

3.1 Notations

The MRST (Maximum Rooted Spanning Tree) problem and HMRST (Hop con-strained Maximum Rooted Spanning Tree) can be formulated as the following binary integer linear program using the notation given below. Here, we assume that all web objects and hyperlinks among them are converted into corresponding directed graph. Also, the directed graph has its root node as one web object that are selected by a user at a search engine from the list of URLs as explained in previous section.

i, j	indices for nodes that represent web objects existing in a web site, $i, j \in$ set of all nodes: $N = \{1, 2, ..., n\}$ (Here, node zero is the root node)
t	index for terminal nodes, $t \in$ set of all terminal nodes: $T \subseteq N$
A	set of all existing arcs
w_{ij}	Weight of arc (i, j) that represents the degree of relevance between two nodes
h_t	Number of allowable arcs from the root node to a terminal node t in the rooted spanning tree obtained
x_{ij}	equals 1 if arc (i, j) is selected to make rooted spanning tree, and 0 otherwise.
y_{ij}^t	equals 1 if arc (i, j) is included in the path for accessing to terminal node t from the root node, and 0 otherwise.

3.2 MRST Problem

Now, we present a binary integer linear programming formulation of the MRST problem.

$$\max \quad \sum_{\substack{i, j \in N, j \geq 1 \\ (i,j) \in A}} w_{ij} x_{ij} \tag{1}$$

subject to

$$\sum_{\substack{i \in N \\ (i,0) \in A}} x_{i0} = 0 \tag{2}$$

$$\sum_{\substack{i \in N \\ (i,j) \in A}} x_{ij} = 1 \qquad \text{for all } j \neq 0 \tag{3}$$

$$x_{ii} = 0 \qquad \text{for all } i \tag{4}$$

$$x_{ij_1} + \begin{cases} x_{j_m i} \leq m & \text{if } m = 1 \\ \sum_{k=1}^{m-1} x_{j_k j_{k+1}} + x_{j_m i} \leq m & \text{if } 2 \leq m \leq |N| - 1 \end{cases}$$

For all directed circuits starting from any node i, and returning to the same node through m intermediate nodes, where a directed circuit can be represented as an ordered list of nodes, $(i, j_1, j_2, ..., j_k, j_{k+1}, ..., j_{m-1}, j_m, i)$

$$\tag{5}$$

$$x_{ij} \in \{0, 1\} \qquad \text{for all } i, j \tag{6}$$

The objective function (1) to be maximized denotes the sum of arc weights. Methods for measuring arc weights used in the objective function are described in Section 3. Constraints (2) to (5) are all required to satisfy conditions for feasible spanning tree. Constraint (2) ensures that any arc toward the root node should not be included in the rooted spanning tree, while constraint (3) ensures that every node should have only one node as its parent. Even though the constraint (1) through (3) are satisfied, however, if there is a circuit and that is selected as a solution, then the solution falls into the degenerate case. It is not the rooted tree any more. So constraints (4) and (5) eliminate the directed circuits including the self-referenced circuit. Note that we should find all directed circuits, which exist in a directed graph, for making the constraint (5). The basic strategy to resolve the circuit is to make the circuit have a bound at most the number of paths. For example, a circuit consists of three arcs (x_{35}, x_{56}, and x_{63},), then the bound will be 2, so the constraint will be: $x_{35} + x_{56} + x_{63} \leq 2$. The constraint (5) ensures that total number of selected arcs, which are included in a directed circuit, should be less than or equal to the intermediate number of nodes for the directed circuit. Constraint (6) represents binary integer decision variables for the MRST problem.

3.3 HMRST Problem

We give another binary integer linear programming formulation in which a special constraint is added to the original formulation for the MRST problem. We call this extended problem as HMRST (Hop constrained Maximum Rooted Spanning Tree) problem. The special constraint is called as hop limits that are the maximum number of allowable arcs from the root node to terminal nodes. A binary integer linear programming formulation of the HMRST problem is given below.

$$\max \sum_{\substack{i, j \in N, j \geq 1 \\ (i,j) \in A}} w_{ij} x_{ij} \tag{1}$$

subject to (2)-(6), and

$$\sum_{\substack{(i,j)\in A \\ j\in N,\, j\geq 1}} y_{ij}^{t} - \sum_{\substack{(j,i)\in A \\ j\in N}} y_{ji}^{t} = \begin{cases} +1 & \text{if } i=0 \\ -1 & \text{if } i=t \\ 0 & \text{otherwise} \end{cases} \quad \text{for all } i \text{ and } t \qquad (7)$$

$$y_{ij}^{t} \leq x_{ij} \quad \text{for all } i, j, t \qquad (8)$$

$$\sum_{\substack{(i,j)\in A \\ j\in N,\, j\geq 1}} y_{ij}^{t} \leq h_{t} \quad \text{for all } t \qquad (9)$$

$$y_{ij}^{t} \in \{0,1\} \quad \text{for all } i, j, t \qquad (10)$$

Constraints (7) and (8) ensure that paths for accessing terminal nodes should be determined in association with a hop constrained rooted spanning tree. Constraints (9) represent the maximum number of allowable arcs (hops) from the root node to a terminal node. Constraints (10) represent binary integer path variables that determine paths from the root node to terminal nodes.

4   Arc Weights Measurement

4.1   PageRank Based Arc Weights

In this research, we develop a new method for determining the arc weights that basically uses PageRank algorithm, well-known web objects (that is, nodes in converted directed graph for a web site) ranking algorithm. In PageRank algorithm, the rank of node i, $R(i)$, is derived with the equation (11) as given below. In the equation, a_{ij} is the elements of Markov transition matrix used in computing ranks for the nodes. $O(i)$ is a set of nodes whose elements (that is nodes in the set) has incoming arcs from node i. Also, d is a damping factor that is used to control the speed of convergence of ranks of nodes when computing the ranks with PageRank algorithm [14].

$$R(i) = (1-d) \times \begin{bmatrix} 1/n \\ . \\ . \\ . \\ 1/n \end{bmatrix}_{n\times 1} + d \times \sum_{\substack{(i,j)\in A \\ j\in O(i)}} a_{ij} R(j) \qquad (11)$$

Although the PageRank algorithm utilizes the arc structures in computing ranks for nodes, as shown in the equation (11), it focuses on computing ranks for nodes not weights for arcs that are required to generate rooted spanning trees for structured web search. Of course, we can compute arc weights using the ranks for nodes. Equation (12) describes how to compute arc weights with ranks for nodes, $R(i)$. Weights of arcs computed as the equation (12) can be interpreted as probabilities that a user visits from a web object to other linked web objects. Note that all outgoing arcs from a node to any other nodes have the same arc weights (that is, the same probability), $R(i)/|O(i)|$, when we compute arc weights according to the equation (12). Here, $|O(i)|$ is the cardinality of the set $O(i)$.

$$w_{ij} = R(i)/|O(i)| \quad \text{for all } i, j \in R(i) \text{ and } (i, j) \in A \tag{12}$$

4.2 Bidirectional Arc Weight

We propose a new method to measure arc weights, named as bidirectional arc weights measurement method. In order for two web pages to share arcs to each other, the authors should know of their existence. The following equation (13) shows the measurement method.

$$w_{ij} = p \cdot R(i) + (1 - p) \cdot R(j) \tag{13}$$

Here, p is a parameter satisfying $0 \le p \le 1$, and $R(i)$ and $R(j)$ are ranks for nodes i and j obtained with PageRank algorithm.

We can overcome the two limitations of PageRank based arc weights by using the parameter p appropriately. If we set p as 0.5, ranks of two nodes are equally considered, while larger weight is multiplied to the page rank of starting node (that is, node i) if p is greater than 0.5. Similarly, if p is less than 0.5, larger weight is multiplied to the page rank of destination node (that is, node j). It may be possible to determine best-suited value of p by comparing effectiveness of web search results with various p values. Note that the determination of p should be related to the domain, and we will not prove here that the matrix with the bidirectional parameter converges since the values are the weighted average of PageRank. Also, other methods for determining node ranks such as *cosine*, *tf-idf* method from the vector space model can also be used instead of HITS [8] or PageRank algorithm [14]. In other words, even though the node weight $R(i)$ and $R(j)$ can be *tf-idf* values, the arc weight of eq. (13) will work well with that semantics.

5 Implementation

We performed a real web site case to evaluate how to find structured search trees (that is, a rooted spanning tree) for given a web object. As mentioned earlier, we assume that this web object was selected from a list of URLs given by a search engine. The problem of indexing and weighting "the indexable web" [3] therefore starts with identifying what constitutes "the usable web."

Before we give results of the case study for a real web site, we first explain how the two binary integer linear programming models can be used to find rooted spanning trees with a small example. Figure 6 shows a directed graph that is assumed to be obtained from converting web objects and hyperlinks of a web site into. Note that the root node corresponds to a web object that may be selected from a list of URLs given by a search engine. As shown in Figure 6, the directed graph has seven nodes (from node 0 to node 6) and some arcs among them. Numbers on the arcs are the arc weights obtained with the method given in section 3. Without loss of generality, we set $p=0.5$ to compute the arc weights in this example.

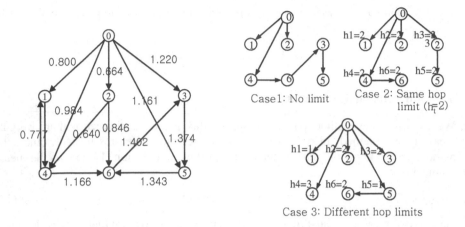

Fig. 6. Example Graph   **Fig. 7.** HMRST for the example

For the example directed graph, we generate structured search trees by solving the two binary integer linear programming models (for the MRST and HMRST problems). Obtained rooted spanning trees, which can be used as structured search trees, are shown in Figure 7. In Figure 7, the rooted spanning tree given in Case 1 is an optimal solution of MRST problem for the example directed graph. That is, Case 1 corresponds to a problem of finding rooted spanning tree without any hop constraints. On the other hand, rooted spanning trees given in Case 2 and Case 3 are optimal solutions of HMRST problem for the example directed graph. Values in the node represent hop limits for the nodes that represent the maximum allowable number of arcs from the root node.

Table 1. Total arc weights and paths for sample cases

		Case 1	Case 2	Case 3
Total Arc Weight		6.390	6.208	6.172
Paths for terminal nodes	Node 1	0→1	0→1	0→1
	Node 2	0→2	0→2	0→2
	Node 3	0→4→6→3	0→3	0→3
	Node 4	0→4	0→4	0→4
	Node 5	0→4→6→3→5	0→3→5	0→5
	Node 6	0→4→6	0→4→6	0→5→6

Table 1 gives optimal objective values (that is, total arc weight) and paths for accessing terminal nodes from the root node. As shown in Figure 7 and Table 1, the objective values and paths change according to the hop constraints. In Case 2, all the terminal nodes appear within two hops, while various hop limits are applied to each terminal node in Case 3. User may not want to go searching further more (that is at least specific number of clicks) from a web object (that be selected from URLs given by search engine). In this case, user can set hop limit when he or she submit search query. Then hop constrained rooted spanning tree can be generated with the

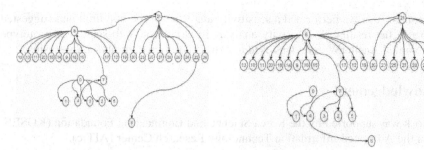

Fig. 8. MRST without hop limits   **Fig. 9.** MRST with a hop limit

hop limit. The hop constrained spanning tree gives the most relevant web objects that can reach within the hop limit from the root web object.

We test our approach of generating rooted spanning trees with real case. In this test, we assume again a user selects a URL of a web site from a search engine and the selected web object (that is selected URL) becomes the root node of a directed graph for the web site. Assume that selected URL is the homepage for a web site of Samsung Electronics, www.samsung.co.kr. The number of only static web objects in Samsung's web site is 31 and number of hyperlinks are 88.

Figure 8 shows an optimal rooted spanning tree when a hop limit for node 6 is set as 2. As shown in Figures 8 and 9, optimal rooted tree changes with hop limit for node 6. We may interpret this change as follows. A user can set a maximum number of clicks (from a selected URL given by a search engine) when he or she submits a search query for relevant web objects. Structured web search approach suggested in this study can support this user, who may not want to go searching further more from a selected URL, by providing hop constrained rooted spanning tree to the user. Hop constrained rooted spanning tree suggests the most relevant web objects to the selected web object (that can be the root web object) satisfying the hop limit set by the user.

Due to the space limitation, we do not show the results. We performed computational tests for several distinguished electronic companies' web sites. Included are Hitachi, Intel, Microsoft, NEC, and Nokia. Their web sites have a number of thousands of web objects and hyperlinks. After identifying nodes and arcs, the two models for these web sites are solved within a few seconds with CPLEX on a personal computer.

6 Conclusions

In this study, we suggested a new approach for effective web searching, defined as structured web search. For the structured web search, we developed two binary integer linear programming models to generate rooted spanning trees and a new method for measuring the relevance among web objects in a web site. In order to achieve hop constraints, it is inevitable to lose an allowable objective cost with the global optimal value. We tested our approach with Samsung's real web site. Results showed that we could find rooted spanning trees, which can be used in structured web search, within a few seconds. Also we performed a sensitivity analysis for the hop limit and suggested how to use the results of sensitivity analysis in structured web search. A prototype system named AnchorWoman was used to extract a directed graph for a web site.

Acknowledgement

This work was supported by the Korea Science and Engineering Foundation (KOSEF) through the Advanced Information Technology Research Center (AITrc).

References

[1] Barabasi A., Albert R., and Jeong H. Scale-free characteristics of random networks: the topology of the world-wide web. Physica A 281 (2000), 69-77
[2] Bharat, K., Chang, B. W., Henzinger, M. R., and Ruhl, M. Who Links to Whom: Mining Linkage between Web Sites. In: Proc. ICDM 2001. 51-58
[3] Eiron, N. McCurley, K., and Tomlin, J. Ranking the web frontier. In Proc. WWW 2004: 309-318
[4] Faloutsos, M., Faloutsos, P., Faloutsos, C. On Power-law Relationships of the Internet Topology. In: Proc. SIGCOMM 1999. 251-262.
[5] Garofalakis, J., Kappos, P. and Mourloukos, D. Web Site Optimization Using Page Popularity, IEEE Internet Computing, 3(4): (1999) 22-29
[6] Gyongyi, Z., Garcia-Molina, H., and Pedersen, J. Combating Web Spam with TrustRank. VLDB (2004), 576-587
[7] Henzinger, M. R., Heydon, A., Mitzenmacher, M. and Najork, M. On Near-uniform URL Sampling, Computer Networks, 33(1) (2000), 295-308
[8] Kleinberg, J. M. Authoritative sources in a hyperlinked environment, Journal of the ACM, Vol.46 (5). (1999) 604-632
[9] Lee, W.: Hierarchical Web Structuring from the Web as a Graph Approach with Repetitive Cycle Proof. In: proc. APWeb Workshops 2006: 1004-1011
[10] Lee, Wookey, Geller, J. Semantic Hierarchical Abstraction of Web Site Structures for Web Searchers, Journal of Res. Practice in Information Technology, 36(1) (2004),71-82
[11] Lee, W., Kim, S., Kang, S.: Structuring Web Sites Using Linear Programming. In: proc. EC-Web 2004: 328-337
[12] Lerman, K., Getoor, L., Minton, S., and Knoblock, C. Using the Structure of Web Sites for Automatic Segmentation of Tables. In: Proc. SIGMOD 2004: 119-130
[13] Najork, M., and Wiener, J.: Breadth-first Crawling Yields High-quality Pages, In: Proc. WWW 2001: 114-118
[14] Pandurangan, G., Raghavan, P. and Upfal, E.: Using PageRank to Characterize Web Structure. In: Proc. COCOON 2002: 330-339

CAMS 2006 PC Co-chairs' Message

Context awareness is increasingly forming one of the key strategies for delivering effective information services in mobile contexts. The limited screen displays of many mobile devices mean that content must be carefully selected to match the users needs and expectations, and context provides one powerful means of performing such tailoring. Context-aware mobile systems will almost certainly become ubiquitous - already in the UK affordable "smartphones" include GPS location support. With this hardware comes the opportunity for "onboard" applications to use location data to provide new services—until recently such systems could only be created with complex and expensive components. Furthermore, the current "mode" of the phone (e.g., silent, meeting, outdoors), contents of the built-in calendar, etc. can all used to provide a rich context for the users immediate environment.

However, there is much to learn from a computer science perspective: context is a plastic and variable concept that can be realized in many ways—from the early notions of location-based services, through social navigation techniques based upon profiling of users, to concepts of work processes and information journeys. Together, these differing forms of context provide a challenging diversity of data which need to be brought together and consistently and rapidly processed. These demands provide a strong testbed of contemporary techniques for modelling context, particularly when the network and processing capacities of mobile systems are considered.

The second Context Aware Mobile Systems (CAMS) workshop had a strong set of paper presentations spread over two days. Building on last years very successful programme, we are sure that workshop attendees were delighted with the breadth and depth of contributions that were discussed. Papers covered the spectrum of context-aware mobile systems: the traditional basis of location, the processes of personalization and profiling, emerging areas such as interface design and ontologies, plus engineering requirements such as development models and architectural frameworks. The global nature of the research in this area is also reflected in the wide spread of countries represented by the paper authors.

The workshop received nearly 40 submissions, and our panel of 16 reviewers closely scrutinized these to select the 13 best papers.

August 2006   Annika Hinze, University of Waikato, New Zealand
George Buchanan, University of Wales Swansea, UK

R. Meersman, Z. Tari, P. Herrero et al. (Eds.): OTM Workshops 2006, LNCS 4278, p. 1883, 2006.
© Springer-Verlag Berlin Heidelberg 2006

An Investigation into a Universal Context Model to Support Context-Aware Applications

Jason Pascoe, Helena Rodrigues, and César Ariza

Information Systems Department, University of Minho, Campus Azurém,
4800-058 Guimarães, Portugal
{jason, helena, cariza}@dsi.uminho.pt

Abstract. If a mobile device is to offer rich context-aware behaviour it must have a good knowledge of the world around us. This paper explores the concept of universal context model, able to represent any form of context information and therefore be an enabler to the full spectrum of context-aware applications. It explores how such a model may accurately represent - as far as practically possible - the multitude of different objects we encounter in our surrounding environment and their many states and interrelationships. Three key propositions are that the context model should be of an object-oriented nature, that location is most appropriately and flexibly represented as a relationship between two objects rather than being considered as a special type of object unto itself, and finally, that objects may be coupled with observer-dependent validity rules that determine if the object is visible within the model.

Keywords: context-aware, location-aware, context model, context, object model, e-government, mobile government services.

1 Introduction

This work was conducted as part of the USE-ME.GOV initiative [1] to develop a platform to enable the easy development and deployment of local government applications/services that citizens can access via their smartphones. A core component of the USE-ME.GOV platform concept was a context model to support context-aware [2] behaviours of the various services through the provision of a model of the surrounding environment. The term *surrounding environment* meaning the physical world in which we all live, the technical environment in which the application resides, or, even, a virtual environment that does not, in reality, exist at all. The aim of this context model was to enable applications to easily sense their surrounding environment so that they could react or adapt to it as appropriate.

Although each application could theoretically construct its own model of the surrounding environment, it is often a complicated and difficult endeavour due to the plethora of data types, formats, sensor systems, and protocols that one must master and work with [5]. It would therefore seem sensible to concentrate these general environment-monitoring and representation capabilities into a shared resource rather than developing these facilities from the ground up for each and every application.

R. Meersman, Z. Tari, P. Herrero et al. (Eds.): OTM Workshops 2006, LNCS 4278, pp. 1884–1893, 2006.

Research into frameworks and models to support context-awareness in applications has tended to concentrate on particular niches. For example, some context-aware research has been application centric with any modelling component embedded in the applications themselves (such as Guide [3]), some has dealt primarily with handling and conversion of sensor data (such as the Context toolkit [4]), some has concentrated on models for specific types of application behaviours (such as stick-e notes [5]), and some has concentrated on particular data types (such as tuple spaces [6]). Two broader approaches to modelling context are SOUPA (Standard Ontology for Ubiquitous and Pervasive Applications) [9] and CoOL (Context Ontology Language to enable Contextual Interoperability) [11]. SOUPA uses semantic web techniques (among others) to exploit context, but is primarily aimed at pervasive computing environments. CoOL employs semantic web techniques in an object-oriented approach but differs from our concept of a context model in that context dimensions form the basis of the model rather than the concepts of a generic object structure and the expression of location as a relationship between two objects.

In the USE-ME.GOV initiative the core idea was that the resulting platform should support the development and deployment of *any* service/application that a local government could care to offer its citizens (example applications later developed included an in-situ complaint service, a healthcare service, a student information service, and a city information service). So by necessity we had to think of our context model in the broadest possible terms in order to support the full spectrum of possible context-aware applications, and to therefore be able to consider anything in the surrounding environment as potentially useful context information.

In this paper we present the key concepts and recommendations of a context model of such universal scope. An implementation based on these concepts has been made in the USE-ME.GOV project, as has an application and usability study. However, in this paper we shall concentrate on an in-depth examination of the key concepts and recommendations underpinning such a universal context model, and we will present a full description of our implementation and test application in a subsequent paper.

2   The Need for an Object Oriented Model

Location is an important and oft-sited example of context. However, we subscribe to the notion that practically any factor in the surrounding environment could be employed in context-aware behaviours. Objects, properties, and relationships are three powerful abstractions with which we can think about and describe most of the things we encounter in our everyday world (and indeed the technical and virtual worlds too) and it forms the underlying nature of our concept for a universally applicable context model.

Note that it is possible, and quite correct, to develop a context model that does not comply with this or many of our other concepts. For example, a simple cell-based location model may serve perfectly well within its remit of modelling the location of the persons in a building equipped with an active badge network. However, our intention in defining these concepts and recommendations is to address the broader scope of a universal context model that is able support any and every type of context information, and for any and every context-aware application.

3 Objects

People, cars, dogs, knives, films, oranges, and bags are all what we would intuitively consider to be objects. Furthermore, each of these entities has a number of attributes such as a name, colour, mood, price, ripeness, etc. But what exactly makes an object an object? It seems to be a rather subjective issue where an apple could be viewed as a fruit or, more fundamentally, as merely a collection of atoms. In constructing our context model we should therefore ensure support for layered views of reality through the constructs of abstraction, containment, and possibly partial containment, of objects.

3.1 Uncertainty, Referencing, and Change

Some characteristics of a particular object may change over time, and some may be uncertain. For example, when exploring a city I may be quite confident of my location but not absolutely sure. I may also talk about another person and say that "I *think* he was about 180cm tall". In such cases we express an object's characteristics with only a degree of certainty or confidence. Additionally, we sometimes might also express a characteristic of an object by referring to another (e.g. her height is the same as his).

These concepts of uncertainty, referencing and change certainly need to be expressible in a context model.

4 Object Types

Unlike the types or classes (we use the two terms interchangeably here) that we may be familiar with in programming languages, in our everyday lives a class/type of object acts as a kind of template or, more accurately, a *stereotype*. That is, it illustrates how an instance of that type of object can typically be *expected* to be. It is comprised of a set of assumptions about the object's "normal" characteristics, i.e. those characteristics that will hold true in the face of many, though not necessarily all, individual cases of that type of object. For example, in our general understanding about people we know that they tend to have a home and a job, even if in some cases this does not hold true. When we encounter a particular individual we can retain our general assumptions about a person that do hold true whilst ignoring the ones that do not, and also adding in any characteristics that are peculiar to the specific individual.

Our model aims to support this notion that types are more like suggestions or stereotypes that can be altered and added to in specific instances of objects, and *not* like rigid rules or templates that must be steadfastly conformed to. We also see the value of an evolutionary construction of types, necessitating a model where objects can be created without a type, and where the nature of the types and objects can develop and change over time. Though in a richly populated and evolved model it may more often be the case that an object has multiple object types rather than none at all.

5 Relationships

Objects normally do not exist in isolation. They are commonly related in many ways to other objects. For example, consider a person who owns a computer, and that computer contains a hard drive and is currently sitting on a table, and that table is within an office, and that office is within a room in the university, etc. In this example we can see relationships between objects that express ownership, containment, and positioning, though there are infinitely more possibilities for types of relationships.

Sometimes it is satisfactory to express relationships as simple linkages between one object and another, but it can also often be the case that a more detailed description of the nature of the relationship is required. If, for example, we consider an is-in relationship then sometimes it may be satisfactory to simply link together the container object with the contained object, but sometimes we may need to know more precisely where the contained object is within the container object. In effect our link becomes parameterised with more information.

Intuitively we tend to view relationships as special constructs set apart from other objects. But perhaps we should actually consider them as only another type of object. We can consider a relationship, at the highest level of abstraction, to be a type of object that involves a reference to one or more other objects. At a lower level of abstraction we may consider particular types of relationship object, such as containment relationships, ownership relationships, etc. which exhibit more specific characteristics. And, naturally, specific instances of relationship objects will describe the characteristics of a particular relationship in concrete form. Furthermore, types and type hierarchies can be similarly constructed as relationships using generic object structures (e.g. via "is-a" and "is-kind-of" objects).

Treating relationships as just another type of object allows us to model and reason about them using the same methods and techniques as we use for any other object.

5.1 Location as a Relationship

Although it is often the case that location is viewed as a special object type, or as the property of another object, we believe it is more appropriately and flexibly thought of as a relationship between two objects. For example, a computer is on the table, the table is in a room, the room is in the university, etc. Even complex co-ordinate based location types can be simply expressed as is-in relationships. For example, latitude and longitude can be expressed as an is-in relationship, parameterised with the specific degree values of latitude and longitude, between a person and the world.

Cell-based location systems (such as a mobile phone cell network) offer at least two possible means of representation in the model. We could consider an is-in relationship between a phone object and a cell network object, where the is-in relationship is parameterised with the ID of the cell in which the phone is currently residing. We could also choose to represent the individual cells as objects in their own right within the model. For example, a phone is-in a cell, and a cell is-in a cell network. We favour the latter solution as it offers interesting possibilities for further linking and reasoning, such as linking the individual cells to a world object with an is-in relationship that is parameterised with a latitude and longitude polygon. This could potentially enable an elegant co-operation of cell and co-ordinate based systems.

Proximity or "is-near" relationships (perhaps parameterised with values that indicate the degree of closeness) are useful in themselves and also in inferring the location of an object, whose location is not known, through its proximity to another object, whose

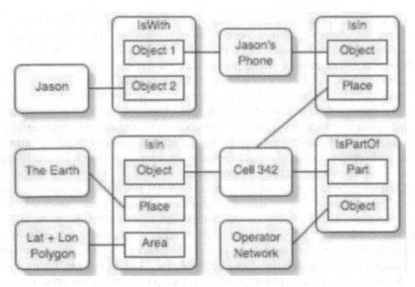

Fig. 1. An Illustration of Location Represented via Relationship Objects

location is known. It is also often the case that we do not know the location of an object directly but rather through the use of a device such as a GPS receiver or mobile phone. As we know that a particular person is *with* a particular phone or GPS receiver then we can infer that the location of the person is the same as that of the device. We believe that these devices, and their relationships with a person, should be included in the model for a more accurate picture of reality. Note that we prefer a "with" relationship for this purpose of "location inference" rather than an is-near, ownership or "using" relationship. Only "with" combines current proximity with the meaning of a higher social or semantic connection. For example, walking down the street next to a friend of mine I would consider myself to be with them, but, on the other hand, I would not consider myself to be with a stranger just because he happens to be walking nearby me in the street. The problem with ownership is that it does not necessarily imply current proximity (I may have left my phone at home), and a "using" relationship is only true for a small percentage of the time that the user's mobile device is with them (i.e. the time in which the user is interacting with the device and not when it is still with them but stowed in their pocket or purse, etc.).

Note that as a result of it being possible to have any type of object as the subject of a location relationship we are able to consider any type of object as being a place. We typically think only of certain things as being places, such as buildings, towns, etc. However, in principle, we do not see any reason why we should not consider tables, cars, and even people to be places too. For example, from a flea's perspective perhaps the name of a dog is the most meaningful way he has to describe his location.

6 Conditional Objects

It can be useful for an object, especially a virtual one, to be defined in such a way that it is only seen to exist in the model when certain conditions hold true. Such conditional objects could potentially provide the basis for context-triggered actions in observing applications [5], and for information filtering/targeting and privacy.

This object-conditionality can be expressed by coupling an object with a logical expression, which we call a *validity rule*. An object is only observable when its validity rule evaluates to true. For example, consider a red rose object that is coupled with the following pseudo-code validity rule:

```
(Jason.isin.place == JasonsGirlfriend.isin.place) &&
(Moon.state == "full") &&
(Jason.mood == JasonsGirlfriend.mood == "romantic") &&
(Jason.isin.place != JasonsXGirlfriend.isin.place)
```

Note the way of expressing the validity rule may differ considerably from this in its implementation (especially for more "fuzzy" forms of location matching).

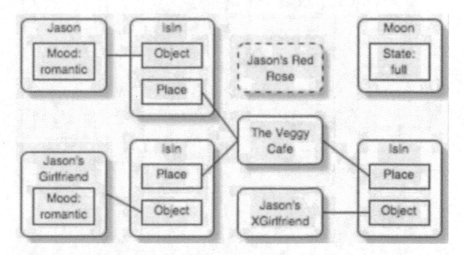

Fig. 2. The red rose is not visible because Jason's ex-girlfriend is present

Given this validity rule a red rose will appear in the model if Jason is in the same place as his girlfriend, the moon is full, both her and he are in a romantic mood, and, for the discretion's sake, his ex-girlfriend is not present. In Figure 2 an example illustration is given where the latter condition is not met.

6.1 Observer Dependency

In this red rose example the validity rule functions well, with the red rose appearing in the correct romantic circumstances. However, all clients of the model will be able to see the red rose whereas Jason's intention is rather more personal: he would like to create a rose for his girlfriend alone. This may be achieved by incorporating the notion of an observer when interacting with the context model (though note that we believe a client should also be free to execute anonymous queries that will yield observer-independent results).

Given the concept of a current observer we can adjust the rose object's validity rule as follows:

```
(Observer.id ==  JasonsGirlfriend.id) &&
(Jason.isin.place == JasonsGirlfriend.isin.place) &&
(Moon.state == "full") &&
(Jason.mood == JasonsGirlfriend.mood == "romantic") &&
(Jason.isin.place != JasonsXGirlfriend.isin.place)
```

In Figure 3 we illustrate a scenario where all the conditions are met and hence the red rose appears visible to the current observer (who *must* be Jason's girlfriend).

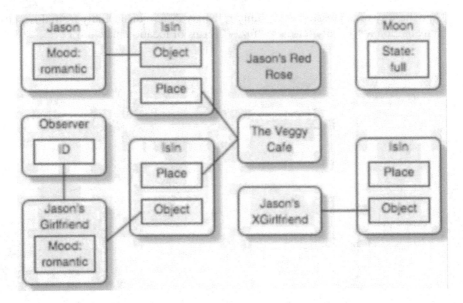

Fig. 3. All conditions are met for the observer to see Jason's Red Rose

For the above validity rule to evaluate to true then the observer must be set to Jason's girlfriend. If the observer was set to any other type of object, or any other individual person, then the validity rule would evaluate to false and so the object would remain invalid and invisible to the observer.

Note that any type of object, such as dogs, phones, pot plants, and so forth, may all be considered equally valid observers (though all presumably having some client software working on their behalf). So an object's validity rule could also check the type of the observer, for example, to only permit person objects to view a specified object. In fact, any other characteristic that we may like to check for in the observer may be included in the validity rule.

7 Functions for Comparing, Testing and Feeding the Model

An extensible function repository is needed to register functions that in some way work with the context model. These functions could be registered with their type, parameters, and type of result. Two particularly useful types of function could be comparators (greater than, less than, equal to, etc.) and converters. Converters could take a parameter of one type of object and yield another type of object as a result. This is often useful, for example, when a client requires a value in a particular format.

"Feeders" are another type of function needed in the model's function repository. A feeder is a function that provides a means to obtain values from the user or a software sensor or a hardware sensor. The results of such functions may then be fed into the model. Of course, unlike comparison or conversion functions, such continually running functions need a means to be configured, started and stopped.

A good example of a feeder is a GPS sensor function that could be initialised with the data necessary to connect it to a specific GPS receiver (e.g. port, data rate, etc.) and the output plugged into an is-in relationship in order to feed it with a current latitude and longitude parameter.

Such sensor functions may provide a single one-off value, but perhaps will more often provide a continuous service. In the case of continuous updates we need to be able to regulate the sensor function so as to strike a balance between keeping the model up-to-date to a satisfactory level whilst taking care not to over-consume processing resources on needless updates. In essence, we need to specify some level of quality of service. In the coarsest terms we could specify whether a sensor function should autonomously and continuously update the model or whether it should only do so on a demand-driven basis (i.e. only updating a characteristic of an object when it is viewed by an observer). If a sensor is autonomously updating an object then the model should offer some further configuration to allow the update process to be appropriately regulated (e.g. by specifying a time interval that defines how often a latitude and longitude object is updated from a connected GPS sensor function).

8 Implementation

We will present the results of our implementation in a separate paper but will give a brief overview here to illustrate the direction we took in developing the context model and applications for a local government services platform (USE-ME.GOV [1]).

Our implementation of the context model is represented using OWL [7]. We also considered adapting ontologies from CONON [8] and SOUPA [9] but found some key differences that made them unsuitable for our concept of a context model. Regardless, a major reason to choose OWL was the relatively straightforward way in which we can represent and evaluate rules and infer knowledge from the model.

Objects within our context model implementation are represented in the form of RDF files, and for our deployment of the context model in the mobile government services platform in Vila Nova de Cerveira (a municipality in the north of Portugal) the model was populated with objects such as streets, squares, points of interest, water mains, hydrants, trash cans, traffic lights, etc. and the various inter-relationships between them. In addition to these physical objects we also represented the local government services as objects within the model, and linked them to their related objects. For example, a parks & gardens complaint service may be linked to the various green areas of the city, whereas the highways complaint service may be linked to the physical road infrastructure that is also represented within the model. In this way many different complaint services could be added to the model in the situations where they would be of use. Therefore finding a complaint service to assist a particular citizen would often be as simple as seeing which services are in the same situation as the citizen in the model (e.g. in the park, walking along the street, etc.)

To manage the population of objects in the model an Object Manager API was created based on Jena [10]. This Object Manager API can either be invoked directly or as a Web Service, and offers functionalities for object creation, relation creation, querying (where Jena is especially helpful), and directly or indirectly feeding the model (i.e. manually entering a value into the model or setting up a feeder function to automatically enter data into the model from a sensor source).

A context-aware complaint application developed for use from a citizen's smartphone uses the Object Manager functionalities to help citizens find complaint services using their current context. Firstly the context model must be populated with objects representing the citizen, their smartphone, the relationships between them, and feeders set-up to automatically update the model (e.g. to ascertain the operator cell location of the smartphone). After this initial setup procedure the application is able to query the Object Manager to, for example, ask about objects related to the user in the real world and to ask about "unreal" objects such as services. These queries are used to perform an automatic identification, or honing down, of objects that the user may like to complain about in their surrounding environment, followed by the identification and connection to the appropriate end-service to handle their complaint.

9 Conclusions and Future Work

In this paper we have presented some key areas for consideration in developing a universal context model that is able to support as broad a range of context types and applications as possible. In particular, we suggest an object-oriented construction that is capable of representing practically any part of our surrounding environment.

Object types in this model may be viewed as commonly occurring characteristics of a particular class of objects rather than precisely defining what each individual's nature will be. Some objects may express a level of uncertainty about their correctness and some may even fade in and out of existence altogether as the validity rules with which they are associated evaluate differently as the surrounding environment changes. Those rules may also take into account the identity, or other characteristics, of the observer of the model, thus enabling a degree of targeting or personalisation of the context model. The same validity rules also provide a basis for a trigger- or event-driven context-aware behaviour in clients.

Practically all the model's elements may be represented using the same generic object construct, including relationships, types, and class hierarchies. More specifically, location, often considered an object or property unto itself, may be modelled as a relationship between two objects, so allowing any object to be considered as a place. A final component of the context model is a repository of functions with which to compare, convert and feed the contents of the model.

In a subsequent paper we will present in-depth our work on the implementation of a context model based on the concepts presented in this paper. We will also detail the practicalities faced in deploying it in a real-world scenario and the advantages and disadvantages perceived by both application developers and application users.

References

1. The USE-ME.GOV Project Web Site, http://www.usemegov.org/
2. Schilit, B.N., Adams, N.I., and Want, R.: Context-Aware Computing Applications. Proceedings of the Workshop on Mobile Computing Systems and Applications. Santa Cruz, CA, USA (1994) 85-90
3. Cheverst, K., Davies, N., Mitchell, K., and Friday, A.: Experiences of Developing and Deploying a Context Aware Tourist Guide: The GUIDE Project. MOBICOM. Boston, MA, USA (2000) 20-31
4. Dey, A.K., Abowd, G.D., and Salber, D.: A Conceptual Framework and a Toolkit for Supporting the Rapid Prototyping of Context-Aware Applications. Human-Computer Interaction   Journal, Vol. 16 (2-4). (2001) 97-166
5. Pascoe, J., Ryan, N., and Morse, D.: Issues in Developing Context-Aware Computing Applications. HUC '99. Karlsruhe, Germany (1999) 208-221
6. Davies, N., Wade, S., Friday, A., and Blair, G.: Limbo: A Tuple Space Based Platform for Adaptive Mobile Applications. International Conference on Open Distributed Processing/Distributed Platforms (ICODP/ICDP'97). Toronto, Canada (1997) 291-302
7. Bechhofer, S., van Harmelen, F., Hendler, J., Horrocks, I., McGuinness, D., Patel-Schneider, P., Stein, L.: Owl Web Ontology Language Reference, www.w3.org/TR/owl-ref/ (2004)
8. Gu, T., Wang, X.H., Pung, H.K., Zhang, D.Q.: An Ontology-based Context Model in Intelligent Environments. Proceedings of Communication Networks and Distributed Systems Modeling and Simulation Conference. San Diego, California, USA (2004) 18-22
9. Chen, H. Perich, F. Finin, T. Joshi, A.: SOUPA: standard ontology for ubiquitous and pervasive applications. First Annual International Conference on Mobile and Ubiquitous Systems: Networking and Services (MOBIQUITOU). Boston, MA, USA (2004) 258-267
10. Jena - A Semantic Web Framework for Java. http://jena.sourceforge.net/ (2006)
11. Strang, T., Linnhff-Popien, C., Frank, K.: CoOL: A Context Ontology Language to Enable Contextual Interoperability. In: 4th International Conference on Distributed Applications and Interoperable Systems (DAIS). Lecture Notes in Computer Science, Vol. 2893. Springer-Verlag (2003) 236-247

A System for Context-Dependent User Modeling

Petteri Nurmi[1], Alfons Salden[2],
Sian Lun Lau[3], Jukka Suomela[1], Michael Sutterer[3],
Jean Millerat[4], Miquel Martin[5], Eemil Lagerspetz[1], and Remco Poortinga[2]

[1] Helsinki Institute for Information Technology HIIT,
P.O. Box 68, FI-00014 University of Helsinki, Finland
firstname.lastname@cs.helsinki.fi
[2] Telematica Instituut (TELIN), P.O. Box 589,
7500 AN Enschede, The Netherlands
firstname.lastname@telin.nl
[3] University of Kassel, Faculty of Electrical Engineering,
Wilhelmshöher Allee 73, 34121 Kassel, Germany
firstname.lastname@comtec.eecs.uni-kassel.de
[4] Motorola Labs, Parc Les Algorithmes, Saint-Aubin,
91193 Gif-sur-Yvette Cedex, France
firstname.lastname@motorola.com
[5] NEC Europe Ltd, Kurfürster Anlage 36,
69115 Heidelberg, Germany
firstname.lastname@netlab.nec.de

Abstract. We present a system for learning and utilizing context-dependent user models. The user models attempt to capture the interests of a user and link the interests to the situation of the user. The models are used for making recommendations to applications and services on what might interest the user in her current situation. In the design process we have analyzed several mock-ups of new mobile, context-aware services and applications. The mock-ups spanned rather diverse domains, which helped us to ensure that the system is applicable to a wide range of tasks, such as modality recommendations (e.g., switching to speech output when driving a car), service category recommendations (e.g., journey planners at a bus stop), and recommendations of group members (e.g., people with whom to share a car). The structure of the presented system is highly modular. First of all, this ensures that the algorithms that are used to build the user models can be easily replaced. Secondly, the modularity makes it easier to evaluate how well different algorithms perform in different domains. The current implementation of the system supports rule based reasoning and tree augmented naïve Bayesian classifiers (TAN). The system consists of three components, each of which has been implemented as a web service. The entire system has been deployed and is in use in the EU IST project MobiLife. In this paper, we detail the components that are part of the system and introduce the interactions between the components. In addition, we briefly discuss the quality of the recommendations that our system produces.

R. Meersman, Z. Tari, P. Herrero et al. (Eds.): OTM Workshops 2006, LNCS 4278, pp. 1894–1903, 2006.
© Springer-Verlag Berlin Heidelberg 2006

1 Introduction

In order to tailor mobile, context-aware applications and services to better match the needs of users, we need to make them able to adapt to the behavior of a user. In other words, we need to *personalize* the applications and services.

Background and related work. A widely used approach for personalization is user modeling [1]. In user modeling, the aim is to construct models that capture the beliefs, intentions, goals, and needs of a user [2]. In context-aware environments, we also need to associate the captured interests (needs, beliefs etc.) with the situation of the user. The main techniques for user modeling are knowledge representation (KR) methods and predictive user models [3]. The former covers traditional expert systems and logic-based systems, whereas the latter includes statistical machine learning techniques such as rule induction, neural networks, and Bayesian networks.

Previous work on context-dependent user modeling has mainly focused on KR methods. The most common approach has been the use of static rules, which are usually handcrafted and provided by the application designer (e.g., [4, 5]). Also the so-called preference approach (e.g., [6]), where users can specify application-specific rules, falls under the scope of KR based methods. In addition to rules, also ontology reasoning (e.g., [7]) and case-based reasoning (e.g., [8]) have been suggested. Finally, many context-aware middlewares provide system-level support for using KR methods (e.g., [9, 10]).

The KR methods suffer from two major problems. First of all, the techniques do not have a way to cope with uncertainty. Secondly, KR methods are not usually able to generalize their performance, i.e., to work well in previously unseen situations. However, in context-aware environments, there are various sources of uncertainty (e.g, the uncertainty about the goals of a user and inaccurate sensor signals) and the number of different situations that are relevant to a user might be very large. As a consequence, predictive user modeling seems the natural way to go. At the moment, however, work on using predictive user models in context-aware settings has been rather limited and all the uses are confined to a single application (e.g., [11]) or to a well defined spatial area such as a smart home (e.g., [12]) or a smart office (e.g., [13]).

Design process. Our work has been conducted within the EU project MobiLife[1]. In MobiLife, we have followed a user-centric design process (UCD). As the first step of the UCD process, we envisioned a set of high-level scenarios and evaluated them with users. With the help of the user feedback, the scenarios were used to construct mock-ups[2] of new, context-aware, mobile applications and services. The mock-ups were evaluated with users and both the feedback and the mock-ups were thoroughly analyzed.

---

[1] See http://www.ist-mobilife.org for more information.
[2] Mock-up: a model of something that is used to show other people how it will work or what it will look like.

While analyzing the mock-ups, we discovered several uses for context-dependent personalization in the application ideas. Examples of the uses include modality recommendations (e.g., switching to speech output when driving a car), service category recommendations (e.g., journey planners at a bus stop) and recommendations of group members (e.g., people with whom to share a car).

Contribution. In this paper, we describe a generic system for context-dependent user modeling. The system can be used with the diverse set of applications described above. We have followed ideas from the field of user modeling and made the system independent of the applications and services that use it [1]. The structure of our system is highly modular; this ensures that the user modeling techniques that are used can be easily replaced. Furthermore, the modularity makes it easier to evaluate how well different techniques perform in different domains. The current implementation supports rule based reasoning and tree augmented naïve Bayesian classifiers (TAN). We have also decoupled learning and inference, which makes it possible to extend the system so that inferences are run on a mobile device. The system consists of three components, each of which has been implemented as a web service. The entire system has been deployed and is in use in the MobiLife project.

Our system is, to our best knowledge, the first generic user modeling system for context-aware settings. By following a UCD design process, we have been able to ensure that our system is suited to the requirements of future mobile, context-aware applications and services. Finally, we are, to our best knowledge, the first to apply predictive user models in context-aware settings in a task independent way.

Structure of the paper. The rest of the paper is organized as follows. Sect. 2 introduces the three application mock-ups that were used in the design process of our system. Sect. 3 details the components that are part of our system, introduces the interactions between different components, and discusses the quality of the recommendations made by our system. Sect. 4 concludes the paper and discusses future work.

2   Application Mock-Ups and Design Goals

In this section, we briefly introduce the application mock-ups that were the main drivers in the design of our system. In addition, we describe the design goals that we derived from the mock-ups.

Multimedia Infotainer is a mobile application that allows users to interact seamlessly with different input and output devices. For example, when the user is driving with a car, the output modality of the phone should be speech. Or, when the user is at home, she could project all her non-confidential messages, e.g., to a plasma screen for easier reading. In order to make the application truly seamless, it needs to be able to infer what input or output modality is best suited for the current situation.

MobiCar is a car sharing application for mobile users. Users ask the application to find them a suitable car for going into a particular location at a specific time. As additional information, the user may choose to include personal preferences related to the car. Examples of potentially relevant user preferences include smoking or non-smoking, pets or no pets, or music and trustworthiness preferences of the user. The goal of the application is to find a suitable allocation, i.e., a set of people whose requests match as closely as possible and who could be willing to share a car. In MobiCar, we need to know which preferences have the most impact on the acceptance of suggestions made by the system. To this end, we need user models that associate *groups* of people and their *preferences* to a particular situation (going by car to X on a weekday night).

Personal Communicator is an application that integrates the interactions between a user and mobile services. The Personal Communicator can be used, among others, for reading RSS news feeds, planning trips using online travel planners, and printing on Bluetooth-based printing services. In order to simplify and make the services more easily accessible to the user, we need to recommend services that might interest the user in her current situation. Thus, the Personal Communicator offers another application where situation-dependent user modeling could significantly reduce the amount of user interactions.

The three mock-ups above are rather diverse and, in order to simplify reuse of machine learning methods, we need a way to provider a *generic* and *unified* approach for context-dependent user modeling. In addition, we should be able to provide (context-aware) personalization support for different entities (individual users or groups) in different and potentially very diverse domains. Finally, as different tasks have traditionally called for different kinds of solutions, we need to be able to replace and easily reconfigure the machine learning algorithms that are used for user modeling. A summary of the main design goals is given below.

- User modeling algorithms are independent of the application and the entity for whom the recommendations are made (user or group).
- User modeling algorithms can be easily replaced and the methods that are used for a particular entity and application can be easily reconfigured.
- The system is applicable (without changes) to diverse domains.

3   System Structure

In this section, we discuss the structure of our context-dependent user modeling system. A component diagram of the system is shown in Fig. 1 and in the following subsections we detail the functionalities of the individual components. The system has been integrated with a context management framework that is based on a service-oriented architecture. To this end, our discussion refers to a specific *instance* of each of the components and in practice there can be multiple instances running.

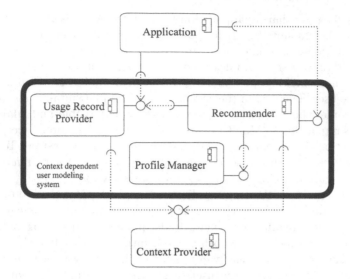

Fig. 1. A component diagram describing the context dependent user modeling system (the box in the middle) and its dependencies to external components

3.1   Usage Record Provider

The first component that we describe is the *Usage Record Provider*, which is a repository that stores information on the behavior of a user and the context in which the behavior takes place. For example, the Multimedia Infotainer stores the selected modality and the corresponding situation of the user. The information that is stored in the Usage Record Provider is then used by the *Recommender* (see Fig. 1 and Sect. 3.2) to learn and update user models.

The entries that the system logs are called *Usage Records*. An example of a Usage Record is shown in Fig. 2. All context information is contained within the XML tag `contextElement`. For privacy reasons, we have removed and obfuscated some of the context parameters in the example.

In our setting, the context information comes from components that are called *Context Providers*. More details on Context Providers and the used context model can be found at [14] and on the website of the MobiLife project[3]. See the list of software components on the website for a number of concrete examples of Context Providers, as well as descriptions of what kind of context information they provide.

The Usage Record Provider also acts as an entry point for applications and services into the system. To get useful information from the system, the applications must send usage information to the Usage Record Provider. The sent information should contain at least unique identifiers for the user and for the action the user performs. When the Usage Record Provider receives usage information, it checks whether it can enrich the context associated to the usage

---

[3] http://www.ist-mobilife.org/

```
<usageRecord
        action="update"
        actor="355023003598706"
        application="Buddy"
        feedback="0.0"
        initiationType="manual"
        recommendationType="action"
        timestamp="2005-12-13T07:51:34.000Z">
    <contextElement>
        <parameter name="location">
            <parameter name="cluster" value="1">
                <parameter name="mcc" value="204"/>
                <parameter name="mnc" value="815"/>
                <parameter name="cellid" value="45960"/>
                <parameter name="latitude" value="32.232845916875"/>
                <parameter name="longitude" value="9.8896758573835"/>
            </parameter>
        </parameter>
    </contextElement>
</usageRecord>
```

Fig. 2. An example of a Usage Record

information. This is done by contacting those Context Providers that are known to contain parameters that are not yet part of the received usage information. This step is especially useful for mobile applications: both the Usage Record Provider and the Context Providers typically reside on a server, reducing the communication costs of the mobile client.

3.2 Recommender

The *Recommender* is responsible for performing all tasks related to user modeling: learning and updating user models and making inferences with the learned models. Within the component, the functionalities have been divided into three kinds of modules: Finders, Mappers and Reasoners.

Finders. The Finders are responsible for finding components and for the interactions that take place between the Recommender and other components. There is a Finder for each component with which the Recommender needs to interact. The reason for separating the interactions with external components is that it offers us more flexibility as the Recommender is not tied to a particular implementation of the external components. Thus, we can modify the external components at any stage and the only thing we need to change in the Recommender is the corresponding Finder.

Mappers. The Mappers are responsible for mapping structured information into a non-structured (flat) form and vice versa. Context and behavior information are often structured (for example, nested context parameters as illustrated in Fig. 2, or references to a tree-like or graph-like ontology of user behavior), whereas common machine learning algorithms can only handle flat data (for example, numeric vectors or name-value pairs).

The requirements of the mappers are two-fold. First, the data formats must be made compatible. Second, the translated data should contain information that makes it as efficient as possible to learn and apply the context-dependent user model. While the first requirement could be handled in an application-independent manner, this is not the case for the second requirement. A good mapping may depend on the application: for example, an application-specific ontology of service categories can be used to map fine-grained identifiers of individual services into higher-level identifiers of service categories; this way the system can make useful predictions with considerably less training data and the predictions generalize to new situations. Furthermore, a good mapping may also depend on the specific machine learning algorithm.

Examples of possible mappings include the following: (i) Flattening structured information; e.g., translating the Usage Record of Fig. 2 into (cluster $= 1$, mcc $= 204, \ldots$, longitude $= 9.89$). (ii) Feature selection, i.e., choosing a subset of input data; e.g., translating the Usage Record of Fig. 2 into (cluster $= 1$). (iii) Extracting higher-level features in an application-specific manner; for example, using an external ontology of context or behavior information. (iv) Technical low-level translations as required by the specific machine learning algorithms; for example, discretizing real-valued data to integral values, or mapping class-valued data to Boolean vectors.

Reasoners. The Reasoners are responsible for encapsulating implementations of individual machine learning algorithms into the Recommender. Thus, the Reasoners are the part of the architecture where the actual learning and inference is done. The Reasoners interact closely with the Mappers: Before usage records are used for learning, the Mappers map the context and behavior information into vectors that are given to the Reasoners. Similarly, when the Reasoners are used for inference, the Mappers take the results of the inference and map them so that the applications can understand the results.

To have a clear separation between learning and inference, we have specified separate interfaces for the components that offer learning functionalities and for the components that offer inference functionalities. The separation of interfaces is crucial as in a mobile device we seldom have enough resources to run the learning phase. However, once we have learned a model, it may be possible to run the inference stage even on the phone. Another advantage of the clearly separated interfaces is that this further improves the reusability of the implementations of individual algorithms.

Once a Reasoner has learned a new model, we store the models into a Profile Manager (see Sect. 3.3). The motivation for this is improved scalability and better distribution of functionalities. Furthermore, by storing the models into a Profile Manager, the user models become part of the user profile and thus all relevant preference-related data is stored in a single place.

In the current implementation of the Recommender, we have support for tree augmented naïve Bayesian classifiers (TAN; see, e.g, [15]) and for rule-based reasoning. The algorithm that is used for learning the TAN classifiers is described in [15] and as the inference method we use so-called quasi-Bayesian inference [16]. Rule learning, on the other hand, has been implemented using the Ripper algorithm [17] and the inference utilizes RuleML-based [18] rule-engines.

3.3   Profile Manager

The third component of the system is the *Profile Manager*. A detailed description of the Profile Manager can be found at [19]; we focus on the functionalities that are relevant for the user modeling system.

The Profile Manager is responsible for managing profiles of different entities such as users and groups. Each entity has a separate profile that is further divided into views that contain data specific to a particular application or a set of applications. In terms of the user modeling system, the role of the Profile Manager is to act as a persistent storage for user models. Whenever new models are learned, the models are sent to the Profile Manager, which stores them in the appropriate user profile. When an application requests for recommendations, the Recommender fetches suitable models from the Profile Manager.

The entity for whom the recommendations are requested uniquely specifies the profile to use; the application specifies the appropriate view within the profile. Since the user modeling system has been designed to be usable in a wide variety of scenarios and potentially with a large number of users, we need to properly index the models that are stored in the Profile Manager. To this end, we use qualifiers, which are collections of (name, value) pairs. Thus, the qualifiers specify a set of index terms for each model, which facilitates finding the appropriate models. As an example, when we store a newly created model, we use the names of context parameters to specify a set of qualifier constraints. When we then want to infer on the models, we can first check what context information is available and to fetch only those models than can be used with the available context information.

3.4   Evaluation of Recommendations

In order to evaluate the quality of the recommendations that our system produces and to ensure that the system works properly, we selected two datasets from the UCI machine learning repository [20]. We exported the data into our system by mapping the data records into usage records. After this, we used leave-one-out cross-validation to test the classification accuracy of the system. In the experiments, we used the TAN, and as the system is able to make probabilistic predictions, we also measured the logarithmic loss ($-\log p_i$, where p_i is the probability assigned to the correct class).

The data sets and the experiment results are summarized in Table 1. The first data set, Vote, consisted of 435 records. The data set contains many records with missing values. In this experiment, we considered only the part of the data set with complete information, leaving us with 232 records. The classification task is a binary task and our system was able to achieve a 94.4 percent accuracy on the data set. The second data, Zoo, consisted of 101 records, each of which had 17 attributes. However, since one of the attributes was a unique identifier, we removed it. On this data set, our system achieved an accuracy of 98 percent.

Table 1. Summary of the used datasets and results of the experiments

Data set	Records	Attributes	Classes	Accuracy	Avg. log-loss
Vote	232 (435)	16	2	94.4%	0.165
Zoo	101	16 (17)	7	98.0%	0.121

4   Conclusions and Future Work

In this paper, we have presented a generic component for context-dependent user modeling. The component has been designed with flexibility in mind and it eases the reuse and the evaluation of different machine learning methods. In the future, our goal is to implement additional machine learning methods, more specifically rule learning and neural networks, to the Recommender. We will also perform user acceptance studies in different settings and test the relevancy of different machine learning methods for these settings.

Acknowledgements

This work has been performed in the framework of the IST project IST-2004-511607 MobiLife, which is partly funded by the European Union. The authors acknowledge the contributions of their colleagues.

References

1. Kobsa, A.: Generic user modeling systems. User Modeling and User-Adapted Interaction **11**(1–2) (2001) 49–63
2. Horvitz, E., Breese, J., Heckerman, D., Hovel, D., Rommelse, K.: The Lumière project: Bayesian user modeling for inferring the goals and needs of software users. In: Proc. 14th Conference on Uncertainty in Artificial Intelligence (UAI), Morgan Kaufmann Publishers (1998) 256–265
3. Zukerman, I., Albrecht, D.W.: Preditive statistical models for user modeling. User Modeling and User-Adapted Interaction **11**(1–2) (2001) 5–18
4. Siewiorek, D., Smailagic, A., Furukawa, J., Krause, A., Moraveji, N., Reiger, K., Shaffer, J., Wong, F.L.: SenSay: A context-aware mobile phone. In: Proc. 7th IEEE International Symposium on Wearable Computers (ISWC), IEEE (2003) 248–249
5. van Setten, M., Pokraev, S., Koolwaaij, J.: Context-aware recommendations in the mobile tourist application COMPASS. In: Proc. 3rd International Conference on Adaptive Hypermedia and Adaptive Web-Based Systems (AH). LNCS, Vol. 3173. Springer-Verlag (2004) 235–244

6. Henricksen, K., Indulska, J.: Personalizing context-aware applications. In: Proc. Workshop on Context-Aware Mobile Systems (CAMS). LNCS, Vol. 3762. Springer-Verlag (2005) 122–131
7. Sadeh, N.M., Gandon, F.L., Kwon, O.B.: Ambient intelligence: The MyCampus experience. CMU-ISRI-05-123, Carnegie Mellon University (2005)
8. Kofod-Petersen, A., Aamodt, A.: Case-based situation assesment in a mobile context-aware system. In: Proc. Artificial Intelligence in Mobile Systems (AIMS), Saarbrücken, Germany, Universität des Saarlandes (2003) 41–48
9. Ranganathan, A., Al-Muhtadi, J., Campbell, R.H.: Reasoning about uncertain contexts in pervasive computing environments. IEEE Pervasive Computing **3**(2) (2004) 62–70
10. Yau, S.S., Karim, F.: An adaptive middleware for context-sensitive communications for real-time applications in ubiquitous computing environments. Real-Time Systems **26**(1) (2004) 29–61
11. Horvitz, E., Koch, P., Sarin, R., Apacible, J., Subramani, M.: Bayesphone: Precomputation of context-sensitive policies for inquiry and action in mobile devices. In: Proc. 10th Conference on User Modeling (UM). LNCS, Vol. 3538. Springer-Verlag (2005) 251–260
12. Tapia, E.M., Intille, S.S., Larson, K.: Activity recognition in the home setting using simple and ubiquitous sensors. In Ferscha, A., Mattern, F., eds.: Proc. 2nd International Conference on Pervasive Computing. LNCS, Vol. 3001. Springer-Verlag (2004) 158–175
13. Oliver, N., Garg, A., Horvitz, E.: Layered representations for recognizing office activity. In: Proc. 4th IEEE International Conference on Multimodal Interaction (ICMI), IEEE (2002) 3–8
14. Floréen, P., Przybilski, M., Nurmi, P., Koolwaaij, J., Tarlano, A., Wagner, M., Luther, M., Bataille, F., Boussard, M., Mrohs, B., Iau, S.: Towards a context management framework for mobilife. In: Proc. IST Mobile & Wireless Communications Summit. (2005)
15. Friedman, N., Geiger, D., Goldszmidt, M.: Bayesian network classifiers. Machine Learning **29** (1997) 131–163
16. Cozman, F.: A derivation of quasi-Bayesian theory. Technical Report CMU-RI-TR-97-37, Robotics Institute, Carnegie Mellon University (1997)
17. Cohen, W.W.: Fast effective rule induction. In: Proc. 12th International Conference on Machine Learning (ICML), Morgan Kaufmann (1995) 115–123
18. Boley, H., Tabet, S., Wagner, G.: Design rationale of RuleML: A markup language for semantic web rules. In: Proc. International Semantic Web Working Symposium (SWWS). (2001) 381–401
19. Coutand, O., Sutterer, M., Lau, S., Droegehorn, O., David, K.: User profile management for personalizing services in pervasive computing. In: Proc. 6th International Workshop on Applications and Services in Wireless Networks (ASWN). (2006)
20. Newman, D., Hettich, S., Blake, C., Merz, C.: UCI repository of machine learning databases. University of California, Irvine, Dept. of Information and Computer Sciences (1998) http://www.ics.uci.edu/~mlearn/MLRepository.html

Granular Context in Collaborative Mobile Environments

Christoph Dorn, Daniel Schall, and Schahram Dustdar

VitaLab, Distributed Systems Group,
Institute of Information Systems,
Technical University of Vienna,
Vienna, Austria
{dorn, schall, dustdar}@infosys.tuwien.ac.at

Abstract. Our research targets collaborative environments with focus on mobility and teams. Teams comprise a number of people working on multiple projects and activities simultaneously. As mobile and wireless technology advances people are no longer bound to their offices. Team members are able to collaborate while on the move. Sharing context information thus becomes a vital part of collaborative environments. However, challenges such as heterogeneous devices, connectivity, and bandwidth arise due to the dynamic nature of distributed, mobile teams. We present a methodology for context modeling and employ a framework that reduces costs such as computing information and usage of network resources by transferring context at relevant levels of detail. At the same time, robustness of the system is improved by dealing with uncertain context information. Our framework is implemented on an OSGi container platform using Web services for communication means.

1   Introduction

A team is a group of people working collaboratively on tasks and activities. In our scenario we consider distributed teams working on activities within projects. Several team forms exist (such as Nimble, Virtual, and Nomadic or Mobile) [1], each featuring distinct characteristics such as shared vision, goals, and time span of existence. In real life, a person may be member of multiple, heterogenous teams at once. In fact, a person may work on more than one task or activity simultaneously. This means that users need to handle a number of activities, switching back and forth between activity context and gather all information relevant for a particular activity. In addition to these challenges, users need to keep track of changes and update their knowledge as information may become updated. Having updated and relevant pieces of information available is essential for decision making and has major impact on how a person assesses a problem or situation. In our research we consider team dynamics and mobility aspects. Nomadic or Mobile teams naturally have laptops or hand-held sized devices. Not only network bandwidth is a scarce resource in a mobile/wireless setting, but also computing power needed to process information, and thus battery consumption

R. Meersman, Z. Tari, P. Herrero et al. (Eds.): OTM Workshops 2006, LNCS 4278, pp. 1904–1913, 2006.
© Springer-Verlag Berlin Heidelberg 2006

of the device. Therefore, one important goal of our architecture is to provide only information needed considering the user's current situation and context.

In addition, using context information to establish team awareness is one major challenge in mobile, distributed teams we intend to solve. The technical and organizational facets of collaboration cover the whole life cycle of context information: sensing, aggregating, storing, provisioning, and reasoning. As these problems are independent of the actual semantic content of context, this work focuses on the general mechanism to manage, process, and access context information.

The next section (2) will outline the problem in more detail. Thereafter, we present our fundamental concepts in Sec. 3 followed by our proof-of-concept implementation (Sec. 4). We then compare our approach to existing work (Sec. 5) and conclude our paper stating future research issues (Sec. 6).

2   Problem Statement

Taking one team member consuming context information, let us look at these challenges in detail. Suppose a team member is part of multiple teams. This person is updated on activities or status of fellow team members, however, his/her current activity should also be considered and provided information customized accordingly. At the same time his/her role such as leader, expert, adviser, observer or regular member influences scope of needed information. In other words, the amount and level of detail, relevant at a particular moment, depends on the context and thus changes continuously. Other related approaches to the issue of relevance such as choosing the best time or the most suitable communication channel are potential extensions for the future. Context plays an important part in all three cases.

Furthermore, team members expect information to be reliable to some degree. This means that decision making should be supported by evidences and data that do not lead to wrong assumptions. Thus, uncertainty has to be taking into account and a fallback mechanism provided, if confidence of data is too low.

Finally, usage of mobile devices limits the amount of information that can be processed and viewed. Transferring only relevant pieces of context information reduces costs such as network bandwidth, but also increases device responsiveness and battery lifetime. Thus, large amounts of context data, which are produced due to the nature of highly dynamic mobile environment, need to be filtered to reduce information being exchanged.

Throughout this paper, we will use the term `context consumer` for indicating the person, device, or software that receives context information, while the object the context information is about is labeled `context entity`. Before we present our concepts, a scenario will motivate our approach.

2.1   Scenario of Distributed Teams

Suppose a scenario where we have two distributed teams that wish to exchange context information. Figure 1 depicts teams at Location A and Location B.

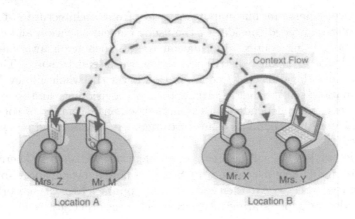

Fig. 1. Context Sharing in Distributed Teams

Team members may be in close proximity at a particular location but not col-located, for instance user Z and M at Location A at different floors in a building. Since both users work in the same team, it is required to share location informa-tion at a detailed level of spatial granularity. In this case both team members re-ceive location information or updates at room level resolution, whereas the team located at Location B only needs to know course grained location information. Thus, higher level location information such as city and street is shared with remote teams. This not only saves bandwidth consumed by location updates, but also reduces unnecessary information being exchanged. The techniques to achieve this are presented in the next section.

3   Context Modeling and Processing

3.1   Hierarchical Context

The main idea of granular context lies in modeling a piece of information at multiple levels of detail. Consequently, the most generic information is found at the highest level, whereas the most detailed information resides at the bottom. Hierarchies consisting of levels are one way to model context granularity. One straightforward example is a location hierarchy, where continents or countries populate the upper parts and streets, floors, and rooms present the lower parts. Depending on the specific problem domain, such a hierarchy features additional levels at the top or bottom. Furthermore, for each level one or more values of varying complexity specify the context structure. To point out the difference between levels and values: the former one describes the granularity and posi-tion within the hierarchy, whereas the latter one contains the actual context information.

When it comes to handling actual context data, we pick up the outlined future work as presented in [2] and now directly include levels. Hence, there is no longer

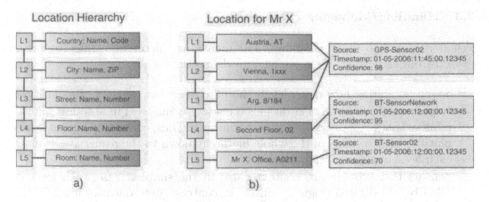

Fig. 2. Storing Hierarchical Location Information

a need for mapping hierarchies to other representational forms of context and vice-versa. Context in such a form allows navigating up and down along the hierarchical structure. In addition, context values in each level are tagged with the sensor source, timestamp of capture and data confidence. Fig. 2 visualizes our context model consisting of hierarchies and actual context information structured accordingly.

3.2   Empowering Collaboration

Structuring context as hierarchies provides the basis for our proposed mechanisms that tackle the outlined problems. Team members no longer receive the full amount of context information continuously, but just the information at the relevant level of detail. Determining what is relevant for a specific problem is outside the scope of this work, yet we present the means to manage relevance.

Furthermore, as outlined in the motivating scenario, varying context granularity is not only empowering awareness at the organizational level but also reduces the required bandwidth for context distribution at the link level. The amount of context flow between collocated team members is higher than between distributed ones. Thus, the sharing of context becomes completely relevance based as members a-priori define under which conditions data is exchanged.

Going beyond reducing bandwidth use, context granularity allows resource constraint devices to focus on their managable level of detail and thus limit processing and storing. Context hierarchies also provide a means to tackle unreliable context information. In order to utilize more coarse grained context information in case of too uncertain detailed levels, we require all confidence values within a hierarchy to be monotonically increasing. Consequently, instead of having to work with uncertain but detailed information, information that is less detailed but more confident allows for more appropriate actions. To establish a reliable confidence value for each level, we have to adapt the way context information is derived. Thus we will analyze the nature of hierarchies in the next subsection before focusing on processing.

3.3   Handling/Managing Hierarchies

When it comes to creating, filling, and managing, hierarchies differ to some extend from each other. First, we need to define the

- Scope for stating how many levels should cover what range of granularity
- Representational Form that decides if context is modeled in absolute values, relative values, numbers, or abstract concepts. Thus, context of a given granularity either consists of the whole hierarchy down to the respective level or each level contains all information.
- Sensors that provide raw context data. In the simplest case, each level is filled by a dedicated (logical) sensor. In contrast, only one sensor might fill all levels by providing the most detailed context. Finally, multiple sensors capture context for a single level.
- Inter-level Mapping Mechanism that describes how to derive the context for each level. Hence, where context information arrives at its most detailed form, values in all higher levels derive from this value.

Taking the location hierarchy as an example, the scope covers countries down to rooms. This also implies to use a representation form known from postal addresses (adding floors and rooms) split to five levels. As exemplary sensors, GPS and Bluetooth beacons provide the corresponding raw data. Finally, between every pair of adjacent levels, a mapping function defines how context information is transferred from one level to the other and vice-versa. For this example, the mapping function is simply adding the lower value or subtracting it. These four concerns are highly interrelated. If for example, purely GPS serves as a location technique, and location itself is merely provided in absolute coordinates. In addition, the levels reflect the precision of the data while the mapping function includes or excludes a digit of the coordinates.

Defining hierarchies that structure context of a single type such as location or time is rather straightforward. This process becomes more complex, once concepts from different domains are included that feature no natural ordering of granularity levels. For example, modeling team status including members, roles, activity and member distribution is nondeterministic, as it depends on the context consumer, whether information on collocated members or their activities describes more detailed information. In this case, either a predefined ordering of levels creates a static hierarchy, or context information (internal or external to the hierarchy) dynamically arranges the levels. In addition, advanced hierarchy forms consist of several other basic hierarchies, but are beyond the scope of this paper.

In contrast to conventional context systems, granular context potentially comprises multiple confidence values instead of a single one. Requiring all confidence values to grow monotonically from the most fine-grained up to the most coarse-grained level, each value reflects the accuracy of a piece of context information and not the sensor supplying raw data. Having confidence values at every level brings another advantage. The application using context information needs no longer know about the implicit confidence characteristics of each sensor but can purely rely on the value for each level. Factors that influence the confidence values are manifold and depend heavily on the hierarchy's characteristics as outlined above.

- Sensor Model: Each sensor class has confidence values associated (e.g., statistically calculated) that describe the sensor's performance. Performance characteristics include a number of factors that limit the sensor's suitability for a particular application domain. Consider wireless sensor technology for context data acquisition. Results and the ability to obtain accurate estimates depend on the actual scene, e.g., spatial arrangement of furniture, dynamics such as open or closed doors, etc.
- Combining Heterogenous Sensors: In case of multiple sensors being used, sensors at different levels mutually improve the precision (e.g., GPS in combination with Bluetooth for localization).
- Context Entities: Accuracy of context data depends on a number of physical attributes and characteristics of the target entity we wish to observer (e.g., walking speed of a person, color, etc.).
- Computation: Accuracy and confidence of hierarchical context data depends on the inter-level mapping function (i.e., confidence increases if we step one level up).

Returning to the examplary location hierarchy, we are able to base our decisions e.g. on the context and confidence provided at the floor level, if the exact position of a person in a certain room (a more detailed level) cannot be determined accurately enough.

3.4 Storing Context

The challenge in storing granular context lies in preserving the hierarchy while enabling efficient access to the actual context value. Pure XML-based technologies provide one solution but are slow for larger amounts of data. We opted to use an object oriented database discussed in more detail in Section 4. Yet, as all our objects and hierarchy are described by means of an XML Schema we are able to compare and combine hierarchies. Allowing for multiple values in each level we can also extend a given hierarchy as described in our previous work [2]. Context itself is exchanged as XML documents also used by the sharing mechanims introduced in the following subsection.

3.5 Sharing Context

Polling for context changes is usually not a suitable option in a resource-restricted environment. Thus, sharing happens on an event basis. Interested context consumers subscribe for context changes in two ways. Using simple rules that are context content independent, they are notified about all changes in a given hierarchy, level or entity. Further restrictions can be made to take metadata such as timestamp, source or confidence into account. Advanced rules are more complex as they cover either multiple entities, and/or are dependent on the context value of other hierarchies. They further allow notification if a certain context state is no longer valid. Unfortunately, we are unable to go into more detail here due to page restrictions. However, we will outline in more detail those rules in our future work where we intend to use RuleML combined with an interaction pattern-based approach.

To evaluate these concepts we designed and implemented a simple context framework targeted at a mobile collaboration environment presented in the following section.

4   Implementation

4.1   OSGi Based Architecture

Having discussed the basic building blocks of our approach we are now going to present our proof-of-concept implementation based on the OSGi container technology. We build a number of software services that are deployed as bundles. Hence they can be discovered and consumed by other bundles residing either in the same or remote containers. A loose coupling of software services using OSGi containers and Web services for communication means among containers allows us to implement a scalable and flexible infrastructure. Figure 3 shows a block diagram of the set of services and components that have been deployed in our infrastructure.

Context Information Acquisition. A Context Sensor Layer abstracts various context sources which can be either software sensors or actual hardware elements such as Bluetooth devices. Each sensor is wrapped as a logical entity, regardless of physical location, and controlled by the Sensor Layer. Measurements are fed into a Context Aggregation and Context Reasoning Component. A Context Reasoning Component is implemented for each context source. The Bluetooth context source requires a Bluetooth Context Reasoner as location measurements may be imperfect or ambiguous. Location information can be acquired from a number of heterogenous sources in order to increase confidence. In our implementation we make observations by scanning the environment with Bluetooth sensors (anchor nodes at well known positions). Mobile entities such as Pocket-PCs and Smartphones, also equipped with Bluetooth, respond to those frequent scans (inquiry method). Thus, we are able to localize entities by resolving the mobile devices location through anchor points. These anchor points are associated with a logical location which is provided by the environment controller (e.g., particular anchor node is located in Floor Y, Room X). The environment controller essentially holds all persistent information needed for our context-aware infrastructure, such as anchor nodes, users, devices belonging to a particular user, etc. In respect to Bluetooth based tracking, locating mobile entities indoors to room level granularity is usually sufficient for collocated teams.

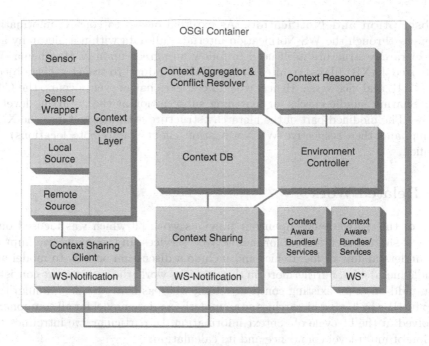

Fig. 3. OSGi Container Architecture

Context Reasoning and Conflict Resolution. The Context Aggregation Component fetches a hierarchy, depending on the context source, from the Context DB and updates the respective hierarchy level values. Each hierarchy holds context knowledge and confidence. In addition, time stamps allow us to save temporal versions of a specific hierarchy. By using previous versions of a hierarchy we can reason about plausibility of obtained information and thus smoothen state information and context. In our first prototype, we implemented three hierarchies relevant to collaborative environments. Besides the above mentioned location context, we are able to process hierarchies covering actions and reachability. The former one consists of levels describing `environment`, `subenvironment`, `project`, `artifact`, and `activity`, whereas the latter one consists of `online status`, `substatus`, `device status`, and `communication capability status`.

Context Database. An object oriented database as db4o[1] enables to dynamically change the context information to be stored; something that is much harder to achieve with a traditional relational database. In order to provide content independence the database requires all objects to implement interfaces for hierarchy, level and value. In doing so, the context reasoner extracts instances of specific context objects while the sharing component is able to focus on levels rather than context content.

---

[1] http://www.db4o.com

Subscription and Notification. As external access to context information happens through the WS-Notification interface, all data within a hierarchy and the hierarchy structure itself need to follow an agreed upon XML schema. We employed JAXB[2] (Java Architecture for XML Binding) to transfer Java objects into XML and vice versa. Hence, when a context change event occurs, the Context Sharing bundle checks for matching subscription at the occurring level or below. The modified part of the hierarchy structure is transferred into the XML format and then respective WS-Notification clients (at remote locations) are notified.

5   Related Work

Part of this paper builds upon our previous work [2] which was focused on a context sharing architecture for mobile Web services. In this paper, we improve the understanding of hierarchies and include a discussion on how to model and handle hierarchies. Furthermore, in this pervious work, the architecture consisted of an add-on to an existing context system, whereas here we take granularity a step further by having hierarchies as an underlying data model for all components involved in the lifecycle of context information. In particular, we introduce the notion of multi-level confidence and its calculation.

Of the many context-aware systems and frameworks, few support distributed context consumers. For a more detailed survey and overview refer to Baldauf et al. [3]. Besides centralized systems, distributed approaches such as the Solar middleware by Chen and Kotz [4] or the WASP Subscription Language by Costa et al. [5] target also mobile devices but lack the support for efficient sharing and processing. Other subscription enabled context frameworks include work by Sørensen et al. [6] and Hinze et al. [7]. Yet, Biegel and Cahill [8] present a framework for developing mobile, context-aware applications that uses a kind of context hierarchy. However, their concept has the notion of a task tree rather than structuring context information into various levels of detail.

A similar notion of context structuring is proposed by the ASC context model by Strang [9]. This ontology-based model introduces aspects, scales, and operations to semantically describe context information. Yet, the ASC model remains at a higher conceptual level, whereas our proposed concepts can be regarded as a light-weight, ready-to-use approach targeted at mobile collaborative environments.

Groupware system on the other hand, focus only on a subset of collaborative environments and issues and thus provide either very limited context support if at all, or target only narrow problem domains.

6   Future Work and Conclusion

We are at an initial stage of evaluating our prototype implementation. As presented in Section 4.1, three hierarchies for collaborative teams (describing a

---

[2] http://java.sun.com/xml/jaxb/

person's location, reachability, and activity) have been implemented and tested as proof of concept. Thorough evaluation and studies of our prototype as well as further improvements are subject of our future research. Furthermore, we will investigate techniques that build upon our framework for modeling and managing of relevance.

Yet, we believe that structuring context information in a granular way will greatly improve effectiveness of mobile, distributed teams as relevant data empowers team awareness, multi-level confidence ensure viable decisions and intelligent sharing reduces the strain on mobile devices.

Acknowledgment

Part of this work was supported by the Austrian Science Fund (FWF) under grant P18368-N04 Project OMNIS and EU STREP Project inContext (FP6-034718).

References

1. van Do, T., Jørstad, I., Dustdar, S.: Mobile Multimedia Collaborative Services. In: Handbook of Research on Mobile Multimedia. Idea Group Publishing (2006) 414–429
2. Dorn, C., Dustdar, S.: Sharing hierarchical context for mobile web services. Technical report, Vienna University of Technology (2006)
3. Baldauf, M., Dustdar, S., Rosenberg, F.: A Survey on Context-Aware Systems. International Journal of Ad Hoc and Ubiquitous Computing (2006) forthcoming
4. Chen, G., Kotz, D.: Solar: An open platform for context-aware mobile applications. In: First International Conference on Pervasive Computing (Short Paper). (2002) 41–47
5. Costa, P.D., Pires, L.F., van Sinderen, M., Filho, J.P.: Towards a service platform for mobile context-aware applications. In: 1st International Workshop on Ubiquitous Computing - IWUC 2004. (2004) 48–61
6. Sørensen, C.F., Wu, M., Sivaharan, T., Blair, G.S., Okanda, P., Friday, A., Duran-Limon, H.: Context-aware middleware for applications in mobile ad hoc environments. In: ACM/IFIP/USENIX International Middleware conference 2nd Workshop on Middleware for Pervasive and Ad-Hoc Computing (online proceedings), Toronto, Canada (2004)
7. Hinze, A., Malik, R., Malik, P.: Towards a tip 3.0 service-oriented architecture: Interaction design. Technical report, Department of Computer Science, University of Waikato (2005)
8. Biegel, G., Cahill, V.: A framework for developing mobile, context-aware applications. In: Second IEEE Annual Conference on Pervasive Computing and Communications, 2004. PerCom 2004. (2004) 361–365
9. Strang, T.: Service Interoperability in Ubiquitous Computing Environments. PhD thesis, L-M University Munich (2003)

Context-Aware Services for Physical Hypermedia Applications

Gustavo Rossi[1,2,*], Silvia Gordillo[1,3], Cecilia Challiol[1], and Andrés Fortier[1]

[1] LIFIA. Facultad de Informática. UNLP. La Plata, Argentina
{gustavo, gordillo, ceciliac, andres}@lifia.info.unlp.edu.ar
[2] Also CONICET, [3] Also CICPBA

Abstract. In this paper we present an approach for designing and deploying context-aware services in the context of physical hypermedia applications, those applications in which mobile users explore real and digital objects using the hypermedia paradigm. We show how to adapt the objects' response to the user's navigation context by changing the role these objects play in the user's travel. We first motivate our research with a simple example and survey some related work; next we introduce the concept of travel object and show that physical objects might assume the role of different type of travel objects. We then present an architectural approach for context-aware services and describe its evolution into a software substrate for physical hypermedia services. We conclude by indicating some further work we are pursuing.

1 Introduction and Background

Physical Hypermedia (PH) applications extend the well-known navigation paradigm, made popular by the Web, in order to support the mobile user and to allow a unified exploration of digital and physical (real-world) objects. In a typical PH application physical objects are augmented with digital information in such a way that when the user is sensed to be facing an object it can access information on this object (as if it were a hypermedia node) in his mobile device. From this point of view, one can consider PH application as a particular case of Location-aware software; however physical objects may also exhibit hypermedia links to other objects (either physical or digital). The user explores these links and might either get digital information (when the link's target object is digital) or some indication on how to "walk" the link to reach the physical target. More elaborated context-aware responses can be provided by personalizing the information (or links) made available to the user, to his actual context, preferences, etc.

This simple but powerful idea can be very appealing in many different domains, such as tourism, entertainment, logistics, etc. In fact every former application of the "old" hypermedia paradigm, in which the user is mobile can benefit from these concepts. Many authors have already shown the feasibility of this kind of software (certainly an evolution of mobile information systems) in different areas such as learning

---

* This work has been partially funded by Project PICT 2003, Nro 13623, SeCyT.

R. Meersman, Z. Tari, P. Herrero et al. (Eds.): OTM Workshops 2006, LNCS 4278, pp. 1914–1923, 2006.

games [16], design [8], tourism [10], collaboration [3], and have built powerful frameworks to support the construction of hybrid information networks in which the real and the digital worlds are glued together with links.

Imagine for example a tourist application for a city (we exemplify here with our city, La Plata). When the user is in front of the Cathedral he accesses the information in the hypermedia node corresponding to this physical object. He can explore links which allow him to read about the building process, the historical context in which it was created, etc. Some links "point" to other buildings by the same architect. These links are called in our modeling approach "walkable" links (WLinks) [6]; when the user selects one of them, he is presented a plan to reach the building. In his tour, he can either reach the target or deviate because he found another interesting place to explore; when facing other physical objects, they can help him to find his way, show him information, etc. An oversimplified schema of this example can be seen in Figure 1. The thick black line indicates the relationship which the user is exploring by walking from the Cathedral to the Town Hall.

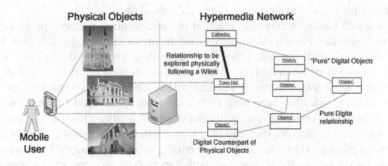

Fig. 1. A Schematic View of Physical Hypermedia

Our research in this area has included the definition of a modeling approach which extends the OOHDM hypermedia design framework [14] to this field [7] and an implementation framework which extends a standard Web application architecture to support physical objects and mobile users [1]. In this paper we present a seamless extension to an architecture for context-aware services [7] to make it PH "compliant", i.e. to support navigation and hypermedia-aware context information; we also discuss the concept of context-aware hypermedia services and show how we materialized these services in our architecture.

The main contributions of our paper are the following:

- We present the concept of context-aware PH services and relate it with the role which physical objects play in a user's journey.
- We present a modular implementation of these ideas stressing the need to keep our base architecture evolvable to support further extensions in this field.

The rest of the paper is organized as follows: In Section 2 we briefly discuss related work. In Section 3, we discuss the idea of physical hypermedia services and present a model of travel objects; In Section 4 we give an overview of our architecture for context-aware services; we focuses on our solution for building physical hyper-media services and show some simple but meaningful examples. Finally, we present our concluding remarks in Section 5.

2 Related Work

The roots of physical hypermedia can be traced to the first mobile tourist guides, such as [2]. Even though not explicitly mentioned, this guide of the city of Lancaster mixed real world objects with their digital counterparts in the same was as PH software does. More recently, in [9] the authors present a powerful framework, HyCon, which supports not only context-aware physical navigation but also allows users to create their own linking structures and trails. In [11] meanwhile, an object-oriented framework (HyperReal) which allows mixing the real and the digital world is presented. Finally, in [10] the authors discuss the idea of "walking" a link and propose a future scenario in which the physical world will be augmented with digital information to make it more accessible to the traveler, particularly a disabled one.

Our research has been certainly inspired in these seminal research projects. There are some differences among our approach and the previously mentioned; first, follow-ing our previous work on model-based hypermedia software building [14], we con-sider the existence of an underlying hypermedia application, in the context of which we provide context-aware services. For example Figure 1 clearly shows a hypermedia schema, which besides has been built on top of a conceptual model (not shown in the Figure) using well-known viewing mechanisms. We also characterize real-world objects according to the role they can play to assist the user's journey; finally from an architectural point of view we chose not to build a software substrate from scratch but to extend a service-oriented architecture with hypermedia services; in this way we can integrate hypermedia behaviors with other context-aware services not directly related with navigation.

3 Physical Hypermedia Services

Physical Hypermedia applications are a particular kind of context-aware mobile soft-ware, which basically aims at enhancing real world objects with digital information and links; this kind of software provides one coarse grained service: HInformation which allows to access the physical object properties and links. Notice that this ser-vice is by definition location-aware because the information which it presents depends on the actual user's position. As indicated in Section 1, HInformation might also ex-hibit more elaborated context-aware features, by filtering the presented information according to the user's profile. The distinctive feature of PH applications however is the notion of physical navigation which underlies the whole user experience. While digital navigation has been widely explored in the literature on hypermedia and the Web (even for context-aware access [15]), research on service support for physical navigation is still in its infancy (See [10] for a good introduction to the problem).

Our research is focused on providing context-aware support for the navigation task. In the following sub-sections we introduce the core ideas of our approach.

3.1 A Model for the Hypermedia Traveler

We have developed a conceptual framework (and implemented it as discussed in Section 4) for understanding context-aware services to aid physical navigation. The framework which has been inspired in [17] defines a set of roles which physical objects may play in the context of the user's journey. While the work in [17] aims to support handicapped users while navigating the Web, we tied to the original concepts in [12] to provide digital help for physical navigation.

The basic idea is simple: when we traverse a physical space (e.g. a city) we constantly face objects which are usually assigned pre-defined, standard roles (i.e. they exhibit certain behaviors). We know which "behaviors" we can wait from traffic lights, signals, street names, etc. However, if we have the chance to augment them with digital information to be presented to the mobile user, the possibilities are enormous and certainly appealing.

Our framework provides an open set of predefined roles which can be assigned to physical objects and a simple model of user navigation through the physical space. These roles exhibit a set of services (their behaviors) which basically allow them to provide different kind of information or guidance to the mobile user. Therefore, by making a physical object play one of these roles we can enrich its behavior according to the user's needs.

Table 1. Travel Objects Roles

Role	Example
Navigation Point	Street, Corridor.
Decision Point	Junction, Corridor, Intersection.
Alert	Traffic Light, Signs
Information Point	Information desk. Monuments
Attention	Advertisements
Landmarks	Distinguished Monuments
Travel Memory	Route Plan

A list of the most important roles, according to the research in [17] is presented in Table 1. In [5], the authors use this classification of travel objects to find similar ones in the context of a Web page, in order to provide assistance to the blinded user. Instead, we aim to assign these roles to physical objects in such a way that the traveler (in this case the mobile user who is traversing a walking link) improves his tour.

Summarizing, when the user traverses the (physical) hyperspace by following links he faces a multitude of objects, which might play those roles shown in Table 1. As part of the role's behavior the objects will provide certain services to help the user complete his task (e.g. know a city, shop a product, etc). Additionally all objects will also provide a set of general purpose hypermedia services such as: *CancelNavigation*, *MapUpdate*, etc, which are fundamental for the trip.

The application designer might decide which roles a particular application object (or class) may play; he may refine the framework by adding new services to a role or eventually new roles according to the application domain. We next describe the rationale for assigning a role to a physical object in the context of physical hypermedia.

3.2   Bridging Role Services with the User's Context

A naïve analysis might conclude that certain physical objects only play some predetermined roles: for example we might never expect that a traffic light acts as an Information Point; however a technician, who repairs traffic lights, will presumably receive information about the object's functioning or the foreseen schedule of reparation. In fact, even the most simple real world object might play different roles (and therefore exhibit different services) according at least to:

- The application context in which it is being accessed (clearly, the technician is not using a tourism application).
- The current user's activity; e.g. whether he is traversing a link to reach a particular place, or if he is just wondering around without a plan in mind.

For the sake of conciseness and precision, we will focus on those services which depend on the actual user's activity.

In our approach, roles are assigned to physical objects dynamically according to the current user's state regarding navigation, which means that for two different users, the object might play (at the same time) different roles.

Suppose, as shown in Figure 2 a tourist in La Plata (user A) who, while being in front of the Museum, chooses a link that directs him to the Government House; while he is traversing the physical space to reach that place, he may interact with intermediate objects to receive assistance in his task. When he faces the Cathedral, and knowing that his actual task is to reach another place, the Cathedral plays the role of Decision Point which indicates him (as one of his services) that he must turn left to reach the target. Meanwhile, another tourist who is beginning his tour (User B in Figure 2), may be facing the Cathedral as regular node.

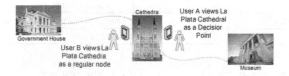

Fig. 2. Physical Objects play different roles according to the user's context

Summarizing, the set of services which a physical object provides depends on the role it is playing, which in turns depends on the current user's context. Additionally, other contextual information might be useful to further filter or elaborate the response of those services. For example, when viewing the Cathedral as a hypermedia object at visit hours, the tourist might be able to buy entrance tickets from his device, etc.

Next we describe how we extended an architecture for context-aware services to support the recording and use of the user's navigation state. The intent in Section 4 is twofold: we aim to show our solution and to emphasize how modularity allows seamless architectural evolution.

4 Architectural Support for Context-Aware Hypermedia Services

In [13] we presented a pure object-oriented approach for specifying and providing context-aware services. The main focus of our presentation was to show how certain well-known design practices such as separation of concerns and treatment of context more as behavioral than as data constructs, helps to achieve seamless evolution when the original requirements change. In the context of our current research to enrich physical objects with context-aware role playing behaviors (in a hypermedia setting) the use of our "old" framework proved to be the best option as explained in the subsections below.

4.1 The Architecture in a Nutshell

A high level schema of the architecture presented in [13] is shown in Figure 3, together with the key hot-spots for adding physical hypermedia behaviors. We ignore the Sensing layer for the sake of conciseness.

In the Application layer, we specify application (digital) objects and behaviors in such a way that they are oblivious with respect to their physical nature or their eventual contextual features. This decoupling allows us to eventually extend legacy software (e.g. objects, behaviors and relationships in the application layer). In our specific domain, the application layer contains the classes which comprise the conceptual model in a hypermedia application [14]. Notice that relationships are considered first-class citizen as they are the conceptual origin of hypermedia links. Hypermedia nodes, meanwhile are, as in OOHDM, views on conceptual classes.

Some objects of these classes will have a physical presence, and we need to sense when the user is in front of them. The Context Layer contains itself a set of sub-layers, particularly a Location Layer which aim to extend conceptual classes with their location information. Location classes act as decorators on their conceptual counterparts and allow freeing the latter from the burden posed by location models (geometric, semantic, etc). This approach also allows adding physical presence at the instance, instead of class level; for example, some instances of class Monument might not have a physical presence, either because we decided not to provide information on them or because they no longer exist, though we still have digital information about them. This layer also contains "purely' physical objects which are relevant for the application though they have not been described in the application model, such as streets, traffic lights, etc. Additionally the context layer partitions the user's context in objects which represent each contextual element which is sensitive to the user dynamics. Physical hypermedia applications need to take into account the user's navigation context (as described in Section 4.2).

The Service layer contains the (context-aware) services that the system provides. Services, are specified as objects and attached to physical areas. The architecture uses dynamic publish/subscribe mechanisms to activate services. In the case of location-aware service as those described here, when the user changes his position, the object representing his position is updated triggering a message to the Service Environment, which in turn determines in which Service Area the user is located and thus which are the current available services. The main extension to the architecture is the specialization of the ServiceProvider component in order to change the way in which the available

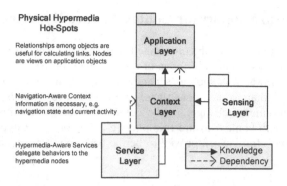

Fig. 3. High-Level View of our architecture

services are determined. This sub-class, named HypermediaServiceProvider, delegates to the physical objects (the "nodes" of the hypermedia network) the responsibility of returning the services which are meaningful in the actual context. This extension involves the assignment of roles to these objects as discussed below.

4.2 Adding Hypermedia Contexts to Our Architecture

The main two differences between the general idea of context-aware services and physical hypermedia services is that while the former are attached to places (locations) and further filtered according to the user's context, hypermedia services are allocated to the different roles played by physical objects; these role depends on the actual user's navigation context.

The simplest hypermedia service is triggered when the user selects a WLink; the response to this user's request, which is delegated to the source of the link (the physical object) may be a plan or map provided by the designer in which the source and target are highlighted; however this behavior can be overridden to provide more elaborated responses, e.g. according to the user's profile or preferences (e.g. if he likes walking), time of the day, etc.

The most interesting services however arise while the user traverses the physical space. Each time he faces a physical object, this object provides those services which are meaningful for the user; this is achieved by making the physical object play the role which corresponds better to the user's context. Figure 4 shows the Role hierarchy together with the relationship with the Physical Object base class.

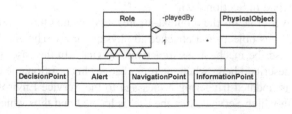

Fig. 4. Enhancing Physical Objects with Roles

The assignment of roles to physical objects is a responsibility of a RoleBuilder object. The RoleBuilder analyzes the user context to determine these roles; in particular it analyzes the current user's activity and navigation state. In Figure 5 we show a simplified diagram of the possible user's activities and states. The user navigation state is represented as an instance of the State pattern [4] as partially shown in Figure 5; the navigation history is recorded as a list of traversed objects and navigation states. In a specific application, the designer may extend the State hierarchy if needed.

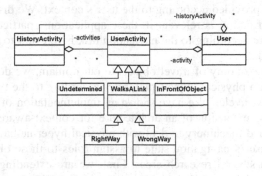

Fig. 5. User navigation state and history

RoleBuilder performs a "double dispatching" interaction with the actual user's activity object which may know which role corresponds to it. For example, if the user is walking a link and his actual position matches a "right way", the actual instance of RightWay in Figure 5 returns the *Navigation Point* Role object which is further assigned to the physical object. As a simplified example we show in Figure 6, the different kind of background information and services which a user who is moving through the city might receive when standing in front of the Cathedral. On the left, user A who is walking a link and is in the right way to his target; in the middle, user B who has lost his way to the target and on the right, user C who is standing in front of

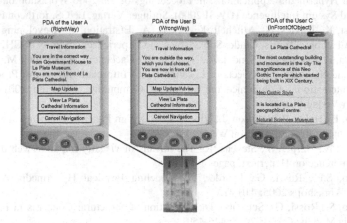

Fig. 6. Relationships among the user state and the response of physical objects

the Cathedral but he is not following a link. In the first and second case the physical object assumes the role of a navigation object, with slight differences according to the actual user's state. In the last case, the physical object behaves as a regular node.

5 Concluding Remarks and Further Work

In this paper we introduced the concept of physical hypermedia services and showed why they must be provided according to the user's context. We discussed which kind of contextual information is relevant in these applications; particularly we analyzed why the user's state according to the navigation task is relevant to determine the kind of services he needs.

By adapting a taxonomy of travel objects to our domain, we defined a conceptual framework in which physical objects play roles according to the type of travel object they exhibit to the traveler. We have shown an implementation of these ideas by describing a seamless extension of an architecture for context-aware services to which we added the needed machinery to deal with physical hypermedia objects and to take into account the user's navigation state to assign roles to these objects. We are currently working on several research areas. First, we are extending the travel objects framework to comprise a broader set of objects which can be specialized according to different application domains; for example we are interested in analyzing the situation in which physical objects move as in [8]. In this sense it is interesting to see how navigation states evolve. We are also adapting the OOHDM approach by defining a set of reusable navigation classes (nodes and links) targeted to physical hypermedia. From the point of view of support tools we are adapting a well-known browser (Mozilla Firefox) to support physical, context-aware navigation in its main menus.

References

1. Challiol, C., Rossi, G., Gordillo, S., De Cristófolo, V.: Designing and Implementing Physical Hypermedia Applications. In Proceedings of the 2006 Workshop on Ubiquitous Web and System Intelligence (UWSI 2006), Springer Verlag, LNCS, forthcoming.
2. Cheverst, K., Davies, N., Mitchell, K., Friday, A., Efstratiou, C.: Developing a Context-Aware Electronic Tourist Guide: Some Issues and Experiences. In Proc. of CHI 2000.
3. Espinoza, F., Persson, P., Sandin, A., Nystrom, H., Cacciatore, E., Bylund, M.: GeoNotes: Social and Navigational Aspects of Location-Based Information Systems. Proceedings of Third International Conference on Ubiquitous Computing (Ubicomp 2001), pp 2-17. Springer Verlag.
4. Gamma, E., Helm, R., Johnson, J., Vlissides, J.: Design Patterns. Elements of reusable object-oriented software, Addison Wesley 1995.
5. Goble, C. A., Harper, S., Stevens, R.: The travails of visually impaired web travellers. In UK Conference on Hypertext, pages 1-10, 2000.
6. Gordillo, S.E., Rossi, G., Lyardet, F.: Modeling Physical Hypermedia Applications. SAINT Workshops 2005: 410-413.
7. Gordillo, S., Rossi, G., Schwabe, D.: Separation of Structural Concerns in Physical Hypermedia Models. CAiSE 2005: 446-459.

8. Gronbaek, K., Kristensen, J., Eriksen, M.: Physical Hypermedia: Organizing Collections of Mixed Physical and Digital Material. Proceedings of the 14th. ACM International Conference of Hypertext and Hypermedia (Hypertext 2003), ACM Press, 10-19.

9. Hansen, F., Bouvin, N., Christensen, B., Gronbaek, K., Pedersen, T., Gagach, J.: Integrating the Web and the World: Contextual Trails on the Move. Proceedings of the 15th. ACM International Conference of Hypertext and Hypermedia (Hypertext 2004), ACM Press. 2004.

10. Harper, S., Goble, C., Pettitt, S.: proXimity: Walking the Link. In Journal of Digital Information, Volume 5, Issue 1, Article No 236, 2004-04-07. http//jodi.ecs.soton.ac.uk/Articles/v05/i01/Harper/.

11. Romero, L., Correia, N.: HyperReal: A Hypermedia model for Mixed Reality. Proceedings of the 14th ACM International Conference of Hypertext and Hypermedia (Hypertext 2003), ACM Press, 2-9.

12. Passini, R.: Wayfinding in Architecture. Van Nostrand Reinhold, New York, 1984.

13. Rossi, G., Gordillo, S.G., Fortier, A.: Seamless Engineering of Location-Aware Services. OTM Workshops 2005: 176-185.

14. Schwabe, D., Rossi, G.: An Object Oriented Approach to Web-Based Applications Design. Theory and Practice of Object Systems (TAPOS), Special Issue on the Internet, v.4#4, October, 1998, 207-225.

15. UWA Project. www.uwaproject.org

16. Weal, M., Michaelides, D., Thompson, M., DeRoure, D.: The Ambient Wood journals: Replaying the experience. In Proceedings of Hypertext and Hypermedia. ACM Press, NY, 2003, 20--27.

17. Yesilada, Y., Stevens, R., Goble, C.: A foundation for tool based mobility support for visually impaired web users. In Proceedings of the Twelfth International Conference on World Wide Web, pages 422–430, 2003.

QoS-Predictions Service:
Infrastructural Support for Proactive
QoS- and Context-Aware Mobile Services
(Position Paper)

Katarzyna Wac[1,2], Aart van Halteren[2], and Dimitri Konstantas[1,2]

[1] University of Geneva, CUI/ASG, 24 rue General-Dufour, 1211 Geneva, Switzerland
[2] University of Twente, EWI/ASNA group, P.O.Box 217, 7500 AE Enschede, The Netherlands
{k.e.wac, a.t.vanhalteren, d.konstantas}@utwente.nl

Abstract. Today's mobile data applications aspire to deliver services to a user *anywhere - anytime* while fulfilling his *Quality of Service* (QoS) requirements. However, the success of the service delivery heavily relies on the QoS offered by the underlying networks. As the services operate in a heterogeneous networking environment, we argue that the generic information about the networks' offered-QoS may enable an *anyhow* mobile service delivery based on an intelligent (proactive) selection of 'any' network available in the user's context (location and time).

Towards this direction, we develop a *QoS-predictions service provider*, which includes functionality for the acquisition of generic offered-QoS information and which, via a multidimensional processing and history-based reasoning, will provide predictions of the expected offered-QoS in a reliable and timely manner.

We acquire the generic QoS-information from distributed mobile services' components quantitatively (actively and passively) measuring the application-level QoS, while the reasoning is based on statistical data mining and pattern recognition techniques.

1 Introduction[1]

The emergence of new wireless broadband networks and diverse miniaturized and personalized networked devices gives rise to a variety of new mobile services in our daily life. Ultimately, these mobile services are envisaged to be delivered as we move: *anywhere anytime* and under different conditions. However, on the move, these services receive a continuously changing information flow from the environment. A management of this information becomes critical for the delivery of the services. *Context-awareness* seems to be a promising paradigm to manage this flow, where *context* denotes any information that characterizes the user's environment and situation, (e.g. location and time), and any object relevant to the interaction between the user and his service [1].

---

[1] This is an ongoing research in frame of the Dutch Freeband AWARENESS project (BSIK 03025), partially supported by the INTEROP Network of Excellence (FP6-IST-508011).

R. Meersman, Z. Tari, P. Herrero et al. (Eds.): OTM Workshops 2006, LNCS 4278, pp. 1924–1933, 2006.

A mobile service operates in a heterogeneous networking environment consisting of diverse wireless and wired networks, owned by different providers. As a result, each network is responsible for only a section of the 'end-to-end' communication path between a mobile user and an application server, as illustrated in Figure 1. In the case of the *wireless access network*, it can be of diverse technologies (e.g. 2.5G/3G/WLAN), and provided by any provider, including a commercial Mobile Network Operator (MNO).

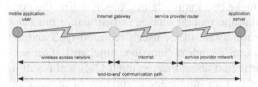

Fig. 1. An 'end-to-end' communication path for a mobile service delivery

Mobile connectivity, that is, persistency of a wireless connection while being mobile, and *Quality of Service* (QoS) *offered* by this connection are critical factors for the success of the service delivery. This success is measured in terms of fulfilment of the user's QoS requirements   (i.e.   *required-QoS*). However, current rules for the wireless network connectivity are rather simple (and imposed by the MNOs): a default wireless connection, provided by an MNO to which the user is 'locked-in', is assumed during the service-design time. As a result, an implicit assumption is made on the network's offered-QoS. Because a wireless link is usually the bottleneck in an end-to-end communication path, the wireless network's offered-QoS defines the *end-to-end offered-QoS* and as a result, the fulfilment level of the user's required-QoS. Furthermore, in today's mobile services, in spite of the user's context changes (location, time etc), the required-QoS is assumed to be static during the service delivery.

In our research we take a different direction based on more realistic (in our view) assumptions. The first assumption is that at any location and time various connectivity possibilities (can) coexist and are accessible, offering different QoS to the user. Although this is true today, because of the user 'lock-in' restrictions imposed by MNOs, current mobile applications are unaware and unable to make use of these offers. Our second assumption is that the user's QoS requirements change during the lifetime of the service delivery, depending on the user's context change. This assumption is valid especially for services that have a long duration, like for example epileptic patients' continuous mobile health monitoring service ([2], [3]), where the required-QoS will change along the health state of the user. In case of emergency, i.e. epileptic seizure, the required-QoS will be stricter (i.e. shorter delays required), than in case of a non-emergency situation [4]. For other mobile services, the required-QoS can change as, e.g., other mobile services (e.g. mobile TV) overlap with the main service (thus changing its execution environment), or as the user changes roles during the service delivery (as a company's employee or a father sharing family moments).

For our first assumption - the availability and accessibility of diverse wireless networks at a user's location and time, we consider not only networks owned by MNOs (2.5/3G) but also other private or public networks (WiFi, WiMax etc). To support the full exploitation of these networks, we make more assumptions. Our third assumption is that a mobile user is empowered to choose amongst the different network providers (and wireless access technologies); he is being able to handover between 'any' one of them, in order to obtain the *best-of the end-to-end offered-QoS* fulfilling his required-QoS[2]. Our fourth assumption is that it is not possible to negotiate end-to-end offered-QoS over the heterogeneous communication path; as a consequence it is possible to obtain only the *best-effort end-to-end offered-QoS*.

With the above four assumptions we overcome the restrictions imposed by the MNOs, and come closer to the reality that the mobile users will face in the future, under the vision of the 4G heterogeneous networking environment [5].

Based on the above assumptions we make two major claims, which define the context of our research. Our first claim is that the mobile service infrastructure must not only be context-aware, but also QoS-aware; aware of the user's required-QoS and the QoS offered by the various networks in user's context (location, time, etc). Our second claim is that the availability of information about these offered-QoS will result in user's intelligent choice of connectivity and an intelligent adaptation of application protocol parameters.

The research concerning our first claim is carried out in the Dutch AWARENESS project [3], and we have already presented it in [4].

In this paper we concentrate on issues related to our second claim. Our starting point is that the availability of run-time generic information regarding the offered QoS by the different available networks may (will, eventually) result in an intelligent (proactive) adaptation of mobile application to the user's environment. From one side, the application will be able to choose 'any' (the best fulfilling required-QoS) suitable network available at his context. From the other side, the application will be able in an intelligent way, to adapt the application protocol according to the network's offered-QoS (for example, by changing the packet size and an inter-packet-delay), in order to obtain best of the best-effort end-to-end offered-QoS. To reach these goals however, we will need *QoS-predictions service provider* as a part of the QoS- and context-aware service infrastructure (or a separate service provider). This service provider will provide generic predictions on the offered-QoS based on historical end-to-end offered-QoS measured and logged by mobile service components (of different users). These predictions will be provided with the use of predictive data mining, pattern recognition techniques, or any other methodology that might be convenient.

A common element for any type of prediction methodology is, nevertheless, the availability of consistent and valid historical data. The focus of this paper is to present our ideas regarding the collection of the end-to-end offered-QoS historical data. Our vision is that the QoS-predictions service provider acquires and aggregates the set of generic end-to-end offered-QoS information that can serve as a basis for predictions for *any* mobile service delivery. The goal is to enable *anywhere anytime anyhow* mobile service delivery obtaining the best of the best-effort end-to-end offered-QoS in an MNO-independent, heterogeneous networking environment, fulfilling the user's required-QoS.

In section 2 we give an overview of the related research, while in section 3 we present the overall system requirements. Section 4 provides our QoS-information model, while section 5 explains information acquisition. The conclusion in section 6 summarizes our research goals and gives an outlook on our research trajectory.

---

[2] Further considerations like e.g. the inter-MNO handover speed, or billing, are outside our research scope.

2 State-of-the-Art

This section presents the most important existing research on QoS- and context-awareness as well as on QoS- prediction techniques.

Considering the QoS-awareness aspect, the closest to our goal is the CELLO project, concentrating on a location-based performance evaluation of wireless access networks. Data regarding networks' performance is stored in a GIS system. However, as a network's performance indicator, this project only considers signal strength and not the end-to-end offered-QoS, as we do. Moreover, the overall goal of the project is to enhance the existing mobile operator network [6] and support efficient network extensions; the data is not used for mobile users, as we propose in our research.

Considering the context-awareness, the recent surveys on advances in this research area ([7], [8]) indicate that it focuses mainly on acquiring, processing and using of user context e.g. his location, time, and some physical characteristics of the user's environment and user's personal preferences, based on which the system must adapt. There exists some research in the context-awareness domain on including networks-related context information at the service infrastructure level [9]; however, there is no solution for the reliable network-related context information acquisition. For example, the publication of [10] provides a framework for network-aware applications and indicates that an application-level monitoring is one of the methods for application to be network-aware. However, this publication only considers the end-to-end bandwidth, and no other QoS parameters, as we propose. Moreover, this publication does not provide a solution for information acquisition.

Similarly, [11] and [12] provide an idea on network resource awareness at the application level; both indicate user context as necessary information for an application to adapt. However, both indicate their focus on the wireless access network and not end-to-end resources availability, as we do. Moreover, the mobile connectivity predictions service provider indicated in [12] is based on the single user's history of connectivity, and is used for a user himself to derive further context information. Hence, it will not be used for other users, as we indicate in our research.

In most cases, the research indicates only a signal strength of a wireless access network and this network's theoretical capacity as an indication for offered QoS ([12], [13]). In contrary, we focus on the practical, application-level, end-to-end offered-QoS as the most significant for the mobile service delivery.

There exists some positioning research for context-awareness and prediction techniques using e.g. data mining techniques, however it is very limited - the research presented in [14] focuses on finding an optimal techniques for an application to adapt to the context, rather than to predict the context itself.

Regarding the QoS-awareness of mobile applications, there is a researched solution in which a mobile user of a streaming video application would obtain some information about the offered-QoS directly from the mobile operator network infrastructure [15] e.g. information about his wireless access network performance and location of the video-replica servers. Proposed solution is MNO-specific and does not solve the end-to-end offered-QoS issue, as we do.

Based on this short representation of the ongoing research, we define the innovative contribution of our research to the existing state of the art as the fact that we take the application-level, i.e. end-to-end QoS characteristics as context information.

Moreover, we research the QoS-predictions service provider created based on generic QoS-information obtained by users for users, to support MNO-independent, *anyhow* mobile services delivery obtaining best-of the best-effort end-to-end offered-QoS in a heterogeneous networking environment.

3 System Requirements

3.1 Requirements on a QoS- and Context-Aware Mobile Service Infrastructure

To introduce QoS-awareness into a context-aware service infrastructure, the infrastructure must fulfill a set of requirements (we described them in detail in [4]). Firstly the infrastructure must support user's QoS requirements specification, secondly, the context-aware mapping of user's QoS requirements into the requirements on end-to-end offered-QoS and thirdly, it has to support the service delivery adaptation to the end-to-end offered-QoS, to best fulfill the user's required-QoS. Additionally to these, the context-aware service infrastructure must support *QoS monitoring*; it must support real-time measurements of end-to-end offered-QoS and log those measurements to the QoS-predictions service provider.

3.2 Requirements on the QoS-Predictions Service Provider

As we explained in the introduction, the QoS-predictions service provider is the source of the predictions of end-to-end QoS offered by the underlying heterogeneous networking environment.

The functional requirements on the QoS-predictions service provider are:

- QoS acquisition and storage – the provider must acquire and aggregate results of real-time end-to-end offered-QoS measurements performed by the mobile users, and estimate the quality of the acquired (and aggregated) information
- QoS processing – the provider must transform the acquired data into a form meaningful for inferring further QoS information; inference rules may be dynamically learned along the acquired QoS information
- QoS predictions provisioning - the QoS-predictions provider must provide generic predictions of end-to-end offered-QoS to mobile users, with estimation of the quality of the prediction (i.e. its probability)

The non-functional requirements on QoS-predictions service provider are (after [8], [16]): heterogeneity, interoperability, support for mobility of users, performance, scalability, security and privacy, cost, traceability and control and fault tolerance.

4 QoS-Information Model

In order to support the QoS-predictions, measured QoS information as well as other context information must be logged. It is thus of major importance to define in details what type of data are needed to develop a generic QoS-predictions service provider. In the following sections we describe in detail structure of the logged generic end-to-end offered-QoS information, and namely a) end-to-end QoS information (section 4.1) and associated context information (section 4.2). All the generic QoS-information needs to be acquired, processed and provided along with its quality measures like e.g. information freshness and accuracy. These quality measures are denoted as a *Quality of Context (QoC)* and they play a significant role in QoS-information processing phase [17].

4.1 QoS-Information Model

Following the classification given in [18] we focus on a generic *network-oriented* and selected *user-oriented* end-to-end offered-QoS information that our QoS-predictions service provider acquires, aggregates, processes and provides:

- network-oriented end-to-end offered-QoS information is the end-to-end communication path's performance [16] expressed in terms of:
  - speed - end-to-end application-level data delay and goodput[3]
  - accuracy - data corruption probability
  - dependability - service availability, service reliability in terms of application-level data loss probability
- user-oriented end-to-end offered-QoS information is:
  - service cost, e.g., per use or per unit cost
  - security level, e.g., authentication, confidentiality, integrity, non-repudiation

The user-oriented perceived QoS, e.g., picture resolution, video rate/smoothness, audio quality, AV synchronization, are outside of the scope of our QoS-predictions provider due to its application-domain dependency. Our vision is that the QoS-predictions service provider deals with the set of *generic* end-to-end offered-QoS information that can serve as a basis for *any* mobile service delivery adaptation.

4.2 Associated Context-Information Model

The network- and selected user-oriented end-to-end offered-QoS information described in the previous section needs to be acquired from, and disseminated to mobile users along with the following service usage's generic context information (non exhaustive list):

- Mobile user's geographical location and time – where (and when) the end-to-end offered QoS was measured or for where (and when) the QoS-predictions are given
- Mobile user's mobility level – velocity of changes of user location in time
- Wireless access network provider used e.g. Vodafone, and wireless access network technology e.g. 3G; associated network's usage cost and security level
- Mobile service used, application-protocol and its traffic model type – we define 1) an interactive, 2) messaging and 3) streaming traffic models described in terms of a) packet size distribution and b) inter-packet-delay distribution

---

[3] Goodput is an application-level throughput.

- Transport-level protocol, e.g. TCP or UDP and its parameters
- Mobile device used and its technical specifications like, e.g. OS and its version, CPU and its load level, memory type/size and its usage level, battery type/size and its level, wireless access networks interfaces supported
- Application server used and its technical specifications like, e.g. OS and its version, CPU and its load level, memory type/size and its usage level

Other type of context information can be included, depending on the specific needs of the mobile application and the prediction service provider.

5 End-to-End Offered-QoS Information Acquisition

The QoS-predictions' service provider acquires and accumulates logs on end-to-end offered-QoS measured by mobile service components of different users. Particularly, the results of run-time quantitative measurements of end-to-end application-level offered-QoS are logged. This can be done in two ways: first, actively by a standalone *evaluation system* – distributed mobile application dedicated in performing the measurements (section 5.1) and second, passively during the execution of a mobile application (section 5.2)

5.1 Active End-to-End Offered-QoS Measurements – The *Evaluation System*

To actively measure the end-to-end QoS offered by the underlying heterogeneous networking environment, we first considered the existing performance evaluation tools as presented in [18]. However, as these tools are mainly fixed-networks oriented they do not fulfill the basic mobility, heterogeneity and distribution requirements. For this reason we have developed our own a scalable distributed non-invasive measurements-based performance evaluation system (described in [19]) consisting of:

- *workload generator* – for generating a controlled application-level workload (i.e. along the application-protocol traffic model type) at ingress points of the heterogeneous networking environment;
- *measurement function* – for acquiring and correlating measurements (i.e. application-level's events-based timestamps), at the ingress and egress points of the heterogeneous networking environment and for generating statistically analyzed end-to-end measurements results in a textual and graphical form.

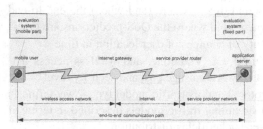

Fig. 2. The evaluation system in the 'end-to-end' communication path

Figure 2 presents the distribution of evaluation system in the end-to-end communication path. The critical requirement for this setup is that the distributed nodes have their time clocks precisely synchronized (by e.g. GPS) in order to get reliable timestamps.

Our evaluation system measures speed-related performance characteristics - one-way end-to-end delays and goodput along with the user context information (section 4.2) e.g. user location, time, wireless access network provider/technology and technicalities of mobile device/application server used. The current implementation of our system used only TCP as a transport protocol and we are expanding it towards use of the UDP protocol.

The system has been used in the measurement of end-to-end offered-QoS for a continuous mobile health monitoring application - the *MobiHealth* application [2] operational in a heterogeneous networking environment with a 3G-UMTS wireless network as a wireless access network, as presented in [20] and [21].

5.2 Application-Level Passive End-to-End Offered-QoS Measurements

To passively measure generic end-to-end QoS offered by the underlying heterogeneous networking environment, we are now working on an instrumentation of our MobiHealth application, developed and operational at the University of Twente, the Netherlands. The application itself acts as a workload generator, and we are currently working on the implementation of a generic measurement function within it.

6 Conclusions and Outlook

In this paper we discussed our ongoing research on QoS- and context-aware service infrastructure that supports the development of mobile applications in a heterogeneous networking environment. Particularly we presented our vision of *anywhere anytime anyhow* mobile service delivery fulfilling the user's required-QoS by using the generic predictions of end-to-end offered-QoS in user's actual context (e.g. his location and time) to obtain the best-of the best-effort end-to-end offered-QoS. We presented issues related to the collection of generic QoS measurements.

The main functionality of the QoS-predictions service provider is the processing of the logged generic QoS-information (i.e. end-to-end offered-QoS) and the provision of generic predictions of the end-to-end offered-QoS to mobile applications. We envision that the QoS-information processing is based on the data mining and patterns recognition techniques. We anticipate that the Quality of Context information associated with the QoS-information will play an important role in the QoS-information processing. However, we have not acquired any concrete results yet as the research is still ongoing.

In our research, the mobile entities are generic wireless sensor/actuator network nodes – logging the generic QoS-information to the QoS-predictions provider and acting upon the generic QoS-predictions, hence changing the heterogeneous networking environment's offered-QoS.

We identify the novelty of our approach as being the expansion beyond the standard QoS management framework, comprising of QoS contracts and QoS negotiation components. We propose a complete user-driven approach, where a mobile user (and particularly an application on the user's behalf) can make an intelligent choice amongst the underlying network providers and technologies to best fulfill the mobile user's required-QoS. We indicate the importance of our eventual findings and its applicability to fulfill required-QoS for any mobile service user, in an *anyhow* manner.

The target audience of our research is any mobile service provider. As more and more applications go mobile, the demand for a generic QoS-information provided in a reliable and timely manner, will be growing. The beneficiaries of our research will be directly mobile users, experiencing their mobile services at the required quality level.

Our research expands beyond the current telecom business model, where the user is locked to one MNO and technologies offered by this operator. In our view, the user should be empowered to make a decision on which network technology offered by which provider is the most convenient for him to use. Moreover, by introducing the generic QoS-predictions service provider we further indicate the user-empowerment; generic QoS-information is acquired by users and it is used exclusively for the users.

References

1. Dey, A. The Context Toolkit: Aiding the Development of Context-Aware Applications. In Workshop on Software Engineering for Wearable and Pervasive Computing. 2000. Limerick, Ireland.
2. van Halteren, A., et al., Mobile Patient Monitoring: The MobiHealth System. The Journal on Information Technology in Healthcare, 2004. 2(5): p. 365-373.
3. Wegdam, M. AWARENESS: A project on Context AWARE mobile NEtworks and ServiceS. In 14th Mobile & Wireless Communication Summit. 2005. Dresden, Germany.
4. Wac, K. Towards QoS-Awareness of Context-Aware Mobile Applications and Services. In On the Move to Meaningful Internet Systems 2005: OTM Workshops, Ph.D. Student Symposium. 2005. Agia Napa, Cyprus: Springer Berlin / Heidelberg.
5. Frattasi, S., Fathi, and F. Fitzek, 4G: A User-Centric System. Wireless Personal Communications Journal (WPC) - Special Issue on Advances in Wireless Communications: Enabling Technologies for 4G, 2006.
6. Horsmanheimo, S., H. Jormakka, and J. Lähteenmäki, Location-Aided Planning in Mobile Networks - Trial Results. Wireless Personal Communications: Special Issue on Cellular and Wireless Location Based Technologies and Services, 2004. 30(2-4): p. 207-216.
7. Chen, G. and D. Kotz, A survey of context-aware mobile computing research, in Technical Report TR2000-381. 2000, Dept. of Computer Science, Darthmouth College.
8. Henricksen, K., et al. Middleware for Distributed Context-Aware Systems. In On the Move to Meaningful Internet Systems 2005. 2005. Agia Napa, Cyprus: Springer Berlin / Heidelberg.
9. Gloss, B. System Architecture of a Mobile Message Transport System. In 11th Open European Summer School - Networked Applications (EUNICE05). 2005. Madrid, Spain.
10. Bolliger, J. and T. Gross, A framework based approach to the development of network aware applications. IEEE Transactions on Software Engineering, 1998. 24(5): p. 376-390.
11. Chalmers, D. and M. Sloman. QoS and Context Awareness for Mobile Computing. In 1st Intl. Symposium on Handheld and Ubiquitous Computing (HUC99). 1999. Karlsruhe, Germany: Springer.
12. Sun, J., J. Sauvola, and J. Riekki. Application of connectivity information for context interpretation and derivation. In 8th International Conference on Telecommunications (ConTEL05). 2005. Zagreb, Croatia.
13. Peddemors, A., H. Eertink, and I. Niemegeers. Communication Context for Adaptive Mobile Applications. In 3rd IEEE International Conference on Pervasive Computing and Communications Workshops (PERCOMW05). 2005.

14. Mähönen, P., et al. Cognitive Wireless Networks: Your Network Just Became a Teenager. In INFOCOM06. 2006. Barcelona, Spain: IEEE.
15. Han, Q. and N. Venkatasubramanian, Information Collection Services for QoS-aware Mobile Applications. IEEE Transactions on Mobile Computing, 2006. 5(5): p. 518-535.
16. ITU-T, General aspects of Quality of Service and Network Performance in Digital Networks, including ISDNs. 1993, ITU.
17. Widya, I., B.J. van Beijnum, and A. Salden. QoC-based optimization of end-to end m-health data delivery services. In 14th IEEE International Workshop on Quality of Service (IWQoS06). 2006. New Haven CT, USA: IEEE Press.
18. Michaut, F. and F. Lepage, Application-oriented network metrology: Metrics and active measurement tools. IEEE Communications Surveys & Tutorials, 2005. 7(2): p. 2-24.
19. Bults, R., A. van Halteren, and K. Wac, Design of a Scalable Distributed End-to-End Performance Evaluation System. 2005, University of Twente, the Netherlands.
20. Wac, K., et al. Measurements-based performance evaluation of 3G wireless networks supporting m-health services. In 12th Multimedia Computing and Networking (MMCN05). 2005. San Jose, CA, USA.
21. Bults, R., et al. Goodput Analysis of 3G wireless networks supporting m-health services. In 8th International Conference on Telecommunications (ConTEL05). 2005. Zagreb, Croatia.

LiteMap: An Ontology Mapping Approach for Mobile Agents' Context-Awareness

Haïfa Zargayouna and Nejla Amara

LIPN, Université Paris 13 - CNRS UMR 7030,
99 av. J.B. Clément, 93440 Villetaneuse, France
firstname.lastname@lipn.univ-paris13.fr

Abstract. Mobile agents' applications have to operate within environments having continuously changing execution conditions that are not easily predictable. They have to dynamically adapt to changes in their context resulting from other's activities and resources variation. To be aware of their execution context, mobile agents require a formal and structured model of the context and a reasoning process for detecting suspect situations. In this work, we use formal ontologies to model the agents' execution context as well as its composing elements. After each agent migration, a reasoning process is carried out upon these ontologies to detect meaningful environmental changes. This reasoning is based on semantic web techniques for mapping ontologies. The output of the mapping process is a set of semantic relations among the ontologies concepts that will be used by the agent to trigger a reconfiguration of its structure according to some adaptation policies.

1 Introduction

With the advent of ubiquitous computing and the proliferation of Internet applications requiring dynamic and possibly mobile access to Internet resources, autonomous mobile agents can be used with significant advantages. They are especially attractive for accessing resources and services distributed through the networks on a large scale and performing complex, tedious or repetitive tasks in open and dynamic systems. Nevertheless, when moving from host to host to perform their tasks, mobile agents are continuously expected to run in heterogeneous and changing execution environments. To survive, they have to be aware of their execution context in order to adapt themselves to the environment where they are running. The adaptation is achieved by dynamically composing an environment-specific version of the agent that assembles the appropriate components, without stopping of the agent. In [1], we proposed a component-based Generic Adaptive Mobile Agent architecture ($GAMA$) that exhibits a minimal mobile agent behavior. $GAMA$ agents have the ability to move from node to node according to an itinerary, in order to fulfill their tasks. Using component-based design increases modularity, reusability and extensibility of our agents. Thus, a $GAMA$ agent structure can be easily adjusted to fulfill requirements of

R. Meersman, Z. Tari, P. Herrero et al. (Eds.): OTM Workshops 2006, LNCS 4278, pp. 1934–1943, 2006.

new execution to which it is continuously faced during its migration. The decision of adapting the agent structure is the result of a reasoning process held by the agent about its context.

In order to enable our agents to carry out the reasoning and the adaptation processes, we enriched the $GAMA$ architecture by two new components: the **context-awareness** for reasoning about the agent context, and the **Reconfiguration** for the adaptation decision making. Meanwhile, the reasoning process requires an adequate representation of the agent context. This representation must provide a formal and well structured means for enabling intelligent agents to reason about contextual information. To do so, the agent need to detect the relationship between the knowledge about its profile and the knowledge about its execution environment. Formal ontologies can provide a judicious representation of contextual information, as they offer a high level representation of knowledge and enables reasoning and inferences. In this work, we model two ontologies (OntoContext and OntoAgent) for describing the agent execution context and its functional components. The $GAMA$ agents' awareness about their execution context is achieved by mapping concepts of their handled data with those of their context. The mapping enables to extract common structures between the two ontologies and thus highlighting semantic relations between their concepts.

In this paper, we will focus on $GAMA$ agents awareness of their execution context. Section 2 presents the notions of context and context awareness. Section 3 is devoted to the use of formal ontologies to represent the context. Section 4 introduce the mapping method we propose illustrated by an example. Section 5 surveys the related works. At last, we conclude and give some perspectives to this work.

2 Mobile Agents: Context and Context-Awareness

2.1 Definitions

As stated in [2], *"context consists in any information that can be used to characterize the situation of an entity where an entity is a person, place, or object that is considered relevant to the interaction between a user and an application, including the user and applications themselves"*. This definition stresses the relation between the system, the context and the user. In our work, by context we mean information about the current execution environment of the mobile agent and we focus rather on how the context influences the agent behavior when executing its assigned tasks. This can be illustrated by a failure of the agent execution process if it moves to a host where the context attributes doesn't fit the agent's requirements. According to these considerations, we propose a definition of the $GAMA$ agents context-awareness as follows:

Definition 1. *A mobile agent GAMA can be context-aware if it is able to detect contextual situations that affect its behavior aiming to achieve its tasks.*

According to this definition, developing context-aware mobile agents requires facilities for recognizing and representing context in order to enable agents to reason on it and take decisions about their execution process (adapt, inform the user, etc.). For *GAMA* agents, sensing and structuring context information is performed at the hosting platforms. Every interaction between agents and the operating systems (of computers and the network) as well as those between agents and their owners (human users) are achieved by the platform.

2.2 The Context Elements

To describe the agents context, we identify three specific context levels: physical context, social context and user context. Physical context refers to physical devices the mobile agent is running on; for example, the host's processing power and the network bandwidth. Social context refers to the local Multi-Agent System (MAS) deployed on the platform with whom the incoming agent has to interact. For instance, information about this context includes the local interaction and coordination protocols. User context refers to the agents owner preferences, such as restrictions about the exchanged files' size or type, the display quality, etc.

2.3 How to Achieve Context-Awareness?

Developing context-aware mobile agents needs capacities to:

1. Capture the contextual parameters by the means of some physical sensors, graphic interfaces and the deployment platform. Currently, this step is outside the focus of our work.
2. Represent the context knowledge in order to be available for use by the agents.
3. Reason on the context model in order to be aware of it. The reasoning process consists in mapping the proposed ontologies in order to detect possible relations which affect the agent behavior.

The result of this process is a notification that enables the agent to take decision about the behavior to adopt in the new context: adapt itself to continue its execution, or alert the user if the adaptation is not possible. Thus, the agent needs not only a model of its context entities but also a comparable model of its own components. Mapping these models allows checking their compatibility degrees. Assuming these requirements, we propose to extend the *GAMA* architecture with new component called **Context-awareness**. This component processes the context model provided by the component *Context Description* of the platform, and the agent model provided by the component *Agent Profile*. The *GAMA* architecture is baptized from now to up $GAMA_{context-aware}$ (see Figure 1).

3 Formal Ontologies for Context Representation

Formal ontologies has regained interest with the emergence of the Semantic Web. The Semantic Web, described by [3], is an extension of the current web in which information is given well-defined meaning.

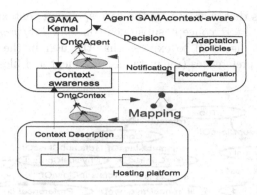

Fig. 1. From GAMA to GAMA$_{context-aware}$

OWL [4] is a language for expressing ontologies on the web. OWL provides three increasingly expressive sublanguages. We concentrate on OWL-Lite which is sufficient for our purposes.

A formal ontology is defined by a set of concepts, a set of roles and a partial order relation applied to these two sets. Formally we define the ontology as:

Definition 2. *An ontology is a tuple* $O = \langle S, R, \leq_R, \leq_S, \top \rangle$[1]

- *S: the set of concepts.*
- *R: the set of roles between the concepts.*
- *$\leq_S$: a partial order relation applied to concepts.*
- *$\leq_R$: a partial order relation applied to roles.*
- *$\top$: the top of the ontology.*

A key idea to realizing the $GAMA_{contexte-aware}$ architecture is the use of ontologies to represent the agent structure and MAS platforms. Agents and platforms need to represent two kinds of knowledge: (i) knowledge about their own structure (Agent Profile for the agent and Context description for the MAS platform) and (ii) knowledge about handled data (such as credit card, auction protocols, etc.).

We present in the following the two ontologies proposed: OntoContext and OntoAgent.

3.1   OntoContext: The Context Ontology

The upper concept in OntoContext ontology is *Context* that represents an abstraction of the agent execution context. This concept subsumes the hierarchy of subconcepts characterizing the agent context. The *context* concept defines three subconcepts: *PhysicalContext*, *SocialContext* and *UserContext* in order to represent the several context aspects stated in section 2. Each one of these subconcepts

---

[1] We choose to reason at the concept level but the instance level can also be considered.

subsumes concepts that characterize the correspondent context feature. For example, the *UserContext* concept subsumes concepts *PreferencePayement* and *PreferenceFile* (see figure 2) to express that the user in the agent context is represented by its preferences (for instance, payement and files).

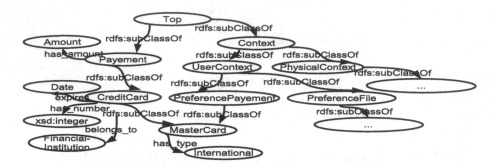

Fig. 2. A graphical representation of an extract of OntoContext. Each oval represents an OWL concept. Labelled arrows represent relations among these concepts.

3.2 OntoAgent: The Agent Ontology

A *GAMA* agent is built by assembling software components, its profile can be described by the descriptions of all its components. The upper level concept of the OntoAgent ontology is *AgentProfile*, which represents an abstraction of informations about the agent structure. It has several subconcepts describing the different functional components (TaskComponent, CoordinationComponent, etc.) of the agent and properties representing relations between theses concepts (See figure 3).

4   LiteMap: A Light Mapping Approach

4.1   Interoperability Problem

The representation of the agent's profile and MAS platforms by ontologies does not resolve the knotty problem of interoperability. Ontologies are seen as the solution to data heterogeneity on the web. However, the available ontologies could themselves introduce heterogeneity: given two ontologies, the same entity can be given different names or simply be defined in different ways, whereas both ontologies may express the same knowledge. The underlying problem, can be described as follows: given two ontologies each one describing a set of discrete entities (classes, properties, predicates, etc.), find the relationships that hold between these entities. These relations can be:

– equivalence: the two entities represent the same knowledge,
– subsumption: an entity subsumes (or is subsumed by) another entity,

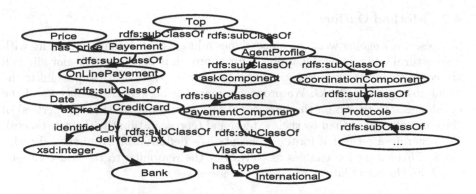

Fig. 3. A graphical representation of an extract of OntoAgent. Each oval represents an OWL concept. Labelled arrows represent relations among these concepts.

- common subsumer: the two entities are subsumed by equivalent entities (the common subsumer must not be high in the ontology),
- mismatch or disjointness: in all the other cases.

Two possible solutions can be considered. First a common reference shared by the two ontologies can be used. This supposes a huge effort made in standardization and the adoption, by the different web components, of these standards. The second alternative consists of the extraction of a new ontology that represents the common structures between the ontologies and references the common elements (concepts, relations, etc).

The second possibility seems more realistic to solve our problem in the actual context of the semantic web. In this case, the ontologies have to be *aligned*. The alignement of concepts is a task that requires understanding the meaning of concepts. It is unrealistic to fully automate this task. In practice, a presence of an *expert* is necessary. We have to deal with this limitation, as the agent cannot interrupt its work to ask for expert intervention. It has to specify a procedure to recover when it has erroneous information. We define a method to map concepts in order to have the relations cited above (equivalence, mismatch, subsumption). To be able to map OntoAgent and OntoContext, we make these assumptions:

- The same representation language: We make the hypothesis that the ontologies share the same representation language because in the other cases a translation is required. The semantic web presents a formal framework that enables us to make such a hypothesis. Both ontologies are supposed to be formalized in OWL-LITE.
- The presence of similar elements: This hypothesis permits to consider a possible solution to the mapping. In absence of shared elements the mapping would be impossible. This hypothesis is not restrictive in case of ontologies of the same domain. Our agents and their hosting platforms share a minimal common vision of the environment in which they evolve and the knowledge they handle.

4.2   Method Outline

We describe ongoing work which combines a linguistic[2] similarity measure with a structural and semantic mapping. Our approach is light as we do not align all the concepts in the two ontologies but a set of concepts that are important to the agent to achieve its tasks. We propose a mapping between leaf concepts of the ontologies. We reason on the intensional representation (by their properties) of the concepts rather than by their extensional representation (by their instances). We generate a saturated form of concepts (see definition 3) from their descriptions. This saturation enables us to restrict the reasoning to the leaf concepts. Let L be the set of labels, we use ℓ_i to range over.

Definition 3. *A saturated concept is represented by a tuple* $C =< \langle \ell, A, RC \rangle$

- *l is the label of the concept, it could be enriched by its natural language definition.*
- *A is a set of the antecedents of the concept C. This set is a transitive closure of the subsumers of the concept.*
- *RC is a set of concepts related with the concept C by a role. This set is a saturation of the related concepts, it contains the related concepts of the concept C and those of its subsumers, as a concept inherits the characteristics of its ancestors.[3]*

To align the concepts at the linguistic level, we define θ-relation as follows:

Definition 4. *Let C_i and C_j be two concepts. A θ-relation : $C_i \times C_j \rightarrow String \cup \{Nil\}$. θ-relation$(C_i, C_j) = \ell_i$ if $Sim(\ell_i, \ell_j) \geq \alpha$*

This relation associates two concepts if the linguistic similarity between their label exceeds a fixed threshold (α), it returns the preferred label (which in this case is always the label of the first concept) and *Nil* in the other cases. For example, *CreditCard* in OntoContext verifies θ-relation with *CreditCard* in OntoAgent, as their linguistic similarity is 1.

Our algorithm tries to find a common structure for each leaf concept C_i in a source ontology (O_S) and a leaf concept (C_j) in a target ontology (O_T). The common structure (that we call C_f) is extracted as follows:

If $Sim(\ell_i, \ell_j) > \alpha$
Then
$\ell_f = \ell_i$
$A_f = \theta$-Intersect(A_i, A_j)
$RC_f = \theta$-Intersect(RC_i, RC_j)
Else return$(Nil, \emptyset, \emptyset)$

---

[2] A terminological similarity can also be performed if a semantic ressource is available in the execution environment.

[3] Initially, we do not consider transitive cyclic definitions (eg. transitive and symmetric roles).

Such as θ-Intersect is defined as follows:

Definition 5. *Let S_1 and S_2 be two sets of concepts.*
$$\theta\text{-}Intersect(S_1, S_2) = \bigcup_{(C_i, C_j) \in S_1 \times S_2} (\theta\text{-}relation(C_i, C_j)).$$

The common structure of two concepts is a concept which is represented by its label (the preferred label), a list of common subsumers and a list of common related concepts. Our method is based on the linguistic similarity of the concepts (by *Sim* a measure of similarity), a structural mapping (by the intersection of their subsumers) and a semantic mapping (by the intersection of their related concepts). As the description of the concept is saturated, it gives all the informations about the shared entities.

4.3   Example

The common structure between *VisaCard* (figure 3) and *MasterCard* (figure 2) is computed as follows. In the following computations, θ-relation is assumed between (CreditCard, CreditCard), (OnLinePayement, Payement), (Payement, Payement), (Price, Amount), (Date, Date) and (Bank, Financial-Institution).

$A_{VisaCard} = \{\text{CreditCard, OnLinePayement, Payement}\}$
$RC_{VisaCard} = \{\text{Price, Date, Bank, International}\}$

$A_{MasterCard} = \{\text{CreditCard, Payement}\}$
$RC_{MasterCard} = \{\text{Amount, Date, Financial-Institution, International}\}$

$\theta\text{-intersect}(A_{VisaCard}, A_{MasterCard}) = \{\text{CreditCard, Payement}\}$
$\theta\text{-intersect}(RC_{VisaCard}, RC_{MasterCard}) = \{\text{Price, Date, Bank, International}\}$

The common concept thus is *VisaCard* that has as common subsumers *CreditCard OnLinePayement* and *Payement*. This Concept points to the concepts *VisaCard* and *MasterCard* in the OntoAgent and OntoContext ontologies. We can then state that *VisaCard* and *MasterCard* are equivalent.

5   Related Work

A number of architectures for ontology-based context-aware systems have been proposed. CoBrA-ONT [5] is an ontology designed for supporting knowledge sharing and context reasoning. The CONON [6] ontology has similar objectives: checking the consistency of context, and deducing high-level, implicit context from low-level, explicit context. In our work, reasoning upon ontologies doesn't aim at deducing new implicit concepts to describe the context. Indeed, our purpose is to enable agents to decide after each migration whether their current structure fits the new execution environment by mapping the OntoAgent and OntoContext ontologies. In fact, we need to discover common areas where the ontologies can have several points of contact. This is a common step for merging and aligning ontologies.

Most of the existing tools and approaches proposed for processing merging or aligning ontologies at a semantic level can not proceed completely automatically. Many semi-automatic approaches exist and make possible to perform some operations automatically and suggest others to the user. An exhaustive state of the art is given in [7]. Ontomorph [8] defines a set of transformation operators that can be applied to an ontology. PROMPT [9] looks for linguistically similar class names, studies the the structure of relations in the vicinity of recently merged concepts, and matches slot names and slot value types. FCA-Merge [10] is a method for merging ontologies guided by the application-specific instances (a set of representative documents) of the given source ontologies. The need of external data, in our sense, limits the use of such approach.

Some automatic mapping approches exist but they are based on strong assumptions. For instance, IF-Map [11], based on the theory of information flow, formalises ontologies as local logics and ontology mappings as logic infomorphisms. Nevertheless, a reference ontology is needed and thus reduce the interoperability problem. We propose an automatic light mapping method that doesn't need any extra knowledge. We insure the autonomy of the agent, but it has to deal with possible matching errors.

6   Conclusion and Future Work

We have described an approach for mobile agent context awareness. A key idea of the architecture proposed is the use of ontologies to represent $GAMA$ agents and MAS platforms. These ontologies are merged by a light mapping method in order to find common substructures. The extracted substructures enable to find different relations between ontologies' elements (equivalence, subsumption, etc.). Experiments are necessary to have a deep insight into the behavior of our mapping algorithm. We plan to make evaluations by computing precision and recall of the proposed matchings compared to a manual one. Ontology Alignment Evaluation Initiative[4] aims at assessing strength and weakness of alignment/matching systems, we plan to evaluate our approach in this context.

The next step of the self-adaptation process is triggered when an incompatibility notification is generated by the "Context-awareness" component towards the "Reconfiguration" component that is in charge of the decision making about the kind of adaptation to be held. This decision is made by referring to some adaptation policies. Concretely, an adaptation policy is a named set of rules of the form: **When** $< event\_desc >$ **if** $< gard >$ **do** $< action >$.

Where $< event\_desc >$ is an event descriptor, $< gard >$ is a boolean expression, and $< action >$ is an action describing the adaptation to undertake, such as replacing an existing component, adding a new component or removing a component. In the case of adaptation by replacement or adding, new components

---

[4] http://oaei.ontologymatching.org/

are retrieved in a "Components Repository" available on the local platform, in order to link them to the core by the "Controller" component.

We plan to specify a recover procedure for the agent. If the extracted relations are erroneous, the agent should be able to go back to a stable state.

References

1. Amara-Hachmi, N., Fallah-Seghrouchni, A.E.: A framework for context-aware mobile agents. In: 4th Workshop on Ambient Intelligence - Agents for Ubiquitous Environments held in conjunction with AAMAS 2005. (2005)
2. Salber, A.D.D., Abowd, G.: A conceptual framework and a toolkit for supporting the rapid prototyping of context-aware applications. Human- Computer Interaction (HCI) Journal **16**(2-4) (2001) 97–166
3. Berners-Lee, T., Hendler, J., Lassila, O.: The semantic web : A new form of web content that is meaningful to computers will unleash a revolution of new possibilities. Scientific American (2001) 35–43
4. Dean, M., Schreiber, G., (eds.): Owl web ontology language: reference. Recommendation, W3C (2004) http://www.w3.org/TR/owlref/.
5. Chen, H., al.: An ontology for context-aware pervasive computing environments. Special Issue on Ontologies for Distributed Systems, Knowledge Engineering Review (2004)
6. Wang, X., al.: Ontology based context modeling and reasoning using owl. In: Workshop on Context Modeling and Reasoning at IEEE International Conference on Pervasive Computing and Communication (PerCom'04). (2004)
7. Euzenat, J., Bach, T.L., Barrasa, J., Bouquet, P., Bo, J.D., Dieng-Kuntz, R., Ehrig, M., Hauswirth, M., Jarrar, M., Lara, R., Maynard, D., Napoli, A., Stamou, G., Stuckenschmidt, H., Shvaiko, P., Tessaris, S., Acker, S.V., Zaihrayeu, I.: State of the art on ontology alignment (2004)
8. MacGregor, R., Chalupsky, H., Moriarty, D., A.Valente: Ontology merging with ontomorph. http://reliant.teknowledge.com/HPKB/meetings/meet040799/Chalupsky/index.htm (1999)
9. Noy, N., Musen, M.: Prompt: Algorithm and tool for automated ontology merging and alignment. In: Seventeenth National Conference on Artificial Intelligence (AAAI-2000). (2000)
10. Stumme, G., Madche, A.: Fca-merge: Bottom-up merging of ontologies. In: 7th Intl. Conf. on Artificial Intelligence (IJCAI '01). (2001) 225–230
11. Kalfoglou, Y., Schorlemmer, M.: If-map: An ontology-mapping method based on information-flow theory. Journal of Data Semantics **1**(1) (2003)

Compressing GPS Data on Mobile Devices

Ryan Lever, Annika Hinze, and George Buchanan

University of Wales, Swansea
r.m.lever.290132@swansea.ac.uk
University of Waikato, New Zealand
a.hinze@cs.waikato.ac.nz
University of Wales, Swansea
g.r.buchanan@swansea.ac.uk

Abstract. In context-aware mobile systems, data on past user behaviour or use of a device can give critical information. The scale of this data may be large, and it must be quickly searched and retrieved. Compression is a powerful tool for both storing and indexing data. For text documents powerful algorithms using structured storage achieve high compression and rapid search and retrieval. Byte-stream techniques provide higher compression, but lack indexation and have slow retrieval.

Location is a common form of context frequently used in research prototypes of tourist guide systems, location-aware searching and adaptive hypermedia. In this paper, we present an exploration of record-based compression of Global Positioning System (GPS) data that reveals significant technical limitations on what can be achieved on mobile devices, and a discussion of the benefits of different compression techniques on GPS data.

Keywords: Compression, GPS, Context-aware.

1 Introduction

Contextual data can take many forms. In this paper, we focus on GPS location data, but many of the lessons we demonstrate here will be pertinent to other structured location data.

GPS data is commonly presented in simple NMEA *sentences* [2] which contain information such as latitude, longitude and altitude. A GPS device can output sentences many times a minute, and therefore a substantial volume of data can aggregate within a single day. Given that a device may be stationary for periods of time, or moving within a very limited distance, it seems natural to exploit this redundancy and trim the data to reduce the total data size required. However, there are both consequences and complications to a simple implementation to this approach: first, it is not clear, given GPS data alone, when localised movement may be significant and require storage; second, the well-reported variability of recorded location complicates the determination of a 'static' location; third, improved precision can be achieved by over-sampling the entire GPS trace, which is clearly compromised by premature loss of data.

R. Meersman, Z. Tari, P. Herrero et al. (Eds.): OTM Workshops 2006, LNCS 4278, pp. 1944–1947, 2006.
© Springer-Verlag Berlin Heidelberg 2006

2 Design Constraints

2.1 Mobile Hardware

Mobile devices have relatively consistent configurations – sharing the same processors, similar memory configurations and storage options. One key factor for our design is that most processors have no floating point (FP) hardware. This is due to the significant price and power consumption differentials between those CPUs with and without FPUs. To provide some level of floating-point capacity, processor manufacturers, e.g. ARM, provide FP libraries, e.g. the ARM-FPE (Floating Point Emulator). Though efficient, such libraries naturally cannot compete with purpose-built hardware.

2.2 Programming Environments

J2ME – Java for mobile applications – is a common platform for building mobile applications. The common CLDC v.1.0 configuration doest not support FP due to the hardware limitations just discussed. The later and rarer CLDC v.1.1 has (usually library-based) FP support. Software–based solutions suffer the same inherent limitations as the ARM-FPE above. A common alternative platform is the use of either C or C++. C–based environments are usually platform-specific, and can provide close fidelity to the hardware capabilities. However, given the general lack of FPUs, the same reservations apply to C as for J2ME.

GPS access libraries are available for both J2ME and C/C++. These only provide *access* to GPS data but do not support *processing* of GPS data.

2.3 GPS Limitations

It is well-known that GPS has a limited window of accuracy and variable coverage [1]. Given the variability of atmospheric and electromagnetic conditions and signal reception, the observed GPS for a stationary person will fluctuate. This can be turned to our advantage. If GPS were accurate to the nearest metre – which it is not – longitudinal positions would need a range of -1x10e7m to +1x10e7m, or approx. 25 bits. This is a much smaller range than the IEEE floating point standard. Representing the degree, minutes, and four-decimal figure sub-minute data supported by most GPS receivers would require 9 bits (for 360 degrees), 6 bits (for 60 minutes) and 14 bits (to contain 10,000 decimal values) – or 29 bits. Both formats fit well within the 32 bits of most mobile CPUs. We therefore created a bespoke GPS library.

3 Compression

Compression of text is well documented, and the upper bounds of achievable compression are well understood [5,3]. What is not widely recognised is the benefit of compression in terms of performance, particularly on devices with slow input/output. To minimise retrieval time, compression schemes must allow the random access of individual texts [5]. Therefore, the compressed documents have, in fact, a record-like structure. Where record-based retrieval is needed, a similar approach can naturally be adopted, exploiting the known performance advantages found in the compression of plain text.

3.1   Distinguishing Movement from Error

Given that the first GPS location in a sequence is at a starting site, A, the first challenge is to distinguish small-scale actual movement (e.g. on foot) from random variations in the detected position. A naive approach would discard new data that falls within the error distance of the last GPS location. However, the greater the actual initial error, the more likely that a subsequent reading from the same point may be erroneously taken to be a movement from A. A better approach is to maintain a rolling average when the rate of movement is small. This method, however, has in turn its problems as slow movement may not be observed when the rate of movement over the sample is less than the GPS margin of error. It is worth remembering that GPS data may be received in short time durations, meaning that several samples may reflect only a couple seconds of time duration.

Therefore, the final method is to aggregate an initial location over several GPS NMEA sentences, and if the deviation between readings is within the known maximum error bounds, the location is fixed and subsequent readings checked against the computed average of the initial readings. Until the rolling average moves outside the initial site, the location is taken to be stationary. Intervening measures may be discarded. This leaves us with, for a "stationary" position, an averaged location (which may improve accuracy) and a *duration* figure as well, to distinguish between a momentary fix on the move and an enduring location fix at a stationary point.

A final factor is highly spurious readings - where there is a temporary but large displacement in the recorded GPS location. Such abberations would result in an apparent movement given the simple approach above. However, we further exploit our buffering of several readings, and a detected movement is only confirmed when successive readings, rather than a single reading, suggest it.

3.2   Rapid Movement

When a device is moving rapidly across the earth, the data on any given point is momentary and fleeting. To achieve compression, we need different approaches than for stationary positions – particularly, we need to use interpolation to discern smooth paths that can be found in the GPS data which can be readily compressed into vectors. Where movement is rapidly changing direction, this may be of limited use, particularly when the GPS sample rate is low. Conversely, when the movement is relatively smooth (e.g. a car on a motorway) and as the sample rate rises, the opportunity for compression increases.

4   Indexation

As the GPS stream is compressed, an index is built over the longitude and latitude data. Limited by the onboard processing power of mobile devices, retrieval
is of items within a minimum/maximum latitude and longitude. Supplementary
indexes are created to identify the beginning and end of stationary periods.

5   Implementation

Much of our work has been the creation of an efficient library for processing
GPS latitude and longitude data. Our GPS–compression library has been built
upon this, providing a complete implementation for stationary sequences and
a simple implementation of the interpolation scheme for periods of movement.
We have tested the implementation on Nokia mobile phones and HP iPaq PDA
devices running IBM's J2ME environment. There was a marked reduction in
the space taken to store GPS sequences on the on-device permanent (Flash)
storage of between 20% (high movement) to 50% (low movement). Storing a
compressed GPS sequence is also quicker. Our results are broadly comparable
to MG's compression of textual and numeric data [5].

6   Discussion and Conclusion

Our primary focus was to obtaini a method for compression of GPS data. We
wish to refine the interpolation techniques, and extend the indexation to cover
directional movement.. Further work will incorporate the system into a broader
network service context – e.g. incorporation into peer-to-peer networks [4].

Compression certainly can create compact and high-performance storage for
GPS data. However, due to a lack of FPUs, achieving this on mobile devices
is problematic. Given the much higher energy consumption, cost and size of
FPUs, these units are unlikely to be added to the CPUs of mobile devices in
the near future. Therefore, for compression specifically, and a whole range of
mobile applications, we must learn to harness a selective use of slow (relative to
'on-board') network communication to reduce the demand for FP operations.

References

1. A. Crabtree, S. Benford, T. Rodden, C. Greenhalgh, M. Flintham, R. Anastasi,
   A. Drozd, M. Adams, J. Row-Farr, N. Tandavanitj, and A. Steed. Orchestrating a
   mixed reality game 'on the ground'. In *Proc. of ACM CHI*, pages 391–398, 2004.
2. National Marine Electronics Association. *NMEA 0183 Standard For Interfacing
   Marine Electronic Devices*, 3.01 edition, 2002.
3. D. Salomon. *A guide to data compression methods*. Springer-Verlag, 2002.
4. M. Scholl and A. V. Marie Thilliez. Location-based mobile querying in peer-to-peer
   networks. *Lecture Notes in Computer Science*, 3762:166–175, 2005.
5. I. H. Witten, A. Moffat, and T. C. Bell. *Managing gigabytes (2nd ed.): compressing
   and indexing documents and images*. Morgan Kaufmann, San Francisco, 1999.

Seamless Service Adaptation in Context-Aware Middleware for U-HealthCare

Eun Jung Ko, Hyung Jik Lee, and Jeun Woo Lee

Post-PC Platform Research Team, Digital Home Division, Electronics and
Telecommunications Research Institute,
161, Ga-Jeong Dong, Yu-Sung Gu, Dae-Jeon, Korea
kej@etri.re.kr, leehj@etri.re.kr, ljwoo@etri.re.kr

Abstract. In ubiquitous computing environment, intelligent context-aware service should be adapted seamlessly to context-aware middleware. Semantic matching between service and middleware is needed for this. To solve the match, ontology is used for context-aware service adaptation. If service description includes service profile, service input, output, service grounding etc, middleware can understand the description describe using some inferences. This paper proposes a seamless service adaptation agent for context-aware middleware in wearable computing environment.

Keywords: Context-aware middleware, ontology, inference, service matching, seamless service adaptation.

1 Introduction

To build the infrastructure using ubiquitous technology, it is important to recognize the current situation of a user. Context-aware system aims at recognizing the surrounding environment of the sensor while providing appropriate high-level context to the service. And context-aware system enables the middleware function in the ubiquitous infrastructure. Also an independent functioning of the enterprise providing the service and context-aware middleware should be guaranteed. There has to be a match function between an application and context-aware middleware. Therefore, ontology which describes the common concept is needed. The ontology can bridge this gap. Thus, ontology guarantees the matching between a service and the context-aware system.

In a service center, service and service description is provided to the context-aware system within a mobile system in a download. If the service and service description are downloaded through a network to the context-aware system in a mobile system, the context-aware system can recognize the downloaded service description. Therefore, an interaction with a service and context-aware system is created. Service metadata, including the required context list is described in the service description. The service adaptation agent in the context-aware system analyzes this description, so that this agent can mediate the context between context-aware system and service.

Thus the context-aware system uses ontology. Its advantages are as follows:

R. Meersman, Z. Tari, P. Herrero et al. (Eds.): OTM Workshops 2006, LNCS 4278, pp. 1948–1955, 2006.

1. Independent functioning of the device sensor and service manufacturing enterprises is enabled.
2. The sensor device manufacturing enterprise can independently provide context by using the sensor device. The service manufacturing enterprise can independently describe the necessary context in a service description.
3. The service adaptation agent of the context-aware system solves the mismatch of the context between sensors through the language arbitration and deduction.

In this research, the context-aware system was designed and developed in the field of ubiquitous health care (U-HealthCare).

2   Context-Aware Systems for U-HealthCare

Because interest in well-being is increasing among the aging population, many individuals are interested in ubiquitous health care [1]. In order for U-HealthCare service to be available to a user anytime and anywhere, the infrastructure for the ubiquitous environment should be prepared. Optimally, the system providing health care service to a user should be based on a wearable computer or a small-sized portable personal computer. Therefore, it is necessary to establish the context-aware middleware appropriate for the embedded environment in order to provide U-HealthCare services.

A U-HealthCare infrastructure providing services for managing users' health anytime and anywhere is shown in Figure 1.

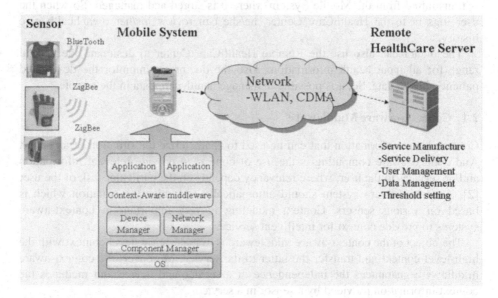

Fig. 1. U-HealthCare infrastructure

It is necessary to have the Mobile System and the Remote HealthCare Center, Sensor Device and communication protocol to support U-HealthCare.

The Sensor Device senses the user's physiological data. This is transferred to the context-aware system of the Mobile System through the communication protocol such as either the BlueTooth or Zigbee.

The Sensor Device is composed of *vest type, wrist type and chest type*. This Sensor Device measures the user's physiological data with body temperature, blood pressure, pulse and respiration.

The Mobile System is portable and this enables the context-aware system installed here to recognize any situation anytime, anywhere. The context-aware system receives the sensor data, and converts it to the context. This transforms the context into a format as specified by the service. The applications of the Mobile System are downloaded from the Remote HealthCare Center and performed. The applications request the necessary context through an interface with the context-aware middleware.

In the remote, the Remote HealthCare Center is the portal server deciding all comprehensive tasks regarding health care. This enables the services such as manufacture and publishing. When a user logs in to the Remote HealthCare Center, and selects the requisite service, it gets downloaded onto the Mobile System. The Component Manager of the Mobile System receives the service and then notifies context-aware middleware of the service and its description. Then, the Service Adaptation Agent analyzes the downloaded service description using ontology. Thus, the service and sensor device develop independently. Moreover, the Remote HealthCare Center creates the user profile to be used in context-aware middleware based on the member information input by a user.

The Remote HealthCare Center manages the users. All health related information is transmitted from the Mobile System where it is stored and managed. So when the user logs in to the HealthCare Center, he/she can review his/her own health care history.

The doctor can also use the Remote HealthCare Center to designate the normal range for all input health information. Also the doctor can monitor the designated patient's health data. So, it is possible to manage health care data in the remote.

2.1 Contexts-Aware Middleware

Context is any information that can be used to characterize the situation of an entity. And context-aware computing is the use of context to provide relevant information and/or services to the user, where relevancy depends on the particular task of the user [2]. A context-aware system should automatically recognize the situation which is based on various sensors. Context modeling is very important in context-aware systems to provide context for intelligent service.

The object of the context-aware middleware is to make a low-level context with the high-level context and transfer the latter to the service. Moreover, the context-aware middleware guarantees the independence of a service and device and mediates the context information provided by a sensor in a service.

Our context-aware middleware is based on this function and is shown in Figure 2.

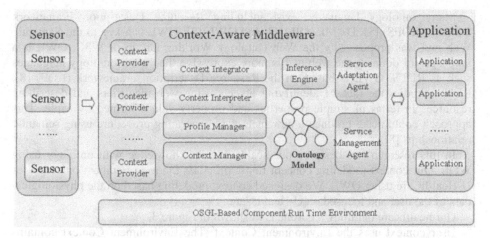

Fig. 2. Context-Aware Architecture

In our research, the context-aware system uses the OSGi-based component management. So, if the bundle is downloaded from the Remote HealthCare, it is immediately practiced on OSGi. All compositional elements and applications of the Context-Aware system make up the bundle in the OSGi-base. Therefore those are managed by OSGi bundle manager with a plug-in and plug-out.

The Context-Aware Middleware is composed of the Context Provider, Context Integrator, Context Interpreter, Profile Manager, Context Manager, Service Adaptation Agent and Service Management Agent.

The Context Provider creates the user's physiological data which is detected by the sensor. If the sensor transmits data to the Context Provider by using the Bluetooth or Zigbee communication protocol, the Context Provider extracts a feature from the user's physiological data and then creates the low-level context. Our system's sensor device can sense the skin temperature, blood pressure, pulse, respiration and falling detection and activity.

The Context Integrator integrates the context coming from the different Context Providers. The Context Integrator then selects the most suitable context among the different context providers. The integrated context is delivered to the Context Interpreter. If two or more Context Providers generate the same context, the Context Integrator selects the best context provider in accordance with the sensor accuracy in the context ontology.

The Context Interpreter plays the roles of converting the low-level context into the high level context. Even in this case, ontology and healthcare related knowledge base are used. For example, the simple low-level context such as skin temperature, blood pressure, pulse, respiration is transferred to the Context Interpreter, which reasons them by using the knowledge base through the Inference Engine. Then, the high-level context creates a result for body temperature, blood pressure, pulse, respiration and emergency determination and whether they are normal or not.

Ontology is a formal, explicit specification of a shared conceptualization of a domain [3]. Ontology shares a common understanding of the structure of descriptive information and enables reuse of domain knowledge [4].

Many ontology languages exist including Resource Description Framework Schema (RDFS) [5], DAML+OIL [6], and OWL [7]. OWL is a key to the Semantic Web and was proposed by the Web Ontology Working Group of W3C. OWL is a language for defining the web and is more expressive than other ontology languages such as RDFS. OWL is based on the Resource Description Framework (RDF) [8]. RDF embodies the idea of identifying objects using web identifiers and describing resources in terms of simple properties and property values formed by triple. This approach could make produce a new meta-data generating procedure using semantic relationships [8].

In this research, we describe our health domain knowledge with ontology using WOL. Our context-modeling concept firstly proposes the use of context ontology for U-HealthCare using OWL. We designed context modeling based on the physiological data of the user and focused on U-HealthCare.

Our healthcare ontology's outline is as shown in Figure 3.

User context uses the Environment Context. The Environment Context contains temporal information like date, time and also has the use's location information. The User context owns Device context. The Device context describes the user's Mobile Device and Sensor Device. The User context has the Profile and Psychological data and Physiological data. The Profile describes the user's profile information, name, age, height, address, phone number. And the Psychological data means the user's emotion like no emotion, angry, hate, romantic love, platonic love, reverence. The Physiological data has the skin temperature, blood pressure, heart rate, respiration, and activity and stress level.

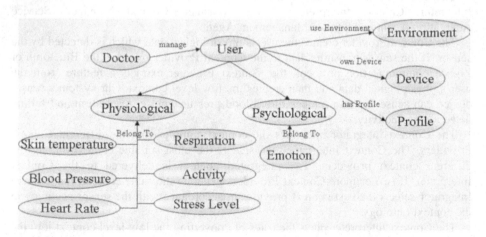

Fig. 3. HealthCare Ontology Outline

The Profile Manager looks after the user profile information. The profiles are auto-downloaded if the user profile is changed in the Remote HealthCare Center. The user profile includes the name, id, home server IP, and normal range of skin temperature, blood pressure, respiration and selected service list.

This profile information can be delivered to an application by the context-aware middle which is reasoned out by the Context Interpreter. If the user profile information is changed, the changed information is notified to the context-aware middleware automatically.

The Context Manager looks into context delivery, the context selection and the context notification. The Context Manager is the bridge between the context producer and context consumer.

The Service Adaptation Agent matches the context between the context provided by the context-aware middleware and the context which a service requests. If service and service description are downloaded into the Mobile System, the OSGi component manager notifies the Agent which analyzes the service description and deduces information. By inference the context-aware middleware understands the service's request context described in the service description.

The Service Management Agent invokes the service and manages the service's life cycle. If there is an application which transmits the user's physiological data in the designated time with the Remote HealthCare Center, the Service Management monitors the invoked time for monitoring service.

2.2 Contexts-Aware Service Adaptation

In the Remote HealthCare Center, a service and service description are downloaded alongside. The service description describes the developing company, and the execution environment of a service, the execution condition of a service, and a needed context.

The Service Adaptation Agent analyzes the service description of a scrvice leading to its download. The context required by a service is analyzed among the service description. The Service Adaptation Agent matches the context between context-aware middleware's context and the context used in the application by using the inference engine.

The Inference Engine uses the knowledge base and ontology to infer context. Ontology is used in order to make explicit assumptions and to separate domain knowledge from operational knowledge. Additionally, ontology has the advantage of sharing of knowledge, logic inference and the reuse of knowledge. If any system uses ontology, the system can provide a general expressive concept and offer syntactic and semantic interoperability. By mapping concepts in different ontologies, structured information can be shared. The Inference Engine applies health care domain so that the Service Adaptation Agent can context between service and context-aware middleware.

The matching algorithm is as follows.

First, service description is downloaded and parsed.

Second, this is analyzed and the service requiring context list is created.

Third, by using the knowledge base defined in ontology throughout the inference engine, context meaning is recognized.

Fourth, the context between the context-aware middleware and service is matched.

Fifth, context delivery between the context-aware middleware and service using the common concept is undertaken.

The matching algorithm of the Service Adaptation Agent is as follow.

```
matchingContext(serviceDownloadEvent service)
  {
    List ContextList;
    ServiceModel serviceDesc;
    InferenceEngine ie;
    OntologyModel ontology;

    serviceDesc = Parsing(service.sDescriptionFile);
    ContextList =MakeContextList(service.desc);
    ie = RunInferenceEngine(ontology);

    Context context[ContextList.length];
    for(int i=0;i<ContextList.length;i++){
       context[i] = matchContext(ContextList[i], ie);
    }
  }
```

2.3 Implementation

We built an experimental testing system, Figure 4, composed of a Remote Health Care Server, a Mobile System like DDA and wearable chest- and wrist-type sensors.

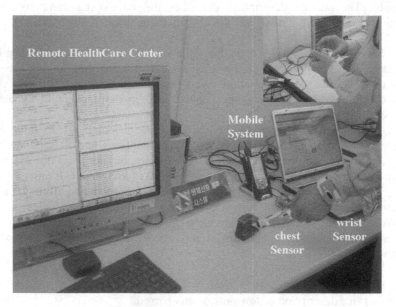

Fig. 4. Experimental Testing System

The development environment is composed of the PDA which operates on a context-aware framework. The Model is IPAQ 5450; the CPU is 400MHz, having 64M of Memory. We installed the familiar 0.7.2 for embedded Linux. We used JENA [9] and JESS [10] as an inference engine in the context-aware framework. The operating system of the HealthCare Portal Server is kernel 2.4.23 and Red Hat Linux 9.0 was installed. The memory size is 1G and the CPU is a Pentium 4.

The HealthCare Portal Server and PDA are connected by WLAN. And The PDA and wearable device are connected BlueTooth Protocol.

3 Conclusion

In ubiquitous environment, it is not necessary that all services should be downloaded and running. With regard to the Mobile System, necessary services may be downloaded from the Remote Service Server when the user selects the service. All services are now adapted and interfaced with the context-aware middleware seamlessly. This system can offer independent functioning between the sensor device and the service.

When a service is downloaded, the service description information is analyzed by using ontology and the knowledge base, so that the context-aware middleware can understand the context that the service wants. Thus, the interface between context-aware middleware and service is guaranteed. The matching algorithm between middleware and service is also presented.

Using ontology to match the context has the following advantages:

Firstly, our system can describe the domain vocabulary, context type and hierarchical layer and relation.

Secondly, dependability between the service developer and the device developer are guaranteed.

Moreover in this research, our system can offer the high-level context to the service automatically according to the deduction rule which infers the situation information.

References

1. H.S Lee, "IBM U-HealthCare" Tutorial of Database Technology for U-HealthCare Bio Medical Industry, Proc. KISS Spring Tutorial, 2006, p. 49-62
2. Dey A. K and Abowd G.D. "Toward a Better Understanding of Context and Context-Awareness," GVU Technical Report, 1999. 2. Bruce, K.B., Cardelli, L., Pierce, B.C.: Comparing Object Encodings. In: Abadi, M., Ito, T. (eds.): Theoretical Aspects of Computer Software. Lecture Notes in Computer Science, Vol. 1281. Springer-Verlag, Berlin Heidelberg New York (1997) 415–438
3. Gruber, T. "A Translation Approach to Portable Ontology Specification," "Knowledge Acquisition, 5(2)", p.199-200 1993.
4. N.F Noy and D.L McGuiness, "Ontology Development 101: A Guide to Creating Your First Ontology", "Stanford Knowledge Systems Laboratory Technical Report KSL-01-05 and Stanford Medical Informatics Technical Report SML-2001-0880," March 2001.
5. W3C, RDFS (RDF Vocabulary Description Language 1.0: RDF Schema), Recommendation 10, February 2004, http://www.w3.org/TR/rdf-schema/
6. http://www.daml.org
7. W3C, OWL Web Ontology Language Overview, Recommendation, 10 February 2005, http://w3.org/TR/2004/RDC-owl-features-20040210/.
8. W3C, "RDF Primer", W3C Recommendation 10, February 2004, http://www.w3.org/TR/rdf-primer/
9. HP Labs Semantic Web Programme, "JENA – A Semantic Web Framework for JAVA."
10. Sandia National University, "JESS – the Rule Engine for the JAVA Platform"

Using Laddering and Association Techniques to Develop a User-Friendly Mobile (City) Application

Greet Jans and Licia Calvi

Centre for Usability Research (K.U.Leuven) - IBBT
E. Van Evenstraat 2A, 3000 Leuven, Belgium
{greet.jans, licia.calvi}@soc.kuleuven.be

Abstract. In this paper, we present an ongoing project on the concept of interaction among people via a mobile (city) application. The focus of our research lies on its usability and sociability, i.e., on all aspects that are related to community forming and development in a city context. In order to analyze them, we have developed a method that combines two techniques that are not common in usability studies: the association technique and the laddering method. We have called this combination the 'connotation chain' technique. In this paper, we will first introduce this technique showing its advantages and disadvantages in a usability study. Then, we will present the results of applying this technique to our specific objective and, finally, we will discuss its implications for the further development of the interface of this application.

Keywords: Mobile communication within a city context, Communities, Association technique, Laddering and User-centered design.

1 Introduction

People interact with each other and some of them do so by sharing or exchanging information. Mobile applications make it possible to do this whenever and wherever people want while they are wandering around in a city [6]. The kind of information they interchange and the ways people communicate in a city context depends, in general, on the intimacy of the contact they are interacting with, but more specifically, on the contingent status of both the sender and the receiver: where they are located, what they are doing, what and how much they want to disclose about themselves to the other. In this setting, not only communication but also information retrieval is important: users indeed need to be able to find information about the city, about the events taking place in the city. It is precisely the aim of the A4MC^3 (Architecture for Mobile Community Creation Content) project to explore the possibilities of community building using state of the art technology, like, i.e., mobile terminals, wireless networks, multimedia and metadata technology, to create a new user-friendly experience.

In this paper, we refer to this but only focus on the research aspects related to the usability (in a wide sense) and sociability of the application to ensure that users can easily add metadata, communicate with other members within the community (who share the same interests) and navigate through its 3D interface. During this project, a

R. Meersman, Z. Tari, P. Herrero et al. (Eds.): OTM Workshops 2006, LNCS 4278, pp. 1956–1965, 2006.

series of demonstrators of this (social mobile) application will be developed and evaluated through an iterative process. The basic principle of user-centered design is that end-users evaluate whether a product is user friendly. We use a combination of two existing techniques - that are quite unusual in this research field - to get to this conclusion.

The paper is structured as follows: Section 2 presents a brief overview about the state-of-the-art in social mobile technology and introduces the topic of community building based on sociability. Section 3 illustrates the methodology that was developed and defines the experimental set-up. Section 4 discusses the results of this study, while Section 5 analyses user values related to the interface. Finally, in Section 6, we draw some conclusions.

2   The Concept of 'Sociability' in a City Environment

The technology available today allows to realize a wealth of services for mobile people. Such services may be very diverse in nature: they may support mobility as such, e.g., by supplying information about transportation or other practical facilities needed by traveling or commuting people, but they may also supply additional services in the form of any sort of information that may be needed while moving, like for instance, shopping facilities, tourism advice, cultural content [4]. It is precisely the combination of these two components (i.e., practical transportation information together with additional move-related services) in the specific context of a mobile city setting that is further investigated in the framework of the project A4MC^3. In this sense, the final system will have many of the features of a mobile guide [2] where, by means of information retrieval techniques, users can find information about the city, or about events taking place in the city.

Because this application encourages the establishment of social relationships, we have to get a good idea of what sociability is. People want to be part of a group of peers whom they respect and like, whose values they share. Their social relationships speak to who they are, say that they are social (human) beings whose existence is not complete unless they care for others, and are in turn cared for by them [5], [7].

From this social perspective, the project identifies four different user categories based on their typology and related goals (see [2] for details). They are: advertisers, professional content providers (like journalists), moderators and end users (i.e., somebody on the street who is using a digital camera, a personal digital assistant or a smart phone). This last group is rather heterogeneous and can be further subdivided into four subcategories with different, although sometimes overlapping goals: (1) the inhabitants of a city, (2) shoppers, (3) tourists, and (4) people who work in the city. After a preliminary analysis, it was decided to study further the city inhabitants, since they seem to be more appropriate for the focus of the current research because they present more social contacts in a city setting than the other subcategories.

A special technique was developed to analyze the needs of this user category. This is presented in the following sections, together with the results of the preliminary evaluation of the interface for a mobile city application.

3 Experimental Setting

3.1 Methodology

In this section, we introduce the 'connotation chain'-technique showing its advantages and disadvantages in a usability study. This is a novel usability methodology that we have derived by combining two existing methods that are not used often in usability research (see further). But before we do this, both techniques will be briefly reviewed.

(1) *The association technique.* By using this method we are looking for the connections that users see between the developed interface and the context in which this application will be used. It is very important to investigate if the functions and relations that are identified by the developers are the same as those that the users have in mind. This qualitative research method is a projective technique to get accurate information about the thoughts and feelings of the respondents. Indirect questions are used to get some answers [3]. Within the usability domain, this is an interesting technique because we can get an idea of the mental model of the users for whom we are developing a certain product. That is why it is very important to check carefully if our interpretations and the relations we see are similar to the one seen by the users of this application.

(2) *The laddering method or 'means-end' approach.* For many products (and the mobile city application we are developing is an example of that), it is not enough to evaluate usability only in the narrow sense of the word, namely to look at how easily it is to use it. It is also important that end users like to use it too. The likeability aspect of a product can be investigated through the laddering method. By looking for the 'attributes' (A) of a product or service and their 'effects' or consequences (C), we try to reveal its expected 'values' (V), its deeper meanings for the users. By asking what characteristics are preferred, what is important for that application or why users (dis)like that certain aspect, a ladder (formed by a list of connected items) is build. 'Why' and 'what' questions are being asked by the reviewer until s/he has found the users' personal values(s) [3], [8]. This is why the laddering method was originally used in marketing research, where the 'sell ability' of a product stands central. In the field of Human-Computer Interaction (HCI) it is less used (see however an example of it in [10]), although it is still very useful to explore what the user prefers, which deeper goals are being solved by using a particular application, what the emotional aspects of the user experience are and the way users perceive it, as in [9]. There are however some drawbacks related to this method. It is possible that the interviewer leads the respondent during the laddering interviews and causes him/her to give wrong connotations. Laddering can also become quite annoying for the respondent, when this method is strictly implemented, because the issues that are questioned can be too personal for a respondent or s/he might not know why that particular attribute or consequence is important for him or her. These 'problems' can be solved often by reformulating the question or ask what s/he would feel when that certain aspect would be missing for this application. Respondents will look then for non-existing relationships between the attitudes and values [3], [8]. In our research, we experienced that we better start with 'why'-questions at the beginning of the interview

and specify them into a 'what'-question later, if we feel a respondent is getting it hard to keep finding an answer, when we ask questions to reveal the underlying feelings. This is in line with results formulated by other researchers (see, for instance, in [9] and [10]).

The combination of these two methods gives us a unique and more complete idea of what users want/expect and what they find usable for that particular product. The first method, i.e., the association technique, focuses more on the usability aspects of the application which are evoked by the user's feelings and mostly elicited by graphical material. The laddering method, instead, investigates the likeability of that same application in a verbal way, i.e., by asking questions, waiting for answers. By combining these techniques, complementary aspects related to the users and their attitudes can become evident. Moreover, because of the different reasoning and learning styles they impinge upon, the whole spectrum of cognitive profiling can be addressed.

3.2 Experimental Setup

The needs of the users identified in Section 2 were translated into a conceptual model (Figure 1). This model already gives a first indication of how the system should look like and what its functionalities, which form the attributes (A) of the ladder, should be.

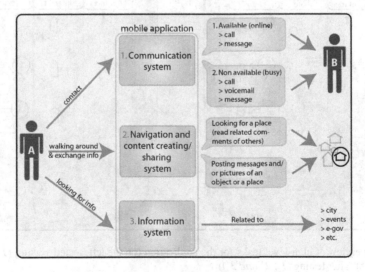

Fig. 1. The 3 major functions of this mobile application based on the user and task analysis

With these indications in mind, a paper prototype of the interface was built for the usability tests. The aim of these tests is twofold: 1) to check if all major functions are available (on the first screen after users have logged in), if all symbols are recognizable, if they are placed logically and if the relationship between the functions is clear; 2) to explore what the users want to accomplish by using this mobile device, which functions they will use mostly, which not and what is missing according to them in its current form to accomplish their goals.

The left Figure 2, which is a direct translation of the conceptual model (see Figure 1) into the first screen of the user interface, was being used during these interviews.

In the first part (where we looked for associations), we asked the ten respondents - which were all inhabitants of a big Flemish city and heterogeneously chosen in terms of gender, age, familiarity with technology and professional background - separately to give word associations to our graphical icons and group them according to what they place together. Then, we asked what they prefer: only textual or graphical labels or a combination of both and this for the first level of functions and some sublevels. In the last part of this test, we asked them to explain what they expect to see when they press a certain button, what they think will happen and what they associate with a mobile city application.

In the second part, we tried to develop a ladder based on the associations users translated out of the attributes of the product through the different questions.

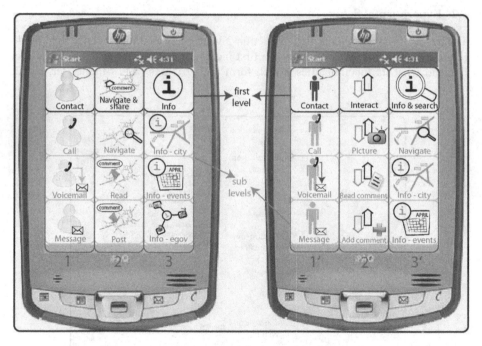

Fig. 2. Overview of high-level tasks for the application (on the left: tested version *(1, 2 and 3)*; on the right: after testing *(1', 2' and 3')*)

4   Preliminary Results

The data, which are presented below, are derived from the analysis of the interviews. Because of the limited space, we will especially focus on the consequences for the interface, which are related to:

(1) *The contact function:* In its current state, the four icons look a bit like chat buttons for some respondents, because of the graphical similarity with MSN Messenger (which is very popular in our country). This wrong connotation can easily be solved by changing 'the MSN-icon' (in the left figure) with a much more common drawing of a unisex person. Because the chosen icons for 'call', 'voicemail' and 'message' are standard, all respondents understand their meaning.

(2) *The options navigate & share (~ interact):* Although we originally combined the navigation through a city function with the option to leave comments in the form of pictures or notes, this combination is not as obvious as we thought. The first function is a bit related to a GPS and the second to a forum or blog where people can interact. Every respondent finds this navigation function very useful (and even necessary) when they visit a town that is not their hometown; not everybody is instead interested to read comments from others or certainly not post them him/herself (what we call 'build a social environment'). It is also not clear in the original interface that there is a possibility to take pictures with this mobile device and upload them on the application itself. That is why we made a new button on the main screen for this function, next to the 'read and add comment' functions, i.e., the two last buttons in row 2'.

(3) *The info (& search) - function:* People who look for a place or other related stuff often want more information about it. That is why it looks much more logical to combine these two aspects. The three most important sub-functions under this are: navigate and zoom (to search for a place); info-city (to what information about e-government belongs) and info-events (to know what is happening when in a city).

In the right drawing of Figure 2, the suggested changes are shown. They will be tested later on, but their look and feel is already based on the one we have used for the original 'info-events'-icon, because most respondents preferred a more pictorial style instead of a detailed one. We also chose to display a graphical image in combination with a text label, because most respondents indicated to prefer this option for functions that are not known very well by everyone (like i.e. the add comment, etc.) or for new functions (i.e., info-events) that are shown on the first 'introduction' screen.

From the test, it became clear that the designers' model is not totally similar to the one that our respondents have in mind (what is already explained in detail above). In Figure 3, the new structure is sketched based on the users' mental model. It differs from the previous one on the level of exploring the city and exchanging content with others. A good overall structure is very important because it will make the application much more logical, and as a consequence of that more usable to work with.

Our results enable us to identify three different groups within the inhabitants community based on their interest and (related to that) the functions they use and require on a mobile application. In Table 1, we give an overview of the characteristics of each group and review which implications this has for the application. The biggest question that will come out of this subdivision is: what makes that most people are not interested in the contributions of online communities (~ *see group 1*), while a smaller

1962   G. Jans and L. Calvi

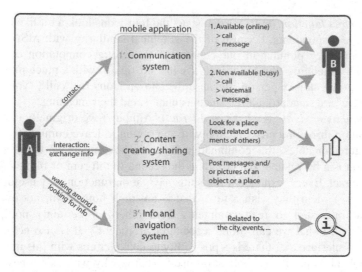

Fig. 3. The 3 major functions of this mobile application based on the mental model of the users

Table 1. High-level tasks for the application based on the characteristics of the community

User group characteristics	Consequences (C) for functions of application.
(1) People who will use the application only to *communicate* with others and to *find their way* i.e.; if they have to be somewhere new where they have never been.	a) Standard mobile phone function, like i.e. the possibility to call someone, leave a message or listen to your voicemail & send/read written messages. b) A GPS function which is combined with an option to get more information about specific city aspects when required. → (a & b): *Basic mobile phone combined with a GPS*
(2) The next one can be subdivided into two subgroups. 2.1. People will read the comments of others, take a look at the uploaded pictures & reviews and maybe let themselves guide to visit a certain place, but will not contribute content themselves. 2.2. People who will read the comments of others; react on some of them and place new posts on the forum.	a) The communication & navigation/info function. b) A read comments option (which gives a possibility to download stuff that others have posted), but without any pressure of personal contribution (~ 2.1). c) An up-/download possibility to add pictures (taken with the device) and text to the virtual city map, with the opportunity to give ratings to places, events, etc. when they are limited in time to write a summery (~ 2.2). → (a, b & c): *The possibility to read comments, look at pictures, and upload own contributions in case they want this.*
(3) People who are acting as a moderator. Their function is related to the one of the moderators that are selected by the city itself, but they do this out of their own interests. This means that they can check posts and look for new info of events or other topics.	a) A basic mobile phone combined with a GPS (= communication & navigation/info function) b) The possibility to share 'stuff'. c) The option to change or delete comments from others (when i.e. the content isn't correct, etc.) and start new topics. → (a, b & c): *An application which makes it possible to read posts, contribute own 'stuff' and moderate.*

group of users are curious enough to look at the comments of people they barely know *(~ group 2.1)*, take the time and effort to write own comments *(~ group 2.2)* or even try to moderate the whole thing *(~ group 3)*? As predicted by many theories (like for instance by [1]), individuals contribute more when they are reminded of their uniqueness and when they are given specific and challenging goals. Otherwise they will maybe read comments of others out of curiosity or do not look at the interaction function at all. This non-contribution can become a problem, because if there is not enough interaction, an online community can fall apart. That is why the moderator function is so important, because moderators are able to keep the community dynamic and others will feel the need to participate as a community is more 'alive'.

Of course this demarcation, into three subgroups, is not so strict, but most people will be able to see themselves as belonging to one of these groups. The important thing of this subdivision is that it has got consequences for the final demonstrator. It would be a good idea to develop one 'basic' version of this application with the possibility to get extra options (like an integrated photo camera) for those (user groups) who want this. This will also change the design of the interface. It would be a waste of screen space to show icons on the main (selection) screen when some user groups are not interested in the functions on it. Because of that particular reason, it should be better that the basic functions are being selected for each group based on their specific needs which is related to the selected 'user-profile' that is asked when the user logs in on his/here device direct when they put it on. Based on this identification, the main functions on the device can change. Future research will show if this is a good approach according to the users.

5 Likeability Aspects Discussed

The values (V) derived from the ladder (Figure 4), which indicate the likeability of the interface, are considering two aspects: first, the abstract consequences for the users when they use this product; then, the preferred habits or goals that users want to reach related to this usage [3]. Our most notable findings (ordered from more important to less according to our respondents and the mentioned values placed between brackets) are:

- People can get the wanted information (contributed by volunteers or employees of the city) almost immediately. If they decide at the last minute to visit a big city like for instance Brussels, they can check if there is still a room for two, what that will cost them and if there is anything special organised when they are interested in; what fits much better with our current lifestyle. The time and efforts that they can save by getting information more quickly gives them more time for other activities and people, what will make them feel more "fulfilled".
- Some get a bigger feeling of freedom, because they can reach others and can be reached via this application whenever they want and wherever they are, and this in a way they prefer ('call, voicemail or message'). This aspect is quite important for some respondents, because some get a bit an uncomfortable 'big brother is

watching you' feeling when they hear that others can see where they are at any time if their status is available. The value that is related to this location-specific content that helps them interact with others is the "(emotional) security".

- They can get new social contacts or find out about activities that take place just by reading stuff that is posted by others who share the same interests. This gives them the opportunity to "build new relationships" or "explore new things".

- People, who are planning to put their own contributions on the mobile application, have the feeling that they can mean something for their city and for others just by looking for interesting things and share that on the computer-mediated communication system. This can give them "satisfaction". The posts that others (especially strangers like i.e. tourists) see can change their opinion of a city in a positive way, which is also related to the possibility to "explore new things".

- They can get more social recognition if other read their posts or take a look at their pictures and give it a good average rating score. This could be a way to "distinguish themselves" for those who find this important.

- And last but not least, in its current form, this application will be most useful for tourists according to our respondents provided by the city as a rent service. They see themselves use it for when they visit a strange city but are not planning to use it all the time. That is why further research, of what is missing for the inhabitants in its current form is necessary.

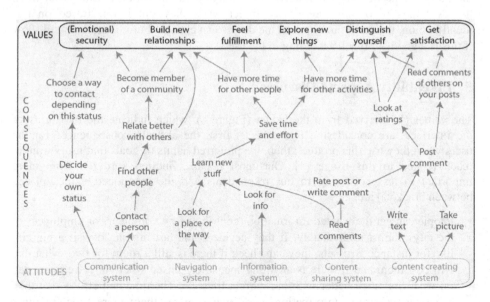

Fig. 4. Hierarchical value map (or ladder) for this application

In the next phase of the design process, a usability test will take place in the natural environment of the users to analyze the impact of the (city) context while they perform real task scenarios. For this field research, we will make use of a mobile lab.

6 Conclusion

In this paper, we have presented a novel methodology that was developed to test a mobile context-aware application for users who move around in a city and the results that we obtained by applying it. These methods are not often used for evaluating the usability of a system but were combined here. Our results were better specified by the association technique where we explored what users see, think and feel while using the device. But we found the laddering method very interesting to complement them, to get an idea of what the inhabitants want, like and dislike. We may conclude that the 'connotation chain'-method is a useful and cost-efficient technique in this research domain because it gives a holistic picture of the users' needs in a very quick way.

Given the heterogeneity of the users (as reported in Table 1), our conclusion is that it would be better to group people who share the main needs and interests and present the same system features to them. This is related to the community building within a user group like (in this case) the inhabitants of a city.

Acknowledgments. The A4MC[3] project (https://projects.ibbt.be/a4mc3/) is co funded by the Interdisciplinary institute for Broad Band Technology (IBBT) and the following companies: Alcatel Bell NV, Androme, Concentra Media NV and Philips. Other (research) partners in the consortium are: EDM (University of Hasselt), CUO (K.U. Leuven), ICRI (K.U. Leuven), MMLab (Ghent University), IMEC/DESICS, SMIT (Free University of Brussels) and ETRO (Free University of Brussels).

References

1. Beenen, G. *et al.*: Using social psychology to motivate contributions to online communities. Journal of Computer-Mediated Communication 10(4), (2005)
2. Calvi, L.: Sociability with Ubiquitous Technologies: A View on Phatic Interactions. In Proceedings of SIGCHI.NL Conference, ACM Press. (2005)
3. Cornelis, M.: Methodologie van het onderzoek: Begrippenkader en onderzoeksmethodes. Handboek Departement Ontwerpwetenschappen (2001), 58.
4. Eisenhauer, M., Oppermann, R. and Schmidt-Belz, B.: Mobile information systems for all. Proceeding of the 10th International Conference on HCI, Heraklion – Crete (2003)
5. Kikin-Gil, R.: Affective is effective: how information appliances can mediate relationships within communities and increase one's social effectiveness. Personal and Ubiquitous Computing 10 (2-3), Springer-Verslag (2006), 77 – 83.
6. Lacohée, H., Wakeford, N. and Pearson, I.: A Social History of the Mobile Telephone with a View of its Future. In BT Technology Journal 21 (3), September (2003), 203 – 211.
7. Monroe, K.: Sociability. In Boston Review 23, 6: 24. December/January (1998-9)
8. Reynolds, T.J. and Gutman, J.: Laddering theory, method, analysis, and interpretation. Journal of Advertising Research. Feb/March (1988)
9. Subramony, D.P.: Why users choose particular web sites over others: Introducing a 'means-end' approach to Human-Computer Interaction, Journal of Electronic Commerce Research 3(3) (2002), 144-161
10. Zaman, B.: Introducing contextual laddering to evaluate the likeability of games with children. Journal Cognition Technology and Work, Special issue Child Computer Interaction: Methodological Research. In press (2006)

A Situation-Aware Mobile System to Support Fire Brigades in Emergency Situations

Kris Luyten[1], Frederik Winters[1], Karin Coninx[1],
Dries Naudts[2], and Ingrid Moerman[2]

[1] Hasselt University – transnationale Universiteit Limburg
Expertise Centre for Digital Media – IBBT
Diepenbeek, Belgium
{kris.luyten, frederik.winters, karin.coninx}@uhasselt.be
[2] Ghent University – INTEC – IBBT
Gaston Crommenlaan 8 bus 201
Gent, Belgium
{dries.naudts, ingrid.moerman}@intec.ugent.be

Abstract. In a firefighter emergency mission it is essential for the members of a fire brigade to get an intelligent and reliable overview of the complete situation, presented according to the role of each member. In this paper we report on the design and development of a system to support a fire brigade on site with a set of mobile services that offers a role-based focus+context user interface. It provides the required overview over the emergency situation according to the user task and context, while life-saving information is emphasized. The implementation of a context-rule-based decision module enhances the visualization of required information. Interaction with the user interface is designed for use in the wild; which in this case comes down to providing a "fat finger" interface that allows firemen to interact with the user interface on site with his gloves on.

1 Introduction

Though mobile crisis management systems have been researched for some time now [1,2], their usage is not very common among intervention teams. We started from the requirements of an actual fire brigade to design and develop a situation-aware mobile system that supports the different members of the brigade and their particular roles. Contextual information plays an important role in the design of the system. Certain parts of the user interface can be emphasized because they contain critical information according to the context (situation).

We had some interviews with firemen of a firebrigade involved in the project that revealed a set of requirements we needed to fulfill to produce a mobile system that could be used during a firefighter emergency mission. Immediate access to site specific information in combination with team communication facilities is highly rated: currently most firebrigades use reliable walkie-talkies to communicate with each other and the site-specific information comes from paper plans

R. Meersman, Z. Tari, P. Herrero et al. (Eds.): OTM Workshops 2006, LNCS 4278, pp. 1966–1975, 2006.
© Springer-Verlag Berlin Heidelberg 2006

that show the floorplan of a building annotated with the places where toxic gases can occur, where the hydrants are located, where the emergency exits are located etc. The system should also provide a quick overview of the situation of the environment (e.g. direction the wind blows) and of the team (e.g. whether there is a team member that has a very low heartrate). This is contextual data that can influence the user interfaces and presentation of data. Furthermore, it should support the coordination of a fire brigade team while they are on the site, and take into account the outfit a firefighter needs to wear during a emergency mission such as thick gloves.

For the design of the user interfaces we used a task-based approach [8]. Task specifications for the different types of users were created and presented to a fire brigade team member. After this iteration mockups of the interface were created: for each task specification a mockup covered the tasks embedded in the specification. The mockups were presented to the firefighters, their feedback was collected and the designs were adapted accordingly. Next, the concrete interfaces were implemented and tested with the users. With this user-centered approach we aimed at creating a complete and usable system first, that fullfilled the complex requirements typical for a mobile crisis management system. Furthermore, the chances for acceptance by the end-users were increased, an important goal for the design of this type of application that deals with critical situations.

The part of the user interface that is created this way has a static structure and navigation: a fireman does not have time to interpret possible changes in the interface because of a change in context. However, a context-aware interface helps to emphasize critical situations and data related with these situations. Jiang et al. already showed the importance of context-sensitive user interfaces for firefighters in the Siren project [5]. The system we present in this paper has many similarities to the work presented in the aforementioned project. The challenge is to add context-awareness without changing the structure or navigation of the user interface, but merely parts of the presentation. This is an important issue; although a context-aware user interface can help in making a quicker assessment of the situation, the interface needs to be predicatable and reliable at all times. Our approach differs from Siren that mainly focuses on context-aware messaging; we integrate different types of information sources in a single user interface that are used during an intervention.

2 Dynamic Mobile Networking Infrastructure

To satisfy the need for real-time information, we implement an advanced mesh networking technology to dynamically build up a network in the disaster area [10]. This mesh network will be connected to an infrastuctured network (wireless or wired), providing permanent access to various sources of information, relevant during the crisis intervention. It is necessary to provide a self-configurable, dynamically adaptable and self-healing mesh network, because one cannot trust the existing infrastructure, in order to maintain communication at each step of the ongoing intervention. Besides transporting different media streams such as voice data and video streams, the mesh network is also responsible for the exchange of context data with other team members and the commanding officer. The former has the highest priority; context data is sent over the network with a lower priority and must not effect the voice communication. An *On The Go-Coverage* service is provided by the mesh network to measure the quality of the network connection for each member of the team. According to the physical location of the firemen, there will be differences in signal strenght and thus bandwidth.

The On The Go-Coverage Indicator (OTG-CI) is a user interface element that is shown at the Personal Digital Assistant (PDA) device of the team member and provides an overview of the quality of the mesh network. The OTG-CI will help to decide when and where to deploy a new wireless node inside the building, in order to maintain a wireless connection with the fire truck. As the team explores the building, the OTG-CI indicates when the wireless signal between the node, that is carried by the first team member, and the nearest node becomes too weak or will die. At that point, a new node, carried by another reconnaissance team member, is deployed in order to extend the mesh network. Since the nodes are battery powered, they can be easily installed by e.g. putting it on a window bench. The new node will automatically register itself within the current mesh network, and new routes are calculated. The integration of a new node is seamless. The OTG-CI will also make an estimation of the end-to-end bandwidth from the reconnaissance team to the fire truck. Whenever a node goes down, the mesh network will automatically try to recover itself, within a minimum amount of time. Thus, it is important that there is a certain redundancy when deploying the nodes. A dynamic channel selection algorithm is implemented to optimize throughput.

3   A Focus+Context Interface

During an intervention, each member of the fire brigade has a specific role. The commanding officer (CO) will coordinate the team, but will not take part in the exploration. It is essential that he has an overview over the situation and knows the status of the different team members of the fire brigade. The other members of the fire brigade have to follow his orders and trust on his insights. The exploratory team members are the first to enter a building to get a detailed overview of the situation. One fireman of the exploratory team carries a camera that transmits a video stream to the fire truck where it is stored and can further be distributed. The fire truck contains a server that allows access to this video stream and secures communication. Finally, there are some stakeholders (e.g. the local governor) who mainly observe the actions of the fire brigade and can decide to send backup.

Focus+context [6] is a central concept used during the design of the user interface. Context is often used to determine the way information is presented (or focused) in a mobile guide: e.g. TIP [4] and GUIDE [3] are both context-aware mobile guides. Context changes in mobile guides are mainly location- and time-based (e.g. when approaching, more information about a hospital appears), whereas in crisis management systems, the interface is influenced by events during the intervention (e.g. the heartrate of a firefigher suddenly drops).

Depending on the role of the person he/she will be equipped with a mobile device. We use two classes of devices: PDAs and Tablet computers. Figures 1 and 2 show the ruggedized devices that are used in the *GeoBIPS* project. On each of these devices, a user interface is implemented that meets the demands of the user depending on its role, as well as the current circumstances. As a tablet PC provides a larger screen space than a PDA, multiple information resources can be visualized simultaneously on the Tablet PC while a PDA interface requires the display of a single information item, to provide a clear and simple overview of the ongoing intervention. Each firefighter is provided with a ruggedized PDA as shown in figure 1. The CO has a ruggedized tablet PC as shown in figure 2.

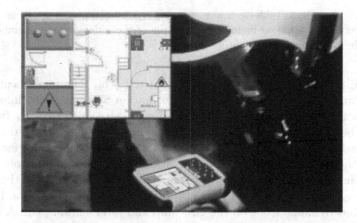

Fig. 1. The ruggedized PDA shows the floorplan and shows the status of the exploration

An easy to understand interface is important in these types of situations. We used a standard icon set as part of the visualizations: currently we are using the ANSI-DIN icons, but these could be easily replaced by the Homeland security set[1]. This makes communication between different team members more effective because of the common understanding of these representations [9].

4 Role-Driven Mobile Crisis Interfaces

4.1 The Commanding Officer

It is of great importance that the CO is provided with information concerning both the crisis location and the environment. Decisions made during the intervention often depend on the amount of information available at the current

---

[1] http://www.fgdc.gov/HSWG/index.html

Fig. 2. The ruggedized tablet computer is used by the commanding officer and gives an overview of the situation including the status of the different team members of the fire brigade at the intervention site

time. The mobile crisis management system relies on four fundamental information sources: relevant Geographical Information Systems (GIS) information, intervention plans, team overview and realtime on-site video streams. Important relations between these information sources, or within one information source, can be predefined to allow easy access while operating the user interface. Figure 2 shows the tablet interface. Basic operations such as panning, zooming and selecting information items are supported by all the four parts of the user interface (the video stream itself does not allow panning). Information items are presented as dynamic icons on the GIS map and intervention plan. A semantic zoom is supported by our system: e.g. information items on the map can change presentation according to the zoom level, thus give an adapted view according to the level of interest in a certain region.

To provide a general overview of the environment, the interface of the CO's Tablet PC implements the presentation of GIS information. The dynamic mobile networking infrastructure provides access to a web service that delivers an environment map with different layers of information. This web service interprets the requests according to the user role requirements and renders a result bitmap accompanied by the user defined information layers. These layers present interactive information items that are important for the specific user. Relations between items presented on the map provide more background information: this allows the user to easily filter out information that is necessary depending on the situation. The semantics of these relations can be visualized, e.g. selecting one information item in a layer on the map can result in highlighting other information items from other layers on the map.

The intervention plans enhance the CO's overview of the current crisis site. Intervention plans provide an overview of the building, together with emergency exits, surrounding hydrants, the locations of dangerous materials (e.g. toxic gases) etc. As elements on the intervention plan are updated, e.g. when a hydrant outside the building appears to be damaged, these updates are automatically updated in the user interface of the CO. These dynamic updates are necessary to maintain a clear and concise overview of the crisis situation. Updates in the user interface should increase the CO's awareness of the situation keep him/her up to date. For example, if the status of one of the members of the exploratory team changes indicates the condition is critical, the ongoing task of the CO should be interrupted by a user interface update that shows this information.

When selecting an information item on a GIS map or intervention plan, detailed information is shown to the user. For example, when clicking on a hospital near a crisis site, other hospitals in the environment could also be highlighted if this relation is emphasized in the configuration. This linking speeds up information querying by the user, and creates an easier way to have a general overview and interpretation of the environment. For each zoom level, the interface will decide if distinct layer elements are separately visualized, or whether an aggregation of different elements within that layer will be shown. Understanding information of a particular layer element is done by exploring and filtering the aggregate representations.

4.2   The Exploratory Team

Each fireman taking part in the site exploration wears a ruggedized PDA that provides an overview of the intervention plan, current team status and the OTG-CI. The PDA interface is shown in figure 1. It is designed in such a way that it supports touch-based interaction with gloves on. We implemented a "fat-finger" interface library: a set of controls for mobile devices that allows an interface designer to add large dynamic widgets to an existing interface. Example widgets that are available are different types of custom buttons, trackbars, selectors, combo-boxes and image-enabled combo-boxes. Informal preliminary tests with firemen have shown the added value of such a widget set. Furthermore, the fact that no other tools are required to interact with the touch sensitive screen increases acceptance by the firemen.

The intervention plan can be panned by moving a finger over the screen. The PDA interface provides two large buttons that can be easily activated by the gloves. A detailed view of the OTG-CI and the intervention plan can be accessed by one of these buttons. The other button is an alarm button that notifies the CO when a life-threatening situation occurs. Activating this alarm triggers an alert in the Tablet PC interface of the CO.

Because the PDA interface is used during an exploration of the site, the amount of information should be limited. The firemen might well be in the middle of a burning house when he needs to access the information. The visualization of information is adjusted to this context. The interface for the PDA allows the firemen to focus on exploring the building and deploying new wireless access points when necessary, and provides the necessary information to ensure a secure intervention.

5   Situation-Awareness

A detailed description of the different user roles taking part in the exploratory intervention was created as part of the design process. They clarify which interaction tasks and visualization features can or must be implemented for each role. We defined the roles of a CO, firemen surrounding the CO, firefighters and the team member carrying the camera who are part of an exploratory team and created a task specification for each role. Next to these roles and tasks there are other team members, like the firemen who monitor the ongoing situation while seated in the fire truck, that we did not take into account here. However, since we are creating a mobile system that needs to support a team of firemen, indirect and direct communication between team members is integrated in the interface. Examples include real-time video streams from the exploratory team to the tablet PC of the CO, the status feedback to the firemen who participate in the team and an overview of each member's situation on the CO's tablet PC. We take advantage of the wireless mesh networking infrastructure that is set up.

The following types of direct style communication are supported:

Verbal communication: A RTP[2]-based VoIP implementation is used. Each firefighter and the CO can be equipped with a Bluetooth earpad connected to their *GeoBIPS* mobile device (e.g. a PDA).

Streaming video: The camera man from the exploratory team permanently films the situation and streams the output via the wireless mesh network towards the video server that is deployed on the fire truck. This video server forwards the video stream towards the mobile device of the CO.

The following types of indirect communication are supported:

Team member context: Each fireman's PDA permanently aggregates incoming data of different personal sensors. These sensors can describe the fireman's blood pressure and heartrate for example. This aggregation of data is pushed towards the CO's interface via the wireless mesh network, allowing for the interface to interpret and visualize the sensor information in a status view of the firefighter.

Team member connectivity status: Because of the particular situation it is important to know the degree of connectivity (using the wireless mesh network) of each team member. This can influence the reliability of data retrieved from the team member device, and can also indicate a problem when the team member goes further out of range of the wireless network.

The implementation of zoomable user interface elements, combined with focus+context visualization techniques [6], provides a detailed view of firemen in trouble, while maintaining a concise overview of the other firefighter in the exploratory team. To enable indirect communication, it is possible for the CO to interact with the team management view. For example, when a fireman has an exceptionally low heartrate, the CO is alerted and can alert the other firemen to

---

[2] http://www.ietf.org/html.charters/avt-charter.html

join the troubled firefighter. The CO can alert the team of firemen through verbal communication, and can appoint a team member to help the troubled fireman. Complementary, this notification is sent towards the PDA of that team member. Verbal communication is always preferred, other communication is complementary but nevertheless also important.

6 Context-Processing Rule System

To further support efficient decision making in crisis management systems, we integrated a rule-based system for context information. Partially based in the idea of event webs introduced by Chandy et al. [7], that considers routes events over a web of connections to the subscribed clients. Clients on the network are represented by knowledge agents that are deployed on mobile devices and communicate over the wireless network. The agents continuously share new or changed context information and interpret incoming context. Each knowledge agent is configured with a predefined set of decision rules which are loaded when the system is prepared for usage. A decision rule might be "If heartrate lower than 75 then send an alert to all other team members and fire truck". This rule can be triggered when context information originating from sensors enters the mobile device of the user. The information is distributed to other devices according to the rule. Each client device can have its own specific set of rules; according to the tasks and role of the user it can be useful to specify additional rules.

Usually, the Tablet PC of the CO is the mobile device which first obtains all time critical information, since he/she makes all strategic decisions during the intervention. Since different predefined sets of rules can be deployed on different devices, rules can also be shared with others when they are triggered on the source device. This automation ensures the context information is spread over the context web, together with the rules that are responsible for this, so an agent can easily deduct the reasoning that was used to send the information. This can be useful if the systems of different intervention teams need to be integrated on the fly, and cooperation between members of different teams is desired. Our interface has fixed parts because of the critical information that must be accessible at all time, the exchange of processing rules will not lead to missing data in the interface. It could lead to confusing information being displayed in the non-fixed parts though: this is an open issue that needs attention. The result of a rule being triggered, does not immediately affect the intervention. Information visualization techniques alter the provision of data, corresponding to the rule, and alert the user of ongoing happenings. This approach allows the user to control the situation, being assisted by tips or notifications which might facilitate the decision making.

Decisions made by the context processing agent result in user interface events that notify the user. As the crisis situation progresses, dynamic updates in overall available information based on changing context like environmental parameters can influence the behavior of the exploratory team. For example, when the direction of wind conditions changes, toxic gases can endanger team members inside a building on fire. The reflection of changing conditions or context in team specific information further emphasizes the importance of this integration. Similarly, team specific information can influence overall information. For example, when a team member collapses because of a critical shortage of oxygen, his location can be interactively visualized on the intervention plan accompanied with a sound and a flashing animation on the map. This feature allows the CO to respond and order other team members to relocate to the firefighter.

7   Future Work

The system described in this paper is not yet tested in a real intervention. However, we used a user-centered approach and informal acceptance tests to validate our approach. An initial demo in realistic settings was done before the public[3], and the pariticipants in the demo were all firemen. This is still different from a real intervention, so additional tests are necessary to have a complete assessment of the system. Software systems that need to handle complex and context-dependent data and that are life-critical systems are probably the hardest to get completely right: there is no room for error. We provide a clean separation between the fixed interface part, and the context-dependent interface parts, since no interference can happen between both.

Currently, there is no integration with a body-sensor network that captures the context data. Although the software system embeds processing rules to handle context and adapt the interface presentation accordingly, we still simulate the contextual data with custom servers that are deployed on the network. In addition, a vocabulary for describing and exchaning contextual data will be created. The different types of components integrated in the system like GIS data, body-network sensors, messaging,... should be able to make use of this vocabulary to exchange information easily and indicate that this information is delivered to the devices invoked by a context-change and not a direct human action.

8   Conclusions

Within the *GeoBIPS* project we present a mobile crisis management system. Our solution allows the user to focus at the task at hand without losing the overview of the situation. Different types of information sources are combined and presented to the user according to the user role, tasks and situation of context. GIS data, intervention plans, streaming video, team status and also different types of communication are integrated into one single system.

Current user tests and practical use indicate that the interface for the mobile devices is intuitive and easy to use. It assists the firefighters with the required information and supports the decision making process by providing a smooth integration with contextual information. The Tablet PC data visualization allows

---

[3] See https://projects.ibbt.be/geobips/index.php?id=183

the CO to consult all necessary intervention and crisis data, while maintaining a clear overview over the current situation. A team status visualization supports monitoring the status of the exploratory firefighters. The interface can emphasize data according to the user context, which is based on different sensors that can be integrated in the environment. However, more realistic testing is required to ensure usability of the entire system in a real-life situation.

The GeoBIPS project web site can be found on http://geobips.ibbt.be/.

Acknowledgments

Part of the research at the Expertise Centre for Digital Media is funded by the ERDF (European Regional Development Fund), the Flemish Government and the Flemish Interdisciplinary institute for Broadband Technology (IBBT). The authors would like to thank the Antwerp Fire Brigade for providing valuable feedback.

References

1. A. Berfield, P. K. Chrysanthis, and A. Labrinidis. Automated Service Integration for Crisis Management. In *Proceedings of the First Workshop on Databases In Virtual Organizations*, Paris, France, June 2004.
2. G. Cai, L. Bolelli, A. M. MacEachren, R. S. nd Sven Fuhrmann, and M. McNeese. GeoCollaborative Crisis Management: Using Maps to Mediate EOC-Mobile Team Collaboration. In *5th Annual NSF Digital Government Conference Proceedings*, Los Angeles, California, May 2004.
3. K. Cheverst, N. Davies, K. Mitchell, and A. Friday. Experiences of developing and deploying a context-aware tourist guide: the GUIDE project. In *Mobile Computing and Networking*, pages 20–31, 2000.
4. A. Hinze and A. Voisard. Location- and timebased information delivery in tourism, 2003.
5. X. Jiang, N. Chen, K. Wang, L. Takayama, and J. Landay. Siren: Context-aware Computing for Firefighting. In *Proceedings of Second International Conference on Pervasive Computing (Pervasive 2004)*, April 2004.
6. Y. K. Leung and M. D. Aerley. A review and taxonomy of distortion-oriented presentation techniques. *ACM Transactions on Computer-Human Interaction*, 1(2):126–160, 1994.
7. K. Mani Chandy, B. Emre Aydemir, E. Michael Karpilovsky, and D. M. Zimmerman. Event-Driven Architectures for Distributed Crisis Management. In *16th International Conference on Parallel and Distributed Computing Systems Proceedings*, Reno, Nevada, August 2003.
8. F. Paternò. *Model-Based Design and Evaluation of Interactive Applications*. Springer, 2000.
9. L. Rothkrantz, D. Datcu, S. Fitrianie, and B. Tatomir. Personal Mobile Support for Crisis Management Using Ad-Hoc Networks. July 2005.
10. B. Tatomir and L. Rothkrantz. Crisis management using mobile ad-hoc wireless networks. In *Proceedings of the 2nd International ISCRAM Conference*, Brussels, Belgium, April 2005.

Context-Based e-Learning Composition and Adaptation

Maria G. Abarca, Rosa A. Alarcon, Rodrigo Barria, and David Fuller

Pontificia Universidad Católica de Chile, Computer Science Department,
6904411, Santiago, Chile
{mgabarca, rabarria}@uc.cl, {ralarcon, dfuller}@ing.puc.cl

Abstract. To be effective, a learning process must be adapted to the learner's context. Such a context should be described at least from pedagogical, technological and learning perspectives. Current e-Learning approaches either fail to provide learning experiences within rich contexts, thus hampering the learning process, or provide extremely contextualized content that is highly coupled with context information, barring their reuse in some other context. In this paper we decouple context as much as possible from content so that the latter can be reused and adapted to context changes. This approach extends the LOM standard by enriching content context, thereby allowing e-Learning platforms to dynamically compose, reuse and adapt educative content provided by third parties (Learning Objects). Three context models are presented together with a multiagent-based e-Learning platform that composes and adapts extended Learning Objects according to learner's context changes.

Keywords: distance learning, ubiquitous learning, learning context, reusable learning object, context-aware computing, adaptive system, reusability.

1 Introduction

Distance Learning (DL) is characterized by a geographical and temporal separation between instructors and students. Interaction between them may be direct but mediated by computer synchronously (e.g., chat) or asynchronously (e.g., e-mail question & answer), or indirectly through the educative content (e.g., Web-course) and learning activities (e.g., reading through a tutorial). Learning becomes even more flexible when students are released from specific platforms and allowed to engage in learning situations at various places through various devices. Such a learning mode is known as "ubiquitous learning" and is characterized by a pervasive and ongoing learning situation that involves interaction among students, faculty, parents, etc. [5, 20]. Ubiquitous learning offers two main advantages: learners can engage in learning situations anywhere, anytime from any device; and learning activities can exploit learners' location or situation. The two properties are particularly appealing when supporting learning experiences for life-long learners, that is, adults seeking to acquire new skills for improving their job qualifications or just satisfy a personal interest. Since these learners tend to have hectic and unpredictable schedules, ubiquitous environments become the most suitable alternative, allowing them to engage in learning situations during their free time, while traveling, etc.

R. Meersman, Z. Tari, P. Herrero et al. (Eds.): OTM Workshops 2006, LNCS 4278, pp. 1976–1985, 2006.

However, some challenges remain unsolved. First, it must be considered the context where the experience takes place. In a broader sense, context describes the circumstances under which something occurs as well as the interrelationships of those circumstances. Such interrelationships provide a semantic perspective that restricts and narrows the meaning of "something" [21, 4, 3]. Researchers in education highlight three kinds of relevant contexts when designing educative experiences: the learner, the technology, and the pedagogical context or learning strategy [17, 11].

The second challenge is the need to adapt learning experiences to the learner context. Some researchers [5, 22] support learner's context by modeling relevant learning situations *a priori*. Yet learner context is the result of the simultaneous occurrence of pedagogical, technological and student perspectives whose possible combinations can be complex and enormous and choosing only a set of predefined scenarios hardly captures the dynamics of learner's context changes [9]. Other approaches to educative content adaptation consider primarily the learners' cognitive properties such as goals, preferences and knowledge [6] and assign them the responsibility of guiding their own learning process.

The third challenge stems from the fact that the increasing demand for education throughout one's life implies a vast diversity in the demanded learning content. A large-scale economy where digital learning resources can be developed, shared and reused by teachers and students around the world is required. The development of such an economy requires not only the participation of business, the education sector and government, but most importantly, the definition of open standards for describing learning context relating technology, education and learners [18]. The "Learning Objects Metadata" (LOM) standard [14] may serve as the basis for satisfying such need. Learning Objects are digital entities supporting learning that are annotated with a set of attributes (object type, author, owner, distribution terms, format, interaction style, grade level, mastery level, and prerequisites). LOM's main drawback is that attributes are too generic for specifying earning context, a certain pre-defined and fixed context is assumed, and context is strongly coupled with the Object itself so that its reuse within some other context is ineffective [23, 19].

In this paper we propose three contexts – technological, pedagogical and learner – that describe learning situations in a ubiquitous learning scenario. The proposal aims at extending LOM definitions in a manner that will permit the automatic composition, reuse and adaptation of educative content (that is, Reusable Learning Objects). We also present a multiagent-based platform that exploits the three contexts plus a LOM database that will make it possible to create and adapt educative content to the learners' situation. This approach involves a multiple-context vision for adapting learning content so that new context models may be added later.

The remainder of this paper is organized as follows: Section 2 discusses our understanding of context, Section 3 contains the conceptual background for the adaptive learning process and our vision of it, Section 4 describes the three contexts represented as ontologies, Section 5 sets out the MAS architecture, and finally, Section 6 presents a discussion and some conclusions.

2 Context

The "context" notion has acquired ever greater relevance with the emergence of ubiquitous and mobile computing, context-aware computing and adaptive systems [1], [10, 7]. Research in "context" also includes areas such as linguistics and artificial intelligence. Although there exists no consensual definition of what constitutes "context", there does seem to be agreement on two main properties. First, context comprehends everything that surrounds "something" (a situation, an activity, an idea, etc.) but is not the "thing" itself [4]. And second, context embraces a set of interrelated elements that maintain a coherent relationship, providing a meaning to the "thing" [4, 21, 3]. Various strategies have been proposed for modeling context. Among them, the most promising technology is ontology [7]. An ontology is a declarative formalism in which the problem domain is described as a set of concepts, describable relationships among those concepts, and formal axioms that restrict the interpretation and proper use of such terms and of concept instances [13]. The concepts may contain a series of attributes or slots.

An ontology is also a common vocabulary that describes a certain domain and defines a unique conceptual frame agreed upon by a community (e.g., teachers, learners, software designers, software agents). This provides a common ground so that ontology-based modeling can facilitate knowledge sharing and reuse. Context expressed through ontologies has enabled the construction of interesting applications that adapt their functionality, user interfaces, and information delivery to the particular needs of each user in areas as diverse as distributed virtual work, learning, entertainment, mobile computing, etc. If contexts describe a situation in which the user is immersed, they can then predict and adapt context-based software in accordance with some ultimate goal (e.g., to achieve an effective and satisfying learning situation) [7]. Contextual information is obtained through both a bottom-up perspective (integrating what the system can detect) and a top-down perspective (interpreting such information in relation to the learner's goals and tasks [8].

3 Adaptive Learning Process

Educative curricula should be adapted to individual differences [12], such differences have an impact on the time required for achieving learning objectives. The most relevant difference is the knowledge already acquired that serves as the basis for acquiring new knowledge (internal condition); external conditions depend on the kind of subject to be learned. Both internal and external conditions should be considered in a learning situation so that new capabilities can be developed and they describe the learner's situation or context. The more detailed and explicit is the learning context, the more a learner can learn and the less time the learning process will require, the result being an improvement in pedagogical effectiveness [23].

It follows, then, that curricular designs which do not consider learners' differences, and learning supporting technologies that do not take into account pedagogical design, will limit the construction of knowledge, disregard learners' culture and assign learners the responsibility of defining and guiding their own learning process. Various ubiquitous learning applications provide educative content developed for a prototypical learner and a relatively static context defined by the system developer. Generally, the unique context aspects regarded as changeable are the learner's location and his or her environmental and physical conditions. But as discussed in the introduction, the technological and pedagogical contexts should also be considered. An educative experience can be seen as a curricular unit whose configuration consists of objectives (why teach), content (what to teach), methods (how to teach) and evaluation (what the benefits of teaching are).

Other approaches similar to ours recognize the need for a technological and pedagogical dimension [5], but propose an *a priori* definition of a set of learning situations. Since context is continually changing [9, 7], context-aware applications should not freeze the learning situation into a set of possibilities but rather should consider and react to context changes. Furthermore, educative content must be adapted at various stages of the learning process, in particular when the knowledge is organized, when the learning resources are chosen, and when the learning sequence of activities are defined. In our approach we model relevant features of learner's context, however, the current instance of the ontology elements depends on learners' action and activity. This approach does not restrict the combination of such elements (predetermined scenarios). Adaptation to such changes are heuristics (rules) recommended by experts for facilitating learning (eg. the content format). A more accurate adaptation process may require learning the appropriateness of such heuristics, such task is part of our future work. In addition, a remaining problem related to the use of an Ontology as a representation language for context, remains, which is the accurateness of the model (did we consider all the possible elements?).

Finally, the development of educative material is costly and reusability of already built material is highly desirable. We propose to annotate current material with context information in the form of XML tags corresponding to the ontology elements. The goal is to decouple the knowledge to be learned from the learning activity and the educative content themselves. The best candidates for the task are Learning Objects, and our aim here is to enrich these objects with the developed ontologies so that they may be used for composing learning content that automatically adapts to learners' internal conditions and their technological and pedagogical situations.

4 Learning Context from a Technological, Pedagogical and Learner Perspective

A learning situation should take account of pedagogical, technological and learners' personal characteristics [17, 11]. Such contexts cannot be considered separately; indeed, the learning situation is the result of their interaction. As an example, the effort demanded by a pedagogical task triggers the learner's recall of concepts [17]. The pedagogical context includes the concepts being taught together with a learning strategy and the educative objective; the learner context defines the learner's situation at the moment of embarking upon the learning experience; and finally, the technological context describes the technological characteristics of the learning environment. Fig. 1 depicts these three contexts and their composition.

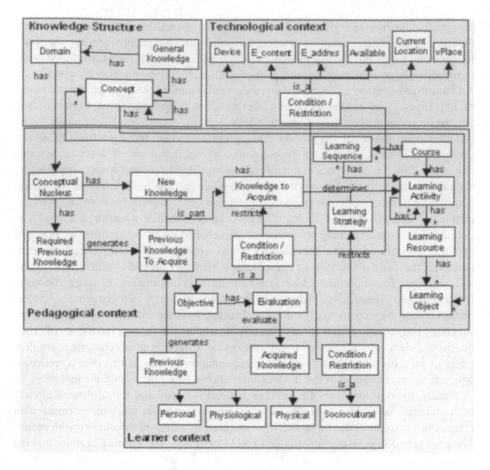

Fig. 1. Learning situation context

Knowledge Structure. The knowledge to be taught is organized into a General Knowledge library that forms a network of semantically related Concepts. A Concept is a knowledge unit, itself composed of one or more Concepts. A subset of such Concepts comprises a conceptual Domain (such as a set of course topics).

As an example, the "programming languages" Domain may include the "Java" and "C" domains. The two share certain concepts such as "control structure" while differing on others like "data type". Java will be cited twice as an example under Pedagogical Context below. The Java domain was designed based on "Java Learning Object Ontology" [15]. In the discussion of the three contexts that follows, knowledge is seen as constituting subsets of Concepts.

Pedagogical Context Ontology. This context contains the Knowledge to Acquire that belongs to a certain Domain. Each Domain has a Conceptual Nucleus that serves as a root for the Knowledge to Acquire. The Conceptual Nucleus is the most important concept to be learned (e.g., Java), and includes all the others. The New Knowledge is what will be learned. Also, it is necessary to specify the Required Previous Knowledge or prerequisites for achieving the New Knowledge. Knowledge may be conceptual (facts and concepts), procedural (heuristic and algorithms), attitudinal (attitudes, values and norms) or strategic (learning strategies) [17].

In addition, it must be determined whether learners satisfy all the prerequisites, that is, whether or not they already have the Previous Knowledge. If they do not, this pre-required knowledge must be taught as well (Previous Knowledge To Acquire), thus extending the definition of the Knowledge to Acquire or learn. According to [17] and [12], learners construct new knowledge by establishing relations with what they already know. Hence, the stimulation or recall of previous knowledge is a relevant event that supports learners' internal processes and should be taken into account at the beginning of each learning unit.

The "Condition/Restriction" entity defines pedagogical constraints on the learning process such as the learning objective (the desired outcome in terms of ability and attitude development and knowledge acquisition), the pedagogical strategy (procedures, ways and forms of education) and evaluation (verification of learning taken place from start to end of process) [16]. A Sequence of Learning is the ordered route followed by the learner depending on the structure of the Course and can have diverse sequencing possibilities.

Finally, learning should occur within the frame defined by a Learning Activity that may itself be composed of sub-activities. Learning activities (e.g., presenting the concept data ordering) depend on Learning Strategies (e.g., conceptual maps, analogies, exercises, etc.) aimed at achieving the pedagogical objectives. A course consists of a set of activities organized in some sequence. Learning activities are implemented through Learning Resources (e.g., code-examples of ordering algorithms) which are made up of one or more Learning Objects. A Learning Object is an independent and self-contained didactic unit predisposed for reuse in diverse educative contexts [19] specified by the LOM standard [2]. In this way, for example, learning the Java programming concept "Relational Operators" may require a Learning Object for defining the main concept, another object for exemplifying the concept, a third for putting the concept into practice, and a fourth for evaluating the concept acquisition.

Learner Context Ontology. The learning process is also influenced by the learner's internal situation. This factor may include a cognitive aspect that consists of knowledge about pre-requisites and knowledge acquired (validated by evaluation) as well as certain properties that are physiological (e.g., learning style) or physical (time available, level of environmental noise) or consist in the learner's personal description (age, language, educational level) or his or her socio-cultural condition (e.g., socioeconomic level).

Technological Context Ontology. A learning situation may also be impacted by the technological conditions in which learning takes place. These include the device the learner uses to access learning content and the learner's current location.

In Fig. 2 we present an extract of the LOM extension. The learningStyle and device tags are examples of the Ontology attributes described in this section (pedagogical, learner, technological).

```
<manifest xmlns:lom = "http://ltsc.ieee.org/xsd/LOM">
    <metadata>
        <schema>ADL SCORM</schema>
        <schemaversion> CAM 1.3</schemaversion>
        <lom:lom>
            <lom:educational>
                <lom:learningStyle>
                    <string language="en"> Recommended learning style type
                        (active, reflexive, theoretician, pragmatic, anyone)</string>
                </lom:learningStyle>
            </lom:educational>
            <lom:technical>
                <lom:otherPlatformRequirements>
                    <lom:device>
                        <lom:type>
                            <string language="en">Principals digital device type
                                (pc, cell phone, pda, anyone)</string>
                        </lom:type>
                        <lom:network>
                            <string language="en">Recommended digital
                                bandwidth (kbs)</string>
                        </lom:network>
                    </lom:device>
                </lom:otherPlatformRequirements>
            </lom:technical>
        </lom:lom>
    </metadata>
</manifest>
```

Fig. 2. LOM Extension

5 Software Architecture

Coutaz [7] has proposed a conceptual framework for Context-Aware Systems that includes both an ontological and an architectural foundation for structuring the adaptation process in a unified way. Under this approach, the defined context (technological, pedagogical and learner ontologies) is the basis for a multiagent system (MAS) that adapts the ubiquitous learning application to the changing learner context. The MAS allows us to simplify the software design by modularizing it and assigning responsibilities to agents that are autonomous, execute concurrently and independently, and collaborate with each other in achieving the system's goals. The components of the architecture are arranged in three layers: the Web interface, the agent server and the information space (see Fig. 3). The layers are briefly described below.

Web Interface and API. In accordance with [1] our ubiquitous learning application permits learners to engage in an educative situation from a range of devices (including unknown ones). The interfaces are written as Web content (html, WAP pages, etc.) in

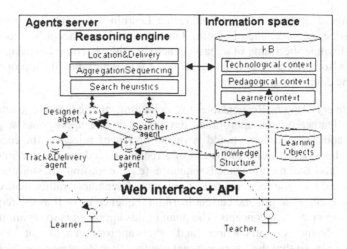

Fig. 3. Multiagent System Architecture

the Web Interface layer and access the agent's layer through messages written in accordance with an API. The API forces callers to specify environmental conditions (such as the device type) described in the technological context as well as the learner's actions (e.g., request a Learning Resource, override system recommendation, etc.). This information represents agents' perceptions.

Agents Server. An agent is an autonomous software process that operates in such a way as to achieve its own goals. Agents are contained in a JADE agent server where they cooperate for understanding the current learner situation and adapting educative content to it. A set of four agents (learner, designer, searcher and track&delivery) are assigned to each learner, providing a natural modularization of the required tasks so that design, implementation and scalability is simplified.

Learner Agent. Responsible for capturing and maintaining information about the learner context. It includes relatively static contextual information such as learners' condition and restrictions (e.g., age, learning style as captured through questionnaires) plus dynamic aspects such as the technological context (e.g., the device type used by the learner for accessing the system), previous knowledge (related to a specific domain) and acquired knowledge (recorded as learners undergo evaluation).

Designer Agent. Responsible for organizing knowledge delivery according to a pedagogical strategy and contextual information provided by the Learner Agent. The designer's goal is to adapt the educative content and sequencing to the learner context (e.g., recommend different types and arrangements of learning objects depending on whether learner is theory-oriented or practice-oriented). This agent reasons using a rule-based reasoning engine (JESS).

Searcher Agent. Responsible for finding the Learning Objects (LO) related to the concepts to be learned. Once Learning Objects are chosen according to the learner context and within the frame of a learning activity, they become Learning Resources. This agent also needs a reasoning engine, using it to determine the appropriateness of an LO in the described conditions.

Track&Delivery Agent. Responsible for delivering the educative content to the appropriate learner on the appropriate device and in the appropriate sequence and format. In addition, learners should have the option of rejecting the recommended LOs (e.g., choosing an exercise instead of a recommended tutorial for studying Java exceptions) and the recommended sequence (e.g., choosing to study class-object theory first and then the recommended flow-control sentences rather than vice versa). The agent therefore records the current learning sequence as well as the requested LO types for learning certain concepts. The point of this approach is to obtain information about the learner's satisfaction and the appropriateness of the system recommendation, so that the Learner Agent can fine-tune its perception of the learner.

Information Space. Contains a knowledge base for storing contextual information. It is updated by the Learner agent and serves as the basis for inferring the appropriate LOs and learning sequence (Aggregation&Sequencing and Location&Delivery rule packages). It also includes databases for storing relatively static contextual information such as learner conditions and limitations (e.g., age, learning style, etc.), and knowledge structure. There is also a local database for storing Learner Objects, but in our view the latter may be acquired (purchased) from remote databases through the Internet as long as they possess enriched context description metadata. Thus, the LOs may be stored in a distributed XML database.

6 Conclusions

Learning experiences should be adapted to the learner context, which is the product of the simultaneous occurrence of pedagogical, technological and student perspectives. We proposed three context models (technological, pedagogical and learner) that describe the learner's learning situation in a ubiquitous learning scenario. The contexts can be implemented as a LOM extension to enable the automatic composition of already created educative content by reusing Learning Objects. This approach involves a multiple-context vision for adapting learning content so that new context models can enrich understanding of the learner's situation. We also presented a multiagent-based architecture that exploits the three contexts to create and adapt educative content to the learner's ubiquitous learning situation. We have implemented the MAS architecture and currently we are refining the adaptation rules.

Our future work includes the refinement of agents' reasoning so that they can learn from the actual learner's choices, identifying such things as best sequencing routes and content format. We plan as well a ubiquitous learning experiment with undergraduate students, in order to validate our proposal. Another challenge consists of automatically generating the Knowledge Domain given that the need to specify Knowledge structures increases the costs of developing educative content. Finally, we would like to explore the inclusion of more context models such as a collaborative work ontology.

Acknowledgments. We would like to thank the Education Ministry of Chile for its contribution to this project.

References

1. Abowd, G., & Mynatt, E.: Charting Past, Present, and Future Research in Ubiquitous Computing. ACM Transactions on CHI Vol. 7 No.1 pp. 29-58. (2000)
2. Advanced Distributed Learning (ADL): SCORM. http://www.adlnet.org/ (2005)
3. Alarcón, R., Guerrero, L., Ochoa, S., Pino, J.: Context in Collaborative Mobile Scenarios. 1st. International Workshop on Context and Group Work. Paris, France, 5-8, Julio. (2005)
4. Brezillon, P.: Context in Artificial Intelligence. C& AI 18 321-340 (1999)
5. Bomsdorf, B.: Adaptation of Learning Spaces: Supporting Ubiquitous Learning. Higher Distance Education. Mobile Computing and Ambient Intelligence (2005)
6. Brusilovsky, P., Peylo, C.: Adaptive and Intelligent Web-based Educational Systems. International Journal of Artificial Intelligence in Education 13 IOS Press, 156-169 (2003)
7. Coutaz, J., Crowley J., Dobson S., Garlan D.: Context is key. ACM (2005)
8. Crowley J., Coutaz J., Rey G., Reignier P.: Perceptual Components for Context Aware Computing. UbiComp 2002, Springer LNCS 2498 pp 117 – 134 (2002)
9. Dourish, P.: We Talk About When We Talk About Context. Personal and Ubiquitous Computing (2004)
10. Dey A., Abowd, G., & Salber D.: A conceptual framework and a toolkit for supporting the rapid prototyping of context-aware applications. HCI. Vol.16. (2001)
11. Downes, S.. The Buntine Oration: Learning Networks. International Journal of Instructional Technology and Distance Learning, Vol 1, No 11, Nov (2004)
12. Gagné, R..: The conditions of learning. McGraw-Hill. (1993)
13. Guarino, N.: Formal ontology and Information Systems. FOIS'98, Trento, Italy. (1998)
14. IEEE LTSC: IEEE Learning Object Metadata. http://www.adlnet.org/ (2005)
15. Lee, M., Yen Ye, D., Wang, T.: Java Learning Object Ontology. IEEE International Conference on Advanced Learning Technologies (2005)
16. Martin, F.: The Didactics before the third millenium. Editorial Síntesis S.A., España. (1999)
17. Monereo, C.: The learning strategies: like incorporating them to the educative practice. Edebe (1997)
18. Paris, M.: Reuse in practice: Learning objects and software development. G.Crisp, D.Thiele, I.Scholten, S.Barker and J.Baron (Eds.), Interact, Integrate, Impact: Proceedings of the 20th Annual Conference of the Australasian Society for Computers in Learning in Tertiary Education (ASCILITE). (2003)
19. Polsani, P.: Las Use and abuse of reusable learning objects. Journal of Digital Information, Volume 3, Issue 4, Article No. 164. Article N°164. (2003)
20. Ogata, H., Yano, Y.: Context-Aware Support for Computer-Supported Ubiquitous Learning. IEEE Inteer. Workshop on Wireless and Mobile Technologies in Education 27-34 (2004)
21. Rittenbruch, M.,: ATMOSPHERE: A Framework for Contextual Awareness.International Journal of Human-Computer Interaction 14(2), 159-180 (2002)
22. Trifonova, A., Ronchetti, M.,: A General Architecture to Support Mobility. Learning. IEEE International Conference on Advanced Learning Technologies, Finland (2004)
23. Wiley, D.: Learning objects: Difficulties and opportunities. Academic ADL Co-Lab News Report: No. 152-030406. [Online]. http://wiley.ed.usu.edu/docs/lo_do.pdf (2003)

Context-Driven Data Filtering: A Methodology*

Cristiana Bolchini and Elisa Quintarelli

Politecnico di Milano, Italy
bolchini@elet.polimi.it, quintare@elet.polimi.it

Abstract. The goal of this paper is the introduction of a methodology for designing context-driven data selection, that is the possibility to tailor the available, usually too rich, data to be held on portable mobile devices, according to *context*. First of all, we will introduce the concept of context and its model, a data structure that expresses knowledge on the user, the environment and the possible scenarios. We will then focus on the proposed methodology for selecting, by means of such information, the relevant data to be made available on a user device. An application of the proposed methodology is the possibility to select data of interest for portable devices, where computation, memory, power and connectivity resources are limited, and thus, tailororing the available, usually too rich, data according to context is a mandatory task.

1 Introduction

Today the amount of available information is growing at high rates, making it difficult to be able to select in a simple way those data that are of interest, discarding all the other ones. Such a task becomes even more significant as the size of the devices devoted to managing such data decreases. Indeed the wide spread of portable devices, with limited resources such as computational power, battery life and memory, poses a quest for applications able to manage the most interesting data, keeping on board only the small portion that – in that moment – the user wants.

In this scenario, the criteria for performing either off-line or dynamic data tailoring plays a relevant role, being it the central element to determine which data should be kept and which should be discarded. In our opinion, such criteria can be expressed by means of the notion of *context*. Our model of context differs from the several ones available in literature, proposed in the past few years; some of them mainly concern the design and implementation of adaptive applications by introducing the notions of user profile and contexts [1,2,3,4,5,6,7]. However, these approaches often provide very specific solutions to data personalization that mainly consider either user preferences [1] or device features [3,5]. In this work we apply a very general notion of context that can include general aspects, at different levels of detail, mainly related to the application scenario. Indeed, our main purpose is to propose a methodology to support the data tailoring task by considering some dimensions as being part of the context and the application as the main point of view of the context description. More in detail, the methodology defines the main steps to identify the relevant portion of information, called *chunk*, on the basis of the current user's context.

---

* This work has been partially supported by MIUR projects Esteem and ARTDECO.

R. Meersman, Z. Tari, P. Herrero et al. (Eds.): OTM Workshops 2006, LNCS 4278, pp. 1986–1995, 2006.
© Springer-Verlag Berlin Heidelberg 2006

Among the possible scenarios that can take advantage from the proposed methodology we mention the Context-ADDICT (Context-Aware Data Design, Integration, Customization and Tailoring) project, aimed at defining and providing a framework for selecting and integrating the relevant information to be delivered on user's devices on the basis of the current context [8].

In this paper we present the methodology supporting *chunk* definition, that can be effectively adopted in such scenario, as well as in others.

The paper is organized as follows. The next section informally introduces our previous work, i.e., the context model used to represent the different aspects for tailoring data within an application scenario, whereas Section 3 presents the methodology for performing such data selection. The proposed approach is exemplified through a running example, discussed in Section 4. The last section draws some conclusions and highlights future research issues.

2   Context Modeling and Usage

The aim of the proposed context model is to allow the designer to express the various criteria that can be adopted to select a portion of the available data, considering the application environment and the active scenario. It is thus important to notice that this notion of context is strictly connected to the considered application and is not meant to model the general knowledge concerning one or more areas of interest, a situation where a data schema, or a domain-ontology may be better suited. In the following a brief description of the model and its representation is presented, for a formal and more detailed discussion please refer to [9].

The knowledge being modeled has neither the goal to be fully comprehensive, nor the necessity to be particularly detailed or homogeneous in its content; the important thing is that it models all the significant criteria that have a relevant impact on the choice of the interesting information within a defined application scenario. The set of primary criteria constitutes the so-called *ambient dimensions* of the context, and includes the following ones, identified throughout our experience as being significant: *holder* (expresses the role the user has within the application, modeling the different person types that may use the device); *interest-topic* (expresses the possible topics that will be considered within the application scenario); *situation* (indicates the different phases/circumstances the user, the environment and the application may be in); *interface* (identifies the kind of interaction with the stored data); *time* (expresses the possibility of filtering data with respect to a time instant, with levels of granularity depending from the specific application scenario); *space* (similarly to the *time* dimension, expresses the possibility of filtering data with respect to a location, with levels of granularity depending from the specific application scenario); *data-ownership* (expresses the type of access that can be performed on the available data based on the ownership permissions).

Owing to the fact that this context is strictly related to the application scenario, it cannot be a-priori defined and, more important, it may happen that not all the listed dimensions are applicable in certain situations, or others could become significant. Let us, for instance, consider a peer-to-peer scenario; the *holder* dimension is not applicable, since there are different roles a peer may assume with respect to the data it is interested in. On the other hand, it could be useful to introduce other dimensions, to model other data selection criteria; in this same scenario it may be of interest to introduce a *service* dimension. Do note that dimensions are orthogonal among themselves, providing independent points of views driving the tailoring of data.

In order to model this kind of context a tree structure has been defined, where the root node represents the entire data space, and the listed ambient dimensions are the first-level nodes, to be further exploded into subtrees. This model has been dubbed the Context Dimension Tree (CDT), aimed at defining the elements used to tailor data; furthermore, the tree structure is then extended to define a Context Dimension Graph (CDG), which includes constraints and relationships among dimension values to remove meaningless combinations of elements, which will be discussed in the following.

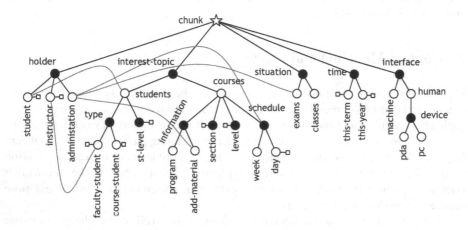

Fig. 1. The Context Dimension Graph for a university application scenario

For each one of the pertinent ambient dimensions a subtree is created, increasing the detail-level adopted to select data, thus allowing a refinement of the knowledge used to tailor data. An example of a Context Dimension Graph for a university application scenario, gathering contents about courses, students and related issues, is reported in Figure 1. Let us consider, as an example, the children of the *holder* dimension: student, instructor, administration; in each moment, and hence for each possible context, the device user may have only one of these roles. The same criterion applies to the children of the other ambient dimensions. For the *interest-topic* dimension the following mutually exclusive values can be envisioned: courses and students. Moreover, when considering the courses node, there are several aspects that can be identified for further refining the selection of interesting data: information, section, level and schedule; these aspects, which are graphically represented as sibling black nodes, are not mutually exclusive, since they provide different characterizations of the same concept.

To differentiate these two main types of nodes in the Context Dimension Tree two colors have been used; black nodes are *dimension nodes*, whereas white nodes are *concept nodes*. A concept may be characterized by several aspects, and each aspect may be constituted by different concepts; as a result, there is an alternating pattern in the levels of the tree and at each level all siblings have the same color. In the context model there are also attribute nodes, which are leaves graphically represented as rectangles, expressing the desire to be able to select data according to a specific run-time generated value. Without considering attributes, leaf nodes are either concept or dimension nodes. When a dimension (black) node has not concept (white) children it must have an attribute child. In this case, it is possible to substitute the single attribute node, with a set of white children enumerating all possible choices, leading to the same information, although expressed in a less-compact form.

In order to identify a portion of data (called *chunk*) to be tailored from the entire data set, to be made available on the user's device, one or more nodes for each possible dimension are selected, choosing a single white sibling and any number of black siblings. This set of selected nodes/values is called *chunk configuration* and refers to a chunk of the entire data. Examples of chunk configurations for the Context Dimension Graph reported in Figure 1 are: $\langle\{student\}, \{schedule, program\}, \{classes\}, \{this\_year\}\rangle$ and $\langle\{instructor\}, \{students\}, \{classes\}, \{this\_year\}\rangle$.

Not all possible combinations of dimension values are worth considering, due to the fact that certain selections would never occur in the application scenario. Consider, as an example, the *interest-topic* dimension and the students value, this is not a significant value when *holder* is student; thus it is not necessary to generate and manage chunk configurations where holder=student ∧ interest-topic=students. This constraint is a *forbid constraint*, used to specify chunk configurations that would not be significant, and defined as a red solid relationships between the involved nodes; it is worth noting that this constraint would also discard all chunk configurations considering descendants from the involved nodes.

As a result, the tree structure is enriched leading to a graph one, to reduce the number of chunk configurations that will be generated, corresponding to the various possible application contexts that will be used. On the portable device, a user will load the portion of data corresponding to one or more configurations.

The proposed context model tree can be specified by means of different formalisms, in OWL-DL [10,11] as well as by means of an XML based (XML-SCHEMA or DTD) representation. The choice between the two possible representations is driven by the application scenario: in a situation where data sources are XML documents referring to an XML schema, an XML-SCHEMA representation may be more suitable and homogeneous (eventually translated from a DTD by means of one of the many available tools, e.g., dtd2xml [12]). On the other hand, in an ontology based application scenario, an OWL description may ease the integration with a Domain Ontology, as well as the possibility to use other available tools for manipulating the context model.

The next section discusses how the Context Dimension Graph is used to produce the significant chunk configurations, to be used to tailor the complete dataset.

3   Data Filtering Methodology

The Context Dimension Graph is the instrument to determine, based on the context, the portion of data to be held on a portable, mobile device. The following guidelines

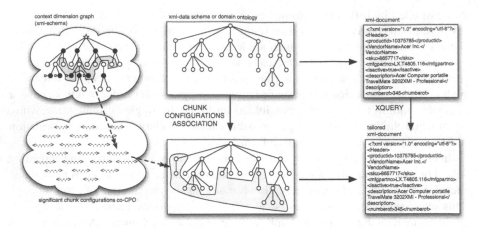

Fig. 2. The methodology flow in an XML data source environment

present the main steps to be followed in order to tailor data; an overall picture of the methodological approach is described in Figure 2. For each step a brief description summarizes the actions to be performed to pursue the final goal. Most of the actions are carried out by the designer, a few can be automated by means of tools that are being developed.

Identification of the CDT ambient dimensions. The set of dimensions modeling the application scenario is determined, referring to the set of common criteria previously listed. Some of them may be omitted, others may be added.

Identification of each dimension sub-tree. For each dimension, a sub-tree of relevant concepts and classes is created, providing an increasing level of detail as the depth of the sub-tree increases.

Introduction of the constraints. Specification of undesired chunk configurations to prevent the generation of insignificant portions of data that would never be used (top left corner of Figure 2).

Generation of significant chunk configurations. By traversing the Context Dimension Graph all chunk configurations, considering one or more values according to the stated rules and constraints roles, are computed. The result is a co-complete partial order (co-CPO) where the greatest (top) chunk configuration is represented by no value per dimension (i.e., the Context Dimension Graph root itself corresponding to the entire data) (bottom left corner of Figure 2). The partial order relation $\succ$ between two chunk configurations is defined as follows: given two chunk configurations $A = \langle A_1, \ldots, A_n \rangle$, $B = \langle B_1, \ldots, B_n \rangle$, we say that $A \succ B$ (A is more abstract (i.e. less detailed) of B) iff $(\forall j \in \{1, \ldots, n\})(\forall a_i \in A_j \exists b_k \in B_j$ such that $b_k \in Descendant(a_i) \cup \{a_i\})$.

Identification of the data schema. The data schema is determined (or designed from scratch), and when more data sources are available their schemata are integrated.

Chunk configurations and XML-data schema areas association. For each one of the derived chunk configurations, an area corresponding to all interesting elements of the XML-data schema is selected (see the bottom center of Figure 2). The designer is in charge of determining the relationships between the chunk configurations and the elements of the schema (domain ontology or entity relationship or relational database/XML schema) of the data to be tailored.

XQuery generation. Given the XML-data schema elements corresponding to a chunk configuration, a set of XQuery expressions is generated to produce tailored data.

XQuery application. The XQueries, derived according the XML-data schema as representing the desired data portions, are applied to XML documents producing a *tailored* XML-data document, that is a chunk (in the bottom right corner of Figure 2).

Chunk collection. One or more chunks are collected, based on the selected applied context, and loaded on the user's device.

The information associating the chunk configuration with the XQuery is stored in a repository called *chunk dictionary*, that can be used on- and off-line to select and load on the portable device the desired chunks.

In three cases it may be necessary to update the loaded data: i) context changes (i.e., the user's interests change, the situation changes, ...) or ii) new data sources are available, or iii) both events occur. In these situations, the chunk dictionary is used to find the set of XQueries to be applied to the available data sources that are assumed to be valid w.r.t. the XML-data schema. It is worth noting that the underlying assumption is that the XML-data documents refer to the XML-data schema used during the association phase between chunk configurations and the schema itself. If this is not the case, the applied query will retrieve unpredictable data, as semantically distant as the document is not valid w.r.t. the used schema and is structurally very different from this schema.

Deriving the association between chunk configurations and the XML-data schema areas is one of the most complex tasks within this methodology. Indeed the number of significant chunk configurations may be relevant and the selection, for each one of them, of the related XML schema portion may be both sensitive and time-consuming. To cope with this issue, we are currently working on the possibility to automate the association between chunk configurations and the XML-data schema, by requesting the designer to perform an association between Context Dimension Tree nodes and XML-data schema elements. More precisely, for each node in the tree, a set of XML-data schema elements are identified independently of the other dimension nodes. The elements corresponding to a chunk configurations are thus derived as a combination (intersection) of the elements associated with the nodes expressing the dimensions' values. The goal is to reduce the complexity of the association phase, because the number of nodes in the tree is smaller than the number of significant chunk configurations. The automated association result can be considered as a starting point to be refined to better tailor data, adding or pruning elements that are not really interesting. More details of this alternative approach will be provided in the application example.

4   Methodology Application: An Example

The application of the proposed methodology to the university scenario, partially introduced in the previous discussion, is now presented.

As a *first step*, the designer of the application has to *produce the Context Dimension Tree of the application*, by means of one of the formalism we have discussed in
Section 2. Figure 1 shows the CDG of our application; we consider three *holders*: the
student, the instructor, and the employee of the administration office.
Two possible *situations* may be relevant for the application: we can immagine to have
the necessity of tailoring relevant information for a given *holder* during the session
when exams are held, or in the other periods. To complete the model, constraints are
introduced, deriving the graph.

Starting from this representation of the context model, as a *second step*, the *relevant
chunk configurations* are automatically extracted by a Java tool. In our scenario, the forbid constraints used to reduce the chunk configurations (504 for the represented CDT)
and remove the meaningless ones are:

$holder$ = student $\leftrightarrow$ $interest\_topic$ = students
$holder$ = instructor $\leftrightarrow$ $interest\_topic$ = faculty_students
$holder$ = administration $\leftrightarrow$ $interest\_topic$ = schedule
$holder$ = administration $\leftrightarrow$ $interest\_topic$ = add_material
$holder$ = administration $\leftrightarrow$ $situation$ = exams

Once the relevant chunk configurations have been extracted (208 in the present example), as *third step*, the designer has to *select, from the global schema of data sources,
for each meaningful chunk configuration the portion of data that are relevant*; in this
way the chunk schema is defined for each chunk configuration. As an example of data
source for the university scenario, we consider in this section an extension of the XML
dataset of the Reed Courses ([13]), whose graphical representation of the XML Schema
of the dataset is shown in Figure 3a.

As anticipated, we are investigating two ways for defining the chunk schemata (the
former is described in Figure 2), described here in the following.

Relevant area per chunk configuration. The designer, for each significant *chunk configuration*, starting for the global schema (e.g., the XML schema) of the data sources,
selects – manually – the relevant sub-schema. As an example, consider the chunk configuration
$$\langle \{\text{instructor}\}, \{\text{course\_student}\}, \{\text{classes}\}, \{\text{this\_year}\} \rangle$$
the portion of the source XML schema that is relevant for the considered combination
of dimension values is depicted in Figure 3a, where grey nodes represent the chunk
schema. This chunk configuration is used by the instructor to collect, for each course
(s)he is teaching during the current year, the list of the students attending it. The following chunk configuration
$$\langle \{\text{instructor}\}, \{\text{course\_student}\}, \{\text{exams}\}, \{\text{this\_term}\} \rangle$$
is used to select for a given instructor all the information about the exams of the courses
(s)he is teaching during the current term, and about students who are attending those
exams. Figure 3b reports the chunk schema for the chunk configuration: note that in this
case the information about the students are those related to an exam (and not a course).

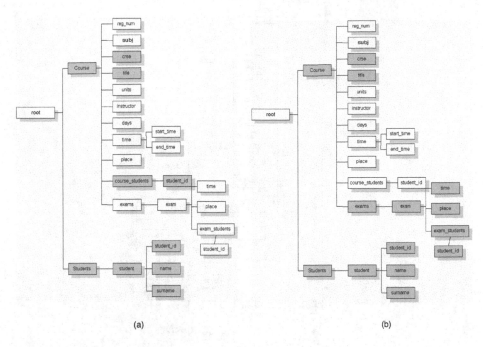

(a)   (b)

Fig. 3. The portions of XML Schema for the chunk configurations (a) $\langle\{\text{instructor}\},$ $\{\text{course\_student}\}, \{\text{classes}\}, \{\text{this\_year}\}\rangle$ and (b) $\langle\{\text{instructor}\}, \{\text{course\_student}\}, \{\text{exams}\},$ $\{\text{this\_year}\}\rangle$

Relevant area per node. Another possibility allows the designer, starting from the CDT, to manually select for each *dimension* value the relevant portion of the global schema, and automatically obtain a first approximation of the chunk schema as intersection of the relevant sub-schemata of each dimension value composing a chunk configuration. In this case, when considering intersection to combine different sets of relevant data, the portion of source schema relevant for each dimension value must include all the data that are relevant for that value. Thus, given the chunk configuration $C = \langle D_1, \ldots, D_n \rangle$, where D_i is the set of values for the i-th ambient dimension, if $Rel(D_i)$ is the subset of the data source schema relevant for the set of values D_i, then the chunk schema of C is obtained as $\bigcap Rel(D_i)$. For example, in Figure 4 we annotated each node with a number 1, 2, 3 or 4 assessing the relevance of that node for the `instructor` value of the *holder* dimension, for the `course_student`, for the `classes` *situation*, and for the value `this_year` of the *time* dimension, respectively. In this last case, we notice that the XML document does not contain information about the validity of the published information, thus, we suppose they refer to the current year. The portion of XML Schema relevant for the chunk configuration

$$\langle\{\text{instructor}\}, \{\text{course\_student}\}, \{\text{classes}\}, \{\text{this\_year}\}\rangle$$

is thus obtained as intersection of the relevant areas and corresponds to the set of grey nodes.

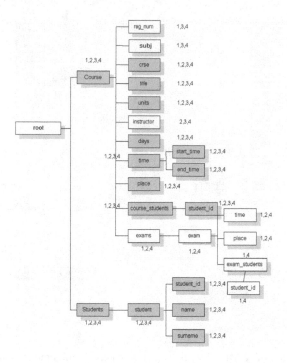

Fig. 4. The annotated xml schema: each number corresponds to a node in the CDT

For the *last step*, given a chunk configuration and its chunk Schema, the XQuery expressions to *retrieve the XML document related to that chunk* are produced. This task can be automatically performed similarly to [14], where a Java tool is presented, a tool that a) selects the chunk schema starting from the E-R representation of the structure of the data source, and b) produces the XQuery expression to retrieve the chunk data.

The XQuery expression to retrieve the data chunk for the chunk configuration

$$\langle \{\text{instructor(VAR)}\}, \{\text{course\_student}\}, \{\text{regular}\}, \{\text{this\_year}\} \rangle$$

where parameter VAR is instantiated at run-time with the instructor name, e.g., I1, is

```
<chunk> {
    for $c in document("reed.xml")//Course[./instructor[text()="I1"]]
    for $s in $c/course_students/student_id
    return <Course>{
            $c/crse
            $c/title
            <Students>
                for $st in document("reed.xml")//Students/student/student_id[text()=$s]
                <Student>
                    $st/student_id
                    $st/name
                    $st/surname
                </Student>
            </Students>
        </Course>
    }
} </chunk>
```

The XQuery expression retrieves for each course taught by the instructor I1 the information about the students attending that course. Note that here the Students element is a sub-element of each Course taught by instructor I1.

The same process is iterated for each significant chunk configuration, leading to a set of data chunks, to be then collected on the user's device.

5   Conclusions and Future Work

In this work we have presented a general methodology to support the designer of context-aware applications in all the phases related to the context definition and the chunk extraction.

As an ongoing work we are integrating the algorithm to extract chunk configurations in the visual tool that automatically generates XQuery expressions to collect data to be stored in the user's device, starting from an Entity Relationship representation of the global schema of the data sources. Moreover, we plan to extend the tool in order to manage XML Schemata and OWL ontologies as well.

References

1. Torlone, R., Ciaccia, P.: Management of user preferences in data intensive applications. In: Proc. of the 11th Italian Symp. on Advanced Database Systems, SEBD. (2003) 257–268
2. Agrawal, R., Wimmers, E.L.: A framework for expressing and combining preferences. In: Proc. of the 2000 ACM SIGMOD Int. Conference on Management of Data, ACM (2000) 297–306
3. De Virgilio, R., Torlone, R.: A general methodology for context-aware data access. In: Proc. of the Int. Workshop on Data engineering for wireless and mobile access, ACM (2005) 9–15
4. Buchholz, S., Hamann, T., Hübsch, G.: Comprehensive structured context profiles (cscp): Design and experiences. In: 2nd IEEE Conf. on Pervasive Computing and Communications Workshops (PerCom 2004 Workshops), (2004) 43–47
5. MAIS: Multi channel adaptive information system (http://www.mais-project.it/)
6. Aberer, K., et al.: Emergent semantics: Principles and issues. In: Invited paper at 9th International Conference on Database Systems for Advanced Applications (DASFAA 2004), Springer-Verlag Lecture Notes in Computer Science (LNCS 2973), (2004) 25–38
7. Ouksel, A.M.: In-context peer-to-peer information filtering on the web. SIGMOD Record 32(3) (2003) 65–70
8. Bolchini, C., Curino, C., Schreiber, F.A., Tanca, L.: Context integration for mobile data tailoring. In: Proc. IEEE/ACM Int. Conf. on Mobile Data Management, (2006)
9. Bolchini, C., Curino, C., Quintarelli, E., Schreiber, F.A., Tanca, L.: Context-addict. Technical Report 2006.044, Dip. di Elettronica e Informazione, Politecnico di Milano (2006)
10. McGuinness, D.L., van Harmelen, F.: OWL Web Ontology Language Overview, W3C Recommendation (2004)
11. Curino, C., Quintarelli, E., Tanca, L.: Ontology-based information tailoring. In: Proc. IEEE 2nd Int. Workshop on Database Interoperability (InterDB 2006). (2006) 5–5
12. dtd2xml: A Conversion Tool from DTD to XML Schema (2004)
13. The XML document of Reed Courses: (http://www.cs.washington.edu/research/xmldatasets/ data/courses/reed.xml)
14. Pigozzo, P.: Metodologia e strumento per la traduzione di diagrammi E-R in Schemi XML normalizzati e la generazione automatica della porzione di dati da memorizzare su un dispositivo mobile. Master's thesis, Politecnico di Milano (2005)

A Contextual Attribute-Based Access Control Model*

Michael J. Covington and Manoj R. Sastry

Corporate Technology Group, Intel Corporation

Abstract. The emergence of ubiquitous mobile devices, such as MP3 players, cellular phones, PDAs, and laptops, has sparked the growth of rich, mobile applications. Moreover, these applications are increasingly "aware" of the user and her surrounding environment. Dynamic mobile environments are generating new requirements – such as allowing users to access real-time, customized services on-demand and with no prior registration – that are not currently addressed by existing approaches to authorization. We investigate using contextual information present in the user's operating environment, such as a user's location, for defining an authorization policy. More precisely, we have defined an access control model that uses contextual attributes to capture the dynamic properties of a mobile environment, including attributes associated with users, objects, transactions, and the environment. Our Contextual Attribute-Based Access Control model lends itself more naturally to a mobile environment where subjects and objects are dynamic. Our authorization model promotes the adoption of many revolutionary mobile applications by allowing for the specification of flexible access control policies.

1 Introduction and Motivation

Rich, context-aware applications are emerging for mobile computing environments that provide new and innovative services to consumers. In order for this vision to be successfully realized, security must be addressed. Mobile computing presents a compelling usage model in which authorization policies could benefit from a more flexible authorization framework. For instance, consider a scenario in which a coffee shop provides access to premium online services – without requiring advance registration – as an incentive to attract paying customers into the shop. In this situation, premium service offerings could be tiered according to the dollar amount each individual customer spent on coffee or food. In such cases, the authorization engine is more concerned with properties of the user (e.g., how much they spent or whether the customer is present in a physical location) than with specific identity information. As a result, we are challenged to define an authorization model that is more appropriate for dynamic mobile computing environments.

In traditional authorization models, users and objects must be known *a priori* to define access policies. Policy that is based on users and objects alone

---

* Copyright ©2006 Intel Corporation.

R. Meersman, Z. Tari, P. Herrero et al. (Eds.): OTM Workshops 2006, LNCS 4278, pp. 1996–2006, 2006.
© Springer-Verlag Berlin Heidelberg 2006

introduces unnecessary administrative complexities by forcing the rules to be rigid. In reality, users and objects possess certain properties, such as location, that change rapidly, thus making traditional policies inflexible and ineffective in dynamic computing environments.

We introduce the concept of *Contextual Attributes* to describe the user and various aspects of her mobile environment, without necessarily disclosing the user's personally identifiable information. New computing paradigms such as mobility provide usage scenarios that can no longer rely on legacy security mechanisms.

The remainder of this paper is organized as follows: Section 2 introduces situation-aware security and contextual attributes. We discuss the limitations of traditional authorization and provide a brief overview of the security-relevant information inherent in a dynamic, mobile environment. In Section 3 we present a detailed model for achieving attribute-based authorization. Finally, Section 4 looks at related work, and we conclude with Section 5.

2 Situation-Aware Security

A significant body of work has emerged around the use of contextual information in computer systems. Context can be used to provide these systems with certain capabilities inherent to human perception and reasoning. As computers become more pervasive, interpreting context becomes an essential requirement for next-generation applications. Context describes a specific situation by capturing the setting in which an event occurs.

These observations have led us to consider the impact of context on security services. In particular, we are interested in how contextual attributes, the fundamental primitives that comprise context, can be used to support and enhance authorization in a dynamic, mobile environment. In this section, we briefly explore contextual attributes and examine how they can be used for security purposes. Through our research, we have identified some possible categories of contextual attributes and provide examples of each. In previous work [1,2], we have described a model for verifying the authenticity of contextual attributes; we provide an overview of that approach here and highlight the necessary logical framework needed to support access policies based on contextual attributes.

2.1 Capturing a Situation Through Contextual Attributes

Policy that is based on users and objects alone introduces unnecessary administrative complexities by forcing the rules to be rigid. In reality, users and objects change, thus making traditional policies inflexible and ineffective in mobile computing environments.

Transactions in a mobile environment involve the user, the mobile platform, the specific resource or service being accessed, and the physical environment of both the user and platform. We propose the use of contextual information to achieve authorization in dynamic computing environments. We introduce the concept of Contextual Attributes to describe the user's mobile operating environment without necessarily disclosing the user's personally identifiable information. Context describes a specific situation by capturing the setting or circumstances in which an event occurs. A contextual attribute represents a measurable contextual primitive (e.g., a user's current location). It is the full set of contextual attributes that comprise the context of a situation (e.g., a transaction that is initiated by a user from a **specific location**, to access a resource that is currently **in state** S, at a particular **time of day**, on a **specified day of the week**).

Examples of context include location, time, temperature, etc. and can be associated with any of the following:

- The user(s) making the access request
- The object or resource being accessed
- The access transaction itself

2.2   Authenticating Contextual Attributes

The traditional approach to authentication is not always well-suited for a mobile environment. We have proposed a new approach for authentication that utilizes contextual information present in the environment, hence making it better suited for a dynamic mobile environment. In [2] we described an attribute-based authentication model that takes into account the contextual attributes pertaining to a specific situation in which an access request was initiated. We have identified assumptions, trust dependencies and described interactions between the various components of the authentication model. Further, we examined the role of trusted platforms in providing security assurances for the contextual attributes used for achieving authentication. Our approach provides several benefits, including protected user privacy, seamless user authentication, and reduced administrative overhead for the service provider. We are currently exploring how this model is made more secure through the use of trusted platforms.

3   A Contextual Attribute-Based Access Control Model

We have developed a Contextual Attribute-based Access Control (CABAC) model for specifying and enforcing authorization policies using contextual information. Our model is not an extension of existing access control models as it removes the need to specify specific "actors" in the system; because we rely heavily on situations to define access policy, contextual attributes serve as the foundation of our model.

In the coffee shop scenario previously presented, a merchant provides premium online services (e.g., news content, digital music, and streaming video) as an incentive for customers to remain on-site while they consume their coffee. The coffee shop maintains a policy that allows paying customers access to three tiers of service based on the amount of their purchase; the service is available to all customers located inside the coffee shop. Consider the following three customer experiences:

1. Alice walks into the coffee shop and makes a $2 purchase. The policy states that customers spending less than $5 have access to an Online News Source for 30 minutes while at that location.
2. Bob walks into the coffee shop and makes an $8 purchase. In addition to news, Bob's purchase allows him access for one day to a digital music repository where he can download one song from that week's "Top 10".
3. Carol is a repeat customer of the coffee shop who visits every day on her way to work and spends approximately $23 during the week. Because she spent over $20, the coffee shop allows her to download 10 songs at any participating retail location and provides unlimited reading of the Online News Source during that week.

The coffee shop provides services based on the amount of purchase (as indicated on an electronic receipt) and the physical location of the customer. In this section, we will use this running example to motivate our approach using contextual attributes and illustrate where CABAC is more useful than previous models when providing security services in a dynamic computing environment.

Using contextual information as the foundation, we present a precise description of the CABAC model that consists of six fundamental components. These components are as follows.

- User Attributes (UA)
- Object Attributes (OA)
- Transaction Attributes (TA)
- Environment Attributes (EA)
- Action (Act)
- Permission Assignments (PA)

As illustrated in Figure 1, our CABAC model does not require a resource administrator to specify specific entities as policy is defined. User attributes (UA) capture properties of the subject that initiated the access request. Object attributes (OA) are properties that describe resources being protected by the access policy. Environment attributes (EA) describe properties of the physical environment at the time a transaction takes place. Finally, transaction attributes (TA) capture information about the transaction as it takes place.

Our model is unique in that it considers attributes to be highly dynamic. At the time an access request is made, attributes must be evaluated and reported to the access control monitor. Figure 2 depicts a transaction taking place and shows where each of the contextual attributes originates. In this case, the user and object each have contextual attributes that must be collected, authenticated, and evaluated. There may also be attributes associated with the transaction that must be presented if required by the policy. Finally, environment attributes must be collected to fully capture the situation in which the access request takes place.

In the following subsections, we further elaborate on these components and their roles in the model.

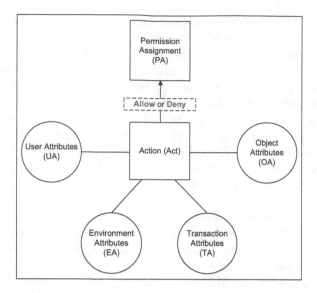

Fig. 1. Contextual Attribute-based Access Control Model Components

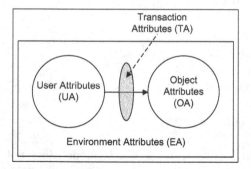

Fig. 2. Transaction Overview using Contextual Attributes

3.1   Core Model Components

User Attributes. User attributes (UA) define the specific properties that must be held or exercised by the user in order to obtain rights to an object or resource. In our contextual attribute-based access control model, user attributes are used to determine access rights for an entity requesting access privileges. Entities requesting access privileges may or may not be required to possess unique user attributes, in which case their privacy is protected at the time of access. Dynamic contextual attributes, such as the user's location in the coffee shop scenario, can be used without unique attributes; however, such attributes require that the contextual information be collected and reported in a secure fashion.

Object Attributes. Object attributes (OA) are properties that define or describe the set of entities that users hold rights on, thus allowing users to access certain resources. As with users, objects may or may not be defined using unique object attributes. In our coffee shop scenario, the third-party service provider is able to label any content as "Premium" and it is immediately protected by the specified access control policy.

Transaction Attributes. Transaction attributes (TA) capture significant properties of transactions that are occurring or have occurred in the past. Specifying transaction attributes as stand-alone components in our model allows the TAs to be delegated between users. In the running example, when Alice makes a purchase, the service provider issues an electronic receipt that denotes proof-of-purchase. Alice could conceivably delegate the TA she receives to another user, Carol, if the service provider allows such attribute sharing.

Environment Attributes. Environment attributes (EA) share many characteristics with the other classes of attributes in our model. For environment attributes, attribute authentication is based on conditions in the environment when a request is made. These could include temperature, ambient noise, or other contextual information that is relevant to access control. The state of the environmental conditions must be captured via sensors that are embedded in the environment. Clearly, the contextual information must be collected securely, in a manner similar to credential collection in user or subject authentication.

Although some environment attributes (EA) can be activated for the duration of an entire session, changing conditions will require other attributes to be evaluated every time. Thus, based on the environmental conditions (EC), a set of environment attributes are activated at the time of a request.

Permission Assignment. Permission assignments (PA) capture the privileged actions that a subject is authorized to hold or exercise on an object. The authorization is determined based on user attributes, object attributes, transaction attributes, and environment attributes. One significant advantage of our contextual attribute-based access control model is that rights can be assigned to attributes only; this allows policy to be specified on mere properties alone. In situations where specific users are incorporated into the policy, our model can support the unique user attributes required for "stronger" policies that enforce access to objects based not only on user identification, but on certain active properties of that user as well.

The following function captures the rights that are assigned to a user when a given set of environment attributes are active and she is attempting to access an object with a particular set of object attributes:

$$(< Act, UA, OA, EA, TA >, Perm) \in PA, \text{ where } Perm = \{Allow, Deny\}$$

As indicated above, the permission assignment (PA) not only associates a permission with the user attribute(s), but makes it conditional on a set of active environment attributes. Clearly, rights may change for the same user accessing a resource if the object attributes, environment attributes, or even user attributes vary between requests.

In our system, a request will be granted access rights if and only if:

1. The policy rule assigning a specified action (Act) to an access request exists with the specified user attributes (UA), object attributes (OA), environment attributes (EA), and transaction attributes (TA) that match those specified in the set of permission assignments (PA)
2. The user attributes (UA) are active for the user making the current request
3. The object attributes (OA) are active for the object being accessed by the user
4. The environment attributes that are made active by the current environmental conditions (EC) are contained in the set EA
5. The transaction attributes (TA) are active for the current transaction

In the most basic sense, rights are used to define authorizations in generic situations. By stating policy using attributes, multiple situations could conceivably be defined using a single line of access policy. For example, policy that defines a user attribute in terms of how much money that user has spent (e.g., Purchase Amount > $5) allows the administrator's policy to cover all situations in which the purchase amount is greater than $5.

Authorizations. Authorizations are functional predicates that must be evaluated in order to return whether the user (requester) is allowed to perform the requested right (operation) on the object (resource). Authorizations evaluate subject attributes, object attributes, transaction attributes, environment attributes, and the requested rights.

The context-aware applications referred to in this document present new and interesting security challenges. The transparency associated with dynamic mobile computing motivates the need for a security architecture that will transparently determine the sources of requests and handle a high degree of context changes. We can no longer assume that user "sessions" will persist for extended periods with the same authentication and authorization credentials. Thus, we are investigating new access control models and authentication techniques that will operate effectively in these next-generation environments.

Attributes specify and capture properties or conditions that are relevant to access control. A contextual attribute-aware authentication service is responsible for evaluating the trustworthiness of all attributes. Attributes are activated when certain conditions are met. These conditions can change dynamically and hence the active attributes are also subject to change. In our model, we assume that the authentication service evaluates attribute status on-demand.

Our authorization policy specification language is created using the following:

- Constant Symbols (e.g., object reference)
- Variable Symbols (e.g., location, time, etc.)
- Operation Symbols (e.g., +, −, /, *, AND, OR, <, >)

3.2   Comparing CABAC with Existing Access Control Models

To better illustrate the advantages of using contextual attribute-based authorization over existing models, we explore the coffee shop scenario using a variety of competing models. Ultimately, we are attempting to answer the following questions: Do contextual attributes help administrators to specify more flexible or meaningful policy statements? If so, what are they able to do with policy using contextual attributes that was not previously possible? We begin with the third-party content provider's policy as indicated at the beginning of Section 3.

Using standard RBAC [3], the policy administrator would be required to assign roles to all customers in the coffee shop. This implies that each customer must be known *a priori* and that the customer's role must be statically assigned.

Unfortunately, standard RBAC provides no mechanism for specifying policy based on dynamic transaction properties, such as how much money the user spends in the coffee shop. The user's role will, therefore, be based on some predefined purchase amount and cannot adjust accordingly. Likewise, standard RBAC does not provide a means of incorporating environmental properties (such as the user's location) into the specified policy. Similarly, standard RBAC does not allow for flexible object protections and requires that specific resources be specified in policy.

Generalized Role-Based Access Control (GRBAC) [4] is an extension to traditional RBAC that incorporates the notion of object roles and environment roles, in addition to subject roles. These new types of roles allow one to define rich, easy-to-understand security policies without having significant technical knowledge of the underlying computer systems that implement those policies. In the coffee shop example, GRBAC is limited by the limiting definition of environment roles. For example, location of the subject would be considered the environment role and, therefore, is decoupled from the subject.

While GRBAC allows policy to be specified using object roles, GRBAC policies do not clearly specify if the environment role (location) is intended to describe the subject, the object, or some other aspect of the transaction. Further, GRBAC suffers from the same subject-centric limitations of RBAC. While it is possible to update the role to "Paying Customer", there is still no means of validating how much money each customer spent in the store in order to dynamically update their access rights.

The Usage Control (UCON) model [5] consists of a family of models built around three decision factors: authorizations, obligations, and conditions. In a usage control policy, authorization is based on the access right and attributes of the requesting subject and the target object. One significant difference between CABAC and UCON is that CABAC defines transaction attributes, which capture the properties of transactions that are occurring or have occurred in the past for an access request. In UCON, it is unclear how to cover access control decisions based on transaction attributes, which are important factors for the context-aware applications we have discussed.

In addition, CABAC defines transaction attributes to capture the results and other properties of a transaction (e.g., the electronic receipt with amount of

the purchase), with which flexible and fine-grained access control policies can
be specified. In UCON, there are no attributes defined to describe obligation
actions. Another important property of CABAC is the delegation of transaction
attributes between users. For example, Alice could delegate the transaction attribute (e.g., the receipt) she receives to Bob, who accompanies her; he can then
access the online content. This mechanism can enable many flexible policies in
contact-aware access control scenarios. In UCON, delegation between subjects
has not been defined.

3.3   Benefits of CABAC

Our model provides several advantages over existing authorization models.

1. **Better suited for rich mobile applications**
   Current authorization models utilize static concepts - such as unique user
   identities, object names, and subject roles - to specify policy. Mobile computing environments, however, have subjects and objects that may not be
   known ahead of time due to the dynamic nature of interactions. CABAC
   supports authorization in these dynamic environments by using contextual
   attributes instead of static concepts in policy specification.
2. **Less administrative overhead for policy specification**
   In contrast to traditional access control models, CABAC does not require the
   definition of static policies based on users, objects or roles. Instead, CABAC
   utilizes contextual attributes that do not limit the policy administrator to
   using pre-defined entities in policy specification. As a result, policy administration requires less management overhead.
3. **Run-time policy evaluation**
   CABAC specifies operations that can be performed on attributes. This results in policy evaluation that occurs at run-time, thus giving the administrator flexibility to specify generic policy that can apply to a variety of
   situations.
4. **User privacy**
   Using attributes instead of user identification information protects the user's
   privacy and allows her to access protected resources without yielding personal information that is unnecessary for the requested access. In the case of
   the coffee shop scenario, this is advantageous because it eliminates the need
   for advance user registration and requires the user present information that
   is relevant to the associated access request.
5. **Enables new business models**
   Consider the example of a WiFi-enabled restaurant that offers free wireless
   Internet to paying customers. In the existing model, all customers get the
   same default level of service. Using CABAC, the restaurant would have the
   flexibility of defining rich, fine-grained access control policies that provide
   different levels of access based on contextual attributes.

4   Related Work

Context-aware security has been studied from various perspectives and research in this area remains active. Our approach using contextual attributes is a continuation of previous work that we contributed to this research space; it addresses deficiencies that other approaches are faced with given our usage model. Further, we maintain that this work represents a significant paradigm shift in access control modeling for dynamic mobile environments.

Giuri and Iglio [6] have proposed an enhancement to the Role-based Access Control (RBAC) model that provides special mechanisms for the definition of content-based policies. By extending the notion of permission, they have allowed for the specification of security policies in which the permissions to an object may depend on the content of the object itself.

Further extending RBAC to constrain subject roles can be achieved through the use of environment roles, as defined by Covington et al. [4,7]. Similar to our definition of an attribute, environment roles were designed to capture the security-relevant context or state of the environment. GRBAC, however, may not be feasible in practice for two reasons. First, it does not address how to establish trust in environmental conditions that are an essential component of the model. Second, environmental conditions such as location are meaningless on their own; instead, they should be bound to an entity (subject, object, etc.) to add clarity to the access policy.

Similar work by Hess et al. [8] provides a general-purpose access control model that was designed to determine if a sender or receiver is authorized to access sensitive information when it is being transmitted. Their model identifies sensitive content, maps the sensitive content to an access control policy, and determines the trustworthiness of the sender or receiver before disclosing the sensitive content.

Hulsebosch et al. [9] have investigated the practical feasibility of using context information for controlling access to services. Based solely on situational context, they claim that users can be granted anonymous access (transparently) to services. While they propose a system architecture for context-sensitive access control, their approach fails to provide adequate security assurances in contextual information. As a result, contextual information can be disassociated from the entity it belongs to, and context can be placed in the control of a third-party.

5   Conclusion

The mobile ecosystem is experiencing rapid growth and, as a result, rich context-aware applications are emerging that provide new and innovative services. As these new, dynamic applications begin to gain traction, it is increasingly important that the appropriate services be in place to secure these rapidly evolving computing environments. Our research has identified limitations with existing authorization models when they are applied to context-aware mobile environments.

In this paper, we have defined an access control model that utilizes contextual attributes to capture the dynamic properties of the mobile environment.

In our model, authorization is based solely on the contextual information associated with users, objects, transactions, and the environment. Our Contextual attribute-based access control model lends itself more naturally to a mobile environment where subjects and objects are dynamic. Further, our approach provides several benefits, including protected user privacy, seamless user authentication, a flexible run-time policy evaluation, and reduced administrative overhead for the service provider.

Acknowledgments

The authors thank Ravi Sandhu and Xinwen Zhang of George Mason University for reviewing our paper and providing valuable feedback.

References

1. Sastry, M.R., Covington, M.J.: Attribute-based authentication using trusted platforms. In: Proceedings of the 8th International Symposium on Wireless Personal Multimedia Communications (WPMC '05), Aalborg, Denmark (2005) Special Session on Platform Security.
2. Covington, M.J., Sastry, M.R., Manohar, D.J.: Attribute-based authentication model for dynamic mobile environments. In: Proceedings of The 3rd International Conference on Security in Pervasive Computing (SPC '06), York, UK, Springer Lecture Notes in Computer Science (2006)
3. Sandhu, R.S., Coyne, E.J., Feinstein, H.L., Youman, C.E.: Role based access control models. In: IEEE Computer. Volume 2. (1996)
4. Covington, M.J., Long, W., Srinivasan, S., Dey, A., Ahamad, M., Abowd, G.: Securing context-aware applications using environment roles. In: Proceedings of the 6th ACM Symposium on Access Control Models and Technologies (SACMAT), Chantilly, Virginia, USA (2001) 10–20
5. Zhang, X., Parisi-Presicce, F., Sandhu, R.: Formal model and policy specification of usage control. In: ACM Transactions on Information and System Security. Volume 8. (2005) 351–387
6. Giuri, L., Iglio, P.: Role templates for content-based access control. In: Proceedings of the Second ACM Workshop on Role Based Access Control, Fairfax, Virginia, USA (1997) 153–159
7. Moyer, M.J., Ahamad, M.: Generalized role based access control. In: Proceedings of the IEEE International Conference on Distributed Computing Systems (ICDCS), Mesa, Arizona, USA (2001)
8. Hess, A., Holt, J., Jacobson, J., Seamons, K.E.: Content-triggered trust negotiation. ACM Transactions on Information and System Security 7 (2004) 428–456
9. Hulsebosch, R.J., Salden, A.H., Bargh, M.S., Ebben, P.W.G., Reitsma, J.: Context sensitive access control. In: Proceedings of the 10th ACM Symposium on Access Control Models and Technologies (SACMAT 2005), Stockholm, Sweden (2005) 111–119

Author Index

Lecture Notes in Computer Science

For information about Vols. 1–4193

please contact your bookseller or Springer